Colombo's Canadian References

One can never finish exploring a people.

Knud Rasmussen

Colombo's
Canadian Reference

John Robert Colombo

Toronto   London   New York
OXFORD UNIVERSITY PRESS
1976

Canadian Cataloguing in Publication Data

Colombo, John Robert, 1936-
  Colombo's Canadian references

ISBN 0-19-540253-7

1. Canada – Dictionaries and encyclopedias.
I. Title. II. Title: Canadian references.

FC23.C64   971'.003   C76-017163-7
F1006.C64

ISBN 0-19-540253-7

1 2 3 4 – 9 8 7 6

Printed in Canada by
JOHN DEYELL COMPANY

Preface

In the course of my involvement in the world of books as an editor, writer and teacher, I have long felt the need for a single wide-ranging source of information on Canadian subjects that would combine facts that were already available in various publications with material that was virtually inaccessible to the general reader. When I finished *Colombo's Canadian Quotations* (1974), I resolved that my next major endeavour would be just such a popular reference work: a mini-encyclopedia that would do for general references what the 'quote book' did for quoted matter. *Colombo's Canadian References* is the result. It is the first book of its kind to be published in Canada.

Far from providing the last word on any subject, as a full-fledged encyclopedia is expected to do, this book aims to *introduce* a great many people, places, and things of Canadian interest that are likely to be encountered by the average person in reading or conversation. The entries—some 6,000 of them—relate to the following fifty categories: Abbreviations, Agriculture, Architecture, Art, Associations, Aviation, Awards, Broadcasting, Business, Canadianisms, Culture, Education, Entertainment, Eskimos, Events, Fauna, Film, Finance, Flora, Food & Drink, Geography, Government, History, Holidays, Indians, Journalism, Labour, Language, Law, Literature, Manufacturing, Military, Mining, Money, Music, Personalities, Places & Regions, Politics, Publications, Railways, Religion, Resources, Ships, Science, Sites, Society, Sports, Technology, Theatre, War.

Let me briefly consider some of the characteristics of *Colombo's Canadian References*. The author's name in the title indicates that the book reflects one person's enthusiasms and interests; nonetheless, care has been taken to ensure that the range is reasonably comprehensive. The adjective 'Canadian' can be taken to mean 'native', or 'relevant to this country'. The noun 'references' implies information on 'things referred to'—excluding elaboration and documentation.

While every attempt has been made to include the principal Canadian references, a good deal of selectivity had to be exercised to keep the project within bounds. In the process of setting limits, I had to make decisions that may seem arbitrary. For example, I thought it unnecessary to give equal treatment to all categories in an informal book of this kind. The degree of comprehensiveness, both in the overall coverage and in the individual entries, has been influenced by the expectations of the general reader rather than the requirements of the specialist. My approach has to some extent been modelled on that adopted by William Rose Benét in his very useful *The Reader's Encyclopedia* (2nd ed., 1965), and I often recalled the question he posed in his Preface: 'What is it that intelligent readers and writers do *not* want to know?' However, though brevity was demanded, this was not employed at the expense of providing useful information and, where necessary, explanations and clarification. The length of an entry does not necessarily relate to the significance of the subject. It often required more words to explain a secondary than a primary reference; this was particularly true in the case of biographies.

A balance had to be struck between current and historical entries; between essential references without which the book would not be complete and relatively inessential ones that could, however, be considered useful, interesting, or simply entertaining. While this book stresses topics of national significance, local references are by no means unrepresented. Fairly extensive coverage is given the mass media and the creative and interpretative arts—including individual entries on the most celebrated films, plays, ballets, books, poems, paintings, musical compositions, buildings, etc.—but the book ranges far beyond these areas, as the list of categories shows. While there are no doubt gaps in the treatment of subjects, the system of cross-referencing—setting in SMALL CAPITALS those topics mentioned that extend the coverage of a subject in entries of their own—enables this alphabetical compilation to reveal and illuminate a network of relationships and interconnections.

Many will feel that it was quixotic for a single person to undertake a reference work of this scope. Nevertheless, any qualms I had were greatly lessened by the assistance I received; by my conviction that the book would meet a genuine need; and by the satisfactions that flowed from being involved in a labour of love—the compilation of facts and accomplishments that I see as having significance for Canadians.

English-speaking Canadians are not very knowledgeable about their country and its heritage. There is an immense amount of information, peculiar to ourselves, that has never become part of our shared knowledge, enriching our feelings of nationality and contributing to a tradition. *Colombo's Canadian References*, which brings a good deal of this information together in one volume, is a kind of inventory of Canadian lore and learning—some of the things we have in common after 450 years of history and more that 100 years of nationhood. I have tried to make it a useful book. But it is my hope that its function will go beyond usefulness—that it will be enjoyed and valued for what it tells us about ourselves.

Acknowledgements

This book could never have been researched and written but for the assistance of many people and the prior publication of many sources of information. During the twenty-four months spent in its preparation, I consulted some 500 separate publications and twice that number of individuals.

Of all the reference books I consulted, I would like to mention those that became my constant companions, the sources that assisted me in compiling information received from other quarters: *A Dictionary of Canadianisms on Historical Principles* (1967) edited by Walter S. Avis *et al.*; *Dictionary of Canadian English: The Senior Dictionary* (1967) edited by W.S. Avis, P.D. Drysdale, R.G. Gregg, and M.H. Scargill; *The Canadian Oxford School Atlas* (3rd ed., 1972) edited by E.G. Pleva and Spencer Inch; *The Oxford Companion to Canadian History and Literature* (1967) by Norah Story; *Supplement to the Oxford Companion to Canadian History and Literature* (1973) edited by William Toye; *The Macmillan Dictionary of Canadian Biography* (3rd ed., 1963) by W. Stewart Wallace; *Creative Canada: A Biographical Dictionary of Twentieth-Century Creative and Performing Artists* (1971-2) compiled by the Reference Division, McPherson Library, University of Victoria; *Contemporary Canadian Composers* (1975) edited by Keith MacMillan and John Beckwith; *The Canada Year Book* (1974); the four published volumes of *The Dictionary of Canadian Biography*; and the ten volumes of the *Encyclopedia Canadiana*.

I am indebted to numerous people who gave me the benefit of their specialized knowledge and in many cases wrote draft entries: G. Abrahamson, Kirwan Cox, Leonard Crainford, William Dendy, Doug Fetherling, David Flint, D.M. Graham, J.L. Granatstein, Cyril Greenland, Winston A. MacIntosh, Elizabeth McLuhan, Ken Macpherson, Sandra Martin, Chloe Prokos, Henry Roxborough, Walter Shankman, Morris Shumiatcher, Quentin Stanford, Sandy Stewart, and Peter Weinrich.

Among many others who provided me with suggestions and various kinds of assistance of a specialized nature, I would like to thank Bruce Affleck, Alexandre L. Amprimoz, Jack Batten, Don Bell, Courtney C.J. Bond, Roger Boulton, Ginny Brass, Wendy Butt, Richard Cleroux, Margaret Collier, Donald Currie, Selwyn Dewdney, Louis Dudek, Dorothy Eber, R.G. Everson, Mark Frank, Robert Fulford, J.D. Griffin, Allan Gould, Sandra Gwyn, David Harrison, Tom Hill, Alan L. Hoover, E. Rex Kearley, John Kellnhauser, Grace S. Lewis, Hugh Hood, Alex Mercer, Stan Obodiac,

E.S. Rogers, Stuart E. Rosenberg, Stuart Ross, Ruth-Ellen Soles, Norah Story, Frazer Sutherland, and Robert Weaver.

I am grateful to the management and staff of the Oxford University Press Canada for devoting considerable time and talent to helping me transform my three-page proposal into a work of 576 pages. I am most indebted to William Toye, Editorial Director of the firm, who was my editor. His contributions, arising out of extensive knowledge, went well beyond those of a skilled editor to become those of a fellow writer and friend. I also depended on members of his department. Tilly Crawley researched and drafted many entries, as did Richard Teleky; Martha Dzioba dealt over a long period with the minutiae of checking, styling, and proofreading; David Densmore combined checking with keeping the 50 binders of typescript organized. Secretarial and typing services were provided by Phyllis Wilson, Barbara Mackay, Donna Dunlop, and Margarite Sullivan.

Most of the research was undertaken at the Metropolitan Toronto Central Library whose staff—especially David Easson—was unfailingly helpful. Research at Metro Central was supplemented by extensive use of the vertical-file material at the reference library of the Canadian Broadcasting Corporation, Toronto, where the outgoing librarian, Margaret (Pat) Cooke, and the incoming librarian, Liz Jenner, were always helpful. I also used the reference libraries of the Canadian Music Centre, the *Globe and Mail*, and the *Toronto Star*, as well as the John P. Robarts Research Library, University of Toronto, and other special libraries, including those of many businesses. Research was also undertaken at the Bathurst Heights Area Branch of the North York Public Library System, where the research librarian, Philip Singer, thrived on difficult assignments. As in the past I made use of borrowing privileges extended to me by Asher Joram of the Acadia Book Store, Toronto.

As for the errors—I almost wrote 'terrors'—that haunt large undertakings of this kind, I would like to blame them on someone or something else—my researchers, editors, or publishers. But I must shoulder the responsibility myself, and do so willingly. Sins of omission and commission brought to my attention will be rectified when the opportunity arises.

As a matter of course I would dedicate this book to someone who not only encouraged me at all times (and drew my attention to any number of possible entries) but also undertook research during the final months: my wife, Ruth Colombo. Yet I feel that a general reference work deserves a public rather than a private dedication, and I should like this book to commemorate the lives of two men, connected in different ways with the cultural life of Canada, whose standards and personal qualities—the spirit of inquiry, the pursuit of excellence—made a lasting impression on me: Nathan Cohen and Peter M. Dwyer.

A

A.J.M. Smith Poetry Prize. Literary award made annually by the American-Canadian Studies Program at Michigan State University '. . . for distinguished achievement in Canadian poetry represented by a volume of new poems published in the previous year'. The prize of $350 is in honour of A.J.M. SMITH, poet and anthologist, who taught at Michigan State in East Lansing for many years. It was first awarded in 1972.

'À la claire fontaine'. Title and first words of a French folksong widely sung in French Canada. 'By the Clear Fountain', a lament for lost love includes the haunting refrain *'Lui y a longtemps que je t'aime,/Jamais je ne t'oublierai'* ('Many long years have I loved you,/Ever in my heart you'll stay'). Marius BARBEAU has written that it is 'a masterpiece of oral literature and melody. For French Canada it has been used as a national anthem.'

A mari usque ad mare. The motto of the Dominion of Canada. The Latin phrase for 'From sea to sea' (the French is *D'un océan à l'autre*) was suggested by Psalm 72:8, 'He shall have dominion also from sea to sea, and from the river unto the ends of the earth', which impressed Leonard TILLEY when a designation for Canada was being discussed in 1866 and DOMINION was chosen.

'À Saint-Malo, beau port de mer'. Title and first words of a French folksong especially popular in Quebec. 'At St Malo, beautiful port of the sea' has nothing to do with the discovery of Canada, but since it celebrates the French seaport on the English Channel, from which Jacques CARTIER sailed in 1534, it is a favourite among French Canadians. The song is about three women who come to St Malo to sell grain. 'But for this song,' Marius BARBEAU has written, 'the name of St Malo might have long disappeared from the memory of Canadian country folk.'

À tout prendre. Feature film directed by Claude JUTRA and photographed by Michel BRAULT. It was produced on a shoestring budget and released in 1963. Jutra himself starred as a man who cannot accept restrictions on his love. The title means, literally, 'Take it all'. 100 min., 16 mm, b & w.

A.V. Roe Canada Ltd. A company formed in 1945 by the Hawker Siddeley Group, London, Eng., to provide Canada with a domestic aircraft design and manufacturing capability. Initially, the company took over the Crown-owned Victory Aircraft plant at Malton on the edge of what is now Toronto International Airport. (Victory Aircraft had built Hampden and LANCASTER bombers.) Avro designed and manufactured 692 CF-100 interceptors; more than 3,800 Orenda engines, which powered the CF-100s and the Canadian-built Sabre aircraft; the CF-102 (Avro Jetliner); the AVRO ARROW; and the saucer-shaped development vehicle known at one point as the AVROCAR. Following cancellation of the Arrow and its associated IROQUOIS engine program in 1959, the company—which had gone public in 1956—ceased aircraft manufacture. Its name was changed to Hawker Siddeley Canada Ltd in 1962.

AAM. Initials of the Art Association of Montreal. See MONTREAL MUSEUM OF FINE ARTS.

AB. Official abbreviation of Able Seaman.

Abbott, Sir John (1821-93). Second prime minister. Born in St Andrews, L.C. (Que.), he became an authority on constitutional law and the dean of the McGill Law School (1855-62). He was elected to the legislative assembly in 1857. As solicitor for Sir Hugh ALLAN in negotiations for the charter for the CPR, he possessed documents that brought about the PACIFIC SCANDAL when they were found in his desk. Appointed to the Senate in 1887, he succeeded Sir John A. MACDONALD in 1891 as prime minister, but resigned for health reasons the following year.

Abel, S.G. (Sid) (b. 1918). Hockey player. Born in Melville, Sask., he became a professional player with the Detroit Red Wings at the age of 20. Through 10 seasons he won many NHL honours and centred for the Howe-Abel-Lindsay line. He later became a television commentator, coach, and general manager of NHL teams. He was elected a member of the Hockey HALL OF FAME in 1969.

Abenake. See ALGONKIAN.

Aberdeen, Lord (1847-1934). GOVERNOR GENERAL of Canada from 1893 to 1898.

Aberhart, William (1878-1943). Premier of Alberta from 1935 to 1943 and founder of the Social Credit movement in Canada. Born in Ontario, he moved to Alberta in 1910 and taught school, becoming principal of a large Calgary high school in 1915. His spare time was devoted to bible classes (hence his sobriquet 'Bible Bill') in his own Prophetic Bible Institute, and to his radio sermons. By 1932 he became convinced that the doctrine of SOCIAL CREDIT could cure the DEPRESSION and in 1935 he led his new Social Credit party to power. Federal powers and economic realities prevented the implementation of straight Social Credit, and there were revolts and grumblings that persisted through to the premier's death in 1943. His successor, Ernest Manning, premier from 1943 to 1968, maintained the religiosity that had characterized the Aberhart style, but there was little of the party ideology remaining beyond the label.

Abominable snowman. See SASQUATCH.

A/C. Official abbreviation of Air Commodore.

AC1. Official abbreviation of Aircraftman, 1st Class.

AC2. Official abbreviation of Aircraftman, 2nd Class.

Académie Canadienne-Française. An organization established 'to serve and defend the French language and culture in Canada'. Founded in Montreal on 7 Dec. 1944, it consists of 24 members who meet regularly and reward works 'which are worthy of it' by the presentation of a medal. The founding members were Victor Barbeau, Marius BARBEAU, Robert Charbonneau, Marie-Claire Daveluy, Léo-Paul Desrosier, Rodolphe Dubé, Guy FRÉGAULT, Alain GRANDBOIS, Lionel GROULX, Louis Lachance, and Philippe Panneton.

Academy of Radio Arts. A training school for actors and announcers founded by Lorne GREENE. The staff included Andrew ALLAN, Eric Christmas, John DRAINIE, Fletcher MARKLE, Mavor MOORE, and Lister SINCLAIR. The only accredited school of its type in the country, it was located on Jarvis St across from the CBC's Toronto studios. Between 1945 and 1951 the Academy gave six months of instruction in acting, speech, announcing, production, radio writing, singing, and sound effects to such 'stars to be' as Anna Cameron, Fred DAVIS, Elsa FRANKLIN, Bruce Marsh, and Gordie TAPP. In 1950-1 a series of lectures on television was introduced.

Acadia or **Acadie.** Name given by France to her Atlantic-seaboard possessions in the New World—an area that lay within the present boundaries of Nova Scotia, New Brunswick, Prince Edward Island, and Maine. The French first settled there in 1598, when the marquis de la Roche placed colonists on SABLE ISLAND. In 1604 an expedition under Pierre Du Gua de Monts (which included CHAMPLAIN) and POUTRINCOURT spent the winter on Dochet's Island, Maine; the settlement was moved to PORT ROYAL in 1605. For 100 years France and England contended for the territory, establishing small colonies there until it was ceded to Britain in 1713 by the Treaty of Utrecht and became Nova Scotia. France retained Île-Royale (Cape Breton), Île-Saint-Jean (Prince Edward Island), and the area north of the Isthmus of Chignecto (New Brunswick) until the cession of New France to Great Britain in 1763.

Acadia University. Located in Wolfville, N.S., it is an outgrowth of the Horton Academy, a Baptist institution erected in 1828. University status was attained in 1891. In 1965 the School of Theology was established as a separate college affiliated with the university.

Acadian Forest Region. Forest area covering the greater part of the Maritime Provinces, with red spruce the characteristic species and balsam fir, yellow birch, and sugar maple also present. The area supports a substantial pulp and paper and lumber industry.

Acadian Trail. Picturesque motor route across northern New Brunswick and through Acadian fishing villages along the eastern coast—a region populated by descendants of the original French settlers.

Acadians, Expulsion of. The French-speaking population in ACADIA grew after 1713, when French ceded the region to Britain under the Treaty of Utrecht, and by the 1750s the British in Nova Scotia considered them an alien and a potentially menacing people—particularly when the SEVEN YEARS' WAR broke out—because they would not take the oath of allegiance to the Crown. In 1755 and 1758 they were expelled—to Massachusetts, Virginia, France, and Louisiana. After the war many returned. The tragic deportation from GRAND PRÉ is the subject of Longfellow's famous narrative poem, *Evangeline: A Tale of Acadia* (1847).

ACCL. Initials of the ALL CANADIAN CONGRESS OF LABOUR.

Accommodation, The. First steamboat in Canada. Promoted by John MOLSON, she was built in three months, entirely of Canadian materials, and was launched on 19 Aug. 1809. On her maiden voyage, 31 Oct. to 6 Nov., she carried 10 passengers from Montreal to Quebec. She remained in service for over four months, making between 9 and 12 round trips, before being replaced by the larger *Swiftsure*.

Achat chez nous. Catchphrase of a movement among French Canadians during the 1930s to 'buy from our own' rather than from Jewish or foreign merchants. The anti-semitic and xenophobic movement, led by small businessmen, died when fascism lost its appeal in the late thirties.

A/C/M. Official abbreviation of Air Chief Marshal.

Acorn, Milton (b.1923). Poet. Born in Charlottetown, P.E.I., and a carpenter by training, he has allied himself to the socialist and revolutionary movements in the country. His publications include *I've Tasted My Blood* (1969), *More Poems for People* (1972), and *The Island Means Minago* (1975)—'Minago' being the Micmac name for Prince Edward Island, the subject of many of Acorn's most moving poems.

Acres Consulting Services Limited. Perhaps the top engineering research and development firm in Canada. Originally incorporated by the engineer Harry G. Acres in Niagara Falls in 1926, it is now a diversified international consulting operation based in Toronto. Acres undertakes on its own initiative feasibility studies—like the MID-CANADA DEVELOPMENT CORRIDOR—that may be of interest to government or industry. In 1969 it paid six carefully chosen individuals $10,000 each to 'think about the future'. One recent undertaking was the power complex at CHURCHILL FALLS.

Acres of snow, A few. See QUELQUES ARPENTS DE NEIGE.

Act of the Heart. Feature film written and directed by Paul ALMOND. Released in 1970, it starred Geneviève BUJOLD, Donald SUTHERLAND, Gilles VIGNEAULT, and Monique LEYRAC. Bujold, married to Almond at the time, played a choir girl who fell in love with a priest and immolated herself. It was not as successful as their previous joint production, ISABEL (1968). The film made use of Harry FREEDMAN's cantata, *The Flame Within*. 103 min., colour.

Act of Union. (i) A bill of 1822 to reunite the provinces of UPPER CANADA and LOWER CANADA. It was not passed in the British Parliament, but its unfairness to French Canadians, who would have been placed in a minority and would have lost their language rights, angered Louis-Joseph PAPINEAU, who

had been sent to England to oppose it. (ii) An Act of Union came into effect on 10 Feb. 1841, reuniting the provinces of Upper and Lower Canada and creating the PROVINCE OF CANADA. It followed upon Lord DURHAM's Report that recommended a union as a means of speeding up the assimilation of French Canadians—a process he thought necessary after the abortive REBELLION OF 1837.

Action française. A Montreal-based nationalistic movement. Developing during the later years of the First World War and after, and expressing the bitterness and resentment then felt by many French Canadians, it blossomed in the 1920s, under the guidance of the priest-historian Abbé Lionel GROULX, who urged French Canadians to recognize the linguistic, economic, social, and political threats to their distinctive way of life. It disintegrated in 1928 but had a lasting effect. Susan Mann Trofimenkoff has studied it in *Action française* (1975).

Action nationale, L'. A nationalistic journal published in Montreal. It was founded as a quarterly by Abbé Lionel GROULX in 1933 as the voice of the Ligue d'Action Nationale, a descendant of the ACTION FRANÇAISE. It is now published monthly and is concerned with the preservation of Quebec values and culture.

Action: The October Crisis of 1970. Documentary film produced by the NFB in 1973. Directed by Robin SPRY, it recreates the OCTOBER CRISIS in Montreal through news footage and commentary. Spry also directed a spin-off, *Reaction: A Portrait of a Society in Crisis* (57 min., 50 sec.; colour; 1973), in which English-speaking groups in Quebec express their reactions to the Quebec crisis. 87 min., 9 sec.; colour.

Actors' Equity. See CANADIAN ACTORS' EQUITY.

ACTRA. Acronym of the ASSOCIATION OF CANADIAN TELEVISION AND RADIO ARTISTS.

ACTRA Awards. Annual awards given by the ASSOCIATION OF CANADIAN TELEVISION AND RADIO ARTISTS to encourage excellence in Canadian broadcasting and film production. The ACTRA Awards were first given at a formal dinner in Toronto in 1971 and are now televised nationally. The award itself is a bronze statuette of a chubby nude, sculpted by William McElcheran. It was nicknamed 'Nellie' by Elizabeth Malone, an ACTRA secretary. Awards have been given in the following categories: Best Sportscaster, Best Writer in the Dramatic Mode in Radio, Best Writer in the Documentary Mode in the Visual

3

ACTRA Awards

Media, Best Performance in a Feature Film, Best Writer in the Dramatic Mode in the Visual Media, Best Writer in the Documentary Mode in Radio, Best Newsbroadcaster, Best Public Affairs Broadcaster in Television, Best Public Affairs Broadcaster in Radio, Best Variety Performer, Best Program of the Year. ACTRA also makes the following special awards: ANDREW ALLAN AWARD, JOHN DRAINIE AWARD, EARLE GREY AWARD, FOSTER HEWITT AWARD, and GORDON SINCLAIR AWARD.

ACUTE. Acronym of the Association of Canadian University Teachers of English, a society that held its first annual meeting in Edmonton in 1958.

Adams, David (b.1928). Dancer. Born in Winnipeg, he trained with Gweneth LLOYD in the Winnipeg Ballet School, danced with the company (now the ROYAL WINNIPEG BALLET) from 1939 to 1946, and became one of the best male dancers on the continent, a performer of physical prowess and excellent dramatic instinct. After dancing in London with the Sadler's Wells Theatre Ballet, the Metropolitan Opera Ballet, and the International Ballet, he returned to Canada in 1951 and was principal dancer of the NATIONAL BALLET OF CANADA until 1961. He danced with the Festival Ballet, London, from 1961 to 1969, and became a soloist with the Royal Ballet in 1970.

Adams, J.J. (Jack) (1895-1968). Hockey player, coach, and manager. Born in Fort William (now Thunder Bay), Ont., he was both an exceptional hockey player and an important coach and manager. He guided the Detroit Red Wings to seven STANLEY CUP victories and later headed the Central Professional Hockey League.

Adamson, Gordon S. (b.1904). Architect. Born in Orangeville, Ont., he trained at the University of Toronto. He was the first prize-winner in the 1952 competition to design a National Gallery for Ottawa. Among the buildings designed by his firm, Adamson Associates, are the New Academic Building and E.J. Pratt Library at VICTORIA COLLEGE, Toronto (c.1961-2), and the ST LAWRENCE CENTRE FOR THE PERFORMING ARTS, Toronto (1965-70). He was also associated in the design of YORK UNIVERSITY'S Keele St campus.

Adanac. Canada spelled backwards. It was a popular business name before the First World War. Canadian soldiers are buried in the Adanac Military Cemetery at Miraumont, near COURCELETTE, France, which was opened in 1916.

Adario. Fictitious Huron chief of the eighteenth century. Called the prototype of the Noble Savage, Adario was the literary creation of the French traveller and writer Baron de LA HONTAN, who used him as a mouthpiece for his own unorthodox opinions about life in New France.

Adaskin, Harry (b.1901). Violinist and educator. Born in Riga, Latvia, he was brought to Toronto in 1902 and studied at the Toronto Conservatory of Music. He was a violinist with the Toronto Symphony Orchestra (1917-22) and was a founding member of the Hart House String Quartet (1923-38) and a concert soloist. He was professor and head of the Department of Music, University of British Columbia, from 1946 to 1973, when he retired. He introduced CBC TUESDAY NIGHT from 1970 to 1974. He is the brother of Murray and John ADASKIN.

Adaskin, John (1908-64). Cellist, conductor, producer. Born in Toronto, he studied cello with George Bruce, Boris Hambourg, and Leo Smith and conducting with Luigi von Kunitz. He was a cellist with the Toronto Symphony Orchestra (1925-36) and the CBC String Orchestra (1926-35). For the CBC he produced over 4,000 radio programs, among them SINGING STARS OF TOMORROW (1944-58) and The HAPPY GANG. He was the brother of Harry and Murray ADASKIN. See also JOHN ADASKIN MEMORIAL AWARD.

Adaskin, Murray (b.1906). Composer. Born in Toronto, he studied violin there and later in New York and Paris. A member of various musical groups and orchestras, including the Toronto Symphony Orchestra (1926-37), he studied composition with John WEINZWEIG, Charles Jones, and Darius Milhaud before becoming a composer. In 1952 he became professor of music and head of the department at the University of Saskatchewan and in 1966 became composer-in-residence until he retired in 1973. Unlike much contemporary music, his work is conservative and lyrical in character (*Serenade Concertante*, 1954; *Fanfare*, 1970). He has used Canadian folklore themes in the *Algonquin Symphony* (1958) and *There Is My People Sleeping* (1970), both for orchestra. He married Frances JAMES in 1931. He and his wife live in Victoria, B.C. He is the brother of Harry and John ADASKIN.

Address, Styles of. *Honourable.* All members of the PRIVY COUNCIL of Canada are styled 'Honourable' and may use the initials 'P.C.' after their names. Members of the Privy Council include all cabinet ministers, past and present, and speakers of the Senate and the House of Commons, plus appointed civilians. In addition, all senators, all premiers and members of the executive councils of provinces, and all justices of the superior courts of Canada and of the provinces are styled 'Honourable'.

Right Honourable. The prime minister of Canada, the chief justice of Canada, and all members of the United Kingdom Privy Council are styled 'Right Honourable'.

Excellency. The style of address for the governor general of Canada.

Adieu Alouette Series. Twelve documentary films about contemporary Quebec society and stereotypes, produced by the NFB in 1972-3. Under the direction of Ian McLaren and with musical introductions by Robert CHARLEBOIS, they examine respectively: theatre (Michel TREMBLAY and André Brassard); the church; journalism (*Le* DEVOIR from Henri BOURASSA to Claude Ryan, in two parts); *haute cuisine* (Le Club Prosper Montagné); community action (at Beauharnois and St-Hubert near Montreal); hockey (Les Nordiques de Québec); film-making; women; humour (Yvon DESCHAMPS); village life (Roch CARRIER on the village of Ste-Justine); and popular music (Gilles VIGNEAULT). 30 min., b & w.

Adm. Official abbreviation of Admiral.

Administrator of the Government of Canada. Title of the governor general's replacement in case of illness, absence (for 30 days or more), or death. In any one of these events the chief justice of Canada, or the senior judge (or next senior judge) of the Supreme Court of Canada, becomes administrator of the Government of Canada and may be addressed as 'His Excellency' for the duration of the appointment.

Adventures of Pierre Radisson. An independently produced CBC-TV series that was dubbed 'Canada's answer to Davy Crockett'. It starred Jacques Godin as Pierre-Esprit RADISSON, the seventeenth-century adventurer in New France, and was filmed in both French and English on Île Perrot in the St Lawrence R., south of Montreal. The executive producer was Jean-Yves Bigras, the writer John Lucarotti. The first half-hour episode appeared on 9 Feb. 1957. The series was sold in the United States, where it was called 'Tomahawk'.

Adventures of Tugboat Annie. A situation comedy produced in Toronto and shown on CBC-TV. The weekly 30-minute programs starred two American actors—Minerva Urecal and Walter Sande as Annie Brennan and

her business rival, Captain Horatio Bullwinkle, characters created by Norman Reilly Raine while he was a writer for MACLEAN'S. The series was launched on 14 Oct. 1957 but failed to catch on.

AECL. Initials of ATOMIC ENERGY OF CANADA LIMITED.

Aerial Experiment Association. Organization founded by Alexander Graham BELL and others to develop 'a practical aerodrome or flying machine driven through the air by its own power and carrying a man'. The other founders were F.W. (Casey) Baldwin, Glen Curtiss, J.A.D. McCurdy, and Thomas Selfridge. Baldwin (1882-1948) was born in Toronto and in 1908 became the first British subject to fly an airplane. He specialized in the study of hydrofoils and became internationally known for such work. He also sat in the Nova Scotia legislature. McCurdy (1886-1961) was born in Baddeck, N.S., and was lieutenant-governor of that province from 1947 to 1952. Although the association was short-lived—from 1907 to 1909—it oversaw the design, production, and testing of CYGNET I, JUNE BUG, RED WING, SILVER DART, and WHITE WING. Former members of the association also built the HYDRODROME-4.

AFC. See AIR FORCE CROSS.

AFM. See AIR FORCE MEDAL.

After the Bath. Painting by Paul PEEL. It is a glowing, sentimental, much-reproduced picture of two naked children standing before a fire. It was coveted by Sarah Bernhardt when first shown in Paris. (1890, AGO)

Agaguk. A novel by Yves THÉRIAULT published in 1958. A story of love and fatherhood among the Eskimos of the Eastern Arctic, it depicts Agaguk's development to maturity and the various conflicts he has with the whites, with his own tribe, and with his harsh environment. It was translated into English by Miriam Chapin in 1963.

AGH. Initials of the ART GALLERY OF HAMILTON.

Agira. Town in Sicily, the scene of severe fighting during the SECOND WORLD WAR, where the 1st Canadian Infantry Division under Maj.-Gen. (later Lt-Gen.) G.G. SIMONDS fought with the British Eighth Army. The last major action of the Division was in the Salso valley from 2 to 6 Aug. 1943. The fighting ended on 17 Aug. with the capture of Messina by American infantry.

Agnes Etherington Art Centre. Art gallery at Queen's University, Kingston, Ont. Located in Windburn, the former home of Agnes Etherington, who gave her estate to the university to be used as a community art gallery in 1957, it boasts a permanent collection that contains contemporary regional art, a survey of historical Canadian art, international graphics, and several representative European works.

AGO. Initials of the ART GALLERY OF ONTARIO.

Agostini, Lucio (b.1913). Pop composer, conductor, arranger. Born in Fano, Italy, he was brought to Canada in 1916, and at 16 was the first cellist with the MONTREAL SYMPHONY ORCHESTRA. Over a 35-year career he became Canada's foremost arranger, composer, and conductor in the broadcasting world, in charge of the music for such major programs as 'Pick the Stars', JULIETTE, and FRONT PAGE CHALLENGE. See also SARAH BINKS.

Agricultural and Rural Development Act. See Department of REGIONAL ECONOMIC EXPANSION.

Agriculture, Department of. Federal government department. It has been in existence since 1867 and is concerned with all aspects of agriculture: research, storage and transportation of grain, farm income and price stability. Among other activities, it operates the CANADIAN GRAIN COMMISSION.

Agyhagayu (b.1937). Eskimo sculptor and printmaker at CAPE DORSET. His first stonecut, *Wounded Caribou*, is one of the most successful Eskimo prints.

Ahearn, T. Franklin (1866-1962). Hockeyteam owner. The Ottawa sportsman assembled and owned an outstanding professional hockey team, the Ottawa Senators, which in 1926-7 won the STANLEY CUP and included many all-time great players. Franklin was elected a member of the Hockey HALL OF FAME in 1962.

AIB. Initials of the Anti-Inflation Board, a regulatory body established by the federal government on 16 Oct. 1975 to apply a program of guidelines to restrict inflationary increases in wages and prices.

Air Canada. Government-owned airline. Established in 1937 as Trans-Canada Air Lines (TCA), the Crown corporation became Air Canada effective 1 Jan. 1965. Seasoned air travellers recall the following TCA and Air Canada planes in particular: DC-3, NORTH STAR (DC-4), LOCKHEED LODESTAR, LOCKHEED SUPER CONSTELLATION, DC-8, DC-9, VANGUARD, and VISCOUNT. In fleet size Air Canada is the eighth-largest airline in the world, flying DC-

8s, DC-9s, Lockheed L1011s, and Boeing 727s and 747s, and carrying passengers and cargo across the country and to Europe, the United States, and the West Indies.

Air Command. One of five functional commands of the CANADIAN ARMED FORCES. It assumed the roles of the Air Defence and Air Transport Commands.

Air Force Cross. Commonwealth decoration for acts of courage or gallantry while flying, but not in the presence of the enemy. It was first awarded to commissioned officers of the Royal Air Force in 1918. The abbreviation is AFC.

Air Force Medal. Commonwealth decoration for acts of courage while flying, but not in the presence of the enemy. It was first awarded to non-commissioned officers and men in the Royal Air Force in 1918. The abbreviation is AFM.

Air of Death. A controversial, award-winning CBC-TV special. The 60-minute documentary, which pre-empted the 'Ed Sullivan Show' on 22 Oct. 1967, dealt with the problems of pollution and charged that the area of Dunville, Ont., suffered an excess of fluoride emission. It was written by George SALVERSON, produced by Larry Gosnell, and hosted and narrated by Stanley BURKE. An Ontario legislative committee met to investigate the accuracy of the charge. In May 1970 a special committee of the CRTC found the program useful and well researched. It has never been rerun.

Air Post. See ALL UP MAIL.

Air Transport Command. See CANADIAN ARMED FORCES.

Aird Commission. A royal commission, chaired by the Toronto banker Sir John Aird, to examine 'the broadcasting situation in the Dominion of Canada'. Appointed on 6 Dec. 1928, it tabled its influential report on 11 Sept. 1929. To promote national unity and combine commercial and non-commercial broadcasting interests, it recommended the creation of a public body that would both regulate private broadcasters and broadcast its own programs. This came about with the creation of the CANADIAN RADIO BROADCASTING COMMISSION in 1932.

Airtransit. See STOL.

Aislin. See Christopher MOSHER.

Aitken, Kate (1891?-1971). Popular lecturer and radio personality. Born in Beeton, Ont., she opened the CNE's first cooking school in

1923. 'Mrs. A.' was a popular broadcaster from 1934 until her retirement in 1957. She wrote a lively column on her travels and thoughts for the GLOBE AND MAIL and published several popular books, including a cook book and her memoirs, *Never a Day So Bright* (1956).

Aitken, Max. See Lord BEAVERBROOK.

Aitken, Robert (b.1939). Flutist and composer. Born in Kentville, N.S., at 19 he became principal flutist of the Vancouver Symphony Orchestra. Later he studied composition in Vancouver and Toronto and the flute with Jean-Pierre Rampal in Europe. He has been a member of the CBC Symphony Orchestra (1959-64) and the Toronto Symphony Orchestra, of which he was co-principal flutist (1965-70), and has concertized internationally. He is an associate professor in the Faculty of Music, University of Toronto, and musical director of the New Music Concerts. His compositions are characterized by experimentation: *Noësis* (1963) and *Music for 'Hamlet'* (1964) employ electronic sound.

Akeeaktashuk (1898-1954). Eskimo sculptor of Arctic Quebec. A Port Harrison artist and hunter, he was one of the first Inuit sculptors to achieve individual recognition. His carving *Hunter with Harpoon* has been widely reproduced.

Aksunait. Eskimo word for 'hail' or 'farewell' in northern Quebec and Labrador. The exclamation is said to mean, literally, 'keep on'.

Alarie, Pierrette (b.1921). Coloratura soprano. Born in Montreal, she studied singing there and with Elisabeth Schumann in Philadelphia. She sang with the Metropolitan Opera, New York, from 1945 to 1947 and thereafter pursued her career in Europe, where she sang with the leading opera companies, including the Opéra Comique, and Paris Opéra, Glyndebourne, and La Scala. She also sang frequently in Canada on radio and television and made numerous recordings. She married the distinguished tenor Léopold SIMONEAU in 1946.

Alaska Boundary Award. The United States purchased Alaska from Russia in 1867, but the boundary remained unclear and this became contentious during the Klondike Gold Rush in 1896, when Canada wanted possession of land at the head of the Lynn Inlet for easy access to the Yukon. The matter was settled in 1903—by three American, one British, and two Canadian commissioners—largely in favour of American interests, a decision that enraged the Canadian public.

Alaska Highway. An all-weather gravel highway built by the United States Army in 1942-3. Almost 1,600 mi. long, extending from Dawson Creek, B.C., to Fairbanks, Alaska, the Alcan Highway connects Fort St George, Fort Nelson, and Whitehorse and was constructed as a military road to supply the forces in Alaska during the Second World War. The part of the highway located within Canada (more than 1,200 mi.) came under Canadian control in Apr. 1946.

Albani, Emma (1847-1930). Soprano. Born Marie Louise Cécile Lajeunesse in Chambly, Que., she moved with her family to Albany, N.Y. (whence her stage name may have derived), and studied singing in Paris and Milan. She made her London début at Covent Garden in 1872 and thereupon pursued a highly successful career until she retired in 1906. She then performed in dance halls before her second and last retirement in 1909. She married Ernest Gye, the son of her impresario.

Alberta. The most westerly of the Prairie Provinces, bounded by British Columbia on the west, the 60th parallel on the north, Saskatchewan on the east, and the 45th parallel on the south. Its name was originally given to the southwestern administrative district of the NORTHWEST TERRITORIES in 1882 (covering most of the southern half of present-day Alberta). As a result of heavy immigration at the turn of the century, Alberta was created a province with its present boundaries in 1905, but control of public lands and natural resources was retained by the federal government until 1930.

With the discovery of large deposits of petroleum and natural gas after 1946 (see LEDUC), the provincial economy has changed from being primarily dependent on agriculture to being resource oriented. This in turn has led to the growth of manufacturing and service industries, concentrated mainly in the major cities of EDMONTON and CALGARY. Alberta has a land area of 248,800 sq. mi., and a population in 1971 of 1,627,874. Its capital is Edmonton; it has no official motto.

Alberta, District of. Area in western Canada created in 1882 as a provisional district of the NORTHWEST TERRITORIES. In 1905 it became part of the province of ALBERTA.

Alberta Heritage Day. See CIVIC HOLIDAY.

Alberta Non-Fiction Award. Annual literary award made to the author of a book concerned with Alberta published in the previous year. With a value of $1,000, it was instituted in 1973 by the government of Alberta

7

Alberta Non-Fiction Award

'to give tangible recognition to Alberta's established authors'.

Alberta Novelist Competition. See SEARCH-FOR-A-NEW-ALBERTA-NOVELIST COMPETITION.

Alberta Tar Sands. See ATHABASKA TAR SANDS.

Albertite. A jet-black bituminous mineral found in Albert Co., N.B. It yields oil and gas and is used as fuel.

Albertosaurus. A giant carnivorous dinosaur of 60 million years ago, similar to the famed *Tyrannosaurus rex*. It walked upright on massive hind legs and reached a length of over 30 ft. Its scientific name derives from the discovery of its fossils in the Alberta BADLANDS in 1884.

Alcan Aluminium Limited. One of Canada's largest industrial enterprises. The multinational corporation, with its headquarters in Montreal, engages, through subsidiary and related companies, in all phases of the world aluminum business, on regional and area bases. It was founded in 1928 as Aluminium Limited to acquire most of the subsidiaries of the Aluminum Company of America (Alcoa) outside the United States, of which the Aluminum Company of Canada, Ltd was the largest, and became Alcan Aluminium Limited in 1966. The trademark Alcan was introduced in Canada in 1944 and gradually became the international trademark beginning in 1959. It is a public company with a large Canadian ownership—under 50%. The word 'aluminium' is the international spelling of the metal's name in English, French, German and other languages. (Only in North America is the metal known as 'aluminum'.) The white powdery substance from which the lightweight metal is extracted is called alumina or aluminum oxide. See also ARVIDA, KITIMAT.

Alcan Highway. See ALASKA HIGHWAY.

Alcock, Norman Z. See CANADIAN PEACE RESEARCH INSTITUTE.

Alert. World's most northern settlement. It is a weather station, 518 mi. from the NORTH POLE, on the northern tip of ELLESMERE ISLAND in the Arctic Ocean.

Alert. Sloop built for the Royal Navy at Pembroke, Wales, in 1856, and converted for the Polar expedition of Capt. George Nares in 1875. She was lent in 1884 to the U.S. government for the relief of Greely's Polar expedition and borrowed by the Canadian government from 1885 to 1894, for use as a

lighthouse supply ship. She was sold for scrapping in 1895.

Alexander, Lord (1891-1969). GOVERNOR GENERAL of Canada from 1946 to 1952.

Alexander Graham Bell National Historic Park. See BADDECK.

Alexander Trophy, The Viscount. See SPORTS FEDERATION OF CANADA.

Alexandra Falls. A cataract on the Hay R. in the Northwest Territories. This waterfall descends 160 ft in two drops just before emptying into Great Slave Lake.

Algoma Central and Hudson Bay Railway. A railway in northern Ontario owned by ALGOMA STEEL. Opened in 1901, it transports freight and passengers between Sault Ste Marie and Hearst, Ont. The AC&HB initials have been dubbed 'All Curves and Hills and Bridges'.

Algoma District. See Stephen B. ROMAN.

Algoma Steel Corp. A major steel complex at Sault Ste Marie. Founded in 1902, the fully integrated company had its origins in the efforts of an American promoter, Francis Clergue, to develop the resources of the Sault and Algoma regions of Michigan and Ontario. Clergue's turn-of-the-century dream involved interlocking projects to tap the waterpower resources of the Soo rapids for power, forest products, coal, iron ore, steel mills, railroads, and major cities. Over the years some of Clergue's dreams became realities on both sides of the border. The 'last of the multimillionaires', Sir James Dunn (1875-1956), was the key figure in putting together in 1935 the basic structure of what is today Algoma Steel Corp. Early operations of the steel complex were closely tied to supplying steel for railroad construction. It now produces a wide range of iron and steel products as well as sintered iron ore, commonly known as Algoma Sinter. Canadian Pacific Investments is the largest shareholder, with a controlling interest of more than 50%.

Algonkian. The most widespread linguistic family of Indians in North America. The various groups moved within circumscribed areas in most of Canada south of the tundra from the Rockies to the Atlantic. The Algonkian Indians of the eastern woodlands possessed the snowshoe, the toboggan, and the versatile birchbark canoe. From west to east the main Algonkian divisions are BLACKFOOT (Blood, Piegan), CREE (Plains), Cree (Woods), OJIBWA, Ottawa, ALGONKIN, MONTAGNAIS-

NASKAPI, Abenake, MICMAC, and Malecite. The Algonkian population in 1970 was 153,594.

Algonkin. ALGONKIAN-speaking Indians who inhabited the Ottawa R. valley.

Algonquin. French name for ALGONKIN Indians.

Algonquin Provincial Park. Ontario's oldest park. Created in 1893, it is on the southern edge of the Canadian Shield, between Georgian Bay and the Ottawa R. Its 2,910 sq. mi. include forests, lakes, and rivers, with facilities for canoeing, hiking, and camping. To interpret nature its educational program maintains a park museum, conducts hikes and a lecture series, and publishes a weekly bulletin called the *Raven*.

All About Us. A play written by Len PETERSON for the CANADIAN PLAYERS' tour of 1964-5. Subtitled 'A New Canadian Vaudeville Play', and made up of snippets of Canadian history treated sarcastically, it was directed by John HIRSCH.

All Canadian Congress of Labour. An association founded to bring together all unions not identified with the international trade-union movement as represented by the AMERICAN FEDERATION OF LABOR and the TRADES AND LABOUR CONGRESS OF CANADA. Founded on 16 Mar. 1927, the ACCL became the CANADIAN CONGRESS OF LABOUR in 1940.

All Red Route. Scheme to supply sea and rail services around the world under the British flag. Long an imperial dream, it became feasible in July 1889 when the British government awarded the Pacific mail contract to the CP LINE. Although discussed at the Ottawa Conference of 1894, and proposed by Sir Wilfrid LAURIER at the Colonial Conference of 1907, the All Red Route, for reasons of capital, never became a reality.

All Up Mail. Philatelic term in use since 1 July 1949, when the Post Office arranged for all domestic first-class mail, and not just mail designated Air Post, to be carried by air when such service expedited its delivery.

Allan, Andrew (1907-74). Actor and director. Born in Scotland and raised in Australia, he came to Canada in 1926. He joined CBC Radio in Vancouver (1939-43) and served as a supervisor of radio drama in Toronto (1943-62). He is remembered for the CBC STAGE series of live dramas, which he created in 1943. He served as artistic director of the SHAW FESTIVAL from 1963 to 1965. His talks and autobiographical sketches were published in *Andrew Allan: A Self-Portrait* (1974).

Allan, Sir Hugh (1810-82). Scots-born financier and founder of the ALLAN LINE. He came to Canada in 1826, settling in Montreal, where in 1831 he joined a shipbuilding firm that he subsequently reorganized and of which he eventually became the head. A promoter of the CPR, he was awarded a contract by the Macdonald government to build the railway, but disclosure of his large election contributions to the Conservatives resulted in the PACIFIC SCANDAL. He was the builder of RAVENSCRAG.

Allan, Sir Hugh Montague (1860-1951). Montreal-born financier and donor of the ALLAN CUP and RAVENSCRAG. He was the son of Sir Hugh ALLAN.

Allan, Ted (b.1916). Author and playwright. 'Ted Allan' is the *nom de plume* of Montreal-born writer Alan Herman, who fought in the Spanish Civil War and, following the Second World War, settled in London, Eng., where he writes for radio, television, and the stage. His Spanish experience is treated in his autobiographic novel *This Time a Better Earth* (1939). With Sydney Gordon, a Canadian-born Communist now living in East Germany, he wrote *The Scalpel, The Sword* (1952; rev. 1971), the biography of Dr Norman BETHUNE and the most widely translated of all Canadian books. An unpublished collection of stories about the author's boyhood on ST URBAIN ST, Montreal, in the 1920s is the basis of the popular film LIES MY FATHER TOLD ME (1975), in which Allan makes a cameo appearance as an elderly Marxist.

Allan Cup. An award emblematic of 'the senior amateur hockey championship of Canada'. It was named after Sir Hugh Montague ALLAN, who donated the silver bowl in 1908. Since 1928 it has been awarded by the Canadian Amateur Hockey Association to the winning amateur team. Its professional counterpart is the STANLEY CUP. See also SENIOR A.

Allan Gardens. A 13-acre botanical garden in downtown Toronto, containing floral displays, fountains, and greenhouses. Originally a 5-acre park donated to the Toronto Horticultural Society by the Honourable George W. Allan, it opened in 1860. The Horticultural Gardens—as they were then called—were turned over to the city in 1888 and renamed Allan Gardens in 1901.

Allan Line. Well-known fleet of steamships owned and operated by the Allan family of Montreal. Sir Hugh ALLAN was awarded the Atlantic mail contract by the Canadian government in 1855, and the following year the

Allan Line

Allan Royal Mail Line began fortnightly (then weekly) sailings between Liverpool and Quebec City. The tricolour of the Allan Line Steamship Co. was raised in 1897. The line operated in the Atlantic and Pacific and even scheduled sailings to South America. The company was taken over in 1915 by its principal competitor, the CP LINE, which gradually amalgamated the two services. But it was not until 1931 that the Allan Line ceased to exist as a corporate body. Among its well-known ships were BUENOS AYREAN, CANADA, CANADIAN, EMPRESS OF FRANCE, and PARISIAN.

Allen, Ralph (1913-66). Journalist and editor. Born in Oxbow, Sask., he worked for the *Winnipeg Free Press* and the Toronto *Globe and Mail*, and served with the Canadian army. He was editor of MACLEAN'S from 1950 to 1960 and inspired a generation of journalists with his fairness and high writing standards. His last years were spent with the *Toronto Star*. He wrote a satire on the CBC, *The* CHARTERED LIBERTINE (1954), among other books. Christina Newman edited *The Man from Oxbow: The Best of Ralph Allen* (1967).

Allen, Robert Thomas (b.1911). Journalist and author. Born in Toronto and educated at the Central Technical School, he has worked for the *Globe and Mail* and *Maclean's*. Since 1948 he has been a free-lance writer of light comic pieces for magazines. He is the author of many books, including *When Toronto Was for Kids* (1961), and was the editor of *A Treasury of Canadian Humour* (1968).

Allen's Theatres. Early motion-picture theatre chain. It was begun by three young American brothers, Jule, Jay-Jay, and Herbert Allen, who opened their Theatorium in Brantford, Ont., in 1906. At the end of the First World War they claimed their theatre circuit was the largest in the Canada. After Adolph Zukor of Paramount withdrew the franchise for his films from the Allens' distributing company—perhaps in a move to acquire Allen's Theatres—he established FAMOUS PLAYERS Canadian Corporation Ltd as a rival circuit, assisted by N.L. Nathanson. The interests of Allen's Theatres were now over-extended, for they had acquired theatres in Cleveland and Detroit, and the company went bankrupt. In 1928 the Allen brothers formed Premier Operating Corporation, in partnership with Famous Players, to operate theatres in small towns in Ontario. Premier now owns 58 theatres, including seven under construction, and is headed by Barry Allen, the son of Herbert Allen.

Alligator Pie. Poetry collection for children written by Dennis LEE, with illustrations by Frank NEWFELD, and published in 1974. It is an attractive book of nonsense rhymes and verses that have an underlying ring of sense.

Alline, Henry (1748-84). Preacher. Born in Newport, R.I., he was brought as a child to Falmouth, N.S. He toured Nova Scotia and what later became New Brunswick as an itinerant evangelist, inspiring a religious revival known as the 'New Light' movement. Many of his converts became Free Christian Baptists when Alline returned to New England the year before his death. His *Life and Journals* (1806) appeared posthumously.

Allo Police. A French-language tabloid published weekly in Montreal. It specializes in a sensational coverage of crime and sex news. The title is French for 'Hello, Police'. Almost single-handedly it made a cult figure of the criminal Richard BLASS.

Allward, Walter Seymour (1876-1955). Sculptor. Born in Toronto, he had no formal art training but learned to model ornamental figures in terra cotta when he worked for a brick company and later became an architect's apprentice. In 1896 he became a sculptor when he won a competition for a monument to the NORTH WEST REBELLION for Queen's Park, Toronto. The creator of numerous commemorative monuments, he is mainly remembered for his imposing VIMY MEMORIAL (1936).

Almanacs. In addition to the CANADA YEAR BOOK there are three annually published compilations of information on the country. The largest, with over 900 pages, is the *Canadian Almanac and Directory*, published by Copp Clark since 1847. Next is *The Corpus Almanac of Canada*, issued since 1965, originally by McGraw-Hill and now by Corpus Publishers Services. Appearing in paperback, and under 200 pages, is *The Canadian Pocket Encyclopedia*, published since 1944 by Quick Canadian Facts.

Almighty Voice (1874-97). CREE hero and martyr. A member of a Cree band that resisted white civilization while it struggled with near starvation, he was arrested in 1895 for slaughtering a cow on the reserve near Duck Lake, N.W.T. (the exact circumstances were unclear even at the time). He escaped from prison without violence, but in a show of power shot and killed his original captor and pursuer, Sgt Colebrook of the NORTH WEST MOUNTED POLICE. The Canadian government offered a $500 reward for the capture of Almighty Voice. During the next two years he became an almost mythical figure on the Saskatchewan prairie, symbolizing for his people the plight of the Cree nation. Pursued by North West Mounted Police he drifted from one reservation to another. On 30 May 1897, after visiting his father's cabin, he and two other Indians were cornered and shot to death in a round of fire exchanged with the police. His story is told in Len PETERSON's play *Almighty Voice* (1970); in the film *Alien Thunder* (1973), starring Donald SUTHERLAND as the Cree hero; and in the title story of *Where Is the Voice Coming From?*, by Rudy WIEBE. Howard O'HAGEN's *Wilderness Men* contains the best account of Almighty Voice.

Almond, Paul (b.1931). Film director. Born in Montreal, he studied at McGill and Oxford and travelled with a repertory company in England. Joining CBC-TV in 1954, he directed many productions for FESTIVAL, WOJECK, RCMP, etc. He wrote, directed, and produced ISABEL (1968), ACT OF THE HEART (1970), and *Journey* (1972), three feature films that starred Geneviève BUJOLD to whom he was then married. His films are noted for their mystical and atmospheric qualities.

Alouette. Series of two satellites designed and built in Canada. *Alouette I*, the first satellite designed and built by a nation other than the Soviet Union or the United States, was launched by NASA at Cape Kennedy on 29 Sept. 1962 into a circular orbit 625 mi. above the earth. *Alouette II* was sent into an elliptical orbit, from 320 to 1,800 mi. up, on 29 Nov. 1965. Both satellites were designed to explore the ionosphere and transmit 'radar maps' back to earth. The satellites were no doubt named after the popular French-Canadian folksong 'ALOUETTE'.

'Alouette'. A French folksong extremely popular in French Canada. The enumerative song begins: '*Alouette, gentille alouette,/Alouette, je t'y plumerai*' ('Alouette, gentle Alouette,/Alouette, I'll pluck your feathers yet'). Marius BARBEAU writes that 'this playful rigmarole' has 'grown into the most popular of the Canadian repertory'. An *alouette* is a meadowlark.

Alphabet. Literary magazine published by James REANEY in London, Ont. It appeared twice a year between 1960 and 1971. Reaney himself edited, designed, handset, printed, and distributed each issue, which was devoted to the presentation of a mythopoetic theme.

Alta. Abbreviation of ALBERTA.

Aluminum Company of Canada, Ltd. See ALCAN ALUMINIUM LIMITED.

A/M. Official abbreviation of Air Marshal.

Ambassador. The highest-ranking diplomatic representative sent by one non-Commonwealth country to another. In 1975 Canada maintained embassies (resident and non-resident) in 101 countries. See also HIGH COMMISSIONER, CONSUL.

Ambassador Bridge. A 1,850-ft bridge that spans the Detroit R. between Windsor, Ont., and Detroit, Mich., erected in 1929.

Ambrose, Tommy (b.1939). Country, gospel, pop, and jazz singer. Born in Toronto, he was a child gospel-singer and by his early twenties had his own CBC-TV show. He sang jazz and blues in clubs and, in 1975, was the star of CBC-TV's 'Celebration'. With lyricist Gary Gray, he has written 'A Point of View' (1974), the GLOBAL TELEVISION NETWORK's theme song, and 'People City' (1975), a quasi-official Toronto theme song.

AMCRO. Partial acronym of Automatic Machine Control by Recorded Action, the name chosen in 1947 by the Toronto-based industrial inventor E.W. Leaver for his invention—the world's first automatically controlled machine tool with a memory system.

Amelia Frances Howard-Gibbon Medal. Annual award made to encourage the publication of well-illustrated children's books in Canada. It was first presented in 1971 by the Canadian Association of Children's Librarians to the artist who best illustrated a book published the previous year. The medal commemorates Amelia Frances Howard-Gibbon (1826-74), an Englishwoman who, while living in Sarnia, Ont., in 1859 drew 'An Illustrated Alphabet', Canada's first picture-book. The manuscript, in the OSBORNE COLLECTION OF EARLY CHILDREN'S BOOKS, was published as *An Illustrated Comic Alphabet* in 1966.

Ameliasburg. Township and village in Prince Edward County, eastern Ontario, settled by Loyalists. It is the home, and frequent subject in his writings, of the poet Al PURDY.

Amerindian. Composite word derived from 'American Indian'. Referring to all the original peoples of North and South America, including Eskimo and Aleut, it is a less ambiguous word than 'Indian' and is frequently abbreviated to 'Amerind'. It may also refer to any of the indigenous languages of the aboriginal peoples. However, it is falling into disuse—at least in ethnographic circles.

11

Amex Canada

Amex Canada. Bimonthly publication concerned with those issues that involve American WAR RESISTERS in Canada. The title of the magazine, which was founded in Toronto in Sept. 1968, is a contraction of 'American' and 'exiles'.

Amherst, Jeffrey, Baron (1717-97). British general. Commander of the expedition that took LOUISBOURG in 1758, he became commander-in-chief of the British forces in North America and took Ticonderoga in 1759. After accepting the surrender of Montreal in 1760, he was made governor general of British North America. He was recalled to England in 1763 after failing to put down the uprising led by PONTIAC.

Amiens. City in northern France near which the Allies won a notable victory and gained the initiative in the struggle with Germany in the FIRST WORLD WAR. The British Fourth Army, the French First Army, the Australian Corps, and the CANADIAN CORPS joined in the general offensive from 8 to 11 Aug. 1918. By 20 Aug. the Canadian Corps had penetrated 14 mi., on a frontage that had widened from 7,500 yards to 10,000 yards, and captured 9,000 prisoners and nearly 200 guns.

Amiituk, Davidialuk (b.1910). Eskimo carver and printmaker, known as 'Davidialuk' or 'Davideealuk'. A POVUNGNITUK artist, considered by many to be a mystic, he depicts stories and legends in his prints and carves strong fantastic figures. He sometimes signs his work 'Big David'.

Amnesty question. Bitter subject of contention after the RED RIVER REBELLION of 1869-70. Amnesty was promised to Louis RIEL and his insurgents in Dec. 1869, but this was opposed in the east when public opinion in Ontario was inflamed over the execution of Thomas SCOTT in Mar. 1870. The amnesty finally granted in Jan. 1875 was a partial one for Riel, Ambroise Lépine, and W.B. O'Donoghue, all of whom were to be pardoned only after five-year's banishment.

Amundsen, Roald (1872-1928). Norwegian Arctic explorer. In 1903 he set sail on the GJOA through Lancaster Sound, spent two winters at Gjoa Haven and a third near Herschel Island, after passing through Queen Maud Gulf, Coronation Gulf, and Amundsen Gulf into the Beaufort Sea. He entered Bering Strait in 1906 and reached Nome, Alaska, on 13 Aug. to complete his negotiation—the first—of the NORTHWEST PASSAGE.

Amyot, Frank (1904-62). Champion paddler. Born in Ottawa, he won six senior Canadian paddling championships. He represented

Canada at the 1936 Olympics in Berlin, where he became Canada's only gold medalist in paddling in Olympic history.

Anahareo. See GREY OWL.

Anaija (b.1913). Eskimo sculptor at SPENCE BAY. He specializes in whalebone sculptures.

Anansi Press, House of. Book publisher specializing in new poetry and fiction. It was founded in Toronto by Dave GODFREY and Dennis LEE in 1967 and named after the African spider-god. It has paid special attention to Quebec writers and has published their novels, plays, and poems in translation.

Anatomy of Criticism. An important book of literary criticism, published in 1957, that helped to establish Northrop FRYE's international reputation as a scholar and critic. Subtitled 'Four Essays', it examines the nature and use of symbol and myth in literature, exploring techniques and methods of criticism in its various modes: historical, ethical, archetypal, and rhetorical.

Anciens Canadiens, Les. Historical novel written by Philippe-Joseph AUBERT DE GASPÉ in 1863 when the author was 73 years old. Based on the burning of the manor house of Saint-Jean-Port-Joli by British troops during the SEVEN YEARS' WAR, it has as its protagonists a French Canadian and a Scot. The story is interspersed with legends, folklore, information about social customs, and other digressions. This classic of French-Canadian literature was translated by Charles G.D. ROBERTS under the title *Canadians of Old* (1890).

Ancre Heights. Ridge above the Ancre R., a tributary of the SOMME, in northern France. It was the scene of much fighting during the latter part of the Battles of the Somme in Oct. and Nov. 1916, which ended when the Fourth Canadian Division took the REGINA TRENCH on 11 Nov. 1916.

Anderson, Patrick (b.1915). Poet. Born in England and educated at Oxford and Columbia, he taught in Montreal between 1940 and 1950, when he returned to England and commenced a new career as a writer of travel books and as the headmaster of a public school. A founder of PREVIEW in 1942, he published three volumes of richly metaphoric poems: *A Tent for April* (1945), *The White Centre* (1946), and *The Colour as Naked* (1953). Inspired by a later generation's interest in his work, he revised his early poems and included them with new ones in *A Visiting Distance* (1976).

André, Brother (1845-1937). Religious mystic. Born Alfred Bissette in St Grégoire d'Iberville, C.E. (Que.), he was a barely educated labourer and school caretaker until, in middle age, he joined the Congregation of the Holy Cross as a lay brother and gained a reputation for piety and for healing miracles. He received permission to build a small shrine to St Joseph, his patron saint, on Mount Royal in Montreal. Before his death it was visited by three million pilgrims, many of whom claimed to be cured of illnesses and physical handicaps. Construction of the present church, known as ST JOSEPH'S ORATORY, which now incorporates the chapel, was begun in 1924. Brother André's preserved heart was stolen from the Oratory in Mar. 1973 and recovered in the basement of a Montreal house in Dec. 1974.

Andrew Allan Award. Awarded annually by ACTRA for the best performance by an actor or actress in radio during the previous year. It was named after the distinguished actor and director, Andrew ALLAN, who died in 1974.

Andrews, John (b.1934). Architect. Born near Sydney, Australia, he studied at the University of Sydney and at Harvard. After a design done with three other students was placed among the finalists in the 1959 competition for the new TORONTO CITY HALL, he joined the John B. PARKIN office in Toronto. His work includes Scarborough College, University of Toronto (1965)—a design in which the massing of the building's poured concrete both extends the contours of the cliff-site and melts into them. He also became involved with the design for the Metro Centre project in Toronto (c.1972-4).

Anerca. Eskimo word meaning 'to breathe' (pronounced 'aniksa'). Edmund Carpenter, in the preface to his collection of Eskimo poems called *Anerca* (1959), relates the word to the verb 'to make poetry' and also to 'soul', which is *aniningnik* in Eskimo.

Angakok. Eskimo word for SHAMAN, conjurer, curer, or medicine man.

Angers, Félicité (1845-1924). Quebec novelist. Born in La Malbaie, C.E. (Que.), she wrote under the pseudonym Laure Conan and is regarded as the first French-Canadian woman novelist. Her best novel is considered to be *Angéline de Montbrun* (1884)— translated into English by Yves Brunelle and published under the same title in 1975.

Anglais, Les. 'The English'. Phrase used by French Canadians to refer to English Canadians.

Anglican Church of Canada. It was formed from the Church of England in Canada, which carried on mission work across the country from earliest British colonial times. In 1971 it had 2,543,175 adherents, most of them in cities and of Irish and English ethnic background. The church is broad in its appeal, with some congregations having a Catholic tradition of liturgical worship and sacramental life while others are more Protestant in their emphasis on evangelical preaching and hymn singing.

Anglo. Abbreviation of 'Anglo-Saxon'. An Anglo is an English-speaking person, especially a Canadian of British origin, in the usage of French Canadians and some English Canadians.

Anglo-Saxons, Les. Term applied in Quebec, mistakenly, to all English-speaking Canadians.

Anglophone. A noun or adjective, it refers to a person whose active, prime language is English, and to a region where the language of major practical use is English. The word has several shades of meaning; it also suggests an English-speaking inhabitant of a country where English is only one of two or more official languages—such as Canada or many African nations. The adjective *anglophonic*, meaning attuned to English, was first used in the Aug. 1968 issue of *Maclean's*. Anglophone grew out of the prior use of FRANCOPHONE.

Anguhadluk, Marion Tudluq (b.1910). Eskimo artist, popularly known as 'Tudluq'. Working at BAKER LAKE, she is an active maker of wall-hangings. Her work was chosen for inclusion in the World Crafts Council's travelling exhibition 'In Praise of Hands' in 1974.

Anguhadluq, Luke (born c.1894). Eskimo printmaker at BAKER LAKE. Sometimes called 'the Grand Old Man of Baker Lake', he is among the most prolific of graphic artists. As a camp leader among the Back R. people of Chantrey Inlet, where he was born, he portrays activities of camp life, such as hunting and fishing, in multi-directional drawings that can often be displayed at different angles. His style is reminiscent of prehistoric Eskimo engravings.

Anhalt, István (b.1919). Composer. Born in Hungary, he studied in Budapest with Zoltan Kodaly and in Paris with Nadia Boulanger before coming to Canada in 1949. He has since taught at McGill University and Queen's University, where he is head of the Music Department. His massive, intricate works are rooted in Schoenberg's 12-tone composition theories. He has also experimented with electronic music. Some of his major pieces are *Fantasia* (1954) for piano; and *Symphony No 1* (1958), *Symphony of Modules* (1967), and *Foci* (1969) for voice and instrumental ensemble.

Anik. Series of three satellites, known as *Anik I*, *Anik II*, and *Anik III*, designed and built by TELESAT CANADA. *Anik I*, launched by NASA at Cape Kennedy on 9 Nov. 1972, maintains a stationary orbit rotating with the earth at 114° W at an altitude of 22,300 mi. The world's first geostationary communications satellite designed for domestic commercial use, it provides telephone communication in the north, supplements existing microwave systems in the south, and improves television transmission across Canada. To extend this service, two virtually identical satellites were launched into similar orbits: *Anik II* on 20 Apr. 1973 and *Anik III* on 7 May 1975. *Anik* is an Eskimo word meaning 'brother of a woman'.

Aniksa. See ANERCA.

Anka, Paul (b.1941). Popular singer and songwriter. Born in Ottawa of Syrian ancestry, he wrote and recorded 'Diana' at 15. (This smash hit was inspired by a friend, Diana Ayoub, then 17.) He became a teen idol, then a very successful club entertainer and songwriter—he wrote 'My Way' for Frank Sinatra—in Hollywood, Las Vegas, and on Broadway.

Annapolis-Cornwallis Valley. The beautiful area of western Nova Scotia famed for its association with the ACADIANS, its scenic attractiveness, and relatively prosperous mixed farming, particularly apple production.

Annapolis Royal. The name given to the settlement at PORT ROYAL, on the south side of the Equille R., after the French fort was captured by British and New England troops in 1710. It was the capital of Nova Scotia until 1749, when Halifax was founded. See also FORT ANNE NATIONAL HISTORIC PARK.

Anne of Green Gables. One of the most popular children's books ever written. L.M. MONTGOMERY's *Anne of Green Gables* (1908) tells the story of the adoption and education of Anne Shirley, an imaginative orphan, by a strict but kindly brother and sister who live in a farm house called Green Gables on the outskirts of the village of Avonlea, P.E.I. Mark Twain described the novel, which was followed by seven sequels, as 'the sweetest creation of child life yet written'. Two feature films based on it were produced by Hollywood studios. A silent version, starring Mary Miles Minter, was released in 1919. The sound version with Anne Shirley (named after the heroine) appeared in 1934, and was followed in 1941 by a sequel, *Anne of Windy Poplars*. A musical based on the novel—with words by Don HARRON and music by Norman CAMPBELL—was written in 1954. It opened the CHARLOTTETOWN SUMMER FESTIVAL in July 1965 and played at the ROYAL ALEXANDRA THEATRE in Toronto in 1967. In a 1971 New York production, the set was designed by Murray LAUFER.

The fictional community of Avonlea is modelled on the village of Cavendish, on the north shore of Prince Edward Island. The charming green-and-white house the author lived in with her grandparents, after the death of her parents, and where she later wrote this children's classic, is now Canada's most popular literary shrine. Green Gables is part of Cavendish National Park and is visited each year by thousands of tourists.

Annex, The. Area of downtown Toronto 'annexed' by the city in 1883. The Annex extends from Avenue Rd west to Bathurst St and from Bloor St north to the CPR tracks. Many of its large homes became boarding houses after 1945. Albert FRANCK painted Annex houses and Hugh GARNER wrote about Annex life in *The Silence on the Shore* (1962).

Annexation manifesto. Signed in the autumn of 1849 by over 1,000 businessmen and politicians in Montreal, it advocated the annexation of Canada to the United States. Disillusionment with the British connection on the part of those who had been its most ardent supporters was the result of Britain's abandonment of mercantilism (and its system of colonial preferences) and Lord Elgin's signing of the REBELLION LOSSES BILL. It aroused very little interest in the general population, however.

Anonymous, Brother. English translation of the pen-name of 'Frère Untel' (literally, 'Brother Nobody'), adopted by Jean-Paul Desbiens, a Quebec Catholic brother later employed by the curriculum branch of the Quebec Department of Education. Desbiens published two books—*The Impertinences of Brother Anonymous* (1962), translated by Miriam Chapin, and *For Pity's Sake* (1965), translated by Frédéric Côté—that constituted a scathing indictment of the Church-dominated educational system in Quebec. In a sarcastic and readable fashion, Desbiens demanded more freedom from officialdom, higher language standards, increased patriotism, more political awareness, and greater administrative efficiency.

'Another world next door'. Description of NEWFOUNDLAND by its department of tourism in the 1960s.

Anse. French word for 'cove' or 'bay', as in Anse au Foulon (WOLFE'S COVE).

Anse aux Meadows, L'. See L'ANSE AUX MEADOWS.

Anson. A twin-engined training and communications aircraft designed in Britain. A Canadian version for RCAF use was built in 1940 by National Steel Car Co. Ltd at Malton, Ont.

Anthem. A song of praise, especially a patriotic song. The Canadian Parliament has recognized two official anthems: the national anthem ('O CANADA') and the royal anthem ('GOD SAVE THE QUEEN').

Anthology. A CBC Radio series devoted to literature and the arts. The hour-long weekly program has been called 'a radio version of the traditional literary magazine—a kind of QUEEN'S QUARTERLY of the air'. Launched in 1953 and edited by Robert WEAVER, it is now heard on Saturday evenings.

Anti-Confederate. An opponent of CONFEDERATION, especially prior to 1867.

'Anti-Confederation Song, An'. Ballad popular in Newfoundland during the pre-confederation debates in 1864. The first verse runs: 'Hurrah for our own native isle, Newfoundland!/Not a stranger shall hold one inch of its strand!/Her face turns to Britain, her back to the Gulf. Come near at your peril, Canadian Wolf!' Newfoundland remained out of Confederation until 1949.

Anticosti Island. A cigar-shaped island, 140 mi. long, situated in the mouth of the St Lawrence. Until recently the world's largest privately owned island, it was sold in 1975 to the Quebec government by Consolidated Bathurst Limited.

Antigonish Movement. A co-operative, self-help movement with world-wide influence that grew out of an extension program at St Francis Xavier University, Antigonish, N.S. It was begun by Father James J. Tompkins (1870-1955) as a six-week course in group action in 1921. In 1929—through the efforts of the head of the extension department, Father Moses Michael Coady (1882-1959) and others—it helped fishermen and farmers in the Maritimes to establish co-operatives, credit unions, etc. The Coady International Institute, which opened in 1960, trains students from foreign lands (particularly the Third World) in social leadership so that men and women may be 'masters of their own destiny'.

Apostrophe to the Heavenly Hosts, An. Composition for unaccompanied choir, written by Healey WILLAN for the TORONTO MENDELSSOHN CHOIR in 1921. Frequently performed, it typifies the lush strain of his early choral music.

Appalachians. A loose collective term for the mountains of the Maritimes. An extension of the eastern United States range, the rocks range in age from Precambrian to Palaeozoic sediments. The highest peak in eastern Canada is Mount Jacques Cartier in the Gaspé Peninsula, rising to an elevation of 4,160 ft.

Applebaum, Louis (b.1918). Composer and arts administrator. Born and educated in Toronto, he joined the National Film Board in 1941. His score for *The Story of GI Joe* (1945) was nominated for an Academy Award. In 1955-60 he was musical director of the Stratford Festival and from 1960 to 1963 music consultant to CBC Television. He has composed numerous orchestral and choral works and scores for many CBC-TV series, including 'Images of Canada' and 'The National Dream'. In 1971 he was appointed executive director of the Province of Ontario Council for the Arts.

Appleyard, Peter (b.1930). Vibraphonist. Born in England, he started playing with dance bands at 14. He settled in Toronto in 1951 and now tours regularly with such figures as Oscar PETERSON, Frank Sinatra, Ella Fitzgerald, and Count Basie. Since 1960 he has played a 15-week engagement each year at the Sutton Place Hotel, Toronto.

Apprehended insurrection. Notable phrase from the WAR MEASURES ACT, 1914, which grants the federal government extraordinary powers during an emergency. Section 3 states that 'this Act shall be in force during war, invasion, or insurrection, real or apprehended'. The War Measures Act was invoked during the OCTOBER CRISIS of 1970, when the federal government saw in the political kidnappings of Pierre Laporte and James R. Cross an 'apprehended insurrection'.

Apprenticeship of Duddy Kravitz, The. Novel by Mordecai RICHLER published in 1959 and considered to be his best work. Set in the Jewish community on ST URBAIN ST in Montreal, it is an entertaining story of an ambitious and amoral youth who develops into a ruthless manipulator of others. It was made into a film of the same title, with a screenplay by the author (who shared credit with Lionel Chetwynd); it was produced by John Kemeny, directed by Ted Kotcheff, and starred Richard Dreyfuss, with Micheline Lanctot, Joseph Wiseman, and Henry Ramer. Shot on

15

location in the Laurentians and in Montreal, and released in 1973, the film cost $910,000 and was a critical and commercial success. 121 min., colour.

Apps, Sylvanus (Syl) (b.1915). All-round athlete. Born in Paris, Ont., he represented Canada in pole-vaulting at the 1936 Olympic Games in Berlin. The same year he began his professional hockey career with the Toronto Maple Leafs, winning the CALDER MEMORIAL TROPHY as the NHL's best first-year player. He played on three STANLEY CUP winning teams, and more recently was an Ontario MPP and cabinet minister. His son, Sylvanus Apps Jr, is an NHL star player.

Aquin, Hubert (b.1929). Quebec novelist. Born in Montreal and a graduate of the Université de Montréal and the Université de Paris, he has been a film producer for the NATIONAL FILM BOARD and an editor of LIBERTÉ. His revolutionary concerns were expressed in his first novel, PROCHAIN ÉPISODE (1965), published in an English translation by Penny Williams in 1967. Alan BROWN has translated two other novels: *The Antiphonary* (1973) and *Blackout* (1974).

Arbutus, Trailing. See MAYFLOWER.

Arcadian Adventures with the Idle Rich. Stephen LEACOCK'S fifth book, published in 1914, and a favourite with many. It satirizes the pretences of big-city life and its institutions—as SUNSHINE SKETCHES satirized small-town life—and contains the memorable 'The Rival Churches of St Asaph and St Osoph'.

Arcand, Adrien (1899-1967). Montreal fascist leader. An effective speaker and arresting personality, he edited a series of newspapers (including *Le Goglu* in 1929, and *Le Patriote* in 1933) and headed a series of fascist parties (Ordre Patriotique des Goglus in 1929, PARTI NATIONAL SOCIAL CHRÉTIEN in 1934, the National Unity Party in 1939) that promoted anti-Communism, anti-Semitism, pro-Catholicism and pro-French-Canadianism. Interned during the Second World War, he was ineffective thereafter.

Arcand, Denys (b.1941). Quebec film director. Born in Deschambault, Que., he studied history at the Université de Montréal, where he helped direct *Seul ou avec d'autres* (with Dénis HÉROUX, 1962), the first feature of the Quebec 'new wave'. His three dramatic features reflect his social commitment: *La Maudite Galette* (1972), *RÉJEANNE PADOVANI* (1973), and *Gina* (1975). His work has a vivacious sense of humour.

Archaic culture. See CLOVIS CULTURE.

Archambault, Louis (b.1915). Sculptor. Born in Montreal, Que., he graduated from the Université de Montréal and the École des Beaux-Arts, Montreal, where he became a teacher. His works—many of them bird forms—are primarily large-scale commissions in bronze and aluminum. Examples can be seen at the City Hall and airport, Ottawa, and the Toronto International Airport. He has exhibited internationally at the Venice Biennale (1956) and in Milan and Brussels.

Arche, L'. A movement to care for mentally handicapped males in small homes as opposed to large institutions. It was founded by Dr Jean Vanier (b.1928), the son of the late Governor General Georges VANIER, who opened the first home for the mentally handicapped at Trosly-Breuil, a French village north of Paris, in the summer of 1964. In 1969 Daybreak House was opened for the treatment of retarded adults on a farm near Richmond Hill, Ont., and six years later Avoca House was started in downtown Toronto. There are now 15 houses at Trosly-Breuil and more than 50 homes for the handicapped around the world. *Arche* is French for ark, an allusion to Noah's refuge.

Archer, Violet (b.1913). Composer. Born in Montreal, she studied with Claude CHAMPAGNE, Béla Bartók, and Paul Hindemith and received degrees from McGill University and Yale University. She currently teaches at the University of Alberta. Her work includes choral music, chamber pieces, songs, and orchestral music. Prominent among her many compositions are *Fanfare and Passacaglia* (1948-9) and *Prelude-Incantation* (1964) for orchestra, *Sonata for Cello and Pianoforte* (1956), and *Concerto for Piano and Orchestra* (1956).

Archibald, Sir Adams G. (1814-92). A FATHER OF CONFEDERATION. As leader of the Liberal Party in Nova Scotia he attended all three conferences at which the terms of Confederation were discussed and agreed upon. He was later lieutenant-governor (the first) of Manitoba, and of Nova Scotia, and a member of the House of Commons from 1888 to 1891.

Architects of Modern Thought. A series of 30-minute talks on world thinkers by Canadian academics commissioned by CBC Radio. Highlights of the first series included John A. Irving (adviser to the series) on Bertrand Russell and Northrop FRYE on Oswald Spengler. The programs were heard from 1955 to 1962 on 'CBC Wednesday Night' (see CBC TUESDAY NIGHT) and the texts were issued by the CBC in booklet form.

ARCT. Abbreviation of Associateship, ROYAL CONSERVATORY OF MUSIC, a diploma awarded to successful candidates in performance, teaching, or composition.

Arctic, The. The northern polar region between the ARCTIC CIRCLE and the NORTH POLE, characterized by such inhospitable conditions as ice, snow, total darkness (midwinter) or a midnight sun (midsummer). In Canada it is sometimes called the Far North.

Arctic archipelago. A term loosely applied to Canada's Arctic islands and including all the territory between Davis Strait, Baffin Bay, and Kane Basin on the east and the Beaufort Sea on the west. The Queen Elizabeth Islands, including Ellesmere Island, lie farthest north and are separated by McClure Strait and Viscount Melville and Lanscaster Sounds from the islands of the District of Franklin, which include Victoria, Banks, and Prince of Wales Islands. In numerous searches for a NORTHWEST PASSAGE the archipelago was gradually explored and charted over a period of 275 years: FROBISHER sighted Resolution Island off BAFFIN ISLAND in 1576 and Cmdre Robert McClure discovered the western entrance to the Passage (northerly route) in 1850.

Arctic char. Coldwater fish native to Canada's northern waters. Its taste resembles a cross between trout and salmon. The fish was popularized during the Centennial Year. The Eskimo name for arctic char is *ilkalupik*. It is also called *ilkalu*.

Arctic Circle. A parallel of latitude at 66° 32′ N. Situated on the Arctic Circle are Fort Yukon, Alaska, and Repulse Bay, N.W.T. The word Arctic derives from the Greek for 'bear', an allusion to the northern constellation *Ursa Major*, which at this latitude does not set. The Arctic Circle represents the most southerly point where the sun does not rise (22 Dec.) or set (21 June) in a 24-hour period.

Arctic Ocean. By far the smallest of the earth's oceans. It occupies the polar basin between Canada, Siberia, and Greenland and is more than half-covered by the Arctic ice cap.

Arctic sovereignty. The concept that Canada has sovereign jurisdiction over the Arctic between 140° and 60° W longitude. The claim that Canada has sovereignty over the mainland and the islands in the Arctic archipelago is not seriously disputed, but claims to sovereignty over the waters between the islands have not been clearly established, and such claims are resisted by the U.S. government because they would place the NORTHWEST PAS-

SAGE under Canadian jurisdiction. The voyages of the American ship SS MANHATTAN through the Passage in 1969 and 1970 were seen by some as challenges to Canadian sovereignty. Canada has never specifically enclosed the waters of the Arctic archipelago as internal waters but it has extended limited jurisdiction through the Arctic Waters Pollution Prevention Act, passed in Apr. 1970.

Arctic Winter Games. A series of competitive events held every two years for residents NORTH OF SIXTY. Competitors from the Yukon, Northwest Territories, Alaska, New Quebec, and Greenland have been involved in these Games since they were first held in Yellowknife, N.W.T., in Mar. 1970. The fourth series was held in Schefferville, Que., in Feb. 1976. It included winter sports such as hockey, curling, and skiing; other southern-type sports, such as badminton and volleyball; and arctic sports and traditional activities of the native people, such as dog-sledding and drum-dancing. See also NORTHERN GAMES.

Ardnainiq. A mythical people believed by the CENTRAL ESKIMOS to live far to the northwest of them. Franz BOAS wrote that the women are supposed to be of ordinary stature. They hunt in KAYAKS and provide for their husbands who are covered with hair and are so tiny that the women carry them about in their hoods.

Area Code. The telephone industry's three-digit numbering system for long-distance dialing. The decision to change the telephone code for North America from a letter-number system to an all-number system was made in 1959. The Area Code, which precedes the seven-digit telephone number and indicates a specific area, came into effect during the early 1960s. A characteristic of the Area Code is that the second digit is always 0 or 1. For example, the number of the governor general is: 1 (for Long Distance), then 613 (the Area Code for Ottawa), followed by 749 5933 (the telephone number for GOVERNMENT HOUSE). The Area Code for Alberta is 403; British Columbia, 604; Manitoba, 204; New Brunswick, 506; Newfoundland, 709; Saskatchewan, 306. Nova Scotia and Prince Edward Island are both 902; the Northwest Territories and Yukon Territory are both 403, the same as Alberta. Ontario has five Area Codes: 416, 519, 613, 705, 807; Quebec has three: 418, 514, 819.

Argillite. A scarce, sedimentary rock associated with HAIDA carvers. Deposits of the dull grey slate-like rock were found near Skidegate, Queen Charlotte Islands, before

17

Argillite

1820, when the curio trade began in argillite. The quarry is the exclusive property of the Skidegate tribe and other Haida carvers. When cut and polished, argillite shines with a bright black sheen and is commonly worked into pendants and sculptures. Powdered argillite is moulded into less valuable miniature totem poles and figurines by Indian artisans.

Argus Corporation Limited. Perhaps the country's most powerful investment and management company. Founded in Toronto in 1945, with its headquarters since 1958 at 10 Toronto St, it was directed from 1945 to 1969 by E.P. TAYLOR. It is now under the direction of John Angus (Bud) McDougald (b.1908). Angus is the dominant shareholder in such large corporations as DOMINION STORES LTD, HOLLINGER MINES LTD, MASSEY-FERGUSON LTD, Standard Broadcasting Corporation Ltd, the Crown Trust Company, and DOMTAR, etc. The Montreal-based POWER CORPORATION OF CANADA attempted to take it over between 1972 and 1975, and this led the federal government to appoint the Royal Commission on Corporate Concentration in 1975.

Ark Project. A self-sufficient home built at Spry Point, P.E.I. This prototype for a family-size food, energy, and housing complex was designed and built in 1976 with federal and provincial funding by the New Alchemy Institute, an association of scientists co-founded in the United States in 1969 and headed by a Canadian. The structure looks like a large greenhouse and windmill. It utilizes solar heat and wind power as sources of fuel, and supplies greenhouse and fish culture as sources of food.

Armistice Day. See REMEMBRANCE DAY,

Arms of Canada. See CANADIAN COAT-OF-ARMS.

Armstrong, George E. (b.1930). Hockey player, nicknamed 'The Chief'. Born in Skead, Ont., he was officially named 'Big Chief Shoot-the-Puck' by his band because of his Scottish-Indian ancestry and his pre-eminent hockey skills. He began hockey as a junior with Stratford and the Toronto Marlboros, then played 21 seasons with the TORONTO MAPLE LEAFS; he was a member of four STANLEY CUP teams. He retired to become a coach of the junior Marlboros, which won the national championship in 1974-5.

Arnaktauyok, Germaine (b.1946). Eskimo graphic artist at Igloolik. Admired for her black-and-white designs, she was commissioned by El Al Airlines to do posters, and she illustrated *Harpoon of the Hunter* (1970) by Markoosie.

Arnasungnak, Vital Makpa (b.1922). Well-known Eskimo sculptor and printmaker at BAKER LAKE. He sometimes signs his work 'Makpaaq'.

Arnhem. Dutch city near the Rhine, scene of fighting during the SECOND WORLD WAR. It was captured on 13 Apr. 1945 by the British 49th (West Riding) Infantry Division, which was under the command of the 1st CANADIAN CORPS.

Aroostook War. Territorial dispute between the province of New Brunswick and the state of Maine. The valley of the Aroostook R. in Maine was the setting for incidents in the 1830s that led to an armed clash in 1839, after which a truce was arranged. The boundary was settled by the WEBSTER-ASHBURTON TREATY of 1842.

Arpent. French linear measurement, now obsolete—about one and a quarter English acres. Voltaire referred to Canada as *quelques arpents de neige* ('a few acres of snow') in *Candide* (1759).

Arras. City in northern France. In the FIRST WORLD WAR the CANADIAN CORPS started an offensive two miles east of Arras on 26 Aug. 1918, advancing towards Cambrai. Hard fighting ensued over difficult broken country and stoutly held trenches.

Arrow. See AVRO ARROW.

Art Bank. A collection maintained by the CANADA COUNCIL to encourage and assist professional Canadian artists by exposing their works in government buildings. Established in 1972, it now owns some 5,000 works in all visual-arts media—paintings, prints, drawings, hangings, sculptures—which are leased to federal departments and agencies for an annual fee of 12% of the cost of the works. Selections of works for the Art Bank are made by travelling juries appointed on an ad-hoc basis. The Bank has a budget of $5 million extended over a five-year period.

Art Gallery of Greater Victoria, The. Founded in 1947, it displays its collection in a house built in 1890 for Alexander Green. The collection is noteworthy in the areas of Oriental painting, ceramics, and textiles, and in woodcuts by Albrecht Dürer. Along with the VANCOUVER ART GALLERY, it is responsible for the Emily CARR Trust.

Art Gallery of Hamilton. It was founded in 1912. Its present building was opened in 1953; in 1977 it will move into a new building. Major bequests include gifts from the Galbreaith and Penman estates. The collection covers early-to-contemporary Canadian art and American, British, and French art.

Art Gallery of Ontario. Incorporated in 1900 as the Art Museum of Toronto, it housed its collection in The GRANGE from 1913 to 1918. The original buildings of the Art Gallery of Toronto (adjoining The Grange) were erected in 1918, 1926, and 1935. The greatly enlarged Art Gallery of Ontario—renamed in 1966—opened in 1974. The Gallery contains Canadian and European paintings and the largest public collection of the work of Henry Moore; selected pieces of his sculpture are displayed in the Henry Moore Sculpture Centre. It also houses the bequest of Ayala and Samuel ZACKS, which consists of 385 works of twentieth-century art. The gallery's directorial post did not formally exist until 1947. Edward R. Grieg was Curator from 1912 to 1927; Fred Haines from 1928 to 1932, when Martin Baldwin was appointed Curator. Baldwin was Director from 1947 to 1960 and William Withrow has been Director since 1961.

Art Ross Trophy. Presented annually 'to the player who leads the NATIONAL HOCKEY LEAGUE in scoring points at the end of the regular season'. The cup for the leading scorer was donated by the late Arthur Howie Ross, former manager-coach of the Boston Bruins, in 1947. The winner receives $1,000 and the runner-up $500.

Arthur, Eric (b.1898). Architect and architectural historian. Born in Dunedin, New Zealand, and educated at the University of Liverpool, he came to Canada in 1923, taught at the University of Toronto, and practised as an architect and consultant, latterly as a senior partner in the firm of Fleury and Arthur, which designed a fine suburban house for J.S. McLean (c.1932) on Bayview Ave in a rough stone-walled Georgian style. He found his vocation as a commentator on Ontario and Toronto architecture of the nineteenth century and his books—*The Early Buildings of Ontario* (1938), *Toronto: No Mean City* (1963), and *The Barn* (1972)—stand as landmarks in the appreciation of Canadian architecture.

Arthur, Jack (1889-1971). 'Mr Showbusiness'. Born in Glasgow, Scot., and brought to Canada at the age of two, he went on tour with Sir Harry Lauder at the age of nine, and at 14 was the youngest violinist in the Toronto Symphony Orchestra. From 1952 to 1967 he was the showman behind the CNE GRANDSTAND SHOW. His wife Margaret (Midge) directed the well-known CANADETTES chorus line.

Arthur, Paul (b.1924). Graphic designer. Born in Liverpool, Eng., the son of the architectural historian Eric ARTHUR, he was educated at the University of Toronto where he published HERE AND NOW. He was assistant editor of *Graphis International* (1952-6), published in Zurich, and became art director of *Canadian Art* (ARTSCANADA) in 1956; he was editor from 1964 to 1967. Now president of Visu-Com Limited, Toronto, he is a consultant to corporations and governments on their communication systems and identity programs.

Artillery Park. An 8.2-acre national historic park in Quebec City. It recalls French military history that goes back to the Dauphine Redoubt, part of the city's fortifications, built in 1712.

Arts and Letters Club. An association founded in Toronto in 1908 for those concerned with the arts. An exhibition of J.E.H. MacDONALD's sketches in the club's quarters in Nov. 1911 led to the formation of the GROUP OF SEVEN in 1920. Over the years many prominent artists and patrons of the arts have been members. It is now primarily a men's luncheon club with premises in downtown Toronto.

Arts councils. Federal or provincial arts bodies. The largest arts-subsidizing body in the country is the CANADA COUNCIL. Provincial bodies include the MINISTÈRE DES AFFAIRES CULTURELLES DU QUÉBEC, the ONTARIO ARTS COUNCIL, the MANITOBA ARTS COUNCIL, the SASKATCHEWAN ARTS BOARD, and the BRITISH COLUMBIA CULTURAL FUND.

Arts of the Raven. An important exhibition—subtitled *Masterworks by the Northwest Coast Indian*—held at the VANCOUVER ART GALLERY from 15 June to 24 Sept. 1967. It presented carvings, sculptures, and textiles by HAIDA, TLINGIT, TSIMSHIAN, and KWAKIUTL artists and by the master Haida carver Charles EDENSHAW. The works were selected by Wilson Duff, Bill Holm, and Bill REID.

artscanada. A leading publication devoted to the visual arts. It first appeared five times a year from Oct. 1940 to Aug. 1943 as *Maritime Art: The Journal of the Maritime Art Association*, edited by Walter Abel, professor of the history of art at Acadia University, Wolfville, N.S. Renamed *Canadian Art* in 1943, it was then published from Ottawa, with Abel eventually retiring in favour of Robert Ayre and Donald W. Buchanan. Alan JARVIS was editor from 1960 to 1964 and Paul ARTHUR was editor from 1964 to 1967. (As art director Arthur had redesigned and enlarged the format in Jan. 1958.) In Jan. 1967 a new editor, Barry Lord, changed the name to *artscanada* and edited monthly issues that appeared in fascicle-form with a sheaf of accompanying materials (records, posters, etc.) until July 1967, when Anne Trueblood Brodzky replaced Lord. Since then *artscanada* has appeared every two months, surveying the Canadian and world art scenes, with a different theme for every issue.

Arvida. City on the south bank of the Saguenay R. near Chicoutimi, Que. It was founded in 1926 by the Aluminum Company of Canada, Ltd. (See ALCAN ALUMINIUM LIMITED). 'Arvida' is composed of the first syllables of the names of the company's then-president, Arthur Vining Davis.

As For Me and My House. Sinclair ROSS's first novel, published in 1941. A sad and disenchanting story of a frustrated artist, Philip Bentley, who enters the ministry and serves in a succession of poor prairie communities, it is told in the form of a diary kept by his wife. It vividly recreates the isolation and desolation of the Prairies during the 1930s.

As It Happens. Popular CBC Radio program that interviews people in the news by telephone. Launched on 18 Nov. 1968 as a 'phone-out' show by producer Val Cleary, with host William RONALD, it gradually evolved into an outlet for investigative journalism. Barbara FRUM joined Harry Brown and producer Mark Starowicz in Sept. 1971. Alan Maitland replaced Brown in Sept. 1974. The 90-minute show is among the few CBC programs heard or seen across the country in each of the six time zones at local time, 6:30 to 8:00 p.m., Monday through Friday.

Asbestos. A town in the Eastern Townships of Quebec noted for the production of asbestos. Over 40% of the world's asbestos comes from Canada and the bulk of this is mined in Asbestos and the nearby towns of Thetford Mines and Black Lake. See also ASBESTOS STRIKE.

Asbestos Corporation Limited. One of the world's largest producers of asbestos. Founded in Montreal in 1925, the company worked the asbestos mines in the Eastern Townships of Quebec. In 1964 it acquired a discovery named Asbestos Hill in the Ungava Peninsula, and the mine went into production in 1972. The majority of the company's shares were acquired in 1968-9 by General Dynamics, an American company, through Canadair Ltd.

Asbestos Strike. A well-known strike by asbestos-workers in the town of ASBESTOS, near Sherbrooke, Que. It broke out on 14 Feb. 1949 over demands for increased wages and better and safer working conditions in the Johns-Manville mines. The Quebec premier, Maurice DUPLESSIS, sent in the provincial police to enforce a back-to-work injunction. The Archbishop of Montreal, Joseph Charbonneau, unexpectedly spoke on behalf of the strikers in his sermon on Sunday, 2 May, at the Church of Notre Dame and collected funds to sustain them. On 5 May the company tried to send in strike-breakers, aided by provincial police, who acted with considerable violence. Mediation finally came through Archbishop Roy of Quebec and the strike ended on 1 July 1949. Pierre Elliott TRUDEAU edited a collection of essays on the issues raised by the strike, *Grève de l'amiante* (1956), translated by James Boake in *The Asbestos Strike* (1974).

Asdic. Acronym of Allied Submarine Detection Investigation Committee, a device for detecting submarines by echoes of sound waves. Conceived in Great Britain, it was much improved during the First World War by the UK Committee but was not put into operation until the Second World War. The RCN was using Asdic from 1939 and Canada began producing the device in 1941 (in CASA LOMA), making useful contributions to its development. The American name for it is Sonar.

Ashevak, Karoo (1940-74). Widely acclaimed Eskimo sculptor at SPENCE BAY. He specialized in fantastic carvings in bone. His work displayed great imagination and humour and he achieved international recognition before his tragic death in a house-fire at the age of 34.

Ashini. A novel by Yves THÉRIAULT published in 1960. It is the story, told in the form of a dramatic monologue, of an old and weary MONTAGNAIS, the last of his tribe to live in accordance with ancestral custom, who summons the prime minister to a parlay. When the meeting fails to take place, he retires to the wilderness and finally kills himself. An English translation by Gwendolyn Moore was published in 1972.

Ashoona, Pitseolak (born *c*.1900). Popular and prolific Eskimo graphic artist at CAPE DORSET. She produces drawings, stonecuts, and engravings that depict her joyful memories of the traditional ways. Her autobiography, *Pitseolak: Pictures Out of My Life* (1971), edited from tape-recorded interviews by Dorothy Eber, is illustrated with her work. She is the subject of *Pitseolak*, an NFB film released in 1970.

Ashoona, Shoroshiluto (b.1941). Eskimo graphic artist, popularly known as 'Shoroshiluto'. A CAPE DORSET artist, she has a lively narrative style and has experimented in animated films.

ASLT. Official abbreviation of Acting Sub-Lieutenant.

Assemblée législative. The lower (elected) house in the Quebec legislature until 1968, when the upper house was abolished and the Quebec legislature was renamed the ASSEMBLÉE NATIONALE.

Assemblée nationale. The Quebec legislature. Prior to 1968 the term Assemblée nationale (National Assembly) embraced both the ASSEMBLÉE LÉGISLATIVE (Legislative Assembly), the lower (elected) house, and the CONSEIL LÉGISLATIF (Legislative Council), the upper (appointed) house. In 1968 the Conseil législatif was abolished and the single (elected) house of the Quebec legislature was termed the Assembléé nationale.

Assiniboia. (i) An administration district of 50 sq. mi. around the junction of the Red and Assiniboine Rivers set up to manage the RED RIVER SETTLEMENT. In 1870, by which time it had been augmented to 13,000 sq. mi., it was erected into the province of Manitoba. (ii) One of four provisional administrative districts erected in the NORTHWEST TERRITORIES in 1882, with its centre at Regina. It was abolished in 1905 when the area was included in the newly created provinces of Saskatchewan and Alberta.

Assiniboine. A branch of the SIOUAN-speaking Dakota Indians. After migrating north from the headwaters of the Mississippi, they hunted from the Assiniboine R. westward almost to the Rocky Mountains. Both the eastern Assiniboine, who lived west of Lake Winnipeg, and the western bands had a Plains culture based on the buffalo. Assiniboine means 'people who cook with stones'; small bands in the Bow Valley are known as Stoneys. The Assiniboine population in 1970 was 1,059.

Associate state. The concept that the French Canadians living in Quebec form a nation; and that Quebec is not a province of Canada but a state that should be treated as independent while retaining certain ties with Canada.

Associated Medical Services Inc. North America's first non-profit, prepaid health-care scheme, established for Ontario residents. It was founded in 1937 by Dr Jason Hannah (b.1899), a Toronto neuro-pathologist, and directed by him until 1972, when the Ontario Health Insurance Plan was introduced. AMS's reserves of $12 million were then set aside to endow chairs in medical history at five Ontario universities and to found the Hannah Institute for the History of Medical and Related Sciences.

Association of Canadian Publishers. An organization of Canadian-owned book publishers. It was formed in Toronto in 1971 as the Independent Publishers Association (IPA)—following the sale of the RYERSON PRESS to McGRAW-HILL, an American company—to represent the interests of Canadian-owned companies and to pressure various levels of government for assistance. The name-change occurred in Mar. 1976. See also CANADIAN BOOK PUBLISHERS' COUNCIL.

Association of Canadian Television and Radio Artists. Performers' and writers' union. Established nationally through the merging of local performers' unions in 1963, ACTRA has 10 branches from Newfoundland to Vancouver. Its head office is in Toronto. In 1976 the total membership was approximately 5,000. The ACTRA AWARDS are made each spring at a gala televised banquet. See also CANADIAN ACTORS' EQUITY.

Assomption sash, L'. A worsted belt, sash or waistband worn by the VOYAGEUR and MÉTIS and having a bright arrow or lightning design. Such sashes were woven at L'Assomption, Que.

Assouyoutidlik. Eskimo word of greeting in southern Baffin Island. It means roughly, 'How go things?'

Astral Bellevue Pathé Ltd. A Canadian-owned mini-film conglomerate. Run by the flamboyant Harold Greenberg, who specializes in foreign co-productions, the Montreal operation includes Astral Films (the largest Canadian-owned film distributor), Bellevue-Pathé (the largest Canadian film laboratory, which goes back to 1923), and Associated Screen News.

Astrolabe. An instrument formerly used for taking altitudes of heavenly bodies and thereby determining latitude. Two astrolabes have been found in Canada. One dated 1603, and thought to have belonged to Samuel de CHAMPLAIN, was found near Renfrew, Ont., in 1867, and since 1943 has been in the collection of the New York Historical Society. The other, dated 1595 and found in 1925 on Christian Island in Georgian Bay, is believed to have been used by Jesuit missionaries.

At the Crease. Popular painting by Ken DANBY. Widely reproduced since it was

21

At the Crease

painted in 1972, it portrays a hockey goal-keeper with all the mystery and foreboding of a medieval jouster. A crease is the marked-off area in front of a goal; any goals scored when the shooter is inside the crease do not count. (Private coll.)

'At The Mermaid Inn'. Weekly column published in the Saturday edition of the Toronto *Globe* from 6 Feb. 1892 to 24 June 1893. It was written by Wilfred CAMPBELL, Archibald LAMPMAN, and Duncan Campbell SCOTT. The title recalls the Mermaid Tavern of the seventeenth century associated with Ben Jonson.

Athabasca River. Important part of the MACKENZIE RIVER system. It measures 765 mi. in length and rises from the glaciers of the same name near the southern end of Jasper National Park, on the border of Alberta and British Columbia, and empties into Great Slave Lake.

Athabasca Tar Sands. Oil-saturated sands along the Athabasca R. near Fort McMurray in northeastern Alberta. Methods of extracting the oil, the existence of which was known to traders and geologists for 200 years, were not devised until 1950. Extraction on a minor scale was begun in 1969 by Great Canadian Oil Sands Ltd, a subsidiary of Sun Oil. Extraction on a major scale, approved by the Alberta government on 18 Sept. 1973, will commence before 1980 through SYNCRUDE CANADA LIMITED. It is claimed that the bituminous sands contain the world's largest supply of oil.

Athabaska, District of. A provisional district of the NORTHWEST TERRITORIES created in 1882. In 1905 most of its territory was divided between the provinces of ALBERTA and SASKAT-CHEWAN.

Athapaskan. After the ALGONKIAN the most widely distributed linguistic family of Indians in Canada. Their name for themselves is *Dene*, 'the people'. They separate into four groups: KUTCHIN, TAHLTAN, CARRIER, and CHIL-COTIN of the Cordilleran interior; HARE, DO-GRIB, Kaska, and SLAVE of lands drained by the Mackenzie R.; Sekani and Beaver of the Peace R. country; and the CHIPEWYAN of the sub-Arctic, north of the Churchill R., from Lake Athabasca to Hudson Bay. A small group of Sarcee, in spite of their Athapaskan tongue, moved into the prairie and adopted the ways of the BLACKFOOT. The population of Athapaskan-speakers in 1970 was 22,657.

Athlone, Lord (1874-1957). GOVERNOR GENERAL of Canada from 1940 to 1946.

Athlone Fellowships. Annual engineering fellowships funded by the British Board of Trade. Tenable for up to two years at a British university or corporation, they are open to Canadian graduates of Canadian universities in any branch of engineering. The stipend of £744 includes travelling expenses. They were named for Lord ATHLONE.

Atigi. Eskimo word meaning 'a covering'. It is traditionally an outer, hooded garment of fur; in modern times it may be a blanket-like garment used to cover an inner heavier material. In olden times it was worn with the fur next to the skin. In areas of Keewatin, *atigi* means a man's undershirt.

Atkinson, Joseph E. See the TORONTO STAR and the ATKINSON CHARITABLE FOUNDATION.

Atkinson Charitable Foundation. It was established in Toronto in 1942 by Joseph E. Atkinson, publisher of the TORONTO STAR, 'to receive and maintain a fund or funds and apply the income thereof, in perpetuity, for religious, charitable, or educational purposes within the Province of Ontario.'

Atlantic, Battle of the. A series of actions fought around convoys bound, in particular, to and from the United Kingdom. The battle may be considered to have begun in earnest in the summer of 1940 and to have been won (though not ended) in the late spring of 1943. Nearly half the burden of escorting these convoys was assumed by ships of the ROYAL CANADIAN NAVY.

Atlantic Acceptance Corporation. Giant trust company whose bankruptcy shook BAY ST and Wall St. It was founded in Toronto in 1953 by C. Powell Morgan (1908-66), a promoter whose interests ranged from the RAC-CAN copying machine to the Lucayan Beach Hotel at Freeport, Grand Bahama Island. It went into receivership on 17 June 1965 with liabilities of approximately $32 million. An Ontario Royal Commission characterized the management as 'either incompetent or thieves'.

Atlantic Advocate. A monthly magazine, it has been published in Fredericton, N.B., since 1956, when it absorbed *Maritime Advocate*, founded in 1949. It publishes articles and literature of a regional and sometimes a general interest.

Atlantic cable. The first submarine cable to link North America and Great Britain for telegraphic communication. Laid in 1858, it connected Trinity Bay, Nfld, and Valentia, Ire. The first message was carried on 5 Aug. 1858. The engineer chiefly responsible was Frederick Newton Gisbourne (1824-92), president of the British North American Telegraph Company.

Atlantic Charter. A declaration signed by Winston Churchill (U.K.) and Franklin Delano Roosevelt (U.S.A.) at a meeting held on board the *Prince of Wales* on 14 Aug. 1941, at a time when the United States was officially neutral in the Second World War. It stated that 'their countries seek no aggrandizement, territorial or other'; that 'they desire to see no territorial changes that do not accord with the freely expressed wishes of the peoples concerned'; that 'all the men in all the lands may live out their lives in freedom from fear and want'; and that 'all of the nations of the world, for realistic as well as spiritual reasons, must come to the abandonment of the use of force.'

'Atlantic community'. A term first used at a NATO Council meeting in Ottawa in Sept. 1951. It embodied the hopes of Canada and other member nations that there would be close political and economic co-operation among western nations working together in a North Atlantic alliance as an Atlantic community rather than as an Atlantic union.

Atlantic Development Council. Government advisory body. Created in 1969, with 11 appointed representatives, it advises the Minister of REGIONAL ECONOMIC EXPANSION on plans and policies for economic expansion and social adjustment in the Atlantic Provinces.

Atlantic Neptune, The. Maritime atlas. It was an elaborate compilation of nearly 200 charts and superbly executed monochrome prints based on surveying trips made from Quebec to the Gulf of St Lawrence and from Nova Scotia to the Gulf of Mexico by the military cartographer J.F.W. DES BARRES. It was published in four volumes between 1770 and 1781.

Atlantic Provinces. The three Maritime Provinces (New Brunswick, Nova Scotia, Prince Edward Island) and Newfoundland.

Atlantic Region or **Appalachia.** One of the five principal GEOGRAPHICAL REGIONS of Canada, it consists of the Atlantic Provinces and southeastern Quebec. It is a rather fragmented array of peninsulas and islands formed from the northern extension of the Appalachian Mountain system. The landscape is diverse, with few large areas of good agricultural land; natural resources are limited; and settlement is scattered, with few large cities and little manufacturing. In relation to the rest of the country the region is economically underdeveloped, with low incomes and relatively high rates of unemployment.

Atlas of Canada, The. Canada's first national atlas and the second in the world after Finland's. It was published in 1906 by the Department of the Interior. A second enlarged edition was issued in 1915; in 1958 a new atlas appeared, followed by a French version two years later. The title of the present edition, the fourth, is *The National Atlas of Canada* (1974).

Atomic Energy of Canada Limited. CROWN CORPORATION concerned with the development of nuclear power for peaceful purposes. Incorporated in 1952, the AEC operates the CHALK RIVER project and other sources of nuclear power, and undertakes scientific research and development in the atomic-energy field.

Atwood, Margaret (b.1939). Poet and novelist. Born in Ottawa and educated at the University of Toronto and at Harvard, she has achieved a wide following for her remarkable body of poetry and fiction in which she explores a threatening universe and ambiguous, conflicting details of everyday life and human relationships. *The Circle Game* (1966), *The Animals in That Country* (1968), *The* JOURNALS OF SUSANNA MOODIE (1970), *Procedures for Underground* (1970), POWER POLITICS (1971), and *You Are Happy* (1974) are all represented in her *Selected Poems* (1976). Her three novels are *The Edible Woman* (1969), *Surfacing* (1972), and *Lady Oracle* (1976). Atwood's examination of the victim theme in Canadian writing, SURVIVAL (1972), has been widely read and discussed.

Aubert de Gaspé, Philippe-Joseph (1786-1871). Seigneur and author. Born in Saint-Jean-Port-Joli, Que., and called to the bar in 1813, he lived from 1841 until his death at the family manor, the scene of his historical novel *Les* ANCIENS CANADIENS (1863). Written in his seventies, it dramatizes an incident in the SEVEN YEARS' WAR and includes considerable lore about eighteenth-century New France—as does his *Mémoires* (1866). *Canadians of Old* (1890) is a translation by Charles G.D. ROBERTS of the novel. Philippe-Ignace-Françoise Aubert de Gaspé (1814-41), his son, wrote one of the earliest Quebec novels, *L'Influence d'un livre* (1837), about a search for buried treasure.

Auditor General. Officer of Parliament who audits expenditures, revenues, public property, etc., and examines government accounts, including those of the CROWN CORPORATIONS, reporting his findings annually to Parliament. The Auditor General's Report is referred to the House of Commons Standing Committee on Public Accounts, which may review it and report findings and recommendations to the HOUSE OF COMMONS. The Office of the Auditor General originated in 1878.

Augustyn, Frank (b.1953). Dancer. Born in Hamilton, Ont., he was a pupil of Betty OLIPHANT and Daniel Seillier at the National Ballet School, joining the company in 1970 and becoming a soloist in 1971. He and Karen KAIN placed first in the duet class at the Moscow International Ballet Festival in 1973 and are considered the most exciting ballet partnership Canada has yet produced. Augustyn has inherited several of the Nureyev roles in the NATIONAL BALLET OF CANADA.

Aulnay, Charles de Menou d'. See Charles de Sainte-Étienne de LA TOUR, and PORT ROYAL.

Aurora Borealis. The proper name for the 'Northern Lights'. Appearing to the unaided eye as multicoloured 'curtains' of wavering lights, they are the result of giant solar storms whose exploding radiation is trapped in the Van Allen radiation belts and channelled towards the polar regions by the earth's magnetic field. The aurorae take place at times of sunspot activity and during magnetic storms that disrupt long-distance radio broadcasts. In North America, during more severe disruptions, they can be seen as far south as the Gulf of Mexico. A similar display in the southern hemisphere is called the Aurora Australis or 'Southern Lights'.

Aurora speech. Celebrated address delivered by Edward BLAKE at Aurora, Ont., on 3 Oct. 1873, in which the Liberal leader maintained that the future of Canada 'depends very largely upon the cultivation of a national spirit'. These sentiments found expression in the CANADA FIRST movement. The speech was reprinted in the *Canadian Historical Review* (Sept. 1921).

Aurore, Les Éditions l'. A publishing house established in Montreal in 1974. Managed by Victor-Lévy BEAULIEU and Léandre Bergeron, it has published since its founding over 100 literary and political books of a leftist or separatist persuasion. It operates its own book club.

Auto Pact. Canadian-American trade agreement in the auto industry, signed in Jan. 1965. It provided for the removal of tariffs and other impediments to trade between Canada and the United States in motor vehicles and their component parts. Built-in safeguards ensure that three-quarters of the vehicles sold in Canada are manufactured there

and that the Canadian content is kept stable with that achieved in 1964.

Automatistes, Les. The name given to a group of French-Canadian painters in Montreal who broke new ground with their Surrealist automatic paintings—chance forms arrived at without premeditation. It included Paul-Émile BORDUAS and six younger followers: Marcel Barbeau, Roger Fauteux, Jean-Paul RIOPELLE, Pierre Gauvreau, Fernand Leduc, and Jean-Paul Mousseau. The name became attached to them after a show—from 15 Feb. to 1 Mar. 1947—in Gauvreau's Montreal apartment, which excluded Riopelle, who had already left for Paris.

Automobiles, Canadian-built. Cars designed or assembled in this country were: Acme, Anhut, Amherst 40, BARTLETT, Belcourt Steam Buggy, Bell, Bennett, BIRMINGHAM FLEXIBLE AXLE SIX, Bourassa Six, BRICKLIN, BRISCOE, Brock Six, BROCKVILLE ATLAS, BROOKS, Canada, Canada Baby Car, CANADIAN, Canadian Standard, Case, CHATHAM, Clinton, COMET, Crow, Dart, Davis, Derby, Dickson-Fetherstonhaugh Electric, Doherty, Dominion, Duplex, Falcon, Fleetwood Knight, Foss, Forster, FRONTENAC, Galt, Gareau, Gilson, Glen, Glover, Gramm, Gray, GRAY-DORT, Guy, Hambrecht, Imp, Iroquois, Ivanhoe, JULES 30, Keeton, Kelly Steam Buggy, Kennedy, La Marne, LAVOIE, Leader, LEROY, Locomobile, LONDON SIX, McKAY, McLAUGHLIN-Buick, Maritime Singer Six, Martin, MAXMOBILE, Menard Auto Buggy, Mercury, Mottette, Neff, OXFORD, PARKER, PECK, Queen, Redpath Messenger, REGAL, Roberts, Ross, RUSSELL, SAGER, Shamrock, Still, Superior, Swift, Tate, Taylor Steam Buggy, TUDHOPE, Victorian, Vinot, Walker, Wel-Doer, WINNIPEG, Wright.

Auyuittuq National Park. Near Pangnirtung in Cumberland Peninsula on Baffin Island, N.W.T., this 8,300-sq.-mi. park is the first national park inside the Arctic Circle. Dominated by long fjords, glacier-filled mountain valleys, and the massive Penny Ice Cap, it has no roads or trails, just four emergency shelters with food and emergency radiotelephones. Originally known as Baffin Island National Park, which was opened in 1972, in Feb. 1975 it was given the Inuit name Auyuittuq, meaning 'land of the big ice' or literally 'the place which does not melt'.

'Avant tout soyons Canadiens'. 'Before all, be Canadians'. Title of the marching song of the *Patriotes* in the REBELLION OF 1837, composed by Sir George-Étienne CARTIER. The patriotic song is sometimes called *'Avant tout je suis*

Canadien' ('Before all I am a Canadian') after the words of the last line. The moving lyrics are reproduced by John Boyd in *Sir George Etienne Cartier, Bart.: His Life and Times* (1914).

Avco World Trophy. Presented annually by the WORLD HOCKEY ASSOCIATION to the winning team at the completion of the WHA season. Established by Avco Financial Services and first awarded in 1973, the trophy is a 'symbol of supremacy in the World Hockey Association'.

'Ave, maris stella'. Title and first words of a Latin hymn sung with special affection by the Acadians. 'Hail, star of the sea' beseeches the Mother of God to grant 'all good things'. It was first sung by French settlers in ACADIA in the seventeenth century, was accepted as a national hymn, and is regarded as such to this day.

Avens, Mountain. A flower with broad white petals and a yellow centre, common throughout most of the central and eastern Arctic, including the Mackenzie delta, Banks and Victoria Islands, and Hudson Bay. It was adopted as the floral emblem of the Northwest Territories in 1957.

Avis, Walter S. See DICTIONARY OF CANADIAN-ISMS.

Avison, John (b.1915). Conductor and pianist. Born in Vancouver, he was educated at the Universities of British Columbia and Washington and studied music in Toronto and New York. He accompanied numerous musicians on tour. He was co-founder of the CBC Vancouver Chamber Orchestra in 1943 and has been its conductor ever since.

Avison, Margaret (b.1918). Poet. Born in Galt, Ont., a graduate of the Universities of Toronto and Chicago, she has published two poetry collections, *Winter Sun* (1960) and *The Dumbfounding* (1966). She writes metaphysical poems—intense examinations of man's relationship to the world and to God that achieve their insights through minute, visionary details.

A/V/M. Official abbreviation of Air Vice-Marshal.

Avonlea. See ANNE OF GREEN GABLES.

Avro Arrow. Popular name of the CF-105. The highly advanced delta-winged supersonic interceptor aircraft, driven by two powerful Pratt and Whitney J-75 engines, was designed and built (in 1953-9) by A.V. ROE CANADA LTD at Malton, near Toronto. The first of five planes was test-flown by Janus Zurakowski on 25 Mar. 1958. The IROQUOIS engine was developed to power the sixth and subsequent Arrows, but both programs were summarily cancelled by the Diefenbaker administration on 20 Feb. 1959, to much public outcry. High costs, together with the belief that bomber threats should be met with missiles rather than planes, were given as reasons for the cancellation.

Avrocar. Popular name of the Avro VZ-9V, an experimental air-cushion vehicle developed during the 1950s by A.V. ROE CANADA LTD at Malton, near Toronto. Funding for the project was provided by the company, the Canadian government, the U.S. army, and the U.S. air force. The two-man saucer-shaped craft was driven by three turbojets. Development work was discontinued in 1961.

AW1. Official abbreviation of Aircraftwoman, 1st Class.

AW2. Official abbreviation of Aircraftwoman, 2nd Class.

Axe-grinder, The. Sobriquet given to Sir John Sandfield MACDONALD, first premier of Ontario (1867-71), for his tendency to bear grudges.

Ayerst Award. An annual award made to a leading Canadian biochemist under 40. It was established by the Canadian Biochemical Society in 1966 and consists of a check for $1,000 from the pharmaceutical firm, Ayerst Laboratories of Montreal.

Ayorama. Eskimo expression in the Baffin and Keewatin regions meaning 'destiny' and used in a way to dismiss misfortune. It was the title of a study of the Eskimo by Raymond de Coccola and Paul King published in 1955. The word literally means 'because I cannot do it' and is correctly spelled *ayogama*.

Ayungnamat. A common Eskimo saying in the eastern Arctic. It is a way of dismissing misfortune and literally means 'because it can't be helped'.

B

B and E. Short form for 'breaking and entering', a phase used to describe the offence of burglary, which is defined as follows in the CRIMINAL CODE OF CANADA, Section 308(b): 'A person shall be deemed to have broken and entered [a place] if (i) he obtained entrance by a threat or artifice or by collusion with a person within, or (ii) he entered without lawful justification or excuse, the proof of which lies upon him, by a permanent or temporary opening.' (R.S.C., 1953-54, c. 52, s. 294)

B.C Initials of BRITISH COLUMBIA.

Babiche. French word, derived from the AL-GONKIAN, for leather strips used by the Indians as cord, a lace, thread etc. It is cut from a moose or caribou hide in a spiral fashion.

Baby Blue Movie. Name given the series of soft-core pornographic feature films shown every Friday midnight on CITY-TV in Toronto from the time the UHF station went on the air on 29 Sept. 1972 to 25 Apr. 1975.

Baby bonus. Popular name for the FAMILY ALLOWANCE.

Baccalaos. Sixteenth-century name for the region that now comprises Newfoundland, Cape Breton, Nova Scotia, and Labrador. The word is derived from the Portuguese for 'codfish'.

Bachman, Randy (b.1944). Rock star. Born in Winnipeg, Man., he composed many international hits with Burton Cummings of the GUESS WHO. Since 1973 he has been the leader, chief guitarist, and main composer of the 'supergroup', BACHMAN-TURNER OVERDRIVE.

Bachman-Turner Overdrive. Rock group. Organized in 1973 by Randy BACHMAN, formerly with the GUESS WHO, this recording and concert 'supergroup' with the 'hard-core sound' is composed of Randy and Bob Bachman, Fred Turner, and Blair Thornton. It is managed by Bruce Allen, who was born in Vancouver in 1945.

Back to God's Country. Early Canadian feature film. It was produced by Ernest Shipman of Canadian Photoplay Productions Ltd and released in 1919 by First National. Based on James Oliver Curwood's best-selling novel of the same name, it is said to have made a 300% profit for its Calgary investors. 6 reels, b & w.

'Backstage at Ottawa'. See MACLEAN'S.

Backwoods. Wild, uncleared forests; bush country; small settlements remote from well-settled areas.

Backwoods of Canada, The. A classic account of pioneer life in Upper Canada (Ontario) by Catherine Parr TRAILL, published in 1836. Composed of letters home, it is a common-sense handbook for emigrating gentlewomen that is interesting, cheerful, and replete with nature lore.

Baddeck. Summer-resort centre in the Bras d'Or region of Cape Breton Island, N.S. The 25-acre Alexander Graham BELL National Historic Park is located there. It includes Bell's summer home, which he called *Beinn Bhreagh* (Gaelic for 'beautiful mountain'), his grave, and the Bell Museum, which incorporates the tetrahedron as a design motif and houses experimental models, inventions etc. representing Bell's work.

Badlands. An arid area in south-central and south-eastern Alberta, particularly along the Red Deer R., consisting of deep gullies, sharp ridges, flat tops, and tall columns caused by river erosion. The resulting canyons and unusual rock formations are among the richest dinosaur-bone locations in the world.

Baffin, William (1584?-1622). Arctic explorer. In 1615 and 1616 he made two voyages with Robert Bylot on the *Discovery* in search of a NORTHWEST PASSAGE. On the second they entered Davis Strait, discovered Baffin Bay, and mapped Smith Sound, Jones Sound, and Lancaster Sound—which, unknown to them, was the entrance to the Northwest Passage.

Baffin Island. Largest of the Canadian Arctic islands—195,928 sq. mi. in area—and part of the Franklin District of the Northwest Territories. Near the North Magnetic Pole, it was named after William BAFFIN, who discovered Lancaster Sound in 1616, although Martin FROBISHER in 1576 and John DAVIS in 1585 had made landfalls on the island.

Baffin Island National Park. See AUYUITTUQ NATIONAL PARK.

Baggataway. A word derived from the AL-GONKIAN for the game once played by the Indians in eastern Canada. Played by as many as 200 to a team, it evolved during the nineteenth century into LACROSSE.

Bahut. A wooden chest, the earliest piece of furniture brought to New France. Used for storing garments and valuables, *bahuts* were made in Quebec of planks held together by dowels, with lids that were either flat or domed. The Quebec chests were more elaborately carved than similar pieces from Acadia.

Bailey, Irwin W. (Ace) (b.1903). Hockey player. Born in Bracebridge, Ont., he starred in both lacrosse and hockey. He became a professional hockey player with the Toronto St Patrick's (predecessor of the TORONTO MAPLE LEAFS), and continued to be an outstanding forward until he received a nearly fatal injury in the Boston-Toronto game of 1934. He is currently a league official at MAPLE LEAF GARDENS and is honoured in the Hockey HALL OF FAME.

Baillairgé, Charles (1826-1906). Architect and engineer. Born in Quebec, the nephew of François BAILLAIRGÉ, he was trained at the Quebec Seminary. For two years he had an assistant-supervisory role in the construction of the PARLIAMENT BUILDINGS and was Engineer to the City of Quebec from 1866 to 1906. His Quebec buildings include the façade of NOTRE-DAME-DE-LA-PAIX DE QUÉBEC (1843-4) and the terrace and pavilions of DUFFERIN TERRACE (1878-9).

Baillairgé, François (1759-1830). Architect, painter, and sculptor. Born in Quebec, he studied art in Paris and in 1781 set up a studio in Quebec, where he taught and painted commissioned portraits, executed sculptures, and practised architecture. He decorated the interior of NOTRE-DAME-DE-LA-PAIX DE QUÉBEC (1785-1802) and the façade of NOTRE-DAME-DES-VICTOIRES (1820). He was also treasurer of Quebec (1812-30).

Baillif, Claude (*c*.1635-98). The leading master-builder in seventeenth-century New France. Among the buildings he worked on were the enlargement of NOTRE-DAME-DE-LA-PAIX DE QUÉBEC (1684); the original NOTRE-DAME-DES-VICTOIRES in Lower Town, Quebec (1688); the bishop's palace (1693); and the renovated church of SAINTE-ANNE DE BEAUPRÉ (1689-95).

Bain, Donald Henderson (Dan) (1876-1962). All-round Winnipeg athlete. Born in Belleville, Ont., he participated in lacrosse, gymnastics, baseball, rowing, cycling, golf, figure- and roller-skating. He excelled in hockey, captaining the Winnipeg Victorias, who won the STANLEY CUP in 1896 and 1901,

and in trap-shooting, winning the Canadian championship in 1903. In later years he sponsored a variety of clubs and was prominent in the social life of Winnipeg. He was elected to the Hockey HALL OF FAME in 1945.

Bakeapple. This yellow-coloured berry, also known as the cloudberry, grows in the bogs of Newfoundland and Labrador. It has an acidic taste and is used for pies and jams.

Baker, Col. Edwin Albert (b.1893). Founder of the CANADIAN NATIONAL INSTITUTE FOR THE BLIND. Born in Kingston and a graduate in engineering from Queen's University, he lost his sight in France in 1915. A founder of the CNIB in 1918, he was managing director of the volunteer organization from 1920 until his retirement in 1962, when the E.A. Baker Foundation for the Prevention of Blindness was established.

Baker Lake. Eskimo settlement in the Northwest Territories (District of Keewatin) on the western tip of the lake of the same name. The community is known for its artists. Carving was introduced in 1961, printmaking in 1969, and wall-hangings in 1970. Eskimo artists working at Baker Lake include Marion Tudluq ANGUHADLUK, Luke ANGUHADLUQ, Vital Makpa ARNASUNGNAK, Luke IKSEETARKYUK, William NOAH, Jessie OONARK, Thomas SIVURAQ, Irene TICKTALA, Simon TOOKOOME, and Paul TOOLOOKTOOK.

Bald eagle. See Bald EAGLE.

Balding, Al (b.1924). Champion golfer. Born in Toronto, he became a professional golfer at 28 and during a long career won the Canadian Open championship and several tournaments in the United States and Mexico. He took the World Cup in Rome in 1967 and, pairing with George KNUDSON, won the team title for Canada.

Baldoon. Settlement of Highlanders near Lake St Clair, U.C. (Ont.), founded in 1804 and sponsored by Lord SELKIRK. It was a failure.

Baldwin, F.W. See AERIAL EXPERIMENT ASSOCIATION.

Baldwin, Robert (1804-58). Lawyer and statesman. The son of William Warren BALDWIN, he was an influential REFORMER in Upper Canada (Ontario) who developed the principles of RESPONSIBLE GOVERNMENT, conceived by his father, which he expounded in a memorandum to the colonial office in 1836 (it attracted the interest of Lord DURHAM) and later presented to the legislative assembly, of which he was a member from 1841 to 1851. He headed two ministries with Louis-H. LA-

Baldwin

FONTAINE, the second of which ('The Great Ministry', 1848-51) established the principles of responsible government.

Baldwin, William Warren (1775-1844). Conceiver of RESPONSIBLE GOVERNMENT. Irish born, he came to Upper Canada (Ontario) in 1798 and practised both law and medicine in York. A member of the legislative assembly (1824-30) and a leader of the REFORMERS, he proposed the principle of responsible government in a letter to the Duke of Wellington in 1828. He was the father of Robert BALDWIN.

Balfour Report. Resolution defining Great Britain and the self-governing dominions as 'autonomous communities within the British Empire, equal in status'. Moved by Arthur Balfour and adopted at the Imperial Conference of 18 Nov. 1926, it was embodied in the STATUTE OF WESTMINSTER of 1931.

Ball, James (b.1903). Noted runner. Unlike most track-and-field athletes, Ball, who was born in Dauphin, Man., matured slowly and won his first intercollegiate title at 22. At 25 he became Canadian 440-yard champion, and the following year he represented Canada at the 1928 Olympics in Amsterdam, where he won the silver medal in this event and the bronze medal as a member of the Canadian 1600-metre relay team.

Ball, Nelson (b.1942). Poet. Born in Clinton, Ont., he attended the University of Waterloo. In 1965 he established Weed/Flower Press and, in 1972, William Nelson Books, a Canadian book service, both in Toronto. His volumes of imagist poetry include *The Pre-Linguistic Heights* (1971).

Ballantyne, R.M. (1825-94). Novelist. Born in Edinburgh, he joined the Hudson's Bay Company in 1841 and served in Rupert's Land until 1847, when he returned to Scotland. *Hudson's Bay; or, Every-day Life in the Wilds of North America* (1848) is a vivid account of his experiences. He became a very successful and prolific writer of boys' adventure stories, of which *The Young Fur Traders* (1856), *Ungava: A Tale of Esquimaux Land* (1857), *The Wild Man of the West* (1863), *The Red Man's Revenge* (1880), and *The Buffalo Runners* (1891) have Canadian settings.

Banana belt. Any region with a relatively mild climate. The name is usually applied facetiously to the Okanagan Valley and the Niagara region where, supposedly, it is hot enough for bananas to grow.

Bancroft Award. Given every two years by the ROYAL SOCIETY OF CANADA for instruction and research in geology. It was established in 1975 by the widow of J.A. Bancroft, a McGill professor who died in 1957. It consists of a presentation scroll and $1,000.

Band, The. A popular five-man rock group. It began as a back-up band named The Hawks with Ronnie HAWKINS in 1964, and the next year joined Bob Dylan in the same capacity. At Woodstock in 1967 it turned from electronic rock to country music with a rock sound and became The Band. The group's first album, *Music from Big Pink* (1968), was an instant hit and The Band has ridden high ever since.

Bandy Papers, The. A series of novels about a horse-faced, wall-eyed preacher's son from the Ottawa Valley whose slapstick exploits are chronicled by Donald Lamont Jack, a Toronto-based playwright and novelist, in *Three Cheers for Me* (1962, 1973), *That's Me in the Middle* (1965), and *It's Me Again* (1975).

Baneful domination. Anti-colonial phrase used by Joseph Hume, a radical British parliamentarian, in a letter to William Lyon MACKENZIE published in the *Colonial Advocate* on 22 May 1834. Hume applauded Mackenzie's own radical stand, 'which will terminate in independence and freedom from the baneful domination of the mother country, and the tyrannical conduct of a small and despicable faction in the colony'. Mackenzie was accused of treason after he published Hume's letter. The relevant documents are reproduced by Margaret Fairley in her edition of *The Selected Writings of William Lyon Mackenzie: 1824-1837* (1960).

Banff Centre, The. Educational centre in Banff, Alta, that began in Aug. 1933 as an experimental summer school called The School of Fine Arts. It was founded on behalf of the University of Alberta through the efforts of Senator Donald Cameron and with the aid of a $10,000-a-year grant (given from 1932 to 1935) from the Carnegie Corporation. In Aug. 1970 David Leighton became director of the School and the following summer staged the first Banff Festival of Arts. Since its establishment it has grown greatly in size and concept and now embraces not only the fine arts—with year-round courses in the visual arts, theatre crafts and design, and French—but also a School of Management Studies, a Conference Division, and a Language Training Program. Its formal name is The Banff Centre for Continuing Education.

Banff National Park. It was established in 1885 amid the Rocky Mountains of Alberta. The oldest of the national parks, Banff is internationally known for its picturesque beauty as well as for its mineral hot springs and ski slopes. It includes the resort town of Banff with its BANFF SPRINGS HOTEL and the BANFF CENTRE. The COLUMBIA ICEFIELD north of Lake Louise is a remnant of a glacial advance. The park, which covers 2,564 sq. mi., was named by Lord Strathcona (Donald A. SMITH) after the town of Banff in Banffshire, near his birthplace in Scotland.

Banff School of Fine Arts. See The BANFF CENTRE.

Banff Springs Hotel. CPR hotel at Banff, Alta. The present hotel, designed in 1912-13 by W.S. Painter, with additions in 1926-8 by J.W. Orrock, is in the CHÂTEAU STYLE and replaces a frame structure (designed by Bruce PRICE) that was built in 1886-8 to exploit the presence nearby of mineral hot springs.

Bank of British Columbia. A chartered bank with its head office in Vancouver. Incorporated in 1967, it commenced operations on 18 July 1968 and in 1976 had 25 branches in British Columbia and three in Alberta.

Bank of Canada. The central bank of Canada. It began operations on 11 Mar. 1935, charged with regulating 'credit and currency in the best interests of the economic life of the nation'. In order to do this it regulates the total amount of Canadian money held by the community in the form of chartered bank deposits and currency and sets the bank rate, which determines the interest rate. The Bank has the sole right to issue paper money for circulation in Canada; it acts as the fiscal agent for the federal government and manages the public debt. It does not accept deposits from individuals or perform any of the other commercial services provided by the chartered banks. It is owned by the federal government and is under the management of a board of directors composed of a governor, a deputy governor, and 12 directors, who are appointed by the Minister of Finance with the approval of the GOVERNOR IN COUNCIL.

Bank of Montreal. The oldest chartered bank in Canada, founded in Montreal in 1817. In 1976 it had 1,263 branches and offices, including 42 outside the country.

Bank of Nova Scotia. A chartered bank with head offices in Halifax and Toronto. Incorporated in 1832 in Nova Scotia, in 1976 it had 982 branches, 79 of which were outside Canada.

Banks, Canadian. The largest chartered banks—the so-called 'Big Five'—are, in order of size: ROYAL BANK OF CANADA, CANADIAN IM-

PERIAL BANK OF COMMERCE, BANK OF MONTREAL, BANK OF NOVA SCOTIA, and TORONTO-DOMINION BANK. Five smaller banks are: BANQUE CANADIENNE NATIONALE, BANQUE PROVINCIALE DU CANADA, MERCANTILE BANK OF CANADA, BANK OF BRITISH COLUMBIA, and UNITY BANK OF CANADA.

Banks, Harold C. Former head of the Seafarers' International Union. Despite a criminal record in the United States, Hal Banks was brought to Canada in 1949 to drive the Communist-dominated Canadian Seamen's Union out of the Great Lakes. As a result of a régime of corruption and terrorism, he was charged and sentenced to five years, but in July 1964, while free on bail, he skipped to the U.S. A request for his extradition was made in 1967, but it was turned down by the U.S. Department of State in 1968.

'Banks of Newfoundland, The'. Title of an old sea ballad. One verse runs: 'I had a dream the other night, I dreamt that I was home./I dreamt that me and my true love were in old Marylebone—/That we were on old England's shore with a jug of ale in hand,/But when I woke my heart was broke on the Banks of Newfoundland.' It is of British origin and is popular in Newfoundland.

Bannerman, James (1902-70). Professional name of John McNaught, Toronto-born critic and broadcaster. A millionaire's son, he was (according to his own admission) successively a squanderer of a fortune, a welterweight boxer called 'The Canadian Hurricane', a gigolo in Vienna, a Yorkshire vaudevillan, a Hollywood scriptwriter, a New York gagman, and an espionage agent with the RCN. Once married to the novelist Gwethalyn Graham, Bannerman was popular with a generation of radio listeners for his deep voice and critical opinions. From Jan. 1949 he was a long-time panelist on the quiz show NOW I ASK YOU. From Oct. 1950 to July 1970 he wrote and delivered his famous 'introductions' to 'CBC Wednesday Night' (see CBC TUESDAY NIGHT). A linguist and musicologist, he possessed an eccentric erudition that covered literature, music, and the arts generally.

Bannock. Staple bread made by settlers and fur trappers. Of Scottish origin, it was originally unleavened.

Banque Canadienne Nationale. A chartered bank with its head office in Montreal. It was incorporated in 1873 and in 1976 had 385 branches and 95 agencies in the country, most of them in the province of Quebec.

Banque Provinciale du Canada. A chartered bank with its head office in Montreal. It was founded in 1861, and in 1976 had 186 branches and 34 agencies in eastern Canada, largely in the province of Quebec.

Banting, Sir Frederick G. (1891-1941). Medical researcher. Born in Alliston, Ont., he graduated from the University of Toronto in medicine in 1922. He practised privately before undertaking original research in diabetes. In the middle of the night, on 30 Oct. 1920, he leapt out of bed and scribbled these words in his notebook: 'Tie off pancreas ducts of dogs. Wait six or eight weeks. Remove and extract.' He convinced J.J.R. MA-CLEOD, professor of physiology at the University of Toronto, that he should lend him laboratory facilities and an assistant (Charles H. BEST). In the summer of 1921 Banting and Best isolated INSULIN and, with the help of J.B. COLLIP, succeeded in purifying the substance. Banting and Macleod were co-recipients of the 1923 NOBEL PRIZE for chemistry, Banting sharing his monetary reward with Best and Macleod sharing his with Collip. Banting, who was granted an annuity by Parliament, occupied a newly endowed chair of medical research at the University of Toronto and presided over the Banting Institute, with its Banting and Best Department of Medical Research, erected in 1930. He was knighted in 1934. A captain in the Canadian Army Medical Corps, he died when his plane attempted a forced landing near Musgrave Harbour, eastern Newfoundland; he was on a 'mission of high national and scientific importance' to Britain. Banting's important and well-publicized award helped to gain public acceptance for medical and scientific research.

Baptist Church. Originating from the United Empire Loyalist migrations, it practises congregational autonomy, stresses adult baptism on profession of faith, and upholds a puritan morality code. The emphasis in worship is on preaching and hymn singing. The census of 1971 identified 667,245 adherents.

Baptiste, Jean. See JEAN BAPTISTE.

Barbeau, Jean (b.1945). Quebec dramatist. Born in St-Romuald, Que., and a graduate of Laval, he is a prolific writer of experimental plays. *Solange*, a monologue, and *Goglu*, a dialogue, were staged in both French and English in 1970. *Le Chemin de Lacroix* (1970) is a two-act political play about an unemployed workman that is divided into 14 'stations' and recalls the OCTOBER CRISIS. It was published in an English translation by Laurence Bérard and Philip W. London called *The Way of Lacross* (1972).

Barbeau, Marius (1883-1969). Folklorist. Born in Sainte-Marie de Beauce, Que., and educated at Université Laval, Oxford, and the Sorbonne, he served as an ethnologist and folklorist at the National Museum of Canada from 1911 to 1958. He wrote almost 100 books and reports in English and French about Indian cultures, Quebec folklore, Canadian arts and crafts, etc., in an impressionistic but knowledgeable manner. Although unsystematic in his approach to folklore and ethnology, he made a considerable contribution to these fields and was for many years regarded as Canada's foremost folklorist. Among his books are *Folk Songs of French Canada* (1925); *The Downfall of Temlaham* (1928), a novel; *The Tree of Dreams* (1955), a collection of French-Canadian legends; and *The Golden Phoenix and Other French-Canadian Fairy Tales* (1958), stories for children retold by Michael Hornyansky.

Barbini, Ernesto (b.1909). Opera conductor. Born in Venice, Italy, he had an extensive European and North American conducting career—including three years at the Metropolitan Opera, New York (1950-3)—before arriving in Toronto in 1953, when he became conductor of the CANADIAN OPERA COMPANY. He has guest-conducted internationally.

Barker, Billy. See BARKERVILLE.

Barkerville. 'Gold Capital of British Columbia'. It grew up during the FRASER RIVER GOLD RUSH around the shafthouse of Billy Barker, who made an important strike in the valley of Williams Creek in Aug. 1862. More than 75 buildings have been reconstructed since 1958 to recreate the mining town as it appeared following the devasting fire of 1868. See also CARIBOO MOUNTAINS.

Barnes, Emery (b.1930). Football player. Born in New Orleans and raised in Oregon, he graduated from the University of Oregon and played with the Green Bay Packers before joining the B.C. Lions in 1957. He played end and tackle for that football team before retiring from the game in 1964. A director of the Civil Liberties Union, the Black athlete represented the NDP in the B.C. legislature from 1972 to 1976. From 1952 to 1971 he was married to LaVerne Barnes, author of *The Plastic Orgasm* (1971), a wife's view of Canadian football.

Barnes Wines. Oldest wine company in Canada. Founded by George Barnes in St Catharines, Ont., in 1873, Barnes Wines is the only Canadian wine sold in every province of Canada.

Barometer Rising. The first novel of Hugh MacLENNAN, published in 1941. Set in Halifax at the time of the explosion that destroyed a good part of the city on 5 Dec. 1917, it is the story of Neil Macrae, a young Canadian officer who has been accused of refusing to obey an order while serving overseas. The evidence that vindicates him is revealed simultaneously with the death of his accuser. See also HALIFAX EXPLOSION.

Baron, Sid (b.1917). Cartoonist. Born in Toronto, he worked as a commercial artist before becoming an editorial cartoonist for the *Victoria Times* in 1958. Since then he was an editorial cartoonist for the *Toronto Star* (1960-74) and the *Calgary Albertan* (1964-70). Also a part-time painter, he has shown his work in most of Canada's major cities.

Baronets of Nova Scotia. A colonizing order founded in 1625 by Sir William Alexander under authority of Charles I. Limited to 150 members, it was formed to create settlements in Nova Scotia.

Barr body. The sex nucleus of a cell. The presence of a small mass of chromatin (the bearer of the hereditary qualities of an organism) in the nerve cells of female (but not of male) cats was recognized in 1949 by Dr Murray Barr (b.1908) of the University of Western Ontario. The sex chromatin, a female characteristic, was named after him.

Barr colony. A settlement of English colonists sent out to the Saskatchewan valley near Battleford in 1903 by Isaac M. Barr. In 1905 the colony was renamed Lloydminster, Sask., in honour of the Rev. George Exton Lloyd, a co-founder.

Barre du jour, La. Literary quarterly devoted to poetry and fiction. Founded in Montreal in 1965, it is committed to the cause of unilingualism in Quebec, a specific identity for Quebec, and the democratization of the arts. Among its editors is Nicole BROSSARD.

Barren Lands. The TUNDRA area of the Northwest Territories. Forming a great triangle with its hypotenuse stretching from Churchill, Man., to the shore of Coronation Gulf (an arm of the Arctic Ocean northeast of Great Bear Lake), the Barren Lands are studded with tens-of-thousands of lakes and hundreds of rivers. The name is apt only as it refers to the absence of trees; there is considerable plant life, although this is now somewhat depleted by indiscriminate hunting and ecological mismanagement. The trapper and explorer John HORNBY referred to the Barrens—where he eventually starved to death—as 'the land of feast and famine'.

Bartlett. Automobile designed by R.C. Bartlett and built in Toronto from 1914 to 1917. The Bartlett came in two models: a $665 roadster and a $995 touring car.

Bartlett, Bob (1875-1946). Seaman and explorer. Born in Brigus, Nfld, he led an adventurous life that was highlighted by the two polar voyages of R.E. PEARY in 1905-6 and 1908-9, on which he commanded Peary's ship *Roosevelt*; by sledging part way to the North Pole with Peary on his 1909 expedition; and by commanding the flagship KARLUK on the Arctic voyage of Vilhjamur STEFANSSON. Setting out in 1913, the *Karluk* sank in the Siberian Sea and a tragic adventure ensued, which Bartlett survived by reaching help in Alaska. He wrote several books, notably an autobiography, *The Log of Bob Bartlett* (1928).

Bartlett, W.H. (1809-54). English artist. As a result of his visits to the United States and Canada in 1836 and 1838 he executed a series of sketches of Upper and Lower Canada, New Brunswick, and Nova Scotia, 117 of which were published as steel engravings in *Canadian Scenery Illustrated* (1840; 2nd ed. 1842) by N.P. Willis. Reflecting a contemporary taste for the picturesque, these handsome scenes—more romantic than accurate—were very popular in their time and are much in evidence today reproduced for various decorative purposes.

Basilica, Quebec. See NOTRE-DAME-DE-LA-PAIX-DE-QUÉBEC.

Bassett dynasty. Three generations of businessmen. It was founded by John Bassett I (1886-1958), an immigrant from Ulster who was associated with the *Montreal Gazette* from 1910 to 1956, latterly as its publisher. His son, John W. Bassett II, was born in Ottawa and educated at Bishop's University. The publisher of the *Toronto Telegram* (1948-71), he is owner of CFTO, the masthead station of the CTV Television Network, and has extensive sporting interests. His oldest son, John F. Bassett III, born in Toronto in 1940 and a graduate of the University of Western Ontario, is a Toronto film producer—*The* ROWDYMAN (1971), *Face-Off* (1971), PAPERBACK HERO (1973)—and sports figure. In 1974 the federal government blocked his attempt to introduce the World Football League into Canada by acquiring for Toronto a team that he called the Northmen, which was affiliated with the League.

Basso, Guido (b.1937). Jazz trumpeter and musical director. Born in Montreal, he was discovered by Vic Damone in a Montreal

31

night club and toured with Damone, Pearl Bailey, and others. Since settling in Toronto in 1960 he has worked with television orchestras as a soloist, composer, conductor, and musical director.

Bata Limited. The largest footwear manufacturing company in the world. The multinational firm was originally founded in 1894 by Tomas Bata at Zlin, Czech. The Canadian operation, which is now the world headquarters, was established in Toronto in 1939 by Czech-born Thomas J. Bata (b.1914), the son of the founder. Bata Limited owns and operates factories and retail outlets in 89 countries and has over 90,000 employees. The Canadian plant is called Batawa, the Pakistan plant Batapur, the French plant Bataville, the Indian plant Batanagar. The company motto is 'Bata—Shoemaker to the World'.

Batoche. Former Métis settlement in Saskatchewan, on the South Saskatchewan R. near Prince Albert. It was the headquarters of Louis RIEL during the NORTH WEST REBELLION and the site of the Battle of Batoche, the principal engagement of the rebellion, fought on 9-12 May 1885. It fell after an attack by troops under Gen. Frederick Middleton. Riel fled, but gave himself up the next day. Little remains of the old settlement today except the rectory, which is a national historic site, and the parish church of St Antoine de Padoue, built in 1884.

Batten, Jack (b.1932). Journalist and author. Born in Montreal, he was raised in Toronto and was a lawyer by profession before becoming a free-lance magazine and newspaper writer. He has covered jazz, rock, and folk music for the *Toronto Star* (1968-70) and rock and jazz for the Toronto *Globe and Mail* (since 1971). The best-known of his many books is on hockey—*The Leafs in Autumn* (1975), a nostalgic look at the TORONTO MAPLE LEAFS.

Batterwood. The country estate of Vincent MASSEY on the outskirts of Port Hope, Ont. It was in the 25-room mansion on the estate that the PORT HOPE CONFERENCE was held in the summer of 1933.

Battle, Rex (1897-1967). Pianist and conductor. Born in London, Eng., he came to Canada in 1922. As musical director and conductor of SINGING STARS OF TOMORROW he 'discovered' Robert GOULET and Lois MARSHALL. For his fast piano-playing style he was called 'King of the Keys'.

'Battle of Queenston Heights, The'. Title of a popular ballad about the death of Sir Isaac

BROCK at Queenston Heights on 13 Oct. 1812. The folksong includes the stirring lines attributed to Brock: 'No foreign flag shall float above the Union Jack' and 'PUSH ON, BRAVE YORK VOLUNTEERS!' See also QUEENSTON HEIGHTS AND BROCK'S MONUMENT.

Battleford, Relief of. An incident in the NORTH WEST REBELLION. This settlement—the capital of the Northwest Territories—at the junction of the Battle and North Saskatchewan Rivers in present-day Saskatchewan, was besieged by the Cree chief POUNDMAKER in Mar. 1885 and the settlers had to take refuge in the NORTH WEST MOUNTED POLICE barracks. It was relieved by Col. William OTTER and the Canadian militia on 23 Apr. 1885. The police buildings that comprised Fort Battleford, erected in 1876, are still to be seen in Battleford National Historic Park. In North Battleford, on the north side of the river, is Western Development Museum, a pioneer village with turn-of-the-century buildings and indoor displays.

Battleford National Historic Park. See Relief of BATTLEFORD.

Bau-Xi Gallery. Commercial art gallery in Vancouver, B.C. Founded by Paul Wong, and named for the Mandarin word meaning 'great fortune', it is devoted to the work of contemporary western-Canadian artists. Branches were opened in Victoria in 1974 and Toronto in 1976.

Bauer, David (b.1925). Top amateur hockey player. Born in Waterloo, Ont., he joined the Oshawa junior hockey team that won the Canadian junior championship in 1943. He considered turning professional but instead joined the Basilian Order where, in addition to teaching and coaching, he recruited several hockey teams that represented Canada at world and Olympic tournaments. He was prominent in the establishment of HOCKEY CANADA.

Bauer, Walter (b.1904). Poet. Born in Merseburg, Germany, he attended teacher's college there and supported himself as a writer until 1952, when he decided to immigrate to Canada. A student at the University of Toronto from 1954 to 1958, he taught in the German department until his retirement in 1976. Over 70 of his books—novels, biography, poetry, essays, and children's stories—have been published in Germany. Henry Beissel translated two collections of his remarkable lyric poetry: *The Price of Morning* (1968) and *A Different Sun* (1976). Humphrey Milnes translated a new selection of his verse, *A Slight Trace of Ashes* (1976), illustrated by Aba Bayefsky. Bauer has recently begun to write poetry in English.

Baum, Gregory (b.1923). Theologian. Born in Berlin of Jewish ancestry and interned in England and Canada during much of the Second World War, he graduated from McMaster University and in 1947 joined the Augustinian Order. He is a professor of theology and religious studies at St Michael's College, University of Toronto, editor of *The Ecumenist: A Journal for Promoting Christian Unity,* and a leading ecumenical scholar and Catholic spokesman who is especially concerned with 'marginalized groups'. He is the author of *That They May Be One* (1958), *The Jews and the Gospel* (1961), *Religion and Alienation: A Theological Reading of Sociology* (1975), and *Journeys: The Impact of Personal Religious Experience on Religious Thought* (1975).

Baxter, Sir Beverley. See LONDON LETTER.

Bay, The. A historical reference to Hudson Bay, and an informal reference to the modern HUDSON'S BAY COMPANY or to one of its department stores.

Bay of Fundy. The picturesque arm of the Atlantic separating southwest Nova Scotia and New Brunswick, whose tides are the highest in the world, the spring tides rising up to 53 ft while the neap tides average 26 ft. Three sites on Fundy—Minas Basin, Shepody Bay, and Cumberland Basin—are considered potential sites for the construction of tidal electric power installations. See also TIDAL BORE.

Bay St. The financial centre of downtown TORONTO on which stands the Toronto Stock Exchange, the second-largest exchange in North America. With ST JAMES ST in Montreal it has come to symbolize the financial interests of central Canada.

Bayeux Memorial. Imposing Second World War memorial near the ancient town of Bayeux in Normandy, France. Across the road from the Bayeux War Cemetery, it is dedicated to the 'soldiers of the Commonwealth and Empire who fell in the assault upon the Normandy beaches, or in the sweep of the Seine, but to whom the fortune of war denied a known and honoured grave'. The words inscribed across the frieze, *Nos a Gulielmo victi victoris patriam liberavimus,* translate as, 'We, once conquered by William, have now set free the Conqueror's native land'. The town is associated with the famous tapestry depicting the Norman Conquest; there is a bronze equestrian statue of William the Conqueror in nearby Falaise.

Bayman. In Newfoundland someone who lives in an OUTPORT or a small isolated community. A bayman is the opposite of a TOWNIE.

BCATP. Initials of the BRITISH COMMONWEALTH AIR TRAINING PLAN.

B/C/P Publicité. Leading advertising agency in French Canada. The first Canadian advertising agency to specialize in original French-language creative work in advertising and marketing, B/C/P was founded in Montreal in 1964. The initials stand for the last names of the founders: Quebec advertising executives Jacques Bouchard, Jean-Paul Champagne, and Pierre Pelletier.

BCR. Initials of the BRITISH COLUMBIA RAILWAY.

Beachcombers, The. A popular comedy-adventure series on CBC-TV. The 30-minute weekly program starred Bruno GERUSSI as Nick Adonias, a Greek-born 'beachcomber' or licensed log salvager who worked along the west coast. Created by Marc and Susan Lynn Strange, the series was produced by Philip Keatley and shot on location at the B.C. fishing village of Gibsons. It was first seen on 1 Oct. 1972.

Beacon Hill Park. Scenic park of 154 acres in downtown VICTORIA, B.C., with descendants of swans brought from England in the 1920s and a 127-ft high totem pole, probably the tallest in the world, carved by Mungo MARTIN.

Bear. See BLACK BEAR, GRIZZLY BEAR, POLAR BEAR.

Beardmore relics. A cache of Norse weapons dating from A.D. 1000, supposedly unearthed near Beardmore in the Lake Nipigon area of northern Ontario. A Port Arthur prospector, J.E. Dodd, claimed that, while blasting for gold on 24 May 1930, he came upon a rusting sword, an axhead, and other iron fragments that he sold for $500 to the ROYAL ONTARIO MUSEUM six years later. Although there is little question of the authenticity of the relics, there is considerable controversy over the location of the find and the presence of Vikings in northern Ontario.

Beardy, Jackson (b.1944). Cree artist. Born at Garden Hill Reserve, Island Lake, Man., he painted for three years before refining his technique at the University of Manitoba's School of Fine Arts. His vividly coloured drawings and paintings interpret the traditional ways of his people and frequently include a sun symbol divided into thirds, one-third dark (or evil) and two-thirds bright (or good). He illustrated John S. Morgan's *When the Morning Stars Sang Together* (1974).

Beau Dommage. A Quebec rock group, combining soft sound and an innovative technique, founded in 1973. The group of four men and one woman—whose first album *Beau Dommage*, was a record-breaking bestseller—is popular in both French and English Canada and has appeared in France. The name is slang for 'of course'.

Beauchemin, Nérée. See Le TERROIR.

Beauchemin Ltée, Librairie. Quebec booksellers and publishers. Founded in Montreal in 1842, it issues books of literary interest and is the oldest publisher in the province.

Beauchesne's Rules of Order. The authoritative work on parliamentary procedure, *Rules and Forms of the House of Commons of Canada* (1922), by Arthur Beauchesne (1876-1959), distinguished clerk of the House of Commons from 1925 to 1949. He also wrote the popular guide, *Procedure at Meetings in Canada* (1954). See also BOURINOT'S RULES OF ORDER.

Beauharnois affair. A scandal involving the purchase of hydro-electric power from the Beauharnois Company, located on the St Lawrence R. at Beauharnois, Que. R.O. Sweezey, president of the power company, admitted to a Special Parliamentary Committee in July 1931 that his company had made substantial contributions to the coffers of the Ontario, Quebec, and federal government parties in exchange for preference in the awarding of contracts. He concluded: 'Gratefulness was always regarded as an important factor in dealing with democratic governments.' The affair was a factor in the defeat of the Ontario administration of George Henry by Mitchell HEPBURN in 1934.

Beaulieu, Victor-Lévy (b.1945). Quebec novelist. Born in Saint-Paul-de-la-Croix, near Rivière-du-Loup, Que., he was literary editor of Les ÉDITIONS DU JOUR, has managed Les Éditions l'AURORE, and recently established his own imprint, V.L.B. He is the author of numerous novels, including *Jos Connaissant* (1970) and *Les Grands-pères* (1972), translated by Marc Plourde and Gil de Cardaillac as *The Grandfathers* (1976). Beaulieu is an enthusiast for the subject of his literary study, *Jack Kerouac: A Chicken-Essay* (1976), translated by Sheila FISCHMAN.

Beautiful Joe. A well-known sentimental animal story for children by Marshall Saunders (1861-1947), published in 1894. About a dog who is maltreated as a puppy but finds a home with a kind family, it has gone through numerous editions and been translated into several languages.

Beautiful Losers. Novel by Leonard COHEN published in 1966. A wild fantasy described by the author as 'a great mad confessional prayer', it touches on such themes as ugliness and evil as a source of beauty, the corruption of love, a mysticism of the flesh, and sainthood in passages about the venerated Mohawk, Kateri TEKAKWITHA.

Beaver. (i) Semi-aquatic mammal found in wooded areas throughout North America. Characterized by thick brown fur, sharp incisors, large webbed hind feet, and a broad flat scaly tail, its average size is about 4 ft long and its weight 40 or 50 lb. It feeds chiefly on bark and twigs and is noted for its ingenuity in building lodges and dams. Gregarious social animals, beavers live in colonies—normally 10 or 12 in a family group—in small streams. See also BEAVER MEAT. (ii) Canada's national emblem. *Castor canadensis*, because of its valuable fur, was a major factor in the exploration and settlement of much of North America and served in early times as a staple of the FUR TRADE. The earliest heraldic use of the beaver was in 1633 when its image appeared, rampant, on the device of Sir William Alexander (see BARONETS OF NOVA SCOTIA). FRONTENAC suggested to COLBERT in 1673 that the beaver appear on the coat-of-arms of New France, but the notion was never taken up. The beaver did appear, building a dam, on the first Canadian postage stamp: the THREE-PENCE BEAVER designed by Sir Sanford FLEMING and issued in 1851. The best-known image of the beaver has graced the obverse of the five-cent piece since 1936.

Beaver. Paddle vessel launched on 2 May 1835 at Blackwall, Eng., for the HUDSON'S BAY COMPANY. Brig-rigged as well, she sailed that fall to Fort Vancouver, where her paddles were fitted. She was the first steamer in the north Pacific and served the Company as a supply vessel until 1874, when she was sold and became a towboat. She was wrecked at the entrance to Vancouver harbour on 26 July 1888.

Beaver. A light, all-purpose airplane, ideal for bush aviation. Built by DE HAVILLAND in Canada in 1947, it was the first STOL aircraft built in Canada and proved to be very popular around the world.

Beaver, The. An illustrated quarterly magazine founded as a house organ of the HUD-

SON'S BAY COMPANY in Oct. 1920. Since the 1950s it has enjoyed a semi-independent status and today publishes free-lance articles on the history, development, and people of Canada's North. It is sometimes referred to as the 'Magazine of the North'.

Beaver, The. Nickname of William Maxwell Aitken, Lord BEAVERBROOK, the Canadian-born British press lord.

Beaver Award. An annual award given 'for distinguished service to Canadian radio . . . beyond fee or salary'. Instituted on an annual basis by the *Canadian Broadcaster*, it was awarded in 16 categories from 1945 to 1950.

Beaver Club. A Montreal dining club associated with the fur trade. Founded in 1785 by partners in the NORTH WEST COMPANY, it restricted membership at first to those who had spent a winter in the Northwest. With a lapse from 1804 to 1807, it lasted until about 1825. It was revived in the 1950s by Donald Gordon when he was president of the CNR and meets in the 'Beaver Club' room of the Queen Elizabeth Hotel.

Beaver Dam, Battle of. An engagement in the WAR OF 1812 on the Niagara Peninsula. A band of Six Nations Indians under Lt-Col. Joseph BRANT ambushed an American force between Queenston, U.C. (Ont.), and a British outpost near Beaver Dam and forced it to surrender on 24 June 1813 to Lt James Fitz-Gibbon. See also Laura SECORD.

Beaver Hall Hill. Street in Montreal named for the mansion and estate of the fur trader Joseph FROBISHER, which was built and enlarged in the late-eighteenth century and burnt down in 1848.

Beaver Hall Hill Group. A group of Montreal painters that formed in the early twenties. Named after the street in Montreal (see entry), they were probably the finest figure painters in Canada in the thirties, all students of William BRYMNER. The group included Randolph Hewton, Edwin HOLGATE, Lilias Torrance Newton, Albert Robinson, Prudence HEWARD, Sarah Robertson, Mabel Lockerby, and Annie Savage.

Beaver House. Name of the building housing the chief offices of the HUDSON'S BAY COMPANY in Great Trinity Lane, London, Eng.

Beaver meat. A dark, fat, tender meat commonly eaten in the nineteenth century. It was often made into a stew called beaver tail soup.

Beaver Pelt, The. A tag that guarantees the authenticity of a piece of art or craft pro-duced by an Indian in Canada. The brown oval shape of the beaver-pelt design, joined to a strong black border, is said to signify all Indian cultures united as one brotherhood with the common aim of producing articles of quality and distinction. Superimposed on the pelt design are the words 'Authentic Canadian Indian Fine Craft' or 'Authentique oeuvre de l'artisanat Indien du Canada'. See also IGLOO TAG.

Beaverbrook, Lord (1879-1964). Canadian industrialist and British press baron. Born William Maxwell Aitken in Maple, Ont., and raised in Newcastle, N.B., he briefly attended the University of New Brunswick. His talent for manipulation came to the fore in a bank merger, in the formation of Canada Cement from 13 smaller companies, and in a steel merger—the latter in association with another New Brunswick magnate, Sir James Dunn (1875-1956)—all before he was 31. He retired from business and left Montreal in 1910 for London, Eng. He became private secretary to the Canadian-born Andrew Bonar Law (1858-1923; prime minister of Great Britain from Nov. 1922 to May 1923) and was a member of Parliament from 1910 to 1916. He oversaw the CANADIAN WAR RECORDS and became minister of information in 1918. He was knighted in 1911, created a baronet in 1916, and raised to the peerage in 1917; he took his title from the Acadian hamlet of Beaver Brook Station, north of Newcastle, and adopted an appropriate motto: *Res mihi non me rebus* ('Things for me, not I for things'). Regarding himself as 'an apprentice in Fleet Street', he formed Beaverbrook Newspapers and acquired the *Daily Express*, founded the *Sunday Express* in 1921, and then bought the *Scottish Daily Express*, the *Scottish Sunday Express*, and the *Evening Standard*, etc. He was an avowed imperialist who continued to refer to the Commonwealth as the Empire. He wielded an immense influence in Britain and in Churchill's Second World War cabinet held various posts, including that of minister of aircraft production. The year before his death he married Marcia Anastasia Christoforides Dunn, the widow of Sir James Dunn. His will was probated at Newcastle ('the town where my heart lies') and his assets were entrusted to the Beaverbrook Canadian Foundation, managed by Lady Beaverbrook, who resides at St Andrews, N.B., and continues 'The Beaver's' notable benefactions to his native province. Max Aitken, Beaverbrook's son by a first marriage, was born in Montreal in 1910. Chairman of Beaverbrook Newspapers in London, he disclaimed the hereditary title in 1964.

Beaverbrook Art Gallery

Beaverbrook Art Gallery. Public art institution in Fredericton, N.B. Incorporated in 1957, it was built by Lord BEAVERBROOK, who endowed it with a trust fund. Its building houses 34 paintings by Cornelius KRIEGHOFF, much British art, and Salvador Dali's immense *Santiago el Grande*.

Beck, Sir Adam. See ONTARIO HYDRO.

Beckwith, John (b.1927). Composer. Born in Victoria, B.C. he studied piano there and in Toronto, graduated from the University of Toronto in music, and studied composition with Nadia Boulanger in Paris. He became a teacher at the University of Toronto—while also writing music criticism for the *Toronto Star* (1952-62, 1963-5)—and since 1970 has been Dean of the Faculty of Music there. His music is in the North American tradition of Ives and Copland. He has written songs, choral music, piano pieces, chamber works, and orchestral compositions, and has often collaborated with the poet James REANEY, notably in the chamber opera NIGHT-BLOOMING CEREUS (1953-8). With Reaney he has created several musical 'collages' for radio, such as *Canada Dash, Canada Dot* (1965-7), notable for its beautiful Sharon section evoked by the Sharon Temple, which also figures in his choral work SHARON FRAGMENTS (1966). (See David WILLSON.) Other compositions include *The Great Lakes Suite* (1949) for voices and instrumental ensemble and *Jonah* (1963), a chamber cantata for choir and instruments.

Beecroft, Norma (b.1934). Composer. Born in Oshawa, Ont., she first studied composition in Toronto and later with Lukas Foss and Aaron Copland. She graduated from the Academy of St Cecilia in Rome in 1961. Her experimental early work is based on the 12-tone system (*Improvvisazioni Concertanti*, 1961). She next studied electronic music, worked as a producer for the CBC's National Music Department and as a free-lance commentator for the CBC-FM series 'Music of Today'. Recent works include the choral piece *Living Flame of Love* (1967) and the *Improvvisazioni Concertanti No 2* (1971), commissioned by the NATIONAL ARTS CENTRE ORCHESTRA.

Beef and 'Red Eye'. Roasted prime rib and baked red kidney beans, a speciality of Calgary, Alta.

Beer. A fermented malt beverage. Over 115 brands are brewed by 44 breweries across the country. Most beer sold in Canada is lager, rather than ale and is light on hops and hence tastes milder than its European counterpart. Canadian ales and lagers, with an alcoholic content of approximately 5%, are only marginally stronger than American brands.

Beer parlour. A hotel room licensed to serve beer, also called a beverage room. It usually has two entrances: 'Men' and 'Ladies and Escorts'.

Beers, William George (1843-1900). 'The father of lacrosse'. Born in Montreal and a surgeon-dentist, he is best known for having revised and brought up to date the rules of LACROSSE in 1867. He organized the first Canadian lacrosse team that visited the British Isles in 1876. Beers published a number of works, including *Lacrosse: The National Game of Canada* (1869), and also gave leadership to two other sports: snowshoeing and tobogganing. He is honoured in the Lacrosse HALL OF FAME.

Begbie, Sir Matthew Baillie (1819-94). Judge. Born in Edinburgh and educated at Cambridge, he was made a judge in British Columbia in 1858. Dispensing justice on horseback or in a tent, he had a reputation for firmness and strict legality—desirable qualities for a judge during the FRASER RIVER GOLD RUSH—and acquired the nickname 'The Hanging Judge'. He was appointed chief justice of British Columbia in 1870 and was knighted in 1874.

Begone Dull Care. A short film made by Norman McLAREN. It was co-directed by Evelyn Lambart and released by the NFB in 1949. Using his camera-less abstraction technique, McLaren created a succession of visuals to accompany a score played by the Oscar PETERSON jazz trio. The title comes from an anonymous Elizabethan song with the refrain: 'Begone, dull Care! I prithee begone from me!/Begone, dull Care! Thou and I shall never agree!' 7 min., 30 sec.; colour.

Beissel, Henry. See Walter BAUER.

Belaney, George Stansfeld. See GREY OWL.

Beliveau, Jean A. (b.1931). Hockey player, nicknamed 'Le Gros Bill'. Born in Trois-Rivières, Que., the 6-ft-3-in., 205-lb athlete began his hockey career with the junior Quebec Aces, then signed professionally with the MONTREAL CANADIENS, with which he played nearly 1,300 games, scored over 500 goals, and won the STANLEY CUP 10 times. Widely esteemed for his talent and sportsmanship, he became a club vice-president and director.

Bell, Alexander Graham (1847-1922). Scientist and inventor of the telephone. Born in Edinburgh, Scot., he was educated there and in London, Eng. He employed 'visible speech' (a system of symbolically illustrating the action of vocal chords), devised by his father Melville Bell (1819-1905), to teach the deaf to talk. A history of tuberculosis brought the family in 1870 to Tutela Heights, then on the outskirts of BRANTFORD, Ont., and now the site of the Bell homestead (a museum furnished with Bell memorabilia). The father taught philology at Queen's University (1870-81), then continued his work on speech in Washington, D.C. The son taught deaf pupils in Brantford and was an instructor in vocal physiology at Boston University. 'The telephone was conceived in Brantford in 1874, and born in Boston in 1875', Bell explained in 1917. 'It was in Brantford that the first transmission of speech to a distance occurred . . . that was in August, 1876.' The Bell Telephone Company was organized in July 1877, and the appeal of this invention eclipsed Bell's many other scientific achievements. In later years he summered at *Beinn Bhreagh*, the Gaelic name (meaning 'beautiful mountain') he gave his estate at BADDECK, Cape Breton, N.S., where he founded the AERIAL EXPERIMENT ASSOCIATION, which produced working models of the tetrahedral kite and the hydrofoil. He died there and is buried in the 25-acre Alexander Graham Bell National Historic Park. His tombstone bears the inscription: 'Died a Citizen of the United States'.

Bell, Dr Leslie (1906-62). Choral arranger and conductor. The Toronto-born Doctor of Music (from the University of Montreal) was an English teacher at Parkdale Collegiate, Toronto, in 1939 when he formed his first all-girl choir, a group of young women from 18 to 22. It grew into the Leslie Bell Singers, which performed in concert, recorded, and broadcast on CBC Radio's 'General Electric Hour' from 1949 and on CBC-TV's 'Leslie Bell Singers' (with Howard Cable and the Orchestra; Charles Jordan, baritone; and John Scott, announcer) from 1952. The group disbanded on Bell's death. He planned to call his unwritten autobiography 'A Man and a Thousand Girls'.

Bell, Marilyn (b.1937). Popular marathon swimmer. The Toronto-born distance swimmer was 16 years old when, on 9 Sept. 1954, under the tutelage of coach Gus RYDER, she became the first person to swim across Lake Ontario from Youngstown, N.Y., to Toronto's CNE shore. In 1955 she became the youngest swimmer to conquer the English Channel and the following year, on her second try, she swam the formidable Strait of Juan de Fuca. She gave up marathon swimming at 18 and is now a New Jersey primary-school teacher and the mother of four children. The slogan of her Lake Ontario swim, which received wide press coverage, was 'We'll win for Canada'.

Bella Coola. A SALISHAN-speaking group of Indians on the Pacific coast. Isolated from the COAST SALISH, they shared the culture but not the language of their coastal neighbours, the KWAKIUTLS. The Bella Coola originally lived in over 40 villages. Their population in 1970 was 597.

Belle Province, La. Unofficial motto of the Province of Quebec. The French phrase (which means 'The Beautiful Province') appears on automobile licence plates and tourist literature. The official motto is JE ME SOUVIENS ('I remember').

Belles-soeurs, Les. Play by Michel TREMBLAY that established him as Quebec's leading playwright. It is about a Montreal housewife who wins a million trading stamps and invites her friends to help her paste them into coupon books. The 15 characters, all women living in working-class Montreal, are frustrated, lonely, and malicious to each other. Their multi-voiced dialogue and choruses— they speak in JOUAL—effectively and entertainingly present a view of life that is both comic and pessimistic. The play was published in French in 1968 and in English— translated by John Van Burek and William GLASSCO—in 1974, and has had successful productions in both languages. It was originally produced by the THÉÂTRE DU RIDEAU VERT in 1968. The English production, directed by André Brassard, at the ST LAWRENCE CENTRE, opened to rave reviews on 3 Apr. 1973.

Bellevue House. Kingston residence of Sir John A. MACDONALD. Built about 1840 in the Tuscan Villa style, it was the home of the future prime minister, who was then a lawyer, from Aug. 1848 to Sept. 1849. Its first owner was a retired tea merchant who dubbed his ornate residence Tea Caddy Castle. Macdonald called it Pekoe Pagoda. Acquired by the federal government and opened in 1964 as a national historic park, the attractive 12-room residence has been restored and contains many of Macdonald's personal effects.

Bellot, Joseph-René (1826-53). French seaman and explorer. In a British expedition of 1851-2 in the search for Sir John FRANKLIN, he and the commanding officer, William Kennedy, made independent discoveries of Bellot Strait, between Somerset Island and Boothia Peninsula—an important link in the southerly route of the NORTHWEST PASSAGE.

Bengough, John Wilson (1851-1923). Cartoonist. Born in Toronto, he founded GRIP, a humorous weekly, in 1873 and for it did political cartoons that made his name well known. In 1842 he moved to the *Montreal Star* and then worked for the Toronto *Globe*. His cartoons were collected in two books, *Grip's Cartoons* (1875) and *Caricature History of Canadian Politics* (2 vols, 1886).

Bennett, R.B. (1870-1947). Twelfth prime minister. Born in Hopewell Hill, N.B., he practised law in the province before settling in Calgary, where he prospered as a lawyer and businessman. He was elected to the federal Parliament as a Conservative in 1911 and became leader of the party in 1927. His prime ministership, from 1930 to 1935, is associated with the Imperial Conference of 1930 that discussed the principles embodied in the STATUTE OF WESTMINSTER, and above all with the problems of the DEPRESSION, which he tried to cure by a number of reform measures that, while they were found to be unconstitutional in 1937, influenced his successors. In 1938 he resigned as leader and the next year he moved to Surrey, Eng. He was created Viscount Bennett of Mickleham, Calgary, and Hopewell in 1941.

Bennett, W.A.C. (b.1900). Premier of British Columbia, 1952-72. Born in Hastings, N.B., he moved to Edmonton as a young man, and to the Okanagan Valley in 1930. There he prospered as a hardware merchant and soon found his way into Conservative politics. Elected to the legislature in 1941, he fought a series of battles that led to increasing disillusionment with his own party and to increasing fear of the CCF. In 1951 he became a supporter of SOCIAL CREDIT and in 1952 he led this party, mostly an anti-CCF coalition, to power. For the next 20 years he *was* British Columbia—loud, aggressive, popular, well-off. The province prospered in the atmosphere of 'Wacky' Bennett's showmanship, but serious issues often were left unresolved. In 1972 the NDP under David Barrett fought a skilful campaign and ousted the Social Credit government. Bennett retired to the Okanagan, but his son William emerged as Social Credit leader shortly thereafter, taking the party back to office in 1975. See also CALONA WINES.

Bennett buggy. A horse-drawn automobile, named after R.B. BENNETT, who was prime minister from 1930 to 1935. Prairie farmers during the DEPRESSION, who owned automobiles but could no longer afford to maintain them, removed the engines and hitched teams to the front bumpers to provide two-horsepower transportation.

Benoit, Jehane (b.1904). A French-Canadian chef and popularizer of Canadian cuisine. Mme Benoit received a degree in food chemistry from the Sorbonne in Paris and is a graduate of the Cordon Bleu school there. In 1931 she established her own cooking school in Montreal. She has written many books on Quebec and Canadian cookery, and appeared on radio and television. Her books include *The Encyclopedia of Canadian Cuisine* (1963), *The Canadiana Cookbook* (1970), and *Enjoying the Art of Canadian Cooking* (1974).

Bentley, D.W. (Doug) (1916-72). Hockey player. He was born at Delisle, Sask. His father excelled in hockey and speedskating, and the five sons played on the same local hockey team. Doug and his brother Max went on to become NHL stars and received many of hockey's highest honours. With Bill Mosienko they formed one of hockey's great forward lines with the Chicago Black Hawks. All were elected to the Hockey HALL OF FAME.

Beny, Roloff (b.1924). Photographer and author. Born in Medicine Hat, Alta, he was educated at the University of Toronto, the State University of Iowa, Columbia University, and New York University. Before turning to photography, he worked as an abstract-expressionist painter. His interest in sensuous colours and exotic images resulted in the desire to preserve the beauty of past and present civilizations in dazzling photographs that have been published in many books, including *The Thrones of Earth and Heaven* (1958); *A Time of Gods* (1962); *Pleasure of Ruins* (1964); *To Everything There is a Season* (1967), a picture essay on Canada accompanied by Canadian poems selected by Milton Wilson; *Japan in Colour* (1967); and *Persia: Bridge of Turquoise* (1975). He lives in Rome.

Beothuk. Indians living in Newfoundland when early European visitors observed them and commented on their custom of painting their bodies with red ochre. This gave rise to the term 'Redskin' and 'Red Indian' for the aboriginal people of North America. They were exterminated by European fishermen and the MICMAC. Although there are periodic reports that Beothuk are not extinct, Nancy Shanawdithit, who died in 1827, has been called the last of the Beothuk.

Berczy, William (1744-1813). Portrait painter. Born Johann Albrecht Ulrich Moll in Saxony, he was in York (Toronto) between 1794 and 1805, when he moved to Montreal and earned his living painting portraits. His best-known paintings are *Joseph* BRANT (*c.*1805, NGC) and *The* WOOLSEY FAMILY (1808, NGC).

Beresford-Howe, Constance (b.1922). Novelist. Born in Montreal and educated at McGill and Brown Universities, she taught in the English department of McGill until the mid-1960s, when she settled in Toronto. Her best-known novel is *The Book of Eve* (1972), which was adapted by Larry Fineberg for the STRATFORD FESTIVAL and first performed on 14 July 1976, with Jessica Tandy taking the role of a determined elderly woman who leaves her husband when her first pension check arrives.

Bergeron, Léandre. See NEW CANADA PRESS.

Berlin, Eugenia (b.1905). Sculptor. Born in Russia, she studied in Geneva before immigrating to Toronto in 1925. She continued her studies at the Central Technical School, Toronto. She sculpts realistic heads and studies of children. She is represented in the National Gallery of Canada by a bronze head of Marius BARBEAU. For 25 years she directed the internationally known children's Saturday Morning Club at the Royal Ontario Museum.

Berliner, Emile (1851-1929). Inventor of the gramophone. Born in Hanover, Germany, he worked in New York in the 1870s as an engineer with Alexander Graham BELL. He took the phonograph, Edison's device to record on cylinders, one step further and in 1888 invented the gramophonic disc, the modern record. He patented the gramophone in Canada and in 1900 began manufacturing, recording, and distributing in Montreal. His company, which handled Victor records and equipment, was the first in the world to use the famous trademark 'His Master's Voice'.

Bernardi, Mario (b.1930). Conductor, pianist. Born in Kirkland Lake, Ont., he lived in Italy from 1936 to 1947 and studied music in Venice, Salzburg, and at the Royal Conservatory of Music, Toronto. He was musical director of the Sadler's Wells Opera Company, London, from 1966 to 1969, when he became the builder and conductor of the NATIONAL ARTS CENTRE ORCHESTRA, Ottawa. Under his guidance it has become a highly polished ensemble and has achieved international recognition.

Bernie Braden Tells a Story. Popular series of 15-minute programs on CBC Radio in which the actor Bernard BRADEN told original stories submitted by listeners. It ran from 16 Aug. 1948 to 1950.

Bernier, Joseph-Elzéar (1852-1934). Arctic explorer. Born in l'Islet, C.E. (Que.), he was a shipmaster at the age of 17. After holding various positions, he joined the Department of Marine and Fisheries and made his first Arctic voyage in 1904; he subsequently commanded patrols in known and uncharted Arctic waters. On 1 July 1909 he claimed the Arctic archipelago for Canada. Bernier was an advocate of the SECTOR THEORY. His memoirs, *Master Mariner and Arctic Explorer*, appeared posthumously in 1939.

Berthon, George Theodore (1806-92). Portrait painter. Born in France, he settled in Toronto in 1844. His best-known paintings are *The Three Robinson Sisters* (1846, AGO)—daughters of John Beverley ROBINSON—and *Mrs Wm Boulton as a Bride* (1847, AGO). Much later Mrs Boulton took as her second husband Goldwin SMITH.

Berton, Pierre (b.1920). Author, journalist, TV personality. Born in Whitehorse, Yukon, and educated at the University of British Columbia, he was city editor of the *Vancouver News-Herald* at 21, feature writer for the *Vancouver Sun* at 26, and an editor of *Maclean's* from 1947 to 1958, when he left to write a five-day-a-week column for the *Toronto Star*. He wrote and narrated the outstanding NFB film CITY OF GOLD in 1958. He became a national celebrity with his appearances on FRONT PAGE CHALLENGE and with a series of popular syndicated television series: The PIERRE BERTON SHOW (1962), UNDER ATTACK (1967), MY COUNTRY (1974), and The GREAT DEBATE (1974). His print journalism has been collected in such books as *Just Add Water and Stir* (1959), and his electronic journalism is the basis of *The Cool Crazy Committed World of the Sixties* (1966). *The Comfortable Pew* (1965) and *The Smug Minority* (1968) are short, best-selling books that launched national debates on the relevance of the church and the nature of the establishment. Berton's reputation as an accomplished writer of serious popular history rests firmly on *The Mysterious North* (1956), KLONDIKE (1958), and his two-volume history of the CPR, *The NATIONAL DREAM* (1970) and *The Last Spike* (1971). He has also found time to write the story and the music of PARADISE HILL (1967), to watch hundreds of old films in the preparation of HOLLYWOOD'S CANADA (1975), and to participate in a number of good causes.

Bessborough, Lord (1880-1956). GOVERNOR GENERAL of Canada from 1931 to 1935.

Bessette, Gérard (b.1920). Quebec novelist. Born in Sainte-Anne-de-Sabrevois, Que., and educated at the Université de Montréal, he is a professor of French at Queen's University and the author of novels that deal with social and psychological problems. Four

Bessette

have appeared in English: *Not for Every Eye* (1962) and *Incubation* (1967), both translated by Glen Shortliffe; *The Cycle* (1971), translated by Charles Strong; and *The Brawl* (1975), translated by Marc Lebel and Ronald Sutherland.

Bessy, The. The award presented annually by the Television Bureau of Canada and the Broadcast Executives Society, the word 'Bessy' being a partial acronym of the latter society's name. Bessies are awarded to the producers of the best television commercials produced in Canada during the previous year. The award itself is an androgynous figure less than a foot high, half kneeling, holding a globe aloft. Bessies were first awarded in the early 1960s and come in gold, silver, and bronze plate, identifying first, second, and third standings.

Best, Charles H. (b.1899). Medical researcher. Born in West Pembroke, Maine, of Nova Scotia-born parents, he was raised in Toronto and graduated in medicine from the University of Toronto in 1925. While a graduate student in physiology, he joined Dr Frederick G. BANTING, Dr J.J.R. MACLEOD, and eventually Dr J. B. COLLIP in a research project in diabetes that succeeded in isolating and purifying INSULIN. The 1923 NOBEL PRIZE for medicine was awarded to Banting and Macleod for this discovery. (Banting shared the prize money with Best, Macleod with Collip.) Best was director of the Insulin Division of CONNAUGHT LABORATORIES (1922-5) and an associate of the Banting and Best Department of Medical Research (1923-41), of which he became head (1941-67) on Banting's death. He is now emeritus director. The Charles H. Best Institute, a diabetes research laboratory at the University of Toronto, was named in his honour in 1951.

Best Damn Fiddler from Calabogie to Kaladar, The. Documentary film produced by the NFB in 1968. Directed by Peter Pearson, it is the story of an itinerant bush worker in a logging community in the Upper Ottawa Valley and studies the effects of isolation and deprivation on family life. Based on a poem by Joan FINNIGAN, it starred Chris Wiggins, Kate REID, and Margot Kidder. 49 min., 6 sec.; b & w.

Bethlehem Copper Corporation Limited. Important copper producer. Production of copper concentrates at the Bethlehem property in the cattle country of the Highland Valley in the interior of British Columbia began in 1962, seven years after the formation of the company by H.H. (Spud) Huestis, a Maritime-born prospector who believed that porphyry copper deposits could be found and developed near Ashcroft, B.C. Bethlehem was the first of many large copper mines developed in the province in the 1960s and early 1970s, and the first to attract Japanese capital from the giant Sumitomo trading company.

Bethune, Norman (b.1890). Medical doctor and hero of Communist China. Born in Gravenhurst, Ont., he graduated from the faculty of medicine of the University of Toronto. He worked with FRONTIER COLLEGE and served as a stretcher-bearer with the Royal Canadian Army Medical Corps at the second battle of YPRES, where he was wounded. He practised medicine in Detroit, recovered from tuberculosis at the Trudeau Sanatorium, Saranac Lake, N.Y., in 1927, and worked at the Royal Victoria Hospital and the Sacred Heart Hospital in Montreal, where he devised some still-used medical instruments. He attended the International Physiological Congress in the summer of 1935 and, impressed with the practice of state medicine in Moscow and Leningrad, secretly joined the Communist Party in Montreal in 1936. He organized the world's first mobile blood-transfusion service at Madrid for the Loyalists during the Spanish Civil War. Early in 1938 he joined the Eighth Route Army of the Chinese Communists in the hills of Yenan and formed the world's first mobile medical unit. He died of septicemia, contracted while operating, on 12 Nov. 1939. With the formation of the People's Republic of China 10 years later, and the publication of Mao Tse-tung's essay 'In Memory of Norman Bethune' (which extols his 'boundless sense of responsibility' and comes to the conclusion that 'every Communist must learn from him'), Bethune emerged as a leading hero and martyr of Communist China. Close by his tomb in Shih-chia Chuang, northern China, are a larger-than-life statue, a pavilion, a museum, and the Norman Bethune International Peace Hospital, all built in his honour. Ted ALLAN and Sydney Gordon wrote the first biography of Bethune, *The Scalpel, The Sword* (1952, 1971). The NFB produced a moving documentary—*Bethune* (58 min., 38 sec.; b & w; 1964), directed by Donald BRITTAIN, John Kemeny, and Guy Glover—which inspired Roderick Stewart to write his biography, *Bethune* (1973). The same year the federal government purchased the Gravenhurst manse where he was born—declaring it a national historic site—for a future Bethune museum.

Beurling, George 'Buzz' (1921-48). Second World War flying ace. Born in Montreal, he enlisted in the Royal Air Force in 1940 and within a year had earned his sergeant's wings. He served as a Spitfire pilot in England before he was posted to Squadron 249 of the RAF in Malta, where he achieved fame during the summer of 1942, when he shot down six enemy fighters and damaged one bomber. In Sept. 1942 he destroyed nine more enemy aircraft. He became a commissioned pilot officer the following year and continued a dramatic career that brought him many military awards. After he was shot down and wounded in Oct. 1942, he transferred to RCAF Squadron 403 and later Squadron 412. He returned to Canada in 1944 but continued flying after the war. In May 1948, while flying a Norseman aircraft to Israel, he crashed in Rome and was killed instantly.

Beverage room. See BEER PARLOUR.

BGen. Official abbreviation of Brigadier-General.

Bi and Bi Commission. See Royal Commission on BILINGUALISM AND BICULTURALISM.

Bible Bill. A nickname for William ABERHART, an evangelist and Social Credit premier of Alberta.

Bibliographie du Québec. Annual checklist, issued by the NATIONAL LIBRARY OF QUEBEC since 1969, of current books published in or about Quebec.

Bibliothèque nationale du Québec. See NATIONAL LIBRARY OF QUEBEC.

Bickerstaff, Isaac. See Don EVANS.

Biéler, Ted (b.1938). Sculptor. Born in Ottawa—the son of the artist André Biéler—he studied sculpture in France with Ossip Zadkine and at the Slade School of Art, London, Eng. His fibreglass moulds and concrete bas-reliefs have been exhibited in Toronto and New York and are represented in collections of the Montreal Museum of Fine Arts and McMaster University, Hamilton, Ont. Important commissions include Expo 67 and sculpture for the Royal Winnipeg Ballet (1970).

Biencourt de Saint-Just, Charles de. See Charles LA TOUR and Jean de Biencourt de POUTRINCOURT.

Bienfait Strike. See ESTEVAN STRIKE.

Big Bear (d.1888). Cree chief who gave leadership to disaffected Indians prior to the NORTH WEST REBELLION. He was unable to prevent them from killing some whites at FROG LAKE and from besieging and burning Fort

Pitt. He and his band were attacked by the militia at Frenchman's Butte, after which the Indians scattered. Big Bear surrendered in July 1885 and was tried and sentenced to two years' imprisonment.

Big Blue Machine. Political phrase used to characterize the Conservative party of Ontario as a sleek, efficient, vote-getting apparatus. It was coined by Claire Hoy in the *Toronto Star* in Apr. 1971 to describe the men surrounding Premier William Davis. The name is an adaptation of the nickname given the Cincinnati Reds baseball team: the Big Red Machine.

Big David. See Davidialuk AMIITUK.

Big Dipper. Trade name of a dark rum from the West Indies, popular in Newfoundland. It took its name from a popular bar at GANDER Airport in the 1950s.

Big Foot or **Bigfoot.** See SASQUATCH.

Big Four Football League. An association of four football clubs that banded together in 1907. They were the Ottawa Rough Riders, the Montreal A.A.A., the Toronto Argonauts, and the Hamilton Tigers. William A. HEWITT presided over the first meeting.

Big Nickel, The. 'The biggest man-made tourist attraction in Northern Ontario'. Located in 'the world's only numismatic park' on the outskirts of Sudbury, which has the world's largest nickel deposits, this immense replica of solid nickel is 30 ft in diameter and 2 ft thick. It was modelled on the 12-sided Canadian nickel minted in 1951 to honour two centuries of nickel mining. Its erection in 1967 was the inspiration of Ted Szilva, a local fireman.

Big Six. The six largest multinational oil companies operating in Canada. The so-called Bix Six are British Petroleum (BP), Gulf, Imperial (Exxon), Shell, Sun Oil (Sunoco), and Texaco.

'Big sky country'. Description of the PRAIRIE PROVINCES, especially Alberta, used in tourist literature during the 1960s.

Big Train, The. Sobriquet of the all-round athlete Lionel CONACHER dating from the 1930s. Earlier it was used to describe 'Smirlie' Lawson, a popular football halfback, in 1912.

Bigelow, Dr William G. See HYPOTHERMIA.

Biggar, H.P. (1872-1938). Historian and archivist. Born at Carrying Place, Ont., he was educated at the University of Toronto and at

Oxford. From 1905 until his death he was Canada's chief archivist in Europe. He translated and edited for the Public Archives of Canada *The Voyages of Jacques Cartier* (1924) and was general editor for the Champlain Society of *The Works of Samuel de Champlain* (6 vols, 1922-33).

Bigot, François (1703-78). Intendant of New France, celebrated embezzler. First at LOUISBOURG, where he was administrator (1739-45), and then as Intendant at Quebec (1748-60), he conducted a system of embezzling government property and funds that grew until it virtually ruined New France. With numerous associates he controlled trade through a storehouse, 'La Friponne' ('the cheat'), profiteering at the expense of the government and cheating the colonists. He was stopped only by the Conquest. In France he was imprisoned in the Bastille for 11 months, fined, forced to make some restitution, and banished. He died in Switzerland.

Bilingual Districts Advisory Board. Federal body reporting on the need for bilingual districts. The OFFICIAL LANGUAGES ACT, 1969, provides that, following each decennial census, the Canadian government is required to constitute a Bilingual Districts Advisory Board to recommend to cabinet the designation of areas in which federal services must be provided in both English and French.

Bilingualism and Biculturalism, Royal Commission on. A commission to inquire into the use of the French language and the status of French Canadians in Canada. It was appointed in July 1963 because of the disturbances in Quebec caused by the separatists. The chairmen were André LAURENDEAU of *Le Devoir* and Davidson Dunton of Carleton University. The Commission issued an interim report in 1965; a final report in six volumes began appearing in 1967. As a result of the Commission's recommendations the OFFICIAL LANGUAGES ACT was passed in 1969.

Bill 22. Popular name of Quebec's language act. The controversial measure, designed to make French the only official language of the province and to extend the use of and instruction in French in the province, was passed by the Quebec legislature in 1974. One of its provisions is that children whose mother tongue is not English must be taught in French-language schools.

Bill Masterton Memorial Trophy. Presented annually 'to the NATIONAL HOCKEY LEAGUE player who best exemplifies the qualities of perseverance, sportsmanship and dedication to hockey'. The winner, who receives $1,000, is selected by the Professional Hockey Writers' Association, which first presented trophy in 1968 to commemorate the late William Masterton, a Minnesota North Stars player who exhibited these qualities.

Bill No. 1. A bill introduced into the Houses of Parliament immediately after the reading of the SPEECH FROM THE THRONE. In the HOUSE OF COMMONS, Bill No. 1 is 'a Bill respecting the administration of the oaths of office'. In the SENATE it is 'a Bill relating to railways'. These bills do not exist except as titles but are introduced at the opening of every session to signify the right of Parliament to attend to its own business first before considering the affairs of the CROWN. The practice derives from a tradition of the British Parliament.

Bill of Rights. See CANADIAN BILL OF RIGHTS.

Bingo. Feature film written and directed by Jean-Claude Lord. Released in 1973, it starred Jean Duceppe, Gilles Pelletier, Manda Parent, and Alexandra Stewart. A student gets caught up in a strike and finds himself involved in a kidnapping and bombing—and deserted by his terrorist mentor. Though criticized as being a political exploitation of recent events in Quebec, the film was a tremendous commercial success. 113 min., colour.

Binks, Sarah. See SARAH BINKS.

Binning, B.C. (1909-76). Painter. Born in Medicine Hat, Alta, he studied at the Vancouver School of Art, the University of Oregon, and the Art Students' League of New York, and taught art and architecture at the University of British Columbia. He exhibited internationally. His abstracts of marine themes, often painted in muted cool shades, are based on tightly constructed, simple geometric shapes. Their thin-lined designs recall his background in architecture. *Ghost Ships* (1949, AGO) is his best-known painting.

Birch. Any of numerous species of deciduous hardwood trees with a thin, papery bark. Of the 10 species native to Canada, the most important is the white birch, widely distributed except for the tundra and southern British Columbia. A prominent staple of the pulp and paper industry, it was once used extensively in birchbark CANOES.

Bird, Will R. (b.1891). Author. Born near Amherst, N.S., and educated at Amherst Academy, he is known for his historical romances about the early settlers in Nova Scotia, including *Here Stays Good Yorkshire* (1945); personal travel books, including *This is Nova*

Scotia (1950); and collections of short stories, including *Sunrise for Peter* (1946). He edited *Atlantic Anthology* (1959) and described his First World War experiences with the Black Watch in *Ghosts Have Warm Hands* (1968).

'Birdcages, The'. Nickname of the legislative buildings of the colony of Vancouver Island. Commissioned by Governor James DOUGLAS and built in Victoria by Gideon Hallcrow, a Scottish handyman, in 1859, they were described by the Victoria *Gazette* as 'the latest fashion of Chinese-pagoda, Swiss-cottage, and Italian-villa birdcages'. They were replaced by the present legislative buildings in 1898. A fire destroyed the last of the buildings in 1957.

'Birdseye Centre'. A weekly half-page cartoon feature that depicted life among farmers and fishermen, urchins and dogs, in a fictitious community somewhere in rural Ontario. The popular feature was created by James (Jimmy) Frise, who was born at Lake Scugog, Ont., in 1891 and died in Montreal in 1948. It was carried by the STAR WEEKLY (originally as 'Life's Little Comedies') from 1921 to 1947, when it began to appear in colour in WEEKEND MAGAZINE (under the title 'Juniper Junction') until Frise's death. Greg CLARK introduced *Birdseye Centre* (1973), a selection of Frise's work.

Birks & Sons Limited, Henry. A chain of 94 silver and china shops founded in Montreal in 1879 by Henry Birks (1840-1928), the son of a Sheffield silversmith. The main store on Phillips Square has been a Montreal landmark since 1893. Birks also sells other quality goods, such as jewellery, crystal, leather goods, etc. Merchandise is packaged in the 'familiar Birks blue box'.

Birmingham Flexible Axle Six. Automobile manufactured at Peterborough, Ont., by Birmingham Motors about 1922. The Birmingham slogan was 'The easiest riding car in the world'.

Birney, Earle (b.1904). 'The Dean of Canadian Poets'. Born in Calgary and brought up in Banff, Alta, he was educated at the Universities of British Columbia, Toronto, and California. He has taught English and creative writing on campuses across the country. A rebel by temperament and a technician by training, he writes poetry that ranges widely and richly in style, place, and subject matter, from the narrative DAVID (1952) to more recent concrete experiments. From his individual collections—*David and Other Poems* (1942), *Now is Time* (1945), *The Strait of Anian* (1948), *Trial of a City and Other*

Verse (1952), *Ice Cod Bell or Stone* (1962), *Near False Creek Mouth* (1964), *Selected Poems* (1966), *Pnomes, Jukollages and Other Stunzas* (1969), *Rag & Bone Shop* (1971)—he fashioned *The Collected Poems of Earle Birney* (2 vols, 1975). He is also the author of two satiric novels, TURVEY (1949, 1976) and *Down the Long Table* (1955); two works of non-fiction, *The Creative Writer* (1966) and *The Cow Jumped Over the Moon: The Writing and Reading of Poetry* (1972); and he edited *Twentieth Century Canadian Poetry* (1953) and *The Selected Poems of Malcolm Lowry* (1962).

Bishop, William A. (Billy) (1894-1956). War ace. Born in Owen Sound, Ont., and educated at the Royal Military College, he distinguished himself in the Royal Flying Corps in France in 1917 and 1918. For his aerial duels he was known to German fliers as 'Hell's Handmaiden'; he is credited with shooting down 72 enemy aircraft. He entered commercial aviation in 1919 and was vice-president of the McCOLL-FRONTENAC OIL COMPANY for 23 years. He was appointed the RCAF's honorary air vice-marshal in 1936 and its honorary air marshal during the Second World War. His son W.A. Bishop wrote *The Courage of the Early Morning: The Story of Billy Bishop* (1965).

Bishop's University. A small, predominantly residential university at Lennoxville, Que., it was founded by the Right Reverend George Mountain, third Bishop of Quebec, in 1843 as a liberal arts college. It continued under the Church of England until 1947, when it became non-denominational. In 1971 Champlain College (CEGEP) was established on the campus in co-operative association with the university.

Bison. Symbol of Manitoba. The largest hoofed animal native to North America, it is characterized by a dark brown coat, large head with short black horns, and a large muscular hump on its shoulders, covered by a shaggy mantle. The American bison, commonly called the buffalo, once roamed the Prairies in vast herds, but millions were slaughtered by Indians and the white man for food and hides, bringing the species to the verge of extinction. Bison can now be found on select tracts of western and sub-Arctic lands, mostly in national parks and wildlife refuges.

Bissell, Claude (b.1916). University administrator and writer. Born in Meaford, Ont., he was educated at the University of Toronto and Cornell University and taught English at Cornell from 1938 to 1941 and at the University of Toronto from 1941 to 1956, when he became president of Carleton University. While president of the University of Toronto from 1958 to 1971, he was also chairman of the CANADA COUNCIL (1960-2), Visiting Professor at Harvard University (1967-8), and president of many academic organizations. He currently teaches at Massey College as one of five University Professors of the University of Toronto. He wrote *The Strength of the University* (1968) and *Halfway Up Parnassus: A Personal Account of the University of Toronto 1932-71* (1974), and edited *Our Living Tradition* (1957) and *Great Canadian Writing* (1966).

Bissett, Bill (b.1939). Poet and artist. Born in Halifax and self-educated, he lives in Vancouver, where he operates the BLEWOINTMENT PRESS. Signing himself 'bill bissett', he composes sound and concrete poems and creates felt-pen drawings and acrylic canvases. His iconoclastic poems—which are experiments in form, sometimes incorporating drawings and reproduced in blurred print with a personal system of spelling—challenge both the sensibility and the assumption of the reader. His publications include *We Sleep Inside Each Other All* (1966) and *Medicine My Mouth's on Fire* (1976). *Nobody Owns th Earth* (1971) is a representative selection of his work edited by Margaret ATWOOD and Dennis LEE.

Bitter Ash. Feature film directed by Lawrence KENT. Released in 1963, it is about sexual games revolving around a Vancouver playwright. It was produced by students at the University of British Columbia and, when shown in Ontario, was seized by the Censor Board. 79 min., b & w.

Biyiasas, Peter (b.1950). Canadian chess champion in 1972 and 1975. Born in Athens and now living in Vancouver, he is an International Master and holds second place on Canada's rating list.

Bjarni, Herjólfsson (active c.986). The first European to sight the east coast of North America. An Icelandic merchant on his way to visit his father in Greenland, Bjarni sailed off course, eventually sighting the shores of what are thought to be Newfoundland, Labrador, and Baffin Island, according to descriptions in *The Sagas of the Icelanders*.

Black bear. The most widely distributed of Canada's three groups of bears, found in forest regions of all the provinces except Prince Edward Island. It has a black coat, brown snout, weighs an average of 300 lbs, measures 5 to 6 ft in length, and hibernates in the winter. See also GRIZZLY BEAR, POLAR BEAR.

Black cod. Pacific codfish, distinct from the Atlantic variety. It is brined and smoked.

Black Creek Pioneer Village. Folk village in northwest Toronto that recreates life in a rural Ontario community 100 years ago. It was opened by the Metropolitan Toronto and Region Conservation Authority in 1967, with five original log buildings of the Stong farm and a Pennsylvania-style barn built in 1809 providing the nucleus. Since then some 25 other buildings—including a general store, gristmill, printing office, and town hall—have been moved to the site and authentically restored and furnished. Other buildings are gradually being added.

Black Diamond Cheese. The label on a wide range of cheeses produced by factories near Belleville, Ont., now owned by BROOKE BOND holding company. Black Diamond Cheese Limited, established in 1933, acquired a number of old cheese factories, including W.S. Cook & Sons Limited, founded in 1874. The original Black Diamond Cheese was a cheddar, the rind of which turned black when dipped in hot paraffin wax to prevent shrinkage and mould-formation. This hard, mild cheddar, regarded as 'a diamond among cheeses', has long been popular in Britain. Black Diamond Cheeses—which now include many process cheeses—are popular in Canada, the United Kingdom, the United States, and the West Indies.

Black Donnellys. See The DONNELLYS.

Black fly. A small biting insect with gauzy wings, short legs, and humped back. Nearly world-wide in distribution, it is found in great swarms throughout the central forests, northern prairies, and tundra of Canada. Only the female fly bites and sucks the blood from her victim, but both sexes harass man and animal alike.

'Black Fly Song, The'. A popular song about the BLACK FLY of northern Ontario. The words and music were written in 1949 by Wade Hemsworth, an Ontario Hydro employee, when he was surveying the Little Abitibi R., which flows into James Bay. The refrain runs: 'And the black flies, the little black flies,/Always the black fly no matter where you go,/I'll die with the black fly a pickin' my bones/In North Ontario-io, in North Ontario.'

Black Friday. Phrase used by Thomas M. Bell, Conservative MP, in the House of Commons on Friday, 1 June 1956, when the Liberal government applied CLOSURE during the PIPELINE DEBATE.

Black gold. An epithet for oil, suggestive of both its colour and value.

Black king. See ROI NÈGRE.

Black Rod. See GENTLEMAN USHER OF THE BLACK ROD.

Black Watch of Canada, The. Canadian army regiment. Also known as the Royal Highland Regiment, it was organized in Montreal in 1862 and served in the SOUTH AFRICAN WAR. In the FIRST WORLD WAR it served in France and Flanders with the 1st, 3rd, and 4th Canadian Divisions, distinguishing itself in many battles. During the SECOND WORLD WAR it was part of the 5th Infantry Brigade and participated in the DIEPPE raid before serving with the 2nd Canadian Infantry Brigade in the Normandy Landing. Battalions have since served in Korea and Germany.

Blackfoot. A confederacy of tribes of ALGONKIAN-speaking Indians who roamed the western plains. Their name is said to be explained by the word for moccasins blackened by walking over burnt prairie grass. With the introduction of the horse in the mid-eighteenth century, the Blackfoot rapidly became superb horsemen and daring raiders. When whisky traders from the south began to compete in the fur trade, the NORTH WEST MOUNTED POLICE force was organized, winning a reputation for fairness that influenced Blackfoot leaders like CROWFOOT to remain aloof from the NORTH WEST REBELLION of 1885. The Blackfoot SUN DANCE and distinctive war bonnet have been adopted by neighbouring tribes. Their population in 1970 was 8,030.

Blackfoot Crossing. A point on the Bow R., 70 mi. east of Calgary, where it was once possible to cross the river by means of a dry stone ridge that extended from one bank to the other. It was the site of the annual SUN DANCE of the BLACKFOOT Indians, whose great chief, CROWFOOT, met there to sign Blackfoot Treaty Number Seven, creating the Blackfoot Reserve, on 22 Sept. 1877. Crowfoot died at Blackfoot Crossing on 25 Apr. 1890 and is buried there.

Blackskin. See MUKTUK.

Blais, Marie-Claire (b.1939). Quebec novelist. Born in Quebec City, she left school at 15 and published her first novel, La Belle Bête— translated by Merloyd Lawrence as MAD SHADOWS (1960)—at 18. She was encouraged in her writing by the Rev. Georges-Henri Lévesque and the American critic Edmund Wilson and went on to become a prolific writer of novels that deal obsessively, sometimes lyrically, with unloved misfits, doomed innocents, evil, and damnation. Her other novels published in English, with their translators' names, are: Tête blanche (1960), Charles Fullman; A Season in the Life of Emmanuel (1966), Derek Coltman; The Manuscripts of Pauline Archange (1969), Derek Coltman; St Lawrence Blues (1974), Ralph Manheim; David Sterne (1973), David Lobdell; and The Wolf (1974), Sheila FISCHMAN. Two novellas, Le Jour est noir (1962) and Les Voyageurs sacrés (1969), have been translated by Derek Coltman in a single volume as The Day is Dark and Three Travellers (1967). Her latest novel, Une Liaison Parisienne (1975), explores the relationship that exists between the French in France and the French in Quebec.

Blaise, Clark (b.1940). Short-story writer. Born in Fargo, N. Dak., of French- and English-Canadian parents, he was raised in Florida and since the 1960s has lived in Montreal, where he teaches at Concordia University. An assured writer of fiction with a vigorous narrative style and a strong sense of characterization, he has written two collections of short stories: A North American Education (1973) and Tribal Justice (1974). He is married to the writer Bharati MUKHERJEE.

Blake, Edward (1833-1912). Lawyer and politician. Educated at Upper Canada College and the University of Toronto, he had a brilliant intellect and was a recognized authority on the constitution. In 1867 he was elected both to the House of Commons as a Liberal and to the legislative assembly of Ontario. He was premier of the province briefly in 1872, when he resigned to hold his seat in Parliament. He left the Liberals in 1873 and joined the CANADA FIRST party, announcing his new loyalty in his famous AURORA SPEECH. He returned to the Liberal fold in 1875, however, and was party leader from 1880 to 1887, when he was succeeded by Wilfrid LAURIER; he resigned from the party in 1891 in opposition to the platform of RECIPROCITY. The next year he left the country and was elected to the British House of Commons as a supporter of Home Rule for Ireland. He returned to Canada in 1907.

Blake, Hector (b.1912). Hockey player. Born in Victoria Mines, Ont., he played amateur hockey and turned professional with the Montreal Maroons. He played with the MONTREAL CANADIENS for 12 seasons and helped form one of hockey's most memorable lines—the Richard-Lach-Blake line. After retiring as a player he coached the Canadiens to eight STANLEY CUP championships. The nickname 'Toe' came from his childhood playmates, who could not pronounce 'Hector'.

Blake

Blake, W.H. (1861-1924). Essayist and translator. Born in Toronto, William Hume Blake graduated from the University of Toronto and was called to the bar in 1885. He published two collections of essays relating to rural Quebec and its landscape: *Brown Waters and Other Sketches* (1915) and *In a Fishing Country* (1922). He translated superbly Louis HÉMON'S MARIA CHAPDELAINE (1921) and Adjutor Rivard's *Chez nous: Our Quebec Home* (1924).

Bland, Salem Goldworth (1859-1950). Methodist minister, author, and social critic. Born in Lachute, Que., he was educated at McGill University and ordained in 1884. He became a controversial churchman who advocated the humanistic and radical 'social gospel'—involvement of the church in politics and labour problems—in his widely read book *The New Christianity* (1920). A famous portrait of him by Lawren HARRIS is in the Art Gallery of Ontario.

Blank cheque. A reference to the attack made by opposition leader Mackenzie KING in the House of Commons, 16 June 1931, on Prime Minister R.B. BENNETT. King claimed that Bennett was asking 'this parliament to give a blank cheque which he might fill in for as much as he wished to draw'.

Blass, Richard (1946-75). Quebec gangster nicknamed *'Le Chat'*. An escapee from St Vincent de Paul Penitentiary, he was wanted by the Montreal Mafia for an alleged double-cross and by the Montreal police for a gang-land-murder and arson at the Gargantua Bar Salon on 21 Jan. 1975. Traced by the police to a ski resort at Val David in the Laurentians, he was shot to death at 4:30 a.m. on 25 Jan.

Blasted Pine, The. Widely read 'anthology of satire, invective, and disrespectful verse, chiefly by Canadian writers'. The collection of over 150 poems, edited by F.R. SCOTT and A.J.M. SMITH, was published in 1957 and revised and enlarged in 1967.

Blatz, William E. (1895-1964). Child psychologist. He was born in Hamilton, Ont., and educated at the Universities of Toronto and Chicago. In 1925 he founded the INSTITUTE OF CHILD STUDY, University of Toronto, to explore children's psychological development. He is known particularly for his Security Theory, which holds that a sense of security in childhood—fostered by the parents' approach to the child—is the most important requirement for healthy psychological growth and will enable the child to pass from a state of dependent security to one of independent security. He was the author of *Understanding the Young Child* (1944).

Bleus. Sobriquet for members of the Conservative Party of Quebec in the nineteenth century. (Blue is the traditional Conservative colour.) The term originated about 1850 and was applied to supporters of Louis-H. LAFONTAINE to distinguish them from the radical ROUGES, who were influenced by the ideas of Louis-Joseph PAPINEAU.

Blewointment Press. Underground press established by Bill BISSETT in Vancouver in 1967 and specializing in poetry publications that are visually and verbally avant-garde.

Bley, Paul (b.1945). Jazz guitarist. Born in Hochfield, Man., he moved to Toronto at 19 and followed a career as a jazz guitarist. He has played with Hagood HARDY, Moe KOFFMAN, Phil NIMMONS, and Ron COLLIER. He performs in clubs and does extensive radio and television work.

Blind River. See Stephen B. ROMAN.

Blinkity Blank. A short film made by Norman McLAREN. Fantastic images—some animated and some scratched directly onto 35 mm film-stock—flash on the screen to the accompaniment of a musical score by Maurice Blackburn, supplemented by McLaren's sound score drawn directly onto the sound track. The film was released by the NFB in 1954. 6 min., colour.

Bloc Populaire Canadien. A Quebec wartime party that operated at provincial and federal levels. It was the successor to La Ligue pour la Défense du Canada, the anti-conscription-ist group that opposed the CONSCRIPTION plebiscite in 1942. Bringing together a coalition of nationalist and anti-DUPLESSIS forces, the Bloc (under Maxime Raymond) had some limited success in federal by-elections during the war and (under André LAURENDEAU) in the 1944 Quebec election. It was progressive in industrial relations and concerned about foreign investment. It soon foundered, however, in divisive squabbling. Gratien GÉLINAS called it the 'flop populaire'.

Blomidon, Cape. Promontory on the north coast of Nova Scotia that forms the abrupt east end of the North Mountain range of Nova Scotia. It is 670 ft high and extends into Minas Basin in the Bay of Fundy. The origin of the name is uncertain but is thought to be a corruption of 'Blow-me-down', a name by which it was known to early sailors. Nova Scotia amethysts are found around the cape, which, by tradition, is the home of GLOO-SCAP.

Blood, breath, spit and urine. Colourful phrase based on sections 236 and 237 of the

46

CRIMINAL CODE OF CANADA. These sections prohibit the driving of a motor vehicle if the driver's alcohol blood content exceeds 80 mg of alcohol in 100 ml of blood. The Bakenstein breathalyzer is used to determine blood-alcohol content by means of a test in which the suspect blows into the machine and a calculation is made by the machine of the alcohol-blood content of the suspect. The code provides that a 'certificate of an analyst making a chemical analysis of a sample of the blood, urine, breath or other bodily substance of an accused may be used to establish alcohol-blood content'. See also .08%.

Blood Is Strong, The. A powerful three-act play by Lister SINCLAIR. Published in 1956, it was earlier produced by JUPITER THEATRE and on CBC Radio by J. Frank WILLIS on 3 Apr. 1957. It is about a Scots immigrant to Cape Breton, N.S., in the early nineteenth century and the problems of different generations. The title comes from *The Lone Sheiling* (see CANADIAN BOAT SONGS).

Bloody Assize. Trials for high treason conducted against marauding bands of settlers who defected to the United States during the WAR OF 1812. At the trials—held in Ancaster, U.C. (Ont.), in May 1814—15 men were condemned to death as traitors. Ultimately eight were executed and seven were exiled.

Bloody Saturday. See WINNIPEG GENERAL STRIKE.

Bloody Sunday. Epithetical description of events that took place on Sunday, 19 June 1938. The Vancouver Post Office was occupied for six weeks until RELIEF CAMP workers and others until a full-scale assault by the RCMP dislodged them on 'Bloody Sunday'. 35 people were wounded.

Bloore, Ronald (b.1925). Painter. Born in Brampton, Ont., he studied at the University of Toronto, the Institute of Fine Arts at New York University, Washington University, and the Courtauld Institute, London, Eng. In 1958 he was appointed director of the Norman MacKenzie Art Gallery at Regina College, and became a member of the REGINA FIVE. He now teaches at York University, Toronto. In the early-1960s he explored pictorial images, often using mandala-like shapes in tinted paint on a white ground. *Painting, June 1960* (1960, NGC) is a beautiful example of this style. To explore fully the values of light, he has since rejected warm colours in favour of white-on-white abstractions that reflect his interest in ancient art. He has also made constructions of wooden spoons that he calls 'sploores'.

Blue baby operation. Surgery to correct the congenital heart defect of a baby or child whose features have a bluish tinge owing to the poor circulation of blood. The first such operation in the British Empire, and one of the world's earliest, was performed by Dr Gordon Murray (1896-1976) at the Toronto General Hospital. During the surgical treatment to correct a case of Tetralogy of Fallot, he made use of the anticoagulant he had discovered, HEPARIN. The results of the successful operation were published in 1947.

Blue Diamond Coal. See McINTYRE MINES.

Blue Mountain Pottery. Trade name of an internationally known artware. The studio was founded in 1949 in a barn on the outskirts of Collingwood, Ont., by Czech-born Jozo Weider. Almost 200 people are now employed producing a line of pottery that is characterized by the use of Georgian Bay clay (from nearby Blue Mountain), slip casting, handpainted surfaces of deep blues and rich greens (though other colours have been introduced), and high, mirror-like glosses.

Blue Ribbon Tea. The brand name of a popular tea. It was blended, branded, and packaged by two brothers, G.F. and J. Galt, wholesale merchants and grocers in Winnipeg, and first sold in 1882. Since 1951 the company has been owned by BROOKE BOND CANADA LIMITED.

Bluenose. Sobriquet of a Nova Scotian. It was 'acquired from a superior potato of that name' grown in the province, according to Thomas Chandler HALIBURTON in 1849.

Bluenose. The most famous sailing ship of the century. The 130-ft fishing schooner, launched in 1921 at Lunenburg, N.S., was the last of the great Nova Scotian clippers. Under Capt. Angus J. Walters, she won the International Fishermen's Trophy that year and successfully defended it in four subsequent races before being sold in 1942; she was lost on a reef off Haiti in 1946. In 1963 Oland's Brewery built a replica, *Bluenose II,* which they donated to the province of Nova Scotia. The likeness of the original has appeared on the obverse of the Canadian 10-cent piece, first minted in 1936.

Bluenose country. Sobriquet of NOVA SCOTIA. See also BLUENOSE.

Blues. Name given the galley proofs of HANSARD, which are made available to members of the House of Commons for their approval before being paged and published as *House of Commons Debates: Official Reports.*

Blunden Harbour

Blunden Harbour. Well-known painting by Emily CARR. A striking and monumental composition of totem figures in profile facing the water, with mountain and sky in the background, it was painted at a KWAKIUTL village on the British Columbia coast about 1928-30. (NGC)

BMI Canada Limited. Performing rights society. Founded in Canada in 1940 by Broadcast Music Inc. of New York, it served as a licensing body for the music of American composers. In 1947 it became an active promoter of Canadian music, and represented Canadian composers, authors, and publishers. On 1 July 1976 it broke away from Broadcast Music Inc. and became an autonomous body; its name will change in late 1976. At an annual dinner it presents the HAROLD MOON AWARD as well as numerous other prizes. See also COMPOSERS, AUTHORS AND PUBLISHERS ASSOCIATION OF CANADA.

BNA Act, 1867. A statute passed by the Parliament of the United Kingdom in Feb. 1867 that created 'one Dominion under the name of Canada' out of the colonies of Canada, Nova Scotia, and New Brunswick, dividing them into four provinces named Ontario, Quebec, Nova Scotia, and New Brunswick. The bill received royal assent on 29 Mar. 1867 and became effective on 1 July. The Act is popularly held to be 'the Canadian constitution', but is in fact a British law that provides for the distribution of legislative powers between the federal Parliament and the provincial legislatures and assures the independence of the judiciary and the provincial ownership of Crown lands. The BNA Act can be amended by an address to the British Parliament upon a resolution and address of the Parliament of Canada—a flexible and technically simple procedure. The federal government, under Prime Minister Pierre Trudeau, is pledged to 'repatriate' the BNA Act once approval has been negotiated with the provinces. The final authority to interpret its terms is vested in the Supreme Court of Canada. It is reprinted in *British North America Acts and Selected Statutes: 1867-1962* (1962) edited by Maurice Ollivier.

Boa, Gilmour S. (Gil) (1924-73). One of the world's best rifle-shooters. The son of James Boa, himself a coach of Canadian rifle teams that competed at Bisley, Eng., he won the King's Prize at Bisley in 1951 and the world's championship in the smallbore carbine event at Caracas, Venezuela, in 1954. At the 1956 Olympics in Melbourne he won the bronze medal. He captured the gold medal at the 1966 British Commonwealth Games in Kingston, Jamaica.

Board of Broadcast Governors. A federal regulatory agency for radio and television. A key recommendation of the FOWLER COMMISSION was the creation of a regulatory agency for public as well as private broadcasting in Canada. Dr Andrew Stewart was appointed head of the BBG, which assumed the CBC's regulatory powers on 11 Nov. 1958. It established CANADIAN CONTENT regulations, issued television licences for 'second stations', and authorized the creation of the CTV Network in 1961. It was replaced by the CANADIAN RADIO-TELEVISION COMMISSION in 1968.

Boas, Franz (1858-1942). Anthropologist. Born and educated in Germany and an American citizen, he was regarded as the leading anthropologist and ethnologist of his day. The first anthropologist to do field work in Canada, he investigated the Eskimos of Baffin Island in 1883-4, then turned his attention in 1886 to the Eskimos and Indians of the Northwest Coast. Among his numerous important publications are *Tsimshian Texts* (1902), *Kwakiutl Tales* (1910), *Bella Bella Texts* (1928), and *Bella Bella Tales* (1932). His seminal study *Primitive Art* (1927) included illustrations of the work of Charles EDENSHAW. Ronald P. Rohner edited *The Ethnology of Franz Boas* (1969), a collection of letters and diaries written by Boas on the Northwest Coast, translated from the German by Hedy Parker.

Bochner, Lloyd (b.1924). Actor. Born in Toronto and a graduate of the University of Toronto, he began his professional training at the age of 10 with Josephine Barrington's Juveniles. He made his CBC Radio début at the age of 11 and has been associated with CBC STAGE, the NEW PLAY SOCIETY, and GM PRESENTS, etc. The tall actor, with a rich baritone voice, appeared at the STRATFORD FESTIVAL in its first three seasons. Since 1960 he has made Hollywood his base, after landing the role of a police commissioner in the 26-episode ABC-TV series *Hong Kong*. He has appeared in a number of films, including *The MEGANTIC OUTLAW* (1971).

Bodsworth, Fred (b.1918). Naturalist and author. Born in Port Burwell, Ont., he became a magazine and newspaper writer. His detailed knowledge of ornithology was used creatively in his novels *The Last of the Curlews* (1954), *The Strange One* (1959), *The Atonement of Ashley Morden* (1964), and *The Sparrow's Fall* (1966).

Boer War. See SOUTH AFRICAN WAR.

Boggs, Jean Sutherland (b.1922). Former director of the NATIONAL GALLERY OF CANADA. Educated at the University of Toronto and

Radcliffe College (Harvard University), she taught in American universities before becoming curator of the Art Gallery of Toronto; Steinberg Professor of Art at Washington University; and, in 1966, the very successful fifth director of the National Gallery. Her resignation as director—which became effective on 1 July 1976—was mostly brought about by the encroachment on gallery autonomy by the NATIONAL MUSEUMS OF CANADA, a Crown Corporation. The author of *Portraits by Degas* (1962) and *The National Gallery of Canada* (1971), she is now professor of fine art at Harvard.

Bohemian Embassy. Toronto literary coffee house. The 'BoEm'—managed by the writer-performer Don Cullen—was open from 1 June 1960 to 1 June 1966 and featured the first regular poetry readings in a Canadian coffee house. Through an error it was listed in the telephone directory under 'Embassies and Consulates'. It was revived at The Harbourfront on 1 June 1974 and closed with the world's longest poetry reading, held on 26-9 Feb. 1976—75 hours and 30 minutes of readings by 150 poets, arranged by the Toronto poet Greg Gatenby.

Bois-brûlé. Nineteenth-century French phrase for a half-breed having Indian and French blood (also called MÉTIS). It means literally 'charred wood' and refers to the dark complexion of the half-breed.

Boky, Colette (b.1937). Coloratura soprano. Born in Montreal, she studied there and in Toronto at the Royal Conservatory of Music. Well established as an opera singer in Canada, Europe, and the United States, she is a member of the Vienna Volksoper and the Metropolitan Opera, New York, where she made her début in 1967.

Bolt, Carol (b.1941). Playwright. Born in Winnipeg, she settled in Toronto in the 1960s and has served as manager of the PLAYWRIGHTS CO-OP and as dramaturge at the Toronto Free Theatre (1973-4). Her best-known play is *Buffalo Jump* (1971), a funny, episodic treatment of the ON TO OTTAWA Trek that was produced by the THÉÂTRE PASSE MURAILLE in May 1972. *Red Emma*, produced by the Toronto Free Theatre in 1974 and published that year, is about Emma Goldman, the anarchist who died in Toronto in 1940. The St Lawrence Centre, Toronto, produced another play, *Shelter*, in 1975.

Bomarc. Acronym of BOeing Michigan Aeronautical Research Center. It is an American-made winged, supersonic, surface-to-air interceptor missile with a range of 400 mi.

Prime Minister DIEFENBAKER announced the acquisition of Bomarcs by the RCAF for NORAD use, but hesitated to arm them with the atomic warheads that alone would make them effective. In 1963 the United States indicated that Canada had made a commitment to accept the warheads, and Lester B. PEARSON reversed his opposition to nuclear weapons and said he would stand by the commitment, a promise he carried out when he came to power after the ensuing general election.

Bon Echo Provincial Park. At Mazinaw Lake in eastern Ontario, the park includes a mile-long granite rock with Indian pictographs and an inscription from Walt Whitman: 'My foothold is tenon'd and mortis'd in granite,/I laugh at what you call dissolution,/And I know the amplitude of time.' This memorial was dedicated in 1919 by Horace Traubel and Flora Macdonald Denison. The park was presented to the Ontario government in 1957 by Merrill DENISON as a memorial to his mother.

Bonanza Creek. A tributary of the Klondike R., it rises 11 mi. southeast of Dawson, Y.T. It was the site of a rich gold strike that sparked the KLONDIKE GOLD RUSH of 1896 and is now a YUKON HISTORIC SITE.

Bonaventure. A modern aircraft carrier. The 704-ft vessel was launched in 1946 and commissioned into the ROYAL CANADIAN NAVY in 1957 as a replacement for the MAGNIFICENT. It could accommodate *Banshee* jet fighters and *Tracker* anti-submarine planes, but required a mid-life refit in 1966-7 that totalled $11 million. Nonetheless the *Bonaventure*—named after the bird sanctuary in the Gulf of St Lawrence, but commonly called 'Bonnie'—was inexplicably sold for scrap three years later on 1 July 1970.

Bonne entente. French phrase meaning 'good will' or 'cordial co-operation'. The *bonne entente* movement, led by business and professional interests, tried to bring the French and English in Canada into a closer relationship. It flourished between the First and Second World Wars, then faltered and was derided in the 1950s.

Bons. Due bills issued by merchants in LOWER CANADA to meet the need for small change. 'Bons' is an abbreviation of *Bon pour* or 'Good for'.

Bonsecours Market. A large building in OLD MONTREAL. Designed by John Footner and begun in 1844, it has a massive iron Greek portico and an impressive dome. Used originally as a market, with two public halls on the upper floor, it was renovated by the city and houses its planning department.

Book Award of the City of Toronto. A literary prize given annually by the City of Toronto to the author or authors of the best book or books touching on Toronto published during the previous year. The award of $3,000 was first made in 1974.

Book-of-the-Year-for-Children Medal. Annual award made to encourage the writing of fine children's books. Two awards are given each year by the Canadian Library Association at its June conference: one in English, established in 1946; and one in French, established in 1950. The medal is engraved with a picture of Marie Hébert, wife of Louis HÉBERT, the first farmer in Canada, reading to her children.

Books Canada. An organization to promote Canadian books abroad. Established in 1972, it is a government agency that operates book distribution outlets in Paris, London, and New York. Titles of the books to be promoted are selected by publisher-members of the Association for the Export of Canadian Books.

Books in Canada. A national review of books. A monthly magazine founded in 1971 and available through subscription or free in bookstores across the country, it is devoted to publishing reviews of current titles and articles of general literary interest.

Bootmakers of Toronto. Canadian counterpart of the Baker Street Irregulars. The Bootmakers was founded in Toronto in 1970 to study the Sherlock Holmes 'canon'. The society's name recalls the passage in *The Hound of the Baskervilles* (1902) in which A. Conan Doyle describes a boot as bearing the mark 'Meyers, Toronto'.

Borden, Camp. See CANADIAN FORCES BASE BORDEN.

Borden, Sir Robert (1854-1937). Eighth prime minister. Born in Grand Pré, N.S., he trained as a lawyer and was elected to Parliament as a Conservative in 1896, becoming leader of the party in 1901 and prime minister in the election of 1911. A coalition of parties took place in 1917 and he headed the Union government until 1920, when he retired. His prime ministership is associated, among other things, with conscription, enforced by the Wartime Measures Act of 1917, and with achieving for Canada a place at the peace conference, at which it was a signatory of the peace treaties, and membership in the League of Nations. He was knighted in 1914.

Borden-Smuts Resolution. Adopted at the Imperial War Conference in London in 1917, Resolution IX affirmed the British Dominions' right to consultation in the development of Imperial foreign policy and recommended that their status as 'autonomous nations' be officially recognized at a conference to be called at the end of the First World War. By this resolution, proposed by the prime ministers of Canada (BORDEN) and South Africa (Smuts), the desire of some British authorities for tighter control of the Dominions was forestalled.

Borden's Canadian Cavalcade. A CBC Radio series that was popular during the Second World War. Lorne GREENE narrated stories involving war heroes, Howard CABLE and his orchestra supplied the music, the announcer was Cy Mack, and the producer was Rai Purdy. The program was sponsored by Borden's Milk Company which, during the war, produced Klim, a milk substitute. The advertising slogan was 'If it's Borden's it's got to be good.'

Border, Canadian-American. Frontier between Canada and the United States. The United States of America is the only country with which Canada shares a border; in fact it shares two borders with the United States. The southern frontier extends across the North American continent for a distance of 3,986.8 mi.; the northern border, which separates British Columbia and the Yukon Territory from Alaska, extends for 1,539.8 mi. The southern frontier has been called 'the longest undefended border in the world'. From the Lake of the Woods west to Vancouver it corresponds to the FORTY-NINTH PARALLEL.

Borduas, Paul-Émile (1905-60). Painter. Born in Saint-Hilaire, Que., he apprenticed as a church decorator with Oziac LEDUC and followed this line of work—with periods of study in Montreal and Paris and of teaching in Montreal—until 1933. Filling a vacancy left by Jean-Paul LEMIEUX, he taught at the École du Meuble in Montreal—a progressive, provincially sponsored school of crafts—from 1937 until he was dismissed in 1948 for writing the REFUS GLOBAL. His figure painting caught the attention of John LYMAN, and when the CONTEMPORARY ART SOCIETY was formed in 1939, Borduas was elected vice-president. (He was elected president in 1948, the year the CAS was dissolved). His great period of creativity began in 1941-2, when he became interested in Surrealism. Two well-known paintings of this period are *La Femme à la mandoline* (1941) in the Musée d'art contemporain, Montreal, and *Sous le vent de l'île* (1947, NGC). A CAS exhibition in 1946 that featured paintings by Borduas and six younger painters—some of them his students—who became known as Les AUTOMATISTES, signaled a revolution in Canadian painting in favour of Surrealism and abstraction, along with a liberating movement that was to affect the culture of Quebec itself, particularly through the publication of Borduas's REFUS GLOBAL. Borduas worked in New York from 1953 and in Paris from 1955 until his death, by which time he had gained an international reputation with one-man shows in Montreal, Toronto, New York, London, Paris, and—in 1960, after his death—in Amsterdam. His international eminence was achieved with a body of rich and resonant abstractions—the living creations of a great artist—produced in oils, gouache, and watercolour, with both brush and palette knife. He is associated particularly with the severe and powerful reductions of his vision in black-and-white studies, of which *L'Étoile noir* (1957, MMFA) is perhaps the best-known example.

Boreal forest region. The largest forest area in the country, and one of the largest in the world. It forms a continuous belt from Newfoundland westward to the Rocky Mountains and northwestward to Alaska. It is largely coniferous, with white and black spruce, tamarack, balsam fir, and jack pine the major species. Along its southern margins are many mills that produce the majority of Canada's pulp and paper.

Botheration scheme. Derisive epithet referring to the federal union of the British North American colonies. First used in 1865 in the title of a pamphlet by William Garvie, editor of the Halifax *Citizen*, it was taken up by Joseph HOWE for the title of 12 anti-Confederation letters he published in Halifax the same year.

Bott, Edward Alexander (1887-1974). Psychologist. Born near Ingersoll, Ont., he was educated at the University of Toronto and McGill. The founder of the Department of Psychology at Toronto, of which he was head for 44 years, he worked in the areas of perception and sensations and introduced physio- and occupational therapy, child study, and social work into the course of studies. He was the founder in 1940 and first president (1940-2) of the Canadian Psychological Association, and its honorary president from 1942 to 1944.

Boucher, Frank (b.1901). Hockey player. Born in Ottawa, he had three brothers who all played professional hockey. He was a member of the Ottawa Senators, Vancouver Maroons, and New York Rangers. With the Rangers from 1926 to 1944, he centred the famed Cook-Boucher-Cook line and won the LADY BYNG MEMORIAL TROPHY so often that the NATIONAL HOCKEY LEAGUE had a copy made and gave him the original in 1936. After retiring as a player, he coached the Rangers to a STANLEY CUP victory.

Bouey effect. Name given to the economic consequences of a wide spread in the interest rates charged by banks in Canada and the United States. The economic term—which takes its name from Gerald K. Bouey, governor of the BANK OF CANADA—was first recorded in 1975.

Boulogne. French seaport on the English Channel, scene of fighting during the SECOND WORLD WAR. It was surrendered on 22 Sept. 1944 after an assault by Allied forces that included the 3rd Canadian Infantry Division.

Bourassa, Henri (1868-1952). Journalist and politician. The grandson of Louis-Joseph PAPINEAU, he was an independent Liberal member of the House of Commons from 1896 to 1899; from 1900 to 1907, when he entered the provincial legislature; and from 1925 to 1935. In 1910 he co-founded Le DEVOIR, which promulgated his nationalist views, and he resisted French-Canadian participation in the First World War. He changed his mind about Quebec nationalism and was forced to resign from Le Devoir in 1932. He came out of retirement to help found the BLOC POPULAIRE in 1943.

Bourgeois. French word for a member of the middle class, used historically in French Canada for the boss or foreman of a group of fur traders or lumbermen.

Bourgeoys, Marguerite (1620-1700). Founder of the Congrégation de Notre-Dame de Montréal. In 1653 MAISONNEUVE brought her to VILLE MARIE, where she opened a day school and founded the religious order. She was beatified in 1950.

Bourget, Bishop Ignace. See INSTITUT CANADIEN and GUIBORD INCIDENT.

Bourinot's Rules of Order. A 'compact and short treatise' on 'the procedure of public bodies in general' by Sir John George Bourinot (1837-1902), clerk of the House of Commons from 1880 until his death. *Rules of Order*, which was published in 1894 and reprinted many times, spread the reputation of its author well beyond historical and legal circles. An abridgement of *Parliamentary Procedure and Practice in Canada* (1884, 1903, 1963), it is divided into three sections: 'Rules and usages of Parliament', 'Rules of order and procedure for public meetings and socieites', and 'Corporate bodies'. See also BEAUCHESNE'S RULES OF ORDER.

Bousille and the Just. Play by Gratien GÉLINAS. It opened in French at the COMÉDIE-CANADIENNE in Montreal, with the playwright taking the lead, on 16 Aug. 1959, and was published the following year. Gélinas also starred in the English version at the ROYAL ALEXANDRA THEATRE, Toronto, in Jan. 1962; it was published in 1961 in a translation by K. Johnstone. Bousille (meaning 'bungler') is the only witness to a murder. His failure to tell the full details at the subsequent trial results in his downfall.

Bow River. The most westerly portion of the NELSON RIVER system. It is 365 mi. long and flows from near Banff National Park eastward through the city of Calgary, and joins the South Saskatchewan R. in south-central Alberta.

Bowell, Sir Mackenzie (1823-1917). Fifth prime minister. Born in England, he came to Canada in 1833 and learned the printing trade on the Belleville *Intelligencer*, which he eventually owned. Elected to the House of Commons as a Conservative in 1867, he held several cabinet posts. He was appointed to the Senate in 1892 and became prime minister in 1894. Disagreement among his ministers over his leadership during the MANITOBA SCHOOLS QUESTION caused him to hand over power to Sir Charles TUPPER; he resigned in Apr. 1896. He was knighted in 1895.

Bowering, George (b.1935). Poet and novelist. Born in Penticton, B.C., and a graduate of the University of British Columbia, where he was a member of the TISH group, he now teaches at Simon Fraser University. The editor of IMAGO, a magazine for long poems, he has published numerous collections of poems that have a kind of tense lyricism—including, most recently, *Touch: Selected Poems, 1960-1970* (1971), *Curious* (1973), and *In the Flesh* (1974). He has also written a novel, *Mirror on the Floor* (1967), and a collection of stories, *Flycatcher* (1974).

Box 99. The federal government's consumer-complaint inquiry service. It was started in May 1968 by the Department of Consumer & Corporate Affairs to protect customers, particularly the poor and elderly, against unfair trade practices. Over 6,000 complaints a month were received at Box 99, Ottawa. Re-gional post boxes were opened in 1969 in Halifax, Montreal, Toronto, Winnipeg, and Vancouver, but the Ottawa office still deals with matters of national concern.

Boxing Day. Statutory holiday observed throughout Canada—except in Ontario, Quebec, and the Yukon Territory—to provide a day of rest on 26 Dec. (It is usually observed in urban Ontario, although it is not a statutory holiday.)

Boyd, Liona (b.1949). Classical guitarist. Born in London, Eng., she grew up in Toronto and began to study the guitar at 14, graduating from the Faculty of Music, University of Toronto, in 1971. She has studied with Julian Bream, Narciso Yepes, and with Alexandre Lagoya in Paris. She made her New York début in 1975 and now tours internationally. *The Guitar—Liona Boyd* (1975) is the first Canadian classical guitar record.

Boyd Gang. Three bank robbers who, on 8 Sept. 1952, made a daring escape from Toronto's Don Jail. Eight days later, following the greatest manhunt in Canadian history, Leonard Jackson, William Russell Jackson, and Edwin Alonzo Boyd were cornered and captured after a shoot-out at a North York barn. Boyd, a policeman's son born in Toronto in 1914, was the leader. Sentenced to life imprisonment, he was parolled in 1966 and now lives under another name somewhere in western Canada.

Boyle, Harry J. (b.1915). Broadcaster and author. Born in St Augustine, Ont., he was an announcer with CKNX in Wingham (1936-41), then a reporter with the *Stratford Beacon Herald* (1941-2). He was a popular and innovative producer with CBC Radio from 1942 to 1968—he created 'CBC Wednesday Night' (see CBC TUESDAY NIGHT) and 'Assignment', among other programs—and was appointed vice-chairman of the CANADIAN RADIO-TELEVISION COMMISSION on 1 Apr. 1968 and chairman in Jan. 1976. His publications include three memoirs—*Mostly in Clover* (1961), *Homebrew and Patches* (1963), and *Memories of a Catholic Boyhood* (1973)—and five novels: *A Summer Burning* (1964), *With a Pinch of Sin* (1966), *Straws in the Wind* (1969), *The Great Canadian Novel* (1972), and *The Luck of the Irish* (1975).

Boyle, Joseph W. (Joe) (1867-1923). Yukon and European adventurer who was dubbed 'King of the Klondike' and 'The Uncrowned King of Romania'. Born in Toronto, he was in the Yukon in 1897 and there founded a gold-dredging operation, which he managed until 1916. As an allied agent in Russia in 1917, he failed in his attempt to rescue the Royal Family. He was a confidant of Queen Marie of Romania and a power behind the Romanian throne. When he died in London, Eng., Queen Marie selected the lines from Robert SERVICE that appear on his tombstone: 'Man with a heart of a Viking/And the simple faith of a child.'

Boys and Girls House. Children's library and home of the special collection of children's books of the Toronto Public Library. A Children's Room was established in the College Street Branch of the Toronto Public Library in 1909. The first Boys and Girls House was opened in Sept. 1922 by Lillian H. Smith, who had been appointed the first children's librarian on joining the Children's Room in 1912. It is believed to be the first library for children in the British Commonwealth. The present building of the Boys and Girls House was opened on 7 May 1964 and houses the OSBORNE COLLECTION OF EARLY CHILDREN'S BOOKS and the Lillian H. Smith Collection.

Bracebridge. Resort town in the Muskoka district of Ontario. Like GRAVENHURST, Bracebridge is said to be named after a fictitious location in Washington Irving's two-volume work *Bracebridge Hall; or The Humourists* (1822).

Bracken, John (1883-1969). Leader of the Progressive Conservative Party from 1942 to 1948. Born in Ellesville, Ont., he was educated at the Ontario Agricultural College and the University of Illinois. He became premier of Manitoba in the farmers' government that had won the provincial election of 1922 and held power for the next twenty years. Generally considered a Liberal (certainly by the Liberals), Bracken nonetheless accepted the challenge of seeking the leadership of the national Conservative Party in 1942, won, and changed the party's name to Progressive Conservative. As national leader he was a failure, in large part because he did not seek entry to the House of Commons until 1945. Disillusionment with Bracken's performance in Parliament led to pressure for his resignation, which came in 1948.

Braden, Bernard (Bernie) (b.1916). Broadcasting personality. Born in Vancouver, the smooth-voiced Braden was an announcer and singer on CJOR in Vancouver before joining CBC Radio in Toronto. Between 1936 and 1949 he acted on the CBC STAGE series and launched his own program, BERNIE BRADEN TELLS A STORY, on 16 Aug. 1948. In the spring of 1949 he left Canada with his wife, the Toronto-born actress Barbara Kelly, for London, Eng., where he established himself as an actor and radio personality ('Breakfast with Braden', 'Bedtime with Braden'). His television shows ('Early to Braden', 'On the Braden Beat') had an immense audience. For GLOBAL TELEVISION on 12 Jan. 1974 he created a Canadian version of 'The Braden Beat', a weekly consumer-and-conversation show (or 'chattire'), with himself as host, and Ed Hailwood, Bernie Zuckerman, and Mary K. Patrick as contributors.

Braithwaite, Max (b.1911). Author. Born in Nokomis, Sask., and a graduate of the University of Saskatchewan, he has written for radio and television. *Why Shoot the Teacher* (1965)—filmed in 1976—*Never Sleep Three in a Bed* (1970), and *The Night We Stole the Mountie's Car* (1971) constitute three reminiscences about his early life on the Prairies. He has also written a novel, *A Privilege and a Pleasure* (1973), and a travel book, *Max Braithwaite's Ontario* (1974). His brother Dennis is the *Toronto Star*'s television columnist.

Brand, Oscar (b.1920). Composer and entertainer. Born in Winnipeg, he was raised in the United States from the age of nine. While a broadcaster and popularizer of folksongs in New York he starred in CBC-TV's 'Let's Sing Out', a half-hour folkmusic show heard weekly from 1966 to 1970, and in other radio and television programs. He wrote 'A Guy's a Guy' for Doris Day in 1951 and 'Something to Sing About', a patriotic song, in 1963. His best-known books are *Bawdy Songs and Backroom Ballads* (1960) and *The Ballad Mongers: Rise of the Modern Folk Song* (1962).

Brandon Strike. A prolonged and violent strike by meat-packers at Brandon, Man. It broke out on 29 Feb. 1960 over a concerted effort to change the basis of wage rates, but it soon widened because of instances of strikebreaking, charges of managerial confusion, and revelations of fraudulent practices. With the promise of an increased settlement, the workers returned to work on 30 Aug. 1960.

Brandon University. Originally a Baptist institution called Brandon College, it was founded in 1899 in Brandon, Man., and offered theology, commerce, and high-school courses. A school of music was added in 1906. It became non-denominational in 1938, ending an affiliation with Ontario's McMaster University that dated from 1911. Until 1967, when it received its university charter, the college was affiliated with the University of Manitoba. Of special significance is the Jeff Umphrey Memorial Centre (1971), a research centre in mental retardation.

Brandy Parliament. A meeting held in 1678

in Quebec to discuss trading liquor with the Indians. The meeting was in favour, but because of opposition from Bishop LAVAL, traders were prohibited the next year from carrying liquor to the Indians.

Brant, Joseph (1742-1807). Mohawk chief, principal chief of the Six Nations Indians (see IROQUOIS). After leading his Indians on the British side in the Seven Years' War and the American Revolution, he brought them to a reserve set aside for them on the Grand R. (Ont.). He himself lived in a large house, Wellington Square, at Burlington Bay (Ont.). On a visit to England in 1787 his portrait was painted by George Romney; it hangs in the National Gallery of Canada. The Brant Museum at Burlington is a replica of his cedar house, which he built about 1800.

Brantford. 'Telephone City' in southern Ontario, founded and named after Joseph BRANT, who led the Six Nations Indians (IROQUOIS) to the Grand R. valley in 1784. A village in 1826, a town in 1847, a city in 1877, Brantford has as its motto *Industria et Perseverantia* ('Industry and Perseverance'). Associated with Brantford is the CHAPEL OF THE MOHAWKS, CHIEFSWOOD, and Glenhyrst Gardens. It has been called 'Combine Capital of the World' for its farm-implement industry and 'Telephone City' for its association with Alexander Graham BELL.

Brascan Ltd. An investment and management company, incorporated in Toronto in 1899 as Sao Paulo Tramway, Light and Power Company, Limited. The present name of the company—which operates public utilities in Brazil and Canada—was adopted in 1969 and is an acronym of the first syllables of Brazil (in Portuguese) and Canada.

Brault, Michel (b.1928). Quebec cinematographer and director. Born in Montreal, he worked on the film magazine *Découpages* (with Pierre JUNEAU and Marc Lalonde) and with the NFB'S CANDID EYE series. A cameraman-director, he acquired an international reputation as a master of *cinéma-verité* with such short films as *Les Raquetteurs* (with Gilles GROULX, 1958) and such feature films as POUR LA SUITE DU MONDE (with Pierre PERRAULT, 1963) and *L'Acadie, L'Acadie* (again with Perrault, 1971). Acknowledged for many years as a premier cameraman (he photographed MON ONCLE ANTOINE and KAMOURASKA), Brault came into his own as a director with *Les* ORDRES (1975).

Braun, Victor (b.1935). Baritone. Born in Windsor, Ont., he studied at the Royal Conservatory of Music, Toronto, and in Vienna.

He was a member of the CANADIAN OPERA COMPANY (1956-63), the Montreal Opera (1963-4), and the Vancouver Opera Association (1963-7). Since 1963 he has based his international concert, opera, and recording career in Germany, where he now lives. He was winner of Vienna's prestigious International Mozart Competition in 1970.

'Brave Wolfe'. Title of a folksong popular in English Canada that celebrates the heroism and dramatizes the death of Gen. James WOLFE, who fell taking Quebec on 13 Sept. 1759. The last stanza runs: 'He raiséd up his head/Where the guns did rattle,/And to his aide he said, "How goes the battle?"/"Quebec is all our own,/They can't prevent it."/He said without a groan,/"I die contented." '

Bravery, Medal of. See MEDAL OF BRAVERY.

Breaking and entering. See B AND E.

Breakneck Stairs. L'Escalier casse-cou, an ancient short-cut in Quebec City from Côte de la Montagne to Petit Champlain Street in Lower Town. There have been stairs there since the seventeenth century, rebuilt from time to time, most recently in 1969. The name is said to be derived from a man's having broken his neck by falling down the stairs on the day they were finished—a story that may be apocryphal, though early visitors invariably remarked on the accidents that were associated with these stairs, particularly in winter.

Brébeuf, Jean de (1593-1649). Jesuit missionary in New France. Born in France, he came to New France in 1625 and founded the missions in HURONIA, near Georgian Bay. During Iroquois raids on the HURON MISSIONS he was martyred at Saint-Ignace. He was canonized with other Jesuit martyrs in 1930. Brébeuf's two accounts of the missions are included in the JESUIT RELATIONS.

Brébeuf and His Brethren. A book-length narrative poem by E.J. PRATT. The unrhymed epic, based on the JESUIT RELATIONS and published in 12 parts in 1940, celebrates the devotion and courage of Jean de BRÉBEUF and Gabriel LALEMANT, who were missionaries to the Huron Indians. The climax of the work is the torture and martyrdom of the two Jesuits on 16-17 Mar. 1649.

Breeze, Claude (b.1938). Painter. Born in Nelson, B.C., he studied with Ernest LINDNER at Regina College, Saskatoon, where he was influenced by the REGINA FIVE, and at the Vancouver School of Art. Influenced by Francis Bacon and British pop culture, he abandoned abstraction for figure painting of socially relevant subjects. A vivid, gruesome image dominates *Sunday afternoon: from an Old American Photograph* (1966, Canada Council), his monumental study of racism. Its lurid colours intensify the scene of two lynched Blacks at a hanging tree. Breeze has recently tended to allegorize his subjects in richly coloured paintings about erotic themes and in abstract-expressionist landscapes. He has exhibited internationally.

Brent Crater. One of Canada's largest and most accessible meteorite craters. Approximately 10,000 ft wide and 3,600 ft deep, it is partially filled with sediment and now contains Gilmour and Tecumseh Lakes in south-central Ontario.

Breskens Pocket. See Battle of the SCHELDT.

Bricker, Calvin David (1884-1963). Track-and-field star. He won the all-round Canadian Intercollegiate championships in 1906 and 1907 and represented Canada in the Olympic Games of 1908 and 1912, during which he won bronze and silver medals in the running-broadjump event. His best Canadian record in that speciality was unbroken for 27 years. He went on to practise dentistry in Regina.

Bricklin. Sports car manufactured by Bricklin (Canada) Ltd with the assistance of the New Brunswick government. The two-seater car was designed and developed by Malcolm Bricklin, a millionaire entrepreneur from Phoenix, Ariz. The first Bricklin rolled off the assembly line late in 1973. The company went into receivership in 1975.

Bridle, Augustus (1869-1952). Journalist and author. Born in Dorset, Eng., he came to Canada as a child and for many years was art, drama, and music editor of the *Toronto Star*. His *Sons of Canada* (1917) is a series of profiles of oustanding Canadians. He also wrote *Hansen* (1925), a novel.

Brig. Official abbreviation of Brigadier.

Briggs, William. See the RYERSON PRESS.

Bright's Wines. Canada's largest winery. It was founded by Thomas Bright and F.A. Shirriff in 1874 as the Niagara Falls Wine Company. The chief winemaker at Bright's, Adhemer de Chaunac, perfected a blended wine that used grape vines imported from New York state, thus improving the quality of Canadian wines. Bright's now bottles 12,000 gallons of wine a day. It has 14 stores throughout Ontario.

Brinco. Acronym of BRItish Newfoundland COrporation Ltd, a consortium of British and Newfoundland interests formed in 1953 to undertake construction of the CHURCHILL FALLS POWER PROJECT.

Brind'Amour, Yvette (b.1918). Quebec actress-manager. Born in Montreal, she acted with Les COMPAGNONS DE ST LAURENT in 1943 and in 1948 co-founded Le THÉÂTRE DU RIDEAU VERT, now Quebec's oldest repertory theatre.

Briscoe. Automobile manufactured in 1916 at Brockville, Ont., by the Canadian Briscoe Motor Company. The touring and roadster models were based on French cars being manufactured in the United States.

Britannia Heights. The name given to CBC Radio's short-wave station outside Ottawa. Established shortly before the Second World War, it was erected to receive rather than to send overseas broadcasts—especially 'This is London Calling' from the BBC—and to monitor short-wave signals for the war effort.

British Columbia. The westernmost province, bounded by Alaska and the 60th parallel on the north, Alberta on the east, and the 49th parallel on the south. The first landing was made by Captain James COOK at Nootka Sound, Vancouver Island, in 1778. The first European overland crossing to the Pacific Coast was made by Alexander MACKENZIE in 1793. The region of British Columbia, known as New Caledonia, was administered by the HUDSON'S BAY COMPANY. In 1846 Britain and the United States agreed on a boundary beginning at the 49th parallel in the Rocky Mountains. Vancouver Island became a British colony in 1851 and the mainland in 1858, the year of the gold strikes that led to the FRASER RIVER GOLD RUSH; the two colonies were united in 1866 and joined Confederation in 1871. In 1885 the province was physically linked with the rest of Canada with the completion of the CPR, terminating in Vancouver.

The present economy of B.C. is a resource-based one with forestry, mining, and fishing being most important. Agriculture, restricted by the rugged landscape of the WESTERN CORDILLERA, occurs mostly in the southwest, particularly in the Fraser delta and Okanagan Valley. The most important manufacturing industries are dependent on forest products (including lumber and pulp and paper) followed by food processing and primary metals. A major producer of copper, zinc, molybdenum, and lead, B.C. is also the largest coal-producing province in Canada and has significant oil and gas reserves.

British Columbia

With a land area of 359,279 sq. mi. and a 1974 population of 2,384,000, B.C. is the second-largest province in area and the third-largest in population, most of which (over 50 per cent in Vancouver and Victoria) is concentrated in the southwestern part of the province. Its capital is VICTORIA and the motto of the province is *Splendor sine occasu* ('Splendour without diminishment').

British Columbia Cultural Fund. Provincial arts body established in 1967. The interest on what is now a $15 million endowment fund is distributed by the Department of Finance on the recommendation of an appointed advisory committee 'for stimulation of the cultural development of the people of the Province'.

British Columbia Railway. New name of the Pacific Great Eastern Railway, a line conceived in 1912 to link Vancouver with Prince George, B.C. The present provincially owned railway's mainline runs from Vancouver through Squamish, Quesnel, Prince George, and Fort St John to Fort Nelson. One branch line runs to Dawson Creek, another to Dease Lake. The initials PGE have been said to stand for: Please Go Easy; Province's Greatest Expense; Progressively Greater Earnings; Past God's Endurance; Prince George Eventually.

British Commonwealth Air Training Plan. A Second World War flying school operated by the ROYAL CANADIAN AIR FORCE. On 17 Dec. 1939 Australia, Canada, New Zealand, and the United Kingdom agreed in Ottawa to establish a training program for pilots. Before the highly successful plan was terminated on 31 Mar. 1945 there were more than 100 schools and depots across the country. Franklin Delano Roosevelt called the BCATP 'the aerodrome of democracy'.

British Empire. A collective term for the territories under the leadership or control of the British CROWN. Britain's overseas empire has been dated from 1583 when Sir Humphrey GILBERT claimed Newfoundland as England's first colony. It reached its apogee in 1897, the year of Queen Victoria's Diamond Jubilee. The passing of the STATUTE OF WESTMINSTER in 1931 is generally taken as the terminal date of the Empire and that of the inception of the COMMONWEALTH OF NATIONS.

British Empire and Commonwealth Games. A series of irregularly scheduled competitions for athletes from countries within the BRITISH EMPIRE and then the COMMONWEALTH. They were first held in London, Eng., in 1911. Canada hosted the games for the first time in Hamilton, Ont., in 1930, and for the second time in Vancouver in 1954, an occasion marked by the running of the famous MIRACLE MILE.

British North America. Collective name for the British colonies in North America from 1783, when the independence of the United States was acknowledged, until Confederation in 1867.

British North America Act. See BNA ACT.

British Preference. The principle and policy of importing British and colonial goods at preferred tariff rates. The policy of maintaining regular and preferred rates was followed from 1897 to 1907. A most-favoured-nation rate, which bridged the gap between regular and preferred rates, was introduced into Canada's tariff schedules in 1907. British Preference might be said to have ended in 1935, when most-favoured-nation status was extended to the United States.

British subject. The official designation of any person born or naturalized within the British Commonwealth. Until the passage of the Canadian Citizenship Act in 1947 a CANADIAN was officially designated as a British subject. Since 1947 a Canadian may be officially described as a Canadian citizen while retaining the status of a British subject.

'British subject I was born—a British subject I will die, A'. A declaration of loyalty made by Sir John A. MACDONALD during his last campaign in 1891 and in his final address to the House of Commons on 7 Feb. 1891. It was a response to the annexationist tendencies of Unrestricted RECIPROCITY, a platform of the Liberals.

Britnell's Book Shop. Well-stocked bookstore in Toronto. The Albert Britnell Book Shop was founded in Toronto by Albert Britnell in 1893. He passed it on to his son Roy who passed it on to his son Barry. The store on YONGE ST, it is said, stocks at least one copy of. every new British, American, and Canadian book.

Brittain, Donald (b.1928). Film director. Born in Ottawa, he joined the NATIONAL FILM BOARD in 1954. He collaborated as a writer and director on many NFB documentaries, including *Bethune* (with John Kemeny, 1964), *Ladies and Gentlemen, Mr Leonard Cohen* (with Don OWEN, 1966), *Never a Backward Step* (with John Hammond and John Spotton, 1967), *Saul Alinsky Went to War* (with Peter PEARSON, 1968), and LABYRINTH (with Colin LOW, 1967). He directed the recent documentary *Volcano: An Inquiry into the Life and Death of Malcolm Lowry* (NFB, 1976). Now a freelance, his work is noted for its stylish editing and fine commentaries.

Brittain, Miller (1913-69). Painter. Born in Saint John, N.B., he studied in New York but spent the rest of his life in his home town except for three years' war service. During the Depression he painted strong, bleak pictures of children and workmen. He became interested in Biblical themes after the war and then moved into Surrealism. A well-known picture of his early period is *Longshoremen* (1940, NGC).

Broadbent, Edward (Ed) (b.1936). Leader of the federal NDP. Born in Oshawa, Ont., and educated at the University of Toronto and the London School of Economics, Ed Broadbent started his career as a university teacher; he was first elected to the House of Commons in 1968. He succeeded David LEWIS as leader of the party in 1975.

Broadcaster. A monthly trade magazine, published in Toronto since 1942, covering all aspects of the broadcasting industry in Canada.

Broadfoot, Barry (b.1926). Journalist and interviewer. Born in Winnipeg and a graduate of the University of Manitoba, he worked for the *Winnipeg Tribune,* the *Vancouver News-Herald,* and the *Edmonton Bulletin.* He has been a journalist in Vancouver since 1953. His vivid memories of the DEPRESSION and his experience with the Canadian Infantry during the Second World War helped him prepare two best-selling volumes of interviews: *Ten Lost Years, 1929-1939: Memories of Canadians Who Survived the Depression* (1973) and *Six War Years, 1936-1945; Memories of Canadians at Home and Abroad* (1974). In 1976 he published a third collection of taped reminiscences, *Pioneer Years.*

Broadfoot, Dave (b.1925). Comedian and satirist. Born in North Vancouver, he created the Senator for Kicking Horse Pass—the dull-witted, loud-mouthed founder of the 'New Apathy Party'—for the 1953 edition of SPRING THAW. Another of his characters is Corporal Renfrew of the Mounties, who 'never gets his man'. With Jean Templeton, to whom he was married (1959-62), he formed an effective dinner-club act. He is the author of *Sex and Security* (1974), humour in words and pictures devoted to the Senator.

Broadus, E.K. (1876-1936). Teacher and author. Born in Alexandria, Va, and educated at the University of Chicago and Harvard, he taught at Harvard until 1908. Requiring a change in climate for reasons of health, he accepted an invitation to be professor of English at the newly formed University of Alberta, where he taught until his death. Among his publications are a collection of essays, *Saturday and Sunday* (1935), and *A Book of Canadian Prose and Verse* (1923), an influential textbook that he edited with his wife Eleanor. One student who remembers him with affection is Lovat DICKSON.

Broadway, Canadians on. The New York stage has attracted many Canadian-born or -bred theatrical personalities. Among them are Margaret Anglin, Margaret Bannerman, David Belasco, John COLICOS, Hume CRONYN, Donald Davis (see DAVIS FAMILY), Colleen Dewhurst, Brian DOHERTY, Marie Dressler, Don Franks, Bill Freedman, Robert GOULET, Lorne GREENE, Tyrone GUTHRIE, Ruth Harvey, Doug HENNING, John HERBERT, John HIRSCH, Walter Huston, Lou Jacobi, Ruby Keeler, Beatrice Lillie, Raymond MASSEY, Galt Mac-DERMOT, Larry Mann, Henry Miller, Mary PICKFORD, Walter Pidgeon, Christopher PLUMMER, Kate REID, Anna RUSSELL, William SHATNER, Madeleine Sherwood, Milton Shulman, Bernard SLADE, Eva Tanguay, Joseph Wiseman, George White, Robert Whitehead, and Ira Withers.

Brock, Sir Isaac (1769-1812). Hero of the WAR OF 1812. A British officer, he was put in command of the forces in Upper Canada in 1810 and the next year was made maj.-gen. and administrator of the province. He led the capture of DETROIT in Aug. 1812—for which he received a knighthood that he never learned about—and died while leading an attack in the Battle of Queenston Heights on 13 Oct. He is buried beneath a monument in his name. See also QUEENSTON HEIGHTS AND BROCK'S MONUMENT, 'PUSH ON, BRAVE YORK VOLUNTEERS!'.

Brock Copper. Numismatic term for a copper coin, worth about a farthing, that was circulated in Upper and Lower Canada after the War of 1812. It honoured Sir Isaac BROCK but was withdrawn from circulation after 1816 because of the appearance of American counterfeits that rendered it worthless. The legend on the obverse read: 'Sir Isaac Brock the Hero of Upper Canada'. The legend on the reverse read: 'Success to Commerce & Peace to the World'.

Brock University. Located on the Niagara escarpment in St Catharines, Ont., it was chartered by the Ontario legislature in 1964. Degree programs are offered in the arts, sciences, administration, education, and physical education.

Brock's Monument. See QUEENSTON HEIGHTS AND BROCK'S MONUMENT.

Brockville Atlas. Automobile manufactured from 1911 to 1915 at Brockville, Ont., by the Brockville Atlas Auto Company. The Atlas, which used many U.S. parts, was one of the first cars to have parking lights.

Broken Jug, The. A play translated by Barker FAIRLEY and adapted by Don HARRON from *Der zerbrochene Krug* (1811), a one-act comedy by Heinrich von Kleist. It was presented by the CANADIAN PLAYERS at the ROYAL ALEXANDRA THEATRE, Toronto, in the week of 24 Feb. 1958. The Fairley-Harron version, in three acts, is set in a pioneer settlement in Upper Canada during the WAR OF 1812 where the citizenry are engaged in what seems to be an innocent collaboration with the invading American army.

Brome Lake duck. Duckling bred in the Brome Lake area of the EASTERN TOWNSHIPS. This international delicacy is similar to Long Island duck.

Bronfman, Samuel. See SEAGRAM CORPORATION.

Brooke, Frances (1724-89). Novelist. Born in England, she married the Rev. John Brooke, who was appointed chaplain to the garrison in Quebec City, where she lived from 1763 to 1768—an experience that inspired her epistolary novel *The* HISTORY OF EMILY MONTAGUE (1769), considered to be the first Canadian novel.

Brooke Bond Canada Limited. The British-owned company, one of the world's largest tea-growers and distributors, dates back to 1869 when Arthur Brooke, a Manchester tea merchant, opened a retail shop to sell tea, coffee, and sugar. He became a pioneer in the blending, branding, and packaging of teas. The business moved into the North American market in 1932 when it acquired RED ROSE TEA; it acquired BLUE RIBBON TEA in 1951. The two Canadian companies were merged in 1957 when Brooke Bond Canada Limited was formed; but the long-established brand names were retained. The company also controls BLACK DIAMOND CHEESE.

Brooker, Bertram (1888-1955). Painter and writer. Born in Croydon Eng., he settled in Portage la Prairie with his family in 1905. He entered the advertising field in Toronto in 1921 and in 1926 took up painting seriously, producing a surprising show of abstracts in 1927; the following year he painted *Sounds Assembling,* now in the Winnipeg Art Gallery, a brilliant conception of tubular and circular forms suggesting the relationships of musical sounds. He abandoned abstractions in 1929 and in the thirties produced a

number of striking realistic studies, of which the most memorable is *Torso* (1937, NGC). This highly creative period in his life included writing—his novel *Think of the Earth* (1938) won the first Governor General's Award for fiction—and the responsibilities of being a business executive.

Brookes, Air Vice-Marshal G.E. (b.1894). Born in Ingleton, Eng., he was brought to Canada in 1910 to settle in Owen Sound, Ont. He joined the Royal Flying Corps in 1916, and was wounded in combat in France in 1917. In 1921 he joined the Canadian Air Force, which became the ROYAL CANADIAN AIR FORCE on 1 Apr. 1924. By 1939 he was a group captain at Headquarters Eastern Air Command, Halifax, planning Canada's coastal defence and convoy patrols. He was appointed Air Officer Commanding the No. 6 (RCAF) Group RAF Bomber Command in Oct. 1942 with the rank of air vice-marshal. For meritorious service in organizing and commanding the RCAF bomber squadrons in his group, he was made a Companion of the Order of Bath. He retired from the RCAF in 1944.

Brooks. Automobile manufactured from 1923 to 1927 by Brooks Steam Motors, Stratford, Ont. A 21-gal. water tank, a 15-gal. gasoline-kerosene tank, and a 600-lb. pressure boiler produced enough steam to drive the car for almost 500 mi. It featured a leather-covered interior.

Brooks, Lela (b.1908). Champion speed-skater. At the age of 17 she competed in Chicago against 200 challengers and won the Silver Skate Derby. At another meet she broke three world records on the same afternoon. She also competed under her married name, Lela Brooks Potter.

Brookside Cemetery. Large cemetery in Winnipeg with the largest Military Plot of its kind in Canada. It was unveiled in 1960 by the Commonwealth War Graves Commission and located at what it called 'the geographical heart of the country'. 6,500 servicemen and -women are buried there, of whom 448 died serving in the First and Second World Wars. It has a CROSS OF SACRIFICE and the only STONE OF REMEMBRANCE in Canada.

Brookwood Military Cemetery. Large Commonwealth cemetery near London, Eng., where 2,716 Canadian soldiers who died in Britain during the First and Second World Wars lie buried. It is located not far from the garrison town of Aldershot.

Brossard, Nicole (b.1943). Quebec poet and novelist. Born in Montreal and educated at the Université de Montréal, she is associated with the magazine *La* BARRE DU JOUR. Her poetry and fiction, written with facility and directness, are deeply committed to the cause of an independent Quebec. An experimental novel-poem, *A Book (Un Livre)* (1975), translated by Larry Shouldice, is her only publication to appear in English.

Brothers in Arms. Popular one-act play by Merrill DENISON. A satire on the rugged individualism of the north woods, the four-character play opened at HART HOUSE THEATRE in Apr. 1941. The plot concerns a businessman and his wife who prove inept when faced with life in a primitive hunting cabin.

Brott, Alexander (b.1915). Conductor, violinist, composer. Born in Montreal, he studied music at the McGill Conservatorium (1928-35) and the Juilliard School of Music, New York. Concert master and assistant conductor of the Montreal Symphony from 1945 to 1958 and a prolific composer, he teaches at McGill University and is musical director of the McGill Chamber Orchestra. He is the father of Boris BROTT; his wife Charlotte and other son Denis are cellists.

Brott, Boris (b.1944). Conductor. Son of Alexander BROTT, he was born in Montreal and was educated there at La Conservatoire and McGill University; he trained also with Igor Markevitch and Pierre Monteux. He was assistant conductor of the Toronto Symphony Orchestra (1964-8); conductor of the Northern Sinfonia Orchestra (1964-8) and the Royal Ballet, Covent Garden (1966-8), both in England; and assistant conductor of the New York Philharmonic (1968). He became the director and conductor of the Hamilton Symphony Orchestra in 1969.

Brown, A. Roy (1893-1944). Air ace. Born in Carleton Place, Ont., he was raised in Ottawa and Edmonton. He learned to fly in 1915 and served in the First World War with the Royal Naval Air Service and the RAF, attaining the rank of captain. He shot down 12 enemy planes, including the Fokker Triplane piloted by Captain Manfred von Richthofen—the 'Red Baron', Germany's leading war hero—on 21 Apr. 1918. Shortly afterwards he went into a severe depression. He entered a paint business in Toronto upon his release from hospital. The year before his death he unsuccessfully contested a provincial election.

Brown, Dr Alan (1887-1960). Renowned pediatrician. Born in Clinton, Ont., and a graduate of the medical faculty of the University of Toronto, he interned at the Hospital for Sick Children, Toronto, before continuing his studies in New York, Munich, Vienna, Berlin, Paris, and London. In 1919 he was appointed chief physician of the Hospital for Sick Children, where he succeeded in halving the mortality rate in the infant ward. He was renowned for his abrasive wit, his fetish for breast-feeding, and his involvement in the development of PABLUM. When he retired in 1951 he was called 'the best baby doctor Canada ever had'.

Brown, Alan (b.1920). Translator. Born in Millbrook, Ont., and a graduate of the University of Toronto, he received a DFC in the Second World War and joined the CBC in 1952 after spending seven years in Europe. He has been the Montreal-based director of RADIO CANADA INTERNATIONAL since 1974. Among his ingenious and spirited translations from the French are Blaise Cendrars's *Moravagine* (1968), Jean Giono's *Two Riders of the Storm* (1967), Jacques GODBOUT's *Hail Galarneau!* (1970), Naim KATTAN's *Reality and Theatre* (1972), Hubert AQUIN's *The Antiphonary* (1973) and *Blackout* (1974), and Anne HÉBERT's *Poems* (1975).

Brown, E.K. (1905-51). Teacher and literary critic. Born in Toronto and educated at the Universities of Toronto and Paris, he taught English literature from 1929 until his death, at the Universities of Toronto and Manitoba and at Cornell and Chicago. While editor of the *University of Toronto Quarterly* (1932-41) he introduced the annual survey 'LETTERS IN CANADA'. The author of studies of Edith Wharton, Matthew Arnold, Willa Cather, and Duncan Campbell SCOTT, he is principally remembered for his important historical and critical essay *On Canadian Poetry* (1943; rev. 1944).

Brown, George (1818-80). Journalist and FATHER OF CONFEDERATION. Born in Scotland, he spent five years in New York before going to Toronto in 1843. He founded the GLOBE there the next year. Through this reformist newspaper, which eventually became a daily, Brown had a great influence on the Liberal Party, advocating among other things REPRESENTATION BY POPULATION. He was elected to the legislative assembly in 1851. As a member of the GREAT COALITION that sought to achieve Confederation, he attended the CHARLOTTETOWN and QUEBEC CONFERENCES, but resigned from the government in 1865 because he could not work with the Conservatives. Appointed to the Senate in 1873, he devoted himself mainly to his newspaper—while remaining a dominant influence on the Liberals—until he was assassinated by a disgruntled ex-employee.

Brown, George (1839-75). Champion oarsman. The Nova Scotia fisherman became a professional sculler and defeated all American and British challengers before his death by stroke at the age of 36. A tablet in St James' Anglican Church, Herring Cove, N.S., identifies him as 'champion oarsman of the world, 1874-75'.

Brown, Dr John. See BROWNDALE.

Brown bread. Steamed molasses bread, popular in the Maritime provinces.

Browndale. A non-profit organization for the treatment of emotionally disturbed children in normalized, functional, extended family settings in ordinary homes on residential streets. Unrelated child-care workers supply 'parenting'. It was established by Dr John L. Brown, a psychiatric social worker, born in the United States in 1922, who settled in Canada in 1948. He was founder and director of the provincially administered WARRENDALE from 1953 until his controversial dismissal in 1966, the year he established Browndale. By the mid-1970s Browndale operated more than 130 homes for more than 700 youngsters between 3 and 18 in Canada, the U.S., and Europe. The Warrendale and Browndale approach emphasizes normal living within the community, active help for the biological parents, and a quick return to the child's family home.

Bruce, Charles (1906-71). Poet, novelist, and journalist. Born in Port Shoreham, N.S., and a graduate of Mount Allison University, he was general superintendent of CANADIAN PRESS from 1945 to 1963. His nostalgia for the way of life in Nova Soctia past and present informed his six books of verse, the best known of which is *The Mulgrave Road* (1951); his novel *The Channel Store* (1954); and his collection of short stories, *The Township of Time* (1959). He also wrote *News and the Southams* (1968), a history of the newspaper chain.

Bruce Nuclear Power Station (Douglas Point). Canada's first nuclear power-generating station, in Bruce Township, Ont. Since opening in 1967 it has used natural uranium fuel to produce electricity, with a total capacity of 200,000 kilowatts. It is now part of the Bruce Nuclear Power Development.

Bruce Peninsula. A long finger of land that extends northward from southwestern Ontario, separating Georgian Bay from Lake Huron, of which the bay is a part. The rugged east coast formed by the Niagara escarpment contrasts with the low-lying sandy coast in the west. See also CYPRUS LAKE PROVINCIAL PARK.

Bruce Trail. Well-known Ontario hiking path opened in 1960. It extends 450 mi. along the top of the NIAGARA ESCARPMENT from Niagara Falls to Tobermory at the tip of the BRUCE PENINSULA.

Bruemmer, Fred (b.1929). Photographer. Born in Riga, Latvia, he came to Canada in 1957 and joined the *Northern Daily News* in Kirkland Lake as a reporter. Later he worked as a free-lance photographer and writer, and as a reporter for the *Chatham Daily News* and the *Montreal Gazette*. Residing in Montreal half of each year, he spends the other half in the Canadian Arctic, where he lives with the Eskimos and records Arctic life in a series of spectacular photographs published in many books, including *The Long Hunt* (1969), *Seasons of the Eskimo* (1971), *Encounter with Arctic Animals* (1972), and *The Arctic* (1974).

Bruhn, Erik (b.1928). Dancer. Born in Copenhagen, he trained at the Royal Danish Ballet School. He entered the company in 1947, becoming soloist in 1949, and went on to become perhaps the greatest male dancer of his generation. For the NATIONAL BALLET OF CANADA he staged *La Sylphide* and danced James in 1964. He danced in his own version of *Swan Lake* in 1966 and performed his most famous character part, Dr Coppelius, in the 1976 winter season. He was resident producer for the National from 1973 to 1976.

Brûlé, Étienne (c.1592-c.1633). Interpreter of the Huron language, the first white man to live among the Indians. He may have come to Quebec with CHAMPLAIN in 1608. In 1615, in company with a party of Indians, he reached the mouth of the Humber R. (in the area of present-day Toronto), the first European to see Lake Ontario (and, in 1621-3, Lake Superior). In obscure circumstances he was killed and eaten by the Hurons among whom he had lived.

Brunet, Michel (b.1917). Quebec historian. Born in Montreal and educated at the Université de Montréal and at Clark University in Massachusetts, he has taught history at the Université de Montréal since 1949. An influential historian whose books attempt to interpret the tragic effects of the Conquest on French Canada and its social development, he has written *Canadians et Canadiens* (1954; rev. 1971), *Les Canadiens après la conquête, 1759-1775* (1969), and other studies.

Brymner, William (1855-1925). Painter and teacher. Born in Scotland, he grew up in Ottawa, the son of the first Dominion archivist.

He studied in Paris from 1876 to 1885 and then became an influential teacher as director of painting classes at the Art Association of Montreal from 1886 to 1921. His painting of four little girls on a hillside, *A Wreath of Flowers* (1884, NGC), is probably his best-known work. He also painted society portraits and scenes of the St Lawrence valley.

Buchan, John. See Lord TWEEDSMUIR.

Buck, Tim (1891-1973). Communist leader. Born in Beccles, Eng., he trained as a machinist and settled in Canada in 1910. A fine speaker and organizer, he served as General Secretary of the COMMUNIST PARTY OF CANADA (under its various names) from 1929 to 1962, a record for a Communist leader in any country. An attempt was made on his life in 1932 while he was serving time in Kingston Penitentiary under Section 92 of the Criminal Code. Among his many publications are *Put Canada First* (1934), *Our Fight for Canada: Selected Writings, 1923-59* (1960), and *Lenin and Canada: His Influence on Canadian Political Life* (1970).

Bucke, Richard Maurice (1837-1902). Physician and author. Born in Methwold, Eng., he was brought the following year to the region of London, U.C. (Ont.). He graduated from McGill in medicine in 1858, practised in Sarnia, C.W. (Ont.), and was superintendent of the Hamilton Asylum in 1876 and of the London Asylum from 1877 until his death, having become recognized as a leading authority in the field of mental illness. A friend of Walt Whitman, he invited the American poet to tour central Canada in the summer of 1880. He wrote (with some help from the poet) *Walt Whitman* (1883), the first formal biography, and was a literary executor. Bucke is also remembered as the author of a pioneer study, COSMIC CONSCIOUSNESS (1901).

Buckler, Ernest (b.1908). Novelist and short-story writer. Born in Dalhousie West, N.S., and educated at Dalhousie University and the University of Toronto, he lives on a farm near Annapolis Royal and writes movingly of life in the Annapolis valley. *The* MOUNTAIN AND THE VALLEY is a classic of its kind. His other books are *The Cruelest Month* (1963), *Ox Bells and Fireflies* (1968), *The Rebellion of Young David and Other Stories* (1975), and a travel book, *Nova Scotia: Window on the Sea* (with the photographer Hans Weber, 1970).

'Bud the Spud'. Popular song written by Tom CONNORS in 1960. It tells of trucking potatoes from the Maritimes to Toronto. The chorus runs: 'It's Bud the Spud, from the bright red mud,/Rollin' down the highway smilin',/The spuds are big, on the back of Bud's rig,/They're from Prince Edward Island.'

Budget Speech. Annual address to the HOUSE OF COMMONS forecasting financial operations of the government for the year ahead. It is delivered by the Minister of Finance, and at the close of the address he tables formal resolutions for changes in the existing tax rates and customs tariff. On occasion there have been two budgets in one year.

Buell, John (b.1927). Novelist. Born in Montreal and educated at Loyola College and the Université de Montréal, he teaches at Concordia University. He has written four psychological thrillers: *The Pyx* (1959), *Four Days* (1962), *The Shrewsbury Exit* (1972), and *Playground* (1976). The first and the third have been turned into popular films.

Buenos Ayrean. Steamship operated by the ALLAN LINE. The 4,005-ton vessel, built at Dumbarton, Scot., in 1896, was the first sizeable steel steamer on the North Atlantic, providing Canadian mail service between Scotland and North America, with an annual voyage to South America. She was scrapped in 1910.

Buffalo. See BISON.

Buffalo. Name of a tactical and utility transport aircraft. The twin turboprop plane was designed and built by DE HAVILLAND, Canada, in 1964 to meet military needs for a plane with STOL characteristics. It flies 285 m.p.h.

Buffalo berry. A thorny shrub with yellow or red berries, native to the Prairies. Its name comes from the Indian custom of eating the berries with buffalo meat.

Buffalo chip. A piece of dried buffalo dung used by the Plains Indians and early settlers for fuel in lieu of wood. Buffalo Chip Lake was the original name of Chip Lake, Alta.

Buffalo jump. The place where buffalo were stampeded over a precipice and slaughtered by Plains Indians.

Buffalo meat. Edible meat of the buffalo, with a rich, beef-like flavour. It is available commercially only when the federal government thins out the herd in WOOD BUFFALO NATIONAL PARK. 'Sweetgrass' is a trade name for the finest-quality buffalo meat.

Bujold, Geneviève (b.1943). Film star. Born in Montreal, she performed in 1962 with the THÉÂTRE DU RIDEAU VERT before being chosen to appear opposite Yves Montand in *La*

Guerre est finie (1965). Her acting skills developed brilliantly as she performed in English (not her native tongue) in Canadian and international films. She married Paul ALMOND and appeared in his films ISABEL (1968), ACT OF THE HEART (1970), and *Journey* (1972). She played opposite Alan Bates in *The King of Hearts* (1966), starred opposite Richard Burton in *Anne of the Thousand Days* (1969), and played Cassandra in the all-star film version of *The Trojan Women* (1971). Now divorced, she lives in Malibu, Calif., and pursues an international film career.

Bullock, Michael (b.1918). Translator and author. Born in London, Eng., and educated at Stowe School, the Hornsey College of Art, and the Regent Street Polytechnic School of Languages, he has translated some 150 full-length books and plays from the German, French, and Italian, including three novels and 11 plays by Max Frisch and numerous works by such authors as Karl Jaspers, Martin Buber, and Wilhelm Worringer. Since 1968 he has been associated with the University of British Columbia's CREATIVE WRITING DEPARTMENT, where he is a professor, director of the translation program, and editor of PRISM INTERNATIONAL. Bullock's own poetry and fiction—including *A Savage Darkness* (1969) and *Randolph Cranstone and the Glass Thimble* (1976)—display a surreal vision.

Bunyan, Paul. A mythical giant lumberjack, the subject of tall tales told in lumbercamps of New Brunswick and Maine in the late-nineteenth century. Accompanied by his 'fabulous blue ox Babe', he was said to have created the tides of the Bay of Fundy, hollowed out the Great Lakes, and raised up the Rocky Mountains, etc. The comic figure and his adventures may be an adaptation of the GLOOSCAP cycle; a corruption of the French-Canadian TI-JEAN, 'Beau Jean', or BONHOMME figures; a tribute to a 'giant warrior ' recalled from the REBELLION OF 1837 in Lower Canada; or an oral-literary creation employed by various American writers from 1910 on. Bunyan's epic exploits are recalled in Esther Shephard's *Paul Bunyan* (1924) and John D. Robins' *Logging with Paul Bunyan* (1957).

Burka, Petra (b.1947). Champion figure-skater. Brought to Canada from Amsterdam at the age of four (her mother had been a Dutch champion), she won the Canadian skating title in 1964. The following year, within one month, she won the Canadian, North American, and world championships, and was voted Canada's top female athlete of the year. She performed for three years in an ice-skating show then retired to become an organizer of skating clubs across Canada.

Burke, Desmond (1904-73). Champion rifleshot. He represented Canada in more than 20 competitions at Bisley, Eng., where at the age of 19 he won the King's Prize. He practised medicine and taught and wrote about the sport of rifle-shooting.

Burke, Edmund (1851-1919). Architect. Born in Ireland, he spent the greater part of his life in Toronto and was educated there. He trained with his uncle Henry Langley and then joined him as a partner—the first of several partnerships. The office designed a few buildings for prominent Methodists and Baptists in Toronto, such as Jarvis Street Baptist Church (1876) in Victorian Gothic and Sherbourne St Methodist Church (1884) in the Romanesque Revival. Burke also designed shingle-styled houses in the ANNEX area of Toronto and the store for the Robert Simpson Co. at Queen and Yonge Sts (begun 1894-5). Burke Horwood & White designed the Eaton's stores in Calgary, Vancouver, and Victoria.

Burke, Stanley (b.1924). Broadcast journalist. Born in Vancouver, he began writing at the age of 13 and served in the Royal Canadian Navy during the Second World War. He has been the CBC's Paris correspondent, the *Vancouver Sun*'s Ottawa correspondent (1953-7), and the CBC's United Nations correspondent. He succeeded Earl CAMERON on The NATIONAL (1966-9) and with his rugged features and abrupt delivery gave it a new character; he left over a union dispute that meant he could write or read the news but not do both, and over a personal concern with the Biafran war. He wrote *Frog Fables and Beaver Tales* (1973) and *The Glorious Revolution* (1974), humorous books illustrated by Roy PETERSON.

Burlap Bags. Controversial 'theatre-of-the-absurd' play by Len PETERSON. Written for CBC STAGE in 1946, it was rebroadcast a number of times and telecast in 1960. It concerns a group of nobodies (with names such as Got and Aintgot) who meet in the rented rooms of a suicide to read their late companion's autobiographical manuscript. The characters don burlap bags to dramatize their indifference to the world around them.

Burnford, Sheila. See INCREDIBLE JOURNEY.

Burns, Lt-Gen. E.L.M. (b.1897). Army commander. Born in Westmount, Que., he was educated at the Royal Military College. He served in the Royal Canadian Engineers during the First World War. In Apr. 1941 he went to England to become the Brigadier General Staff, 1st Canadian Corps. After commanding the 4th Canadian Armoured Brigade in England for 15 months, on 6 May 1943 he was promoted major-general to command the 2nd Canadian Infantry Division. He assumed command of the 5th Canadian Armoured Division in Italy on 30 Jan. 1944 and on 20 Mar. became General Officer Commanding the 1st Canadian Corps. He commanded this corps during operations in the Liri Valley and in the advance to Rimini. In Dec. 1944 he was appointed Officer in Charge, Canadian Section, General Headquarters 1st Echelon, 21 Army Group. He retired from the Canadian Army on 26 June 1947. Thereafter he had a distinguished career as a public servant and from 1970 to 1975 was Professor of Strategic Studies, School of International Affairs, Carleton University.

Burns, Tommy (1881-1955). Champion boxer. Born Noah Brusso at Hanover, Ont., the young sportsman changed his name in 1900 when he became interested in professional boxing. Although 5 ft 7 in. in height and weighing only 175 lbs, he won both the world's light- and heavyweight boxing championships, losing the latter title to Jack Johnson in 1908. During two decades in the ring he fought 58 bouts and lost only four. In later years he became an evangelist. He died in Vancouver.

Burns Meats Ltd. One of the world's largest meat-packing operations. It was founded as P. Burns & Co. in Calgary in 1890 by the colourful Oshawa-born Pat Burns (1856-1937), the 'cattle king' and later senator, who provisioned the prospectors in Dawson City in 1898, was the first to introduce canned meats into Canada in 1928, and saw his small operation grow into a chain of packing houses across Canada, with markets around the world. Burns products are advertised as 'Pride of Canada Products'.

Burroughs, Jackie (b.1940). Actress. Born in Lancashire, Eng., she was brought to Toronto when she was 12 and educated at Trinity College, University of Toronto. Her parents opened the OBAN INN at Niagara-on-the-Lake, Ont. The lean, amber-haired actress performed at HART HOUSE THEATRE and with the CREST THEATRE, then studied under Uta Hagen in New York, where she met the composer Zalman YANOVSKY (they were married from 1966 to 1970). She is identified with TEN LOST YEARS produced by TORONTO WORKSHOP PRODUCTIONS in 1974. In 1975 she joined the STRATFORD FESTIVAL's touring group, The Young Company; she played Portia in the Festival's 1976 production of *The Merchant of Venice.*

Burton, Dennis (b.1933). Painter. Born in Lethbridge, Alta, he studied at the Ontario College of Art and the University of Southern California and now lives in Toronto, where he co-founded the NEW SCHOOL OF ART in 1965. His early interest in abstract expressionism, acquired from the PAINTERS ELEVEN, is seen in *Intimately Close-in* (1958-9, NGC). Determined experimentation has resulted in a style that now ranges from realism to abstraction. His bold, inventive sense of design is evident in a series of paintings of the female torso called 'Garterbeltmania', which uses pop elements to criticize the stereotyping of woman. At present he is exploring welded sculpture based on found objects. He has exhibited internationally.

Bush, Jack (b.1909). Painter. Born in Toronto, and largely self-taught, he worked as a commercial artist and was a founding member of PAINTERS ELEVEN. After rejecting his cubist-like landscapes and figurative work because of the influence of abstract expressionism, he developed a highly simplified abstract style that emphasized colour and direct composition. In the early 1960s this refinement led to the lyrical colour-field style of raw canvas surfaces painted in arcylic with bold, brilliant colour forms. *Dazzle Red* (1965, AGO) is one of his most impressive and subtle modulations of colour. He exhibits internationally.

Bush Garden, The. Retrospective collection of articles on Canadian literature and its creators by Northrop FRYE, published in 1971. Subtitled *Essays on the Canadian Imagination,* it includes his important 'Letters in Canada' series—10 years of reviews of poetry books published in this country during the 1950s—and his masterly analysis of Canadian literature written as the conclusion to the *Literary History of Canada* (1965; rev. 1976) edited by Carl F. Klinck.

Bush pilot. Someone who flies freight or passengers into or out of the northern bush and barrens. Early bush pilots—like C.H. 'Punch' Dickens, 'Wop' May, and Grant McConachie—were figures of daring and resourcefulness. The romantic era of the bush plane began in 1920 with the first commercial flight into the North, and may be said to have ended with the more dangerous flying demanded by the Second World War.

Businesses, Canada's largest. See Canada's largest COMPANIES.

Buster Keaton Rides Again

Buster Keaton Rides Again. See The RAILROD-DER.

Busza, Andrzej (b.1938). Emigré poet writing in Polish. Born in Poland, he settled in Canada in the 1960s. He teaches in the English department of the University of British Columbia. His *Astrologer in the Underground* (1970) consists of poems translated by Jagna Boraks and Michael BULLOCK.

Butchart Gardens. Well-known floral gardens and tourist attraction near Victoria, B.C. Around 1910 Robert Butchart, a cement manufacturer, and his wife developed the extensive gardens in one of his company's abandoned quarries. They are planned to flower the year round and sections include an English rose garden, an Italian garden with sculptured trees and Florentine arches, and a Japanese garden.

Butler, Sir William Francis (1838-1910). Soldier and author. Born in Tipperary, Ire., he was commissioned in 1858 in the 68th Foot and served with his regiment in Canada against the FENIANS in 1867. Three years later, learning that a former associate, Col. Garnet Wolseley, was mounting the RED RIVER EXPEDITION, he cabled him to 'REMEMBER BUTLER'. He joined the expedition and arranged a secret interview with Louis RIEL at Fort Garry. Sent to report on the HUDSON'S BAY COMPANY posts on the Saskatchewan R. later in 1870 and, in 1872, on conditions in the Lake Athabasca country, he described his travels in two classics of the Northwest: *The* GREAT LONE LAND (1872) and *The Wild North Land* (1873). He left Canada in 1873.

Butler's Rangers. Corps of Loyalist refugees raised by John Butler (1725-96), an American-born Loyalist, at Fort Niagara (N.Y.) in 1777. They conducted many raids in the Mohawk and Wyoming valleys during the American Revolution. When they were disbanded in 1784 many settled in the Niagara Peninsula. Butler—who had been appointed commissioner of Indian affairs at Niagara (which remained in British hands until 1796)—is buried at Butler's Burying Grounds, Niagara-on-the-Lake.

Butter tarts. Nationally popular pastry. Made with raisins, butter, brown sugar, eggs, and corn syrup, the recipe is an adaptation of the English treacle tart.

Button, Sir Thomas (d.1634). Welsh naval officer and explorer. Sent in search of Henry HUDSON in 1612 and of the NORTHWEST PASSAGE, with Robert Bylot and Abacuk Pricket in his company, he named the island at the entrance of Hudson Strait after his ship, the *Resolution,* and wintered at the mouth of the Nelson R. (which he named after the ship's master, who died there) in Hudson Bay; he made further explorations in the spring and summer. For a time thereafter the bay was called Button Bay. His voyage was described in *North-West Fox* (1635) by Luke FOX.

Buxton Settlement. Village for fugitive Black slaves founded in 1849 by William King, the American emancipator. Descendants of these settlers live to this day in the village of South Buxton and environs in Kent Co., Ont.

By, John (1781-1836). Military engineer. Born in England and educated at the Royal Military Academy, he came to Canada (for the second time) in 1826 to design and construct the RIDEAU CANAL, settling at a spot near the junction of the Ottawa and Rideau Rivers that came to be called Bytown—now Ottawa. He returned to England in 1832.

Bylot, Robert. See Henry HUDSON, William BAFFIN, and Sir Thomas BUTTON.

Byng, Lord (1862-1935). Julian Hedworth George Byng, Viscount Byng of Vimy, was GOVERNOR GENERAL of Canada from 1921 to 1926. As Lt-Gen. (later Gen.) Sir Julian Byng he commanded the officers and men of the CANADIAN CORPS—'Byng Boys'—from 29 May 1916 to June 1917. He is associated with a constitutional crisis at the end of his term when he refused to grant Mackenzie KING dissolution of Parliament.

Byng Trophy. See LADY BYNG MEMORIAL TROPHY.

Bystander. 'A Monthly Review of Current Events, Canadian and General', appearing monthly and sometimes weekly between Jan. 1880 and Sept. 1890. It was published in Toronto and edited by Goldwin SMITH, whose articles appeared with the byline 'A Bystander'. Its motto was 'Not Party, But the People'.

Bytown. The name of OTTAWA from 1827 to 1855. It was named after Col. John BY who built the RIDEAU CANAL.

C

C1. Official abbreviation of Chief Petty Officer 1st Class.

C2. Official abbreviation of Chief Petty Officer 2nd Class.

C.D. Howe Research Institute. A private, non-profit organization founded in Montreal in Jan. 1973. This centre for independent economic policy analysis is the result of a merger of the C.D. HOWE Memorial Foundation and the Private Planning Association of Canada. It undertakes research into Canadian economic policy issues, especially in the areas of international trade policy and major federal government programs. Its findings are published in the form of Special Studies and are the basis for public discussion.

C.E. Abbreviation of CANADA EAST.

C.S.A. Initials and certification mark of the CANADIAN STANDARDS ASSOCIATION.

C.W. Abbreviation of CANADA WEST.

CAA. Initials of the CANADIAN AUTHORS ASSOCIATION.

CAAE. Initials of the CANADIAN ASSOCIATION FOR ADULT EDUCATION.

CAATs. Acronym of Colleges of Applied Arts and Technology—community colleges established during the 1960s to meet the need for post-secondary vocational and technological education. In Quebec they are called CEGEPS (Collèges d'Enseignement Général et Professionnel).

CAB. Acronym of CANADIAN ASSOCIATION OF BROADCASTERS.

Cabbagetown. District in Toronto between Sherbourne St and the Don R., south of Carlton and north of Queen. It was settled in the 1860s, 70s, and 80s by working-class people from Ireland and England who grew cabbages in their front yards. It became a slum but is now the site of subsidized housing and selective renewal schemes, and almost all the old houses have been torn down (see REGENT PARK). *Cabbagetown* (1950, 1968) is the title of a realistic novel by Hugh GARNER about the working-class people who lived in the area between the two world wars.

Cabinet. An executive committee of elected members of the legislature chosen by a prime minister or a premier. Most members of a

cabinet are the political heads of government departments, but a cabinet can also include ministers without portfolio who have no department to administer. See also MINISTRY.

Cable, Howard (b.1920). Popular conductor and arranger. The Toronto-born musician had his own dance band, Howard Cable's Cavaliers (1935-40), but he is best known for his CBC work. He conducted and arranged for the LESLIE BELL SINGERS Orchestra (1948-55) and 'General Electric Showtime' (1952-9). He is now retired and lives in Bala, Ont.

Cabot, John (*c.*1450- *c.*1498). Italian mariner and explorer. A Venetian citizen, possibly of Genoese birth, he went to England in 1495, becoming a naturalized citizen in 1496. For Bristol merchants he undertook a voyage westwards in 1497 in the ship *Matthew*, coasting the shores of North America from Maine or southern Nova Scotia (in either of which regions his famous landfall on 24 June may have been made) to Cape Race in Newfoundland, thinking he had reached Asia. With five ships he made another voyage in 1498 from which he did not return.

Cabot Memorial Tower. Museum on SIGNAL HILL overlooking St John's, Nfld. Raised in 1897-8 to celebrate Queen Victoria's Jubilee, the Tower commemorates the 400th anniversary of Newfoundland's discovery. It is not certain, however, that John CABOT made a landfall in Newfoundland.

Cabot Strait. The entrance from the Atlantic Ocean into the Gulf of St Lawrence between Cape Breton Island, N.S., and Newfoundland. It was named after John CABOT.

Cabot Trail. One of the most scenic drives in North America. The 184-mi. trail, which skirts the rugged coastline of the northern half of Cape Breton Island, N.S., offers vistas of sea and highland. ACADIAN and Scottish settlements may be visited along the way, and excursions include BADDECK, Bras d'Or Lakes, Glace Bay, and LOUISBOURG. The Cabot Trail was named after John CABOT, who sighted the Cape Breton coast in 1497.

Cache. A hiding place, especially one used by explorers and fur traders to store and conceal provisions, implements, etc., from foraging animals and inclement weather. From the French *cacher*, 'to hide'.

Cadborosaurus

Cadborosaurus. Name given to a fabulous sea monster sighted in the Straits of Georgia off Cadboro Bay, near Victoria, B.C., in 1933. Although known to the Chinook Indians, Cadborosaurus ('Caddy' for short) was first reported following the sighting of Scotland's Loch Ness monster. Caddy has been spotted many times, often accompanied by his mate Amy. Another native sea monster is OGO-POGO.

Cadets. See CANADIAN ARMED FORCES CADETS.

Cadieux, Jean. See PETIT ROCHER.

Caen. City in northern France, scene of fighting in the Second World War. An allied objective of the NORMANDY INVASION, the city was taken and occupied by the troops of the 1st British Corps (including the 3rd Canadian Division) on 9 July 1944.

CAF. Initials of the CANADIAN ARMED FORCES.

Caibaiossi, Lloyd (1947-75). Ojibwa artist. Born on the Spanish River Indian Reserve in north-central Ontario, he studied at the University of Windsor. His Indian name is Nawhguakgeiig (When the Sun Stands at its Zenith). He did much of his vivid painting, which depicts the myths and symbols of his people, at the reserve at Brocket, Alta. He died in a car accident.

Caisse populaire. French for 'people's bank'. A caisse populaire is a credit-union—a co-operative savings and loan society in Quebec. It was first introduced to Canada in 1900 by Alphonse Desjardins (1854-1920), a journalist.

Cajun. Corruption of 'Acadian'—a person who lived in ACADIA. In Louisiana a Cajun is anyone who claims Acadian ancestry.

Calais. French port on the English Channel, scene of fighting during the SECOND WORLD WAR. It was captured after an assault by allied forces, which included the 3rd Canadian Infantry Division, on 1 Oct. 1944.

Calder, Frank (1877-1943). Hockey president. Born in Scotland, he was president of the NATIONAL HOCKEY LEAGUE from 1917 to 1943. In 1936 he donated the Calder Trophy, together with a cash award, for annual presentation to the outstanding first-year player in the NHL. See also CALDER MEMORIAL TROPHY.

Calder Memorial Trophy. Presented annually 'to the player selected as the most proficient in his first year of competition in the NATIONAL HOCKEY LEAGUE'. The selection is made by the Professional Hockey Writers'

Association. It commemorates the long service of Frank CALDER as president of the NHL (1917-43) and was first presented in 1944. The winner receives, in addition to the trophy, $1,500; the runner-up, $750.

Calèche. French for a light four-wheeled horse-drawn carriage with a folding hood. Calèches are still used for sightseeing in Quebec City.

Calgary. The second-largest city in Alberta. It originated in 1875 as a NORTH WEST MOUNTED POLICE post, Fort Brisebois (renamed Fort Calgary the following year), to combat American whisky traders. Its future was secured in 1883 when it became a divisional point along the CPR; it was incorporated as a city in 1893. It also served as a market and processing town for the surrounding agricultural population, and with the discovery of nearby oil and gas fields, notably at TURNER VALLEY in 1914, Calgary has been the administrative headquarters of those industries. Close to 50% of the city's total employment is related in some way to the petroleum industry, largely in the areas of production, exploration, and development. The 1971 CMA population was 403,319. See also CALGARY STAMPEDE.

Calgary Albertan, The. A morning newspaper published in Calgary. The product of a merger of two semi-weekly papers in 1902, it has been published by FP PUBLICIATIONS since 1959.

Calgary Eye Opener. See EYE OPENER.

Calgary Herald, The. An evening newspaper published in Calgary. Established in 1883, it has been published by SOUTHAM PRESS since 1908.

Calgary red-eye. A popular western drink. It contains equal amounts of beer and tomato juice.

Calgary Stampede. An internationally famous annual exhibition of rodeo events, amusements, and livestock shows held for 10 days each July in Stampede Park, Calgary, Alta. Known as 'the greatest outdoor show on earth', it was founded in 1912 by Guy Weadick, an American promoter and showman. It came into its own in 1923 when it was amalgamated with the old Calgary Industrial Exhibition and added the now-famous CHUCKWAGON races to a growing list of attractions.

Callaghan, Morley (b.1903). Novelist and short-story writer. Born in Toronto and a graduate of the University of Toronto and

Osgoode Hall, he worked summers on the *Toronto Star*, where he was encouraged in his short-story writing by Ernest Hemingway. After spending eight months in Paris in 1929, he returned to Toronto and has lived there since. Referred to in 1965 by the American writer Edmund Wilson as 'perhaps the most unjustly neglected novelist in the English-speaking world', he has pursued a writing career for nearly 50 years, remaining faithful to his standard of literary artistry and to his vision of the lonely, vulnerable people who exist on the fringes of society and of acceptance. His early collections of finely crafted stories—*A Native Argosy* (1929) and NOW THAT APRIL'S HERE AND OTHER STORIES—were brought together in *Morley Callaghan's Stories* (1959). His novels are *Strange Fugitive* (1928), *It's Never Over* (1930), *No Mans' Meat* (1931), *A Broken Journey* (1932), SUCH IS MY BELOVED (1934), *Luke Baldwin's Vow* (1948), *They Shall Inherit the Earth* (1935), *More Joy in Heaven* (1937), *The* LOVED AND THE LOST (1951), *The Many Coloured Coat* (1960), *A Passion in Rome* (1961), and *A Fine and Private Place* (1975). He also wrote *The Varsity Story* (1948), about the University of Toronto, and THAT SUMMER IN PARIS: *Memoirs of Tangled Friendships with Hemingway, Fitzgerald and Others* (1963).

Calona Wines. The largest winery in British Columbia, founded in 1931 by Pasquale Capozzi in the Okanagan Valley, B.C. Its name was changed from Domestic Wines and By-Products Ltd to Calona Wines Ltd in 1934. The first president was W.A.C. BENNETT, later a premier of British Columbia.

Calumet. The French-Canadian word for a peace pipe, a ceremonial pipe smoked by Indians to symbolize the commencement of peaceful relations and other ceremonial events. See also CASSE-TÊTE À CALUMET.

Camboose. The central fireplace in log shanties built by voyageurs and lumbermen; the name became associated with the shanties themselves. Lumber camps were sometimes called 'camboose camps' after the 'camboose shanty', which could house as many as 60 men. The name is derived from the French word *cambuse* for 'store-room' or 'hut'.

Cambrai. Town in northern France liberated by the CANADIAN CORPS on 9 Oct. 1918, at the end of the FIRST WORLD WAR.

Cambridge. New city in southwestern Ontario. Created on 1 Jan. 1973 from the city of Galt and the towns of Hespeler and Preston, it has an estimated population of 70,082.

'Came-from-aways'. Mildly pejorative term used by Newfoundlanders to describe residents of that province who were not born there. It is most frequently applied to federal planners. Often shortened to CFA, the usage dates from the late 1960s and was given wide currency by Ray GUY, a columnist with the *St John's Evening Telegram*.

Camerata. The Italian word for 'companion', the name of a chamber ensemble of youthful musicians who perform in period costumes. Camerata made its début at the St Lawrence Hall, Toronto, on 12 Apr. 1973 and since then has performed lesser-known classical compositions in concerts at the SHAW FESTIVAL and across the country. It consists of Adele Armin, violin; Suzanne Shulman, flute; James Campbell, clarinet; Coenraad Bloemendal, cello; Kathryn Root and Elyakim Taussig, piano.

Cameron, Donald (b.1937). Cultural journalist. Born in Toronto but raised in Vancouver, he took his M.A. at the University of California (Berkeley) and his Ph.D. at the University of London (England). He has taught English at the University of New Brunswick, but since 1971 has been a free-lance writer living in D'Escousse, N.S., contributing to publications as various as *The* MYSTERIOUS EAST, which he founded in 1969, and WEEKEND MAGAZINE. Cameron is the author of *Faces of* LEACOCK (1967), the first critical study of the humorist, and of a two-volume collection of interviews, *Conversations with Canadian Novelists* (1973). In 1976 he began signing his articles Silver Donald Cameron, an allusion to the colour of his hair.

Cameron, Earl (b.1915). Popular CBC-TV newscaster. Born in Moose Jaw, Sask., he joined CBC Radio in 1944. He read The NATIONAL on television from 1959 to 1966 with avuncular detachment. Replaced by Stanley Burke, he was the announcer on VIEWPOINT until its cancellation in 1976, the year of his retirement from the CBC.

Cameron, George Frederick (1854-85). Poet. Born in New Glasgow, N.S., and educated at the Boston Law School and at Queen's University, he was appointed editor of the Kingston *News* two years before his early death. Eschewing patriotism and nature, he wrote poems celebrating the spirit of independence and democracy that were published posthumously in *Lyrics on Freedom, Love and Death* (1887).

Cameron, John Allen (b.1939). Folksinger and guitarist. Born and educated in Cape Breton, N.S., a former priest and high school teacher, Cameron sings, fiddles, and strums old Irish and Scottish ballads in a contemporary way, with humour. He has acquired a following for his concert and festival appearances as well as for his CBC-TV work.

Cameron Highlanders of Ottawa, The. Canadian army regiment. Organized in 1861, it served in the SOUTH AFRICAN WAR. During the FIRST WORLD WAR it served in France and Flanders at the battles of the SOMME, VIMY, and YPRES. In the SECOND WORLD WAR it was active in the NORMANDY INVASION as part of the 3rd Canadian Infantry Division and distinguished itself in many battles.

Camp, Dalton (b.1920). Advertising executive and Conservative spokesman. Born in Woodstock, N.B., and a graduate of Columbia University, he was a Beaverbrook Overseas Scholar to the London School of Economics. He began his advertising-public relations career as a copywriter with J. Walter Thompson in 1950 and eventually established his own agency, Travel Directions (Public Relations) Limited. He was president of the PROGRESSIVE CONSERVATIVE PARTY (1964-9) and led the battle to depose the P.C. leader, John G. DIEFENBAKER. A political commentator and columnist, he is the author of *Gentlemen, Players, and Politicians* (1970).

Camp Borden. See CANADIAN FORCES BASE BORDEN.

Campbell, Sir Alexander (1822-92). A FATHER OF CONFEDERATION. Born in England, he trained as a lawyer in Canada West (Ontario) and became a partner and life-long friend of John A. MACDONALD. Appointed to the legislative council in 1858, he attended the QUEBEC CONFERENCE and at Confederation was appointed to the Senate. In later years he headed numerous ministries and was lieutenant-governor of Ontario from 1887 to his death.

Campbell, Clarence S. (b.1905). Long-time president of the NATIONAL HOCKEY LEAGUE. Born in Fleming, Sask., he attended the University of Alberta and Oxford University as a Rhodes Scholar and had a distinguished war record. Campbell has served as president of the NHL since 1946.

Campbell, Douglas (b.1922). Stage actor. Born in Glasgow, Scot., he acted with the Old Vic (1942-53), married the actress Ann Casson in 1947, and settled in Canada in 1953 to join the STRATFORD FESTIVAL, in which he took leading roles until 1961. He co-founded the CANADIAN PLAYERS (1954-65). In 1963 he became artistic director of the Tyrone Guthrie Theatre in Minnesota.

Campbell, Marjorie Wilkins (b.1901). Popu-

lar historian. Born in London, Eng., she was brought up in the Qu'Appelle Valley, Sask., and educated at Swift Current and Toronto. Among her books are *The Saskatchewan* (1950), *The North West Company* (1957), and *McGillivray: Lord of the Northwest* (1962).

Campbell, Norman (b.1924). Television producer. Born in California and raised in Los Angeles and Vancouver, he graduated from the University of British Columbia in mathematics and physics and spent a year as a meteorologist on Sable Island. He was a producer and composer of popular music for CBC Radio in Vancouver before going to Toronto, where he produced the first English-language CBC-TV program, seen on 8 Sept. 1952. He wrote the music and Don HARRON the lyrics for ANNE OF GREEN GABLES (1954). His wife Elaine Campbell wrote the lyrics, Don Harron the book, and he the music for *The Wonder of It All*, a 90-minute musical about Emily CARR shown on CBC-TV in Oct. 1972 and starring Catherine McKINNON. Campbell's work is characterized by its technical competence and he is recognized for his U.S. and U.K. variety and comedy shows. He has televised more ballet than any other person, beginning in 1956 with the NATIONAL BALLET'S full-length production of *Swan Lake*.

Campbell, Wilfred (1858-1918). Poet. Born in Berlin, C.W. (Kitchener, Ont.), he graduated from the University of Toronto and the Episcopal Theological School, Cambridge, Mass. He was a clergyman in New Brunswick and Ontario from 1886 and a civil servant in Ottawa from 1891 until his death. Campbell expressed his patriotism and imperialism in prose and poetry and even aspired to be the first 'poet-laureate of the British Empire'. He wrote numerous books of verse and acquired a following, but never excelled the poems in his first book, *Lake Lyrics and Other Poems* (1889), which contains the well-known 'INDIAN SUMMER' and 'How One Winter Came in the Lake Region'. He was the editor of the first *Oxford Book of Canadian Verse* (1913). See also 'AT THE MERMAID INN'.

Campeau, Robert (b.1924). Ottawa builder and developer. Born in Sudbury, Ont., and educated by correspondence, he moved at 25 to Ottawa, where he built his first house, which he then sold for a handsome profit. Within a year he had nearly 100 houses under construction. Campeau Corporation Limited was established in 1968 and rapidly diversified. Among Campeau's notable buildings are Place de Ville in downtown Ottawa and the multi-million-dollar Harbour

Castle Hotel, Toronto, which opened in 1975.

Campobello Island. Largest of a group of small islands in Passamaquoddy Bay, which flows into the Bay of Fundy. Politically a part of New Brunswick, the island is closer to the United States and is linked with Maine by the Roosevelt International Bridge. It was originally granted in 1767 to Admiral William Owen, a Welshman of the Royal Navy, and was held by his descendants until 1881. It is now the site of the 2,600-acre Roosevelt Campobello International Park, which was opened in 1964 in memory of the American President Franklin Delano Roosevelt. The park includes the 32-room summer home used intermittently by FDR between 1883 and 1938—now a memorial museum.

Can. Unofficial abbreviation of CANADA.

Canada. In area the second largest country in the world (after the Soviet Union), Canada occupies the northern half of the North American continent: 3,223 mi. from east to west and 2,875 mi. from north to south—a total of 3,851,809 sq. mi. Its most southerly point is Middle Island, Lake Erie; its most northerly, Cape Columbia, Ellesmere Island; it most easterly, Cape Spear, Nfld; its most westerly, Mt St Elias, Y.T. A constitutional monarchy, Canada was founded on 1 July 1867. Its population on 1 June 1971 was estimated by the census to be 21,569,000.

The word Canada may have derived from the Iroquoian word *kanata*, which means 'village' or 'community'. It first appeared in print in Jacques CARTIER'S account of his voyage of 1535, in which it designated a region along the St Lawrence R. from Grosse Ile in the east to a point between Quebec and Trois-Rivières in the west. Canada's motto is A MARI USQUE AD MARE.

Canada. Sailing ship operated by the ALLAN LINE. A 330-ton wooden vessel, she was built in Scotland in 1831 and was the Line's first full-rigged ship, sailing in the Quebec City-West Indian trade as opportunity offered.

Canada. A Portuguese liquid measure that varies according to locality. In Lisbon it equals 1.38 litres; in Rio de Janeiro, 2.81 litres.

Cañada. A word derived from the Spanish, chiefly used in the western United States, for a dry riverbed, a deep canyon, or a small glen. Three towns in central Argentina are called: Cañada de Gomez, Cañada Honda, and Cañada Verde.

'Ca-na-da'. Hit song of Canada's Centennial Year written by Bobby GIMBY, composer and bandleader, who spent most of 1967 travelling across the country with his band playing 'Ca-na-da'. It is officially called 'A Centennial Song: Canada'. All royalties from the use of the song go to the Boy Scouts of Canada.

Canada, Province of. See PROVINCE OF CANADA.

Canada A.M. Early-morning CTV Network program devoted to information. Launched in the fall of 1971, it is seen across the country at 7:00-8:30 a.m. five mornings a week, and is the only live-network public-affairs show in Canada. Devoted to news, interviews, conversation, weather, and sports, it is hosted by Norm Perry and Helen Hutchinson.

Canada/A Year of the Land. Title of a 'coffee table book' superbly illustrated with photographs of Canada arranged by seasons, with a text by Bruce HUTCHISON. It was produced by Lorraine MONK of the NATIONAL FILM BOARD in 1967 as the federal government's official gift during Centennial Year. A trade edition sold more than 80,000 copies.

Canada: An Encyclopedia of the Country. The first general encyclopedic work published in Canada. It appeared in six volumes in Toronto between 1898 and 1900, edited by John Castell Hopkins and written by 'a corps of eminent specialists'.

Canada and Its Provinces. A 23-volume reference work subtitled 'A history of the Canadian people and their institutions'. Published between 1914 and 1917, it was in its time an important work of national, provincial, and regional history. It was edited by Arthur G. DOUGHTY and Adam SHORTT.

Canada Assistance Plan. Plan to provide aid to people in need. It was enacted in 1966 to provide basic requirements such as food, shelter, and clothing; the maintenance of children in the care of welfare agencies; items necessary for the safety, well being, or rehabilitation of persons in need or handicapped persons; maintenance in a home for special care such as a home for the aged or a nursing home; health-care services; and welfare services. Under an agreement with the provinces and territories, the federal government contributes a minimum of 50% of the cost of this aid. Any person or family who is in need is eligible for assistance under the plan.

Canada at War. Series of 13 documentary films produced by the NFB in 1962. Filmed in black and white and under 30 minutes each, they were produced by Stanley Clish, Peter

Jones, and Donald BRITTAIN. Through footage taken at home and on the battlefronts, they examined Canada's role in the SECOND WORLD WAR.

Canada balsam. A viscous, yellowish resin, exuded by the balsam fir of North America. Both transparent and adhesive, it is used for cementing glass in optical instruments and for mounting specimens between glass slides for microscopic examination. It is also called Canada turpentine.

Canada Bay. A natural harbour on the eastern shore of northern Newfoundland. No other site in the country is called 'Canada'.

Canada-Belgium Literary Prize. Annual award given alternately to a French-language writer from Belgium or Canada. The $2,000 prize is awarded on the basis of a writer's body of work. It has been co-sponsored since 1971 by the Canadian and Belgian governments and is financed in Canada by the Cultural Affairs Division of the Department of External Affairs and the Canada Council.

Canada buffalo berry. A species of the BUFFALO BERRY, this shrub is thornless and its fruit is unpalatable. It grows on wooded banks from Newfoundland to Alaska.

Canada Carries On. An important series of propaganda newsreels released once a month by the NFB during and after the Second World War. The one- and two-reel films were distributed to 1,000 Canadian theatres by Columbia Pictures and to theatres in Commonwealth countries by other Hollywood companies. The series was originally produced by Stuart Legg, who was replaced by Stanley Hawes when Legg moved on to the WORLD IN ACTION series in 1942. At the end of the war Sydney NEWMAN succeeded Hawes as producer. The series was narrated by Lorne GREENE, with music written and arranged by Lucio AGOSTINI. The first film was *Atlantic Patrol* (released Apr. 1940) and the last was *Wheat Country* (released Jan. 1960). Some of the best-known films were CHURCHILL'S ISLAND (1941), *War Clouds in the Pacific* (1941), *Battle for Oil* (1942), *Quebec, Path of Conquest* (1942), and *Target Berlin* (1944). *En Avant Canada* was the title of the French-language version of the series.

Canada Company. A land and colonization company in Upper Canada (Ontario). Founded in 1824, in London, Eng., it bought over two million acres on which the towns of Guelph, Galt, and Goderich were founded. Its first superintendent was John GALT. The company's contract expired in 1843.

Canada Council. Independent body created to encourage the arts, humanities, and social sciences. It was established in 1957 by Parliament, to which it reports through the secretary of state. The Council consists of 21 members, appointed by the government for three-year terms, and a permanent staff in Ottawa. It advises the government on cultural matters, maintains the Canadian Commission for UNESCO, and administers a broad program of fellowships and grants to both individuals and institutions. The Council's income derives from an annual grant from the Canadian government, an Endowment Fund established when the Council was created, and private funds willed or donated to the Council; its annual income from all sources now amounts to over $35 million. The larger part of the budget is spent on assistance to the humanities and social sciences. The Humanities and Social Sciences Division awards M.A. fellowships, doctoral fellowships, leave and research fellowships, and research grants; arranges cultural exchanges; and is of direct assistance to university research programs. Grants are made to the HUMANITIES RESEARCH COUNCIL and the SOCIAL SCIENCE RESEARCH COUNCIL for their activities, including supporting the publication of scholarly works. The Council also gives substantial support to the arts. The Arts Division awards senior arts grants, arts grants, short-term grants, project cost grants, and travel grants to individuals, and directly aids cultural organizations and institutions. The creation of such a body was the principal recommendation of the MASSEY COMMISSION in 1951. Its influence on the arts and on research and education has been enlightened and substantial. For other activities of the Council, see: ART BANK, CANADA-BELGIUM LITERARY PRIZE, CANADIAN CULTURAL INSTITUTE, EXPLORATIONS PROGRAM, GOVERNOR GENERAL'S LITERARY AWARDS, KILLAM PROGRAM, MOLSON PRIZES, PETER DWYER SCHOLARSHIPS, QUEEN'S FELLOWSHIPS, STANLEY HOUSE, TOURING OFFICE, TRANSLATION PRIZES, VICTOR LYNCH-STAUNTON AWARDS, VINCENT MASSEY AWARDS, and WATKINS FELLOWSHIPS.

Canada Council Medal. Award made annually since 1961 by the CANADA COUNCIL to acknowledge distinguished achievement and excellence over an extended period of time in the arts, humanities, or social sciences. The bronze medal is accompanied by a check for $2,500.

Canada Day. Event held annually on no special day, but usually in the spring, to celebrate Canadian sovereignty and culture. The first Canada Day—held in the spring of 1970 at Port Colborne High School, Ont.—was organized by James (Jim) FOLEY, English teacher and Canadian-literature enthusiast. The celebration now embraces grade schools and community colleges and is organized on a local basis across the country. See also DOMINION DAY.

Canada Development Corporation. It was established in 1971 to develop and maintain Canadian corporations and to encourage Canadians to invest in the economic development of Canada. It is administered by a board of 21 directors and is not an agency of the Crown. It is part or full owner of a number of private Canadian corporations, including CONNAUGHT LABORATORIES.

Canada Dock. The name of the chief dock of the Liverpool, Eng., dockyards.

Canada Dry. The trade name for a ginger ale. John J. McLaughlin, a chemist and pharmacist and founder in 1890 of a Toronto bottling plant for soda water, perfected an extract of ginger that he patented in 1907 as 'Canada Dry ginger ale'. His company rapidly expanded, acquiring an American subsidiary in 1922. After McLaughlin's death in 1924 the subsidiary purchased the original Canadian company. Through large-scale advertising, Canada Dry products became popular in the U.S. and are now marketed in over 60 countries.

Canada East. The name of present-day Quebec between 1841 and 1867 when, with CANADA WEST (present-day Ontario), it comprised the PROVINCE OF CANADA.

Canada Emergency Measures Organization. Federal body concerned with co-ordinating the civil aspects of defence policy to meet the threat of nuclear war. On 1 Apr. 1974 CEMO was renamed the NATIONAL EMERGENCY PLANNING ESTABLISHMENT to ensure a co-ordinated response to any national emergency.

Canada Evidence Act, The. A federal statute, a counterpart of which is enacted by each province, governing the rules for the admission of evidence in court proceedings. For a witness to 'claim the protection of the Canada Evidence Act', he must make the request of the presiding judge. When such protection is requested and granted, any statement made by the witness may not be used in evidence against him in any other proceeding, but if the evidence he gives is false, he may be prosecuted for perjury.

Canada First. Patriotic movement. It was founded in Ottawa in 1868 by a group of young enthusiasts who wanted to foster national pride and to encourage maturity in the arts and in political development. The Toronto branch was headed briefly by Goldwin SMITH and attracted Edward BLAKE. Though it lasted for less than 10 years, its nationalist sentiments influenced the founding of Smith's journal *The Nation* (1874-6), the two political parties, and a literary flowering associated with Charles MAIR, Charles G.D. ROBERTS. Bliss CARMAN, Wilfred CAMPBELL, Archibald LAMPMAN, and D.C. SCOTT.

Canada for Canadians. Slogan of the Conservative Party in the election of 1861.

Canada Games. A series of amateur sports events for Canadian athletes held every two years in summer and winter in different cities. The first Canadian Winter Games were held in Quebec City in 1967. The first Canadian Summer Games were held in Halifax-Dartmouth in 1969.

Canada Gazette. Official publication of the federal government, published in French and English in three parts. Part 1 is published every Saturday and contains notices of a general character, including official appointments, bankruptcy notices, certain orders-in-council, and glosses on statutory notices. Part 2 is published every second and fourth Wednesday of each month (special editions are published when required) and contains regulations of the STATUTES OF CANADA. (Acts of Parliament outline legislation in broad terms; the appropriate department or board that is to implement the legislation provides for its detailed application through the regulations.) Part 3 was started in 1975 to publish public acts as soon as possible after they receive ROYAL ASSENT, to counter the delay in issuing the Statutes of Canada. The *Canada Gazette* was issued as the official paper of the united provinces of Upper and Lower Canada from 2 Oct. 1841. As the official paper of the Dominion a new series was started on 29 June 1867.

Canada goose. Unofficial national bird of Canada. A common wild goose, one of the largest waterfowl, it has a wing span that may reach 5½ ft. The plumage is greyish-brown on the wings and back, lighter below; the feet, bill, head, and neck are black and it has a white chin strap. It mates for life. Migrating in v-formation flocks, it winters in western Canada, northern Quebec, and the Maritimes, and summers in the central and southern United States and Mexico. Now a seasonally protected game bird, its flights reach heights of 3½ mi. and speeds of 34 m.p.h.

Canada Grading. A food-grading system used by the Canada Department of Agriculture. The grades applied to the following foods indicate decreasing levels of quality.

Butter, Cheese, and Milk Powder: Canada First Grade, Canada Second Grade, Canada Third Grade, Below Canada Third Grade.

Beef: Canada A, classes 1,2,3,4 (red ribbon brand); Canada B, classes 1,2,3,4 (blue ribbon brand); Canada C, classes 1,2 (brown ribbon brand); Canada D, classes 1,2,3,4 (black ribbon brand); and Canada E (black ribbon brand).

Lamb: Canada A, classes 1,2,3,4 (red); Canada B (blue); Canada C, classes 1,2 (brown).

Mutton: Canada D, classes 1,2,3,4 and Canada E (both black ribbon brand).

Pork: Pork is graded by indices: Canada Indices 112, 110, 109, 107, 105, 103, 102, 100, 98, 97, 95, 92, 91, 88, 87 (heavy and light), 85 (extra-heavy), 82 (extra-heavy), 80, 67 (ridgling). In addition there are Canada Stag and Canada Sow classes 1 and 2.

Veal: Canada A (red), Canada B (blue), Canada C (brown), Canada D and Canada E (black).

Poultry: Canada Grade Special (purple), Canada Grade A (red), Canada Grade B (blue), Canada Grade Utility (blue), Canada Grade C (yellow), Canada Grade D (brown). In addition there may be an inspection stamp: 'Canada Approved' or 'Canada'.

Eggs: Canada Grade A1, Canada Grade A, Canada Grade B, Canada Grade C. Sizes for Grades A1 and A are: Extra Large Size, Large Size, Medium Size, Small Size, Peewee Size.

Apples: Canada Extra Fancy, Canada Fancy, Canada Commercial (also called Canada CEE or Canada 'C').

Apricots, Crabapples, Cranberries, Grapes, Peaches, Plums, Prunes, Rhubarb: Canada No. 1, Canada Domestic.

Blueberries, Cantaloupe, Strawberries: Canada No. 1.

Cherries: Canada No. 1, Canada Domestic, Canada Orchard Run.

Pears: Canada Extra Fancy, Canada Fancy (or Canada No. 1), Canada Commercial (or Canada CEE, Canada 'C', or Canada Domestic).

Asparagus, Beets, Brussels Sprouts, Cabbage, Cauliflower, Cucumber, Lettuce, New Potatoes, Tomatoes: Canada No. 1, Canada No. 2.

Carrots, Parsnips: Canada No. 1 and Canada No. 1 Cut Crowns, Canada No. 2.

Celery: Canada No. 1 and Canada No. 1 Heart, Canada No. 2.

Onions: Canada No. 1 and Canada No. 1 Pickling, Canada No. 2.

Potatoes: Canada No. 1 and Canada No. 1 Large and Small, Canada No. 1 New Potatoes, Canada No. 2.

Rutabagas, Sweet Corn: Canada No. 1.

Canned Fruits and Vegetables: Canada Fancy, Canada Choice, Canada Standard.

Tomato Juice, Apple Juice: Canada Fancy, Canada Choice.

Frozen and Dehydrated Fruits and Vegetables: Canada Fancy, Canada Choice.

Honey: Canada No. 1, Canada No. 2, Canada No. 3. There are four classes of colour: White, Golden, Amber, Dark.

Maple Syrup: Canada Fancy, Canada Light, Canada Medium, Canada Dark.

Canada House. The name given the residences or offices maintained for consular and cultural purposes by the Department of External Affairs in London, Paris, and other world capitals. In a FRANCOPHONE country such a residence or office is known as *Maison du Canada*.

Canada jay. A grey crestless jay with a dark cap and white throat and forehead. Found in northern coniferous forests, it is also called whiskey-jack, moosebird, and camp robber—a nickname acquired because of its boldness in stealing food.

Canada Labour Relations Board. Board to administer provisions of the Canada Labour Code with respect to workers under federal jurisdiction. Established in 1970, it consists of a chairman, a vice-chairman, an additional vice-chairman when necessary, and not less than four and not more than eight other members.

Canada Lakes. A chain of small lakes fed by the East Canada Creek south of Lake Pleasant in Upper New York State, U.S.A.

Canada lynx. A wild feline found in the forested regions of Canada's North. Second in size only to the mountain lion, its average length is 34 in. Silvery grey with a short black-tipped tail, long legs, and long tufts on its ears, it is valued for its long, soft fur.

Canada Manpower Centres. An employment service for workers and employers administered by the Department of MANPOWER AND IMMIGRATION. There are about 400 centres across Canada that provide up-to-date information on jobs available and workers looking for jobs, help in transferring workers to areas where jobs are available, labour counselling, and placement services for immigrants. The Canada Manpower Training-on-the-Job Program, under the Special Employment Plan introduced in 1971, arranges for contracts with employers to hire trainees.

Canada Medal. Award for outstanding service to Canada. Created in 1943 by the Canadian government, it was approved by King George VI but never actually awarded.

Canada Park. A 7,500-acre park midway between Tel Aviv and Jerusalem in the most densely populated part of Israel. On what was bare, rocky ground in 1970 now grow five million trees, planted by the Jewish National Fund of Canada (at the cost of $3.00 a tree). Dedicated in Mar. 1976, it is used by 35,000 visitors on peak days, many of whom drive along DIEFENBAKER Parkway, named in honour of the former prime minister of Canada, a friend of the Jewish people.

Canada Pension Plan. National retirement plan. The Act proclaiming the Canada Pension Plan received Royal Assent on 3 Apr. 1965, and the first benefits to contributors were paid out in Jan. 1967. The CPP, which is self-supporting, pays out retirement pensions, survivor benefits, and disability benefits in relation to the contributions people have made to it. Provision is made for escalation of pensions to meet the rise in the cost of living. The Plan is compulsory throughout Canada, except in Quebec where a comparable pension plan has been established. See also OLD AGE SECURITY PENSION.

Canada Post. Official short form for the Canada Post Office Department.

Canada Steamship Lines. Formed in 1913 through the merger of a number of companies, notably the Richelieu & Ontario Navigation Co., Montreal Transportation Co., Northern Navigation Co., and Niagara Navigation Co. The fleet grew to more than 100 ships of all kinds, operating from the head of Lake Superior to the Saguenay R. CSL also owned the MANOIR RICHELIEU and the Tadoussac Hotel (sold in 1967). With the retirement of SS *Cayuga* in 1957 the company's passenger traffic ended. The concentration on fewer and larger ships has reduced the fleet to 29.

Canada Student Loans Plan A federally guaranteed program of bank loans to university students, repayable at low interest rates over an extended period after graduation. They were first offered in 1964.

Canada Studies Foundation. A privately supported association, established in Toronto in 1970, to improve the quality of Canadian studies programs in primary and secondary schools across the country. It is headed by A.B. Hodgetts, the author of *What Culture? What Heritage? A Study of Civic Education in Canada* (1968). It commissions reports and prepares learning materials for use in schools.

Canada Temperance Act, 1878. A federal statute, which could be invoked by any province, prohibiting the sale of intoxicating liquor except for sacramental or medicinal purposes. Popularly known as the Scott Act, it remained in force in most parts of Canada until the 1930s. Its constitutionality was tested in the famous case of *Russell v. The Queen* (1882) in which it was contended that the regulation of the use of liquor was a local or provincial and not a federal matter. But the legislation was upheld because it 'is clearly meant to apply a remedy to an evil which is assumed to exist throughout the Dominion. Accordingly, Parliament has authority to deal with the matter under its power to enact laws for the "peace, order and good government" of Canada.' Since the 'peace, order and good government' clause of the BNA ACT can be invoked only in unusual circumstances, it is said that the Canada Temperance Act was upheld only because drunkenness was considered to have reached such an alarming state in the 1870s that 'it was a menace to the national life of Canada so serious and pressing that the National Parliament was called on to intervene to protect the nation from disaster.' See also PROHIBITION, DUNKIN ACT.

Canada turpentine. See CANADA BALSAM.

Canada West. The name of present-day Ontario between 1841 and 1867 when, with CANADA EAST (present-day Quebec), it comprised the PROVINCE OF CANADA.

Canada Year Book. Official statistical annual published by the Canadian government. It has appeared each year under this title since 1905, and under other titles since 1867.

Canadair Limited. It was founded in 1944 from the nucleus of Vickers Aircraft Co., Montreal, to assume production of the Canso (PBY-5), which was used by the RCAF (called the 'Canso'), the RAF (called the 'Catalina'), and the U.S. Air Force (called the 'PBY-5 Amphibian'). It was a Crown corporation from 1944 to 1947 and later became a subsidiary of the General Dynamics Corporation of St Louis. Canadair's production has included the following series of planes: the CL-44, CL-84, CL-215, and CL-13. On 5 Jan. 1976 it was purchased by the federal government.

Canadas, The. A reference either to UPPER CANADA and LOWER CANADA between 1791 and 1841 or to CANADA EAST and CANADA WEST between 1841 and 1867.

Canada's Atlantic Playground. Description of NOVA SCOTIA by its department of tourism in the 1960s.

Canada's Golden Gateway. Unofficial motto of VANCOUVER, B.C. Another is 'Gateway to the Orient'.

Canada's Sports Hall of Fame. See HALLS OF FAME.

Canadaway. Original name of Fredonia, a town southwest of Buffalo, N.Y. It was founded in 1804 and renamed Fredonia in 1817.

'Canaday-i-o'. A lumberjack's song popular among workers recruited in Maine to work in winter camps along the St Lawrence in the 1850s. It is attributed to Ephraim Braley, and the last verse is: 'And now the winter's over, it's homeward we are bound,/And in this cursed country we'll never more be found./Go back to your wives and sweethearts, tell others not to go/To that God-forsaken country called Canaday-i-o.'

Canadensis. A town in northeastern Pennsylvania, U.S.A.

Canader. A slang term used at Oxford University at the turn of the century for the Canadian CANOE.

Canadettes. A well-known chorus line that performs as part of the CNE GRANDSTAND SHOW. Created in 1952 and developed and choreographed by Margaret (Midge) Cousins, the wife of the showman Jack ARTHUR, they have been called 'the world's longest precision line of dancers'. The Canadettes are composed of from 32 to 60 female dancers, all between the ages of 13 and 24.

Canadian. A citizen of Canada. Before the passage of the Canadian Citizenship Act, which came into force on 1 Jan. 1947, a Canadian could not call himself or herself a Canadian citizen because the official designation for a person born or naturalized within the British Commonwealth was BRITISH SUBJECT. The Act created the distinct nationality of a Canadian citizen: someone born in Canada or born of a Canadian father outside of Canada, or a British subject or alien who has become naturalized according to the provisions of the Act. A Canadian citizen still retains the status of a British subject.

Canadian. A small railway town in northeastern Texas near the Oklahoma border, on the CANADIAN RIVER.

Canadian. The name of three steamships operated by the ALLAN LINE. *Canadian I*, built

in Scotland in 1854, took troops to the Crimea and was wrecked in 1856 below Quebec City. Also Scottish-built, *Canadian II* was constructed in 1860 and sank the next year, after striking an iceberg near Belle Isle. *Canadian III*, built at Liverpool in 1873, was employed on the Liverpool and Glasgow run to Canada, and from 1892 to South America.

Canadian. Automobile manufactured in 1921 by Colonial Motors, Walkerville, Ont. The touring model sold for $2,600. Its advertising slogan was 'All Canadian Car'.

Canadian, The. The name of the CPR's transcontinental passenger train on the Montreal-Toronto-Vancouver run. Inaugurated on 24 Apr. 1955, *The Canadian* boasted new stainless-steel, scenic-domed passenger cars and was advertised as 'the longest dome-train ride in the world'. See also VISTA DOME.

Canadian Actors' Equity. An association of professional performers. It was so named on 1 Apr. 1976, having been the Canadian chapter—founded in Toronto on 19 Sept. 1954—of the American stage performers' union, which goes back to 1919. Canadian Actors' Equity is concerned with the stage; ACTRA covers television and radio performers. Some actors belong to both associations.

Canadian and Catholic Confederation of Labour. See CONFEDERATION OF NATIONAL TRADE UNIONS.

Canadian Annual Review. A yearbook devoted to politics and public affairs edited by John Saywell and published annually by the University of Toronto Press. The first volume, covering events in Canada during 1960, appeared the following year. *CAR* is modelled on an earlier annual of the same name, edited by J. Castell Hopkins (1864-1923), which covered the period 1901 to 1938.

Canadian Architect and Builder, The. Canada's first major architectural journal. Published in Toronto from 1888 to Apr. 1908, it inevitably reflected a Toronto-Montreal bias but illustrated a wide variety of work, in both photos and engravings, by architects from coast to coast. The monthly magazine also crusaded for recognition of the professional and artistic status of Canadian architects.

Canadian Arctic Co-operative Federation Limited. It was formed on 22 Feb. 1972, with headquarters at Yellowknife, to represent Eskimo art co-operatives in the Northwest Territories. Each community where art is produced has its own co-operative, which arranges the manufacture and sale of its products. The active members include the following co-operatives, with their locations in parantheses: West Baffin (CAPE DORSET), Kikitaoyak (Port Burwell), Coppermine (Coppermine), Resolute Bay (Resolute Bay), Grise Fiord (Grise Fiord), Holman (Holman Island), Ekaloktotiak (Cambridge Bay), Ikaluit (Frobisher Bay), Issatik (Whale Cove), Aklavik (Aklavik), Igloolik (Igloolik), Great Bear (Fort Franklin), Pangnirtung (PANGNIRTUNG), Koomuit (Pelly Bay), Kekertak (Gjoa Haven), Paulatuk (Paulatuk), Naujat (Repulse Bay), Kissarvik (Rankin Inlet), Kapami (Colville Lake), Metiq (Sanikiluaq), Nanuk (Tuktoyaktuk), Toonoonik-Sahoonik (Pond Inlet), Lac La Martre (Lac La Martre), Ikahuk (Sachs Harbour), Kooneak (Arctic Bay), Katudgevik (Coral Harbour), Pitsiulak (Chesterfield Inlet), Sanavik (BAKER LAKE), Dene (Fort Simpson), Padlei (Eskimo Point), Paleajook (Spence Bay), Hanayee (Baker Lake), Tulugak (Broughton Island), Inuivik (Inuvik), Petanea (Fort Wrigley), Jean Marie River Community (Jean Marie), Tetlit (Fort McPherson), Kimik (Lake Harbour), Snowdrift (Snowdrift), Hall Beach (Hall Beach), Res Logging (Fort Resolution), Raven (Yellowknife). See also La FÉDÉRATION DES COOPÉRATIVES DE NOUVEAU-QUÉBEC.

Canadian Arctic Producers Limited. The central arts-and-crafts marketing agency that services the Eskimo and Indian people of northern Canada. Established as a private company in 1965 and restructured with the help of the Department of INDIAN AFFAIRS AND NORTHERN DEVELOPMENT in 1970, CAP is now owned and controlled by the Eskimo people.

Canadian Armed Forces. World's first unified fighting force. UNIFICATION of the ROYAL CANADIAN NAVY, the CANADIAN ARMY, and the ROYAL CANADIAN AIR FORCE became effective on 1 Feb. 1968. The CAF is headed by the CHIEF OF DEFENCE STAFF, who is responsible to the Minister of National Defence. There are five functional commands to the CAF: Maritime, Mobile, Air, Communications, and Canadian Forces Europe. Canadian Forces Headquarters assumed the roles of Materiel and Training Commands in 1970 and 1975 respectively. Air Command was formed late in 1975 and it assumed the roles of Air Defence and Air Transport Commands.

The following three Force formations and 14 units are observed: *Naval Formations:* Fleet, Squadrons, Ships; *Field Formations:* Division, Brigades, Regiments, Battalions, Squadrons, Companies; *Air Formations:* Division, Groups, Wings, Squadrons, Units. Members of the CAF wear a common uniform. The following ranks are observed:

OFFICERS. *General Officers:* General, Lieutenant-General, Major General, Brigadier General; *Senior Officers:* Colonel, Lieutenant-Colonel, Major; *Junior Officers:* Captain, Lieutenant, 2nd Lieutenant; *Subordinate Officers:* Officer Cadet.

OTHER RANKS. Chief Warrant Officer, Master Warrant Officer, Warrant Officer, Sergeant, Master Corporal, Corporal, Private.

Canadian Armed Forces Cadets. A program of training in the fundamentals of citizenship and leadership sponsored by the CANADIAN ARMED FORCES and civilian agencies, with the support of the Department of National Defence. Its three leagues—Army Cadet, Air Cadet, and Navy—maintain summer camps where boys between the ages of 13 and 18 can become familiar with the elements of the armed forces and pursue a program of physical fitness. There are currently over 62,000 cadets enrolled in approximately 960 Corps across the country. In July 1975 Royal Assent given to Bill C-16 authorized an amendment to the National Defence Act to support female cadets.

Canadian Army. Until 1940 it was known at the Canadian Militia, one of the oldest institutions in Canada, which originally consisted of both volunteers and men compulsorily enrolled. Volunteers served in the WAR OF 1812 and the REBELLION OF 1837. The Militia Act of 1846 marked the first time that the Canadian authorities recognized the volunteer principle. The Militia Act of 1855 provided for 5,000 volunteers to be equipped and trained for 10 days a year at public expense. The first federal Militia Act of 1868 authorized an active militia of 40,000 volunteers, which increased to 45,000 in 1871. The First Permanent Active Militia units—'A' and 'B' Batteries, Canadian Artillery—were formed on 20 Oct. 1871. Permanent cavalry and infantry units were formed in 1883. Other permanent corps were formed subsequently. The Canadian militia served during the FENIAN Raids (1866-70), and in the RED RIVER REBELLION (1870) and the NORTHWEST REBELLION (1885). Over 7,000 members of the militia, mainly the Non-Permanent Active Militia, served in the SOUTH AFRICAN WAR (1899-1901). By 1914 the militia consisted of 3,000 permanent and 60,000 non-permanent members. The Canadian Expeditionary Force—619,636 men and women—suffered 59,544 fatal casualties and 172,950 wounded during the FIRST WORLD WAR. (See also CANADIAN CORPS.) In 1939 the Permanent Force strength was 4,000 and the Non-Permanent Active Militia 52,000. The Canadian Army Active Service Force—730,159—had 22,917 fatal casualties and 52,679 wounded during the SECOND WORLD WAR. Canadian Army formations served in Hong Kong, Sicily, Italy, and Northwest Europe. (See also FIRST CANADIAN ARMY and NORMANDY INVASION.) In 1950 Canada provided an infantry brigade group for United Nations service in Korea until 1953 and in 1951 another infantry brigade group was sent to Germany as part of Canada's continuing NATO commitment. The Canadian Army (Regular) also provided personnel for United Nations peace-keeping tasks from 1954 onwards. On 1 Feb. 1968 the Canadian Army was unified with the ROYAL CANADIAN NAVY and the ROYAL CANADIAN AIR FORCE to form the CANADIAN ARMED FORCES.

Canadian Art Club, The. A private exhibiting society of painters of atmospheric landscapes that existed in Montreal from 1907 to 1915. Among its members were Homer WATSON, its first president, Horatio WALKER, William BRYMNER, Maurice CULLEN, Clarence GAGNON, and James Wilson MORRICE.

Canadian Artists' Representation. Professional association of practising artists. CAR was founded by Jack CHAMBERS in London, Ont., in 1968 to help visual artists solve day-to-day problems. It has lobbied in favour of exhibition rental fees, increased copyright protection, artists as appointees to arts institutions, and against censorship.

Canadian Association for Adult Education. A voluntary association to 'represent the interest of adult learning in Canada and in the world community'. Founded in Toronto in 1935, its first director was Edward A. (Ned) Corbett (1887-1964), a former teacher. He retired in 1950 and was succeeded by J.R. (Roby) Kidd (b.1915), a former YMCA secretary. He retired in 1962 and was succeeded by Alan M. Thomas (b.1928), a professional educator. The CAAE co-sponsored the NATIONAL FARM RADIO FORUM and CITIZENS' FORUM on CBC Radio in the 1940s and has published such journals as *Food for Thought* and *Continuous Learning*. It is associated with the Institut Canadien d'Éducation des Adultes (ICEA), its Quebec counterpart.

Canadian Association of Broadcasters. A trade association representing the interests of privately owned radio and television stations in Canada. Founded in Ottawa in 1926, the CAB in 1976 spoke on behalf of 267 AM radio stations, 61 FM stations, 60 television stations, 79 associate members, and several privately owned networks.

Canadian Author and Bookman, The. A quarterly publication of the CANADIAN AUTHORS ASSOCIATION. Founded in 1921, it supplies news to members and publishes—especially since it absorbed the CAA's *Canadian Poetry Magazine* (founded in 1936) in 1968—members' poetry.

Canadian Authors Association. National organization for writers in Canada, founded in Montreal in 1921 'to foster and develop a climate favourable to the creative arts, to promote recognition of Canadian writers and their work'. There are more than 900 full and associate members and more than a dozen branch associations across the country. The CAA published *Canadian Poetry* from 1936 to 1968, when it was merged with the CANADIAN AUTHOR AND BOOKMAN, which has appeared since 1921. From 1936 to 1960 it administered the GOVERNOR GENERAL'S LITERARY AWARDS. At its national conventions the CAA oversees the GIBSON LITERARY AWARD, the ROTHMANS MERIT AWARD FOR LITERATURE, the VICKY METCALF AWARD and, since 1975, the CAA Medals for fiction, non-fiction, poetry, and drama 'to honour writing which achieves literary excellence without sacrificing popular appeal'. Funded by HARLEQUIN Enterprises Limited, the CAA awards consist of four silver medals each accompanied by a cheque for $1,000. They are presented at the CAA's annual summer meeting. The CAA does not represent all writers in Canada. See also the WRITERS' UNION OF CANADA and the LEAGUE OF CANADIAN POETS.

Canadian Authors' Foundation. See CANADIAN WRITERS' FOUNDATION.

'Canadian Authors Meet, The.' Satirical poem by F.R. SCOTT, inspired by a meeting of the CANADIAN AUTHORS ASSOCIATION in Montreal and written in 1927. It first appeared in the McGILL FORTNIGHTLY REVIEW on 27 Apr. 1927.

Canadian bacon. Cured, smoked back bacon. Cut from a boned strip of pork loin, it is leaner than side bacon.

Canadian Basic Books. Annual catalogue of about 900 popular Canadian books. The titles for the main annotated list of books from Canadian-owned publishing houses and for the supplementary checklist of other publishers' books are selected by booksellers from across the country. The catalogue, published each June, first appeared in 1975.

Canadian Bill of Rights. An Act of Parliament that guarantees rights and freedoms to Canadians. Its full title is 'An Act for the Recognition and Protection of Human Rights and Fundamental Freedoms'. It was given

76

Royal Assent on 10 Aug. 1960 after passing Parliament under the leadership of Prime Minister John G. DIEFENBAKER. It guarantees the rights of life, liberty, security of person and enjoyment of property, equality before and protection of the law, freedom of religion, of speech, of assembly, and of the press, 'without discrimination by reason of race, national origin, colour, religion, or sex'.

Canadian black. Marijuana grown in Canada—a slang term.

Canadian blueberry. Low-growing shrub with hairy foliage, white flowers, and sweet bluish-black fruit. It grows in abundance from Newfoundland to Saskatchewan.

Canadian boat songs. There are several songs in French—such as *'M'en revenant de la vendée'*—associated with the voyageurs who paddled the canoes of the western fur brigades in the eighteenth and nineteenth centuries. One in English—'Canadian Boat-Song (from the Gaelic)', known by its sub-title, 'The Lone Shieling'—is said to have been sung by Hebrideans who settled in Canada and was published anonymously in *Blackwood's Magazine* in 1829. It boasts a lovely refrain: 'Fair these broad meads—these hoary woods are grand/But we are exiles from our fathers' land'. The text may be found in *The Lone Shieling* (1941) by G.H. Needler, who attributed it to David Macbeth Moir, a Scot. Another boat song in English, by the Irish poet Thomas Moore who visited Canada in 1804, was never sung, but it celebrates the departure of the annual fur brigades from Sainte-Anne's, near Montreal. The refrain of 'A Canadian Boat Song: Written on the River St Lawrence' runs: 'Row, brothers, row, the stream runs fast/The rapids are near and the daylight's past'. It appears in *The Poetical Works of Thomas Moore* (1910).

Canadian Book Publishers' Council. Established in 1910, it grew out of the Canadian Textbook Publishers' Institute (CTPI), a department of the Toronto Board of Trade, and originally comprised 12 publishers and a semi-autonomous affiliate—the Book Publishers' Association of Canada (BPAC). Its present name was adopted on 12 Apr. 1961. Committee groups—made up of volunteers from 40 Canadian, American, and British member publishers, and, since 1968, a member of the Council's secretariat—actively promote topics of interest to the Canadian book publishing industry and act as a liaison body with government and industry. The Council is currently concerned with the de-

velopment of international markets, conversion to the SI SYSTEM, professional development, and copyright etc. See also ASSOCIATION OF CANADIAN PUBLISHERS.

Canadian Books in Print. Annual checklist of books published in Canada. A working guide for the book trade, *CBIP* indexes new publications by author and title for ordering and reference purposes. It has been published annually by the University of Toronto Press since 1967. A companion volume, *Subject Guide to Canadian Books in Print*, which indexes titles by subject, has appeared annually since 1973. Some French-language titles are included, but the complete annual listing of books and pamphlets issued by Quebec publishers is *Répertoire de l'édition au Québec* published by Édi-Québec since 1972. See also CANADIANA.

Canadian Books of Prose and Verse. See the RYERSON PRESS.

Canadian Booksellers Association. Organization of trade stores and university and community-college bookstores, founded in 1951. Its 300 members—representing approximately 375 stores—are governed by an elected council. In 1975 Randall Ware was appointed the first full-time executive director.

Canadian bouncer. Inferior Seconal from Canada—a slang term.

Canadian Brass, The. A musical ensemble formed in Toronto in 1970. It is composed of Eugene Watts (trombone), Charles Daellenback (tuba), Ronald Romm (trumpet), Frederick Mills (trumpet), and Graeme Page (French horn). Though the group plays serious music superbly, it delights in adding comic touches to its performances.

Canadian Broadcasting Corporation. The largest broadcasting system in the world. Created on 2 Nov. 1936 to replace the CANADIAN RADIO BROADCASTING COMMISSION, the publically owned corporation operates four national radio networks (AM and FM, both in English and French) and two national television networks (in English and French), in addition to the NORTHERN SERVICE and RADIO CANADA INTERNATIONAL. The Trans-Canada Network, which dates from 1936, and the Dominion Network, which dates from 1944, were consolidated by the CBC into the CBC RADIO NETWORK in 1962. FM broadcasting was introduced in 1946. Separate FM networks in French and English were formed in 1960 and FM stereo networks in 1975. Television, authorized in 1949, commenced from CBFT in

Canadian Broadcasting Corporation

Montreal on 6 Sept. 1952 and from CBLT in Toronto two days later. The two CBC Television Networks date from that year. Colour television was introduced to both networks in 1966. On 10 Dec. 1974 the CBC introduced a new corporate identification symbol, globular in shape, to convey the corporation's international responsibilities as well as its national role. The French name of the Corporation is Société Radio-Canada.

Canadian Broadcasting League. An association formed to promote national broadcasting in Canada. Founded in Ottawa as the Canadian Radio League by Alan. B. Plaunt (1904-41) and Graham SPRY, it supported the recommendations of the AIRD COMMISSION (1929) and lobbied for legislation that resulted in the creation of the CANADIAN BROADCASTING CORPORATION in 1936. It reappeared under its present name in 1962 and is still active. In 1974 it made its first annual CYBIL AWARD.

Canadian Brotherhood of Railway Employees and Other Transport Workers. A labour union founded in 1908, in Moncton, N.B., covering freight-handlers, clerks, and station servicemen. It was involved in some important early strikes. It gained affiliation with the TRADES AND LABOUR CONGRESS in 1917, was expelled from it in 1921, and joined the ALL CANADIAN CONGRESS OF LABOUR in 1927.

Canadian Business. A monthly magazine published in Montreal since 1930. It publishes articles of general interest to businessmen on employee relations, executive development, marketing, management, finance, promotion, and advertising.

Canadian Cameos. A series of short films produced by Associated Screen News in Montreal between 1932 and 1954. Each of the 85 subjects was intended as a 'little gem carved in high relief', thus the series title. During the 1930s these 10-minute films were practically alone in bringing Canada to the world's screens. Gordon Sparling, initiator of the series, was director of most of the films. Among the most remarkable shorts in the series were *Grey Owl's Little Brother* (1932), RHAPSODY IN TWO LANGUAGES (1934), *The Thousand Days* (1942), and *Sitzmarks the Spot* (1948).

Canadian Cardinals. A cardinal is a high ecclesiastic, second only to the pope, appointed to the College of Cardinals in Rome. A list of the Canadian Cardinals, with the years of appointment, follows.

Elzear-Alexandre Cardinal Taschereau (1820-98). 1886.

Louis Nazaire Cardinal Begin (1840-1925). 1914.

Raymond-Marie Cardinal Rouleau (1866-1931). 1927.

J.M. Rodrigue Cardinal Villeneuve (1883-1947). 1933.

Maurice Cardinal Roy (b.1905). 1965.

James Charles Cardinal McGuigan (1894-1974). 1946.

Paul-Émile Cardinal Léger (b.1904). 1953.

George B. Cardinal Flahiff (b.1905). 1969.

Canadian Centenary Series, The. A history of Canada in 18 volumes published by McCLELLAND & STEWART. The executive editor of the series, each volume of which is an independent work by a historian of note, is W.L. MORTON. The advisory editor is Donald CREIGHTON.

1. *Early Voyages and Northern Approaches: 1000-1632* (1963) by Tryggvi J. Oleson.

2. *The Beginnings of New France: 1524-1663* (1973) by Marcel TRUDEL.

3. *Canada under Louix XIV: 1663-1701* (1964) by W.J. ECCLES.

4. *New France: 1702-1743* (in preparation) by Jean Blain.

5. *New France: The Last Phase: 1744-1760* (1968) by G.F.G. STANLEY.

6. *Quebec: The Revolutionary Age: 1760-1791* (1966) by Hilda NEATBY.

7. *Upper Canada: The Formative Years: 1784-1841* (1963) by Gerald M. Craig.

8. *Lower Canada, 1792-1841* (in preparation) by Fernand OUELLET.

9. *The Atlantic Provinces: The Emergence of Colonial Society, 1712-1857* (1965) by W.S. MacNutt.

10. *The Union of the Canadas: The Growth of Canadian Institutions, 1841-1857* (1967) by J.M.S. CARELESS.

11. *The Fur Trade and the Northwest to 1857* (1967) by E.E. Rich.

12. *The Critical Years: The Union of British North America, 1857-1873* (1964) by W.L. MORTON.

13. *Canada, 1874-1896: Arduous Destiny* (1971) by P.B. Waite.

14. *Canada, 1896-1921: A Nation Transformed* (1974) by Robert Craig Brown and Ramsay COOK.

15. *Canada: 1922-1939* (in preparation) by Roger Graham.

16. *The Opening of the Canadian North: 1870-1914* (1971) by Morris Zaslow.

17. *The North: 1914-1967* (in preparation) by Morris Zaslow.

18. *The Forked Road: Canada 1939-1957* (1976) by Donald CREIGHTON.

Canadian Churchman. A monthly publication of the Anglican Church of Canada. It has been published in Toronto since 1871 and includes religious news, social comment on national and international concerns, and book reviews, etc.

Canadian Club. One of the world's most popular whiskies. It is distilled by HIRAM WALKER-GOODERHAM AND WORTS LTD. Known as 'the world's lightest whisky' and as 'the Best in the House', Canadian Club was first marketed as Club Whisky in 1880 and is sold in 87 countries. Part of its popularity is due to the effective advertising campaign originated by a New York agency that shows Canadian Club being enjoyed by adventurers in out-of-the-way places. The Canadian Club World Adventure Series, the longest sustained advertising campaign of its kind, has appeared in magazines since 1946.

Canadian Clubs, The Association of. A national association of luncheon clubs established 'to foster throughout Canada an interest in public affairs and to cultivate therein an attachment to Canadian institutions'. The first Canadian Club was founded by a group of businessmen in Hamilton, Ont., in 1892. Within a decade and a half there were Canadian Clubs in principal cities across the country. Each week some 25,000 members, in over 50 cities and towns, meet for lunch and listen to a speaker discourse on national or international affairs. Women were introduced as members in 1971.

Canadian coat-of-arms. Heraldic arms of Canada, officially proclaimed by George V on 21 Nov. 1921. Among the many elements that appear on the Canadian coat-of-arms are St Edward's (imperial) Crown; a crowned lion raising a MAPLE LEAF; a lion supporting the UNION JACK; a unicorn supporting the FLEUR-DE-LIS; a chaplet of roses, thistles, shamrocks, and lilies; a scroll inscribed with the Latin motto A MARI USQUE AD MARE; and a shield bearing emblems of the four countries from which the original settlers of Canada were chiefly drawn—the three lions of England, the lilies of France, the lion rampant of Scotland, the harp of Ireland—together with a branch carrying three maple leaves, the special emblem of Canada.

Canadian College of Dance. Inaugurated in Montreal in 1968 by Sonia Chamberlain, it provides professional qualifications for teachers of dance. By 1971 the College had earned an international reputation for excellence and in that year Ryerson Polytechnical Institute, Toronto, invited it to become an integral part of its new Theatre Department. The three-year course offers a widely based

training in teaching dance in its several forms and in acquiring knowledge of allied and academic subjects and other arts necessary to the understanding of sound methods of teaching. Students take their dance examinations with the Royal Academy of Dancing and the Imperial Society of Teachers of Dance.

Canadian Commentator. 'An independent journal of Canadian opinion'. Published by W.H. Baxter in Toronto from Jan. 1957 to Oct. 1971, and called simply *Commentator* from Oct. 1962, the monthly specialized in political and social coverage of Canadian and world scenes. It was edited by Marcus Long (from Jan. 1957), Paul Fox (from Oct. 1961), John Gellner (from Oct. 1964), and Gordon Donaldson (from June 1971).

Canadian Committee for Industrial Organization. A Canadian affiliate of the CIO, founded on 4 Oct. 1939 by representatives of the American organization. Its goal was to co-ordinate the work of CIO unions in Canada and 'to organize the unorganized'. It merged to form the CANADIAN CONGRESS OF LABOUR in 1940.

Canadian Conference of the Arts. National association committed to 'the encouragement and advancement of the arts in Canada'. From 1945 to 1958 it was known as the Canadian Arts Council. It sponsored the first Canadian Conference of the Arts at the newly opened O'Keefe Centre in Toronto on 3-7 May 1961. The CCA, with executive offices in Toronto, has as members over 400 individual artists and art supporters as well as some 250 arts organizations, and is funded entirely by the Department of the Secretary of State. Largely concerned with increased government and community participation in the arts scene, it awards the DIPLÔMES D'HONNEUR and publishes a monthly magazine, *Bulletin*.

Canadian Congress of Labour. An association founded in 1940 through the amalgamation of the ALL CANADIAN CONGRESS OF LABOUR and the CANADIAN COMMITTEE FOR INDUSTRIAL ORGANIZATION. Its merger in Apr. 1956 with the TRADES AND LABOUR CONGRESS created the CANADIAN LABOUR CONGRESS.

Canadian Constitution. See BNA ACT, 1867.

Canadian Consumers Council. Advisory body on consumerism. The Council of 19 members was established in 1968 to advise the Minister of Consumer and Corporate Affairs on all facets of consumer affairs.

Canadian content. The proportion of Canadian to imported content on a radio or television schedule. The Broadcasting Act of 1958, which created the BOARD OF BROADCAST GOVERNORS, required this regulatory agency to maintain programming that was 'basically Canadian in content and character'. The BBG insisted that television stations, as of 1 Apr. 1962, broadcast '55 per cent Canadian content', a ruling that was subsequently relaxed. The CANADIAN RADIO-TELEVISION COMMISSION has policed the 'Canadian content' regulations of both radio and television programming more effectively.

Canadian Corps. Central command of the Canadian officers and men of the Canadian Expeditionary Force serving in Europe during the First World War. The Corps, formed on 13 Sept. 1915, was commanded successively by Maj.-Gen. E.A.H. Alderson, Lt-Gen. Sir Julian BYNG, and Lt-Gen. Sir Arthur CURRIE (a Canadian who assumed command on 23 June 1917). The Corps consisted of four infantry divisions.

Canadian Culture Centre in Paris/Centre Culturel Canadien. Showplace for Canadian culture in France. Established in 1970, it is financed and staffed by French-speaking members of the Cultural Affairs Division of the Department of External Affairs. It was created to demonstrate the diversity of Canadian cultural life by arranging concerts, lectures, literary evenings, film shows, and art exhibitions. It also provides an orientation service for Canadian students in France.

Canadian Cultural Institute. Created by the Government of Canada in Rome to promote exchanges and strengthen cultural ties between Canada and Italy. Chaired by the Canadian Ambassador in Rome, it has awarded each year since 1969 senior fellowships to outstanding Canadian artists and scholars to pursue in Italy advanced studies or research in any areas of the arts or humanities. Today the fellowships are worth 11,500,000 lire each (approximately $17,000) and are financed by the income from a fund of approximately half a million dollars provided by the Italian government and administered by the CANADA COUNCIL to repay Canada for its assistance to Italian civilians in the Second World War.

Canadian Dimension. A magazine of the left published eight times a year in Winnipeg. Founded by Cy Gonick in 1963, it includes articles on politics, society, and culture, and takes a socialist and militant view of current events.

Canadian edition. A periodical whose editorial content is lifted in whole or in part from a parent edition published outside Canada and then used in a Canadian-produced edition to attract Canadian advertising—thus competing for advertising on the same basis as Canadian periodicals. See also READER'S DIGEST and TIME CANADA.

Canadian Education Association. It was founded in 1890 as the Dominion Education Association to co-ordinate educational policies at a national level, since the BNA Act gave educational autonomy to the provinces. The association now supports the provincial educational systems by its research studies and publishes the journal *Education Canada*.

Canadian English. The English spoken as a native language by Canadians.

Canadian Eskimo Arts Council. Advisory body, founded by the federal government and appointed by the Minister of INDIAN AFFAIRS AND NORTHERN DEVELOPMENT, to recommend policies and initiate projects to achieve an orderly development of Eskimo arts and crafts. Formed in 1964, it sponsored the international exhibition SCULPTURE/INUIT.

Canadian Expeditionary Force. See CANADIAN CORPS.

Canadian Federation of Labour. An association formed in 1908 by a change of name from NATIONAL TRADES AND LABOUR CONGRESS. Joined by the PROVINCIAL WORKMEN'S ASSOCIATION in 1910 and the ONE BIG UNION in 1919, it continued the policy of the NTLC until joining with the CANADIAN BROTHERHOOD OF RAILWAY EMPLOYEES AND OTHER TRANSPORT WORKERS in the formation of the ALL CANADIAN CONGRESS OF LABOUR in 1927.

Canadian Fiction Magazine. Literary quarterly devoted to the publication of new fiction, critical studies, reviews, and interviews. It was founded in 1971 by Jane Kennon and R. Wayne Stedingh in Vancouver and is particularly concerned with innovative techniques. See also JOURNAL OF CANADIAN FICTION.

Canadian Film Awards. An annual festival to 'celebrate, honour, and promote the films and the people of the Canadian film industry'. The awards were first given at the Elgin Theatre, Ottawa, in 1949 under the aegis of the CANADIAN ASSOCIATION FOR ADULT EDUCATION to recognize Canadian accomplishments and raise standards of production. The jury consisted of representatives of the public, and awards took the form of original Canadian paintings, including those by the GROUP OF SEVEN. In 1967 the CFA were taken over by the film industry itself and the awards changed from certificates (which replaced the paintings) to ETROG sculptures. The jury was made up of internationally known film celebrities. Quebec film-makers boycotted the proceedings in 1973 and no festival was held in 1974. The awards were re-established at the SHAW FESTIVAL at Niagara-on-the-Lake in 1975. The films to receive 'best feature' awards are: 1949—*The* LOON'S NECKLACE; 1952—*Newfoundland Scene*; 1953—TIT-COQ; 1954—*The Seasons*; 1955—*The Stratford Adventure*; 1958—CITY OF GOLD; 1961—UNIVERSE; 1963—*Lonely Boy*; 1964—*Pour la suite du monde*; 1965—*The* LUCK OF GINGER COFFEY; 1966—*Mills of the Gods*; 1967—WARRENDALE; 1968—*A* PLACE TO STAND; 1969—*The* BEST DAMN FIDDLER FROM CALABOGIE TO KALADAR; 1970—*Psychocratie*; 1971—MON ONCLE ANTOINE; 1972—WEDDING IN WHITE; 1973—*Slipstream*; 1974—*The* APPRENTICESHIP OF DUDDY KRAVITZ; 1975—*Les* ORDRES.

Canadian Film Development Corporation. Crown corporation to promote the development of a feature-film industry. Formed in 1967 and consisting of a Government Film Commissioner and six other appointed members, the CFDC fosters the development of a feature-film industry in Canada through investment in productions, loans to producers, and grants to film-makers. It assists in the distribution of feature films and organizes their exhibition abroad. Michael Spencer, a former NATIONAL FILM BOARD administrator, has been the executive director from its inception. Playwright Gratien GÉLINAS is chairman of the board.

Canadian Film Institute. Non-profit, non-governmental organization promoting and developing the use of film and television in Canada. Founded in Ottawa in 1935 as the National Film Society to provide an outlet for foreign films that were blocked from commercial exhibition, it became the CFI in 1950. Under Peter Morris it developed the Canadian Film Archives, which the CFI housed from 1950 to 1974, when they were transferred to the National Film Archives. The CFI is supported by the CANADA COUNCIL, the SECRETARY OF STATE, and the NATIONAL RESEARCH COUNCIL. It has the country's largest film library (some 6,500 titles) and operates the Film Distribution Library, the National Film Theatre, and a Publications Division.

Canadian Flag. See NATIONAL FLAG OF CANADA.

Canadian football. A game—a cross between British rugby and American football—played by two 12-man teams on a field 165 by 65 yds.

Canadian Football League. Association of professional football teams in Canada. The CFL, a 1960 amalgamation of the Eastern and Western Conferences, organizes the championship games and, since 1966, has been custodian of the GREY CUP. The Eastern Conference consists of four teams: Hamilton Tiger-Cats, Toronto Argonauts, Ottawa Rough Riders, and Montreal Alouettes. The Western Conference consists of five teams: British Columbia Lions, Edmonton Eskimos, Calgary Stampeders, Saskatchewan Roughriders, and Winnipeg Blue Bombers. The CFL gives the CANADIAN PACIFIC DICK SUDERMAN AWARD and the LABATT AWARDS.

Canadian Forces Base Borden. Beginning as a Militia training camp in 1916, Camp Borden, Ont., was capable of accommodating 30,000 troops in tents. In Jan. 1917 the Royal Flying Corps established a training station there from which nearly 2,000 pilots graduated during the FIRST WORLD WAR. In the 1930s Permanent Force armoured, signals, infantry, and several administrative corps schools were established at Camp Borden, which expanded greatly during the SECOND WORLD WAR: 185,000 soldiers were trained there. The Canadian Air Force (predecessor of the RCAF) conducted refresher courses at Camp Borden in 1920 and it became an RCAF Station in 1924. During the Second World War the station was called No. 1 Service Flying Training Centre and trained hundreds of pilots under the British Commonwealth Air Training Plan. In 1946 No. 2 Technical Training School was re-formed. In 1968 both Army and Air Force establishments were integrated to form CFB Borden.

Canadian Forces Base Esquimalt. Beginning as a Royal Navy hospital and stores depot in 1857, Esquimalt, B.C., became an official Royal Navy dockyard in 1865. It was transferred to the ROYAL CANADIAN NAVY in 1910. In 1922 a shore establishment, HMCS Naden, was commissioned. It gradually expanded to include a torpedo school and a signal school. During the SECOND WORLD WAR it expanded rapidly as the principal naval training establishment in western Canada. HMC Dockyard and HMCS Naden became CFB Esquimalt in 1966.

Canadian Forces Base Shearwater. Shearwater, N.S., began as a United States Navy seaplane base in 1918 and the Canadian government took it over later in the year. It was handed over to the Air Board in 1921 and used to erect and repair seaplanes until 1926. From 1927 to 1933 it served only as a base for RCAF photographic operations during the summer. It was reopened in 1934 and in 1937 further development commenced to accommodate landplanes as well as seaplanes. It expanded rapidly during the SECOND WORLD WAR and in 1942 the Royal Navy established a Naval Air Section, which was taken over by the ROYAL CANADIAN NAVY in 1945. RCAF activity diminished and RCN activity increased so that by 1 Dec. 1948 it was designated HMCS Shearwater. In 1966 it became CFB Shearwater.

Canadian Forces Base Valcartier. Valcartier, Que., started as a militia training camp in 1913 and was rapidly expanded to serve as the concentration area for the Canadian Expeditionary Force during the FIRST WORLD WAR. Subsequently it was used very little until 1930, when Militia infantry units of eastern Quebec began to train there in the summer. During the SECOND WORLD WAR it was an infantry training centre and a concentration area for units mobilized for overseas service; in 1945 it was a demobilization centre. It was used on a year-round basis from 1946 onwards and greatly expanded during and after the Korean War (1950-3). In order to permit all arms training, both for firing and manoeuvre, approximately 42,000 acres were expropriated in 1966-8. In Aug. 1968 the 5e Groupement de combat, an infantry formation of the Canadian Forces, was formed there.

Canadian Forces Council. Advisory body to the CHIEF OF DEFENCE STAFF. Created in Aug. 1966, it makes available the advice and opinions of the senior commanders of the three functional commands of the CANADIAN ARMED FORCES: Maritime, Mobile, and Air.

Canadian Forces Europe. One of five functional commands of the CANADIAN ARMED FORCES, located at Lahr in the Federal Republic of Germany.

Canadian Forum, The. 'An independent journal of opinion and the arts'. The monthly was founded in Toronto in 1920 by F.H. UNDERHILL, C.B. Sissons, Barker FAIRLEY, and other writers and academics. It has maintained a consistent interest in progressive politics, civil liberties, artistic freedom, political dissent, and has published new and established writers with poems, stories, articles, and reviews, illustrating these contributions in the beginning with black-and-white reproductions of works by the GROUP OF SEVEN and later by other artists. Among its editors have been F.H. Underhill, Northrop FRYE, Milton Wilson, Abraham ROTSTEIN, and Denis Smith. J.L. GRANATSTEIN and Peter Stevens edited *Forum: Canadian Life and*

Letters from 1920-70: Selections from 'The Canadian Forum' (1972).

Canadian French. The French spoken as a native language by French Canadians, especially in Quebec.

Canadian Geographical Journal. Published six times a year in Ottawa since 1930 by the Royal Canadian Geographical Society, it contains illustrated articles on every phase of geography—historical, human, physical, and economic.

Canadian Girls in Training. A non-denominational Christian ecumenical movement for girls between the ages of 12 and 17. CGIT—which consists of a camping program, community projects, and work with the handicapped—is directed by the National CGIT Committee of the Canadian Council of Churches. It began in 1915 and for years the initials were rumoured to mean 'Cutest Girls in Town'.

Canadian Grain Commission. Federal body that supervises the physical handling of grain. Formed in 1971, it replaced the former Board of Grain Commissioners of Canada and consists of three commissioners.

Canadian Grenadier Guards, The. Canadian army regiment. Also known as the 6th Battalion and the Canadian Guards, it originated in 1859 and served during the FENIAN Raids. In the FIRST WORLD WAR it served as part of the 87th Battalion in France and also with the 4th Canadian Division, distinguishing itself in many battles. During the SECOND WORLD WAR it was converted to an armoured regiment, serving in England and at the Normandy Landing with the 4th Armoured Brigade.

Canadian Group of Painters. A group of artists who exhibited together and whose policy was 'to encourage and foster the growth of Art in Canada which has a national character'. Founded in Toronto as a successor to the GROUP OF SEVEN, it held its first exhibition in Atlantic City, N.J., in the summer of 1933 and its second at the Art Gallery of Toronto the following November, the month of its annual exhibitions, which ceased in 1969 when it disbanded. The 28 founding members were: Bertram BROOKER, Franklin CARMICHAEL, Emily CARR, A.J. CASSON, Charles COMFORT, LeMoine FITZGERALD, Lawren HARRIS, Prudence HEWARD, Randolph Hewton, Edwin HOLGATE, Bess Houser, A.Y. JACKSON, Arthur LISMER, J.W.G. (Jock) MACDONALD, Thoreau MacDONALD, Mable May, Yvonne McKague, Isabel McLaughlin, Lilias Newton, Will Ogilvie, George Pepper, Sarah

Robertson, Albert Robinson, Ann Savage, Charles Scott, F.H. VARLEY, William Weston, and W.J. Wood. The Group expanded and many of the best-known names in Canadian painting from the thirties to the sixties exhibited with it.

Canadian Historical Review, The. A scholarly quarterly founded in Toronto in 1920 with W. Stewart WALLACE as its first editor. Since 1922 the *CHR* has been the official publication of the Canadian Historical Association.

Canadian History Series. A popular history of Canada in six volumes edited by Thomas B. COSTAIN. The volumes are complete in themselves and stress the romantic and heroic elements in the country's past. The six titles, published by Doubleday in New York and Toronto, are: *The White and the Gold: The French Régime in Canada* (1954) by Thomas B. Costain; *Century of Conflict: The Struggle between the French and British in Colonial America* (1956) by Joseph Lister Rutledge; *The Path of Destiny: Canada from the British Conquest to Home Rule, 1763-1850* (1957) by Thomas H. RADDALL; *From Sea Unto Sea: Canada, 1850 to 1910, The Road to Nationhood* (1959) by W.G. HARDY; *Ordeal by Fire: Canada, 1910-1945* (1961) by Ralph ALLEN; and *The Search for Identity: Canada, 1945-1967* (1967) by Blair FRASER.

Canadian Home Cook Book, Compiled by Ladies of Toronto and Chief Cities and Towns in Canada, The. The most comprehensive early cookbook of Canadian cuisine, published in 1877 (reprinted 1970). Though cookbooks of American and English origin were published in Canada as early as 1831, *The Canadian Home Cook Book* was the first significant Canadian culinary guide.

Canadian Home Journal. A consumer magazine of special interest to women, published monthly in Toronto between 1904 and June 1958, when it was absorbed by CHATELAINE. In its heyday it claimed the highest circulation of any magazine in the country.

Canadian Homes and Gardens. A consumer magazine of special interest to women, published monthly in Toronto between 1925 and July 1962 by MACLEAN-HUNTER. During its last two years it appeared as *Canadian Homes*.

Canadian Illustrated News. A weekly that was published in Montreal from 30 Oct. 1869 to 29 Dec. 1883. It was founded and published by Georges-Edouard Desbarats (1838-93), with a format and title reminiscent of the better-known *London Illustrated News*. The Canadian publication pioneered in the use of lithographic reproduction. The Montreal-born author and television personality, Peter Desbarats, a descendant of the original publisher, edited a selection from the publication in 1970.

Canadian Imperial Bank of Commerce. A chartered bank with its head office in Toronto. It was formed in 1961 through the amalgamation of the Imperial Bank of Canada, founded in 1875, and the Canadian Bank of Commerce, founded in 1867. The Canadian Imperial Bank of Commerce in 1976 had 1,695 offices, including 82 outside the country. It is one of the world's largest banks. See also COMMERCE COURT.

Canadian Indian Marketing Service. A wholesale marketing agency. Originally operated by the Department of INDIAN AFFAIRS AND NORTHERN DEVELOPMENT, it was turned over to the Indians themselves on 3 June 1975 for the marketing of their arts and crafts.

Canadian Institute of International Affairs. The only private voluntary organization in Canada concerned with the study of foreign policy. It was founded in Toronto in 1928 and now has more than 20 branches. The CIIA organizes seminars and sponsors speakers across the country. Its publications include *International Journal* (a separate French edition of the monthly appears as *Études internationales*); *Behind the Headlines*, a series of popular pamphlets issued six times a year; and *Canada in World Affairs,* a series of books covering two-year periods. Identified with the CIIA is John W. Holmes—born in London, Ont., in 1910—who has been its secretary, president, director general, and research director intermittently from 1941 to the present. Since 1971 the executive director has been Robert W. Reford, a former journalist and editorial writer who was born in England of Canadian parents in 1921. See also the CANADIAN INSTITUTE ON PUBLIC AFFAIRS.

Canadian Institute on Public Affairs. Educational organization founded in 1932 by the National Council of the YMCA. The Toronto-based body was known as the Canadian Institute on Economics and Politics until it was incorporated as the CIPA on 21 Nov. 1952. Its main function is to sponsor the COUCHICHING CONFERENCES. See also the similarly named CANADIAN INSTITUTE OF INTERNATIONAL AFFAIRS.

Canadian International Development Agency. Government organization responsible for aid to developing countries. Established in 1960, and known until 1968 as the

External Aid Office, CIDA has a staff of 900 and is headed by a president who reports to Parliament through the Secretary of State for EXTERNAL AFFAIRS. CIDA's budget for 1974-5 was $733 million, which was spent on multilateral programs (involving organizations like the UNITED NATIONS) and bilateral programs (involving grants and loans and technical training) with developing countries.

Canadian Journal of Economics and Political Science. A scholarly quarterly published by the Canadian Political Science Association since Feb. 1935. In Nov. 1967 *CJEPS* was superseded by two journals: the *Canadian Journal of Economics* and the *Canadian Journal of Political Science.*

Canadian Junior College. A co-educational private school in Switzerland at Lausanne—also called the Academy of Lausanne—founded in 1968. Enrolment is limited to 130 and it provides instruction for Grades 12 and 13. In 1972 a second campus of marine studies was opened on the island of Carriacou in the Grenadines, B.W.I., which emphasizes environmental studies; its enrolment is 40. A Toronto campus is scheduled to open in Sept. 1976.

Canadian Labour Congress. An association of labour unions. It was founded in 1956 as a result of the merger of the TRADES AND LABOUR CONGRESS and the CANADIAN CONGRESS OF LABOUR. It includes both industrial and craft unions, both national and international, and represents over 70% of Canadian unions.

Canadian Labour Defence League. A group founded in Sept. 1925 after a strike in Drumheller, Alta. Following increased use of SECTION 98 of the Criminal Code against trade unionists, the CLDL expanded in 1931 under the leadership of A.E. Smith. The object was to provide legal advice and aid in the defence of any worker charged under this and similar legislation.

Canadian Labour Party. A political group founded in Winnipeg in 1921 to nationalize public utilities and campaign for social legislation to improve the conditions of the workers. It ran candidates in the federal elections of 1925 and 1926 but declined rapidly after 1928.

Canadian Labour Union. An effective early association of unions. Founded by the TORONTO TRADES ASSEMBLY on 23 Sept. 1873, and lasting little more than four years, this Ontario-based organization was effective in agitating for the benefit of the working class and in effecting the repeal of oppressive legislation.

Canadian League of Composers. National association of composers formed in Toronto in 1951 to encourage the composition, appreciation, and performance of contemporary music. From 1953 to 1956 the League functioned as the Canadian Section of the International Society for Contemporary Music, arranging concerts, issuing records and catalogues, and helping to establish the CANADIAN MUSIC CENTRE. In 1960, at the Stratford Festival, it organized the International Conference of Composers, the first in North America. Since 1967 the CLC has awarded the Canadian Music Citation to 'outstanding performers who have shown special artistry in performances of contemporary Canadian repertoire'.

Canadian Legion. See ROYAL CANADIAN LEGION.

Canadian Liberation Movement. See NEW CANADA PRESS.

Canadian Library Association. Professional association with headquarters in Ottawa, Ont. It is a national organization devoted to improving the quality of library and information services in Canada and to developing higher standards of librarianship. It was founded in 1946, with the assistance of the Canadian Library Council, and dates back to a resolution passed by a Canadian group attending the annual meeting of the American Library Association in Montreal in 1900. Among its publications are the *Canadian Library Journal* (the official bimonthly journal), *Canadian Materials* (the annotated critical bibliography of current print and non-print materials produced in Canada for schools), and the CANADIAN PERIODICAL INDEX. The CLA has five divisions: the Canadian Association of College and University Libraries (CACUL); of Public Libraries (CAPL); of Special Libraries and Information Services (CASLIS); the Canadian Library Trustees Association (CLTA); and the Canadian School Library Association (CSLA).

Canadian Library Week. National program to encourage reading and to stress the importance of libraries. It was held annually each spring from 1959 to 1967, after which it was discontinued for financial reasons. Sponsored by the CANADIAN LIBRARY ASSOCIATION, the CANADIAN BOOK PUBLISHERS' ASSOCIATION, and La Société des Éditeurs Canadiens des Livres Français, it included displays, talks, and meet-the-author programs.

Canadian Literature. A quarterly published by the University of British Columbia. It was founded in 1959 by George WOODCOCK, who is still editor, and is devoted exclusively to criticism, publishing articles on, and reviews of, letters in Canada.

Canadian Magazine. 'A Canadian magazine of politics, science, art, and literature'. The most long-lived of the early magazines, it was published monthly in Toronto from Mar. 1893 to Apr. 1939. It absorbed *Massey's Magazine* (a monthly founded in Toronto and published from Jan. 1896 to June 1897), and two years before its demise it was renamed *The Canadian.* A general-interest periodical, it published many of the prominent and most of the minor writers of its period. Its policy, as defined by the founding editor J.G. Mowat, was one of 'cultivating Canadian patriotism and Canadian instincts'.

Canadian Magazine, The. The weekly supplement to the Saturday editions of 13 newspapers. Founded in 1965 by Southstar Publishers (jointly owned by SOUTHAM PRESS and the TORONTO STAR), it has the largest circulation of any Canadian publication—just over two million copies a week. It publishes well-illustrated articles of general interest and has had four editors since its founding: Harry Bruce, Michael Hanlon, Denis Harvey, and Donald Obe. The managing editor is Alan Walker.

Canadian Materials. See CANADIAN LIBRARY ASSOCIATION.

Canadian Mental Health Association. See MENTAL HEALTH CANADA.

Canadian Mercury, The. 'A monthly journal of literature and opinion'. It was founded by F.R. SCOTT and Leo Kennedy and appeared in seven issues between Dec. 1928 and June 1929. It published many of the contributors to the McGILL FORTNIGHTLY REVIEW, along with such writers as Stephen LEACOCK and B.K. SANDWELL.

Canadian Military Colleges. Institutes for military study. The three Canadian Military Colleges are the ROYAL MILITARY COLLEGE OF CANADA, ROYAL ROADS MILITARY COLLEGE, and Le COLLÈGE MILITAIRE ROYAL DE SAINT-JEAN. The role of the Colleges is to educate and train officer cadets and commissioned officers for a career in the Canadian Forces. 'Truth, Duty, Valour' is the motto of both RMC and RRMC; 'Verité, Devoir, Vaillance' is the motto of CMR. All three admit students in one of two officer-training plans (see RETP and ROTP). They accept Canadian citizens who are single, male, and between the ages 16 and 21.

Canadian Mite, The. The largest round of cheese on record. Manufactured in Perth, Ont., the 6-ft high, 22,000-lb. cheese was exhibited in 1893 at the Chicago World's Fair.

Canadian Monthly and National Review. A serious magazine of general interest published monthly in Toronto from Jan. 1872 to June 1878, when it went bankrupt and united with *Belford's Monthly Magazine* (1876-8), appearing between July 1878 and June 1882 as *Rose-Belford's Canadian Magazine and National Review.* It was edited by Graeme Mercer Adam until 1879 and expressed the aspirations of the CANADA FIRST movement.

Canadian Mounties vs Atomic Invaders. A 12-episode serial produced by Republic Pictures, directed by Franklin Adreon and released in 1953. Starring Bill Henry and Susan Morrow, it was one of 14 serials on Canadian subjects produced by Hollywood studios between 1917 and 1956. It had a Mountie sergeant and a woman undercover agent battling sinister foreign operatives intent on constructing rocket sites in the Yukon.

Canadian Music Centre. National organization founded in Toronto in 1959 to promote the performance of works by Canadian composers. It was brought into being through the efforts of the Canadian Music Council in collaboration with the CANADIAN LEAGUE OF COMPOSERS under three-year grants assured from the CANADA COUNCIL and CAPAC. The Centre and its Montreal division, established in Oct. 1973, maintain a library of the published and unpublished musical scores of some 4,500 works, as well as a collection of disc tape cassettes. It encourages various publication projects and administrates the JOHN ADASKIN MEMORIAL AWARD and the Creative Arts Award, an annual award of the Canadian Federation of University Women. The first president was Sir Ernest MacMILLAN; his son Keith has been executive secretary since 1964.

Canadian Music Citation. See CANADIAN LEAGUE OF COMPOSERS.

Canadian Nation, The. A political and social journal, six issues of which appeared between Feb. 1928 and May-June 1929. It was edited by Graham SPRY and published by the Association of CANADIAN CLUBS. Members of the editorial board included Marius BARBEAU and Frederick Philip GROVE.

Canadian National Exhibition. The world's largest annual exhibition. It was originally an agricultural fair, called the Toronto Exhibition, first held in 1846. It became the CNE in 1878. It now has a permanent site covering 350 acres, many exhibition buildings, and its own services—police, fire, communications, etc. The average annual attendance is about three million. See also CNE GRANDSTAND SHOW and CONKLIN SHOWS.

Canadian National Institute for the Blind

Canadian National Institute for the Blind.
Volunteer organization established in
Toronto in 1918 to rehabilitate the blind and
to prevent blindness. The CNIB serves 30,000
blind and near-blind Canadians. See also
Col. Edwin Albert BAKER.

Canadian National Railways. One of the
world's major transportation and communications systems. It is Canada's largest
railroad and has its head office in Montreal.
Created as a CROWN CORPORATION in 1919,
over the next four years it acquired the assets
of five financially embarrassed railroad systems: CANADIAN NORTHERN RAILWAY, Grand
Trunk Pacific, GRAND TRUNK RAILWAY, INTER-
COLONIAL RAILWAY, and National Transcontinental. In 1960, to stress the company's involvement in communications, it unveiled its
familiar CN logo (designed by Allan FLEMING).
In 1976 there were six operating divisions: CN
Rail, CN Trucking and Express, CN-CP TELE-
COMMUNICATIONS, Grand Trunk Corporation
(for U.S. operations), CN Passenger Services
(including CN hotels and the CN TOWER), and
CN Marine. The company holds the capital
stock of AIR CANADA. See also LRC, PLACE VILLE
MARIE, RAPIDO, RED WHITE & BLUE DAYS, TURBO.

Canadian Nature Federation. National non-
profit organization representing provincial
naturalists' federations, local societies, and
interested individuals. It developed out of
the Canadian Audubon Society in 1971 and
from Ottawa publishes a quarterly journal,
Nature Canada.

Canadian News Facts. 'An indexed digest of
Canadian current events'. This news service
appears twice monthly in the form of an
eight-page pamphlet of news abstracts that
can be inserted into a binder. The monthly
index is cumulated quarterly and annually.
It has been published by Marpep Publishing
Limited since 16 Jan. 1967.

Canadian Northern Railway. An important
railway company that once operated in
northern Ontario and northern Manitoba. It
began in 1896 with the acquisition by William
Mackenzie (1849-1923) and Donald Mann
(1853-1934) of a charter for the construction
of a line from Gladstone through Dauphin to
Lake Winnipegosis. The Canadian Northern
opened the following year and continued to
expand, acquiring the Northern Pacific Railway in 1901. Heavily subsidized, it was acquired by the federal government in 1917
and, with the GRAND TRUNK RAILWAY, ultimately formed part of the CANADIAN NATIONAL
RAILWAYS.

Canadian Notes and Queries. An irregularly

issued journal devoted to the sharing of specialized information. Sponsored by Bernard
Amtmann, Inc. of Montreal, and edited since
its inception in July 1968 by William F.E.
Morley of the Douglas Library, Queen's University, it publishes, approximately three
times a year, 100-word notes ('those little
discoveries encountered, often by serendi-
pity, in the course of scholarly investigation')
and queries ('when you are confronted with
a problem which is beyond your present resources to solve'). *Canadian Notes and Queries*
is modelled on the British *Notes and Queries*
(established in 1849) and *American Notes and
Queries* (established in 1962).

Canadian Open Golf Championship. See
PETER JACKSON TROPHY.

Canadian Open Tennis Championship. See
ROTHMANS CANADIAN OPEN TENNIS CHAMPION-
SHIP.

Canadian Opera Company. The Royal Con-
versatory of Music Toronto Opera School
was founded by Dr Arnold WALTER in 1946; in
1950 an opera festival was presented in
Toronto's ROYAL ALEXANDRA THEATRE, with
Herman GEIGER-TOREL as director/producer;
and in 1951 Dr Boyd NEEL and Edward JOHN-
SON encouraged the formation of an Opera
Festival Association. By 1954 the Opera Festival Company of Canada was fully professional and in 1958 became the Canadian
Opera Company under Geiger-Torel as general director. That year the company toured
36 communities, which by the mid-sixties
had increased to 100. In the 1970s, with a
chamber-size orchestra added, the touring
company became an autonomous operation.
The Toronto company now has an annual
six-week fall season in Toronto at the O'KEEFE
CENTRE, with another week in Ottawa's NA-
TIONAL ARTS CENTRE. From 10 performances in
1950 the Canadian Opera Company has increased its annual season to 40 performances
in 1975. In 26 seasons in Toronto alone it has
staged 568 performances of 51 operas including world premières of the following Canadian works: DEIRDRE by Healey WILLAN (1960),
The LUCK OF GINGER COFFEY by Raymond PAN-
NELL (1967), LOUIS RIEL by Harry SOMERS
(1967), and *Héloise and Abelard* by Charles
Wilson (1973). A list of the Company's
Toronto seasons follows:

1950 *La Bohème, Rigoletto, Don Giovanni*
1951 *Faust, Madama Butterfly, The Marriage of
Figaro*
1952 *The Bartered Bride, Manon, The Magic
Flute*
1953 *Madama Butterfly, The Consul, Così Fan
Tutte*

1954 *La Bohème, Rigoletto, The Consul, School for Fathers*

1955 *The Marriage of Figaro, La Traviata, Die Fledermaus*

1956 *Madama Butterfly, Don Giovanni, Carmen*

1957 (i) *Hansel and Gretel, Tosca, The Abduction from the Seraglio*
(ii) *Die Fledermaus, The Merry Widow, Carousel*

1958 *La Bohème, The Tales of Hoffman, Un Ballo in Maschera*

1959 *The Barber of Seville, The Love for Three Oranges, La Forza Del Destino*

1960 *The Marriage of Figaro, Otello, A Night in Venice, Deirdre*

1961 *Tosca, Carmen, The Bartered Bride, Cavalleria Rusticana, I Pagliacci*

1962 *Rigoletto, Madama Butterfly, Hansel and Gretel, Die Walküre*

1963 *Hansel and Gretel, La Bohème, Don Giovanni, Aida, Der Rosenkavalier*

1964 *Aida, Madama Butterfly, Carmen, La Traviata, Die Fledermaus*

1965 *La Bohème, Rigoletto, The Barber of Seville, Mavra, Salome, Turandot*

1966 *Faust, La Traviata, Cavalleria Rusticana, I Pagliacci, Macbeth, Deirdre*

1967 *Madama Butterfly, The Barber of Seville, Tales of Hoffman, Louis Riel, Il Trovatore, The Luck of Ginger Coffey*

1968 *Tosca, La Bohème, Aida, Louis Riel, Salome*

1969 *Die Fledermaus, Rigoletto, Turandot, La Forza Del Destino, Elektra*

1970 *Don Giovanni, Carmen, La Traviata, Faust, Fidelio*

1971 *The Merry Widow, Madama Butterfly, Die Walküre, Macbeth, Lucia Di Lammermoor*

1972 *Tosca, Aida, La Bohème, Siegfried, Eugene Onegin*

1973 *Rigoletto, The Merry Widow, Fidelio, The Barber of Seville, Die Götterdämmerung, Héloise and Abelard*

1974 *Bluebeard's Castle, L'Heure Espagnole, The Flying Dutchman, Boris Godunov, La Traviata, Carmen, Faust*

1975 *I Pagliacci, Il Tabarro, Madama Butterfly, Die Fledermaus, Louis Riel, Manon Lescaut, Salome*

1976 *La Bohème, Tosca, Die Walküre, The Grand Duchess of Gerolstein*

Canadian Overseas Telecommunications Corporation. See TÉLÉGLOBE CANADA.

Canadian Pacific. Feature film produced by 20th Century-Fox in 1949. Directed by Edwin L. Marin, it starred Randolph Scott, Jane Wyatt, Victor Jory, and Nancy Olson. Exteriors were produced on location in the West. Randolph Scott single-handedly overcame the greedy villains who would stand to make millions should the CPR fail. 90 min., colour.

Canadian Pacific Airlines. See CP AIR.

Canadian Pacific Dick Suderman Award. Annual award made by the CANADIAN FOOTBALL LEAGUE to the outstanding Canadian player in the GREY CUP game. Named after the first winner in 1971, the award, a silver bowl, is accompanied by the air fare for two to any point on the CP system.

Canadian Pacific Limited. A privately owned, widely diversified transportation system, second in size only to the publicly owned CANADIAN NATIONAL RAILWAYS. Formerly known as the CANADIAN PACIFIC RAILWAY, it acquired its present name in 1971 when it designated its operations as: CP AIR, CP Express, CP Hotels, CP Investments, CP Rail, CP Ships, CP Telecommunications, and CP Transport. See also EMPRESS LINE, CN-CP TELECOMMUNICATIONS.

Canadian Pacific Railway. A privately owned, widely diversified transportation system, which changed its name to CANADIAN PACIFIC LIMITED in 1971. Promised in 1871 as a condition of British Columbia's entry into Confederation, and completed on 7 Nov. 1885, the transcontinental railway provided an essential link for the scattered population of Canada. Initial arrangements to build the railway, made with Sir Hugh ALLAN, lapsed when the PACIFIC SCANDAL of 1873 forced Sir John A. MACDONALD to resign as prime minister. The new Liberal prime minister, Alexander MACKENZIE, whose term (1873-8) coincided with a world-wide depression, allowed only such construction as could be financed by very limited public funds. Back in office, Macdonald awarded the CPR contract in 1880 to a new private group, which included officials of the HUDSON'S BAY COMPANY and the Bank of Montreal. Though government subsidies promised to the new company included $25 million and 25 million acres, these proved insufficient and several additional grants had to be made. It was incorporated as the Canadian Pacific Railway on 16 Feb. 1881. In 1882 William VAN HORNE was made general manager and he pushed the railway to completion: it ran from Montreal to Port Moody, B.C. The LAST SPIKE was driven home on 7 Nov. 1885. See also CANADIAN PACIFIC STEAMSHIP CO., EMPRESS LINE.

Canadian Pacific Steamship Co. The first seagoing ships owned by this extension of the CPR were the famous 'White Empresses', which entered service in 1891. Named *Em-*

press of China, Empress of India, and *Empress of Japan,* they provided a luxurious link between Vancouver and the Orient. In 1903 a transatlantic service was inaugurated with the purchase of the 16-ship Beaver Line, a fleet further augmented in 1915 by the taking over of the 16 ships of the ALLAN LINE. Many other ships were built or acquired between the wars, but the Second World War ended the company's pre-eminence as a passenger line. It is now known as CP Ships.

Canadian Peace Congress. A body founded in Toronto by Dr James Endicott, a United Church missionary born in 1898 in Szechwan Province, China, and other Communists after Endicott's return from the World Peace Congress held in Paris in Apr. 1949. Like the parent body, the Canadian organization attempted to arouse public opinion against the threat of war. It sponsored 'ban the bomb' demonstrations in the early 1950s. Endicott, who called himself 'a Christian Marxist', was awarded the Stalin Peace Prize in 1952. He refused to exchange it for the Lenin Prize in 1962, saying, 'That would be rewriting history.' The Canadian Peace Congress has published the *Canadian Far Eastern Newsletter* since 1971.

Canadian Peace Research Institute. A private, independent organization for the purpose of conducting research into the causes of war and the conditions for peace. Founded in 1961 in Oakville, Ont., by the research scientist Norman Z. Alcock (b.1918), it has undertaken studies of arms races, UN voting patterns, civil and international conflicts, and attitudes in relation to war and peace.

Canadian period. Obsolete geological term for PRECAMBRIAN PERIOD.

Canadian Periodical Index. A reference guide to magazines. Published monthly and cumulated annually since 1938 by the CANADIAN LIBRARY ASSOCIATION, the CPI indexes approximately 100 English- and French-Canadian magazines by author and subject.

Canadian Players. A national touring company founded by Tom PATTERSON and Douglas CAMPBELL of the STRATFORD FESTIVAL. Sometimes referred to as the 'winter company' of the Festival, it opened in Ottawa on 6 Oct. 1954 with the eight-member troupe performing a modern-dress version of Shaw's *Saint Joan,* starring Ann Casson and her husband Douglas Campbell. An 'Eskimo' *King Lear* was directed by David Gardner and opened in Toronto on 24 Oct. 1961. The troupe took Len PETERSON'S ALL ABOUT US,

directed by John HIRSCH, on its 1964 tour. Marigold Charlesworth and Jean Roberts assumed artistic and administrative directorship in 1965, until it merged with the CREST THEATRE in 1966 and ceased as a touring company.

Canadian Press. A co-operative news agency. CP operates a wire service to supply domestic and international news to 108 Canadian newspapers, the CBC, and 320 privately owned broadcast outlets. Co-operatively owned, it was formed in Sept. 1917 and took its present name in Mar. 1923. It subscribes on an exchange basis to such news services as Reuters (U.K.), The Associated Press (U.S.), and Agence France-Press (France). It began its broadcast service in 1941 and its French-language service in 1951. Located in Toronto, it has 19 bureaux across the country and abroad.

Canadian Quotations and Phrases. First dictionary of quotations published in Canada. Edited by Robert M. Hamilton, this pioneering work appeared in 1952, with 3,500 quotations, arranged topically, by 800 contributors.

Canadian Radio Broadcasting Commission. The forerunner of the CBC. A key recommendation of the AIRD COMMISSION, much lobbied for by the Canadian Radio League (later the CANADIAN BROADCASTING LEAGUE), the CRBC was established on 26 May 1932 to supervise all public and private broadcasting in Canada. It commenced public radio broadcasting in English and French at its Montreal station for one hour a day in May 1933. It was succeeded by the CANADIAN BROADCASTING CORPORATION in 1936.

Canadian Radio League. See CANADIAN BROADCASTING LEAGUE.

Canadian Radio-Television Commission. A federal regulatory agency for radio and television broadcasting. A recommendation of the FOWLER COMMITTEE, it was established under the Broadcasting Act on 1 Apr. 1968 to replace the BOARD OF BROADCAST GOVERNORS. Under the aggressive chairmanship of Pierre JUNEAU, private broadcasters were called upon to increase their CANADIAN CONTENT, especially in the area of music. The CRTC consists of an executive of five full-time members and a committee of 10 part-time members chosen on a regional basis and appointed by the GOVERNOR IN COUNCIL. It issues licences, holds public hearings, and regulates and supervises all private and public broadcasting in Canada—radio, television, and cable.

Canadian Red Ensign. The recognized flag of Canada abroad from 1924 to 1965. It has a red ground, a Union Jack in the upper left corner, and carries the CANADIAN COAT-OF-ARMS in the fly. It was flown over Canadian buildings abroad, raised by Canadian troops abroad, and flown at the United Nations. In 1965 it was replaced by the NATIONAL FLAG OF CANADA.

Canadian River. American river that drains the eastern slope of the Rocky Mountains in New Mexico and flows southeasterly through Texas and past the town of CANA-DIAN into Oklahoma, where it empties into the Arkansas R.

Canadian Scene. An information service for editors of the ethnic press and producers of foreign-language radio and television programs. Founded in Toronto in Apr. 1951, and funded by the IODE and various corporations, it commissions articles of Canadian interest and issues them every two weeks in the form of a newssheet. Selected articles, translated into 14 languages, are supplied to specific language groups. A selection of articles was made by Marcus Van Steen and published as *Glimpses of Canada* in 1973.

Canadian Schenley Football Awards. A gold cup has been presented to the most outstanding player in the CANADIAN FOOTBALL LEAGUE each November since 1953 by Canadian Schenley Distributors Ltd. Engraved gold-and-ebony plaques are given to the outstanding Canadian player, rookie, offensive lineman, and defensive lineman. Each award is accompanied by a Canada Savings Bond. Winners are decided by ballots cast by sportswriters and sportscasters.

Canadian Seamen's Union. A Canadian-based union important in the struggle for Canadian union sovereignty. Founded in 1936 and affiliated with the TRADES AND LABOUR CONGRESS OF CANADA, under the leadership of J. A. (Pat) Sullivan, it resisted the jurisdiction over all North American waters granted the rival Seafarers International Union by the AMERICAN FEDERATION OF LABOR in 1944. This evoked the celebrated TLC slogan 'CO-OPERATION, YES. DOMINATION, NO!'

Canadian Shield. The largest of the five principal geographical regions of Canada, it is a rolling, lake-dotted region of rock, forest, and water, that covers about 42% of the land area of Canada. Geologically very old and complex, it is of Precambrian age (and is also known as the Precambrian or Laurentian Shield), meaning that geologic events affecting its surface, such as periods of mountain building, began with the formation of the earth's crust over 4.5 billion years ago and ended more than 600 million years ago. Shorn of most sedimentary deposits by successive continental glaciers, it is exposed through most of the Northwest Territories, northern Saskatchewan, Manitoba, Ontario, Quebec, Labrador, and Baffin Island, forming a ring, as it were, around Hudson Bay. The use of the word 'shield' in this context is obscure but may derive from its shape (a breast-plate), its hardness (a protective covering), or its unyielding quality (a barrier against man). The population of the Shield, less than 10% of the Canadian total, lives in scattered communities that produce the majority of Canada's metallic minerals (copper, nickel, lead, zinc, iron, uranium, etc.), pulp and paper, and hydro electricity. Agriculture is not an important activity, but the southern part of the Shield, particularly in Ontario and Quebec, serves as an important recreation region for the densely populated areas. See also PRECAMBRIAN PERIOD.

Canadian Speakers' and Writers' Service. Literary agency and lecture bureau. Established in Toronto in 1950 by Matie Molinaro, this is the oldest and largest such organization for authors and celebrities in the country.

Canadian Standards Association. A private organization founded in Toronto in 1919 to certify goods. Since 1940 it has allowed its 'certification mark' (C.S.A.) to appear on commercial, consumer, industrial, and scientific products and equipment that meet its standards.

'Canadian Sunset'. Popular song celebrating the natural beauty of Canada. It was written in 1956 by two Americans, Norman Gimbel (words) and Eddie Heywood (music). Best-selling recordings were made later that year by Hugo Winterhalter and his Orchestra (instrumental) and Andy Williams (vocal).

Canadian Talent Library. A music service for radio stations and a production house for Canadian recording talent. It was established as a co-operative venture in Toronto in 1962 by J. Lyman Potts. 250 radio stations across Canada subscribe to the service, which makes available new recordings of popular musicians and groups. These records are often released by commercial record companies.

Canadian Teachers' Federation. Founded in 1919, it includes all but one of the 15 provincial and territorial teacher organizations and represents 210,000 teachers (1973)—about

75% of all those teaching in Canadian elementary and secondary schools. The CTF is 'dedicated to the improvement of the quality of education in Canada and, to this end, to the maintenance and improvement of the status of teachers.'

Canadian Television Network. See CTV.

Canadian Theatre of the Air. A series of original plays produced live on CBC Radio. Sponsored by Ironized Yeast, it was broadcast from 4 Oct. 1940 to 2 Jan. 1942. 47 of the 65 hour-long scripts were by Canadian playwrights.

Canadian Tire Corporation, Limited. 'The largest direct automotive supply house in Canada'. It was founded in 1922 by two Toronto-born brothers, John W. and Alfred J. Billes (both tire repairmen), as Hamilton Tire and Garage Limited, after its location at the intersection of Hamilton and Gerrard Sts, Toronto. It acquired its present name in 1927 and the following year issued its first catalogue. The low-price policy on supplies, sporting goods, small appliances, and tools, etc., was introduced in 1930. Canadian Tire catalogues are distributed in English and French semi-annually to four million homes. There are 295 franchise dealers in all provinces except British Columbia, where transportation costs would make difficult Canadian Tire's one-price policy.

Canadian Transport Commission. A federal commission to regulate railways, commercial air lines, the merchant marine, telecommunications, and pipelines. Established in 1967 by the National Transportation Act, it replaces the Board of Transport Commissioners, the Air Transport Board, and the Canadian Maritime Commission. The CTC consists of a president, two vice-presidents, and not more than 14 members appointed by the GOVERNOR IN COUNCIL for a maximum of 10 years. It reports to Parliament through the Minister of Transport and the Minister of Communications. There are six committees: Railway Transport, Air Transport, Water Transport, Telecommunication, Motor Vehicle Transport, and Commodity Pipeline Transport.

Canadian Tribune, The. Weekly newspaper published by the COMMUNIST PARTY OF CANADA. It has appeared under several names since its founding in Toronto: as *The Worker* (1922-36), *The Daily Clarion* (1936-9); *The Clarion* (1939); *The Toronto Clarion* (1940-1); and *The Canadian Tribune* (from 1941). From May to Nov. 1947 it appeared six times a week. A regional edition, *The Pacific Tribune*, with additional west-coast news, has been published since the mid-1960s.

Canadian True Blue. See LOYAL TRUE BLUE ASSOCIATION.

Canadian University Service Overseas. Volunteer service for young Canadians in developing countries. Founded in 1961 (one year before the U.S. Peace Corps, which it resembles), CUSO arranges assignments in developing countries for volunteers—often recent university graduates with skills in such areas as education, health, renewable resources, and technology, but volunteers may include men and women from all walks of life who have needed skills. They are supplied with rent-free housing and are paid the same as their counterparts in the host country. CUSO is funded by the CANADIAN INTERNATIONAL DEVELOPMENT AGENCY and by universities and other interested groups across Canada.

Canadian War Art Collections. Paintings and drawings of artistic and archival interest depicting Canada's contributions during the FIRST and SECOND WORLD WARS. Lord BEAVERBROOK originated this collection by commissioning English and Canadian artists on a scale never undertaken before in any country to document the First World War. Canadian artists who painted in the field included Maurice CULLEN, F. H. VARLEY, A. Y. JACKSON, and David MILNE. The original collection was known as the Canadian War Memorials 1914-18. The Second World War art collection was initiated by the late H. O. McCurry, director of the National Gallery, and A. Y. Jackson in 1943. War artists of this war included Charles COMFORT, Will Ogilvie, Alex COLVILLE, Carl SCHAEFFER, and Michael Forster. These two collections, formerly held by the NATIONAL GALLERY OF CANADA, are now held by the CANADIAN WAR MUSEUM in Ottawa.

Canadian War Museum. A museum to collect and display mementos of Canada's military past. Opened in 1942, it is part of the NATIONAL MUSEUM OF MAN. It includes the CANADIAN WAR ART COLLECTIONS, and in 1973 began a series of publications.

Canadian Wheat Board. Federal body that controls the movement and marketing of wheat. Incorporated in 1935, it may purchase and control the interprovincial and export marketing of designated grains.

Canadian Whites. Comic books produced in Canada during the Second World War. When the importation of full-colour American comic books was restricted by the War Exchange Conservation Act from 1940 to 1945, Canadian writers, artists, and manufacturers produced comic books in black and white. See also NELVANA OF THE NORTHERN LIGHTS.

Canadian Who's Who, The. 'A Biographical Dictionary of Notable Canadian Living Men and Women'. First published in 1910, and edited since 1931 by Arthur L. Tunnell, who acquired the Canadian rights to *Who's Who* from Lord Northcliffe, it appears every three years and includes detailed biographical information on some 8,000 notable living Canadians. A separate publication lists the entries by 40 professional categories. It is not to be confused with WHO'S WHO IN CANADA.

'Canadian Wolf, Come near at your peril'. Last menacing line of 'An ANTI-CONFEDERATION SONG', popular in Newfoundland in the 1860s. Newfoundland entered CONFEDERATION some 75 years later.

Canadian Women's Educational Press. Publishers of feminist books. Known colloquially as The Women's Press, it was founded on a LIP grant in Toronto in 1972 by the publishing collective of the Toronto Women's Liberation in order to issue books to meet the needs of Canadian women.

Canadian Writers' Foundation. An independent body established in 1931 to support distinguished but indigent Canadian writers. It was incorporated in 1945 as the Canadian Authors' Foundation and its first chairman was Pelham Edgar. Under its present name it is funded by federal grants and private donations.

Canadian Writer's Market, The. Standard guide to the Canadian literary market. Edited by Eileen Goodman and published by McCLELLAND & STEWART in revised editions since 1970, this handbook lists courses in journalism and creative writing, publications, advertising agencies, prizes and awards, and book publishers. It also includes information on copyright, libel, manuscript preparation, and market requirements.

Canadiana. Checklist of Canadian books issued monthly and consolidated annually by the NATIONAL LIBRARY OF CANADA. The current national bibliography includes books published by Canadian authors in this country and elsewhere as well as all books relating to Canada. It also includes information on a selection of pamphlets and theses, as well as new periodicals, government publications, records, audiotapes, films, and filmstrips. It first appeared in 1952, superseding the *Canadian Catalogue of Books, 1921-1949* (compiled by the Toronto Public Libraries) and *Canadian Catalogue, 1950* and *Canadiana 1951* (issued by the Canadian Bibliographic Centre, which became the National Library in 1953). See also the specialized BIBLIOGRAPHIE DU QUÉBEC and the book trade's CANADIAN BOOKS IN PRINT.

Canadians of Old. See *Les* ANCIENS CANADIENS.

Canadien, Canadienne. A French-speaking Canadian male, female.

'Canadien errant, Un'. A moving lament, popular to this day in Quebec, for those who fled or were exiled for taking part in the REBELLION OF 1837. The song was composed shortly after the Rebellion by Antoine Gérin-Lajoie. The French lyric appears in *The Oxford Book of Canadian Verse* (1960) edited by A.J.M. SMITH. An English version, 'The Canadian Exile' by John Boyd, appears in *Canadian Poetry in English* (1954) edited by Bliss CARMAN, Lorne PIERCE, and V.B. Rhodenizer.

Canadienne. In French argot, a sheepskin jacket. *Une canadienne en sapin* (literally, 'a pine overcoat') is slang for a coffin.

Canal du Nord (Capture of Bourlon Wood). Narrow canal and part of the supposedly impregnable 'Hindenburg Line' between Quéant and CAMBRAI in northern France, crossed during the FIRST WORLD WAR by the CANADIAN CORPS on 27 Sept. 1918. Part of the canal crossed was under construction and dry. The casualties were light; it was the subsequent fighting around Bourlon Wood that caused much loss of life.

Can-Am Cup. Prize for the 'world's fastest auto racing'. The Canadian American Challenge Cup, sponsored by the Sports Car Club of America, was first awarded in 1966 to the owner-driver of the fastest two-seat sports-racing car. Each year six races are held in the United States and two in Canada on various routes.

Candid Eye. A series of half-hour documentary films produced by the NFB for CBC-TV in the late fifties and early sixties. Experimenting with hand-held cameras and location-synchronized sound, the UNIT B film-makers who produced it developed a journalistic style later called *cinéma-vérité*. They were influenced by the photographer Henri Cartier-Bresson, who attempted to capture the significance of a real-life event at the 'decisive moment'. The first seven films, seen on CBC-TV between 26 Oct. and 7 Dec. 1958, were *Blood and Fire, A Foreign Language, Country Threshing, Pilgrimage, Memory of Summer, Police,* and *The Days Before Christmas.*

CANDIDE. Acronym of CANadian Disaggregated InterDepartmental Econometric, the large-scale computerized model of the Canadian economy. Undertaken by the ECONOMIC COUNCIL OF CANADA in 1970, it is used to review the state of the economy and its future prospects. The model provides the basis for the annual reports of the ECC.

CANDU. Acronym of CANada-Deuterium-Uranium, a nuclear reactor of Canadian design using as fuel natural rather than enriched uranium. Developed by ATOMIC ENERGY OF CANADA during the 1950s and installed during the 1960s, Canada's nuclear-power stations employ atomic reactors that make use of heavy water (deuterium oxide) to moderate the flow of neutrons to maintain a fission-chain reaction. Because natural uranium is more economic and more widely available than enriched uranium, the CANDU system possesses distinct advantages over those that consume processed uranium. There are three such Nuclear Power Demonstration stations in Ontario (Rolphton, Pickering, Douglas Point) and one in Quebec (Gentilly) that generate electric power. Three 'generations' of reactors are represented; their cooling ingredients range from pressurized heavy-water through boiling light-water to organic (light-oil) systems. The CANDU reactor has been exported, notably to India, where the Rajasthan Atomic Power Project, contrary to agreements, enabled the Indian government to produce its first atomic device in 1974. There were eight CANDU Power Reactors in operation in three countries in 1975.

CanLit. Contraction of 'Canadian Literature' as an academic discipline. CanLitCrit is a contraction of 'Canadian Literary Criticism'. Both barbarisms date from the late sixties.

Canoe. A lightweight watercraft propelled by paddles. Commonly associated with the North American Indian, it was built with various materials, ranging from the birchbark used in the Eastern woodlands—named after the bark from which it was constructed—to simple dug-outs and their more sophisticated variants used by west-coast tribes. They also ranged in size from small canoes for one or two paddlers to larger craft that carried hunting parties and transported a tribe's possessions. Canoes were used in the fur trade as the principle means of transporting pelts from inland posts to ocean ports. Measuring approximately 40 ft in length and 6 ft in width and accommodating 4 tons of freight plus a crew of 10, they were of two basic types that varied in dimension: the *canot de maître* and the *canot du nord*; the *canot bâtard* was midway between the two in size. A loaded freighter was known as a *canot de charge;* an unburdened canoe a *canot allège.* The latter was often used as an express canoe or a *canot du gouverneur.* The Eskimo canoe is known as a KAYAK or UMIAK. Today's canoes, manufactured for pleasure and sport, average 16 ft in length, 2 ft in width, and are made of wood, aluminum, or plastic.

Canrail Pass. A travel plan that allows residents of the United States and European countries to purchase up to one month's travel time on Canadian railroads. Introduced on 1 Dec. 1964 and still in use, it is the Canadian counterpart of Eurorail.

Canso Causeway. A road and rail link across the Strait of Canso connecting Cape Breton Island with mainland Nova Scotia. Completed in 1955, it has a total length of 7,000 ft.

Canton. See TOWNSHIP.

Canuck. A light-hearted reference to a Canadian. When the word first appeared in print in 1849, it referred to an English Canadian. Six years later it meant a French Canadian. Canuck today refers to a Canadian of either French or English ancestry, but the reference has a facetious or sarcastic edge. The personification JOHNNY CANUCK dates from 1909.

Canuck. Name given to three aircraft: the CF-100, the Canadian version of the JENNY, and the Fleet Canuck.

Canuck, Johnny. See JOHNNY CANUCK.

Caouette, Réal (b.1917). Leader of the RALLIEMENT DES CRÉDITISTES. Born and educated in Quebec, he first won a seat in the House of Commons as a member of the SOCIAL CREDIT party at a by-election in 1946, but was defeated in the subsequent general election in 1949. In 1962 he led a large contingent of *Créditistes* to Ottawa and has retained a federal seat at every election since, although he broke with the English-speaking Social Crediters in 1963.

CAPAC. Acronym of COMPOSERS, AUTHORS AND PUBLISHERS ASSOCIATION OF CANADA.

Cape Ann. A rain hat with a broad back flap, especially popular among the fishermen of Newfoundland. The name is said to derive from Cape Ann, Mass.

Cape Breton Highlands National Park. Established in 1936 on Cape Breton Island, on tableland overlooking the Atlantic coast of Nova Scotia, it covers 367 sq. mi. It includes coastline and forests and is traversed by the CABOT TRAIL.

Cape Breton Island. Part of the province of Nova Scotia. Located between the Gulf of St Lawrence and the Atlantic, it is connected to the mainland by the mile-long CANSO CAUSE-WAY. One of the first parts of North America known to Europeans, it was occupied by the French after they ceded ACADIA to Great Britain in 1713 and called by them Île-Royale. Their fortress city, LOUISBOURG, was captured by New England forces in 1745, returned to France in 1748, and retaken by the British in 1758. LOYALISTS settled there and founded Sydney in 1784 and changed the island's status to that of a separate colony; but it was re-annexed to Nova Scotia in 1820. Descendants of the Highland Scots who settled there in the early 1800s still speak Gaelic. Fishing, small farming, and lumbering have been major sources of the economy; coal mining and steel are the island's two modern industries. CAPE BRETON HIGHLANDS NATIONAL PARK covers most of the island's northern area and contains the CABOT TRAIL. The population in 1971 was 170,007.

Cape Columbia. Canada's farthest northern land, at the tip of Ellesmere Island. An unnavigable polar ice cap, frozen solid the year round, begins almost immediately north of the Cape.

Cape Diamond. Bold promontory on the north shore of the ST LAWRENCE RIVER upon which stands the CITADEL of Quebec City. It was given this name in 1608 by CHAMPLAIN, who mistook the quartz crystals he found there for diamonds (see Kingdom of SA-GUENAY).

Cape Dorset. Eskimo settlement in the Northwest Territories on the south coast of Foxe Peninsula, Baffin Island. It is famous for the fine quality of its Eskimo arts. Carving was introduced in 1951, and in 1959 Cape Dorset became the first community to acquire printmaking facilities. Among the many Eskimo artists associated with Cape Dorset are AGYHAGAYU, Pitseolak ASHOONA, Shoroshiluto ASHOONA, EEGYVADLUK, IYOLA, JAMASIE, JOHNNIEBO, KANANGINAK, KENOJUAK, KIAKSHUK, LATCHOLASSIE, LUCY, LUKTAK, NI-VIAKSIAK, OSOWETUK, PARR, PAUTA, PUDLO, Joanassie SALOMONIE, and TUDLIK.

Cape Spear National Historic Park. A 121-acre park in Newfoundland, the easternmost point of North America. It includes the first major lighthouse in Newfoundland, built in 1836, and the site of a Second World War coastal battery.

Capilano Suspension Bridge. World's longest suspension bridge, erected in 1899. It swings 230 ft above and 450 ft across the Capilano R. and Canyon in North Vancouver.

Capital Report. Long-running CBC Radio news program. A roundup of national and international news by leading correspondents, it was first heard in Feb. 1946. The Sunday afternoon program had its format expanded in Apr. 1969 from 30 to 60 minutes with the addition of another popular feature, 'Looking Through the Papers'—a commentary, with quotations from the week's press coverage of current events.

Caplan, Rupert (b.1896). Actor and radio producer. Born in Montreal, he acted in the historic ROMANCE OF CANADA radio series in 1931 and produced for CBC Radio the 'Victory Loan Shows' (1939-45). He has also produced and directed for the THÉÂTRE DU NOU-VEAU MONDE and the COMÉDIE-CANADIENNE.

Capt. Official abbreviation of Captain.

Captain Al Cohol. Comic-strip character created in 1973 by Maurice Metayer, an Oblate missionary at Cambridge Bay, N.W.T. Eskimo readers followed the antics of the Captain, a blundering drunkard, in government publications devoted to discouraging the consumption of alcohol in the North.

Capt(N). Official abbreviation of Captain (Naval).

CAR. Acronym of CANADIAN ARTISTS' REPRE-SENTATION and the CANADIAN ANNUAL REVIEW.

Cara Operations Limited. A 'fast-food' service. Established in Toronto in 1961 for inflight meals on planes, Cara has branched out into restaurant and fast-food concessions across the country, including service for airlines, railroads, and hotels. 'Cara' is Gaelic for 'friend' or 'companion'.

Caravan, Metro International. Annual nine-day, multi-cultural food and entertainment festival sponsored by non-commercial ethnic community organizations and held in June in 'pavilions' throughout Toronto. Each pavilion adopts the theme of a country and a culture, with appropriate entertainment, food, decorations, folk costumes, exhibitions, and bazaars. Caravan '75 registered close to two million visits.

Carbide. A greyish-black, lumpy, crystalline powder, usually derived from coke or anthracite by reaction with limestone or quicklime. Calcium carbide, as it is more properly called, is chiefly used in the generation of acetylene gas. The discoverer of the first commercial process for its production was Thomas Willson (1860-1915)—an electrical engineer, born in Woodstock, C.W. (Ont.), and trained in Hamilton—who discovered the process at Spray, N.C., in 1892, thus earning the nickname Carbide Willson.

Carcajou. A WOLVERINE or small wolf. The word came into Quebec French from the Algonkian; when applied to a person it has the overtones of 'thief' or 'rogue'.

Card money. A form of currency used in New France from 1685 to 1721 and from 1741 to 1763 when specie was scarce. Whole playing cards, or pieces of them, when marked and signed were redeemable in supplies when these arrived from France.

Careless, J.M.S. (b.1919). Historian. Born in Toronto and educated at the University of Toronto and Harvard, he joined the history department of the University of Toronto in 1945. As an author he is best known for his biography of George BROWN—*Brown of the Globe: The Voice of Upper Canada: 1818-1859* (1959) and *Statesman of Confederation: 1860-1880* (1963); for his general history, *Canada: A Story of Challenge* (1959; rev. 1970); and for *The Union of the Canadas: The Growth of Canadian Institutions: 1841-1857* (1967). As a historian he is associated with the 'metropolitan thesis', which expresses the idea that the metropolis—as the centre of business, political, and cultural life—had a determining effect on the hinterland.

Cariboo Country. A popular CBC-TV series of 30-minute dramas. The 13-part weekly programs, written by Paul ST PIERRE and produced in Vancouver by Philip Keatley, began on 2 July 1960. Set and shot in the Chilcotin Plateau region of British Columbia, in the fictitious community of NAMKO some time in the past, it dramatized the interaction of native Indians and white settlers. The series introduced Chief Dan GEORGE as OL' ANTOINE. A four-part series and a nine-part series, also called 'Cariboo Country', were produced in 1964, 1965 (a repeat), and 1966 by the CBC. A two-part episode, 'The Education of Phyllistine', also starred Dan George and was produced on 12 and 19 Mar. 1964 and again in 1965 and 1967.

Cariboo Gold Rush. See FRASER RIVER GOLD RUSH.

Cariboo Mountains. A range in east-central British Columbia. The Cariboo District in the western foothills was the scene of a gold rush when a strike was made in 1860 at Keithley Creek, and in 1862 at Williams Creek (BAR-

KERVILLE). See also CARIBOO ROAD, FRASER RIVER GOLD RUSH.

Cariboo Road. Wagon road built in 1862-5 connecting Yale with BARKERVILLE, in the Cariboo Mountains, and covering almost 400 mi. A spectacular piece of construction, partly cut out of the rock of the Fraser Canyon and sometimes resting on pilings or cribwork, it was travelled by thousands of miners, wagons, pack-trains, and coaches on their way to the FRASER RIVER GOLD RUSH.

Caribou. The North American reindeer, a large hoofed mammal with long legs, a dense brownish-to-greyish coat with white markings, and short ears and tail; both sexes have antlers. Ranging in weight from 200 to 700 lb., the caribou, because of its flesh and hide, once figured prominently in the lives of Indians and Eskimos. Two species in North America are the western barren-ground caribou of Alaska and northern Canada—a migratory species that follows well-defined paths—and the larger woodland caribou found in wooded regions from Newfoundland to British Columbia.

Caribou. A twin-engined plane manufactured by DE HAVILLAND. A twin-engined successor to the OTTER with some STOL ability, it went into production in 1958 and was adopted by the U.S. Army.

Caribou Eskimos. One of five groups of ESKIMOS. They inhabit the BARREN LANDS of the Northwest Territories and feed on caribou.

Carignan-Salières Regiment. Eight companies of this regiment were sent to Canada in 1665 to quell the Iroquois. They built three forts along the Richelieu R. and in 1666 wiped out five Mohawk villages, with the result that the Iroquois made peace with the French. The regiment was recalled in 1668 but over 400 men chose to remain in Canada, including some 30 officers who accepted seigneuries near Montreal and on the Richelieu R. Such family names as Chambly, Contrecoeur, St Ours, and Verchères were thus established in New France. See also KING'S GIRLS.

Cariole. French word for a light open sleigh, drawn by horses or dogs, carrying one or two passengers and a driver. Used in Quebec in the nineteenth century, it has been fancifully called 'carryall' in English.

Carl Tapscott Singers. A 12-voice male choir, led by the Toronto-born arranger and conductor Carl Tapscott, frequently heard on CBC Radio from 1954 to 1970. It specialized in spirituals and popular numbers.

Carle, Gilles (b.1929). Quebec film director. Born in Maniwaki, Que., and with a background as a lumberjack and artist, he joined the NATIONAL FILM BOARD as a researcher in 1960. His first feature, *La* VIE HEUREUSE DE LÉOPOLD Z (1965), was the first NFB feature to achieve popular success in Quebec movie houses. As a partner in Les Productions Carle-Lamy, he has been prolific and eclectic. His features include *Le Viol d'une jeune fille douce* (1968), *Les Males* (1970), *La* VRAIE NATURE DE BERNADETTE (1972), *La Morte d'un bûcheron* (1973), *Les Corps celestes* (1973), *Red* (1969), and *La Tête de normande St-Onge* (1975).

Carleton, Sir Guy (1724-1808). Governor-in-chief of British North America. As governor of Quebec (1768-78) his recommendations to the Colonial Office led to the QUEBEC ACT of 1774. His forces repelled the American invasion of 1775-6, for which he was knighted. As Lord Dorchester he was governor-in-chief of British North America from 1786 to 1798.

Carleton Library. A paperback series of reprinted and original books published under the auspices of the Institute of Canadian Studies at CARLETON UNIVERSITY by McCLELLAND & STEWART. It was launched in 1963 with Gerald M. Craig's edition of *Lord* DURHAM'S *Report*. In 1976 there were almost 100 volumes of Canadian interest published in anthropology, economics, geography, history, law, political science, and sociology.

Carleton Martello Tower. National historic site at Lancaster, opposite Saint John, N.B. Built to defend Saint John during the WAR OF 1812, this circular fort represents a type of coastal fortification much used by the British in the early part of the nineteenth century.

Carleton University. Founded in 1942 as Carleton College, it initially gave only evening classes in introductory university subjects and public administration. In 1945 day classes for veterans were started and a Faculty of Arts and Science was established. Full university powers were conferred in 1952 and in 1957 the name was changed to Carleton University. The present campus on the outskirts of Ottawa was established in 1959. St Patrick's College (1927), offering an alternative undergraduate education through integrated and interdisciplinary programs, has been integrated with Carleton since 1967.

Carling O'Keefe Breweries. The original O'Keefe Brewery was founded in Toronto by Eugene O'Keefe in 1862, becoming the first brewery in Canada to produce lager beer. Its most popular beers are Old Vienna Lager and O'Keefe Ale. Carling's Brewery was founded in London, Ont., by Tom Carling in 1840. Red Cap Ale and Black Label Lager are its most popular products. In 1930 Carling's joined Canadian Breweries—a newly incorporated holding company—followed by O'Keefe in 1934. Together they were known as Canadian Breweries Ltd until 1973, when their name was changed to Carling O'Keefe Ltd. They and their subsidiaries brew ale, lager, and stout in Canada, the United States, and Ireland, and are engaged in the production of wine, oil, and gas in Canada. ROTHMANS OF PALL MALL CANADA LTD, affiliated with the multi-national Rothman Group, holds majority shares.

Carman, Bliss (1861-1929). Poet. Born in Fredericton, N.B., a cousin of Charles G.D. ROBERTS, he was educated at the Universities of New Brunswick and Edinburgh and at Harvard. In 1890 he settled in New York, though he visited Canada regularly, and worked intermittently as a journalist and professional poet. His romantic poems—with their impressionistic and symbolic landscape imagery, gentle mysticism, and uncontrolled word music—appeared in many books and gained him a reputation as a quintessential poet; but few of his poems have endured. The title poem in his first collection of nature lyrics, LOW TIDE ON GRAND PRÉ (1893), is probably his best. Other titles associated with Carman are *Songs from Vagabondia* (1894) and *The Pipes of Pan* (1906). Lorne PIERCE edited *The Selected Poems of Bliss Carman* (1954).

Carmichael, Franklin (1890-1945). Landscape painter and member of the GROUP OF SEVEN. Born in Orillia, Ont., he worked as a designer for Grip Limited and Rous & Mann, Toronto; he studied art there and in Antwerp. He became a teacher at the Ontario College of Art in 1932. His rich, effective *Autumn Hillside* (1920, AGO) was in the first Group show.

Carnarvon terms. Arbitration by Lord Carnarvon, the British colonial secretary, in 1874 between British Columbia and the Canadian government. To avoid British Columbia's secession, he supported the promise of railroad construction between Fort Garry and British Columbia—made when the province entered Confederation in 1871—by increasing the amount of money to be spent on the railroad and setting 1890 as its completion date. See also CANADIAN PACIFIC RAILWAY.

Carnaval. See QUEBEC WINTER CARNIVAL.

Carnival Overture. Frequently performed orchestral piece composed by Oskar MORAWETZ in 1946. Its gay rhythms and lush melodies are reminiscent of Dvořák.

Caroline. American steamer used during the REBELLION OF 1837. She carried supplies from the American shore to Upper Canadian rebels on Navy Island above Niagara Falls. On 29 Dec. 1837 some Canadians cut her adrift from her mooring on Schlosser's Landing and set her on fire; the figurehead and some planks were swept over the Falls. From this incident came the rallying cry: 'Remember the *Caroline*!'

Carr, Emily (1871-1945). Painter and writer. Born in Victoria, B.C., she studied painting in San Francisco for five years, taught in Victoria for four, and studied in England (1899-1904) and France (1910-11). She drew her creative inspiration mainly from the Indian communities and carvings she saw in North Vancouver and the Queen Charlotte Islands and the 'woods and skies' of the interior, which she interpreted in powerful paintings of Indian artifacts, sculptural forests, and huge, pulsating skies bursting with light and energy. Three of her most famous paintings are INDIAN CHURCH (*c*.1930), BLUNDEN HARBOUR (*c*.1928-30, NGC), and *Scorned as Timber, Beloved of the Sky* (*c*.1936, Vancouver Art Gallery). Carr was also an exceptional writer who wrote three books in her lifetime that are a highly regarded part of Canadian literature. KLEE WYCK (1941) was followed by *The Book of Small* (1942) and *The House of All Sorts* (1944). Published posthumously were her autobiography, *Growing Pains* (1946), *The Heart of a Peacock* (1953), *Pause: A Sketch Book* (1953), her journals, *Hundreds and Thousands* (1966), and *Fresh Seeing* (1973).

Carrier. Salmon-eating ATHAPASKAN Indians of the Upper Fraser R. in British Columbia. The name is derived from the fact that widows were obliged to carry the ashes of their husbands on their backs. Their population in 1970 was 4,549.

Carrier, Roch (b.1937). Quebec novelist. Born in Sainte-Justine-de-Dorchester, Que., he attended the Université de Montréal and the Sorbonne. He is the author of four effective novels about Quebec in the present and the recent past—in which conventional realism, violence, and humour all combine—that have been translated into English by Sheila FISCHMAN: *La* GUERRE, YES SIR! (1970), *Floralie, Where Are You?* (1971), *Is It the Sun, Philbert?* (1972)—linked novels about 'Quebec's dark ages'—and *They Won't Demolish Me!* (1974). He adapted *La Guerre, Yes Sir!* for the THÉÂTRE DU NOUVEAU MONDE, of which he is secretary-

general, in 1970. The first production in English was at the STRATFORD FESTIVAL in 1972.

Carry On, Canada! A CBC Radio series devoted to the war effort. Written by William Strange and produced by J. Frank WILLIS, the 60-minute program, heard live on Sunday evenings from 18 Feb. 1941 to Feb. 1942, took listeners 'on visits to armament and munitions factories, to mines, shipyards, docks, granaries and other centres of production, to hear for themselves accounts of the operations, processes, tests and demonstrations which were making Canada's emergence as "the arsenal of democracy".'

Carry On, Sergeant. Early Canadian feature film. Produced in 1958 by W.F. Clarke of Canadian International Films Ltd and directed by Gerald Thomas at Trenton, Ont., it is a eulogy of the men who died at YPRES. It was budgeted at $500,000 and was an extravagant failure. 10 reels, b & w.

Carson, Clarice. Soprano. Born in Montreal, she studied singing there and was the only member of the 1966 Metropolitan Opera National Company chosen to join the Met itself. Since then she has also become a member of the Scottish Opera. She has sung at the Stratford Festival (1969), in *Tosca* on CBC-TV, with the Vancouver Opera (1972-3), and the CANADIAN OPERA COMPANY.

Carter, Sir Frederick (1819-1900). A FATHER OF CONFEDERATION. Born in St John's, Nfld, and educated as a lawyer, he was elected to the House of Assembly in 1855. An advocate of Confederation, he attended the QUEBEC CONFERENCE, but his stand did not gain favour in Newfoundland. He was premier from 1865 to 1869 and from 1875 to 1878.

Carter, Wilf (b.1904). Country singer. Born in Caysborough, N.S., he began recording such songs as 'Swiss Moonlight Lullaby' and 'The Capture of Albert Johnson' in 1932. Sometimes called 'The Yodelling Cowboy', he has written more than 500 songs, sold millions of singles and albums, and enjoys an international reputation.

Carter Commission. The Royal Commission on Taxation under Kenneth Carter. It was established in Sept. 1962 and its report was tabled in massive detail in Parliament in Feb. 1967. The report attacked the existing tax system, said that 'a buck is a buck' and should be taxed as such, and proposed to establish equity—taxation according to the ability to pay. In particular the Carter Commission urged taxation of capital gains.

Cartier. Typeface designed by Carl DAIR. The first type designed in Canada since James EVANS published his Cree Syllabic Hymn Book in 1841, it was named after Jacques CARTIER. It was released on 1 Jan. 1967, the year of Dair's death, and dedicated 'to the Canadian people on the occasion of the Centenary of Confederation'. Especially suited to photo-setting, Cartier is a highly legible, well-proportioned face characterized by a strong base line. This entry is set in Cartier.

Cartier, Sir George-Étienne (1814-73). A FATHER OF CONFEDERATION. Born in Saint-Antoine, L.C. (Que.), he fought in the REBELLION OF 1837 as a rebel and had to flee the country. Returning in 1838, he practised as a lawyer and was elected to the legislative assembly in 1848. He became leader of the French-Canadian section of the Conservative government in 1857. When the MACDONALD-Cartier ministry fell in 1858, it was replaced by the Cartier-Macdonald ministry by means of the DOUBLE SHUFFLE. As attorney-general in the GREAT COALITION, he attended all three conferences that led to CONFEDERATION, paving the way for this by persuading French Canadians of its value. He was involved in the PACIFIC SCANDAL, but died in England the year after it broke out. He was created a baronet in 1868.

Cartier, Jacques (1491-1557). Navigator, discoverer of the St Lawrence R.; one of the heroes (along with CHAMPLAIN) of French Canada. He was born in Saint Malo, France. In search of a route to Asia in 1534, he passed Labrador, which he described as 'the land God gave Cain', explored the Gulf of St Lawrence, which appeared to him to be a large lake, and raised a cross on the Gaspé Peninsula. He took two Iroquois Indians, Taignoagny and Domagaya, back to France. In his second voyage of 1535 he sailed in the GRANDE HERMINE, which was accompanied by the *Petite Hermine* and the *Émérillon*. He entered the St Lawrence R. and visited Stadacona (Quebec City) and the island of Hochelaga (Montreal), where Cartier named the great hill behind the village 'Mont Royal'. After spending the winter near Stadacona, Cartier returned to France with some captured Indians, among them DONNACONA. He made a third voyage in 1541 as part of a colonizing expedition led by ROBERVAL, who did not leave France until the following year. Cartier built two forts at the mouth of the Cap Rouge R., calling the post Charlesbourg Royal. It was abandoned the next June when he sailed for France. *The Voyages of Jacques Cartier* (1924) edited by H.P. Biggar presents contemporary accounts of the voyages in French and English. See also Kingdom of SAGUENAY, ST LAWRENCE RIVER, SCURVY.

Cartier-Brébeuf Park. National Historic Park in Quebec City. Two significant sites are preserved in this 22-acre park: the spot where Jacques CARTIER moored the GRANDE HERMINE for the winter of 1535-6 (a 78-ft replica is moored there today) and the site of the missionary headquarters erected by Jean de BRÉBEUF in 1626.

CAS. Acronym of the CONTEMPORARY ART SOCIETY.

Casa Loma. A Toronto landmark, this architectural fantasy of a castle was designed by E.J. LENNOX for Sir Henry Pellatt and built in 1911-14. It contains 98 rooms, including a marble-floored conservatory, a library for 100,000 volumes, secret passageways, and an 800-ft tunnel that leads to towered stables. Pellatt lived in the castle for only 10 years. In the 1920s it reverted to the city for unpaid taxes, and since 1937 it has been restored by the Kiwanis Club of West Toronto and operated as a tourist attraction.

Casavant Frères Limitée. An organ-building firm of international repute. It was founded in 1879 at Saint-Hyacinthe, Que., by Joseph-Claver Casavant and Samuel-Marie Casavant, sons of Joseph Casavant, a blacksmith who began repairing organs in 1837 and building them in 1850. The brothers established their reputation with their first electro-pneumatic pipe organ, which was installed in NOTRE-DAME DE MONTRÉAL in 1890. The firm has remained innovative and the leader in the field.

Casse-tête. French-Canadian word meaning 'head-breaker'—a TOMAHAWK.

Casse-tête à calumet. French for 'tomahawk pipe', a combination tomahawk (CASSE-TÊTE) and peace pipe (CALUMET) made by Indians in the nineteenth century for ceremonial and trade purposes. It was perhaps a dual symbol of war and peace.

Cassiar Asbestos Corp. Ltd. Important asbestos mine. The mystery of 'the mountain with the white plume' was solved in the late forties when asbestos was found on McDame Mountain in the Cassiar Range in northern British Columbia, near the Yukon border. The ALASKA HIGHWAY provided access to the site and production of asbestos commenced in 1953. The Cassiar company operates two mines, one at Cassiar and another at Clinton in the Yukon Territory.

Cassino War Cemetery. In the SECOND WORLD WAR the lst Canadian Infantry Division broke through the Hitler Line between Pontecorro and Aquino—4 mi. to the rear of Cassino—

on 23 May 1944, suffering very heavy casualties. This opened the way to Rome, which fell to the Allies on 4 June 1944. The rebuilt abbey on the summit of Monte Cassino overlooks the large Cassino War Cemetery, where 855 Canadian soldiers are buried.

Casson, A.J. (b.1898). Landscape painter and member of the GROUP OF SEVEN. Born in Toronto and educated in Hamilton and Toronto, he worked as design assistant to Franklin CARMICHAEL at Rous & Mann. He moved to the printing firm of Sampson-Mattthews Limited and was its vice-president for 20 years. A late member of the Group—he joined in 1926 as a replacement for Frank JOHNSTON who had resigned—he specialized in well-designed, sun-drenched paintings of Ontario villages. His best-known painting is *Anglican Church at Magnetawan* (1933, NGC).

Castle Hill National Historic Park. A 60-acre park overlooking the town of Placentia, Nfld, it includes the ruins of seventeenth-century French fortifications, ceded to the British in 1713, as well as later British batteries.

Castonguay Commission. A Quebec royal commission of inquiry into health and social welfare in the province. It was chaired by Claude Castonguay (b.1929) and its multi-volume reports appeared between 1967 and 1972. Since 1970 Castonguay has been Minister of Social Affairs in the Quebec government.

Castor. French word for beaver or beaver pelt; nickname for the right wing of the Conservative Party in Quebec that derived from the founding of the party newspaper (*L'Etendard*), which bore the beaver emblem, in 1883. See also ULTRAMONTANE.

Castor canadensis. See BEAVER.

CAT. Acronym of Canadian Anti-acoustic Torpedo Gear, a noise-making device. Towed astern of each escort vessel in Atlantic convoys, it was designed to attract the acoustic torpedos of the enemy submarines in the North Atlantic. CATs were manufactured in Canada after Sept. 1943.

Catawba. An inexpensive wine produced in the Niagara Peninsula, Ont. It is made from a reddish grape native to the banks of the Catawba R. in South Carolina.

Catherwood, Ethel (b.1909). Well-known track-and-field star. Born in Toronto but trained in Saskatchewan, she was called 'The Saskatoon Lily' for her statuesque beauty. She represented Canada at the women's track-and-field events that were included for the first time in the 1928 Olympics in Amsterdam, where she won the gold medal in the women's high-jump competition. The following year she accompanied her sister to the United States and retired from competition.

Catholic Church. See ROMAN CATHOLIC CHURCH.

CATV. Abbreviation of CAble TeleVision. Privately owned but regulated by the CANADIAN RADIO-TELEVISION COMMISSION, cable companies improve the range and quality of television reception by connecting subscribers' sets to an antenna and booster system.

Caucus. A regular meeting of the elected legislators of a political party. While the legislature is in session, the caucus of each party usually meets once a week.

Caughnawaga. Indian reserve on the St Lawrence R. opposite LACHINE, Que. The land was set aside by Louis XIV for Christian Iroquois to settle on in 1676, when it was known as Sault-Saint-Louis, and for a Jesuit mission. The saintly Kateri TEKAKWITHA, who was declared venerable in 1941, lived and died there in the seventeenth century. In the 1920s men from Caughnawaga gained fame as steelworkers in New York—'The Mohawks in High Steel'—when they helped build the George Washington Bridge and Rockefeller Center, etc.

CAUT. Abbreviation of the Canadian Association of University Teachers, an association founded in Ottawa in 1951 to promote the interests and rights of teachers and researchers in Canadian universities and colleges. It defends academic freedom, handles grievance procedures, advances the standards of the profession, and tries to raise the quality of higher education.

Cavendish, P.E.I. See ANNE OF GREEN GABLES.

Caviar. Sturgeon roe. Poorer-grade salmon or lumpfish roe is often marketed as Canadian caviar.

Cayuga. See IROQUOIS.

CBA Book Award. Annual award given to the author of 'the Canadian book which the Canadian Booksellers Association feels has not generated the popular interest it merits'. The award of $1,000, given at the CBA's annual convention, was first made in 1975.

CBC Ideas. A series of adult-education programs heard on CBC Radio's FM network. Talks and discussions by specialists are organized around themes of current intellectual interest. Launched on 25 Oct. 1964, it is now heard for 60 minutes five times a week on the CBC FM network. Forerunners of 'CBC Ideas' are 'University of the Air', which was heard from 1953 to 1962, and 'The Learning Stage', heard from 1962 to 1964.

CBC National News. Newscasts on CBC Radio and CBC-TV. The first CBC news bulletin was a bilingual radio report heard in Montreal on 2 Nov. 1936. The CBC News Service was inaugurated on 1 Jan. 1941 when DAN McARTHUR, chief news editor, had Wells Ritchie prepare for the announcer Charles Jennings a national report at 8:00 p.m. based on copy from the national newsroom in Toronto and on dispatches from regional newsrooms in Halifax, Montreal, Winnipeg, and Vancouver. Readers who followed Jennings were Lorne GREENE, Frank Herbert, and Earl CAMERON. Current radio news reports include the WORLD AT SIX and the WORLD AT NINE. On English-language television the first newscast, part of CBC NEWSMAGAZINE, was given on 8 Sept. 1952 on CBLT (Toronto), the only English station then telecasting. Later that year the 'CBC National News' took its present television form—19 minutes at 11:00 p.m. seven nights a week—with Larry Henderson. Other news readers have included Earl Cameron (from 1959), Stanley BURKE (from 1966), and Lloyd Robertson (from 1970). In Aug. 1970 the title was changed from 'CBC National News' to The NATIONAL.

CBC Newsmagazine. A long-running CBC-TV program devoted to news stories and features. It was the first program to be televised in English Canada—from 7:30 to 10:00 p.m., 8 Sept. 1952, on CBLT in Toronto—and carried the first English-language news report. It began as a selection of newsreels and gradually changed into an independent news program treating the day's major stories. It appears once a week throughout the year on Monday evenings.

CBC Opera Company. One of the most important chapters in Canadian opera history began in 1952 when the CBC commissioned two operas for radio (*Transit Through Fire* and *DEIRDRE of the Sorrows*), both by Healey WILLAN, with libretti by John COULTER. Their performances led to an active CBC Opera Company that was in existence from 1948 to 1951.

CBC Radio. See CANADIAN BROADCASTING CORPORATION.

CBC Radio Canada/Canada Council Awards for Young Composers. Competition held every second year since 1973 to encourage composers under 29 years of age. At the discretion of the jury as many as four equal prizes of $3,000 each, with a possible runner-up prize of $1,000, are awarded by the CANADIAN BROADCASTING CORPORATION and the CANADA COUNCIL. Award-winning competitions are then performed at a CBC Radio public concert. In addition the ONTARIO ARTS COUNCIL awards $3,000 for the best work by an Ontario composer and the MINISTÈRE DES AFFAIRES CULTURELLES DU QUÉBEC does the same for the work of a Quebec composer.

CBC Radio Network. A national hookup of CBC stations, both public and private, created on 1 Oct. 1962. It consolidated two separate national hookups: the Trans-Canada Network and the Dominion Network. The Trans-Canada Network, the original hookup inherited from the CRBC, consisted in 1949 of 44 stations. It received its name only on 2 Jan. 1944 when a second hookup, the Dominion Network, was created to supply an alternative service for 45 stations. The two networks were consolidated in 1962 as an economy measure. See also CANADIAN BROADCASTING CORPORATION.

CBC Stage. General title of the flagship drama series of CBC Radio. The oldest series of weekly radio dramas heard in North America, it began on 23 Jan. 1944 as 'Stage 44', a 30-minute program produced by Andrew ALLAN. The 'Stage' series was extended to 60 minutes in Sept. 1946 and rechristened 'CBC Stage' when Esse W. LJUNGH took over production in 1955. The Andrew Allan years of live broadcasts correspond to the GOLDEN AGE OF CANADIAN RADIO and set a pattern for commissioning from Canadian writers either original radio scripts or adaptations and dramatizations of suitable literary works. Two notable programs were 'Mr. Arcularis', a dramatization of Conrad Aiken's short story, and Reuben Ship's original satire The INVESTIGATOR. Playwrights identified with the 'Stage' series include Harry J. BOYLE, Charles Israel, Fletcher MARKLE, Len PETERSON, Joseph SCHULL, Lister SINCLAIR, and Tommy TWEED. Among the actors who formed this 'radio repertory group' were Andrew Allan, John Bethune, Robert CHRISTIE, Eric Christmas, John DRAINIE, Alice Hill, Alan King, Bud Knapp, and Ruth Springford. Original musical scores were composed and conducted by Lucio AGOSTINI and Morris Surdin.

CBC Symphony. Consisting largely of musicians from the TORONTO SYMPHONY ORCHES-

CBC Symphony

TRA, it was organized by CBC producer Terence Gibbs in 1952. It performed almost weekly on radio, with a different conductor for each performance, and was highly regarded—the only full-sized orchestra supported entirely by a broadcasting network. It was disbanded in 1964 when the CBC began using the TSO for symphonic broadcasting.

CBC Talent Festival. Annual music competition open to young Canadian artists between the ages of 15 and 30. Established by the CANADIAN BROADCASTING CORPORATION, it was first heard on radio on 4 Oct. 1959 under the direction of Sir Ernest MacMILLAN. The Festival is judged in four categories: voice; piano; string; woodwind and brass. Winners in each category receive $3,000 and a CBC recital broadcast in Toronto or Montreal; second-place winners receive $1,500 each.

CBC Television Network. See CANADIAN BROADCASTING CORPORATION.

CBC Times. Semimonthly publication giving schedules for the CBC's English-language radio and television programs, plus features on shows and stars. Launched on 16 July 1948, it was terminated on 28 Dec. 1969.

CBC Tuesday Night. The current title of CBC Radio's prestige series of cultural programs. Modelled on the BBC's 'Third Program', it has been described as 'an evening of serious music, drama, and the spoken word'. It was launched as 'CBC Wednesday Night' on 3 Dec. 1947—beginning with a talk by Arthur L. PHELPS—with the première of a musical comedy called 'The Gallant Greenhorn', with words by Ray Darby and music by Morris Surdin. It continued on Wednesday nights until 23 Oct. 1963. Shifted to Sunday evenings, it was called 'CBC Sunday Night' from 27 Oct. 1963 to 17 Oct. 1965. It has been heard for a minimum of two hours on Tuesdays as 'CBC Tuesday Night' since 26 Oct. 1965. The program was introduced by James BANNERMAN from the fifties until his death; his duties were assumed by Harry ADASKIN on 6 Oct. 1970. Both ANTHOLOGY and 'Cohen's Choice' (a series of neglected plays chosen and sometimes adapted for radio by Nathan COHEN and broadcast intermittently between 1966 and 1970) were heard in conjunction with 'CBC Tuesday Night', which always included classical concerts as well as the spoken word. The series was terminated in Oct. 1976.

CBC-TV. See CANADIAN BROADCASTING CORPORATION.

CBL. See CJBC.

CBRE. Abbreviation of CANADIAN BROTHERHOOD OF RAILWAY EMPLOYEES AND OTHER TRANSPORT WORKERS.

CC. See Companion of the ORDER OF CANADA.

CCA. See CANADIAN CONFERENCE OF THE ARTS.

CCCL. Initials of the Canadian and Catholic Confederation of Labour. See CONFEDERATION OF NATIONAL TRADE UNIONS.

CCF. Co-operative Commonwealth Federation, a democratic socialist political party formed in Calgary in 1932. A number of labour and farm groups came together to establish 'a co-operative commonwealth in which the basic principle regulating production, distribution, and exchange will be the supplying of human needs instead of the making of profits.' Its first leader was J.S. WOODSWORTH. In 1933 at Regina the party adopted the REGINA MANIFESTO. With farm and labour organizations it founded in 1958 NEW PARTY clubs, which led to the founding of the NEW DEMOCRATIC PARTY in 1961. Though having small electoral success at the federal level, the CCF was elected to power in Saskatchewan, with T.C. DOUGLAS as premier, in 1944; and for some time in the 1940s it was the official opposition in British Columbia, Manitoba, and Ontario.

CCIO. Initials of the CANADIAN COMMITTEE FOR INDUSTRIAL ORGANIZATION.

CCL. Initials of the CANADIAN CONGRESS OF LABOUR.

CCM. Initials of the Canadian Cycle and Motor Company, a manufacturing operation founded in Toronto in 1896. As well as designing and building the popular lines of CCM bicycles, it manufactured the Ivanhoe electric car in 1903 and the RUSSELL in 1907-8. It supplies a complete line of hockey and lacrosse equipment and advertises itself as 'good sports'.

CD. Initials of the *Corps diplomatique*. A plaque with these initials fastened to an automobile licence plate identifies the vehicle as the property of the diplomatic corps.

CDC. Initials of the CANADIAN DEVELOPMENT CORPORATION.

CDN. Official abbreviation of 'Canada'. The letters CDN were first used by the Canadian Army in the First World War and were subsequently registered with the League of Nations as the distinguishing sign for Canada. CDN is most commonly seen alongside automobile licence plates. In Europe all cars operating outside the country of registration are required to carry an oval white plaque on the rear panel, near the licence plate, bearing in black letters the identification initial or initials of the country of registration. Thus CDN identifies Canada; F, France; GB, Great Britain; and USA, the United States of America.

Cdr. Official abbreviation of Commander.

Cedar, Red. An evergreen tree called 'cedar' in Canada but actually an *arbor-vitae* and not related to the true cedars of the Old World. Up to 200 ft in height and 8½ ft in diameter, this species of the British Columbia coast and islands and the Rocky Mountain foothills is best known for its light reddish wood that was carved by west-coast Indians into totem poles and canoes, the former often several storeys high, the latter up to 60 ft long.

CEF. Initials of the Canadian Expeditionary Force (see CANADIAN CORPS).

CEGEPs. Acronym of Collèges d'Enseignement Général Et Professionnel. These initials are used in Quebec to identify what in English Canada are called CAATs (Colleges of Applied Arts and Technology), or community colleges.

CELDIC. Acronym of Commission on Emotional and Learning Disorders In Children. See ONE MILLION CHILDREN.

Celestial city. Unofficial motto of FREDERICTON, N.B.

Celia. An award made by the NATIONAL BALLET OF CANADA to a person who has made a distinguished contribution to ballet in Canada. It has been made irregularly since 1971 and honours Celia FRANCA, the Ballet's founder and artistic director from 1951 to 1974. It takes the form of a stylized metal sculpture of a dancing girl executed by the Toronto sculptor Sasha G. Ulbricht.

CEMO. Initials of the CANADIAN EMERGENCY MEASURES ORGANIZATION.

Census. A survey of the population—of its numbers and characteristics. In Canada a census is taken every 10 years by STATISTICS CANADA. It includes the sex, age, ethnic origin, occupation, etc., of the population, and a survey of agriculture. The original purpose of the census was to determine the distribution of the population so that federal electoral districts could be revised to ensure REPRESENTATION BY POPULATION.

Census Metropolitan Area. A unit employed in the census for measuring population in and around large urban centres with a population over 100,000. In general CMA includes the main labour-market area, or the daily commuting area, around these cities. In the 1971 census the population of 22 Canadian cities was measured in this way.

Centennial Medal. Medal awarded by the secretary of state during CENTENNIAL YEAR to honour Canadians of some distinction in all walks of life. Approximately 40,000 medals were presented. The abbreviation is C.M.

Centennial Year. One hundredth anniversary of Confederation, celebrated in 1967. Festivities held during the Centennial (or Centenary) Year included the DOMINION DAY ceremony on Parliament Hill to mark Confederation and the opening of EXPO 67 in Montreal.

Central Bank. See BANK OF CANADA.

Central Eskimos. One of five groups of ESKIMOS. They inhabit the Arctic shores north of HUDSON BAY, especially Southampton Island and northwest BAFFIN ISLAND.

Central Mortgage and Housing Corporation. Federal CROWN CORPORATION that makes loan funds available for housing. Incorporated in 1945, the CMHC makes loans and contributions for new housing, home improvements, urban renewal, new development, and low-income housing.

Central Provinces. Ontario and Quebec. These provinces lie between the ATLANTIC PROVINCES and the WESTERN PROVINCES.

Centre Block. See PARLIAMENT BUILDINGS.

Centre Culturel Canadien. See CANADIAN CULTURAL CENTRE IN PARIS.

Centre for Culture and Technology. A centre within the University of Toronto 'to study the psychic and social consequences of technology and media', directed by Marshall McLUHAN. Established in 1963 as an interdisciplinary seminar among the faculties of the university, it operates out of a coachhouse near St Michael's College. In the 1970s the Centre undertook the study 'The Laws of the Media'. In the words of the director, 'This has led to the discovery that the most human thing about people is technology.'

CF-100. A twin-jet-engined, all-weather interceptor, designed and built by A.V. ROE CANADA LTD at Malton, near Toronto. It was the first modern military aircraft to be produced in Canada specifically to Canadian requirements. Design work started in 1946 and the first prototype flew in Jan. 1950. A total of 692 CF-100s of different types were built, including 53 for the Belgian Air Force. The Orenda engines that powered the CF-100 were also designed and manufactured by A.V. Roe Canada.

CF-101B Voodoo. A supersonic fighter-interceptor and nuclear-weapons carrier flown by Canada's NORAD squadrons. A version of the McDonnell F-101B, the Voodoo was acquired in the 1960s by direct purchase from the United States. It is capable of being armed with Falcon missiles and Genie nuclear rockets.

CF-102. An Avro Jetliner designed and built by A.V. ROE CANADA LTD. The first jet transport to fly in North America and the second in the world (after the De Havilland Comet), it made its initial flight on 10 Aug. 1949. It set many records, but development was shelved with the outbreak of the Korean War.

CF-104 Starfighter. A supersonic fighter plane capable of nuclear-weapons delivery, flown by Canada's NATO squadrons. A version of the Lockheed F-104 Starfighter, the CF-104 was Canadian-built by CANADAIR, Montreal, and modified for a strike-reconnaissance role. Acquisition was announced on 2 July 1959; the first overseas delivery was accepted in Oct. 1962.

CF-AAA. Specimen registration for Canadian civil aircraft. The CF designation was assigned to Canada by the Radio-Telegraph Convention in Washington in 1927, replacing the earlier G-CAAA system, to permit radio call letters to correspond to registration marks on aircraft. The system went into effect 1 Jan. 1929. The last three letters are assigned by the Civil Aviation Branch of the Department of Transport. Identification marks were issued as C-FTNI, C-FTNJ, etc. until Jan. 1974 when the series C-GAAA was introduced.

CFCF. See XWA.

CFDC. Initials of the CANADIAN FILM DEVELOPMENT CORPORATION.

CFE. Initials of CANADIAN FORCES EUROPE.

CFI. Initials of the CANADIAN FILM INSTITUTE.

CFL. Initials of the CANADIAN FEDERATION OF LABOUR.

CFRB. Call letters of the Toronto radio station with 'the largest radio audience in Canada'. It was started in 1927 by E.S. (Ted) Rogers who perfected, in Apr. 1925, the AC radio tube, which made modern broadcasting possible, all previous broadcasting being accomplished by DC current from batteries. CFRB has therefore been known as the world's first batteryless broadcasting station. Its call letters commemorate the invention: CF is the once-standard broadcasting prefix for 'Canada'; RB stands for 'Rogers Batteryless'. Its programming in the 1960s and 1970s has been identified particularly with Betty KENNEDY and Gordon SINCLAIR.

CGIT. Initials of CANADIAN GIRLS IN TRAINING.

CGM. See CONSPICUOUS GALLANTRY MEDAL.

Ch. Official abbreviation of Chaplain.

Chabanel, Noël. See JESUIT MARTYRS.

Chairy Tale, A. A short film made by Norman McLAREN. Co-directed by Claude JUTRA, it was released by the NFB in 1957. A man dances a *pas de deux* with a chair to Eastern music played by Ravi Shankar. McLaren photographed live action frame-by-frame to create the effect of animation. 9 min., 30 sec.; b & w.

Chalk River. Site of Canada's first nuclear reactor. The decision to build a pilot plant for the production of plutonium from uranium, using heavy water as a moderator, on the Chalk R. (near Pembroke, Ont.), was made by ATOMIC ENERGY OF CANADA LIMITED on 19 Aug. 1944. See COBALT THERAPY UNIT, DEEP RIVER, ELDORADO MINES, MACDONALD PHYSICS LABORATORY, PORT RADIUM. See also CANDU, NRU, NRX, NUCLEAR POWER DEMONSTRATION, PTR, ZED-2, ZEEP.

Challenge for Change. The NATIONAL FILM BOARD's program for community action. Working with other government departments and agencies, the NFB offers its films and film-making facilities as resource materials and catalysts and recorders of social action. Three films on Saul Alinsky and five on his method of organizing communities into effective action units based on participatory democracy, produced during the 1960s, are characteristic of the program. In French it is known as *Société nouvelle*. See also FOGO PROCESS.

Chalmers Award. Annual award made since 1972 to encourage the writing and producing of Canadian plays. A cash prize of $5,000 is made to the playwright and $2,500 to the production company of the best drama mounted in Canada during the previous year, as judged by the Toronto Drama Bench (an independent group of theatre critics). The award is administered by the Ontario Arts Council with funds provided by the Floyd S. CHALMERS FOUNDATION (established by the former head of the Maclean-Hunter Publishing Company).

Chalmers Foundation, The Floyd S. It was established in Toronto in 1968 by Floyd S. Chalmers, a retired MACLEAN-HUNTER executive, to promote and develop the performing arts in Canada. It commissioned the opera LOUIS RIEL and established the annual $5,000 CHALMERS AWARD.

Chamberland, Paul (b.1939). Quebec poet. Born in Longueuil, Que., and educated at the Université de Montréal and the Sorbonne, he was a co-founder of PARTI PRIS in 1963. He supplied the title of Malcolm Reid's study of poets of Chamberland's generation and persuasion—*The Shouting Signpainters: A Literary and Political Account of Quebec Revolutionary Nationalism* (1972), in which some of his outspoken poems appear—and is the author of several poetry collections, including *Terre-Québec* (1964) and *L'Afficheur hurle* (1965).

Chambers, Jack (b.1931). Painter. Born in London, Ont., he studied there at Beal Technical School and at the Royal Academy of Fine Arts, Madrid. His early works were symbolic figurative pictures having a dreamlike quality. *Messengers Juggling Seed* (1962, NGC) exemplifies this style with its use of repeated images of smiling faces that float in bubbles against a hilly surrealistic landscape. He developed this lyrical, nostalgic strain in fragmented-image pictures like *Olga and Mary Visiting* (1964-5, London Public Library). In the late sixties he began to paint scenes drawn from the familiar southern-Ontario environment that are photographic in their realism but in their intensity and feeling transcend photographs. Two of his best-known paintings in this vein are 401 TOWARDS LONDON, #1 (1968-9, Northern & Central Gas Corporation Ltd) and SUNDAY MORNING, #2 (1969-70, Mr & Mrs E.A. Schwendau Collection). He has exhibited internationally and lives in London, Ont., where he founded CANADIAN ARTISTS' REPRESENTATION in 1967.

Champagne, Claude (1891-1965). Composer. Born in Montreal, he was self-taught before studying in Paris. Later he taught at the Conservatoire of Music and Dramatic Arts of Quebec in Montreal. His work is characterized by its romanticism, modified by the elegance of French music. Important works include *Symphonie gaspésienne* (1945), and *Suite canadienne* (1927) and *Altitude* (1959), both for choir and orchestra.

Champlain, Hélène Boullé de (1598-1654). Wife of Samuel de CHAMPLAIN, whom she married at 14 (her husband being 31 years her senior). She lived with him at Quebec from 1620 to 1624. Île-Sainte-Hélène off Montreal is named after her.

Champlain, Samuel de (c.1570-1635). Geographer, explorer, 'Father of New France'. Born in Brouage, France, he accompanied the fur-trading expedition of François Gravé Du Pont to New France in 1603, visiting TADOUSSAC, journeying up the St Lawrence R. as far as the rapids, and visiting Gaspé. In 1604, under Pierre du Gua de Monts and POUTRINCOURT, he sailed for ACADIA where, in search of a place to start a settlement, he explored the east coast. He wintered at Île-Sainte-Croix (Dochet's Island, Maine) and moved with the colony to PORT ROYAL, where he spent two winters. In 1606 he founded the ORDER OF GOOD CHEER (Ordre de bon temps). Returning to France in 1607, he led an expedition to the St Lawrence R. in 1608 as lieutenant to du Monts and on 3 July started to build the HABITATION at Quebec. With this its history began. In the years that followed, until he died at Quebec in 1635, Champlain laid the foundations of New France, latterly as the unofficial governor. Between 1609 and 1616 he made journeys of exploration, including one that took him south to Lake Champlain and another—by way of the Ottawa R., Lake Nipissing, and the French R.—in which he reached Georgian Bay and Lake Huron. He saw Quebec pass into English hands temporarily (1628-32) and made many trips to France in the interests of organizing the fur trade and maintaining French presence on the river through settlement and the missionary work of the Jesuits. Accounts of his voyages can be read in *The Works of Samuel de Champlain* (CHAMPLAIN SOCIETY, 6 vols, 1922-36).

Champlain Society. An imprint on books dealing with the history of Canada, issued on a subscription basis. It was founded in Toronto in 1905 to publish scholarly editions of historical journals and documents. Some 200 titles have appeared, including the standard six-volume edition of the *Works* of Samuel de CHAMPLAIN. Manufacturing and distribution are handled by the University of Toronto Press.

Chandler, Edward Barran (1800-80). A FATHER OF CONFEDERATION. A member of the legislative assembly of New Brunswick from 1827 to 1836, and then a member of the legislative and executive councils, he attended all three conferences that led to CONFEDERATION. He was lieutenant-governor of the province when he died.

Chantecler. Breed of white poultry developed by the Trappist monks at Oka, Que.

Chantecler

The first all-Canadian chicken, it was bred by Brother Wilfred between 1908 and 1918 by crossing the Cornish, White, Leghorn, Rhode Island Red, Wyandotte, and White Plymouth Rock chickens. Also spelled Chanticler, the name derives from Chanticleer, the cock in the medieval *Reynard the Fox;* it is spelled 'Chantecler' in Rostand's drama of that name (1910).

Chapais, Jean-Charles (1811-85). A FATHER OF CONFEDERATION. Elected to the legislative assembly as a Conservative from Canada East in 1851, he attended the QUEBEC CONFERENCE. After Confederation he was minister of agriculture from 1867 to 1869 and receiver-general from 1869 to 1873.

Chapel of the Mohawks. Small white frame church outside Brantford, Ont. Named St Paul's, Her Majesty's Chapel of the Mohawks, in 1788, it is the only Indian Royal Chapel in the world. The Chapel owns part of the Queen Anne Communion Service and Bible, which dates from 1712 and bears the inscription 'The Gift of Her Majesty Anne by the Grace of God, Queen of Great Britain, France and Ireland and Her Plantations in North America, to her Indian Chapel of the Mohawk'. Buried in the churchyard is Joseph BRANT.

Chapman, Christopher (b.1927). Film director. Born in Toronto, he achieved success with his first short film, *The* SEASONS, in 1953. He has worked intermittently with CBC-TV, the NATIONAL FILM BOARD, and Crawley Films, but he thrives best on his own, with a corporate sponsor. Chapman is internationally known for his poetic and innovative multi-screen film *A* PLACE TO STAND (1967), which he directed and photographed for the Ontario Pavilion at EXPO 67. For the world's fair at Osaka he was equally innovative with *Ontario* (1970).

Chaput, Marcel. See RIN.

Charbonneau and Le Chef. A realistic three-act play by John T. McDonough, a former Catholic priest living in Toronto. It dramatizes the conflict between Joseph Charbonneau, the Archbishop of Montreal, and Maurice DUPLESSIS, the Premier of Quebec, over the ASBESTOS STRIKE of 1949. Stage, radio, and television productions and a recording followed its publication in 1968.

Chargex. An all-purpose charge-card system whereby consumers may purchase goods or services from participating consumer outlets or obtain cash from branches of participating banks on presentation of their Chargex card. Originating with the Bank of America, it was introduced in Canada in 1968 when four Canadian banks were licensed to launch the Chargex program: Canadian Imperial Bank of Commerce, The Royal Bank of Canada, the Toronto-Dominion Bank, and Banque Canadienne Nationale. The Bank of Nova Scotia joined in 1973. The system is international—any card, whatever its name, that bears the three-colour band of blue, white, and gold may be used in any participating outlet anywhere in the world. There are in excess of five million card holders in Canada and 42 million in the world; there are 119,000 participating outlets in Canada and 1.9 million in the world.

Charlebois, Robert. (b.1944). Quebec rock singer. Born in Montreal, he attended the NATIONAL THEATRE SCHOOL in the early sixties and emerged as a sensational pop singer with his *Lindbergh* album in 1968. Dressed in a MONTRÉAL CANADIENS hockey sweater and wearing his hair in an Afro style, he performed his 'baroque and roll' or *le jazz libre du Québec* across Canada and in Europe. He gradually discarded such attention-getting effects and emerged as a more popular singer in the 1970s. Each of his 10 albums has sold over a million copies. Since 1974 he has been making 'spaghetti westerns' in France.

Charles Edwards Awards. Annual awards, one in radio and one in television, given to recognize enterprise and thoroughness in spot-coverage reporting of a news story in a regular newscast. Sometimes called the 'Charlies'—after Charles B. Edwards, who was at the time general manager of the Canadian Press's Broadcast News—they were first made in 1967 by the Radio Television News Directors Association of Canada (RTNDA). See also DAN McARTHUR AWARDS.

Charlesworth, Hector (1872-1945). Journalist. Born in Hamilton, Ont., he was city editor of the *Mail and Empire* (1904-10), Toronto, and associate editor and then editor-in-chief of *Saturday Night* (1910-32). Appointed first chairman of the Canadian Radio Broadcasting Commission, he was forced to resign four years later and returned to journalism as a music and drama critic. He was staunchly conservative and took a dim view of the work of the GROUP OF SEVEN, members of which referred to him as 'Old Heck'. He was music critic of the Toronto *Globe and Mail* when he died. His reminiscences appear in *Candid Chronicles* (1925), *The Canadian Scene* (1927), *More Candid Chronicles* (1928), and *I'm Telling You* (1937).

Charlevoix, Pierre-François-Xavier de (1682-1761). Jesuit priest, author of the first general history of the French settlements in North America. He taught in Quebec from 1705 to 1709. Sent west to investigate a possible 'western sea', between 1720 and 1723 he travelled as far as Michilimackinac and down the Mississippi to its mouth. His *Histoire et description générale de la Nouvelle France* and his *Journal* of his trip, published together in 1744, are highly regarded for their historical and literary value. Both have been translated into English.

Charlie Conacher Memorial Trophies. Two hockey tropies awarded since 1969 by the Charlie Conacher Research Fund, established in honour of Charles CONACHER. The Memorial Trophy is awarded to a player who has made an outstanding contribution to humanitarian causes and the public service. The Team Trophy is awarded to the Canadian team in the NATIONAL HOCKEY LEAGUE with the best seasonal record against other Canadian teams. No cash awards accompany the trophies.

'Charlies, The'. See CHARLES EDWARDS AWARDS.

Charlottetown. Capital city of Prince Edward Island. Originally a French settlement called Port-la-Joie, its name was changed to honour the consort of George III when the island was ceded to Britain in 1763; when the colony separated from Nova Scotia in 1769, Charlottetown was made the capital. It was incorporated as a city in 1875 and has been called 'the cradle of Confederation' (its motto) because the first discussions of a union of British North America took place in PROVINCE HOUSE in Sept. 1864—the CHARLOTTETOWN CONFERENCE. It is the home of the CONFEDERATION CENTRE OF THE ARTS. The 1971 CMA population was 19,133.

Charlottetown Conference. A meeting held at Charlottetown, P.E.I., in Sept. 1864 by delegates from Nova Scotia, New Brunswick, and Prince Edward Island to discuss Maritime union. It was attended by delegates from the Province of Canada, including John A. MACDONALD and other FATHERS OF CONFEDERATION who put forward a convincing case for British North American union, thus paving the way for CONFEDERATION. See also PROVINCE HOUSE (Charlottetown).

Charlottetown Summer Festival. A program of plays and musicals held each summer in the 946-seat theatre of the CONFEDERATION CENTRE arts complex in Charlottetown, P.E.I. Founded by Mavor MOORE, it opened in July 1965 with ANNE OF GREEN GABLES, a musical that has been revived as the Festival's fea-

tured presentation every year. In 1968 Alan LUND succeeded Moore as artistic director.

Charpentier, Gabriel (b.1925). Composer. Born in Richmond, Que., he studied classics and music at Brébeuf College, Montreal, and composition with Nadia Boulanger and others in Paris. His work is primarily for the theatre, including scores for Le THÉÂTRE DU NOUVEAU MONDE and the STRATFORD FESTIVAL. It is based on collaboration with all aspects of a production and often unites them with a counterpoint style similar to Gregorian chant. He is a program organizer at the CBC and artistic adviser for television musical broadcasts.

Chartered bank. A bank licensed by Parliament under the Bank Act to operate in Canada. There are 10 privately owned chartered banks in Canada, each with many branches across the country.

Chartered Libertine, The. Novel by Ralph ALLEN published in 1954. It is a satire on the publicly owned CBC and its desire for a broadcasting monopoly.

Chasse-galerie, La. The French-Canadian legend of a young voyageur who makes a 'flying visit' to his girlfriend. He is transported there and back in a 'flying canoe' propelled by the devil who, in exchange, claims the young man's soul. The devil is outwitted in the end. The legend is said to be based on the old French story of a 'Monsieur Galéry' who, as punishment for hunting rather than attending Mass on Sunday, was condemned to hunt through the skies at midnight until the world ended.

Chat dans le sac, Le. Feature film written and directed by Gilles GROULX and released in 1964. Starring Barbara Ulrich, Claude Godbout, Manon Blain, and Veronique Vilbert, it is the love story of two people who question the meaning of life, the hypocrisy of the world, and their responsibility to themselves. It was a harbinger of the political concerns of the new Quebec cinema. 74 min., b & w.

Château cabinet. Nickname for a group of federal Conservative MPs with rightist leanings. Some distinguished backbenchers met frequently at the CHÂTEAU LAURIER in Ottawa after the 1974 election, when Robert STANFIELD failed to lead the Conservative Party to power. The name is a pun on the British 'shadow cabinet'.

Château Clique. An epithet referring to the appointed officials in Lower Canada (Quebec) before 1841, derived from the name of the governor's residence, the CHÂTEAU ST LOUIS.

Château de Ramezay. Historic building and museum in Montreal. It is on the site of a house—the Hôtel de Ramezay—built about 1720 by Claude de Ramezay, governor of Montreal (1702-24). It became the official residence of the Intendant in 1727. Sold in 1745, it was enlarged, sold again, and purchased by the government in 1763. From 1875 to 1895 it housed the Université Laval, then was bought by the city, which sold it in 1929 to the Numismatic Society, its present owners, who gave it its present name. Almost nothing of the original structure has survived.

Château Frontenac. CP hotel in Quebec City. Located near the historic site of the CHÂTEAU ST LOUIS overlooking the St Lawrence R., it was designed in 1890 by the American architect Bruce PRICE in a picturesque late-Victorian style based on the traditions of late medieval French château architecture. It was built in 1892-3, with later additions (1897-1924) by Price, E. & W.S. MAXWELL, and W.S. Painter. A pupil of the American architect Henry Hobson Richardson, Price based his design on Richardson's 1872 design for the Lunatic Asylum in Buffalo, N.Y. Perhaps the best example of what came to be called the CHÂTEAU STYLE, it is one of the most dramatically sited buildings in Canada. There are 665 guest rooms.

Chateau Gai Winery. One of Ontario's major wineries, founded in 1890 as the Stamford Park Wine Company near Niagara Falls, Ont. Chateau Gai is the only Canadian wine sold outside Canada, in Barbados and Great Britain.

Château Lake Louise, The. CP hotel sited at Lake Louise, Alta, to take advantage of the spectacular scenery. The present building—designed in 1912-13 by W.S. Painter, with additions by Barott & Blackader in 1924-5, in a simplified version of the CHÂTEAU STYLE—replaces a half-timbered wooden building of 1900. It has 360 guest rooms.

Château Laurier, The. CN hotel in Ottawa. Built in 1908-12, it was designed in the CHÂTEAU STYLE by Ross & MacFarlane to complement the Parliament Buildings. The additions of 1927-9 were by Archibald & Schofield. It has 480 guest rooms.

Château Montebello, Le. A CP hotel on the north shore of the Ottawa R. in Quebec, midway between Ottawa and Montreal. Originally the Seigniory Club, it became a public hotel in Oct. 1970, though the Club still exists as part of the hotel. There are 198 guest rooms. The main building, a handsome log structure, was erected in 1930 on land that became the seigniory of the Papineau family in 1801. 'Montebello', the manor house built by Louis-Joseph PAPINEAU in 1850, is maintained as a museum on the hotel grounds.

Château St Louis. The residence of the governors of New France and of British North America (now demolished), situated where the upper station of the elevator stands on DUFFERIN TERRACE. The first building on this site was Fort St Louis, begun by CHAMPLAIN in 1620, pulled down in 1629, and rebuilt on a larger scale. His successor, Huault de Montmagny, built stone fortifications in 1636 and in 1647 a one-storey Château with a terrace across the river façade. In 1694 the Château was rebuilt by FRONTENAC to plans by Gédeon de Catalogne, who designed a two-storey building with a steep roof, two pavilions, and an impressive terrace. In 1808-11 it was rebuilt again and raised one storey. It was destroyed by fire in 1834 and replaced by the Durham (later Dufferin) Terrace in 1838 and after.

Château Style. The architectural style that in the first half of the twentieth century came to be considered Canada's national style. It was established in the picturesque design of several wooden CPR hotels built in the Rockies in the late 1880s. The first stone-and-brick building in this style was the CHÂTEAU FRONTENAC in Quebec City. Begun in 1893 by the American architect Bruce PRICE, it was given a medieval French character in response to that of Quebec City and to its prominent site on the St Lawrence. The high-roofed Château Style was adapted in CPR and CNR hotels across the country, most literally in the CHÂTEAU LAURIER, Ottawa. It was then used for federal buildings, especially in the Ottawa area, because of its similarity to the High Victorian Gothic of the Parliament Buildings: it was seen to be romantically and functionally 'in character with a northern country'. It finally died in public and private architecture because of its unsuitability for post-war needs, but the buildings in the Château Style remain among the best in the history of Canadian architecture.

Châteauguay, Battle of. An engagement in the WAR OF 1812. On 26 Oct. 1813 the 'Hero of Châteauguay', Lt-Col. Charles de Salaberry, deploying his French-Canadian troops on the banks of the Châteauguay R. opposite Lachine, L.C. (Que.), turned back a numerically superior American invading force advancing on Montreal.

Chatelaine. A monthly magazine of interest to women, published by MACLEAN-HUNTER in Toronto since 1928. It carries general-interest articles, fiction, consumer reports, film and book reviews, and helps the Canadian woman define her role as a homemaker or breadwinner. The editor is Doris Anderson. A French edition was launched in 1960. See also MISS CHATELAINE.

Chatham. Automobile manufactured from 1906 to 1909 by Chatham Motor Car Company, Chatham, Ont. It was a four-passenger open touring car with right-hand steering.

Chaussegros de Léry, Gaspard-Joseph (1682-1756). Chief engineer of Quebec. Sent to Canada in 1716, he stayed for the rest of his life, putting his stamp on the architecture of the time in forts, fortifications, and public buildings. He was responsible for the fortified walls of Montreal (begun 1722); the façade of the old Church of Notre Dame in Montreal (designed 1721, completed 1725)— a remodelling of the 1672 building, it was the forerunner of the present NOTRE-DAME-DE-MONTRÉAL; the Château Vaudreuil, Montreal (1723, demolished); a pavilion of the CHÂTEAU ST LOUIS, Quebec (1724); and a rebuilding of NOTRE-DAME-DE-LA-PAIX, Quebec (1744-9).

Chauveau, Pierre-Joseph-Oliver. See CHAUVEAU MEDAL.

Chauveau Medal. Awarded every two years by the ROYAL SOCIETY OF CANADA for a distinguished contribution to knowledge in the humanities other than Canadian literature and Canadian history. The award was established in 1951 to honour the memory of P.-J.-O. Chauveau (1820-90)—first premier of Quebec (1867-73), senator, professor of law, and past president of the Society. It consists of a silver medal and $1,000.

Chebucto. See HALIFAX.

Cheddar. A hard, smooth cheese. Though cheddar originated near Bristol, Eng., it is known as a Canadian speciality. It was first commercially produced in Canada in Ingersoll, Ont., in the 1860s, where the distinctive Canadian flavour was developed. Summer cheddar is richer than the winter variety because the cows have eaten grass instead of fodder, thus producing better milk. Cheddar must age 18 months to two years before achieving its sharp taste and crumbly texture. See also BLACK DIAMOND CHEESE and COLBY.

Chee Chee, Benjamin (b.1944). Ojibwa artist. Born in Temagami, Ont., he attended a training school for four years, hitchhiked around northern Ontario, and settled down in Montreal in 1965. His first exhibition was at the Nicholas Gallery in Ottawa in 1973. He has developed a free-flowing lyrical style in his drawings and a modernist style in his acrylics, both of which often depict birds and animals in an imaginative way.

Cheechako. Word for 'newcomer' in the CHINOOK JARGON. Inexperienced goldseekers who came to the KLONDIKE as a result of the Gold Rush of 1898 were called cheechakos or 'greenhorns' by the experienced prospectors or SOURDOUGHS who greeted them. *Ballads of a Cheechako* (1909) is the title of Robert W. SERVICE's third book.

'Cheese Poet, The'. See James McINTYRE.

Chef, Le. Sobriquet of Maurice DUPLESSIS—in English 'the chief'.

Chemical Institute of Canada Medal. Awarded annually since 1951 by the Chemical Institute of Canada 'as a mark of distinction and recognition to the person making an outstanding contribution to the science of chemistry or chemical engineering in Canada.' The paladium medal is donated by INCO.

Chemical Valley. The area around and south of Sarnia, Ont., where a number of chemical industries—including Polymer and Don Chemical Ltd—produce such products as ammonia, synthetic rubber, ethylene, fertilizers, etc., based principally on petroleum and natural gas.

'Chénier, Brave like'. Descriptive phrase that recalls the courage of Jean-Oliver Chénier, a *patriote* leader in the REBELLION OF 1837 who was killed at SAINT-EUSTACHE, on 14 Dec. 1837.

'Chénier Cell'. The name assumed by the FLQ members who were responsible for the kidnapping of James R. Cross during the OCTOBER CRISIS. See also 'Brave like CHÉNIER'.

Cherry, Zena. Newspaper columnist. Born in Prince Albert, Sask., an eighth-generation Canadian and a descendant of a colonel in James Wolfe's regiment, she was educated at Bishop Strachan School and the University of Toronto. She is married to a prominent Toronto business executive. Since the fall of 1958 she has written 'After a Fashion', a column that records top-drawer social events and appears six days a week in the GLOBE AND MAIL.

'Chesapeake and the Shannon, The'. Title of a popular ballad that celebrates the victory of the SHANNON over the USS Chesapeake on 1 June 1813, an exciting naval engagement in the WAR OF 1812.

Chess Federation of Canada. Highest authoritative chess organization in the country. Founded on 24 Sept. 1872 in Hamilton, Ont., it now has its headquarters in Ottawa. With a membership of over 2,600, it is the national affiliate of the Fédération Internationale des Échecs and is responsible for Canada's participation in Chess Olympics, the World Junior Championship, and the Interzonal, the first qualifying tournament towards the world title. In addition it publishes the bimonthly *Bulletin*, a bilingual magazine of chess news and games. Owing primarily to the CFC's work, Canada is by far the strongest chess nation in the Commonwealth and has the only two International Grandmasters. See also Duncan SUTTLES and Daniel Abraham YANOFSKY.

Chesterfield. A sofa. The word, widely used in Canada, is frequently singled out as a Canadianism but is not unknown in parts of England and the United States. It derives from Lord Chesterfield, the eighteenth-century patron and man of letters.

Chevalier, Leo. Fashion designer. Born in Montreal, he was educated at Loyola College and the École des Beaux-Arts, Montreal, before beginning a career as a designer of women's and men's ready-to-wear fashions. In 1973 he opened the first exclusive boutique devoted to clothes by a Canadian designer in the T. EATON CO. LIMITED (Montreal); he now has nine such shops in Eaton's across Canada. He has designed uniforms for Bell Canada, the National Arts Centre, and Air Canada, for which he is permanent designer and consultant. A co-founder of the FASHION DESIGNERS ASSOCIATION OF CANADA, INC., and the current president, he was part of the team (with Marielle Fleury, Michel ROBICHAUD, and John WARDEN) that designed Canada's uniforms for the Montreal Olympics in 1976.

Chewett, James Grant (1793-1862). First English-speaking, Canadian-born architect. Born in Toronto, he was trained by his father, who was Deputy Surveyor General in Upper Canada. In 1831 he acted as Clerk of the Works on the reconstruction of ST JAMES' CATHEDRAL, to the plans of Thomas Rogers. He also designed the Upper Canada Legislative Buildings at Front St W. and Simcoe St (1829, demolished) and Toronto's second market building (1831), on the site of the present ST LAWRENCE HALL.

Chez Bardet. Montreal restaurant specializing in traditional French cuisine. Many gourmets consider it one of the finest restaurants on the continent. It opened on 1 Nov. 1958. The owner, André Bardet, is an award-winning chef.

Chez Hélène. Popular bilingual children's program on CBC-TV. Produced in Montreal from 1958 to 1973, it taught preschoolers oral French for 15 minutes five days a week. Hélène Baillargeon spoke in that language to Louise (played by Madeline Kronby), who replied in English.

Chicora. Well-known vessel. Built at Liverpool, Eng., in 1864 as a blockade-runner for the Confederate navy, she was purchased and brought to the Great Lakes in 1868 by N. Milloy & Co. of Niagara. She carried Wolseley's RED RIVER EXPEDITION to Fort William two years later, and served Lord Dufferin as a vice-regal yacht in 1874. In 1878 she was put on the Toronto-Queenston run with the *Chippewa, Corona,* and *Cayuga.* She remained in service until 1913, when she was cut down for a barge.

Chief, The. Sobriquet of John G. DIEFENBAKER and title of Thomas Van Dusen's 1968 biography of the former prime minister.

Chief electoral officer. An officer responsible for the conduct of all federal elections. In addition the officer is responsible for elections to the Northwest Territories Council and the Yukon Council and conducts any vote taken under the CANADA TEMPERANCE ACT. The office was established in 1920 under the Dominion Elections Act, now the Canada Elections Act. The chief electoral officer is responsible directly to the House of Commons.

Chief Justice. A judge who acts as the chairman of a group of judges in a court—the Chief Justice of the Supreme Court of Canada, the chief justices of the high courts of the provinces and territories, and the chief justices of other superior courts. The chief justice of the Supreme Court of Canada is called the Chief Justice of Canada. Appointed by the GOVERNOR IN COUNCIL, he holds office during good behaviour and meets with eight other puisne (junior) judges, who are also appointed by the Governor in Council. The Right Honourable Mr Justice Bora Laskin was appointed Chief Justice of the Supreme Court of Canada on 27 Dec. 1973. The formal style of address of a chief justice in conversation is 'Sir' or 'Madam', the informal, 'Chief Justice'. In formal usage the Chief Justice of the Supreme Court of Canada is addressed as The Rt Hon. the Chief Justice of Canada; the chief justice of a province or territory as The Hon. the Chief Justice of—; the chief justice of other high courts as The Hon. Mr Justice—.

Chief of Defence Staff. Appointed official responsible to the Minister of National Defence for the control and administration of the CANADIAN ARMED FORCES. The position was created on 1 Aug. 1964 as a prelude to UNIFICATION.

Chiefswood. Birthplace of the Mohawk poet Pauline JOHNSON. This attractive two-storey frame house, which stands on the bank of the Grand R. near Brantford, Ont., was erected about 1853 by the poet's father, G.H.M. Johnson, a chief of the Six Nations Indians, as a wedding present to his wife. Chiefswood is now a provincial museum.

Chieftain, The Old. Sobriquet of Sir John A. MACDONALD.

Chien d'or, Le. See The GOLDEN DOG.

Chignecto Canal. A scheme dating back to 1822 to cut a canal across the CHIGNECTO ISTHMUS, the narrow neck of land at the New Brunswick-Nova Scotia border that separates the Gulf of St Lawrence from the Bay of Fundy. A 20-mi. canal would have reduced the sailing distance between Saint John and Quebec City by more than 1,000 mi. Work on a canal-railroad progressed in 1889-95 but the promoters ran out of funds.

Chignecto Isthmus. The track of land between Northumberland Strait and the Bay of Fundy. Formerly the north limit of Acadia, it now forms the border between Nova Scotia and New Brunswick.

Chilcotin. The southernmost ATHAPASKAN-speaking Indians of the British Columbia interior. They carried on an active trade with the neighbouring Pacific Coast Indians, which led to cultural interchanges. Their population in 1974 was 1,352.

Chilcott, Barbara. See DAVIS FAMILY.

Children of Peace. See SHARON TEMPLE.

Chilkat. See TLINGIT.

Chilkat blanket. A polygonal woollen blanket with symbolic designs, woven from the hair of the mountain goat and shredded cedar bark by the Chilkat (TLINGIT) Indians. In colour it is bluish-black and yellow on white. Tradition indicates that this famous ceremonial dancing blanket originated in historic times among the TSIMSHIAN.

Chilkoot Pass. Route to the Yukon through the Coast Mountains across the international boundary between the Alaska Panhandle and British Columbia. In the KLONDIKE GOLD RUSH of 1896 it was used by prospectors trekking overland from Skagway to the Yukon and is now a YUKON HISTORIC SITE.

Chimo. Mixed Indian and Eskimo word of salutation. It is pronounced either 'chee-mo' or 'chy-mo'. Although it is sometimes used as a toast (in place of 'cheers'), it means 'greetings'.

Chinese Pacific. Nickname given the CANADIAN PACIFIC RAILWAY, which was completed in 1885 with much oriental labour.

Chiniquy, Charles-Paschal-Télésphore (1809-99). Clergyman and author. Born at Kamouraska, L.C. (Que.), and ordained a priest in 1833, he became curé of Beauport and of Kamouraska and began a temperance crusade in the 1840s that made him a national figure. Following two scandals involving women and excommunication in 1856, he became a Presbyterian minister and began an anti-Catholic campaign in Canada, Great Britain, India, and Australia. Among his sensational publications—some in print to this day—are *The Priest, the Woman, and the Confessional* (1875), *The Murder of Abraham Lincoln Planned and Executed by Jesuit Priests* (1893), and *The Perversion of Dr. Newman to the Church of Rome* (1896).

Chinook. (i) A small group of west-coast Indians who lived near the mouth of the Columbia R. in the nineteenth century. See also CHINOOK JARGON. (ii) A dry, warm southwest wind in southern Alberta and British Columbia. Commonest during the winter, it causes a rapid rise in temperature. It occurs when outbursts of Pacific air crossing the Rockies are forced to descend on the lee side, with the result that the air is heated and dried. While it is a welcome break from sub-zero winter temperatures, the Chinook is said to contain large numbers of positive air ions that may be hazardous to health. It was first described by fur traders at Fort Astoria, who noted that it seemed to come from the direction of the villages of the Chinook Indians. It is similar to the Swiss *Föhn* or the *sirocco* of the Sahara.

Chinook jargon. A form of the language spoken by the CHINOOK. It incorporated English, French, Chinook, and other Indian words and was used by Indians and whites for conducting the fur trade in the nineteenth century.

Chipewyan. Largest ATHAPASKAN-speaking

Chipewyan

Indian group in Canada. Prominent in the fur trade with the HUDSON'S BAY COMPANY in the eighteenth and early nineteenth centuries, they hunted, fished, and trapped in an enormous region northwest from Hudson Bay (near Churchill, Man.) to Great Bear Lake and beyond and made summer excursions to hunt caribou in the neighbouring tundra. Their population in 1970 was 5,098.

Chipmunk. Lightweight single-engine plane designed and built by DE HAVILLAND, Canada. Used extensively for primary training, it lent its name to the Chipmunk Project, a refresher flying course for reserve RCAF pilots sponsored by the Royal Canadian Flying Clubs Association between 1950 and 1958.

Chippewa, Battle of. An engagement in the WAR OF 1812 on 5 July 1814, near Chippewa Creek on the west bank of the Niagara R. Gen. Phineas Riall led some 2,000 British regulars and Canadian militia against an invading army of 4,000 American soldiers, under Generals Jacob Brown and Winfield Scott, and was badly beaten.

Chiriaeff, Ludmilla (b.1924). Artistic director and choreographer. Born in Riga, Latvia, she studied dancing in Berlin and danced with Col. de Basil's Ballet Russes and the Berlin Opera Ballet. She came to Montreal in 1952 and founded Les Ballets Chiriaeff, the first Canadian television ballet company, which gave its first stage performance in 1955. Since 1957 it has been known as Les GRANDS BALLETS CANADIENS. As the company's artistic director, Chiriaeff has choreographed over 600 CBC-TV productions and many others for the stage.

Chiropractic. Term for spinal manipulation, coined by its leading practitioner, Daniel David Palmer, a native of Port Perry, Ont., in 1903.

Chisholm, Dr Brock. See PULHEMS.

Chitty's Law Journal. A periodical for lawyers published 10 times a year in Toronto since 1950. It was edited until 1963 by Robert Michael Willes Chitty, QC. (1893-1970), who then edited the *Ontario Law Reports.* In 1974 Hugh W. Silverman became chief editor, succeeding J. de N. Kennedy. *Chitty's* publishes articles of current interest to the legal profession, with case comments, etc.

Chlorpromazine. See LARGACTIL.

Chouayens, Les. Derogatory term applied to the French Canadians who, although sympathetic to the aims of the REBELLION OF 1837, sided with the CHÂTEAU CLIQUE. The usage may derive from the description *Chouauens* given to the militia who deserted MONTCALM during the attack on OSWEGO (*Chouagüen*) in 1756. It may also derive from Chouans ('screech-owls' in Breton)—smugglers in the west of France who fought as Royalists during the French Revolution.

CHR. See CANADIAN HISTORICAL REVIEW.

Christian Guardian, The. See the UNITED CHURCH OBSERVER.

Christie, Robert (b.1913). Actor. Born and educated in Toronto, he has become a well-known actor on CBC Radio and was in several productions of the STRATFORD FESTIVAL. From the fifties to the seventies he made a specialty of impersonating Sir John A. Macdonald on radio, television, and the stage. He is the father of Dinah Christie, the singer and entertainer.

Christmas carol, The first. See HURON CAROL.

Christmas Day. Statutory holiday observed throughout Canada on 25 Dec. It celebrates the birth of Christ.

Christopher's Movie Matinee. Feature film produced by the NFB in 1968. The director, Mort Ransen, put movie cameras in the hands of 14 Toronto high school students, who made this film about themselves—the flower-power generation—and their world. It took a dramatic turn when the NFB stopped further filming and the students reacted on camera. 87 min., 28 sec.; colour.

Chronicles of Canada. A series of historical and biographical monographs devoted to the development of Canada. The 32 volumes were edited by George M. WRONG and H.H. Langton and published in Toronto between 1914 and 1916. The authors and titles are:

1. Stephen LEACOCK. *The Dawn of Canadian History: A Chronicle of Aboriginal Canada* (1915).

2. Stephen Leacock. *The Mariner of St. Malo: A Chronicle of the Voyages of Jacques Cartier* (1915).

3. Charles W. Colby. *The Founder of New France: A Chronicle of Champlain* (1915).

4. Thomas Guthrie Marquis. *The Jesuit Missions: A Chronicle of the Cross in the Wilderness* (1916).

5. William Bennett Munro. *The Seigneurs of Old Canada: A Chronicle of New-World Feudalism* (1915).

6. Thomas Chapais. *The Great Intendant: A Chronicle of Jean Talon in Canada, 1665-1672* (1914).

7. Charles W. Colby. *The Fighting Governor: A Chronicle of Frontenac* (1915).

8. William Wood. *The Great Fortress: A Chronicle of Louisbourg: 1720-1760* (1915).

9. Arthur G. DOUGHTY. *The Acadian Exiles: A Chronicle of the Land of Evangeline* (1916).

10. William Wood. *The Passing of New France: A Chronicle of Montcalm* (1915).

11. William Wood. *The Winning of Canada: A Chronicle of Wolfe* (1915).

12. William Wood. *The Father of British Canada: A Chronicle of Carleton* (1916).

13. W. Stewart WALLACE. *The United Empire Loyalists: A Chronicle of the Great Migration* (1914).

14. William Wood. *The War with the United States: A Chronicle of 1812* (1915).

15. Thomas Guthrie Marquis. *The War Chief of the Ottawas: A Chronicle of the Pontiac War* (1915).

16. Louis Aubrey Wood. *The War Chief of the Six Nations: A Chronicle of Joseph Brant* (1915).

17. Ethel T. Raymond. *Tecumseh: A Chronicle of the Last Great Leader of His People* (1915).

18. Agnes C. LAUT. *The 'Adventurers of England' on Hudson Bay: A Chronicle of the Fur Trade in the North* (1914).

19. Lawrence J. Burpee. *Pathfinders of the Great Plains: A Chronicle of La Vérendrye and his Sons* (1915).

20. Stephen Leacock. *Adventurers of the Far North: A Chronicle of the Arctic Seas* (1914).

21. Louis Aubrey Wood. *The Red River Colony: A Chronicle of the Beginnings of Manitoba* (1915).

22. Agnes C. Laut. *Pioneers of the Pacific Coast: A Chronicle of Sea Rovers and Fur Hunters* (1915).

23. Agnes C. Laut. *The Cariboo Trail: A Chronicle of the Gold-Fields of British Columbia* (1916).

24. W. Stewart Wallace. *The Family Compact: A Chronicle of the Rebellion in Upper Canada* (1915).

25. Alfred D. De Celles. *The 'Patriotes' of '37: A Chronicle of the Lower Canadian Rebellion* (1916).

26. William Lawson Grant. *The Tribune of Nova Scotia: A Chronicle of Joseph Howe* (1915).

27. Archibald MacMechan. *The Winning of Popular Government: A Chronicle of the Union of 1841* (1916).

28. A.H.U. Colquhoun. *The Fathers of Confederation: A Chronicle of the Birth of the Dominion* (1916).

29. Sir Joseph Pope. *The Day of Sir John Macdonald: A Chronicle of the First Prime Minister of the Dominion* (1915).

30. Oscar D. Skelton. *The Day of Sir Wilfrid Laurier: A Chronicle of Our Own Times* (1916).

31. William Wood. *All Afloat: A Chronicle of Craft and Waterways* (1915).

32. Oscar D. Skelton. *The Railway Builders: A Chronicle of Overland Highways* (1916).

Chuckwagon. A wagon equipped with a stove, cooking gear, water-barrel, and provisions necessary during a roundup or while camping on the range. Chuckwagon races have been a popular feature of the CALGARY STAMPEDE since 1923.

Church union. See UNITED CHURCH OF CANADA.

Churchill Falls. A 245-ft waterfall on Labrador's Churchill R., one of the largest sources of electrical power in Canada with a capacity of 5,225 megawatts. Several hydro-electric plants have been developed along the river, the largest being the CHURCHILL FALLS POWER PROJECT.

Churchill Falls Power Project. The largest single-site power station in the western world. As early as 1894 the hydro-electric potential of Churchill Falls in central Labrador was recognized, but it was not until 1953, with the creation of BRINCO, that steps were taken to harness the flow of water. Much of the initial planning, which included diverting the Churchill R. above its falls, was undertaken by ACRES CONSULTING SERVICES LIMITED. Work commenced once Hydro-Québec agreed on 13 Oct. 1966 to purchase the electrical power. The giant power project was completed 16 months ahead of schedule in Sept. 1974.

Churchill River. The major river of northern Saskatchewan and Manitoba. It flows over 1,000 mi. from the central Saskatchewan lake district to empty into Hudson Bay on the coast of northeastern Manitoba. There is a second Churchill R. in Labrador.

Churchill's Island. A theatrical newsreel produced by the NATIONAL FILM BOARD in its CANADA CARRIES ON series. Produced, directed, edited, and written by Stuart Legg, the film was a study of Winston Churchill and the Battle of Britain. It was released internationally in 1941 with a narration by Lorne GREENE and was the first Canadian film to win an Academy Award. 22 min., b & w.

Chuvalo, George. (b.1937). Boxer. Born in Toronto and of Croatian descent, he began to fight at the age of 15 and turned professional in 1957. He won the Canadian heavyweight championship the following year and has been called the greatest Canadian heavyweight since Sam LANGFORD and Tommy

BURNS. Although he never took the world heavyweight championship, he outboxed Floyd Patterson, went 15 rounds with Cassius Clay, and has always conducted himself with dignity.

CIC. See COMMITTEE FOR AN INDEPENDENT CANADA.

CIDA. Acronym of the CANADIAN INTERNATIONAL DEVELOPMENT AGENCY.

Cider. Beverage made from apples. 'Hard' cider is a fermented alcoholic drink, while 'sweet' cider is unfermented. The cider-making process was brought to Quebec by early settlers from Normandy. Cider is now produced in Quebec, southern Ontario, and the Okanagan Valley of British Columbia.

CIIA. Initials of the CANADIAN INSTITUTE OF INTERNATIONAL AFFAIRS.

C-I-L. Initials of Canadian Industries Limited, a Hamilton-based chemical manufacturing company. Dating back to the founding of the Hamilton Power Company in 1862, it became Canadian Explosives Ltd (CXL) in 1910 and Canadian Industries Limited (C-I-L) in 1927. It now manufactures, directly and through subsidiaries, heavy and industrial chemicals, explosives, ammunition, and paints, etc.

Cinderella of Confederation. Term applied to Manitoba by Premier John Norquay in his budget speech of 1884.

Cinderella of the Empire. Term applied to Newfoundland by Lord Rosebery, prime minister of Great Britain (1894-5).

Cinema Canada. A monthly film magazine published in Toronto. Originally called *Canadian Cinematographer*, it acquired its present name in 1972. It concentrates on Canadian film information, analysis, and opinion. See also MOTION.

Cinémathèque québécoise, La. An important film archive in Montreal. Founded by Guy Côté as Connaissance du Cinéma in 1962, it became La Cinémathèque canadienne in 1964 and acquired its present name in 1972. Directed by Robert Daudelin, it maintains an impressive collection of Canadian and world animation material.

CIPA. Initials of the CANADIAN INSTITUTE ON PUBLIC AFFAIRS.

Cipaille. Fowl and game pie. The traditional Quebec and Maritime recipes use five layers of crust.

'Circle Game, The'. Title of Joni MITCHELL'S first big hit song. Sung at the MARIPOSA FOLK FESTIVAL in 1966, the song's refrain runs: 'And the seasons they go 'round and 'round/Painted ponies they go up and down./We're captive on the carousel of time;/We can't return, we can only look/Behind from where we came and go 'round/And 'round and 'round in the circle game.' It is also the title of Margaret ATWOOD'S first book of poems, published in 1966.

Circumpolar Sea. Fabulous river depicted by imaginative cartographers of the past as circling a great island on which was situated the NORTH POLE.

Cisco. One of several varieties of small white fish found in the Great Lakes and in eastern Canadian rivers. The word is derived from the Ojibwa.

Citadel, Halifax. A massive British fortification on Citadel Hill overlooking HALIFAX, N.S. It was built between 1828 and 1856 on the spot where Cornwallis erected a fort in 1749. Although never attacked, the Citadel was manned by British troops until 1900. It gives its name to a national historic park. The Town (or Garrison) Clock, set in a tower on the hill, was designed in Classical fashion by the Duke of KENT.

Citadel, Quebec. Situated 320 ft above the St Lawrence on CAPE DIAMOND and dominating the river at a narrows, it contains 25 buildings, only two of which date from the French régime: a small redoubt in the King's Bastion begun in 1693—the first 'citadelle'—and a powder magazine in the Cape Diamond Bastion, built in the early 1750s. Further buildings were added in 1797-9 and 1801-4. The main building program took place from 1820 to 1832, including the officers' quarters (1828-31)—since 1872 the summer residence of the GOVERNOR GENERAL—and the main powder magazine (now the chapel). An armoury was built in the late 1830s and the hospital in 1848.

Citadel Hill. See Halifax CITADEL.

Citadel Theatre. Regional repertory theatre in Edmonton, Alta. Created and managed by Joseph Shoctor, an Edmonton lawyer and producer, the Citadel takes its name from a Salvation Army meeting hall that was completely renovated for its opening production, Edward Albee's *Who's Afraid of Virginia Woolf?*, on 8 Nov. 1965. A touring company, Citadel-on-Wheels, was organized in 1968.

Cité libre. A quarterly journal published in Montreal from 1950 to 1966. Founded by a group that included Gérard PELLETIER, Pierre Elliott TRUDEAU, and Pierre VALLIÈRES, it was concerned with civil liberties and social problems in Quebec and took a moderate reformist, anti-clerical, anti-separatist stand. Trudeau, its chief editor, turned over control to Vallières in 1964, but reassumed control when Vallières began publishing material of a separatist nature. From 1967 to 1971 its imprint appeared on a series of *Cahiers* that treated topics of a socio-economic nature.

Citizens' Coalition. A political-action group. Founded in Toronto in 1972 by Colin Brown, an insurance agent from London, Ont., it campaigns against government bureaucracy and spending, largely through regular advertisements in newspapers headed 'Ouch . . . pass it on', followed by an instance of alleged federal-government mismanagement.

Citizens' Forum. Title of an important series of adult-education programs on CBC Radio and CBC-TV. Produced with the assistance of the CANADIAN ASSOCIATION FOR ADULT EDUCATION, which established across the country discussion groups called 'listening groups' and published literature to accompany the series, it presented weekly talks and discussions on perennial problems and the issues of the day. The urban counterpart of the NATIONAL FARM RADIO FORUM, it began as a segment of that series on 10 Nov. 1941, and later became known as 'Of Things to Come'. Half-hour panel and discussion shows—and even an early 'open-line' program—were broadcast on radio through the 1940s and 1950s. In Feb. 1945 it acquired its present name. A series of 13 half-hour discussions was produced simultaneously for television and radio, the TV series beginning on 25 Oct. 1955, the radio series two days later. 'Citizens' Forum' was seen and heard intermittently until the mid-1960s.

Citizenship. Status conferred by birth on natural-born Canadians and, by the Canadian Citizenship Act of 1952, on naturalized Canadians. For an immigrant to acquire Canadian citizenship, he or she must gain admission as a LANDED IMMIGRANT for permanent residence; meet the RESIDENCE REQUIREMENT of five years; speak at least one of the two official languages; be of good character; possess a knowledge of the responsibilities and privileges of citizenship; intend to live in Canada permanently; and be ready to take the OATH OF ALLEGIANCE.

Citizenship Act, Canadian. See CANADIAN.

City Bank. See MERCANTILE BANK OF CANADA.

City Magazine. A publication that has ap-

peared eight times a year since 1974 in Toronto. It reports on controversial urban issues across Canada in a lively, critical style and includes articles that deal with city politics, architecture, planning, community organization, and land development.

City of Gold. Documentary film on DAWSON, written and narrated by Pierre BERTON and produced by the NFB in 1957. Directed by Wolf KOENIG and Colin LOW and produced by Tom DALY, it is a nostalgic recreation of Dawson during the KLONDIKE GOLD RUSH and in its later 'ghost-town' phase. The film uses vintage photographs and won many awards. 21 min., 40 sec.; b & w.

'City of the End of Things, The'. Poem by Archibald LAMPMAN. It appeared in his first collection of verse, *Among the Millet* (1888). A philosophical poem, it is a nightmarish vision of lifeless industrialism.

Civic holiday. Holiday observed in Alberta, Manitoba, Ontario, and the Northwest Territories. In Alberta it is known as Alberta Heritage Day. It is held on the first Monday in August and was proclaimed solely to create a long summer weekend between DOMINION DAY weekend in July and LABOUR DAY weekend in September.

Civil Elegies. Poetry collection by Dennis LEE first published in 1968. It was expanded from seven to nine poems and republished as *Civil Elegies and Other Poems* in 1972. From the vantage point of Toronto's Nathan Phillips Square, Lee documents his own complicity in the country's 'failures of nerve and sellouts'.

Civil Service Commission. See PUBLIC SERVICE COMMISSION.

CIV/n. An important 'little magazine' of poetry and reviews, seven issues of which appeared in 1953-4. Published in Montreal by Aileen Collins, it included poems by Louis DUDEK, D.G. JONES, Irving LAYTON, Raymond SOUSTER, Phyllis WEBB, etc. The title is a contraction of 'civilization' and alludes to a line by Ezra Pound: 'Civ/n not a one-man job'.

CJBC. Call letters of CBC Radio's French network station in Toronto, one of two CBC Radio outlets in the city. CJBC was originally a commercial station of Jarvis Street Baptist Church, but became the flagship station of the CBC's Dominion Network in 1944. In 1964, two years after the Dominion Network folded, CJBC was turned into a full French-language network station to much controversy. BC in the call letters stands for 'Baptist Church'.

CJBC Views the Shows

CJBC Views the Shows. A magazine-format program on the arts carried weekly by CJBC in Toronto from Oct. 1949 to Sept. 1964. The CBC Radio program, originally produced by Helen James, featured three regular reviewers: Nathan COHEN on theatre, Doris Mosdell on movies, and William Krehm on music. Other contributors included Gerald PRATLEY and George ROBERTSON. It was not only a training ground for critics but a major source of literate and informed criticism of the arts in Toronto for over a decade. The 30-minute program was the local equivalent of the national CRITICALLY SPEAKING.

CJEPS. Acronym of the CANADIAN JOURNAL OF ECONOMICS AND POLITICAL SCIENCE.

CL-13 (The Sabre). A series of jet fighters built by CANADAIR LIMITED, Montreal, under licence from North American Aviation. Basically the F-86-E, the aircraft was developed through several marks. Later versions, powered by the Canadian Orenda engine, were markedly superior to the American counterpart. From 1950 to 1958, 1,815 aircraft were produced for the RCAF and NATO countries.

CL-44. A series of turboprop airliners built by CANADAIR LIMITED, Montreal, and based on the British Britannia. The CL-44-6 Long Range Transport served with the RCAF as the Yukon. From this the CL-44D4 Swing Tail Cargo Transport was developed. The latter was later 'stretched' to become the CL-44J, carrying 189 passengers transatlantic. The first flight of this aircraft was in 1960. Powered by the Rolls-Royce Tyne 12 turboprop engine, it has a payload of 64,000 lb.

CL-84. A series of aircraft designed and built by CANADAIR LIMITED, Montreal, the prototype of which first flew in May 1965. A tilt-wing feature enables the aircraft to achieve vertical take-off and transition to forward flight at a cruising speed of 350 m.p.h. Three CL-84-1 tilt-wing VSTOL operational evaluation aircraft were produced for the Canadian Armed Forces.

CL-215. A series of twin-engined multi-purpose amphibious aircraft designed and built by CANADAIR LIMITED, Montreal, and used by four countries in forest protection (with a payload of 12,000 lb. of water or retardent) as a crop-spraying utility transport, and for search, rescue, and patrol. The prototype flew in Oct. 1967, and the aircraft is still in production. It is capable of scooping a full payload from a body of water in under 20 seconds.

CLA. Initials of the CANADIAN LIBRARY ASSOCIATION.

Clancy, Frank Michael (King) (b.1903). Colourful hockey figure. Born in Ottawa, the son of a notable OTTAWA ROUGH RIDERS football player who bore the same nickname, 'King' Clancy became a professional hockey player at the age of 18, first with the Ottawa Senators and then with the TORONTO MAPLE LEAFS. He retired after 16 seasons and became coach, referee, manager, and then executive vice-president of the Leafs. His long experience, genial wit, and verbal fluency have made him a popular public speaker, especially for charitable functions. He was elected to the Hockey HALL OF FAME in 1958.

Clarence S. Campbell Bowl. Presented annually to 'the team finishing in first place in the Western Division at the end of the regular championship schedule' by the NATIONAL HOCKEY LEAGUE. The silver bowl, crafted in 1878, was first presented in 1968 in recognition of the services of Clarence S. Campbell, League president since 1946. The Clarence S. Campbell Bowl is to the Western Division what the PRINCE OF WALES TROPHY is to the Eastern Division.

Clark, Charles Joseph (b.1939). Leader of the Opposition. Born in High River, Alta, and educated at the University of Alberta and Dalhousie University, he was a journalist and university lecturer until he became first special assistant to Davey Fulton and then executive assistant to Robert STANFIELD. Joe Clark first entered federal politics in 1972 as a Progressive Conservative and was elected leader of the party at a convention on 22 Feb. 1976.

Clark, Gregory (b.1892). Newspaperman and humorist. Born in Toronto, the son of Joseph T. Clark, editor of *Saturday Night* and later of the *Toronto Star*, he became one of the *Star*'s best-known reporters and feature writers. His career at the *Star* and the STAR WEEKLY—which included the period in the 1920s when Morley CALLAGHAN, Ernest Hemingway, and Gordon SINCLAIR were also on staff—extended from 1911 to 1947. He then accompanied Jimmy FRISE to the *Montreal Herald* and WEEKEND MAGAZINE, for which he still writes his light, humorous, story-like articles. These have been collected in numerous volumes, the most recent being *Greg's Choice* (1968), *May Your First Love Be Your Last* (1969), and *The Bird of Promise* (1973).

Clark, Paraskeva (b.1898). Painter. Born in Leningrad, she studied and worked in theatre decoration there. In 1923 she moved to Paris, where in 1931 she married Philip Clark, a Canadian, and moved to Toronto.

She came into her own as a dynamic painter in Canada, producing a memorable and well-known *Self-portrait* (1933, the artist), landscapes, and still lifes.

Clark, S.D. (b.1910). Sociologist. Born in Lloydminster, Alta, he joined the University of Toronto in 1938 to lecture in sociology and became the department's first chairman in 1963. He was a pioneer in obtaining recognition for sociology as a separate discipline and in relating sociology and history. His major works are *The Social Development of Canada* (1942); *Church and Sect in Canada* (1948); *Movements of Political Protest in Canada* (1959); *The Developing Canadian Community* (1962; rev. 1968); and a book of essays, *The Suburban Society* (1966).

Clarke, Andy. See NEIGHBOURLY NEWS.

Clarke, Austin C. (b.1932). Novelist. Born in Barbados, he settled in Canada in 1956 and graduated from the University of Toronto. His lively fiction, rich with the rhythms of Barbadian speech, combines bitterness and humour. His first two novels studied the lot of the discontented in Barbados: *The Survivors of the Crossing* (1964) and *Among Thistles and Thorns* (1965). His trilogy—*The Meeting Point* (1967), *Storm of Fortune* (1973), and *The Bigger Light* (1974)—recreates the experiences of Barbadians living in Toronto. His stories are collected in *When He Was Free and Young and He Used to Wear Silks* (1971).

Clarke, Irwin and Company Limited. Educational and trade publishing house. It was founded in Toronto in 1930 by W.H. Clarke, his wife Irene, and her brother John C. Irwin (who later left the business to found the Book Society of Canada), principally to publish textbooks. Gradually the firm moved into trade publishing. It is now headed by Dr W.H. Clarke, the son of two of the founders.

Clarkson, Adrienne (b.1939). Television personality and author. Born in Hong Kong of Chinese ancestry, she was brought to Ottawa in 1941 and was educated at the University of Toronto. She was co-host with Paul Soles on CBC-TV's TAKE 30 (1965-73) and, with Warner Troyer, is the regular on-camera personality on 'The Fifth Estate', which made its début on 16 Sept. 1975. In addition she has written two wry romances, *A Lover More Condoling* (1968) and *Hunger Trace* (1970).

Clarkson, Gordon & Co. The country's oldest, largest, and leading firm of chartered accountants. It was established in Toronto in 1864 by Thomas Clarkson, an English trustee and receiver. Toronto-born Col. H.D.L. Gordon joined the firm in 1913. Clarkson, Gordon, with branches in major cities across Canada, has been called 'the Eton of Canadian commerce'. There are two related firms: Woods, Gordon & Co., Management Consultants, formed with J.D. Woods Co. Ltd in 1939; and The Clarkson Company Limited, a firm of trustees and receivers, established in 1954.

Classic Bookshops. Bookstore chain founded by Louis Melzack. Born in Montreal in 1914, Melzack opened a second-hand magazine and book shop on Bleury St, Montreal, when he was 13 and a bookstore on St Catherine St W. in 1938. He began to expand the business in 1952. In 1976 there were 54 stores across the country—including 12 in Montreal proper and 7 in Toronto—and two in New York.

Clayton-Thomas, David (b.1945). Rock singer. Born in Toronto, he became known in the late sixties as 'the voice' of the American-based rock group 'Blood, Sweat and Tears'. His baritone growl was the highlight of such hits as 'Spinning Wheel' and 'Lucretia MacEvil'. The group's album, *Spinning Wheel* (1971), sold nine million copies.

CLC. Initials of the CANADIAN LABOUR CONGRESS.

CLDL. Initials of the CANADIAN LABOUR DEFENCE LEAGUE.

Clear Grits. See GRITS.

Cleghorn, Sprague (1890-1956). Hockey player. Born in Montreal, he was famed for his robust style and effective defensive play in 17 seasons with the New York Crescents, Renfrew Millionaires, Montreal Wanderers, Ottawa Senators, and MONTREAL CANADIENS. His brother 'Odie' Cleghorn was also an excellent player and had a notable career.

Clergy reserves. Crown lands set aside in UPPER CANADA (Ontario) and LOWER CANADA (Quebec) under the CONSTITUTIONAL ACT OF 1791 'for the support and maintenance of a Protestant clergy'. This was interpreted by some as meaning that the revenue from the sale of these uncultivated tracts would support the Church of England. The clergy reserves remained a contentious issue until they were secularized in 1854.

Clerk of the House. Title of the chief administrative officer of the HOUSE OF COMMONS. The Clerk is responsible for all officers and papers and records of the House, records divisions when votes are taken, and is consulted on procedural and other matters.

Clockmaker

Clockmaker, The. See SAM SLICK.

Close-Up. A CBC-TV series of 'personal journalism'. It ran for 30 minutes on Sunday evenings from 6 Oct. 1957 to 25 Aug. 1963. It was originated and produced for four years by Ross McLEAN and starred such TV regulars as Pierre BERTON, Elaine Grand, Percy SALTZMAN, and J. Frank WILLIS.

Closure. Motion by a cabinet minister in the HOUSE OF COMMONS to shorten debate on a bill. An extreme measure, closure was first invoked to ensure the speedy passage of the Naval Aid Bill in 1913, and has been used on other occasions, including the PIPELINE DEBATE of 1956.

Cloutier, Cécile (b.1930). Poet. Born in Quebec City and a graduate of Université Laval and the Sorbonne, she is a professor of French at the University of Toronto. Her poems, which are imaginative and personal responses to the world's contradictions, appear in such collections as *Mains de sable* (1960), *Cuivre et soies* (1964), *Cannelles et craies* (1969), *Paupières* (1970), and *Cablogrammes* (1972).

Clovis culture. Archaeological term for the culture of the first inhabitants of parts of North America. Remains of Clovis man, who may have emigrated from Asia about 10,000 B.C., have been found in eastern Canada. Plano man, his descendant, immigrated to western Canada. Archaic man, the descendant of Plano man, settled in southern Ontario about 3,500 B.C.; from Archaic man came the native Indian and Eskimo peoples and their cultures. Both Clovis and Plano are names of cities in Texas where traces of these early cutlures were first found and described. The word Archaic is used by anthropologists for early cultures that were not fully developed.

CLP. Initials of the CANADIAN LABOUR PARTY.

CLU. Initials of the CANADIAN LABOUR UNION.

Clubs, Private. According to Peter C. Newman in *The Canadian Establishment: Volume One* (1975), there are in Canada only seven private clubs for business executives and others that rank as 'national institutions', these being the MOUNT ROYAL CLUB, NATIONAL CLUB, RIDEAU CLUB, ST JAMES'S CLUB, TORONTO CLUB, VANCOUVER CLUB, and YORK CLUB. Of somewhat lesser importance are the following: Halifax Club (Halifax), Union Club (Saint John), Garrison Club (Quebec City), St Denis Club (Montreal), Mount Stephen Club (Montreal), Montreal Racket Club (Montreal), Hamilton Club (Hamilton), Albany Club (Toronto), University Club (Toronto), London Club (London), Manitoba Club (Winnipeg), Assiniboia Club (Regina), Edmonton Club (Edmonton), Ranchmen's Club (Calgary), Petroleum Club (Calgary), Terminal City Club (Vancouver), Lawn Tennis and Badminton Club (Vancouver), Union Club (Victoria). Three exclusive hunting and fishing clubs are FIVE LAKES FISHING CLUB, LONG POINT COMPANY, and RISTIGOUCHE SALMON CLUB. See also ARTS AND LETTERS CLUB, BEAVER CLUB, ROYAL CANADIAN YACHT CLUB.

Clutesi, George (b.1905). Nootka artist and writer. Born on the west coast of British Columbia, he worked for 21 years as a pile driver operator before turning to painting in 1962. Before her death in 1945, Emily CARR donated brushes, oils, and canvas to Clutesi, who gradually emerged as a painter, writer, and spokesman for the Nootka and other Indian people. He completed a 40-ft mural for the Indian Pavilion at EXPO 67 and has illustrated his own two books: *Son of Raven, Son of Deer: Fables of the Tse-shaht People* (1967) has been called the first book of legends written by a Canadian Indian; *Potlatch* (1969) combines the oral tradition of his people with his own experiences in terms of the POTLATCH custom. He lives in Alberni on Vancouver Island.

CM. Member of the ORDER OF CANADA.

CMA. Initials of CENSUS METROPOLITAN AREA.

CmdO. Official abbreviation of Commissioned Officer.

Cmdre. Official abbreviation of Commodore.

CMHA. Initials of the Canadian Mental Health Association, now MENTAL HEALTH CANADA.

CMHC. Initials of the CENTRAL MORTGAGE AND HOUSING CORPORATION.

CMM. Commander of the ORDER OF MILITARY MERIT.

CMR. Initials of the COLLÈGE MILITAIRE ROYAL DE SAINT-JEAN.

CN. See CANADIAN NATIONAL RAILWAYS.

CN-CP Telecommunications. Canada's principal communications system, jointly run since 1947 by CANADIAN NATIONAL RAILWAYS and CANADIAN PACIFIC LIMITED. In addition to sending and receiving telegrams and cables, it operates such communications systems as Telex (1956), Telenet (1964), DataTelex (1966), Info-Fax (facsimile reproduction),

Telemetering (control at a distance), Broadband Exchange Service (1967), Telepost (1972), Infodat (1973), and Info-Switch (1976). Telepost, the only one of these systems used by the general public, is the telexing of messages to terminals in post offices for next-day postal delivery. CN-CP Telecommunications owns and operates the trans-Canada microwave transmission network, which consists of transmission towers located 30 mi. apart along the 5,000-mi. system between St John's and Vancouver, completed in 1964. It is also a founder of TELESAT CANADA.

CN Tower. Tallest free-standing structure in the world. Built of poured concrete and completed in 1976, it rises 1,815 ft. This soaring landmark near Toronto's harbourfront contains a restaurant, three observation decks, and radio and TV transmission facilities. It was built by CANADIAN NATIONAL RAILWAYS.

CNE. See CANADIAN NATIONAL EXHIBITION.

CNE Grandstand Show. A musical variety entertainment, the featured attraction at the CANADIAN NATIONAL EXHIBITION. The 2½-hour show, held twice daily for two weeks in the CNE grandstand before 20,000 spectators, was produced from 1952 to 1967 by Jack ARTHUR, who used to refer to the annual summer spectacle as 'the biggest show on the biggest stage on this earth'. The Arthur period was associated with the use of big-name·American acts. His wife Midge Arthur created and choreographed the well-known CANADETTES chorus line.

CNIB. Initials of the CANADIAN NATIONAL INSTITUTE FOR THE BLIND.

CNoR. Abbreviation of the CANADIAN NORTHERN RAILWAY.

CNR. Initials of CANADIAN NATIONAL RAILWAYS.

CNRV Players. The first radio drama group in Canada. In 1927 they began producing original scripts and music for radio plays from the CNR radio station in Vancouver. By 1936, the year the CBC was created, they had broadcast locally more than 250 half-hour or one-hour dramas.

CNTU. Initials of the CONFEDERATION OF NATIONAL TRADE UNIONS.

Coach House Press. Printers and publishers. Founded in Toronto in 1965 as a publishing collective by Stan Bevington, Victor COLEMAN, Frank DAVEY, and others, and originally associated with ROCHDALE COLLEGE, Coach House has specialized in fine, innovative printing and design, issuing books of poetry and fiction of an experimental, underground, avant-garde, or 'way-out' nature.

Coach House Theatre. 'Oldest little theatre group in Canada'. Founded as the University College Alumnae Dramatic Club in 1918, the all-female non-professional group chose Molière's Les Femmes savantes for its first production. Engaging men to fill the male roles, it has produced its plays in a Toronto coach house, a garage, a synagogue, and—since 1972, when it changed its name to the Fire Hall Theatre—in an abandoned fire-hall on Berkeley St. From the 1920s to the late fifties it was virtually the only non-commercial playhouse in Canada producing the works of Canadian, American, and European playwrights in both classical and experimental genres.

Coady, Father M.M. See ANTIGONISH MOVEMENT.

Coaffee, Cyril (1897-1945). Outstanding sprinter. The Winnipeg athlete, despite a crippled arm, not only won the 100-yard dash in the 1922 Canadian championships but equalled the world record of 9.6 seconds, unbeaten by any Canadian in the succeeding 25 years. He suffered a leg injury while training for the 1928 Olympics and retired.

Coal oil. See Abraham GESNER.

Coast Forest Region. Forest area on the Pacific coast. Essentially coniferous, it consists principally of western red cedar and western hemlock, with Sitka spruce in the north and Douglas fir in the south. It is an extremely important resource area, supporting a lumber industry whose output in 1970 (8 billion board feet) was the equivalent of the lumber needed to build one million wood-frame houses.

Coast Mountains. Part of the Western Cordillera, forming a wide (up to 199 mi.) range along the west coast of British Columbia. The range has many peaks over 9,800 ft, all of which have been severely glaciated. Deep fjords have been formed along the western margin of these mountains, producing a beautiful, rugged, relatively inaccessible coastline.

Coast Salish. SALISHAN-speaking Indians of the Pacific coast. There were six Coast Salish language groups: STRAIT, spoken on Vancouver Island; Halkomelen, spoken by Indian groups of the lower Fraser Canyon, and by the COWICHAN and Nanaimo; SQUAMISH; Sechelt; Pentlatch (extinct as a separate language since 1935); and COMOX. (The BELLA

COOLA speak a separate and isolated Coast Salish language.) The northern Gulf of Georgia Salish are another culturally distinct group. The Coast Salish of southern Vancouver Island, the Lower Mainland and the Fraser Valley, and northern Washington maintain a very active and growing social and ceremonial community involving winter spirit dancers and summer festivals, the highlight of which is canoe races. (These Indian summer festivals are quite distinct and separate from the many summer festivals held by neighbouring white communities.) See also INTERIOR SALISH.

Coat-of-arms. See CANADIAN COAT-OF-ARMS.

Cobalt Silver Stampede. Famous silver rush in northern Ontario. The discovery of the world's richest silver vein in Sept. 1903 led to the influx of thousands of prospectors over the next two years. The site of a major strike was named Cobalt, after the element found in the silver ore.

'Cobalt Song, The'. Title of the most widely known Canadian mining song. The words were written in 1910 by a mining engineer, L.F. Steenman, to a popular tune, 'Oh You Rosseau'. The song's refrain begins: 'For we'll sing a little song of Cobalt,/If you don't live there it's your fault.' Cobalt is a silver-mining city in northern Ontario.

Cobalt Therapy Unit. A form of radiation therapy perfected in Canada. The radioactive isotope cobalt 60, sometimes referred to as the 'cobalt bomb', was first used to treat a patient with deep-seated tumours in London, Ont., on 27 Oct. 1951. The isotopes were produced by the NRU atomic reactor at CHALK RIVER.

Coboconk. Village near Lindsay, Ont.; the name is the Algonkian word for 'swift water'. *The Political Experiences of Jimuel Briggs, D.B.* (1873) by Phillips Thompson is a political satire in the form of letters supposedly written to the *Coboconk Irradiator* by Jimuel Briggs, D.B., graduate of Coboconk University.

Cockburn, Bruce (b.1945). Singer-composer. Born in Ottawa, he played improvisational jazz in Paris before studying at the Berklee School of Music in Boston, Mass. Known for his tender and often melancholy lyrics and for a musical style based on the techniques of jazz and traditional folk idioms, he has achieved a wide North American following. He wrote the powerful score for GOIN' DOWN THE ROAD (1970).

Cockburn, James (1819-83). A FATHER OF CON-FEDERATION. Born in England, he came to Canada in 1832, trained as a lawyer, and practised law in Cobourg, C.W. (Ont.). Elected to the legislative assembly in 1861, he was a delegate to the QUEBEC CONFERENCE and at Confederation became first speaker of the House of Commons. He held this office until 1874.

Cockburn, James Pattison (1779-1847). British officer-artist. Trained in watercolour painting by Paul Sandby at the Royal Military College, Woolwich, Eng., he was stationed at Quebec from 1826 to 1836 as lieutenant-colonel in the Royal Artillery. He produced a large number of attractive, pale-toned, carefully drawn watercolours that form an accurate and wide-ranging visual record of landscapes, buildings, and people, particularly in and around Quebec as well as in Upper Canada and west to Niagara. His Quebec pictures were published in *Quebec and Its Environs* (1831). Twelve aquatint engravings—including the well-known *The Falls of Montmorency* (a picnic scene) and *The Ice Pont Formed Between Quebec and Point Levi*—appeared in 1833.

Cockfield, Brown and Company Limited. The first publicly owned Canadian advertising agency. One of the largest in Canada—with offices in Toronto, Montreal, Vancouver, London, and Winnipeg—it was formed in Toronto in 1928 as the result of a merger between Advertising Services Limited (founded by H.R. Cockfield in 1913) and National Publicity Limited (founded by G. Warren Brown in 1918). It was responsible for the publicity for EXPO 67 and went public in 1970.

Cod, Atlantic. Valuable food fish. It is found most abundantly in the northern Atlantic, especially on offshore banks. Occasionally attaining very large size, cod fished commercially usually average from 10 to 35 lb. Cod tongues and cheeks are considered a delicacy in Newfoundland. Cod develops an unpleasant odour unless cooked immediately after being caught. See also GRAND BANKS.

CODA Magazine. One of the world's leading jazz publications. This monthly trade paper, published and edited by John Norris and Bill Smith, who operate the Jazz and Blues Record Store in Toronto, combines inside information and fine critical writing on all aspects of jazz, including records and concerts. It was founded in 1958.

Codco. A contraction of 'Cod Company', the name of a lively satirical group of performers from Newfoundland. It consists of seven members—Andy Jones, Cathy Jones, Bob Joy, Greg Malone, Diane Olsen, Tommy Sexton, Mary Walsh, plus their manager Maisie Rillie—born in the 1950s in St John's, who met at Memorial University's Drama Society (MUDS). Codco first performed in Toronto in the fall of 1973, gently mocking the life-styles of their fellow Newfoundlanders. This 'commedia dell'outport' has the avowed aim of making St John's 'the centre for comedy in North America'.

Code civil. The statutory civil law enacted by the legislature of the Province of Quebec, based on the Code Napoléon. Quebec is the only province to have French civil law and English criminal law; in all other provinces non-statutory civil and criminal law derive from the COMMON LAW.

Coffin murder case. A widely reported murder trial that resulted in the hanging of Wilbert Coffin on 10 Feb. 1956. The Gaspé prospector was the last man to see three bear hunters from Pennsylvania in June 1953. When their remains were discovered, Coffin was charged with their murder in 1954. Found guilty on circumstantial evidence, he maintained his innocence to the end but was hanged in Montreal. Jacques Hébert, the Montreal publisher, wrote *I Accuse the Assassins of Coffin* (1963) in which he maintained that the Quebec government, anxious for a conviction, had railroaded Coffin to his death. A one-man Quebec Royal Commission reviewed the case in 1964 but upheld the original verdict.

Coghill, Joy (b.1926). Actress and director. Born in Findlater, Sask., and raised in Glasgow, Scot., she settled in Vancouver in 1941 and won a DOMINION DRAMA FESTIVAL acting award in 1947. She taught at the drama department of the University of British Columbia and was the founder-director in 1952 of Holiday Theatre, a troupe that takes dramatic presentations into primary and secondary schools. A director of the VANCOUVER INTERNATIONAL FESTIVAL in 1960, she succeeded Malcolm Black as artistic director of the Playhouse Theatre in Vancouver in 1967. She has continued to act on CBC Radio and TV.

Cogswell, Fred (b.1917). Poet and editor. Born in East Centreville, N.B., he graduated from the University of New Brunswick and Edinburgh University. He was associated with the FIDDLEHEAD from 1945 to 1969, for most of this period as editor. As publisher of FIDDLEHEAD POETRY BOOKS from 1959 to 1976 he provided encouragement to many new poets. He is the author of several short poetry collections, including the recent *Light*

Bird of Life: Selected Poems (1974), and the editor and translator of *Poems of Modern Quebec: An Anthology* (1975).

Cohen, Leonard (b.1934). Poet and singer. Born in Montreal and educated at McGill and Columbia Universities, he attracted considerable attention with his second book of poems in 1961 and, after his appearance at the Newport Folk Music Festival in Aug. 1967 became an international pop hero for his songs (including the popular SUZANNE) and performances. His rich, lyrical poems, which combine romanticism and anarchism, have been collected in *Let Us Compare Mythologies* (1956), *The Spice-Box of Earth* (1961), *Flowers for Hitler* (1964), *Parasites of Heaven* (1966), *Selected Poems* (1968), and *The Energy of Slaves* (1972). His novels are *The Favourite Game* (1963) and BEAUTIFUL LOSERS (1966), the former a series of stories about love, the latter a surreal novel in which Kateri TEKAKWITHA figures. His record albums include *Songs from a Room* (1968), *Songs of Leonard Cohen* (1969), and *Songs of Love and Hate* (1970). In 1965 the NATIONAL FILM BOARD produced a 41-minute film portrait of Cohen the performer: *Ladies and Gentlemen . . . Mr. Leonard Cohen*, directed by Donald BRITTAIN and Don OWEN.

Cohen, M. Charles (b.1926). Radio and television playwright. Born in Winnipeg, he has lived in Montreal as a free-lance writer since 1955. The author of many teleplays and adaptations, he is widely remembered for DAVID: CHAPTER 2 (1963) and *David: Chapter 3* (1966). He also wrote the script for *The* DRYLANDERS (1962), the first feature film in English produced by the NATIONAL FILM BOARD. He is married to the economist Dian Cohen.

Cohen, Matt (b.1942). Novelist. Born in Kingston, Ont., and educated at the University of Toronto, he has emerged as a novelist of power who writes about individuals menaced by society and their past. His novels include *Korsoniloff* (1969), *Johnny Crackle Sings* (1971), *The Disinherited* (1974), and *Wooden Hunters* (1975). His stories appear in *Columbus and the Fat Lady* (1972).

Cohen, Morris (General 'Two-Gun') (1887-1970). Canadian Jewish general in the Chinese Army. Born in London, Eng., he was sent at 16 by his father to Canada, where he worked as a ranch-hand, peddler, gambler, and real-estate speculator. Ward boss in the Chinese quarter of Edmonton in 1913, he lobbied successfully for the repeal of the head-tax clause in the Chinese Immigration Act. Three years earlier Cohen had met Sun Yat-sen, the Chinese nationalist leader then in exile, and acted as Sun's bodyguard in Edmonton in 1911. He joined Sun in China as an aide in 1922 and, after his death, advised his successor Chiang Kai-shek in 1926. Cohen helped to organize the Kuomintang Army, which awarded him the rank of general, and from 1926 to 1928 he functioned in all but name as the Nationalist war minister, taking part in military campaigns against both Communist rebels and the Japanese invaders. Captured by the Japanese at Hong Kong in 1941, he was repatriated to Canada two years later and subsequently settled in Manchester, Eng.

Cohen, Nathan (1923-71). Drama critic, broadcaster, and columnist. Born in Glace Bay, N.S., he attended Mt Allison University in Sackville, N.B., and edited the one-man labour paper, *Glace Bay Gazette* (1942-4). He worked in Toronto as an editor and writer on politics and the arts for a Communist Jewish weekly, *Vochenblatt,* and from 1948 to 1959 was the theatre critic on several CBC radio programs, including 'Across the Footlights', 'Theatre Week', CRITICALLY SPEAKING, 'Audio', and CJBC VIEWS THE SHOWS. He also published and wrote for the CRITIC (1950-4). He was moderator of FIGHTING WORDS, a CBC Radio and TV debate program, from 1953 to 1962, and later, in 1970-1, on CHCH-TV, Hamilton, Ont. He was script editor for 'Ford Radio Theatre' and 'General Motors Theatre' (1953-9), and weekly theatre critic of the TORONTO TELEGRAM (1957-9). He then joined the TORONTO STAR, where he was drama and dance critic and sometime entertainment editor until his death from kidney failure in Mar. 1971. He combined knowledgeability, intelligence, and social conscience with a provocative and outspoken manner on radio, television, and in his widely read drama columns. He judged Canadian theatre with the same rigorous standards with which he measured world drama, and helped awaken the country to the growth of regional theatres.

Coho salmon. A commercialy important species of large Pacific fish commonly found from northern California to Alaska. It is 3 ft long and weighs over 25 lb.

Coinage. See ROYAL CANADIAN MINT.

Coins, Rare. The following is a list of some of the rare Canadian decimal coins.

1936 dot 1¢ and 10¢. After the accession of Edward VIII in 1936 it was planned to put his portrait on the 1937 coins. However, he abdicated and was succeeded by George VI late in 1936. Because of a shortage of coins before the new dies of George VI were ready, the old dies of George V and date 1936 were used,

but with a raised dot under the date. Only four of each coin are known to exist; the value of each is around $5,000.

1921 5¢ silver. After this coin had been minted the government decided to issue a larger nickel coin instead of this small coin. Almost all the issue was melted and only about 400 are known still to exist.

1921 50¢. Almost the entire issue of over 200,000 was melted down in 1928, owing to a lack of demand. Only about 100 are known to exist. Their value could range from $20,000 to $40,000 each.

1911 silver dollar. Originally three silver and two bronze specimens were known to exist, all purchased by King Farouk of Egypt. When Farouk was exiled his stamp and coin collection was sold by the Egyptian government. One of these coins is in the Royal Mint Museum, one is owned by an Ontario collector, and one was in the British Museum but was stolen. Each coin could be worth over $50,000.

A useful reference work is the *Standard Catalogue of Canadian Coins, Tokens and Paper Money* (24th ed., 1976) edited by J.E. Charlton.

COJO. Acronym of the Comité Organisateur de Jeux Olympiques, the organizing committee for the OLYMPIC GAMES held in Montreal in 1976.

Col. Official abbreviation of Colonel.

Colborne, Sir John (1778-1863). Lieutenant-governor of Upper Canada from 1828 to 1836 and founder in 1829 of UPPER CANADA COLLEGE in York (Toronto). Appointed commander of the forces in 1835, he put down the REBELLION OF 1837 in Lower Canada. He was briefly governor-in-chief of British North America before returning to England in 1839. He was raised to the peerage as Baron Seaton.

Colby. A mild Canadian cheese, similar to CHEDDAR.

Coldwell, M.J. (b.1888). Leader of the Co-operative Commonwealth Federation (CCF) 1940-58. Born in Seaton, Eng., he came to Canada in 1910 and settled in Saskatchewan, where he taught school. His active involvement in politics began in the 1920s in Regina municipal politics, in teachers' federation business, and in the various farmer and labour parties that sprang up in his province. Coldwell was elected to Parliament in 1935 for Rosetown-Biggar, a seat he held for the CCF until the 1958 election. He succeeded J.S. WOODSWORTH as leader of the CCF in 1940. He presided over the party's great wartime gains, and the subsequent post-war disillusionment, with force and dignity.

Coleman, James (Jim) (b.1911). Sportswriter and commentator. Born in Winnipeg and educated at McGill University, he began his journalistic career with the *Winnipeg Tribune*. He later wrote for the *Edmonton Journal*, the Toronto *Globe and Mail*, the *Toronto Telegram*, and the *Toronto Sun*. He writes a daily sports column, syndicated by SOUTHAM PRESS, that is the most widely read in Canada. Although he covers all sports with knowledge and affection, he reserves a special warmth for horse racing, his first love. His autobiography is called *Hoofprints on My Heart* (1971).

Coleman, Victor (b.1944). Poet. Born and raised in Toronto, he was the publisher of *Island*, a 'little magazine' published in 1964-6, and the editor of COACH HOUSE PRESS from 1967 to 1973. His impressionistic, fragmentary poems appear in such collections as *Light Verse* (1969), *America* (1972), and *Speech Sucks* (1974).

Coles, George H. (1810-75). A FATHER OF CONFEDERATION. Born in Prince Edward Island, he was elected to the legislative assembly in 1842 and became premier of the province in 1851. As leader of the Opposition he attended the QUEBEC CONFERENCE but turned against the province's joining Confederation, which it did not do until 1873.

Coles Book Stores Limited. A chain of book stores established in Toronto in 1960 by Jack Cole, a specialist in the sale of publishers' remainders. The stores—of which there were 100 across Canada, with another 15 in the United States, in 1976—are directly owned or operated through associates. The chain publishes and sells COLES NOTES and 'Coles Canadian Collection', a series of paperback reprints of nineteenth-century Canadiana.

Coles Notes. Study and review aids for students. They are probably the most popular and profitable Canadian publishing venture to date. The first *Coles Note* (on Prosper Mérimée's *Colomba*) appeared in 1947. Currently 450 different titles are available. Some 30 million copies have been printed.

Colicos, John (b.1929). Actor. Born in Toronto, he acted with the Montreal Repertory Theatre before leaving for London, where he acted with the Old Vic Theatre Company from 1951 to 1953. Understudying King Lear, he replaced the principal to great acclaim on 20 Mar. 1952. He played with the STRATFORD FESTIVAL before embarking on an international film career from Hollywood in 1964. Perhaps his most celebrated role was that of Churchill in the world première in Toronto of Rolf Hochhuth's drama *Soldiers* on 28 Feb. 1968.

Collected Works of Billy the Kid, The. An award-winning book by Michael ONDAATJE published in 1970. It is a collage of lyrics, ballads, short prose narratives, and 'found' poems about the American outlaw William H. Bonney (1859-81). The first of many stage productions was at the ST LAWRENCE CENTRE on 23 Apr. 1971 in a dramatic adaptation by Martin Kinch.

Collège Militaire Royal de Saint-Jean, Le. Opened at Saint-Jean, Que., in 1952 as a triservice military school for French-speaking cadets, it is now one of three CANADIAN MILITARY COLLEGES that provide scientific and military education for future officers in the Canadian armed forces. Each year CMR graduates at the baccalaureate level some 50 Officer Cadets. See also ROYAL MILITARY COLLEGE OF CANADA, ROYAL ROADS MILITARY COLLEGE.

Collège Universitaire de Saint-Boniface. St Boniface College originated in 1818 when Bishop Provencher founded a Latin school for boys of the RED RIVER SETTLEMENT. It was incorporated as a university by the legislature in 1871 and in 1877 joined with St John's and Manitoba Colleges to form the UNIVERSITY OF MANITOBA. Today St Boniface is an affiliated college of the latter university and maintains its French Roman Catholic traditions.

Collèges d'enseignement général et professionnel. See CEGEPs.

Colleges of Applied Arts and Technology. See CAATs.

Collier, Ron (b.1930). Jazz composer, arranger, conductor. Born in Coleman, Alta, he arrived in Toronto in 1951 and founded and directed the Ron Collier Quartet in 1955 and the Ron Collier Tentet in 1960. A composer, trombonist, and conductor for radio, films, theatre, and television, he became the first jazz composer to receive a CANADA COUNCIL award in 1965.

Collip, J.B. (1892-1965). Medical researcher. Born near Belleville, Ont., he graduated from the University of Toronto with a Ph.D. in biochemistry in 1916. Asked by J.J.R. MACLEOD to work with Frederick G. BANTING and Charles H. BEST on the purification of INSULIN, he did so in 1921, claiming that his contribution to the successful project was no more than that of an ordinary biochemist. When Banting and Macleod were awarded the 1923 NOBEL PRIZE in chemistry, Banting shared his monetary award with Best, and Macleod his with Collip. The modest biochemist returned to the University of Alberta, where he developed PARA-THOR-MONE, and then moved to McGill and finally to the University of Western Ontario.

Colombo's Canadian Quotations. Dictionary of quotations published in 1974. Compiled by John Robert Colombo, it includes 6,000 remarks made by 2,500 contributors and an extensive topical and keyword index.

Colonial Advocate, The. A weekly newspaper edited and published by William Lyon MACKENZIE to further the reform cause in Upper Canada. It was published from 18 May 1824 to 4 Nov. 1834 in Queenston (in the first year) and thereafter in York (Toronto). Its often abusive attacks on the FAMILY COMPACT so angered a group of young men that on 8 June 1826 they raided the office, destroyed the press, and pitched the type into Toronto Bay. Damages of £625 enabled Mackenzie to recommence publication.

Colonial period. Period during which the colonies that eventually united to form Canada were subject to French or British governments. At the end of the SEVEN YEARS' WAR, under the Treaty of Paris of 1763, that part of North America that was called NEW FRANCE ceased to be French and became British. When the independence of the United States was recognized in 1783, Quebec (in 1791 Upper and Lower Canada), Nova Scotia (in 1784 the two provinces of Nova Scotia and New Brunswick), and the Island of St John (later Prince Edward Island) were designated BRITISH NORTH AMERICA. With CONFEDERATION on 1 July 1867 colonial status ended for the PROVINCE OF CANADA (formerly Upper and Lower Canada, now Ontario and Quebec), Nova Scotia, and New Brunswick. Manitoba joined Confederation in 1870; British Columbia in 1871; Prince Edward Island in 1873; Alberta and Saskatchewan in 1905; and Newfoundland in 1949. See also RUPERT'S LAND, NORTHWEST TERRITORIES.

Colonist cars. Second-class 'sleeping cars' on CPR trains that left Montreal each week for points on the Prairies or Vancouver from the 1880s to the 1910s. They differed from first-class cars (or Pullmans) in that the seats were not upholstered, etc. Colonists could purchase a non-returnable mattress, pillow, and blanket from the CPR agent for $2.50.

Colony to Nation. A widely read history of Canada by A.R.M. LOWER, published in 1946 (rev. 1964). Rather than a systematic general history it is more of a series of reflections whose theme is Lower's belief in the power

of nationalism to create a true communal feeling in the country and to foster its growth.

Columbia Department (or District). Administrative district of the HUDSON'S BAY COMPANY in the nineteenth century. It extended over the watershed of the Columbia R. and included the states of Washington and Oregon. Its headquarters were Fort Vancouver (now Vancouver, Wash.) on the north bank of the Columbia.

Columbia Forest Region. Forest area covering a large part of the Kootenay Valley, the upper valleys of the Thompson and Fraser Rivers, and other British Columbia lake areas. Western red cedar and western hemlock are the characteristic species in this interior 'wet belt'.

Columbia Icefield. One of several small glacier areas along the British Columbia-Alberta border. Owing to its situation in Jasper National Park, it has become better known than larger fields, like the Logan-Hubbard Icefield.

Columbia Mountains. Part of the WESTERN CORDILLERA, they consist of four parallel ranges—the Purcell, Selkirk, Monashee, and Cariboo Mountains—and are located in the southern half of British Columbia between the Rocky Mountains and the Fraser plateau.

Columbia River. Rising in Columbia Lake in the Rocky Mountains, B.C., it flows 460 mi. through Canada before entering the United States, where for part of its course it forms the Washington-Oregon boundary. Its total length is 1,200 mi. See also COLUMBIA RIVER TREATY.

Columbia River Treaty. A treaty for the co-operative development of the Columbia R. signed by Canada and the United States in 1961 and ratified in 1964. Under its terms Canada agreed to build three dams on the Canadian portion of the river: Duncan, Keenleyside, and Mica; they were completed in 1967, 1968, and 1973 respectively. Of these dams, only Mica is used to generate electricity; the others regulate and store water, making possible increased electrical power generation in the U.S. While the U.S. paid in advance for the project, it is generally conceded that Canada made a very poor bargain.

Colville, Alex (b.1920). Painter. Born in Toronto, he studied at Mount Allison University, where he taught from 1946 to 1963 after serving as a war artist. A pioneer of contemporary high realism, he is exhibited and collected internationally. His haunting and precisely composed pictures—with their hazy, sensual texture and meticulous, detailed brushwork—depict people and animals isolated in a frozen moment. They convey an element of the mystery of daily life, showing their subjects on the verge of an expected movement that captures and suspends the viewer's attention. Among his best-known paintings are *Hound in Field* (1958, NGC) and HORSE AND TRAIN (1959, AGH).

Combines Act. A federal statute that provides for the investigation of combines, monopolies, trusts, and mergers. The Combines Investigation Act (RSC, 1970, cap. C-23) was based on the Sherman anti-trust legislation in the United States.

'Come all you bold Canadians'. Title and first line of a popular ballad celebrating the victory in the WAR OF 1812 of Isaac BROCK over the American general, William Hull, at the little town of Sandwich, U.C. (Ont.), on 16 Aug. 1812. The first stanza goes: 'Come all you bold Canadians, I'd have you lend an ear/Concerning a fine ditty that would make your courage cheer,/Concerning an engagement that we had at Sandwich town,/The courage of those Yankee boys so lately we pulled down.'

Comédie-Canadienne, Théâtre de la. A leading repertory theatre founded by Gratien GÉLINAS in Montreal for the production of plays in both French and English. It opened at the Gaiety Theatre, a former vaudeville house (485 seats), on 22 Feb. 1958 with Jean Anouilh's *L'Alouette*, followed by its English version, *The Lark*. It was originally founded as 'a centre for the creation of a Canadian theatrical life', but its role was later defined 'to serve, first and foremost, the development of a national identity in the performing arts in French Canada'. Its final production was Gélinas's play YESTERDAY THE CHILDREN WERE DANCING, which opened on 11 Apr. 1966.

Comet. Automobile manufactured from 1906 to 1908 by Comet Motor Company, Montreal. It was a four-passenger open touring car, painted maroon, that sold for $5,000.

Comfort, Charles (b.1900). Painter. Born in Edinburgh, he immigrated to Winnipeg with his family in 1912, studied there and in New York, and settled in Toronto in 1925. While working as a commercial artist he developed as a serious painter of great facility, producing portraits in oil and watercolour, landscapes, and murals. In 1938 he joined the Fine Art Department of the University of Toronto and returned there after serving as a war artist from 1943 to 1946. He was director of the NATIONAL GALLERY OF CANADA from 1960 to 1965. His best-known paintings are *Young Canadian* (1932), a watercolour portrait of the painter Carl SCHAEFER in Hart House, University of Toronto, and *Tadoussac* (1935, NGC), in which the simplified forms of the church and village and the curving peninsula in the Saguenay R. make a striking design.

Cominco Ltd. The name since 1966 of the Consolidated Mining and Smelting Company of Canada Ltd, of which it is a partial acronym. The mining, metallurgical, and chemical company was formed in 1906 in Trail, B.C.—where the Sullivan base-metal mine had been discovered—as an amalgam of British Columbia mines. The head office is in Vancouver.

Commentator. See CANADIAN COMMENTATOR.

Commerce Court. Head office of the Canadian Imperial Bank of Commerce in Toronto. Designed by I. Mario Pei and built in 1972-4, it preserves the old Canadian Bank of Commerce Building (1929-31, F. DARLING and J.A. PEARSON)—at 34 storeys the tallest building in the British Empire for many years. Commerce Court includes four towers (the tallest, the West Tower, is 57 storeys) and an underground shopping mall.

Commissioner. Head of a commission; the chief executive officer who presides over a council or commission. In the NORTHWEST TERRITORIES and YUKON TERRITORY the Commissioner is the chief executive officer, appointed by the federal government, and together with a Council is responsible for the administration of the Territory. The present commissioners are James Smith (Y.T.), appointed in 1966, and S.M. Hodgson (N.W.T.), appointed in 1967.

Commissioner of Official Languages. Watchdog charged with ensuring equal status for the French and English languages. The first appointment was made in 1970. Holding office for seven years, the Commissioner is empowered to receive complaints from the public and on his own initiative to conduct investigations into alleged violations of the OFFICIAL LANGUAGES ACT, 1969. He reports annually to Parliament on the state of bilingualism in the federal government.

Committee for an Independent Canada. Nationalist organization founded in Toronto in

Committee for an Independent Canada

1970 by Walter L. GORDON, Peter C. NEWMAN, and Abraham ROTSTEIN. Aims of the CIC include more government control of foreign business operations in Canada, increased CANADIAN CONTENT of the media, more Canadian studies programs in educational institutions, a strengthened CANADA DEVELOPMENT CORPORATION, etc.

Committees of the House. Committees created by the HOUSE OF COMMONS to perform various tasks. There are five categories: Standing Committees (to study business from session to session); Special Committees (to consider and report on particular bills); Joint Committees (which meet with members of the Senate to consider specific subjects); Joint Standing Committees (combining the characteristics of Standing and Joint Committees); and the Committee of the Whole (which comprises all members of the Commons functioning as a committee).

Common law. Unwritten law, established by custom and judicial decision over many centuries, as opposed to statute or written law. Common law, both civil and criminal, was developed in England and is in use across Canada except in Quebec, where the civil law, the CODE CIVIL, is statutory only. See also LAW REPORTS.

Commoner. A member of the HOUSE OF COMMONS.

Commonwealth Air Forces Ottawa Memorial. Impressive bronze globe commemorating 822 men and women of the air forces stationed in North America who died during the SECOND WORLD WAR and have no known graves. Rising above the northeastern tip of Green Island in front of Ottawa City Hall, it was unveiled by Queen Elizabeth II on 1 July 1959.

Commonwealth citizen. Any person born or naturalized within the Commonwealth; a BRITISH SUBJECT.

Commonwealth Day. See VICTORIA DAY.

Commonwealth of Nations. A free association of sovereign independent states—together with colonies, protectorates, protected states, mandated and trust territories—united by a common allegiance to the British Crown. An outgrowth of the BRITISH EMPIRE, the Commonwealth embraces more than 30 sovereign nations, including Canada, and covers one-quarter of the earth's surface. The Commonwealth is usually dated from the passing of the STATUTE OF WESTMINSTER in 1931. The Commonwealth Secretariat, with Toronto-born external-affairs officer Arnold Smith as secretary general, was established at Marlborough House, London, in 1965.

Commonwealth Scholarships. Annual postgraduate awards. Open to all citizens of the Commonwealth, they allow unrestricted areas of study and include tuition, travel expenses, and a maintenance allowance. They are administered by the Commonwealth Scholarships Commission of the Association of Commonwealth Universities, London, Eng., and are tenable in any Commonwealth country other than the candidate's own.

Communications, Department of. Federal government department responsible for all aspects of communications in Canada. Established in 1969, it is responsible for the orderly operation of communications, the introduction of new facilities, the administration of the radio frequency spectrum, and the protection of Canadian interests in international telecommunications.

Communications Command. One of five functional commands of the CANADIAN ARMED FORCES.

Communications Technology Satellite. Experimental satellite designed and built in Canada and launched by NASA at Cape Kennedy in late 1975. CTS was sent into orbit, 22,000 mi. above the earth's surface at 116°W, as a forerunner of a new generation of high-powered satellites that will meet future communications needs.

Communist Party of Canada. A Marxist party formed in Guelph, Ont., in May-June 1921. The formation of the party took place in secret because of government repression; for much of its history the party operated in similar conditions, harassed by the government and police and largely scorned by Canadians. The period of greatest influence came during the DEPRESSION when Communists were crucial in organizing unions among the unskilled and the unemployed. Banned under the WAR MEASURES ACT, it operated from 1943 to 1959 as the LABOUR-PROGRESSIVE PARTY and supported the war effort. In co-operation with the Liberal Party, the LPP attempted to divide the socialist vote in the election of 1945, but the advent of the Cold War and of growing hostility towards the Soviet Union weakened any chances the party had for electoral success. Its national leaders were: Jack Macdonald (1922-9); Tim BUCK (1929-62); Leslie Morris (1962-4); and William Kashtan (from 1964).

Communist Party of Canada (Marxist-Len-

inist). Political group better known as 'Maoists'. It was founded in the late 1960s in Toronto by Hardial Baines as a result of the schism in theory and practice in the international Communist movement. The CPC(M-L) follows the line of Chairman Mao Tse-tung of the People's Republic of China, which is rejected by other Communist parties, including the COMMUNIST PARTY OF CANADA.

Community Colleges. Junior colleges. Community colleges generally offer a two-year program in any one of three different streams: academic, technical, or continuing adult education. The first two demand high-school qualifications: entrance can also be provided via the third stream. In Quebec they are known as CEGEPs, in Ontario as CAATs.

Comox. The more northerly of the COAST SA-LISH Indians. They live on Vancouver Island and the adjacent mainland and are strongly influenced by the neighbouring KWAKIUTL culture. Their population in 1970 was 828.

Compact Theory of Confederation. Interpretation of the BNA ACT, 1867, as a pact or agreement rather than as a federal union. This was argued especially by the province of Quebec in the late 1880s. Donald CREIGHTON has maintained, in *Canada's First Century: 1867-1967* (1970), that Confederation was 'a political union of several provinces, not a cultural compact between two ethnic communities, English and French'.

Compagnons de St Laurent, Les. Theatrical group founded by Père Émile Legault in Montreal in 1938. It grew out of a presentation of a mystery play on the steps of l'Église Saint-Laurent on the outskirts of Montreal. The company, which included Jean GASCON and Jean-Louis ROUX, remained active until 1952.

Companies, Canada's largest. Each year *The FINANCIAL POST* compiles a list of the largest Canadian companies, based on financial statements for the previous year filed with the Department of Consumer and Corporate Affairs. The following list, which appeared in greater detail in the issue of 26 July 1975, should be examined with the following provisos in mind: (i) since only federally chartered companies are required to report their assets and incomes, some provincially chartered companies may be missing from the list; (ii) some parent companies consolidate the assets and incomes of their subsidiaries, so even major subsidiaries may appear on the list only in the guise of their parent companies; (iii) no Crown corporations are listed.

HUNDRED LARGEST MANUFACTURING, RESOURCE, AND UTILITY COMPANIES
1. Ford Motor Co. of Canada
2. IMPERIAL OIL LTD
3. General Motors of Canada Ltd
4. CANADIAN PACIFIC LTD
5. Bell Canada
6. ALCAN ALUMINIUM LTD
7. Chrysler Canada Ltd
8. MASSEY-FERGUSON LTD
9. INTERNATIONAL NICKEL CO. OF CANADA LTD
10. Shell Canada Ltd
11. Gulf Oil Canada Ltd
12. Canada Packers Ltd
13. NORANDA MINES LTD
14. MacMILLAN BLOEDEL LTD
15. Steel Co. of Canada
16. MOORE CORP.
17. DOMTAR LTD
18. SEAGRAM Co.
19. BRASCAN LTD
20. Texaco Canada Ltd
21. Canadian General Electric Co.
22. Consolidated-Bathurst Ltd
23. Dominion Foundries & Steel Ltd
24. IBM Canada Ltd
25. Genstar Ltd
26. MOLSON COMPANIES LTD
27. BURNS Foods Ltd
28. TransCanada PipeLines Ltd
29. Imasco Ltd
30. Abitibi Paper Co.
31. International Harvester Co. of Canada
32. Canadian Industries Ltd (See C-I-L)
33. HIRAM WALKER-GOODERHAM & WORTS LTD
34. John LABATT LTD
35. FALCONBRIDGE NICKEL MINES LTD
36. Swift Canadian Co.
37. BP Canada Ltd
38. Husky Oil Ltd
39. Mobil Oil Canada Ltd
40. Westinghouse Canada Ltd
41. ROTHMANS OF PALL MALL CANADA LTD
42. RIO ALGOM MINES LTD
43. Anglo-Canadian Telephone Co.
44. Dominion Bridge Co.
45. Du Pont of Canada Ltd
46. Petrofina Canada Ltd
47. Northern & Central Gas Corp.
48. Crown Zellerbach Canada Ltd
49. Union Carbide Canada Ltd
50. Dominion Textile Ltd
51. Canada Cement Lafarge Ltd
52. Maple Leaf Mills Ltd
53. Canron Ltd
54. Hawker Siddeley Canada Ltd
55. Ensite Ltd
56. Price Co.
57. Dow Chemical of Canada Ltd
58. Reed Paper Ltd
59. Consumers' Gas Co.
60. Kraft Foods Ltd

Companies

61. Goodyear Canada Inc.
62. British Columbia Forest Products Ltd
63. Sun Oil Co.
64. Amoco Canada Petroleum Co.
65. Weldwood of Canada Ltd
66. Westcoast Transmission Co.
67. American Motors (Canada) Ltd
68. Hugh Russel Ltd
69. Jannock Corp.
70. Celanese Canada Ltd
71. Comstock International Ltd
72. General Foods Ltd
73. Continental Can Co. of Canada
74. Union Gas Ltd
75. Canadian Hydrocarbons Ltd
76. Neonex International Ltd
77. Lever Brothers Ltd
78. Canadian Corporate Management Co.
79. Pacific Petroleums Ltd
80. Silverwood Industries Ltd
81. Standard Brands Ltd
82. Redpath Industries Ltd
83. CANADA STEAMSHIP LINES LTD
84. White Motor Corp. of Canada Ltd
85. SOUTHAM PRESS LTD
86. Texaco Exploration Canada Ltd
87. Hudson Bay Mining & Smelting Co.
88. Total Petroleum (North America) Ltd
89. Uniroyal Ltd
90. J.M. Schneider Ltd
91. Robin Hood Multifoods Ltd
92. SHERRITT GORDON MINES LTD
93. Interprovincial Pipe Line Ltd
94. Canadian Johns-Manville Co.
95. Canadian Cellulose Co.
96. Firestone Tire & Rubber Co. of Canada
97. Rockwell International of Canada Ltd
98. Hudson's Bay Oil & Gas Co.
99. Atco Industries Ltd
100. THOMSON NEWSPAPERS LTD

Not included in the above list are the following major subsidiaries (with parent companies): Aluminum Co. of Canada (Alcan Aluminium Ltd), Northern Electric Co. (Bell Canada), COMINCO LTD (CANADIAN PACIFIC LTD), ALGOMA STEEL CORP. (Canadian Pacific Ltd), British Columbia Telephone Co. (Anglo-Canadian Telephone Co.), Canadian Pacific Air Lines Ltd (Canadian Pacific Ltd), BACM Industries Ltd (Genstar Ltd), CARLING O'KEEFE LTD (Rothmans of Pall Mall Canada Ltd), Ogilvie Flour Mills (John Labatt Ltd).

TEN LARGEST MERCHANDISERS
1. George WESTON LTD
2. DOMINION STORES LTD
3. Canada Safeway Ltd
4. Simpsons-Sears Ltd
5. STEINBERG'S LTD
6. HUDSON'S BAY CO.
7. M. Loeb Ltd
8. Oshawa Group Ltd
9. F.W. Woolworth Co.
10. WOODWARD STORES LTD

Missing from the above list is the T. EATON CO., a private firm that does not publish financial statements.

TWENTY-FIVE LARGEST FINANCIAL INSTITUTIONS
1. ROYAL BANK OF CANADA
2. CANADIAN IMPERIAL BANK OF COMMERCE
3. BANK OF MONTREAL
4. BANK OF NOVA SCOTIA
5. TORONTO DOMINION BANK
6. Sun Life Assurance Co. of Canada
7. Banque Canadienne Nationale
8. Royal Trust Co.
9. Manufacturers Life Insurance Co.
10. Banque Provinciale du Canada
11. Huron & Erie Mortgage Corp.
12. Canada Permanent Mortgage Corp.
13. London Life Insurance Co.
14. IAC Ltd
15. Great-West Life Assurance Co.
16. Canada Life Assurance Co.
17. Mutual Life Assurance Co. of Canada
18. Confederation Life Insurance Co.
19. Crown Life Insurance Co.
20. General Motors Acceptance Canada
21. Victoria & Grey Trust Co.
22. Guaranty Trust Co. of Canada
23. National Trust Co.
24. Traders Group Ltd
25. North American Life Assurance Co.

Companion of the Order of Canada. See ORDER OF CANADA.

Company, The. A reference to the HUDSON'S BAY COMPANY.

Company of New France. A means of colonization founded by Cardinal Richelieu in 1627 (also called the Company of One Hundred Associates). In return for title to all the lands claimed by NEW FRANCE and a monopoly of the fur trade, the 100 or more shareholders were supposed to establish 4,000 settlers in the colony by 1643. The population was only 2,500 when their charter was revoked in 1663.

Company of Young Canadians. A domestic peace corps. The CYC was established in 1966 as a CROWN CORPORATION and consisted of full-time paid volunteers between the ages of 18 and 28 who worked with community groups on projects concerned with such matters as legal aid, welfare, native rights, and education. The volunteers were chosen directly by the community group seeking CYC support. The program was discontinued in 1975. See also CUSO.

Comparisons Series. 14 films produced by the NFB between 1959 and 1964. Each film compares similar aspects of life in Canada and in two or three other countries. The one on cities finds similarities and contrasts in city squares in Montreal, Athens, and Bangkok. The one on fishermen compares fishing in the Aegean, the Gulf of Siam, and the Atlantic Ocean. Many of the films were directed by Julian Biggs. 30 min., b & w.

Composers, Authors and Publishers Association of Canada. Non-profit organization established to administer performing rights. CAPAC, founded in Toronto as the Canadian Performing Rights Society in 1925, is owned by 3,500 Canadian composers, lyric writers, and publishers. Its main function is to arrange for international copyright protection and to license the public performance of music. See also BMI CANADA LIMITED.

Comrades in Arms. A CBC Radio series devoted to the war effort. Produced by J. Frank WILLIS from 2 Oct. 1942 to May 1945, it dramatized Second World War incidents involving the army, navy, and air force.

Conacher, Charles (1909-67). Hockey player. Born in Toronto, the younger brother of Lionel CONACHER, he played professional hockey for 13 years, nine of them with the TORONTO MAPLE LEAFS, and was a member of the famed 'Kid' line composed of Harvey (Busher) Jackson, Joe Primeau, and Conacher. For four consecutive seasons he was leading scorer in the NHL and is still reputed to have had the hardest shot in all hockey history.

Conacher, Lionel (1900-54). Outstanding sports figure who was dubbed 'The Big Train'. The Toronto-born athlete participated in eight different sports and starred in five (boxing, baseball, lacrosse, football, and hockey). In one GREY CUP football game he scored 15 points; in two successive hockey seasons he played on STANLEY CUP winning teams, each with a different club. He became chairman of the Ontario Athletic Commission and was elected to both the provincial and federal Parliaments. In 1950, four years before his death during a parliamentary-press football game, he was voted 'Canada's all-round athlete of the half-century'. In 1963 he was elected to the Football HALL OF FAME and in 1965 to the Lacrosse HALL OF FAME. He was the brother of Charles CONACHER.

Conan, Laure. Pseudonym of Félicité ANGERS.

Concession. A division of land. In NEW FRANCE the seigneuries were divided into concessions that fronted on a river or a road. In UPPER and LOWER CANADA the unit of survey

was a TOWNSHIP, and these were divided into concessions for settlement. The size and layout of the concessions within a township varied at different times and places, but concession roads were laid between parcels of lots in a grid pattern, and side roads were built along the boundaries of concessions at right angles to the concession roads. Front concessions were the lots laid out along the baseline marking the beginning of a township; back concessions were the lots behind these and came to signify a rural region. The term comes from the French word *concession*, meaning 'grant'.

Concordia University. Created by order-in-council on 24 Aug. 1974, it is an amalgamation of two local colleges: Sir George Williams University (founded by the YMCA in downtown Montreal in 1873, becoming independent in 1929) and Loyola College (founded for Catholic instruction in Montreal's west end in 1899 and affiliated with the UNIVERSITÉ DE MONTRÉAL). 'Concordia' is Latin for 'harmony'. Protesting unproved charges of racial discrimination, 93 West Indian and Canadian students rioted and occupied the Computer Centre of Sir George Williams in the Henry F. Hall building in downtown Montreal on 29 Jan. 1969. They held off the police for 13 days and finally smashed and burned the main computer to an estimated damage of $2 million. The ringleaders were charged and, by 1976, had been fined, imprisoned, or deported.

Coneybeare, Rod (b.1930). Writer and performer of humorous material on CBC Radio. Born in Belleville, Ont., he delights in a pixieish sense of satire. 'Thanks, I think I deserve this,' he said, accepting a NELLIE as best radio documentary writer at the 1974 ACTRA AWARDS.

Confederation. The creation on 1 July 1867 of the Dominion of Canada by an act of the British Parliament known as the BNA ACT. The union of the British colonies of North America had been proposed at various times. In the minds of its proponents it would increase trade and economic prosperity, strengthen the colonies militarily in case of attack from the United States, create a government capable of securing and developing the Northwest, and make possible the building of a railway that would contribute to the realization of all these ambitions. North American union was first openly discussed at the CHARLOTTETOWN CONFERENCE in Sept. 1864. At the QUEBEC CONFERENCE in Oct. 1864 delegates adopted the SEVENTY-TWO RESOLUTIONS, which outlined the principles of federation later incorporated in the BNA Act. Con-

Confederation

federation was given final form at the LONDON CONFERENCE in Dec. 1866. Because of strong local loyalties, John A. MACDONALD'S arguments for a unitary system were rejected. Even the federal system, which had been adopted by the delegates at Quebec, was rejected by the governments of Prince Edward Island and Newfoundland. The newly created Dominion, therefore, consisted of the Province of Canada (now divided into the provinces of Ontario and Quebec), Nova Scotia, and New Brunswick. Manitoba joined in 1870, British Columbia in 1871, Prince Edward Island in 1873, Alberta and Saskatchewan in 1905, and Newfoundland in 1949.

Confederation, Only living Father of. See ONLY LIVING FATHER OF CONFEDERATION.

Confederation Centre of the Arts. Nonprofit arts centre at Charlottetown, P.E.I. It was built to celebrate the centenary of the CHARLOTTETOWN CONFERENCE that preceded Confederation. The cost of the building, of which Dimitri Dimakopoulos of Montreal was the chief architect, was shared by provincial and federal grants. Officially opened by Queen Elizabeth II in 1964, it contains a 946-seat theatre that houses the CHARLOTTETOWN SUMMER FESTIVAL, which opened in July 1965. The Music Department has a 40-voice choir, a Boys' Choir, and a Madrigal Choir, directed by Mark La Roux. An Art Gallery and Museum, which opened in 1964, is directed by Dr Moncrieff Williamson and exhibits primarily works by Canadian artists—notably Robert HARRIS—and contemporary fine crafts.

Confederation Day. See DOMINION DAY.

Confederation Debates. See SEVENTY-TWO RESOLUTIONS.

Confederation of National Trade Unions. An association of Catholic unions, mostly in Quebec. Its French name is Confédération des Syndicats Nationaux. Its origins go back to Quebec City in 1901, when a union of shoe workers accepted the social doctrine of the Catholic Church. The first union to restrict membership solely to Catholics was La Fédération Ouvrière Mutuelle du Nord de Chicoutimi in 1912. Other unions accepted as a guide the encyclical *De rerum novarum* (*The Conditions of the Working Classes*) of Pope Leo XIII, published on 15 May 1891. The National Central Trades and Labour Council of the District of Quebec was formed in 1918 from two major unions, and in September of that year a provincial conference was called that developed into an annual convention. From

this grew the Canadian and Catholic Federation of Labour, or Confédération des Travailleurs Catholiques du Canada, on 1 Jan. 1922. It has been known as the Confederation of National Trade Unions (CNTU) since 1960 and no longer accords the Church such a dominant role.

Confederation Square. Central square in OTTAWA. The area of two acres was given its present name in 1912. Dominating the Square is the NATIONAL WAR MEMORIAL and from it may be seen the CHÂTEAU LAURIER, the LORNE BUILDING, the NATIONAL ARTS CENTRE, the PARLIAMENT BUILDINGS, and the RIDEAU CANAL.

Congé. A permit to enter Indian country issued by the governor of NEW FRANCE, from the French word for 'leave' or 'permission'.

Conklin Shows Ltd. Largest midway concessionaires in the world. The company was founded in Winnipeg in 1929 by J.W. (Patty) Conklin (1892-1970), a Brooklyn-born carnival operator who, in 1924, went into partnership with Speed Garrett, the operator of shows in western Canada. In 1937 Conklin bid successfully for the midway franchise to the CANADIAN NATIONAL EXHIBITION and in that year he supplied new rides and other concessions and opened the world's first Kiddieland. The company also supplies midways to the Western Ontario Fair in London, the Amusement Park at Crystal Beach, and to 10 county fairs in Ontario and Quebec. Since 1970 it has been managed by J.F. (Jim) Conklin, Patty's son, who was born in Toronto in 1933.

Conn Smythe Trophy. Presented annually 'to the most valuable player for his team in the entire playoffs' by the NATIONAL HOCKEY LEAGUE. It was presented by MAPLE LEAF GARDENS in 1964 to honour Conn SMYTHE, former coach, manager, and president and owner-governor of the TORONTO MAPLE LEAFS. The winner, who is chosen by the Professional Hockey Writers' Association, receives a cup and $1,500.

Connaught, Duke of (1850-1942). GOVERNOR GENERAL of Canada from 1911 to 1916.

Connaught Laboratories. World-famous publically owned pharmaceutical house. Established by the University of Toronto and named after the governor general, the Duke of Connaught, in 1913, it manufactures vaccines and anti-toxins for international use. Since 1921 it has had the franchise for INSULIN in Canada. Connlab—or Connaught Medical Research Laboratories—was acquired by the

CANADA DEVELOPMENT CORPORATION in June 1972.

Connaught Tunnel. Railway tunnel at ROGERS PASS. Cut for the CPR line that crosses the Selkirks, it is 5 mi. in length and the longest in Canada. It was named after the Duke of Connaught, governor general from 1911 to 1916, and was officially opened on 9 Dec. 1916.

Connolly, Joseph (1839-1904). Architect. Born in Limerick, he trained in the office of McCarthy of Dublin, Ireland's most prolific church architect. In the 1860s he came to Toronto, where his work was almost exclusively for the Roman Catholic Church—in an elaborately correct French Gothic style—and included additions to St Michael's Cathedral, Toronto; St Mary's Bathurst St, Toronto (1885); St Mary's, Guelph (designed 1863, built 1876-1926); the façade and tower of the Cathedral in Kingston (1890); St Peter's Cathedral, London; St Paul's, Power St, Toronto (1890—but Florentine Renaissance rather than Gothic); and numerous other churches across the province.

Connor, Ralph (1860-1937). Novelist. 'Ralph Connor' was the pseudonym of Charles William Gordon, who was born in Glengarry County, C.W. (Ont.), and educated at the University of Toronto and Edinburgh University. He was ordained into the Presbyterian ministry in 1890, and became the minister of St Stephen's Church, then outside Winnipeg, in 1894. He served as the senior Protestant chaplain to the Canadian forces in the First World War and as moderator of the Presbyterian Church in 1921 prior to its becoming part of the UNITED CHURCH OF CANADA. Under his pen name he published more than 30 novels, many of them bestsellers in their time and some of them of interest today—he may well be the most popular novelist Canada has ever had. His romantic stories—excitingly and vividly told with lively characterizations and unashamed emotionalism—celebrate the commitment to religion of strong men and women. Among his best-known books are *Black Rock* (1898), a tale of the Selkirks; *The* SKY PILOT (1899); *The* MAN FROM GLENGARRY (1901); and GLENGARRY SCHOOL DAYS (1902). His autobiography, *Postscript to Adventure* (1938), was edited by his son J. King Gordon.

Connors. Newfoundland name for inshore sea bass. This fish is seldom eaten by Newfoundlanders but is popular with visitors from the mainland.

Connors, Stompin' Tom (b.1934). Country singer. Born in Skinner's Pond, P.E.I., he held down odd jobs until his first single, 'BUD THE SPUD', was a great success in 1969. A popular performer, he enlivens the songs he writes by making them very local in reference.

Conscription. The popular term by which compulsory military service is known in Canada. Although there had been various forms of conscription in the statutes from the French régime through to and after Confederation, compulsory military service was not a major issue until the First World War. After high casualties and declining enlistments threatened to deplete the Canadian divisions in France, Sir Robert BORDEN's government introduced the Military Service Act in 1917. It passed Parliament and led to the creation of a UNION GOVERNMENT of Liberals and Tories. English Canadians in general supported the measure; French Canadians in particular opposed it. The measure produced very few men for the front lines.

Conscription again became an issue in the Second World War. The Mackenzie KING government, pledged not to impose compulsory overseas service, first introduced conscription for home service in the NATIONAL RESOURCES MOBILIZATION ACT of 1940. Early in 1942 the government conducted a plebiscite seeking release from its promises against conscription. English Canada granted release by a large majority; French Canadians opposed it bitterly. As it turned out there was no military need of any kind for conscription until the late fall of 1944, when casualties in France, Italy, and the Low Countries temporarily outran infantry reinforcements. After a cabinet crisis, King agreed to send 16,000 home-defence conscripts overseas. Very few of these men made it to the front before the war ended in May 1945.

Conscription became a subject of concern in 1951 once more when the ST LAURENT government flirted with the idea in the event of a major anti-Soviet war. More recently the subject has been mentioned for its 'therapeutic' values, its ability to 'straighten out' today's youth. But given the unhappy U.S. experience with the draft in the Viet Nam war, the practicality of conscription in Canada seems limited indeed.

Conseil législatif. The upper appointed house in the Quebec legislature, abolished in 1968. See ASSEMBLÉE NATIONALE.

Conservative Party. See PROGRESSIVE CONSERVATIVE PARTY.

Consolidated Revenue Fund. Aggregate of

all public money on deposit to the credit of the RECEIVER GENERAL FOR CANADA. The BANK OF CANADA and chartered banks are the custodians of such public money, and no payment out of this fund may be made without parliamentary authority.

Conspicuous Gallantry Medal. Commonwealth decoration for acts of pre-eminent bravery, first awarded to non-commissioned officers and men of the Royal Navy in 1874. The abbreviation is CGM.

Constitution, Canadian. See BNA ACT, 1867.

Constitutional Act of 1791. An act dividing Quebec into the provinces of UPPER and LOWER CANADA and providing government institutions that superficially resembled those of Britain. It was enacted as a result of the migration of some 10,000 Loyalists into Quebec following the American Revolution. Each province was given a bicameral legislature. However, the popularly elected branch of the legislature had little power, since the executive council was responsible only to the governor, who appointed it, while the governor was responsible only to the British colonial office.

Constitutional Crisis. A political crisis that developed in June 1926 over the right of the governor general to act independently of the prime minister. Governor General Lord BYNG, having denied Prime Minister Mackenzie KING's request to dissolve a newly elected Parliament that might bring in a vote of censure, acceded to the request for dissolution of his successor, Arthur MEIGHEN, a few days later. In the election that followed, King campaigned on the issue of political interference and was returned with greater strength.

Constitutional monarchy. The principle that the monarch is able to do virtually nothing without the authorization of his or her constitutional advisers, the cabinet, who are accountable to Parliament. Since the constitutional monarch may not act on his or her own authority, he or she cannot be held to account for his or her actions. In Canada the sovereign delegates most of the powers of the CROWN to the GOVERNOR GENERAL.

Consul. The head of a consulate or consulate-general. A consul promotes the commercial and economic interests of his or her country in a foreign state. In 1975 Canada maintained consulates in 15 cities. See also AMBASSADOR, HIGH COMMISSIONER.

Consumer and Corporate Affairs, Department of. Department of the federal government concerned with all aspects of consumer affairs; corporations; combines, mergers, monopolies, and restraint of trade; bankruptcies; and patents, copyrights, trademarks, and industrial design not assigned to any other government department or agency. Established in 1967 to replace the Department of the Registrar-General of Canada, it has five main sections: the Bureau of Consumer Affairs, the Bureau of Corporate Affairs, the Bureau of Intellectual Property, the Field Operations Service, and the Bureau of Competition Policy. The Restrictive Trade Practices Commission (Combines Investigation Act) reports to the Minister of Consumer and Corporate Affairs, who is also the Registrar-General of Canada.

Contact Press. Underground publishing house for contemporary Canadian poetry that flourished in Toronto between 1952 and 1967. It was named after Raymond SOUSTER'S mimeographed poetry magazine *Contact* and managed by Souster, Louis DUDEK, and Irving LAYTON, joint authors of the first book published, *Cerberus* (1952). The last publication was Harry Howith's *Total War* (1967).

Contant, Alexis (1858-1918). Composer. Born in Quebec, he was a church organist for over 30 years in Montreal. He studied briefly with Calixa LAVALLÉE. His compositions include *salon* pieces for piano, songs, and sacred works for chorus and orchestra. His *Cain* (1905) was the first Canadian oratorio to be performed. His work shows the strong influence of Gounod and Wagner.

Contemporary Art Society. Group founded by John LYMAN in 1939 to promote the interests and work of the most advanced painters in Montreal. The first vice-president was Paul-Émile BORDUAS, who succeeded Lyman as president in 1948, the year the CAS was dissolved when Borduas resigned over disagreements among his young followers and those of Alfred PELLAN, who had already resigned.

Contemporary Literature in Translation. A literary quarterly devoted to contemporary prose and poetry from round the world in English translation. It was founded by Andreas SCHROEDER and J. Michael YATES in Vancouver in 1968.

Contemporary Verse. 'A Canadian quarterly'. It was founded in Sept. 1941 by Alan CRAWLEY, a British Columbia lawyer whose judgement and catholicity of taste in poetic matters were unaffected by the fact that he was slowly going blind. It appeared until Mar. 1953, publishing important work by the leading poets of the country. One of its principal contributors, Dorothy LIVESAY, helped revive its successor *CV/II* in the fall of 1975.

Content. Monthly tabloid for media people offering news and views on newspapers, radio, TV, public relations, advertising, government, and education. It was founded by Dick MacDonald in Montreal in Oct. 1970 and since Jan. 1975 has been published by Barrie Zwicker in Toronto.

Continental Divide. The height of land that separates the drainage basins of a continent; also called the Great Divide in North America. In Canada it corresponds to the ROCKY MOUNTAIN Range, extending from the FORTY-NINTH PARALLEL to a region north of the YELLOWHEAD PASS in the Northwest Territories. Thus in part it corresponds to the boundary between Alberta and British Columbia. It has been noted that there is one spot—an ice-cap—in North America where the drainage is divided among three oceans. At the Snow Dome, in the icefield where BANFF NATIONAL PARK meets JASPER NATIONAL PARK, one's cup of tea could be spilled to flow eventually into the Arctic Ocean, the Atlantic Ocean (via Hudson Bay), and the Pacific Ocean.

Continental Limited, The. The CANADIAN NATIONAL RAILWAYS' first transcontinental train. A daily service was introduced between Montreal and Vancouver on 12 Dec. 1920. In 1955 it was superseded by The SUPER CONTINENTAL.

Continental Shelf. A land area, actually part of a continental landmass, that has become submerged along ocean coasts. The true ocean floor does not begin until after such shelves drop in submarine cliffs (continental slope) to almost 10 times their previous depth after the 600-ft mark. Most fishing is done on these shelves since they offer a spawning ground for many otherwise widely distributed species. Shelves may be a few miles or a few hundred miles wide. The GRAND BANKS off Newfoundland constitute part of one of the world's most important continental shelves. The presence of oil deposits on these shelves and the overfishing of these areas have led the Canadian and other governments to advocate a 200-mi. economic zone.

Contractual link. A principle of foreign policy first advanced by Prime Minister Pierre Elliott TRUDEAU in 1969. It implies that Canada should seek a special trade and cultural relationship with countries and economic communities other than Great Britain and

the United States. The principle is sometimes referred to as the 'third option', Great Britain being the first option and the United States the second.

Cook, Frederick A. See NORTH POLES.

Cook, James (1728-79). Navigator. A master in the Royal Navy, he was at the siege of LOUISBOURG in 1758 and at QUEBEC in 1759. On the last of three voyages to the Pacific in 1778, he explored the west coast of Canada as far north as Bering Strait and entered Nootka Sound on the west coast of Vancouver Island, taking possession of the land for Great Britain. He was killed the following year in Hawaii. Cook's *A Voyage to the Pacific Ocean* appeared in 1784.

Cook, Ramsay (b.1931). Historian. Born in Saskatchewan, and educated at the University of Manitoba and at Queen's, he taught at the University of Toronto from 1958 to 1969 and is now professor of history at York University, Toronto. His first book was *The Politics of John W. DAFOE and the Free Press* (1963). His special interest is the political and social history of modern Quebec and the cultural duality of Canada. Among his other books are *Canada and the French-Canadian Question* (1966) and *The Maple Leaf Forever: Essays on Nationalism and Politics in Canada* (1971). He edited *French-Canadian Nationalism: An Anthology* (1969).

Cooke, Jack Kent (b.1912). Millionaire. Born in Hamilton, Ont., he acquired Northern Broadcasting and Publishing in 1935 and, between 1937 and 1952, was in partnership with Roy THOMSON. During the 1940s he acquired control of LIBERTY, SATURDAY NIGHT, CANADIAN HOME JOURNAL, and CKEY in Toronto. By a special act of the U.S. Congress he was made an American citizen in 1960. He built the Los Angeles Forum in 1967, and has extensive hockey, basketball, broadcasting, and cable-television interests in that city.

Cool Sound from Hell, A. Feature film directed by Sidney J. FURIE and released in 1959. It starred Anthony Ray, Carolyn Dannibale, Madeline Kronby, and Ronald Taylor. A young man leaves his girl-friend for the beat life and then goes straight. The director settled in England when the film was well received there. The musical score was composed by Phil NIMMONS. 71 min., b & w.

'Co-operation, Yes. Domination, No.' Celebrated statement of Canadian labour-union sovereignty. The slogan was used by Percy Bengough, president of the TRADES AND LABOUR CONGRESS, in Mar. 1949, when the AMER-

ICAN FEDERATION OF LABOR, recognizing the jurisdiction of the Seafarers International Union at the expense of the CANADIAN SEAMEN'S UNION, attempted to disenfranchise its Canadian members.

Co-operative Commonwealth Federation. See CCF.

Copp Clark Limited. Educational publishers. Like many publishing houses, Copp Clark grew out of a book and stationery business—in this case one founded in Toronto in 1841 by the Scottish newspaperman Hugh Scobie. Messrs Copp and Clark bought the firm a few name-changes later, in 1869, retaining the stationery line but greatly expanding the textbook publishing; even today the company distributes games and other trade items. In 1963 the firm was purchased by Sir Isaac Pitman and Sons, the British publishers, and soon became linked with Hunter, Rose & Company, an old Toronto printing firm, under the corporate name Copp Clark Limited. The president is Michael Pitman.

Copper. The leading non-fuel mineral produced in Canada in 1974, with production valued at over $1,400 million. Canada ranks fifth in the world as a producer of copper, with 10% of the world production. The most important mines are located in the Sudbury area, Ont.; Murdochville, Que.; Timmins, Ont.; Thompson, Man.; and in Highland Valley, Peachland, and Babine Lake, B.C.

Copper Eskimos. One of five groups of ESKIMOS. They inhabit the Arctic Coast near the Coppermine R. These Eskimos, some of whom are fair-haired and blue-eyed, were studied by Vilhjamur STEFANSSON in 1908 and by Diamond JENNESS in 1913-18.

Copper Indians. See YELLOWKNIFE.

Copyright Act. Protection of original literary, dramatic, musical, and artistic works. Under the Copyright Act (RSC 1970, c. C-30), in force since 1924, copyright protection in Canada is automatic without any formality, although a system of voluntary registration is provided by the Commissioner of Patents, Ottawa. The Act states: 'The term for which the copyright shall subsist shall, except as otherwise expressly provided by this Act, be the life of the author and a period of fifty years after his death.' Canada subscribes to the Universal Copyright Convention, by which works of Canadian authors are protected in the United States and other signatory countries without formality of compulsory registration or the obligation of printing in the United States, provided that, from the first publication, the work bears in a prominent place the copyright symbol, followed by the name of the proprietor and the year of publication.

Coq d'or. Award given annually since the early 1960s by the Publicité Club de Montréal to the producer of the best French television commercial produced the previous year.

Corbeil, Claude (b.1940). Bass. Born in Rimouski, Que., he studied singing in Montreal and became established as an opera singer in his middle twenties, singing at the Royal Opera House Covent Garden, London; the New York City Opera; in Philadelphia, Pittsburgh, New Orleans; and widely in Canada. He has sung leading roles with the CANADIAN OPERA COMPANY in seven operas, including *Don Giovanni* (1970), *Carmen* (1970, 1974), and *Bluebeard's Castle* (1974).

Corbett, Edward A. (Ned). See CANADIAN ASSOCIATION FOR ADULT EDUCATION.

Corbin Strike. A strike by miners for union recognition at Corbin, B.C., from Jan. to Mar. 1935. When the mine owners tried to open the mine with strikebreakers, miners and their wives paraded to the mine, where they were met by police and strikebreakers on a narrow ledge. A general riot ensued when police drove a bulldozer several times into the parade. 25 strikers were injured and 17 were arrested. The strike ended with union recognition for the Mine Workers of Canada.

Corduroy road. A road of logs laid side by side over swampy or muddy terrain. Associated with rural southern Ontario in the nineteenth century, it got its name from its resemblance to the ribbed surface of corduroy cloth.

Corktown. District in Ottawa, Ont., inhabited in the mid-nineteenth century by Irish labourers and loggers. It was probably named for Cork, Ire.

Corn or **maize.** North and South American kernel grain. Jacques CARTIER found it in the fields at Hochelaga and CHAMPLAIN saw it growing from Nova Scotia to the Ottawa Valley. Though it was cultivated as a food staple by the Indians and early settlers, corn was not adopted on a large scale in Canada because of the country's harsh climate. Its cultivation for use as a grain and food is restricted to southern Ontario, Manitoba, and small areas in Quebec.

Cornell. A single-engined monoplane used for training purposes. Designed by Fairchild and built by Fleet Aircraft in Fort Erie, Ont., during the Second World War, it supplanted the TIGER MOTH at the BCATP flying schools.

'Corporate welfare bums'. Epithetical description of large corporations that avoid paying taxes and seek government subsidies. It was first used by NDP leader David LEWIS in a speech at New Glasgow, N.S., on 3 Aug. 1972.

Corps of Royal Canadian Engineers, The. Canadian army corps. Militia Engineer companies existed as early as 1861. The Corps was authorized in 1903 and took its present name in 1936. During the FIRST and SECOND WORLD WARS it served with field companies, transport units, and tunnelling companies. It has recently served in the Far East, Europe, the Middle East, and Indo-China.

Corriveau, La. The nickname of Marie-Josephte Corriveau (1733-63). On 15 Apr. 1763, at a trial in the Ursuline Convent, Quebec, she was condemned to death for murdering her second husband after she confessed to hitting him on the head twice with an axe while he was asleep. She was hanged near the Plains of Abraham on 18 Apr. 1763 and her body was exposed in an iron cage across the river at Pointe-Lévy (Lauzon), until about 25 May. Because of the nature of her crime—which may have been the last of several murders she committed—and the discovery of the iron cage in the Lauzon cemetery in 1850, she entered the oral and written tradition of Quebec. AUBERT-DE GASPÉ related one of numerous embellished versions of her story in Les ANCIENS CANADIENS.

Corte-Real, Gaspar (c.1450-c.1501). Portuguese explorer. In two voyages he reached Greenland (1500) and the east coast of Newfoundland (1501). He did not return from the second voyage.

Corvette. A class of coastal escort ship developed early in the SECOND WORLD WAR that came to typify the ROYAL CANADIAN NAVY in the Battle of the Atlantic. 123 corvettes served with the RCN. A typical unit displaced 950 tons on a length of 205 ft, with the main armament one 4-in. gun. Its sea-keeping qualities made it invaluable in its unintended role as an ocean escort.

Cosmic Consciousness. Title of 'a study in the evolution of the human mind', first published in 1901. Written by the physician and author Richard Maurice BUCKE, this mammoth work is a case-history analysis recording instances of individuals (ranging from Buddha and Jesus to Whitman and Emerson) who experienced 'a higher form of consciousness than that possessed by the ordi-

nary man'. The phrase 'cosmic consciousness' was first used by Bucke in a paper read before the American Medico-Psychological Association's meeting in Philadelphia on 18 May 1894.

Costain, Thomas B. (1885-1965). Popular historian and historical novelist. Born in Brantford, Ont., he was editor of *Maclean's* (1915-20) and was associated with the *Saturday Evening Post* (1920-34); he then became story editor for Twentieth-Century Fox (1934-6) and advisory editor for Doubleday (1939-65). He did not write his first book until he was 57, but during the next 23 years he published 13 novels, two biographies, five histories, and five anthologies. His best-known historical novel is *The Black Rose* (1945), which was filmed; he also wrote the fictionalized 'Pageant of England' series in four volumes (1949-62). His Canadian background informed *High Towers* (1953), set in Montreal, and *Son of a Hundred Kings* (1950), set in the Brantford area. For Doubleday he edited the four-part CANADIAN HISTORY SERIES called *The White and the Gold* (1954-61).

Côte. French word for 'slope', often found in the names of settlements or districts, like Côte des Neiges in Montreal.

Côté, Gérard (b.1913). Noted long-distance runner. Born at St Barnabé, Que., he became a four-time winner of the Boston Marathon and the victor in three United States Marathon championships, winning in all 112 long-distance races. He lit the Olympic urn on Mount Royal when the Olympic flame was welcomed to Montreal on 16 July 1976, prior to the opening of the Games on the 17th.

Côteau. French word for 'hillock' or 'hillside', often found in the names of settlements or districts, like Côteau Station, Que. In western Canada the word describes a plateau.

Coteau-du-Lac National Historic Park. At Coteau-du-Lac, Que., it includes the remains of the first canal built on the St Lawrence R. and of a British military post dating from the WAR OF 1812.

Cotton Debates. Three unofficial volumes of debates in the House and Commons and the Senate, covering the years 1870, 1871, and 1872. Named after John Cotton, the reporter for the *Ottawa Times* who covered the sessions, they were preceded by the SCRAP-BOOK DEBATES and followed by HANSARD.

Couchiching Conferences. Series of summer and winter conferences held at GENEVA PARK, on the shore of Lake Couchiching, 9 mi. from

Couchiching Conferences

Orillia, Ont. They are sponsored by the CA-NADIAN INSTITUTE ON PUBLIC AFFAIRS to provide 'an open forum for discussion of Canadian social and economic problems in international settings'. Specialists from Canada and abroad speak on a designated theme and members of the public engage in Round Table discussions. The first summer conference was held in Aug. 1932. The first winter conference was held on a weekend in Feb. 1954. Since 1953 the conferences have been jointly sponsored by the CBC, which has broadcast or telecast the highlights of each series.

Coughtry, Graham (b.1931). Painter and sculptor. Born in St Lambert, Que., he studied at the Montreal Museum of Fine Arts School and the Ontario College of Art, Toronto, where he later taught. After completing a series of romantic interior studies based on common furniture pieces (*Interior Twilight*, 1957, Winnipeg Art Gallery), he was influenced by the New York expressionist style to create imaginary portraits almost sculpted on canvas in thickly congealed paint. This resulted in his finest work, a dramatic series of strongly coloured abstract-expressionist paintings using the two-figure motif of lovers (*Two Figure Series No. 10*, 1963, University of Toronto). His many commissions include a mural for the Toronto International Airport (1962) and a 16-ft bronze stylized figure sculpture for Yorkdale Plaza, Toronto (1963), both showing the influence of Francis Bacon and Giacometti on his figurative style. He has exhibited internationally and lives on the Mediterranean island of Ibiza.

Coulee. In western Canada, a deep gulch or ravine formed by heavy-rain erosion or melting snow. It is usually dry in summer. The French-Canadian *coulée* comes from the French *couler*, 'to flow', and is thought to have originated with French-Canadian fur traders.

Coulter, John (b.1888). Playwright. Born in Belfast, he was associated with both the Abbey Theatre in Dublin and John Middleton Murry's *The New Adelphi* in London. He married a Canadian and settled in Toronto in 1936. He was commissioned by CBC Radio to write librettos for two operas by Healey WILLAN—*Transit through Fire* (1942) and DEIRDRE (1946). Coulter's best-known work is RIEL, written in 1950 and published in 1962, a three-act pageant of a play that turns the Métis leader into a figure of tragic proportions. The actual courtroom proceedings are the subject of *The* TRIAL OF LOUIS RIEL (1968), first staged in the actual courtroom in Regina

in 1967 and repeated annually since then. A third Riel play, the two-act *The Crime of Louis Riel*, was published in 1976. Mavor MOORE's libretto for the opera by Harry SOMERS, LOUIS RIEL (1967), owes much to Coulter's conception and handling of the Riel story.

Coulthard, Jean (b.1908). Composer. Born in Vancouver, she studied composition at the Royal College of Music in London, Eng., and now teaches at the University of British Columbia. Her music shows the influence of Ralph Vaughan Williams, one of her teachers, and reflects her interest in solo and choral vocal music; for example *Spring Rhapsody* (1958), for voice and orchestra, written for Maureen FORRESTER, and the cantata *This Land* (1967).

Council bluff. Prairie term for a natural elevation, like a hill or bluff, that afforded a vantage-point for Indians to hold a pow-wow or to search for herds of buffalo, etc.

Council for Business and the Arts in Canada, The. An organization founded 'to encourage and stimulate business support of the arts'. It was established in Toronto in 1974 by a one-time grant from the CANADA COUNCIL and since then has operated on its corporate membership fee of $1,000. The president is Arnold EDINBOROUGH.

Country and Eastern. A name for 'Country and Western' music in Canada, suggested by Peter GZOWSKI in 1975. Most of the 'Western' music that originates in Canada comes from the Maritimes in the East and not the Prairies in the West. See also DON MESSER'S JUBILEE.

Country Calendar. A long-running CBC-TV series of farm and gardening interest. The 30-minute Sunday afternoon programs began in 1954 and ran to 3 Jan. 1971, when the series was renamed 'Country Canada'. It is now a program of urban interest with commentaries from across Canada and a 'rural cameo segment'. It is the TV counterpart of COUNTRY MAGAZINE.

Country Magazine. Title of a CBC Radio series devoted to news, discussions, and interviews of interest to farmers. The 30-minute weekly series, which began on 1 Nov. 1965, is actually a continuation of the pioneer adult-education series, NATIONAL FARM RADIO FORUM. It is the radio counterpart of COUNTRY CALENDAR.

County. A geographical subdivision of a province. Prince Edward Island, New Brunswick, Nova Scotia, Quebec, and Ontario have geographical counties. The municipal county, which usually covers the same extent as the geographical county, occurs only in Nova Scotia, New Brunswick, Quebec, Ontario, and Alberta. In Nova Scotia and New Brunswick the municipal county is the sole rural municipal unit of government; in Alberta counties were created as large-area rural MUNICIPALITIES as an experiment; in Ontario and Quebec the southerly part of the provinces are divided into geographical counties that are also municipal counties, but there are no municipal counties in the northern parts of these provinces.

Courage, Star of. See STAR OF COURAGE.

Courcelette. Village in northern France, scene of fighting in the FIRST WORLD WAR. With dash and daring the Second and Third Divisions attacked and captured this German-held village near the SOMME on 15 Sept. 1916. Tanks, a British invention, were used for the first time in this battle.

Coureurs de bois. 'Runners of the woods'— the unlicensed fur traders of NEW FRANCE. They journeyed by canoe to the western trading posts, often living for long periods with the Indians and assuming their ways. They were later called VOYAGEURS.

Court of Opinion. Popular panel show on CBC Radio. Chairman Neil LeRoy moderated a group of four non-expert panelists, who discussed subjects submitted by listeners and then reached a yes-or-no verdict. Early panelists included Kate AITKEN, Lotta Dempsey, John FISHER, and Lister SINCLAIR. The 30-minute weekly program was in session on radio from 1946 to 1968. Subjects the public deemed controversial remained roughly the same over two decades. One analysis of listeners' mail made in the mid-1960s revealed the subjects that were thought to be most debatable (in order of priority): divorce, capital punishment, taxation, lotteries and legalized gambling, teenage problems, women's role in society, moral decline, education, treatment of Indians and Eskimos, immigration, politics, censorship, pensions, English-French relations, international affairs, and birth control. The program was transferred to television in 1952 but lasted there only one season.

Courteau, Johnny. See JOHNNY COURTEAU.

Courts of Canada. Under the provisions of the BNA ACT the federal government has authority to establish a general court of appeal and 'any additional courts for the better administration of the laws of Canada'; and the provinces have the right to establish courts of civil and criminal jurisdiction. Judges of the SUPERIOR COURTS in the provinces are ap-

pointed by the federal government, as are judges of the County or District Courts and the Surrogate Courts; judges of the INFERIOR COURTS are appointed by the provincial governments.

Federal courts: the SUPREME COURT OF CANADA and the FEDERAL COURT OF CANADA.

Provincial courts. The structure of the courts in all provinces is similar, although the names may differ. The most important court in each province is the Court of Appeal, sometimes referred to as the Appellate Division of the Supreme Court of the province. It hears appeals from lower courts, the principal one being the Trial Division of the Supreme Court or the Court of Queen's Bench. These are superior courts that hear trials and, in certain cases, appeals from lower courts.

County Courts or *District Courts* have similar authority to that of the superior courts but in money matters their jurisdiction is generally less and they may not try certain very serious criminal cases.

Surrogate Courts deal with cases arising from wills and the probate of estates. Frequently a district or county court judge will preside over the Surrogate Court.

Provincial courts (criminal division or jurisdiction) are sometimes referred to as *Magistrates' Courts.* They deal with criminal matters of a less serious nature than the higher courts and with preliminary hearings of more serious offences. They also deal with domestic matters in the family division where this exists.

Small Claims Courts. County Court judges or provincial magistrates may sit in these courts with jurisdiction to deal with claims for small amounts of money.

The provincial courts are constituted as follows:

Alberta: The Supreme Court of Alberta: Appellate Division and Trial Division; The District Court of Alberta; The Juvenile Court; The Family Court.

British Columbia: The Court of Appeal for British Columbia; The Supreme Court of British Columbia; The County Court of British Columbia; Judges of the Provincial Court; The Family and Children's Court; Divisions of the Provincial Court: the Family Division and a Small Claims Division.

Manitoba: The Court of Appeal for Manitoba; The Court of Queen's Bench for Manitoba; County Court; The Surrogate Court; Magistrates' Court; Family Court.

New Brunswick: The Supreme Court of New Brunswick: Appeal Division and Queen's Bench Division; The County Court of New Brunswick; Magistrates and Justices of the Peace.

Newfoundland: The Supreme Court of Judicature for Newfoundland: Court of Appeal, Trial Division; The Family Court; The District Court; Magistrates' Court.

Nova Scotia: The Supreme Court of Nova Scotia: Appeal Division, Trial Division; The Court of Divorce and Matrimonial Causes; Magistrates and Justices of the Peace; The County Court.

Ontario: The Court of Appeal; The Supreme Court; Magistrates' Court; Juvenile Court; Justices of the Peace.

Quebec: The Court of Appeal: (a) Montreal, (b) Quebec City; The Supreme Court of Quebec; Municipal Judges.

Prince Edward Island: The Supreme Court of Prince Edward Island: appellate and original jurisdiction; Provincial Judges.

Saskatchewan: The Court of Appeal for Saskatchewan; The Court of Queen's Bench for Saskatchewan; Judges of the Magistrates' Court.

Northwest Territories: Court of Appeal for the North West Territories; Supreme Court of the North West Territories.

Yukon Territory: Court of Appeal for the Yukon Territory; Supreme Court; Magistrates' Court; Juvenile Court.

Cousineau, Yves (b.1932). Dancer. Born in Montreal, he trained there as an actor with Les Compagnons de St Laurent from 1949 to 1952 and studied ballet with Mme E. Leese in 1952-3. After working briefly on television, he joined the NATIONAL BALLET OF CANADA in 1953, becoming a soloist in 1959 and their principal character dancer in 1963, when he performed one of his most memorable roles, Tybalt, in *Romeo and Juliet.* He left the National in 1972 and since 1970 has taught mime and ballet at York University, Toronto, while also acting as president of Graphics Studio, a Toronto workshop for printmakers.

Couture, Guillaume (1851-1915). Composer. Born in Montreal, he studied in Paris, where his early compositions were performed. He was also choirmaster at Ste-Clotilde Church, where César Franck was organist. After returning to Montreal, he worked as a choral conductor, formed the Société des Symphonistes, and developed the Philharmonic Society. All of his music is religious. Its finest example is the oratorio *Jean le Précurseur* (1914).

Cowan, Gary (b.1938). Amateur golfer. Born in Kitchener, Ont., he won the Ontario juvenile championship at 14 and took many national amateur titles. He won the United States amateur tournaments in both 1966 and 1971 and was the leading medallist in world amateur competition in Japan in 1962. He has resisted becoming professional and plays in the important amateur tournaments.

Cowichan. One of the COAST SALISH Indian groups. They live on Vancouver Island in the Duncan area. Their population in 1970 was 6,031.

Cowichan sweater. A heavy sweater of grey unbleached wool, knitted by the COWICHAN Indians with black-and-white symbolic designs.

'Cows' breakfasts'. Wide-brimmed hats worn by farmers for protection against the sun in the nineteenth century. The stetson-like hat was made of straw and frequently eaten by cows.

Cowtown. Nickname of Calgary, Alta, and of other western cities and towns that do business in cattle.

Cox, E.B. (b.1914). Sculptor. Born in Botha, Alta, Elford Bradley Cox graduated from the University of Toronto and taught languages before turning to a career in sculpture. He is self-taught and works in wood, steel, and stone, producing large-scale abstract human and animal forms. His pieces include miniature carvings in semi-precious Canadian stones and the headstones for the graves of members of the GROUP OF SEVEN on the grounds of the McMICHAEL CANADIAN COLLECTION.

Cox, Kirwan (b.1946). Boston-born, McGill-educated, Toronto-based free-lance film producer. He produced *Dreamland* (1974), which was directed by Donald BRITTAIN.

Coy, Eric (b.1914). Versatile athlete. Born in Manitoba, he won the North American title in snowshoe racing and many other honours. He competed in weight-lifting events at both British Commonwealth and Olympic Games and in 1938 was voted 'Canada's outstanding athlete of the year'.

Coyne affair. A dispute in 1961 between the federal government under John DIEFENBAKER and the governor of the BANK OF CANADA, James E. Coyne. The government claimed that it did not control the Bank of Canada's monetary policies, which were counter to government policy, that Coyne was making controversial public speeches, and that the Governor's pension was increased by the Board of Directors without informing the Minister of Finance. The government demanded Coyne's resignation six months before his term was due to expire. Coyne refused to resign because he claimed that he had been appointed during 'good behaviour' and the government had made no case against him, because he felt that the government would make him the scapegoat for its economic policies in the next general election, and because if he resigned the position of future governors would be untenable. The government introduced a bill into Parliament to remove the governor and refused to accede to Opposition demands that Coyne be given a hearing. However, the Liberal-dominated Senate rejected the bill. Immediately thereafter Coyne resigned. As a result of the Coyne affair an amendment to the Bank Act was passed that requires the Bank of Canada to follow the government's monetary policy if directed to do so.

CP. Initials of CANADIAN PRESS and of CANADIAN PACIFIC LIMITED.

CP Air. Privately owned airline. Canadian Pacific Airlines was formed in 1942, five years after the creation of the government-owned TCA (now AIR CANADA). The parent company, CANADIAN PACIFIC LIMITED, had gained aviation experience with the initial phases of the TRANS-ATLANTIC FERRY SERVICE and by the amalgamation of 12 small airlines that serviced mainly the West and the North. Like Air Canada, CP Air is one of the world's largest passenger and freight carriers, ranking twenty-fourth in passenger miles flown.

CP Line. The ocean services of CANADIAN PACIFIC STEAMSHIPS Limited. This subsidiary of the CPR was formed in 1891 with the acquisition of the *Empress of India*, the first ship of the famous EMPRESS LINE to ply the Pacific and Atlantic.

CP Rail. See CANADIAN PACIFIC LIMITED.

CP Telecommunications. See CN-CP TELECOMMUNICATIONS.

CPC. Initials of the COMMUNISTY PARTY OF CANADA.

CPC(M-L). Initials of the COMMUNIST PARTY OF CANADA (MARXIST-LENINIST).

Cpl. Official abbreviation of Corporal.

CPP. Initials of the CANADA PENSION PLAN.

CPR. Initials of the CANADIAN PACIFIC RAILWAY, now CANADIAN PACIFIC LIMITED.

CPR strawberries. Railway slang for prunes, dating from the early twentieth century.

CQMS. Official abbreviation of Company Quartermaster Sergeant.

Cradle of Confederation. Motto of CHARLOTTETOWN, P.E.I., a reference to the important conference that was held there in 1864 that eventually led to CONFEDERATION.

Craigellachie. See LAST SPIKE, 'STAND FAST, CRAIGELLACHIE'.

Craigs, The. A long-running CBC Radio serial about 'the triumphs, trials and tribulations of an Ontario farm family'. It chronicled the domestic life of Martha and Tom Craig and their children Bill and Janice who lived on Briarwood Farm somewhere in central Canada. The series, created and written by Dean Hughes, was heard in the Ontario region from 1 May 1939 to 31 July 1964 in 10-minute episodes at 12:40 Monday through Friday as part of the 'CBC Farm Broadcast'. It was the model for similar programs in other regions.

Cranston, Toller (b.1950). Figure skater and painter. Born in Kirkland Lake, Ont., and raised in Montreal, he was trained by Ellen Burka, the mother of Petra BURKA, and became the Canadian men's figure-skating champion in 1971. Cranston has been called the 'greatest free skater in history' and his style has been likened to 'painting on ice'. He won a bronze medal in the Winter Olympics of 1976. Examples of his individual and highly ornate painting style can be seen in *Toller* (1975) by Elva Oglanby. In May 1976 he turned professional with the Sol Hurok Agency of New York; he is president of Theatre On Ice Productions.

Crawford, Isabella Valancy (1850-87). Poet. Born in Dublin, she was brought to Canada West (Ontario) as a child and grew up in the Peterborough area. The possessor of a remarkable sensibility and great energy, she contributed poems and fiction to Toronto newspapers and published *Old Spookses' Pass, Malcolm's Katie, and Other Poems* at her own expense in 1884. She was accorded a significant place in Canadian poetry when John Garvin edited *The Collected Poems* (1905).

Crawley, Alan (1887-1975). A Victoria-based lawyer, blind since 1933, who was a mentor to poets and published CONTEMPORARY VERSE from 1941 to 1952.

Crawley, Frank Radford (Budge) (b.1911). Film producer. Born in Ottawa, he became, like his father, a chartered accountant, but produced his first sponsored film in 1931. With Judith Crawley (b.1914) he founded Crawley Films in 1939 to make military training pictures for the NFB during the war. From then until 1976 the company has made more than 2,400 sponsored films for over 400 clients. Its best-known shorts include *The* LOON'S NECKLACE (1948), NEWFOUNDLAND SCENE (1951), and LEGEND OF THE RAVEN (1957). Films shot for television series include *Au Pays de Nouvelle France* (1960) and *R.C.M.P.*

(1959-60). Notable feature films include *Amanita Pestilens* (1964); *The* LUCK OF GINGER COFFEY (1964); *Hamlet* (1972); *The* ROWDYMAN (1971); *Janis* (1974); *The Man Who Skied Down Everest* (1975), which won an Academy Award as the best feature-length documentary in 1976; and WHO HAS SEEN THE WIND? (in production, 1976). Many leading filmmakers and technicians learned their trade at Crawley Films in Ottawa.

CRBC. Initials of the CANADIAN RADIO BROADCASTING COMMISSION.

Creative Writing Department, University of British Columbia. The first such department—as distinct from a program—within a Canadian university, it was established by Earle BIRNEY in 1965 and its first head was Robert HARLOW, who resigned in 1976. It grants M.A. degrees and publishes PRISM INTERNATIONAL. The second such department in Canada was formed in 1973 by Robin SKELTON at the University of Victoria.

Créditiste. Member of the RALLIEMENT DES CRÉDITISTES, the Quebec wing of the SOCIAL CREDIT Party.

Cree. The largest and most widespread group of ALGONKIAN-speaking Indians, formerly active in the French and British fur trade. They divide into several sub-dialects: the Plains Cree of the Saskatchewan prairie, the Woods Cree of sub-Arctic Saskatchewan and Manitoba; the Swampy Cree living in northern Manitoba and in sub-Arctic Ontario; the James Bay Cree; and the Mistassini Cree of the Quebec interior. Their population in 1970 was 70,403. They were called *Cristinois* or *Knistinois* by the French.

Cree syllabics. See SYLLABICS.

Creeps. Play by David FREEMAN. A bitter comedy about a group of cerebral palsy victims set in the washroom of a 'sheltered workshop'. Its first production, directed by William GLASSCO, opened the TARRAGON THEATRE on 5 Oct. 1971.

Creighton, Donald G. (b.1902). Historian. Born in Toronto and educated at the University of Toronto and at Oxford, he joined the history department of the University of Toronto in 1927, was its chairman from 1954 to 1959, and taught there until 1970. He is a scholar who undertook the writing of history as a literary art, evoking character, setting, and the shape of events with the flair of a nineteenth-century novelist, while adhering to the findings of meticulous research. His major works are on the economic and political influences of the St Lawrence R. system,

brilliantly examined in *The Commercial Empire of the St Lawrence* (1937; reissued 1956); and on the age of Macdonald and Confederation, about which he wrote a notable two-volume biography of John A. MACDONALD: *The* YOUNG POLITICIAN (1952) and *The* OLD CHIEFTAIN (1955); *British North America at Confederation* (1939; rev. 1963); and *The Road to Confederation* (1964). His other books are *Dominion of the North* (1944; rev. 1957); *Canada's First Century* (1970); *Towards the Discovery of Canada* (1972), a collection of essays and speeches; and *Canada: The Heroic Beginnings* (1974), a pictorial history; and *The Forked Road: Canada 1939-1957* (1976). He is married to Luella CREIGHTON.

Creighton, Helen (b.1899). Folklorist. Born in Halifax, N.S., she is a self-taught pioneer in the collecting of the oral tradition of the Maritimes. She has compiled such basic works as *Ballads and Sea Songs of Nova Scotia* (1928) and *Songs and Ballads from Nova Scotia* (1932). *Bluenose Ghosts* (1957) and *Bluenose Magic* (1968) reflect her interest in the supernatural. In her autobiography, *A Life in Folklore* (1975), she describes how she first rescued from oblivion the lilting words and music of 'FAREWELL TO NOVA SCOTIA', subsequently popularized by Catherine McKINNON.

Creighton, Luella (b.1901). Historical novelist. Born in Stouffville, Ont., she is the author of two historical novels, *High Bright Buggy Wheels* (1951) and *Turn East, Turn West* (1954); *The Elegant Canadians* (1967), a study of manners and customs in the Confederation era; and two children's books, *Tecumseh: The Story of the Shawnee Chief* (1965) and *The Hitching Post: A Story Dealing in Magic* (1969). She married Donald CREIGHTON in 1926.

'Cremation of Sam McGee, The'. Popular ballad by Robert SERVICE, first published in *The Spell of the Yukon* (1907). Service tells how he attempted to cremate the corpse of his friend McGee, 'from Tennessee', only to find that he was very much alive and grateful for the heat.

Crémazie, Octave (1827-79). Quebec poet. Born in Quebec City and educated at the Quebec Seminary, he opened a bookshop there in 1847 that became the meeting place for a school of writers. When the shop failed in 1862, Crémazie immigrated to France, where he wrote little and died. He has been called 'the father of French-Canadian poetry' for his patriotic verse, often rhetorical in style, celebrating such subjects as MONTCALM's defence of Fort Carillon in '*Le Drapeau de Carillon*', a popular poem written in 1858 on the centenary of that event. His poems, letters, journal, and essays were collected by Henri-Raymond Casgrain and J.-H.-B. Chouinard in *Oeuvres complètes de Crémazie* in 1882.

Crerar, Gen. H.D.G. (1888-1965). Army commander. Born in Hamilton, Ont., he was educated there and at Upper Canada College, Toronto, and the ROYAL MILITARY COLLEGE, Kingston. Commissioned in 1910, he served in France and Belgium during the FIRST WORLD WAR, attaining the rank of lieutenant-colonel. After service with the army in the United Kingdom and Italy during the SECOND WORLD WAR, he was appointed General Officer Commanding-in-Chief, First Canadian Army, which he commanded during the operations in Northwest Europe in 1944-5. This was the largest field formation Canada had ever provided and it achieved an enviable fighting record. Crerar was the first Canadian to gain the rank of general while in a theatre of war; he was promoted on 21 Nov. 1944. He retired in Oct. 1946.

Crerar, T.A. (1876-1975). Cabinet minister and farm leader. Born in Molesworth, Ont., and raised in Manitoba, he farmed for a time. In 1907 he became president of the Grain Growers' Grain Co., a post he held until 1929. As a leader of Manitoba farm opinion, he was brought into the UNION GOVERNMENT in 1917 as Minister of Agriculture. Resigning in 1919, he became the *de facto* head of dissident farmer MPs and in 1921 led the PROGRESSIVE PARTY to 64 seats in Parliament. But Crerar was really just a Liberal in a hurry and he found his task of leadership over an undisciplined farmers' party too onerous. He resigned in 1922. He joined the Mackenzie KING government in 1929 as Minister of Railways and, after King returned to power in 1935, he served in the cabinet in several portfolios until he was called to the Senate in 1945.

Crest Theatre. A Toronto theatrical company managed by Murray and Donald Davis (see DAVIS FAMILY). It opened on 5 Jan. 1954 with a production of Gordon Daviot's *Richard of Bordeaux* and closed with Henrik Ibsen's *Hedda Gabbler* in 1966, after support had dwindled with the appearance of other theatres in Toronto. Among its many productions of classical and modern plays, ranging from the excellent to the mediocre, it is remembered for *The* GLASS CAGE, written by J.B. Priestley for the Davis brothers and their sister Barbara Chilcott, the world première of which took place on 5 Mar. 1957. In 1962 Barbara Chilcott headed the Theatre Hour Company to bring live professional theatrical entertainment to Ontario secondary schools, a

function assumed in 1970 by the ST LAWRENCE CENTRE. The 822-seat theatre on Mount Pleasant Rd reverted to being a cinema.

Cretaceous Inland Sea. A sea, now extinct, that once covered the greater part of western North America. It joined the Arctic Ocean with the Gulf of Mexico and was inhabited by varieties of giant marine reptiles over 60 ft long. It was formed after the SUNDANCE SEA during the Upper Mesozoic era 63-132 million years ago, the last age of the dinosaurs.

Creton. A mild pork pâté, made with onions and mixed spices. It is popular in Quebec.

Crewcuts, The. A popular singing group composed of four ex-choir boys from Toronto. It had a big hit with the nonsense song 'Sh-Boom' in 1955 but broke up in 1964.

Criminal Code of Canada. A statute of the Parliament of Canada that identifies crimes, defining them and prescribing the penalties imposed upon conviction for them. The Code also provides for procedures in relation to arrests, bail, trials, and sentencing. It is the statutory branch of the criminal law that is supplemented by the body of the common law, the whole comprising the criminal law of Canada. Criminal law generally consists of legislation of a prohibitive character relating to infractions for which punitive sanctions are attached, having for its purpose the preservation and advancement of public morality.

Crimson Route. A little-used aviation corridor connecting the western United States and Europe via the Arctic Circle. It was named after the staging route flown by the Red Cross during the Second World War that went from the United Kingdom, across Iceland, Greenland, Baffin Island, Hudson Bay, and Manitoba to northern California. The Crimson Route required the construction of airbases (the Crimson Project) at The Pas and Churchill, Man.; Coral Harbour, Southampton Island; Fort Chimo, Que.; and Frobisher, Baffin Island.

Critic, The. A six-page review of the arts, 17 issues of which appeared between Mar. 1950 and Jan. 1954. Published monthly in Toronto by Nathan COHEN (then a free-lance drama critic for CBC Radio), it covered radio, films, music, ballet, and drama. Cohen wrote on ballet and drama, Ron Hambleton on music, Robert WEAVER on Canadian books, Gerald PRATLEY on film, George ROBERTSON on art, and G.B. Roman on radio and television. It was important for its literate printed coverage of major Canadian cultural events, documenting the rise of television drama, the related fall of radio drama, the rise of the CREST THEATRE, and the fall of the JUPITER THEATRE.

Critically Speaking. A national radio magazine of the arts, heard in the late 1940s through the 1950s. Clyde GILMOUR, as its original and permanent member, and other critics, including Nathan COHEN on a visiting basis, commented for 30 minutes each week on new plays, books, films, and concerts, etc. It was the national equivalent of the local Toronto program CJBC VIEWS THE SHOWS. In the 1960s it became 'The Arts This Week', with Ralph Hicklin as host of the national edition and Peter GZOWSKI and later Robert FULFORD hosting it in Toronto. In 1967 it was replaced by the hour-long 'Arts and Science Journal', the first half for Toronto only, the second half on the national network.

Crocus. A fictitious community in southern Saskatchewan, the setting for JAKE AND THE KID. Through W.O. MITCHELL's popular stories and CBC scripts, one learned that Crocus had a population of 739 in the forties. Variously set 'on the CPR line' or 'on the CNR line', one writer even located it 'on the banks of the Broken Shell River in the heart of the bald-headed prairie, deep in the imagination of W.O. Mitchell'. The author was born in Weyburn and resides in High River, so both Saskatchewan cities have been called the original of Crocus.

Crocus, Prairie. A white six-petalled flower, Manitoba's floral emblem since 1906. It is related to the buttercup and was portrayed on the 1970 silver dollar.

Croker Land. A mountain range on ELLESMERE ISLAND, later found to be an apparition. Named in 1906 by Robert E. PEARY after George Croker, a backer of his polar expedition, the 'peaks' were subsequently dismissed as an Arctic mirage or *fata morgana*, caused by the atmosphere's moisture acting as a lens to exaggerate slight irregularities in the horizon.

Cronyn, Hume (b.1911). Actor. Born in London, Ont., to a family prominent in finance, he was nominated to the Canadian Olympic Boxing Team in 1932, and educated at Ridley College, McGill University, and the New York School of Theatre. He planned to study law but was attracted to the stage. The slim, slightly built actor made his professional début in Washington, D.C., in 1931, his Broadway début in 1935, his television début in 1939, and his motion-picture début in 1943. In 1942 he married Jessica Tandy (b.1909 in London, Eng.) and they have frequently acted together. Cronyn played the STRATFORD FESTIVAL in 1969 (as the lead in the memorable *Hadrian VII*), and returned in 1976 to play Shylock in *The Merchant of Venice* and Bottom in *A Midsummer Night's Dream*. Jessica Tandy played Hippolyta and Titania in the latter play and created the title role in Larry Fineberg's *Eve*, based on Constance BERESFORD-HOWE's novel *The Book of Eve* (1972).

Cross, James. See OCTOBER CRISIS.

Cross-Canada Hit Parade. A popular CBC-TV show. Top tunes were played and sung each week, usually by Winnipeg-born Wally Koster (1923-75) and Joyce Hahn, backed by Bert NIOSI's Orchestra, with Austin WILLIS as announcer. Originally 30 minutes in length, it was expanded to 60 minutes in 1960. It was seen from 5 Oct. 1955 to 11 July 1960.

Cross of Sacrifice. Official name for the memorial cross of stone found in cemeteries for the war dead. It was designed by the British architect Sir Reginald Blomfield for the Imperial (since 1960 Commonwealth) War Graves Commission. Rudyard Kipling's description, a 'stark sword brooding on the bosom of the Cross', fits the austere memorial.

Cross of Valour. A Canadian honour awarded to mark instances of extraordinary heroism in circumstances of extreme peril. The abbreviation is CV.

Crothers, William (b.1940). Noted runner. A specialist in middle-distance running, he was born in Markham, Ont., and won the silver medal in the 800-metre event at the 1964 Olympics in Tokyo. Owing to muscular ailments he was unable to compete in the 1968 Olympics in Mexico City, but he has assisted many clubs and helped many young athletes.

Crow Memorial Trophy, The Norton H. See SPORTS FEDERATION OF CANADA.

Crowbar. A hard-rock band that played rock, rock-and-roll, blues, country, and every combination of these. The six-man group from Ancaster, Ont., flourished between 1970 and 1974. Its hit recording was 'Oh, What a Feeling'.

Crowfoot (c.1830-90). Chief of the Blackfoot Indians. He was influential in maintaining peace between Indians and whites, co-operating with the NORTH WEST MOUNTED POLICE when they arrived on the Prairies in 1874, and restraining his Indians when the CPR moved into their lands (for which he received a railway pass). Though his adopted son POUNDMAKER took part in the NORTHWEST REBELLION, Crowfoot did not. See also BLACKFOOT CROSSING.

Crown, The. The supreme executive authority of the state. The BNA ACT of 1867 provides that 'authority of and over Canada is . . . vested in the Queen.' In Canada, as in Britain, the Crown is a formal institution whose powers are exercised through responsible officials acting in the monarch's name. The individual sovereign is a CONSTITUTIONAL MONARCH. In Canada the formal functions and most powers of the sovereign are discharged by the GOVERNOR GENERAL, who is appointed by the sovereign on the advice of the Canadian cabinet. However, some powers—the granting of honours or the conduct of foreign relations—are carried out directly by the monarch acting on the advice of the Canadian cabinet. If the monarch is paying a ROYAL VISIT to Canada, he or she may participate in those ceremonies usually carried out in his or her name by the governor general.

Crown attorney. Title of the prosecutor of criminal and quasi-criminal cases in courts in Ontario and Manitoba. 'Crown attorney' is a Canadianism. The public prosecutor is called the 'district attorney' in the United States and the 'Crown council' in the United Kingdom; and the 'attorney-general' in Alberta, British Columbia, Newfoundland, and Prince Edward Island; the 'prosecuting officer' in Nova Scotia; and the 'procureurgénéral' in Quebec.

Crown corporation. A publicly owned corporation accountable to Parliament. The Canadian government has found it advantageous to conduct some of its business through corporations rather than through federal departments, special boards, and commissions. Some degree of free enterprise with public accountability is combined in Crown corporations, of which there are four types. A Departmental Crown Corporation—for example, the UNEMPLOYMENT INSURANCE COMMISSION—carries out work of an administrative, supervisory, or regulatory nature on behalf of the government. An Agency Crown Corporation—for example, the ROYAL CANADIAN MINT—carries out work of a quasi-commercial nature on behalf of the government. A Proprietary Crown Corporation—for example, AIR CANADA—is responsible for financial operations or for operations involving the production of goods or services to the public. There are unclassified Crown corporations, such as the BANK OF CANADA and the CANADA COUNCIL, that are governed by their individual Acts of incorporation. The government has also established for specific purposes corporations that are not agencies of the Crown and do not report to Parliament. PANARCTIC OILS and TELESAT CANADA are two examples of government-established non-Crown corporations.

Crown lands. See CROWN RESERVES.

Crown prerogative. The right of the CROWN to intervene in any action between subject and subject that may affect Crown rights. It is the basis for bringing an action to assert such rights, and to this end it may stay proceedings in the court. The right is exercised through the attorney general.

Crown reserves. Lands owned by the federal or provincial governments on which specific rights may be leased. In colonial times Crown reserves were tracts of land set apart to assure the Crown a source of revenue free from the control of the colonial legislatures. Less than 12% of the land area of Canada is privately owned; the rest is Crown lands.

Crow's Nest Pass. Route through the Rocky Mountains between Alberta and British Columbia, 4,450 ft above sea level. The CPR built a branch line through the pass in 1898.

Crow's Nest Pass Agreement. An agreement between the federal government and the CPR, passed in 1897. The CPR had been exempt from government regulations of its freight rates until it had earned a certain profit, but by the agreement of 1897 it reduced its rates on certain goods inbound into the prairie west and on grain outbound to eastern ports in return for a subsidy to build its branch line through the Crow's Nest Pass. Western farmers were thus able to overcome the high costs of exporting grain to world markets. The Crow's Nest rates were later extended to grain shipped to western ports.

CRTC. Initials of the CANADIAN RADIO-TELEVISION COMMISSION.

Crum, George (b.1926). Conductor. He came to Toronto at the age of three from Providence, R.I., and was educated at Trinity College School, Port Hope, Ont.; he also studied piano with Mona Bates in Toronto. He made his professional début as an opera conductor at 21, conducting *Faust* for the Royal Conservatory Opera and later was chorus master and a conductor for the CANADIAN OPERA COMPANY. He became conductor of the newly formed NATIONAL BALLET OF CANADA in 1951 and has been its musical director and conductor ever since. He has conducted internationally in both symphony and opera.

Crush International Limited. A world-wide

Crush International Limited

soft drink company based in Toronto. Beginning as Orange Crush Bottlers in 1921 and incorporated as Crush International Limited in 1927, it steadily acquired other bottling concerns and in the 1970s operates in more than 60 countries. Its line of beverages includes Orange Crush, Hires, Sun-Drop, Pure Spring, American Dry, Kik, Wilson's, Sussex, Gurd's, Vée de Vée, Old Colony, Gini, Uptown, Honee, Brio Chinotto, India Express, and Denis.

Cry of the Wild. Documentary feature film directed by Bill Mason and produced by the NFB in 1972. Mason, as the narrator, shares his love of wildlife, especially wolves, with the audience. The film was shot in the Northwest Territories, British Columbia, and the Arctic, and became a box-office hit through aggressive American promotion. 88 min., 4 sec.; colour.

Crysler's Farm, Battle of. An engagement in the WAR OF 1812. On 11 Nov. 1813, on a farmer's field on the north shore of the Upper St Lawrence, a British force of some 800 regulars, militia, and Indians under Lt-Col. Joseph W. Morrison defeated a numerically superior force of American troops under Gen. James Wilkinson that was advancing on Montreal.

CSU. Initials of the CANADIAN SEAMEN'S UNION.

CTCC. Initials of the Confédération des Travailleurs Catholiques du Canada. See CONFEDERATION OF NATIONAL TRADE UNIONS.

CTS. Initials of the COMMUNICATIONS TECHNOLOGY SATELLITE.

CTV. Call letters of the Canadian Television Network, a private network inaugurated on 1 Oct. 1961, with eight newly licensed television stations in Vancouver, Edmonton, Calgary, Winnipeg, Toronto, Ottawa, Montreal, and Halifax. On 1 Jan. 1976 there were stations in 17 cities in addition to 107 rebroadcast transmitters. The head office and main production studio, CFTO-TV, are in Toronto. CTV is sometimes called the 'second network', having been formed after the public CBC-TV NETWORK.

CUCND. Initials of the Combined Universities Campaign for Nuclear Disarmament, a student movement in Canada during the sixties. See also OUR GENERATION.

Cullen, Maurice (1866-1934). Painter. Born in St John's, Nfld, he settled with his family in Montreal in 1870 and studied painting in Paris. Returning to Canada in 1895, he

painted brightly coloured winter landscapes—such as *Logging in Winter* (1896, AGH)—in an Impressionist style, revelling in the possibilities of depicting snow. He resorted later to a more conventional, naturalistic style of painting.

Culture. A literary quarterly published in Quebec City from 1940 to 1971. It was edited by Edmond Gaudron and carried articles on the humanities in English or French.

Cultus coulee. West-coast Indian expression with the approximate meaning of wandering aimlessly but pleasurably, a 'crazy trip'. *Cultus* is CHINOOK JARGON for 'useless'; COULEE is an Anglicised form of the French word for 'gulch', *coulée*.

Cumberland, Frederick William (1821-81). Toronto architect. Born and trained in England, he came to Canada in 1847. In partnership with W.G. STORM, he designed some of Toronto's finest nineteenth-century buildings, notably UNIVERSITY COLLEGE (completed 1859), ST JAMES' CATHEDRAL (begun 1850), and the central portion of OSGOODE HALL (1857-60). His house, Pendarvis (1856), at St George and College Sts, became Baldwin House—the history department of the University of Toronto—and is now the university's International Student Centre.

CUPE. Acronym of the Ottawa-based Canadian Union of Public Employees. The largest union in the country, it was formed in 1963 when the National Union of Public Service Employees (founded in 1924) and the National Union of Public Employees (founded in 1955) dissolved their separate memberships and merged into one large union.

Curnoe, Greg (b.1936). Painter. Born in London, Ont., he studied there at Beal Technical School and later at the Ontario College of Art, Toronto. Influenced by the Dada aesthetic, he staged the first Canadian happening, 'The Celebration', in London in 1962, founded the Nihilist Party (1962), and wrote several anti-American manifestos. He creates inventive, brightly coloured hard-edge compositions that embody elements of pop art; their strong graphic qualities are often emphasized by the inclusion of a text in block letters. He brings both irony and whimsy to his treatments of nationalism, social criticism, and personal events—as in the powerful *Family Painting No. 1—In Labour* (1966, private coll.), a hospital scene inspired by the birth of his child. He lives in London and has exhibited internationally.

Currency. See BANK OF CANADA.

Currie, Gen. Sir Arthur (1875-1933). Army commander. Born at Napperton, Ont., he attended Strathroy Collegiate Institute and Model School, taught school for six years, and in 1900 opened an insurance and brokerage office in Victoria, B.C. In 1897 he joined the Militia, was commissioned in 1900, and by 1909 was commanding his regiment. At the outbreak of the FIRST WORLD WAR he assumed command of the 2nd Canadian Infantry Brigade, which withstood the onslaught at St Julien (near YPRES) in Apr. 1915. In Sept. 1915 he was appointed General Officer Commanding the 1st Canadian Infantry Division, and commanded this division during the Battles of the SOMME and VIMY Ridge. In June 1917 he was appointed GOC Canadian Corps. Currie distinguished himself as the commander of a superb fighting corps that maintained high morale despite the appalling conditions of trench warfare. On 15 Nov. 1919 he was promoted general and appointed Inspector-General Canadian Militia. After retiring from the army he became the principal and vice-chancellor of McGill University. He was knighted in 1917.

Curtiss JN-4. See JENNY.

CUSO. Acronym of CANADIAN UNIVERSITY SERVICE OVERSEAS.

Cut Knife Hill, Battle of. An engagement in the NORTH WEST REBELLION. POUNDMAKER'S camp at Cut Knife Hill, west of BATTLEFORD in present-day Saskatchewan, was the scene of a battle fought on 2 May 1885. Commanding his Cree, Poundmaker was able to check the advance of the Canadian militia under Col. William OTTER, who retired to Battleford.

CV. Initials that the holder of the CROSS OF VALOUR is entitled to place after his name.

CVO. Commander of the Royal Victorian Order, a British decoration for chivalry.

CWAC. Acronym of the Canadian Women's Army Corps.

CWO. Official abbreviation of Chief Warrant Officer.

Cybil Award. The CANADIAN BROADCASTING LEAGUE gives this award annually 'for a contribution by a person or program [that], in the opinion of the League, has been instrumental in upholding and promoting the public interest in broadcasting'. It was first awarded in 1974. Its name is formed from the initial letters of the CBL and recalls the sibyl of antiquity.

CYC. Initials of the COMPANY OF YOUNG CANADIANS.

Cygnet I. An immense tetrahedral kite built by the AERIAL EXPERIMENT ASSOCIATION and designed by Alexander Graham BELL as a means of carrying passengers. It kept Thomas Selfridge, a researcher, aloft at a height of 168 ft for seven minutes at Baddeck, N.S., on 6 Dec. 1907, but it had to be towed and no means of controlling its movement was ever devised.

Cypress Hills. A hilly region 60 mi. wide in the Prairies, straddling the border between southern Saskatchewan and Alberta. Rising from 400 to 500 ft above sea level, they contain fossils, pre-Ice Age ants, toads, rodents, and pine—not cypress trees.

Cyprus Lake Provincial Park. 1,818-acre park near the tip of the BRUCE PENINSULA, Ont. It includes forests, swamps, lakes for fishing, and wildlife. The steep cliffs of the Niagara Escarpment provide ideal lookout points over a part of Georgian Bay where rock formations and wrecks attract skin-divers.

Cyr, Louis (1863-1912). 'The strongest man in the world'. Born at St Cyprien de Napierville, C.W. (Ont.), he worked as a policeman before he capitalized on his strength. He won the world championship in weight-lifting and established several world records in London, Eng., in 1892. He travelled with the Ringling Brothers and Barnum and Bailey from 1894 to 1899 and was always one of Quebec's favourite sons.

D

D-Day. See NORMANDY INVASION.

Dafoe, John W. (1866-1944). Journalist. Born in Combermere, C.W. (Ont.), he became a parliamentary correspondent for the *Montreal Star* in 1884 and a convert to Liberalism. He moved to Winnipeg in 1886 to work for the *Manitoba* (later *Winnipeg*) *Free Press* and, after an interlude in Montreal, was its editor until his death. He was the leading Canadian journalist of his time, whose opinions were influential and widely respected. Among his books were studies of Wilfred LAURIER and Clifford SIFTON, who had owned the *Free Press*.

Dair, Carl (1912-67). Typographic designer. Born in Welland, Ont., he was a 'printer's devil' and salesman under Louis Blake Duff, editor of the Stratford *Beacon-Herald*, from 1922 to 1925. Acquiring the art and craft of typographical design through his association with various printing firms in Montreal and Toronto, he emerged as an internationally recognized typographer and designer in the 1950s. He was awarded the Silver Medal of the Leipzig International Book Fair in 1959, and taught at the ONTARIO COLLEGE OF ART from 1959 to 1962. He was the author of *Design with Type* (1952, 1967) and in the year of his death introduced CARTIER, the first typeface designed in Canada since 1841.

Dakota. See SIOUAN.

Dalhousie Review. An academic journal published by Dalhousie University, Halifax, appearing quarterly since 1920. It is specially concerned with political, social, and cultural life in Canada.

Dalhousie University. The provincial university of Nova Scotia, it was founded in Halifax in 1818 by Lord Dalhousie, then lieutenant-governor of the province. The largest university in the Atlantic provinces, it is the regional headquarters of the Institute of Public Affairs, established in 1937. It publishes the DALHOUSIE REVIEW. In 1969 Mount Saint Vincent University became a college within Dalhousie; co-operative arrangements are also maintained with the Nova Scotia Technical College and the UNIVERSITY OF KING'S COLLEGE.

Daly, Tom (b.1918). Film producer. Born in Toronto and educated at the University of Toronto, he joined the newly formed NATIONAL FILM BOARD in 1940. With Stuart Legg he edited the WORLD IN ACTION series, and from 1950 to 1964 he was executive producer for UNIT B and produced some of the Board's notable films, including the CANDID EYE television series. He is associated with such award-winning documentary features as UNIVERSE (1960), which won an Academy Award, and LABYRINTH (1967), a multi-screen film produced for Expo 67.

Dan McArthur Awards. Annual awards, one in radio and one in television, given to recognize enterprise and thoroughness in reporting a news story or community problems in greater detail and with a more meaningful background than can be done in a regular newscast. The documentary awards, sometimes called the 'Dans', after the late Dan C. McArthur, the CBC's first chief news editor, were first made in 1967 by the Radio Television News Directors Association of Canada (RTNDA). See also CHARLES EDWARDS AWARDS.

Danby, Ken (b.1940). Painter. Born in Sault Ste Marie, Ont., he studied at the Ontario College of Art with Jock MACDONALD and worked as a commercial artist. Painting in the *quattrocento* method, mixing pigment with egg yolk instead of oils, he creates intensely nostalgic rural Ontario scenes. His high realism is associated with the style of Alex COLVILLE and Andrew Wyeth. He is also attracted to sports for his subject matter. His powerful and skilfully painted study of a hockey goalkeeper, AT THE CREASE (1972, private coll.), has been widely reproduced. He is exhibited and collected internationally and lives near Guelph, Ont.

Dandelion wine. A popular rural fermented beverage. The Indians used spruce gum and saliva to activate fermentation, while settlers and farmers made the wine with yeast cake. May or June is the best time for dandelions.

Dandy Lion, The. Children's musical with words and music by Pat Patterson and Dodi Robb, Toronto broadcasters. It had its première in Toronto in Jan. 1965 and has been revived frequently in Canada and abroad. A young boy and a funny friendly lion decide to break into the real world of the circus. The script and score were published in 1972 as *The Dandy Lion: A One-Act Musical Play for Children*.

Dangerous Age, A. Feature film directed by Sidney J. FURIE and released in 1957. It starred Ben Piazza, Anne Pearson, Kate REID, J. Austin WILLIS, and Barbara HAMILTON. An underage boy and girl run off to the United States to get married. They are picked up by the police and eventually decide they should wait until they can marry legally in Canada. The director was only 24 years old at the time. The musical score was composed by Phil NIMMONS. 70 min., b & w.

Daniel, Antoine. See JESUIT MARTYRS.

'Dans, The'. See DAN McARTHUR AWARDS.

Daoust, Sylvia (b.1902). Sculptor. Born in Montreal, she studied there at the École des Beaux-Arts, where she later taught. The creator of wood carvings, bronze portrait busts, liturgical sculpture, and trophies, she was awarded a medal by the Royal Architectural Institute of Canada in 1961.

DAR. Initials of the Dominion Atlantic Railway.

Darling, Frank (1850-1923). Architect. Born in Scarborough, Ont., and educated at Upper Canada College and Trinity College, he trained in the offices of Henry Langley in Toronto and in London with G.E. Street, one of Britain's finest Gothic-Revival architects, and Sir Arthur Blomfield, architect to the Bank of England. When Darling returned to Toronto he practised with Alan Macdougall, S.G. Curry, and J.A. PEARSON (1895-1923). Darling's finest buildings—most of which are banks—were influenced by the Classical traditions of the English Georgian period and the manner of the École des Beaux-Arts in Paris. The Bank of Montreal at 30 Yonge St, Toronto (1885-6) is exuberantly and eclectically detailed in the manner of the French Beaux-Arts and incorporates the grandest early banking hall in Canada—octagonal, with a stained-glass dome. For the Bank of Commerce the firm of Darling and Pearson designed main offices and branches across the country and a series of prefabricated branches that could be erected in a few days but were dignified in a classical manner consistent with an image of wealth and power. The firm also designed for other Canadian banks—for example, the Dominion Bank Head Office, 1-5 King W., Toronto (1914)—and homes for several prominent bankers, notably 'Holwood' for Sir Joseph Flavelle at 78 Queen's Park Crescent W., Toronto (1901)—now the Faculty of Law, University of Toronto. In 1916 Darling was awarded the Royal Gold Medal of the Royal Institute of British Architects, the first 'colonial' architect

to be so honoured, in recognition of his importance to, and influence on, Canadian architecture.

Daulac. See DOLLARD DES ORMEAUX.

Davey, Frank (b.1940). Poet and critic. Born in Vancouver, he was founding editor of TISH while still a student at the University of British Columbia. On the staff of York University, Toronto, since 1970, he is editor of OPEN LETTER, a quarterly of poetics. His lyric poetry has appeared in some 12 volumes, several of them privately printed, including *Four Myths for Sam Perry* (1970), *L'An trentième: Selected Poems 1961-70* (1972), and *The Clallam* (1973). Among his critical writings are *Earle* BIRNEY (1971) and *From There to Here: A Guide to English-Canadian Literature Since 1960* (1974).

Davey, Keith. (b.1926). Senator and prominent Liberal spokesman. Born in Toronto, he graduated from the University of Toronto in 1948 and was sales manager of CKFH in Toronto (1949-60). National organizer of the Liberal Party of Canada from 1961 to 1966, he was appointed to the Senate in 1966. That year the columnist Scott Young dubbed Davey 'The Rainmaker' for his uncanny ability to predict the outcome of federal elections. He prepared 'The Davey Report' of the Special Senate Committee on Mass Media in 1971.

'David'. Well-known narrative poem by Earle BIRNEY. It tells of a tragic incident involving two students who attempted, one 'sunalive weekend', to scale 'the Finger of Sawback' in the Rocky Mountain range in Banff National Park. David saves Bob's life but in the process falls and is paralysed. He begs Bob to roll him over the ledge to a certain death, and Bob complies. Though the 184-line poem, brilliantly executed in stress scansion and half rhyme, dramatizes an instance of mercy killing, it does not advocate the practice. But this did not stop certain schools from refusing to teach the poem when it was listed as required reading in upper-school courses. Written in 1940, it was published in *David and Other Poems* (1942) and gave Birney the ill-deserved reputation of 'the man who would push his best friend over a cliff'.

David: Chapter 2. 90-minute CBC-TV play by M. Charles COHEN. Directed by Harvey HART and shown on 28 Jan. 1963, it is about a Jewish youth beset by rebelliousness and indecision in Winnipeg during the summer of 1948. David was played by Donnelly Rhodes, his girl friend Lilith by Toby Tarnow. Hart also directed the sequel, *David: Chapter 3*, shown on 5 Oct. 1966, with Mark Richman playing the lead—David is now a lawyer, 39, a husband and a father—and Toby Tarnow playing his wife. These plays are based on chapters from Cohen's semi-fictionalized, still-unpublished autobiography.

David Dunlap Observatory, The. Research centre for studies in astronomy and astrophysics. Located in Richmond Hill, Ont., it was presented to the University of Toronto in 1935 by Jessie Dunlap. It advances theoretical and observational research, trains students from the university, and fosters public interest in astronomy. Housing Canada's largest telescope (the mirror is 74 in. in diameter), it is open to the public by appointment.

David Mirvish Gallery. Commercial art gallery in Toronto. Founded in 1963 by David Mirvish, the son of Edwin MIRVISH, it shows primarily North American post-war abstract painting and sculpture, including works by both Americans and Canadians.

Davidialuk. See Davidialuk AMIITUK.

Davidson, Joyce. See TABLOID.

Davidson, Robert (Bob) (b.1947). Haida carver. Born at Masset in the Queen Charlotte Islands, B.C., and a member of the Eagle clan, he is the great-grandson of Charles EDENSHAW. He had a one-year apprenticeship with Bill REID and studied for one year at the Vancouver Art School. Since 1969, when one of his totem poles was raised in his native village, he has been recognized as a leading carver. He lives at Whonnock in the Fraser Valley.

Davies, Robertson (b.1913). Novelist, playwright, and man of letters. Born in Thamesville, Ont., and educated at Oxford, he was literary editor of *Saturday Night* (1940-2), editor of the Peterborough *Examiner* (1942-60), and is now Master of MASSEY COLLEGE. His first three novels—*Tempest Tost* (1951), LEAVEN OF MALICE (1954), and *A Mixture of Frailties* (1958)—are witty social comedies set in SALTERTON, a fictitious community identified with Kingston, Ont. Davies achieved true distinction and international recognition as a novelist in the 1970s with his trilogy: FIFTH BUSINESS (1970), *The Manticore* (1972), and *World of Wonders* (1975). Intricately plotted (though highly readable) and informed by the principles of Jungian psychology, they unfold and illuminate the mysteries of human motives and character as the narratives move from a small Ontario town called Deptford to Europe and South America. Davies' plays include *Eros at Breakfast* (1949),

FORTUNE MY FOE (1949), *At My Heart's Core* (1950), *A* JIG FOR THE GYPSY (1954), and *Hunting Stuart* (1972). *Love and Libel*, an adaptation of *Leaven of Malice*, was first performed in 1957, and his most recent play, *Question Time*, was produced in 1975. In the 1940s Davies created SAMUEL MARCHBANKS, whose trenchant comments on twentieth-century life appear in *The Diary of Samuel Marchbanks* (1947), *The Table Talk of Samuel Marchbanks* (1949), and *Samuel Marchbanks' Almanack* (1968). Davies' occasional essays are collected in *A Voice from the Attic* (1960), in which he gives a name to the readership he writes for: the 'clerisy'—those who enjoy books but are not professionally involved with them. He has also written *Stephen Leacock* (1970), a study of the humorist, and edited *The Feast of Stephen* (1970), a collection of lesser-known Leacock pieces.

Davies, Thomas (*c*.1737-1812). English officer-artist. Trained in watercolour painting by Paul Sandby at the Royal Military Academy, Woolwich, Eng., he was the most gifted of the officers who depicted the Canadian landscape in watercolours. He spent four tours of duty in North America: in 1757-63, 1764-7, 1776-9, and 1786-90, when he was lieutenant-colonel in command of the artillery at Quebec. Among his most admired landscapes—which are vibrantly alive with glowing colours, minutely detailed foliage, and rhythmic, somewhat stylized compositions—are two views of Montreal made in 1762 and 1812 (his last watercolour, based on a sketch made many years earlier) and *The Falls of Ste Anne* (1790)—all in the NGC.

Davin, Nicholas Flood (1843-1901). Journalist and politician. Born in Kilfinane, Ire., and educated at London University, he came to Canada in 1872, wrote for the Toronto *Globe* and later the *Mail* and the *Empire*. In 1883 he established the Regina *Leader*, the first newspaper issued in ASSINIBOIA, and from 1887 to 1900 he represented West Assiniboia in the House of Commons. Although he published books of poetry, drama, political satire, and polemics and a study of the Irish in Canada, he is principally remembered for gaining entrance, disguised as a priest, to the Regina prison where Louis RIEL was awaiting execution. Davin's exclusive interview appeared in the *Leader* on 16 Nov. 1885.

Davis, Fred (b.1921). Television personality. Born in Toronto, he began in show business as a trumpeter in one of Howard CABLE's bands. A graduate of the ACADEMY OF RADIO ARTS, he was co-host (with Anna Cameron), starting in 1956, of *Open House* for four seasons, and became the host of the long-running FRONT PAGE CHALLENGE in 1957. Affable and unflappable, he has been dubbed 'Mr Nice Guy'.

Davis (Davys), John (c.1550-1605). English navigator and explorer, discoverer of DAVIS STRAIT. In search of a NORTHWEST PASSAGE he made three voyages—in 1585, 1586, and 1587—in which he charted stretches of the Greenland, Baffin Island, and Labrador coasts.

Davis Family. A theatrical trio consisting of Donald, Murray, and Barbara Davis (who acts under her mother's name of Chilcott). All three were born in Newmarket, Ont.— Donald in 1928, Murray in 1925, Barbara in 1923—and acted at HART HOUSE, managed the STRAW HAT PLAYERS (1948-55), and founded the CREST THEATRE (1953-66), where they made a 'grand entrance' in J.B. Priestley's play The GLASS CAGE (1957), written specially for them. Donald and Barbara both acted in the STRATFORD FESTIVAL in 1955; Donald, who also appeared at the Festival in 1956, acted in New York for 10 years from 1959 and now works mainly as a director. Murray taught at the NATIONAL THEATRE SCHOOL and is now retired from the theatre. Barbara, who married the composer Harry SOMERS in 1967, still acts occasionally on stage and television.

Davis Strait. The northern arm of the Atlantic Ocean, which separates Baffin Island from Greenland (part of Denmark), named after its discoverer, John DAVIS. With Baffin Bay at its north end, it is usually frozen from November to April. In late spring it is a major source of icefloes carried south by the Labrador Current.

'Dawn to Dusk Across Canada'. Romantic name of an early trans-Canada flight. The Department of Transport arranged the well-publicized demonstration hop on 30 July 1937. C.D. HOWE, the Minister of Transport, C.P. Edwards, Deputy Minister, and H.J. Symington, a director of TRANS-CANADA AIRLINES, left Montreal aboard a DOT Lockheed 12A, CF-CCT and, with refuellings at Gilles, Sioux Lookout, Winnipeg, Regina, and Lethbridge, landed in Vancouver the same day. Travelling 200 m.p.h., the elapsed time was 17 hours 35 minutes. Its purpose was to demonstrate confidence in the newly created transcontinental airway system.

Dawson. City on the east bank of the Yukon R. at the confluence of the Klondike R. Known as the Yukon's 'City of Gold', it sprang up after the discovery of gold on BONANZA CREEK in 1896 and boasted a population of 25,000 at the peak of the KLONDIKE GOLD RUSH. As accessible gold was removed, the population dwindled and today it has fewer than 750 permanent residents. It is the site of several restored gold-rush buildings, including the Palace Grand Theatre, which is part of KLONDIKE GOLD RUSH INTERNATIONAL HISTORIC PARK.

Dawson, Sir John William (1820-99). Geologist and writer. Born in Pictou, N.S., he was educated at the Pictou Academy and the University of Edinburgh. A voluminous writer, he was a noted geologist and naturalist who wrote many popular books on his subjects as well as scientific papers. He was president of McGill University from 1855 to his retirement in 1893, was first president of the Royal Society of Canada (1882) and president of both the British (1886) and American (1892) Associations for the Advancement of Science.

Dawson City Gold Rush Festival. The first and last attempt of the federal government to bolster tourism in the YUKON TERRITORY through a summer festival. The highlight of the celebration, from 1 July to 17 Aug. 1962, was the world première of the musical Foxy, starring Bert Lahr, in Dawson's Palace Grand Theatre, which was built in 1899.

Day, Clarence (Hap) (b.1901). Hockey player, coach, and manager. Born in Owen Sound, Ont., he played amateur hockey before he graduated in pharmacy. He began his professional career with the Toronto St Patricks (later the TORONTO MAPLE LEAFS) and launched a 33-year career as hockey player, captain, coach, manager, and referee. During his playing career he teamed up with 'King' CLANCY to form an all-time great defence. He retired from hockey in 1958.

Daylight Saving Time. Method of conserving daylight. Daylight Saving Time was first introduced by the federal government in 1918 and has been used intermittently ever since. The departure from STANDARD TIME permits the maximum use of sunlight during the non-winter months. The mnemonic device 'Spring forward, fall back' is a reminder that at a designated hour and day in the spring, clocks are set forward one hour, and in the fall backwards one hour.

Dayliner. A self-propelled railway passenger car built by the Budd Company and introduced to CPR service in 1953. It is also the popular name for a train consisting of one or more of these cars.

DC-3. A popular aircraft flown by TRANS-CANADA AIR LINES from 1945 to 1963. Built by Douglas Aircraft in the United States as a military aircraft (C-47s) and converted to passenger use in Canada for TCA, it seated from 21 to 28 passengers in an unpressurized cabin and flew 160 m.p.h.

DC-4. See NORTH STAR.

DC-8. A turbojet aircraft introduced by TRANS-CANADA AIR LINES in 1960. Built by Douglas Aircraft in the United States, it carried 127 passengers at 550 m.p.h. TCA later introduced the Super (or Stretched) DC-8, which carried 198 passengers at 550 m.p.h.

DC-9. A turbojet aircraft introduced by AIR CANADA in 1966. Built by Douglas Aircraft in the United States, it carries 95 passengers at 530 m.p.h.

DCB. See DICTIONARY OF CANADIAN BIOGRAPHY.

DCM. See MEDAL FOR DISTINGUISHED CONDUCT IN THE FIELD.

DDF. See DOMINION DRAMA FESTIVAL.

De Cosmos, Amor (1825-97). Premier of British Columbia. Born William Alexander Smith in Windsor, N.S., he left Nova Scotia for California in 1851 and in 1854 had his name legally changed in Sacramento. In 1858 he went to Vancouver Island, where he founded a newspaper, the *British Colonist*, in Victoria. An eccentric figure, he had a brief 13-year prominence in British Columbia affairs as an agitator for the union of Vancouver Island and mainland British Columbia, for the entry of the united British Columbia into Confederation, and for the achievement of responsible government for the province—all of which were won. A member of the legislative assembly of the Island from 1863 to 1866 and of the legislative council of the united colony from 1867 to 1871, he was elected to the House of Commons in 1871 and was premier of the province from 1872 to 1874. He retired in 1882.

De Havilland Aircraft of Canada. Well-known manufacturer of leading military and civilian aircraft. A subsidiary of the British company, it was formed in 1928 and began by servicing the parent company's aircraft at Downsview, near Toronto. It is active in the STOL field and was bought by the Canadian government in 1975. Planes manufactured by the parent company are identified by DH followed by the model number; planes manufactured by the Canadian company by DHC followed by the model number. Many DHC planes are well known by name, including BEAVER, BUFFALO, CARIBOU, CHIPMUNK, Dragonfly, Fox Moth, GYPSY MOTH, MOSQUITO, OTTER, TIGER MOTH, TWIN OTTER, and Vampire.

de la Roche, Mazo (1885-1961). Novelist. Born in Toronto, where she lived, she was the author of three novels—*Explorers of the Dawn* (1922), *Possession* (1923), and *Delight* (1926)—before she achieved fame by winning a well-publicized *Atlantic Monthly* prize with JALNA (1927). It was so popular that it was followed by *Whiteoaks of Jalna* (1929), *Finch's Fortune* (1931), *The Master of Jalna* (1933), *Young Renny* (1935), *Whiteoak Harvest* (1936), *Whiteoak Heritage* (1940), *Wakefield's Course* (1941), *The Building of Jalna* (1944), *Return to Jalna* (1946), *Mary Wakefield* (1949), *Renny's Daughter* (1951), *The Whiteoak Brothers* (1953), *Variable Winds at Jalna* (1954), and *Morning at Jalna* (1960). The matriarch who built Jalna and celebrated her hundredth birthday there was Adeline Whiteoak, played by Kate REID in CBC-TV's dramatization WHITEOAKS OF JALNA (1972). Other books by Mazo de la Roche were eclipsed by the success of the Jalna series: novels about young children growing up, tales about animals and birds for young readers, several plays, including *Whiteoaks* (1936)—a West End and Broadway success in 1936-7—and an autobiography, *Ringing the Changes* (1957).

De Mille, James (1836-80). Novelist. Born in Saint John, N.B., and educated at Acadia University and Brown University, Rhode Island, he taught classics at Acadia and then English at Dalhousie University from 1860 until his death. He wrote many popular novels for the North American market but is mainly remembered for A STRANGE MANUSCRIPT FOUND IN A COPPER CYLINDER, a utopian novel published posthumously in 1888. He also wrote four children's books about a band of boys—the B.O.W.C. (Brothers of the White Cross)—and 'Sweet Maiden of Passamaquoddy', a light poem, published in 1870, that rhymes melodious New Brunswick place-names.

de Pédery-Hunt, Dora (b.1913). Medallist and sculptor. Born in Budapest, Hungary, she graduated from the Royal School of Applied Arts before coming to Canada in 1948. She specializes in the medallic arts and has exhibited her finely designed and executed medals internationally. Among her many commissions are the CENTENNIAL MEDAL and the medal for Expo 70 at Osaka. A book illustrating her work, *Medals*, was published in 1974.

de Tonnancour, Jacques (b.1917). Painter. Born in Montreal, he studied there at the École des Beaux-Arts and the Montreal Museum of Fine Arts School. Turning from abstract landscapes in oil to a realistic style, he painted warmly coloured and powerfully designed studies of the Laurentians before moving to spare collages in which the feeling of archaeological ruins comes from minimal elements and muted colours. *Edge of the Forest* (1957, private coll.) is one of his finest works. He is exhibited and collected internationally, and lives in Montreal, where he has taught at the École des Beaux-Arts.

Deacon, William Arthur (b.1890). Writer and critic. Born in Pembroke, Ont., he graduated from the University of Manitoba in 1918 and practised in Winnipeg as a lawyer. A writer for the *Winnipeg Free Press*, he served as book-review editor of *Saturday Night* (1922-8) and as literary editor of the *Globe and Mail* (1928-60). His book column, 'The Fly Leaf', appeared until his retirement in 1963. Deacon, who now lives in Hamilton, Ont., was Canada's first full-time book reviewer and is the author of several books, including the classic *The* FOUR JAMESES (1927).

Death of Wolfe, The. Famous Neo-Classical painting by Benjamin West of James WOLFE expiring on the Plains of Abraham after taking Quebec on 13 Sept. 1759. West was a Pennsylvania-born historical painter who died in London, Eng., in 1820. His monumental canvas, a fantasized depiction of the event, shows the dying hero surrounded by officers and a crouching Indian. It was completed in 1770. (West was commissioned to paint three other versions, one for George III.) It was given to the National Gallery of Canada by the Duke of Westminster, through Lord Beaverbrook, as a tribute to Canada's role in the First World War.

Debassige, Blake (b.1956). Ojibwa artist. Born on the West Bay Reserve, Manitoulin Island, Ont., he attended the Manitou Arts Foundation's Schreiber Island Program of instruction in the summer of 1972 and then Laurentian University in Sudbury. He completed in 1973 eight bas-relief carvings for the entrance to the Chingaucousy Centennial park in Bramalea, Ont. His acrylic paintings interpret the legends of his people.

Deciduous Forest Region. Forest area that extended from the United States into southwestern Ontario between Lakes Huron, Erie and Ontario. Sugar maple, beech, white elm, and other deciduous trees were common to the region. Very little of this forest remains.

Decoration Day. A day formerly set aside to deck the graves of the war dead with flags and floral tributes. Between the two World Wars it was observed on a local basis by members of the IODE and the ROYAL CANADIAN LEGION in late May. It has been largely superseded by REMEMBRANCE DAY ceremonies.

Deep Bay Crater. One of Canada's two-dozen meteorite craters. Located on Reindeer Lake in northern Saskatchewan, it is 5.9 mi. wide and, excluding fill, nearly 2,000 ft deep. Fossils in sedimentary rocks within the crater indicate that it is about 100 million years old.

Deep River. Town built for atomic-energy workers on the Ottawa R., north of Pembroke, Ont. It was named on 22 Jan. 1945 when the site was selected to house personnel connected with the nuclear reactor at nearby CHALK RIVER.

Deer, White-tailed. Species of Canadian deer with a long white tail, forward-arching antlers, and weighing about 200 lb. full grown. Its colour changes from a reddish brown in summer to greyish brown in winter. Widely distributed in woodlands from Nova Scotia to southeastern British Columbia, it is the most important game animal in North America and was once the source of food and buckskin to Indians and white settlers.

Defence Council. Principal policy group within the Department of National Defence concerned with military, scientific, financial, and foreign-policy matters. It was reactivated in July 1964 as a prelude to the integration (1966-7) and UNIFICATION (1968) of the CANADIAN ARMED FORCES.

Defence Research Board. Statutory agency in the Department of National Defence responsible for defence research and for advising the Minister of National Defence on all matters relating to scientific, technical, and other research and development that, in its opinion, may affect national defence. The DRB was established on 1 Apr. 1947.

Defence Scheme No. 1. A reference to guidelines for the Canadian Army in case of a U.S. military invasion of Canada. Various scenarios were drawn up by Col. J.S. (Buster) Brown, Director of Military Operations and Intelligence, Department of National Defence, between 1921 and 1931, when the operation was cancelled. One such document is reproduced in the Jackdaw *Canadian-American Relations* (1975), compiled by Wilfried Neidhardt.

Defence Staff. See CHIEF OF THE DEFENCE STAFF.

Defendo. A system of self-protection based on the immediate administration of pain. It was created in 1907 by W.F. (Bill) Underwood, who as a youth in England worked with Houdini and acquired the art of ju-jitsu.

Defendo

Since 1931 he has taught Defendo in Toronto—although he is now advanced in years—but the system is better known outside the country than within it.

Degaussing. A procedure used during the Second World War to demagnetize ships. To protect Allied vessels from magnetic mines, they were first neutralized by being encircled with giant coils in which electrical currents were flowing. Then copper degaussing cables, carrying electric currents, were wired throughout their hulls. Some 2,000 Allied ships were degaussed at Halifax and other ports in May and June of 1940. The procedure was devised by Charles Goodeve, a Winnipeg scientist who received an OBE for his work the following year. A gauss is a unit of magnetic induction, named after the nineteenth-century German mathematician Karl Friedrich Gauss.

Deichman pottery. Highly valued and widely exhibited pottery. The bowls, vases, plates, etc., designed and crafted by Kjeld and Erica Deichman at their studio at Moss Glen, N.B., were characterized by delicate blue and green glazes. Copenhagen-born Kjeld and Wisconsin-born Erica were married in Canada in the 1930s. The business was sold in 1963, following the death of Kjeld.

Deirdre. An opera by Healey WILLAN, composed in 1943-5 and originally called *Deirdre of the Sorrows.* It was the first opera commissioned by the CBC and one of the earliest of Canadian operas. With a libretto by John COULTER, it is based on a famous story of ill-fated lovers from the *Tales of the Red Branch Knights of Ulster.* It was broadcast by CBC Radio on 20 Apr. 1946 and was performed by the CANADIAN OPERA COMPANY at the O'Keefe Centre, Toronto, in 1966.

Dekanahwideh. A semi-legendary IROQUOIS hero. According to tradition, he was a HURON, born to a virgin mother, near the present site of Kingston, Ont., and was raised by a Mohawk family. His name may mean 'two river currents flowing together'. Dekanahwideh is the traditional founder of the IROQUOIS Confederacy, established in 1459 or later. In bringing the 'Great Peace' to the Six Nations Indians, he was assisted by the semi-legendary HIAWATHA. Shortly before his death Dekanahwideh promised the Iroquois: 'If the Great Peace should fail, call on my name in the bushes, and I will return.'

Delamont, Gordon (b.1918). Jazz composer, teacher, and trumpeter. Born in Moose Jaw,

Sask., he moved to Toronto in 1937 and played trumpet on CBC Radio and in several dance orchestras. From 1945 to 1959 he was head of his own band and in 1949 opened the Gordon Delamont Studios in Toronto, where he teaches composition and arranging. Among his compositions is the *Ontario Suite,* a commission from the Ontario government for EXPO 67.

Delaney, Marshall. See Robert FULFORD.

Delta. 'A magazine of poetry'. Founded by Louis DUDEK in Montreal in 1957, it appeared quarterly until 1966, publishing poems and criticism, especially work with social relevance, by the leading poets of the day.

Delta Canada. Small poetry-publishing house founded in Montreal by Louis DUDEK, Glen Siebrasse, and Michael Gnarowski in 1964. It issued books and booklets of contemporary poetry until 1972, when it was succeeded by three presses: Glen Siebrasse's Delta Books, Louis Dudek's D.C. Books, and Michael Gnarowski's Golden Dog Press.

Demara, Ferdinand Waldo (b.1921). Imposter. Born in Lawrence, Mass., to an American mother and an Irish-French father of Canadian ancestry, he became notorious in the 1950s as 'the Great Imposter' or 'alter-egoist' when it was discovered that he had successfully assumed a number of identities, some of them of Canadians. He posed as a Trappist in Montreal in 1943 and as a Royal Canadian Navy surgeon from Mar. to Nov. 1951 abroad the HMCS *Cayuga* (where he performed an emergency appendectomy). His last Canadian imposture was as an associate professor of psychology at Lakehead University, Thunder Bay, from 1963 to 1966. Demara then found his true vocation as an evangelist in Oregon.

Demonstration woodlot. Term used in Ontario by the Department of Lands and Forests from the 1930s to the 1950s to identify a tract of land in its natural state where trespassers were not allowed. The Woodlot Improvement Act (1966) provides for agreements with private landowners whereby the Ministry of National Resources plants trees and manages the lot for a 15-year period, after which time the owner assumes full responsibility.

Dene. ATHAPASKAN word for 'the people', the name of a proposed separate Indian nation in the Northwest Territories. The proposal, made by the Indian Brotherhood and Métis Association of the Northwest Territories in July 1975, was that Indians of Chipewyan,

Cree, Dogrib, Loucheux, and Slavey ancestry constitute the Dene nation.

Denison, Merrill (1893-1975). Playwright and company historian. Born in Detroit, he settled in Toronto in 1919 as the first art director of HART HOUSE THEATRE, where his first plays were produced. Such satires on the he-man cult of the North as *Marsh Hay* appeared in *The Unheroic North* (1923). Other works about the North are *Boobs in the Woods* (1927) and KLONDIKE MIKE (1943). His scripts for the ROMANCE OF CANADA radio series were published as *Henry Hudson and Other Plays* (1931). He moved to New York, where he wrote a similar series for American radio, and returned to Montreal in the mid-1950s. Denison's company histories are *Harvest Triumphant* (Massey Harris, now MASSEY-FERGUSON, 1949), *The Barley and the Stream* (MOLSON, 1955), *The People's Power* (ONTARIO HYDRO, 1960), and *Canada's First Bank* (BANK OF MONTREAL, 2 vols, 1966, 1967). He married Muriel DENISON in 1926.

Denison, Muriel (1885-1954). Author of children's books. Born in Winnipeg, she married Merrill DENISON in 1926. A film made in 1939 starring Shirley Temple, SUSANNAH OF THE MOUNTIES, was based on the first of four books about the bright nine-year-old girl who is 'adopted' by a North West Mounted Police detachment near Regina in the 1880s: SUSANNAH, A LITTLE GIRL WITH THE MOUNTIES (1936), *Susannah of the Yukon* (1937), *Susannah at Boarding School* (1938), and *Susannah Rides Again* (1940).

Denison Mines Limited. See Stephen B. ROMAN.

Denison's Ice Road. An Arctic truck route in the Northwest Territories. Covering more than 300 mi. of snowy ground and frozen lakes, it exists only in winter. It connects Rae, the northern terminus of the Yellowknife Highway on the northwestern tip of Great Slave Lake, with Port Radium on the eastern shore of Great Bear Lake, travelling over a chain of lakes. There are plans to run another road over Great Bear Lake to Coppermine on Coronation Gulf. The ice road is named after its supervising engineer, John Denison, an ex-Mountie turned trucker.

deNiverville, Louis (b.1933). Painter. Born in Andover, Eng., he is entirely self-taught. He worked with the CBC graphics department before devoting himself to painting. The wry grotesqueries of his richly coloured early paintings, almost child-like in their imaginative fantasy, were the basis of the surrealistic vision of human isolation that now dominates his work. A painter of the subconscious, who often returns to the symbolic garden motif, he has simplified textural details by using acrylic and air-brush techniques to create blurred surfaces around brilliantly coloured figures that are compelling and ominous. One of his finest works is *The Enclosure* (1975, AGO). He lives in Toronto, where he teaches part-time at the Ontario College of Art, and has exhibited internationally.

DePoe, Norman (b.1917). Broadcaster. Born in Portland, Oregon, he was brought to Vancouver in 1923 and joined CBC Radio in 1948 as a newscaster. As host of CBC NEWSMAGAZINE in 1959 and an Ottawa-based national affairs commentator from 1960 to 1968, he achieved popularity with his informality and his gravelly voice.

Depression, The. A 10-year period of world economic disaster that began with the stock-market crash on Wall St, New York, in Oct. 1929. Canada's economy was severely affected, especially in the West, and at the same time the Prairies were hit by unprecedented drought that produced 'dust bowl' conditions and ruined many farmers. High unemployment caused great hardship as workers turned to local relief for the means to keep themselves alive; others travelled across the country, hitchhiking or 'riding the rods' on freight trains to look for work; many single men ended up in RELIEF CAMPS. Finally the ON-TO-OTTAWA trek was organized to protest against these conditions. New political parties were founded, among them SOCIAL CREDIT and the CCF. The prime minister, R.B. BENNETT, brought in 'new deal' legislation to handle the economic problems, which was disallowed by the Judicial Committee of the Privy Council. The Depression ended only after the outbreak of the Second World War stimulated both industry and agriculture.

Deputy minister. The civil-service head of a government department, e.g., 'Deputy Minister of Finance'. He manages the department for the minister, who is a member of the CABINET. The American equivalent is 'Under-Secretary'.

Des Barres, J.F.W. (1722-1824). British military cartographer. Educated at the Royal Military College, Woolwich, Eng., he surveyed for the British admiralty the St Lawrence R. from Quebec to the Gulf and the east coast from Nova Scotia to the Gulf of Mexico between 1763 and 1773. As a result of this work he produced *The* ATLANTIC NEPTUNE, four volumes of charts and superb monochrome prints, which appeared between 1770 and 1781. He was lieutenant-governor of Prince Edward Island from 1805 to 1812.

Desbarats, Peter. See CANADIAN ILLUSTRATED NEWS.

Desbiens, Jean-Paul. See Brother ANONYMOUS.

Deschambault, rue. Street in St Boniface, Man., where Gabrielle ROY lived at number 375. She wrote about it in the novel *Rue Deschambault* (1955), known as *Street of Riches* in its English translation by Harry Binsse.

Deschamps, Yvon (b.1934). Quebec performer. Born in Montreal and a Grade X drop-out, he made his début in a Montreal cabaret in 1967 with the then-unknown singer Robert CHARLEBOIS. Deschamps has since become an increasingly important singer and stand-up comedian in Quebec revues, concerts, recordings, and films. He delivers witty monologues, which he writes himself, about the 'little guy' from the East End whose main concerns are *une bonne job et un bon boss* ('a good job and a good boss'). In 1974, in place of the unnamed labourer, he introduced one Roger Lalumière, a *gars de la shoppe* ('a guy from the factory') who lives in the suburbs and hates his boss as much as he loves his union.

Design Canada. See NATIONAL DESIGN COUNCIL.

Desmarais, Paul. See POWER CORPORATION.

Desmarteau, Étienne (1877-1905). Champion weight-thrower. At the 1904 Olympics in St Louis, Mo., the Montreal policeman threw a 56-lb. weight a distance of 34 ft 4 in. to become the only non-American to win a gold medal in a track-and-field event in those games that year. He died of typhoid fever the following year.

Detroit, Capture of. An engagement in the WAR OF 1812. On 16 Aug. 1812 Gen. William Hull surrendered the American-held fort without a fight to Gen. Isaac BROCK, half of whose men were Indians under TECUMSEH.

Detroit River. It connects Lake St Clair and Lake Erie, forming part of the international border between Canada and the United States.

Detroit-Windsor Tunnel. A vehicular tunnel under the Detroit R. that connects Detroit, Mich., and Windsor, Ont. Construction of the tube tunnel, which is almost a mile in length, commenced in 1928.

'Devil in the hair'. Unintentional image on federal bank notes. Shortly after the 1954 issue appeared, the 'devil' was discovered in the Queen's hair. Certain unshaded portions of her hair created the illusion of an ugly face behind the ear. All denominations were issued using the 'devil' plates, but before too long new plates with a re-done coiffure eliminated the apparition.

Devil's field. The *champ du diable*, a rocky pasture at Rigaud, Que. According to a legend common in the Lac des Deux Montagnes country, a certain farmer provoked God's wrath by tending his fields on Sunday only to find that his potato crop had turned to stone. Rigaud also boasts the Shrine of Our Lady of Lourdes.

Devoir, Le. A morning newspaper published in Montreal. Founded by the Quebec nationalist Henri BOURASSA and first issued on 10 Jan. 1910, it is the province's most influential publication, although in circulation it is easily outstripped by its rival *La* PRESSE. Among the important editors of *Le Devoir* have been Bourassa, Gérard Filion, and André LAURENDEAU. Claude Ryan is the present editor. Its motto is *Fais ce que dois* ('Let's get on with it').

Devonshire, Duke of (1868-1938). GOVERNOR GENERAL of Canada from 1916 to 1921.

DEW Line. Distant Early Warning Line. It consists of some 50 tracking, warning, and control stations constructed by the United States, but operated and manned by Canadians since 1959. This part of a system of continental defence extends across the northern limits of the Arctic Islands from Greenland to Alaska, roughly along the 70th parallel. The undertaking was announced in a joint communiqué of the defence departments of Canada and the United States on 27 Dec. 1954. See also MID-CANADA LINE and PINE TREE LINE.

Dewar, Phyllis (1916-61). Noted swimmer. She trained in Vancouver and represented Canada in the 1934 British Empire Games in London, Eng., where she won four gold medals in swimming.

Dewart, Leslie (b.1922). Theologian. Born in Madrid, Spain, and educated in Havana, Cuba, he immigrated to Canada in 1942 and is a graduate of the University of Toronto. Since 1956 he has taught at St Michael's College, University of Toronto, and has been a professor in its Institute of Christian Thought since 1969. A distinguished Roman Catholic intellectual, he is the author of *Christianity and Revolution* (1963), *The Future of Belief* (1966), *The Foundations of Belief* (1969), and *Religion, Language and Truth* (1970).

DFC. See DISTINGUISHED FLYING CROSS.

DFM. See DISTINGUISHED FLYING MEDAL.

Dhârâna. Canvas by F.H. VARLEY painted in Vancouver in 1932. The title refers to a Buddhist state of spiritual union with nature and the painting shows a seated girl whose exalted state and relationship with nature are expressed in the elongation of her torso, her uplifted head, and the soft greens, blues, and purples of both the background and the girl herself. (AGO)

Diamond, A.J. (b.1932). Architect. Born in South Africa, he was educated at the University of Cape Town, Oxford, and the University of Pennsylvania, where he studied with Louis Kahn; he also worked in the London office of Sir Hugh Casson. He came to Canada in 1965. With Barton MYERS he designed the Ontario Medical Association building (1968) and York Square (1969), both in Toronto, and the student housing for the University of Alberta, Edmonton (1969)—all acknowledging and respecting the existing urban fabric without compromising a strongly contemporary character. The Dundas-Sherbourne project, Toronto (1973-6), was both innovative and influential in its combination of sympathetically renovated period houses and relatively high-density infill housing to serve the city's need for low- and moderate-income housing in the core area. The building for Innis College, University of Toronto—designed independently in 1975—continues his development into the field of institutional design.

Diamonds of Canada. See Kingdom of SAGUENAY.

D'Iberville. A CBC-TV series about the adventures of Pierre Lemoyne, Sieur d'IBERVILLE. The French soldier and explorer of early Canada was played by Albert MILLAIRE. The series was shot on the Île d'Orléans and produced by the French network through co-production arrangements with French, Belgian, and Swiss television networks. The first of the 39 half-hour weekly episodes was shown on the English network on 7 Oct. 1968.

Dick murder case. Sensational murder trials involving Evelyn Dick, a beautiful woman scandalously linked with prominent Hamilton men. A jury found her not guilty of murdering her husband John Dick, whose body—minus arms, legs, and head—was found on the Hamilton escarpment on 16 Mar. 1946. When the body of her infant son was discovered embedded in cement in an attic bedroom, a jury convicted her of manslaughter. Mrs Dick served 11 years at Kingston Penitentiary and was paroled in 1958. The full story of the dramatic murder trials is told by Marjorie Freeman Campbell in *Torso* (1974).

Dickens. Township in the Nipissing district of northern Ontario, named in 1894 in honour of the British novelist Charles Dickens (1812-70).

Dickey, Robert B. (1811-1903). A FATHER OF CONFEDERATION. Born in Amherst, N.S., he trained as a lawyer, sat on the legislative council of Nova Scotia from 1858 to 1867, and was a delegate to the QUEBEC CONFERENCE. At Confederation he was appointed to the Senate.

Dickson, James. American adventurer who, with a dishevelled group of supporters, arrived in the RED RIVER SETTLEMENT in 1836 to recruit halfbreeds to go to Sante Fe as an 'army of liberation'. He left the Red River ignominiously in 1837. See also Pierre FALCON.

Dickson, Lovat (b.1902). Author and publisher. Born in Mitta Mitta, Victoria, Australia, and educated at the University of Alberta, where he lectured from 1927 to 1929, he settled in London, Eng., where he edited the *Fortnightly Review* and the *Review of Reviews* from 1929 to 1932. That year he founded the publishing firm of Lovat Dickson Ltd, which he operated until 1938, when he joined Macmillan and Company, where he was editorial director until his retirement in 1964. He returned to Canada in 1967. *The Ante-Room* (1950) and *The House of Words* (1963), written with high style, constitute his autobiography. Among his other books are two biographies: *H.G. Wells* (1969) and *Wilderness Man* (1973). The latter tells the story of GREY OWL, whom Dickson introduced to Britain through publication and lecture tours.

Dickson, Roy Ward (b.1910). Radio and television quizmaster. Born in England, before he was 11 he had read through the entire *Encyclopaedia Britannica*. He settled in Canada at the age of 16 and began a quiz column in the *Toronto Star* in 1930. He created the radio quiz-show format with 'Professor Dick and His Question Box', broadcast privately on 15 May 1935, and went on to devise, produce, and conduct well over 5,000 audience-participation radio and television shows. He was the smooth-talking emcee of 'Double or Nothing' (written by Frank Deaville) and the 'Fun Parade' (1938-55), the latter on CFRB. He created 'Abracadabra' in London, Eng., in 1956. His program 'Take a Chance,' launched on CFTO-TV on 9 Oct. 1961, was phenomenally successful. Since 1968 he has lived in semi-retirement in Victoria, B.C. He is the author of *The Greatest Quiz Book Ever* (1975).

Dictionary of Canadian Biography. Projected 12-volume biographical dictionary of notable Canadian figures, called 'the most ambitious work of scholarship ever undertaken in Canada'. It was made possible by the bequest to the University of Toronto of James Nicholson (1861-1952), Toronto manufacturer of Brock's Bird Seed, who wished to bring into being a Canadian reference work similar in principles and scope to the British *Dictionary of National Biography*. (His will also gave instructions for the partial payment of the British debt and the purchase of park benches for Toronto.) Work commenced on the *DCB* at the University of Toronto Press in July 1959 and on the French edition, *Dictionnaire biographique du Canada (DBC)*, at Les Presses de l'université Laval in Mar. 1961. At this time the editorial committee was headed by George W. Brown (general editor), Marcel Trudel (directeur adjoint), and André Vachon (secrétaire général). The volumes are compilations of biographies by leading scholars in English and French Canada and are arranged according to death dates. Thus far four have appeared: Volume I: 1000-1700 (1966), Volume II: 1701-1740 (1969); Volume III: 1741-1770 (1974); and Volume X: 1871-1880 (1972). It is hoped that all volumes documenting the lives of those associated with Canada from the earliest days to the end of the nineteenth century will appear before 1984, when the editorial committee will move into the twentieth century.

Dictionary of Canadianisms, A. Historical record of words and expressions characteristic of English-Canadian life. Produced in 1967 by the Lexicographical Centre for Canadian English, University of Victoria, it was compiled by an editorial board headed by Walter S. Avis. The entries include etymologies and range from Abegweit to ZOMBIE.

Dictionnaire biographique du Canada. See DICTIONARY OF CANADIAN BIOGRAPHY.

Diefenbaker, John G. (b.1895). Thirteenth prime minister of Canada. Born in Grey County, Ont., he was taken to Saskatchewan at the age of eight and was educated at the University of Saskatchewan as a lawyer. He entered politics early in his career, first provincially and then federally, was elected leader of the federal Conservative Party in Dec. 1956, and after the federal election in 1957 became prime minister on 21 June 1957—the first Conservative prime minister in 22 years. In the general election the next year, he won the largest majority ever obtained by a Canadian prime minister. He owed his success to his impassioned rhetoric and his populist approach to fighting for the underdog. His government was defeated in the election of 1963, and he remained leader of the Opposition until 1967. *One Canada* is the general title of his three-volume memoirs, two volumes of which have so far appeared: *The Crusading Years: 1895-1956* (1975) and *The Years of Achievement: 1956-1962* (1976).

Dieppe. Seaport in northern France, site of the controversial Dieppe Raid of the SECOND WORLD WAR. On 19 Aug. 1942 an Allied force of 4,963 Canadian soldiers of the 2nd Canadian Division and more than 1,000 British commandos launched a large-scale raid on the German-occupied stronghold. It lacked surprise and the invading force withdrew under fire. The Canadians in their first fighting suffered 3,367 casualties, the Germans 333. It was later said that what was learned on that 'brave and bitter day' ensured the success of the NORMANDY INVASION two years later.

Dietz, 'Dutch Bill'. See FRASER RIVER GOLD RUSH.

Digby chicken. Local nickname for a small smoked herring popular in Digby, N.S.

Digby scallop. Large scallop found in Nova Scotia. It is less sweet than the smaller bay scallop found outside Canada.

Dingman's discovery. One of the earliest oil strikes in Alberta, known also as Royalite No. 1. It was named after Archibald Wayne Dingman, an employee of the Royalite Company in charge of the drilling rig along Sheep Creek, Turner Valley, Alta. Made on 25 Jan. 1913, the strike established Turner Valley, south of Calgary, as Alberta's chief oil field until the LEDUC strike in 1947 opened up oil fields near Edmonton.

Dinosaur Provincial Park. Located 30 mi. northeast of Brooks, Alta, this 22,000-acre park in Alberta's BADLANDS is the world's richest burial ground of prehistoric creatures. Skeletons of 70-million-year-old dinosaurs are displayed where they were found.

Dionne quintuplets. Five daughters born on 28 May 1934 to Oliva and Elzire Dionne, a French-Canadian farming couple living at Callander, Ont. Cécile, Yvonne, Emilie, Annette, and Marie were put in the care of the Toronto pediatrician Dr Alan Roy Dafoe, who 'kept the girls alive'. Their birth created a sensation in the 1930s and during their childhood 'the quints' were 'the world's most famous youngsters'. Emilie died in 1954, Marie in 1970. Dr Dafoe died in 1943.

Diplômes d'Honneur. Annual awards made to persons who have contributed outstanding service to the arts in Canada. The first Diplôme d'Honneur was awarded in 1954 by the CANADIAN CONFERENCE OF THE ARTS to Vincent MASSEY in recognition of his contribution to the MASSEY COMMISSION.

Directories. See ALMANACS.

Dirty Thirties. A Prairie reference to the DEPRESSION years of the 1930s, especially evoking the dust storms and drought.

Disallowance. The action of the GOVERNOR IN COUNCIL in disallowing a statute passed by a provincial legislature. This is a power contained in Sections 55 and 90 of the BNA ACT, 1867. These provisions impose on the LIEUTENANT-GOVERNOR of a province, representing the Queen, the duty to declare that he or she assents to a bill that is presented, or withholds assent or reserves the bill for the signification of the governor general. The lieutenant-governor must act 'according to his discretion, but subject to the provisions of the British North America Act and to instructions' of the governor general. It has been held that there is nothing controlling this discretion nor is there any other statute having any relevancy to this power. The question of whether this power still exists is subject to some debate.

Disc Numbers. See ESKIMO IDENTIFICATION DISC NUMBERS.

Discovery. (i) The vessel in which Henry HUDSON made his voyage of exploration to Hudson Bay and James Bay where, on 24 June 1611, he was set adrift by his mutinous crew. She was piloted back to England by Robert Bylot. (ii) A 337-ton sloop built in 1789 on the Thames R., Eng., and used in Capt. George VANCOUVER's exploration and survey of the northwest coast of North America. Sold in 1816, she later became a convict hulk.

Discovery claim. A mining term for the first claim staked on a creek, all subsequent claims being recorded as 'above discovery' or 'below discovery'.

Discovery Day. A statutory holiday in two widespread parts of the country. In Newfoundland it is observed on 24 June or the closest Monday. It celebrates a landfall believed to have been made by John CABOT at Cape Bonavista, Nfld, on 24 June 1479, which is the feast day of St John the Baptist;

hence Discovery Day is sometimes called John Cabot Day or St John's Day. There is, however, no certain historical evidence for Cabot's landfall in Newfoundland. In the Yukon it is celebrated on 17 Aug., the anniversary of the first gold strike at BONANZA CREEK in 1896, which precipitated the KLONDIKE GOLD RUSH and opened up the Yukon and Northwest Territories.

Disorderly house. A phrase used in the CRIMINAL CODE OF CANADA meaning a common bawdy-house, a common betting house, or a common gaming house, as defined in the Code.

Distinguished Flying Cross. Commonwealth decoration for acts of courage or gallantry, first awarded to commissioned officers of the Royal Air Force in 1918. The abbreviation is DFC.

Distinguished Flying Medal. Commonwealth decoration for acts of courage while flying in the presence of the enemy, first awarded to non-commissioned officers and men in the Royal Air Force in 1918. The abbreviation is DFM.

Distinguished Service Cross. Commonwealth naval decoration for acts of courage, first awarded to commissioned officers of the Royal Navy in 1914. The abbreviation is DSC.

Distinguished Service Medal. Commonwealth naval decoration for acts of bravery, first awarded to non-commissioned officers and men of the Royal Navy in 1914. The abbreviation is DSM.

Distinguished Service Order. Commonwealth military decoration, first awarded in 1886 to officers of the British Army and Royal Navy for distinguished service in modern warfare. The abbreviation is DSO.

Distribution of powers. The way in which power was divided between the federal and provincial levels of government by the BNA ACT. Matters of general interest were given to the federal government and those of a particular or local interest to the province. The federal government was to 'make laws for the peace, order, and good government of Canada', and 31 specific powers were listed, including the regulation of trade and commerce, 'any mode or system of taxation', postal services, penitentiaries, defence, navigation and shipping, fisheries, marriage and divorce, currency, banks and banking, naturalization, criminal law, and jurisdiction over railways, canals, telegraphs, etc., extending beyond the limits of a province or for the advantage of Canada or two or more provinces.

Distribution of powers

Both federal and provincial governments were given jurisdiction over immigration and agriculture, but the federal government had all residual powers—all powers not specifically mentioned by the Act. The federal government has jurisdiction over foreign relations since the STATUTE OF WESTMINSTER. For provincial powers see PROVINCIAL AUTONOMY.

District. A subdivision of the country. Districts were created for the administration of justice from the beginning of British rule in Canada. Today in Ontario and Quebec only the northern parts of the provinces are divided into districts for judicial purposes; in the south the county is the unit for both municipal and judicial purposes. In the West the Northwest Territories were divided into districts, out of which the provinces of Manitoba, Alberta, and Saskatchewan were later formed. In British Columbia the MUNICIPALITIES that were established were called districts. Today the use of the term 'district' varies from province to province: a district may be a municipality, an unincorporated local-improvement district, or a regional district—a second-tier local government unit extending over a number of municipalities.

Dixon, George (1870-1909). Prizefighter. The Nova Scotia-born Black fighter, nicknamed 'Little Chocolate', made his home in Boston. He began a fighting career that lasted 20 years, during which he won both the featherweight and the bantamweight world titles. In his day he was called 'the greatest little fighter the black race has ever produced'.

Dmytruk, Peter. See PIERRE LE CANADIEN.

Dobbs, Fred. See Mike MAGEE.

Dobbs, Kildare (b.1923). Author. Born in Meerut, India, and educated at Cambridge University, he was a colonial officer in Tanganyika before he immigrated to Canada in 1952. He has worked as an editor for Macmillan's and as book editor for the *Toronto Star*. He is the author of *Running to Paradise* (1962, reissued 1974), a popular collection of autobiographical essays; *Reading the Time* (1968), a second essay collection; and *The Great Fur Opera* (1970), a light-hearted look at the history of the Hudson's Bay Company, with drawings by Ronald Searle.

Doc Snider's House. Painting by LeMoine FITZGERALD. Created over two winters and finished in 1931, it is one of the notable Canadian paintings. It shows a house seen through bare trees that rise from the snow-covered ground in an artful arrangement of 'plastic' forms, and evokes an atmosphere of reverent stillness that is characteristic of Fitz-Gerald. (NGC)

Doctors' Strike. See SASKATCHEWAN DOCTORS' STRIKE.

Dofasco. Acronym of DOminion FOundaries And Steel (COmpany) Limited, a steel mill founded in Hamilton, Ont., in 1912. Its motto is: 'Our product is steel. Our strength is people.'

Dog Who Wouldn't Be, The. Popular story by Farley MOWAT published in 1957. An animal biography written for adults and adopted by children, it is about Mutt, the Prince Albert retriever, an eccentric character who possesses human intelligence and emotions.

Dogrib. ATHAPASKAN-speaking Indians. Caribou hunters and fishermen, they occupied the territory between Great Bear and Great Slave Lakes. Their population in 1970 was 1,202.

Dog-train. A sled pulled by a team of dogs, a method of transportation used in the North. The word 'train' may be a corruption of *traîneau,* French for 'sled'.

Dogwood. Family of shrub-trees, of which about 20 species are native to North America. The white six-petalled flower of the Pacific dogwood has been the floral emblem of British Columbia since 1956. The alternate name 'Dagwood' derives from the use of its wood in skewers or dags (derived from the French *dague,* 'dagger').

Doherty, Brian (1906-74). Theatre enthusiast and founder. The Toronto-born lawyer's adaptation of Bruce Marshall's novel *Father Malachy's Miracle* (1931) was the hit of the 1937 Broadway season. He retired to the Niagara area, where he founded the SHAW FESTIVAL in 1962. Other theatres he was associated with include the STRAW HAT PLAYERS, the RED BARN THEATRE, the Canadian Mime Theatre, and the Irish Arts Theatre. He wrote a memoir, *Not Bloody Likely: The Shaw Festival, 1962-1973* (1974).

Dollar-a-year-men. A reference to successful businessmen who were employed by the federal government doing war work from 1939 to 1945. They were recruited by C.D. HOWE and paid a token salary. Peter C. Newman in *The Canadian Establishment: Volume One* (1975) names 128 dollar-a-year-men who worked in the Department of Munitions and Supply under Howe, as well as 75 dollar-a-year-men who worked on the Wartime Prices and Trade Board under Donald Gordon.

Dollard des Ormeaux, Adam (1635-60), sometimes called Daulac. Hero of New France. Dollard was commander of the garrison at Ville Marie (Montreal) and leader of 'The Seventeen'. On 1 May 1660, Dollard and 16 companions, joined by 44 Hurons and Algonkins, laid an ambush for some Iroquois in an abandoned fort at the Long Sault on the Ottawa R. The Iroquois, after being joined by a reinforcement of 500, took the fort some 10 days later. The Frenchmen lost their lives and the Indian allies were killed or captured. RADISSON came across their bodies a short while later. For many years the incident was regarded as an exploit that saved the colony and the Frenchmen were considered martyrs for the faith. It inspired Archibald LAMPMAN's narrative poem 'At the Long Sault' and a patriotic essay by the nationalist Abbé GROULX, *Si Dollard revient* (1919), which Ramsay COOK included in *French-Canadian Nationalism: An Anthology* (1969) under the title 'If Dollard Were Alive Today'. The purpose and significance of the expedition are discussed by André Vachon in the *Dictionary of Canadian Biography: Volume I, 1000-1700* (1966).

Dollier de Casson, François (1636-1701). Sulpician priest, first historian of Montreal. Arriving at Montreal in 1666, until 1670 he made several missionary journeys, including one of nearly a year (1669-70) in which his party proved that Lakes Ontario, Erie, and Huron were all connected. On his return he became superior at Montreal and performed the duties of a seigneur, organizing the town, laying out the first streets, and supervising the building of a parish church. Dollier wrote a history of Montreal from 1640 to 1672, using eyewitness accounts wherever possible and making certain episodes in the narrative memorable with vivid descriptions, as in his report of the first mass at Montreal for which fireflies—'hung by threads in a beautiful and marvellous manner'—provided illumination. *A History of Montreal: 1640-1672*, translated by Ralph Flenley, was published in 1928. See also MAISONNEUVE.

Domagaya. See DONNACONA.

Dome Mines Ltd. The pioneer gold producer in the Porcupine area of northern Ontario. Going into production in 1910, it is still producing from its original property 5 mi. from Timmins. The discovery of the original lode is said to have occurred when the prospector Harry Preston slipped on a rocky knoll and his boot heel stripped the rock clean of moss, exposing free gold. The present company controls two other important gold producers: Sigma Mines in the Bourlamaque area of Quebec and Campbell Red Lake in the Red Lake district of northwestern Ontario. An affiliated company is Dome Petroleum, a pioneer in oil and gas exploration in the Far North.

Dominion. 'Sovereignty' or 'territory subject to a king or a ruler'; the title that Great Britain granted to Canada in 1867. According to the BNA ACT, 1867, 'The Provinces of Canada, of Nova Scotia, and New Brunswick shall form and be One Dominion under the name of Canada.' John A. MACDONALD wanted to call the new country a Kingdom, but it was thought that such a monarchical title would be resented by the United States. 'Dominion' was chosen after Leonard TILLEY found the word in Psalm 72:8: 'He shall have dominion also from sea to sea, And from the river unto the ends of the earth'. The word 'dominion' is used in the sense of 'federal' as opposed to 'provincial' in such phrases as 'Dominion government' and 'Dominion-provincial conference'.

Dominion Day. Statutory holiday observed throughout Canada on 1 July. It celebrates the birthday of the Dominion of Canada, which is the anniversary of CONFEDERATION, on 1 July 1867. Dominion Day has also been called Canada Day, Confederation Day, the First of July, and July the First. It is the principal Canadian holiday, marked by pomp and circumstance in Ottawa and in the capitals of the provinces and territories.

Dominion Drama Festival. An association of amateur and semi-professional theatrical groups from across Canada. Inaugurated on 29 Oct. 1932, the first annual competitive Festival was held in the week of 24 Apr. 1933, with little-theatre and community-theatrical groups competing for awards and recognition. Until 1939 only one-act plays were presented in the regional and national competitions; after the war activities resumed in 1947 with full-length plays. In 1949 the 14 geographical regions were reduced to four zones (Maritimes, Quebec, Ontario, West). Commercial sponsors of the DDF have been Calvert Distillers, the CANADIAN BROADCASTING CORPORATION, the CANADIAN ASSOCIATION OF BROADCASTERS, and ROTHMANS OF PALL MALL. The last national competitions were held in the week of 24 May 1969, when the DDF became THEATRE CANADA.

Dominion Gallery, The. Commercial art gallery in Montreal. Founded in 1940 by Dr Max Stern, an art historian, it held the first successful exhibition of Emily CARR's work in 1944. It currently shows the finest interna-

Dominion Gallery

tional art of all periods and specializes in modern sculpture.

Dominion Network. See CBC RADIO NETWORK.

Dominion Observatory Time Signal. See NATIONAL RESEARCH COUNCIL OFFICIAL TIME SIGNAL.

Dominion Police. A federal police force created by an Act of Parliament in 1868. Its duties entailed guarding public buildings in Ottawa and Canadian government stockyards in Halifax, N.S., and Esquimalt, B.C. In 1920 it merged with the Royal NORTH WEST MOUNTED POLICE to become the ROYAL CANADIAN MOUNTED POLICE.

Dominion Stores Limited. A food retailing organization with a chain of groceterias. It was incorporated on 3 Oct. 1919 with its head office in Toronto. In 1965 it launched its advertising campaign with the slogan 'It's mainly because of the meat', and in 1970 its 'Deep Discount' campaign. There were 387 Dominion Stores across Canada in May 1976.

Domtar. The name of the Dominion Tar and Chemical Company since its reorganization in 1971. The Montreal-based operation, through subsidiaries, manufactures and sells pulp-and-paper products. It is controlled by the ARGUS CORPORATION.

Don Messer's Jubilee. A popular weekly CBC-TV series of 'Down East' music. It starred Don Messer (1909-73), an old-time fiddler from New Brunswick whose first radio broadcast—from CFBO in Saint John, N.B.—was on 29 Mar. 1929 and called 'New Brunswick Lumberjacks'. In 1939 he moved with his expanded band, the Islanders, to Charlottetown, where he broadcast three nights a week from a private station, CFCY. The show switched to the Halifax CBC-TV station in 1956. Featuring Marg Osburne, Charlie Chamberlain, Johnny Forest, the Buchta Dancers (under the direction of the Hungarian-born choreographer Gunter Buchta), and host Don Tremaine, it was seen on national television under a new name—'Don Messer's Jubilee'—for 30 minutes on Friday evenings from 1958 to 1969, when it was cancelled amid a storm of complaints. It was revived by CHCH-TV in Hamilton for one season in 1970.

Don Mills. Planned community built in the 1950s northeast of the City of Toronto that introduced new concepts in neighbourhood organization, housing and road design, and parks. It was one of the first communities in Canada to combine a variety of residential units, from single-family to apartment dwellings; shopping facilities; a wide range of service and recreation facilities; and a diversity of offices and manufacturing operations. The focal point of the suburb is Don Mills Centre, an innovative shopping plaza designed by John B. PARKIN Associates. The first phase of it was completed in 1955, an extension by Fisher, Tedman & Fisher was added in 1959, and further changes have been made.

Don Wright Chorus. Popular weekly program heard over the CBC Radio Dominion Network and the Mutual Network in the United States. It was created in 1946 by Don Wright, manager of the privately owned radio station CFPL in London, Ont., where it originated. Wright prepared the musical arrangements. The chorus—with Max McGee featured on piano, organ, and celeste—was so successful that the program attracted Westinghouse as a sponsor in 1949 and was renamed 'Westinghouse Presents', which became a television program in 1952.

Donalda, Pauline (1882-1970). Soprano. Born Pauline Lightstone in Montreal, she studied opera and oratorio at the Royal Victoria College and later was coached by Massenet and Puccini. She had a brilliant opera career in Europe and the United States, singing mainly with the Covent Garden Opera House, London, and the Manhattan Opera House, New York. In 1937 she returned to Montreal, where she did much voluntary work for musical organizations, becoming founder and first president of the Opera Guild. She also taught singing.

Donnacona (died c.1539). Chief of STADACONA. Jacques CARTIER first met Donnacona, an Iroquois chief, at Gaspé Bay in 1534, and persuaded him to let him take his two sons, Domagaya and Taignoagny, to France. They returned with Cartier in 1535 when he sailed up the St Lawrence. He met Donnacona again at Stadacona (Quebec City). The following May, Cartier seized Donnacona, his sons, and some other Indians and sailed with them to France. Donnacona was interviewed by the king, Francis I, about the fabulous Kingdom of SAGUENAY. He died in France.

Donnellys, The. An Irish-Catholic family that lived in Lucan, Biddulph Township, near London, Ont. On the night of 4 Feb. 1880 unidentified vigilante nightriders descended on the Donnelly farm and slaughtered James and his wife Johannah, their sons Thomas and John, and their niece Bridget—continuing a blood feud introduced into Canada from Tipperary, Ireland. Six men were charged with murder. One, James Carroll, was brought to trial but the prosecution resulted in a hung jury. It is estimated the feud brought about 20 subsequent violent deaths. The original black gravestone, which stated that the Donnellys had been 'murdered', was replaced in 1966 with a granite marker that identified them as having 'died'. Thomas P. Kelley's *The Black Donnellys* (1954) has kept the story alive. James REANEY wrote a series of three plays on the subject under the general title *The* DONNELLYS.

Donnellys, The. Over-all title of three plays by James REANEY inspired by the blood feud that was climaxed by the murder of the DONNELLYS in Biddulph Township, near London, Ont., in 1880. Under the direction of Keith Turnbull the plays were first produced by the TARRAGON THEATRE, Toronto. *Sticks and Stones* opened on 24 Nov. 1973; *The St Nicholas Hotel* on 16 Nov. 1974; and *Handcuffs* on 29 Mar. 1975. All three were performed on the same day on 14 Dec. 1975. Written with great poetic and theatrical power, the trilogy constitutes an 'epic of southwestern Ontario' in the words of one critic.

Donner Canadian Foundation. It was established in Toronto in 1950 by William H. Donner—an American industrialist who lived in Montreal and died there in 1953—to aid in legal and penal reform, to help the native peoples, and to develop the North, etc.

Dora Hood's Book Room. A Canadiana book service. At the suggestion of W. Stewart WALLACE, the Toronto widow Dora Hood began supplying antiquarian and used books, especially Canadiana, to collectors and institutions from the back room of her house in 1928. She retired in 1954 and Wallace, when he retired from the University of Toronto library, continued the operation. His former secretary, Julia Jarvis, acquired it from him and ran the service—which includes a subscription agency for foreign libraries—with Jean Tweed, who now operates the concern with Lawrence R. Cooper.

Dorchester, Lord. See Sir Guy CARLETON.

Dorion Report. An inquiry and report prepared by Frédéric Dorion, Chief Justice of the Quebec Supreme Court, tabled on 29 June 1965. It found that Guy Favreau, as Minister of Justice, had shown poor judgement in not proceeding towards prosecution when the RCMP supplied him with evidence that the prime minister's parliamentary secretary and other well-placed Liberals had attempted, through bribery, to arrange bail for Lucien Rivard. Guy Favreau promptly resigned, a broken man. See also the RIVARD AFFAIR.

Dorset. The name given the palaeolithic Eskimo culture that followed the Arctic Small Tool culture (a microblade technology) and flourished in the Central Arctic between 800 B.C. and A.D. 1000. It was described in 1925 by Diamond JENNESS, who uncovered its remains at Cape Dorset on the southwest coast of Baffin Island.

Dorval. The name of the Montreal International Airport from its founding in 1941 (replacing the earlier airport at Saint-Hubert) to 15 Dec. 1960, when it received its present name.

Dosco. Acronym of DOminion Steel and COal Company. See SIDBEC.

DOT. Acronym of the Department Of Transport, now the Ministry of TRANSPORT.

Double Hook, The. Novel by Sheila Watson (b.1919) published in 1959. Experimental in its form and making much use of symbols, it examines the social relationships of a small isolated community in British Columbia. With the murder of the life-fearing Mrs Potter, the characters experience a liberation and rebirth. Life is a double hook: 'When you fish for the glory you catch the darkness too.'

Double majority. Principle advocated for passing legislation in the PROVINCE OF CANADA from 1854 to 1864. John Sandfield MACDONALD was one of the proponents of the idea, which was that legislation affecting CANADA EAST only or CANADA WEST only would not be passed unless it received majority support from the members having constituencies in the section in question. The principle was never implemented because it was unworkable.

Double or Nothing. See Roy Ward DICKSON.

Double shuffle. Audacious expedient employed by the Cartier-Macdonald ministry of the PROVINCE OF CANADA to maintain power. When the Macdonald-Cartier ministry fell on 29 July 1858 over a disagreement about the location of the capital city, it was replaced by a government led by George BROWN. Under a law of the day, a newly appointed minister lost his seat in Parliament and had to seek re-election. While the new ministers absented themselves from the House for this purpose, John A. MACDONALD defeated the government. Brown asked the governor general to dissolve Parliament, which he refused to do, and his two-day government (the shortest in Canadian history) came to an end. A new government was formed by George-Étienne CARTIER and Macdonald—the Cartier-Macdonald ministry. Disinclined to face a by-

Double shuffle

election and risk Brown's fate, Macdonald made use of a statutory provision whereby a minister may resign his office and accept another without seeking re-election should this be done within one month. He appointed his cabinet ministers to new posts on 6 Aug., just before midnight, which did not necessitate a by-election (the 'shuffle'); about a half hour later, on the 7th, each minister resigned and was sworn into his old post (the 'double shuffle'). The Cartier-Macdonald ministry remained in power.

Doubleday Canada Ltd. The Canadian wing of Doubleday and Company Inc. of New York. When Doubleday moved into Canada in 1944 with the purchase of a small Canadian distribution operation, two of the original owners, J. Wilfred Ford and George E. Nelson, were retained to develop branch operations. In 1976 the Toronto-based firm had 6,000 titles in print, of which 250 were by Canadian authors.

Doughty, Sir Arthur George (1860-1936). Archivist and historian. Born in Maidenhead, Eng., he came to Canada in 1886 and entered the Quebec civil service in 1897. Dominion Archivist from 1904 to 1936, he instituted a systematic search for collections of historical material, opened branch offices in London and Paris to transcribe records pertinent to the history of Canada, and initiated a series of Archives publications, including *Documents Relating to the Constitutional History of Canada: 1759-1828* (1907-35). With Adam SHORTT he edited CANADA AND ITS PROVINCES (23 vols, 1913-17) and with L.J. Burpee he compiled the *Index and Dictionary to Canadian History* (1911) for the MAKERS OF CANADA SERIES. It was revised and enlarged as *The Oxford Encyclopaedia of Canadian History* (1926).

Douglas, J.J. See J.J. DOUGLAS.

Douglas, Sir James (1803-77). 'Father of British Columbia'. Born in British Guiana and educated in Scotland, he entered the service of the NORTH WEST COMPANY in 1819 and of the HUDSON'S BAY COMPANY in 1821. He was sent to Fort Vancouver on the Columbia R. in 1830, and in 1843 founded Fort Victoria on Vancouver Island, the Company's new western headquarters, of which Douglas became chief factor. He became governor of the island in 1851 and of the mainland colony of British Columbia as well in 1858, when the FRASER RIVER GOLD RUSH began. Two years later he laid plans for the CARIBOO ROAD. He was knighted in 1863 and retired in 1864.

Douglas, T.C. (b.1904). Premier of Saskatchewan, 1944 to 1961; leader of the New Democratic Party, 1961-71. Born in Falkirk, Scot., he was brought to Canada in 1910. He was educated at Brandon College, McMaster University, and the University of Chicago, and became a Baptist minister in 1930, moving to Weyburn, Sask. After an unsuccessful run for the provincial legislature of Saskatchewan as a Farmer-Labour candidate in 1934, he was elected to Parliament in 1935 for the CCF. In 1944 he returned to Saskatchewan to lead the CCF to victory, forming North America's first socialist government. As premier he headed the most innovative and one of the most successful provincial régimes, implementing path-breaking social reforms. He was called to lead the newly formed NEW DEMOCRATIC PARTY in 1961 and in 1962 was elected to Parliament again. As leader his success was limited in electoral terms, but his party projected its views with clarity and forthrightness. In 1971 Douglas turned over the leadership to David LEWIS but continued to sit in Parliament.

Douglas Day. 19 Nov., the birthday of Sir James DOUGLAS, the first governor of British Columbia (1858-64). It is observed in B.C. but is not a statutory holiday.

Douglas fir. Immense coniferous evergreen of which two types are native to Canada. Not a true fir, it is one of the most commercially valuable timber trees and has been known to grow to a height of 300 ft with a 15-ft diameter, living over 1,000 years. It is native to coastal British Columbia and the Rockies, but owing to the wide variety of uses for its wood, it has been introduced into large areas of Europe and Australia. It was named after David Douglas (1799-1834), a Scots-born botanist who spent two years in the Pacific Northwest.

Doukhobors. A pacifist Christian sect that in 1899 emigrated en masse from Russia to the Yorkton-Prince Albert area of present-day Saskatchewan, where they established communal villages and practised vegetarianism and non-violence. About 1910, after the federal government confiscated most of their prairie lands, they moved to British Columbia—though some stayed in Saskatchewan and assimilated. The majority of the 12,000 more identifiable Doukhobors now live in the Kootenay and Kettle Valley regions of the interior. The Sons of Freedom—numbering at most 2,500—abhor the modern technological society and seek to maintan religious purity by living simply in isolated British Columbia mountainside Doukhobor villages. They have often protested against B.C.'s compulsory education laws and the growing assimilation of their co-religionists by parading publicly in the nude; on numerous occasions some extremists have conducted waves of terrorism by bombing and burning private homes—often their own—and public buildings, usually schools. See also Peter VEREGIN.

Down East music. See DON MESSER'S JUBILEE.

Downchild. A 'high-energy blues band', established in Toronto in 1965. A popular band that uses Black American rhythms, it has a reputation for being cheerfully rowdy.

Doyle Bulletin, The. A radio series immensely popular in Newfoundland. The daily program, heard at 7:45 p.m. for 15 minutes, was the only sponsored news bulletin carried by the CBC after Newfoundland joined Confederation in 1949. Written and delivered by journalist Gerald S. Doyle (1892-1956), it has been called 'an intriguing hodgepodge of news, folklore, personal messages, steamer and train schedules, and weather reports'. It originated in St John's in Nov. 1932, was pronounced 'The Dile Bulletin', and promoted such patent medicines as 'Doyle's Codliver Oil in the Familiar Blue Bottle'. It outlasted its originator by a few years. This was a typical item: 'Here is a message from Sarah Greening at Muscle Cove to her husband James in St John's: Glasses broken. Cow not giving milk. Lucy passed exams. Salt scarce. No sign of fish. Love.'

Draft-dodgers. See WAR RESISTERS.

Drainie, John (1916-66). Well-loved actor. An announcer and actor in Vancouver, his home town, from 1937 to 1941, he moved to the CBC in Toronto in 1943 and was associated with the ACADEMY OF RADIO ARTS, the NEW PLAY SOCIETY, JUPITER THEATRE, and the EARLE GREY PLAYERS. A versatile performer with a readily identifiable style, he was one of the mainstays of the CBC STAGE series, starring in The INVESTIGATOR in 1954. He took the lead in the film The INCREDIBLE JOURNEY (1963), did many imitations of Stephen LEACOCK, and at the time of his death had his own radio program, STORIES WITH JOHN DRAINIE. See also JOHN DRAINIE AWARD.

Drapeau, Jean (b.1916). Mayor of Montreal. Born in Montreal and educated at the Université de Montréal, he was first elected mayor in 1954. When he was defeated in 1957 by a Union Nationale opponent, he founded the Montreal Civic Party in 1960 and was re-elected with huge majorities in that year and in each subsequent election. During his tenure as mayor, Drapeau was responsi-

ble for the erection of the PLACE DES ARTS, for conceiving the highly successful EXPO 67, and for securing the XXI Olympiad for Montreal in 1976. He claimed that the games could be self-financing—that 'The Montreal Olympics can no more have a deficit than a man can have a baby'. Owing to escalating costs and labour troubles, however, the province was forced to take over construction of the facilities late in 1975. (See also OLYMPIC GAMES.)

DRB. Initials of the DEFENCE RESEARCH BOARD.

Dreamer's Rock. Tall quartzite rock near Little Current, Manitoulin Island, Ont. Before the arrival of the white man, Indian youths were fastened to its summit and through dreams would receive powers from the spirit world. The rock offers an incomparable view of the surrounding countryside.

DREE. Acronym of the Department of REGIONAL ECONOMIC EXPANSION.

Drenters, Yosef (b.1931). Sculptor. Born in Belgium, he came to Canada in 1951. His regal, abstract human images in wood, sometimes embellished with pieces of beaten metal, often have characteristics of religious art. His work has been exhibited in Toronto, Winnipeg, Regina, New York and at EXPO 67.

Drew, George. (1894-1973). Leader of the Progressive Conservative Party, 1948-56. Born in Guelph, Ont., he was educated at the University of Toronto and Osgoode Hall. After a career in local politics and in various legal and appointive posts, he ran for and won the leadership of the Ontario Conservative Party in 1938. In 1943 the Conservatives under his leadership formed a minority government and two years later won a sweeping victory, crushing the CCF in a scandal-filled campaign. As premier, Drew laid the foundations of modern Ontario and established the Tory dynasty that has ruled the province ever since. He was selected to lead the national party shortly after his election victory in Ontario in 1948, but his appeal could not be transmitted to the national stage and he was defeated by Louis ST LAURENT in the 1949 and 1953 federal elections. Nonetheless his leadership did prepare the party for his successor, John DIEFENBAKER, and for electoral success in 1957. Diefenbaker appointed Drew High Commissioner in London, a post he filled until 1964.

Drinkwater, Charles Graham (1875-1946). Football and hockey star. Born in Montreal, he never played professionally but was an outstanding member of teams representing the Montreal Amateur Athletic Association,

McGill University, and the Montreal Victorias. With the latter club he played on four STANLEY CUP championship teams. He was elected to the Hockey HALL OF FAME in 1950.

Drocourt-Quéant. Line of defence manned by the Germans during the FIRST WORLD WAR. The two villages of Drocourt and Quéant in northern France were part of the supposedly impregnable 'Hindenberg Line', which was cracked by the CANADIAN CORPS on 2 Sept. 1918.

Drumlins. Elliptical-shaped hills moulded during the retreat of the last continental glacier (Wisconsin) and all aligned in the direction in which the ice retreated. Often found in large groups (e.g., the Peterborough drumlin fields), they vary in size from 15 ft high to slight undulations.

Drummond, William Henry (1854-1907). Poet. Born in County Leitrim, Ire., he was brought to Canada as a child. He graduated from McGill and from the medical school at Bishop's University in 1884, setting up practice at Lac Megantic, Que., and 10 years later in Montreal, where he also taught at McGill. He began to compose humorous affectionate verse in broken English about the French-Canadian lumbermen, canoemen, and farmers he had met. Some readers felt they verged on ridicule, but Louis FRÉCHETTE disagreed and wrote an introduction to *The Habitant and Other French-Canadian Poems* (1897), which proved so successful that it was followed by other collections, including JOHNNY COURTEAU *and Other Poems* (1901). Fréchette introduced as well *The Poetical Works of William Henry Drummond* (1912) and Arthur Phelps made a selection for *Habitant Poems* (1926, 1959).

Dry belt. On the Prairies, a region with little rainfall, located between Moose Jaw, Sask., and Medicine Hat, Alta. In British Columbia, a tract of arid country from the U.S. border to Prince George. See also PALLISER'S TRIANGLE.

Drybones. A treaty Indian of the Northwest Territories who, on 10 Apr. 1967, pleaded guilty to 'being an Indian unlawfully intoxicated off a reserve, contrary to Section 94(b) of the INDIAN ACT'. He was fined $10 and costs or three days in jail. Upon an appeal his conviction was quashed by the Supreme Court of Canada because the section of the Indian Act under which he was found guilty was held to conflict with the CANADIAN BILL OF RIGHTS, which guarantees 'the right of the individual to equality before the law and the protection of the law . . . without discrimination by reason of race, national origin, col-

our, religion or sex'. Section 94(b) of the Indian Act placed Indians in a different position from other persons in Canada. It was held that the section could not stand in the face of Section 2 of the Canadian Bill of Rights, which provides that if any statute of Canada contravenes the freedoms enunciated in the Bill, the statute will not apply. This was the first time the Canadian Bill of Rights had been cited and shown to be effective.

Dryland farming. Term applied to farming methods used in the southern Prairies to conserve moisture. Most grain farms are used for crops only every other year; during the fallow year moisture is stored for the succeeding crop.

Drylanders. The first English-language NFB feature film. Directed by Don Haldane and produced by the NFB in 1962, it tells the story of a family that homesteads on unproved land on the Prairies between 1907 and the 1930s. The script was written by M. Charles COHEN, and the principal roles were played by Frances HYLAND, William FRUET, James Douglas, and Don Francks. 69 min., 24 sec.; b & w.

DSC. See DISTINGUISHED SERVICE CROSS.

DSM. See DISTINGUISHED SERVICE MEDAL.

DSO. See DISTINGUISHED SERVICE ORDER.

du Maurier Council for the Performing Arts, The. The largest single source of non-government funding for the performing arts. The du Maurier Council—formed by Imperial Tobacco in 1971 and named after the popular cigarette—makes grants to supplement existing sources of income to give ballet, opera, theatre, modern-dance, and music groups the opportunity to present innovative programming without financial risk. The objectives of the Council are to help performing groups to help themselves; to encourage development of Canadian talent; and to broaden public interest in the performing arts.

Dubé, Marcel (b.1930). Quebec playwright. Born in Montreal and a graduate of the Université de Montréal, he writes for Radio-Canada as well as for the stage and has been called Canada's most prolific playwright. Among his plays are *Zone* (1955), *Le Temps des lilas* (1958), and *Les Beaux Dimanches* (1968). *The White Geese* (1972)—a translation by Jean Remple of *Au Retour des oies blanches*—is the only Dubé play to be published in English.

Ducharme, Noel (b.1923). Ojibwa artist.

Born in Fort William, Ont., of mixed ancestry (his father was part French and part English, his mother a full-blooded Ojibwa), he learned both reading and writing and the crafts and lore of his people in a tuberculosis sanatorium. He worked as a fireman-oiler on Great Lake boats until 1967. His acrylic paintings on paper recreate the traditional tales and images of the Ojibwa. His work hangs in the McMICHAEL CANADIAN COLLECTION's Woodland Indian Gallery.

Ducharme, Réjean (b.1942). Quebec novelist. Born in Saint-Félix-de-Valois, Que., he created a literary sensation with the publication of *L'Avalée des avalés* (1966), a novel about a girl's rejection of her cruel parents. A blend of fantasy and realism, it was translated by Barbara Bray as *The Swallower Swallowed* (1968). His other novels have not yet been translated.

Duck Lake, Battle of. The first engagement in the NORTH WEST REBELLION, on 26 Mar. 1885. At this small settlement on the South Saskatchewan R., Gabriel DUMONT defeated a North West Mounted Police detachment under Supt L.N.F. Crozier in a half-hour skirmish that forced the police to retreat.

Duddy Kravitz. See *The* APPRENTICESHIP OF DUDDY KRAVITZ.

Dudek, Louis (b.1918). Poet and man of letters. Born in Montreal and educated at McGill and Columbia Universities, he has taught literature at McGill since 1951. He helped edit FIRST STATEMENT in 1942, co-founded CONTACT PRESS in 1952, and launched his own magazine DELTA (1957-66) and a series of small-press publications under the Delta Press imprint. Selections from his books—*East of the City* (1946), *Twenty-four Poems* (1952), *The Searching Image* (1952), *The Transparent Sea* (1956), *En México* (1958), *Laughing Stalks* (1958), and *Atlantis* (1967)—appear in his *Collected Poetry* (1971), which is chronologically ordered to show his evolution from a social poet to a poet whose philosophical and intellectual interests have made him a social philosopher. He analysed the history of printing and its relation to literature in *Literature and the Press* (1960), theorized about subjectivism in the modern age in *The First Person in Literature* (1967), and published a collection of aphorisms in *Epigrams* (1975).

Dufferin, Lord (1826-1902). GOVERNOR GENERAL of Canada from 1872 to 1878.

Dufferin Terrace. A wide boardwalk southeast of the CHÂTEAU FRONTENAC, Quebec City.

It was begun in 1838 under the direction of Governor Lord DURHAM. Governor General Lord Dufferin ordered an extension with pavilions. These were designed by Charles BAILLAIRGÉ and built in 1878-9. Fort St Louis, built by CHAMPLAIN, stood on this site: see CHÂTEAU ST LOUIS.

Duke, Daryl (b.1932). Television and film director. Born in Vancouver, he joined the NATIONAL FILM BOARD in Montreal in 1950 as a writer. Three years later he returned to Vancouver to join the new CBC Film Unit there that included Ron KELLY, Gene Lawrence, Allan KING, Arla Saare, and Stan Fox. For CBC-TV Toronto he produced CLOSE-UP, 'Explorations', and QUEST from 1958 to 1964, before leaving for the United States. Among the feature films he has directed are *God Bless the Children* (1970), *The Cradle of Hercules* (1971), *The President's Plane Is Missing* (1971), and *Payday* (1972). He now lives in Vancouver, where he is program director for a new station, CKVU-TV.

Duke of Edinburgh's Award in Canada. An award for young adults between the ages of 14 and 21 to encourage civics, fitness, and the pursuit of a hobby. Established by the Duke of Edinburgh in the United Kingdom in 1956, in Canada in 1963, and now in 40 other COMMONWEALTH countries, it consists of Gold, Silver, and Bronze certificates and badges, 45 of which are awarded each year.

Dumbells, The. A popular First World War vaudeville group formed from the Canadian Army's Third Division Concert Party. Named 'The Dumbells' after the symbol of the division, it was formed by Captain Merton Plunkett to entertain troops near VIMY Ridge in Aug. 1917. The eight original players were enthusiastically received and an enlarged group played in London for four weeks and in New York for 12 weeks. Canadian and other tours were arranged until the troop disbanded in 1929. The Dumbells included Captain Plunkett's brother Al Plunkett, Red Newman, Ross Hamilton, Fraser Allan, Stan Bennett, Jack Ayre, and Jack McLaren.

Dumont, Gabriel (1838-1906). Colourful rebel in the NORTH WEST REBELLION. Born at Red River (Man.), he moved to the Saskatchewan valley after the RED RIVER REBELLION, in which he did not take part. He was in the group that went to St Peter's, Montana, to invite Louis RIEL to lead the discontented people in his valley. He became Riel's brilliant 'adjutant-general', gaining victories in skirmishes at DUCK LAKE and FISH CREEK and defending BATOCHE on 9-12 May 1885. He fled to the United States and worked in Buffalo Bill's Wild West Show, but returned to Canada and died at Batoche.

Dumping. Goods imported for resale at less than their normal value. An Anti-dumping Tribunal is empowered to levy an anti-dumping duty on goods equal to the difference between the imported price and the normal value as a means of protecting Canadian manufacturers.

Duncan, Douglas (1902-68). Collector and gallery owner. Born in Toronto and educated at Victoria College, University of Toronto, he trained as a bookbinder in Paris and returned to Toronto in 1928. In 1936 he was cofounder, and eventually proprietor, of the Picture Loan Society to encourage artists and collectors with regular showings and picture rentals. His impeccable artistic judgement and taste influenced the art scene in Toronto from the thirties through to the sixties as well as the artists he presented—including David MILNE, whose sole agent he was—and put their stamp on his remarkable collection of paintings, which was dispersed at his death among 41 galleries and museums across the country, the largest number going to the National Gallery of Canada and the Art Gallery of Ontario.

Duncan, James (1806-81). Artist. Born in Ireland, he immigrated to Canada in 1825 and in 1827 settled in Montreal, where he became active as an artist, taught drawing, and had a photography and then a lithographic printing business. Best known for his paintings of Montreal, he published nine views of the city as lithographs between 1847 and 1878.

Duncan, Sara Jeannette (1862-1922). Novelist. Born in Brantford, C.W. (Ont.), and educated there and at the Normal School in Toronto, she wrote for the Toronto *Globe*, the *Week*, the Memphis *Appeal*, and the Washington *Post* under the pseudonym 'Garth Grafton'. Appointed parliamentary reporter for the MONTREAL STAR in 1888, she married Charles Everard Cotes three years later and went to live in India, where he was curator of the Indian Museum at Calcutta. She died in England, the author of 19 novels and travel books. Her only novel with a Canadian setting, *The* IMPERIALIST (1904), is a witty portrayal of life in a small Ontario town, named 'Elgin', but easily identified as Brantford.

Dundonald incident. Lord Dundonald, who came to Canada in 1902 to command the militia, wrote in 1903 a report recommending an enormous program of militia expansion.

As much of it was considered unacceptable, he gave vent to bitter remarks, which were climaxed by his public reference to 'political interference'. His dismissal aroused some political controversy.

Dundurn Castle. Regency villa overlooking the harbour at Hamilton, Ont., built in 1832 by Sir Allan Napier MacNAB. Named after the MacNab family seat in Scotland, Dundurn is Gaelic for 'fort on the river'. In 1967 the mansion was restored to its former elegance and opened to the public. A sound-and-light show is presented on the grounds.

Dunkin Act. An act passed in 1864, sponsored by Christopher Dunkin, to permit local option for alcoholic beverages in municipalities in Canada East (Quebec) and Canada West (Ontario). It remained in force in Quebec and Ontario after Confederation and was extended to all provinces by the CANADA TEMPERANCE ACT.

Dunlop, 'Tiger'. See William DUNLOP.

Dunlop, William (1792-1848). Physician, soldier, pioneer settler, and author. Born and educated in Scotland, he was in Canada in 1813-15 as an army surgeon, serving in the WAR OF 1812. After a period in India and Scotland, where he wrote for *Blackwood's Magazine* under the pseudonym 'Tiger', he returned to Upper Canada (Ontario) in 1826 as an employee of the CANADA COMPANY and was appointed 'Warden of the Forests'. In 1827 he felled the first tree where Guelph now stands and founded Goderich, where he built his home 'Gairbraid'. He was a member of the legislative assembly from 1841 to 1846, when he became superintendent of the Lachine Canal. A lively and whimsical writer, he was the author of numerous essays, written for English and Canadian periodicals, a famous will, and two books: *Statistical Sketches of Upper Canada, for the Use of Emigrants* (1832), by 'A Backwoodsman', and *Recollections of the American War, 1812-14*, written for magazine publication in 1847 and published as a book in 1905.

Dunn, Sir James. See ALGOMA STEEL CORP. and Lord BEAVERBROOK.

Dunnell, Milt (b.1905). Sports writer. Born in St Mary's, Ont., he began his career in journalism in 1929, writing for the *Stratford Beacon-Herald*. In 1942 he joined the *Toronto Star*, has served as its sports editor since 1949, and has his own column. He is a member of the selection committee of the Hockey HALL OF FAME.

Dunning, George (b.1920). Film animator.

Born in Toronto, he worked in film animation for the NATIONAL FILM BOARD (1943-56),
where he trained Richard WILLIAMS, before
settling in London, Eng. His studio produces
clever commercials and amusing cartoons,
including *The Wardrobe* (1960) and *Canada Is
My Piano* (1966). He directed *The Yellow Submarine* (1968), a full-length cartoon featuring
the Beatles that popularized pop-art graphics.

Dunsmuir. The estate in Hatley Park, near
Victoria, B.C., of Sir James Dunsmuir, now
part of ROYAL ROADS MILITARY COLLEGE.

Duplessis, Maurice (1890-1959). Founder of
the UNION NATIONALE and premier of Quebec,
1936-9, 1944-59. Born in Trois-Rivières,
Que., he became a Conservative and was
first elected to the legislature in 1927, becoming leader of the provincial party in 1933. In
an effort to drive out the entrenched and corrupt Taschereau Liberal administration, Duplessis allied his Conservatives with break-
away Liberals led by Paul Gouin in 1935. The
Union Nationale, as the coalition was called,
narrowly lost the 1935 election but came to
power in 1936. The new government was
Duplessis's own, Gouin having been forced
out. The premier was a *nationaliste*, a conservative, a strong supporter of provincial
rights, and was soon involved in fights with
Ottawa. The election of 1939 saw Duplessis
defeated, but he regained power in 1944 and
held it to his death in 1959. His governments
were characterized by a lavish, skilful use of
patronage, strong-arm methods, and effective electoral campaigning. The result was to
slow the growth of reformist ideas in the
province. But after Duplessis's death, the
QUIET REVOLUTION flowered in the 1960s.

Dupuis case. Yvon Dupuis was a cabinet
minister in the PEARSON government. He was
fired on 23 Jan. 1965, the only Canadian minister to be discharged to face charges under
the Criminal Code. He was accused of accepting a $10,000 bribe in 1961, before being
made a cabinet minister, to obtain a licence
for a racetrack in his home riding in Quebec.
He was found guilty, but was acquitted on
appeal in 1968.

Durham, Lord (1792-1840). Governor general and high commissioner of British North
America. Arriving in Canada in 1838 to investigate the circumstances surrounding the
REBELLION OF 1837, he stayed just over five
months. In his detailed and famous *Report on
the Affairs of British North America* (1839)—in
which he stated: 'I found two nations warring in the bosom of a single state: I found a
struggle, not of principles, but of races'—he

recommended a modified form of RESPONSI-
BLE GOVERNMENT and a legislative union of
Canada and the Maritime provinces. In spite
of defects of judgement, which included the
downgrading of French Canadians, the *Report*'s eloquent proposals for constitutional
reform and self-government make it an enduring document in Canadian history.

Durham boat. A large vessel used in the
nineteenth century on the St Lawrence R. for
freight and passengers. It was propelled by
sails or poles and was almost 100 ft in length.
The name is said to derive from that of Robert Durham, an eighteenth-century boat-
builder in Philadelphia.

Durham Report. See Lord DURHAM.

Durnan, W.R. (Bill) (1915-72). Hockey goalkeeper. Born in Toronto, he participated in
many sports but excelled as a goalie, particularly with the MONTREAL CANADIENS. He was a
member of six teams that won the VEZINA
TROPHY and was voted all-star NHL goalkeeper
on six occasions.

Dust Bowl. The area of southwestern Saskatchewan and southeastern Alberta that experienced drastic erosion of topsoil and sand
storms during the great drought of the 1930s.
See also DEPRESSION and PALLISER'S TRIANGLE.

Duthie, George (1902-68). Sports director of
the CANADIAN NATIONAL EXHIBITION. Born in
Scotland and brought to Toronto at an early
age, he became a YMCA leader and basketball
coach. He was sports director of the CNE, a
position he held with distinction for 35 years,
while also occupying executive posts in national sports bodies. His daughter Carol Ann
Duthie was a world-champion water-skier.

Dutton, Mervyn (Red) (b.1898). Hockey
player and executive. Born in Montreal, he
began his professional hockey career in 1921
after recovering from First World War
wounds. He played with the Montreal
Maroons and later with the New York Americans. In 1943 he succeeded Frank CALDER to
become president of the NATIONAL HOCKEY
LEAGUE for three years.

Dwyer, Peter M. (1914-72). Arts administra-
tor. Born in London, Eng., he edited the
Cherwell at Oxford and, according to an offi-
cial press release, 'joined the European Story
Department of Twentieth Century Fox Film
Corporation, working in London and Paris'.
According to subsequent reports, however,
this was pre-war cover for British intelligence
activities. In 1939 he served as a British
Foreign Service Officer in France, Latin

America, and the United States. According to the double-agent Kim Philby, Dwyer exposed the atomic spy Klaus Fuchs in Washington. He first visited Canada in 1942 and later joined the NATIONAL RESEARCH COUNCIL and then the PRIVY COUNCIL OFFICE. Appointed to the newly created CANADA COUNCIL'S staff in Apr. 1958 as supervisor of the arts program, he was named associate director in 1965 and director in 1969. He suffered a stroke in Apr. 1971, resigned in Nov. 1971, and died on 31 Dec. 1972. Dwyer combined a civilized outlook with broad cultural interests and an administrative expertise that had a lasting effect on the Canada Council. His concern for the arts is commemorated in the PETER DWYER SCHOLARSHIPS.

Dye, Cecil H. (Babe) (1898-1962). Hockey player. He played baseball and football but was an especially good professional hockey player. He began his professional hockey career with the Toronto St Patricks (later the TORONTO MAPLE LEAFS) and played briefly with the Chicago Black Hawks and the New York Americans. While not a fast skater, he had such a hard, accurate shot that he was a four-time leading NHL scorer and recorded the highest goals-per-game average in League history. He later coached and refereed.

Dying Waters, The. A hard-hitting CBC-TV documentary on water pollution. Produced by Larry Gosnell, written by George SALVERSON, and narrated by Stanley BURKE—the team that produced the controversial AIR OF DEATH program—it was telecast on 30 Oct. 1969.

Dynavert. See CL-84.

E

E.M. Abbreviation frequently found on brass tokens issued to trappers by the HUDSON'S BAY COMPANY around 1854. E.M. stands for East Main, the Bay's trading district south and east of Hudson Bay.

Eagar, William (c.1796-1839). Artist. Born in Ireland, he was in St John's, Nfld, from 1831 to 1834, when he moved to Halifax. He executed a series of 19 lithographs of Halifax and environs, published in 1839, as well as some watercolour sketches.

Eagle, Bald. A large bird of prey with a dark brown body and a white head and tail when full grown. Although it is the national symbol of the United States, it is found in most of Canada's North.

Earle Grey Award. A medal presented annually by ACTRA to the actor or actress who gave the best acting performance in television or in a non-feature film during the previous year. First awarded in 1972, it honours Earle Grey, an ACTRA president in the 1940s who founded the EARLE GREY PLAYERS.

Earle Grey Players. A theatrical group founded by Earle Grey and his wife Mary Godwin. English actors who toured Canada with Maurice Colbourne and Barry Jones, they remained in Toronto and produced the first of many Shakespearean plays 'according to the intention of Shakespeare' in the quadrangle of Trinity College, University of Toronto, in 1939. As the Earle Grey Shakespeare Festival Company, they staged festivals in the quadrangle and in HART HOUSE from 1946 to 1959, with fall and winter tours of Ontario and the Maritimes. Unable to find a suitable home for their company, the Greys returned to England in 1960.

'Early Mornin' Rain'. The first big hit song by Gordon LIGHTFOOT, written in 1964, about the loneliness of a man 'with no place to go'.

Earnscliffe. Ottawa residence of Sir John A. MACDONALD. Built in 1855-7, it was the home of the first prime minister from 1870 to 1871 and from 1883 until his death in 1891. The attractive limestone mansion on Sussex Drive was acquired by the British government in 1930 and is now the residence of the British High Commissioner. Earnscliffe is Old English for 'eagle's cliff'.

Earth and High Heaven. Novel by Gwethalyn Graham (1913-65) published in 1944. The story of a young Montreal couple and the anti-semitic forces that threaten to keep them apart, it was written at a time when anti-semitism was not much talked about and was very widely read. Plans to film the novel were scrapped when *Gentlemen's Agreement* was released in 1948.

East Block. See PARLIAMENT BUILDINGS.

Easter Monday. Statutory holiday observed throughout Canada. It occurs between late March and late April on the Monday following Easter Sunday. Easter celebrates the resurrection of Christ and falls on the first Sunday following the full moon that occurs on or after the vernal equinox (21 Mar.).

Easterly point, The most. Cape Spear, Nfld, 52° 37' W.

Eastern Canada. Geographic division. It consists of the Atlantic Provinces plus Ontario and Quebec.

Eastern Provincial. Regional airline. Established in 1963, with its headquarters at Halifax, Eastern Provincial Airways Limited offers scheduled services in the Atlantic Provinces.

Eastern Shore. The Atlantic seaboard of Nova Scotia stretching from Halifax to Canso.

Eastern Townships. 11 Quebec townships south of the St Lawrence R. and east of the Richelieu R. *Les Cantons de l'Estrie*, famous for their rural charm, have been called 'the Garden of Quebec'. Originally settled by the United Empire Loyalists, the area is predominantly French-Canadian today. See also WESTERN TOWNSHIPS.

Eastmain, The. The eastern shore of Hudson Bay. The term was used in the fur trade and dates from 1689. See also The WESTMAIN.

Eastview case. A case involving the dissemination of birth-control information. Dorothea Palmer, a nurse employed by the Parents' Information Bureau of Kitchener, Ont., was arrested on 14 Sept. 1936 in Eastview, Ont., for contravening the Criminal Code by disseminating information on preventative techniques. The trial lasted 19 days. When she was acquitted six months later, the way was cleared for the legal dissemination of such information.

Eaton, Cyrus. See PUGWASH CONFERENCES.

Eaton Co. Limited, The T. Chain of department stores. It was established in 1869, the year after Timothy Eaton (see EATON DYNASTY) opened his first Toronto store to sell goods for cash at fixed prices. EATON'S CATALOGUE, published from 1884 to 1976, was 'the homesteader's bible' and revolutionized the

mail-order business with its 'Goods satisfactory or money refunded' guarantee. In 1976 Eaton's owned and operated 62 department stores, 17 house-furnishing stores, 13 Horizon (discount department) stores, and numerous clearance outlets. The firm is owned by Eaton's of Canada Limited, a family holding company.

Eaton dynasty. A family so pre-eminent in English-Canadian life that it has been dubbed (by Peter C. NEWMAN) 'a quasi-aristocracy'. Notable descendants of Timothy Eaton (1834-1907), who founded the T. EATON CO. LTD in 1869, and his wife Margaret Beattie, are his son (Sir) John Craig Eaton (1876-1922), who married Flora McCrae (1901-70); his grandson John David Eaton (1909-73), who married Signy Stephenson; and his great-grandsons: John Craig Eaton (b.1937), who married Catherine Farr; Fredrik Stefan Eaton (b.1938), who married Catherine Martin; and George Ross Eaton (b.1945), who married Theresa McIntosh. Since 1967 the great-grandsons have been directors of Eaton's of Canada Limited, the family holding company.

Eaton's Catalogue. Mail-order catalogue of the T. EATON CO. LIMITED. First issued in 1884 as an unillustrated 32-page booklet, it appeared regularly from that time in a varying number of editions (12 editions were issued in 1975, the last full year of publication). It was called 'the wish book' by Indians and 'the homesteader's bible' by settlers. The last Spring-Summer issue (Jan. 1976) had a print-run of two million copies, was nearly 900 pages in length, three-quarters of them in full colour, and featured approximately 15,000 items.

Eaton's Santa Claus Parade. Annual pre-Christmas parade sponsored by the T. EATON CO. LIMITED. Travelling through downtown Toronto streets on a Saturday morning in late November since 1904 (though the first parades were in the afternoon), it attracts three-quarters of a million people and is covered by national television.

Eayrs, James (b.1926). Political scientist and author. Born in London, Eng.—the adopted son of Hugh Eayrs, president of the MACMILLAN COMPANY OF CANADA—he was educated at the University of Toronto, Columbia, and the London School of Economics. He has taught in the department of political economy of the University of Toronto since 1951. A witty, incisive, graceful writer on international relations in books and occasional journalism, he is the author of *The Art of the Possible: Government and Foreign Policy in Canada* (1961);

Eayrs

Northern Approaches: Canada and the Search for Peace (1961); the important three-volume work *In Defence of Canada* (1964, 1965, 1972); *Diplomacy and Its Discontents* (1971), which includes *Fate and Will in Foreign Policy* (1967); *Right and Wrong in Foreign Policy* (1966); *Minutes of the Sixties* (1968); and *Greenpeace and Her Enemies* (1973)—among other volumes.

ECC. Initials of the ECONOMIC COUNCIL OF CANADA.

Eccles, W.J. (b.1917). Historian. Born in Yorkshire, Eng., and educated at McGill University and the Sorbonne, he has taught in the history department of the University of Toronto since 1963 and is the leading English-speaking scholar of New France, a social historian who has eradicated all romantic conceptions of the French period. He is best known for his definitive biography *Frontenac: The Courtier Governor* (1959), and for *Canada Under Louis XIV: 1603-1701* (1964) in the CANADIAN CENTENARY SERIES, *The Canadian Frontier: 1534-1760* (1969), and *France in America* (1972).

École Littéraire de Montréal. An association of French-Canadian writers that flourished in Montreal in 1895-1900, 1913-20, and 1925-30. Led by Jean Charbonneau, Albert Ferland, and others, it held some public sessions at the CHÂTEAU DE RAMEZAY. The École differed from the Mouvement littéraire de Québec, which was patriotic and rhetorical, in savouring poetry that presented imaginatively and romantically the rural and traditional elements of Quebec life, as expressed by the school of Le TERROIR—'the soil' or 'the homeland'.

Economic Council of Canada. Advisory body on economic matters. Established in 1963, the ECC consists of one chairman, two directors, and 25 part-time members chosen to represent labour, agriculture, primary industry, secondary industry and commerce, and the general public. Through annual reviews of Canada's medium- and long-term economic prospects, the Council recommends to the government measures to ensure high employment and efficient production that will raise the standard of living.

Economic nationalism. A movement—having not only economic but political, social, and cultural implications—to assert the country's sovereignty and independence from the United States and other foreign countries. J. Bartlet Brebner wrote in 1940: 'The most substantial Canadian nationalism in times of peace has been economic nationalism.' The COMMITTEE FOR AN INDEPENDENT CANADA was formed in 1970 to press for the goals of economic nationalism.

Écrits du Canada français. A publication devoted to the printing or reprinting of unusual French-language literary, social, and historical texts. It was founded and first published in 1954 in Montreal by Jean-Louis Gagnon and is now issued quarterly by Claude Hurtubise of Éditions HMH.

Ecstasy of Rita Joe,The. A play about Indian-white relations by George RYGA, and a ballet. First performed at the Vancouver Playhouse on 23 Nov. 1967 the play was directed by George Bloomfield and starred Frances HYLAND, with Chief Dan GEORGE as the father. Rita Joe leaves a west-coast reservation to live in a big city, where she becomes a prostitute and is raped and murdered. A cross between a social documentary and a lyric poem, the script was published in 1971, the year the Manitoba Indian Brotherhood commissioned the ROYAL WINNIPEG BALLET to adapt it. Norbert Vesak choreographed the multimedia ballet—employing film clips and a recorded narration by Chief Dan George—which was first produced at the NATIONAL ARTS CENTRE, Ottawa, in July 1971.

Eddy Company, E.B. One of the world's largest matchmaking operations. It was established at Hull, Que., in 1851, by Ezra Butler Eddy (1827-1906), who over the years merchandised his friction matches under the names 'Telegraph' (for the speed of ignition), 'Parlour' (because they did not smell up the parlour), and 'Eddy Matches' (to honour the founder). The company, which includes widespread lumbering interests, introduced the book match into Canada in 1928.

Edel, Leon (b.1907). Literary scholar and writer. Born in Pittsburgh, Pa, he was brought to Yorkton, Sask., about 1912 and was educated there and at McGill University and the Sorbonne. While at McGill he was involved with the McGILL FORTNIGHTLY REVIEW and has maintained his contacts with Canada, especially his friendship with A.J.M. SMITH, F.R. SCOTT, and John GLASSCO. Working in journalism before entering the academic world—he was a professor of English literature at New York University and is now at the University of Hawaii—he has received many honours for his literary scholarship and as the foremost authority on Henry James. His five-volume biography of James (1953-72) is considered by many to be the most distinguished biography in English written in the twentieth century.

Edenshaw, Charles (1839-1920). Master

168

HAIDA carver. Born at Skidegate in the Queen Charlotte Islands, B.C., he acquired the traditional Haida carving skills and, although he never signed his work, produced carvings that were highly esteemed by captains and traders who plied the North Pacific coast. He began by carving totem poles and masks and went on to produce boxes, chests, and dishes; silver jewellery; small wooden totem poles and figures; and the black Haida slate figures, pipes, dishes, chests, poles, etc. for which he was best known. Franz Boas reproduced his designs in his *Primitive Art* (1927), and the exhibition ARTS OF THE RAVEN (1967) singled out his work for special recognition. Edenshaw's nephew Charles GLADSTONE continued the Haida tradition.

Edge. A literary magazine that appeared from 1963 to 1969. Called by its editor, Henry Beissel, 'the most controversial publication in Canada', and published from Edmonton and other cities, it appeared twice a year and was devoted to new writing and dissent.

Edinborough, Arnold (b.1922). Journalist. Born in Donington, Eng., and educated at Cambridge University, he came to Canada in 1947. He taught at Queen's University and became editor of the *Kingston Whig-Standard* in 1954 and of *Saturday Night* in 1958, purchasing the latter magazine in 1963 and acting as publisher and editor intermittently until 1970. The author of a weekly column on books in the *Financial Post* and a monthly column on society in the *Canadian Churchman*, he collected his columns in *Some Camel, Some Needle* (1974). He became president of the COUNCIL FOR BUSINESS AND THE ARTS IN CANADA in 1974 and is editor of *Performing Arts in Canada*, a quarterly.

Edinburgh, Duke of. See ROYAL FAMILY.

Éditions du Jour, Les. A French-language publishing house in Montreal. Established in 1963 by Jacques Hébert, a former journalist, it specializes in paperback editions of topical books and serious literature. Hébert left the firm in 1975.

Edmonton. The capital of Alberta and, as the most northerly of Canada's major cities, 'The Gateway to the North'. While fur-trading posts called Fort Edmonton existed on the site from 1795, settlement did not begin until 1864. It was incorporated as a town in 1892 and as a city in 1904. Its most rapid period of expansion began after the 1946 discovery of oil at LEDUC. It is an important retail, wholesale, and transportation centre. The major pipelines begin near Edmonton. It also serves the petroleum industry as the largest refining centre in western Canada. Edmonton hosts KLONDIKE DAYS and was selected to be the home of the 1978 BRITISH EMPIRE AND COMMONWEALTH GAMES. It is the home of the UNIVERSITY OF ALBERTA. The 1971 CMA population was 495,702. Its official motto is 'Industry, Integrity, and Progress'.

Edmonton Bulletin, The. The first newspaper in what became the Province of Alberta. Founded in 1880 by Frank Oliver with a total capitalization of $21.00, it flourished until 1951, when its assets were assumed by the EDMONTON JOURNAL.

Edmonton Grads. The world's leading women's basketball team. It was coached by Dr Percy PAGE, who taught at McDougall Commercial High School in Edmonton. Page founded the team in June 1915, and when it won the Canadian championship in 1922 and the international championship in 1923, it included both undergraduates and graduates of the high school. The Grads retained the international championship for 17 years, finally disbanding in 1940. They toured widely and lost only 20 of their 522 games.

Edmonton Journal, The. An evening newspaper published in Edmonton, Alta. Founded in 1903, it has been owned by SOUTHAM PRESS since 1912. It employs a northern reporter who files stories from Northwest Territories.

Edmonton Oilers. See WORLD HOCKEY ASSOCIATION.

'Education of Phyllistine, The'. See OL'ANTOINE.

Edwards, Charles B. See CHARLES EDWARDS AWARDS.

Edwards, Robert Chambers (Bob) (1864-1922). Satirist and publisher of the Calgary EYE OPENER. Born in Edinburgh, Scot., and educated at Glasgow University, he immigrated to Canada in 1895 and settled in Calgary, where he published the weekly *Eye Opener* from 1902 to 1922. His unconventional paper specialized in broadly humorous treatments of politicians, prohibitionists, and public figures generally. He was an independent member of the Alberta legislature in 1921-2. Hugh A. Dempsey edited *The Best of Bob Edwards* (1975).

Eedee Awards. Annual awards given by the Ontario government to encourage 'excellence of design', of which 'Eedee' is a quasi-abbreviation. The Eedee Fashion Awards were first given in 1965, the Eedee Furniture Awards in 1967, the Eedee Craft Awards in

Eedee Awards

1973. The award itself is a clear acrylic rectangular object with a gold-coloured ED medallion suspended in the acrylic. It is presented to manufacturers to focus attention on Ontario-manufactured and Canadian-designed products. The award is made on the basis of design, quality, and consumer appeal.

Eegak. Eskimo word for snow-glasses. Made of bone or ivory with a narrow horizontal slit to see through, they protect the eyes against snowblindness.

Eegyvadluk (b.1931). Eskimo stone-cutter and printer at CAPE DORSET. He was the draughtsman of KENOJUAK'S The ENCHANTED OWL in 1960.

Eelalee. Eskimo word commonly used in the south Baffin Island region for 'You're welcome'.

Eh? Colloquial expression meaning 'What did you say?', known in Britain in 1837. In *Canajan, Eh?* (1973), Mark M. Orkin wrote: 'Rhymes with hay. The great Canadian monosyllable and shibboleth, "eh?", is all things to all men.'

Eight Men Speak. An 'agit-prop' dramatization of the plight of eight Communists who were sentenced in Toronto in Nov. 1931. The Progressive Arts Club was formed to produce the group-written play in Dec. 1931. It was banned by the Toronto police after its first performance.

8th Canadian Hussars (Princess Louise's). Canadian army regiment. It originated in 1866 when the 'New Brunswick Regiment of Yeomanry Cavalry' was formed. It was first associated with the wife of the Marquis of LORNE in 1884 and received its present name in 1960. In the FIRST WORLD WAR it provided one squadron for the 6th Regiment and was important in the Battle of the SOMME (1916). During the SECOND WORLD WAR it was active in England and Italy in numerous battles and since then has served in Germany.

Eldorado Nuclear Limited. One of the world's principal suppliers of uranium. Much of the uranium used in the bombs dropped over Hiroshima and Nagasaki in the Second World War came from a mine discovered by the Ontario-born prospector and mine developer Gilbert A. LaBine (b.1890). His principal discovery was made on 16 May 1930 at what is now PORT RADIUM in the Great Bear Lake district of the Northwest Territories. The mine that produced the original radium ore (called pitchblende) became Eldorado Mining and Refining Limited. The first ounce of radium was not produced until 1936; the original mine was exhausted and closed in 1960. For national security reasons Eldorado became a CROWN CORPORATION in 1944. It operates uranium mines at Uranium City in the Beaverlodge area of northern Saskatchewan, as well as one of the world's largest uranium refineries at Port Hope, Ont. Eldorado supplies uranium to CHALK RIVER.

Elections, Federal. What follows is a list of federal elections held since Confederation, with the elected party and date. (C, Conservative; L, Liberal; PC, Progressive Conservative; U, Unionist.)

1867 (C) 7 Aug.-20 Sept.
1872 (C) 20 July-12 Oct.
1874 (L) 22 Jan.
1878 (C) 17 Sept.
1882 (C) 20 June
1887 (C) 22 Feb.
1891 (C) 5 Mar.
1896 (L) 23 June
1900 (L) 7 Nov.
1904 (L) 3 Nov.
1908 (L) 26 Oct.
1911 (C) 21 Sept.
1917 (U) 17 Dec.
1921 (L) 6 Dec.
1925 (L) 29 Oct.
1926 (L) 14 Sept.
1930 (C) 28 July
1935 (L) 14 Oct.
1940 (L) 26 Mar.
1945 (L) 11 June
1949 (L) 27 June
1953 (L) 10 Aug.
1957 (PC) 10 June
1958 (PC) 31 Mar.
1962 (PC) 18 June
1963 (L) 8 Apr.
1965 (L) 8 Nov.
1968 (L) 25 June
1972 (L) 30 Oct.
1974 (L) 8 July
See also PRIME MINISTERS.

Electric Gallery, The. The world's only commercial art gallery exclusively exhibiting electric art. Founded in Toronto by Sam and Jack Markle in 1970, it promotes the experimental art form of non-functional decorative machines.

Electron microscope. An instrument for magnification that employs a stream of electrons and a magnetic field instead of light waves and optical lenses. Particularly valuable for medical technology and general microscopy, it was first built commercially by research scientists in the McLennan Laboratories of the University of Toronto in 1935-9. The working model was produced in Apr. 1938 by a team that included E.F. Burton,

C.E. Hall, James Hillier, and Albert Prebus. Commercial production of the electron microscope was undertaken by Carl Zeiss and other firms.

Eleventh of November. See REMEMBRANCE DAY.

Elgin, Lord (1811-63). Governor of the Province of Canada from 1846 to 1854. His period is associated mainly with the granting of RESPONSIBLE GOVERNMENT and the REBELLION LOSSES BILL.

Elgin-Marcy Treaty. RECIPROCITY agreement between the colonies of BRITISH NORTH AMERICA and the United States. The treaty, establishing free trade, was negotiated in Washington in 1854 by the governor of the Province of Canada, Lord ELGIN, and the United States representative, W.L. Marcy. It was terminated by the United States in 1866.

Elizabeth II. See ROYAL FAMILY.

Elizabethans. Philatelic term for Canadian postage stamps issued from 1952, when Elizabeth II became Queen, to the present time. They are sometimes called 'Elizabethan Issues'.

Elk Island National Park. Near Edmonton, Alta, it was established as a game preserve in 1906 and became a national park in 1930. It covers 76 sq. mi. of rolling landscape—aspen and spruce forestland—that is in contrast with the flat farmlands surrounding it.

Ellesmere Island. The most northerly island in the Canadian Arctic. Part of the Queen Elizabeth Islands and 75,765 sq. mi. in area, it lies in the extreme northeastern Arctic. Much of its surface is covered with permanent ice-fields.

Elliot Lake. A planned community in Algoma District, Ont., north of Lake Huron. Built in the 1950s to serve the nearby uranium mines, it has one of the largest uranium reserves in the world. The Elliot Lake Centre is a summer school of the arts that opened in 1965. See also Stephen B. ROMAN.

Ellipse. A literary journal, published three times a year, devoted to the translation of French-Canadian literature into English and English-Canadian literature into French. It was founded by D.G. JONES and others at the University of Sherbrooke. Each issue presents a pair of writers—one from French Canada, the other from English Canada—in the other's language.

Ellis, Arthur. Pseudonym of Arthur Bartholomew English, an executioner. He came to Canada from England in 1913 at the invitation of the Department of Justice as someone competent to carry out hangings, although there was no official position to offer him and there were several other executioners. English performed many executions, the last in 1935. He died in obscurity in 1938. One of his successors also worked under the same pseudonym.

Elmer the Safety Elephant. Symbol of a national safety program for school children. Elmer—a grey elephant who wears a green suit with an orange hat and tie—'never forgets the safety rules'. The initial concept dates from 1946-7 and is credited to Vernon Page, an inspector with the Toronto police force. Elmer was promoted by the *Toronto Telegram*, which turned the copyright over to the non-profit, Ottawa-based Canada Safety Council. The figure of Elmer is based on designs made about 1949 by the Winnipeg artist Charles Thorson, who was trained in the Disney Studios. Elmer appears on a flag, pamphlets, posters, crests, puppets, booklets, etc. His Six Safety Rules are: 'Look always before you cross the road. Keep away from all parked cars. Ride your bike safely and obey all signs and signals. Play your games in a safe place away from traffic. Walk, don't run, when you cross the road. Where there are no sidewalks, walk off the road to the left and face oncoming traffic.'

Emblem Books. A series of poetry chapbooks published by Jay MACPHERSON in Toronto from 1954 to 1962. The series began with a book by Daryl HINE and ended with a collection by Al PURDY.

Emerak, Mark (b.1901). Eskimo sculptor and printmaker at HOLMAN. Noted for his sculpture and drawings, he produced his first prints in 1968.

Emergency Measures Organization. See CANADIAN EMERGENCY MEASURES ORGANIZATION.

Emma Lake. Lake and summer camp north of Prince Albert, Sask., the site of an influential artists' workshop. Under the direction of Kenneth Lochhead of the Regina College School of Art, such prominent painters and critics of the New York and Canadian schools of Abstract Expressionism and Post Painterly Abstraction as William Barnett, Clement Greenberg, Barnett Newman, Jules Olitski, Jack SHADBOLT, and Frank Stella conducted workshops there from 1955 to 1960, influencing the work of Ronald BLOORE, Roy KIYOOKA, and Arthur McKay. The Emma Lake experience sparked the important REGINA FIVE ex-

Emma Lake

hibition in 1961. The workshop is currently run by the University of Saskatchewan.

Emmanuel College. A United Church college offering instruction for the ministry. Federated with the UNIVERSITY OF TORONTO, it came into being in 1928 from a merger of Union College (Presbyterians from KNOX COLLEGE who voted to join the United Church at church union in 1926) and the Faculty of Theology of VICTORIA COLLEGE. Since 1969 it has been a participant in the TORONTO SCHOOL OF THEOLOGY.

EMO. See CANADIAN EMERGENCY MEASURES ORGANIZATION.

Empire Club of Canada. A luncheon club 'dedicated to the interests of Canada and the Commonwealth, in partnership, for peace and progress, with our friends and allies throughout the world'. Founded in Toronto on 18 Nov. 1903, it meets weekly at the Royal York Hotel from October through April. The luncheons are addressed by prominent people who speak with authority on the issues of the day. The addresses are published annually.

Empire Day. See VICTORIA DAY.

Empress Hotel. Stately hotel set in gardens overlooking the Inner Harbour of Victoria, B.C. Built on the reclaimed mudflats of James Bay, it was one of the last of the CPR's chain of CHÂTEAU-STYLE hotels. The centre block, designed by F.M. Rattenbury and built in 1904-8, was followed by additions in 1912 and 1929. High tea at the Empress is a west-coast tradition.

Empress Line. A celebrated fleet of Pacific steamships operated by the CANADIAN PACIFIC STEAMSHIP CO. The *Empress of India*, acquired in 1891, was followed by the *Empress of Japan* in 1927 and the *Empress of China* in 1931. They docked at Victoria and Vancouver and made possible the SILK TRAINS. The oceanliners travelled to the Orient via Suez and advertised the tour as 'Around the World in 80 Days—$610.00'. On account of their dazzling whiteness they were sometimes referred to as the 'White Empresses'. Later Canadian Pacific *Empresses* on the Pacific included *Asia* and *Russia*. Those on the Atlantic included *Britain, Scotland, Ireland, Australia,* and *Canada*, the CP's last ocean passenger liner, which was withdrawn from service in 1971. See also EMPRESS OF BRITAIN, EMPRESS OF FRANCE, EMPRESS OF IRELAND.

Empress of Britain. The largest of the CANADIAN PACIFIC STEAMSHIP fleet, this 42,348-ton liner was launched on the Clyde in 1930. She

carried King George VI and Queen Elizabeth home from their tour of Canada in 1939 and shortly thereafter became a troopship. She was bombed on 26 Oct. 1940 and two days later was torpedoed and sank.

Empress of France. A well-known liner. Built in 1914 for the ALLAN LINE and originally named the *Alsatian*, she served during the First World War as an armed merchant cruiser and was renamed in 1919 by her new owners, the CANADIAN PACIFIC STEAMSHIP CO. A favourite with Atlantic travellers, the 18,400-ton vessel was broken up in 1935.

Empress of Ireland. A 14,191-ton liner of the CANADIAN PACIFIC STEAMSHIP CO. completed in 1906. She sank in the St Lawrence R. near Father Point on 29 May 1914, after being rammed by the Norwegian collier *Storstad*. Over 1,000 passengers and crew lost their lives in this disaster—the worst marine disaster in Canadian history.

'En roulant ma boule'. Title and refrain of a medieval French song popular in Quebec. 'While rolling my ball', which served as both a paddling song and a dance song, tells of a young prince who took his shining gun and went out to shoot a duck. 'So characteristically Canadian is *En roulant ma boule'*, explained Marius BARBEAU, 'that we are apt to forget that it is an old-country possession as well.'

Enchanted Owl, The. Most famous of all Eskimo prints, drawn by KENOJUAK and engraved by EEGYVADLUK in 1960. It depicts a proud owl, the symbol of wisdom, with spreading plumage and tail. 50 prints were made at CAPE DORSET—25 in black and red, 25 in black and green. In 1970 the design was used for the six-cent postage stamp commemorating the Centennial of the Northwest Territories. That same year one print was sold for $10,000.

Encyclopedia Canadiana. A 10-volume illustrated reference work. Based in part on W. Stewart WALLACE's The ENCYCLOPEDIA OF CANADA (1935-7), it was launched in 1957 and has been reissued with various changes at intervals of from one to three years. Originally edited by Dr John E. Robbins (editor-in-chief) and Dr W. Kaye LAMB (chief editorial consultant), it is issued by Grolier Limited and remains the only Canadian encyclopedia on the market.

Encyclopedia of Canada, The. A six-volume reference work edited and partly written by W. Stewart WALLACE and published in Toronto between 1935 and 1937. Biographies of living Canadians were excluded. It was re-

172

printed in 1948 and a 'Newfoundland Supplement', edited by Robert H. Blackburn, was issued the following year, when the colony joined Confederation. It provided the basis for parts of the ENCYCLOPEDIA CANADIANA.

End of steel. Railroading phrase for the terminus of service, whether temporary or permanent.

Endicott, Dr James. See CANADIAN PEACE CONGRESS.

Energy, Mines and Resources, Department of. Federal government department. Established in 1966, it is organized in three sections: the Energy Development Sector is responsible for all forms of energy, and for developing a national energy policy; the Mineral Development Sector is responsible for non-renewable resources; the Science and Technology Sector includes the GEOLOGICAL SURVEY OF CANADA, the Surveys and Mapping Branch, and the POLAR CONTINENTAL SHELF PROJECT.

Enfant au pain, L'. Painting by Ozias LEDUC. Executed over the years 1892-9, it is a study of a boy playing a mouth-organ, seated before an empty porridge bowl and a half-eaten slice of bread. It transcends the meticulous realism of its subject matter to become a memorable work of art. (NGC).

Engel, Marian (b.1933). Novelist. Born in Toronto and educated at McMaster and McGill Universities, she was the first chairperson of the WRITERS' UNION OF CANADA. Her novels are *No Clouds of Glory* (1968); reissued in 1974 as *Sara Bastard's Notebook*); *The Honeyman Festival* (1970); *Monodromos* (1973; reissued as *One Way Street*, 1975); *Joanne* (1975), a novel written in diary form as a CBC Radio serial; and *Bear* (1976), a remarkable narrative about the erotic relationship between a woman and a bear. *Inside the Easter Egg* (1976) is a collection of short stories.

Ensign, Red. See CANADIAN RED ENSIGN.

Enutsiak. See INUTSIAK.

Environment, Department of the. Federal government department responsible for pollution and for the management of Canada's resources. Established in 1971, it is organized in two sections: Fisheries and Marine Services and Environmental Services. The latter is responsible for the Atmospheric Environment Service, which provides meteorological information and weather forecasts, and the Environmental Protection Service, which is concerned with pollution.

Epiphany in the Snows. Altar-piece in the Cathedral Church of All Saints at Aklavik, N.W.T. Executed by Violet Teague, an Australian portrait-painter, and installed in the newly built 'Cathedral of the Arctic' in 1939, it illustrates the theme that Christ is for all people by depicting the Madonna and Child dressed in regal ermine wearing Eskimo boots. A Cree offers a live beaver, an Eskimo offers walrus tusks. HBC and RCMP officers kneel before the infant, and in the background reindeer appear among the camels.

Epitaph for Moonlight. Choral work for youth choir composed by R. Murray SCHAFER in 1968. It is frequently performed by student groups.

Equal Rights Association. A pressure group formed by D'Alton McCarthy (1836-98) in 1889 to press for the supremacy of the English language in Canada. McCarthy was a leading Conservative politician and crusader against separate schools who almost singlehandedly precipitated the MANITOBA SCHOOLS QUESTION, which bedevilled politics in the 1890s. His association of militant bigots ran a few candidates in the 1891 federal election and in 1896 other supporters ran as 'McCarthyites'. While there was no electoral success, the impact of McCarthy's doctrine was severe.

Equal status. Political phrase associated with the rise of Canadian nationhood. Robert BORDEN, at the Imperial War Conference of 1907, requested 'an increasingly equal status between the Dominions and the mother country'. After W.L. Mackenzie KING became prime minister in 1921, he pressed for equal status, which in principle was affirmed by the BALFOUR REPORT of 1926. Equality and sovereignty were formally declared by the STATUTE OF WESTMINSTER in 1931.

Equalization payments. A tax-sharing agreement whereby poorer provinces receive a larger share of tax revenue from the federal government than the wealthier provinces. This meaning of the word 'equalization' is said to date from 1956, although the principle is as old as Confederation.

Erebus and *Terror.* Famous naval vessels that carried Sir John FRANKLIN'S Arctic expedition. The two ships were trapped in the ice off King William Island in Sept. 1846 and abandoned the following April. All the members of the expedition subsequently perished and the ships were never found.

Eric the Red. See LEIF ERICSSON and L'ANSE AUX MEADOWS.

Erickson, Arthur (b.1924). Architect. Born in Vancouver, he trained at the University of British Columbia and McGill University. His work includes SIMON FRASER UNIVERSITY in Vancouver (1963-5), the University of Lethbridge, and the Canadian Pavilion at the 1970 World's Fair, Osaka, Japan. It shows a strong feeling for dramatic siting and geometric form.

Ericsson, Leif. See LEIF ERICSSON and L'ANSE AUX MEADOWS.

Ermite. A strongly flavoured blue cheese, produced by Benedictine monks at St Benoit-du-lac, Que.

Ernie Game, The. Feature film directed by Don OWEN and produced in 1967 by the NFB in a co-production arrangement with the CBC. It tells the story of a mid-winter romance in Montreal involving a youth who has left his parents' home but has not yet made his own. For Ernie, played by Alexis Kanner, life is a game. 88 min., 10 sec.; colour.

Eskimo Identification Disc Numbers. A system devised by the federal government to permit the individual identification of each Eskimo in the Canadian Arctic. For the 1941 census, a four-digit number stamped on a thin fibre disc slightly larger than a quarter was prepared by the federal government for each Eskimo. The disc had two small holes punched in it and could be worn around the neck or on the wrist. In 1945, to allow for the introduction of FAMILY ALLOWANCES, the Canadian Arctic was divided into three Western and nine Eastern districts, and replacement discs—bearing the designation of the district as well as of the individual—were supplied. The disc system was discontinued in 1971 with the implementation of Project Surname, under which most Eskimos agreed to adopt family names.

Eskimo syllabics. A modified form of Cree SYLLABICS.

Eskimos. The original inhabitants of the Arctic shores of Greenland, Canada, Alaska, and northeastern Siberia. The word 'Eskimo' is a misnomer, being ALGONKIAN for 'eaters of raw flesh', a word considered to be derogatory. The Eskimos cook their fish and game and refer to themselves as the INUIT, 'the people'. Archaeologists have revealed the existence of two Eskimo cultures prior to the present culture: the palaeolithic DORSET followed by the THULE. There are estimated to be 80,000 Eskimos living in the world today. The Eskimo population of Canada in 1971 was approximately 18,000, of whom 12,000 live in the North West Territories, 4,000 in New Quebec, 1,000 in Labrador, and 1,000 in northern Ontario. See also LABRADOR ESKIMOS, CENTRAL ESKIMOS, CARIBOU ESKIMOS, COPPER ESKIMOS, and MACKENZIE ESKIMOS.

Esquimalt. See CANADIAN FORCES BASE ESQUIMALT.

Estevan. Town in southern Saskatchewan, the name of which is an acronym of GeorgE STEphen and William VAN Horne (see entries). They were important figures in the building of the CPR, which passes through the town.

Estevan Strike. A bitter strike by coal miners for union recognition at Bienfait, near Estevan, Sask. For six years the Mine Workers Union of Canada pressed for union recognition. The strike broke out on 8 Sept. 1931, and on 29 Sept. a solidarity parade to nearby Estevan was met on the highway by the RCMP and the fire brigade. Although unarmed, three strikers were killed, 23 wounded, and 22 arrested. The strike was ended on 8 Oct. The final report of the Wylie Commission contained 17 recommendations, including improved working conditions, but excluded recognition of the union.

Ethel and the Terrorist. Novel by Claude JASMIN published in French in 1964 and translated into English by David Walker in 1965. Based on the first fatal FLQ incident, in Apr. 1963, it contains the reflections of a man trapped by the leaders of the organization and forced to kill despite his efforts to live a life of love and understanding.

Ethier-Blais, Jean (b.1926). Quebec man-of-letters. Born in Sturgeon Falls, Ont., and educated at the Université de Montréal and abroad, he is well known in Quebec for his stringent literary criticism and reviews in Le DEVOIR and elsewhere. His stories appear in *Mater Europa* (1968), his poems in *Asies* (1969), and his criticism in *Signets* (1967) and *Littératures: mélanges littéraires* (1971).

Etrog, Sorel (b.1933). Sculptor. Born in Jassy, Romania, he studied painting there before immigrating to Israel in 1950, to New York in 1958, and to Toronto in 1962. His mainly large curvilinear sculptures in bronze and marble show the influence of Sumerian, Aztec, and Egyptian art. He has exhibited internationally and his works are in many public and private collections. One of his finest pieces—*War Remembrances*—is in the Montreal Museum of Fine Arts. See also The ETROG.

Etrog, The. The Canadian counterpart of the Oscar. It has been awarded annually since

1968 at the Canadian Film Awards banquet, sponsored by the CANADIAN FILM INSTITUTE, for outstanding achievements in Canadian film-making during the previous year. The statuette is named after its sculptor, Sorel ETROG.

Evangeline. First Canadian feature film. It was produced with the co-operation of the CPR by Canadian Bioscope, a Halifax-based company of American expatriates. Based on Longfellow's poem *Evangeline: A Tale of Acadie* (1847), and photographed in the Annapolis Valley, it was released in 1914 and was both a critical and a financial success. As with almost all very early Canadian films, there are no known prints or negatives. 5 reels, b & w.

Évangéline, L'. A French-language evening tabloid published in Moncton, N.B. Established in 1887 by Valentine Landry as a weekly, it became a semi-weekly, a tri-weekly, and since 1949 has appeared five times a week. It describes itself as *Le seul quotidien français de Maritimes* (the only French-language daily in the Maritimes) and represents the special interests of the ACADIANS. It is North America's only French-language daily outside the province of Quebec.

Evangeline Country. Picturesque region around GRAND PRÉ, N.S., inhabited by the ACADIANS until they were deported by the British in 1755. It is named after the heroine of Henry Wadsworth Longfellow's poem *Evangeline: A Tale of Acadie* (1847). Longfellow's model, Emmeline Labische, died of shock when she located her lover in Louisiana and found him engaged to another woman.

Evangeline Trail. Historic and scenic drive through those parts of Nova Scotia that are associated with the ACADIANS and their expulsion in 1755. The 209-mi. trail, which includes the coastal villages along the FRENCH SHORE and the towns of the ANNAPOLIS-CORNWALLIS VALLEY, culminates at the church at GRAND PRÉ. It was named after the heroine of Longfellow's poem *Evangeline: A Tale of Acadie* (1847).

Evans, Don (b.1936). Caricaturist. Born in Toronto and educated at the Ryerson Polytechnical Instutute and the University of Western Ontario, he is a self-taught cartoonist and caricaturist. His sharp and witty work appears regularly in *Maclean's* and *Books in Canada*, where it is signed 'Isaac Bickerstaff', after the pseudonym adopted by the satirist Jonathan Swift.

Evans, James (1801-46). Inventor of a Cree syllabic alphabet. An English Methodist minister who became superintendent of the missions in the Northwest, he hand-printed a *Cree Syllabic Hymn Book* in 1841 (issued in a facsimile edition in 1954). His alphabet is still in use. See also SYLLABICS.

Everson, R.G. (b.1903). Poet. Born in Oshawa, Ont., and educated at the University of Toronto and Osgoode Hall, he was one of the country's leading public-relations advisers in Montreal until his retirement in 1968. His clear-eyed poetry is informed with a feeling for history and humanity. His best-known book is *Selected Poems: 1920-1970* (1970).

Evidence. A literary quarterly published in Toronto from 1960 to 1967. Each issue contained stories, poems, and art work by new and emerging writers and artists. It was edited by Allan Bevan.

Ewing, Walter H. (born *c.*1880). Champion trapshooter. The Montreal rifleman competed in trapshooting at the 1900 Olympics in Paris and won the gold medal in that event at the 1908 Olympics in London (with another Canadian, G.S. Beattie, finishing second).

Excellency. The style of address of the GOVERNOR GENERAL of Canada. His full title is His Excellency the Right Honourable.

Exchange. A magazine of ideas and the arts, three issues of which appeared in the winter of 1961-2. It included stories, poems, essays, and reviews of wide interest and was edited by Stephen VIZINCZEY in Montreal.

Excuse My French. Situation-comedy series dealing with the English-French problem seen on the CTV Network. Produced from the fall of 1974 to the spring of 1976, the 30-minute weekly program starred Stu Gillard and Lise Charbonneau as Peter and Marie-Louise, young marrieds whose parents create complications and humorous situations. It was produced in Montreal by Paul Wayne, with Arthur Weinthal as the executive producer.

Executive. A magazine for senior management in Canadian business, industry, and government published monthly since 1958 by SOUTHAM Business Publications. Articles deal with major political and economic issues and trends, and each issue includes a monitor of the economy and a market analysis.

Executive Council. A provincial MINISTRY. Each of the 10 provinces has an executive council composed of elected members of the

Executive Council

legislature who have been appointed by a premier to compose a ministry. The term was originally applied to the council appointed by the governor or lieutenant-governor in each of the colonies of BRITISH NORTH AMERICA. With the granting of responsible government, ministers responsible to the legislature came to compose the executive council. See also PROVINCIAL GOVERNMENT.

Exile. A literary quarterly devoted to writing from Canada and abroad, founded in 1972 by Barry Callaghan at Atkinson College, York University, Toronto. Each issue includes stories and poems by leading writers.

Exovedate. The name given by Louis RIEL to the council of a provisional government he established at Batoche, N.W.T., in 1885. It is a pseudo-Latin word meaning 'chosen from the flock'. See also NORTHWEST REBELLION.

Expansion. The sudden growth of professional hockey. Expansion came about with the formation in Nov. 1971 of the WORLD HOCKEY ASSOCIATION. Until that time professional hockey teams were franchised by the NATIONAL HOCKEY LEAGUE. The number of teams doubled in one season, and long-established traditions and practices were called into question by the new, largely American interest in the game.

Explorations. An annual publication devoted to media research edited by Edmund Carpenter and Marshall McLUHAN, both of the University of Toronto, and founded in 1953. Each issue was devoted to a theme that was explored by well-known anthropologists, linguists, and literary critics in an interdisciplinary manner. The typography and production were of a high order. The final issue was the book *Eskimo* (1959) by Carpenter, Robert FLAHERTY, and Frederick H. VARLEY. Carpenter and McLuhan edited *Explorations in Communications: An Anthology* (1960).

Explorations. A series of dramas, documentaries, and discussions on CBC-TV. The 60-minute weekly shows were produced by Mavor MOORE and ran from 23 Oct. 1956 to 21 Sept. 1964.

Explorations Program. Assistance for projects dealing with Canada's cultural and historical heritage, and for projects that explore new forms of expression in the arts, humanities, and social sciences. An extension of the Canadian Horizons Program, established in 1971, it was renamed Explorations two years later. Unlike other CANADA COUNCIL programs, which are directed towards professional artists and scholars, Explorations provides grants to any Canadian individual or

organization whose project is judged to be deserving of assistance. The program has an annual budget of $1,200,000. There are three annual competitions judged by five regional juries.

Expo 67. The brilliantly successful World's Fair of 1967, held in Montreal and commemorating the centenary of Confederation. It took place from 28 Apr. to 27 Oct. on the islands in Montreal harbour, among them Île Notre-Dame, a man-made island. It included exhibits from over 70 countries and was visited by over 50 million people. Its theme was 'Man and His World'. After Expo closed, MAN AND HIS WORLD became a permanent annual exhibition on Île Sainte-Hélène.

Export A. See MACDONALD TOBACCO INC.

External Affairs, Department of. Government department concerned with the protection and advancement of Canadian interests abroad. Established in 1909, the minister responsible is the Secretary of State for External Affairs. The senior permanent officer, with a rank of deputy minister, is the Under-Secretary of State for External Affairs. Officers serving abroad are formally designated as HIGH COMMISSIONERS (in Commonwealth countries); AMBASSADORS (in non-Commonwealth countries); ministers, counsellors, first secretaries, second secretaries, third secretaries, and attachés (at diplomatic posts); and consuls general, CONSULS, and vice-consuls (at consular posts). Canada maintains approximately 177 diplomatic, consular, and other missions, 63 of which are non-resident.

Exxoneration. A political thriller by Richard ROHMER, published in 1974, in which the Canadian government successfully repels an American invasion and asserts its sovereignty and control of energy reserves. *Exxoneration* is a sequel to the same author's best-selling novel ULTIMATUM (1973). The title is a play on the 'exoneration' of Canadian honour and on the Exxon Corporation, the new name of Esso, the multi-national U.S. oil company, the Canadian branch of which is known as IMPERIAL OIL.

'Eye of Glooscap'. Poetic description of the amethyst in legends about GLOOSCAP, the supernatural hero of the MICMAC Indians.

Eye Opener, The A weekly newspaper written and published by Bob EDWARDS, mainly from Calgary. It appeared between 4 Mar. 1902 and 29 July 1922, with anthologies called *Summer Annuals* appearing from 1920 to 1924. Boasting a national circulation of

35,000, Edwards used the *Eye Opener* as a vehicle to satirize politicians and society. One of his fictitious characters, Peter J. McGonigle, editor of the non-existent *Midnapore Gazette*, was so popular that in 1910-11 a rival publisher actually published just such a paper. *The Best of Bob Edwards*, edited by Hugh A. Dempsey, appeared in 1975.

F

Fabre, Edouard (1885-1939). Champion distance runner. Born in Montreal, he competed in more than 300 races during a 30-year career. He represented Canada at the 1912 Olympic Games in Stockholm and was the winner of the 1915 Boston Marathon. He later competed professionally and, when over 40, won a 200-mi. snowshoe marathon.

Fackenheim, Emil L. (b.1918). Philosopher. Born in Halle, Germany, he was ordained a rabbi in 1939 and was granted a Ph.D. in 1945 from the University of Toronto, where he has been a professor of philosophy since 1961. A contributor to *Commentary* and a spokesman for post-Holocaust Jewry, he is the author of *Paths to Jewish Belief* (1960), *Metaphysics and Historicity* (1961), and *God's Presence in History* (1970).

Factor. The manager of a trading post of the HUDSON'S BAY COMPANY.

Factory Theatre Lab. Toronto theatrical workshop founded in 1969 by Ken Gass and John HERBERT to produce Canadian plays.

Faggot. In Newfoundland, codfish so stacked as to shed rain.

Fairley, Barker (b.1887). Man-of-letters and painter. Born in Barnsley, Yorkshire, Eng., he was educated at the Universities of Leeds and Jena and has taught in the German departments of the University of Alberta (1910-15) and the University of Toronto (1915-57). The author of a scholarly classic, *A Study of Goethe* (1947), he has also written books on Charles Doughty (1927) and Heinrich Heine (1954). *The* BROKEN JUG, his translation of a Kleist play, was staged, as was his translation of Goethe's *Faust* (1970). His verse has been collected in *Poems of 1922 or Not Long After* (1972). An early friend of the GROUP OF SEVEN, he was encouraged by Robert FINCH to take up painting in middle age and now devotes himself to painting acrylic portraits and landscapes, which are exhibited regularly.

He was married to Margaret FAIRLEY.

Fairley, Margaret (1885-1968). Socialist. Born in England and educated at Oxford, she dedicated her life to the socialist cause. She edited *Spirit of Canadian Democracy* (1945), a prose and verse anthology expressing a Marxist interpretation of the growth of democratic ideas; the Communist magazine NEW FRONTIERS (1952-7); and *The Selected Writings of William Lyon Mackenzie: 1824-1837* (1960). She was married to Barker FAIRLEY.

Fairweather Mountain. The highest Canadian peak outside of the Yukon and the sixth highest overall. It rises 15,300 ft at the tip of the 'thumb' of northwest British Columbia.

Faith, Percy (1908-76). Composer and arranger of popular music. The Toronto-born musician made a national reputation as a composer and arranger for CBC Radio (1933-40), and then went on to his big break, 'The Carnation Contented Hour', in Chicago (1940). He conducted and arranged music for top American radio programs, composed many popular songs, and recorded with the top names in American music. He also conducted pop concerts for various symphonies. He wrote the words and music of 'My Heart Cries for You' (1951) and 'The Song from "Moulin Rouge" ' (1953).

Falaise. French town in Normandy, scene of repeated attacks during the SECOND WORLD WAR. Canadian troops met a disastrous reverse at VERRIÈRES RIDGE on 25 July 1944, but took Falaise itself and sealed off much of the so-called 'Falaise Gap' on 14 Aug. 1944. Almost 600 Canadian soldiers are buried in the Calais Canadian War Cemetery, on the coastal road between Boulogne and Calais, within sight of England.

Falcon, Pierre (1793-1876). Composer of folkballads. A Métis, he was born at Elbow Fort, Rupert's Land, a NORTH WEST COMPANY post. He was educated at La Prairie (Que.) and joined the company at 15. He was present at the Massacre of SEVEN OAKS (1816) and wrote a famous ballad about it (*'La Ballade des sept chênes'*) on the evening after the affair. Among his other ballads are *'Le Général Dickson'* and *'Les Tribulations d'un roi malheureux'* about William McDOUGALL. The brother-in-law of Cuthbert GRANT, he became a farmer near Grantown.

Falconbridge Nickel Mines Ltd. A pioneer nickel-producing company. Although the original mineral property at Falconbridge in the Sudbury district of northern Ontario was known as early as 1898, the mine and the company did not expand into a major corporation until 1928, when it was taken over by Thayer Lindsley (1882-1976). Born in Yokohama, Japan, of American missionary parents, Lindsley was called 'the man with the x-ray eyes' for his ability to 'read rocks'. He guided Falconbridge into nickel at Sudbury, and into gold, base metals, iron and many other minerals across Canada.

Fall. Autumn, the season between summer and winter. The word is widely used in Canada, less so in the United States, and hardly at all in the United Kingdom.

Fall Fair. Lively program piece for orchestra by Godfrey RIDOUT, composed in 1961. It is considered the most popular Canadian orchestral work.

Fall fair. An agricultural fair held each fall, usually around LABOUR DAY, in small communities. The CANADIAN NATIONAL EXHIBITION began as a fall fair in 1846.

Fall wheat. Wheat sown in the fall, ripening during the following spring.

Faludy, George (b.1910). Emigré poet and man-of-letters who writes in Hungarian. Born in Budapest, imprisoned by both Fascists and Communists, he has lived in Toronto since 1968. Three of his books have appeared in English: *My Happy Days in Hell* (1962), *Karoton* (1966), and *Erasmus of Rotterdam* (1970).

Fameuse. The French name of the 'famous' SNOW APPLE.

Family Allowance. A monthly payment, popularly called 'the baby bonus', paid to parents with children under 18. The Family Allowance Act was passed in Aug. 1944 and the first payments were made in July 1945. A revised Act came into effect in 1974, when the federal monthly allowance stood at $20 per child, though the provinces may vary this amount within certain limits. The Family Allowance is taxable.

Family Compact. The Tory clique that controlled policy and patronage in UPPER CANADA. The term is attributed to Thomas Dalton, editor of the Kingston *Patriot*, and was taken up by William Lyon MACKENZIE in the pages of his *Colonial Advocate*. Certain family names—e.g., Boulton, Jarvis, and Robinson—*were* prominent among the government officials in the early decades of the nineteenth century; but they were virtually the only men who were educated and their appointment to positions of influence was inevitable. The equivalent term in Lower Canada was CHÂTEAU CLIQUE.

Famous Players Ltd. Canada's largest theatre chain. It was begun in 1920 as a subsidiary of Paramount Pictures under N.L. Nathanson (1886-1943), who resigned in 1941 to join ODEON THEATRES. In 1975 it owned or controlled approximately 309 theatres in Canada, 120 of which were partnership operations. It is 51.15% owned by the U.S. conglomerate Gulf and Western, which also owns Paramount. In recent years, under its president George Destounis, it has been investing in Canadian feature films.

Far North. The ARCTIC and sub-Arctic regions of Canada.

Far West. The region of Canada west of the Prairies.

'Farewell to Nova Scotia'. Popular title of a traditional song of Nova Scotia. It was first recorded by Helen CREIGHTON and sung by the Jubilee Singers on the CBC-TV show SINGALONG JUBILEE. The nostalgic refrain goes: 'Farewell to Nova Scotia, the sea-bound coast!/Let your mountains dark and dreary be./For when I am far away on the briny ocean tossed,/Will you ever heave a sigh and a wish for me?' It is identified with Catherine McKINNON.

Farm Forum. See NATIONAL FARM RADIO FORUM.

Farmer-Labour Alliance. A political alliance between Saskatchewan farmer and labour groups. It was never able to achieve power in Saskatchewan, as did the UNITED FARMERS OF ALBERTA, the UNITED FARMERS OF MANITOBA, and the UNITED FARMERS OF ONTARIO in their provinces. But the alliance was active in the formation of the CCF in 1932.

Farmer premier. Sobriquet of E.C. Drury (1878-1968), who created the UNITED FARMERS OF ONTARIO. Drury was premier of Ontario from 1919 to 1923.

Farnon, Robert (b.1917). Composer and arranger. Born in Toronto, he was a trumpeter on CBC Radio's HAPPY GANG from 1936 to 1944, when he became musical director of the 'Canadian Army Show'. He settled in London, Eng., after the war and worked as conductor and arranger for such performers as Gracie Fields and Vera Lynn. He wrote the score for the film *Expresso Bongo* and the novelty song 'Mexican Jumping Bean'.

Farquharson, Charlie. See Don HARRON.

Fashion Designers Association of Canada, Inc. Monreal-based organization to safeguard and promote design standards. Founded in 1974 by 13 designers—including Leo CHEVALIER, Claire HADDAD, Michel ROBICHAUD, and John WARDEN—it encourages and trains new designers. Members must have studied at a recognized school of fashion design or have had equivalent training in the fashion industry; they must also have designed under their own label for at least two years.

Father of British Columbia. Sobriquet of Sir James DOUGLAS.

Father of Canadian geology. Sobriquet of Abraham GESNER (1797-1864), the author of *Remarks on the Geology and Mineralogy of Nova Scotia* (1836).

Father of Confederation. Sobriquet granted Sir John A. MACDONALD, the first prime minister of Canada. See also FATHERS OF CONFEDERATION.

Father of Standard Time. Sobriquet of Sir Sandford FLEMING.

Fathers of Confederation. Delegates of the British North American colonies to one or more of the conferences at which the terms of CONFEDERATION were agreed upon: the CHARLOTTETOWN CONFERENCE (C) on 1 Sept. 1864; the QUEBEC CONFERENCE (Q) on 10-29 Oct. 1864; and the LONDON CONFERENCE (L), which began on 4 Dec. 1866. The list of delegates follows: Adams G. ARCHIBALD, N.S. (C,Q,L); George BROWN, Canada (C,Q); Alexander CAMPBELL, Canada (C,Q); Frederick B.T. CARTER, Nfld (Q); George-Étienne CARTIER, Canada (C,Q,L); Edward B. CHANDLER, N.B. (C,Q); Jean-Charles CHAPAIS, Canada (Q); James COCKBURN, Canada (Q); George H. COLES, P.E.I. (C,Q); Robert B. DICKEY, N.S. (C,Q); Charles FISHER, N.B. (Q,L); A.T. GALT, Canada (C,Q,L); John Hamilton GRAY, N.B. (C,Q); John Hamilton GRAY, P.E.I. (C,Q); Thomas Heath HAVILAND, P.E.I. (Q); William A. HENRY, N.S. (C,Q,L); William P. HOWLAND, Canada (L); John M. JOHNSON, N.B. (C,Q,L); Hector L. LANGEVIN, Canada (C,Q,L); Jonathan

McCULLY, N.S. (C,Q,L); A.A. MACDONALD, P.E.I. (C,Q); John A. MACDONALD, Canada (C,Q,L); William McDOUGALL, Canada (C,Q,L); Thomas D'Arcy McGEE, Canada (C,Q); Peter MITCHELL, N.B. (Q,L); Oliver MOWAT, Canada (Q); Edward PALMER, P.E.I. (C,Q); William H. POPE, P.E.I. (C,Q); John W. RITCHIE, N.S. (L); J. Ambrose SHEA, Nfld (Q); William H. STEEVES, N.B. (C,Q); Sir Étienne-Paschal TACHÉ, Canada (Q); Samuel Leonard TILLEY, N.B. (C,Q,L); Charles TUPPER, N.S. (C,Q,L); Edward WHELAN, P.E.I. (Q); R.D. WILMOT, N.B. (L). See also the entry on Robert HARRIS for the painting by this name.

Fathers of Responsible Government. Sobriquet extended to Robert BALDWIN and Louis LAFONTAINE, who helped bring about RESPONSIBLE GOVERNMENT in the Province of Canada.

Fauna. The native animal life of an area, in Canada that of the boreal (northern) and austral (temperate) regions. Throughout Canada all species have been drastically reduced in numbers and range; several, among them the Maritime sea mink and the passenger pigeon, are now extinct. The original forest fauna of all of Ontario and of southern Quebec have been almost totally destroyed; probably that of the most inaccessible inland pockets of British Columbia remain the closest to their natural state prior to the arrival of Europeans. See: ALBERTOSAURUS, BEAVER, BISON, BLACK BEAR, BLACK FLY, CANADA GOOSE, CANADA JAY, CANADA LYNX, CARIBOU, COD (ATLANTIC), COHOE SALMON, DEER (WHITE-TAILED), EAGLE (BALD), GRIZZLY BEAR, LOON, MASSASAUGA RATTLESNAKE, MOOSE, MOUNTAIN BEAVER, MUSK OX, NARWHAL, OTTER, OWL (ARCTIC), POLAR BEAR, PTARMIGAN, SALMON, SEAL (HARP), SEA OTTER, SNOWSHOE HARE, SOCKEYE SALMON, WHOOPING CRANE, WINNIPEG GOLDEYE, WOLVERINE.

F/C. Official abbreviation of Flight Cadet.

Federal. Under the jurisdiction of the government of Canada; Dominion as opposed to provincial. See also FEDERALISM.

Federal building. A building in a city or town housing the regional offices of such federal government departments as the post office, etc.

Federal Court of Canada. A SUPERIOR COURT having civil and criminal jurisdiction. Authorized by the BNA ACT of 1867 and established in 1875 as the Exchequer Court of Canada, the Federal Court of Canada was so named in 1970. It sits in Ottawa, has appeal and trial divisions, and has jurisdiction in claims by and against the Crown, in matters involving interprovincial and federal-provincial disputes, patents and copyrights, maritime law, aeronautics, and certain cases involving federal boards and commissions.

Federal government. See HOUSE OF COMMONS, SENATE, CROWN, GOVERNOR GENERAL.

Federalism. The name given to a form of political organization in which a number of smaller political units give up certain powers to a central government while retaining certain rights. See also DISTRIBUTION OF POWERS, PROVINCIAL AUTONOMY.

Fédérastes. French portmanteau word, a combination of 'federalist' and 'pederast'. The insulting epithet was used of French-Canadian politicians in Ottawa by their Quebec colleagues during the 1960s.

Fédération des coopératives du Nouveau-Québec, La. A federation formed on 20 May 1967 to represent Eskimo art co-operatives in the Province of Quebec. Each community where art is produced has its own co-operative, which arranges the manufacture and sale of its products. Those that are located in NEW QUEBEC include George River, Fort Chimo, Great Whale River (Poste-de-la-Baleine), Inoucdjouac (Port Harrison), Ivujivic, Payne Bay (Bellin), Povungnituk, Sugluk, Wakeham Bay (Maricourt), and Wemindji. See also CANADIAN ARCTIC CO-OPERATIVE FEDERATION LIMITED.

Feldbrill, Victor (b.1924). Conductor and music director. Born in Toronto, he studied at the Royal College of Music and the Royal Academy of Music, London, and at the Royal Conservatory of Music, Toronto; he also studied conducting with Pierre Monteux and William van Otterloo. In 1973 he was appointed resident conductor of the TORONTO SYMPHONY ORCHESTRA. He is also conductor of the University of Toronto Symphony Orchestra and, since July 1974, of the Toronto Symphony Youth Orchestra.

Fenerty, Charles (1821-92). Inventor, farmer, poet. He was born in Upper Sackville, N.S., near a mill at Bedford, where paper was manufactured in the standard way, out of rags. He began experimenting from 1839 and produced paper from sprucewood pulp, whether through chemical or mechanical means is unknown. His firm, white, durable paper was exhibited in 1844. Fenerty could hardly have known that his 'invention', produced in isolation, was not a world first. He regarded his experiment as being of interest to 'the scientific or the curious'—it had no influence on the history of papermaking. Fenerty visited Australia, wrote but apparently never published a long epic poem, 'Essay on

Progress', resumed farming in Nova Scotia, and died in Lower Sackville.

Fenians. A militant Irish-American society organized in New York in 1859 for the purpose of promoting Irish independence. With their ranks swelled by Irish-American veterans of the American Civil War, they were, by 1865, preparing to launch attacks on Canada, hoping that the British might as a result be forced to divert troops from Ireland. Various raids carried out in 1866, and the threat of further raids, produced a feeling of uneasiness in British North America and lent urgency to the plans for CONFEDERATION. The most serious raid was the Battle of RIDGEWAY.

Ferguson, Elmer W. (Fergy) (1885-1972). Sports promoter. A native of Prince Edward Island, he lived in Moncton, N.B., and Montreal, where he established a national reputation as a sports editor, athletic commissioner, racetrack judge and steward, and sports promoter; he was also the first publicity agent employed by the NATIONAL HOCKEY LEAGUE. He was a member of the nationally televised 'Hot Stove League' (see HOCKEY NIGHT IN CANADA) and a selector for both the Sports and Hockey HALLS OF FAME.

Ferguson, Graeme (b.1929). Film director. Born in Toronto, he was a summer student with the NATIONAL FILM BOARD in 1950 before he left for the United States. He returned to Canada in 1970 and set up Multi-Screen Corporation with Roman KROITER to market the revolutionary IMAX PROCESS, which is in use at ONTARIO PLACE. He directed *Man and the Polar Regions* for EXPO 67 and NORTH OF SUPERIOR (1971) for Ontario Place.

Ferguson, Max (b.1924). Popular CBC personality and satirist. Born in Crook, Durham, Eng., he was brought to Canada at the age of three. After graduating from the University of Western Ontario in 1946, he joined the CBC as an announcer and disc-jockey at their Halifax studios. He created the Rawhide Little Theatre Group, in which he assumed a dozen voices including the rough voice of Old Rawhide, the scratchy voice of Ol' Granny, and the mellifluous cadences of Marvin Mellobell—in satiric commentaries on events of the day. He wrote *And Now . . . Here's Max* (1968), which won the Stephen LEACOCK MEDAL FOR HUMOUR. 'The Max Ferguson Show', which has had various formats in its 30 years on CBC, ended in 1976 when Ferguson retired to his home at Neil Harbour, Cape Breton Island, N.S.

Ferguson, Maynard (b.1929). Jazz trumpeter. Born in Montreal, he joined Stan Kenton's band in 1950 and made an international name for himself with his sensational 'high-note' trumpet. He has since toured the world with his own bands.

Fern, Ostrich. See FIDDLEHEAD.

Ferron, Jacques (b.1921). Quebec man of letters. Born in Louiseville, Que., and educated at Université Laval, he has practised medicine since 1949 in Ville Jacques-Cartier, a working-class suburb of Montreal. In Dec. 1970 he was designated by the Chénier Cell of the FLQ and accepted by the Quebec government to negotiate with the Rose brothers, who were being hunted as the kidnappers and killers of Pierre Laporte. After being active in the separatist RIN, he formed the satirical political movement, the RHINOCEROS PARTY, in 1972. A prolific author of plays, short stories, and novels, Ferron writes about the oppressed with special humour and love. His fiction has been published in English under the following titles, with the names of their translators: *Tales from the Uncertain Country* (1972), Betty Bednarski; *Dr. Cotnoir* (1973), Pierre Cloutier; *The Saint Elias* (1975), Pierre Cloutier; and *The Juneberry Tree* (1975), Raymond Chamberlain.

Ferry, Quebec, The. Painting by James Wilson MORRICE. First exhibited in Paris in 1909, it is one of the masterpieces of Canadian art. The everyday scene of the dock at Lévis and the cliff at Quebec, with the ferry in the ice-strewn river between, is painted impressionistically and is brought alive by its design and its cold, subtle, winter coloration. (NGC)

Fessenden, Reginald Aubrey (1866-1932). Inventor and radio pioneer. Born in Quebec, the son of Clementina Fessenden (the woman responsible for VICTORIA DAY), and educated at Bishop's College, he worked with Thomas Alva Edison in New Jersey in 1886 and was launched on a frequently contentious career as an inventor and radio pioneer. On 23 Dec. 1900 he successfully transmitted the sound of a human voice between two 50-ft towers on Cobb Island, Potomac R., near Washington. On 25 Dec. 1906 he beamed the first radio broadcast to the astonished crews of ships in the Atlantic and the Caribbean—the first mixed broadcast of carol-singing, Bible-reading, and violin-playing, all performed by Fessenden. He died in Bermuda, where his epitaph reads: 'I am yesterday and I know tomorrow'.

Festival. CBC-TV's banner series of 90-minute dramas. The weekly programs began with the STRATFORD FESTIVAL's production of *H.M.S. Pinafore* on 10 Oct. 1961 and ended on 26 Mar. 1969 with Paul ST PIERRE's original teleplay *Sister Balonika*. It was produced by Robert ALLEN and claimed a million viewers a week. It succeeded GM PRESENTS and was the last series of live programs mounted for Canadian television.

Festival Canada. A program of performing arts held each summer at the NATIONAL ARTS CENTRE in Ottawa. It grew out of the nationwide, year-long program arranged by the Centennial Commission for 1967, when such groups as the STRATFORD FESTIVAL and Les FEUX-FOLLETS toured the country and supplied continuous entertainment in Ottawa at a cost of $3 million.

Festival Lennoxville. A six-week summer festival of Canadian plays and other theatrical and musical entertainments held in the 600-seat Centennial Theatre at Bishop's University, Lennoxville, Que. The first production was a revival of *The OTTAWA MAN* by Mavor MOORE, directed by Frances HYLAND, which opened on 8 July 1972. The artistic director of the festival is William Davis, a cousin of Murray and Donald Davis (see DAVIS FAMILY).

Festival of Spring. See TULIP FESTIVAL.

Festival Singers of Canada. Professional choir. Founded in Toronto in 1954 by Elmer ISELER, their conductor, this 60-to-100-voice mixed choir became the first professional choir in North America and a major force in Canadian music. They have brought an excellent choral repertoire to large audiences and also have commissioned many works by Canadian composers. Igor Stravinsky pronounced the Festival Singers the finest choir on the continent. He conducted them and the CBC SYMPHONY in a recording of his *Symphony of Psalms* in Jan. 1962 (the performance, taped by the CBC, was broadcast on 13 June 1962 in honour of Stravinsky's 80th birthday the following week). An NFB film documentary of Stravinsky conducting this same program at a second recording session in MASSEY HALL (Mar. 1962) was directed by Roman KROITER and Wolf KOENIG, with commentary by Donald BRITTAIN. On 29 Apr. 1962 Stravinsky conducted a special concert of his own music for the Dag Hammarskjold Scholarship Fund—including the world première of his anthem *The Dove Descending Breaks the Air*—with the Festival Singers and the CBC Symphony at Massey Hall. In 1968 the Singers became the professional corps of the TORONTO MENDELSSOHN CHOIR.

Festubert. A village in northern France, the scene of a bloody battle during the FIRST WORLD WAR by the First Canadian Division in May 1915 that brought negligible gains.

Fetherling

Fetherling, Doug (b.1949). Journalist and poet. 'Please remember that I was not born anywhere', explains Fetherling, who has worked in Toronto since 1963. He has written on books and films in the *Toronto Star*, the *Canadian Forum*, and *Saturday Night*. Among his poetry collections are *Our Man in Utopia* (1971) and *Achilles' Navel* (1974). He is also the author of a critical study, *Hugh* GARNER (1973).

Feux-Follets, Les. Dance troupe. Started in 1952 by Michel Cartier to involve the boys in his working-class Montreal suburb, it performs strikingly choreographed and staged Canadian folk dances, ranging from Eskimo walrus hunts to square dances, and is considered to be the nation's official folk ensemble. It has been acclaimed across Canada and in Europe and the United States. Its name means 'fireflies'.

Feyer, George (1921-67). Cartoonist. Born in Budapest, he forged his exit visa and (first-class) airplane tickets out of Hungary in 1946. In 1948 he settled in Toronto, where he was highly successful as a commercial artist, greatly admired for his witty caricatures. For CBC-TV he devised the 'Mobiline' process that permits a rapid-sketch artist to draw in ink on the back of a sheet of paper so that the illustration appears on the front as if drawn by itself. In 1965 he left for Los Angeles, where his caricatures and cartoons were popular on television, and where he took his own life. He wrote and illustrated *The Man in the Red Flannel Suit* (1965).

Fiddle-De-Dee. A short film made by Norman McLAREN. A spirited rendition of 'Listen to the Mocking Bird' by an old-time fiddler from the Gatineau Valley supplied the sound track for a succession of rich visual images created by McLaren through his camera-less abstraction technique. The film was released by the NFB in 1947. 3 min., 30 sec.; colour.

Fiddlehead. The edible frond of the ostrich fern. This green spring vegetable grows in North America from Newfoundland to Alaska and south to Missouri. It resembles the curled head of a fiddle, hence its name. Fiddleheads are now marketed frozen across Canada.

Fiddlehead, The. A literary quarterly published by the University of New Brunswick. Founded by the Bliss Carmen Society of Fredericton in 1945 and identified throughout the fifties and sixties with Fred COGSWELL, it has offered first publication to many young poets and story writers.

Fiddlehead Poetry Books. Series of poetry chapbooks edited by Fred COSWELL first in association with the FIDDLEHEAD and then on his own. The first book issued was Cogswell's own *The Stunted Strong* (1954). Some 200 titles appeared between 1954 and 1974, many of them 'first publications' by young poets.

Fiddler. In the Maritimes, an Atlantic salmon weighing less than 8 lb.

Fides, Corporation des Éditions. Quebec publishers. The largest publishing house in French Canada, it was founded in Montreal in 1937. It has a large trade and educational list and has strong links with the Catholic church.

Field of Honour. See LAST POST FUND.

Fife wheat. Spring WHEAT developed by David Fife, a farmer near Otonabee, C.W. (Ont.), about 1851. This variety, later known as Red Fife, was the first Canadian wheat to be resistant to rust.

Fifth Business. A best-selling novel by Robertson DAVIES, published in 1970. It is the first novel in a trilogy—completed by *The Manticore* (1972) and *World of Wonders* (1975)—that illuminates the mysteries of human motives and character and is infused with elements of the miraculous. Set in an Ontario town called Deptford, and moving to Toronto and Europe, it is related by Dunstan Ramsey—who becomes the 'fifth business', the person through whom the dénouement takes place—and begins with a childhood episode when Percy Boy Staunton throws a snowball packed around a small stone at Ramsay and hits instead the Baptist minister's wife, thus setting in motion an intricate sequence of events.

Fifty-eighter. A prospector who joined the FRASER RIVER GOLD RUSH in 1858.

'Fifty-four Forty, or Fight'. Slogan of the Democratic Party in the United States elections of 1844 expressing American claims to the whole Pacific Coast north to Alaska. It is attributed to William Allen, who used it in a speech on the dispute over the boundary between Canada and the District of Oregon (now the states of Oregon and Washington) in the U.S. Senate in 1844. Britain and the United States compromised on the question when the present western boundary between Canada and the United States (the 49th parallel) was established in 1846.

Figgy duff. A boiled raisin pudding, traditional to Newfoundland.

Fighting Navy. A CBC Radio series that was popular during the Second World War. Produced by Bill Strange, it dramatized true adventures of war heroes, setting them aboard the mythical destroyer HMCS *Missinaibi*. Actors who took part included Lloyd BOCHNER and John DRAINIE.

Fighting Words. A popular and fondly remembered CBC series of 'spontaneous and unrehearsed' opinion. The weekly 30-minute panel show was moderated by Nathan COHEN, who challenged the three or four panelists (regulars included Dr William E. BLATZ, Morley CALLAGHAN, Irving LAYTON, and J.B. McGEACHY) to identify and then discuss provocative quotations submitted by listeners. Created for CBC Radio by Mavor MOORE, titled by Stuart Griffiths, and produced by Harvey HART, it was heard on radio from Dec. 1952 to July 1962. It was equally successful on television, from Feb. 1953 to July 1963, and was then produced by Cliff Solway. It was revived for 13 weeks by CHCH-TV in Hamilton as 'Nathan Cohen's Fighting Words' and syndicated, beginning 27 June 1970.

Filion, Hervé (b.1940). Jockey. Born in Angers, Que., he is one of eight brothers, all involved in one form of racing or another. The 5'6" harness racer turned pro at 13 and moved to the United States at 31. He has won all the major harness races and, in 1974, raced an average of eight times a day seven days a week, earning the nickname 'Iron Man'. He once said: 'The only race I can't win is the one I'm watching.' He operates Capital Hills Farms in Montreal.

Filipovic, Augustin (b.1931). Sculptor. Born in Davor, Yugoslavia, he graduated from the Academy of Fine Arts in Rome before coming to Canada in 1959. His bronze free-form and portrait sculptures have been exhibited in Canada's major cities.

Filles du roi. See KING'S GIRLS.

Fils de la liberté. 'Sons of Liberty'. The name of a Montreal group of French-Canadian PATRIOTES that met and drilled openly for three months in 1837. Their clash with a Tory group was a prelude to the REBELLION OF 1837 in Lower Canada (Quebec).

Finance, Department of. A department of the federal government responsible for economic and financial affairs. Created in 1869, and under the Minister of Finance, this senior department carries out its work in six branches: Tax Policy and Federal-Provincial Relations; Economic Programs and Govern-

ment Finance; Tariffs, Trade and Aid; Economic Analysis, Fiscal Policy and International Finance; Financial Operations; and Long-Range Economic Planning. Such agencies as the BANK OF CANADA report to Parliament through the Minister of Finance.

Financial Post, The. A national newspaper covering the world of business, investment, the economy, and public affairs. It appears each Thursday and has been published by MACLEAN-HUNTER in Toronto since 1907. Associated with the magazine since 1919 was Floyd S. Chalmers, who was editor from 1925 to 1942, and president of Maclean-Hunter from 1952 to 1964, when he became chairman of the board. Of particular interest are 'special feature' reports that cover a wide range of topics in depth. The magazine supplement, which appears 10 times each year, includes general-interest articles slanted to a professional audience. Five *Financial Post Annual Surveys* are published each year, covering Funds, Industrials, Markets, Mines, and Oil.

Financial Times of Canada. A national newspaper covering investment, business, and the economy, published by SOUTHAM PRESS each Monday. It was founded in Montreal in 1912 and has been published from Toronto since Nov. 1975. Special features include: 'Portfolio', brief descriptions of public companies; 'The Top One Hundred', a numerical listing of the 100 most active stocks on the Toronto Stock Exchange; and 'Perspective on Money', a quarterly magazine supplement that discusses taxation and personal investment.

Finch. A single-engine biplane. It was built by Fleet Aircraft at Fort Erie, Ont., and acquired by the RCAF in 1939 for use as a trainer in the BRITISH COMMONWEALTH AIR TRAINING PLAN.

Finch, Robert (b.1900). Poet. Born at Freeport, Long Island, and educated at the University of Toronto and in Paris, he taught in the French department of the University of Toronto until his retirement. His delicate and aesthetically fastidious poems have appeared in several collections, including *Poems* (1946) and *Silverthorn Bush and Other Poems* (1966). He has had many showings of his paintings in gouache and he edited, with Eugène Joliat, *French Individualist Poetry* (1971), an anthology of work from the seventeenth and eighteenth centuries.

Findley, Timothy (b.1930). Novelist and TV writer. Born in Toronto, he worked as a stage actor in London and New York before turning to television writing. He has written two novels—*The Last of the Crazy People* (1957) and *The Butterfly Plague* (1969)—and contributed as a writer to the CBC-TV series WHITEOAKS OF JALNA and The NATIONAL DREAM.

Finlayson Point. A point of land on the outskirts of Victoria, B.C., overlooking the Strait of Juan de Fuca. It was named after the HBC factor Roderick Finlayson (1859-72). A monument there today marks the sites of a fortified Indian village and an armed battery erected in 1878-92 for protection against an expected Russian invasion.

Finnigan, Joan (b.1928). Poet. Born in Ottawa and educated at Carleton and Queen's Universities, she is a librarian in Kingston, Ont., and the author of several collections of poems, including *Entrance to the Greenhouse* (1968), *It Was Warm and Sunny When We Set Out* (1970), and *Living Together* (1976). She has also written *Kingston: Celebrate this City* (1976) and The BEST DAMN FIDDLER FROM CALABOGIE TO KALADAR (1968), an NFB documentary.

FIRA. Initials of the FOREIGN INVESTMENT REVIEW AGENCY.

Firebrand, The. Sobriquet given William Lyon MACKENZIE for his radical views and his fiery personality, which was complemented by a red wig. It is also the title of a biography of Mackenzie by William KILBOURN.

Fire-proof house. Phrase associated with Canadian isolationism. Before the League of Nations on 2 Oct. 1924 Senator Raoul Dandurand, a member of the Canadian delegation to the League, declared, 'We live in a fire-proof house, far from inflammable materials.' His address is included in *Documents on Canadian Foreign Policy: 1917-1939* (1962) selected and edited by Walter A. Riddell.

Fire-reels. Nineteenth-century word for 'fire engines' or 'fire trucks', still used in Toronto and some other cities.

Firewater. The name given to cheap whisky or brandy used as barter by fur traders and settlers. In early Canada alcoholic beverages were often imported with an undiluted alcohol content of 90%.

Fireweed. A tall leafy perennial with rosepink flowers, found in the sub-Arctic and on the mainland tundra. After mistakenly choosing a related species, the willow herb, of the northern archipelago as its floral emblem, the Yukon adopted the native fireweed in 1957.

First Canadian Army. The Canadian Army Overseas, commanded by Gen. A.G.L. McNAUGHTON. A Canadian Corps was formed on 25 Dec. 1940. Headquarters for the First Canadian Army came into existence on 6 Apr. 1942, when the Canadian Corps was redesignated the 1st Canadian Corps. The 2nd Canadian Corps was formed on 14 Jan. 1943.

First of July. See DOMINION DAY.

First Person Singular. A 13-part CBC-TV series subtitled 'The Memoirs of a Prime Minister'. The late Lester B. PEARSON reminisced on camera about his life (and saw the completed series two days before his death). The half-hour episodes, produced by Cameron Graham and written and directed by Munroe Scott, first appeared on 23 Oct. 1974.

First Statement. A poetry magazine issued in Montreal and edited by John SUTHERLAND. Appearing irregularly from Sept. 1942 to July 1945, it published the poetry of Louis DUDEK, Irving LAYTON, Raymond SOUSTER, and Sutherland himself, all of whom felt themselves at odds with the more cosmopolitan air of PREVIEW, with which it merged in Dec. 1945 to form NORTHERN REVIEW.

First Union Flag. The British flag of 1606 associated with the early history of Canada. It was flown by Henry HUDSON in 1610 and James COOK in 1779, carried into UPPER CANADA by the LOYALISTS and flown by John Graves SIMCOE at the Parliament in NEWARK on 17 Sept. 1792. It symbolizes the union of England and Scotland in 1606 and combines ST GEORGE'S BANNER (a red cross on a white field) and ST ANDREW'S BANNER (a diagonal white cross on a blue field). With the addition of ST PATRICK'S BANNER in 1801, it became the second (or royal) union flag, the UNION JACK.

First World War. Often called 'The Great War'. Canada entered when Britain signed the declaration of war against Germany on 4 Aug. 1914. The armistice was signed on 11 Nov. 1918, and hostilities officially ceased at 11:00 a.m., the hour marked by annual REMEMBRANCE DAY services. In all, with a population of 8,075,000, Canada contributed to the Great War 626,636 officers and men from all services, of whom 59,769 lost their lives. For Canada's military contribution, see CANADIAN CORPS and also the sites of individual battles: AMIENS, ANCRE HEIGHTS, ARRAS, CAMBRAI, CANAL DU NORD, COURCELETTE, DROCOURT-QUÉANT, FESTUBERT, GIVENCHY, HILL 70, MONS, MONT HOUY, MURMANSK 'MISSION', PASSCHENDAELE, REGINA TRENCH, ST ELOI, The SOMME, VALENCIENNES, VIMY, VLADIVOSTOK 'MISSION', and YPRES.

Fischman, Sheila (b.1937). Translator. Born in Moose Jaw, Sask., and educated at the University of Saskatchewan, she has worked as an editor at the University of Toronto Press and was a founding editor of the bilingual magazine ELLIPSE. She lives in Montreal and has translated works by Marie-Claire BLAIS, Roch CARRIER, and Roland GIGUÈRE, as well as Jacques Benoit's *Jos Carbone* (1975), Max Gros-Louis's *First Among the Hurons* (1974), and Jules-Paul Tardivel's *For My Country* (1975).

Fish and brewis. A traditional Newfoundland dish: salt cod, served with 'brewis' or hard bread cooked in water, with a topping of fried salt pork.

Fish Creek, Battle of. An engagement in the NORTH WEST REBELLION on 24 Apr. 1885. Gabriel DUMONT, commanding the Métis forces of Louis RIEL, intercepted Canadian troops under Gen. Frederick Middleton at Fish Creek near the South Saskatchewan R. The skirmish was inconclusive and Dumont withdrew to BATOCHE.

Fisher, Charles (1808-80). A FATHER OF CONFEDERATION. Born in Fredericton, N.B., he trained as a lawyer and was elected to the legislative assembly of New Brunswick in 1837, becoming premier in 1851; he resigned in 1861. He was a delegate to the QUEBEC and LONDON CONFERENCES and at Confederation was elected to the House of Commons.

Fisher, John W. (b.1912). 'Mr Canada'. A native of Sackville, N.B., and a graduate in law from Dalhousie University, he rose to national prominence as a broadcaster and booster of things Canadian. From 1939 to 1949 'John Fisher Reports' was a popular Sunday-evening CBC Radio feature, and Fisher earned the sobriquet 'Mr Canada'. He was briefly the commissioner of Expo 67 and now runs his own public-relations firm in Toronto.

Fishing Admiral. Title given in the seventeenth and eighteenth centuries to the captain of the first fishing vessel to reach a Newfoundland harbour each year. It carried with it the authority of a magistrate for that fishing region. The captain of the second vessel was considered the 'Vice Admiral' and the captain of the third vessel the 'Rear Admiral'. All three received numerous benefits.

FitzGerald, LeMoine (1890-1956). Painter, teacher, and a late member of the GROUP OF SEVEN. Born in Winnipeg, he studied there and in New York. He taught at the Winnipeg School of Art from 1924 and was a founding member of the CANADIAN GROUP OF PAINTERS.

Particularly noteworthy in his paintings are the quiet reverence and the carefully arranged and sculpturally modelled forms of his landscapes and still lifes—in such paintings as DOC SNIDER'S HOUSE (1931, NGC), *From an Upstairs Window* (1949, NGC), and *The Jar* (1938, Winnipeg Art Gallery). FitzGerald was also a sensitive painter of nudes, self-portraits, and abstractions, and produced many fine drawings.

Five-BX. The first of two programs of physical fitness developed by the RCAF in the 1950s. Both were immensely popular and contributed to the public's awareness of the need to 'maintain desirable levels of physical fitness'. 5BX (or VBX) is a series of 'Five Basic Exercises for Men', taking 11 minutes a day to perform a selection of the 30 exercises that are arranged on six charts. 10BX (or XBX) is a series of 'Ten Basic Exercises for Women', taking 12 minutes a day to perform a selection of the 48 exercises that are arranged on four charts. Credit for developing the concept of brief but progressive daily exercises has been given to the following RCAF personnel: P.J. Carey, arts and crafts specialist, W.A.R. Orban (5BX), and N.J. Ashton (10BX). The health craze was launched in 1958 with the publication of 5BX as a 50-cent booklet by the Queen's Printer. Both 5BX and 10BX appeared as *Royal Canadian Air Force Exercise Plans for Physical Fitness* (1962).

Five-cent speech. Address in the HOUSE OF COMMONS on 3 Apr. 1930 in which Prime Minister Mackenzie KING declared he would not give 'a five-cent piece' to 'any Tory government' for 'these alleged unemployment purposes', the point being that unemployment was a provincial and not a federal responsibility.

Five Islands. Small islands in Minas Basin visible from Parrsboro, N.S. A MICMAC legend tells that they were created when GLOOSCAP, angry with a beaver, pitched five lumps of mud into the sea.

Five Lakes Fishing Club. Private recreational club for senior civil servants. Founded in 1941, with a small lodge in the Gatineau Hills, it has fewer than 50 members, all of whom hold or held important civil-service posts.

Five Songs of Newfoundland Outports. Traditional regional folksongs collected by Kenneth Peacock and arranged by Harry SOMERS in 1969. They are especially popular with music students.

F/L. Official abbreviation of Flight Lieutenant.

185

Flag of Canada, National. See NATIONAL FLAG OF CANADA.

Flaherty, Robert (1884-1951). Documentary film-maker. Born in Iron Mountain, Mich., the son of a gold prospector in northern Ontario and Quebec, he attended Upper Canada College in Toronto and the Michigan College of Mines before making four geological expeditions to the Hudson Bay and Ungava regions in 1910-15. Later Flaherty drew on his Ungava experiences in writing two novels, *The Captain's Chair* (1938) and *White Master* (1939), but it was a casual remark made by the railroad builder Sir William Mackenzie in 1915 that set his new course. Mackenzie suggested that Flaherty acquire a camera, and this led to the filming of NANOOK OF THE NORTH (1920-2). Flaherty, a romantic with an openness to primitive and exotic cultures, followed this with *Moana* (1926) in the South Seas, *Man of Aran* (1934) in the North Atlantic, *Elephant Boy* (1937) in India, and *Louisiana Story* (1938) in the deep South—among other features.

Flanders Fields. CBC Radio series devoted to reminiscences of the First World War. Interviews with 600 survivors were recorded and edited by Frank Lalor, and the series of 17 hour-long episodes, first heard on 11 Nov. 1964, was written, narrated, and produced by J. Frank WILLIS. The first and last episodes were written by Joseph SCHULL, and the VIMY Ridge episode was later released as a two-disc album.

Flash. A weekly tabloid published between 1936 and 1960 by John Blunt Publications in Toronto. It specialized in exposés and sensational journalism and was distributed across the continent.

Flashbacks. See MACLEAN'S.

Flavelle Medal. Awarded every two years by the ROYAL SOCIETY OF CANADA for an outstanding contribution to biological science during the preceding 10 years or for significant additions to a previous outstanding contribution. The award was established in 1925 by the financier and businessman Sir Joseph Flavelle (1858-1939) and consists of a gold medal and $1,000.

Fleming, Allan (b.1929). Typographic designer. Born in Toronto, he studied at Western Technical School and in London, Eng., learning the discipline of classical typography while developing his skill as a modern typographic designer. In a career that has included teaching at the Ontario College of Art, working for Cooper & Beatty, a Toronto type house, *Maclean's*, and McLaren Advertising, he became one of the leading graphic designers in North America, winning many awards. A noted book designer—he designed CANADA/A YEAR OF THE LAND (1967)—he was chief designer of the University of Toronto Press from 1968 to 1976. He is best known for the striking corporate symbols he created for the CN in 1960 and the CBC in 1974.

Fleming, Robert (b.1921). Composer. Born in Saskatchewan, he studied in England and Toronto. From 1958 to 1970 he was musical director of the NATIONAL FILM BOARD and is now teaching at Carleton University. A prolific composer, his lyrical style combines dissonant tonality with melodic writing. He has received commissions from the ROYAL WINNIPEG BALLET (SHADOW ON THE PRAIRIE, 1955), the Saskatoon Symphony Orchestra (*Summer Suite*, 1957), and the NATIONAL ARTS CENTRE ORCHESTRA (*Hexad*, 1972).

Fleming, Sir Sandford (1827-1915). Civil engineer. Born in Scotland, he came to Canada in 1845 and began a distinguished career in surveying and engineering. Chief engineer for the construction of the INTERCOLONIAL RAILWAY, he was appointed chief engineer for construction of the CPR in 1871 and surveyed a northerly route (now used by the CNR) and a southerly route through the Kicking Horse Pass. He retired from government service in 1880 to pursue various public activities and scientific studies. The adoption of international STANDARD TIME in 1884 grew out of his papers on time reckoning. He also designed the first Canadian stamp, the THREE-PENCE BEAVER, issued in 1851. He was knighted in 1897.

Fleur-de-lis. Heraldic lily, associated with the royal houses of France and appearing on both the Quebec shield and the Quebec flag. The device represents three lilies, the centre one erect and the other two curved outwards. The provincial flag of Quebec, adopted on 21 Jan. 1948, is a white cross on a blue ground with a fleur-de-lis in each corner.

Flin Flon Strike. A strike by miners working for the HUDSON BAY MINING AND SMELTING COMPANY LIMITED at Flin Flon, Man., between 11 June and 14 July 1934. The miners were protesting a wage reduction and demanding the eight-hour day and union recognition. On 30 June a mass meeting to vote on whether to continue or end the strike resulted in a riot after the leaders were arrested. Arbitration later partially restored the wage cuts.

Flint and Feather. The collected poems of Pauline JOHNSON published in 1912. The book

186

includes such musical and romantic poems as 'The SONG MY PADDLE SINGS'.

Flood Gate, The. Famous painting by Homer WATSON. Windswept trees and clouds dominate a small group of oxen and a man operating a flood gate in a canvas that—unlike Watson's earlier paintings, which evoked comparisons with John Constable—was actually influenced by the work of the English landscape painter. (1900, NGC)

Flora. Wild plants native to a given area. Many thousands of species of plant life flourish across Canada's seven floralistic zones: Arctic, sub-Arctic, Mixed-Forest, Western, Prairie, Hardwood, Carolinian. See AVENS (MOUNTAIN), BIRCH, CEDAR (RED), CORN, CROCUS (PRAIRIE), DOGWOOD, DOUGLAS FIR, FIDDLEHEAD, FIREWEED, LADY'S SLIPPER, LILY (PRAIRIE), LILY (WHITE GARDEN), MAPLE, MAYFLOWER, MENZIES SPRUCE, MOCCASIN FLOWER, PINE (JACK), PITCHER-PLANT, PRAIRIE GRASS, ROSE (WILD), SASKATOON-BERRY, TAMARACK, TRILLIUM (WHITE), VIOLET, WHEAT.

Flos. Township in Simcoe Co., Ont., named in 1822 after one of three pet dogs of Lady Sarah, wife of Sir Peregrine Maitland, lieutenant-governor of UPPER CANADA from 1818 to 1828. See also TAY and TINY.

Flower Pot Island. A 300-acre island 4 mi. offshore from Tobermory, Ont., in the BRUCE PENINSULA. Water erosion has created two 'flower pots' from the limestone, one 50 ft high, the other 30 ft high. According to Indian legend, the formations are the stone spirits of two young Indian lovers. They were described as 'flower pots' by the earliest explorers.

Floyd S. Chalmers Foundation. See CHALMERS AWARD.

FLQ. The Front de Libération du Québec, a terrorist organization dedicated to obtaining Quebec SEPARATISM. In 1960 George Shoesters, an economics student at the Université de Montréal and a member of the Rassemblement pour l'Indépendance Nationale, led a small group within the RIN that in 1963 became the FLQ. Its slogan (in translation) was 'Revolution by the people, for the people; independence or death', the final line of a manifesto written in Apr. 1963 at the time of the first bombings in Montreal and made public on 17 May 1963, during the next wave of 15 bombings in the Westmount district. It rejected 'Anglo-Saxon colonization' of French Canada and insisted that Quebec's natural resources belong to Québécois. The kidnapping of James Cross, followed by the killing of Pierre Laporte, brought on the OCTOBER CRISIS of 1970.

Flying boxcar. Slang term for a freight plane, especially the C-119, which was flown by the RCAF during the Second World War.

'Flying Saucer'. See AVROCAR.

F/O. Official abbreviation of Flying Officer.

Fogo Process. Term commonly applied to a community-development technique in which film and/or videotape cameras are used as a means of stimulating individual and group action. The name derives from Fogo Island, off the northeast coast of Newfoundland, where, in 1967, the technique was first applied as a joint experiment of the Extension Service of Memorial University and the CHALLENGE FOR CHANGE unit of the NATIONAL FILM BOARD. Since then the process has been used extensively throughout Canada and the United States and has aroused considerable interest in Asia and Africa, notably in India and Tanzania. The Fogo Process has been described as 'a kind of marriage between "the medium is the message" and the NFB's long proud tradition of social documentary'. One observer has written: 'Confronting himself on camera gradually helps a person to develop an internal image of himself . . . the emotional dilemma induced by the gap between the image on the screen and the subjective feeling of the viewer produces a crisis in which the person attempts to bring the two aspects into harmony, thus increasing his self-knowledge.'

Foley, James (Jim) (b.1922). Teacher. Born in Toronto and educated at Columbia University, he is an English teacher and Canadian literature enthusiast who arranged the first CANADA DAY celebration at Port Colborne High School, Ont., in 1970. Since 1976 he has taught at Mohawk College in Hamilton, Ont.

Food Prices Review Board. A board to inquire into increases in food prices. Established on 28 May 1973 and consisting of a chairman, Mrs Beryl Plumptre, and four members, it made public any increases in food prices and offered recommendations to the government. It was discontinued on 16 Oct. 1975 when the Anti-Inflation Board was set up.

Football Awards, Canadian Schenley. See CANADIAN SCHENLEY FOOTBALL AWARDS.

Foothills. Rolling hills of grassland lying between the Prairies and the Rocky Mountains in southern Alberta.

For the Sake of Argument. See MACLEAN'S.

Forbes, Kenneth (b.1892). Artist. Born in

Toronto, he studied in Scotland and England, notably at the Slade, and won numerous prizes. He has been a sought-after painter of agreeable society portraits since 1924. He resigned from the ONTARIO SOCIETY OF ARTISTS in 1951, deploring its emphasis on modern art, and from the ROYAL CANADIAN ACADEMY in 1959 for similar reasons. *The Canadian Who's Who* lists his 'pet aversion' as 'modernist art'.

Ford, R.A.D. (b.1915). Poet and ambassador. Born in Ottawa and a graduate of the University of Western Ontario and Cornell, he joined the Department of External Affairs in 1940 and since 1964 has been the Canadian Ambassador to the U.S.S.R. His two books of poetry—*A Window on the North* (1956) and *The Solitary City* (1969)—are notable for their inclusion of translations from the Portuguese, French, Serbo-Croat, and Russian (including early poems by Pasternak and recent ones by Voznesensky).

Foreign Investment Review Agency. Federal screening body created to review and advise the cabinet on possible takeovers of large Canadian firms by foreign corporations. Established in 1974 under the provisions of Bill C-132, it was charged with requiring any foreign firm to demonstrate that its acquisition of an established Canadian enterprise, with minimum assets of $250,000 or annual sales of $3,000,000, would bring 'significant benefit' to Canada.

Forest City. Sobriquet of London, Ont., in the nineteenth century, when it was surrounded by woods.

Forest regions. There are eight fairly well-defined forest areas and one related non-forest region in Canada. See BOREAL FOREST REGION, GREAT LAKES—ST LAWRENCE FOREST REGION, SUBALPINE FOREST REGION, MONTANE FOREST REGION, COAST FOREST REGION, ACADIAN FOREST REGION, COLUMBIA FOREST REGION, DECIDUOUS FOREST REGION, GRASSLANDS.

Forges du Saint-Maurice, Les. A national historic site at Trois-Rivières Que., where the ruins of Canada's first ironworks—established in 1729 and operated until 1883—can be seen.

Forgotten Footsteps. A 30-minute radio series created for the CANADIAN RADIO BROADCAST COMMISSION from Toronto. Written by Don Henshaw and produced by Stanley Maxsted, it dramatized situations that might have arisen in connection with specific objects in the ROYAL ONTARIO MUSEUM. It originated in 1930, was heard Sunday evenings at 9:00, and ended before the Second World War.

Forillon National Park. Established in 1970 on the tip of Forillon Peninsula at the eastern end of the Gaspé Peninsula, Que., it includes 93 mi. of coastline and has as its theme 'harmony between man, land and sea'.

Forks, The. A reference to Winnipeg, which was established at the forks, or juncture, of the Red and Assiniboine Rivers.

Forrester Maureen (b.1931). Contralto. Born in Montreal, she studied singing there with Bernard Diamant. She was a well-known singer in Montreal and Toronto when she made her recital début at Town Hall, New York, in 1956, after which she went on to a brilliant international career, singing under virtually all the leading conductors and becoming one of the foremost lieder singers and recitalists in the world. Her career also includes many recordings, teaching, and opera: she made her New York opera début with the American Opera Society in 1958, singing Cornelia in *Julius Caesar*, which she sang with the New York City Opera in 1966. She made her Metropolitan Opera début in 1974.

'Forsaken, The'. Poem by Duncan Campbell SCOTT, first published in *New World Lyrics and Ballads* (1905). Written in two long stanzas, it tells of an Indian mother baiting a hook with her own flesh to catch fish to feed her baby, and of her last hours when she is deserted by her son and his family and is covered with snow and left to die.

Forsey, Eugene (b.1904). Authority on constitutional law. Born in Grand Bank, Nfld, was educated at McGill University and Oxford. He was Director of Research for the Canadian Congress of Labour from 1942 to 1956, for the CANADIAN LABOUR CONGRESS from 1956 to 1966, and was one of the authors of the REGINA MANIFESTO. He was appointed to the Senate in 1970. He is the author of *The Royal Power of Dissolution of Parliament in the British Commonwealth* (1943; reissued 1968) and of a collection of essays, *Freedom and Order* (1974).

Forst, Judith. Mezzo soprano. Born in Vancouver, she graduated in music from the University of British Columbia. She joined the Metropolitan Opera, New York, in 1968; sang with the CANADIAN OPERA COMPANY in 1972, 1973, and 1975; and was widely praised for her performance as Hansel in the award-winning CBC-TV production of *Hansel and Gretel* in 1970.

Forsyth. Manufacturers of men's apparel. Founded by J.D.C. Forsyth in Kitchener,

Ont., in 1903, John Forsyth Co. Limited remained a private operation until 1973, when it was acquired by Dylex Limited of Toronto. Forsyth produces and sells men's shirts, ties, woven and knitted sportswear, pajamas, boxer briefs and shorts, and scarves. The main manufacturing plant is in Kitchener, Ont.; another plant is at St-Jean, Que.

Fort Amherst National Historic Park. Small park across the harbour from CHARLOTTETOWN, P.E.I. It includes the earthworks of the French settlement of 1720 that was captured by the British in 1758. Fort Amherst is not to be confused with Crown Point in New York State, also called Fort Amherst.

Fort Anne National Historic Park. 30-acre park at ANNAPOLIS ROYAL, N.S., that includes the remains of the French PORT ROYAL, constructed in 1636 and occupied by the British after 1710, when it was renamed Fort Anne. It became the first national historic park in 1917.

Fort Beauséjour. A military post on the Isthmus of Chignecto, N.B. Built by the French on the boundary between French ACADIA and British NOVA SCOTIA in 1751, it was taken by the British in 1755 and renamed Fort Cumberland. Abandoned after the WAR OF 1812, the fort has been partly restored and is in Fort Beauséjour National Historic Park.

Fort Chambly. French fort on the left bank of the Richelieu R. at Chambly, Que. It was erected on the site of an earlier French fort in 1709-11 to guard the southern frontier. Captured by the British in 1760, it surrendered to American invaders in 1775, during the American Revolution, but was returned in 1776. It was garrisoned until 1851. In 1921 it was restored and made part of Fort Chambly National Historic Park.

Fort Churchill. See FORT PRINCE OF WALES.

Fort Erie, Battle of. An engagement in the WAR OF 1812. An American force under Gen. Winfield Scott took the British fort on the Niagara R. on 3 July 1814 and defended it against attacks by Sir Gordon Drummond on 15 Aug. and 17 Sept. On 5 Nov. the Americans withdrew to American territory, blowing up the fort.

Fort Garry. Fur trade post built by the HUDSON'S BAY COMPANY between 1817 and 1822 at the junction of the Red and Assiniboine Rivers, and around which the city of Winnipeg has grown. It replaced the NORTH WEST COMPANY's Fort Gibraltar, built in 1809-10, and was named after Nicholas Garry, a deputy governor of the HBC who helped arrange

the union of the two companies in 1821. Badly damaged by floods in 1826, the fort was re-established in 1831-3 on a new site 19 mi. down the Red. R. and renamed LOWER FORT GARRY. In 1835 construction was begun on Upper Fort Garry at a site just west of the first Fort Garry and in 1836 it became the administrative centre of ASSINIBOIA and for the fur trade of the Red River district. A stone gateway of this fort still stands.

Fort George. Military post on the Niagara R., near Niagara-on-the-Lake, Ont., erected between 1796 and 1799. On 27 May 1813, during the WAR OF 1812, it was taken by Gen. Winfield Scott and occupied by American invading forces for seven months. Severely damaged, it was rebuilt, garrisoned until 1845, and then closed. The bastions and powder magazine have survived and other buildings have been restored and reconstructed. It is now a museum in Fort George National Historic Park.

Fort Henry. A military post overlooking the harbour of Kingston, Ont. Built in 1813, it was rebuilt in 1832-6 and was garrisoned until 1890. It has been restored and is now a museum.

Fort James. This 100-ft HUDSON'S BAY COMPANY schooner was the first vessel to complete the circumnavigation of the North American continent. With St John's, Nfld, as her point of departure, she sailed 'counterclockwise' to King William Island in 1928 and 'clockwise' to the same place in 1934.

Fort Langley. Trading post built in 1827 for the HUDSON'S BAY COMPANY on the south bank of the Fraser R. near Langley, B.C. In 1839 it was moved about 2 mi. upstream to its present site. It has been partially restored to the period of the 1840s and is in Fort Langley National Historic Park.

Fort Lennox. Originally Fort Île-aux-Noix on the island of that name in the Richelieu R., Que. The fortifications built by the French in 1759, during the SEVEN YEARS' WAR, were taken by the British in Aug. 1759 and occupied by the Americans in 1775-6. After 1782 a British garrison occupied the fort. The creation of a new complex of stone buildings began in 1819 and was named Fort Lennox after Charles Gordon Lennox, Duke of Richmond, who was governor general in 1818-19. It now stands in the 210-acre Fort Lennox National Historic Park.

Fort Malden National Historic Park. On the east bank of the Detroit R., near Amherstburg, Ont. The fort was built in 1797-9 and served as an important base during the WAR

Fort Malden National Historic Park

OF 1812. It has been refurbished in the period of the 1830s.

Fort Niagara, Battle of. An engagement in the WAR OF 1812. On 19 Dec. 1813 the fort on the east bank of the Niagara R., in present-day New York State, was taken by British troops under Col. John Murray.

Fort Pitt. (Sask.) See BIG BEAR.

Fort Prince of Wales. The most northerly fortress on the continent, built by the HUDSON'S BAY COMPANY at the mouth of the Churchill R. A fort begun near this site in 1689 was destroyed by fire before completion. It was rebuilt 5 mi. upstream in 1717 and given the name Fort Churchill, but was commonly called Fort Prince of Wales. Between 1733 and 1771 a new fort was built at the nouth of the river. It was commanded by Samuel HEARNE, who surrendered it to the French in 1782, at which time it was heavily damaged. It has been partially restored and is now part of a 66-acre national historic park at Churchill, Man.

Fort Rodd Hill National Historic Park. In Victoria, B.C., this park is the site of the three turn-of-the-century coastal defence batteries and Fisgard Lighthouse, built in 1860—the first lighthouse on the Pacific coast of Canada.

Fort St James. NORTH WEST COMPANY fort established by Simon FRASER and John Stuart at the east end of Lake Stuart in 1806. It became the chief HUDSON'S BAY COMPANY headquarters for the New Caledonia district in 1821, when the two companies amalgamated. Partially restored and refurnished in the period of the mid-1890s, it gives its name to a national historic park and to Fort St James, one of the oldest settlements in British Columbia.

Fort St Joseph National Historic Park. On the southwest tip of St Joseph's Island, Ont., 36 mi. east of Sault Ste Marie, this 800-acre park is the site of the most westerly British post in Canada from 1796 to 1812. It served as a garrison and as a fur-trade and Indian centre. Temporarily abandoned for Fort Michilimackinac in 1812, it was burned to the ground by American forces in 1814. An archaeological dig begun at the site in 1963, and still under way, has uncovered portions of the blockhouse, guardhouse, and other buildings.

Fort Témiscamingue National Historic Park. At Ville-Marie, Que., it includes the site of the final fort in a series of fur-trade posts maintained on Lake Témiscamingue since the late seventeenth century by the French,

the NORTH WEST COMPANY, and the HUDSON'S BAY COMPANY.

Fort Walsh. It was established by Maj. James Morrow Walsh (1840-1905) of the NORTH WEST MOUNTED POLICE in the CYPRESS HILLS, Sask., in 1875. (These barracks were moved to Maple Creek, Sask., in 1883.) The fort has been reconstructed and gives its name to a national historic park, which also contains a reconstructed fur-trade post.

Fort Wellington National Historic Park. 13-acre park at Prescott, Ont., that includes a British stone fort, built in 1838-9 on the site of an earlier wooden fortification dating from 1812. Fort Wellington, which guarded the upper St Lawrence R., has been restored to the period of the 1840s.

Fort Whoop-up. A fort (originally called Fort Hamilton) built by traders from Montana in 1869 in the CYPRESS HILLS area of the Canadian Prairies. It derived its name from the lawless behaviour of the American traders who sold whisky to the Indians and in 1873 killed 80 Assiniboine accused of stealing horses. This was one of the factors that led to the formation of the NORTH WEST MOUNTED POLICE in 1874, after which Fort Whoop-up was no longer used and eventually became a ranch house.

Fort William. See THUNDER BAY.

Fort William Strike. A strike, accompanied by violence, of railway freight-handlers at the Lakehead from 9 to 24 Aug. 1909. It arose over a claim for a wage increase above 17.5 cents an hour and reached its apogee in a near riot in which many strikers and 11 specially armed CPR constables were injured. The militia was called in to restore order.

Fort York. Military post built at York (Toronto) in 1793. It was captured and burned by American troops in 1813, and was rebuilt in 1816. The fort was restored in the 1930s and includes eight original buildings of 1816. Now surrounded by railway tracks and expressways, it is operated by the city as a museum.

Fortress of Louisbourg National Historic Park. See LOUISBOURG.

Fortune and Men's Eyes. Play about prison life by John HERBERT. A comedy-drama, it deals unsentimentally with homosexuality in an Ontario reformatory. After a single dramatic reading at the STRATFORD FESTIVAL on 1 Oct. 1965, it had its off-Broadway première under the direction of Mitchell Nestor at the Actors' Playhouse on 23 Feb. 1967, the year it was published and the year that also saw the founding in New York of the Fortune Society to help in the rehabilitation of former inmates. The title comes from Shakespeare's Sonnet 29, which begins, 'When in disgrace with fortune and men's eyes . . . '. A 1971 film adaptation, based on a screenplay by Herbert, was shot in Montreal and released through MGM. Directed by Harvey HART, it starred Wendell Burton, Michael Greer, Zooey Hall, Danny Freedman, Larry Perkins, and Jon Granik. It was a successful presentation (like the play) of the role of homosexuality in prison life. 102 min., colour.

Fortune My Foe. Comedy by Robertson DAVIES. First produced in Kingston in the summer of 1949, it deals wittily with philistinism in Canada and the 'brain drain' to the United States.

48th Highlanders of Canada. Canadian army regiment. It was organized in 1891 and served in the SOUTH AFRICAN WAR. In the FIRST WORLD WAR it was part of the 15th Battalion in France and Flanders (with the 3rd Infantry Brigade, 1st Canadian Division), distinguishing itself at YPRES, The SOMME, and VIMY. During the SECOND WORLD WAR it served in Sicily with the 1st Infantry Brigade and in numerous battles throughout Europe.

Forty-ninth parallel. Degrees of latitude north of the equator. This parallel corresponds to the Canadian-American border from the Lake of the Woods to Vancouver.

Forty-Ninth Parallel, The. Feature film produced in Britain in 1941. A propaganda film, it was directed by Michael Powell and starred Eric Portman, Leslie Howard, Glynis Johns, Raymond MASSEY, Anton Walbrook, and Laurence Olivier. Exteriors were shot on location across Canada. Sponsored by the Canadian government, the story concerns several German submarine sailors stranded in Hudson Bay who try to escape across Canada to the then-neutral United States. 123 min., b & w.

Forty-rod whisky. A slang reference in the West and Northwest in the late nineteenth century to cheap but strong spirits, which apparently could kill a man at 40 rods.

Forum, The. Home of the MONTREAL CANADIENS hockey club. The 18,500-seat arena was opened in 1924 and rebuilt and enlarged in 1968. It houses hockey, wrestling, circuses, ice shows, lacrosse, and rock concerts.

Foster, Harry (Red). See FOSTER ADVERTISING LIMITED.

Foster Advertising Limited. A leading Candian advertising agency. It was founded in Toronto in 1944 by Harry (Red) Foster (b.1905), a colourful sports broadcaster turned advertising executive, who has been honoured both for his industry work and for his work with retarded children. Foster Advertising, one of the fastest-growing agencies in the mid-sixties, has five offices across the country.

Foster Hewitt Award. Awarded annually by ACTRA for distinguished contributions to sports broadcasting. Named after the famous sportscaster Foster HEWITT, the award was inaugurated in 1965 by MacLaren Advertising and incorporated into the ACTRA AWARDS in 1975.

Foulkes, Gen. Charles (1903-69). Army commander. Born in Stockton-on-Tees, Eng., he was educated at the Central Collegiate Institute, London, Ont., and at the University of Western Ontario. Commissioned in 1926, in Apr. 1943 he became Brigadier General Staff, First Canadian Army. He commanded the 2nd Canadian Infantry Division in the U.K. and in Northwest Europe until Nov. 1944, when he assumed command of the 1st Canadian Corps in Italy. His brilliant planning and leadership led to the capture of Ravenna and extensive areas around Lake Commachio. This corps moved to Northwest Europe in Feb. 1945 and, as part of the First Canadian Army, completed the liberation of Holland. Foulkes became Chief of the General Staff in Aug. 1945 and was promoted to the rank of general in Jan. 1954. He retired in Jan. 1960.

401 Towards London, #1. Painting by Jack CHAMBERS of Highway 401 being travelled by a single truck under a huge expanse of sky. The meticulous realism with which it is painted is transcended by the artist's intense feeling for the commonplace scene. (1968-9, Northern & Central Gas Corporation Ltd)

Four Horsemen. Group of four experimental poets who perform their 'sound poems' publicly. Formed in Toronto in 1970, the group consists of bp NICHOL, Steve McCaffery, Rafael Barreto-Rivera, and Paul Dutton. They issued one recording of their rich and perplexing work, *Nada Canadada*, in 1972.

Four Jameses, The. Widely admired literary satire by William Arthur DEACON, first published by GRAPHIC PUBLISHERS LIMITED in 1927. The four poetasters whose works are amusingly studied are James GAY, 'Poet Laureate of Canada', and Master of all Poets'; James McINTYRE, 'The Cheese Poet'; James P. GILLIS,

Four Jameses

'A Man of Parts'; and James MacRAE, 'The Man from Glengarry'. This gem of a book was reissued in 1953 and again in 1974 with an introduction by Doug FETHERLING.

Four-Minute Mile. See MIRACLE MILE.

'Four Strong Winds'. A hit song with words and music written in 1963 by Ian TYSON.

Fournier, Claude (b.1931). Quebec film director. Born in Waterloo, Que., he has worked as a cameraman and director for the NATIONAL FILM BOARD and for Leacock-Pennebaker in 1962. He directed *Deux Femmes en or* (1970), a sexploitation comedy that has been a top-grossing film. Other features include *Le Dossier Nélligan* (1968), *Les Chats bottes* (1971), and *Alien Thunder* (1972), the saga of ALMIGHTY VOICE.

Fourteenth Colony, The. An American designation for Canada at the time of the American War of Independence. The Second Continental Congress, on 27 June 1775, so addressed an invitation to the English and French inhabitants of Quebec to defy England and unite with the Thirteen Colonies.

Fowke, Edith (b.1913). Folklorist. Born in Lumsden, Sask., she is a leading collector of folklore and folksongs in Ontario and Quebec for the NATIONAL MUSEUM OF MAN. She has edited such popular books as *Folk Songs of Canada* (4th ed. 1954); *Sally Go Round the Sun* (1969), a collection of children's lore; *The Penguin Book of Canadian Folk Songs* (1974); and *Folklore of Canada* (1976). She is associate professor of English at York University, Toronto.

Fowler Commission. A royal commission on the state of broadcasting in Canada, chaired by Robert MacLaren Fowler, a business executive. Appointed on 2 Dec. 1955, it tabled a report on 15 Mar. 1957 that recommended the establishment of a broadcast authority independent of the CBC. The BOARD OF BROADCAST GOVERNORS was created the following year. See also FOWLER COMMITTEE.

Fowler Committee. An advisory committee to the secretary of state to study the CBC. Appointed on 25 May 1964, it was headed by the business executive Robert MacLaren Fowler, who had earlier chaired the FOWLER COMMISSION. It tabled a report on 1 Sept. 1965 that recommended, among other things, the formation of 'an independent authority' to succeed the BOARD OF BROADCAST GOVERNORS. Three years later the CANADIAN RADIO-TELEVISION COMMISSION was formed.

Fox, Beryl (b.1931). Film-maker. Born in Winnipeg, she was a producer with CBC-TV (1960-6) and with CBS (1966-7). She created a personal and committed style in such television documentaries as *One More River* (1963), The MILLS OF THE GODS: VIETNAM (1965), and *Last Reflections on a War*, a 44-minute plea for the Vietnamese people that was shown on CBC-TV on 10 Mar. 1968. In 1976 she became a Toronto-based film producer for the NATIONAL FILM BOARD.

Fox, Luke (1586-c.1635). English navigator and explorer. Sent in search of the NORTHWEST PASSAGE, he entered Hudson Strait in June 1631 and explored the western shore of Hudson Bay, leaving for home in the autumn. His voyage removed the possibility of Hudson Bay's being a passage to the West. His important and amusing book, *North-West Fox* (1635), a defence of his negative discoveries, recorded the voyage of Sir Thomas BUTTON, relics of which he had found.

Fox populi. Nickname given Sir John A. MACDONALD on account of his cunning and popularity. The phrase is a variant of the Latin tag *vox populi*, 'voice of the people'.

Foxy ice. Rotten, discoloured ice.

Foyer Canadien, Le. See *Les* SOIRÉES CANADIENNES.

FP Publications Limited. A chain of newspapers and other communications interests. The initials 'FP' represent the WINNIPEG FREE PRESS, the first newspaper acquired by Clifford SIFTON in 1898. The chain was founded in 1959 following a merger of the newspaper holdings of the Sifton family and G. Maxwell (Max) Bell (1911-72). In 1976 the company published the following eight newspapers: CALGARY ALBERTAN, GLOBE AND MAIL, *Lethbridge Hearld*, MONTREAL STAR, OTTAWA JOURNAL, VICTORIA DAILY TIMES, VICTORIA DAILY COLONIST, and *Winnipeg Free Press*. The largest Canadian newspaper group in terms of circulation, it also publishes WEEKEND MAGAZINE and the *FP Report on Farming*, a national farm paper issued weekly from Winnipeg.

Franca, Celia (b.1921). Dancer, choreographer, artistic director. Born in London, Eng., she studied at the Guildhall School of Music and the Royal Academy of Dancing. She danced with the International Ballet, the Ballet Rambert, and the Sadler's Wells Ballet before being invited to Toronto to advise on the foundation of a ballet company. She became artistic director of the new NATIONAL BALLET OF CANADA in 1951 and later co-founder with Betty OLIPHANT of the NATIONAL BALLET SCHOOL. She danced with the National in the early years and as director was the driving force behind the many successes of the company in Canada, the U.S., and England. She retired in 1975 and lives in Ottawa. See also CELIA.

France Bringing the Faith to the Indians of New France. Well-known early-Canadian painting, attributed to Frère LUC, the French title of which is *La France apportant la foi aux Indiens de la Nouvelle France*. The figure of France (resembling Anne of Austria), pointing heavenwards to a scene of the Holy Trinity surrounded by the Holy Family, instructs a kneeling Indian in the Christian faith, with the help of a painting of the Holy Family. Painted around 1675, it is in the URSULINE CONVENT, Quebec.

Franchise. The right to vote in elections. During the nineteenth century numerous franchise reforms took place across Canada, altering the colonial franchise system that was linked to property, possessions, and even religion. Voting rights were administered by the provinces until 1885, when the first national franchise was established. In 1898 the franchise reverted to provincial control for federal elections. Federal franchise based on universal suffrage was established by Parliament in 1920, though Indians did not receive complete franchise until 1 July 1960. It is now conferred upon all Canadian citizens who have attained a designated age (18 years for federal elections; from 18 to 21 years for provincial and municipal elections) and who comply with the residence requirements in the electoral district on the date fixed for the beginning of the enumeration for the election. See also WOMEN'S SUFFRAGE.

Franck, Albert (1899-1973). Painter. Born in Middleburg, Holland, he came to Canada in 1926 and began painting while working as a picture restorer. His realistic watercolours of houses, backyards, and street scenes in Toronto's ANNEX and other old sections became very popular and are reproduced in *Albert Franck* (1974) by Harold TOWN.

Franco-Ontarian, Franco-Ontarien. French-speaking native or resident of Ontario.

Francophone. A noun or adjective, it refers to a person whose active prime language is French, and to a region where the language of major practical use is French. A French word derived from the Greek word *phone*, for 'voice', it can also refer to a French-speaking inhabitant of a country where French is only one of two or more official languages—such as Canada, Belgium, or many African nations. The adjective *francophonic* was first used by *The Times* of London in 1970. See also ANGLOPHONE.

Franglais. (i) Portmanteau word characterizing the Americanized French language spoken in France today. Combining elements of *Français* (French) and *Anglais* (English), the word was coined by the Paris grammarian 'Étiemble' in his study *Parlez-vous franglais?* (1965). English-speaking Quebeckers sometimes refer to Quebec French as Franglish. (ii) A furniture style common in nineteenth-century Quebec. A mingling of English and French elements of furniture construction and design, it is found only in the work of rural French-Canadian cabinetmakers.

Frank slide. The worst rock slide in Canadian history. More than 80 people died when rock from Turtle Mountain broke loose and covered much of the town of Frank, near Crow's Nest Pass, B.C., on 29 Apr. 1903. The tragic event was recalled in 'Ballad of the Frank Slide', written by Robert Gard 40 years later.

Franklin, Elsa (b.1930). TV producer. Born in Ottawa, a graduate of the ACADEMY OF RADIO ARTS in Toronto in 1947 and of the Martha Graham School of the Dance in New York (1948-9), she operated a chain of four bookshops in British Columbia before settling in Toronto as a public-relations consultant to McCLELLAND & STEWART in 1962. She was a producer for Screen Gems (Canada) Ltd from 1964, and an executive producer for GLOBAL TELEVISION NETWORK from 1973, being responsible for *The* PIERRE BERTON SHOW, MY COUNTRY, The GREAT DEBATE, and UNDER ATTACK (which she devised and created). She has been called 'Canada's foremost woman television producer' and is married to the journalist Stephen Franklin.

Franklin, Sir John (1786-1847). Explorer. He made three expeditions to the Arctic in 1819-22, 1825-7, and 1845-6. On the third voyage, from which he did not return, he was in command of an expedition in search of the NORTHWEST PASSAGE and sailed on the ships EREBUS and *Terror*, which got caught in the ice off KING WILLIAM ISLAND. Over the next 10 years a great many search parties—several of which were financed by Lady Franklin—failed to find remains of the expedition until 1854, when Dr John Rae located some relics. In 1859 a member of Dr John McClintock's search party found a cairn at Victory Point, King William Island, containing a note giving the date of Franklin's death and other details. Franklin published books on his first two Arctic journeys. He was knighted in 1829.

Franks Flying Suit. A pressurized suit for airplane pilots, the ancestor of the astronaut's space suit. The world's first pressurized suit, devised in 1941, it was constructed in 1943 by a team at the Banting and Best Medical Research Institute of the University of Toronto, headed by Dr William R. Franks, who has been called 'the father of the space suit'. The Franks Flying Suit encased the Allied pilot in a pressurized rubber garment with water pads laced onto the legs. It acted as an anti-gravity suit to minimize the effects of acceleration and deceleration on the human body.

Franquet, Louis (1697-1768). Military engineer. Associated with improving the fortifications at LOUISBOURG, he was posted there from Aug. 1750 to Oct. 1758 (the year the fortress was surrendered to the British), with time out in 1751, 1752, and 1753 for tours of the eastern colonies and Quebec, Trois-Rivières, and Montreal, about which his reports contain valuable observations and descriptions.

FRAP. Acronym of FRont d'Action Politique, a municipal party of reformist tendencies with trade-union ties that competed against Jean DRAPEAU's Civic Party in Montreal elections in the late 1960s. During the OCTOBER CRISIS of 1970 it was falsely accused of being 'a moral shield for the FLQ' and lost the election of that year disastrously.

Fraser, Blair (1909-68). Journalist. Born in Sydney, N.S., and educated at Acadia University, he worked for the English daily newspapers in Montreal before joining MACLEAN'S in 1943 as Ottawa editor. He filed the highly regarded 'Backstage at Ottawa' reports and covered the principal post-war news events from world capitals with objectivity and dedication, for the magazine and often for the CBC. From 1960 to his untimely death in 1968, the result of a canoe accident, he was editor of *Maclean's*. He was the author of *The Search for Identity: Canada, 1945-1967* (1967). '*Blair Fraser Reports': Selections* (1969) was edited posthumously by John and Graham Fraser, his sons, both journalists.

Fraser, Simon (1776-1862). Fur-trader and explorer. Born in Vermont, he joined the NORTH WEST COMPANY in 1792 and was sent in 1805 to the Ròcky Mountains, where he established several fur-trading posts. In 1808 he explored the FRASER R. from Fort George, near the junction of the Fraser and Nechako Rivers, to tidewater, thinking it was the Columbia—an impressively dangerous and difficult journey. His *Letters and Journals* (1960) is an important record of western exploration.

Fraser, Sylvia (b.1935). Novelist. Born in Ha-

milton, Ont., and educated at the University of Toronto, she worked as a journalist before writing her two novels: the autobiographical *Pandora* (1972) and the expressionistic *The Candy Factory* (1975).

Fraser Canyon. Deep canyon carved by the FRASER RIVER through the Coast Mountains between Yale and Lytton in British Columbia. Cliffs that rise 3,000 ft and the dramatic HELL'S GATE are part of the spectacular scenery for which the canyon is noted.

Fraser River. With the Columbia, one of the most important of Canada's western rivers. It rises in the Rockies on the British Columbia-Alberta border near Jasper National Park and flows 850 mi. northwest before making a great 'U-turn' south through the Columbia Mountains to reach the Strait of Georgia and the Pacific Ocean at Vancouver. It was named in honour of Simon FRASER, who first explored it, by David THOMPSON.

Fraser River Gold Rush. A rush for gold in British Columbia that began in Apr. 1858 after deposits had been found the year before on the Thompson and Fraser Rivers. It extended northeast into the foothills of the CARIBOO MOUNTAINS, where strikes were made in 1860 at Keithley Creek; in 1861, at William Creek—named for 'Dutch Bill' Dietz; and in 1862 by Billy Barker (see BARKERVILLE), further down the canyon of the now-named Williams Creek. The Rush lasted into the 1870s. The influx of many thousands of miners led to the creation of the province of British Columbia. See also CARIBOO ROAD.

FRCP(C). Fellow of the Royal College of Physicians of Canada, a national non-teaching college to confer degrees, incorporated in June 1929.

FRCS(C). Fellow the Royal College of Surgeons of Canada, a national non-teaching college to confer degrees, incorporated in June 1929.

Fréchette, Louis-Honoré (1839-1908). Quebec poet. Born at Lévis, L.C. (Que.), he was educated at Université Laval and called to the bar in 1864. He was a member of the House of Commons (1874-8) and from 1889 until his death was clerk of the legislative council. He was called '*le lauréat*' following the publication of the ebullient poems that appeared in *Les Fleurs boréales* (1879), which includes '*La Découverte du Mississippi*', a major historical poem. *La Légende d'un peuple* (1887) is a cycle of patriotic poems celebrating historical figures and events in French-Canadian history. He was the author of several prose works, one of which, *Christmas in*

194

French Canada (1899), he wrote in English then rewrote in French. His *Poésies choisies* (1908) was published in three volumes.

Fredericton. The capital of New Brunswick. Laid out for settlement by Loyalists in 1785, it was incorporated as a city in 1848. As the birthplace of Bliss CARMAN, Charles G.D. ROB-ERTS, and other poets who were born in or near Fredericton, it is known as the POETS' CORNER OF CANADA. Employment depends on government work. It is the home of the UNI-VERSITY OF NEW BRUNSWICK, the BEAVERBROOK ART GALLERY, and Christ Church Cathedral (1845-53), the first cathedral in the Anglican communion built in a new location since the Norman Conquest. Its 1971 CMA population was 24,254. Its official motto is *Fredericopolis silvae filia nobilis* ('Fredericton, noble daughter of the forest').

Fredrickson, Frank (born *c.*1890). Hockey player. Born in Winnipeg, Man., he captained the Winnipeg Falcons which, in 1920, won both the ALLAN CUP and the first world tournament at Antwerp. He then played professionally in Victoria, Detroit, Boston, and Pittsburg, after which he coached with the RCAF and the University of British Columbia.

Free trade. See RECIPROCITY.

Freedman, Harry (b.1922). Composer. Born in Lodz, Poland, he came to Canada with his family at the age of three and grew up in Winnipeg. He studied at the Royal Conservatory of Music, Toronto, and played English horn with the TORONTO SYMPHONY OR-CHESTRA from 1946 to 1971; he was the Symphony's first composer-in-residence. His work uses a modification of the 12-tone system but he has composed in the neo-Impressionistic style and also shows the influence of jazz. *Tangents* (1967), written for the National Youth Orchestra, is one of his finest works. He has also received commissions from the ROYAL WINNIPEG BALLET—for which he wrote the scores for ROSE LATULIPPE (1966), *Five Over Thirteen* (1969), and *The Shining People of Leonard* COHEN (1970)—and for films: his cantata *The Flame Within* was used in ACT OF THE HEART (1970) and he composed the score for ISABEL (1968).

Freedomites. See DOUKHOBORS.

Freedoms, Fundamental. See CANADIAN BILL OF RIGHTS.

Freeman, David. See CREEPS.

Frégault, Guy (b.1918). Quebec historian. Born in Montreal and educated at the Uni-versité de Montréal and the University of Chicago, he taught history at the Université de Montréal and the University of Ottawa until 1969, when he became Quebec's Deputy Minister of Cultural Affairs. He has written many substantial studies of New France, notably biographies of IBERVILLE and BIGOT; *La Civilisation de la Nouvelle France* (1944; 2nd ed. 1969); *La Société canadienne sous le régime français* (1954); and *La Guerre de la conquête* (1955), which was translated by Margaret Cameron as *Canada: The War of the Conquest* (1969).

French, David (b.1939). Playwright. Born in Coley's Point, Nfld, he grew up in Toronto and studied acting at the Pasadena Playhouse, Calif. He sold his first drama to the CBC in 1962. William GLASSCO directed, and TARRAGON THEATRE produced, two of his powerful, realistic plays: LEAVING HOME (1972) and *Of the Fields, Lately* (1974), which is a continuation of the saga of the Mercer family two years after its initial breakup.

French, William (b.1926). Journalist. Born in London, Ont., and a graduate of the University of Western Ontario, he joined the Toronto *Globe and Mail* as a general reporter in 1948. He held a Nieman Fellowship to Harvard in 1954 and with the retirement of William Arthur DEACON became the *Globe's* literary editor in 1960. Since 1971 he has written intelligent and often witty columns devoted to book reviews and book news.

French-Canadian pea soup. Traditional soup of Quebec, usually made from a salt pork stock. Its distinctive ingredient is dried whole yellow peas rather than the green variety.

French Shore. In Newfoundland, the north-eastern and western shores where France was granted the right to dry and cure fish by the British in the eighteenth century; this right was extinguished by purchase in 1904. In Nova Scotia the stretch of the coast on the Bay of Fundy between Yarmouth and Digby, inhabited by Acadian French, is also referred to as the French Shore. See also PETIT NORD.

Frenchman's Butte. See BIG BEAR.

Frère Untel. See Brother ANONYMOUS.

Fricker, Sylvia. See Ian and Sylvia TYSON.

Fridolin. A comic character created by Gratien GÉLINAS. Fridolin was the star attraction in a series of annual revues called *Fridolinons* (Fridolinades) at the Cabaret Mon Paris in Montreal each May between 1938 and 1946. Gélinas, as producer and principal actor, delivered his own monologues dressed as a 14-year-old-street rowdy in short pants, a MONTREAL CANADIENS sweater, running shoes, a peak cap, and a slingshot. He lovingly ridiculed Quebec society, especially such shibboleths as 'our master, the past' (NOTRE MAÎTRE, LE PASSÉ), which he called 'Our Master, the Present Conditional', and the BLOC POPULAIRE CANADIEN, which he called the 'flop populaire'.

Friml, Rudolf. See ROSE-MARIE.

Frise, Jimmy (1891-1948). Cartoonist and creator of BIRDSEYE CENTRE. Born near Lake Scugog, Ont., the self-taught artist with a gentle sense of humour drew a popular series of half-page cartoons that satirized rural Ontario life and appeared weekly in newspapers from the 1920s until his death. A selection appeared in *Birdseye Centre* (1973), introduced by Frise's friend Gregory CLARK.

Frobisher, Joseph (1740-1810). Fur trader. Born in Yorkshire, Eng., he spent several winters in the Northwest in the 1770s. As one of the founders of the NORTH WEST COMPANY and a partner in McTavish, Frobisher and Co., which virtually ran the NWC, he was one of the most powerful figures in the fur trade. He was a member of the legislative assembly of Lower Canada from 1772 to 1796. His log mansion and estate in Montreal, Beaver Hall, gave its name to BEAVER HALL HILL. He was a founding member of the BEAVER CLUB.

Frobisher, Sir Martin (1539?-94). Explorer. In search of a NORTHWEST PASSAGE he made three Arctic voyages. In 1576 he sailed into a bay in Baffin Island that he thought was a strait and named it for himself. Finding a stone there that he thought contained gold, he was sent back in 1577 and 1578 to mine the ore. It was proved worthless in England.

Frog Lake, Massacre at. An incident in the NORTH WEST REBELLION. On 2 Apr. 1885, Wandering Spirit, with a band of BIG BEAR'S Cree, murdered the Indian agent, several white men, and two priests at Frog Lake, north of the North Saskatchewan R.

From Sea to Sea. See A MARI USQUE AD MARE.

Fromage Île d'Orléans. A strong-smelling cheese. Since 1679 it has been made according to a secret family recipe on the ÎLE D'ORLÉANS, Que.

Front Page Challenge. The longest-running entertainment show on Canadian television. The CBC series began as a summer replacement on 24 June 1957 and has appeared ever since for 30 minutes weekly. The format was devised by writer John Aylesworth. The host-moderator (Fred Davis) challenges the four panelists (three regulars—Pierre BERTON, Betty KENNEDY, and Gordon SINCLAIR—and a visitor) to identify the 'mystery guest' whose identity is gradually revealed through clues about his or her association with a headline-making news event from the past or present.

Frontenac, comte de (1622-98). Governor general of NEW FRANCE from 1672 to 1682 and from 1689 until his death. Louis de Buade de Frontenac, a member of the nobility and a soldier, was an autocratic governor who engaged in many quarrels with the INTENDANT and the bishop. He thought nothing of defying orders and was recalled at the end of his first term of office as a result of his intemperate behaviour. But he fostered French expansion in North America with the building of fur-trade posts in the West and defended New France against attacks of the Iroquois and the English colonies. When an emissary of an expeditionary force from Boston under Sir William PHIPS demanded the surrender of Quebec in 1690, Frontenac said: 'I have no reply to make to your general other than from the mouths of my cannon and muskets.' The force eventually withdrew. In 1696, as an old man of 74, he commanded a final campaign against the Iroquois that removed them as a threat to New France.

Frontenac. British-registered steamship that was the first steamer on the Great Lakes. She was launched at Bath, near Kingston, Ont., on 7 Sept. 1816, and for a decade carried passengers between Kingston and Niagara-on-the-Lake, with several stops en route. She was irreparably damaged by fire at Niagara on 29 Sept. 1827 and shortly afterward was scrapped.

Frontenac. Automobile manufactured from 1931 to 1933 by Dominion Motors, Toronto. The Frontenac Six came as a sedan and sold for $975.

Frontier College. A voluntary, funded organization founded in Toronto in 1899-1900 by Alfred Fitzpatrick, a Presbyterian minister from Nova Scotia, and incorporated by an Act of Parliament in 1922. Through correspondence courses and field teachers, it provides educational opportunities for workers in isolated mining, lumber, and railway camps. College students on summer vacation work by day with the labourers and in the evening offer free instruction in subjects of mutual interest.

FRSC. Fellow of the ROYAL SOCIETY OF CANADA.

Fruet, William (b.1933). Film director and writer. Born in Lethbridge, Alta, he acted in DRYLANDERS (1962). He studied at UCLA and worked in Los Angeles from 1960 to 1965 and then wrote the scripts of GOIN' DOWN THE ROAD (1970), *Rip-Off* (1971), and *Slipstream* (1973). He directed WEDDING IN WHITE (1972) and *Death Weekend*(1976).

Frum, Barbara (b.1938). Broadcaster. Born in Niagara Falls, Ont., she honed her investigative talents as a free-lance journalist before joining in Sept. 1971 CBC Radio's AS IT HAPPENS, where her incisive questioning attracted widespread attention. 'The Barbara Frum Show', a 30-minute weekly interview program for CBC-TV, appeared in 1974-5. She is the author of *As It Happened* (1976).

Frye, Northrop (b.1912). Distinguished literary scholar and social critic. Born in Sherbrooke, Que., and brought up in Moncton, N.B., he was educated at the University of Toronto and at Oxford. He was ordained to the ministry of the United Church of Canada in 1936 and three years later began his long association with the English department at Victoria College, University of Toronto, of which he was principal from 1959 to 1966, when he became the first University Professor. His examination of the nature and use of myth and symbol in literature and of the techniques and methods of criticism—in *Fearful Symmetry: A Study of William Blake* (1947) and ANATOMY OF CRITICISM: *Four Essays* (1957)—established his international eminence as a scholar and critic. His writings on literature—including Canadian literature—education, culture, and the interaction of imagination and society, represent collectively a notable work of the scholarly imagination, informed by profound learning, illuminating generalizations, and a writing style graced by wit, clarity, and directness. From 1950 to 1960 he wrote the poetry survey in the annual LETTERS IN CANADA feature of the *University of Toronto Quarterly;* these have been included in *The* BUSH GARDEN: *Essays on the Canadian Imagination* (1971), along with the celebrated 'Conclusion' originally written for the *Literary History of Canada* (1965) edited by Carl F. Klinck. Among his other books are *Culture and the National Will* (1957), *By Liberal Things* (1960), *The Well-Tempered Critic* (1963), *The Educated Imagination* (1963), *A Natural Perspective* (1965), *The Modern Century* (1967), *The Stubborn Structure* (1970), *The Critical Path* (1971), and *The Secular Scripture: A Study of the Structure of Romance* (1976).

FS. Official abbreviation of Flight Sergeant.

Fuddle-duddle. Popular euphemism and genuine Canadianism coined by Pierre Elliott TRUDEAU in the House of Commons on 16 Feb. 1971. Responding to criticism, the prime minister mouthed but did not utter 'a four-letter word'. Outside the House he explained that he had said 'fuddle-duddle'. An Opposition member later opined: 'The Prime Minister wishes to be obscene and not heard.' The euphemism is now the Canadian equivalent of the American expression 'Expletive deleted'.

Fulford, Robert (b.1932). Journalist and editor. Born in Ottawa, he was raised in Toronto, where he began his career in journalism as a copy boy on the *Globe and Mail* in 1949, later rising to city hall reporter. In 1957 he was appointed editor of *Canadian Homes and Gardens*, commencing a magazine career that has included editorial positions on *Maclean's*, *Mayfair*, the *Canadian Forum*, and *Saturday Night*. In 1960-2 and 1964-8 he wrote a daily column on books and culture generally—lively, intelligent pieces on a wide range of topics—in the *Toronto Star*, to which he now contributes a weekly syndicated column. Since 1968 he has been editor of *Saturday Night*, for which he writes its most popular columns, including film reviews under the *nom de plume* Marshall Delaney, derived from his second name and the surname of a great-uncle. He has written *This was Expo* (1968); *Crisis at the Victory Burlesk: Culture, Politics, & Other Diversions* (1968), a collection of his newspaper pieces; and *Marshall Delaney at the Movies* (1974). With Dave GODFREY and Abraham ROTSTEIN he edited *Read Canadian* (1972) and with Morris Wolfe, *A Saturday Night Scrapbook* (1972).

Fuller, Thomas (1823-98). Architect. Born in Bath, Eng., he trained in architects' offices in Bath and London and immigrated to Toronto (from Antigua) in 1857. His most important work was the Centre Block of the PARLIAMENT BUILDINGS, Ottawa (1860-6, with Augustus Laver), which was destroyed by fire in 1916, a design of occasionally eccentric but magnificent Victorian Gothic, of which an example can be seen in the surviving Library. The building and the flanking departmental blocks rank among the most important buildings of the period in North America, both individually and as a group. From 1881 to 1897 Fuller served as Dominion architect, designing over 140 buildings.

Fulton-Favreau Formula. The name given to the proposals for the REPATRIATION OF THE CONSTITUTION. Advanced initially by E. Davie

Fulton-Favreau Formula

Fulton, Minister of Justice in the DIEFENBAKER government, and then picked up and modified by Guy Favreau, Minister of Justice in the PEARSON administration, the formula aimed at devising a suitable amending procedure for certain sections of the BNA ACT that would be agreeable to the provincial and federal governments. Although it was initially acceptable to all the provinces, Quebec had second thoughts and by 1965 the scheme was a dead letter.

Fun Parade. See Roy Ward DICKSON.

Fund for Rural Economic Development. See Department of REGIONAL ECONOMIC EXPANSION.

Fundy National Park. Established in 1948 on the BAY OF FUNDY, N.B., it covers 80 sq. mi. and includes rugged shoreline, sandstone cliffs, forested landscape, and the highest tides in the world (rising to 53 ft). The word 'Fundy' probably derives from *Rio Fondo*, Portuguese for 'deep river'.

Fundy Trail. Scenic motor route on the south coast of New Brunswick. It offers many views of the tides of the BAY OF FUNDY and includes SAINT JOHN, FUNDY NATIONAL PARK, and Moncton.

Fungy. Nova Scotian name for a deep-dish blueberry pie.

Funny money. Pejorative term applied to SOCIAL CREDIT monetary theories.

Furie, Sidney J. (b.1933). Film director. Born in Toronto, he studied at the Carnegie Institute of Technology in Pittsburgh and returned to Canada, where he worked as a free-lance television writer. In Toronto he made two features, *A* DANGEROUS AGE (1957) and *A* COOL SOUND FROM HELL (1959). When his work was panned or ignored, he left for England where he made numerous features, including *The Snake Woman* (1960), *Doctor Blood's Coffin* (1960), *Wonderful Life* (1964), and *The Ipcress File* (1965). Then he moved to Hollywood, where he made *The Appaloosa* (1966), *The Naked Runner* (1967), *Lady Sings the Blues* (1972), *Sheila Levine* (1975), and *Gable and Lombard* (1976).

G

G. Initial letter of 'Government'. From 1950 to 1964 the letter G was overprinted on postage stamps supplied to federal government departments for prepayment of postage on official mail that was ineligible for franking. See also OHMS.

Gaboury, Étienne (b.1930). Architect. Born in Swan Lake, Man., he was educated at the University of Manitoba and the École des Beaux-Arts, Paris. His church for the Paroise de Précieux Sang, St Boniface, Man. (1961-7), exhibits his 'special and personal regionalism' in design, using natural materials such as shingle and brick to associate the building with its environment.

Gage Limited, W.J. Educational and trade publishers. Established in Montreal in 1844, it opened a branch in Toronto in 1860 that was bought in 1880 by William (later Sir William) Gage. It consisted of textbook, envelope, and stationery divisions, and this structure remained until 1970 when the divisions were separated. In 1971 Scott, Foresman and Company, an American educational publisher, purchased a minority of the shares of Gage Educational Publishing. A trade publishing program was initiated in 1974.

Gagging Bill. A bill passed in UPPER CANADA (Ontario) in 1819 that prohibited the holding of political meetings. 'The Act to prevent certain meetings within the Province' was repealed the following year.

Gagnon, Clarence (1881-1942). Painter. Born in Montreal, he studied in Paris, where he lived for some 16 years. He worked as a book illustrator—he illustrated a famous edition of Louis HÉMON'S MARIA CHAPDELAINE in 1933—and his cheerful decorative paintings of Quebec villages have the look of illustrations.

GAINS. Acronym of Guaranteed Annual Income Supplement, an Ontario program allowing basic old-age payments to be supplemented, in addition to the GUARANTEED INCOME SUPPLEMENT, upon application and proof of need. It was introduced in July 1974.

Gairdner Foundation International Awards. A series of annual prizes awarded in the medical field since 1959. They are sponsored by the Gairdner Foundation, established in Toronto in 1957 with funds derived from the personal gifts of James Arthur Gairdner (1893-1971), a Toronto underwriter, and his family. In a typical year one Award of Merit and four Annual Awards are made to scientists, irrespective of country, 'who have made contributions in the conquest of disease and the relief of human suffering' in order 'to assist in focussing public, professional and scientific attention upon significant achievement in the medical field'. The Award of Merit is $25,000; the Annual Awards are each worth $10,000.

Galbraith, John Kenneth (b.1908). Economist and author. Born at Iona Station, Ont., he was educated at the Ontario Agricultural College, Guelph, and the University of California. Among his many activities, he has served as an editor of *Fortune Magazine* and been the U.S. Ambassador to India and a professor at Harvard University; he is also the author of numerous books. His neo-Keynesian ideas, which have influenced Prime Minister TRUDEAU among others, include curbing the monopoly control of large corporations and labour. His rural upbringing in Elgin County is the subject of a delightful memoir, *The Scotch* (1964). Galbraith identifies himself as 'an advisory Canadian', as distinct from 'a practising Canadian'.

Gallant, Mavis (b.1922). Novelist and short-story writer. Born in Montreal, she has lived in France since 1951 and contributes frequently to the *New Yorker*. Her fiction is remarkable for its keenly intelligent, lightly probing examination of people and relationships. Her short stories are collected in *The Other Paris* (1956), *My Heart is Broken* (1959), and *The Pegnitz Junction* (1973). *The End of the World and Other Stories* (1974) contains a selection edited by Robert WEAVER. Her two novels are *Green Water, Green Sky* (1959) and *A Fairly Good Time* (1970).

Gallie living suture. The use of human tissue in surgical repair work. The suture is fashioned from a strip of fascia that is usually removed from the patient's thigh. A graft-like operation, it is identified with Dr Edward A. Gallie (1882-1959), a prominent Toronto surgeon who pioneered the procedure in the 1920s and 1930s.

Galloping Gourmet. Sobriquet of Graham Kerr, a dashing cooking instructor known for his speed of presentation. The 'guru of gastronomy' was born in London, Eng., in 1934, and raised in Australia. He settled in Ottawa, where he began syndicating his cooking programs on radio and television in 1970. 'The Galloping Gourmet', produced by his wife Treena Doorne, first appeared on CBC-TV as a half-hour program on 30 Dec. 1968.

Galt. An automobile manufactured by Canadian Motors when it was the Galt Motor Company, Galt, Ont., from 1911 to 1915. It came as a roadster and as a five-passenger touring car and had a 35 h.p. motor and an automatic starter that proved troublesome.

Galt, Sir Alexander Tilloch (1817-93). A FATHER OF CONFEDERATION. The youngest son of John GALT, he was born in England, spent two years in Lower Canada as a child, and returned to stay in 1835 as a clerk for the British American Land Company at Sherbrooke, C.E. (Que.); he later became involved in railway development. As a member of the legislative assembly and of the GREAT COALITION ministry, he attended all three conferences on Confederation. He became Minister of Finance in July 1867 but resigned in October and retired from Parliament in 1872. He was the first Canadian High Commissioner in London, from 1880 to 1883. He was knighted in 1869.

Galt, John (1779-1839). Scottish novelist. He promoted the CANADA COMPANY and visited Upper Canada (Ontario) in 1825 and 1826-9, when he superintended settlement in the HURON TRACT. He founded the town now of Guelph in 1827 and the town of Galt (now CAMBRIDGE) was named after him. He was the father of Sir Alexander Tilloch GALT. See also William DUNLOP.

Gander. International airport in Newfoundland, well known during the Second World War and in the immediate postwar years. North America's most easterly airport, located on the northeast coast of the island, it opened in 1938 and was operated by the RCAF from 1940 to 1945 as the first terminus of the TRANS-ATLANTIC FERRY SERVICE. The base then served as an airport for transatlantic passenger flights until jet planes, able to make the transatlantic hop without refuelling, bypassed it. Military and civilian personnel speak of Gander's bleak weather and its Big Dipper bar, open 24 hours a day. A new terminal of modern design was opened at Gander in 1959.

Ganglia. Underground press and magazine founded in Toronto in 1964 by bp NICHOL and others to publish booklets and pamphlets of concrete and other innovative poetry.

Ganong Bros Limited. Manufacturer of confectionery and chocolates. Founded as a small bakery and candy shop in St Stephen, N.B., in 1872 by James H. Ganong (1841-88), it is still located there. The family business expanded rapidly and by 1910 had invented the five-cent chocolate bar. It is the only privately owned, large confectionery company in Canada.

Gants du Ciel. A literary quarterly published in Montreal between 1943 and 1946. It was edited by Guy Sylvestre (b.1918), now the National Librarian, and it published, in French, important articles on French- and English-Canadian literature and writers. The title, 'Gloves of Heaven', is a phrase used by Jean Cocteau in a letter to Jacques Maritain.

Garant, Serge (b.1929). Composer. Born in Quebec City, he is a self-taught musician, learning the clarinet, saxophone, and piano and playing in local dance bands and as a clarinetist in the Sherbrooke Symphony before studying in Paris. His compositions are serial and influenced by Pierre Boulez, with whom he shares an interest in musical mathematics. In 1969 his *Anerca* (1961) for voice and instrumental ensemble was performed with acclaim in the International Week of Today's Music. Afterwards he received commissions from the Quebec Symphony Orchestra and began conducting. In 1966 he was named director of La Société de Musique Contemporaine du Québec; he also teaches at the Université de Montréal. His three *Offrandes* (1969-71) for orchestra are complex abstractions of the theme of Bach's *Musical Offering.*

Gard, Robert. See FRANK SLIDE.

Garden of the Gulf. Unofficial motto of the Province of Prince Edward Island, which is situated in the Gulf of St Lawrence.

Garneau, François-Xavier (1809-66). Quebec historian. Born in Quebec City, L.C. (Que.), and educated at the Quebec Seminary, he was licensed as a notary in 1830. Goaded by the passage in the DURHAM *Report* that dismisses the French Canadians as 'a people with no history, and no literature', he wrote *Histoire du Canada* (3 vols, 1845-8). This classic of French-Canadian social history was objected to by Church authorities—though it went through many editions—because it criticized French emigration policies and the involvement of the Church in civil matters.

Garneau, Hector de Saint-Denys- (1912-43). Quebec poet. The great-grandson of François-Xavier GARNEAU, he was born in Montreal but raised at Sainte-Catherine-de-

Fossambault, the family estate north of Quebec City, to which he retired a few years before his early death. He produced most of his writing between 1935 and 1939. His abstract, symbolic poetry grew out of spiritual and identity crises that now seem to apply to both a society and a culture. John GLASSCO has brilliantly translated *The Journal* (1962) and the *Complete Poems* (1975).

Garner, Hugh (b.1913). Novelist and short-story writer. Born in England, he came to Toronto as a child. He fought in the Spanish Civil War and his naval experiences in the Second World War provided the background for his novel *Storm Below* (1949). His fiction conveys a strong feeling of life in Toronto (or Ontario), usually as it is lived by people who are losers or outsiders. His novels are CABBAGETOWN (1950; enlarged 1968); *Waste No Tears* (1950), published under the pseudonym 'Jarvis Warwick'; *Present Reckoning* (1951); *The Silence on the Shore* (1962); *A Nice Place to Visit* (1970); and *The Intruders* (1976). *The Sin Sniper* (1970) and *Death in Don Mills* (1975) are thrillers. His well-crafted short stories are collected in *The Yellow Sweater* (1952), *Hugh Garner's Best Stories* (1963), *Men and Women* (1966), *The Violation of the Virgins* (1971), and *The Legs of the Lame* (1976). *Author! Author!* (1963) contains magazine pieces and *One Damn Thing After Another* (1973) is autobiographical. *Three Women: Plays* (1973) is a collection of one-act plays.

Garnier, Charles. See JESUIT MARTYRS.

Garrard, Don. Bass. Born in Vancouver, he won a scholarship to the ROYAL CONSERVATORY OF MUSIC, Toronto, in 1952. Basing his career in the United Kingdom—singing at Covent Garden, the Scottish Opera, the Glyndbourne Festival, and the Welsh National Opera—he has sung frequently with the CANADIAN OPERA COMPANY, notably in the title role of *Boris Godunov* in 1974.

Gascon, Jean (b.1921). Quebec actor and director. Born in Montreal, he acted with Les COMPAGNONS DE ST LAURENT (1940-5), worked in France, then joined the THÉÂTRE DU NOUVEAU MONDE (1951-66). A consummate actor of great depth and precision in both French and English productions, he was also a founder of the NATIONAL THEATRE SCHOOL and artistic director of the STRATFORD FESTIVAL from 1968 to 1974.

Gaspé. A peninsula and region of southeastern Quebec, characterized by scattered farms and picturesque fishing villages along the coast and a very hilly and sparsely populated area in the interior.

Gastown. An area of downtown Vancouver. It was given its nickname in 1867 by its first saloon-keeper, John 'Gassy Jack' Deighton, whose statue stands in the square today. Reclaimed from its former slum condition, it is now a lively area, with boutiques and office buildings restored to the 1880s period.

Gateway City. Unofficial motto of WINNIPEG and an allusion to the important role played by the Manitoba capital in the opening of the Canadian West.

Gateway to Canada. Unofficial motto of Fort Erie, Ont., across the Niagara R. from Buffalo, N.Y.

Gateway to the Dominion. Unofficial motto of HALIFAX, N.S., an important Atlantic port.

Gateway to the North. Unofficial motto of several northern cities, including Brandon, Man., and EDMONTON, Alta.

Gateway to the Orient. Unofficial motto of VANCOUVER, B.C., an important Pacific port. Another is 'Canada's Golden Gateway'.

Gatineau. The Gatineau Hills are an extension of the LAURENTIAN MOUNTAINS and part of the CANADIAN SHIELD west and north of Hull, Que., across the Ottawa R. from the city of Ottawa. Gatineau County occupies the greater part of the valley of the Gatineau R., which empties into the Ottawa. The lakes and rolling hills of Gatineau Park form a wilderness and recreation area of 88,000 acres. Gatineau, Que., is a town 6 mi. east of Hull. See also HARRINGTON LAKE and KINGSMERE.

Gatling gun. An early machine gun named after its American inventor, Richard Jordan Gatling (1818-1903). A mounted, multiple-firing gun, it was demonstrated in the United States as early as 1862; it was first used north of the border in the NORTH WEST REBELLION during the Battle of BATOCHE, 9-12 May 1885.

Gaucher, Yves (b.1934). Painter. Born in Montreal, he studied printmaking there at the École des Beaux-Arts and turned to painting in the 1960s. His free, geometric-shaped compositions use muted colour fields with minimal texture and simplified spatial design, bringing painting as close as possible to non-painting in a visual equivalent of silence. *Le Cercle de Grande Reserve* (1965, AGO) is one of his finest experimental paintings. He has exhibited internationally and lives in Montreal.

Gaudaur, Jacob Gill (Jake) (1858-1937). Champion sculler. The Orillia-born oarsman defeated the world title-holder, William Beach, on the Thames R. in 1896 and retained the title for five years. Gaudaur, who inspired the youth of his generation, was elected to the Sports HALL OF FAME. His son, Jake Gaudaur, a noted football player with the Hamilton Tigers, is commissioner of the CANADIAN FOOTBALL LEAGUE.

Gay, James (1810-91). Poetaster who called himself 'Poet Laureate of Canada and Master of All Poets'. The eccentric bard's verse is examined humorously by William Arthur DEACON in *The* FOUR JAMESES (1927).

GC. See GEORGE CROSS.

G/C. Official abbreviation of Group Captain.

G-CAAA. Specimen identification mark borne by Canadian civil aircraft from 1919 to 1927. By the Paris Air Convention of 1919, G was assigned to the British Empire and C to Canada. The three remaining letters were assigned by the Civil Aviation Branch of the Department of National Defence. This form of identification was replaced by the CF-AAA system in 1927; in 1974 this was superseded in turn by the C-GAAA system.

Geddes, Gary (b.1940). Poet, critic, and anthologist. Born in Vancouver, B.C., he was educated at the University of British Columbia and the University of Toronto. His poetry publications include *Snakeroot* (1973), *Letter of the Master of Horse* (1973), and *War & Other Measures* (1975). He edited *20th Century Poetry & Poetics* (1969; 2nd ed. 1973) and *Skookum Wawa: Writings of the Canadian Northwest* (1975) and co-edited with Phyllis Bruce *15 Canadian Poets* (1971).

Geiger-Torel, Herman (b.1907). Producer and stage director. Born in Frankfurt, Germany, he directed operas in the leading opera houses in Europe and South America from 1930 to 1948, when he came to Canada to direct the Opera School at the ROYAL CONSERVATORY OF MUSIC, Toronto, where he still teaches. In 1950 he was co-founder of the CANADIAN OPERA COMPANY and became its stage director and producer. From 1959 through 1976 he was the COC's general director, staging 568 performances of 51 operas in its 26 seasons in Toronto.

Gélinas, Gratien (b.1909). Canada's leading man-of-the-theatre. Born in Saint-Tite de Champlain, Que., he has enjoyed an active theatrical career in Montreal as a writer, actor, producer, director, and film executive. He created the well-loved character FRIDOLIN for a series of one-man revues (1938-46) and

Gélinas

is the author of three notable plays, produced in French and English, that were created as vehicles for himself: *Tit-coq, Bousille et les Justes,* and *Hier les enfants dansaient.* They were produced and published in English as: TIT-COQ, BOUSILLE AND THE JUST, and YESTERDAY THE CHILDREN WERE DANCING. He founded the THÉÂTRE DE LA COMÉDIE-CANADIENNE (1958-66). In 1969 he was appointed chairman of the CANADIAN FILM DEVELOPMENT CORPORATION.

Gen. Official abbreviation of General.

Gendarmerie royale du Canada. French name for the ROYAL CANADIAN MOUNTED POLICE.

General Electric Hour. See Dr Leslie BELL.

General Motors Presents. See GM PRESENTS.

General Publishing Company Ltd. A trade publishing house with mass-market distribution for its paperbacks. It was established in Toronto in 1923 by Norman Wittet to sell *The People's Home Library,* a family encyclopaedia. Its present structure was formed in 1957 when the company was bought by Jack Stoddart, who had extensive sales experience. In 1967 Stoddart added the Musson Book Company, which had been founded in Toronto before the turn of the century, but which by 1967 was owned by the British firm, Hodder & Stoughton Ltd. In 1974 Stoddart acquired NEW PRESS and one-third of its founding editorial team, James Bacque. General launched PaperJacks, a line of mass-market paperback books, both original and reprint, by Canadian authors, and in 1976 TrendSetter Books, inexpensive hardcover editions of books by Canadian authors. The firm represents a number of leading British and American publishers in Canada.

Genereux, George Patrick (b.1935). Champion trap-shooter. Born in Saskatoon, Sask., he outshot 39 other competitors in the clay-pigeon event at the 1952 Olympics at Helsinki—at the age of 17. He was elected to the Sports HALL OF FAME.

Genest, Dr Jacques. See HYPERTENSION.

Geneva Park. A 120-acre park on the shore of Lake Couchiching, 9 mi. from Orillia, Ont. Opened in 1909 as a training centre for YMCA leaders, this vacation spot is the site of the summer COUCHICHING CONFERENCES.

Gentleman Usher of the Black Rod. Ancient title of the usher to the House of Lords; in Canada a ceremonial official of the SENATE. One of his principal duties is to summon

members of the HOUSE OF COMMONS to the Senate chamber to hear the SPEECH FROM THE THRONE at the opening of Parliament. His staff of office is an ebony stick surmounted by a gold lion.

Geographical regions. The principal geographical regions of Canada from east to west are: ATLANTIC REGION, GREAT LAKES-ST LAWRENCE PLAIN, CANADIAN SHIELD, INTERIOR PLAINS, and WESTERN CORDILLERA.

Geological Survey of Canada. An organization that maps and studies the geology of Canada. Under the Department of ENERGY, MINES AND RESOURCES, it sends out about 100 parties each year to various regions to examine the potential existence and probable distribution of the country's natural resources and ways to preserve the natural environment. The Surveys and Mapping Branch has produced accurate topographical maps at a medium scale of the whole of Canada and is now preparing large-scale topographical maps for much of the country. It has led the world in rapid mapping techniques, using helicopters and other aircraft, especially in the Arctic regions.

George, Chief Dan (b.1899). Indian spokesman and actor. He acquired the traditional crafts and ways on the Burrard Reserve in North Vancouver, B.C., where he was born, and became a logger and longshoreman. He worked on the Vancouver docks from 1920 to 1947, when an injury ended his work there. He became a musician and entertainer and was later elected chief of the Squamish Indians. He created the role of OL' ANTOINE on the CBC television program CARIBOO COUNTRY in 1960. In 1969 he appeared in the Walt Disney feature *Smith,* based on HOW TO BREAK A QUARTER HORSE. In 1971 he was nominated for an Academy Award for his performance in *Little Big Man* (1970), a Hollywood film in which he portrayed an aged Cheyenne chief. He played the father in George RYGA'S play *The* ECSTASY OF RITA JOE (1970) and in the ballet based on it. A man of considerable dignity and a noble spokesman for his race, he published a collection of meditations on the Indian and the modern world called *My Heart Soars* (1974).

George Cross. Highest civilian decoration in the Commonwealth, first awarded for civilian valour in modern warfare by George VI in 1940. The abbreviation is GC.

George Medal. Commonwealth decoration for a civilian act of bravery (less conspicuous than that for which the GEORGE CROSS is awarded). It was first awarded to civilians for valour in modern warfare in 1940. The abbreviation is GM.

Georgia Straight. An 'underground' newspaper published weekly from Vancouver. The tabloid was founded in 1967 by Dan McLeod and Milton ACORN to report from a radical point of view on society and the arts.

Georgian Bay Islands National Park. Established in 1929 along the coast of Georgian Bay between Macey Bay and Moose Deer Point, Ont., it covers 5.4 sq. mi. and is composed of nearly 50 picturesque islands, including Beausoleil Island, associated with CHAMPLAIN, and FLOWER POT ISLAND.

Gerard, E.G. (Eddie) (1890-1937). All-round athlete. Born in Ottawa, he played football, cricket, tennis, and lacrosse but excelled in hockey. He became a professional in 1913 with the Ottawa Senators, which won the STANLEY CUP three times during the next 10 years. Upon retirement in 1924 he continued coaching or managing in Montreal, New York, and St Louis.

Gérin, Léon. See INNIS-GÉRIN MEDAL.

Gerrymander. A redistribution of parliamentary seats that produces an advantage for one party over another. Sir John A. MACDONALD made a redistribution in 1882 that 'hived' the Liberals—combining strong Liberal townships in such a way that they had few seats. Called the Great Gerrymander, this was possible because at that time the federal government determined the boundaries of constituencies. Since 1963 constituency boundaries have been drawn by electoral boundary commissions, which have the final say over objections by Parliament. The name derives from that of Elbridge Gerry—governor of Massachusetts in 1811 when election districts were redistributed in the Republicans' favour—and salamander.

Gerussi! A popular CBC Radio program. Starring actor-turned-broadcaster Bruno GERUSSI, it featured talk and music and was heard Monday to Friday for two hours each morning. It was produced by Alex Frame and heard from 1 July 1967 to 4 Oct. 1971, when it was succeeded by THIS COUNTRY IN THE MORNING.

Gerussi, Bruno (b.1928). Actor and broadcaster. Born in Medicine Hat, Alta, of Italian parentage, he attended the Banff School of Fine Arts (BANFF CENTRE) and joined the STRATFORD FESTIVAL and the CANADIAN PLAYERS in the mid-1950s. He played the lead in the CBC-TV première of RIEL in 1961. His radio show, GERUSSI!, was heard from 1967 to 1971, and he starred in the CBC-TV series The BEACH-COMBERS.

Gesner, Abraham (1797-1864). Geologist and inventor. Originally trained in medicine, he turned to scientific studies and made a geological survey of New Brunswick from 1838 to 1843. In 1852 he patented a process for distilling kerosene and a year later moved to the U.S. and introduced its use there. Kerosene replaced whale, animal, and vegetable oils as a source of light and heat. In Canada it is known as 'coal oil', as it is distilled from coal.

Giant Yellowknife Mines Limited. A goldmining company located in Yellowknife, N.W.T. In Feb. 1944 drilling on its property reached a large deposit of ore and caught the public's imagination. This resulted in the 'Yellowknife boom', which established the mine as a leading producer of gold in 1949 and was the first of the post-war mining rushes.

Giant's Tomb. See SLEEPING GIANT.

Gibbon, John Murray (1875-1952). Author. Born in Ceylon and educated at Aberdeen, Oxford, and Göttingen, he was appointed director of European publicity for the CANADIAN PACIFIC RAILWAY in 1907. He was director of all its publicity in Montreal from 1913 until his retirement in 1945. A founder and the first president of the CANADIAN AUTHORS ASSOCIATION, he published numerous books of fiction and non-fiction, including *Steel of Empire* (1935), a history of the CPR; *Canadian Mosaic* (1938), a celebration of the country's ethnic composition; and *Canadian Folk-Songs, Old and New* (1927).

Gibraltar of America, Gibraltar of Canada. References to QUEBEC CITY.

Gibson, George (Mooney) (1880-1967). Noted baseball player. Born in London, Ont., he played professional baseball with the New York Giants and later managed major-league clubs, including the Toronto Club in the International League, before retiring to his farm near London at 54.

Gibson, Graeme (b.1934). Novelist. Born in London, Ont., and educated at the University of Western Ontario, he was active in the formation of the WRITERS' UNION OF CANADA, of which he became chairperson. His two experimental novels are *Five Legs* (1969) and *Communion* (1971). His radio interviews with fellow writers were collected in *Eleven Canadian Novelists* (1973).

Gibson Literary Award

Gibson Literary Award. Annual award to the Canadian author of the best first novel published during the previous year. It was first offered by the CANADIAN AUTHORS ASSOCIATION and Canadian Gibson Distillery Ltd in 1976 and consists of $1,000.

Giguère, Roland (b.1929). Quebec poet and printer. Born in Montreal, he trained at the École des Arts Graphiques and was associated with the French Surrealists from 1955 to 1963, when he returned to Montreal and established an atelier from which he issued, under the imprint of Éditions Erta, beautifully illustrated books of poetry and portfolios of art. Giguère's dynamic, passionate poetry was collected in *L'Age de la Parole* (1965). His only book in English, *Mirror and Other Poems* (1975), was translated by Sheila FISCHMAN.

Gilbert, Sir Humphrey (*c.*1537-83). English explorer who claimed Newfoundland for England. In search of a NORTHWEST PASSAGE he sailed westward in 1583 with five ships, including the *Squirrel* (his own) and the *Golden Hind*. He took formal possession of Newfoundland on 5 Aug. On the return voyage, at midnight on 9 Sept., his ship sank in heavy seas. That day he had been seen sitting in the stern holding a book and shouting repeatedly: 'We are as near to heaven by sea as by land!'

Gilhooly, David (b.1943). Ceramic sculptor. Born in Auburn, Calif., he studied at the University of California. He came to Canada in 1968 and has taught at the University of Saskatchewan and York University. His richly detailed ceramic frogs—which make up a fantasy Frog World with its own complex cosmology and history and include pieces such as Frog Victoria and Madonna-and-Frog—show both a nonsense element of playfulness and an imaginative satire achieved by replacing familiar human images, heroes, and mythical figures with frogs. He is exhibited and collected internationally.

Gillam, Zachariah. See RUPERT'S HOUSE.

Gillis, James P. (1870-1930?). Poetaster and author of an inadvertently amusing biography of Angus MacASKILL called *The Cape Breton Giant: A Truthful Memoir* (1899). The work of Gillis is humorously examined by William Arthur DEACON in *The* FOUR JAMESES (1927).

Gilmour, Clyde (b.1912). Film critic. Born in Calgary, Alta, he began reviewing films for the *Medicine Hat News* and then for the *Edmonton Journal*, the *Vancouver Province*, and the *Vancouver Sun*. He became North America's first regular film reviewer on radio with 'Movie Critic' in 1947, and then with appearances on CRITICALLY SPEAKING, both CBC Radio. He joined the *Toronto Telegram* as film critic in 1954, and with its demise in 1971 moved to the *Toronto Star*. A noted record collector, he began 'Gilmour's Albums' on CBC Radio on 2 Oct. 1956. This series of hour-long weekly programs has continued as the longest-running radio program in Canada.

Gimby, Bobby (b.1921). Composer and arranger. Born in Cabri, Sask., he acquired a national following as a regular on the HAPPY GANG from 1948 to 1959. He wrote the official CENTENNIAL YEAR theme, 'CA-NA-DA'. Gimby (who pronounces his name Jim-bee) travelled with the Centennial Train in 1967, leading local children with his trumpet in the singing of this song; he was thereafter referred to as 'the Pied Piper of Canada'. Less well known is the fact that in 1961 one of his tunes was given new words and, as 'Malaysia Forever', became that country's national anthem.

Ginger Group. Term for an active group within a political party. The phrase was applied in Canada to Conservative members within the UNION GOVERNMENT (1917-21). The best-known Ginger Group was composed of MPs who championed farm and labour interests within the PROGRESSIVE PARTY until they seceded from it in 1924. The Group helped form the CCF in 1932.

'Girls, The'. See Frances LORING and Florence WYLE.

GIS. Acronym of GUARANTEED INCOME SUPPLEMENT.

Gitche Manitou. See MANITOU.

Gitksan. A division of the TSIMSHIAN Indians living in the Upper Skeena R. valley, near Hazelton, B.C. They speak a dialect of Nass-Gitksan, to which the Tsimshian language of the Coast Tsimshian is closely related. The name comes from the word for 'people' (*Git*) and 'river of mists' (*Ksan*). The word Skeena is an anglicization of 'Ksan for the river.) Gitksan legends were included in *Tsimsyan Myths* (1961) by Marius BARBEAU. Their rich artistic tradition is now preserved at the 'KSAN INDIAN VILLAGE.

Givenchy. A village in northern France, the scene of an attack during the FIRST WORLD WAR by the First Canadian Division in June 1915 that was as futile as it was bloody.

Gjoa. The first ship to navigate the NORTHWEST PASSAGE. She took Roald AMUNDSEN from the Atlantic to the Pacific in 1903-6. Her name is commemorated by Gjoa Haven, Amundsen's wintering-place on KING WILLIAM ISLAND.

Glace Bay and Springhill Strikes. A series of miners' strikes in Nova Scotia from 1901 to 1911. They were caused by an intense inter-union rivalry between the PROVINCIAL WORKMEN'S ASSOCIATION, which enjoyed closed-shop privileges with the mine owners, and the United Mine Workers of America, whose members were fired by the mine owners. During these strikes hundreds of families were evicted, dozens of union leaders were arrested, and the army was called in to break up meetings and demonstrations. Owing to the recommendations of the Dominion Royal Commission Report of 1917, the two groups merged to form the Amalgamated Mineworkers of Nova Scotia, which became District 26 of the UMWA.

Glacier National Park. Established in 1886 in the Selkirk Mountains of British Columbia, it covers 521 sq. mi. and includes over 100 glaciers.

Gladstone, Charles (1877-1947?). Master Haida carver. He was born in Skidegate in the Queen Charlotte Islands, B.C., like his uncle Charles EDENSHAW, and acquired the traditional arts of the Haida people, which he refined in his carvings of wood, ARGILLITE, and silver. His work is highly valued. Favourite themes were the shark and the killer whale, the latter often depicted with a human face.

Gladstone, Gerald (b.1929). Sculptor. Born in Toronto, he is self-taught. His welded sculpture uses technical methods developed in industry, often including pre-fabricated parts. He has executed many public and private commissions, including a 28-ft fountain for the Winnipeg International Airport, a fountain for the Australian government (1975), and the first piece of modern sculpture commissioned by Harvard University. Notable among the sculptures he created for EXPO 67 was a hydraulically operated sea-monster. In 1962 he mounted a one-man show in London, Eng.

Glass Cage, The. Play by the British playwright J.B. Priestley, written for Barbara Chilcott and her brothers Donald and Murray Davis (see DAVIS FAMILY). Under the direction of Henry Kaplan, it opened at the Davises' CREST THEATRE, Toronto, on 5 Mar. 1957. Described by Brooks Atkinson as 'part melodrama, part mystery, part morality', it is set in Toronto in 1906 and traces the effects of hatred on an old family.

Glassco, John (b.1909). Man of letters. Born in Montreal, he left McGill University in 1928 to go to Paris, where he stayed for three years. His MEMOIRS OF MONTPARNASSE (1970), written shortly afterwards and published almost 40 years later, is a notable record of this period. In this book, as in his fiction, poetry, and translations from the French, Glassco is a writer of elegant precision and quiet authority. He chose 34 of his poems—mostly from *A Deficit Made Flesh* (1958) and *A Point of Sky* (1964)—to appear in his *Selected Poems* (1971), which was followed by *Montreal* (1973). *Four Fatal Women* (1974) is a collection of four stories. He completed Aubrey Beardsley's unfinished erotic classic *Under the Hill* (1959) and wrote the erotic bestseller *The English Governess* (1960) under the pseudonym 'Miles Underwood'; it was revised and reissued in 1976 as *Harriet Marwood, Governess.* He edited *The Poetry of French Canada in Translation* (1970) and has produced impeccable translations of the writings of Hector de Saint-Denys-GARNEAU in the *Journal* (1970) and *Complete Poems* (1975) and of Monique Bosco's novel, *Lot's Wife* (1975).

Glassco, William (Bill) (b.1935). Director. Born in Toronto, a graduate of Victoria College, University of Toronto, and of New York University, he managed the RED BARN THEATRE in 1970. He established the TARRAGON THEATRE in 1971 and opened with a revised version of CREEPS, which he had first directed for FACTORY THEATRE LAB in 1970. Glassco is respected for his directorial skills and his close work with such writers as David Freeman and Michel TREMBLAY, whose plays he translated with John van Burek and produced at the Tarragon Theatre. He directed *The Merchant of Venice* at the STRATFORD FESTIVAL in 1976.

Glazebrook, G.P. deT. (b.1899). Political scientist and social historian. Born in London, Ont., and educated at the University of Toronto and Oxford, until his retirement in 1963 he alternated between teaching in the history department of the University of Toronto and undertaking duties in the Department of External Affairs. His principal publications are the two-volume *History of Transportation in Canada* (1938, 1964), *Canadian External Relations* (1942; 2nd ed. 1950; rev. 1964), *Canada at the Paris Peace Conference* (1940), *A History of Canadian Political Thought* (1966), *Life in Ontario: A Social History* (1968), and *The Story of Toronto* (1971).

Glenbow-Alberta Institute. Museum and archive. Located in Calgary, Alta, this complex was founded on 15 Apr. 1966 by an Act of the

Glenbow-Alberta Institute

Alberta legislature. It incorporates all the holdings, buildings, and properties of the Glenbow Foundation, which had been established in 1955 by the oil magnate Eric L. Harvie (1892-1975) to collect paintings, books, documents, Indian and archaeological specimens and pioneer artifacts relating to the Canadian West. It is divided into three sections: History (Library, Archives, Extension), Exhibitions (Glenbow-Alberta Art Gallery and Museum, Display and Art Department), and Collections (Ethnology, Cultural History, Museum). It is the custodian of over 95,000 photographs of Indians, ranching, and farm life illustrating the historical development of western Canada.

Glenbow Foundation. See GLENBOW-ALBERTA INSTITUTE.

'Glengarry, A Native of County'. See James MacRAE.

Glengarry Fencibles. The Glengarry Light Infantry Fencibles, a regiment raised from Glengarry Co., Ont., that distinguished itself in the WAR OF 1812. It has handed down a military tradition to the STORMONT, DUNDAS, AND GLENGARRY HIGHLANDERS of today.

Glengarry Schooldays. The fourth in a succession of internationally popular novels by Ralph CONNOR, published in 1902. It is a series of linked stories concerning young Hughie Murray and his experiences of growing up and is based on Connor's own schooldays in Glengarry County in eastern Ontario. It opens with a well-known set-piece, 'The Spelling-Match'.

Glick, Srul Irving (b.1934). Composer. Born in Toronto, he was educated in the Faculty of Music of the University of Toronto. He is a producer of music programs for CBC Radio and conducts a synagogue choir. Of his works for orchestra, instrumental ensemble, piano, and voice—many of them brooding, lyrical pieces and some evoking Jewish folk materials—one of the best known is I NEVER SAW ANOTHER BUTTERFLY (1968), a song-cycle commissioned by the CBC for Maureen FORRESTER.

Global Television Network. A private mini-network consisting of a Toronto production centre and six transmitter sites across southern Ontario. It went on the air on 6 Jan. 1974.

Globe, The. A daily newspaper once published in Toronto. Founded by George BROWN, it appeared between 1844 and 1936, when it merged with the MAIL AND EMPIRE to form the GLOBE AND MAIL.

Globe and Mail, The. A morning newspaper published in Toronto. Born in 1936 of a merger effected by C. George McCullagh of two nineteenth-century newspapers, the GLOBE and the MAIL AND EMPIRE, since 1965 it has been the flagship paper of FP PUBLICATIONS. Although outstripped in circulation by the TORONTO STAR, it is read from coast to coast and calls itself 'Canada's National Newspaper'. It excels in business reports and regional and international coverage. Its motto is 'The subject who is truly loyal to the Chief Magistrate will neither advise nor submit to arbitrary measures' (Junius). Journalists and columnists who write for the paper include Richard Cleroux, William FRENCH, Jonathan Manthorpe, Martin O'Malley, Richard Needham, Geoffrey Stevens, Norman Webster, and John Fraser. It is the only Canadian newspaper sold in the Soviet Union. See also the GLOBE MAGAZINE.

Globe Magazine, The. A weekly supplement published with the Saturday edition of the GLOBE AND MAIL. Published between 1957 and 1971, it differed from WEEKEND MAGAZINE and other weekend supplements in that it specialized in publishing long, thoughtful articles on society, politics, and culture. It was edited successively by Richard Doyle, Colin McCullough, Ted Bolwell, Don Nichol, Norman Webster, Oliver Clausen, and Kenneth Bagnell.

Glooscap. The culture hero of the MICMAC Indians of eastern Canada. His adventures are well told by Cyrus MacMillan in *Glooskap's Country and Other Indian Tales* (1955). Glooscap arrived from across the sea in a great stone canoe. He created the Indians, the first of men, and all the animals. He killed his wicked brother in self-defence. He seized the queen Summer from the south and married her to the giant Winter. He battled the Spider Man and brought happiness to the Indians. He made his home on Cape BLOMIDON in Nova Scotia. Then, promising to return and singing a strange sad song, he sailed away again in his great stone canoe. See also WHISKEY JACK.

Glooscap Trail. Scenic drive around Minas Basin and the BAY OF FUNDY, N.S., through country associated with the Micmac culture hero GLOOSCAP. The 223-mi. drive from the border town of Amherst to the capital city of Halifax includes a side-trip to BLOMIDON Mountain, where Glooscap is said to have made his home.

Glover, Elwood. See LUNCHEON DATE.

GM. See GEORGE MEDAL.

GM Presents. CBC-TV's banner drama series. Original 60-minute dramas were presented live each week from 1 Dec. 1953 to 30 July 1961 under the direction of Ed Moser and Esse W. LJUNGH, with Nathan COHEN as story editor. It presented original teleplays by new authors (notably *Flight into Danger* by Arthur HAILEY) and adaptations of classics. It was sponsored by General Motors of Canada and was succeeded by FESTIVAL.

'God Save the Queen'. The royal anthem. It was not until 1967 that Parliament officially designated the words and music of 'God Save the Queen' as constituting the royal anthem. The traditional English lyrics and melody, first published in 1744, constitute the national anthem of Great Britain. In the United States the tune has been known since 1831 as 'America'. The English and French words appear in *Colombo's Canadian Quotations* (1974). 'God Save the Queen' is the royal anthem; 'O CANADA' is the national anthem.

Godbout, Jacques (b.1933). Quebec novelist, poet, and film-maker. Born in Montreal and a graduate of the Université de Montréal, he was a founder of LIBERTÉ and joined the staff of the NATIONAL FILM BOARD in 1958, where since 1970 he has been Director of French Production. Godbout is the author of several collections of poems and a clever novelist of the revolutionary sentiments that have arisen in Quebec society. Two of his novels have been translated into English: *Knife on the Table* (1968) by Penny Williams and *Hail Galarneau!* (1972)—which has been turned into a musical comedy—by Alan BROWN. For the NFB he directed a brilliant short, *Paul-Émile Borduas* (1963), and four interesting features: *YUL 871* (1966), *Kid Sentiment* (1968), *IXE-13* (1971), and *La Gimmick* (1975). In 1975 his *'textes tranquilles'* appeared in *Le Réformiste*, a collection of essays on topical subjects.

Godfrey, Dave (b.1938). Novelist and literary activist. Born in Toronto and educated at the Universities of Toronto and Iowa, he spent 18 months in Ghana where he was employed by CUSO. He has taught English at Trinity College, University of Toronto, helped found the House of ANANSI PRESS (which he named after the African spider-god), NEW PRESS, and Press PORCÉPIC, which he now runs. He is an accomplished writer of short stories, which were collected in *Death Goes Better with Coca-Cola* (1968). His novel *The* NEW ANCESTORS (1970), set in Africa, won a Governor General's Award. With William M. McWhinney, he edited *Man Deserves Man: CUSO in Developing Countries* (1968) and with

Melville Watkins *Gordon to Watkins to You* (1970), a book of readings inspired by the ECONOMIC NATIONALISM of Walter GORDON. With Robert FULFORD and Abraham ROTSTEIN he edited *Read Canadian: A Book about Canadian Books* (1972). In 1970 he helped found the Independent Publishers' Association (now the ASSOCIATION OF CANADIAN PUBLISHERS) to promote the interests of Canadian-owned publishing firms.

Godless coins. Currency minted by the Canadian government in 1911 honouring George V but omitting the customary legend *Dei Gratia* ('By the Grace of God'). There was a public outcry at this seemingly irreligious break with tradition, so the following year the legend on all coins—one, two, five, twenty-five, and fifty-cent pieces—was reworked to read: *Georgivs V Dei Gra: Rex et Ind: Imp* ('George the Fifth by the Grace of God King and Emperor of India').

God's country. Epithet first applied to the Yukon by the Michigan novelist James Oliver Curwood. According to Pierre BERTON, 'he made God's country a household word' with such novels as *The River's End: A New Story of God's Country* (1919) and the screenplays for numerous Hollywood movies set in 'the unsullied north', which lacked civilization but not crime.

Goin' Down the Road. Feature film produced and directed by Don SHEBIB and released in 1970. Written by William FRUET and photographed by Richard LEITERMAN, with music by Bruce COCKBURN, it starred two non-professionals, Doug McGrath and Paul Bradley, as drifters from Newfoundland who arrive in Toronto to better themselves. They leave to escape the law, debts, and marriage. Produced for only $87,000, it is the best and most successful English-Canadian film made to date. 87 min., colour.

Golden age of Canadian radio. Period of vitality and variety in national CBC Radio broadcasting, especially in live radio drama. The so-called Golden Age is generally dated from 1940, before the commencement of the national news broadcasts, to 1955, with the advent of television and its high costs. Associated with this peak period are Lorne GREENE and Andrew ALLAN, among others.

Golden Boy, The. Winnipeg landmark. The gilded bronze figure of a youth—carrying a torch in his right hand and a sheaf of wheat in his left—is perched on top of the dome of the Legislative Building, which opened on 15 July 1920. The work of the French sculptor

Golden Boy

Charles Garde, it is 13 ft 6 in. high and stands 240 ft above the ground. It was described as representing 'Eternal Youth' and 'The Spirit of Enterprise'.

Golden Dog, The. *Le chien d'or,* a carved stone block, perhaps dating from the seventeenth century, now above the entrance to the Quebec Post Office. It bears the gilded figure of a dog gnawing a bone and a four-line inscription that ends *'Je mordrai qui m'aura mordu'* ('I'll bite him who once bit me'). It is associated with a probably apocryphal legend about a family feud, which William KIRBY made use of in his novel *The* GOLDEN DOG.

Golden Dog, The. Historical romance by William KIRBY that first appeared in print without the author's permission in 1877 and was revised for an authorized version published in 1896. Set in the Quebec of 1748, prior to the downfall of NEW FRANCE, it is a tale of love and murder against a background that includes François BIGOT, the corrupt intendant; the sinister La CORRIVEAU; and into which the legend of the GOLDEN DOG is woven.

Golden Hawks, The. A touring aerobatic team of RCAF pilots. Flying SABRES, it thrilled crowds at annual Air Force Day celebrations between 1959 and 1963.

Golden Horseshoe. A crescent of land forming the western tip of Lake Ontario, stretching from St Catharines in the south to Oshawa in the northeast, and including Hamilton and Toronto. The area contains approximately four million people, the majority of whom are located in and around Metropolitan Toronto. It is also called Mississauga, Conurbation Canada, and the Canadian Megalopolis.

Golden Sheaf. The best-film award of the YORKTON INTERNATIONAL FILM FESTIVAL.

Golden Sheaf Trophy. See INTERNATIONAL DOCUMENTARY FILM FESTIVAL.

Goldsmith, Oliver (1794-1861). Poet. Born in St Andrews, N.B., the grand-nephew and namesake of the Irish poet and dramatist, he worked as a civil servant in Halifax and died in Liverpool. In imitation of his grand-uncle's *The Deserted Village* (1770), Goldsmith wrote the sentimental, descriptive poem *The Rising Village* (1825), which records stages in the Loyalist settlement of ACADIA. It is a work of historic interest.

Golf Championship, Canadian Open. See PETER JACKSON TROPHY.

Gomez, Avelino (b.1929). Cuban-born jockey. Born near Havana, he first rode professionally at the age of 15. His first Canadian race was in Vancouver in 1945. Since 1955 he has lived in Toronto, where he has ridden four QUEEN'S PLATE winners. Voted top rider in North America in 1966, he has a spirited way of vaulting off his horse in the winner's enclosure. He is now a leading trainer in Etobicoke, Ont.

Good Friday. Statutory holiday observed throughout Canada. It commemorates the Crucifixion of Christ and is observed on the Friday immediately preceding Easter, which never occurs before 22 Mar. or after 25 Apr.

Gooderham, William. See HIRAM WALKER-GOODERHAM AND WORTS LTD.

Gooderham and Worts. See HIRAM WALKER-GOODERHAM AND WORTS LTD.

Goodis, Jerry (b.1929). Advertising executive. Born in Toronto, he graduated from the Central Technical Institute. He began working as a designer in 1950, was a founding member of The TRAVELLERS singing group in 1954, and two years later became president of Goodis, Goldberg, Soren, a highly creative advertising agency in Toronto. In 1975 it merged with MacLAREN ADVERTISING LIMITED to form MacLaren Intermart Inc. Goodis is the author of an amusing book about the agency business, *Have I Ever Lied to You Before?* (1972).

Goods Satisfactory or Money Refunded. Famous guarantee of the T. EATON COMPANY. These five words, which are familiar to Canadians from coast to coast through EATON'S CATALOGUE, were first used in 1913. But the guarantee was expressed in similar words as early as 1884 by Timothy Eaton, the company's founder.

Goose Bay. International airbase on Churchill (formerly Hamilton) Inlet, Labrador. It was opened in Dec. 1941 and was operated jointly by the RAF Ferry Command and the U.S. Air Force for the TRANS-ATLANTIC FERRY SERVICE as an alternative to the airport at GANDER, Nfld. A nearby residential community is called Hamilton River, or Happy Valley.

'Gooseberries and Radishes'. See 'RADISHES AND GOOSEBERRIES'.

Gopher ranch. Satiric reference to a ranch or farm having more gophers than cattle.

Gordon, Charles William. See Ralph CONNOR.

Gordon, Walter (b.1906). Former cabinet

208

minister and economic nationalist. He started his career in CLARKSON, GORDON, the family accounting business. In 1955 he was named chairman of the Royal Commission on Canada's Economic Prospects, the GORDON COMMISSION. Elected to the House of Commons in 1962, he was appointed Minister of Finance after the Liberals were returned as a minority government in 1963. Gordon's first budget led him into difficulties. The Opposition accused him of not respecting budget secrecy because in its preparation he had used three advisers not in the government service; and under pressure from the business community and the U.S. he was forced to amend his provisions for control of foreign ownership in Canada. After the 1965 election, when the Liberals failed to win a majority, Gordon resigned as Minister of Finance because he had recommended the election. Gordon returned to the cabinet as a Minister without Portfolio in 1967, but resigned in 1968 shortly before the Liberal leadership convention and returned to business life. He has remained a convinced economic nationalist and is a prominent figure in the COMMITTEE FOR AN INDEPENDENT CANADA. Among his books are *A Choice for Canada: Independence or Colonial Status* (1966) and *Storm Signals: New Economic Policies for Canada* (1975).

Gordon Commission. The name by which the Royal Commission on Canada's Economic Prospects (1955-8) is usually known. Under the chairmanship of Walter L. GORDON, and with Douglas LEPAN in charge of the research work, it was an exercise in economic futurology. The Commission's Preliminary Report, presented to the cabinet in Dec. 1956, forecast substantial economic growth for the next quarter-century; the Final Report, published in Apr. 1958, was more cautious but still remained a testament to the economy of growth. Initiated under the ST LAURENT administration but completed in the DIEFENBAKER years, the Gordon Commission was largely ignored by the government and few of its recommendations were implemented.

Gordon Sinclair Award. Awarded annually by ACTRA 'for outspoken opinions and integrity in broadcasting'. It was established in 1970 to mark the seventieth birthday of the Toronto reporter and broadcaster Gordon SINCLAIR.

Gore. In Upper Canada (Ontario), a parcel of land remaining after a region has been surveyed; in Great Britain, a triangular-shaped piece of land.

Gore, The Men of. Militia commanded by Sir Allan Napier MacNAB to quell the REBELLION OF 1837. Figuratively, the Men of Gore are those whose loyalty is such that they will fight bravely for their cause. Gore Township and Gore Park in Hamilton, Ont., are named after Francis Gore, the outspoken lieutenant-governor of Upper Canada (Ontario) from 1806 to 1817.

Gorman, Charles (1897-1940). Champion speed-skater. He was born in Saint John, N.B., the home of many oustanding speed-skaters, and although wounded in the leg during the First World War, he persevered. In 1927 he not only retained his title of national amateur champion of Canada and the United States, in both indoor and outdoor competition, but also established world records that were unbroken for a decade. He retired in 1928 and was elected to the Sports HALL OF FAME.

Gorman, T.P. (Tommy) (1886-1963). Coach and sports editor. The Ottawa-born athlete was a member of Canada's 1908 Olympic lacrosse team. He helped found the NATIONAL HOCKEY LEAGUE in 1917 and managed seven STANLEY CUP champion teams in Ottawa, Chicago, and Montreal. For many years sports editor of the *Ottawa Citizen*, he was elected to the Hockey HALL OF FAME in 1963.

Gotlieb, Phyllis (b.1926). Poet and novelist. Born in Toronto, she was educated at the University of Toronto. Her richly imaginative poems have appeared in *Within the Zodiac* (1965), *Ordinary, Moving* (1969), and *Dr. Umlaut's Earthly Kingdom* (1974). She also writes science-fiction stories and has published one such novel, *Sunburst* (1964). *Why Should I Have all the Grief?* (1969) is a novel about a survivor of the Holocaust.

Gougou. Fabulous female giant, twice the height of a ship, who catches sailors and stores them in her huge pocket before devouring them. CHAMPLAIN, in his account of his voyage of 1603, described the Gougou, which was said to live on an island near the Bay of Chaleurs; but LESCARBOT dismissed the Indian myth, saying that it expressed the terror of those who 'see and hear things which are not'.

Gould, Glenn (b.1932). Pianist. Born in Toronto, and taught the piano by his mother and then by Alberto Guerrero at the Royal Conservatory of Music, Toronto, he was a child prodigy, making his début with the Toronto Symphony Orchestra when he was 15. He made his New York début in Town Hall in 1955, the year he recorded Bach's

Goldberg Variations for Columbia Records, which made recording history. He thereupon entered upon a concert career—as one of the top pianists in the world—that he cut short in 1962 to devote himself to recordings, radio and television productions, and writing. His subsequent recordings have penetrated brilliantly and deeply into the works of Bach, Mozart, and Beethoven as well as Arnold Schoenberg.

Goulding, George Henry (1885-1966). Champion walker and runner. The English-born Toronto resident (since 1904) recorded the fastest-ever one-mile walk in 1911. At the 1912 Olympics at Stockholm he won the 10,000-metre gold medal and set a record that took 30 years to break. He was elected to the Sports HALL OF FAME.

Goulet, Robert (b.1933). Popular singer. Born in Lawrence, Mass., and the possessor of a rich baritone voice, he lived in Edmonton and Toronto and studied singing at the Royal Conservatory of Music. After his Broadway début in Lerner and Lowe's *Camelot* in 1961, he entered American show business and has not looked back.

Goupil, René. See JESUIT MARTYRS.

Gourlay, Robert (1778-1863). Political agitator. Born in Scotland, he arrived in Kingston, U.C. (Ont.), in 1817. Observing signs of discontent in the province, he published *To the Resident Land Owners of Upper Canada* (1818), which criticized the administration and attacked members of the executive council. For this, and for subsequent activities, he was arrested, found guilty of sedition, and deported. Though subject to fits of insanity, he wrote two successful books on Upper Canada and a semi-autobiographical work, *The Banished Briton and Neptunian* (1843-6). In 1856, when the sentence placed on him had been declared unconstitutional, he returned to Canada. He stood for election in 1860, was defeated, and went back to Scotland.

Gouzenko, Igor (b.1919). Soviet defector. Born in Russia and posted to the Soviet Embassy in Ottawa in 1943, the cypher clerk defected on 5 Sept. 1945, taking with him 109 carefully selected documents that established conclusively the existence of a Soviet spy ring in North America. Gouzenko's revelations led to the conviction of Sam Carr, Fred Rose, Klaus Fuchs, Alger Hiss, and others. Gouzenko wrote a biography, *This Was My Choice* (1948)—filmed as *The* IRON CURTAIN—and a novel, *The Fall of a Titan* (1953). His wife, Samarkand-born Svetlana, wrote *Before Igor: Memoirs of My Soviet Youth* (1960). The Gouzenkos live on a farm somewhere in southern Ontario. As an authority on international Communism he appears on television and in court rooms wearing a hood as a disguise. He is writing his memoirs.

Government. The power or authority within a country, or the persons holding such power or authority. In common usage 'the government' usually refers to the leading members of the party in power in the House of Commons. See also CABINET, MINISTRY, PROVINCIAL GOVERNMENT, TERRITORIAL GOVERNMENT.

Government House. Official residence of the Governor General of Canada. In 1865, when Ottawa became the capital, Rideau Hall was rented by the government for the governor general, Lord MONCK, and purchased three years later. The original house was built in 1838 by Thomas MacKay; the wings at both ends were added later, and there have been many subsequent additions and modifications. The official residence of a LIEUTENANT-GOVERNOR is also called Government House.

Government leader. The spokesman for the party in power in either of the two chambers of Parliament. The government leader in the Senate is a senior senator, in the House of Commons a cabinet minister.

Governor. The officer who represents the CROWN in a colony. NEW FRANCE was ruled by a succession of military governors and administrators (who acted in case of the governor's absence). The colonies of BRITISH NORTH AMERICA were also ruled by governors appointed by the Crown in England.

Governor and Company of Adventurers of England trading into Hudson's Bay. Official title of the HUDSON'S BAY COMPANY, from the letters patent that were signed on 2 May 1670.

Governor General. The representative of the CROWN in a self-governing Dominion and the head of state. The governor general—a symbol of national unity and of the continuity of institutions and national life—is appointed by the Queen usually for five years on the advice of the cabinet. The office-holder, as the chief executive officer of the state, is 'above politics'. In its earliest form of governor-in-chief, the office dates from 1786, and in its modern form from 1838. The title of a governor general is 'His (Her) Excellency'; the greeting is 'Your Excellency', followed by 'sir' ('madam'). Vincent Massey was the first native-born governor general. A list of the governors general, including their dates of office, follows: Lord MONCK 1867-8; Sir John YOUNG (Lord Lisgar) 1869-72; Lord DUFFERIN 1872-8; Lord LORNE 1878-83; Lord LANSDOWNE 1883-8; Lord STANLEY 1888-93; Lord ABERDEEN 1893-8; Lord MINTO 1898-1904; Lord GREY 1904-11; Duke of CONNAUGHT 1911-16; Duke of DEVONSHIRE 1916-21; Lord BYNG 1921-6; Lord WILLINGDON 1926-31; Lord BESSBOROUGH 1931-5; Lord TWEEDSMUIR 1935-40; Lord ATH-LONE 1940-6; Lord ALEXANDER 1946-52; Vincent MASSEY 1952-9; Major General Georges-Philias VANIER 1959-67; Daniel Roland MICHENER 1967-74; Jules LÉGER 1974- . See also LIEUTENANT-GOVERNOR.

Governor General's Horse Guards, The. Canadian army regiment. It was organized in 1889 and served in the SOUTH AFRICAN WAR. During the FIRST WORLD WAR it distinguished itself in numerous battles, including VIMY and YPRES. In the SECOND WORLD WAR it served as the 3rd Armoured Reconnaissance Regiment in Italy and Northwest Europe.

Governor General's Literary Awards. Awards given annually by the CANADA COUNCIL for the three best English and three best French books written and published by Canadians during the previous year. The awards were instituted in 1937 by the CANADIAN AUTHORS ASSOCIATION—with the agreement of the then Governor General Lord TWEEDSMUIR (the novelist John Buchan)—and administered by it until 1959. Each winning author receives a cash prize, which is now $5,000, and a specially bound copy of his or her book, presented by the governor general at a ceremony. A list of award winners follows:

1936
Bertram BROOKER: *Think of the Earth.* Fiction.
T.B. Robertson: *T.B.R.*—Newspaper pieces. Non-fiction.

1937
Laura G. SALVERSON: *The Dark Weaver.* Fiction.
E.J. PRATT: *The Fable of the Goats.* Poetry.
Stephen LEACOCK: *My Discovery of the West.* Non-fiction.

1938
Gwethalyn Graham: *Swiss Sonata.* Fiction.
Kenneth LESLIE: *By Stubborn stars.* Poetry.
John Murray GIBBON: *Canadian Mosaic.* Non-fiction.

1939
Franklin D. McDowell: *The Champlain Road.* Fiction.
Arthur S. Bourinot: *Under the Sun.* Poetry.
Laura G. SALVERSON: *Confessions of an Immigrant's Daughter.* Non-fiction.

1940
Ringuet (Philippe Panneton): THIRTY ACRES. Fiction.
E.J. PRATT: BRÉBEUF AND HIS BRETHREN. Poetry.
J.F.C. Wright: *Slava Bohu.* Non-fiction.

1941
Alan Sullivan: *Three Came to Ville Marie.* Fiction.
Anne Marriott: *Calling Adventurers.* Poetry.
Emily CARR: KLEE WYCK. Non-fiction.

1942
G. Herbert Sallans: *Little Man.* Fiction.
Earle BIRNEY: DAVID AND OTHER POEMS. Poetry.
Bruce HUTCHISON: *The* UNKNOWN COUNTRY. Non-fiction.
Edgar McInnes: *The Unguarded Frontier.* Non-fiction.

1943
Thomas H. RADDALL: *The Pied Piper of Dipper Creek.* Fiction.
A.J.M. SMITH: *News of the Phoenix.* Poetry.
John D. Robins: *The Incomplete Anglers.* Non-fiction.
E.K. BROWN: *On Canadian Poetry.* Non-fiction.

1944
Gwethalyn Graham: EARTH AND HIGH HEAVEN. Fiction.
Dorothy LIVESAY: *Day and Night.* Poetry.
Dorothy Duncan: *Partner in Three Worlds.* Non-fiction.
Edgar McInnes: *The War: Fourth Year.* Non-fiction.

1945
Hugh MacLENNAN: TWO SOLITUDES. Fiction.
Earle BIRNEY: *Now is Time.* Poetry.
Evelyn M. Richardson: *We Keep a Light.* Non-fiction.
Ross Munro: *Gauntlet to Overlord.* Non-fiction.

1946
Winifred Bambrick: *Continental Revue.* Fiction.
Robert FINCH: *Poems.* Poetry.
Frederick Philip GROVE: IN SEARCH OF MYSELF. Non-fiction.
A.R.M. LOWER: COLONY TO NATION. Non-fiction.

1947
Gabrielle ROY: *The* TIN FLUTE. Fiction.
Dorothy LIVESAY: *Poems for People.* Poetry.
William Sclater: *Haida.* Non-fiction.
R. MacGregor Dawson: *The Government of Canada.* Non-fiction.

1948
Hugh MacLENNAN: *The Precipice.* Fiction.
A.M. KLEIN: *The Rocking Chair and Other Poems.* Poetry.

Governor General's Literary Awards

Thomas H. RADDALL: *Halifax: Warden of the North.* Non-fiction.
C.P. STACEY: *The Canadian Army, 1939-1945.* Non-fiction.

1949
Philip Child: *Mr Ames against Time.* Fiction.
James REANEY: *The Red Heart.* Poetry.
Hugh MacLENNAN: *Cross-country.* Non-fiction.
R. MacGregor Dawson: *Democratic Government in Canada.* Non-fiction.
R.S. Lambert: *Franklin of the Arctic.* Juvenile.

1950
Germaine GUÈVREMONT: *The Outlander.* Fiction.
James Wreford Watson: *Of Time and the Lover.* Poetry.
Marjorie Wilkins CAMPBELL: *The Saskatchewan.* Non-fiction.
W.L. MORTON: *The Progressive Party in Canada.* Non-fiction.
Donalda Dickie: *The Great Adventure.* Juvenile.

1951
Morley CALLAGHAN: *The* LOVED AND THE LOST. Fiction.
Charles BRUCE: *The Mulgrave Road.* Poetry.
Josephine Phelan: *The Ardent Exile.* Non-fiction.
Frank MacKinnon: *The Government of Prince Edward Island.* Non-fiction.
John F. Hayes: *A Land Divided.* Juvenile.

1952
David WALKER: *The Pillar.* Fiction.
E.J. PRATT: TOWARDS THE LASK SPIKE. Poetry.
Bruce HUTCHISON: *The Incredible Canadian.* Non-fiction.
Donald G. CREIGHTON: *John A. Macdonald: The* YOUNG POLITICIAN. Non-fiction.
Marie McPhedran: *Cargoes on the Great Lakes.* Juvenile.

1953
David WALKER: *Digby.* Fiction.
Douglas LePAN: *The Net and the Sword.* Poetry.
N.J. Berrill: *Sex and the Nature of Things.* Non-fiction.
J.M.S. CARELESS: *Canada: A Story of Challenge.* Non-fiction.
John F. Hayes: *Rebels Ride at Night.* Juvenile.

1954
Igor GOUZENKO: *The Fall of a Titan.* Fiction.
P.K. PAGE: *The Metal and the Flower.* Poetry.
Hugh MacLENNAN: *Thirty and Three.* Non-fiction.
A.R.M. LOWER: *This Most Famous Stream.* Non-fiction.
Marjorie Wilkins CAMPBELL: *The Nor'westers.* Juvenile.

1955
Lionel Shapiro: *The Sixth of June.* Fiction.
Wilfred Watson: *Friday's Child.* Poetry.
N.J. Berrill: *Man's Emerging Mind.* Non-fiction.
Donald G. CREIGHTON: *John A. Macdonald: The* OLD CHIEFTAIN. Non-fiction.
Kerry Wood: *The Map-maker.* Juvenile.

1956
Adele WISEMAN: *The Sacrifice.* Fiction.
Robert A.D. FORD: *A Window on the North.* Poetry.
Pierre BERTON: *The Mysterious North.* Non-fiction.
Joseph Lister Rutledge: *Century of Conflict.* Non-fiction.
Farley MOWAT: *Lost in the Barrens.* Juvenile.

1957
Gabrielle ROY: *Street of Riches.* Fiction.
Jay MACPHERSON: *The Boatman.* Poetry.
Bruce HUTCHISON: *Canada: Tomorrow's Giant.* Non-fiction.
Thomas H. RADDALL: *The Path of Destiny.* Non-fiction.
Kerry Wood: *The Great Chief.* Juvenile.

1958
Colin McDougall: *Execution.* Fiction.
James REANEY: *A Suit of Nettles.* Poetry.
Pierre BERTON: KLONDIKE. Non-fiction.
Joyce Hemlow: *The History of Fanny Burney.* Non-fiction.
Edith L. Sharp: *Nkwala.* Juvenile.

1959
Hugh MacLENNAN: *The* WATCH THAT ENDS THE NIGHT. Fiction.
Irving LAYTON: *A Red Carpet for the Sun.* Poetry.
André Giroux: *Malgré tout, la joie.* Fiction (French).
Félix-Antoine Savard: *Le Barachois.* Non-fiction (French).

1960
Brian MOORE: *The Luck of Ginger Coffee.* Fiction.
Frank UNDERHILL: *In Search of Canadian Liberalism.* Non-fiction.
Margaret AVISON: *Winter Sun.* Poetry.
Paul Toupin: *Souvenirs pour demain.* Non-fiction (French).
Anne HÉBERT: *Poèmes.* Poetry (French).

1961
Malcolm LOWRY: *Hear us o Lord from Heaven Thy Dwelling Place.* Fiction.
T.A. Goudge: *The Ascent of Life.* Non-fiction.
Robert FINCH: *Acis in Oxford.* Poetry.
Yves THÉRIAULT: ASHINI. Fiction (French).
Jean LE MOYNE: *Convergences.* Non-fiction (French).

1962

Kildare DOBBS: *Running to Paradise*. Fiction and autobiographical writing.

Marshall McLUHAN: *The* GUTENBERG GALAXY. Non-fiction.

James REANEY: *Twelve Letters to a Small Town* and *The Killdeer and Other Plays*. Poetry and drama.

Jacques FERRON: *Contes du pays incertain*. Fiction (French).

Gilles MARCOTTE: *Une Littérature qui se fait*. Non-fiction (French).

Jacques LANGUIRAND: *Les Insolites et Les Violons de l'automne*. Drama (French).

1963

Hugh GARNER: *Hugh Garner's Best Stories*. Fiction.

J.M.S. CARELESS: *Brown of the Globe*. Non-fiction.

Gatien Lapointe: *Ode au Saint-Laurent*. Poetry (French).

Gustave Lanctot: *Histoire du Canada*. Non-fiction (French).

1964

Douglas LePAN: *The Deserter*. Fiction.

Phyllis Grosskurth: *John Addington Symonds*. Non-fiction.

Raymond SOUSTER: *The Colour of the Times*. Poetry.

Jean-Paul Pinsonneault: *Les Terres sèches*. Fiction (French).

Réjean Robidoux: *Roger Martin du Gard et la religion*. Non-fiction (French).

Pierre PERRAULT: *Au Coeur de la rose*. Poetry (French).

1965

Alfred PURDY: *The Cariboo Horses*. Poetry.

James EAYRS: *In Defence of Canada*. Non-fiction.

Gilles VIGNEAULT: *Quand les bateaux s'en vont*. Poetry (French).

Gérard BESSETTE: *L'Incubation*. Fiction (French).

André-S. Vachon: *Le Temps et l'espace dans l'oeuvre de Paul Claudel*. Non-fiction (French).

1966

Margaret LAURENCE: *A Jest of God*. Fiction.

George WOODCOCK: *The Crystal Spirit: A Study of George Orwell*. Non-fiction.

Margaret ATWOOD: *The Circle Game*. Poetry.

Claire MARTIN: *Le Joue droite*. Fiction (French).

Marcel TRUDEL: *Histoire de la Nouvelle-France*: vol. II, *Le comptoir, 1604-1627*. Non-fiction (French).

Réjean DUCHARME: *L'Avalée des avalés*. Poetry and theatre (French).

1967

Eli MANDEL: *An Idiot Joy*. Poetry.

Alden A. NOWLAN: *Bread, Wine and Salt*. Poetry.

Norah STORY: *The* OXFORD COMPANION TO CANADIAN HISTORY AND LITERATURE. Non-fiction.

Jacques GODBOUT: *Salut Galarneau*. Fiction (French).

Robert-Lionel Séguin: *La Civilisation traditionelle de 'l'habitant' aux* XVIIᵉ *et* XVIIIᵉ *siècles*. Non-fiction (French).

Françoise Loranger: *Encore cinq minutes*. Drama (French).

1968

Alice MUNRO: *Dance of the Happy Shades*. Fiction.

Mordecai RICHLER: *Cocksure* and *Hunting Tigers Under Glass*. Fiction and essays.

Marie-Claire BLAIS: *Manuscrits de Pauline Archange*. Fiction (French).

Fernand Dumont: *Le Lieu de l'homme*. Non-fiction (French).

Leonard COHEN: *Selected Poems 1956-68* (declined).

Hubert AQUIN: *Trou de mémoire* (declined).

1969

Robert KROETSCH: *The Studhorse Man*. Fiction.

George BOWERING: *Rocky Mountain Foot* and *The Gangs of Kosmos*. Poetry.

Gwendolyn MacEWEN: *The Shadow-maker*. Poetry.

Louise Maheux-Forcier: *Une Forêt pour Zoé*. Fiction (French).

Jean-Guy PILON: *Comme eau retenue*. Poetry (French).

Michel BRUNET: *Les Canadiens après la conquête*. Non-fiction (French).

1970

Dave GODFREY: *The* NEW ANCESTORS. Fiction.

Michael ONDAATJE: *The Collected Works of Billy the Kid*. Prose and Poetry.

bp NICHOL: *Still Water, The True Eventual Story of Billy the Kid, Beach Head, The Cosmic Chef: An Evening of Concrete*. Poetry.

Monique Bosco: *La Femme de Loth*. Fiction (French).

Jacques Brault: *Quand nous serons heureux*. Drama (French).

Fernand OUELLETT: *Les Actes retrouvés* (declined).

1971

Mordecai RICHLER: ST URBAIN'S HORSEMAN. Fiction.

John GLASSCO: *Selected Poems*. Poetry.

Pierre BERTON: *The Last Spike*. Non-fiction.

Gérard BESSETTE: *Le Cycle*. Fiction (French).

Paul-Marie LAPOINTE: *Le Réel absolu*. Poetry (French).

Gérald Fortin: *La Fin d'un règne*. Non-fiction (French).

Governor General's Literary Awards

1972

Robertson DAVIES: *The Manticore.* Fiction.

Dennis LEE: *Civil Elegies.* Poetry.

John NEWLOVE: *Lies.* Poetry.

Antonine MAILLET: *Don l'Orignal.* Fiction (French).

Gilles Hénault: *Signaux pour les voyants.* Poetry (French).

Jean Hamelin and Yves Roby: *Histoire économique du Québec 1851-1896.* Non-fiction (French).

1973

Rudy WIEBE: *The Temptations of Big Bear.* Fiction.

Miriam Mandel: *Lions at Her Face.* Poetry.

Michael Bell: *Painters in a New Land.* Non-fiction.

Réjean DUCHARME: *L'Hiver de force.* Fiction (French).

Albert Faucher: *Québec en Amérique au dix-neuvième siècle.* Non-fiction (French).

Roland GIGUÈRE: *La Main au feu.* Special Award (declined).

1974

Margaret LAURENCE: *The Diviners.* Fiction.

Ralph GUSTAFSON: *Fire on Stone: A Collection of Poetry.* Poetry.

Charles Ritchie: *The Siren Years.* Non-fiction.

Victor-Lévy BEAULIEU: *Don Quixote de la di-manche.* Fiction (French).

Nicole Brossard: *Mécanique Jongleuse suivi de masculin grammaticale.* Poetry (French).

Louise Déchêne: *Habitants et marchands de Montréal au dix-septième siècle.* Non-fiction (French).

1975

Brian MOORE: *The Great Victorian Collection.* Fiction.

Milton ACORN: *The Island Means Minago.* Poetry.

Anthony Adamson, Marion MacRae: *Hallowed Walls.* Non-fiction.

Anné HÉBERT: *Les Enfants du sabbat.* Fiction (French).

Pierre PERRAULT: *Chouennes.* Poetry (French).

Louis-Edmond Hamelin: *Nordicité canadienne.* Non-fiction (French).

Governor in Council. The GOVERNOR GENERAL acting with the advice and consent of the PRIVY COUNCIL of Canada as a formal instrument for legalizing cabinet decisions. In practice the phrase refers to the cabinet acting with the formal approval of the governor general.

Governor's Lady, The. Novel by Thomas RADDALL published in 1960. A historical romance, it centres on the ambitious wife of Sir John Wentworth, lieutenant-governor of Nova Scotia from 1792 to 1808.

Governors of New France. The following list includes administrators who assumed the government in the case of the illness, absence, or death of the governor: Samuel de CHAMPLAIN (lieutenant-general of the Viceroy), 1612-29; Samuel de Champlain (commandant), 1633-5; Marc-Antoine Bras-de-Fer de Château, administrator, 1635-6; Charles Huault de Montmagny, governor, 1636-48; Louis d'Ailleboust de Coulonge et d'Argentenay, governor, 1648-51; Jean de Lauzon, governor, 1651-6; Charles de Lauzon, sieur de Charny, administrator, 1656-7; Louis d'Ailleboust de Coulonge et d'Argentenay, administrator, 1657-8; Pierre de Voyer, Vicomte d'Argenson, governor, 1658-61; Pierre du Bois, baron d'Avaugour, 1661-3; Augustin Saffray, chevalier de Mézy, governor, 1663-5; Jacques Le Neuf de La Potherie, administrator, 1665; Daniel de Rémy de Courcelle, governor, 1665-72; Louis de Buade, comte de FRONTENAC, governor, 1672-82; Joseph-Antoine Lefebvre de La Barre, governor, 1682-5; Jacques-René de Brisay, marquis de Denonville, governor, 1685-9; Louis de Buade, comte de Frontenac, governor, 1689-98; Louis-Hector, chevalier de Callières, administrator, 1698-9; Louis-Hector, chevalier de Callières, governor, 1699-1703; Philippe de Rigaud, marquis de VAUDREUIL, governor, 1703-25; Charles Le Moyne, 1st baron de Longueuil, administrator, 1725-6; Charles, marquis de Beauharnois, governor, 1726-47; Roland-Michel Barrin, comte de La Galissonière, provisional governor, 1747-9; Jacques-Pierre Taffanel, marquis de La Jonquière, governor, 1749-52; Charles Le Moyne, 2nd baron de Longueuil, administrator, 1752; Ange, marquis Duquesne de Menneville, governor, 1752-5; Pierre de Rigaud, marquis de VAUDREUIL-CAVAGNAL, governor, 1755-60.

Grade XIII. The thirteenth and final year of pre-university instruction characteristic of the Ontario school system. Primary- (or elementary-) school instruction extends from Grade I to Grade VIII; secondary (or high) school instruction, from Grade IX to Grade XIII. From 1871-2 to 1931-2 the thirteenth year was equivalent to first-year university and could be taken at high school or at university. In 1931-2 the University of Toronto set the Ontario pattern by declining to teach the thirteenth year, thus requiring university-bound students to complete that year in high school. Over the years the thirteenth year was called 'Upper School', 'Fifth Form', 'University Entrance', 'Senior Matriculation', etc., and its climax was the 'departmentals'—province-wide examinations administered in all Grade XIII subjects and graded by the Department of Education. Departmental exams were last written in 1967.

Grading. See CANADA GRADING.

Graham, Gwethalyn. See EARTH AND HIGH HEAVEN.

Grain. The most widely read of Robert STEAD's novels, published in 1926. It is a realistic study of life on a farm settlement in Manitoba from the 1890s to the 1920s. The central character, Gander Stake, takes up 'that unending routine' of the farmer's life and, through shyness and waywardness, refuses to enlist during the First World War.

Grain elevators. The most common landmark of the Prairies. These wooden buildings, first built in the 1880s, provide storage for the grain crop along the railway lines. Their height and brilliantly coloured painted exteriors, which distinguish their various owners, make the elevators the landmarks they are and aptly symbolize the grain economy. The larger poured-concrete elevators in Vancouver, Montreal, Toronto, and especially Thunder Bay—in which the wheat is stored before it is transferred to ships—were hailed in *Towards a New Architecture* (1927) by Le Corbusier for their clustered cylindrical shapes, which simply and purely expressed the material in a massive, unornamented form.

Graisse de rôti. A snack of bread and cold fat drippings from a roast, generally pork. First eaten by settlers and then during the Depression, it is still popular in French Canada.

Granatstein, J.L. (b.1939). Historian. Born in Toronto and educated at the Royal Military College, University of Toronto, and Duke University, he teaches at York University in Toronto. He has been a member of the editorial board of the *Canadian Forum* (1968-75) and its book-review editor (1973-5). He was active in city politics from 1970 to 1974. Among his books are *The Politics of Survival: The Conservative Party of Canada 1939-45* (1967); *Marlborough Marathon: One Street against a Developer* (1971); *Canada's War: The Politics of the Mackenzie King Government, 1939-45* (1975); and (with R.D. Cuff) *Canadian American Relations in Wartime: From the Great War to the Cold War* (1975). He edited, with Peter Stevens, *Forum: Canadian Life and Letters 1920-1970, Selections from the Canadian Forum* (1972).

Grand & Toy Limited. Stationers and office suppliers. It was founded in Toronto in 1882 by James Grand, who was joined by his brother-in-law Samuel Toy. Now controlled and operated by the Grand family, it has 24 stores across the country, 12 of them in Toronto.

Grand Banks. The shallow area (under 50 fathoms) of the continental shelf in the Atlantic Ocean off Newfoundland, it is the largest of several banks (LaHave, St Pierre, Sable, Banquereau). A spawning area for many species of ocean fish, it is one of the richest fishing areas in the world, although in recent years—owing to overfishing by Russians, Norwegians, and Canadians—the numbers of fish have dropped to a fraction of what they were formerly.

Grand Portage. French for 'Great Carrying Place', a village on the northwest shore of Lake Superior in present-day Minnesota. Until 1805 it was the headquarters of the NORTH WEST COMPANY for trade between Montreal and the Rockies and the terminus of the 9-mi. portage from the Kaministikwia R. to the Pigeon R., a favoured route to the Northwest in the eighteenth century. See also PORTAGE.

Grand Pré. Near Minas Basin at the head of the Bay of Fundy, it was the scene of a battle in 1747 when some 500 New England soldiers were attacked by French troops and Indians. A 14-acre national historic park at Grand Pré, N.S., commemorates the expulsion of the ACADIANS, the original French settlers of what is now Nova Scotia. During the 1920s a chapel that functions as a museum was erected on the site of the original church from which the order for expulsion was read in 1755. Grand Pré, which means 'great meadow', gave its name to Bliss Carmen's poem LOW TIDE ON GRAND PRÉ.

Grand prix littéraire de la ville de Montréal. Annual award to the author of a book published the previous year in French in Montreal. The $3,000 prize was first awarded in 1965 by the Conseil des Arts de la Région de Montréal.

Grand Trunk Pacific. The western division of the GRAND TRUNK RAILWAY.

Grand Trunk Railway. An important railway company in present-day Ontario and Quebec. Chartered in 1852-3, it opened its Montreal-Toronto line in 1856 and, through expansion and amalgamation, became the key railroad in the country. National Transcontinental, its eastern division, consolidated the Moncton-to-Winnipeg line in 1915. Grand Trunk Pacific, its western division, consolidated the Winnipeg-to-Prince Rupert line in 1919. Both were heavily subsidized and taken over by the federal government, as was the Grand Trunk Railway itself in 1923. They formed the main part of the CANADIAN NATIONAL RAILWAYS.

Grandbois, Alain (1900-75). Quebec poet and traveller. Born in Saint-Casimir de Portneuf, Que., he studied law at Laval and travelled widely on an inheritance. He is highly regarded in Quebec as the leading poet of his generation and the most influential. Of his numerous books of verse and prose, only two have appeared in English: *Selected Poems* (1965) translated by Peter Miller and *Born in Quebec* (1964), a biography of Louis JOLLIET translated by Evelyn Brown.

Grande Hermine. The ship on which Jacques CARTIER made his second voyage to North America in 1535; she was used again in the voyage of 1541. A full-scale replica—commissioned by the Department of Indian Affairs and Northern Development as a Centennial project—is berthed at the junction of the St Charles and Lairet Rivers in CARTIER-BRÉBEUF PARK, Quebec City.

Grand-pères. Maple dumplings, an early Quebec speciality.

Grands Ballets Canadiens, Les. Canada's third largest ballet company began when Ludmilla CHIRIAEFF arrived in Montreal from Switzerland in 1953 and choreographed for television. By 1955 she had a semi-professional group of 16 dancers, Les Ballets Chiriaeff, which performed publicly. In 1957 it took the name Les Grands Ballets Canadiens; choreographers were Chiriaeff and Eric Hyrst, a leading dancer. The company presented *La Fille mal gardée* in 1962, staged by Edward Carter, for the first time in Canada. It toured Europe in 1969 and appeared at Sadler's Wells Theatre in London. Ferrand Nault's ballets *Carmina Burana* and *Catulli Carmina* brought the dancers fame. Its biggest success in the 1970s was the rock ballet TOMMY, created by Nault to the music of a movie rock opera of the same name. It toured Canada and the United States and had three separate runs in New York, where it was extraordinarily popular. An offshot of the company, Les Compagnons de la Danse, tours schools in the province.

Grange, The. Toronto mansion built in 1817 by D'Arcy Boulton Jr, in the style of a Georgian manor house, outside of York on 100 acres that stretched from Queen St north to Bloor. It remained in the Boulton family for nearly 100 years. In 1875 Mrs W.H. Boulton married Goldwin SMITH, for whom changes were made and a library was added. She

willed the Grange to the Art Museum of Toronto and it housed the Museum's collection from 1913 to 1918. It is part of the ART GALLERY OF ONTARIO and was restored in 1973 to represent a gentleman's house of 1835.

Grannan, Mary. See JUST MARY.

Grant, Cuthbert (1793-1854). 'Warden of the Plains'. A halfbreed clerk in the NORTH WEST COMPANY, he was the captain of a group of MÉTIS who harrassed the RED RIVER SETTLEMENT, a belligerent course that culminated in the massacre of SEVEN OAKS in 1816. He founded Grantown, a Métis settlement, and in 1828 was made Warden of the Plains by the HUDSON'S BAY COMPANY. See also Pierre FALCON.

Grant, George Munro (1835-1902). Prominent churchman and educator. Born at Albion Mines, N.S., educated at Glasgow University, and ordained in the Church of Scotland in 1860, he served as a minister in Halifax until 1877, when he became principal of QUEEN'S UNIVERSITY, Kingston, a position he held until his death. In 1899 he was elected moderator of the Presbyterian Church in Canada. In the summer of 1872 Grant accompanied Sir Sandford FLEMING, as his secretary, on an exploratory journey from the Great Lakes to the Pacific in search of a route for a trans-continental railway. His OCEAN TO OCEAN (1873), a travel classic that went through many editions, is a record of this experience.

Grant, George P. (b.1918). Social philosopher. Born in Toronto, the grandson of George Munro GRANT, he was educated at Queen's University and Oxford. He taught philosophy at Dalhousie University from 1947 to 1960 and since 1961 has been chairman of the department of religion at McMaster University. Grant's LAMENT FOR A NATION: *The Defeat of Canadian Nationalism* (1965) is perhaps the most influential Canadian book of the 1960s and 1970s and had a marked influence on the proponents of ECONOMIC NATIONALISM. In *Technology and Empire: Perspectives on North America* (1969) his perceptions of liberalism and technology led him beyond nationalism to an examination of their effects on the nature of existence.

Grant, Michael (Mike) (c.1870-1961). Hockey player. Born in Montreal, he was a speedskating champion in three divisions before captaining junior hockey teams. In 1894 he joined the Montreal Victorias, which won the STANLEY CUP several times during the decade. In the course of his senior amateur career he captained the Montreal Crystals,

Shamrocks, and Victorias, and when not participating frequently refereed matches.

Graphic Publishers Limited. 'An all-Canadian company . . . for the purpose of producing and marketing all-Canadian books by Canadian-writers'. Founded by Henry C. Miller, an Ottawa printer, in 1923, it issued a number of novels and collections of essays, including *A Search for America* (1927) by Frederick Philip GROVE, who was employed as a Graphic editor from Dec. 1929 to Oct. 1931. It sponsored a $2,500 Canadian Novel Contest in 1930, and although first prize was awarded to Raymond KNISTER for *My Star Predominant* (ultimately published by RYERSON in 1934), the novelist was unable to collect the full amount. Graphic operated the Carillon Book Club, one of whose judges was the Ottawa littérateur L.J. Burpee. Although Graphic issued distinctively designed books of some quality, the company was undercapitalized and mismanaged and went into liquidation in May 1932.

Grasslands. Non-forest area covering the southern part (about one-sixth) of the Prairie Provinces (Manitoba, Saskatchewan, and Alberta) with grasses such as spear, blue grama, June, and wheat grass, differentiated on the basis of height, the shortest being in the driest areas in south-west Saskatchewan and southern Alberta. Tree and shrub growth occurs along the northern margins in river valleys, and on the uplands where precipitation is higher. Much of this natural vegetation has been destroyed in the conversion of this region to farmland.

Grassy Narrows. An Indian reserve near Kenora in northern Ontario. In the spring of 1970 the rivers on the reservation were found to be contaminated with unacceptably high levels of mercury. Some Ojibwa who fished the rivers were found to be suffering from the Minimata Disease, named after the Japanese town where mercury poisoning was first detected in 1956.

Gravenhurst. Resort town in the Muskoka district of Ontario where Norman BETHUNE was born. Like BRACEBRIDGE, Gravenhurst is said to be named after a fictitious location in Washington Irving's two-volume work *Bracebridge Hall; or The Humorists* (1822).

Graveyard of the Atlantic. Sobriquet of SABLE ISLAND.

Gray, Gary. See Tommy AMBROSE.

Gray, George R. (1865-1938). Shot-put champion. Born in Coldwater, Ont., into a family that excelled in athletics (and that in-

cluded a cousin, Harry Gill, who in 1900 became an all-round champion athlete), Gray broke many world records in shot-putting, winning 188 first prizes in the course of 11 years in the late-nineteenth and early-twentieth centuries.

Gray, Jack (b.1927). Playwright. Born in Detroit, Mich., and educated at Queen's University and the University of Toronto, he was assistant editor of MACLEAN'S (1953-7), secretary-general of the Canadian Theatre Centre (1971-3), and is now the active head of the ACTRA Writers' Council. Among his stage plays are *Bright Sun at Midnight* (1957), about the NORMAN INCIDENT; *Chevalier Johnston* (1964), about French attempts to defend the fortress of LOUISBOURG; and *Striker Schneiderman* (1970), a satire on social action. He is married to the actress Araby Lockhart.

Gray, James H. (b.1906). Popular historian. Born in Whitemouth, Man., he worked as a journalist and then as a public-relations executive for an oil company in Calgary until his retirement. His first book, *The Winter Years* (1966), an autobiographical account of the DEPRESSION on the Prairies, established him as a popular social historian. Subsequent books include *Men Against the Desert* (1970), *The Boy from Winnipeg* (1970), *Red Lights on the Prairies* (1971), *Booze* (1972), and *The Roar of the Twenties* (1975).

Gray, John Hamilton (1812-87). A FATHER OF CONFEDERATION (P.E.I.). Born in Prince Edward Island, he was elected to the legislative assembly in 1858 and was premier of the province from 1863 to 1865. He attended the CHARLOTTETOWN and QUEBEC CONFERENCES on Confederation, which was rejected by the province until 1873.

Gray, John Hamilton (1814-89). A FATHER OF CONFEDERATION (N.B.). Born in Bermuda and educated in Nova Scotia, he was called to the bar of New Brunswick in 1837. He was elected to the legislative assembly in 1850 and attended the CHARLOTTETOWN and QUEBEC CONFERENCES as an advocate of Confederation. Elected to the House of Commons in 1867, he resigned his seat in 1872 to become a puisne judge of the Supreme Court of British Columbia.

Gray-Dort. Automobile manufactured from 1915 to 1925 by Gray-Dort Motors, Chatham, Ont. It was a quality car and some 26,000 were sold at prices ranging from $1,275 to $3,000.

Gray Report. Popular name of *Foreign Direct Investment in Canada*, a report released in May 1972 under the auspices of the Hon. Herb

Gray, Minister of National Revenue. Leaked by the CANADIAN FORUM in Dec. 1971, it analysed the extent and influence of foreign investment in Canada and urged governmental action in reviewing new foreign acquisitions and investments in the Canadian economy. Its findings and recommendations (together with those of the WATKINS REPORT [1968] and the Wahn Report [1970]) led directly to the establishment in Apr. 1974 of the FOREIGN INVESTMENT REVIEW AGENCY.

Grayling. An Arctic fish of the trout family.

GRC. Initials of Gendarmerie royale du Canada, the French name for the ROYAL CANADIAN MOUNTED POLICE.

Grealis, Walt (b.1929). Music editor. Born in Vancouver and a former RCMP constable, he founded RPM WEEKLY, the Canadian recording industry's only important trade paper, in 1964. His weekly lists of important releases have had a great influence on the choice of records played by radio stations. In 1969 he established the JUNO Awards, which did much to bring the star system to the music business in Canada.

Great Bear Lake. The largest lake lying entirely within Canada. It is 12,096 sq. mi. in area and lies in the northwestern part of the Northwest Territories. It is connected to nearby Mackenzie R. through the marshes and channel of the Great Bear R. See also PORT RADIUM.

Great Clay Belt of Northern Ontario. A fairly flat plain formed by clays and silts deposited under glacial lakes Barlow and Ojibway. A marginal farming area around the town of Cochrane, it is strikingly different in its landscape from the surrounding Canadian Shield.

Great Coalition. A union government of the PROVINCE OF CANADA formed in 1864 to secure CONFEDERATION, which came about in 1867. The coalition joined the Conservatives under John A. MACDONALD and George-Étienne CARTIER and the Clear GRITS under George BROWN.

Great Company, The. A reference to the HUDSON'S BAY COMPANY.

Great Confederacy. See IROQUOIS.

Great Debate, The. A 60-minute weekly television series. Pierre BERTON moderates a debate on an issue of the day between two leading personalities in the presence of an audience that votes for or against the resolution. Created by My Country Productions,

Inc., for the GLOBAL TELEVISION NETWORK and first broadcast in Jan. 1974, the show has since been nationally syndicated. The producer is Elsa FRANKLIN.

Great Divide. See CONTINENTAL DIVIDE.

Great Divide. The best-known canvas by Harold TOWN, painted in 1966. A landscape of black-centred golden discs tumbles into a dark valley that is cut by a highly controlled irregular white line whose nervous energy divides the canvas into two shimmering fields. The compulsive quality of the painting is seized and held in check by two side-rows of angled white bars. (AGO)

Great Intendant. See Jean TALON.

Great Island, The. Unofficial motto of NEWFOUNDLAND.

Great Lakes. The five fresh-water lakes in the central part of North America between Canada and the United States (the international boundary passes approximately through the centre of all of them except Lake Michigan). The Great Lakes, with a combined area of about 95,000 sq. mi., are the largest group of lakes in the world. In order of size they are Lake Superior, Lake Michigan, Lake Huron, Lake Erie, and Lake Ontario. They were first called 'these great lakes' by Pierre-Esprit RADISSON in 1665.

Great Lakes—St Lawrence Forest Region. Mixed forest area. It extends inland from the edges of the GREAT LAKES and the ST LAWRENCE RIVER. Species found throughout are eastern white pine, red pine, eastern hemlock, yellow birch, maple, oak, and basswood. Much of this forest has been cut down over the past 300 years as the land was converted to agricultural uses.

Great Lakes—St Lawrence Plain. One of the five principal GEOGRAPHICAL REGIONS of Canada, this area is the economic heartland of Canada. Most of the country's major manufacturers, financial institutions, and other service industries are concentrated in this area in cities stretching along the GREAT LAKES and the ST LAWRENCE RIVER from Windsor in the west to Quebec City in the east, and dominated by the cities of Toronto and Montreal. Underlain by sedimentary rocks and covered with thick glacial deposits, this region is, next to the Prairie Provinces, the second most important agricultural region in Canada.

Great Lone Land, The. William Francis BUTLER's classic book on the Northwest, subtitled *A Narrative of Travel and Adventure in the*

North-West of America, published in 1872. After being involved in the RED RIVER REBELLION in 1870 as a British intelligence officer, Butler was sent to the Saskatchewan R. to report on HUDSON'S BAY COMPANY posts there. The book grew out of the experience of his long winter journey from FORT GARRY.

Great Ministry, The. See Robert BALDWIN.

Great Ring of Canada, The. A mammoth crystal and steel sculpture, a Centennial gift 'from the people of the United States of America for the People of Canada on the Centenary of Canada's Nationhood'. It was designed by Donald Pollard of Steuben Glass and consists of crystal plaques, supported by rhodium-plated steel rods, arranged in two rings and surmounted by a fountain-like structure of crystal balls. On the lower ring a dozen plaques are engraved with the crests of the provinces and territories; on the upper ring, four plaques are engraved with maple leafs and other federal motifs. The imposing sculpture has been displayed across Canada.

Great Shadow, The. Early Canadian feature film warning of the evils of Bolshevism. It was made by Adanac Producing Company and released by Lewis Selznick in 1920. Subsidized by the CPR, it was the first film produced at Trenton, Ont., and was a critical and financial success. It starred Tyrone Power Sr. 5 reels, b & w.

Great Slave Lake. The second-largest lake lying entirely within Canada. A link in the Mackenzie R. system situated in the south-central Northwest Territories, it covers an area of 11,170 sq. mi. It was named after the SLAVE Indians.

Great War. See FIRST WORLD WAR.

Great white land. A reference to the FAR NORTH. Robert SERVICE used the phrase in his novel *Trail of '98* (1910).

Green Chamber. Traditional name for the HOUSE OF COMMONS, derived from the colour of the carpeting and other appointments.

Green Gables. See ANNE OF GREEN GABLES.

Green paper. Document prepared by the government and tabled in the HOUSE OF COMMONS. Its purpose is to encourage discussion of a particular subject, not to present policy proposals. The Green Paper on Immigration Policy was tabled by Robert K. Andras, Minister of Manpower and Immigration, on 3 Feb. 1975. See also WHITE PAPER.

Greene, Lorne (b.1915). Actor. Born in Ottawa, as chief news announcer for CBC Radio (1939-42) he earned the sobriquet 'The Voice of Doom' for his portentous delivery of war news. He founded the ACADEMY OF RADIO ARTS and co-founded the JUPITER THEATRE. As an actor he has appeared in the STRATFORD FESTIVAL in *Julius Caesar* (1955), but his greatest acting success came with the role of Ben Cartwright—the *pater familias* of the Ponderosa Ranch—on NBC-TV's 'Bonanza', the most popular weekly television program of all time, which lasted from 12 Sept. 1959 to 23 Jan. 1972. He narrated CBC-TV's series TO THE WILD COUNTRY, which began on 18 Nov. 1973.

Greene, Nancy (b.1944). Champion skier. Born in Rossland, B.C., she won the Canadian junior skiing championship at the age of 15. In 1967 she became the world's champion female skier and at the 1968 Winter Olympics in Grenoble, France, she won a gold and a silver medal. In both 1967 and 1968 she was voted 'Canada's outstanding female athlete of the year'. She then retired from competition to serve on the Task Force on Sport.

Greenpeace Foundation. Radical organization founded in Vancouver to protest extreme depredations of the environment, notably nuclear testing and the slaughter of whales. The name *Greenpeace* was chosen by David McTaggart and has been applied to a series of vessels employed in its well-publicized encounters. *Greenpeace I* approached Amchitka Island in the Aleutian chain and forced the American government to delay the detonation of a 5.2-megaton hydrogen bomb there. *Greenpeace II* failed to reach the same site in time to stop the rescheduled blast, the largest underground explosion to date, which took place on 6 Nov. 1971. *Greenpeace III* made a gallant attempt to sail into the French nuclear testing zone around Mururoa Atoll in the South Pacific, but was rammed by a French warship on 30 June 1972 and the explosion took place as scheduled. The following year *Greenpeace IV* was illegally boarded by French sailors in the same vicinity on 15 Aug., and McTaggart was beaten in the encounter. He is seeking redress through the French courts. *Greenpeace V* was dubbed 'Project Ahab' because it sought to bring about a moratorium on whaling. It intercepted Soviet whaling vessels off the California coast—the first encounter was on 27 June 1975—to publicize the slaughter of this endangered mammal. In Mar. 1976, the Greenpeace Foundation turned its attention to the SEAL HUNT and, with helicopters, attempted to obstruct the annual slaughter of harp seals in Newfoundland.

Greenwich, Sonny (b.1936). Jazz guitarist. This Toronto-born, Montreal-based performer received critical acclaim and recognition in New York in 1967-9 for his wildly improvisational guitar style. He has since played with Miles Davis, Fred Stone, Don Thompson, and others.

Grenfell, Sir Wilfred (1865-1940). Medical missionary. Born in Parkgate, Eng., he studied at the London Hospital and was licensed to practise medicine in 1886. Learning that resident Labrador fishermen were half-starved and lacking in medical assistance, he established the first of many small hospitals—at Battle Harbour, on the eastern tip of Labrador—in 1893. Hospitals and nursing stations were soon opened along the Labrador and Newfoundland coasts, and Grenfell visited them annually until he retired from active missionary work in 1935 to spend his last five years lecturing to raise funds for the International Grenfell Foundation. He wrote many books, including *Adrift on an Ice-pan* (1909), *A Labrador Doctor* (1919), and *Forty Years for Labrador* (1932).

Greve, Felix Paul. See Frederick Philip GROVE.

Grey, Earle. See EARLE GREY AWARD.

Grey, Lord (1851-1917). GOVERNOR GENERAL of Canada from 1904 to 1911.

Grey Cup. Highly coveted trophy awarded annually to the best professional football team in eastern or western Canada. The silver cup was donated by the governor general, Lord GREY, in 1909 and has has been a national challenge cup since 1921. Champion teams from eastern and western Canada have competed for the trophy in the GREY CUP GAME since 1954. At a special ceremony in Vancouver in 1966 the CANADIAN FOOTBALL LEAGUE became the custodian of the cup. The original trophy (worth $48 in 1909) is on permanent display at the Canadian Football HALL OF FAME in Hamilton, Ont. A replica (which cost $350) resides with the winning team for a year. A list of winners follows.

1909	University of Toronto
1910	University of Toronto
1911	University of Toronto
1912	Hamilton Alerts
1913	Hamilton Alerts
1914	Toronto Argonauts
1915	Hamilton Tigers
1916	No games to 1920
1920	University of Toronto
1921	Toronto Argonauts
1922	Queen's University
1923	Queen's University
1924	Queen's University
1925	Ottawa Senators
1926	Ottawa Senators
1927	Toronto Balmy Beach
1928	Hamilton Tigers
1929	Hamilton Tigers
1930	Toronto Balmy Beach
1931	Montreal Winged Wheelers
1932	Hamilton Tigers
1933	Toronto Argonauts
1934	Sarnia Imperials
1935	The Winnipegs
1936	Sarnia Imperials
1937	Toronto Argonauts
1938	Toronto Argonauts
1939	Winnipeg Blue Bombers
1940	Ottawa Rough Riders
1941	Winnipeg Blue Bombers
1942	Toronto RCAF Hurricanes
1943	Hamilton Flying Wildcats
1944	Montreal Donnacona Navy
1945	Toronto Argonauts
1946	Toronto Argonauts
1947	Toronto Argonauts
1948	Calgary Stampeders
1949	Montreal Alouettes
1950	Toronto Argonauts
1951	Ottawa Rough Riders
1952	Toronto Argonauts
1953	Hamilton Tiger-Cats
1954	Edmonton Eskimos
1955	Edmonton Eskimos
1956	Edmonton Eskimos
1957	Hamilton Tiger-Cats
1958	Winnipeg Blue Bombers
1959	Winnipeg Blue Bombers
1960	Ottawa Rough Riders
1961	Winnipeg Blue Bombers
1962	Winnipeg Blue Bombers
1963	Hamilton Tiger-Cats
1964	British Columbia Lions
1965	Hamilton Tiger-Cats
1966	Saskatchewan Roughriders
1967	Hamilton Tiger-Cats
1968	Ottawa Rough Riders
1969	Ottawa Rough Riders
1970	Montreal Alouettes
1971	Calgary Stampeders
1972	Hamilton Tiger-Cats
1973	Ottawa Rough Riders
1974	Montreal Alouettes
1975	Edmonton Eskimos

Grey Cup Game. Final championship game in the series of east-west football playoffs organized by the CANADIAN FOOTBALL LEAGUE. The game that culminates Grey Cup Week is held during the last week of November or the first week of December and the winning team is awarded the Grey Cup. Broadcast by CBC Radio since 1933, it is now televised. See GREY CUP for a list of winners.

Grey Nuns. A Catholic congregation of nuns founded in Montreal by Mère d'YOUVILLE in 1755. They wear a grey habit and are dedicated to social service.

Grey Owl (1888-1938). Naturalist and writer. Grey Owl is the assumed name of George Stansfeld Belaney, an Englishman born and educated in Hastings, Eng., who immigrated to Canada in 1903 and became a guide and trapper in northern Ontario. He posed as a half-breed and gradually passed for an Ojibwa, taking Anahareo as his common-law wife in 1925. Appointed an honorary ranger in Saskatchewan in 1931, Grey Owl and Anahareo lived in Prince Albert National Park, where Grey Owl wrote his popular studies of the bush and its animal life: *The Men of the Last Frontier* (1931), PILGRIMS OF THE WILD (1934), *The Adventures of Sajo and Her Beaver People* (1935), *Tales of an Empty Cabin* (1936), and *The Tree* (1937). *A Book of Grey Owl: Pages from the Writings of Wa-Sha-Quon-Asin* (1941), edited by E.E. Reynolds, appeared posthumously. Two lecture tours, arranged by his British publisher Lovat DICKSON, were promotional and theatrical successes. It was only after Grey Owl's death that his background as an Englishman was revealed. The most recent biographies are *Devil in Deerskins* (1972) by Anahareo and *Wilderness Man* (1973) by Lovat Dickson.

Grierson, John (1898-1972). First commissioner of the NATIONAL FILM BOARD. Born in Kilmarnock, Scot., and educated at the Universities of Glasgow and Chicago, he coined the word 'documentary' in 1926 to describe a non-dramatic film, appropriating the word *documentaire*, used in French to describe travel films. He later characterized the documentary mode as 'the creative treatment of actuality'. The Canadian government, anxious to establish a centre for the production of propaganda films prior to the impending war, appointed Grierson the first commissioner of the newly created National Film Board in 1939. He also served as head of the War Information Board from 1943 to 1945, when he resigned from both positions, having seen the NFB staff of six grow to 800 and leaving it an enduring stylistic legacy. In 1969-70 he taught film-making at McGill and Carleton Universities, where he was treated as the 'father of documentary'. His writings were collected by H. Forsyth Hardy in *Grierson on Documentary* (1956, 1966). David Bairstow of the NFB produced *Grierson* in 1973, a tribute to the man and his method. (57 min., 50 sec.; colour)

Griffin, J.D.M. See MENTAL HEALTH CANADA.

Griffis, S.S. (Si) (1883-1950). Outstanding athlete. He excelled in rowing, golf, and bowling, but especially in professional hockey. He played on two STANLEY CUP championship teams in Kenora and Vancouver. He was elected to the Hockey HALL OF FAME in 1950.

Griffon. A barque built by LA SALLE in the Niagara R., above the falls, in 1679. The first sailing vessel ever built above Lake Ontario, she made one trip to the mouth of present-day Green Bay, Wisc., started back on 18 Sept. 1679, and was never seen again. Wreckage found at several widely separated locations has been claimed to be that of the *Griffon*.

Grignon, Claude-Henri. See *Un* HOMME ET SON PÉCHÉ.

Grip. A humorous weekly tabloid published in Toronto from 24 May 1873 to 29 Dec. 1894 and named after the raven in Dickens's *Barnaby Rudge*. It was founded, edited, and illustrated by J.W. BENGOUGH until two years before its demise. It poked fun at the dignitaries, especially political, of the day, but is mainly remembered for Bengough's superb cartoons, which were collected in *Caricature History of Canadian Politics* (1886).

Grits. A reference to the LIBERAL PARTY. The advanced wing of the reform party in Canada West (Ontario) came to be called the Clear Grit Party—a phrase coined by Peter Perry ('We want only men of clear grit') and popularized by George BROWN in the Toronto *Globe* on 13 Dec. 1849. The Liberals are sometimes called Grits today, as the Conservatives are called TORIES. In 1956 Blair FRASER coined the word 'Gritterdämmerung', or Twilight of the Grits.

Grizzly bear. One of three groups of bears found in Canada, widely distributed in the mountain and coastal regions of British Columbia and in the Yukon Territory. It is typically brownish yellow in colour, weighs up to 1,103 lb., and hibernates in the winter. Powerful and largely carnivorous, it is noted for its ferocity. See also BLACK BEAR, POLAR BEAR.

Gros Morne National Park. Established in 1970 on the western coast of Newfoundland northwest of Corner Brook, it covers 750 sq. mi. It includes a spectacular section of the Long Range Mountains, which rise dramatically from the low coastal plain. The name means 'big hill'.

Groseilliers, Médard Chouart, sieur des (1618-96?). Explorer and coureur de bois, one

Groseilliers

of the originators of the HUDSON'S BAY COMPANY. He arrived in Canada in 1641 and made two journeys to the fur-trading regions in the West: to Lake Michigan and, in 1659-60, with his brother-in-law RADISSON, to Lake Superior. On their return from this voyage, after their furs were seized and they were fined (and Groseilliers was imprisoned), they left the colony. They were in England in 1665 and were engaged three years later by a group of merchants, the nucleus of the Hudson's Bay Company, to make a voyage to the Bay. They journeyed there several times until 1675, when they deserted to France. In 1682 they went to Hudson Bay for France, establishing Fort Bourbon on the Hayes R. While Radisson went back to the HBC after this expedition, Groseilliers spent the rest of his life in Quebec. See also RADISHES AND GOOSEBERRIES.

Groulx, Gilles (b.1931). Quebec film director. Born in Montreal, he worked as a newsreel editor before joining RADIO-CANADA and then the NATIONAL FILM BOARD in 1956. He made *Les Raquetteurs* (with Michel BRAULT, 1958), a documentary that marked the beginning of Quebec production at the NFB. He is best known for his first feature, *Le CHAT DANS LE SAC* (1964), which celebrated the political and cultural awakening of a young Québécois. Other features include *Où êtes-vous donc?* (1969), *Entre tu et vous* (1969), and *Vingt-quatre heures ou plus* (1972), which the NFB banned because of its radical political and social message.

Groulx, Lionel-Adolphe (1878-1967). Quebec historian and nationalist. Born in Chenaux, Que., he was ordained a priest in 1903. He was an influential professor of Canadian history at the Université de Montréal and founded in 1920 the ACTION FRANÇAISE, a nationalistic movement. His first interest was to make French Canadians aware of their cultural past to prevent their assimilation by the English; he often proclaimed the slogan *Notre maître le passé* ('Our master the past'). Of his many books, the best known are the novel *L'Appel de la race* (1922), about the difficulties of intermarriage between French- and English-speaking Canadians, and *Si Dollard revient* (1919), which grew out of his attempt to make DOLLARD DES ORMEAUX the symbol of the willingness of French Canadians to fight to the last for their culture.

Groundhog Day. 2 Feb. It is a North American tradition that the groundhog emerges from his burrow on this day to determine the length of time remaining until spring. If the groundhog sees its shadow, there remain six weeks of hard winter; if not, mild weather lies ahead.

Group of Seven. Influential art movement that found inspiration in northern-Ontario landscapes—notably Algonquin Park, Georgian Bay, Algoma, and the North Shore of Lake Superior—to represent the unique character of Canada. A group of like-minded painters began to form in 1911 after a show of sketches by J.E.H. MacDONALD at the Arts and Letters Club, Toronto. He found a champion in another artist, Lawren HARRIS, with whom he shared the impact of a show of Scandinavian painting in Buffalo (Jan. 1913) that revealed a fresh, direct way of painting the North. They attracted other artists to them, all of whom worked as designers at Grip Limited: Tom THOMSON, Frank CARMICHAEL, Frank JOHNSTON, and Arthur LISMER. Early in 1914 the new STUDIO BUILDING formed a working and living centre for Harris (who was part-owner), MacDonald, Thomson, and A.Y. JACKSON. The war then intervened. The Group was not officially formed until Feb. or Mar. 1920. The first exhibition was in the Art Gallery of Toronto in May 1920 and the last was held there in Dec. 1931. The original seven members were Carmichael, Harris, Jackson, Johnston, Lismer, MacDonald, and F.H. VARLEY. Tom Thomson, whose tragic death in 1917 precluded his membership, was an inspiration to the Group. Later additions were A.J. CASSON (1926), Edwin HOLGATE (1930), and LeMoine FITZ GERALD (1932). A gallery dedicated to the Group—the McMICHAEL CANADIAN COLLECTION in Kleinburg, Ont.—was formally opened on 8 July 1966. In 1970 the National Gallery of Canada mounted a major exhibition with an extensive and scholarly catalogue, *Le Group des Sept/The Group of Seven*, by Dennis Reid. *The Group of Seven* (1970) by Peter Mellen is another useful reference.

Grouse Mountain. A 3,974-ft mountain in North Vancouver. Its summit, which can be reached by Canada's largest aerial tramway, offers a commanding view of Vancouver and the surrounding coastal area.

Grove, Frederick Philip (1879-1948). Novelist and short-story writer. Born Felix Paul Greve in Radomno on the Polish-Prussian border, he was a writer and translator in Germany before coming to North America in 1909-10. These facts were gleaned from the research of Douglas O. Spettigue and presented in his revisionist biographical inquiry, *FPG: The European Years* (1973), which corrects the autobiographical fabrications in Grove's IN SEARCH OF MYSELF (1946), in which he claimed he was born of Swedish parents

222

in Russia in 1871 and that he came to North America in 1892. Grove began teaching school in Manitoba in 1912 and in 1929 moved to Ottawa, where he was an editor of GRAPHIC PRESS; he moved again after a year to a farm north of Simcoe, Ont., where he died. He is a towering figure among early modern Canadian novelists, not because his novels were great but because of their ambitious creative aims and the cumulative significance of his laborious but frequently compelling and subtle explorations of universal themes and human relationships. His first two books, OVER PRAIRIE TRAILS (1922) and *The Turn of the Year* (1923), are nature essays. His novels are SETTLERS OF THE MARSH (1925), A SEARCH FOR AMERICA: *The Odyssey of an Immigrant* (1927), *Our Daily Bread* (1928), *The Yoke of Life* (1930), *Fruits of the Earth* (1933), *Two Generations: A Story of Present Day Ontario* (1939), *The Master of the Mill* (1944), and *Consider Her Ways* (1947), a fantasy about ants that satirizes human society. *It Needs to be Said* (1929) is a collection of essays based on speeches. Desmond PACEY has edited a collection of previously unpublished stories, *Tales from the Margin* (1971), and *The Letters* (1976).

Grundy. See SOLOMON GRUNDY.

Grunt. A steamed fruit or berry pudding made in the Maritime provinces.

GTPR. Initials of the Grand Trunk Pacific Railway, now CANADIAN NATIONAL RAILWAYS.

GTR. Initials of the GRAND TRUNK RAILWAY, now CANADIAN NATIONAL RAILWAYS.

GTWR. Initials of the Grand Trunk Western Railroad, now CANADIAN NATIONAL RAILWAYS.

Guaranteed Income Supplement. A federal program allowing basic old-age payments to be supplemented, upon application and proof of need. See also OLD AGE SECURITY PENSION.

Guelph Spring Festival. Classical music festival. Founded in 1968 by Dr Murdo Mackinnon, Dean of Arts at the University of Guelph, who wanted to revive Edward JOHNSON's idea of a musical festival in his native city, it takes place in April-May and has become the leading classical music festival in the country. It stresses innovation and commissions original works from Canadian composers each year. The director of music is Nicholas Goldschmidt.

Guerre, Yes Sir!, La. The first book of a trilogy by Roch CARRIER. Published in French in 1968 and in English in 1970, it is an account of personal and national tensions in a small Quebec village in the early years of the Second World War. It revolves around the funeral wake of Corriveau, a young soldier who died in action and whose body has been brought home for burial. A dramatic version was staged in both French and English in 1972. The other books of the trilogy, in their English titles, are *Floralie, Where Are You?* (1971) and *Is It the Sun, Philibert?* (1972). All three were translated by Sheila FISCHMAN.

Guess Who, The. The first Canadian rock group to become an international success. This 'supergroup' was formed in Winnipeg where it was known as Chad Allan and the Expressions. As The Guess Who from 1962 to 1975, the group included Gary Peterson, Kurt Winter, Don McDougall, Randy BACHMAN, Chad Allan, Burton Cummings, and Jim Kale. It had one major hit after another, including 'Shakin' All Over' (1964) and 'American Woman' (1969). The latter was the first Canadian single to hit the number-one spot on the American hit-parade charts.

Guest, John Schofield (Jack) (b.1906). Amateur sculling champion. At the age of 23 the Montreal-born oarsman, representing the Don Rowing Club, won the Diamond Sculls at Henley, Eng., the greatest honour in amateur sculling. He was president of the Canadian Association of Amateur Oarsmen and managed two Canadian rowing teams at British Empire Games in 1962 and 1966.

Guèvremont, Germaine (b.1896). Quebec novelist. Born in Saint-Jérôme, Que., she settled in Montreal in 1935 and worked as a journalist. She is principally known for two novels that portray the demise of *habitant* life: *Le Survenant* (1945) and its sequel *Marie-Didace* (1947), which were translated together as *The Outlander* (1950) by Eric Sutton.

Guibord incident. A *cause célèbre* in Quebec involving the Church and the courts. Joseph Guibord was a member of the INSTITUT CANADIEN and the printer of its *Annuaire* when he died suddenly on 18 Nov. 1869. Since the Institut was under a papal ban and members were automatically excommunicated, Guibord was refused burial in consecrated ground by Bishop Bourget. His widow had recourse to the courts and, six years later, on 16 Nov. 1875, Guibord's body was reburied under military escort—in ground declared profane by the bishop.

Gulf Islands. A group of more than 100 islands in the Strait of Georgia between Vancouver Island and the British Columbia mainland. The name derives from the fact that the strait was originally called the Gulf of Georgia. The lovely islands are the northern extension of an archipelago known as the San Juan Islands, which belong to the State of Washington.

Gulf of St Lawrence. Canada's eastern inland sea, forming the mouth of the St Lawrence R. An extension of the Atlantic Ocean bordered by Quebec, the Maritimes, and Newfoundland, much of it has a depth greater than that of the Continental Shelf.

Gumbo. Term applied to prairie soils that become very sticky when saturated, particularly in the spring.

Gunny sack parade. Epithetical description of unemployed married men who lined up with bags (or gunny sacks) to receive their quota of food and shelter-and-food tokens. This was a common sight in Vancouver during the DEPRESSION.

Gurik, Robert (b.1932). Quebec playwright. Born in France of Hungarian parents, he settled in Montreal in 1951 and trained as an engineer. He is a prolific dramatist who became well known with his *Hamlet, Prince du Québec* (1968), an allegorical play, based on Shakespeare's drama, propagandizing Quebec independence. The four Gurik plays available in English, with their translators' names, are *The Hanged Man* (1972), Philip London and Laurence R. Bérard; *Api 2967* (1974), Marc F. Gélinas; *The Trial of Jean-Baptiste M.* (1974), Allan Van Meer; and *Hearts* (1976), Marc F. Gélinas.

Gustafson, Ralph (b.1909). Poet and anthologist. Born near Sherbrooke, Que., and educated at Bishop's College and Oxford, he lived in New York for many years and now teaches in the English department at Bishop's University, Lennoxville, Que. His career as a highly intellectual, often metaphysical poet has covered 40 years and produced numerous collections, which are represented in *Selected Poems* (1972). For Penguin Books he has edited *Anthology of Canadian Poetry* (1942), *Canadian Accent* (1944), and *The Penguin Book of Canadian Verse* (1958; rev. 1967; rev. 1975).

Gutenberg Galaxy, The. A study of the communications media by Marshall McLUHAN published in 1964. It analyses the pre-print oral/aural culture, its destruction by Gutenberg's invention of moveable type, and the change in values produced by the print culture that resulted.

Guthrie, Tyrone (1900-71). Irish director. Born in Tunbridge Wells, Eng., he was a director of the Old Vic-Sadler's Wells from 1933 to 1945. He made two contributions to Canadian theatre. He produced the important ROMANCE OF CANADA series for radio in 1931 and was the guiding spirit and first artistic director of the STRATFORD FESTIVAL (1953-5). He then became the founder and director of the Tyrone Guthrie Theatre, Minneapolis, Minn.

Guttman, Irving (b.1928). Opera director. Born in Chatham, Ont., he was educated in Montreal and at the Royal Conservatory of Music, Toronto. After being assistant to Herman GEIGER-TOREL at the Canadian Opera Company from 1949 to 1954, he was guest director at the Montreal Festival from 1953 to 1962 and went on to direct widely in Canada and the United States, including six productions for the Canadian Opera Company. He was founder of the Vancouver Opera Association and artistic director from 1960 to 1973.

Guy, Ray (b.1939). Journalist and author. Born at Come By Chance, Placentia Bay, Nfld, and educated at Memorial University and the Ryerson Polytechnical Institute, he has written for the ST. JOHN'S EVENING TELEGRAM since 1963, latterly as a columnist. Guy's humorous essays, collected in *You May Know Them as Sea Urchins, Ma'am* (1975), catch the quirky spirit of life on 'the Great Island' in an individualistic fashion.

Gwynne, Horace (Lefty) (b.1913). Champion boxer. Toronto born and a retired jockey, he won the Canadian bantamweight title in 1932. Then he represented Canada at the 1932 Olympics in Los Angeles, where he won the gold medal in his class.

Gyles, John (c.1680-1755). Captive of the Indians. At the age of nine he was captured at Pemaquid (Maine) by Malecite Indians and taken to ACADIA (near Woodstock, N.B.), where he lived as a slave for six years. His graphic account of this experience was published many years later as *Memoirs of Odd Adventures, Strange Deliverances, etc. in the Captivity of John Gyles Esq.* (1736).

Gypsy Moth. A small, light aircraft, suitable as a trainer for flying clubs. Designed in Britain, it was assembled by DE HAVILLAND in Canada in 1928. It was the forerunner of the TIGER MOTH.

Gzowski, Peter (b.1934). Broadcaster and journalist. Toronto-born and Galt-raised, the great-grandson of Sir Casimir Gzowski, he became at 26 the youngest managing editor of MACLEAN'S. The 'boy wonder of Canadian journalism' went on to be the last editor of the STAR WEEKLY in 1969. He then broke into broadcasting and hosted the popular CBC Radio program THIS COUNTRY IN THE MORNING from 1971 to 1974. CBC-TV introduced his late-night talk-and-variety show, 'Ninety Minutes Live', nationally in the fall of 1976.

H

Habakkuk. A top-secret research project carried out in Canada during the Second World War. The object was to produce a man-made iceberg with a flat top 2,000 ft long and 300 ft wide and anchor it in the middle of the Atlantic Ocean to make a staging stop for airplanes. During the winter of 1942-3 small-scale ice stations were built on Lake Louise, Alta. The project, which proved expensive and impracticable, was named after the apocryphal book of the Bible, which includes the passage: 'For I will work a work in your days which ye will not believe though it be told you.'

Habitant. French word for 'inhabitant'. It was used in NEW FRANCE for a peasant or farmer who worked land owned by a seigneur. See also SEIGNEURIAL TENURE.

Habitant and Other French Canadian Poems, The. A collection of poetry by W.H. DRUMMOND published in 1897. Written in the broken English speech of French-Canadian lumbermen, canoemen, and backwoods farmers, these humorous, affectionate poems were once very popular and widely recited, but came to be resented, not surprisingly, by French Canadians.

Habitat. A multi-level 155-unit apartment complex on Cité du Havre in MONTREAL. One of the star attractions of EXPO 67, it earned a world-wide reputation for its Israeli-born, McGill-educated architect, Moshe SAFDIE. Minutes away from downtown Montreal, with a magnificent view of the harbour, it features pre-cast modular buildings for on-site assembly.

Habitat. A magazine founded in 1958 and published six times a year by CENTRAL MORTGAGE AND HOUSING CORPORATION. Articles, written in either English or French, are devoted to the general themes of housing and the environment.

Habitation. French word meaning 'residence' or 'dwelling'. It is associated with Samuel de CHAMPLAIN, who described the *habitation* that was built at PORT ROYAL in 1605 and in 1608 at Quebec, where three buildings were joined by a second-floor gallery that was part of a continuous wall. A moat, crossed by a drawbridge and a palisade, surrounded this miniature fortress, which was erected at the base of CAPE DIAMOND.

Habs. Abbreviation of *Habitants*—a sportswriter's nickname for the MONTREAL CANADIENS.

Hackmatack. Alternative name used in the Maritime provinces for the TAMARACK.

Haddad, Claire. Fashion designer. Born in Toronto and of Lebanese descent, she studied at the Ontario College of Art and at the Fashion Academy in New York before marrying Albert A. Haddad in 1944. In 1964 they established the Toronto firm of Claire Haddad Limited to design and manufacture lingerie and leisure wear. Claire Haddad was the first Canadian designer to break into the American and European markets, which she did with stylish loungewear designs that aimed to be 'functional, versatile and, above all, attractive'.

Hagen, Betty-Jean (b.1930). Violinist. Born in Edmonton, Alta, she trained in Calgary, Toronto, and New York, and was first violinist with the Edmonton Philharmonic from 1945 to 1949. She made her New York début in Town Hall in 1950 and then began appearing as a soloist with major orchestras—including the New York Philharmonic, London Philharmonic, the Concertgebouw in Amsterdam—and made annual tours of Canada, the U.S.A., and Europe. She won the Leventritt Foundation Award, New York, in 1955.

Hahn, Emanuel Otto (1881-1957). Sculptor and teacher. Born in Germany, he came to Canada with his parents in 1888 and studied at the Central Ontario School of Art and Design. In 1910 he began to teach sculpture at the ONTARIO COLLEGE OF ART and became head of the department in 1922. In 1926 he married Elizabeth Wyn WOOD. His realistic commemorative sculptures are well known in the Toronto area—for example, the statues of Ned HANLAN (1926) and Sir Adam Beck (1934)—but he also designed coins, including the 1935 silver dollar, and medals, and a marble portrait bust of his wife in the National Gallery of Canada. He was the first president of the Sculptors Society of Canada in 1928.

Haida. A linguistic group of Indians who occupy the QUEEN CHARLOTTE ISLANDS. In historic times they built huge cedar dug-out canoes—some holding as many as 50 people. They are also well known for their ARGILLITE carvings and TOTEM POLES. Their population in 1970 was 1,367.

Haida. A well-known Second World War destroyer. A member of the Tribal Class, designed for an offensive rather than a defensive role, she was commissioned into the ROYAL CANADIAN NAVY on 30 Aug. 1943. She served on Russian convoys in 1944 and won fame later that year in a series of night actions in the English Channel. After the war she served the NATO force and did a tour of duty in Korean waters. 'Paid off' on 11 Oct. 1963, the *Haida* was acquired by a citizens' group, restored to her former state, and exhibited in Toronto Harbour. Since 1970 she has been owned by the Ontario government and berthed at ONTARIO PLACE, where a visit to the *Haida* is one of the attractions.

Haig-Brown, Roderick (b.1908). Author. Born in Lancing, Eng., and educated at Charterhouse School, Surrey, he worked on the Pacific Coast as a logger, trapper, guide, fisherman, and farmer in British Columbia from 1926 to 1929. He is an accomplished nature writer many of whose books were written while he was magistrate and judge of the family and children's court at Campbell River, B.C. Some of his books on rivers, fish, and fishing are *Silver: The Life of an Atlantic Salmon* (1931), *Return to the River* (1941), *A River Never Sleeps* (1946), *Measure of the Year* (1950), *The Living Land* (1961), *Fisherman's Spring* (1951), *Fisherman's Winter* (1954), *Fisherman's Summer* (1959), and *Fisherman's Fall* (1964). He has written several fine children's books, notably *Starbuck Valley Winter* (1943), *Saltwater Summer* (1948), and *The Whale People* (1962).

Hailey, Arthur (b.1920). Popular novelist. Born in Lutton, Eng., and now a resident of Lyford Cay, New Providence, Bahamas, he came to Canada in 1947 and worked in

Toronto as an editor for MACLEAN-HUNTER (1947-53). His first success was *Flight into Danger*, a 60-minute teleplay shown by CBC-TV on GM PRESENTS on 3 Apr. 1956. The suspense drama launched his career as a popular writer who combines fact and fiction in such a way that critics call the finished result 'faction'. His novels are *Flight into Danger* (1958); *The Final Diagnosis* (1959); *In High Places* (1962), the only one that has a specific Canadian setting; *Hotel* (1965); *Airport* (1968); *Wheels* (1971); and *The Money-Changers* (1975). He also wrote *Close-Up: On Writing for Television* (1960).

Haileybury Fire. A number of small forest fires that, fanned by strong winds, united and all but gutted the town of Haileybury in northern Ontario on 4 Oct. 1922, forcing many of the inhabitants to take refuge in Lake Timiskaming.

Haisla. See WAKASHAN.

Half-breed. A person of mixed Indian and European ancestry. The French equivalent is MÉTIS.

Half-section. In western Canada, 320 acres of land. (A SECTION is 640 acres.)

Haliburton, Thomas Chandler (1796-1865). Humorist. Born in Windsor, N.S., he was educated at King's College and called to the bar in 1820. He practised law in Annapolis, which he represented in the House of Assembly (1826-9), served as a judge of the provincial Supreme Court (1841-56), then settled in England, where he was elected to the British House of Commons (1859-65). In his first work, *A General Description of Nova Scotia* (1829), his sympathetic treatment of the ACADIANS influenced Longfellow's poem *Evangeline* (1847). As a satirist—the creator of the famous comic character SAM SLICK—'Judge Haliburton' attracted a large Anglo-American readership. Slick, a loquacious Yankee clock pedlar, travels Nova Scotia selling his wares and making pithy, homespun comments about human nature in *The Clockmaker: The Sayings and Doings of Sam Slick of Slickville*, three volumes of which appeared in 1836, 1838, and 1840. He is the principal character in *The Attaché; or, Sam Slick in England* (1843-4), *Sam Slick's Wise Saws and Modern Instances* (1853), and *Nature and Human Nature* (1853). Haliburton wrote a number of other books, including *The Old Judge* (1849), and edited the three-volume anthology, *Traits of American Humour by Native Authors* (1852).

Haliburton County. Village and county in the resort area of Ontario, named in 1875 in honour of Thomas Chandler HALIBURTON, the eminent author who was also first chairman of the Canada Land and Emigration Company, which settled the region.

Halifax. Capital of Nova Scotia and the leading city of Atlantic Canada. Founded in 1749 as a fortified British settlement (called Chebucto by the Indians) and later settled by United Empire LOYALISTS, it served for many years as little more than a military garrison. Throughout its history its economy and distinctive character have been related to its superb deepwater harbour and its close association with the sea. The city grew slowly during the nineteenth and twentieth centuries as it became the predominant commercial and administrative centre for Nova Scotia, a national port, and the headquarters of the Royal Canadian Navy. Today 25% of the total labour force of the metropolitan area—including Dartmouth across the harbour—is employed in national defence. The city was devastated by the HALIFAX EXPLOSION in Dec. 1917 and in 1945 was damaged by the HALIFAX RIOT on V-E Day and after. It is the seat of DALHOUSIE UNIVERSITY and the home of the NEPTUNE THEATRE. Its 1971 CMA population was 222,637. Its official motto is *E Mari Merces* ('Wealth from the Sea'). See also Halifax CITADEL, Duke of KENT, PRINCE OF WALES MARTELLO TOWER, PRINCE'S LODGE, PROVINCE HOUSE.

Halifax III. A huge four-engine bomber that was used in the Second World War. The long-range heavy aircraft was built by Handley-Page in England and became operational in 1941. After the war it was used in Canada for coastal reconnaissance.

Halifax Chronicle-Herald, The. A morning newspaper published in Halifax. Dating back to the founding of the NOVASCOTIAN in 1824, it has since 1949 been owned by The Halifax Herald Limited, which publishes it in tandem with the HALIFAX MAIL-STAR. The *Chronicle-Herald* has both a motto ('What will you do today for Nova Scotia?') and a slogan ('If it is good for the Maritimes, *The Chronicle-Herald* is for it').

Halifax Explosion. The collision in Halifax harbour of a Norwegian freighter, the *Imo,* and a French munitions ship, the *Mont Blanc,* caused the latter to catch fire at 9:05 a.m. on 5 Dec. 1917. The resulting explosion and its consequence devastated the entire city, and an estimated 2,000 people died. There have been several books about the disaster, the best being Hugh MacLENNAN's novel BAROMETER RISING (1941). The Halifax Relief Commission, established in 1918, was finally wound up in 1975.

Halifax Gazette, The. The first newspaper published in what is now Canada. It was issued in Halifax as a two-page weekly from 23 Mar. 1752 and 'printed by John Bushell at the Printing Office, Grafton St, where advertisements are taken in'. Bushell, who had come to Halifax from Boston, died in 1761 and was succeeded by German-born Anthony Henry, under whom the *Gazette* became in 1770 the *Nova Scotia Gazette and Weekly Chronicle.*

Halifax Mail-Star, The. An evening newspaper published in Halifax. Dating back to the founding of the NOVASCOTIAN in 1824, it has since 1949 been owned by The Halifax Herald Limited, which publishes it in tandem with the HALIFAX CHRONICLE-HERALD. The publishing company explains that its papers 'stand for the Atlantic Provinces' progress and development and are dedicated to the service of the people that no good cause shall lack a champion and that wrong shall not thrive unopposed.'

Halifax Memorial. A monument commemorating Canadian war dead who have no grave but the sea. Originally erected by the Imperial (later Commonwealth) War Graves Commission in Point Pleasant Park, Halifax, after the First World War, it was moved after the Second to Citadel Hill, and back again in 1956 to Point Pleasant Park. Its cross of sacrifice stands 40 ft above the harbour and is visible to all ships entering.

Halifax Riot. Plans by the military authorities to keep servicemen off the streets of Halifax, a city they disliked, during the V-E Day celebrations were not successful. Extensive damage and looting occurred in the business districts of Halifax and Dartmouth, commencing on the evening of 7 May 1945 and continuing into the next day. Naval ratings, soldiers, airmen, and civilians joined in the rampage.

Hall, Glenn H. (b.1931). Hockey player. Born at Humboldt, Sask., he became a professional NHL goalkeeper who played 18 seasons with Detroit, Chicago, and St Louis, during which time he led the League in the most shutouts and the most consecutive games. He took part in 13 all-star annual matches and won every League trophy available to a goalkeeper.

Hall Commission. The Royal Commission on Health Services under Mr Justice Emmett Hall. Created by the DIEFENBAKER government on 20 June 1961 and reporting in 1964, it proposed a 'health charter' for Canadians and the creation of a universal health-services program, including physicians' services,

Hall Commission

dental services, and pharmaceutical benefits. The Canadian Medical Association in response argued that such a program would lead to the deterioration of medical care; only the public wanted the Hall Commission's recommendations. Little was implemented.

Hall-Dennis Report. A three-year government-sponsored study of the aims and objectives of Ontario education. It was co-chaired by Mr Justice Emmett M. Hall and Lloyd Dennis, a former school principal. Their published report was entitled *Living and Learning* (1968). It recommended inter-disciplinary, continuous education attuned to the needs of individuals. Grades, exams, failures, and centralized curricula were to be abolished in favour of liberal electives and pupil participation in choice of content and methods of instruction. The implementation of many recommendations of this report by the Ministry of Education has radically changed the Ontario school system and has resulted in widespread criticism from both teachers and parents.

Halls of Fame. Galleries that honour men and women of achievement in a field of endeavour, a concept that goes back to the first Hall of Fame, established in the United States in 1901. In Canada the best-known are the Hockey Hall of Fame and Canada's Sports Hall of Fame, both housed in one building, which opened on 26 Aug. 1961 in Exhibition Place, Toronto. In addition there are sports halls of fame in Cornwall, Edmonton, Halifax, Ottawa, Thunder Bay, and Vancouver. Other halls of fame devoted to specific sports are: aquatic (Winnipeg), curling (Toronto), equine (Toronto), flying (Edmonton), football (Hamilton), hockey (Toronto, Kingston), lacrosse (New Westminster).

Halton, Matthew (1906-56). War correspondent and broadcaster. Born in Pincher Creek, Alta, he joined the CBC in Apr. 1943 and became its principal war correspondent, reporting from London in a characteristically breathless yet eloquent fashion. Some of Halton's broadcasts are transcribed by A.E. Powley in *Broadcasts from the Front* (1975).

Hambourg, Boris (1884-1954). Cellist and teacher. Born in Voronezh, USSR, he settled in Toronto in 1910 and in 1914 co-founded the Hambourg Conservatory of Music, of which he was principal until his death. He was an original member of the HART HOUSE STRING QUARTET. His brother Clem founded the House of HAMBOURG.

Hambourg, House of. An 'after-hours' jazz club founded in Toronto by the late Clem

Hambourg, the brother of Boris HAMBOURG, who co-founded the Hambourg Conservatory of Music. The House of Hambourg, which flourished from 1957 to 1964, was an important meeting-place for such newcomers as Ron COLLIER, Hagood HARDY, and Rob McCONNELL.

Hamilton. Founded in 1813 at the foot of the Niagara Escarpment, it grew to become the second city of southern Ontario after Toronto. The presence of the large, smoke-shrouded iron and steel plants of STELCO and DOFASCO have given Hamilton the name 'Steel City'. Its economic specialization and its proximity to, and domination by, Metropolitan Toronto account for a lack of social and cultural amenities, which HAMILTON PLACE is now alleviating. The 1971 CMA population was 498,523. Its official motto is 'Commerce, Prudence, Industry'.

Hamilton, Barbara (b.1928). Comedienne. Born in Toronto, she acted with HART HOUSE THEATRE, the STRAW HAT PLAYERS, and SPRING THAW, where she acquired a devoted following for her strong skits and effective mime. She appeared as an actress in LOVE AND LIBEL and as Aunt Marilla in ANNE OF GREEN GABLES (1965). A mainstay of such CBC Radio programs as 'Inside from the Outside', she has been called 'the funniest woman in Canada'.

Hamilton, Robert M. See CANADIAN QUOTATIONS AND PHRASES.

Hamilton Place. Community cultural centre in HAMILTON, Ont. Designed by Trevor Garwood-Jones, it opened in 1973. Its Great Hall for theatrical and symphonic performances seats 2,183, while the Studio Theatre seats 400 and is used for small productions and community events. It also houses five rooms for meetings.

Handcuffs. See The DONNELLYS.

Hands Across the Seas. Movement to encourage the exchange of teachers among British Empire (and later British Commonwealth) countries. It originated in Canada, was endorsed by the League of Nations, sponsored by the British Empire, and went into effect immediately following the FIRST WORLD WAR. The phrase, now used semi-seriously as an expression of friendship with peoples or nations abroad, comes from a poem by the British versifier Byron Webber that was popular before the turn of the century.

Handy, Arthur (b.1933). Sculptor. Born in New York, he came to Canada in 1960 to head the ceramics department of the ONTARIO

COLLEGE OF ART. Of his abstract-expressionist work in ceramics, wood, and fibreglass, his *Aphrodite Yawns*—a fibreglass and polyester resin pierced sphere—created a sensation when it was exhibited in the Sculpture 67 show at Toronto's City Hall. He has exhibited internationally.

Hanging Judge, The. Sobriquet of Matthew Baillie BEGBIE.

Hanlan, Edward (Ned) (1855-1908). World-champion sculler and popular sportsman. Toronto born, and nicknamed 'The Boy in Blue', he won the world-championship sculling event in 1880 and over the next four years defended the title seven times. He retired after a professional career of 20 years and became a Toronto alderman. Hanlan's Point on TORONTO ISLAND, where he owned a hotel, was named after him. A memorial erected on the CNE grounds attests to his popularity: 'Edward Hanlan: most renowned oarsman of any age, whose victorious career has no parallel in the annals of sports. Victor in three hundred consecutive races, his achievements are all the more worthy of commemoration by his display of true sportsmanship, which is held in honour in all fields of sport.'

Hannah, Jason A. See ASSOCIATED MEDICAL SERVICES INC.

Hansard. The verbatim printed record of the debates of the House of Commons. Named after Luke Hansard (1752-1828), who began printing the proceedings of the British House of Commons in 1774, *Hansard* is now only an established familiar title; the official title is *House of Commons Debates: Official Reports*. The daily printed report of the debates is as accurate as the shorthand reporters in the chamber can make it. Hansard includes what was said, or what the reporters understood to have been said, with obvious errors edited out. Corrections to improve sense and correct grammar may be made, but the House is jealous of the integrity of *Hansard* and will permit substantial changes only under grave circumstances. See also SCRAP-BOOK DEBATES, COTTON DEBATES, and BLUES.

Hanson, Richard Burpee (1879-1948). Leader of the Opposition and Conservative House leader, 1940-3. Born in Bocabec, N.B., and a lawyer, he was first elected to the House of Commons for York-Sunbury, N.B., in 1921. He was named to the cabinet as Minister of Trade and Commerce by Prime Minister BENNETT in 1934. His tenure of office was competently handled but inglorious and Hanson went down to defeat with most of the Bennett Tories. Re-elected in 1940, he succeeded

R.J. MANION as Conservative leader. For the next three years Hanson, with one or two others, struggled successfully to keep Canadian Conservatism alive in the face of a powerful and competent Mackenzie KING government and a revivified CCF.

Hanson, Willy Blok (b.1916). Dance and movement instructor. Born in Java (now Indonesia), she made her début in London, Eng., with Ram Gopal's company in 1939, and settled in Toronto in 1951. She choreographed a ballet based on *The* LOON'S NECKLACE and popularized a woman's exercise known by the title of her book *The Pelvic Tilt: Master Your Body in Seven Days* (1973).

Happy Gang, The. The most popular of all CBC Radio programs. Beginning as a summer replacement on 14 June 1937, it captured an estimated 2.5 million listeners at its peak in the late 1940s and lasted until 5 June 1959. The 30-minute music-and-comedy program, heard five days a week in the early afternoon, was created by Bert Pearl, 'the king of happiness', who acted as master of ceremonies, and was produced by George Temple from 1937 to 1956. It featured trumpeter Bob Farnon, violinist Blain Mathé, and organist Kathleen (Kay) Stokes. Other performers through the years included announcers Hugh Bartlett and Barry Wood, accordionist and singer Eddie Allen, vibraphonist Jimmy Namarro, clarinetist Bert NIOSI, bass-player Joe NIOSI, accordionist Les Foster, the trumpeter Bobby GIMBY. The show began: 'Knock, knock. Who's there? It's the Happy Gang! Well, com'on in!' It was sponsored by Colgate-Palmolive-Peet. Pearl, who was billed as 'that five-foot-two-and-a-half of sunshine', left for Hollywood in 1955. He returned for a CNE GRANDSTAND SHOW starring the surviving Happy Gang entertainers in the summer of 1975.

Happy Time, The. A collection of stories about a youngster growing up in Ottawa in the 1910s. Published in 1945, it was written by Robert Fontaine (1907-65), who was born in Massachusetts but raised until his fifteenth year in Ottawa. It was dramatized as a radio series in 1945, turned into a Broadway musical (with songs by Rogers and Hammerstein) in 1950, and filmed by Stanley Kramer in 1952. Fontaine's sequel, *Hello to Springtime* (1955), was equally charming but less successful.

Hardy, Hagood (b.1937). Jazz vibraphonist, pianist, bandleader. Born in Toronto, he became a top vibraphonist and joined Herbie Mann's band in New York in 1961. He founded his own group, The Montage, on

229

his return to Toronto in 1967. His composition 'The Homecoming', written as background music for a popular Salada Tea commercial in 1972, was released in an album of the same name in 1975 and became an instant success.

Hardy, W.G. (b.1896). Novelist. Born near Lindsay, Ont., and educated at the Universities of Toronto and Chicago, he taught classics at the University of Alberta until his retirement. He wrote historical novels—including *Father Abraham* (1935), *Turn Back the River* (1938), *All the Trumpets Sounded* (1942), *The City of Libertines* (1957)—and one contemporary novel, *The Unfulfilled* (1951). Two works of popular history are *From Sea Unto Sea* (1960) and *Alberta: A Natural History* (1967).

Hare. ATHAPASKAN-speaking Indian group named for their reliance on rabbits for their meat and skins, supplemented by fish and occasional caribou. Reputed to have been a timid people, living in fear of the more aggressive KUTCHIN and Yellowknife, they lived west and northwest of Great Bear Lake. Their population in 1970 was 715.

Harlequin Books. Inexpensive paperback novels sold on a mass-market basis. Invariably about romantic encounters in modern hospitals or gothic castles, they are considered to appeal mainly to women, especially older women, and are sold in 80 countries in 15 languages. The series was launched from Winnipeg in 1949 but has been published in Toronto since the 1960s. Since the 1970s 12 new books have been published each month. In Sept. 1975 Harlequin launched a second series, Laser Books, which offers three titles a month of low-grade science-fiction. Also in 1975 the *Toronto Star* became a majority shareholder.

Harlow, Robert (b.1923). Novelist and teacher. Born in Prince Rupert and raised in Prince George, B.C., he was educated at the University of British Columbia and attended the Iowa Writers' Workshop in 1950. He was a producer with CBC Vancouver until 1964 and then became head of the CREATIVE WRITING DEPARTMENT, UNIVERSITY OF BRITISH COLUMBIA, resigning in 1976. He has published three novels—*Royal Murdoch* (1962), *A Gift of Echoes* (1965), and *Scann* (1972)—and wrote the screenplay for Larry Kent's feature film *When Tomorrow Dies* (1967).

Harman, Jack (b.1927). Sculptor. Born in Vancouver, he studied at the Slade, Hammersmith, and Central Schools of Art in London, Eng. His bronze figure sculptures in-

clude commissions from churches—for example, Corpus Christi Church in Vancouver, for which he did a 9-ft crucifix, murals, an exterior mosaic, and 12 apostles—universities, and hospitals. He did the stylized bronze figure sculpture (1964) in Lothian Mews, Toronto.

Harold Moon Award. Annual award to the person who 'has generated the greatest international influence for Canadian music in the past calendar year'. It was established in 1974 by BMI CANADA LIMITED and honours its first managing director, Wm Harold Moon.

HARP. Acronym of HIGH ALTITUDE RESEARCH PROJECT.

Harper, Henry Albert. See SIR GALAHAD.

Harrington Lake. Official summer home of the prime minister since 1959. The house and 13.4 acres of land were part of the property on Harrington Lake (now Lac Mousseau), Que., acquired by the federal government in 1951 to enlarge GATINEAU Park.

Harris, Alanson. See MASSEY-FERGUSON LIMITED.

Harris, Lawren (1885-1970). Painter and prime mover of the GROUP OF SEVEN. Born in Brantford, Ont., into the Harris half of the Massey-Harris firm, manufacturers of farm implements, he left Canada in 1904 to study and work in Europe, returning to Toronto in 1909. He was one of the first enthusiasts for painting the north country and was co-owner of the STUDIO BUILDING, Toronto. He painted numerous effective portraits of houses and other buildings, as well as the Algoma landscape, but is particularly identified with a striking series of Lake Superior landscapes that were created at a time when he was concerned to inject spiritual values into his painting, which acquired abstract qualities. (It became totally abstract in the late 1930s.) Among his best-known works are NORTH SHORE, LAKE SUPERIOR (1926, NGC); a similarly stylized but more forceful and impressive painting done in the Rockies, *Maligne Lake, Jasper Park* (1924, NGC); and a powerful and accomplished realistic portrait of Dr Salem BLAND (1925, AGO).

Harris, Robert (1849-1919). Painter. Born in Wales, he immigrated with his parents to Charlottetown, P.E.I. He spent two periods in Paris studying painting and in 1879 settled in Toronto, where he became an academic portrait painter. He also executed several of the best-known Canadian genre paintings of the time: MEETING OF THE SCHOOL TRUSTEES (1885, NGC) and *Harmony* (1886, NGC), a memorable study of his wife at the harmonium. His *Fathers of Confederation*, a group portrait of the delegates to the QUEBEC CONFERENCE commissioned by the government, was destroyed in the Parliament Building fire of 1916; an oil sketch is in the Art Gallery of the CONFEDERATION CENTRE OF THE ARTS, Charlottetown.

Harrison Prize. Awarded every three years by the ROYAL SOCIETY OF CANADA for the best work on a bacteriological subject, excluding medical bacteriology. It was endowed by F.C. St Barbe Harrison, FRSC, in 1952 and consists of a presentation scroll and $150.

Harron, Don (b.1924). Actor and writer. Born in Toronto and educated at Victoria College, University of Toronto, he acted with the Village Players, the HART HOUSE THEATRE, and the CBC STAGE series before going on to perform on Broadway, in London's West End, and in Shakespearean festivals in three countries, including the STRATFORD FESTIVAL. He created and impersonated Charlie Farquharson, a rustic farmer from Parry Sound, Ont., for the 1952 edition of the revue SPRING THAW, and is now closely identified with this fictional character from performances on television and through his books: *Charlie Farquharson's Histry of Canada* (1972) and *Charlie Farquharson's Jogfree of Canada* (1974). He adapted *The* BROKEN JUG (1958) and co-authored with Norman CAMPBELL the libretto for ANNE OF GREEN GABLES (1965). In 1969 he married Catherine McKINNON. See also SARAH BINKS.

Hart, Harvey (b.1928). Television and film director. Born in Toronto, he formed one of CBC-TV's first production units in Toronto with Norman JEWISON, Sydney NEWMAN, Arthur HILLER, Paul ALMOND, and Robert Allen. He produced 'Folio', QUEST, and FESTIVAL; directed CBC-TV's DAVID: CHAPTER 2 and *David: Chapter 3* by M. Charles COHEN; and directed stage productions for the CREST THEATRE and the Civic Square Theatre in Toronto. He left for the United States in 1964 and directed two features there: *Bus Riley's Back in Town* (1964) and *The Sweet Ride* (1968). In Canada he directed the films FORTUNE AND MEN'S EYES (1971) by John HERBERT and *The Pyx* (1973) by John BUELL.

Hart House. Accomodating athletic, social, and dining facilities for University of Toronto students, it was given to the university by the Massey Foundation and planned by Vincent MASSEY as a memorial to his father Hart Massey. It is a Gothic Revival building—intended to evoke the atmosphere and ideals of Oxford and Cambridge—designed by SPROATT AND ROLPH and built in 1911-19. Soldier's Tower (1924) next to it, dedicated to students who died in the First World War, is modelled on Magdalen Tower, Oxford. Originally a centre for men, it is now open to women also.

Hart House Orchestra. Chamber orchestra. The group of 18 players was founded in 1954 by Boyd NEEL, who was its permanent conductor. Its annual seasons were all held in the Great Hall of HART HOUSE, University of Toronto, until it disbanded in 1971.

Hart House String Quartet. Founded in 1923-4 by Mr and Mrs Vincent MASSEY and associated with HART HOUSE in the University of Toronto, it was the first Canadian chamber group to develop an international reputation. Its four original members—Harry ADASKIN, Boris HAMBOURG, Milton Blackstone, and Géza de Kresz—played in the leading cities of the United States and Europe. It disbanded in 1945.

Hart House Theatre. An 800-seat theatre in the University of Toronto's HART HOUSE. A centre for local and student dramatic activity and training, it has been identified with a succession of directors, including Roy Mitchell (1919-21), Edgar Stone (1929-34), and Robert Gill (1949-66). Under Mitchell, Merrill DENISON and other student playwrights flourished. Under Gill, an entire generation of student actors emerged. A memorable Gill production was *Saint Joan*—starring Charmion King, supported by Donald and Murray Davis (see DAVIS FAMILY), David Gardner, William HUTT, and Henry Kaplan—which opened on 27 Jan. 1947. Subsequent productions launched the careers of Anna Cameron, Kate REID, and others. The theatre now operates under the aegis of the Graduate Centre for the Study of Drama.

Hart Memorial Trophy. Presented annually by the NATIONAL HOCKEY LEAGUE 'to the player adjudged to be most valuable to his team'. He is selected by the Professional Hockey Writers' Association. The trophy was donated in 1923 by Dr David A. Hart, father of Cecil Hart, former manager-coach of the MONTREAL CANADIENS. In addition to the trophy, the winner receives $1,500; the runner-up, $750.

Hartford of Canada. Unofficial motto of Waterloo, Ont. Like Hartford, Conn., it boasts the head offices of several insurance companies.

Hartland Bridge. The longest covered bridge in the world. Completed in 1897 and rebuilt

Hartland Bridge

in 1920, the 1,282-ft wooden structure crosses the St John R. at Hartland, N.B.

Harvest House. Publishing company, established by Maynard Gertler in Montreal in 1960, that specializes in books on topical issues and in translations of Quebec literature.

Harvey, Douglas (b.1924). Hockey player. Born in Montreal, he participated in many sports but was an outstanding defenceman in professional hockey. During 21 seasons, mostly with the MONTREAL CANADIENS, he was voted for seven consecutive years the best player in his position. He played on six STANLEY CUP teams.

Harvey, Jean-Charles (1891-1967). Quebec journalist and author. Born at Murray Bay, Que., and educated at Université Laval, he was the editor of *Le Soleil* from 1926 to 1934, when he was dismissed from the Quebec daily for publishing *Les Demi-civilisées* (1934). A sympathetic treatment of the young who experiment with new social and sexual norms, it aroused both the clergy and the lay public. It was translated by Lukin Barette as *Sackcloth for Banner* (1938). The publisher of *Le* JOUR from 1937 to 1946, Harvey fought both the separatist and the fascist movements. Among his last publications was *Pourquoi je suis anti-séparatiste* (1967), an 'answer' to Marcel Chaput's best-selling polemic that appeared in English as *Why I Am a Separatist* (1962), translated by Robert A. Taylor.

Harvie, Eric L. See GLENBOW-ALBERTA INSTITUTE.

Harwood, Vanessa (b.1947). Dancer. Born in Cheltenham, Eng., she was a pupil of Betty OLIPHANT and Nancy Schwenker at the NATIONAL BALLET SCHOOL from 1959. She joined the NATIONAL BALLET OF CANADA in 1965, became soloist in 1967, and a principal in 1970.

'Hasty P's'. Nickname of the Hastings and Prince Edward Regiment, formed of older militia battalions in 1920. Farley MOWAT has praised its spirit in *The Regiment* (1955).

Hat trick. Term used in hockey when a player scores three goals in a single game. It derives from the custom in cricket of rewarding the bowler who takes three wickets in three successive balls with a hat.

Hatchet. See TOMAHAWK.

Hatch's Mill. A 10-week series of one-hour comedy-adventure dramas on CBC-TV. Produced by Ron Weyman and shot at Klein-

berg, Ont., it made its début on 24 Oct. 1967 and was the television network's first dramatic production filmed in colour. It depicted pioneer life in Upper Canada (Ontario) in the 1830s and starred Robert CHRISTIE as Noah Hatch, owner of a mill and founder of the fictitious pioneer community of Hatch's Mill, and Cosette Lee as his wife, with Marc Strange and Sylvia Fiegel as their children.

Hatley Park. See DUNSMUIR.

Haviland, Thomas Heath (1822-95). A FATHER OF CONFEDERATION. Born in Prince Edward Island, he trained as a lawyer and was elected to the legislative assembly in 1847. He was a delegate to the QUEBEC CONFERENCE and was a delegate to Ottawa in 1873 to arrange terms for the Island's entry into Confederation. He then was appointed to the Senate, from which he resigned in 1879 to become lieutenant-governor of the province.

Hawkins, Rompin' Ronnie (b.1934). Country rock singer. Born in Arkansas, he moved to Toronto in 1958 and played with what later became The BAND in 1964. He has a strong personal following and has helped launch from his club, The Hawk's Nest, the careers of David CLAYTON-THOMAS and many others.

Hawley, Sandy (b.1949). Jockey. Born in Oshawa, Ont., he went to work for WINDFIELDS Farms at 16 and within two years was riding regularly on the Ontario circuit. Hawley—who is 5 ft 2 in. and is so gentlemanly that he has been dubbed 'Sir Lancelot'—was leading rider in Canada from 1969 to 1974, winning the Joe Perlov Trophy. He was the first rider in racing history to win more than 500 races in a single season, setting a world record in 1973 with 515 wins. In 1976 he received the George WOOLF Memorial jockey award.

Hay, William (1818-88). Architect. Born in Cruden, Scot., he trained in the office of John Henderson of Edinburgh before becoming assistant to George Gilbert Scott. In 1848 he came to St John's, Nfld, to supervise the construction of the Anglican Cathedral to Scott's designs. From 1852 to 1864 he lived in Toronto, where his works include the first sections of St Basil's Church and St Michael's College (1856); the church school (1857) and rectory (1861) of Holy Trinity, Trinity Square; and Yorkville Town Hall (1860). He also designed St George's, Newcastle (c.1855), and St Andrew's, Guelph (1857), in a Gothic style reminiscent, as were many of his buildings, of the work of Scott. He left Canada in 1864 and in 1872 settled in Edinburgh, where until his death he worked on the restoration of St Giles Cathedral.

Hayden, Melissa (b.1923). Dancer. Born Mildred Herman in Toronto, she studied with Boris VOLKOFF, making her début in Volkoff's Canadian Ballet, and with George Balanchine in New York, where she joined the Ballet Theatre in 1945 and became a leading dancer with the New York City Ballet in 1950. She danced for Claire Bloom in Charles Chaplin's *Limelight* (1952). She was a guest artist with the NATIONAL BALLET OF CANADA and the Royal Ballet in 1963, and with Les GRANDS BALLETS CANADIENS in 1969. As a star of American ballet, she continued dancing with the Ballet Theatre and the New York City Ballet until her retirement in 1973. She now teaches at Skidmore College, N.Y.

Hayden Formula. The procedure that permits the Senate to refer an important bill tabled before the House of Commons to the Senate's Banking, Trade and Commerce Committee for simultaneous study. Before Senator Salter Hayden devised this procedure in 1969, the Senate could deal with a bill only after it had received Commons approval.

Head, Sir Francis Bond (1793-1875). Lieutenant-governor of Upper Canada (Ontario). Appointed in 1835, he soon took a reactionary stand against the REFORMERS and stubbornly refused to heed warnings of an impending uprising. He had sent troops to Lower Canada (Quebec) when he was surprised by the gathering of rebels at MONTGOMERY'S TAVERN—a prelude to the REBELLION OF 1837 in Upper Canada. He accompanied the militia to the tavern on 7 Dec. and ordered it to be burned. The rebellion was crushed, but his behaviour has earned him some blame for what transpired.

Headless Valley. 'Valley of mystery' on the South Nahanni R., Y.T. The decapitated body of a prospector was discovered there in 1917, and since then legends of this virtually inaccessible 'land that time forgot' have abounded. Imaginative details were supplied by Pierre BERTON in an article in *Maclean's* on 15 Mar. 1947. It was reworked for inclusion in *The Mysterious North* (1956).

Health insurance. See MEDICARE.

Hearne, Samuel (1745-92). Explorer. After service in the Royal Navy he joined the HUDSON'S BAY COMPANY and was sent across the BARREN LANDS in search of copper. On his third journey of 1771-2 he found the Coppermine R. and became the first white man to reach the Arctic Ocean overland. He built the

company's first inland post, Cumberland House (Sask.). in 1774. He retired in 1787 and wrote his famous *Journey from the Prince of Wales Fort in Hudson's Bay to the Northern Ocean* (1795). A modern edition, edited by Richard Glover, appeared in 1958.

'Heat'. Well-known poem by Archibald LAMPMAN that appeared in his first collection of verse, *Among the Millet* (1888). Rich in precisely observed details of sound, colour, and movement, it is a fine example of the poet's power to convey a sense of the order and harmony, the peace and goodness of nature.

Heavysege, Charles (1816-76). Poet and dramatist. Born in Huddersfield, Yorkshire, Eng., he came to Canada in 1853 and settled in Montreal, where he worked as a cabinetmaker and later as a journalist and a writer of verse. He was highly praised in his day for his rhetorical drama in blank verse, *Saul* (1857)—Longfellow called Heavysege 'the greatest dramatist since Shakespeare'. Among his other works are a second Biblical drama, *Jeptha's Daughter* (1865), and *Sonnets* (1855).

Hebb, Donald Olding (b.1904). Psychologist. Born in Chester, N.S., and educated at Dalhousie, McGill, Chicago, and Harvard, he taught at McGill from 1948 to 1958. His experimental and theoretical work on the relation between the brain and behaviour—presented in *The Organization of Behaviour* (1949)—gained him international recognition. He has been president of both the Canadian and American Psychological Associations.

Hébert, Anne (b.1916). Quebec poet and novelist. Born at Sainte-Catherine-de-Fossambault, Que., like her cousin Hector de Saint-Denys-GARNEAU, she worked as a writer for the NATIONAL FILM BOARD, dividing her time between Paris and Montreal. Her impressive symbolist poems—including the memorable 'Le Tombeau des rois' ('The Tomb of the Kings')—can be read in English in *St-Denys-Garneau and Anne Hébert* (1962) translated by F.R. SCOTT and in *Poems* (1975) translated by Alan BROWN. Her best-known work of fiction is KAMOURASKA (1970), translated by Norman Shapiro and filmed by Claude JUTRA. Her most recent novel, *Les Enfants du Sabbat* (1976), is about sorcery in a Quebec convent in 1944. *The Torrent* (1967), translated by Gwendolyn Moore, and *The Silent Rooms* (1974), translated by Katherine Mezei, are collections of short stories.

Hébert, Henri (1884-1950). Sculptor. Son of Louis-Philippe HÉBERT, he studied in Montreal and Paris and accepted a teaching position in McGill's Department of Architecture in 1909. He specialized in commemorative sculpture and completed the famous *Evangeline* statue at GRAND PRÉ, which his father had designed before his death. Examples of his work are two First World War Monuments at Outremont, Que., and Yarmouth, N.S. He was one of the founders of the Sculptors Society of Canada in 1928.

Hébert, Jacques. See Les ÉDITIONS DU JOUR.

Hébert, Louis (1575?-1627). French apothecary; the first Canadian settler to support himself from the soil. He had spent two periods at PORT ROYAL when, in 1617, he brought his wife and three children to Quebec, where they became the first settlers. He received title to land in the present-day Upper Town of Quebec City. Hébert cultivated the earth with handtools—a plough did not arrive until a few months after his death.

Hébert, Louis-Philippe (1850-1917). Sculptor. Born in Sainte-Sophie d'Halifax, Que., he became Canada's first commemorative sculptor in the 1880s. Three of his most famous statues are the monuments to Queen Victoria, John A. MACDONALD, and George-Étienne CARTIER on Parliament Hill, Ottawa.

Heggtveit, Anne (b.1939). Champion skier. Born in Ottawa, where her father and two uncles had been champion skiers, she showed such early talent that when only seven she won a senior slalom event. At the 1960 Winter Olympics in Squaw Valley, Calif., she defeated 41 competitors to win the women's slalom event and to become recognized as the world's best female skier.

Heiltsuk. See WAKASHAN.

Heintzman. The best-known name in Canadian pianos. Heintzman & Co. Ltd (Piano Mfgrs) was established in Toronto in 1860 by Theodore August Heintzman (1817-99), a Berlin-born piano-maker who trained in New York alongside Heinrich Steinway. When Heintzman set up shop in Toronto, there were 20 other piano firms in the city. Heintzman is the largest manufacturer of the instrument in Canada.

Helicopter Canada. Documentary film photographed and directed by Eugene Boyko and produced by the NATIONAL FILM BOARD. It is narrated by Stanley Jackson. The topography of the 10 provinces was stunningly photographed from the vantagepoint of a helicopter to give everything a strange and engrossing appearance. 50 min., 8 sec.; colour.

Hell's Gate. A name applied to a number of river valleys where a narrow tortuous constriction causes tumultuous rapids, notably on the South Nahanni R. below Virginia Falls, B.C., and on the Fraser R. where it enters Fraser Canyon, 17 mi. north of Yale, B.C. Here the Airtram permits a remarkable view of the Fraser and a closeup of a salmon fishway.

Helluland. 'Flagstone land' in Icelandic sagas. It has been identified with numerous locations, the most likely of which is BAFFIN ISLAND. Helluland was named by LEIF ERICSSON in A.D. 1001. See also L'ANSE AUX MEADOWS.

Hellyer, Paul. See UNIFICATION.

Helmcken, John Sebastian (1824-1920). Prominent early resident of Victoria, B.C. Born in London, Eng., and educated as a surgeon, he joined the HUDSON'S BAY COMPANY as a doctor and arrived in Victoria in 1850. He was a member of the legislative assembly of Vancouver Island and British Columbia from 1855 to 1871, helped arrange the terms of union with Canada (though he had previously opposed Confederation), and declined John A. MACDONALD's offer of the premiership of the new province. In 1852 he married Cecilia, the daughter of James DOUGLAS. His house of 1852, near the Parliament Buildings in Victoria, is preserved as a heritage home within the Provincial Museum complex.

Helwig, David (b.1938). Poet and novelist. Born in Toronto, and a graduate of the Universities of Toronto and London, he taught at Queen's University until his appointment as literary editor for CBC-TV under John HIRSCH (1974-6). His books of lyric poetry include *Figures in a Landscape* (1968), *The Silence of the Gunman* (1965), *The Best Name of Silence* (1972), and *Atlantic Crossing* (1974). *The Streets of Summer* (1969) is a collection of stories. *The Day before Tomorrow* (1971), an espionage novel with serious overtones, was reissued as *Message from a Spy* (1975). His most recent novel is *The Glass Knight* (1976). From 1971 to 1975 Helwig edited the annual short-story anthologies published by OBERON PRESS.

Hémon, Louis (1880-1913). French novelist. Born in Brest, France, he worked in England as a journalist before going to Montreal in 1911. He spent the winter of 1912 at Peribonka, Saint-Gédéon, and Roberval among the settlers of the Lac St-Jean region, working on a farm and on surveys. He was killed in a railway accident at Chapleau, Ont., in the summer of 1913 after he had mailed the manuscript of his novel MARIA CHAPDELAINE to *Le Temps* (Paris), which published it as a serial in Jan.-Feb. 1914. It appeared in book form in Montreal two years later and in W.H. BLAKE's translation in 1921. Arthur Richmond was the translator of *My Fair Lady* (1923) and William Aspenwall Bradley of *Battling Malone and Other Stories* (1925), *Monsieur Ripois and Nemesis* (1925), and *The Journal of Louis Hémon* (1924).

Hemsworth, Wade. See 'The BLACK FLY SONG'.

Henday (Hendry), Anthony (active 1750-62). Explorer. While in the employ of the HUDSON'S BAY COMPANY at YORK FACTORY as a netmaker and labourer, he made an important exploratory journey (1754-5)—travelling farther west than any other European—to an Indian encampment near present-day Red Deer, Alta. His journal of his trip, describing the Indians he met and the French competition in the fur trade, was lost, but a copy was used in the publication of *York Factory to the Blackfeet Country* (1929) edited by L.J. Burpee.

Hendry, Tom (b.1929). Playwright and theatre founder. Born in Winnipeg, Man., he attended the University of Manitoba and qualified as a chartered accountant in 1955. Two years later, with John HIRSCH, he founded Theatre 77, which became the MANITOBA THEATRE CENTRE the following year. He was administrative director of this model for regional theatres from 1958 to 1963, and then first general director of the Canadian Theatre Centre (1964-9). In 1969 the STRATFORD FESTIVAL staged the musical *Satyricon*, which he wrote to music by Stanley Silverman. It played off-Broadway as *Dr. Selavy's Magic Theatre* from Oct. 1972 to Mar. 1973. Hendry has written a number of plays, the principal one being *Fifteen Miles of Broken Glass*. A founder of the PLAYWRIGHTS' CO-OP and the Toronto Free Theatre, both in the fall of 1971, he established in 1974 the Playwrights' Workshop of the BANFF CENTRE and created its Playwrights' Colony in the summer of 1976.

Hennepin, Louis (1626-c.1705). Recollet priest, missionary, and explorer. In New France from 1675 to 1681, he accompanied LA SALLE to Niagara in 1678 and was with the explorer until 1680, when he was captured by Sioux Indians. He later wrote *Description de la Louisiane* (1683), in which he gives the first eye-witness description of Niagara Falls, *Nouvelle Découverte d'un très grand pays* (1697), and *Nouveau Voyage d'un païs plus grand que l'Europe* (1698). In the last two he claimed to have made a trip to the mouth of the Mississippi.

Henning, Doug (b.1947). Magician. Born in Fort Garry, near Winnipeg, he was raised in Oakville, Ont., and graduated in psychology from McMaster University. Long fascinated by prestidigitation, he was the first person to receive, in 1970, a CANADA COUNCIL grant to study magic (under Dai Vernon, an Ottawaborn American master of the sleight-ofhand). He was the star of 'Spellbound', a magic-and-rock show that opened in Toronto in Dec. 1973 to an excellent press. Private backers took him to Broadway in 'The Magic Show', which opened in June 1974 and did land-office business, establishing both Henning and his style (jeans and long hair instead of top hat and black tie) as the 'new wave' for illusionists.

Henry, Alexander (1739-1824). Fur-trader and author. Born in New Jersey, he traded on Lake Superior and in the valley of the Saskatchewan. He is best known for his important book, *Travels and Adventures in Canada and the Indian Territories, between the Years 1760 and 1776* (1809). He was the uncle of another Alexander Henry (d.1814), also a furtrader, and is referred to as 'the elder'.

Henry, Ann (b.1914). Playwright. Born in Winnipeg, she was the first woman reporter to cover the Winnipeg police court and the Manitoba legislature, which she did for the *Winnipeg Tribune*. She went on to become the city's chief drama and film critic, winning a *Maclean's* fiction prize in 1955 and a Hollywood writing award in 1959. Her play *Lulu Street*, a comic treatment of a Winnipeg riot, was produced by the MANITOBA THEATRE CENTRE in 1967 and published in 1976. Her autobiography, *Laugh, Baby, Laugh*, appeared in 1970. She is the mother of the actor Donnelly Rhodes. See also Martha HENRY.

Henry, Martha (b.1938). Actress. Born in Detroit and raised in Greenville, Mich., she graduated from the Carnegie Institute of Technology, Pittsburgh, in 1959. She played summer stock and acted with the CREST THEATRE and CBC-TV. In 1960 she attended the NATIONAL THEATRE SCHOOL, where she met the actor Donnelly Rhodes, the son of the writer Ann HENRY. They were married in 1961 and she adopted the name Henry, having acted up to that point under her maiden name of Buhs. They separated when Rhodes headed for Hollywood and she went to the STRATFORD FESTIVAL in 1962. There she played principal roles, marrying Douglas RAIN, whom she accompanied in 1969 to London, Eng. She played in the BBC-TV serial 'Daniel

Deronda' in 1970. Since then she has made numerous appearances at Stratford—most recently as Isabella in the 1975 and 1976 productions of *Measure for Measure*—and on CBC-TV.

Henry, William A. (1816-88). A FATHER OF CONFEDERATION. Born in Halifax, N.S., he trained as a lawyer and was elected to the House of Assembly of Nova Scotia in 1841. A leading advocate of Confederation, he attended all three of the Conferences that led up to it. He was appointed to the Supreme Court of Canada in 1875.

Henry Marshall Tory Medal. It is awarded every two years by the ROYAL SOCIETY OF CANADA for oustanding research in a branch of astronomy, chemistry, mathematics, physics, or an allied science, carried out mainly in the eight years preceding the date of the award, although all the research work of the candidate is taken into account. The award was established by Henry Marshall TORY, founder of the NATIONAL RESEARCH COUNCIL, in 1941. It consists of a gold medal and $1,000.

Henson, Josiah (1789-1883). Black clergyman. Born a slave at Port Tobacco, Md, he became overseer of a plantation in Kentucky and was ordained in the Methodist church in 1828. On learning that his family was to be broken up, he escaped to Canada with his wife and four small children in 1830. Near Dresden, U.C. (Ont.), he helped in the founding of Dawn, a settlement for fugitive slaves. The year his autobiography, *The Life of Josiah Henson* (1849), appeared, he was visited by Harriet Beecher Stowe, who used him as the prototype of Uncle Tom in *Uncle Tom's Cabin* (1852). Fame ensued and Henson travelled widely. He is buried near his two-storey house, built of tulipwood about 1842, which is part of Uncle Tom's Cabin Museum at Dresden, Ont.

Heparin. A substance extracted from the liver and lungs of domesticated animals which, when injected into the bloodstream, prevents thrombosis. The discoverer of the anticoagulant properties of heparin was Dr Gordon Murray (1896-1976), a prominent heart surgeon at the Toronto General Hospital who first published his findings in the *Canadian Medical Association Journal* in 1936. Heparin was later used by Dr Murray in his well-known 'BLUE BABY' OPERATION.

Hepburn, Douglas (b.1926). Champion weight-lifter. Born in Vancouver with a badly twisted leg, he overcame this handicap and at Los Angeles in 1949 captured the U.S.

heavyweight weight-lifting championship. In Aug. 1953, at Stockholm, he became the world's heavyweight and weight-lifting champion, and on his return to Vancouver was voted 'Canada's best athlete of the year'. He competed as a professional wrestler but is remembered as a weight-lifter.

Hepburn, Mitchell (1896-1953). Premier of Ontario, 1934 to 1942. He was born in St Thomas, Ont., farmed there, and served in the infantry and air force during the First World War. Elected to the federal Parliament as a Liberal in 1934, he simultaneously led the Ontario Liberal Party (from 1930), not resigning his seat in Ottawa until 1934, the year he came to power in the province. A mercurial figure with enormous public appeal, he did not suceed as premier. The DEPRESSION hung over the land, and Hepburn and his cronies seemed more concerned with fighting Mackenzie KING, the CIO, and the workers of the province. In 1942, without real explanation, he resigned as premier but stayed in the cabinet as provincial treasurer until 1943. His successors, Gordon Conant and Harry Nixon, could never overcome the problems he had left them, and Liberalism went down to a smashing defeat in the 1943 Ontario election. It has never recovered from Mitch Hepburn's malign effects on the party.

Hepburn's Hussars. Contemptuous term for the task force of special constables organized by Ontario Premier Mitchell HEPBURN to break the OSHAWA STRIKE of Apr. 1937. The Eglinton Hunt Club supplied the horses for the riders. The task force was also known as 'Sons of Mitch's'.

HEPC. Initials of the Hydro-Electric Power Commission of Ontario. See ONTARIO HYDRO.

Her Majesty. Title of the Queen of Canada. In addressing the monarch, 'Your Majesty' is used first and 'Ma'am' is used thereafter.

Herbert, John (b.1926). Playwright. Born Jack Brundage in Toronto, he served six months in the Guelph Reformatory when he was 19 and assumed the name John Herbert when he began to write for the stage. He is internationally known for FORTUNE AND MEN'S EYES, his play about homosexuals in prison, which opened on Broadway on 23 Feb. 1967 and was subsequently published and filmed.

Herbie. A cartoon character that satirized regimentation in the Canadian army, popular during the Second World War. 'Pte Herbie Canadian' was created in the spring of

1944 for *The* MAPLE LEAF, the Canadian Army's newspaper overseas, by two staff members: the cartoonist William Garnet Coughlin (known as Bing) and James Douglas MacFarlane (who used the byline J.D.M.), both Ottawa-born. Herbie was a dopey-looking private with messed-up hair and a nose so bulbous it disguised the absence of a chin or mouth. Rather like Good Soldier Schweik or Private TURVEY, he was always saying or doing the wrong thing, yet he survived. 'What I want to git most out of this war . . . is me!' he once said. A collection of cartoons with a commentary was published as *Herbie!* in 1946 and reprinted three times.

Here and Now. A short-lived literary magazine, three issues of which appeared between Dec. 1947 and June 1949. Edited and designed with typographic flair by Paul AR-THUR, it published a wide range of pieces, including stories and poems by many Canadian writers who are now well known.

'Here Before Christ'. A playful interpretation of the initial letters of the HUDSON'S BAY COMPANY that dates at least from 1872.

Heriot, George (1766-1844). Artist. Born in Scotland, he studied watercolour painting with Paul Sandby at the Royal Military Academy, Woolwich, Eng. He was at Quebec from 1791 to 1816, latterly as deputy postmaster general of British North America. On tours that took him from Montreal to Niagara and from Quebec to Halifax, he produced many small, decorative watercolour sketches and finished watercolours. His *Travels Through the Canadas* (1807), an excellent early travel book, is illustrated with aquatint engravings of some of these paintings.

Heritage. A CBC-TV series of religious dramas and documentaries. The 30-minute programs on subjects related to religion and belief were seen weekly from 12 Oct. 1958 to 19 Feb. 1967.

Heritage Canada. Federal conservation body. Established in 1970, it is a national trust concerned with the conservation of buildings, sites, and scenic areas of importance to the country's heritage.

Heritage Court. Museum and archives complex in Victoria, adjoining the British Columbia Legislative Buildings. Opened in 1968, it is a joint federal-provincial undertaking that commemorates Confederation.

Heritage Day. Proposed holiday to celebrate the Canadian heritage. The suggestion that the third Monday in February be declared a national holiday was made by the Standing Committee on Justice and Legal Affairs in 1973 and endorsed by HERITAGE CANADA. It would give Canadians a mid-winter break and a chance to acknowledge the multi-cultural background of the country. A Private Member's Bill was introduced in the House of Commons in 1974 to establish the statutory holiday, but it was not acted upon.

Heritage Highways. Tourist routes through Ontario and Quebec marked by road signs that carry the symbol of a pioneer's wagon wheel in white against a brown background. This interprovincial tour of historic and scenic points, called *Sur la route des pionniers/Heritage Highways*, extends from Windsor in southern Ontario to Percé on Quebec's Gaspé Peninsula.

Heritage Park. A 60-acre museum community in Calgary, Alta, recreating various aspects of prairie life in the period 1740-1914. This collection of Indian dwellings, farms, banks, shops, and houses was reconstructed and opened in 1964 and was financed by grants of $150,000 from the Woods Foundation and the City of Calgary, respectively.

Heritage Village. Outdoor museum at Burnaby. Opened in 1971, it recreates a typical village on the lower British Columbia mainland between 1890 and 1920.

Héroux, Dénis (b.1940). Quebec film director. Born in Montreal, he helped direct SEUL OU AVEC D'AUTRES (1962), Canada's first student feature, with Denys ARCAND. His most notable film is VALÉRIE (1968). This was followed by *L'Initiation* (1969), *L'Amour humain* (1970), and *Sept Fois par jour* (1971). He directed the political exploitation film *Quelques Arpents de neige* (1972); a slapstick comedy, *J'ai mon voyage* (1972); and an international co-production with the American Film Theatre, *Jacques Brel Is Alive and Well and Living in Paris* (1974).

Herring-choker. A slang reference to a Maritimer, especially a New Brunswicker. So plentiful are herring in the North Atlantic that the Atlantic Ocean was known in England in the late-seventeenth century as a 'herring-pond'.

Herzberg, Gerhard (b.1904). Scientific researcher. Born in Hamburg, Germany, and educated at Darmstadt, Göttingen, and Bristol, he had to leave his teaching post at the Darmstadt Institute of Technology in 1935. He was appointed research professor of physics at the University of Saskatchewan (1935-45) and then professor of spectroscopy, Yerkes Observatory, University of

Herzberg

Chicago (1945-8). He joined the NATIONAL RE-
SEARCH COUNCIL in 1948 and has been a Distinguished Research Scientist there since
1969. Herzberg, who first observed the spec-
tral bands of molecular oxygen (the 'Herzberg Bands'), has been called 'the founding
father of molecular spectroscopy'. Among
his numerous publications is *The Spectra and
Structure of Simple Free Radicals: An Introduction to Molecular Spectroscopy* (1971). In 1971
he was awarded the NOBEL PRIZE for Chemistry 'for his contribution to the knowledge of
electronic structure and geometry of mole-
cules, particularly free radicals'. In 1974 the
NRC announced plans to open The Herzberg
Institute of Astrophysics. Herzberg is an outspoken critic of both technologically directed
research and its bureaucratization by politicians and non-scientists.

Herzberg Medal. A silver medal for 'high
achievement in physics' awarded to a Canadian scientist who is no more than 30 years
old. The presentation is made each June by
the Canadian Association of Physicists to
honour Gerhard HERZBERG, a NOBEL PRIZE
LAUREATE. It was first awarded in 1970 on Dr
Herzberg's sixty-fifth birthday.

Hétu, Jacques (b.1938). Composer. Born in
Trois-Rivières, Que., he studied with Clermont PÉPIN at the Conservatoire in Montreal
and in Paris. He teaches at Université Laval.
His compositions for piano, voice, and orchestra, as well as his chamber music, show
the strong influence of post-romantic composers and use traditional classical structures. *Variations* (1967) for piano and *Passa-
caille* (1970) and *Symphonie No 3* (1972) for
orchestra are characteristic of his best work.

Heward, Prudence (1896-1947). Painter.
Born in Montreal, she studied there and in
Paris. She was a member of the CANADIAN
GROUP OF PAINTERS and achieved prominence
as a figure painter. Two of her best-known
paintings are *Dark Girl* (1935, Hart House,
University of Toronto), and *Farmer's Daugh-
ter* (c.1945, NGC).

Hewitt, Foster (b.1904). 'The voice of
hockey'. Born in Toronto, the son of the
sports editor W.A. (Bill) HEWITT, he distinguished himself as intercollegiate boxing
champion while a student at the University
of Toronto. He announced his first hockey
game in his thin, penetrating voice on radio
23 Mar. 1923 and has continued to cover
sports events longer than any other broadcaster in history. He is the author of a
number of books and the owner of radio station CKFH in Toronto (the FH stands for Foster
Hewitt). Associated with Hewitt are the ex-

clamations 'He shoots! He scores!', first ut-
tered on 4 Apr. 1933. See also FOSTER HEWITT
AWARD.

Hewitt, William A. (1875-1961). Well-known
sports figure. Born in Cobourg, Ont., he
grew up in Toronto, where he was sports editor of the *Toronto Star* for more than 30 years
as well as an officer of many football, rugby,
and hockey associations. The manager of
three Olympic hockey championship teams
and the author of *Down the Stretch* (1958), he
was associated with his son Foster HEWITT in
broadcasting games on both radio and television. Both father and son are members of the
Hockey HALL OF FAME.

Hexagone, Les Éditions de l'. The imprint of
a small publishing outlet for poets. Established in Montreal in 1953 by Gaston MIRON
and others, Hexagone issues beautiful limited editions illustrated by important Quebec
artists and often designed by the printer-
poet Roland GIGUÈRE.

HH. See HRH.

Hiawatha. A semi-legendary IROQUOIS hero.
By tradition he was born an Onondagan,
raised a Huron, and adopted by Mohawks.
His name may mean 'he who combs [out
knots]' or 'he makes rivers'. Hiawatha is credited with the invention of WAMPUM and with
assisting DEKANAHWIDEH in the creation of the
IROQUOIS Confederacy, which was established as early as 1459. In the nineteenth century the scholar Henry Schoolcraft confused
Hiawatha with NANABOZHO, an OJIBWA trickster hero, and Schoolcraft's account was
used by Henry Wadsworth Longfellow in the
writing of his epic *The Song of Hiawatha*
(1855). By Longfellow's account, Hiawatha
was an Ojibwa reared by Nokomis, daughter
of the Moon, on the south shore of Lake Superior, in present-day Wisconsin. He married Minnehaha and brought civilization to
his people before departing for the Isles of
the Blest in Keewaydin to rule over the kingdom of the Northwest Wind.

Hibbs, Harry (b.1943). Folk singer. Born on
Bell Island, Nfld, he was a press operator in
Toronto until 1969, when he began to sing
Newfoundland ballads and accompany himself on the accordion. His 'back home' music
became popular. He has made records, and
the 'Harry Hibbs Show'—a television program independently produced in Hamilton,
Ont., since 1970—has made many friends.

Hiebert, Paul (b.1892). Humorist. Born at
Pilot Mound, Man., he was professor of
chemistry at the University of Manitoba for
28 years. As a writer he is known for the sat-

238

ire SARAH BINKS (1947), which has a sequel, *Willows Revisited* (1967). He has also written a philosophical work, *Tower in Siloam* (1966).

High Altitude Research Project. A program designed to send space probes into the upper atmosphere by means of modified naval cannon rather than by conventional rocket launches. Directed by Dr Gerald V. Bull of McGill University's Space Research Institute, it was started in 1964 and operated test facilities and firing ranges at Highwater, Que., and Barbados, B.W.I. When it was given up by McGill in 1968, the project went to the University of Vermont.

High Commissioner. The highest-ranking diplomatic representative of one Commonwealth country to another. Canada was the first country within the British Empire to post a High Commissioner to London in the 1880s. In 1975 Canada maintained high commissions (resident and non-resident) in 31 countries. See also AMBASSADOR, CONSUL.

High Park. The largest park in the City of Toronto, located in the west end and covering 398 acres. It contains nature trails, gardens, a small zoo, and Grenadier Pond, where bands play from a barge during the summer. John G. HOWARD, a Toronto architect and city engineer, gave much of the present park to the city, which acquired it in 1876 in return for a lifetime annuity for Howard and his wife. His house, Colborne Lodge (1836), still stands and is open to the public.

Highland Lassie, The. A blonde Scottish majorette, trademark of MACDONALD TOBACCO INC.. Painted by Rex Woods, the portrait appeared on Macdonald's Cigarettes packages and advertising from 1934 to 1975.

Highway Book Shop. Bookstore and publishing operation on the outskirts of Cobalt, Ont. It began to issue booklets devoted to local lore in 1971.

Hill, Dan (b.1954). Folk singer and composer. Born in Don Mills, Ont., he is one of the fastest-rising popular performers in the country. His album *You Make Me Want to Be* (1971) has attracted a wide North American following.

Hill, The. A reference to PARLIAMENT HILL.

Hill, Tom (b.1943). Seneca artist. Born on the SIX NATIONS RESERVE near Brantford, Ont., he attended Carleton University and the ONTARIO COLLEGE OF ART. His drawings and acrylic paintings are figurative and contemporary and illustrate traditional Iroquois subjects. In 1967 he designed *The Tree of Peace*, a mural in the Indian Pavilion at Expo 67. He co-ordinated the important Canadian Indian Art '74 exhibition at the Royal Ontario Museum from 4 June to 14 July 1974. He currently works with the Department of INDIAN AFFAIRS AND NORTHERN DEVELOPMENT.

Hill Sr, William (Red) (1882-1942). Celebrated 'Riverman of Niagara'. Born in Niagara Falls, Ont., he performed innumerable dangerous rescues and rode the Niagara rapids and whirlpool in a steel barrel on 30 May 1930. He died in bed, leaving two sons who were obsessed with the desire to be Niagara daredevils. Red Hill Jr (1913-51) rode the rapids and whirlpool but died in an attempt to shoot the Horseshoe Falls on 5 Aug. 1951. Major Hill (1916-71) attempted to shoot the Falls in 1950 and threatened to do so in 1970; he never took the plunge, although he did ride the rapids and whirlpool in a steel barrel of his own design five times between 1949 and 1956.

Hill 70. Promontory on the outskirts of Lens in northern France, the scene of a successful assault during the FIRST WORLD WAR by the CANADIAN CORPS under Gen. A.W. CURRIE on 15-25 Aug. 1917.

Hill 145. See VIMY.

Hill 187. See KOREAN WAR.

Hiller, Arthur (b.1923). Film director. Born in Edmonton, Alta, he became a radio actor there in 1946 and in 1949 moved to Toronto, where he joined CBC Radio as a drama producer. His credits include for CBC Radio JAKE AND THE KID and for CBC-TV the 'On Camera' series. Since 1955 he has worked in Hollywood, where he is known as the 'actor's director'. Aside from work on such television series as 'Perry Mason', 'Gunsmoke', and 'Alfred Hitchcock Presents', etc., he has directed numerous feature films, including *The Careless Years* (1957), *Tobruk* (1966), *Love Story* (1970), and *The Man in the Glass Booth* (1974).

Hincks, Clarence E. See MENTAL HEALTH CANADA.

Hincks, Sir Francis (1807-85). Politican. Born in Ireland, he settled in York (Toronto) in 1832 and entered the banking business. In 1841 he was elected to the legislative assembly of the PROVINCE OF CANADA and 10 years later formed a government with A.N. MORIN, which lasted until 1854. In 1862 he was made governor of British Guiana, but he returned to Canadian politics the year he was knighted, in 1869, and joined Sir John A. MACDONALD's cabinet. He resigned in 1873 and retired the next year.

Hind

Hind, Henry Youle (1823-1908). Geologist. Born and educated in England, he became a professor of chemistry at the University of Toronto in 1853 and was employed as a geologist by the PROVINCE OF CANADA for the Canadian Exploring Expeditions of 1857 and 1858, exploring the agricultural possibilities of the Northwest. He was accompanied by his brother, the painter William G.R. HIND, on a geological survey of Labrador in 1861.

Hind, William G.R. (1833-89). Artist. Born in Nottingham, Eng., he studied painting in London and came to Canada in 1852. He taught drawing in Toronto and in 1861 accompanied his brother, the geologist Henry Youle HIND, on a trip to Labrador, producing some remarkable watercolours and drawings. The next year he went to the Cariboo with the OVERLANDERS OF '62. The sketches he made on this expedition were the basis for compelling, detailed watercolours and oils in which he interpreted scenes of the rough trip and the Fraser River Gold Rush with a Pre-Raphaelite sensibility. *Bar in Mining Camp* (1862)—in the McCord Museum, McGill University—is often reproduced. Hind died in Sussex, N.B.

Hindmarsh, Harry Comfort. See the TORONTO STAR.

Hine, Daryl (b.1936). Poet and editor. Born in Burnaby, B.C., he is a graduate of McGill and the University of Chicago, where he teaches. Since 1969 he has edited the well-known monthly *Poetry*. His recent collections of poetry are *Minutes* (1968); *The Homeric Hymns* (1972), translations; and *Resident Alien* (1975). He has also written a novel, *Prince of Darkness & Co.* (1961), and *Polish Subtitles: Impressions from a Journey* (1963).

Hiram Walker-Gooderham and Worts Ltd. Producers of Canadian and Scotch whiskies. The original distillery was founded in Toronto by William Gooderham (1790-1881) and his brother-in-law James Worts (1818-82) in 1837. Hiram Walker & Sons Limited was founded in 1858 by the Massachusetts-born Hiram Walker (1816-99). Now one of the world's largest distilleries, the amalgamated company is located in Walkerville, Ont., where it manufactures a variety of liquor products, including the famous CANADIAN CLUB, Ballantine's Scotch, Lauder's Scotch, Royal Canadian, and several cordials. More than 80% of its sales are in the United States. See also David ROBERTS.

Hirsch, John (b.1930). Stage and television director. Born in Siófok, Hungary, he came to Winnipeg in 1948 and was educated at the University of Manitoba. With Tom HENDRY he was co-founder of the MANITOBA THEATRE CENTRE, with which he was associated from 1958 to 1967—a period in which he established his international reputation as an imaginative and skilful director. His production of *The Dybbuk* at the MTC in 1974 was highly praised. He directed with Jean GASCON at the STRATFORD FESTIVAL in 1968-9 and was appointed chief of CBC-TV drama in 1974.

Hirshhorn, Joseph. See RIO ALGOM LTD.

His Majesty's Yankees. Novel by Thomas RADDALL published in 1942. A convincing historical romance set during the American Revolution, it stresses the desire of early colonists in Nova Scotia to remain neutral.

His Worship. Title of a mayor of a city, the female form being 'Her Worship'. The formal style of address is 'Sir' or 'Madam'; the informal style is 'Mr Mayor' or 'Madam Mayor'.

Historic Sites and Monuments Board of Canada. Federal body responsible for historic plaques and markers. Established in 1919, the Board—composed of 12 provincial and two federal officials, all appointed—advises the Minister of Indian Affairs and Northern Development on matters of national historic importance. It commemorates persons and events of significance through the erection of blue-and-gold plaques and markers.

History Makers Series, The. A series of 17 documentary films produced by the NATIONAL FILM BOARD between 1961 and 1964. The executive director was Julian Biggs. The films were grouped in three sub-series called 'Explorations', 'Prelude to Confederation', and 'The Struggle for Self-government'. 30 min., b & w.

History of Emily Montague, The. The first Canadian novel. It was written by an Englishwoman, Frances BROOKE, and published in 1769. Inspired by the author's life in Quebec, the story is told in 228 letters and provides a good description of the life of a garrison-based society. It reflects contemporary views on the potential of Canada, on French Canadians, and on the Indians.

Hiving the Grits. Phrase used by Sir John A. MACDONALD to describe the effect of the Redistribution Act of Apr. 1882, which reduced the strength of the Liberals (or GRITS) in Ontario. See also GERRYMANDER.

HMCS. Abbreviation of Her [His] Majesty's Canadian Ship, a naval designation.

Hochelaga. Palisaded Iroqouis town on the site of Montreal. Jacques CARTIER visited Hochelaga in Oct. 1535.

Hochwald Ridge. Ridge of land in Holland between two forests, the Hochwald and the Balbergerwald, the scene of vicious fighting during the SECOND WORLD WAR. Canadian and British troops gained possession of the kidney-shaped ridge in late Feb. 1945, prior to crossing the Rhine in March.

Hockey. See ICE HOCKEY.

Hockey Canada. Federal body established in Feb. 1969 to develop, manage, and operate a national team or teams to represent Canada in international tournaments and to foster and support the playing of hockey in Canada. Among other things, it arranges the amateur and professional games played against U.S.S.R. teams.

Hockey Hall of Fame. See HALLS OF FAME.

Hockey Night in Canada. National radio and television coverage of NATIONAL HOCKEY LEAGUE games during the hockey season. This venerable institution began with Foster HEWITT's radio coverage of games played by the TORONTO MAPLE LEAFS in the season of 1931-2, although on a purely local basis play-by-play coverage of amateur games began with Norman Albert's commentaries on 8 Feb. 1923. Canada's first-ever hockey telecast was transmitted in French over CBFT in Montreal on 11 Oct. 1952 when the MONTREAL CANADIENS played the Detroit Red Wings; René Lecavalier was the commentator. The first English-language telecast was carried on CBLT in Toronto on 1 Nov. 1952 when the Toronto Maple Leafs played the Boston Bruins, with Hewitt reporting the game. 'Hockey Night in Canada' is the most popular program on Canadian radio or television. For many years an intermission feature was the 'Hot Stove League', in which sports personalities such as Wes McKnight, Bobby Hewitson, Elmer FERGUSON, Syl APPS, and Harold Cotton sat around a pot-bellied stove in a general-store setting and talked about the game. See also MacLAREN ADVERTISING.

Hodgson, George (b.1893). Champion swimmer. Born in Montreal, he represented Canada at the 1912 Olympics in Stockholm, where he won the 1,500-metre swim event and, by continuing to one mile, broke three world records in a single event. He also broke the world record in the 400-metre event.

Hoffer, Dr Abram. See PSYCHEDELIC.

Hog town or **Hogtown.** Uncomplimentary reference to Toronto. Its origin and meaning—whether it refers to hogs or to 'hogging' the wealth of Canada—are not known.

Holey Dollar. The name and description of a coin circulated in Prince Edward Island about 1810. The coin in general circulation, a large silver 'Spanish Dollar', was mutilated by the governor to keep it on the island. The centre was punched out and the outer rim passed for five shillings, the centre for one shilling.

Holgate, Edwin H. (b.1892). Painter and a late member of the GROUP OF SEVEN. Born in Allandale, Ont., and educated in Montreal and Paris, he settled in Montreal, where he taught. More of a figure than a landscape painter, he was a member of the Group only briefly, being invited to join in 1930. He is known for his full-bodied female nudes, posed outdoors, of which *Nude* (1930, AGO) is an example.

Holiday Theatre. See Joy COGHILL.

Holidays. Days set aside each year by law or custom to mark specific events or occasions. Statutory holidays are established by act of the federal government, by the provincial legislatures, or proclaimed by municipalities. Non-statutory holidays are observed by custom among certain groups, but have no official status. The following holidays are observed by federal employees throughout Canada by federal statute (in addition to the 52 Sundays each year): NEW YEAR'S DAY, GOOD FRIDAY, EASTER MONDAY, VICTORIA DAY, DOMINION DAY, LABOUR DAY, THANKSGIVING DAY, REMEMBRANCE DAY, and CHRISTMAS DAY.

Additional statutory holidays in the provinces are: *Alberta*, BOXING DAY, Alberta Heritage Day; *British Columbia*, Boxing Day, British Columbia Day; *Manitoba*, Boxing Day, CIVIC HOLIDAY; *New Brunswick*, Boxing Day; *Newfoundland*, ST PATRICK'S DAY, ST GEORGE'S DAY, Commonwealth Day, DISCOVERY DAY, MEMORIAL DAY, ORANGEMAN'S DAY, Boxing Day; *Nova Scotia*, Boxing Day; *Ontario*, Civic Holiday; *Prince Edward Island*, Boxing Day; *Quebec*, Fête de Saint-Jean-Baptiste; *Saskatchewan*, Boxing Day; *Yukon Territory*, Discovery Day; *Northwest Territories*, Civic Holiday, Boxing Day.

Hollinger Mines Limited. Well-known gold mining company. The original discovery of gold at what is now TIMMINS in northern Ontario was made by Benny Hollinger, a barber from Haileybury, in Sept. 1909. The company that brought the gold mine into production was created in 1910 by Noah Timmins (1867-1936) and his brother Henry. The original mine was operated until 1968. The

Hollinger Mines Limited

Timmins family broadened the gold base to include iron ore from the Labrador-Quebec 'iron trough'. Hollinger, whose largest single stockholder is ARGUS CORPORATION, is the major shareholder of NORANDA MINES, since Noah Timmins provided the key financing to put Noranda into production.

Hollywood, Canadians in. There has been a 'Canadian colony' in Hollywood from the days of silent movies to the nights of television series. The list that follows is composed of names of those movie personalities (performers, writers, directors, producers, etc.) who have some connection with Canada. Since the world of Hollywood is an international one, a few Canadians (or former Canadian or new Canadians) who have made a larger contribution to European than to Canadian film-making have also been included. Lloyd BOCHNER, Geneviève BUJOLD, Jack Carson, Susan Clark, John COLICOS, Yvonne De Carlo, Edward Dmytrik, Marie Dressler, George DUNNING, Deanna Durbin, Allan Dwan, Robert FLAHERTY, Glenn Ford, Don Francks, Sidney FURIE, Elinor Glyn, Lorne GREENE, Monty Hall, Arthur Hill, Arthur HILLER, Walter Huston, Norman JEWISON, Victor Jory, Peter Kastner, Ruby Keeler, Margot Kidder, Ted KOTCHEFF, Rich LITTLE, Gene Lockhart, Bert Lytell, Larry Mann, Raymond MASSEY, Louis B. Mayer, Leslie Nielsen, Sidney Olcott, Walter Pidgeon, Mary PICKFORD, Gordon PINSENT, Harold Russell, Ann Rutherford, Harry Saltzman, Michael SARRAZIN, Mack Sennett, William SHATNER, Douglas Shearer, Norma Shearer, Joanna Shimkus, Bernard SLADE, Alexis Smith, Ned SPARKS, Alexandra STEWART, Donald SUTHERLAND, Eva Tanguay, John VERNON, Jack L. Warner, Richard WILLIAMS, Austin WILLIS, Joseph Wiseman, Fay Wray, Alan Young. See also Canadians on BROADWAY.

Hollywood's Canada. Title of a book by Pierre BERTON. Published in 1975 and subtitled *The Americanization of Our National Image*, the study analyses 575 Hollywood films made between 1907 and 1975 that are specifically set in Canada. Berton notes how the images of the Northwest, the Métis, French Canadians, the RCMP, etc. have been 'blurred' and 'distorted' as a result of these films' misrepresentations.

Holman. Eskimo settlement in the Northwest Territories, located on Holman Island in King's Bay, Amundsen Gulf, on the west coast of Victoria Island. There has been a co-operative printmaking studio at Holman since 1967. Artists who work there include Mark EMERAK, Helen KALVAK, and Agnes NANOGAK.

Holmes, Harry (Hap) (1889-1940). Hockey player. Born in Aurora, Ont., he became a professional goalkeeper and in 15 years played with five clubs. He was a member of four STANLEY CUP winning teams—Toronto (twice), Seattle, and Victoria—and was elected to the Hockey HALL OF FAME.

Holmes, Sherlock. See the BOOTMAKERS OF TORONTO.

Holt Renfrew and Company Ltd. A chain of high-fashion stores specializing in sports wear, furs, women's accessories, and men's wear. The present company, formed in Montreal in 1909, dates back to 1837 when W.S. Henderson, an Irish entrepreneur, arrived in Quebec City with a cargo of fur caps and hats, which he proceeded to merchandise. Since 1947 Holt Renfrew has held exclusive Canadian rights to Christian Dior's *haute couture*. Now American owned, it operated in 1976 through 22 specialty stores from Quebec City to Vancouver.

Homburger, Walter (b.1924). Impresario. Born in Karlsruhe, Germany, he arrived in Canada during the Second World War as a friendly enemy alien. In 1947 he became founder and director of International Artists, Toronto, a branch of the American agency, and was the first person to bring international artists to Toronto's MASSEY HALL on a regular basis. He discovered Glenn GOULD at a Kiwanis Club Music Festival and as Gould's manager became the first Canadian to manage the international career of a Canadian concert artist. He was the NATIONAL BALLET'S first general manager and in 1962 took over the management of the TORONTO SYMPHONY ORCHESTRA.

Home Bank failure. The Home Bank, a chartered bank, was forced to close its doors on 17 Aug. 1923. This was the first chartered bank to fail since the closing of the Farmers Bank in 1911. The failure was unexpected because the report to the stockholders issued two months earlier had shown a good financial standing. In October the president, vice-president, five directors, the general manager, the chief accountant, and the chief auditor were arrested and charged with signing or approving false statements respecting the Bank's standing. It was claimed that they had manipulated the books so that dividends were paid out of depositors' cash, not out of earnings. The president died three months before the beginning of the trials in 1924; the others were found guilty on various counts. The convictions against the vice-president and other directors were quashed on appeal in 1925 because the directors had no direct knowledge that the statements were false but relied on the management of the Bank. The Bank had 71 branches, the majority in Ontario. Not only the shareholders but the depositors lost money over the failure, a rare event in Canadian banking history and the cause of great hardship, as most of the depositors were working people.

Home District. The counties of York, Ontario, Peel, and Simcoe. A judicial division, it existed from 1792 until 1849, when the Province of Canada ceased to be divided into districts.

Home of the Klondike. Unofficial motto of the YUKON TERRITORY.

Homebrew. A slang term for a native-born (or local) hockey or football player. A 'homebrew' is the opposite of an 'IMPORT'.

Homestead Act. Act of Parliament passed in 1872, called the Free Land Homestead Act. It governed the conditions under which government land was to be settled, especially in the West, by homesteaders.

Homesteader's Bible. Colloquial name for a mail-order catalogue, especially EATON'S CATALOGUE.

Homme et son péché, Un. The most popular French-language CBC Radio series in its day. The *homme* (man) was Séraphin Poudrier, an old *habitant*, and his *péché* (sin) was miserliness. Conflict was created by his young and saintly wife Donalda. The series, based on the novel by Claude-Henri Grignon (1894-1976) published in 1933, was heard for 15 minutes a day, Monday through Friday, beginning in 1940. It made a brief transition to CBC-TV in the mid-1950s and then was dropped.

Hon. Member for Kingston, The. A reference associated with Sir John A. MACDONALD, Prime Minister of Canada, who represented the Kingston riding in Parliament almost continuously from his first election in 1844 to his death in 1891.

Honest Ed's. Well-known discount department store in Toronto, said to be the first such discount outlet in North America. It was opened in 1948 by Ed MIRVISH, Toronto businessman and philanthropist.

Honest John rocket. See BOMARC.

Honeymoon Bridge. A suspension bridge that spanned the Niagara R. between Niagara Falls ('The Honeymoon Capital of the World'), Ont., and Niagara Falls, N.Y. Its 1,400-ft span was the longest in its day.

Erected in 1898, it was destroyed by ice and collapsed at 4:10 p.m. on 27 Jan. 1938. It was replaced by the RAINBOW BRIDGE.

Honeymoon capital of the world. Unofficial motto of Niagara Falls, Ont.

Hong Kong. British island and free port off the coast of southeast China, occupied by the Japanese during the SECOND WORLD WAR. At the request of the British government, Canada sent two battalions—The Royal Rifles of Canada and the Winnipeg Grenadiers—under Brigadier J.K. Lawson, to reinforce the British and Indian troops garrisoned there. On 8 Dec. 1941, three weeks after the arrival of the Canadians, the Japanese attacked the garrison, which surrendered on Christmas Day. The men were imprisoned for four years. Of the 1,975 Canadians who were sent, 557 never returned. See also HONG KONG INQUIRY.

Hong Kong Inquiry. The popular name for the 'royal commission to inquire into and report upon the organization, authorization and dispatch of the Canadian Expeditionary Force to the Crown Colony of Hong Kong'. It was created in 1942 with Sir Lyman Duff, Chief Justice of Canada, as commissioner. Duff was charged with determining whether the Canadian forces sent to HONG KONG and taken prisoner when the colony fell to the Japanese on Christmas Day 1941 had been properly equipped and trained. His report fixed blame on some military officers but generally absolved the government of blame, a finding that provoked political debate during and after the war.

Honker. A colloquial name for the CANADA GOOSE, whose cry is a kind of honk.

Honourable, The. Style of address, in Canada, of all members of the Privy Council of Canada, all senators, all premiers and members of the executive councils of the provinces, and all justices of the superior courts of Canada and the provinces. It precedes the name of the official and is generally abbreviated to 'The Hon.' See also The RIGHT HONOURABLE.

Honourable Company, The. Sobriquet applied to the HUDSON'S BAY COMPANY, sometimes sarcastically. The phrase served as the title of a history of the Company by Douglas MacKay, published in 1936.

Honourable Member, The. Designation of a member in the House of Commons. When one member refers to another, he is identified not by his name but by his honorific and constituency, as 'The Honourable Member

Honourable Member

for Nanaimo-Cowichan-The Islands' or 'The Honourable Member for Bonavista-Trinity-Conception'. When there is agreement in the House, HANSARD reports it as, 'Some hon. Members: Hear, hear!' Disagreement is reported as, 'Some hon. Members: Oh, oh!'

Honourable Member of Parliament for Kicking Horse Pass, The. Humorous caricature of a western MP created by comedian Dave BROADFOOT in 1952. Familiar to radio, television, and stage audiences, the bombastic MP is a member of the New Apathetic Party whose slogan is 'Apathy is on the March!'

Honours, Canadian. An exclusively Canadian honours system was first introduced in 1967. Canadian honours are the ORDER OF CANADA; the ORDER OF MILITARY MERIT; the CROSS OF VALOUR; the STAR OF COURAGE; and the MEDAL OF BRAVERY.

Hood, Dora. See DORA HOOD'S BOOK ROOM.

Hood, Hugh (b.1928). Novelist and short-story writer. Born in Toronto and a graduate of the University of Toronto, he joined the English department of the Université de Montréal in 1961. His admirable short stories have been collected in *Flying a Red Kite* (1962), *Around the Mountain: Scenes from Montreal Life* (1967), *The Fruit Man, the Meat Man, and the Manager* (1971), and *Dark Glasses* (1976). His novels are *White Figure, White Ground* (1964), *The Camera Always Lies* (1967), *A Game of Touch* (1970), *You Can't Get There from Here* (1972), and *The Swing in the Garden* (1975)—the first in a projected 12-volume series, 'The NEW AGE/Le Nouveau·Siècle', that is intended to document the experience of living in Canada for the better part of a century. He has also written *Strength Down Centre: The Jean BÉLIVEAU Story* (1970) and *The Governor's Bridge Is Closed* (1973), a collection of personal essays.

Hoodless, Adelaide Hunter (1857-1910). Founder of the Federation of WOMEN'S INSTITUTES of Canada. Born on a farm near St George, Ont., she raised a family in Hamilton, Ont. After the youngest of her four children died from drinking contaminated milk—then sold from house to house in open containers—she devoted her life to educating mothers in all the home-making skills. She founded the Institute in 1897 and assisted in forming the national YWCA (1893), the National Council of Women (1894), the VICTORIAN ORDER OF NURSES, and was instrumental in founding the Ontario Normal School of Domestic Science and Art in Hamilton in 1900. Her efforts led to the formation of de-

gree-granting programs in household-science courses in universities and, through gaining the interest of Sir William MACDONALD, in the founding of colleges for this purpose. Her family home in St George, Ont., has been designated a historic site.

Hoodoo. A tall column of earth, often 20 to 30 ft high and capped by a large boulder, caused by erosion. Frequently occurring in mountain valleys, hoodoos can be found in Big Muddy Valley, Sask., the Alberta BADLANDS, and in Hoodoo Valley in YOHO NATIONAL PARK.

Hootch. A cheap but powerful homemade whisky. Distilled in coal-oil cans from the fermentation of sour dough and sugar, it was popular during the KLONDIKE GOLD RUSH.

Horn, Kahn-Tineta (b.1942). Mohawk activist. Born at CAUGHNAWAGA, Que., she adopted her Indian name (which means 'Green Meadows') and became a Montreal fashion model. She was named the first 'Miss Canadian Indian' in 1963 and the following year designed the Princess Kanata Indian Doll for the International Toy and Trade Fair. Since then she has agitated for Indian rights.

Hornby, John (1880-1927). Trapper and explorer. Born in England, he became identified with the BARREN LANDS after he spent several periods exploring them before and after the First World War. Hornby, his 17-year-old cousin Edgar Christian, and Harold Adlard died in a cabin from starvation on the last such trek in 1926-7. Christian left behind a diary, published as *Unflinching: A Diary of Tragic Adventure* (1937). See also *The Legend of John Hornby* (1962) by George Whalley.

Horne, Cleeve (b.1912). Portrait painter and sculptor. Born in Jamaica, he was brought to Toronto by his parents in 1913 and studied at the ONTARIO COLLEGE OF ART. His portrait of John DIEFENBAKER (1968) hangs in the House of Commons. His bronze portrait sculptures include a bust of Shakespeare in the city gardens at Stratford, Ont., and the Benchers' Memorial in Osgoode Hall, Toronto (1951).

Horse and Train. Famous painting by Alex COLVILLE of a bare-backed horse running along a railway track towards an onrushing train—a meticulously detailed image that might be seen in a dream. (1954, AGH).

Horsemen, The. A reference to the ROYAL CANADIAN MOUNTED POLICE who are noted for their equestrian ability. The epithet was the title of the autobiography of C.W. Harvison, a former Commissoner of the Force, published in 1967.

Horwood, Harold (b.1923). Journalist and novelist. Born in St John's, Nfld, he was associated with Joey SMALLWOOD in his movement to bring Newfoundland into Confederation and in 1949 was the first member for Labrador to sit in the House of Assembly. An editorial writer for the St John's *Evening Telegram*, he has written three novels—*Tomorrow Will Be Sunday* (1966), *The Foxes of Beachy Cove* (1967), *The White Eskimo* (1972)—and one travel book, *Newfoundland* (1969). He edited *Voices Underground* (1972), a collection of poems by young poets on the island.

Hospital insurance. See MEDICARE.

'Hot Mush School, The'. The title of an article by H.F. Gadsby in the *Toronto Star* on 12 Dec. 1913 describing an exhibition of Georgian Bay sketches by A.Y. JACKSON and the work of all the younger artists of the time, some of whom later formed the GROUP OF SEVEN.

Hot Stove League. See HOCKEY NIGHT IN CANADA.

Hôtel de Ville, Montreal. The city hall in OLD MONTREAL, on rue Notre-Dame across from Place Jacques-Cartier. The first building was erected in 1874-8. It was designed by Maurice Perrault and A.C. Hutchison in the high-roofed style of the French Second Empire and modelled on the seventeenth-century Château de Maisons. It was destroyed by fire in 1922 and rebuilt in a simplified form. From its balcony in the summer of 1967 Charles de Gaulle, then President of France, gave his now-famous cry, *'Vive le Québec libre'* ('Long live free Quebec') to cheering *séparatistes* below.

Hôtel-Dieu de Montréal. One of the earliest hospitals on the North American continent north of Mexico. It was founded in the fall of 1642 by Jeanne MANCE, the first secular nurse in North America, who began treating three patients in MAISONNEUVE's fort. The construction of a separate hospital began in 1645. The institution has been in continuous operation ever since.

Hôtel-Dieu de Québec. The first hospital on the North American continent north of Mexico. Founded by the Duchesse d'Aiguillon, a niece of Cardinal Richelieu, at Quebec in 1639, its first building was completed in 1644. A second building went up in 1695-8. The present building—containing elements of the rebuilding that took place after the fire of 7 June 1755 and after further damage done in 1759—has 700 beds. A modern wing includes the Jesuit Chapel, a museum with many relics from the Old Régime.

Hotel Fort Garry. Famous hotel in Winnipeg. Since opening in 1913 near the historic FORT GARRY, its Gothic architecture has been a landmark of the city. There are 265 guest rooms.

Houde, Camillien (1889-1958). Former mayor of Montreal. He was first elected mayor of Montreal in 1928, and retained this position except for brief intervals until he retired in 1954. He was also a member of the Quebec legislature during the 1920s and won a federal seat in 1949. He was summarily interned by the federal government under Mackenzie KING 1940-4 because he advised French Canadians not to register under the National Resources Mobilization Act, a wartime act to register men for service within Canada, seen by many French Canadians as the first step towards CONSCRIPTION. He was a lively and colourful figure, recalled in many witty anecdotes.

Houle, Robert (b.1947). Saulteaux painter. Born at St Boniface, Man., he graduated in fine art from the University of Manitoba and in art education from McGill. His vividly coloured canvases are reminiscent of abstract expressionism; however, his traditional culture emerges in content and title. His work was exhibited in the Canadian Indian Art '74 Exhibition at the Royal Ontario Museum, Toronto. He lectures on Native American Art at the Université de Montréal and Concordia University.

House, Eric (b.1923). Actor. Born in Toronto, he acted with the STRAW HAT PLAYERS and at HART HOUSE THEATRE before studying at New York University in 1951. He spent the 1952-3 season with the Canadian Repertory Theatre in Ottawa and joined the STRATFORD FESTIVAL as a character actor in 1953—appearing in five seasons thereafter. In the fall of 1974 he was seen on national television in a chocolate company's commercial asking, 'Are you getting enough?'

House of Anansi Press. See House of ANANSI PRESS.

House of Assembly. Term for a colonial legislature. In colonial times the House of Assembly was taken to mean the lower elected house (the LEGISLATIVE ASSEMBLY), but on occasion it was also taken to include the upper appointed house (the LEGISLATIVE COUNCIL). Since CONFEDERATION the name House of Assembly has been retained in only two provinces, Newfoundland and Nova Scotia, where it designates the provincial legislature.

House of Commons

House of Commons, The. The lower house of the legislature; the house of Parliament whose members are elected, not appointed. Because its members are elected, it can be said to represent the will of the electorate. It was agreed at CONFEDERATION that the number of seats each province could elect to the House of Commons would be based on REPRESENTATION BY POPULATION. There were 264 seats following the 1971 census. The number awarded to each province is: Ontario 91, Quebec 72, Nova Scotia 10, New Brunswick 10, Manitoba 12, British Columbia 26, Prince Edward Island 4, Saskatchewan 12, Alberta 19, Newfoundland 6, Yukon Territory 1, Northwest Territories 1. All members of the House of Commons are elected from single-member constituencies whose boundaries are determined from time to time by a boundary commission that reports to Parliament. The maximum period between elections is five years, but a Parliament may be dissolved and new elections called at any time. Parliament is summoned and dissolved by the GOVERNOR GENERAL, on the advice of the prime minister, and must hold at least one session a year, which may be of any length; extra sessions may also be held.

The government is responsible to the House of Commons, and when it loses the confidence of the House—when it is defeated on a motion of non-confidence or on a money bill or other vote on which it has staked its life—it must resign or the prime minister must request the governor general to dissolve Parliament and call a general election. All acts of the government must be authorized by laws passed by Parliament.

The House of Commons is competent to legislate on all matters placed under federal jurisdiction by the BNA ACT. MONEY BILLS must be introduced first in the House of Commons, but PUBLIC BILLS or PRIVATE BILLS may originate in either the House of Commons or the SENATE. Bills are given three readings in each House, and if passed go to the governor general for his formal signature before becoming law. The business of the House of Commons is presided over by the SPEAKER, who is elected by the members.

Houston, James (b.1921). Author, designer, and arts administrator. Born in Toronto, he attended the ONTARIO COLLEGE OF ART and Yale University and studied art in Paris. On a sketching trip on the east coast of Hudson Bay in 1948 he acquired Eskimo soapstone carvings, which were sold by the Canadian Handicrafts Guild (now the Canadian Guild of Crafts) in Montreal. In 1951 he went to Baffin Island for the Guild and continued to encourage the Eskimo artists who, under his guidance, made more and more of their carvings available in the south. With his first wife Alma (born in Ottawa in 1926), he lived at Cape Dorset in the fifties as a Northern Service Officer of the Department of Northern Affairs. He spent 1958 in Japan studying print-making techniques, which he introduced to the eastern Arctic with impressive results. Since 1962 he has been an associate director of Steuben Glass. The author of numerous popular children's books, which he illustrated himself, he edited *Eskimo Prints* (1967) and wrote the best-selling novel *The* WHITE DAWN: *An Eskimo Saga* (1971); he also worked on the screenplay for the feature film based on his novel that was released in 1974.

How to Break a Quarter Horse. A moving teleplay by Paul ST PIERRE. Produced and directed by Philip Keatley and shown by CBC-TV on 19 Jan. 1966, it starred Chief Dan GEORGE as OL'ANTOINE, who harbours an Indian accused of murder and figuratively breaks the white man's laws to bring about justice. It was partly the basis of a novel, *Breaking Smith's Quarter Horse* (1966), which gave rise to the Walt Disney film *Smith* (1969).

Howard, John George (1803-90). Architect and watercolourist. Born John Corby near London (he changed his name in 1832), he was trained in various London architectural offices and in Maidstone, Kent. In 1832 he immigrated to York (now Toronto), where he held the position of drawing master at Upper Canada College from 1833 to 1856. As an architect Howard practised in a wide variety of styles, all related to the forms current in Late Georgian and Regency England. His churches in the Gothic style apply romantic details to basically Classical buildings: Holy Trinity, Chippewa (1840); St John's, York Mills (1843); and Christ Church, Holland Landing (1843). The designs for the Lunatic Asylum, 999 Queen St W., Toronto (1846, demolished 1976), one of the most advanced buildings of its day in North America, owed much to William Wilkins' National Gallery in London. Howard's own home, Colborne Lodge, Toronto (1836), is perhaps the first picturesque Italianate villa in North America, and today forms the centre-piece of HIGH PARK, the country estate he gave to the City of Toronto.

Howard-Gibbon, Amelia Frances. See AMELIA FRANCES HOWARD-GIBBON MEDAL.

Howe, Clarence Decatur (1886-1960). Former cabinet minister. Born in Massachusetts and educated at the Massachusetts Institute of

Technology, he came to Canada in 1907 to teach at Dalhousie University and subsequently became a successful businessman. He entered federal politics as a Liberal in 1935 and was immediately taken into Mackenzie KING's cabinet. Howe was responsible for establishing the CANADIAN BROADCASTING CORPORATION and Trans-Canada Air Lines (now AIR CANADA), and during the war, as Minister of Munitions and Supply, for Canada's war production. As Minister of Trade and Commerce he introduced the bill concerning Trans-Canada Pipelines, which led to the PIPELINE DEBATE. He was defeated in the election of 1957 and returned to a business career for the remainder of his life. See also C.D. HOWE RESEARCH INSTITUTE.

Howe, Gordon (Gordie) (b.1928). Hockey player. Born in Floral, Sask., he began playing professional hockey with the Detroit Red Wings and, through 25 seasons, established NHL records for most goals, most points, most trophies, and most selections to all-star teams. At 48 he continues to play and is joined on the WORLD HOCKEY ASSOCIATION's Houston, Texas, team by his two sons—Mark and Marty—both of whom are potentially great players.

Howe, Joseph (1804-73). Statesman, known as 'the tribune of Nova Scotia'. Born in Halifax, N.S., he learned the printing trade and in 1828 was able to buy the NOVASCOTIAN, which became a prominent newspaper and first published the SAM SLICK narratives by T.C. HALIBURTON. He made a famous two-day speech in defence of an 'unshackled press' in May 1835. Howe was elected to the House of Assembly as a reformer in 1836 and displayed his growing oratorical and literary powers by speaking out in favour of RESPONSIBLE GOVERNMENT and, in 1839, writing four long, masterly letters on the subject to the colonial secretary. He was premier from 1861 to 1863. As imperial fishery commissioner from 1863 to 1866 he did not assist the province's entry into CONFEDERATION but rather opposed it, notably in a series of articles, written early in 1865, in which he referred to the proposed federal union as the 'BOTHERATION SCHEME'. Converted from this point of view in 1869 by tactful persuasion and an increased annual subsidy for the province, he joined the Dominion cabinet as president of council and was later Secretary of State. He died shortly after taking office as lieutenant-governor of Nova Scotia.

Howland, Sir William P. (1811-1907). A FATHER OF CONFEDERATION. Born in Pauling, N.Y., he came to Upper Canada (Ontario) in 1830 and eventually started a wholesale gro-

cery business in Toronto. Elected to the legislative assembly in 1857, he was a member of the GREAT COALITION ministry and attended the LONDON CONFERENCE on Confederation. He was lieutenant-governor of Ontario from 1868 to 1873 and was knighted in 1879.

HRH. Abbreviation of His Royal Highness or Her Royal Highness, the style of address for the son or daughter of a monarch. HH is used to refer to a prince or princess who is not a member of the reigning family.

Hub of the North. Unofficial motto of Sudbury, Ont.

Hub of the West. Unofficial motto of Medicine Hat, Alta.

Hudson, Henry (active 1607-11). English navigator and explorer. Searching for the route to China on a voyage of 1609, he ascended the Hudson R. as far as Albany. In 1610 he sailed westward in the *Discovery*, entering Hudson Strait (first entered by Martin FROBISHER in 1578). A poor leader, and with a very mixed crew, Hudson was subjected to a mutiny in Ungava Bay, but order was restored and Hudson Bay was entered. The winter was spent near the mouth of the Rupert R. in James Bay, while relations with the crew worsened. On the night of 23 June 1611 Hudson, his son John, and seven others were set adrift in a shallop. The ship returned to England under Robert Bylot. An account of the voyage was published by one of the members, Abacuk Pricket.

Hudson Bay. One of the most distinctive and predominant water features on the entire planet when viewed from space. Situated between the Northwest Territories and Manitoba on the west, Ontario on the south, Quebec on the east, and the Arctic Islands to the north, this body of salt water covers an area of over 317,501 sq. mi. It is properly a 'bay' of neither the Arctic nor Atlantic Oceans but rather an 'inland sea' in its own right.

Hudson Bay Mining and Smelting Company Limited. Mining company. It had its origins in the discovery in 1915 of deposits of various minerals in the Manitoba-Saskatchewan border area. In 1930 the company opened a complex of plants and mines with the financial resources of the Whitney family of the United States and by agreement with the provincial government the town of Flin Flon was developed (it was incorporated in 1946). In 1962 the company was acquired by the South African corporate giant, Anglo-American Corp. See also FLIN FLON STRIKE.

Hudson Bay Railway. The first railway to

247

service the Canadian North, completed in 1932 and extending from The Pas to Churchill, Man., on Hudson Bay. It is also known as the Muskeg Express, the Highball Express, the Muskeg Limited, and the Muskeg Special.

Hudson's Bay blanket. See POINT BLANKET.

Hudson's Bay Company. Historically important fur-trading company and modern retail organization. It was founded by royal charter in 1670—as 'The Governor and Company of Adventurers of England trading into Hudson's Bay'—by a group of English merchants who had sent RADISSON and GROSEILLIERS to the Bay in 1668. (Radisson had to turn back, but Groseilliers returned with a cargo of furs the next year.) The HBC received title to 'Rupert's Land'—the drainage basin of Hudson Bay extending as far west as the valley of the Saskatchewan—and built posts on Hudson Bay and James Bay, letting the Indians come to them, though its rivals—French fur-traders and, later, independent British and American traders who formed the NORTH WEST COMPANY—went into the interior to meet the Indians. In 1774 Samuel HEARNE built the HBC's first western inland post, Cumberland House (Sask.). In 1816 conflict with the North West Company broke out in the RED RIVER SETTLEMENT, which was on land granted by the HBC to Lord SELKIRK. The two companies united, however, in 1821 and the expanded HBC was reorganized. In 1869 it surrendered Rupert's Land to Canada for £ 300,000, one-twentieth of the arable land within the designated fertile belt, and retained its posts. In the 1880s the company entered the retail trade and now has department stores in Victoria, Vancouver, Calgary, Edmonton, Saskatoon, Regina, Winnipeg (its headquarters), Ottawa, Toronto, and Montreal, and over 300 smaller stores in the North and numerous Shop-Rite catalogue stores. In addition it has large wholesale operations and extensive fur-trade and oil interests.

Hull, Bobby (b.1939). Hockey star. Born at Point Anne, Ont., he weighed 12 lb. at birth and learned to skate at the age of four. From 1957 to 1972 he played with the Chicago Black Hawks, where he was known as 'Gentlemanly Bobby' for his courteous manner and the 'Golden Jet' for his skating speed. In 1972 he joined the Winnipeg Jets. Associated Press voted him Player of the Decade, narrowly edging out Gordie HOWE and easily defeating Bobby ORR.

Human Rights. See CANADIAN BILL OF RIGHTS.

Humanities Research Council of Canada. A non-governmental voluntary association that encourages the development of the humanities, particularly in Canadian universities, and represents the interest of the humanities in Canada. Founded in 1943, the Council is composed of representatives of the LEARNED SOCIETIES and individual scholars. It is an advisory body and does not fund research activities. See also its parallel organization, the SOCIAL SCIENCE RESEARCH COUNCIL OF CANADA.

Humphrey, Jack W. (1901-67). Painter. Born in Saint John, N.B., he studied in Boston and Provincetown, Mass., for nine years, and in Munich with Hans Hofmann, before returning to Saint John, which gave him the subjects for a lifetime of painting. These included memorable children's portraits of the 1930s and postwar watercolours of New Brunswick scenery, which embraced both figurative and abstract treatments and sometimes the two combined. Two well-known Humphreys are a Cubist-influenced self-portrait, *Draped Head* (1931), in Hart House, University of Toronto, and *Portrait of a Girl* (1947), in the New Brunswick Museum, Saint John.

Hundred Associates. See COMPANY OF NEW FRANCE.

Hungerford, George (b.1944). Champion oarsman. The British Columbia athlete, paired with Roger JACKSON, competed in the 'two-thousand-metres pairs without coxswain' at the 1964 Olympics in Tokyo and earned the gold medal over more experienced scullers.

Hungry Thirties. A reference to the DEPRESSION (1929-39) when many were unemployed and on relief. See also DIRTY THIRTIES.

Hunt, Dora de Pédery. See Dora DE PÉDERY-HUNT.

Hunt, Tony (b.1942). Kwakiutl carver. Born in British Columbia, he learned wood carving in Victoria from his adoptive grandfather, Mungo MARTIN. A master carver himself, he lives in Victoria, B.C., where he makes jewellery, totem poles, and lyrical silkscreens. In 1970 he opened the Arts of the Raven Gallery in Victoria. In the summer of 1975 he carved a 10-ft totem pole at the CANADIAN NATIONAL EXHIBITION in Toronto.

Hunter, George (b.1921). Photographer. Born in Regina, Sask., he worked as a press photographer for the *Winnipeg Tribune* and a still photographer for the National Film Board before specializing in industrial and international travel photography in 1950. He lives in Toronto but travels across the country four times each year to record Canadian scenes in photographs that have appeared in most major North American magazines.

Hunters' Lodges. Secret society organized in Vermont in 1838 in support of the REBELLION OF 1837. With lodges in border states, they were dedicated to making the British North American colonies independent of British rule and undertook raids on Upper Canada (Ontario), including one near Prescott (Battle of the WINDMILL) and another at Windsor towards the end of the year.

'Hunting in couples'. Political phrase used to describe Sir John A. MACDONALD's practice of fighting an election after having secured the allegiance of a provincial government. It is associated with the period from CONFEDERATION to 1871, when members of the Ontario provincial legislature could also sit in the federal House of Commons.

Hurley, Robert (b.1894). Painter. Born in London, Eng., he came to Canada in 1923 as a farm labourer and studied painting at the Saskatoon Technical College with Ernest LINDNER. His prairie watercolours ignore human figures to concentrate on the flat, empty landscape. Luminous colour relationships are established by a strong design sense, which is also seen in his acrylic paintings of the British Columbia landscape.

Huron. IROQUOIAN-speaking Indians with an agricultural economy who lived in villages between Georgian Bay and Lake Simcoe when first encountered in the seventeenth century. They developed strong trading relationships with the neighbouring Algonkin and other ALGONKIAN groups, such as the Nipissing, and in the early fur-trade period combined with them to resist raids by the IROQUOIS League, with French support. Many were killed by the League in 1648-9. Some moved to the west and a small remnant moved to Quebec, where they remained as a distinctive group on a single reserve. Their population in 1970 was 1,041. See also HURONIA, HURON MISSIONS.

'Huron Carol, The'. The first Canadian Christmas carol. It was written in the Huron tongue by Jean de BRÉBEUF about 1641 and sung by the Indians in HURONIA. Sometimes known by its Huron title *'Jesous ahatonhia'*, it was transcribed in the 1700s, translated into French before 1800, and into English by J.E. Middleton in 1926. The tune is reminiscent of 'God Rest You Merry Gentlemen'. It celebrates the birth of Jesus in North American Indian terms: the infant is wrapped in 'a robe of rabbit skin', and three 'chiefs' come bearing 'gifts of fox and beaver pelt'.

Huron Missions. Seventeenth-century missionary establishments of the Jesuits in HURONIA, near Georgian Bay (Ont.), where the HURON Indians lived. Jean de BRÉBEUF began the first Jesuit mission to the Hurons in 1626. Several missions were founded, including SAINTE-MARIE-AUX-HURONS, Ihonatiria, Saint-Joseph I and II, Saint-Ignace, and Saint-Louis. In the Iroquois raids of 1648-9 they were destroyed, though the priests themselves set fire to Sainte-Marie. See also JESUIT MARTYRS.

Huron Tract. A million-acre tract of land fronting on Lake Huron in western Upper Canada (Ontario). It was opened for settlement by the CANADA COMPANY in 1828, the year Goderich was founded.

Huronia. A fertile area in southern Ontario extending from Nottawasaga and Georgian Bays eastward to Lake Couchiching and Lake Simcoe. Peopled by the HURON Indians in the seventeenth century, it received the missionary attention of the Jesuits who founded several HURON MISSIONS there. They existed until 1648-9, when they were destroyed by the Iroquois and many of the Hurons were killed. Interest in the remains of the Indian villages and the missions was sparked in the nineteenth century, and since then archaeological work has been carried out and one of the Indian villages, SAINTE-MARIE-AUX-HURONS, reconstructed near Midland. See also MARTYRS' SHRINE.

Hurricane X. A famous single-engine fighter of the SECOND WORLD WAR. The backbone of the Battle of Britain in 1940, it was designed by Hawker in Britain and manufactured by Canadian Car and Foundry in Fort William, Ont. It used the Rolls-Royce Merlin engine. Some Hurricanes were used for home defence.

Hurtig Publishers. An Edmonton publishing company. It was founded in 1967 by Mel Hurtig (b.1932), who owned a chain of three Edmonton bookstores (founded in 1956), which he sold in 1972 to devote himself to book publishing. Beginning with reprints of Western and Arctic Canadiana, the company has moved into the public's eye with strong nationalistic and topical books. Hurtig is a charter member of the COMMITTEE FOR AN INDEPENDENT CANADA and a vocal critic of the foreign-owned oil industry.

Hurtubise, Jacques (b.1939). Painter. Born in Montreal, he studied there at the École des Beaux-Arts and was resident-artist at Dart-

Hurtubise

mouth College, N.H., in 1967. His use of the splashed-paint technique in colourful and highly controlled action paintings led to a deeper experiment with colour in 1965, when he developed a hard-edge abstract style that later incorporated pop elements like flashing neon lights. He has now refined the style of Op colour painting by using jig-saw-puzzle shapes and black-and-white optical forms. *Marielle* (1970, private coll.) represents his best work. He has exhibited internationally and lives in Montreal.

Hurtubise-HMH, Éditions. Quebec publishers. Founded in 1960 in Montreal by Claude Hurtubise, it specializes in sociology, history, and fiction. It publishes ÉCRITS DU CANADA FRANÇAIS.

Hush. A weekly tabloid published in Toronto between 1928 and 1973. Concentrating on sex-and-crime news, with the occasional sensational scoop, it boasted an immense North American newsstand circulation.

Husky. A word used by southerners to refer to a dog employed by Eskimos to pull their sleds, etc. The Eskimo word is QIMMIK.

Hutchison, Bruce (b.1901). Newspaper editor and author. Born in Prescott, Ont., and raised in British Columbia, he entered journalism as a sports writer but joined the Parliamentary Press Gallery in 1925 and became editor successively of the Winnipeg *Free Press*, the *Victoria Times*, and the *Vancouver Sun*. He tapped a nationalistic vein with two widely read books about Canada: *The UNKNOWN COUNTRY* (1942; rev. 1948) and *Canada: Tomorrow's Giant* (1957). Among his other books are *The Incredible Canadian* (1953), a biography of Mackenzie KING, and a novel, *The Hollow Men* (1944). He also wrote the text for CANADA/A YEAR OF THE LAND (1967). His autobiography, *The Far Side of the Street*, was published in 1976.

Hutt, William (b.1920). Actor and director. Born in Toronto, he graduated from the University of Toronto and acted with the HART HOUSE THEATRE (1947-9). An actor of great accomplishment, he has performed internationally and has been associated with the STRATFORD FESTIVAL since its inception in 1953, undertaking with distinction a wide range of roles, including Richard II, Tartuffe, Argan in *The Imaginary Invalid*, Prospero in *The Tempest*, and Lady Bracknell in *The Importance of Being Earnest*. He also appeared with great success as Sir John A. MACDONALD in CBC-TV's *The NATIONAL DREAM*. He is director of the Festival Stage at Stratford and in 1976 was appointed Artistic Director of Theatre London.

Hutterites. A pacifist German-speaking Christian sect living since 1918 in farming communities called colonies in Alberta, Saskatchewan, and Manitoba. They were originally an offshoot of the sixteenth-century Swiss Anabaptist movement.

Hydro Blackout, The Great. An electrical power failure that blacked out an area from Ontario to Florida and from Chicago to New York. At 5:27 p.m. on 9 Nov. 1965 a back-up relay at the Sir Adam Beck power-generation station at Queenston, Ont., failed and overloaded the power grid, sending electrical current along four rather than five lines. Thirty million people were affected for from three to 11 hours. The Doris Day film, *Where Were You When the Lights Went Out?*, was about the humorous side of the blackout.

Hydro-Electric Power Commission of Ontario. See ONTARIO HYDRO.

Hydrodrome-4. Experimental hydrofoil, fourth in a series, built by former members of the AERIAL EXPERIMENT ASSOCIATION. Designed by Alexander Graham BELL and F.W. (Casey) Baldwin, it reached a speed of 70.85 m.p.h. on Lake Baddeck, N.S., on 9 Sept. 1919.

Hyland, Frances (b.1927). Actress. Born at Shaunavon, Sask., she attended the Royal Academy of Dramatic Arts in London, Eng., and made her début as Stella in Tennessee Williams' *A Streetcar Named Desire* at the Aldwych Theatre in June 1950. A radiant actress of delicate sensibility and a somewhat mannered way of speaking, she has undertaken a wide variety of roles. She appeared in eight seasons of the STRATFORD FESTIVAL and took the lead in Shaw's *Saint Joan* in the first touring production of the CANADIAN PLAYERS in 1955. One of her best performances is in the NFB film DRYLANDERS (1964).

Hypermarché Laval. A giant supermarket that sells food and general merchandise. It was opened in the Montreal suburb of Laval on 31 Oct. 1973 by The Oshawa Group. The first store of its kind in North America, covering the area of four football fields, it innovated bulk handling and has 49 electronic computerized checkout terminals.

Hypertension. High blood pressure, the study of which is identified with Dr Jacques Genest. Born in Montreal in 1919, and a graduate of the Université de Montréal, Genest has headed the Clinical Research Institute of the HÔTEL-DIEU DE MONTRÉAL since 1952. His studies documenting the interrelationship between physiology and hypertension are recognized internationally.

Hypothermia. The artificial reduction of body temperature to slow metabolic processes, usually to facilitate open-heart surgery. The technique was developed by Dr William G. Bigelow at the Toronto General

Hospital between 1948 and 1952 and is identified with him.

Hy's. Restaurant chain. Founded by Hy Aisanstatt in Calgary, Alta, in 1955, it operates 'steak houses' in Calgary, Toronto, Vancouver, and Winnipeg, and in Chicago, Ill.

I

i never saw another butterfly. Song cycle by Srul Irving GLICK. Commissioned by the CBC for Maureen FORRESTER and written in 1968, it is based on poems by children from the concentration camp at Terezin.

Iberville, Pierre Le Moyne, Sieur d' (1661-1706). Ship's captain, adventurer, trader, hero of NEW FRANCE. The third of 12 sons of Charles LE MOYNE, he took part with great bravery and ruthlessness in numerous expeditions against the English. In 1686 he captured Moose Fort, Charles Fort, and Albany Fort on James Bay and commanded them until 1689. In 1690, with two of his brothers, he took part in a raid on Corlaer (Schenectady, N.Y.). He returned to Hudson Bay in 1690 and again in 1694, when he captured the most lucrative fur-trading station of the HUDSON'S BAY COMPANY, York Fort (YORK FACTORY), renamed Fort Bourbon. In 1695 he saw action in Acadia and the next year in Newfoundland, where he took St John's and destroyed the English fisheries on the eastern shore. In 1697 he was put in command of the PÉLICAN, one of four French ships sent back to the Bay to confront the English, who had regained control. Separated from the other ships, the *Pélican* engaged three English warships and sank one but had to abandoned. The French ships rescued the crew and brought about the surrender of York Factory. In 1698 Iberville was in Louisiana, sailing there by way of the Gulf of Mexico to the mouth of the Mississippi, where he built Fort Maurepas; he returned in 1700 and 1701. In 1706, in command of a fleet that was to attack the English in the West Indies, he captured the island of Nevis. He died a few months later in Havana. See also the television series D'IBERVILLE.

ICBC. Initials of the Insurance Corporation of British Columbia, which permits motorists

of that province to insure their automobiles through the low-cost Autoplan, established in 1973.

ICBM. Acronym of InterContinental Ballistic Missile. This supersonic surface-to-air guided missile, with a range of over 3,500 nautical miles, was developed for use by NORAD. See also IRBM.

Ice Ages. Geological epochs in which glaciers covered large areas of the continents. The most recent epoch occurred during the Pleistocene, which lasted from approximately 1 million to 8,000 years ago and during which there were four major glacial advances and retreats. The last of these major advances, which covered and scarred most of the surface of Canada, is called the Wisconsin. There is some evidence that another glacial advance may begin within the next few centuries—a slow process in which great walls of ice would advance southward over thousands of years, but whose major effect upon Canada would be in the initial stage, as weather changes would render most of the land now under cultivation useless for food crops.

Ice hockey. Game of Canadian origin played on skates by six-man teams consisting of a goalkeeper, two defencemen, and three forwards. There is evidence that a form of the game was played by Canadian Indians centuries ago. On 25 Dec. 1855 a regiment of the Royal Canadian Rifles at Kingston cleared an expanse of snow in the harbour for a game played on ice using field-hockey sticks and a LACROSSE ball. Ice hockey, as a game having a separate identity from field hockey, was recognized in 1860 when, for the first time, a puck was used. In 1879 two McGill students—W.F. Robertson and R.F. Smith—devised a set of rules and in 1880 the first official team, the McGill Hockey Club, was

Ice hockey

formed. Canada is recognized as the first country to organize the game on a national basis. It is the world's fastest team sport.

Ice-railway. A winter railway line built across the frozen St Lawrence R. between Montreal and Longueuil, Que. The tracks were laid in November and taken up the following April, between 1880 and 1882, by the GRAND TRUNK RAILWAY.

Ice Wagon. Popular name for the flying icing laboratory operated by the NATIONAL RESEARCH COUNCIL from 1949 to 1954. It consisted of a NORTH STAR, equipped with special safety and experimental devices, and was flown for study purposes into areas of atmospheric icing that regular aircraft skirted.

Ice-worm. Imaginary worm said to inhabit ice fields. Although a worm of the *Oligochaeta* family does live on mountain snow and ice fields, the ice-worm encountered in the Yukon is likely to be a bit of spaghetti with eyes painted on it added to a cocktail. 'I will meet thee when the ice-worms nest again' is a line from Robert W. SERVICE'S novel, *The Trail of '98* (1911).

ICR. Abbreviation of the Intercolonial Railway, now the CANADIAN NATIONAL RAILWAYS.

Idea of North, The. An impressionistic CBC documentary by Glenn GOULD. Shown on CBC-TV on 5 Aug. 1970 and heard two days later on CBC Radio, it preserved the sounds and sights of a train journey from Toronto to Churchill, Man. Its theme was that 'going North' tests one's courage. Scripted and recorded by Gould and produced and directed by Judith Pearlman of National Educational Television (NET) in New York, the program discovered Wally McLean, an Arctic surveyor and natural actor who did much of the talking.

Ideas. See CBC IDEAS.

IDIA. Acronym of INDUSTRIAL DISPUTES INVESTIGATION ACT.

Igloo. A snow shelter. The word is used by non-Eskimos for the domed structure built entirely of blocks of hard snow that was formerly inhabited by Eskimos during the winter months. Eskimos refer to this dwelling of olden days as an *igloovigak*. During the summer, Eskimos used to live in a TUPEK.

Igloo tag. Guarantee of authenticity and quality attached to an Eskimo art or craft object, in use since 20 Sept. 1958. It assures the purchaser that the carving was handmade by a Canadian ESKIMO at an Art Centre presided over by the Department of INDIAN AFFAIRS AND NORTHERN DEVELOPMENT. The black-and-white tag includes, within a cartouche, the words 'Canada' and either 'Eskimo Art' or 'Art Esquimau', as well as an igloo design. Added by hand are registered details: the name and community of the artist, the year the carving was made, and its description or name. The carving itself may be inscribed with the Eskimo's name (in Roman letters or Eskimo SYLLABICS) and an ESKIMO IDENTIFICATION DISC NUMBER. See also The BEAVER PELT.

Ikseetarkyuk, Luke (b.1909). Eskimo sculptor at BAKER LAKE. Best known for his stark carvings of skeletal human figures in bone and horn (such as a caribou antler), he portrays aspects of traditional life, including fishing, family gatherings, and SHAMAN.

Île d'Orléans. Island in the St Lawrence a few miles below Quebec City. Originally named Bacchus by Jacques CARTIER because of its wild grapes, it was subsequently renamed after the Duke of Orléans. First settled in 1648, the island was the site of one of Gen. James WOLFE'S camps prior to his attack on Quebec in 1759. Several eighteenth-century buildings—including Sainte-Famille Church, built in 1749—still stand. The island has been designated an *arrondissement historique*.

Île-Saint-Jean. French name for PRINCE EDWARD ISLAND until it was ceded to Britain in 1763, when it was called the Island of Saint John. It acquired its present name in 1799.

Îles-de-la-Madeleine. A 60-mi.-long archipelago of about 12 major islands discovered by Jacques CARTIER in 1534. Situated in the centre of the Gulf of St Lawrence and part of the province of Quebec, they are known for their soft red sandstone cliffs and beautiful beaches.

Illustrated Natural History of Canada. A series of well-illustrated books devoted to the fauna, flora, and geology of Canada. Nine volumes were published by McClelland & Stewart, under the advisory editorship of Pierre BERTON, between 1970 and 1975: *The Arctic Coast, The Pacific Coast, The Mountain Barrier, The Western Plains, The Great Lakes, The St. Lawrence Valley, The Atlantic Coast, The Natural History of Mammals,* and *The Nature of Birds.*

Images. Orchestral piece composed by Harry FREEDMAN in 1958. Inspired by Canadian painting, this popular work has become part of the standard orchestral repertoire in Canada.

Images of Canada. Eight 60-minute CBC-TV

documentaries on Canadian history. The executive producer of the program, which was described as a 'visual journey in time and place', was Vincent Tovell. The series made its début on 21 Feb. 1972.

Imago. A magazine devoted to long poems, issued semi-annually by George BOWERING from 1964 to 1974.

IMAX Process. A film technique designed and developed in Canada. Dramatically increasing the frame size of regular 35-mm film tenfold, the system employs 70-mm film in a horizontal position, using a rolling loop to advance the huge frames through the gate in a super-fast caterpillar-like wave-motion. IMAX and its offspring, the 180° fish-eye lens called OMNIMAX, were designed by William Shaw who, with Robert Kerr and Graeme FERGUSON, is a partner in Imax Entertainment Ltd of Cambridge, Ont. As of 1976 there are six theatres equipped to show IMAX films—two in museums (in Washington and Philadelphia), two in parks (ONTARIO PLACE in Toronto, Circus World in Florida), one in an amusement park (Sandusky, Ohio), and one in a planetarium (San Diego, Calif.). Eight IMAX films, all under 30 minutes in length, are in release: Donald BRITTAIN's *Tiger Child* (1970); Graeme Ferguson's NORTH OF SUPERIOR (1971), *Man Belongs to the Earth* (1974), and *Snow Job* (1974); David Mackay's *Catch the Sun* (1973); Christopher CHAPMAN's *Volcano* (1974); Roman KROITER's *Circus World* (1974); and Len Casey's *Energy* (1975).

Immigrant status. See LANDED IMMIGRANT STATUS.

Immigration Appeal Board. A court of record empowered to admit immigrants who appeal against the provisions of the Immigration Act. Established in 1967, the Board consists of nine permanent members and some temporary members.

Imperial Oil Limited. The largest oil company in Canada. Formed by a group of Canadian businessmen in Toronto in 1880, it is affiliated with Exxon Corporation (formerly Standard Oil of New Jersey), its largest shareholder, and markets its products under the Esso trademark. The company has produced *The* LOON'S NECKLACE and LEGEND OF THE RAVEN, sponsored HOCKEY NIGHT IN CANADA, preserved the C.W. JEFFERYS collection, and published the IMPERIAL OIL REVIEW. To mark its hundredth anniversary in 1980 it has commissioned an ambitious series of seven hour-long educational films to be broadcast by CBC-TV, beginning Nov. 1977, under the title *The Newcomers: Inhabiting a New Land.*

Imperial Oil Review. A magazine published six times a year since 1917 by IMPERIAL OIL LIMITED in Toronto. Well researched and illustrated, it includes articles on the oil industry, business, the arts, and Canadian life generally.

Imperial Order Daughters of the Empire. A women's patriotic and philanthropic organization. The first provincial chapter was formed in Fredericton on 13 Feb. 1900 and supplied comforts to Canadian soldiers fighting in the Boer War. Its motto is 'One Flag, One Throne, One Empire'.

Imperial Penny Postage Commemorative Issue of 1898. Famous 'Map Stamp' issued to mark the establishment of Imperial Penny Postage throughout the British Empire. Issued by Postmaster General William Mulock and marked 'Xmas 1898', the stamp depicts a Mercator projection of the world with the British Empire identified in red. The text, a line from Queen Victoria's Diamond Jubilee Ode by the Welsh poet Sir William Morris, reads: 'We Hold a Vaster Empire Than Has Been'.

Imperialist, The. Novel by Sara Jeannette DUNCAN published in 1904, more than a dozen years after the author had left Canada. The only Duncan novel with a Canadian setting, it is an entertaining and skilful portrayal of life in the small Ontario town of Elgin (Brantford) having to do with an election campaign in which a naïve young man is carried away by his belief in the imperialist movement, which would draw the self-governing dominions together in a federation of the Empire. It captures the ambivalence of Canadians in their sentimental attachment to Great Britain and their feelings of national identity.

Import. A slang term for an imported (or non-local) hockey or football player. An import is the opposite of a 'HOMEBREW'.

Improved Britisher. A humorous reference in the late-nineteenth and early-twentieth centuries to a British immigrant, especially an Englishman, who has lived in Canada long enough to have lost some of his Old Country characteristics. An 'improved Scotsman', however, is a slang reference to a HALF-BREED with Indian and Scots blood.

'In Flanders Fields'. The most famous of all war poems, composed by Lt-Col. John McCRAE in 20 minutes on 5 May 1915, during the second battle of YPRES, while mourning the death of a friend. It appeared anonymously in *Punch* on 8 Dec. 1915 and was re-

'In Flanders Fields'

cited at the first Armistice Day service on 11 Nov. 1918. There are minor textual discrepancies between various versions of the poem, but the standard (first) version appears in *The Oxford Book of Canadian Verse* (1960) edited by A.J.M. SMITH.

In Search of Myself. The autobiography of Frederick Philip GROVE published in 1946. It is now seen to give a fictitious account of the author's life before he came to Canada.

Inco. Acronym of the International Nickel COmpany of Canada Limited. Also known as 'Big Nickel', Inco Limited is the world's largest producer of nickel, a leading producer of copper, and a major supplier of platinum, palladium, cobalt, selenium, and other important industrial minerals. The original nickel and copper discovery was made by a blacksmith in 1883 when he collected some discoloured rocks 3 mi. west of the new railraod station at Sudbury in northern Ontario. The International Nickel Company of Canada Limited was incorporated in 1916 and expanded in 1928 through a merger of independent producers. Inco has also developed nickel mines around Thompson, Man., and in other countries. The company controls ESB, Inc., one of the world's largest producers of batteries (some of which are marketed as Exide, Ray-o-vac, and Willard batteries).

Income Tax. A tax payable on the incomes of individuals. Under the BNA ACT the provinces were to derive their revenues from direct taxation within the province, and the federal government had jurisdiction over direct and indirect taxes of all kinds. Income tax is a direct tax; that is, it is paid directly by the person taxed, and therefore falls within the jurisdiction of both federal and provincial governments. The first provincial income tax was levied in British Columbia in 1876, and the first federal income tax during the First World War. By the beginning of the Second World War income tax was being levied by the federal government, by seven of the nine provinces (Alberta, British Columbia, Manitoba, Ontario, Prince Edward Island, Quebec, and Saskatchewan), and by many municipalities authorized by the provinces to levy taxes, including some in New Brunswick and Nova Scotia. During and after the Second World War various fiscal arrangements were in effect, under some of which various provincial governments agreed not to levy income tax in return for subsidies from the federal government. But now all provincial governments levy an income tax, the rate varying in each province, and all but Quebec have arranged to have their income taxes collected by the federal government and remitted to the provincial government.

All Canadian residents are liable for income tax and must pay tax on their net income—their income after certain allowable deductions have been made. Most income tax paid in Canada is deducted at source—by the employer at the time of payment. Federal income tax is a progressive tax: the larger a person's net income, the greater a percentage of income tax he or she pays. The annual deadline for filing the previous year's income tax form is 30 Apr.

Incredible Journey, The. Subtitled *A Tale of Three Animals*, it is a popular children's book (that was also read by adults when it was published in 1960) about two dogs and a cat who made a 250-mi. trek through the northern-Ontario wilderness. It was the first publication of Sheila Burnford (b.1918), who was born in Scotland and came to Canada in 1948. In 1963 it was made into a Walt Disney film starring John DRAINIE and directed by Fletcher MARKLE.

Independent Publishers' Association. See ASSOCIATION OF CANADIAN PUBLISHERS.

Indian. A person designated by the federal government to be of Indian status on the basis of the fact that he or she has been registered on the band rolls; a person who claims descent from the original inhabitants of North America, whether registered with the federal government or not. Registered Indians belong to one of 558 bands and have the right to live on their own reserve, but today large numbers have emigrated and often live in urban centres. See also RED INDIAN and NATIVE PEOPLES. Eskimos are of Indian stock.

Indian Act, The. A statute of the Parliament of Canada passed pursuant to the federal authority vested in Parliament over 'Indians and land reserved for the Indians' under the BNA ACT. The statute and its regulations provide special status for Indians (including Eskimos) to the exclusion of provincial authority.

Indian Affairs and Northern Development, Department of. A department of the federal government concerned with native peoples and the Far North. Established in 1966, superseding the Department of Northern Affairs and National Resources, it has three distinct areas of responsibility: Indian and Eskimo Affairs, Northern Development, and the Conservation Program. The commissioner of the Northwest Territories and the commissioner of the Yukon Territory report to Parliament through the Minister of Indian Affairs and Northern Development, who is also responsible for the National Battlefields Commission and the HISTORIC SITES AND MONUMENTS BOARD OF CANADA.

Indian Church. Canvas by Emily CARR, painted about 1930. A plain, white, steepled church, with grave markers on either side, is seen against a green tapestry of foliage painted as generalized plastic shapes. The church seems to stretch heavenwards, like the tall tree trunks behind it. (AGO)

Indian Claims Commission. Grievance body. Established in 1969, it consists of a commissioner who studies Indian grievances and claims and reports to the GOVERNOR IN COUNCIL on means for settlement.

Indian Days. Annual exhibitions of Indian crafts and customs held throughout the Prairie West in the summer and fall. The first Indian Days is said to have been arranged at Banff about 1889 to entertain CPR passengers who were detained because of a bridge wash-out.

Indian ice-cream. A pink, frothy delicacy having a somewhat bitter taste, prepared by beating soapberries to a lather. It is made by Indians on the west coast.

Indian John Memorial Shoot. One of the leading archery contests in North America, held in Brantford, Ont., on the third Saturday and Sunday in June. It is sponsored by the Brant Bowmen archery club. Indian John Trophies, named in memory of Cayuga chieftain and Six Nations archer John Van Every, are awarded to top men and women archers.

Indian list. A list of persons under legal restraint in the buying, consuming, or selling of liquor. All Indians were under such restraint, except in special circumstances, until recently.

Indian Pageant. Dramatic re-enactment of famous events in Six Nations history, staged in an open-air amphitheatre on the SIX NATIONS RESERVE near Brantford, Ont. It is held on the second and third weekends (Friday and Saturday nights) in August.

Indian paint-brush. Figurative description of various wild flowers, particularly those having bright scarlet to orangey floral bracts.

Indian reserve. A tract of land set aside by the government, usually by treaty, for the exclusive use of a band of Indians (except when it is leased to whites).

Indian slipper. See MOCCASIN FLOWER.

Indian summer. A period of mild and some-times misty weather in late fall or early winter. It occurs across Canada and in the northern United States. The phenomenon is not unknown in England where, in October, it is called St Luke's summer (St Luke's Day being 18 Oct.), and in November St Martin's summer (St Martin's Day being 11 Nov.). Wilfred CAMPBELL'S 'INDIAN SUMMER' poetically describes the phenomenon.

'Indian Summer'. Three-stanza lyric by Wilfred CAMPBELL—beginning 'Along the line of smoky hills / The crimson forest stands'— that has been memorized by generations of schoolchildren. It was included in *Lake Lyrics and Other Poems* (1889).

Industrial Development Bank. A federal CROWN CORPORATION. The IDB was established in 1944 as a subsidiary of the BANK OF CANADA to provide capital assistance, with particular emphasis on small businesses, in developing new businesses or helping businesses to expand. The president is the Governor of the Bank of Canada. The IDB has 67 branches across Canada.

Industrial Disputes Investigation Act. An act passed by the federal government in 1907 for the settlement of labour-management disputes. It provided for compulsory federal intervention upon application of either party through the appointment of a tripartite board to hold hearings and recommend a settlement. The IDIA was passed following the LETHBRIDGE STRIKE and was in force until the Second World War.

Industrial Workers of the World. A labour association founded in the United States in 1905 to establish revolutionary industrial unionism, including the abolition of the wage system. It led a number of bloody strikes in British Columbia before the First World War and was declared unlawful by the federal government on 24 Sept. 1918, but the ban was lifted on 2 Apr. 1919 after an amendment was made to SECTION 98 of the Criminal Code. The IWW (also called the Wobblies) was re-established in Vancouver in 1922 but achieved negligible success.

Industry, Trade and Commerce, Department of. Department of the federal government concerned with manufacturing, processing, tourism, and trade. The present department, a merging of others, dates from 1969. ITC has six major functional groups: Tourism, Industry Development, Industrial Policies, Export Development, International Trade Relations, and Administration. In 1973 it operated eight regional offices across Canada and the Trade Commissioner Service, which has 82 trade offices in 57 countries.

Inferior court. A court with more limited jurisdiction than a SUPERIOR COURT, the jurisdiction of the latter being absolute. Inferior courts include Magistrates' Courts (called in Quebec the Court of Sessions), County and District Courts, Surrogate Courts, Courts of Probate, and Military Courts (e.g., a court martial).

InfoCan. Abbreviation of INFORMATION CANADA.

Information Canada. Central clearing-house for facts about the federal government, its policies, programs, and services. When it was created in 1970, it opened regional inquiry centres across the country and assumed the publishing and bookselling functions of the QUEEN'S PRINTER. The program was discontinued on 1 Apr. 1976. The Queen's Printer now operates under the Department of Supply and Services.

Ingstad, Helge. See L'ANSE AUX MEADOWS.

Innis, Harold Adams (1894-1952). Economist and historian. Born near Otterville, Ont., and educated at McMaster and the Universities of Toronto and Chicago, he joined the staff of the University of Toronto, where he taught economics from 1920; he became head of the department in 1937 and dean of graduate studies in 1947. A truly creative scholar, he wrote two seminal books: *The Fur Trade in Canada* (1930), which explains Canada's development from the early sixteenth century to the 1920s in terms of the exploitation of its staples and the interplay of geographical, technological, and economic forces; and *Empire and Communications* (1950), a study of the dominant influence of communications on institutions and cultures—an exploration that was continued by Marshall McLUHAN. He also wrote *The Cod-Fisheries: The History of an International Economy* (1940) and *The Bias of Communication* (1951). *Essays in Canadian Economic History* (1956), edited by his wife, Mary Quayle Innis, was published posthumously. See Donald CREIGHTON's movingly written biographical sketch, *Harold Adams Innis: Portrait of a Scholar* (1957).

Innis-Gérin Medal. Presented every two years by the ROYAL SOCIETY OF CANADA for a distinguished and sustained contribution to the literature of the social sciences, including human geography and social psychology. The award was established in 1966 to honour the economist Harold Adams INNIS and the sociologist Léon Gérin, both past presidents of the Society. It consists of a bronze medal and $1,000.

Innuit. See INUIT.

Inook and the Sun. A short play, popular with children, about an Eskimo lad's maturity. The poetic fantasy for puppets, masks, and actors was written by Henry Beissel, had its première at the STRATFORD FESTIVAL on 1 Aug. 1973, and was published the following year. An impatient youth, Inook decides against his father's advice to hunt and capture the sun, but learns to appreciate his father's advice, expressed in the word AYORAMA—'all things have their season'.

Institut Canadien. A literary and philosophical society that became politically active and led to the formation of the *parti rouge* (see ROUGES). The liberal views of its members—of which Wilfrid LAURIER was one—earned the displeasure of the Church and its representative, Bishop Bourget. The Institute's chapters outside Montreal had closed by 1858, but the Montreal headquarters, despite a papal ban, remained open until the turn of the century. See also GUIBORD INCIDENT.

Institute of Child Study. Established in 1926 at the University of Toronto, with Dr W.E. BLATZ as its first director, it is the oldest centre in Canada for the scientific study of child development. Its laboratory school, accommodating children from nursery school to Grade 6, has permitted important studies of individual children over a long period of their development. Among its many significant contributions to the field of child-studies are Blatz's Security Theory and its extensions by Michael Grapko; Mary Northway's work in sociometrics; Karl Bernhardt's work in parent education; Carol Davis's studies of family relations; and Betty Flint's studies of infancy. In addition to its research functions it has provided a graduate program in child study since 1944.

Insulin. The drug extracted from the islets of Langerhans in the pancreas of cattle, used in the treatment of diabetes. It was isolated in 1921 by Drs Frederick G. BANTING and Charles BEST working at the University of Toronto under the direction of Dr J.J.R. MacLEOD. Dr J.B. COLLIP joined the team in the work of purifying the substance. Derived from the Latin *insula* for 'island', plus the preposition 'in', the name means 'within the islands' (i.e., the islets of Langerhans). A name occasionally used is 'isletin'.

Insurance. See MEDICARE.

Insurance, Department of. Federal government department concerned with federally incorporated insurance, trust, loan, and investment companies. Established as a separate department in 1910, it is responsible to the Minister of Finance.

Integration. See UNIFICATION.

Intendant. French administrative officer. The intendant of New France was responsible for commerce, finance, and police. There were 12 intendants in all. The first was Jean TALON, who arrived at Quebec in 1665, and the last was François BIGOT, who held office from 1748 to 1760.

Inter-City Limited. The overnight train between Montreal and Toronto. CANADIAN NATIONAL RAILWAYS introduced the daily train service on 27 June 1926. It was phased out in 1964.

Intercolonial Railway. An important early railway company linking the Maritime provinces. Growing out of the Halifax-Truro line, established in 1858, it expanded and amalgamated independent lines until the First World War, when its deficits were met by the federal government, which took it over. In 1923, along with the GRAND TRUNK RAILWAY, it became part of the CANADIAN NATIONAL RAILWAYS.

Interdicted person. A person to whom the sale of liquor is prohibited by order of a court or other authority authorized to make such an order under a statute, the Liquor Control Act.

Interior, The. A reference to the interior of British Columbia, the area of the province from the Alberta border to, but not including, the Pacific Coast.

Interior Plains or **Prairie Region, The.** One of the five principal GEOGRAPHICAL REGIONS of Canada. It includes that part of the Prairie Provinces between the CANADIAN SHIELD and the WESTERN CORDILLERA. Underlain by relatively flat sedimentary deposits, the Prairie region forms the largest tract of agricultural land in the country and is the principal source of petroleum, natural gas, and potash. While economic development has been closely tied to these resources in the past, considerable diversification has taken place in recent years, particularly in the growth of secondary manufacturing.

Interior Salish. SALISHAN-speaking Indians of British Columbia and the northwestern United States. They comprise four major groups and a number of minor ones that speak different dialects. The main groups today are the LILLOOET of the Lillooet valley; the SHUSWAP to the northeast; the THOMPSON Indians; and the OKANAGAN to the south. The population of the Interior Salish in 1970 was 10,631. See also COAST SALISH.

International Boundary Commission. Advisory body concerned with the Canadian-United States border. The Commission, which consists of one Canadian and one American commissioner, has met alternately in Ottawa and Washington since 1925 to maintain at all times an effective boundary line.

International Documentary Film Festival. Biennial competition for 16-mm documentary films less than 30 minutes in running time. The IDFF—held at Weyburn, Sask., since 1950—calls its main prize the Golden Sheaf Trophy.

International Joint Commission. Advisory body concerned with boundary waters between Canada and the U.S. Established in 1911, with three Canadian and three American members, the IJC has authority to consider any matter in dispute between the two countries, but in practice it deals primarily with matters affecting rivers and lakes that involve the two countries jointly.

International Nickel Company of Canada, Limited. See INCO.

International Service of the CBC. See RADIO CANADA INTERNATIONAL.

International Standard Book Numbering. A system for assigning to books computer-standardized codes for ordering purposes, etc. It was evolved in the United Kingdom in 1967 and provides a unique ISBN for every title published. This appears on the copyright page as a 10-digit number composed of a group identifier, publisher prefix, title number, and check digit. The ISBN for *Colombo's Canadian References* is 0-19-540253-7, where 0 stands for Canada, 19 for the Oxford University Press, 5402 for the Canadian Branch, 53 for the title, and 7 for the check digit. The group identifier 0 is the same for Canada, Australia, South Africa, Eire, the United Kingdom, and the United States. The Canadian ISBN Agency is part of the Cataloguing Branch of the National Library of Canada in Ottawa. There is also an ISSN (International Standard Serial Number) for periodicals, established in Paris in 1971, that assigns an eight-digit number to each serial title. Registration of Canadian serials by the National Library commenced in Jan. 1974.

Interprovincial Pipeline. A crude-oil pipeline that originates in Edmonton, Alta, and extends 1,930 mi. across Canada and the U.S.A., terminating in Port Credit, Ont. It is currently being extended eastward to Montreal. The Trans Mountain pipeline completes the network from Edmonton to Vancouver.

Introduction, Passacaglia and Fugue. Composed by Healey WILLAN in 1916, it is a rich, complex organ work that shows his virtuosity as an organist and his mastery of a neoromantic style.

Inuglagit. The Eskimo word for ancestors of the modern-day INUIT. It means 'those people who were wearers of fur clothing'.

Inuit. The word used by the Eskimo people to refer to themselves or to other groups of people. It means 'the people' or 'mankind' and is the plural form of INUK, which means 'man'. The widely used word 'Eskimo' is Algonkian for 'raw-flesh eater' and is considered derogatory. The language the Eskimos speak is often called *Inuit* but is properly called *Inuktituut*.

Inuit Tapirisat of Canada. The National Eskimo Brotherhood, founded in Ottawa in Oct. 1971 by Eskimo (INUIT) delegates representing 18,000 Eskimos from the Northwest Territories, northern Quebec, and Labrador. Funded mainly by the Department of the SECRETARY OF STATE, the ITC has objectives that include uniting all the Inuit of Canada, encouraging Inuit leadership, and promoting their language and culture.

Inuk. Eskimo word for 'man' (one man), especially a superior man. The Eskimos refer to themselves by the plural word *Inuit*, 'men' or 'the people'. Before they were aware of other groups in the world, Eskimos considered themselves to be 'the only people'.

Inukpuk, Johnny (b.1911). Eskimo artist, considered the foremost sculptor of NEW QUEBEC. A Port Harrison artist, he is best known for his mother-and-child themes executed in monumental proportions.

Inukshuk. A human-like form constructed of stone blocks by Eskimos to serve as a landmark. The Eskimo word means 'in lieu of a man' and is derived from INUK. See also TUNIT.

Inuktituut. The word Eskimos themselves use for their language. See INUIT.

Inutsiak (1896-1967). Eskimo sculptor, whose name is also spelled 'Enutsiak'. Working at Frobisher Bay on Baffin Island, she was renowned for her detailed sculptures that depict the traditional ways, especially childbirth through midwifery.

Inutweenat. An Eskimo word that refers to those who are the pure, original or real INUIT.

Inuvik. Town in the Mackenzie R. delta in the Northwest Territories, 100 mi. north of the Arctic Circle. It was established in 1955 to replace Aklavik as the government administrative centre and the major transport and service centre in the North. Its name is from an Eskimo word meaning 'place of man'.

Investigator, The. Political satire on McCarthyism broadcast by CBC Radio to much controversy. The 60-minute production was written by Reuben Ship, a blacklisted American writer then living in Toronto and now working in London, Eng. Directed by Andrew ALLAN, it was broadcast on CBC STAGE on 30 May 1954, the last program in the 'Stage 54' series. An unnamed demagogue, played by John DRAINIE, dies and goes to heaven, where he finds evidence 'for a thousand years of treason'. The powers-that-be reluctantly conclude that the only way to save heaven itself is to return the demagogue to earth. The play is a devastating satire on the mannerisms and tactics of the Communist-baiting U.S. Senator Joseph McCarthy, then at the height of his power. An unauthorized recording was popular in the United States, and the script, in a semi-novelized form, was published in the U.K.

Investors Overseas Services. The world's largest offshore mutual fund. It was founded in the late 1950s by the American mutual-fund salesman Bernard Cornfeld and registered in Panama. Deciding to go public in 1969, Cornfeld re-established IOS in New Brunswick, taking advantage of its lax regard for non-resident operations, and opened the head office in Saint John. Although controlling assets of $2.5 billion, IOS faced innumerable problems, and control of the conglomerate was seized by Robert Lee Vesco, a New Jersey manipulator, who, between 1970 and 1972, stripped IOS of $280 million in assets. IOS went into liquidation in 1973. Cornfeld was imprisoned in Geneva and Vesco took sanctuary in Costa Rica.

Involvement the Key to Better Schools. The report of a four-person Commission on Education established by the British Columbia Teachers' Federation in 1968. Based on 266 briefs, 189 recommendations were made calling for humanizing and personalizing education, and for more community involvement in schools. Many of its proposals were similar to those in Ontario's HALL-DENNIS REPORT.

IOCO. See IRON ORE COMPANY OF CANADA LTD.

IODE. See the IMPERIAL ORDER DAUGHTERS OF THE EMPIRE.

IODE Seventy-Fifth Anniversary Annual Children's Book Award. It is awarded annually by the IODE and the Toronto Public Library to the author of the best book for children published the previous year. The award includes an honorarium of $500. It was first awarded in 1975.

IOS. See INVESTORS OVERSEAS SERVICES.

IPA. Abbreviation of India Pale Ale, a popular beer made by LABATT'S; and also of the former Independent Publishers' Association, now the ASSOCIATION OF CANADIAN PUBLISHERS.

IRBM. Abbreviation of Intermediate Range Ballistic Missile. This supersonic surface-to-air guided missile, with a range of between 800 and 1,500 nautical miles, was developed for use by NORAD. See also ICBM.

Irish Rovers, The. A popular group of five singers and musicians. Led by Will Millar, who came to Canada from Northern Ireland in 1964 and established the group with five other immigrants from Ulster in Vancouver in 1971, it was an overnight television and concert success. Popular numbers written by Millar and identified with the group include 'The Unicorn' and 'Child of Hate', the latter about violence in Northern Ireland.

Iron Curtain, The. Feature film directed by William A. Wellman for 20th Century-Fox in 1948. Starring Dana Andrews, Gene Tierney, and June Havoc, it was produced on location in Ottawa and Montreal. It dramatized the plight of Igor GOUZENKO and was based on his autobiography, *This Was My Choice* (1948), the American title of which was *The Iron Curtain*. 87 min., b & w.

Iron ore. Canada is fourth in the world output of iron ore and exports over 75% of its production. The principal mines are found in the southern part of the LABRADOR TROUGH, including Schefferville and Gagnon in Quebec, and Carol Lake and Wabush in Labrador. There are other important mines at Atikokan, Red Lake, Wawa, and Kirkland Lake in Ontario, and at Shawville, Que.

Iron Ore Company of Canada Limited. The first company to produce iron ore successfully from the Quebec-Labrador 'iron trough' (see LABRADOR TROUGH). Although the presence of iron ore had been known in this region since 1929, it was not until July 1954 that a consortium of Canadian and American interests managed to line up markets, financ-

ing, construction, and production of the first iron ore. The town of Schefferville in northern Quebec was created following IOCC's activity in the region.

Iroquoian. In historical times, a linguistic group of Indian tribes that had an agricultural economy. It was composed of the League of the IROQUOIS and HURON, Neutral, Petun, and other groups. These tribes occupied arable lands in the eastern Great Lakes region of Canada and the United States.

Iroquois. A group of tribes of IROQUOIAN Indians that had an agricultural economy and were associated in a league (sometimes called a confederacy). Originally made up of five tribes in present-day New York State, the league became the Six Nations in 1720 when the Tuscarora were added to the original union of Mohawk, Oneida, Onondaga, Cayuga, and Seneca. In the seventeenth century the Iroquois were enemies of the French and their Indian allies. In their attempt to control the beaver lands in the Northwest, they attacked French settlements along the St Lawrence and destroyed the HURON villages east of Georgian Bay. As effective allies of the British against the French, and later the rebelling colonies, the Six Nations were rewarded with a large land grant in 1784 and moved to the Grand R. (Ont.), led by Joseph BRANT, and to the Bay of Quinte (Deseronto, Ont.). As early as 1676, however, Christian Iroquois were settled at CAUGHNAWAGA, near Montreal. The Iroquois population in 1970 was 21,263.

Iroquois. A powerful turbojet engine. It was designed, built, and first tested in Canada in Dec. 1954 by A.V. ROE CANADA LTD at Malton, Ont., and intended for use in the ill-fated AVRO ARROW. See also ORENDA.

Irvin, J.D. (Dick) (1892-1957). Hockey player and coach. Born in Hamilton, Ont., he moved with his family to Winnipeg, where he began an amateur hockey career with the Winnipeg Monarchs, for whom he scored nine goals in a single game. He played professionally in Regina and Chicago and then became an outstanding coach with the Toronto, Chicago, and Montreal teams, all of whom won the STANLEY CUP.

Irving, K.C. (b.1899). Capitalist. Born at Buctouche, N.B., he attended Dalhousie and Acadia Universities for a year each. He represented Imperial Oil and the Ford Motor Company in New Brunswick until 1928 when, from Saint John, he organized the Irving Oil Company. This provided the basis for his expansion into lumber, pulp and paper,

Irving

smelting, transportation, and publishing, until he became what one critic called 'a one-man conglomerate'. A reclusive millionaire, he retired to Nassau in 1972, leaving his interests in the hands of his three sons: James, Arthur, and John. He once said: 'New Brunswick is too small for politics.'

Is It the Sun, Philibert? See *La* GUERRE, YES SIR!

Isaacs Gallery, The. Commercial art gallery in Toronto. Owned by Avrom Isaacs (b.1926), it began as the Greenwich Gallery on Bay St in 1955, when the work of young contemporary artists was receiving very little exposure, and acquired its present name when it moved to Yonge St in 1961. With regular exhibitions of the work of artists who are now prominent—and, in the fifties and sixties, poetry readings, underground film showings, and mixed-media concerts—it achieved a central place in the evolution of contemporary Canadian art. Among the painters the Gallery represents are Joyce WIELAND, Michael SNOW, Greg CURNOE, and William KURELEK. In 1969 Isaacs opened The Innuit Gallery of Eskimo Art, devoted to the work of Eskimo artists.

Isabel. Feature film written and directed by Paul ALMOND and produced by Paramount in 1968. It starred Geneviève BUJOLD, Marc Strange, Ratch Wallace, and Gerrard Parkes. Isabel, played by Bujold—who was then Almond's wife—returns to her birthplace on a farm in the Gaspé and is haunted by memories of violence in the past. The first truly Canadian film financed by Hollywood, it is a sensitive and attractive production, more successful than the Almonds' subsequent collaboration, ACT OF THE HEART (1970). The musical score was composed by Harry FREEDMAN. 108 min., colour.

ISBN. See INTERNATIONAL STANDARD BOOK NUMBERING.

Iseler, Elmer (b.1927). Choral conductor. Born in Port Colborne, Ont., and educated at the University of Toronto, he was a high-school music teacher in Toronto before becoming conductor of the FESTIVAL SINGERS, which he co-founded, in 1955, and of the TORONTO MENDELSSOHN CHOIR in 1964.

ISIS. See SATELLITES FOR IONOSPHERIC STUDIES.

Island, The. A reference to PRINCE EDWARD ISLAND.

Island of St John. The English name after 1763 of the Île-Saint-Jean. It became PRINCE EDWARD ISLAND in 1799.

Issei. Japanese word for 'first generation', applied to someone born in Japan who settled in Canada. See also KIKANISEI and NISEI.

ISSN (International Standard Serial Number). See INTERNATIONAL STANDARD BOOK NUMBERING.

'It Happened in Canada'. Newspaper cartoon feature. Researched, drawn, and written by Gordon JOHNSTON, the daily cartoon first appeared in newspapers in 1967 and is now syndicated by some 30 papers. It depicts curious and forgotten aspects of Canadian history and society. Numerous compilations have been published since 1967.

Ivey Foundation. The name of three foundations established for charitable, religious, and educational purposes. The first was founded by Richard Ivey in London, Ont., in 1947; the second by Charles H. Ivey in Toronto in 1957; the third by Richard and Jean Ivey in London in 1965.

Iwaniuk, Waclaw (b.1915). Emigré poet who writes in Polish. Born in Poland, in 1948 he settled in Toronto, where he works as a translator. His *Collected Poems* was published in Polish in 1964 in London, Eng.

IWW. See INDUSTRIAL WORKERS OF THE WORLD.

Iyola (b.1933). Eskimo sculptor and stonecutter at CAPE DORSET. He was one of the first four artists to specialize in stone-cutting and stone-printing when the arts were introduced to Cape Dorset.

J

J.J. Douglas. West-coast publishing company. Founded as a wholesale business in Vancouver in 1964 by J.J. Douglas, a Scotsborn book salesman, it began publishing general and western-interest titles in earnest in 1973. The company's chief officers are Douglas and Scott McIntyre.

Jack, Donald Lamont. See The BANDY PAPERS.

Jack Pine, The. Famous oil painting by Tom THOMSON based on sketches made at Lake Cauchon, ALGONQUIN (PROVINCIAL) PARK, Ont. Executed in 1916-17 in an Art Nouveau design, it depicts a scraggly, drooping tree against deep-blue, snow-covered islands and a lake and sky painted in soft-coloured horizontal strokes. Arthur LISMER claimed many of his art students were under the impression that 'Jack Pine' was a member of the GROUP OF SEVEN. (NGC). See also *The* WEST WIND.

Jackson, A.Y. (1882-1974). Landscape painter, member of the GROUP OF SEVEN. Born in Montreal, Alexander Young Jackson studied in Montreal, Chicago, and Paris before settling in Toronto in 1913—at the instigation of J.E.H. MacDONALD and others who later formed the Group of Seven—and soon afterwards moved into the STUDIO BUILDING. The creator of vigorous and colourful paintings of the north country—among them *Terre Sauvage* (1913, NGC), *The* RED MAPLE (1914, NGC), and *Frozen Lake, Early Spring, Algonquin Park* (1914, NGC)—before the actual Group was formed, he quickly established his prominence and went on to become both a very popular artist and a propagandizer for the Group. He travelled widely across the country and painted most of it, including the Arctic; he is particularly identified with paintings of the rolling hills and old buildings of the Quebec countryside, such as *Quebec, Early Spring* (1926, AGO). Jackson's last years were spent in the care of Robert and Signe McMichael at the McMICHAEL CANADIAN COLLECTION, Kleinburg, Ont. His autobiography, *A Painter's Country* (1958), is a lively and enduring work.

Jackson, Donald (b.1940). Champion figure-skater. Born in Oshawa, Ont., he won the bronze medal for figure-skating at the 1960 Winter Olympics at Squaw Valley, Calif. At the 1962 World Tournament at Prague, Czech., he won the gold medal and was re-cognized as the world's best men's figure-skater. He later starred in a professional ice show.

Jackson, Roger (b.1942). Champion oarsman. Paired with George HUNGERFORD, the Ontario athlete competed in the 'two-thousand-metres pairs without coxswain' at the 1964 Olympics in Tokyo and won the gold medal over more experienced scullers.

Jacobs, Joe (b.1934). Cayuga sculptor. Born on the Six Nations Reserve near Brantford, Ont., he is a self-taught artist who was influenced by miniature ivory carvings from China. Most of his stone sculpture is done in steatite or soapstone. He is a traditionalist, both in life-style and art, and brings to his work the deep feeling of the longhouse faith, of which he is very much a part. His work was first presented in the Canadian Indian Art '74 Exhibition at the Royal Ontario Museum.

Jacques and Hay. Nineteenth-century furniture manufacturers in Toronto. The partnership of two English cabinet-makers, John Jacques and Robert Hay, extended from 1835 to 1885, during which time the firm mass-produced elaborately designed High Victorian furniture and some furniture that was grotesquely hand carved.

Jacquet House. The only surviving example of a seventeenth-century house in the Upper Town of Quebec City. It was built about 1675 for François Jacquet *dit* Langevin, a slate-roofer, and enlarged in 1699. It was subsequently owned by the architect Gaspard-Joseph CHAUSSEGROS DE LÉRY and the novelist Philippe-Joseph AUBERT DE GASPÉ.

Jago, Mary (b.1946). Dancer. Born in Henfield, Eng., she studied at the Royal Ballet School, London, and joined the Covent Garden Opera Ballet in 1965. She was invited to join the NATIONAL BALLET OF CANADA in 1966, became a soloist in 1968, and has been a principal dancer for that company since 1970.

Jake and the Kid. A series of radio and television plays and a collection of stories by W.O. MITCHELL. Jake Trumper, a 60-year-old hired hand, instructs the 12-year-old 'kid' and his widowed mother in the mysteries of life in the fictitious community of CROCUS in southern Saskatchewan during the 1940s. (The characters figure in Mitchell's novel

Jake and the Kid

WHO HAS SEEN THE WIND (1947) under other names.) The 'Jake and the Kid' stories first appeared in MACLEAN'S on 15 Aug. 1942; the collection *Jake and the Kid* was published in 1962. On CBC Radio the series starred John DRAINIE and ran from 27 June 1950 to 26 Apr. 1956. Drainie also appeared in one CBC-TV episode, 'Honey and Hoppers', on 7 Nov. 1957. The role of Jake was played by Murray Westgate in the NFB pilot shown on CBC-TV on 4 July 1961, which became the basis of a television series that ended on 19 Sept. 1961.

Jalna. (i) Novel by Mazo DE LA ROCHE published in 1927. The first book in a highly popular family saga, it established the author's international reputation. It is the story of an upper-class family ruled by a matriarch, Adeline Whiteoak, who is mistress of 'Jalna' (see below), the home she built and whose household she dominated throughout her life. This novel was followed by 14 other Jalna books. (ii) The ancestral home of the Whiteoaks in *Jalna* and its numerous sequels. It was modelled on 'Benares', a country house built by a Loyalist in 1837 that still stands at Clarkson, Ont.; set amid a grove of trees, it is privately owned but has been willed to the Ontario Heritage Foundation. The name 'Jalna' was chosen at random from a list of British posts in India. It is unlikely that Mazo de la Roche ever set foot inside 'Benares', which she made into the best-known Canadian house around the world.

Jamasie (b.1910). Eskimo sculptor and graphic artist at CAPE DORSET. He is known for his soapstone carvings of figures, birds, and animals, and especially for his many drawings, which are inspired by memories of camp life.

James, Frances (b.1903). Soprano. Born in Saint John, N.B., she studied singing in Toronto, New York, and Boston (with Roland Hayes). She was Canada's leading soprano in the 1930s and 1940s, performing widely in oratorios and concerts, and was prominent in the CBC's great music productions on radio (1942-53), singing the soprano leads in Canadian premières of Healey WILLAN's *Transit Through Fire* and DEIRDRE, Benjamin Britten's *Peter Grimes* and *Albert Herring*, and Igor Stravinsky's *The Rake's Progress*. She made the first authoritative recording of Hindemith's *Das Marienleben* (1953). She married Murray ADASKIN in 1931.

James Bay. The southern extension of HUDSON BAY.

James Bay Project. A mammoth hydro-electric power development in northern Quebec based on the La Grande R. and adjoining systems and first announced by Quebec Premier Robert Bourassa in Apr. 1971. Power generated will exceed 8 million kilowatts when the entire project is completed in the 1980s. A significant factor in this development was an agreement in 1975 between the local people, principally Cree and Inuit, and the federal and Quebec governments by which certain aboriginal rights have been recognized and $225 million will be paid over 20 years in compensation for lost hunting grounds. Bourassa has called it 'the project of the century'.

James Lorimer and Company. Book publishers. The company was founded in Toronto in 1969 by James LORIMER, Bruce Lewis, and Alan Samuel. The name change in 1974 from the original James Lewis and Samuel reflected a previous change in ownership. The company specializes in publishing highly topical paperback editions in the areas of Canadian history, politics, and urban studies.

James Norris Memorial Trophy. Presented annually 'to the defence player who demonstrates throughout the season the greatest all-round ability in the position'. The trophy is awarded by the NATIONAL HOCKEY LEAGUE and the winner is chosen by the Professional Hockey Writers' Association. It was presented in 1953 by the four children of the late James Norris in memory of the former owner-president of the Detroit Red Wings. In addition to the trophy, the winner receives $1,500; the runner-up, $750.

Jameson, Anna Brownell (1794-1860). Author. Born in Dublin and raised in Hanwell, near London, Eng., she contracted an unhappy marriage to the lawyer Robert Jameson in 1825 and lived apart from him. A number of books stem from this period, including *Celebrated Female Sovereigns* (1831) and *Characteristics of Women* (1832). Three years after Jameson's appointment as Attorney General of Upper Canada (Ontario), in 1836, she visited him in Toronto and travelled on her own in Upper Canada. She recorded her impressions in the classic WINTER STUDIES AND SUMMER RAMBLES IN CANADA (1838). She returned to England in 1837, resumed her writing career, pursued her friendships with Ottilie von Goethe and Lady Byron, popularized German literature in Britain, and completed several important handbooks on Italian art, notably the four-volume *Sacred and Legendary Art* (1852-61).

Janvier, Alex (b.1935). Chipewyan artist. Born at Le Goff, Alta, and a member of the Cold Lake Band, he graduated from the

Southern Alberta College of Art, Calgary, and held the first of his annual one-man shows in Edmonton in 1964. He works in pastels, watercolours, acrylics, and oils, abstracting organic forms in a manner that recalls traditional Navaho art as well as the fantastic imagery of Joan Miró and others. He has been an arts and crafts consultant with the Department of INDIAN AFFAIRS AND NORTHERN DEVELOPMENT and signs his works with both his name and his treaty number (287).

Japanese, Evacuation of the. On 26 Feb. 1942, by order-in-council, all persons of Japanese origin (about 22,000) were ordered evacuated from a 'protected area' about 100 mi. wide along the British Columbia coast. Long-existing racial animosities in this area had been intensified by Japan's entry into the Second World War and by the fear that local Japanese might engage in espionage or sabotage. The evacuees, who included native Canadians and naturalized Canadians as well as aliens, were moved to internment camps in the interior of B.C. or to farming areas in other 'safer' parts of Canada. Property that could not be carried with them was confiscated and sold. Despite the general consensus that such extreme measures were necessary, no charge of disloyalty was laid against any person of Japanese origin during the war.

Jaques, Edna (b.1891). Versifier. Born in Collingwood, Ont., and a resident of Toronto and the Prairies, she found a loyal readership for her rhymes, which recall the subjects of Edgar Guest and the sentiments of Ella Wheeler Wilcox, beginning with her first publication in 1935. *The Best of Edna Jaques* appeared in 1966 and went into its third edition in 1974.

Jarvis, Alan (1915-72). Art administrator and sculptor. Born in Brantford, Ont., and educated at the University of Toronto and New York University, he studied sculpture under Elizabeth Wynn WOOD. In London, Eng., he was private secretary to Sir Stafford Cripps during the Second World War and wrote *The Things We See* (1946), the first volume in a series on design published by Penguin Books. He was also a portrait sculptor of considerable skill. A popular director of the NATIONAL GALLERY OF CANADA from 1955 to 1959 who did much to arouse interest in the arts and the Gallery, he resigned after cabinet approval for the purchase of a Breughel from the Liechtenstein collection was withdrawn owing to a mistake about the availability of funds. Jarvis was editor of *Canadian Art* (ARTS CANADA) from 1960 to 1964.

Jarvis, Judy (b.1941). Dancer and choreographer. Born in Ottawa, she studied in Berlin with Mary Wigman and later achieved in Canada a style of dancing and choreography uniquely her own. Winner in 1974 of the Chalmers Choreography Award, she now directs the Judy Jarvis Dance and Theatre Company in Toronto.

Jarvis, Lilian (b.1931). Dancer. Born in Toronto, she studied with Mildred Wickson and Boris VOLKOFF. She joined the newly formed NATIONAL BALLET OF CANADA in 1951 and later became a principal dancer.

Jasmin, Claude (b.1930). Quebec novelist. Born in Montreal and trained at the École des Arts Appliqués, he has pursued a career that embraces both art and literature as a television designer for Radio-Canada and a writer of stories, plays, and novels. His best-known novel has been published in English as ETHEL AND THE TERRORIST (1965), translated by David Walker. It is about an FLQ-inspired bombing in Montreal.

Jasper. See MACLEAN'S.

Jasper National Park. Established in 1907 in the ROCKY MOUNTAINS of Alberta, it is noted for its beautiful valleys, peaks, icefields, and lakes (notably Maligne Lake), as well as for its resort town of Jasper—the administrative headquarters of the Park—and the nearby CNR summer-resort hotel, Jasper Park Lodge (built in 1922). The Park covers 4,200 sq. mi. and was named for Jasper House, a trading post opened by Jasper Hawes of the NORTH WEST COMPANY in the early nineteenth century. It is one of the largest parks in North America.

Jawbone. Slang term formerly used in the West for credit. It was apparently a reference to the fast talking, or 'jawing', required to secure credit terms. 'No Jawbone' was a sign in the lobby of the Fort Macleod Hotel in Alberta in the 1880s.

Jay's Treaty. Signed in 1794, between the United States and Great Britain, it mainly had to do with the British withdrawal from posts in American territory and with boundary problems in the Northeast. It was named after John Jay, an American diplomat.

Jean A. Chalmers Theatre Apprentice Awards. Scholarships given annually since 1965 by the STRATFORD FESTIVAL to talented apprentices in the company in the name of Mrs Floyd S. Chalmers, wife of the publishing executive. See also TYRONE GUTHRIE AWARDS.

Jean Baptiste

Jean Baptiste. Personification of French Canada, popular in English Canada in the nineteenth century. A roughly dressed HABITANT wearing a toque and smoking a pipe, he is frequently depicted as a lumberjack, a trapper, or a riverman. See also JOHNNY COURTEAU.

Jean Bonhomme. A 7-ft snowman, the personification of the QUEBEC WINTER CARNIVAL. Jean Bonhomme (literally, John Goodfellow) is a traditional name for the French-Canadian peasant.

Jefferys, C.W. (1869-1952). Artist widely known for his line drawings of episodes in Canadian history. Born in Rochester, Eng., he settled in Toronto in 1880 and became a commercial artist, working in New York from 1892 to 1899. In Toronto he worked as a newspaper and book illustrator, developing a lean style verging on caricature. His permanent legacy is *The* PICTURE GALLERY OF CANADIAN HISTORY, which appeared in three volumes between 1942 and 1950. After his death some 1,200 drawings and paintings—including 102 illustrations for *Sam Slick in Pictures,* published in 1956—were acquired by IMPERIAL OIL LIMITED when it appeared that the collection would be sold outside the country. In 1970, when the NEW CANADA PRESS, a Marxist-Maoist publishing house, wanted to reproduce Jefferys' famous drawing of the marching farmers of the REBELLION OF 1837 on the cover of the English translation of Léandre Bergeron's *The History of Quebec* (1971), the American-owned oil company refused permission. It then donated the collection to the National Gallery of Canada, which gave it to the Public Archives of Canada in 1972.

Jehovah's Witnesses case. See RONCARELLI CASE.

Jelinek, Maria (b.1942) and **Otto** (b.1940). Champion figure-skaters. Born in Czechoslovakia, they immigrated to Canada in 1949 and continued training as a sister-and-brother figure-skating pair. They won the Canadian junior title in 1955 and in 1960 captured the senior North American title. They achieved their greatest success in the 1962 World Tournament in their native Prague, where they were recognized as the world's champion figure-skating pair. Retiring from amateur skating, they spent six years with the Ice Capades. Maria then opened a women's boutique and Otto turned to manufacturing skates and other sporting equipment; he was elected to the federal Parliament in 1972 and 1974.

Jenness, Diamond (1886-1969). Anthropologist. Born in Wellington, N.Z., and educated there and at Oxford, he joined the Canadian Arctic Expedition of 1913-18 as an anthropologist. His findings appeared in *The Copper Eskimo* (1922), the standard work in the field, and his reminiscences in *The People of the Twilight* (1928; rev. 1959) and *Dawn in Arctic Alaska* (1957). He uncovered archaeological remains of a culture predating the contemporary Eskimo (or THULE) culture on Baffin Island, and named it the DORSET culture in 1925 after the site, near Cape Dorset. Chief of the anthropological division of what has become the NATIONAL MUSEUM OF MAN, from 1926 to 1946, he wrote *The Indians of Canada* (1932), a basic textbook. More popular is *The Corn Goddess and Other Tales from Indian Canada* (1956).

Jenny. The Curtiss JN-4, a popular two-seater biplane used in the FIRST WORLD WAR. Strictly speaking, Jenny was the name of the original British model, the JN-3. The Canadian modification, built by Glenn Curtiss at Canadian Aeroplanes Ltd in Toronto, was called the Canuck, though it was often referred to as the Jenny. Curtiss produced 2,900 Canucks between Dec. 1916 and the end of the war.

Jerky. Dried strips of caribou, moose, or other game, commonly eaten in the Yukon.

Jerome, Harry (b.1940). Noted runner. Born in Prince Albert, Sask., and raised in Vancouver, he tied the world record in both 100-yard (in 1966) and 100-metre sprints (in 1959) as a member of Olympic and British Commonwealth teams. He is now a physical-education teacher and coach.

Jest of God, A. A novel by Margaret LAURENCE published in 1966. Rachel, a spinster approaching middle age and caught in a narrow existence by a neurotic and dependent mother, is set free to make her own life after the failure of a summer affair. The novel succeeds in being both moving and ironical. It was made into a feature film, *Rachel, Rachel* (1968), which was directed by Paul Newman and starred Joanne Woodward; the setting was moved from the Canadian Prairies to the American mid-west. (101 min., colour)

Jesuit martyrs. Jesuit priests or lay brothers killed by Indians in 1642-9 while serving in the HURON MISSIONS or in Iroquois territory: Jean de BRÉBEUF, Noel Chabanel, Antoine Daniel, Charles Garnier, Gabriel LALEMANT, René Goupil, Isaac JOGUES, and Jean de La Lande (the last three of whom died in present-day New York State). They were canonized in 1930 and are honoured at the MAR-

264

TYRS' SHRINE near Midland, Ont. See also SAINTS.

Jesuit Relations. A series of reports written by Jesuit priests in New France. Published annually in France from 1632 to 1673, they are of immense historical importance, providing information about the missionary work of the priests and about the Indians—their lore, religion, mythology, morals, and customs. They were edited, with texts in French and English, by the American scholar R.G. Thwaites in *The Jesuit Relations and Allied Documents* (73 vols, 1896-1901).

Jesuits. Members of a Roman Catholic religious order, the Society of Jesus. In the seventeenth century, after 1633, they were very active in NEW FRANCE as missionaries and teachers—and, through their missionary work, as explorers. The order was suppressed by the pope in 1773, was reconstituted in 1814, and the Jesuits resumed their educational work in Canada in 1842. See also JESUIT MARTYRS, HURON MISSIONS.

Jesuits' Estates Act. An act passed by the Quebec legislature in 1888 to provide some compensation to the Society of Jesus (see JESUITS) for the confiscation of its property by the Crown, following the abolition of the order by the papacy in 1773. When the Society was reinstated in Canada in 1842, the Jesuits pressured the government either for the return of the property or for some sort of indemnity. Designed to win the support of the Catholic Church for the government of Honoré Mercier, the Act did not ignore the feelings of Anglo-Saxons. Of the $400,000 at which the estates were valued, $60,000 was set aside for the support of Protestant schools in Quebec. The Pope was asked to divide the remainder among the Jesuits and other Catholic bodies. It was this last provision, more than anything else in the Act, that led to the great racial acrimony that was to dominate the press and the hustings, especially in Ontario. To the Ontario MP D'Alton McCarthy—who broke with the Conservative Party over the Act—and to the Orange Order, the Pope's involvement in Canadian politics was convincing evidence of a French-Catholic plot against the Queen's sovereignty and her English-speaking subjects.

Jeunes-Canada, Les. Fascist and racist student organization in Montreal in the 1930s. The 'Young Canada' movement was founded by students of the UNIVERSITÉ DE MONTRÉAL in the summer of 1933 and soon died out. See also André LAURENDEAU.

Jeunesses Musicales du Canada, Les. A non-profit organization to bring music to youth and to further the careers of aspiring young musicians. Founded on 24 Aug. 1949, it sponsors over 600 concerts each year and operates the JMC Orford Arts Centre, a 222-acre music complex in Mount Orford Provincial Park, and its annual Summer Festival. Les Jeunesses Musicales invites 100 musicians (between 18 and 23) from 25 foreign countries to join its world orchestra. It also sponsors such smaller groups as Quartet Tarrago, Quintette à Vent du Québec, and Quintonal Jazz in tours of schools across Canada. See also ORFORD STRING QUARTET.

Jewinski, Hans (b.1946). Poet. Born in Oberammergau, West Germany, he was brought to Toronto at the age of 10 and is a graduate of Waterloo College. He joined the Metropolitan Toronto Police Force in 1968 and shortly afterwards established Missing Link Press. His first book—a mass-market paperback called *The Poet Cop* (1975)—has sold some 30,000 copies.

Jewish Dialogue. A literary quarterly published in Toronto since 1970. Edited by David Cohen and Joe ROSENBLATT, it publishes articles and literature of Canadian, and specifically Jewish, interest.

Jewison, Norman (b.1926). Film director. Born in Toronto, he worked in the Royal Canadian Navy's entertainment unit during the last years of the Second World War and then graduated from the University of Toronto. He worked in London, Eng., from 1949 to 1951, as a CBC-TV drama producer in Toronto from 1951 to 1958, and has been a television and film director in the U.S. since then. His highly commercial feature films include *Forty Pounds of Trouble* (1963), *The Cincinnati Kid* (1965), *The Russians are Coming, The Russians are Coming* (1966), *In the Heat of the Night* (1967), *The Thomas Crown Affair* (1968), *Fiddler on the Roof* (1971), *Jesus Christ Superstar* (1973), and *Rollerball* (1975).

Jig for the Gypsy, A. Play by Robertson DAVIES written for Donald and Murray Davis and their sister Barbara Chilcott (see DAVIS FAMILY). Opening at the CREST THEATRE in Toronto on 14 Sept. 1954, it is set in North Wales in 1885 and is about a gypsy woman who is persuaded to tell the fortune of a local candidate in such a way as to influence the voters. It was published the same year.

Joanassie. See Joanassie SALOMONIE.

Jobin, Louis (1845-1928). Wood-carver. Born in Quebec, he learned the craft from an uncle who specialized in ships' figureheads. His work is in the tradition of medieval and Renaissance carving, and he created mainly religious statues, though he was known to carve cigar-store Indians. The 25-ft *Our Lady of the Saguenay* (1881), on the top of Cape Trinity, is his most famous carving (it is sheathed in lead). Many of his works are unsigned.

Jobin, Raoul (1906-76). Tenor. Born in Quebec City, he trained there and in Paris, where he made his opera début in 1930 and embarked on an international career, performing a very large repertory of roles. He was a leading tenor at the Metropolitan Opera, New York, from 1940 to 1950. From 1961 he taught at the Conservatoire de Musique de Québec, of which he was director.

Joe Beef's. Old Montreal waterfront tavern. Popular with English-speaking sailors for over 150 years, it acquired its name from the original owner, Jos Leboeuf.

Joey. Nickname of Jospeh R. SMALLWOOD, first premier of Newfoundland.

Jogues, Isaac (1607-46). Jesuit missionary. Arriving in New France in 1636, he served in the HURON MISSIONS. In 1642 he was captured by Iroquois on the St Lawrence, taken prisoner, and tortured; he escaped the next year and wrote a *Relation* about his captivity. On his way to establish a mission with the Mohawks in 1646 he was captured again and killed. He was canonized in 1930.

John Adaskin Memorial Award. Annual award made since 1965 by the CANADIAN MUSIC CENTRE to encourage original musical composition. Canadian universities recommend student composers who submit scores in competition, and the composer of the best score is awarded $500 and a performance of the work. The award honours John ADASKIN, who was executive secretary of the Centre from 1961 until his death in 1964.

John C. Webster Memorial Trophy. Aviation trophy 'to do honour to the airmen of Canada'. It was donated by five members of the Webster family of Shediac, N.B., to recall a young flier who was killed in a flying accident in 1931. The trophy itself, a winged Mercury, was designed by R. Tait McKENZIE. It was awarded by the Canadian government from 1932 to 1954, when it was discontinued.

John Cabot Day. See DISCOVERY DAY.

John Drainie Award. Medal awarded annually since 1968 by ACTRA for distinguished service to broadcasting. It was designed by Dora DE PÉDERY-HUNT and portrays John DRAINIE, the distinguished actor who died in 1966.

Johnniebo (1921-72). Eskimo hunter and carver at CAPE DORSET. He was famous for his prints, which depict mythological beings, a subject he shared with his wife KENOJUAK.

Johnny Belinda. Play by the New York playwright Elmer Harris, a hit of the 1940-1 Broadway season. It is set in Souris, a northshore fishing village on PRINCE EDWARD ISLAND, in 1894, and deals in a melodramatic way with the consequences of the rape of a deaf-mute girl when Johnny Belinda, the child of the union, is taken from her. Harris summered at Bay Fortune in the 1930s and may have based his play on an incident that took place in the village of Digwell's Mills. A Hollywood film version starring Jane Wyman was produced in 1948 and set on Cape Breton Island. The play served as the basis of a successful musical, *Johnny Belinda*, with lyrics by Mavor MOORE and music (based on Maritime folksongs) by John Fenwick. Choreographed by Alan LUND, it opened at the CHARLOTTETOWN SUMMER FESTIVAL on 1 July 1968.

Johnny Canuck. (i) A personification of Canada. Although editorial cartoonists have depicted Canada in the person of a wholesome, clean-cut young man—wearing an habitant's logger's, farmer's, or rancher's outfit—since 1869, the eponymous name first appeared in print in 1909. Johnny Canuck may be either French or English. (ii) The wartime comic-book hero of this name, a strong man, was created by artist Leo Bachle in 1941. In one sequence, later reproduced as a poster, he is shown bursting the fetters that bind him, roaring: 'They had better start making stronger rope—if they want to hold Canadians captive!' See also CANUCK.

Johnny Courteau. A personification of French Canada. He is the subject of a poem by this name written by W.H. DRUMMOND in 1901. See also JEAN BAPTISTE.

Johnson, Albert. See MAD TRAPPER.

Johnson, Edward (1881-1959). Tenor. Born in Guelph, Ont., he studied singing in New York, Paris, and Florence. He was a leading tenor at La Scala, Milan (1914-19), and then at the Metropolitan Opera, New York (1921-35), of which he was general director from 1935 to 1950. Moving to Toronto, he was chairman of the board of the Toronto Opera Festival Company and the ROYAL CONSERVATORY OF MUSIC (1945-58). The Edward Johnson Building in the University of Toronto was named for him in 1962. His daughter Fiorenza (d.1965) married George DREW.

Johnson, John Mercer (1818-68). A FATHER OF

CONFEDERATION. Born in Liverpool, Eng., he trained as a lawyer in New Brunswick and was elected to the legislative assembly in 1850. He attended the QUEBEC and LONDON CONFERENCES on Confederation and was elected to the House of Commons in 1867.

Johnson, Pauline (1862-1913). Poet. Born at CHIEFSWOOD on the Six Nations Indian Reserve near Brantford, C.W. (Ont.), daughter of the marriage of a hereditary chief of the Mohawks and an English woman, she began publishing romantic verse at the age of 23. Dressed in buckskin and using her Indian name Tekahionwake, she gave popular recitals of her work across North America and in Great Britain. Her rhythmical and picturesque verse about Indian life appeared in *The White Wampum* (1895), which included the well-known poem 'The SONG MY PADDLE SINGS', and *Canadian Born* (1903), before being collected in FLINT AND FEATHER (1912). She retired from the stage in 1909 and settled in Vancouver where, from Chief Joseph Capilano, she learned the lore of the Squamish Indians, which she retold in *Legends of Vancouver* (1911). *The Shagganappi* (1913) and *The Moccasin Maker* (1913) are other collections of tales. A selection of prose and poetry was made by Marcus Van Steen for *Pauline Johnson: Her Life and Work* (1965).

Johnston, Bill (1782-1870). Smuggler. He grew up in Bath (Ont.), and because of his smuggling activities was forced to move to Sackett's Harbour, N.Y. He and his gang conducted raids in the Kingston area from hideouts in the Thousand Islands and in May 1838 they emptied the steamer *Sir Robert Peel* of passengers, cut her loose, then set her on fire. Johnston was captured by Americans in 1838 and imprisoned, but he escaped. He obtained a pardon in 1840 and became a lighthouse keeper, while doing some smuggling on the side.

Johnston, Frank or **Franz** (1888-1949). Landscape painter, member of the GROUP OF SEVEN. Born in Toronto, he worked there as a commercial artist for Grip Limited (1908-10), studied in Philadelphia, and worked in New York. His connection with the Group was not strong; he painted with Group members in Algoma, but exhibited only in the first Group show in 1920. The next year he became principal of the School of Art in Winnipeg, where he remained for three years. He resigned from the Group in 1924. In 1927 he changed his first name to Franz. His best-known Group paintings are *Fire-Swept Algoma* (1920, NGC) and an aerial panorama, *The Fire Ranger* (c.1920, NGC). He went on to work independently, giving his work a decorative character that found a ready public.

Johnston, George (b.1913). Poet and translator. Born in Hamilton, Ont., and educated at the University of Toronto, he has taught at Carleton University since 1950. He has been called 'the Canadian Betjeman' for his wise, witty, lightly profound verse, first published in *The Cruising Auk* (1951) and collected in *Happy Enough: Poems 1935-70* (1972). He reads Old Norse and translated *The Saga of Gisli* (1963) and *The Faroe Islanders' Saga* (1973).

Johnston, Gordon (b.1920). Cartoonist and creator of 'IT HAPPENED IN CANADA'. Born in Tillsonburg, Ont., and a graduate of the Ontario College of Art, he has worked as a reporter on British newspapers and as a political cartoonist on Canadian newspapers. He created the syndicated cartoon feature 'It Happened in Canada' in 1967.

Johnstone, James, chevalier de (1719-1800?). Soldier. Born in Edinburgh, Scot., an aide-de-camp to Bonnie Prince Charlie, he fled to France in 1746, joined the army, and was sent to LOUISBOURG in 1752. When it fell in 1758, he escaped and eventually became aide-de-camp to MONTCALM; he was at the battle of the PLAINS OF ABRAHAM. He returned to France in 1760. His memoirs were published in English in 1870-1.

Jolliet, Louis (1645-1700). Explorer, discoverer of the Mississippi R. Born in Quebec, he was sent in 1672 by TALON and FRONTENAC to sight and explore the Mississippi R., then known to white men only from second-hand accounts. Leaving Michilimackinac with Father Jacques Marquette (1637-75) and others in 1673, he entered the Mississippi a month later, descending it to the mouth of the Arkansas and establishing that it flowed south. His house in Quebec still stands on Petit Champlain St, though it was altered about 1762.

Jonas, George (b.1935). Poet and television producer. Born in Budapest, Hungary, he settled in Toronto in 1956 and joined the CBC, where he is a television producer. He is the author of three volumes of urbane poems— *The Absolute Smile* (1967), *The Happy Hungry Man* (1970), and *Cities* (1974)—and wrote the libretto (and Hungarian-born Tibor Polgar the music) for the CANADIAN OPERA COMPANY'S productions of *The European Lover* (1965-6) and *The Glove* (1975-6).

Jones, D.G. (b.1929). Poet and critic. Born in Bancroft, Ont., and educated at McGill and Queen's Universities, he teaches at the University of Sherbrooke, where he helped found the bilingual literary magazine, EL-LIPSE. His meditative lyrics have been published in *Frost on the Sun* (1957), *The Sun is Axeman* (1961), and *Phrases from Orpheus* (1967). *Butterfly on Rock: A Study of Themes and Imagination in Canadian Literature* (1970) is an important critical study. Jones has also translated a selection of poems by Paul-Marie LA-POINTE called *The Terror of the Snows* (1976).

Josie, Edith (b.1921). Journalist. A Loucheux Indian of the Vuntakutchin tribe at Old Crow in the Yukon Territory, she sent her first columns of 'Old Crow News' to the *Whitehorse Star* in the fall of 1962. Writing in a vivid, laconic, ungrammatical style, she caught the flavour of the northern community of 200, located 8 mi. north of the Arctic Circle, and the columns have had a wide readership through syndication. A collection, *Here Are the News*, appeared in 1966. Her reports usually begin and end with the statements 'Here are the news' and 'This is end the news.'

Joual. An uneducated form of the French language spoken in Quebec. It is a mixture of French, Anglicisms, slang, mispronunciations, and the elision or omission of words and syllables. André LAURENDEAU noted its existence in a now-famous editorial in *Le Devoir* on 21 Oct. 1959: 'The word *joual*', he wrote, 'is a summary description of what it is like to talk *joual*, to say *joual* instead of *cheval*, horse. It seems to me we used to speak better, not so slurred, not so coarse, not so screechy, not so *joual*.' A number of poems, stories, plays—notably *Les* BELLES-SOEURS (1968) by Michel TREMBLAY—and novels written in *joual* appeared in the 1960s.

Joubin, Franc. See RIO ALGOM LTD.

Joudry, Patricia See TEACH ME HOW TO CRY.

Jour, Le. (i) A journal published in French in Montreal from 1937 to 1946. Founded and edited by Jean-Charles HARVEY, it appeared weekly, attracted conservative Quebec spokesmen as contributors, and argued against separatism and fascism. (ii) A morning newspaper currently published in Montreal. Launched by members of the PARTI QUÉBÉCOIS on 28 Feb. 1974, it takes a strong separatist line. Its best-known contributor is René LÉVESQUE. Internal dissension forced it to cease publication in mid-August 1976.

Journal of Canadian Fiction. A literary quarterly devoted to the publication of new fiction, critical studies, reviews, and interviews. It was founded in 1972 by John G. Moss and David Arnason in the English De-

partment of the University of New Brunswick. See also CANADIAN FICTION MAGAZINE.

Journal of Canadian Studies. A scholarly quarterly concerned with Canadian history, politics, society, culture, and identity. It has been published by Trent University in Peterborough, Ont., since its founding in 1966.

Journals of Susanna Moodie, The. A sequence of poems by Margaret ATWOOD, published in 1970, composed of the imaginary reflections of the English pioneer, Susanna MOODIE, from the time of her arrival in Upper Canada to her death and beyond. The experience of the wilderness that is examined in these poems was continued in the author's novel *Surfacing* (1972).

Jubilee. A special anniversary—especially a 25th (silver), 50th (golden), and 60th (diamond)—and its celebration. The Silver Jubilee of 1935 celebrated the 25th anniversary of King George V's accession to the throne. The Diamond Jubilee of 1897, which marked the 60th year of Queen Victoria's reign, was widely celebrated throughout Canada and the rest of the British Empire. Canada's Diamond Jubilee of 1927, which marked 60 years of CONFEDERATION, included live radio broadcasts from Parliament Hill.

Judge. The title of a judge of a county or district court. A judge is addressed in conversation as Judge _____ and formally as His or Her (Your) Honour Judge _____. See also JUSTICE.

Judicial Committee of the Privy Council. A committee composed of British privy councillors who hold or have held judicial office. Until 1933 it was the final court of appeal for Canada; but as a result of the STATUTE OF WESTMINSTER the Canadian legislature was enabled to enact legislation abolishing appeals to the Judicial Committee, and did so in respect of appeals in criminal cases in 1933. There was considerable controversy for some time over abolishing appeals to the Judicial Committee in civil cases, because it had a long history of rendering decisions in constitutional issues between the federal and provincial governments, but in 1949 a Canadian statute made the SUPREME COURT the court of final appeal for Canada in all cases.

Judy Award. An award made annually for merchandising excellence. Each year since 1958 the Ontario Fashion Exhibitors Inc. (formerly the Garment Salesmen—Ontario Market) has given up to 15 Judys to garment manufacturers and retailers in Canada—selected by an independent panel drawn from the industry—who have shown excellence in merchandising. The award takes the form of a gold miniature of an apparel manufacturers' dummy, on which material is draped—called a 'judy'.

Jules 30. Automobile manufactured in 1911-12 by Jules Motor Car Company, Guelph, Ont. It was named after its engineer, Julius (Jules) Haltenberger, and had a 30 h.p. motor.

Julien, Henri (1854-1908). Illustrator, cartoonist, and painter. Born in Quebec City, he worked for both the Montreal *Standard* and then the *Montreal Star* until his death. He was a distinguished draughtsman—135 of his drawings in several media were exhibited at the NATIONAL GALLERY OF CANADA—who is particularly remembered for his political cartoons, including a memorable sketch of Sir Wilfrid LAURIER making a speech.

Julien, Pauline (b.1933). Quebec singer. Born in Trois-Rivières, Que., the youngest of 12 children, she went to Paris to study acting on a scholarship from the provincial government. From 1951 to 1957 she established a European reputation as a strong-voiced cabaret singer. Jean Genêt wrote about her: 'One gets the impression that you're the author of all the songs you sing.' On her return to Quebec she discovered the songs of the Quebec chansonniers—especially Gilles VIGNEAULT and Claude LÉVEILLÉ—and in 1968 wrote her first lyrics, 'Bonjour, Bonsoir', with music by Stéphane Venne. She created a fuss at a francophone conference at Niamey, Niger, in 1969 by yelling 'Vive le Québec libre' when Secretary of State Gérard Pelletier was speaking. While incarcerated during the OCTOBER CRISIS of 1970, she wrote 'Eille' about freedom.

Juliette (b.1927). Popular singer. Born Juliet Sysak in St Vital, a suburb of Winnipeg, she was the star of the CBC Radio show 'Here's Juliette' (1943-4). Her television career took off with appearances on CBC-TV's 'The Billy O'Connor Show' (1954-6). Her own 'Juliette Show' was seen on Saturday night following the hockey game on CBC-TV from 1956 to 1966, when its cancellation caused a national furor. Dubbed 'Canada's Pet, Juliette', she used the sign-off 'Goodnight, Mom' as a comfort to her mother following the death of her father.

July the First. See DOMINION DAY.

June Bug. A well-known biplane produced by the AERIAL EXPERIMENT ASSOCIATION. It was designed and first flown by Glen Curtiss at Baddeck, N.S., on 21 June 1908. It carried

Curtiss two miles and in its day was the most famous aircraft in North America.

Juneau, Pierre (b.1922). First chairman of the CANADIAN RADIO-TELEVISION COMMISSION. Born in Verdun, Que., he joined the NATIONAL FILM BOARD in 1949. He was appointed vice-chairman of the Board of Broadcast Governors in 1966 and chairman of the CRTC on 1 Apr. 1968. He insisted on strong CANADIAN CONTENT regulations and was particularly effective in establishing them for broadcast music. Resigning in Aug. 1975, he was appointed to the cabinet but failed to be elected to the House of Commons in Oct. 1975. The JUNO Award was named partly after him.

Junior A. One of two hockey series for non-professional players organized by the Canadian Amateur Hockey Association. Players first competed for the Memorial Cup when the series was established in 1918-19. See also SENIOR A.

Junior Matriculation. See MATRICULATION.

Juniper Junction. See BIRDSEYE CENTRE.

Juno, The. Top award of the Canadian recording industry. From 1969 to 1975 it was awarded annually for excellence in the industry by Walt Grealis of *RPM Magazine*. It was named after the Roman queen of the gods and Pierre JUNEAU, chairman of the CANADIAN RADIO-TELEVISION COMMISSION. It is now an important award presented by the record industry itself.

Jupiter Theatre. A professional theatrical group active in Toronto from 1951 to 1954. Founded by Glen Frankfurter, Lorne GREENE, Len PETERSON and others to produce contemporary plays, it opened on 14 Dec. 1951 with *Galileo*, the second English-language production of Brecht's play. Other productions of note were the premières of Nathan COHEN's *Blue Is for Mourning* (1953) and Lister SINCLAIR's *The Blood Is Strong* (1953). Its greatest success was Christopher Fry's *The Lady's Not for Burning*, starring Christopher PLUMMER, which opened on 16 Jan. 1953, with sets designed by Harold TOWN. Its most ambitious production was Jean Anouilh's *Ring Round the Moon*, which opened at the ROYAL ALEXANDRA THEATRE on 19 Oct. 1953 with Douglas RAIN in the lead and Sydney NEWMAN as its designer; it was directed by Leonard Crainford, who was the general manager when the theatre folded in the spring of 1954.

Just Mary. A series of children's stories written and read on CBC Radio by Mary Grannan (1902-75), a Fredericton schoolteacher. The first program was heard on Sunday, 15 Oct.

Just Mary

1939, and continued until 1962. Another Grannan series, devoted to her 'Maggie Muggins' stories, was carried by CBC Radio from 1946 to 1953 and by CBC-TV from 1953 to 1962. The 'Just Mary' and 'Maggie Muggins' stories were collected and published in several books in the 1940s and 1950s.

Just society, The. Campaign slogan of the LIBERAL PARTY under Pierre Elliott TRUDEAU in 1968.

Justice. The title of a member of the Supreme Court of Canada, a member of a provincial or territorial Supreme Court, or a member of other superior courts—the Federal Court of Canada, Courts of Appeal, Courts of the Queen's Bench. A Justice is addressed in conversation as Mr (Madam) Justice _____. In formal usage a justice is addressed as The Hon. Mr (Madam) Justice _____ . See also CHIEF JUSTICE.

Justice, Department of. The department of the federal government responsible for ensuring that the administration of public affairs is in accordance with law and for super-intending all matters connected with the administration of justice in Canada not within provincial government jurisdiction. Established in 1868, it is under the Minister of Justice, who is the official legal adviser of the governor general, the legal member of the Queen's Privy Council for Canada, and *ex officio*, Her Majesty's Attorney General of Canada. One of his (her) duties is to regulate and conduct all litigation for or against the CROWN in the right of Canada.

Jutra, Claude (b.1930). Quebec film director. Born in Montreal, he graduated in medicine and then joined the NATIONAL FILM BOARD, where he was involved in the production of *A* CHAIRY TALE (1957), directed by Norman McLAREN. He directed his first feature, À TOUT PRENDRE (1963), an independently produced autobiographical film that marked a turning-point in the Quebec cinema. His most critically successful film to date is MON ONCLE ANTOINE (1970). Other deft and moving features include *Comment savoir* (1966), *Wow* (1969), KAMOURASKA (1972), and *Pour le meilleur et pour le pire* (1975).

K

Kabloona. Eskimo word for a European or white man. It means, literally, 'person with big [thick] eyebrows'. There are various spellings. In Eskimo, *Kabluna* (or *Kablunak*) is singular, and *Kablunet* is plural. In English, the word is usually uninflected, so *Kabloona* may be singular or plural.

Kagige, Francis (b.1929). Odawa artist. Born on the Wikwemikong Reserve on Manitoulin Island, he developed his own style while employed making Indian-type souvenirs and has exhibited his paintings since 1964. His work, which was seen in the Indian Pavilion at EXPO 67, interprets the legends of his people and his love of the northern woods. He illustrated *Tales of Nokomis* (1970) by Patronella Johnson.

Kahane, Anne (b.1924). Sculptor. Born in Austria, she came to Canada with her parents in 1925 and studied art in Montreal and at the Cooper Union Art School in New York. She began to sculpt in 1949 and in 1953 won an award in the Unknown Political Pris-oner Competition, organized by the Institute of Contemporary Arts, London, Eng. Her semi-abstract sculptures, primarily in wood, are influenced by medieval and early Quebec folk carving. She has exhibited in Canada and abroad and is represented in numerous public collections.

Kain, Karen (b.1951). Dancer. Born in Hamilton, Ont., she studied at the NATIONAL BALLET SCHOOL and joined the NATIONAL BALLET in 1970. She became a principal dancer in 1971 and, partnered by Frank AUGUSTYN, won a silver medal in the duet class at Moscow's International Ballet Competition in 1973. She has been hailed as 'one of the most talented ballerinas in the western world', the first successful partner for Rudolf Nureyev since Margot Fonteyn. After performing demanding leading roles with acclaim in the National Ballet's 1976 season, she fulfilled engagements with the Paris Opera Ballet and the Roland Petit Ballet, with which she danced the title role in *Nana* (based on Zola's novel), specially created for her by Petit. It was first performed on 6 May 1976.

Kakegamic, Joshim (b.1953). Cree artist. Born at the Sandy Lake Reserve in northern Ontario, he has shown his paintings since 1969 in group and one-man shows. He interprets the legendary beliefs and practices of the Cree and Ojibwa and works with his family (which includes his brother Goyce Kakegamic, born in 1948, also a talented painter in acrylics) at the Triple K, a silk-screening company in Red Lake, Ont. He is the brother-in-law of Norval MORRISSEAU.

Kalm, Peter (1716-79). Botanist and early traveller in North America. Born in Sweden, he visited New France and went as far west as Lake Ontario in 1749-50. His journal of this trip is particularly valuable for its detailed descriptions of pre-conquest Quebec. It was published in a modern translation, *The America of 1750: Peter Kalm's Travels in North America* (1937), edited by Adolph B. Benson.

Kalvak, Helen (b.1901). Eskimo graphic artist at HOLMAN. A noted storyteller, she began drawing in the 1960s to illustrate the tales she was telling. Many ancient Eskimo legends and shamanistic practices have been illustrated in Kalvak's prints.

Kamik. Eskimo word for a warm knee-length boot made of sealskin. It is waterproof; if greater warmth is desired, it is made of caribou. Nowadays the fur inner sock has been replaced by the 'duffle sock', which is longer than the *kamik* by about 8 in. and is folded over the top; it is usually vividly embroidered. Horizontal strips or motifs of differently coloured skin are used only on a female's *kamiks*; males wear *kamiks* with vertical designs only. *Kamiks* are worn in the eastern, Keewatin, Labrador and central regions of the Arctic. The MUKLUK is characteristic of the far-western Arctic only.

Kamloops trout. A game fish of varied size and colouration found in the Kamloops area of British Columbia. It has firm flesh and is excellent fresh or smoked. Usually inhabiting inland lakes and streams, it has been described as a landlocked STEELHEAD.

Kamouraska. Novel by Anne HÉBERT published in French in 1970 and in an English translation by Norman Shapiro in 1973. Based on a nineteenth-century Quebec murder case in the Kamouraska region of the EASTERN TOWNSHIPS, it is the story of a woman who, while watching over the deathbed of her husband, reflects on her earlier marriage to a sadistically cruel man; the murder of her husband by her lover, who is forced to leave

her after the killing; her own trial and acquittal; and her second marriage to the man who is now dying. A feature film based on the novel was released in 1973. Produced by Pierre Lamy and directed by Claude JUTRA, it starred Geneviève BUJOLD and Richard Jordan.

Kananginak (b.1935). Eskimo stone-cutter and printer at CAPE DORSET. One of the earliest artists working there, he began to do stone-cuts in 1962, specializing in Arctic birds.

Kane, Paul (1810-71). Painter. Born in Ireland, he came to York (Toronto) as a child and studied portrait painting as a young man. After living and working in Detroit, Mich., and Mobile, Ala, he spent two years in Europe. He developed an interest in the western Indians and arranged to visit their territories, leaving Toronto in May 1846, travelling as far west as Fort Vancouver on the Lower Columbia R., and returning in Oct. 1848. The result of this trip was 100 canvases of Indian life, painted from sketches in Toronto over six years. They not only include some treasures of Canadian art but are of great documentary value. The Royal Ontario Museum, Toronto, has many beautiful sketches in pencil, watercolour, and oil, as well as such memorable oil paintings as *The MAN THAT ALWAYS RIDES* (1849-55, ROM). Kane's *Wanderings of an Artist Among the Indians of North America* (1859), a classic Canadian travel book, was illustrated with reproductions of some of his sketches and paintings.

Kantaroff, Maryon (b.1933). Sculptor and feminist. Born in Toronto of Bulgarian-born parents, she graduated from the University of Toronto in art and archaeology and was assistant curator of the ART GALLERY OF ONTARIO (1957-8). She studied at the Chelsea Art College and Berkshire College in London, Eng., from 1959 to 1962, exhibiting her works widely. She returned to Toronto in 1969 and took up feminism and sculpture. Operating her own foundry, she casts immense bronze sculptures, commissioned by developers, and smaller pieces. Her work is characterized by its polish and its rich, rounded forms.

Kapelsche Veer. A town in Holland, the scene of fighting during the SECOND WORLD WAR. Canadian and British troops eliminated the German bridgehead there in Jan. 1945.

Karluk. Built in San Francisco in 1884 and owned by the National Geographic Society, she was placed under the control of the Royal Canadian Navy for the Canadian Arc-

Karluk

tic Expedition of 1913 led by Vilhjalmur STE-FANSSON. She became icebound that Aug. and on 11 Jan. 1914 was crushed and sank.

Karoo. See Karoo ASHEVAK.

Karsh, Yousuf (b.1908). Portrait photographer. Born in Mardin, Armenia, he came to Canada in 1924 and later studied photography in Boston under John Garo. In 1933 he opened his studio in Ottawa, where he still lives. Brought to international prominence in 1949 by a famous photograph of Winston Churchill without a cigar, he later photographed such prominent figures as Shaw, Einstein, Picasso, and Queen Elizabeth II. His striking portraits have appeared in *Faces of Destiny* (1947), *Portraits of Greatness* (1959), *Faces of Our Time* (1971), and *Portraits* (1976).

Kasemets, Udo (b.1919). Composer. Born in Tallinn, Estonia, he was educated in Germany before coming to Canada in 1951. He has taught piano and theory in Toronto and Hamilton and has also been a conductor, accompanist, organist, and critic. He is a prolific composer of works that have links with the musical avant-garde in the United States and include orchestral, choral, solo vocal, and chamber pieces. He has recently lectured on music and the mixed media at the Ontario College of Art and has developed experimental techniques associated with John Cage.

Kattan, Naïm (b.1928). Writer and arts administrator. Born in Baghdad, Iraq, he settled in Montreal in 1954 and in 1962 joined the Canada Council, becoming its chief literary officer. He is best known for *Reality and Theatre* (1972), six essays translated by Alan BROWN that distinguish between oriental and occidental modes of perception. His novel *Farewell, Babylon* (1976) was also translated by Alan Brown.

Kawartha Lakes. A group of 14 lakes extending across Victoria and Peterborough counties in central Ontario. They are Scugog, Sturgeon, Cameron, Balsam, Pigeon, Bald, Sandy, Buckhorn, Chemong, Deer, Lovesick, Stony, Clear, and Katchewanooka.

Kayak. A light, sealskin, Eskimo canoe completely covered except for a cockpit, which accommodates a single person who propels the craft with a double-bladed paddle. Freight and passengers are conveyed in the UMIAK.

Kazan River. The most important of the great rivers of the Barren Lands. Properly called *Inuit Ku*, 'The River of Men', it flows through the former heartland of the Ihalmuit

people, from Ennadai Lake in southern Northwest Territories northward 455 mi. to join the Thelon R. at Baker Lake; from there both rivers reach Hudson Bay through Chesterfield Inlet.

KC. See QC.

Keaton, Buster. See *The* RAILRODDER.

Keewatin. Algonkian word for 'the north wind', the most chilling of winds, or for 'northwest'. It is the most easterly district of the three NORTHWEST TERRITORIES.

Kejimkujik National Park. It was established in 1968, in the interior of Nova Scotia, to protect Micmac petroglyphs. It covers 147 sq. mi. of rolling countryside, forests, lakes, and islands.

'Kelligrews Soirée, The'. A popular song in Newfoundland dealing with hijinks at a jamboree in Kelligrews, a village near St John's. It was written by John Burke. The last of five different refrains goes: 'There was birch rhine, tar twine, cherry wine, and turpentine,/Jowls and cavalances, ginger beer and tea,/Pigs' feet, cats' meat, dumplings boiled in a sheet,/Dandelion and crackies' teeth at the Kelligrews Soirée.'

Kelly, Leonard Patrick (Red) (b.1927). Hockey player. Born in Simcoe, Ont., he became a professional hockey player with the Detroit Red Wings when only 19. After 12 seasons he joined the TORONTO MAPLE LEAFS. During eight years with the Leafs he won many honours, including the LADY BYNG MEMORIAL TROPHY four times. He played on eight STANLEY CUP championship teams, and while still a player served three years as a Member of Parliament. He later served as a coach in Los Angeles, Pittsburgh, and Toronto. He is married to Andrea McLaughlin, a former world-champion and professional figure-skater.

Kelly, Ron (b.1929). Television and film director. Born in Vancouver, he joined CBC-TV's Vancouver Film Unit in 1954 and in 1959 directed the drama *A Bit of Bark*. He pioneered in the dramatic use of the hand-held camera in OPEN GRAVE (1964). He directed two feature films: WAITING FOR CAROLINE (1967) for NFB-CBC and *King of the Grizzlies* (1969) for Walt Disney. Kelly's feature-length CBC-TV dramas include *The* MEGANTIC OUTLAW (1970) and *Springhill* (1971).

Kelsey, Henry (c.1667-1724). Explorer, governor of the HUDSON'S BAY COMPANY. His career with the HBC lasted from 1684 to 1722, the last four years as governor. In 1690 he left

YORK FACTORY to embark on a memorable journey with Indians lasting two years, in which he was the first white man to see the Prairies and might have reached the site of The Pas on the Saskatchewan R. His journals of this trip have been published in *The Kelsey Papers* (1929) edited by A.G. DOUGHTY and Chester Martin.

Kemano. See KITIMAT.

Kenins, Talivaldis (b.1919). Composer. Born in Liepaja, Latvia, he studied for a diplomatic career in France before turning to musical studies at the Paris Conservatoire. He came to Canada in 1951 and now teaches at the University of Toronto. As a composer whose contrapuntal musical style was formed by a combination of Russian lyricism and the French classical ideal, he has wirtten many choral works—including *Chants of Glory and Mercy* (1970)—chamber works, and solo pieces for both piano and organ. His *Sawan-Oong, The Spirit of the Winds* (1973), a symphonic cantata for baritone, choir, and orchestra, is based on an Ojibwa-Cree legend.

Kennedy, Betty (b.1926). Broadcaster. Born in Ottawa, she has worked on newspapers in Montreal, Calgary, Ottawa, and Toronto. Her first appearance on FRONT PAGE CHALLENGE was in 1957; she joined the show as a regular panelist in 1962. Since 1959 she has hosted her own top-rated, five-day-a-week program—the 60-minute 'Betty Kennedy Show'—on CFRB in Toronto. Following the death of her husband, a prominent business executive concerned with wildlife preservation, she wrote *Gerhard: A Love Story* (1976).

Keno. The stern-wheel steamer that took passengers and supplies from Whitehorse to Dawson during the KLONDIKE GOLD RUSH of 1898. It was restored for the DAWSON CITY GOLD RUSH FESTIVAL in 1962 and is a Yukon Historic Site.

Kenojuak (b.1927). Perhaps the most celebrated of Eskimo artists. A CAPE DORSET printmaker and sculptor, she specializes in graphic images of fantastic owls. She began drawing in the late 1950s and was among the first Inuit artists to achieve personal recognition, which came about through her world-famous print *The* ENCHANTED OWL, executed in 1960. The artist is the subject of *Eskimo Artist—Kenojuak*, an NFB film (19 min., 49 sec.; colour; 1964), directed by John Feeney and produced by Tom DALY, and was the recipient of the ORDER OF CANADA in 1967. With her late husband JOHNNIEBO, she created an enormous carved wall panel for the Canadian Pavilion at Expo 70 in Osaka, Japan.

Kenora Trench. See REGINA TRENCH.

Kensington Market. (i) Lively ethnic market area in Toronto. Located south of College St and west of Spadina Ave, it was once predominantly Jewish but is now about half Portuguese. (ii) Toronto rock group. Formed by Bernie Finklestein in 1966, it brought together some of the city's best rock musicians: Jimmy Watson, Gene Martynec, Luke Gibson, Keith McKie, and Alex Darew. It was a popular performing and recording group, especially liked by the critics, until it disbanded about 1972. It was named after the ethnic market area described above. See also KING OF KENSINGTON.

Kent, Duke of (1767-1820). Commander-in-chief of the forces in British North America. Edward Augustus, Duke of Kent and Strathearn, was the fourth son of George III. He was at Quebec in 1791-3 and at Halifax in 1794 and again in 1799-1800. He is remembered for contracting a morganatic marriage with Julie de Montgenet, by whom he had two sons; for building the Town Clock (see Halifax CITADEL) and the PRINCE'S LODGE in Halifax; and, after his marriage in 1818 to Victoria Mary Louisa, widow of the Prince of Leiningen, for becoming the father of the future Queen Victoria. Prince Edward Island was named for him.

Kent, Lawrence (b.1938). Film director. Born in South Africa, he immigrated to Vancouver in 1957. While a student at the University of British Columbia, he directed Canada's second student feature-length film, BITTER ASH (1963), which immediately became a *succès de scandale* when banned and seized by two censor boards. His later feature films include *Sweet Substitute* (1964), *When Tomorrow Dies* (1965), *High* (1967), *Façade* (1968), *The Apprenticeship* (1971), and *Keep It in the Family* (1972).

Kermode bear. A subspecies of the black bear, found only in northern Pacific Coast regions, named after Francis Kermode (1874-1946), former director of the British Columbia Provincial Museum.

Kerosene oil. See Abraham GESNER.

Kerr, Graham. See GALLOPING GOURMET.

Kerr, Robert (1882-1963). Champion runner. Born in Ireland and brought to Hamilton, Ont., as a child, he won the trophy awarded to the outstanding athlete at the British championship games held in London in 1908. He then won the bronze medal in the 100-metre event and the gold medal in the 200-metre race at the 1908 Olympics, also in

London. He retired from competition in his 30th year, after winning nearly 400 races, but he continued to coach, promote, and officiate for the rest of his life.

Kerr-Addison Mines. The largest gold mine in Canada in the 1950s and 1960s. It went into production in 1938 in the Krikland Lake/Lardner Lake area of northern Ontario and in 1960 produced a record $20 million of 'the money metal'. It was named after H.L. Kerr, a geologist, and William H.F. Addison, a medical doctor. By the 1970s Kerr-Addision had diversified into copper and zinc and had a uranium mine under development.

Khaki College. Junior college and extension department operated in Britain for Canadian troops stationed there during the First and Second World Wars. Originated by the National Committee of the Canadian YMCA, it offered academic and vocational instruction to members of the Canadian Armed Forces in 1917-19 and 1945-6. The name is derived from the dust-coloured uniforms worn by soldiers.

Khaki Election. A reference to the WARTIME ELECTIONS ACT.

Kiakshuk (*c*.1888-1965). Eskimo graphic artist and sculptor at CAPE DORSET. His drawings record the traditional ways. His superb sculpture is not well known because it is unsigned. He built the giant INUKSHUKS that were reassembled at Toronto International Airport in the 1960s, and appeared as a storyteller in the NFB film *The Living Stone*, released in 1958. His son is the sculptor LUK-TAK.

Kicking Horse Pass. Well-known pass through the Rocky Mountains northwest of Banff, Alta, the route used by the CPR in the building of the first transcontinental railway. It was named when a geologist with the Palliser expedition (see PALLISER'S TRIANGLE) was kicked by his own horse. See also HONOURABLE MEMBER OF PARLIAMENT FOR KICKING HORSE PASS.

Kicking Horse Pass Tunnels. A system of spiralling tunnels that reduces the gradient on the CPR line through KICKING HORSE PASS in the Rocky Mountains. Completed in 1911, the system twice crosses its own line through Mt Ogden and Mt Cathedral.

Kidd, Bruce (b. 1943). Runner and sports advocate. The Ottawa-born, middle-distance runner won the bronze medal in the 3-mi. event and the gold medal in the 6-mi. event at the 1962 Commonwealth Games in Perth, Australia. He was chosen 'Canadian athlete

of the year' in 1962 and 1963. Troubled with physical ailments, he competed unsuccessfully in the 1964 Olympics in Tokyo and eventually dropped out of competition. He is the subject of *Runner*, a short NFB film released in 1962, with an impressionistic commentary by W.H. Auden read by Don Francks. The author of *The Death of Hockey* (1972), Kidd teaches in the School of Physical and Health Education at the University of Toronto.

Kidd, J.R. (Roby). See CANADIAN ASSOCIATION FOR ADULT EDUCATION.

Kikanisei. Japanese word for a Canadian-born Japanese who spent the Second World War in Japan and then resettled in Canada. See also ISSEI and NISEI.

Kilbourn, William (b.1926). Writer, teacher, civic politician. Born in Toronto and educated at the Universities of Toronto, Oxford, and Harvard, he became first chairman of the Humanities Division of York University in 1962 and a Toronto alderman in 1969. His best-known book is a biography of William Lyon MACKENZIE, *The Firebrand* (1956). He also wrote the company history of STELCO, *The Elements Combined* (1960), and *Pipeline* (1970), the story of the PIPELINE DEBATE. He edited *Canada: A Guide to the Peaceable Kingdom* (1970) and *The Toronto Book* (1976), two anthologies.

Killam Program. Scholarships awarded annually by the CANADA COUNCIL to support scholars of exceptional ability engaged in research projects of far-reaching significance in the humanities, social sciences, interdisciplinary studies, or studies embracing the natural sciences, medicine, or engineering. They have been made possible since 1973 by a gift and bequest of the late Dorothy J. Killam, widow of I.W. Killam, the succession duties on whose estate had earlier helped to establish the Canada Council itself.

Killdeer, The. Play by James REANEY. It opened at the COACH HOUSE THEATRE, Toronto, on 13 Jan. 1960. A verse-drama that merges fantasy, comedy, and murder, it is set in a small Ontario town where the lives of children from different families are hopelessly entangled. There are recurring references to the killdeer, a wild bird with a haunting cry. Reaney's first play, it was published in 1962 and in a revised version, in *Masks of Childhood*, in 1972.

Kimik. See QIMMIK.

Kindred of the Wild, The. The first collection of animal stories by Charles G.D. ROBERTS, published in 1902. Told realistically with poetic imagination, these wildlife stories were the first in a genre that imparted feeling and reason to animals.

King, Allan (b.1905). Actor and writer. Born at Southend, Eng., and educated in China, he immigrated to Canada in 1927. He held down a variety of jobs in Victoria and Toronto before becoming an actor and then a writer for CBC Radio in 1941. He has contributed to the CBC STAGE series and excelled as a writer and performer with Barry MORSE in 'A Touch of Grease Paint', a half-hour weekly series devoted to the world of theatre, first heard on CBC Radio in May 1954. He researched and wrote the 26-part series of dramatic documentaries on parliamentary government called 'A Man at Westminster', heard on radio in 1965-6 and published in 1967. As an actor he appeared as 'Doc James' in the CBC-TV series 'Corwin' in 1970.

King, Allan (b.1930). Film director. Born in Vancouver, he joined the CBC's Vancouver Film Unit, which produced his first film, *Skid Row* (1956). In 1962 he established Allan King Associates in Toronto. For CBC-TV he directed WARRENDALE (1967), about emotionally retarded children, which the Corporation rejected before this classic of *cinéma-verité* went on to claim international awards. He applied the same technique to a modern marriage with *A* MARRIED COUPLE (1969). Since his last commercially released film, *Come on Children* (1972), he has been working on a film adaptation of W.O. MITCHELL'S novel WHO HAS SEEN THE WIND.

King, William Lyon Mackenzie (1874-1950). Tenth prime minister of Canada. A grandson of William Lyon MacKENZIE, he was born in Berlin (Kitchener) Ont., and educated at the University of Toronto. In 1900 he became the first deputy minister of the newly created federal department of labour. He first entered Parliament as a Liberal in 1908 and in 1909 was appointed Minister of Labour by Sir Wilfrid LAURIER. He lost his seat in 1911. Engaged to study labour questions by the Rockefeller Foundation in 1914, he wrote *Industry and Humanity: A Study in the Principles Underlying Reconstruction* (1918), which grew out of this work. In 1919 he was chosen leader of the Liberal Party and became Prime Minister on 29 Dec. 1921. He was involved in the CONSTITUTIONAL CRISIS of 1926, the year he attended the Imperial Conference that produced the Balfour Declaration and subsequently resulted in the STATUTE OF WESTMINSTER. The Liberal Party was defeated in the general election of 1930, but was returned

with substantial majorities in 1935, 1940, and 1945. King held power longer than any other Canadian prime minister.

In 1939 King signed the ORDER-IN-COUNCIL by which Canada declared war independently of Great Britain, the first time it had ever done so. During the war years he was responsible for establishing the WARTIME PRICES AND TRADE BOARD to control the Canadian war economy. But his most difficult task was to deal with the pressure for conscription for the armed forces from English Canada and resistance to it from French Canada. Though he pledged in 1939 that there would be no conscription for overseas service, in 1942 he was forced to hold a national referendum on conscription, during which he promised 'conscription if necessary but not necessarily conscription'; he avoided implementing conscription for overseas service until 1944. King retired from public life in 1948. His papers, which are gradually being released for public scrutiny, have confirmed that he believed in a spiritual world; was guided by the influence of his dead mother and his famous grandfather; and, as a bachelor, led (in a phrase from his diary) 'a very double life'.

King George's War (1744-8). The North American phase of the War of the Austrian Succession between England and France. Troops from LOUISBOURG and Quebec attacked Nova Scotia and Saratoga, N.Y. Louisbourg was captured by British forces but was returned to France by the TREATY OF AIX-LA-CHAPELLE in 1748.

King of Kensington. A situation comedy produced by CBC-TV. The popular half-hour weekly series, which made its début on 25 Sept. 1975, is set in KENSINGTON MARKET, an ethnic market area in Toronto. It features Al Waxman as Larry King, a cheerful Jewish variety-store owner. Fiona Reid plays his wife, Helene Winston his mother. It is produced by Norman Rosemond.

King of the fur-traders. Sobriquet of Sir George SIMPSON.

King of the Gatineau. Sobriquet of Alonzo Wright (1825-94), who represented the GATINEAU region in Parliament.

King of the Klondike. Sobriquet of Joseph W. BOYLE.

King William Island. It is in the Franklin District of the Northwest Territories, lying north of the mainland between the Boothia Peninsula to the northeast and Victoria Island to the northwest. It was first sighted by

King William Island

James Clark Ross in 1830 and later became connected with the search for the NORTHWEST PASSAGE. In 1846 Sir John FRANKLIN's ships became icebound in Victoria Strait off the west coast of the island, and he and the members of his expedition perished there. On his voyage of 1903-6 through the Passage, Roald AMUNDSEN anchored in a harbour on the southeast coast of the island; he remained there for 23 months and named the place Gjoa Haven.

King William's War (1689-97). The North American phase of the War of the League of Augsburg, which involved England after 1689. The main fighting between England and France took place over control of Hudson Bay and in the attacks by French forces, sent out by FRONTENAC, on English colonies. Sir William PHIPS took PORT ROYAL in 1690 but not Quebec. IBERVILLE made raids on Maine, Newfoundland, and Hudson Bay. Port Royal was relinquished by England in the terms of the TREATY OF RYSWICK in 1697.

King's Bench. See QUEEN'S BENCH.

King's Counsel. See QC.

King's Domain. The *Domain du Roi*, a vast tract of land lying north of the lower St Lawrence R. and originally belonging to the French kings, who leased the trading rights at the King's Posts, a practice taken over by the British government after 1760.

King's Girls. *Filles du roi*, girls sent out to New France by Louis XIV between 1665 and 1671 as brides for unmarried settlers and for officers and men of the CARIGNAN-SALIÈRES REGIMENT.

King's Landing Historical Settlement. A restoration of more than 50 buildings—threatened by construction of a dam—depicting colonial life in New Brunswick from 1790 to 1870. Situated 23 mi. west of Fredericton and opened in 1973, King's Landing is a 300-acre site containing farms, a sawmill, a church, a school, a store, and other mementoes of early Canadian pioneer life.

King's Printer. See QUEEN'S PRINTER.

Kingsmere. Summer home of W.L. Mackenzie KING from 1902 until his death in 1950. It was given its name, which means 'king's lake', by an early surveyor; King sometimes referred to it as Moorside. He bequeathed his 18-room cottage and 500-acre estate to the government as a summer home for the prime minister. As HARRINGTON LAKE meets that need, Kingsmere was opened to the public as a memorial to Mackenzie King, who was re-sponsible for importing rubble from Europe and elsewhere, and erecting mock medieval ruins, which King called 'The Cloisters', among the rolling Gatineau Hills. It is now part of GATINEAU Park.

Kingsmill, Admiral Sir Charles Edmund (1855-1935). First Director of Naval Service. Born in Guelph, Ont., he joined the Royal Navy as a midshipman in 1869. After a long and distinguished career, which included service in the Sudan in 1884, he retired as a rear admiral in 1908, when he took charge of the Marine Service of the Department of Marine and Fisheries of the Canadian government. He was promoted vice admiral soon after. He played a prominent part in the negotiations resulting in the formation of the ROYAL CANADIAN NAVY in 1910 and was the first Director of Naval Service. He was promoted to the rank of admiral in Apr. 1917 and was knighted the following year. He retired in 1920.

Kinsmen Clubs, Association of. A service club for businessmen and professionals between the ages of 21 and 40. The only service club to originate in Canada, it was founded by a First World War veteran, Harold A. Rogers, in Hamilton, Ont., on 20 Feb. 1920. There are over 300 clubs across the country.

Kirby, William (1817-1906). Author. Born in Kingston-upon-Hull, Eng., and taken by his parents to the United States in 1832, he settled in 1839 at Niagara-on-the-Lake, where he edited the Niagara *Mail*. From 1871 to 1895 he was Collector of Customs. He wrote *The U.E.: A Tale of Upper Canada* (1859), composed in Spenserian stanzas; the work for which he is chiefly remembered, *The* GOLDEN DOG *(Le Chien d'or)* (1877; rev. 1896), a romantic novel set in eighteenth-century New France; and *Annals of Niagara* (1896).

Kirkconnell, Watson (b.1895). Scholar. Born in Port Hope, Ont., and educated at Queen's University and Oxford, he was president of Acadia University, Wolfville, N.S., from 1948 to 1963. A linguist and the author of many books and translations, he covered foreign-language publications for the *University of Toronto Quarterly*'s LETTERS IN CANADA for 20 years. His most recent publications are *Centennial Tales and Selected Poems* (1965); his memoirs, *A Slice of Canada* (1967); and *Awake the Courteous Echo* (1973), a study of selected themes in world literature.

Kirke, David (c.1597-1654). Adventurer. He assisted English efforts to capture New France by taking Quebec in 1629, while CHAMPLAIN was in command. Knighted in

1633, he was governor of Newfoundland from 1637 to 1651.

Kirkland Lake. A town in Timiskaming District, northern Ontario, that had its origin in the gold discoveries of 1910. Located nearby were such famous gold mines as Lake Shore (see OAKES MURDER CASE), Wright-Hargreaves, and Teck Hughes. Today few gold mines are left and iron-ore is being mined in the area. The main street is known as the 'Golden Mile' as a result of work crews' using gold ore instead of waste rock from the mines to build the road.

Kirkland Lake Strike. A protracted strike of gold miners for union recognition. It broke out at Kirkland Lake in northern Ontario on 18 Nov. 1941, with the operators refusing arbitration under the INDUSTRIAL DISPUTES INVESTIGATION ACT 10 days later. The strike was terminated on 11 Feb. 1942 without union recognition.

Kiska. One of the Aleutian Islands near Amchitka, held by the Japanese during the SECOND WORLD WAR. A Canadian brigade group assisted the Allied force that landed there on 15 Aug. 1943 to find that the Japanese had abandoned it two weeks earlier.

Kit of the Mail. Sobriquet of Kathleen Blake Watkins (1864-1915), who for 20 years wrote a weekly 'Woman's Kingdom' page in the Toronto MAIL. She was the world's first accredited woman war correspondent, covering the Spanish-American War in 1898.

Kit-Wat. See TWIN CITIES.

Kitimat. Site of a giant smelter and town at the head of Douglas Channel, southeast of Prince Rupert, on the west coast of British Columbia. It was carved out of the wilderness in 1951-4 by ALCAN ALUMINIUM LIMITED for the production of metallic aluminum from bauxite. The electrolytic process is powered by giant hydro-electric generators built some 50 mi. southeast at Kemano, on the Kemano R. Kitimat and Kemano are the names of Indian settlements.

Kiwanis Music Festival. An annual musical competition sponsored for two weeks each February since 1944 by the Kiwanis Clubs of Greater Toronto. One of the largest festivals of its kind in the world, it offers scholarships and cash awards to young amateur musical performers in such categories as singing, piano, accordian, strings, wind instruments, senior and junior choirs, bands, and orchestras.

Kiyooka, Roy (b.1926). Painter. Born in Moose Jaw, Sask., he studied at the Alberta Institute of Technology and Art and the Instituto Allende, Mexico. He taught at the Alberta Institute and the Regina College of Art. In the 1950s he explored an abstract expressionist style that developed into the oval series of abstract patterns represented by *Aleph #2* (1964, NGC). He has recently worked on large-scale canvases in an elegant hard-edge style with serene colours and lyrically elliptical shapes. He lives in Vancouver and has published a number of books of avant-garde poetry.

'K-K-K-Katy'. See Geoffrey O'HARA.

KL. See KNIGHTS OF LABOUR.

Klanak Press. Small publishing house devoted to issuing handsomely designed and printed books of prose and poetry. It was founded by the lawyer William McConnell and his wife Alice in Victoria in 1958. *Klanak* is the Salish word for 'a gathering of people for the purpose of good talk'.

Klee Wyck. Nootka name for Emily CARR, meaning 'the laughing one', and the title of her first book, a collection of west-coast Indian sketches published in 1941.

Klein, A.M. (1909-72). Poet. Born in Montreal, he was educated at McGill and the Université de Montréal, where he studied law; he was called to the bar in 1933. He was editor of *The Canadian Jewish Chronicle* from 1939 to 1954 and was active as a Labour Zionist and with the CCF in the 1940s. A learned man who was proficient in five languages, he was also a humanist whose sympathies embraced minorities—not only the Jew, but the French Canadian, the Indian, and the poet (one of his finest poems is 'Portrait of the Poet as Landscape'). His poetry was collected in *Hath Not a Jew* (1940), *Poems* (1944), *The Hitleriad* (1944), and *The Rocking Chair and Other Poems* (1941). *The Second Scroll* (1951) is a rich parable about a spiritual pilgrimage to the Promised Land. His career as a prominent and respected poet came to a halt in the mid-1950s when he suffered a breakdown. *The Collected Poems* (1975) was edited by Miriam WADDINGTON, who has also written a critical study, *A.M. Klein* (1970).

Kleinburg. See McMICHAEL CANADIAN COLLECTION.

Klondike. (i) A region in the southwestern part of the Yukon Territory that includes the Klondike R. and its tributary creeks, the scene of the KLONDIKE GOLD RUSH of 1896. The name is derived from the Kutchin word (meaning 'hammer river') for the Klondike R.

Klondike

(ii) The title of a history of the gold rush by Pierre BERTON published in 1958. It vividly recreates the drama and the personalities who were attracted from the corners of the world, from 1896 to 1903, by the possibility of discovering gold. An American edition was entitled *Klondike Fever.*

Klondike, King of the. See Joseph W. BOYLE.

Klondike Days. Popular festival held in Edmonton, Alta, in late July. Since the Edmonton Exhibition incorporated a Klondike theme in 1962, the Klondike Exposition Grounds have been open for an annual 10-day celebration of entertainment, regattas, races, and parades. Gold-rush traditions and 1890s' clothing styles set the colourful tone.

Klondike Gold Rush. It was started by a rich strike made at Rabbit (renamed Bonanza) Creek, a tributary of the Klondike R. in the Yukon Territory, on 17 Aug. 1896. Made by George Washington Carmack and two Indians, Skookum Jim and Tagish Charlie—acting on directions given by Robert Henderson, a prospector who received only a $200-a-month pension for being co-discoverer of the Klondike goldfields—the strike attracted many thousands of prospectors from all over the world, many of whom became millionaires, and gave birth to DAWSON. The gold rush began to decline in 1900.

Klondike Gold Rush International Historic Park. A joint project of Canada and the United States begun in 1961, this park, with designated sites in both the Yukon and Alaska, is being developed to commemorate the KLONDIKE GOLD RUSH. For the Canadian sites see YUKON HISTORIC SITES.

Klondike Mike. A biography by Merrill DENISON, published in 1943 and widely translated, of Michael 'Mike' Mahoney, a colourful figure whose exploits during the KLONDIKE GOLD RUSH became legendary. Mahoney boasted that he carried a grand piano over the White Pass in 1898.

Kluane National Park. Established in 1972 in the southwest corner of the Yukon Territory, it covers 8,500 sq. mi. and includes MOUNT LOGAN, the highest peak in the country and one of the world's largest non-polar glacier systems.

Kneebone, Tom (b.1934). Performer. Born in New Zealand and educated at the Bristol and London Old Vics, he settled in Toronto in 1956. A deft performer in revues and plays, he has appeared with Pat Galloway, Dinah Christie, and Barbara HAMILTON. His comic style has been described as 'Pixie Rose Lee'.

Knights of Labour. A union that played an important role in early union history, founded in Philadelphia, Pa, in 1869. The first Canadian local assembly was held in Hamilton, Ont., in 1881. Expelled from the TRADES AND LABOUR CONGRESS OF CANADA at a meeting in Berlin (now Kitchener), Ont., in Sept. 1902, the Knights of Labour immediately established the NATIONAL TRADES AND LABOUR CONGRESS.

Knister, Raymond (1900-32). Novelist and poet. Born in Blenheim, Ont., and educated at the University of Toronto and Iowa State University, he drowned off Stoney Point, Lake Erie, before reaching his full literary powers. His poetry appeared in several well-known American literary magazines and he wrote two promising novels, *White Narcissus* (1929), a love story set in rural Ontario, and *My Star Predominant* (1934), an account of Keats's life. Dorothy LIVESAY introduced his *Collected Poems* (1949) and Peter Stevens edited a collection of his stories, *The First Day of Spring* (1976).

Knowles, Dorothy (b.1929). Painter. Born in Unity, Sask., she studied at the BANFF CENTRE and the University of Saskatchewan, where she currently teaches. By using brushwork associated with watercolour sketching, she gives her colourful oil landscapes of the Prairies an impressionistic quality.

Knox, Walter (1878-1951). All-round track-and-field star. Born in Listowel, Ont., he once won five Canadian championships the same afternoon. In 1913 he won the all-round professional American track-and-field championship; the following year, after defeating the British champion, he became the world title-holder. He collected more than 400 first prizes over the years, and coached many groups, including Canada's 1920 Olympic team.

Knox College. Presbyterian theological college in Toronto, founded in a minister's house in 1844; the present building was erected in 1915. It is federated with the UNIVERSITY OF TORONTO and is a member of the TORONTO SCHOOL OF THEOLOGY.

Knudson, George (b.1937). Golfer. Trained in Winnipeg, Man., he turned professional at 21 and won several important tournaments around the world. In 1968, in Italy, he combined with Al BALDING to win the World Cup. Knudson is an exceptional stylist who has been called 'Canada's finest professional golfer'.

Koch, Eric (b.1919). Novelist and broadcasting executive. Born in Frankfurt/Main, Germany, he immigrated to Canada in 1935 and is a graduate of the University of Toronto. Since 1944 he has been associated with the CBC as a producer and an administrator. He was appointed director of English Services, Montreal, in 1971. His publications include the play *Success of a Mission* (1961), with Vincent Tovell, and three novels: *The French Kiss* (1969), *The Leisure Riots* (1973), and *The Last Thing You'll Want to Know* (1976).

Koenig, Wolf (b.1927). Film director. Born in Germany, he joined the NATIONAL FILM BOARD in 1948 and became a mainstay of UNIT B and CANDID EYE as its cinematographer, editor, scriptwriter, director, producer, animator, and administrator. Among his better-known films are *The Romance of Transportation* (1952), CITY OF GOLD (with Colin LOW, 1957), *The Days before Christmas* (1958), *Lonely Boy* (1961), and *The House that Jack Built* (1967)—all produced with other noted film workers.

Koerner Foundation, Leonard and Thea. It was established in Vancouver in 1955 to foster higher education, cultural activities, and public welfare in British Columbia. Leon Koerner is one of four brothers, born in Moravia, who made a fortune in lumber on the west coast.

Koffman, Moe (b.1928). Flutist, saxophonist, composer. Born in Toronto, where he studied at the Conservatory, he toured the United States with bands led by Sonny Dunham and Jimmy Dorsey but returned to Toronto, where he recorded 'Swingin' Shepherd Blues' (1957), which became an international hit. He has achieved great success with his brilliant record albums devoted to jazz improvisations on works by Bach and Vivaldi.

Komagata Maru incident. Episode involving racial discrimination. Permission was denied the *Komagata Maru*—a Japanese ship that carried 376 prospective immigrants, mainly Sikh veterans of the Indian Army from Hong Kong and Shanghai—to dock at Vancouver on 23 May 1914. A situation of racial tension already existed in British Columbia because federal restrictions prohibiting East Indian immigration had been successfully challenged by some Indian immigrants in 1913. Owing to widespread protest in B.C., new provincial barriers on Indian immigration were effected, and the previous federal regulations were reinstated in 1914. The *Komagata Maru* remained anchored in Vancouver harbour until a federal deportation order was upheld in the provincial Supreme Court. She returned to Hong Kong on 23 July.

Komatik. Eskimo word for an open sled pulled by dogs hitched in a fan position. It is common in the eastern, central, and Keewatin regions, where there are no trees.

Kootenay. A linguistic group of Indians occupying the southeast corner of British Columbia. Their language has distant affinities with ALGONKIAN. Formerly a prairie people, they were driven over the mountains by the BLACKFOOT. They engaged in the fur trade and later turned to farming and ranching. Their population in 1974 was 382.

Kootenay Highlander, The. See TURVEY.

Kootenay National Park. Established in 1922 on the western slopes of the ROCKY MOUNTAINS in southeastern British Columbia, it covers 543 sq. mi. and includes high glaciers and deep canyons, icy lakes and hot springs.

Korean War. A confrontation between North and South Korea involving world powers. It began on 25 June 1950 with the invasion of South Korea by North Korea. The Canadian Army Special Force, a volunteer brigade, fought as part of the United Nations Command under Gen. Douglas MacArthur and his successor, Lt-Gen. Matthew B. Ridgway. Canadians helped free Seoul and the Yap'yong Valley in Apr. 1951 and the Imjin R. in August. The Chinese assault near Hill 187 was repulsed with Canadian losses in May 1953. Canada sent 21,940 soldiers to serve in Korea, plus 7,000 following the cease-fire to the end of 1955. The armistice was signed at Panmunjom on 27 July 1953.

Koster, Wally. See CROSS-CANADA HIT PARADE.

Kotcheff, Ted (b.1931). Film director. Born in Toronto of Bulgarian parents, he joined CBC-TV in 1952 as a stagehand before graduating from the University of Toronto. Sydney NEWMAN elevated him when he was 24 and he became the Corporation's youngest television producer. He followed Newman to ABC-TV in London in 1957 and went on to direct dramas for BBC-TV. The peripatetic film-maker has directed such features as *Tiara Tahiti* (1963), *Life at the Top* (1965, to Mordecai RICHLER's screenplay), *Two Gentlemen Sharing* (1968), *Outback* (1970), *Edna: The Inebriate Woman* (1972), *Billy Two Hats* (1973, with Norman JEWISON as producer), *The* APPRENTICESHIP OF DUDDY KRAVITZ (1974, to Richler's screenplay), and *Dick and Jane* (1976).

Kouchibouguac National Park

Kouchibouguac National Park. Established in 1969 along the northern section of NORTH-UMBERLAND STRAIT, N.B., it covers 87 sq. mi. and includes a sweep of offshore sandbars, quiet lagoons, and bays ideal for protected swimming.

Kraul, Earl (b.1929). Dancer, choreographer, and ballet master. Born in London, Ont., he studied with Bernice Harper, Betty OLIPHANT, and Celia FRANCA in Canada and with Stanislas Idzikowski in London, Eng. He joined the NATIONAL BALLET OF CANADA for its first season in 1951, becoming soloist in 1954 and principal dancer in 1965. With Martine VAN HAMEL he won an award at the Varna International Ballet Competition in 1966. He now teaches at the NATIONAL BALLET SCHOOL.

Kraut Line. Nickname given to the powerful forward line of the Boston Bruins from 1939 to 1941. The Kraut Line was made up of three Canadian-born hockey players of German ancestry: Bobby Bauer, Woody Dumart, and Milt Schmidt.

Kreiner, Kathie (b.1958). Skier. Born in Timmins, Ont., and like her older sister Laurie a skier since her earliest years, she took the World Cup at Pfronten, West Germany, in 1974, when she won the giant slalom in a rainstorm. She was Canada's only Gold Medal winner at the 1976 Winter Olympics in Innsbruck, Austria, in the same event. Her sister Laurie (b.1955) is an outstanding skier too, having taken the Canadian championship at Whistler Mountain in 1969.

Kreisel, Henry (b.1922). Novelist. Born in Vienna, he came to Canada in 1941 and is a graduate of the University of Toronto and the University of London. Since 1947 he has been associated with the University of Alberta, as a professor of English and as vice-president. He has written two novels: *The Rich Man* (1948), about a Jewish immigrant's return to Vienna 33 years after his arrival in Canada; and *The Betrayal* (1964), about the need for revenge growing out of an incident in the Second World War.

Krieghoff, Corneluis (1815-72). Painter. Born in Amsterdam, he spent three years in the United States before coming to Canada and settling eventually in Montreal in 1849 and in Quebec in 1853. He is best known for his many genre paintings of *habitants* and Indians most of them produced for the tourist market. The finest of these, a masterpiece, is the popular MERRYMAKING (1860, Beaverbrook Art Gallery), one of his paintings of the Jolifou Inn. He also painted dramatic, technically accomplished landscapes, such as *Owl's*

Head, Lake Memphramagog (1859, NGC). Krieghoff left Canada in 1867 and died in Chicago, where his daughter lived.

Kroetsch, Robert (b.1927). Novelist. Born in Heisler, Alta, and educated at the University of Alberta and McGill, he teaches English at the State University of New York, Binghamton, N.Y. His novels—which effectively combine vigorous action, comedy, and lively characters—are *But We Are Exiles* (1965), *The Words of My Roaring* (1966), *The Studhorse Man* (1969), *Gone Indian* (1973), and *Badlands* (1975). He has also written a travel book, *Alberta* (1968), and two poetry collections: *The Stone Hammer Poems* (1975) and *The Ledger* (1975).

Kroiter, Roman (b.1926). Film director. Born in Yorkton, Sask., he joined the NATIONAL FILM BOARD in 1949. He worked in UNIT B and on the CANDID EYE series and was in charge of the LABYRINTH project for EXPO 67. He joined Graeme FERGUSON in founding Multi-Screen Corporation to develop the IMAX PROCESS. Among his better-known films are *Paul Tomkowicz, Street-Railway Switchman* (1954), *Glenn Gould: Off the Record* (1959), and UNIVERSE (with Colin LOW, 1960).

'Ksan Indian Village. Indian museum and craft village at Hazelton, B.C., on the Skeena R. Officially opened in 1970, it displays the architecture and arts of the northern Northwest Coast Indians of the pre- and post-European periods and includes the reproduction of an Indian village as it would have appeared a century ago. The work done by Indian craftsmen at the Carving House is influenced by traditional GITKSAN art, with its expressive masks and carved reliefs. 'Ksan is the Gitksan word for the Skeena R.

Kudlik. Eskimo word for a lamp. Crescent in form and made of soapstone, it burns seal or other oil on a moss wick for purposes of illumination and cooking.

Kuerti, Anton (b.1935). Pianist. Born in Vienna, he was named artist-in-residence of the University of Toronto when he first arrived in Canada in 1965. An artist of world repute, he performed the remarkable feat of giving two complete Beethoven sonata cycles in Ottawa and Toronto in 1974-5, playing them with distinction.

Kuletuk. Northern Quebec Eskimo word for a woman's fur parka. It is now manufactured commercially out of orlon, with a hood trimmed with fur. It is pronounced 'quleetok'.

Kurelek, William (b.1927). Painter. Born in

La Pierre

Whitford, Alta, he graduated from the University of Manitoba and briefly studied at the Instituto Allende, Mexico. In a style reminiscent of sophisticated folk art, he began painting narrative watercolour scenes drawn from his prairie childhood while he was a picture-framer working for the ISAACS GALLERY. After experiencing anew his Catholicism he entered a social-realism phase based on a dark vision of man's original sin. His appealing re-creations of everyday scenes from his past have been incorporated in the popular children's books, *A Prairie Boy's Winter* (1973), *Lumberjack* (1974), and *A Prairie Boy's Summer* (1975). He also wrote and illustrated *O Toronto* (1973), *Kurelek's Canada* (1975), *The Passion of Christ* (1975), and *Kurelek Country*

(1975). He has exhibited internationally and lives in Toronto.

Kutchin. The most northerly of the ATHAPASKAN-speaking Indians. They live in the Yukon and are closely related to the Loucheux of the Mackenzie delta and lower Peel R. Together the two groups had a population in 1970 of 2,334.

Kwakiutl. WAKASHAN-speaking Indians occupying the northeastern third of Vancouver Island and adjacent coastland. Their name is said to mean 'smoke of the world'. One of the most complex of the Pacific Coast tribes, they are known for their highly developed art-forms and secret societies. Their population in 1970 was 2,715.

L

L'Anse aux Meadows. A remote fishing village on Épaves Bay, near Cape Bauld, on the north-east tip of Newfoundland. On these grassy plains, in the summer of 1960, the Norwegian explorer Helge Ingstad (b.1899) came upon the remains of 'the first indisputable Norse settlement so far found in North America'. Eight house-sites (including a smithy), four boatsheds, and other evidence of pre-Columbian Norse occupation were uncovered by seven archaeological expeditions between 1961 and 1968. Carbon-14 tests have dated the findings about A.D. 1000, which corresponds to dates suggested by the *Greenlander's Saga* and other epic poems. In *Westward to Vinland* (1969), translated from the Norwegian by Erik J. Frilis, Ingstad identified L'Anse aux Meadows with VINLAND and surmised that the Norse colony was founded here by the Greenlander LEIF ERICSSON (called The Lucky), son of Erik the Red, about A.D. 1000. He further identified HELLULAND with Cape Dyer, Baffin Island, and MARKLAND with Cape Porcupine, Labrador. Newfoundlanders today pronounce the name of the site 'Lancy Meadows'. The name is part French and part English for 'bay of meadows'.

L Cpl. Official abbreviation of Lance Corporal.

L for Lanky. A CBC Radio series devoted to the war effort. Written by Don Bassett and

produced by Alan Savage, it dramatized actual RCAF incidents through the bombing crew of an RCAF Lancaster during the Second World War. The 30-minute programs were heard on Sunday evenings from 1942 to 1944. A program note stated that 'Neil LeRoy is the voice of the aircraft'.

L Sgt. Official abbreviation of Lance Sergeant.

La Hontan, Baron de (1666-1715). French soldier and author. Stationed in New France from 1683 to 1691, he published a three-volume work on his travels, in English and French—*New Voyages to North America . . .* (1703)—that mixes vivid real-life descriptions with fabrications. See also ADARIO.

La Lande, Jean de. See JESUIT MARTYRS.

La Mauricie National Park. Established in 1970 in the Grand'Mère and Shawinigan areas of the LAURENTIAN MOUNTAINS, midway between Montreal and Quebec City, it covers 200 sq. mi. It is traversed by the St Maurice R. and includes a forest and many lakes.

La Pierre, Laurier (b.1929). History professor and television personality. Born at Lac Mégantic, Que., he graduated from the University of Toronto with a doctorate in history in 1962. He joined the department of history at McGill University in 1965, where he heads the French-Canadian Studies Program. La

La Pierre

Pierre rose to national prominence as the emotional pipe-smoking co-host of CBC-TV's THIS HOUR HAS SEVEN DAYS in 1965. He is frequently seen on national television, where his special role is 'interpreting' the mood of Quebec for non-Quebeckers. His own 60-minute weekly variety-and-talk show, 'Midnight', was launched by CBC-TV in Montreal in Oct. 1974. He is the author of two collections of talks, *The Apprenticeship* (1967) and *Genesis of a Nation* (1967), and the co-editor of *Essays on the Left* (1971).

La Potherie, Claude-Charles Le Roy de (1663-1736). Historian. Usually referred to as Bacqueville de La Potherie, he was born in Paris and became a writer. Appointed to the Marine, he was a member of IBERVILLE's expedition to Hudson Bay in 1697. He arrived in Quebec in May 1698—in time to attend the funeral of FRONTENAC—as comptroller of the fortifications. He left New France in 1701, spending the rest of his life in Guadeloupe. He is remembered for his *Histoire de l'Amérique septentrionale* (4 vols, 1722), which provides well-observed descriptions of New France at the turn of the century, including eye-witness accounts of the Iberville expedition; of the government of Quebec, Trois-Rivières, and Montreal; and of peace parleys with the Iroquois. It is not, however, a history of North America as the title says.

La Roque, Marguerite de. Early heroine. A relative of Jean-François de la Roque de ROBERVAL, she accompanied him on his voyage of 1542-3. When he learned that her lover was aboard, she was left on the Île des Démons in the Gulf of St Lawrence. Joined by her lover, she gave birth to a child, who died, as did the lover. She managed to survive until she was picked up by fishermen two years later.

La Salle, René-Robert Cavelier de (1643-87). Explorer, discoverer of the mouth of the Mississippi. Born in Rouen, France, he came to Montreal in 1667 and was given a seigneury on Montreal Island, which he later sold; it was called LACHINE in mockery of his dream of discovering a route to China. He obtained the grant of Fort Cataracoui (Kingston), which he renamed Fort Frontenac. In 1679 he launched the GRIFFON on the Niagara R. and sailed her to Michilimackinac. In 1682 he set out for the Mississippi R., which he descended to its mouth, formed by three channels. He took possession of the region for France and named it Louisiana. Sailing from France in 1684 to found a colony there, he landed on the coast of Texas. Two and a half years later he was murdered by some of his men. See also Henri (de) TONTY.

La Tour, Charles de Saint-Étienne de (1593-1666). Trader, governor of ACADIA. He sailed for Acadia in 1610 with his father Claude (see entry) as part of an expedition to re-establish the settlement of PORT ROYAL under POUTRINCOURT and his son Biencourt, who was made administrator of the colony in 1611. When Port Royal was destroyed by Samuel Argall in 1613, Biencourt and Charles stayed in Acadia to engage in the fur trade. Biencourt died in 1623 and Charles, his heir, became responsible for the colony. He built a fort (Lomeron) at Cap de Sable, which after the capture of Quebec by the English in 1629 was the only French stronghold in New France. When France recovered Acadia and Canada in 1632 a commission as governor of Acadia was given to Isaac de Razilly, who died in 1635, the year Charles moved his headquarters to Fort Sainte-Marie (Fort La Tour) on the north bank of the mouth of the Saint John R. The next 10 years in Acadia were marked by the conflict, sometimes armed, between the ambitious Charles de Menou d'Aulnay, lieutenant to Razilly's successor, and the equally ambitious La Tour, both of whom had been given different areas of authority in Acadia. During one attack by d'Aulnay on Fort Sainte-Marie, it was defended by Françoise-Marie LA TOUR in her husband's absence; not long after she was forced to capitulate, she died. D'Aulnay died in 1650 and in 1653 La Tour combined the interests of the two factions by marrying his widow. Taken prisoner by the English in 1654, he received recognition as a Baronet of Nova Scotia, a title he inherited from his father. He retired to Cap de Sable, where he died.

La Tour, Claude de Saint-Étienne de (*c.*1570-after 1636). Fur trader and colonist. He arrived in Acadia in 1610 with POUTRINCOURT to found a settlement at PORT ROYAL. After it was destroyed by Samuel Argall in 1613, he built Fort Pentagouet (Maine), a fur-trading post and fishing station. On a voyage back from France in 1628 his vessel was captured by the English and he was taken to England, where he met Sir William Alexander, who had been granted ACADIA—called Nova Scotia in England—by James I. In 1629 La Tour explored Acadia with Alexander's son and oversaw the building of Charles Fort, near Port Royal. Back in England, he was made a 'Baronet of Nova Scotia', in recognition of his assistance, which brought him a large grant of land. With some colonists and soldiers and two warships he sailed for Acadia in 1630, visiting his son Charles (see entry), whose fort at Cap de Sable (Fort Lomeron) was the only French stronghold in New

France at the time. Claude tried to persuade his son to hand over his lands to the English king, but Charles refused and his father attacked the fort in a battle that lasted for two days and a night. Unsuccessful, Claude moved on to Port Royal, but in 1631 he returned to his son at Cap de Sable, where he died.

La Tour, Françoise-Marie Jacquelin (1602-45). Heroine of ACADIA. She sailed to PORT ROYAL in 1640 to marry Charles de LA TOUR and lived at Fort Sainte-Marie (Fort La Tour), on the north bank of the mouth of the Saint John R. In 1645, during her husband's absence, the fort was attacked by Charles de Menou d'Aulnay. Madame La Tour, in command of 45 men, defended it courageously until she was forced to capitulate on the fourth day. The captured soldiers (except for one who acted as executioner) were hanged in the presence of Madame La Tour, who, it is said, had to witness the executions with a noose around her neck. She died three weeks later.

La Vérendrye, Pierre Gaultier de Varennes, sieur de (1685-1749). Fur trader and explorer. Born in Trois-Rivières, he served in the colonial troops from 1696 until 1712. He then engaged in the fur-trade and in 1728 was put in command of the post at Kaministiquia (Thunder Bay, Ont.). He became driven by the ambition to discover the 'western sea', which he conceived to be beyond Lake Winnipeg further to the west than the French had yet gone. On four voyages to the west, between 1731 and 1743, with the assistance of his four sons, he established a string of eight posts—the first two at Rainy Lake and Lake of the Woods. From Fort La Reine (Portage La Prairie), he sent his son Louis-Joseph on a westward journey that took him to the Big Horn mountains of Wyoming (1742-3). The La Vérendryes penetrated further west than any previous explorers and directed the traffic of furs from the Saskatchewan and Assiniboine areas to the St Lawrence.

Labatt Awards. Two awards made annually by the CANADIAN FOOTBALL LEAGUE at the GREY CUP Dinner to the outstanding offensive and defensive players of the GREY CUP GAME. Each winner receives a $1,000 Canada Savings Bond and an Eskimo carving from LABATT'S Ltd.

Labatt's. Major Canadian brewery. It was founded in 1847 when John Labatt (1803-66) purchased the Simcoe St Brewery in London, Ont. It was renamed after Labatt in 1853. His sons continued to expand the family business by acquiring further breweries.

In 1975 Labatt Breweries of Canada supplied 36.2% of the Canadian beer market. Among its holdings are LAURA SECORD CANDIES, CHATEAU GAI WINERY, and Chateau Cartier Wines. Labatt's 'Blue' is the best-selling lager beer in Canada. Labatt's Pioneer Brewery in London is a reconstruction of the original plant.

Labelling. See CANADA GRADING.

Laberge, Albert (1871-1960). Quebec novelist. Born in Beauharnois, Que., he studied at the Collège Sainte-Marie in Montreal and worked as a sportswriter and art critic for *La Presse*. All his works—seven volumes of stories, two collections of sketches, three books of memoirs and criticism, and one novel—were privately printed. Laberge was called variously 'the father of pornography in Canada' and 'the author of the first naturalistic novel written by a Canadian' for his realistic novel *La Scouine* (1918), about the misery and degradation of the Beauharnois peasants, cheated by their social betters. It was translated by Conrad Dion as *Bitter Bread* in 1976. Gérard BESSETTE edited the *Anthologie d'Albert Laberge* (1963).

LaBine, Gilbert A. See ELDORADO NUCLEAR LIMITED.

Labour, Department of. Government department concerned with labour legislation. Established in 1900, it administers legislation dealing with working conditions for government employees; promotes joint consultation with industries; and publishes the monthly *Labour Gazette*. The CANADA LABOUR RELATIONS BOARD reports to Parliament through the Minister of Labour.

Labour Day. Statutory holiday observed throughout Canada to honour organized labour. The official date is 1 Sept., but it is observed on the first Monday in September— the last long weekend of summer. The contribution of organized labour to Canadian society has been recognized since 1872 when parades and rallies were held in Ottawa and Toronto. In 1889 the Second Socialist International proclaimed 1 May to be Labour Day, thereby merging the traditional May Day festivities with Labour celebrations. This spring date was briefly observed in Canada, as it continues to be throughout continental Europe. But the North American need for a long weekend at the end of summer brought about the fall observance by parliamentary act in 1894. Canadians preceded Americans in honouring organized labour, for the earliest American parades were not held until 1882.

Labour-Progressive Party. The name of the COMMUNIST PARTY OF CANADA from 1943 to 1959.

Labrador. Comprising the easternmost part of the Canadian mainland, it now refers to those lands drained by rivers flowing into the Atlantic Ocean. In 1763 Labrador was united with NEWFOUNDLAND; it was annexed to Quebec from 1774 until 1809, when it was again placed under the jurisdiction of Newfoundland because its fisheries had been neglected. In 1825 a compromise was reached: the area north of the Strait of Belle Isle was administered by Newfoundland and the north shore of the Gulf of the St Lawrence came under Quebec. A dispute between Quebec and Newfoundland over the western boundary was settled in 1927 by a Privy Council decision, establishing its present boundaries, although Quebec has not entirely accepted them. While many of the native Indians and Eskimos are still occupied in fishing and trapping, the region entered a new era in the 1950s with the development of the large iron-ore reserves of the LABRADOR TROUGH and later the largest hydro-electric plant in Canada at CHURCHILL FALLS. Of the 1971 population of 28,166 about 3,000 are Indians and Eskimos and the remainder are largely involved in resource activities. The rugged character of the CANADIAN SHIELD and the harsh climate of the region indicate that any substantial increase in the population will depend upon the discovery or development of new mineral resources.

Labrador. An icebreaker that entered service in 1954. The largest ship hitherto built in Canada for the ROYAL CANADIAN NAVY, she immediately made history, not only as the first naval vessel to navigate the NORTHWEST PASSAGE, but as the first to circumnavigate the continent. On her second voyage she carried personnel and equipment for the DEW Line. She was transferred to the Department of Transport in 1957.

Labrador current. A cold current flowing south from the Arctic Ocean through Davis Strait into the northwest Atlantic Ocean. The primary delivery system of icefloats and Greenland icebergs into the Atlantic, it may carry these as far south along the Canadian coast as the Bay of Fundy.

Labrador Eskimos. One of five groups of ESKIMOS. They inhabit the coasts of Labrador, Hudson Strait, and southeastern BAFFIN ISLAND.

Labrador Retriever. A breed of sporting dog that originated in Labrador. Compact but powerful, courageous and intelligent, and having either short, black, or long yellow hair, it was introduced to England in the mid-nineteenth century. Once used by Newfoundland fishermen to retrieve wildfowl and catch fish likely to be lost off the hook, it is effective as a gun dog, a guide dog, and in drug detection.

Labrador tea. A drink brewed from evergreen shrubs that grow in Labrador. It was also called Hudson Bay tea and swamp tea by the early settlers who made it.

Labrador Trough. An ancient basin of sedimentary rock extending in a north-south direction through Labrador and northern Quebec. It is the source of very large deposits of iron such as those at Schefferville, Que.

Labrecque, Jean-Claude (b.1938). Quebec cinematographer. Born in Quebec City, he worked on Claude JUTRA'S À TOUT PRENDRE (1963), Gilles GROULX's Le CHAT DANS LE SAC (1964), Gilles CARLE's La VIE HEUREUSE DE LÉOPOLD Z (1965), and many other important Quebec feature films. He both photographed and directed 60 Cycles (1964) and Essai à la mille (1970). Feature films he directed include La Nuit de la poèsie (1970), Les Smattes (1972), and Les Vautours (1974).

Labrusca. A coarse-tasting grape native to North America. Also called the 'fox grape', it was once the only grape used in Canadian wine. The mellower Vinus vinifera from Europe is now grafted to it, producing a subtler wine.

Labyrinth. The pavilion of the NATIONAL FILM BOARD at EXPO 67 that offered 'a remarkable audio-visual entertainment tailored to an architectural surround, a real use of film as environment'. Spectators in four balconies saw a short film projected on two 38' × 20' screens, and another film shown on five screens. The theme was 'the essential story of man'. The $4.5-million project was conceived by Roman KROITER, Colin LOW, and Hugh O'Connor. Tom DALY served as supervisor and Harry Vandelman as architect.

LAC. Official abbreviation of Leading Aircraftman.

Lachine. A city on the south shore of the island of Montreal, part of Metropolitan Montreal. As a seigneury called Saint-Sulpice it was given to LA SALLE by the Sulpician Order in 1667; it became known as La Chine in mockery of La Salle's dream of discovering the route to China. In 1669 La Salle sold it back to the Sulpicians. Settlement began in 1675 and it was the scene of a famous Iroquois attack in 1689. In the era of the northwestern fur trade, Lachine became the departure point for the annual fur brigades. To bypass the rapids below Montreal the Lachine Canal was built from Montreal harbour to Lachine between 1821 and 1824, and later enlarged. It was incorporated as a city in 1909. Its motto is *Union et Progrès* ('Union and Progress').

Lachine Rapids. Heavy rapids on the St Lawrence off the south shore of Montreal Island. During early settlement days they marked the farthest point of unassisted navigation, and were primarily responsible for the location of the city of Montreal at its present site; they gave rise to the building of the Lachine Canal (1821-4). They are now bypassed by the ST LAWRENCE SEAWAY.

Lacombe, Albert (1827-1916). Famous missionary in the West. Born in Lower Canada (Quebec), he was ordained a priest in 1849 and joined the Oblate Order in 1854. In the Northwest he organized a MÉTIS community at Saint-Albert, northwest of Fort Edmonton, and ministered to the mutually antagonistic CREE and BLACKFOOT Indians. He assisted the foundation of French-speaking settlements in Manitoba and was chaplain of the CPR construction camps from 1880 to 1882. He translated the New Testament into Cree and compiled a Cree dictionary and grammar.

Lacrosse. A field game played by two teams; traditionally Canada's national game. The name comes from *la crosse*, the word the French used to describe the hooked and racquetted stick employed by the Indians of eastern Canada to play BAGGATAWAY, which evolved into lacrosse during the nineteenth century. The game was promoted by Dr George BEERS in 1867. The Canadian Lacrosse Association, founded in Winnipeg in 1925, annually awards the MANN CUP to the senior championship team and the MINTO CUP to the junior championship team. See also Patrick Joseph LALLY.

Ladoo, Harold Sonny (1945-73). Novelist. Born in Trinidad, he wrote *No Pain Like This Body* (1972) and *Yesterdays* (1974) while living in Toronto. He died under mysterious circumstances on a visit to Trinidad.

Lady Byng Memorial Trophy. It is presented annually by the NATIONAL HOCKEY LEAGUE 'to the player adjudged to have exhibited the best type of sportsmanship and gentlemanly conduct combined with a high standard of playing ability'. The winner is selected by the Professional Hockey Writers' Association.

The cup was presented by Marie Evelyn, Lady Byng, wife of Governor General Lord BYNG, in 1925. After Frank Boucher of the New York Rangers won the Lady Byng Trophy seven times in eight seasons, he was given it to keep, and Lady Byng donated another in 1936. With her death in 1949, the word 'Memorial' was added to its title. In addition to the cup, the winner receives $1,500; the runner-up $750.

'Lady of the Snows, Our'. See OUR LADY OF THE SNOWS.

Lady's slipper. A white-and-pink wild orchid found from Ontario to the Maritimes; the floral emblem of Prince Edward Island. Its species name was incorrectly identified in government legislation of 1947; two additional bills, in 1952 and 1965, were needed to establish the correct name (*Cypripedium acaule*) for the provincial symbol.

Lafontaine, Sir Louis-Hippolyte (1807-64). Politician. Born in Lower Canada (Quebec), he trained as a lawyer and was elected to the legislative assembly in 1830. At the union of 1841 he was the leader of the French-Canadian members of the assembly of the Province of Canada. He shared a ministry with Robert BALDWIN in 1842-3 (the Lafontaine-Baldwin ministry). The Baldwin-Lafontaine ministry of 1848-51—sometimes called the Great Ministry—achieved RESPONSIBLE GOVERNMENT. Lafontaine resigned in 1851, was appointed chief justice of Canada East (Quebec) in 1853, and was made a baronet in 1854.

Laidlaw Foundation. It was established in Toronto in 1949 by W.C. and R.A. Laidlaw of the Laidlaw Lumber Company for the improvement of services, programs, and policies affecting health and welfare in Canada.

Laing Galleries. Commercial art gallery in Toronto. Founded in 1931, it exhibited Canadian artists before the Second World War and has since shown modern European painting and sculpture and early Canadian painting, in addition to its continued promotion of contemporary Canadian artists.

Lake Agassiz. During the PLEISTOCENE EPOCH, a shallow glacial lake left in the wake of the retreating icebergs that blocked the normal drainage outlet of the southern Prairies (the Nelson R.). It covered 110,000 sq. mi. and occupied parts of Saskatchewan, Manitoba, and Ontario in Canada, and Minnesota and North Dakota in the United States. Its successors include Lake Winnipeg and Lake of the Woods.

Lake Algonquin

Lake Algonquin. A glacial lake, now extinct, that formerly united Lakes Superior, Michigan, Huron, and Nipigon. It existed between 10,900 and 12,500 years ago.

Lake Athabasca. A medium-large lake on the border of Alberta and Saskatchewan in the sub-Arctic. Part of the Mackenzie River System, it forms the link between the Peace and Athabasca Rivers from the south, with the Slave R. continuing the drainage towards the Arctic Ocean.

Lake Champlain, Battle of. See Battle of PLATTSBURG.

Lake Diefenbaker. It is located south of Saskatoon, Sask., and was formed in the late 1960s by the damming of the South Saskatchewan R. by the Gardiner Dam. Named after John DIEFENBAKER, it stabilizes the flow of the river, stores water for power generation, and provides water for irrigation.

Lake Erie. The most southerly of the GREAT LAKES bordering on Canada, between Lakes Huron and Ontario. Slightly under half of its surface area of 9,884 sq. mi. is claimed by Canada.

Lake Erie, Battle of. An engagement in the WAR OF 1812. The Americans gained control of Lake Erie when nine vessels under Capt. Oliver Perry defeated six under Capt. Robert Barclay near Put-in-Bay on 10 Sept. 1813.

Lake Huron. The second-largest of the GREAT LAKES (exceeded only by Lake Superior), its surface area is 23,870 sq. mi. The portion lying within Canada, comprising with Georgian Bay over 65% of the lake's entirety, is one-and-a-half times the surface area of Lake Superior that lies within Canada, making it Canada's largest lake.

Lake Indians. See OKANAGAN.

Lake Michigan. See GREAT LAKES.

Lake of the Woods. A large lake on the borders of Ontario, Manitoba, and the state of Minnesota.

Lake Ontario. The most easterly of the GREAT LAKES. It is 7,313 sq. mi. in surface area. Just over half of the lake lies within Canada.

Lake St Clair. Part of the St Lawrence system that, with the Detroit R. and the St Clair R., separates southwestern Ontario from the United States.

Lake Superior. The most westerly of the GREAT LAKES and the largest in total area. Over two-thirds of its surface area of 32,483 sq. mi. lies in the United States.

Lake Winnipeg. The largest lake lying entirely within Canada south of the sub-Arctic. It is 9,416 sq. mi. in surface area and stretches across a third of the latitude of Manitoba from near the province's centre to just north of Winnipeg in the south.

Lakehead, The. A reference to the head of navigation at THUNDER BAY on the northwest shore of Lake Superior.

Lakehead University. Located in Thunder Bay, Ont., it was founded in 1965 after evolving from the Lakehead Technical Institute, established in 1946, and the Lakehead College of Arts, Science and Technology, founded in 1957. It has 6,000 students, half of whom are full-time, and offers both undergraduate and graduate degree programs and several diploma programs with specific professional orientations. Its Black Sturgeon Research Centre—located about 100 mi. away from the main campus on Black Sturgeon Lake—is used for interdisciplinary research in the natural sciences.

Lakes of the Shield. A loose collective term for the lakes on or at the edges of the CANADIAN SHIELD, including GREAT BEAR, GREAT SLAVE, ATHABASCA, Reindeer, WINNIPEG, and Nipigon, as well as tens of thousands of smaller lakes that dot the tundra and northern areas of Manitoba, Ontario, and Quebec. They hold nearly a quarter of all fresh water on the planet; with the addition of the GREAT LAKES themselves (which hold nearly 20% of all fresh water) and non-Shield lakes, Canada likely contains within its borders over half the world's fresh water.

Lalemant, Charles (1587-1674). First superior of the Jesuit missions in Quebec. The brother of Jérôme LALEMANT and uncle of Gabriel LALEMANT, he arrived in 1625 with Jean de BRÉBEUF and served until 1638.

Lalemant, Gabriel (1610-49). Missionary, one of the JESUIT MARTYRS. The nephew of Charles LALEMANT and Jérôme LALEMANT, he arrived at Quebec in 1646. He was sent to the HURON MISSIONS and was tortured and killed during an Iroquois raid. He was canonized in 1930.

Lalemant, Jérôme (1593-1673). Jesuit missionary. The brother of Charles LALEMANT and the uncle of Gabriel LALEMANT, he arrived at Quebec in 1638. He was superior of the HURON MISSIONS, where he built SAINTE-MARIE-AUX-HURONS, until 1645 and then was superior of the Jesuits at Quebec from 1645 to 1650 and from 1659 to 1665.

Laliberté, Alfred (1875-1953). Sculptor. Born in Quebec, he studied at L'École des Beaux-

Arts, Paris. He produced many commemorative monuments to historical and religious subjects, including the statue of DOLLARD DES ORMEAUX in Lafontaine Park, Montreal, and the monument to St Joseph at the entrance to ST JOSEPH'S ORATORY in Montreal.

Lally, Patrick Joseph (1868-1956). Lacrosse enthusiast and equipment manufacturer. The Cornwall-born athlete and businessman was prominent in lacrosse as player, referee, and executive. With his older brother Frank, he founded the company that supplied lacrosse sticks that were used throughout the world. (These handmade hickory sticks were made by Iroquois Indians at the St Regis Reserve on the Quebec-New York border.) Lally was prominent in reviving the Canadian Lacrosse Association in 1945 and was elected to the Lacrosse HALL OF FAME in 1965.

Lalonde, Edouard (Newsy) (1888-1960). Famed lacrosse and hockey star. Born in Cornwall, Ont., he played lacrosse so well that he was voted 'the outstanding lacrosse player of the half-century'. As a hockey player he scored 38 goals in 11 games during one season alone. He was always an aggressive player, probably the roughest in his day. He was elected to both the Lacrosse and Hockey HALLS OF FAME. His nickname 'Newsy' derives from his early employment as a reporter and typesetter for the weekly *Cornwall Freeholder*.

Lalonde, Michèle (b.1937). Quebec poet. Born in Montreal and educated at the Université de Montréal, she published two much-admired collections of lyric poetry in the 1950s but has chosen to reach her public through recitations and readings. She recited her long poem *Terre des hommes* (1967) at the opening of EXPO 67 to music by André Prevost performed by a choir and orchestra. Her much-discussed poem 'SPEAK WHITE' asserts the need for a French culture in North America.

LaMarsh, Judy (b.1924). Former Secretary of State and popular radio broadcaster. Born in Chatham, Ont., she was a draughtswoman and Japanese linguist during the Second World War. She graduated from OSGOODE HALL Law School and practised criminal law in Niagara Falls, which district she represented as a Liberal MP from 1960 to 1968. She was Minister of Health and Welfare from 1963 to 1965, and Secretary of State from 1965 to 1968, thus presiding over the CENTENNIAL YEAR. A popular personality, she wrote her political memoirs, *Memoirs of a Bird in a Gilded Cage* (1968), and hosted 'The Judy Show', following THIS COUNTRY IN THE MORN-

ING, from 1975 to Mar. 1976. In 1975 she was appointed chairwoman of the Ontario Royal Commission of Inquiry into Violence on Television and in the Movies.

Lamb, W. Kaye (b.1904). Archivist. Born in New Westminster, B.C., and educated at the University of British Columbia, the Sorbonne, and the University of London, he served as Librarian and Archivist of British Columbia from 1934 to 1940, then taught at the University of British Columbia from 1940 to 1948, when he was appointed DOMINION ARCHIVIST in the PUBLIC ARCHIVES OF CANADA (1948-69). He was also National Librarian, the first, from 1953 to 1968, when he retired. He edited *The Letters and Journals of Simon Fraser 1806-1808* (1960) and *The Journals and Letter of Sir Alexander Mackenzie* (1970).

Lament for a Nation. An influential book by George P. GRANT. Subtitled *The Defeat of Canadian Nationalism*, it is a personal and philosophical 'lament' for the loss of humanistic values of the past in the face of progress, continentalism, and technology, mostly American. It was published in 1965 and reissued with a new introduction in 1970.

Lampman, Archibald (1861-99). Poet. Born in Morpeth, C.W. (Ont.), and raised in the Rice Lake district, he graduated from Trinity College, University of Toronto, and from 1883 until his death worked as a postal clerk in Ottawa. The two collections of his poetry that appeared in his lifetime—*Among the Millet* (1888) and *Lyrics of Earth* (1893)—contain the finest Canadian nature poems from the post-Confederation period. 'HEAT', 'Solitude', and 'The CITY OF THE END OF THINGS' are among his best-known poems. His friend Duncan Campbell SCOTT prepared editions of his *Poems* (1900) and *Lyrics of Earth* (1925) and, in collaboration with E.K. BROWN, published an unfinished narrative poem on the stand of Adam DOLLARD DES ORMEAUX against the Iroquois in 1660: *At the Long Sault and Other New Poems* (1943). David Bairstow produced and directed for the NFB in 1961 a beautiful film called MORNING ON THE LIÈVRE (13 min., colour) inspired by Lampman's poem about a September canoe trip down the Lièvre R. in Quebec. See also AT THE MERMAID INN.

Lamy, André (b.1932). Film commissioner. Born in Montreal, he attended both the Université de Montréal and McGill University and, from 1957 to 1962, was a salesman of pharmaceutical products. He joined his brother Pierre Lamy in the organization of Onyx Films in 1964. In 1970 he was appointed assistant film commissioner of the

NATIONAL FILM BOARD under Sydney NEWMAN, whom he succeeded on 21 Aug. 1975.

Lancaster. A famous Second World War bomber. A four-engine plane, the largest flown by the RAF, it was built by Victory Aircraft (later A.V. ROE CANADA LTD) at Malton, near Toronto. The first Canadian-built Lancaster was flown across the Atlantic in 1943. After the war some were converted to 10-passenger airlines and sold to commercial airlines, where they were known as 'Lancastrians'.

'Land God gave to Cain, The'. Jacques CARTIER's memorable description of the desolate shore of Labrador in the Gulf of St Lawrence. It appears in Cartier's account of his first voyage to Canada in the summer of 1534 and is the earliest known image ever applied to Canada.

Land of the Little Sticks, The. Transitional country between the forests and the BARREN LANDS of northern Canada, a sub-Arctic zone of stunted spruce and dwarf willow.

Land of the Midnight Sun. A poetical description of the FAR NORTH where, in the summer, the days are long and the nights are short. 'It's bright enough to read a newspaper outdoors at midnight,' is a frequent saying. The image is also identified with the YUKON because of Robert W. SERVICE's 'The CREMATION OF SAM McGEE', published in 1907, the refrain of which begins: 'There are strange things done in the midnight sun/By the men who moil for gold. . . .'

Land of the North Wind. See KEEWATIN.

Landed immigrant status. Legal status of those admitted to the country for permanent residence but not yet citizens, as defined by the Immigration Act of 1962. A 'landed immigrant' must reside in the country for a period of five years before applying for CITIZENSHIP. See also VISITOR STATUS.

Lane, Henry Bower (1787-d.?). Architect. Born in London, Eng., he trained there at the Royal Academy Schools and in the office of William Inwood. He practised in Toronto from 1840 to 1847, when he returned to England. His work in Toronto includes Little Trinity Church (1843), St George the Martyr (1844—only the tower survives), and Holy Trinity Church, Trinity Square (1846) in 'a flexible, romantic, late-mediaeval idiom' of the Gothic revival. He also designed additions to OSGOODE HALL (1844) and Toronto's first City Hall (1844) in an equally charming Late Georgian classicism.

Lane, Pat (b.1939). Poet. Born in Nelson, B.C., he was a founding editor of Very Stone Press in Vancouver. His poems about the West, expressing a sensibility that is both tough and delicate, have appeared in numerous collections, including *Letters from the Savage Mind* (1966), *Mountain Oysters* (1971), *Beware the Months of Fire* (1974), and *Unborn Things* (1976). He lives in Vernon.

Langevin, André (b.1927). Quebec novelist and dramatist. Born in Montreal, where he is a producer for Radio-Canada, he is an important writer of quasi-existential novels about life in Quebec today. The best of them appeared in English as *Dust over the City* (1955), translated by John Latrobe and Robert Gottlieb. He has also written stage plays and television dramas.

Langevin, Sir Hector-Louis (1826-1906). A FATHER OF CONFEDERATION. Born in Quebec City, he trained as a lawyer and was elected to the legislative assembly in 1856. He was a member of the GREAT COALITION ministry and attended all three conferences that preceded Confederation. In 1867 he was made Secretary of State and became the successor, as leader of the Quebec Conservatives, of George-Étienne CARTIER (in whose office he had studied law). He headed various ministries until he resigned in 1891 because of charges of corruption against his department in the granting of railway contracts; he was exonerated but found guilty of negligence.

Langevin Block. Building on Wellington St, Ottawa, erected in the 1880s when the Civil Service had grown too large for the PARLIAMENT BUILDINGS. It was designed by Thomas FULLER and named after Sir Hector-Louis LANGEVIN. The executive offices, including the prime minister's office, were moved from the East Block to the Langevin Block in July 1976.

Langford, Samuel (1880-1956). Black boxer known as the 'Boston Tar Baby'. Born in Weymouth, N.S., he ran away to Boston at the age of 12. A strong boxer, he fought through all weight divisions up to heavyweight against bulkier opponents. During his 21-year career, he won 138 bouts but lost his sight and retired in Boston, virtually penniless.

Langham, Michael (b.1919). British director. Born in Bridgewater, Eng., he was director of the Birmingham Repertory from 1948 to 1950 before succeeding Tyrone GUTHRIE as artistic director of the STRATFORD FESTIVAL in 1955, the year he directed his first play for the Festival, *Julius Caesar*. He left Stratford in 1967 and was appointed artistic director of the LaJolla Repertory Theatre of California in 1968.

Langley, Henry (1836-1906). Architect. Educated at the Toronto Academy (Knox College) and in the office of William Hay, he was Ontario's most prolific church architect in the nineteenth century, designing 70 churches and altering many more in 44 years of practice for many denominations. The style of his buildings in Toronto was strongly influenced by the work of George Gilbert Scott, Hay's teacher, and includes St Peter's, Carlton St (1865); the spire of St Michael's Cathedral (1866); the spire of St James' Cathedral (1874); Metropolitan Methodist Church, 'the cathedral of Methodism' (1875); and Jarvis Street Baptist Church (1876). Among his secular works are the Second-Empire-styled Eighth Post Office on Adelaide St (1872, demolished) and the head office of the Bank of British North America at 49 Yonge St (1874).

Languirand, Jacques (b.1930). Quebec playwright. Born in Montreal, he has been associated with the THÉÂTRE DU NOUVEAU MONDE and Radio-Canada and, as a teacher, with McGill University and the NATIONAL THEATRE SCHOOL. His plays, written in the 1950s and 1960s, established him as a major Québécois playwright. They include *Les Grands Départs* (1958), *Les Insolites* (1962), *Le Gibet* (1960), and *Les Violons d'automne* (1962). *Klondyke* (1971) is a historical musical comedy, with music by Gabriel CHARPENTIER. Languirand abandoned the theatre in 1967. He teaches at the National Theatre School.

Lansdowne, Fenwick (b.1937). Naturalist, painter. Born in Hong Kong of British parents, he came to Victoria, B.C., at the age of three. Stricken by polio as a child, he is entirely self-taught. His watercolour paintings of North American and English birds are recognized internationally for combining ornithological and botanical accuracy with strong aesthetic appeal. His first exhibition was sponsored by the Audubon Society at the Royal Ontario Museum when he was 19. The Canadian government sponsored exhibitions of his paintings at the Smithsonian Institute in Washington, D.C., in 1963 and 1969. His work is published in *Birds of the Northern Forest* (1966) and *Birds of the Eastern Forest* (Vol.1, 1968; Vol.2, 1970).

Lansdowne, Lord (1845-1927). GOVERNOR GENERAL of Canada from 1883 to 1888.

LaPalme, Robert (b.1908). Cartoonist. Born in Montreal, and self-taught, he has drawn editorial cartoons for *L'Action Catholique, Le Devoir* from 1950 to 1959, and *La Presse* since

1959. The winner of numerous awards, he has appeared on television, organized the International Pavilion of Humour at MAN AND HIS WORLD, and is Director of its International Salon of Cartoons.

Lapointe, Paul-Marie (b.1929). Quebec poet. Born in Saint-Félicien in the Lac Saint-Jean region of Quebec, he studied at St Laurent College and l'École des Beaux-Arts in Montreal, then worked in journalism with *L'Evénement-Journal, La Presse,* and *Le Nouveau Journal*. He became editor of *Le Magazine Maclean* in 1964 and in 1969 joined Radio-Canada, where he is director of the French-language news service. *Le Réel absolu* (1970) is a collection of lyric poems written between 1948 and 1965. This was followed by *Tableaux de l'amoureuse* (1975) and *Bouche rouge* (1976). D.G. JONES translated a selection of his poems called *The Terror of the Snows* (1976).

Laporte, Pierre. See OCTOBER CRISIS.

Largactil. Trade name of chlorpromazine, a major tranquillizer, used primarily to reduce symptoms of severe psychosis. Its full practical significance was revealed in a scientific paper published in Feb. 1954 by Dr Heinz E. Lehmann (b.1911), a German-born medical scientist associated with McGill University and Douglas Hospital. Lehmann's discovery has been called 'a major contribution to American psychiatry'.

Larrigan. A type of moccasin made of cowhide with laced uppers reaching almost to the knee. The origin of the word is unknown.

Larsen, Henry A. See NORTHWEST PASSAGE and ST ROCH.

Laskin, Bora (b.1912). CHIEF JUSTICE of Canada. Educated in law at Osgoode Hall Law School, Toronto, and Harvard University, he taught law at Osgoode Hall and the University of Toronto until 1965. He was made a QC in 1956 and a Fellow of the Royal Society of Canada in 1964. He was appointed to the Court of Appeal of Ontario on 1 Sept. 1965, to the Supreme Court of Canada on 23 Mar. 1970, and became Chief Justice on 27 Dec. 1973.

Lasnier, Rina (b.1915). Quebec poet. Born in Saint-Grégoire, Que., she has been writing lyric poems for over 30 years. They have been published in numerous collections and have brought her a distinguished reputation. Two anthologies of her work have appeared: *Rina Lasnier: textes choisis* (1964) edited by Jean Marcel and *La Part du feu* (1970) introduced by Guy Robert.

Lassy tart. A Newfoundland pie. Made with molasses, egg, and soft bread crumbs, it is similar to the Mennonite shoofly pie.

Last Post, The. A news magazine founded in Montreal in 1969 and since 1972 published eight times a year in Toronto. Produced by an editorial collective, it features investigative articles on social, political, and economic issues of the day. It is written from a leftist and sometimes nihilistic point of view.

Last Post Fund. Society to provide decent burials for destitute and friendless ex-servicemen who fought on active service. It was founded in Montreal in 1909 by the late Arthur H.D. Hair, a veteran and a hospital orderly, who was appalled to learn that no veterans' association provided this service. Since 1922 the Last Post Fund's activities have been nationwide and under Dominion charter. Since 1930 it has operated its own garden-like cemetery, The Field of Honour, at Pointe Claire, 14 mi. west of Montreal.

Last Spike, The. The iron spike that was driven into the final rail of the CANADIAN PACIFIC RAILWAY at a place named Craigellachie, B.C., at 9:22 a.m. on 7 Nov. 1885. After Donald A. SMITH bent the first spike, he hammered in a second one, observed by a group that included William VAN HORNE and Sandford FLEMING. *Towards the Last Spike* (1952) is the title of a narrative poem by E.J. PRATT about the building of the CPR. *The Last Spike: The Great Railway, 1881-1885* is the title of the second volume of Pierre BERTON's history of the CPR. See also 'STAND FAST, CRAIGELLACHIE'.

Latcholassie (b.1919). Eskimo sculptor at CAPE DORSET. He specializes in imaginative bird forms with shamanistic influences that appear sophisticated and contemporary. He is the son of TUDLIK.

Laufer, Murray (b.1929). Set designer. Born in Toronto, he trained at the Ontario College of Art and became resident designer of the CREST THEATRE in 1956. A brilliant and inventive craftsman, he has worked for the CANADIAN OPERA COMPANY (LOUIS RIEL, 1967), the CHARLOTTETOWN FESTIVAL (JOHNNY BELINDA, 1968), and has been resident designer of the ST LAWRENCE CENTRE, Toronto, since it opened in 1968.

Laura Limited. A popular CBC Radio soap opera. It featured the trials of Laura Scott (played by Eileen Clifford), who ran her own dress shop and had to deal with business and personal problems. The 15-minute serial was heard at 11:45 a.m. five days a week from 24 June 1946 to 1957.

Laura Secord Candies. Manufacturer of confectionery and chocolates. The original shop in Toronto was opened in 1913 by Frank T. O'Connor, who named it after the Upper Canadian heroine, Laura SECORD. Business expanded rapidly and a Montreal shop was opened in 1917. In 1926 it was incorporated in Toronto as the Laura Secord Candy Shops Ltd. The chain now includes 250 outlets. LABATT'S Breweries acquired majority shares in 1969.

Laurence, Margaret (b.1926). Novelist. Born in Neepawa, Man. (the model for the MANAWAKA of her novels), she was educated at United College, Winnipeg, and lived in Somaliland and Ghana with her husband from 1949 to 1957. She then divided her time between England and Canada until 1970, when she settled near Peterborough, Ont. An impressive writer of fiction that is built on the inner and outer lives of her strongly delineated characters, she has written a modern classic, *The STONE ANGEL* (1964); *A JEST OF GOD* (1966), filmed as *Rachel, Rachel*; *The Fire-Dwellers* (1969); *A Bird in the House* (1970), made up of linked short stories; and *The Diviners* (1975)—all with a Canadian setting. Her residence in Africa resulted in five books: *A Tree of Poverty* (1954), an anthology of Somali literature; *The Prophet's Camel Bell* (1963), an account of her two years in Somaliland; *This Side Jordan* (1960), her first novel, and a short-story collection, *The Tomorrow-Tamer* (1963), both set in Ghana; and *Long Drums and Cannons* (1971), a study of Nigerian literature. *Jason's Quest* (1970) is a children's book.

Laurendeau, André (1912-68). Quebec spokesman. Born in Montreal and educated at the Université de Montréal, the Sorbonne, and l'Institut Catholique, he was secretary in 1932 of Les JEUNES-CANADA, a Quebec nationalistic youth movement opposed to foreign ownership, and of the anti-conscription BLOC POPULAIRE (which he represented in the legislative assembly in 1944-8), while editing *L'Action nationale* (1937-44), a monthly review of politics and foreign affairs. As editor of *Le Devoir* (1947-63), he popularized the view that Quebec was governed by a ROI NÈGRE (1958) and that Canada required a royal commission on bilingualism (1962). The following year he and E. Davidson Dunton were appointed co-chairmen of the Royal Commission on Bilingualism and Biculturalism. Laurendeau died before the Commission could prepare its final report. Philip STRATFORD translated and edited a selection of his writings in *André Laurendeau: Witness for Quebec* (1973).

Laurentia. The name of an ideal French and Catholic state separate from Canada—a separatist notion that has been identified with Abbé Lionel GROULX since 1937.

Laurentian Mountains. The wooded hills (not properly mountains) of Quebec north of the St Lawrence. Actually the area of the CANADIAN SHIELD exposed by the last retreating glaciers, they contain some mineral deposits, although their greatest fame has come from the numerous tourist resorts that occupy their southern edge.

Laurentian Shield. See CANADIAN SHIELD.

Laurentian University. Non-denominational bilingual university in Sudbury, Ont., established in 1960. Federated with it are the church-related University of Sudbury (Roman Catholic), Huntington University (United Church), Thorneloe University (Anglican), and the non-denominational University College. There are three affiliated colleges in northeastern Ontario: Algoma in Sault Ste Marie, Nipissing in North Bay, and Collège de Hearst in Hearst.

Laurentians. See NATIONAL LIBRARY OF QUEBEC.

Laurier, Sir Wilfrid (1841-1919). Seventh prime minister. Born at St Lin, C.E. (now Laurentides, Que.), he trained as a lawyer at McGill University; as a student he associated himself with the progressive ROUGES, followers of Louis-Joseph PAPINEAU. He sat in the Quebec legislature from 1871 to 1874, when he was elected to the House of Commons as a Liberal; he remained a member until his death. An eloquent speaker, he gave a famous address on political liberalism in June 1877 in which he stated his opposition to party divisions along religious and linguistic lines. He was made leader of the party in 1887 and became the first French-Canadian prime minister in 1896. Personally very popular, he led the country through a period of prosperity that was helped by an aggressive immigration policy. He remained prime minister until the election of 1911, which was lost to the Conservatives. He was knighted at the Jubilee celebrations for Queen Victoria in June 1897.

Laurier and the larger Canada. Slogan of the LIBERAL PARTY under Sir Wilfrid LAURIER in the election of 1904.

Laurier House. Ottawa residence of two prime ministers. Built in 1878, this three-storey stone house was owned by Sir Wilfrid LAURIER from 1897 to 1911. Laurier's widow bequeathed it to W.L. Mackenzie KING, who resided there from 1923 to 1950. King willed it to the nation and it is now a museum.

Laut, Agnes (1871-1936). Popular historian. Born in Stanley, Ont., and educated at the University of Manitoba, she became a writer for the *Manitoba* (later *Winnipeg*) *Free Press*, then settled in the United States. She wrote extensively about Canadian and American history and frontier life, notably a dramatic novel about the fur trade, *Lords of the North* (1900), and *Pathfinders of the West* (1904), a carefully researched account of exploration in the Northwest. She contributed three volumes to the CHRONICLES OF CANADA series. She died in Wassaic, N.Y.

Laval, François de (1623-1708). First bishop of Quebec. Born in France, he arrived at Quebec in 1659 as vicar general of the pope in New France; he became bishop in 1674. He founded the Quebec seminary in 1663 for the education of a native clergy. Strongly opposed to the sale of spirits to the Indians and determined to defend the important role the Church had been given in the civil affairs of New France, he quarrelled with successive governors, notably FRONTENAC. He retired in 1688, becoming the revered Monseigneur l'Ancien. He was buried under the cathedral at Quebec. See also UNIVERSITÉ LAVAL.

Laval University. See UNIVERSITÉ LAVAL.

Lavallée, Calixa (1842-91). Composer. Born in Quebec, he studied in Montreal and Paris, travelled as a piano accompanist, taught in New Orleans, and worked as conductor and artistic director of the New York Grand Opera House before returning to Quebec. After composing 'O CANADA' in 1880, he returned to the United States. He died in Boston and his body was transferred to Montreal's Church of Notre Dame in 1933. His works include *The Widow* (1882), a melodic comic opera, two symphonies, piano studies, and many lively, tuneful overtures and patriotic marches for band.

Laviolette, Jean-Baptiste (Jack) (1879-1960). Lacrosse and hockey star, nicknamed 'The Speed Merchant'. Born in Belleville, Ont., he succeeded in lacrosse with the Nationales of Montreal and in hockey with the MONTREAL CANADIENS. He played with the latter until 1918, when he lost his left foot in a motor accident and was forced to retire. He was elected to both the Hockey and Sports HALLS OF FAME.

Lavoie. Automobile manufactured in 1923 by Lavoie Automotive Devices, Montreal. A five-passenger sedan that sold for $1,800, it was said to be technically ahead of its time.

LAW. Official abbreviation of Leading Air-craftwoman.

Law, Andrew Bonar. See Lord BEAVER-BROOK.

Law Reform Commission of Canada. Advisory body charged with reviewing systematically the laws of the country. Established in 1970, it reports to Parliament, through the Minister of Justice, on measures to improve, modernize, and reform the laws and statutes of Canada.

Law Reports. The most significant judgements of the courts, which are printed and published weekly by various companies. Collected and bound, they constitute the commentaries on STATUTES and on pronouncements of the law that may not be based on statutes. All may be referred to as the COMMON LAW.

Layton, Irving (b.1912). Celebrated poet. Born in Romania, he was brought by his parents to Montreal at the age of one, and was educated at Macdonald College and McGill University. In Montreal he first published with FIRST STATEMENT and NORTHERN REVIEW and, in 1952, helped found CONTACT PRESS, with Louis DUDEK and Raymond SOUSTER. He settled in Toronto in 1969 as professor of English at York University. His almost 30 collections of poetry include lyrical celebrations of joy in life, sensual beauty, love, and, in the prefaces to them, vigorous expressions of anger and contempt for all the life-diminishing, uncreative, hypocritical elements in society. *A Red Carpet for the Sun* (1959) was his first book to receive wide distribution and acclaim. He published a *Collected Poems* in 1965 and a *Selected Poems* in 1969. Since the appearance of *The Collected Poems of Irving Layton* (1971)—and its companion volume, *Engagements: The Prose of Irving Layton* (1972), edited by Seymour MAYNE—he has published *Lovers and Lesser Men* (1973), *The Pole-Vaulter* (1974), *Seventy-Five Greek Poems* (1975), *The Unwavering Eye: Selected Poems 1969-1975* (1975), and *For My Brother Jesus* (1976).

Lazare. Painting by Jean-Paul LEMIEUX. Executed in oil on masonite in 1941, it is an allegory of isolationism and resurrection in Quebec shown in multiple images of a cutaway view of a church congregation, a family being shot down by parachutists, and a funeral procession winding its way to a cemetery where the Lazarus of whom the priest is speaking rises from the dead. (AGO)

LCBO. Abbreviation of Liquor Control Board of Ontario.

LCDR and **LtCdr.** Official abbreviations of Lieutenant-Commander. Both forms are used.

LCol. Official abbreviation of Lieutenant-Colonel.

Le Havre. French seaport on the English Channel, scene of fighting during the SECOND WORLD WAR. It was taken by British troops under Canadian command in mid-Sept. 1944.

Le Jeune, Paul (1591-1664). Jesuit missionary, the first and most prolific editor of the JESUIT RELATIONS. He served in New France from 1632 to 1649 and was superior of the Jesuit mission from 1632 to 1639.

Le Moyne, Charles, Sieur de Longueuil et de Châteauguay (1626-85). Soldier, trader, seigneur. He came to New France at 15 and in 1646 settled at VILLE MARIE, which he helped to defend against Indian attacks. He saw service as a soldier and an interpreter for the Indians and was rewarded by MAISONNEUVE with a grant of land and property on rue Saint-Paul, where he lived for 30 years in a comfortable house. He received letters patent of nobility in 1668, and in 1672 and 1673 was given title to the seigneuries of Longueuil and Châteauguay by FRONTENAC. He had two daughters and 12 sons, one of whom was Pierre Le Moyne d'IBERVILLE.

Le Moyne, Jean (b.1914). Quebec essayist. Born in Montreal and educated at the Collège Sainte-Marie, he has been a journalist, editor of *La* RELÈVE, a producer with the NATIONAL FILM BOARD, and is now a member of the prime minister's staff. His highly acclaimed essays on French-Canadian life, especially on the role of the Church, were translated by Philip STRATFORD as *Convergence* (1966).

Leacock, Stephen (1869-1944). Humorist. Born in Swanmoor, Eng., he was brought to the Lake Simcoe district of Ontario at the age of six and was educated at the Universities of Toronto and Chicago. He taught economics and political science at McGill University from 1903 to his retirement in 1936, and his first publication, *Elements of Political Science* (1906), was a standard textbook for some years. He wrote many other scholarly books but became world famous as a humorist—a writer of sketches, like his famous 'MY FINANCIAL CAREER', that masterfully combine controlled exaggeration and an inspired sense of the incongruous. The setting of his classic SUNSHINE SKETCHES OF A LITTLE TOWN (1912) is MARIPOSA, a fictional community modelled on the Ontario town of Orillia, where Lea-

Leader

cock had his summer home (now a museum) on Brewery Bay, Lake Couchiching. Leacock's remark that Lord Randal 'rode madly off in all directions' has entered the language; it appears in 'Gertrude the Governess' in *Nonsense Novels* (1911).

As Leacock has more books in print than any other Canadian author, living or dead, and as new paperback reprints appear from time to time, what follows is a complete list of his works of humour: LITERARY LAPSES (1910), *Nonsense Novels* (1911), *Sunshine Sketches of a Little Town* (1912), *Behind the Beyond* (1913), ARCADIAN ADVENTURES WITH THE IDLE RICH (1914), *Moonbeams from the Larger Lunacy* (1915), *Further Foolishness* (1916), *Frenzied Fiction* (1918), *The Hohenzollerns in America with the Bolsheviks in Berlin* (1919), *Winsome Winnie* (1920), *My Discovery of England* (1922), *Over the Footlights* (1923), *College Days* (1923), *Short Circuits* (1924), *The Garden of Folly* (1924), *Winnowed Wisdom* (1926), *The Iron Man and the Tin Woman* (1929), *Wet Wit and Dry Humour* (1931), *Afternoons in Utopia* (1932), *The Dry Pickwick* (1932), *The Perfect Salesman* (1934), *Too Much College* (1934), *Hellements of Hickonomics* (1936), *Funny Pieces* (1936), *Here are My Lectures and Stories* (1937), *My Discovery of the West* (1937), *Model Memoirs and Other Sketches* (1938), MY REMARKABLE UNCLE AND OTHER SKETCHES (1942), *Happy Stories Just to Laugh At* (1943), *How to Write* (1943), and *Last Leaves* (1945).

'Humour may be defined as the kindly contemplation of the incongruities of life, and the artistic expression thereof,' Leacock wrote in *Humour and Humanity* (1937). Other books that contain his theory of humour are: *The Greatest Pages of American Humor* (1916), *Humor: Its Theory and Techniques* (1935), and *How to Write* (1943). *The Boy I Left Behind Me* (1946), the beginning of Leacock's unfinished autobiography, was published posthumously. Anthologies of his work—not one of which is truly representative—are *Laugh with Leacock* (1930), *Laugh Parade* (1940), and *Leacock Roundabout* (1946). J.B. Priestley compiled *The Best of Leacock* (1957) and Robertson DAVIES presented some of the lesser-known Leacock pieces in *A Feast of Stephen* (1974). Ralph L. Curry, the curator of the Leacock Museum in Orillia, has written the standard biography, *Stephen Leacock: Humorist and Humanist* (1959).

As a historian, Leacock contributed one volume to the MAKERS OF CANADA series and three volumes to the CHRONICLES OF CANADA series. *Canada: The Foundation of Its Future* (1941), commissioned by the House of SEAGRAM, was distributed free of charge to schoolchildren across the country. *Montreal: Seaport and City* (1942) was reprinted as *Lea-*

cock's *Montreal* (1963) edited by John Culliton.

Leacock Medal for Humour, Stephen. Annual award for the best humorous book published in Canada the previous year. It was established by the Stephen LEACOCK Associates in 1946 to honour the famous writer. The medal, engraved with Leacock's smiling features, is awarded at a banquet held each summer at Leacock's summer home in Orillia, Ont. Since 1973 the medal has been accompanied by a prize of $1,000, made possible by the Manufacturer's Life Insurance Company. Ralph L. Curry, curator of the Leacock Museum, edited *The Leacock Medal Treasury: Three Decades of the Best Canadian Humour* (1976). A list of the award-winners follows:

1949 Angeline Hango, *Truthfully Yours*
1950 Earle BIRNEY, TURVEY
1951 Eric NICOL, *The Roving I*
1952 Jan Hilliard, *The Salt Box*
1953 Laurence Earl, *The Battle of Baltinglass*
1954 Joan Walker, *Pardon My Parka*
1955 Robertson DAVIES, LEAVEN OF MALICE
1956 Eric NICOL, *Shall We Join the Ladies?*
1957 Robert Thomas ALLEN, *The Grass is Never Greener*
1958 Eric NICOL, *Girdle Me a Globe*
1959 No award
1960 Pierre BERTON, *Just Add Water and Stir*
1961 Norman Ward, *Mice in the Beer*
1962 William O. MITCHELL, JAKE AND THE KID
1963 Donald Lamont Jack, *Three Cheers for Me*
1964 Harry J. BOYLE, *Homebrew and Patches*
1965 Greg CLARK, *Gregory Clark's War Stories*
1966 George Bain, *Nursery Rhymes to be Read Aloud by Young Parents and Old Children*
1967 Richard J. NEEDHAM, *Needham's Inferno*
1968 Max FERGUSON, *And Now . . . Here's Max*
1969 Stuart Trueman, *You're Only as Old as You Act*
1970 Farley MOWAT, *The Boat Who Wouldn't Float*
1971 Robert Thomas ALLEN, *Children, Wives and Other Wildlife*
1972 Max BRAITHWAITE, *The Night We Stole the Mountie's Car*
1973 Don Bell, *Saturday Night at the Bagel Factory*
1974 Donald Lamont Jack, *That's Me in the Middle*
1975 Morley Torgov, *A Good Place to Come From*
1976 Harry J. BOYLE, *The Luck of the Irish*

Leader, Government. See GOVERNMENT LEADER.

293

League for Democratic Rights

League for Democratic Rights. Organization founded in Toronto on 21 Apr. 1950 to defend and extend civil rights. Founding bodies were the Montreal Civil Liberties Union, the Timmins Labour Defence Committee, and the Toronto Civil Rights Union (successor to the Emergency Committee for Civil Rights, established in 1946).

League for Social Reconstruction. An organization founded in Jan. 1932 by a group of university professors and others from Toronto and Montreal. Its manifesto stated that it was 'working for the establishment in Canada of a social order in which the basic principle regulating production, distribution and service will be the common good rather than private profit.' Modelled on the Fabian Society of Great Britain, the League aimed to educate the public in economic problems. Its members gave speeches, wrote articles and pamphlets, and jointly produced *Social Planning for Canada*, published in 1935 (reissued 1975). F.H. UNDERHILL, F.R. SCOTT, Eugene FORSEY, and other members were active in founding the CCF and in preparing its REGINA MANIFESTO. The League ceased its activities during the Second World War.

League for Socialist Action. One of the many Trotskyist political groups that emerged during the 1960s and 1970s, affiliated with the Fourth International.

League of Canadian Poets. Professional association of published poets, established in Toronto in 1968 by Raymond SOUSTER and others. The League exists to arrange readings, co-ordinate national tours, and further the cause of poetry and poets in Canada.

Learned Societies, The. An annual gathering of Canadian academics largely from the fields of the humanities and social sciences. The formation of individual learned societies and their collective annual meetings developed from the annual meeting of the ROYAL SOCIETY OF CANADA, which was founded in 1882. There is no accepted definition or criteria for a learned society. The annual meetings, though they currently involve over 50 associations, have no continuing organization or structure. Each year the meetings are held at a different university campus. In 1975 they attracted over 4,000 participants to the University of Alberta. Not all learned societies meet at the time of the annual meetings.

Learning Stage. See CBC IDEAS.

Leaven of Malice. Serio-comic novel by Robertson DAVIES published in 1954. Set in the small university city of SALTERTON (Kingston), Ont., it is about the repercussions that ensue when a false announcement of an engagement appears in a local newspaper. It was dramatized as *Love and Libel*, of which Tyrone GUTHRIE directed the world première at the ROYAL ALEXANDRA THEATRE, Toronto, on 2 Nov. 1959. On 7 Dec. 1960 it opened on Broadway with a Canadian cast and did poorly, nor was it well received in its revival (under the novel's title) at the SHAW FESTIVAL on 29 May 1975.

Leaver, E.W. See AMCRO.

Leaving Home. Play by David FRENCH. It depicts the breakup of a Newfoundland family, the Mercers, who live in Toronto in the 1950s. Under the direction of Bill GLASSCO, it opened at the TARRAGON THEATRE on 16 May 1972.

Leclerc, Félix (b.1914). Poet, Quebec's first chansonnier. Born at La Tuque, Que., he was an announcer with the CBC from 1934 to 1942, reading and singing his own material. He acted with the COMPAGNONS DE SAINT-LAURENT from 1942 to 1945 and from 1951 to 1953 lived in Paris, where his performances as 'le Canadien' were (and still are) popular. His publications include stories, poems, memoirs, and plays. *Allegro*, a book of fables, first published in 1944, appeared in English in 1974 in a translation by Linda Hutcheon.

LeDain Commission. A Commission of Inquiry on the Non-Medical Use of Drugs, headed by Gerald LeDain, then dean of the Osgoode Hall Law School, York University. Appointed in 1969, it issued its final report on 14 Dec. 1973. It revealed the extent of drug abuse in Canada and recommended, among other liberal measures, that possession of cannabis (marijuana and hashish) be decriminalized.

Leduc. The most important oil discovery in Canadian history, known also as Imperial Leduc No. 1. After 10 weeks of drilling, an IMPERIAL OIL crew headed by Vernon Hunter encountered large quantities of high-quality crude oil a few miles northeast of the town of Leduc, 13 mi. south of Edmonton. The oil strike on 13 Feb. 1947 ushered in Alberta's post-war oil boom. The well went dry in 1974.

Leduc, Ozias (1864-1955). Painter. Born in Saint-Hilaire, C.E. (Que.), he lived there all his life while working as a church decorator. For his own pleasure he produced many remarkable still lifes. The beautiful *L'*ENFANT AU PAIN (1892-9, NGC) is one of the most familiar images of nineteenth-century Canadian art.

Lee, Dennis (b.1939). Poet. Born in Toronto and educated at the University of Toronto, he was a founder of ROCHDALE COLLEGE and wrote about the experience in *The University Game* (1968), which he edited with Howard Adelman. He was also a founder in 1967 of the House of ANANSI PRESS, where he launched the careers of several new novelists and poets. His first book of verse was *Kingdom of Absence* (1967). It was followed by CIVIL ELEGIES (1968), which was expanded into *Civil Elegies and Other Poems* (1972), lyrical meditations on the loss of nerve in today's society that are deeply informed by George Grant's LAMENT FOR A NATION (1965). He has since had great success as a poet for children, beginning with *Wiggle to the Laundromat* (1970), some poems of which appear in the very popular ALLIGATOR PIE (1974) and *Nicholas Knock and Other People* (1974).

Lee-Enfield Rifle. See ROSS RIFLE.

Lefèbvre, Jean-Pierre (b.1941). Quebec film director. Born in Montreal, he was known as a poet and film critic before becoming Quebec's most prolific film-maker. He worked at the NATIONAL FILM BOARD before organizing his own production company. His features include *Le Révolutionnaire* (1965), *Il ne faut pas mourir pour ça* (1967), *Les Maudites sauvages* (1971), and *Les Dernières Fiançailles* (1973). He produced and appeared in Denys ARCAND'S RÉJEANNE PADOVANI (1973) and performed also in Cousineau's *L'Île jaune* (1974).

Left Turn, Canada. An influential book by M.J. COLDWELL, national president of the CCF. Published in 1945, it urged Canadians to adopt socialist policies.

Légaré, Joseph (1795-1855). Pioneer landscape painter. Born in Quebec, he worked as a copyist, but he also executed some memorable oil paintings of notable events such as fires—for example, *L'Incendie du quartier Saint-Roch* (1845) in the Musée du Québec.

Legend of the Raven. A popular short feature produced by Crawley Films for IMPERIAL OIL. The film was directed by Judith Crawley, edited by René Bonnière, and released in 1957. It retells, through soapstone carvings, the Eskimo legend of how the raven lost its ability to talk when it broke its promise to direct starving Eskimos to food that was near at hand. It is a companion to *The* LOON'S NECKLACE. 15 min., 16 mm; colour.

Léger, Jules (b.1913). GOVERNOR GENERAL of Canada. Born in Saint-Anicet, Que., he was educated at the Université de Montréal and the Sorbonne. He was associate editor of *Le Droit* from 1934 to 1939 and joined the De-partment of External Affairs in 1940. He was appointed ambassador to Mexico (1953), Italy (1962), France (1964), and Belgium and Luxembourg (1973) before becoming governor general in 1974. He is the brother of Paul-Émile LÉGER.

Léger, Paul-Émile (b.1904). Former cardinal. Born in Valleyfield, Que., he was educated in Montreal and Paris and was ordained a Sulpician priest in 1930. He was rector of the Pontifical Canadian College in Rome from 1947 to 1950, consecrated archbishop of Montreal in 1950, and created a cardinal in 1953—a position he gave up in 1967 to be a missionary priest with lepers in Africa.

Legion. See ROYAL CANADIAN LEGION.

Legislative assembly. A body of members elected to govern a colony or a province. The term was used in colonial times to designate the lower elected house of the legislature. Since CONFEDERATION it has been used to designate the legislature in seven of the ten provinces. In Newfoundland and Nova Scotia the provincial legislature is called the HOUSE OF ASSEMBLY; in Quebec it is called AS-SEMBLÉE NATIONALE.

Legislative council. The former upper house in some of the provinces. Under the colonial constitutions of Nova Scotia, Prince Edward Island, New Brunswick, Lower Canada, Upper Canada, and British Columbia, the governor appointed members to the legislative council for life. After Confederation, Ontario, Alberta, and Saskatchewan did not have legislative councils, and the other provinces eventually discontinued them.

Legislature, The. Institution with the power to make laws for the government of the country. The federal legislative authority is vested in the Parliament of Canada, consisting of the Queen or the Queen's representative, the GOVERNOR GENERAL; the SENATE; and the HOUSE OF COMMONS. The provincial legislative authority is vested in the LEGISLATIVE ASSEMBLY, the HOUSE OF ASSEMBLY, or the AS-SEMBLÉE NATIONALE, and in the Queen or the Queen's representative, the LIEUTENANT-GOV-ERNOR.

Lehmann, Heinz E. See LARGACTIL.

Leif Ericsson or **Leif the Lucky** (died *c.*1020). First European to land on mainland North America. The son of Eric the Red, who settled Greenland, he sailed west in *c.*1000, in a ship he bought from BJARNI, and visited HEL-LULAND, MARKLAND, and VINLAND—probably Baffin Island, Labrador, and Newfoundland (at L'ANSE AUX MEADOWS).

Leiterman, Douglas (b.1927). Television producer. Born in South Porcupine, Ont., and the brother of Richard LEITERMAN, he joined CBC-TV in 1958. With Patrick WATSON he was responsible for THIS HOUR HAS SEVEN DAYS. He produces documentaries for TV on a freelance basis.

Leiterman, Richard (b.1935). Camerman with CBC-TV experience. Born in South Porcupine, Ont., and the brother of Douglas LEITERMAN, he was the cinematographer of *A MARRIED COUPLE* (1969), GOIN' DOWN THE ROAD (1970), and WEDDING IN WHITE (1972). He specializes in *cinéma-vérité*.

Leliefontain, Battle of. See SOUTH AFRICAN WAR.

Leméac, Éditions. Quebec publisher. Established in Montreal in 1957, it publishes a wide assortment of trade books.

Lemelin, Roger (b.1919). Quebec novelist. Born in Saint-Sauveur de Québec, he attended the Académie Commerciale in Quebec City but, being the oldest of 10 children, went to work at the age of 14. Since 1973 he has been editor-in-chief of *La Presse*, where he instituted a $5,000 annual literary prize. His first novel, *Au Pied de la pente douce* (1944)—*The* TOWN BELOW (1948) in its English translation by Samuel Putnam—was a landmark in Quebec realistic literature for its depiction of working-class life. Characters from its successor, *Les* PLOUFFE (1948)—*The Plouffe Family* (1950) in its English translation by Mary Finch—appeared in popular radio and television series in both French and English. Lemelin also wrote *Pierre le magnifique* (1951)—translated by Harry Binsse and published in English as *In Quest of Splendour* (1955)—about a young man's vocation for the priesthood. *Fantasies sur les Péchés capitaux* (1948) is a collection of stories. The most humorous one, 'The Stations of the Cross', translated by Mary Finch, appears in *Canadian Short Stories* (1960) edited by Robert WEAVER.

Lemieux, Jean-Paul (b.1904). Painter. Born in Quebec City, he studied and taught in Montreal and in 1937 took a teaching position at the École des Beaux-Arts in Quebec City, from which he retired in 1965. After painting conventional landscapes, he turned to satire—see his LAZARE—and in the 1950s entered upon the highly simplified depictions of figures, and figures in landscapes, with which he is now associated—haunting, muted, timeless images evoking solitude, space, and memory, of which *Le* VISITEUR DU SOIR (1956, NGC) is a famous example.

Lennox, E.J. (1855-1933). Architect. Born and educated in Toronto, he is primarily associated with the Romanesque Revival in such picturesque buildings as the Old City Hall, Toronto (1884-99); but he also designed a classical building for the Bank of Toronto at 205 Yonge St (1904) and the wildly Edwardian baronial CASA LOMA—all of which are among the most important Canadian buildings of their periods.

Lens. See HILL 70.

Leonard, Stanley (b.1915). Vancouver golfer who has probably won more provincial and national amateur titles than any other Canadian. He joined the company of touring professionals and became so successful that, in 1958, he won the prestigious Tournament of Champions at Las Vegas. In 1971 he retired to play for pleasure.

LePan, Douglas (b.1914). Poet and teacher. Born in Toronto and educated at the University of Toronto and Oxford, he taught at Harvard before joining the Department of External Affairs, where he became Assistant Under-Secretary of State. He returned to the academic life in 1959 and was principal of University College, Toronto, from 1964 until 1970, when he became a University Professor. In addition to his uncollected essays, he has written two books of verse—*The Wounded Prince and Other Poems* (1948) and *The Net and the Sword* (1953)—and one novel about his wartime experiences, *The Deserter* (1964).

Leprohon, Rosanna Eleanor (1832-79). Novelist. Born and educated in Montreal and married to Dr J.L. Leprohon, the Spanish vice-consul there, she was a regular and popular contributor of verse and serial novels to the LITERARY GARLAND. Her romantic novels include *Antoinette de Mirencourt* (1864) and *Armand Durand* (1868). Her verse was collected in *The Poetical Works of Mrs Leprohon* (1881).

LeRoy. Automobile built in Kitchener (then Berlin), Ont., from 1899 to 1902. It was designed by Nelson and Dr Milton Good and boasted a one-cylinder 4-h.p. engine.

Léry, Gaspard-Joseph Chaussegros de. See Gaspard-Joseph CHAUSSEGROS DE LÉRY.

Lesage, Jean (b.1912). Former cabinet minister and premier of Quebec, 1960-6. Born in Montreal and educated in law at Université Laval, he was first elected to the House of Commons in 1945 and entered the cabinet as Minister of Northern Affairs and National Resources in 1953. At the end of May 1958 he was elected head of the Quebec Liberal Party and two weeks later resigned from the House of Commons. He entered the Quebec legislature in 1960 as nineteenth premier, also holding the portfolio of Minister of Finance. Defeated in the election of 1966, he served as leader of the Opposition until 1969, when he resigned as party leader and returned to practising law. During his tenure of office Lesage presided over the QUIET REVOLUTION in Quebec.

Lescarbot, Marc (c.1570-1642). French lawyer and writer who spent the winter of 1606-7 at PORT ROYAL, Acadia. His book, *Les Muses de la Nouvelle-France* (1609), contained 12 poems—probably the first poems written in America north of the Spanish Empire—and a masque, *Le Théâtre de Neptune*, which was written and acted at Port Royal in Nov. 1606—the first theatrical presentation in North America. In the same year he published a history, which has been translated and edited, with the *Muses*, by W.L. Grant: *The History of New France by Marc Lescarbot* (3 vols, 1907-14).

Leslie, Kenneth (1892-1974). Poet. Born in Pictou, N.S., and educated at Dalhousie, Nebraska, and Harvard Universities, he wrote formal poems about Nova Scotia life. These were collected from four books in *The Poems of Kenneth Leslie* (1971).

Leslie Bell Singers, The. See Dr Leslie BELL.

Lest We Forget. Educational film produced by the MOTION PICTURE BUREAU in 1935. Directed by Frank C. Badgley and sponsored by the Department of National Defence, it was a somewhat bombastic compilation of footage depicting Canada's role in the First World War. 102 min., b & w.

Lester and Orpen Limited. Publishing house. Founded in Toronto in 1973 by the editor Malcolm Lester and the publicist Eve Orpen, the company is known for the personalized attention it gives to authors and titles, which are usually of the popular variety with international appeal. Among their successful publications are Morley Torgov's *A Good Place to Come From* (1974) and *You and I, and Love* (1975) by Terry ROWE.

Lester B. Pearson College. See PEARSON COLLEGE OF THE PACIFIC.

Lester Patrick Trophy. Presented annually 'for outstanding service to hockey in the United States' by the NATIONAL HOCKEY LEAGUE. The winner, who is selected by a Canadian-American award committee and receives a miniature of the trophy, may be a hockey player, official, coach, executive, or referee. The trophy was donated by the New York Rangers in 1966 to honour the late Lester PATRICK, the Rangers' Canadian general manager and coach.

Letendre, Rita (b.1929). Painter. Born in Drummondville, Que., she studied at the École des Beaux-Arts, Montreal, exhibiting first with the AUTOMATISTES and later internationally. She is known for large paintings that use colourful optical designs to create a feeling of speed and energy and that suggest boundaries beyond the edge of the canvas. *Sunmist* (1970, private coll.) is an example of her finest work. She lives in Toronto.

Lethbridge Strike. A strike by coal miners at Lethbridge, Alta, for union recognition, the eight-hour day, and wage increases. It lasted from 9 Mar. to 2 Dec. 1906 and resulted in a serious coal famine in Alberta. The federal government intervened and negotiated a settlement. The strike led to the establishment of the INDUSTRIAL DISPUTES INVESTIGATION ACT of 1907.

Let's all hate Toronto. Catch-line common from 1945 to 1960. Lister SINCLAIR made use of it in his radio play 'We All Hate Toronto', published in *A Play on Words and Other Radio Plays* (1948), in which one character explains: 'That's just it. We *all* hate Toronto! It's the only thing everybody's got in common.'

'Letters in Canada'. Annual review feature in the UNIVERSITY OF TORONTO QUARTERLY on the preceding year's publications by Canadian writers. Begun in 1932 by E.K. BROWN, it is composed of chronicle reviews by numerous critics. The poetry chronicles of Northrop FRYE, which appeared from 1950 to 1959, are included in *The* BUSH GARDEN (1971).

Léveillé, Claude (b.1941). Quebec chansonnier. The Montreal-born singer, composer, author, and actor was discovered by Edith Piaf in France in 1959. He wrote several songs for her before returning to Quebec, where he established himself as a chansonnier and composer of musical-comedy and film scores.

Lévesque, Georges-Henri. See UNIVERSITÉ LAVAL.

Lévesque, René (b.1922). Quebec separatist. Born in New Carlisle, Gaspé, Que., he was educated at Université Laval. With RADIO CANADA INTERNATIONAL he gained prominence with his coverage of the Second World War and the Korean War and acquired a wide following in Quebec with his weekly RADIO-CANADA television public-affairs show, 'Point de Mire' ('Focal Point'). He was radicalized during the 68-day strike of Quebec producers for collective-bargaining rights, which broke out on 29 Dec. 1958. He joined the Liberal party of Jean LESAGE and served as a cabinet minister in the Quebec government, nationalizing Hydro-Québec and taking an increasingly separatist stand. He was drummed out of the party by Eric Kierans and others in 1967. He sat as an independent and in 1968 established his own PARTI QUÉBÉCOIS, which was defeated in Robert BOURASSA's Liberal landslide of 1970. Lévesque—a charming and eloquent public figure—has been called 'the long lean tribune' of the Quebec people.

Levine, Les (b.1936). Sculptor. Born in Dublin, he studied art in London before coming to Canada in 1957. The motif of chairs was central to his mixed-media and plastic work in the early 1960s. He also created environments by filling small spaces with lights and closed-circuit television, or by making a large transparent plastic bubble to encase the viewer. He developed the concept of 'disposable art' and is currently experimenting with photography and video tape. His innovative work has been exhibited in Toronto, Ottawa, and New York City, where he lives.

Levine, Norman (b.1924). Short-story writer. Born in Ottawa, he has lived in Cornwall, Eng., since the late-forties. The author of two novels and a book of verse, he is best known for the hard look he took at the country in *Canada Made Me* (1958) and for three short-story collections: *One Way Ticket* (1961), *I Don't Want to Know Anyone too Well* (1971), and *Selected Stories* (1975).

Lévis, duc de (1720-87). French army officer. Second-in-command to MONTCALM in the SEVEN YEARS' WAR, François-Gaston, duc de Lévis, succeeded to the command on Montcalm's death and defeated the British forces under James MURRAY in the Battle of SAINTE-FOY on 28 Apr. 1760. He left Canada in October of that year.

Lewis, David (b.1909). Leader of the NEW DEMOCRATIC PARTY, 1971-5. Born in Poland, he grew up in Montreal and was educated at McGill University and Oxford. He became a leading labour lawyer, but his primary devotion was to the CO-OPERATIVE COMMONWEALTH FEDERATION. As the party's national secretary from 1937 to 1950, he created the organizational basis of the CCF. In electoral politics his career was less successful and he lost elections in 1943, 1945, and 1949. His first success came in 1962, when he won the election in York South, Ont. Lewis immediately established a reputation as one of the country's leading parliamentary orators, but he lost his

seat in the election of 1963. He regained it in 1965, held it in 1968, and in 1971 succeeded Tommy DOUGLAS as leader of the NDP. In 1972, with a brilliant campaign that focused on the tax and other concessions that were received by 'CORPORATE WELFARE BUMS', Lewis led the NDP to its best position ever, holding the balance of power in a minority Commons. But in the election of 1974 the NDP fell back and Lewis lost his seat; he resigned the leadership the next year and retired from active politics. His son, Stephen, is leader of the Ontario NDP, and others in his family play active roles in party affairs.

Leyrac, Monique (b.1932). Quebec chansonnière. Born in Montreal, she made her acting début playing Ste Bernadette in a play on RADIO-CANADA in 1944. She was associated with the THÉÂTRE DU NOUVEAU MONDE, with which she had a great success as Polly Peachum in *The Beggar's Opera*, and established herself as a singer of international calibre when she sang the prize-winning 'MON PAYS' by Gilles VIGNEAULT at the International Song Festival in Sopot, Poland, in 1965 and won first prize at the song festival in Ostend, Belgium, that same year. A singer of dramatic intensity, she is also a Quebec nationalist. As an actress she has most recently distinguished herself in a one-woman play, *Mademoiselle Marguerite* by Roberto Athayde, adapted from the Portuguese by Michel TREMBLAY.

LGen. Official abbreviation of Lieutenant-General.

Liberal Party. One of the two major parties in Canada. Under the leadership of LAURIER, KING, ST LAURENT, PEARSON, and TRUDEAU, Liberalism has held power for all but 21 years in this century. The party originated out of a union of Clear GRITS (hence the party's sobriquet of 'the Grits') and George BROWN's independent reformers in the legislature of the Province of Canada in the mid-1850s. Links were gradually formed with Quebec ROUGES, and after CONFEDERATION other opposition groups also found themselves coalescing with the Liberals. In 1873 Alexander MACKENZIE became the first Liberal prime minister and retained that post until 1878. But real success did not come until Laurier became party leader and led the Grits, by this time a fully functioning national party, to victory in 1896. Under the francophone Laurier, one of the most attractive politicians in Canadian history, the Liberals established themselves as a party in favour of French-English unity, increased independence within the Empire, and both the NATIONAL POLICY and freer trade. With deft variations on these themes, Liberal politicians have almost continuously beguiled the public ever since.

Laurier was defeated by Robert BORDEN's Conservatives in 1911 and the party was out of power until Mackenzie King re-established 'winning' ways in 1921. With the exception of a few months in 1926 and the Depression years of 1930 to 1935, King held power until he retired in 1948. His governments established the social-welfare state, fought and won the Second World War, checked the rise of the CCF, and crushed a legion of Tory leaders. With the exception of the brief DIEFENBAKER interlude, his successors Louis St Laurent, Lester Pearson, and Pierre Trudeau have kept the party in power.

The Liberal party's success has come about through skilful leadership, pragmatism carried to its highest level, and a solid base in the province of Quebec.

Liberté. A literary magazine published six times a year in Montreal since 1959. Among its editors are Hubert AQUIN, Jacques GODBOUT, and Jean-Guy PILON. It is an outlet for new Quebec poets and story-writers and takes a socialistic and nationalistic stand. Every summer it sponsors the Rencontre des Écrivains, a conference of poets and writers in Montreal.

Liberty. (i) A mass-circulation magazine, published in New York and Chicago from May 1924 to July 1950, of which Bernard Macfadden was publisher and Fulton Oursler was editor. It described itself as 'A weekly for everybody'. Selections from back issues were republished in 1971-2 as *Liberty: The Nostalgia Magazine.* (ii) From 1932 to 8 Mar. 1947 a Canadian edition of *Liberty* was published in Toronto. It differed marginally from the American edition but in 1939 was able to describe itself as 'Canada's largest weekly magazine'. Acquired by the businessman Jack Kent COOKE, who renamed it *The New Liberty* on 15 Mar. 1947, it was Canadianized and published such writers as Hugh GARNER and Frank RASKY (who served as editor from 1954 to 1960). Cooke sold the magazine in 1960 and it ceased publication in Aug. 1964. The 'reading time' of each piece was given. At the end of James REANEY's short story, 'The Box Social'—reprinted from a college magazine on 19 July 1947—was the line: 'Reading Time: 4 minutes 50 seconds.'

Liberty of the press. The right to print without any previous licence, but subject to the consequences of the law. The right to a free press in early Canada was reaffirmed in May 1835 when it took a jury 10 minutes to acquit

Joseph HOWE of publishing libellous material in his newspaper the *Novascotian*. It was reaffirmed in 1938 when the Supreme Court of Canada declared that an Alberta statute that sought to compel newspapers to publish government comments on critical articles published by them violated the Canadian parliamentary system that rested on the right of free expression.

Library of Parliament. An information and research library that serves the governor general and members of the two Houses of Parliament. It is run by the Parliamentary Librarian, who is responsible to the Speakers of the Senate and the House of Commons. Its collection includes HANSARD and both the British statutes and debates and the American Congressional Papers. The building—designed by Thomas FULLER (1859) and built in 1860-6—is attached to the Centre Block of the PARLIAMENT BUILDINGS and escaped destruction in the fire of 1916. It is an impressive circular room, with a statute of Queen Victoria by Marshall Wood in the centre, roofed by a 140-ft-high dome with Gothic-style vaulting whose ribs form a radiating star pattern. It was restored to its original form after being damaged by fire in 1952.

Lies My Father Told Me. A popular film based on the boyhood experiences of Ted ALLAN. It was directed by Jan Kadar in 1975 and is a charming depiction of a youngster's growing up on Cadieux St in Montreal's East End during the 1920s. Allan's script is based on a story he wrote in the 1950s and adapted for radio and TV; it is the basis of a novel by his son Norman, published in 1976.

Lieutenant-Governor. The representative of the CROWN in the province of a self-governing Dominion. The lieutenant-governor, appointed by the Queen normally for five years on the advice of the federal ministry, is the chief executive officer of the provincial government and is 'above politics'. The office dates from the appointment in 1712 of the governor of Nova Scotia, the first in British North America. With Confederation in 1867 the governor of a province became a lieutenant-governor under the GOVERNOR GENERAL. The lieutenant-governor is referred to as 'His (Her) Honour' and is greeted as 'Your Honour' followed by 'sir' or 'madam'. The first woman to hold vice-regal office was Pauline McGibbon, who became lieutenant-governor of Ontario in 1974. Canadians use the British pronunciation of 'lieutenant': 'lef-tenant' not 'loo-tenant', which is American. A list of lieutenant-governors since Confederation, including their dates of office, follows:

Lieutenant-Governor

Alberta. George Hedley Vicars Bulyea, 1905-15; Robert George Brett, 1915-27; William Egbert, 1927-31; William Legh Walsh, 1931-6; Philip Carteret Hill Primrose, 1936-7; John Campbell Bowen, 1937-50; John James Bowlen, 1950-9; J. Percy Page, 1959-66; John Walter Grant MacEwan, 1966-74; Ralph Garvin Steinhauer, 1974- .

British Columbia. Joseph J.W. Trutch, 1871-6; Albert Norton Richards, 1876-81; Clement Francis Cornwall, 1881-7; Hugh Nelson, 1887-92; Edgar Dewdney, 1892-7; Thomas Robert McInnes, 1897-1900; Joly de Lotbinière, 1900-6; James Dunsmuir, 1906-9; Thomas Wilson Paterson, 1909-14; Frank Stillman Barnard, 1914-19; Edward Gawler Prior, 1919-20; Walter Cameron Nichol, 1920-6; Robert Randolph Bruce, 1926-31; John William Fordham Johnson, 1931-6; Eric Werge Hamber, 1936-41; W.C. Woodward, 1941-6; Charles Arthur Banks, 1946-50; Clarence Wallace, 1950-5; Frank Mackenzie Ross, 1955-60; George Randolph Pearkes, 1960-8; John Robert Nicholson, 1968-73; Walter Stewart Owen, 1973- .

Manitoba. A.G. Archibald, 1870-2; Alex Morris, 1872-6; Joseph Ed. Cauchon, 1876-82; James C. Aikins, 1882-8; John Schultz, 1888-95; J.C. Patterson, 1895-1900; D.H. McMillan, 1900-11; Douglas C. Cameron, 1911-16; J.A.M. Aikins, 1916-26; Theodore Arthur Burrows, 1926-9; James Duncan McGregor, 1929-34; W.J. Tupper, 1934-40; R.F. McWilliams, 1940-53; John Stewart McDiarmid, 1953-60; Errick French Willis, 1960-5; Richard S. Bowles, 1965-70; W. John McKeag, 1970- .

New Brunswick. C.H. Doyle, July-Oct. 1867; F.P. Harding, 1867-8; L.A. Wilmot, 1868-73; S.L. Tilley, 1873-8; Ed. Baron Chandler, 1878-80; Robert Duncan Wilmot, 1880-5; L. Tilley, 1885-93; John Boyd, Sept.-Dec. 1893; John J. Fraser, 1893-6; A.R. McClelan, 1896-1902; J.B. Snowball, 1902-7; Lemuel J. Tweedie, 1907-12; Josiah Wood, 1912-17; Gilbert White Ganong, June-Nov. 1917; William Pugsley, 1917-23; William F. Todd, 1923-8; Hugh Havelock McLean, 1928-35; Murray MacLaren, 1935-40; William George Clark, 1940-5; David Laurence MacLaren, 1945-58; J.L. O'Brien, 1958-65; J.B. McNair, 1965-8; Wallace S. Bird, 1968-71; Hédard J. Robichaud, 1971- .

Newfoundland. Albert Walsh, Apr.-Sept. 1949; Leonard Outerbridge, 1949-57; Campbell L. Macpherson, 1957-63; Fabian O'Dea, 1963-9; Ewart John Arlington Harnum, 1969-74; Gordon Arnaud Winter, 1974- .

Nova Scotia. F.W. Williams, July-Oct. 1867; C. Hastings Doyle, 1867-73; Joseph Howe, May-July 1873; A.G. Archibald, 1873-83;

Matthew Henry Richey, 1883-8; A.W. McLelan, 1888-90; Malachy Bowes Daly, 1890-1900; A.G. Jones, 1900-6; D.C. Fraser, 1906-10; J.D. McGregor, 1910-15; David MacKeen, 1915-16; MacCallum Grant, 1916-25; James Robson Douglas, Jan.-Oct. 1925; James Cranswick Tory, 1925-30; Frank Stanfield, 1930-1; Walter Harold Covert, 1931-7; Robert Irwin, 1937-40; Frederick Francis Mathers, 1940-2; H.E. Kendall, 1942-7; John Alexander Douglas McCurdy, 1947-52; Allistair Fraser, 1952-8; E.C. Plou, 1958-63; Henry P. MacKeen, 1963-8; Victor de Bedia Oland, 1968-73; Clarence L. Gosse, 1973- .

Ontario. H.W. Stisted, 1867-8; H.P. Howland, 1868-73; John W. Crawford, 1873-5; D.A. Macdonald, 1875-80; John Beverly Robinson, 1880-7; Alexander Campbell, 1887-92; George A. Kirkpatrick, 1892-7; Oliver Mowat, 1897-1903; W. Mortimer Clark, 1903-8; John M. Gibson, 1908-14; John Strathearn Hendrie, 1914-19; Lionel Herbert Clarke, 1919-21; Henry Cockshutt, 1921-7; William Donald Ross, 1927-32; Herbert Alexander Bruce, 1932-7; Albert Matthews, 1937-46; Ray Lawson, 1946-52; Louis Orville Breithaupt, 1952-7; John Keiller MacKay, 1957-63; William Earl Rowe, 1963-8; William Ross MacDonald, 1968-74; Pauline Emily Mills McGibbon, 1974- .

Prince Edward Island. W.C.F. Robinson, 1873-8; Robert Hodson, 1878-9; Thomas T. Haviland, 1879-84; Andrew A. Macdonald, 1884-9; Jedediah S. Carvell, 1889-94; George William Howland, 1894-9; P.A. McIntyre, 1899-1904; D.A. Mackinnon, 1904-10; Benjamin Rogers, 1910-15; Augustine Colin Macdonald, 1915-19; Murdock Mackinnon, 1919-24; Frank Richard Heartz, 1924-30; Charles Dalton, 1930-3; G. des Brisay De Blois, 1933-9; Bradford Lepage, 1939-45; Joseph Alphonsus Bernard, 1945-50; T. William L. Prowse, 1950-8; F.W. Hyndman, 1958-63; William J. MacDonald, 1963-9; J. George MacKay, 1969-74; Gordon Lockhart Bennett, 1974- .

Quebec. N.F. Belleau, 1867-73; René Edouard Caron, 1873-6; Luc Letellier de St Just, 1876-9; Théodore Robitaille, 1879-84; L.F.R. Masson, 1884-7; A.R. Angers, 1887-92; J. Adolphe Chapleau, 1892-8; Louis Amable Jetté, 1898-1908; C.A.P. Pelletier, 1908-11; François Langelier, 1911-15; P.E. LeBlanc, 1915-18; Charles Fitzpatrick, 1918-23; L.P. Brodeur, 1923-4; Narcisse Perodeau, 1924-9; Sir Lomer Gouin, Jan.-Apr. 1929; H.G. Carroll, 1929-34; E.L. Patenaude, 1934-40; Eugène Fiset, 1940-50; Gaspard Fauteux, 1950-8; Onésime Gagnon, 1958-61; Paul Comtois, 1961-6; Hugues Lapointe, 1966- .

Saskatchewan. Amédée Emmanual Forget,

1905-10; George William Brown, 1910-15; Richard Stuart Lake, 1915-21; Henry William Newlands, 1921-31; Hugh Edwin Munroe, 1931-6; Archibald Peter McNab, 1936-45; Thomas Miller, Feb.-June 1945; Reginald John Marsden Parker, 1945-8; John Michael Uhrich, 1948-51; William John Patterson, 1951-8; Frank Lindsay Bastedo, 1958-63; Robert Leith Hanbridge,1963-70; Stephen Worobetz, 1970-

The chief executive officer of a Territory is a COMMISSIONER.

Lieutenant-Governor in Council. The lieutenant-governor acting with the advice and consent of the provincial cabinet·as a formal instrument for legalizing provincial cabinet decisions.

'Lièvre, Morning on the'. See 'MORNING ON THE LIÈVRE'.

'Life in a Prairie Shack'. A song satirizing remittance men on the Prairies in the 1880s. The first verse runs: 'Oh, a life in a prairie shack, when the rain begins to pour!/Drip, drip, it comes through the roof, and some comes through the door./The tenderfoot curses his fate and faintly mutters, "Ah!/This blooming country's a fraud, and I want to go home to my Maw!"'

Life in the Clearings Versus the Bush. Susanna MOODIE'S second book about pioneering in Canada, published in 1853, a year after her ROUGHING IT IN THE BUSH appeared. Written after she moved to Belleville, C.W., where life was less difficult than before, it reflects a change from the critical attitude of her previous book: she came to accept Canadian ways and to admire the country's prospects.

Life Times Nine. A short film produced in 1973 by nine children between the ages of 11 and 16: Jordon Hole, Paul Shapiro, Marilyn Becker, Melissa Franklin, Celia Merker, Andy File, Robi Blumenstein, Kimmie Jensen, and Rick Clark. Asked to sell 'life' as if it were a product, they scripted and directed nine 'commercials for life', using professional technicians. The result was a whimsical film—produced by Pen Densham and edited by John Watson—that won 12 awards, including an Academy Award nomination for the best short film. 15 min., colour.

'Life's Little Pleasures'. See Jimmy FRISE.

Lightfoot, Gordon (b.1939). Singer and composer. Born in Orillia, Ont., he began writing and singing his own country and folk songs in Toronto coffee houses in 1963. Such early hits as 'EARLY MORNIN' RAIN' and 'For Lovin'

Me' were recorded in 1964 and launched perhaps the single most successful career in Canadian popular music. Lightfoot performs to sell-out audiences in both Canada and the United States.

Lighthouse. A popular rock band. The 13-musician rock band, with an electrified string and horn section, was formed by Skip Prokop, a Hamilton-born member of the Paupers, in 1968. The group performed, recorded, and popularized its electric jazz-rock sounds until it broke up in 1975.

Lightstone, Marilyn (b.1940). Actress. Born and raised in Montreal, where she attended Baron Byng High School and McGill University, she is a graduate of the NATIONAL THEATRE SCHOOL (1961-4). She has appeared with the CREST THEATRE'S Hour Company and with the STRATFORD FESTIVAL. Two roles that capitalized on her 'ethnic' looks brought her to national attention. These were Leah in the MANITOBA THEATRE CENTRE'S memorable production of S. Ansky's *The Dybbuk*, directed by John HIRSCH, which opened in Winnipeg on 11 Jan. 1974 and subsequently toured; and the mother in the film LIES MY FATHER TOLD ME (1975), directed by Jan Kadar. She recently performed the one-character play *Miss Margarida* by the Brazilian playwright Roberto Athayde, who translated the Portuguese text for her and directed its English-language première in Toronto on 25 May 1976.

Ligue pour la Défense du Canada, La. See BLOC POPULAIRE CANADIEN.

Like Father, Like Fun. A three-act comedy by Eric NICOL about a father who tries to solve his son's sexual problems. It was well received in Vancouver, Toronto, and Montreal but, retitled *Minor Adjustment*, opened and closed on Broadway on 6 Oct. 1967. Nicol described the episode in *A Scar Is Born* (1968).

Lillian H. Smith Collection of Children's Books. See OSBORNE COLLECTION OF EARLY CHILDREN'S BOOKS.

Lillooet. INTERIOR SALISH Indians of the Lillooet R. basin of British Columbia. The name means 'wild onion'. The Lillooet traded with and were strongly influenced by their Pacific Coast neighbours. Their population in 1970 was 2,494.

Lily, Prairie. A long-petalled, orange-red wild flower, now also common in city gardens. It was adopted as the floral emblem of Saskatchewan in 1941.

Lily, White garden. A long-petalled wild flower. There was considerable controversy

Lily

when it was chosen as the floral emblem of Quebec in 1963, for it is not native to Canada, and the previous provincial flower, the blue iris, is native. But the white garden lily won 'the war of the lilies', for it was seen as 'a symbol of unity with the past'.

Limited. Legal term included in the name of a federally or provincially incorporated company. It gives notice that the obligations of the company are limited to its assets and subscribed capital. The abbreviation is Ltd. The term 'Incorporated' (the abbreviation of which is 'Inc.') is principally used in the United States to indicate the same type of company.

Lindner, Ernest (b.1897). Painter. Born in Vienna, he came to Canada as a farm labourer in 1926 and became head of the Art Department of the Saskatoon Technical College in 1936. His early traditional watercolour studies of nature evolved into finely rendered acrylic and watercolour close-ups of tree stumps, lichen, and vegetation. *Decay and Growth* (1964, Norman MacKenzie Art Gallery) is an example of his concentration on the cyclical process of nature.

Lindsley, Thayer. See FALCONBRIDGE MINERAL MINES LTD.

Line, William (1897-1964). Psychologist. Born in Wycombe, Eng., he was educated at the Universities of Alberta and London. He was professor of psychology at the University of Toronto from 1929 to 1964, introducing several generations of students to his humanistic view of psychology. He established the system of personnel selection and intelligence testing used by the Canadian Army during the Second World War and became a major figure in the development of organizations to promote the application of scholarly humanism to the solution of practical problems, founding the International Institute of Child Study, a UNESCO body, and co-founding the World Federation for Mental Health, of which he was later president.

Lines Vertical. A short film made by Norman McLAREN. Assisted by Evelyn Lambart, McLaren ruled vertical lines directly onto film-stock so that they appear to move against a background of changing colours in response to a musical score by Maurice Blackburn. It was released by the NATIONAL FILM BOARD in 1960. It is frequently shown with *Lines Horizontal,* a sequel released in 1962 for which McLaren and Lambart optically turned each frame of *Lines Vertical* by 90 degrees so that they appear to move to Pete

Seeger's musical score. 5 min. 50 sec.; colour.

Lions Gate Bridge. Graceful mile-long suspension bridge that spans the First Narrows of Burrard Inlet and connects Vancouver with North and West Vancouver. It was opened by King George VI in 1939 and takes its name from the two noble stone lions that guard each end of the bridge.

LIP. Acronym of LOCAL INITIATIVES PROGRAM.

Liquor licences. Licences issued by provincial governments to permit the retail sale of alcoholic beverages. The regulations under which licences are issued vary from province to province, but most provinces permit the sale of spirits by the glass in licensed outlets, and all provinces issue licences to private clubs.

Lisgar, Baron. See Sir John YOUNG.

Lismer, Arthur (1885-1969). Painter, art teacher, and member of the GROUP OF SEVEN. Born in Sheffield, Eng., he studied art there and in Antwerp and in 1911 came to Toronto, where he worked as a designer for Grip Limited. As a member of the Group he was a painter of Georgian Bay and later of Algoma—he is remembered for *A* SEPTEMBER GALE, GEORGIAN BAY (1920, NGC)—but he was best known as a teacher with special skills in teaching art to children. He was vice-principal of the ONTARIO COLLEGE OF ART from 1919 to 1927, when he became education supervisor of the Art Gallery of Toronto (the ART GALLERY OF ONTARIO). He became education supervisor of the Art Association of Montreal (the MONTREAL MUSEUM OF FINE ARTS) in 1940.

Literary Garland. A literary quarterly published in Montreal between 1838 and 1851. 'Entirely the produce of Canadian talent', the genteel magazine attracted such writers as Susanna MOODIE and Major John RICHARDSON.

Literary Lapses. The first of Stephen LEACOCK's celebrated collections of humorous sketches, published in 1910. It includes his best-known piece, 'MY FINANCIAL CAREER'.

Little, Rich (b.1938). 'King of impersonators'. Born in Ottawa, he made his début at 11 and in the early 1960s had his own CBC-TV show on which he developed his impressionistic abilities with political figures. His first album, *My Fellow Canadians* (1963), sold out. In 1964 his appearance with Judy Garland launched his American career. He now lives in Hollywood.

Little Emperor. Sobriquet of Sir George SIMP-SON, the autocratic governor of the HUDSON'S BAY COMPANY from 1826 until his death in 1860.

Little Sticks, Land of the. See LAND OF THE LITTLE STICKS.

Livesay, Dorothy (b.1909). Poet. Born in Winnipeg and educated at the University of Toronto and the Sorbonne, she has been a social worker and teacher of English and creative writing in Zambia (1960-3) as well as Canada. Her work ranges from the short, imagist poems reprinted in *Selected Poems: 1926-1956* (1957), to long reportorial poems such as those collected in *The Documentaries* (1968)—which includes *Call My People Home* (1950) about the evacuation of the JAPA-NESE—to the more personal poems in *Plainsongs* (1969; 1971). Since the appearance of these collections she has published *Disasters of the Sun* (1971), *Collected Poems: Two Seasons* (1972), and *Ice Age* (1976). Her stories were collected in *A Winnipeg Childhood* (1973). She co-edited, with Seymour MAYNE, the anthology *Forty Women Poets of Canada* (1972).

Liveyere. A year-round resident of Labrador or, by extension, of the Newfoundland outports. It might be a contraction of 'live here' or a form of the local English word 'livier' (one who holds a tenement on a lease for a life or lives).

Living and Learning. See the HALL-DENNIS REPORT.

Living tree doctrine, The. A phrase used by Lord Sankey of the JUDICIAL COMMITTEE OF THE PRIVY COUNCIL in the famous PERSONS CASE. In describing the manner of interpreting the BNA ACT, on 18 Oct. 1929, he wrote: 'The *British North America Act* planted in Canada a living tree capable of growth and expansion within its natural limits. The object of the Act was to grant a constitution to Canada. Like all written constitutions it has been subject to development through usage and convention.'

Livres et auteurs québécois. Annual publication devoted to surveys of Quebec books and authors. Edited by Adrien Thério, it has been published in Montreal since 1969.

Ljungh, Esse W. (b.1904). Radio producer. Born in Malmö, Sweden, he settled in western Canada in 1927. He was CBC Radio's drama supervisor in Winnipeg from 1942 to 1946 and network drama supervisor in Toronto from 1946 until his retirement in 1969. He succeeded Andrew ALLAN as the producer of the CBC STAGE series.

Lloyd, Gweneth (b.1901). Ballet teacher and choreographer. Born in Eccles, Eng., she studied at the Ginner-Mawer school in London and opened with her partner, Betty Farrally, the Torch Studio of Dance in Leeds. Coming to Winnipeg in 1938 to start the Canadian School of Ballet, and opening a Sunday-afternoon ballet club for parents and patrons, this hard-driving and prolific teacher soon found she had started the Winnipeg Ballet, Canada's first professional company. She choreographed 35 original, indigenous ballets between 1939 and 1958—notably SHADOW ON THE PRAIRIE—and established the company, which became the ROYAL WINNIPEG BALLET in 1951, as the source of original Canadian ballet choreography. She also founded the ballet division at the Banff School of Fine Arts (BANFF CENTRE) and was its director from 1949 to 1968. A teacher of international renown, she has taught in Kelowna, B.C., since the 1960s.

Loblaw Companies Ltd. A public holding company 80% owned by George Weston Ltd (see W.G. WESTON). It dates back to 1900 when the food merchant T.P. Loblaw (1872-1933) opened his first groceteria in Toronto. Loblaw Companies Ltd operates, through local subsidiaries, chains of retail food outlets that include Loblaws and Zehr's in Ontario; Dionne and Economart in Quebec; Super-Value in British Columbia; Super-Value and Economart in Alberta; O.K. Economy in Saskatchewan; Economart in Manitoba; Atlantic Wholesale (a distributor) in the Maritimes; and Bells and National in the United States. In Oct. 1972 the Ontario subsidiary launched a 'new image' campaign with William SHATNER, who explained that at Loblaws 'More than the price is right'.

Lobster lad. A slang term for a native of PRINCE EDWARD ISLAND.

Lobstick. A tall, conspicuously situated tree with all but its topmost branches stripped or lopped off. 'Lobsticks' or 'lopsticks' were fashioned from spruce or pine trees by northern Indians and later by the voyageurs as talismanic tributes to individuals or as landmarks. Early travellers compared the lobstick to the maypole.

Local Initiatives Program. A program begun in 1971 to create jobs by funding community-improvement plans. Under the LIP plan, local citizens can conceive, organize, and manage a community project for which funds will be provided by the Department of MANPOWER AND IMMIGRATION. In 1975 the program was reduced in size and aimed at high-unemployment areas of the country.

303

Lockheed Lodestar. A propeller-driven aircraft in TCA service from 1941 to 1949. Built by Lockheed Aircraft in the United States, these 14-seat aircraft were modified to carry an additional gross weight of 1,000 lbs and could fly a distance of 2,000 mi. at 200 m.p.h.

Lockheed Super Constellation. A four-prop passenger aircraft widely used by TCA from 1954 to 1962. It was manufactured by Lockheed Aircraft in the United States and carried 68 passengers at 315 m.p.h.

Logan-Hubbard Icefield. A glacier-group in the southwestern Yukon, extending into western Alaska, which tops the St Elias Range. Broken only by Canada's highest mountain peaks, these ice-sheets form the largest and most visually impressive glacier-span on mainland North America. Owing to their inaccessibility to all but mountaineers, they have not become as widely known as much lesser glacier fields farther south.

Loganberry. A hybrid of the blackberry and raspberry. It grows plentifully in only three places: a southern part of Vancouver Island, Tasmania, and South Africa. About 75% of the annual British Columbia crop is used for loganberry wine.

Lombardo, Carmen (1901-71). Songwriter and musical director of The Royal Canadians. Born in London, Ont., the brother of Guy LOMBARDO, he was the author of such hit songs as 'Sweethearts on Parade', 'You're the Sweetest Girl This Side of Heaven', 'It Seems Like Old Times', and 'Powder Your Face with Sunshine'.

Lombardo, Guy (b.1902). Leader of The Royal Canadians. Born in London, Ont., he formed in 1921 the Canadians, a jazz band, with his three brothers Carmen (flute), Liebert (trumpet), and Victor (saxophone); Guy himself played the violin. The name was changed to the 'Royal Canadians' after the crack Canadian Regiment (not the Mounted Police). In 1928 Ashton Stevens, a Chicago critic, described the group as 'the softest and sweetest jazzmen on any stage this side of heaven'. This was simplified for promotion purposes to 'the sweetest music this side of heaven'. Lombardo's band played at the Roosevelt Hotel in New York from 1929 to 1959 and—playing at the Waldorf Astoria, New York, on New Year's Eve—has greeted the New Year annually on North American television since 1960.

London, George (b.1920). Bass. Born George Burnstein in Montreal, he moved with his family to Los Angeles in 1937. He studied singing there and in New York and in the 1940s began a career that was to make him one of the leading operatic basses of his time. He was a member of the Vienna Opera from 1949 to 1964 and of the Metropolitan Opera, New York, from 1951 to 1965 and made many recordings. His notable roles were Boris Godunov (which he sang with the Bolshoi Opera in 1960), Don Giovanni, and Wotan. He is now artistic administrator of Washington's John F. Kennedy Centre for the Performing Arts.

London Conference. A conference held in London, Eng., in Dec. 1866 and chaired by John A. MACDONALD. At these meetings CONFEDERATION was given final form, the name 'Dominion of Canada' was chosen for the new country, and its framework was established. The BNA ACT was passed by the British Parliament on 8 May 1867.

'London Letter'. General title of a series of columns written by the Toronto-born British MP Sir Beverley Baxter (1891-1964) in England and published in MACLEAN'S from 1935 to 30 July 1960. Baxter dropped names of notables, promoted appeasement, dramatized the war effort, extolled the virtues of the monarchy, and informed Canadians generally about British character and institutions.

London Six. Automobile manufactured by London Motors, London, Ont., from 1921 to 1925. It had a six-cylinder engine and came as a sedan, a roadster, a convertible, and perhaps the continent's first metal hardtop.

'Lone Shieling, The'. See CANADIAN BOAT SONGS.

'Lonely Land, The'. A much-anthologized poem about Canada by A.J.M. SMITH. It first appeared in the McGILL FORTNIGHTLY REVIEW in Jan. 1926 and was revised for its appearance in the CANADIAN FORUM in July 1929. It was published in a new form in the *Dial* of June 1929 and since then has been revised further. The memorable last stanza is: 'This is the beauty/of strength/broken by strength/and still strong.'

Lonergan, Bernard (b.1904). Jesuit theologian. Born in Buckingham, Que., he entered the Society of Jesus in 1922. The widely honoured scholar teaches at Regis College, Toronto, and is the author of numerous studies of Aquinas and other thinkers. His *Collected Papers* appeared in 1967.

Long Point Company. A sportsmen's hideaway. This exclusive Ontario club, owned by a group of North American business executives, is located on the Long Point peninsula, which juts out from the north shore of Lake Erie. There are only 20 members, each of whom has his own lodge on the grounds.

Long Range Mountains. A chain of rugged forested peaks running the length of western Newfoundland and still inaccessible in many areas. See also WESTERN BROOK POND.

Long Sault. New community near Cornwall, Ont. It was created from the former communities of Milles Roches and Moulinette as a result of flooding the 9-mi. Long Sault Rapids in the St Lawrence R. for the ST LAWRENCE SEAWAY. See also DOLLARD DES ORMEAUX.

Longboat, Tom (1887-1949). Indian athlete. An Onondaga Indian who was born on the Six Nations Reserve near Brantford, Ont., he was a long-distance runner and in 1906 performed the remarkable feat of outrunning a horse over a 12-mi. course. The following year he won the 25-mi. Boston marathon in record time. He turned professional and ran his last important race in 1912, setting a new record. He served during the First World War with distinction in the Sportsmen's Battalion and died on the Six Nations Reserve where he was born.

Longboat Memorial Trophy, The Tom. See SPORTS FEDERATION OF CANADA.

Longden, Johnny (b.1910). Famous jockey. Born in England, he was brought to Tabor, Alta, at the age of two. At 13 he worked in coal mines but also rode horses at local fall fairs. In 1926 he began riding full time in the United States, where he was so successful that, in 1943, he rode Count Fleet, a notable TRIPLE CROWN winner. He retired in 1966, having ridden over 6,000 winners.

Long-distance telephone. See Alexander Graham BELL.

Longest undefended border in the world. Rhetorical reference to the Canadian-American BORDER. It was used admiringly in the 1920s and derisively in the 1960s.

Longhouse. A communal dwelling and council chamber erected by IROQUOIS tribes and HURONS; it was also used for political and religious gatherings. It was long and narrow and had a semi-circular roof. The longest known was 1,000 ft.

Longhouse Bookshop. First retail outlet to devote itself exclusively to Canadian books. This Toronto store was founded by Dutch-born Beth Appeldoorn and Toronto-born Susan Sandler and opened its doors on 11 Mar. 1972. Longhouse carries 17,500 Cana-

dian titles, in addition to a selection of children's books from around the world.

Longueuil, Barony of. Ancient and still-existing Canadian barony. The first Baron of Longueuil, created by Louis XIV in 1700, was Charles LE MOYNE. The title passed to the Grant Family in 1781. Queen Victoria gave it official recognition in 1881.

Look of Books Award, The. Annual awards for the best-designed books published the previous year in Canada. Sponsored by the Canadian Book Design Committee Inc., the NATIONAL DESIGN COUNCIL, and the Federal Department of Industry, Trade and Commerce, the Awards recognize design achievement in the Canadian book industry. The first competition was held in 1970. Cash awards to designers—first prize, $1,500; second, $1,000; third, $500—were instituted in 1974.

Looking Through the Papers. See CAPITAL REPORT.

Loon. One of several species of diving birds, four of which are native to Canada. The common loon has a black back spotted with white; an incomplete white colour with a white bar across the throat; and a greenish-black head that turns dark grey in winter. Its haunting, piercing call, like a lament, is heard over many northern lakes.

Loon's Necklace, The. A popular short feature produced by Crawley Films for IMPERIAL OIL LIMITED. It was directed by F.R. CRAWLEY, edited by Judith Crawley, scripted by Douglas Leechman, with camerawork and animation by Graham Crabtree, and released in 1950. Authentic ceremonial masks, carved by west-coast Indians, are the 'actors' in this retelling of the Indian legend of how the loon, the beautiful water bird, received its distinguishing neckband. *The Loon's Necklace* makes use of masks in the same manner that the LEGEND OF THE RAVEN makes use of soapstone carvings. 11 min., 16 mm, colour.

Loose fish. Phrase used by Sir John A. MACDONALD to describe members of Parliament not subject to party discipline. See also TRAINED SEALS.

Lorcini, Gino (b.1923). Sculptor. Born in Plymouth, Eng., he came to Canada in 1947 and studied at the Montreal Museum of Fine Arts School before teaching at McGill University. He lives in Montreal and is represented in collections across Canada. Cubistic structurist forms dominate his work, which has evolved from painted wood reliefs to polished-aluminum and stainless-steel geometric shapes often piled on one another. His classical sense of design, emphasizing planes and angles, is represented by the aluminum rectangles of his mural for the National Arts Centre in Ottawa (1968).

Lord, Jean-Claude (b.1943). Quebec film director. Born in Montreal, he directed his first feature, *Délivrez-nous du mal*, in 1965, and then worked on various projects before directing *Les Colombes* (1972). He is identified with the popular political-exploitation film BINGO (1974).

Lord and lady. Fanciful folkname of the harlequin duck, an allusion to its handsome plumage.

Lord Beaverbrook Scholarships. Academic scholarships tenable at the UNIVERSITY OF NEW BRUNSWICK. Ten scholarships, valued at $4-5,000 ($1,000 a year), are awarded annually to male and female undergraduates for four to five years' study in any discipline. They are granted for scholastic attainment, moral character, and financial need. In addition, the Lord BEAVERBROOK Scholarships in Law, valued at a maximum of $2,500 a year for three years, are awarded to male and female graduates who intend studying law at UNB. Both scholarships were established under the Beaverbrook Canadian Foundation.

Lord Strathcona's Horse. Canadian regiment. It originated with the 'A' squadron of 'The Canadian Mounted Rifles' in 1901 and was first redesignated its present name in 1911 to perpetuate an army regiment that served in the SOUTH AFRICAN WAR. During the FIRST WORLD WAR it served as infantry with the 1st Canadian Division in 1915, and later in the Canadian Cavalry Brigade, distinguishing itself at the SOMME in 1916. In the SECOND WORLD WAR it fought as a unit of the 5th Armoured Brigade in numerous battles in Italy. Squadrons of the regiment have also served in Korea, Germany, and the Middle East.

Lord's Day, The. Sunday, the 'day of rest'. The Lord's Day Alliance was founded in 1888 by interdenominational Christian groups to preserve Sunday as a day of rest. The Lord's Day Act, to prevent non-essential commerce and commercial entertainment on Sunday, was passed by the federal government in 1906. During the 1960s it was liberalized to permit commerce and entertainment on Sundays.

Lorimer, James (b.1942). Writer and publisher. Born in Regina, he is a graduate of the London School of Economics. In 1970 he established a publishing house in Toronto, now called JAMES LORIMER & COMPANY. A radical nationalist, he is the author of the *The Real World of City Politics* (1970); *Working People: Life in a Downtown City Neighbourhood* (1971), illustrated with photographs by his wife Myfanwy Phillips; *A Citizen's Guide to City Politics* (1972); and *The Ex: A Picture History of the Canadian National Exhibition* (1973).

Loring, Frances (1881-1968). Sculptor. Born in Wardnor, Idaho, she studied in Europe. In 1913 she opened a studio in Toronto and was joined by her friend Florence WYLE; the two sculptors, known as 'the Girls', eventually moved into a converted church, which was much visited by creative Torontonians. Loring preferred to work on large-scale pieces and accepted many commissions for monuments and portrait sculptures, including the war memorial for Osgoode Hall, Toronto; the stone lion at the entrance to the Queen Elizabeth Way, Toronto; and the Sir Robert BORDEN Monument in Ottawa. She was a founding member of the Sculptors Society of Canada in 1928.

Loring Lion. Large cement statue of a noble lion that guarded the eastern approach to the Queen Elizabeth Way from 1939 to 1973. The imperial-looking beast, sculpted by Frances LORING, was moved to nearby Lakefront Park, Toronto, to permit the widening of the highway.

Lorne, Lord (1845-1914). GOVERNOR GENERAL of Canada from 1878 to 1883.

Lorne Building. An office building in downtown Ottawa built in 1958, the temporary quarters for the NATIONAL GALLERY OF CANADA. It was named after Lord LORNE.

Lorne Pierce Medal. It is awarded every two years by the ROYAL SOCIETY OF CANADA for an achievement of special significance and conspicuous merit in imaginative or critical literature, written in either English or French, with special attention given to Canadian subjects. The award was established in 1926 by the distinguished editor Lorne PIERCE and consists of a gold medal and $1,000.

Lotteries, Canadian. Illegal until 1 Jan. 1970, the first sweepstakes were introduced into Canada when Mayor Jean DRAPEAU, to help Montreal finance its OLYMPIC GAMES, launched in 1968 his so-called 'voluntary tax contribution'—a lottery in all but name. This was so successful that federal legislation was passed to legalize lotteries and Quebec began to operate both the Olympic Lottery and Loto-Québec (with tickets ranging in value from Loto-Perfecta through Mini-Loto and Inter-Loto to Super Loto). Manitoba launched the Western Canadian Lottery in

1975 and Ontario its Wintario in 1975. Other provinces and regions followed suit with lotteries that pay out approximately 35% of their revenue in prizes.

Lou Marsh Trophy, The. A silver memorial cup awarded to Canada's most outstanding male or female athlete (amateur or professional) of the year. It is named after Lou Marsh, a longtime sports editor for the *Toronto Star*. The winner, announced each December, is selected by a committee of five sports editors chaired by Harry (Red) Foster (see FOSTER ADVERTISING LTD). It was first presented in 1936.

Louis Riel. Opera by Harry SOMERS, based on the fall of Louis RIEL, the Métis leader. With a libretto by Mavor MOORE, French passages by Jacques LANGUIRAND, and the leading role sung by Bernard TURGEON, it was given its première, to much acclaim, by the CANADIAN OPERA COMPANY at the O'KEEFE CENTRE, Toronto, on 23 Sept. 1967. In 1975 it was revived in Toronto and was also performed at the Kennedy Centre, Washington. It was commissioned by the Floyd S. Chalmers Foundation, with the assistance of the Centennial Commission and the CANADA COUNCIL.

Loucheux. See KUTCHIN.

Louisbourg. Huge walled French fortress near the eastern tip of Île-Royale (Cape Breton, N.S.). Begun in 1713, the garrison at one time had some 5,000 men and was the largest in North America. It was captured by New England forces in 1745, returned to France in 1748, and retaken by British forces under Jeffrey Amherst in 1758. It was destroyed in 1760. A massive reconstruction project, begun in 1961, will recreate and refurnish 50 buildings by 1980—about one-fifth of the garrison area and town. Most of the 45 buildings already completed have nothing to do with the military, but include inns, shops, and residences. Set in 20 sq. mi., it is part of the Fortress of Louisbourg National Historic Park.

Louisiana. One of the United States of America. The vast territory that includes the present state was named by LA SALLE in 1682, colonized by d'IBERVILLE in 1699, and settled between 1760 and 1790 by the influx of ACADIANS or Cajuns. France sold the land to the United States in 1803 for approximately $15 million. The Louisiana Purchase doubled the size of the American republic and left France bereft of North American possessions except for the islands of ST PIERRE AND MIQUELON.

Louisiana Purchase. See LOUISIANA.

Lount, Samuel (1791-1838). Rebel. Born in Pennsylvania, he settled in Simcoe County, U.C. (Ont.), in 1811 and became a blacksmith. He sat in the legislative assembly from 1834 to 1836. A supporter of William Lyon MACKENZIE in the REBELLION OF 1837, he was in charge of a contingent of men who rendezvoused at MONTGOMERY'S TAVERN and took part in the skirmish north of York (Toronto) on 6 Dec. 1837. He was captured, tried for treason, and hanged—with Peter Mathews—on 12 Apr. 1838.

Loup-garou, Le. French for 'werewolf'. Legends about loups-garous were popular during the eighteenth and nineteenth centuries in French Canada, where werewolves were sometimes described as men cursed or punished for not having been to confession for 10 years. The curse was supposed to be lifted or the punishment ended with the shedding of blood or a religious exorcism.

Love and Libel. See LEAVEN OF MALICE.

Love and Maple Syrup. 'A Canadian musical entertainment' based on poems and songs by Canadian writers. The material was adapted by the performer Louis Negin for a production in London, Eng., in Jan. 1968. It was revised and produced at the NATIONAL ARTS CENTRE, Ottawa, from 8 Sept. to 3 Oct. 1970, and subsequently toured.

Loved and the Lost, The. Novel by Morley CALLAGHAN published in 1951. It contrasts the worlds of industrial power and academia with the Black cabaret life of Montreal, which attracts the novel's heroine, Peggy Sanderson. Her rejection of social conventions is continually thwarted. She cannot be saved from herself by Jim McAlpine, a former professor who became a newspaper columnist, and their story ends with her death.

Low, Colin (b.1926). Film director. Born in Cardston, Alta, he joined the NATIONAL FILM BOARD as an animator in 1945. He was associated with UNIT B and the CHALLENGE FOR CHANGE project, and with Roman KROITER produced LABYRINTH, the NFB's contribution to EXPO 67. Among his best-known films are *Corral* (1953), CITY OF GOLD (with Wolf KOENIG, 1957), UNIVERSE (with Roman Kroiter, 1960), *The Days of Whiskey Gap* (1961), and *The Winds of Fogo* (1970). Through Memorial University's Extension Department, he produced 28 community-affairs films as part of the FOGO Island Project, calling for social action in Newfoundland.

'Low Tide on Grand Pré'. Title poem of Bliss CARMAN's first poetry collection, published in 1893. With its sensitivity to landscape and mastery of metre and diction, it has remained the best known of the nature lyrics on which the poet's reputation rests.

Lower, A.R.M. (b.1899). Historian. Born in Barrie, Ont., and educated at the University of Toronto and Harvard, he taught history at United College, Winnipeg, and since 1944, at Queen's University, where he is Professor Emeritus. His two most widely read books— COLONY TO NATION: *A History of Canada* (1946; rev. 1964), on the development of Canada as a national community, and *Canadians in the Making: A Social History of Canada* (1958), on the characteristic attitudes of Canadians in the past—respectively exemplify his nationalistic concerns and his personal approach to history writing, which he laces with opinions, anecdotes, and witticisms. His other books include *The Most Famous Stream: The Liberal Democratic Way of Life* (1954); *Great Britain's Woodyard: British America and the Timber Trade, 1763-1867* (1973), a culmination of 35 years' interest in the subject; and *My First Seventy-Five Years* (1968), an autobiography. W.H. Heick edited his occasional papers: *History and Myth: Arthur Lower and the Making of Canadian Nationalism* (1975).

Lower Canada. The area east of the Ottawa River—present-day Quebec—formed by the CONSTITUTIONAL ACT OF 1791. Lower Canada became CANADA EAST in 1841 as a result of the ACT OF UNION; it became Quebec in 1867.

Lower Chamber. See HOUSE OF COMMONS.

Lower Fort Garry. Former HUDSON'S BAY COMPANY post on the west bank of the Red R., about 19 mi. north of Winnipeg. Built between 1831 and 1833 to replace FORT GARRY, it was the most elaborate of the Company's posts and served as its headquarters from 1832 to 1837. A reconstruction of the fort stands in Lower Fort Garry National Park at Selkirk, Man.

Lower house. Members of a legislature elected to govern a colony or a country. In colonial times the lower house was known as the LEGISLATIVE ASSEMBLY, the name still used to describe the legislatures of seven provinces (in two provinces, Nova Scotia and Newfoundland, the legislature is known as the HOUSE OF ASSEMBLY and in Quebec as the ASSEMBLÉE NATIONALE). Since Confederation the lower house of the federal Parliament has been known as the HOUSE OF COMMONS. See also UPPER HOUSE.

Lower Town. The area of a town nearest the waterfront and often the oldest. Quebec City's Lower Town, where its earliest settlement began, includes business and industrial sections. Ottawa's Lower Town is the French section below the junction of the Rideau Canal and the Ottawa R. See also UPPER TOWN.

Lowry, Malcolm (1909-57). Novelist. Born in Birkenhead, Eng., he graduated from Cambridge in 1932 and was encouraged to write by the American poet and novelist Conrad Aiken. He based his first novel, *Ultramarine* (1933), on the experience of shipping aboard a freighter bound for the Orient at the age of 19. He travelled widely in Europe and the United States, and a short stay in Mexico in 1936 inspired the hallucinatory passages of his famous novel, UNDER THE VOLCANO (1947), which is about the murder of an alcoholic British consul and at the same time is a surreal expression of the darker aspects of Mexican, and human, existence. He moved to Canada in 1939 and lived with his second wife, Margerie Bonner—whom he married in 1940—mainly in a beach shack at Dollarton, outside Vancouver. The Lowrys left Canada in 1954 and Lowry died in his sleep in England, leaving behind manuscripts that were assembled by his widow and published posthumously. These are: *Hear Us O Lord from Heaven Thy Dwelling Place* (1961), *Lunar Caustic* (1963), *Dark as the Grave Wherein My Friend is Laid* (1968), and *October Ferry to Gabriola* (1970). Earle BIRNEY edited Lowry's *Selected Poems* (1962) and Harvey Breit and Margerie Bonner Lowry the *Selected Letters* (1965).

Lowther, Pat (1935-75). Poet. Born in Vancouver, she wrote *This Difficult Flowring* (1968), *The Age of the Bird* (1972), and *Milk Stone* (1974). She had begun a one-year teaching appointment at the University of British Columbia, was co-chairman of the LEAGUE OF CANADIAN POETS, and was on the verge of wide public recognition for *A Stone Diary*, which had been accepted for publication, when she was murdered in Sept. 1975. The assured and memorable poems in *A Stone Diary* contain perceptions of violence that are both ironic and sad in view of her tragic death.

Loyal True Blue Association. Fraternal organization for Protestant men and women. Founded in Toronto in 1867 as Canadian True Blue, it acquired its present name four years later. It maintains three orphanages and shares with The Loyal Orange Association of British America the desire for the 'entire separation of Church and State'.

Loyalist City. Unofficial motto of Saint John, N.B., which was settled by LOYALISTS in 1783.

Loyalist Province, The. A reference to New Brunswick, which was first settled by LOYALISTS.

Loyalists. Citizens of the Thirteen Colonies who immigrated to the provinces of BRITISH NORTH AMERICA during or immediately after the American Revolution of 1775-83. Those who had arrived by 1783 were given the name United Empire Loyalists, which passed to their descendants; those who arrived after 1783 were called 'Late Loyalists'. It has been estimated that 60,000 Loyalists settled in Canada, 5,000 in the West Indies, and 5,000 in Great Britain.

Loyola College. See CONCORDIA UNIVERSITY.

LPRT. Initials of the Low Power Relay Transmitter, a small unmanned radio station employed by CBC Radio to relay but not originate broadcasts to a specific isolated area.

LRC. A high-speed inter-city passenger train whose name stands for Light, Rapid, and Comfortable. It was developed jointly by three Canadian companies between 1968 and 1975 and tested by CN on its Sarnia-Toronto run on 3 Mar. 1975; it ceased operation on 7 Nov. 1975. Combining a low-profile design with an innovative 'banking' system that allowed it to take curves at high speeds, the LRC reached a top speed of 90 m.p.h. Its purchase, for use by CN, is being considered by the federal government.

LS. Official abbreviation of Leading Seaman.

LSA. Abbreviation of LEAGUE FOR SOCIALIST ACTION.

LSM. Initials of Letter Sorting Machines, used by the Post Office to sort electronically 23,500 letters an hour. Envelopes that do not meet standard dimensions are rejected by the machine and are hand-sorted at a slower rate.

LSR. See LEAGUE FOR SOCIAL RECONSTRUCTION.

Lt. Official abbreviation of Lieutenant.

Lt/Cmdr. Official abbreviation of Lieutenant-Commander.

Lt(N). Official abbreviation of Lieutenant (Naval) after UNIFICATION.

Luc, Frère (1614-85). Painter and architect in New France. Born Claude François in Amiens, France, he became a court painter and, in 1645, a Recollet friar. In 1670 he went to Quebec, where he drew the plans for the chapel of the Recollet monastery and painted the *Assomption* (1671) for the retable, which still stands in the Hôpital-Général. It is the only surviving work, of the many attributed to Frère Luc, that he definitely completed in New France. Other religious paintings for churches there were executed in France. The widely reproduced FRANCE BRINGING THE FAITH TO THE INDIANS OF NEW FRANCE (*c*.1675) is merely attributed to him. Frère Luc returned to France after 15 months.

Luck of Ginger Coffey, The. Feature film produced by Crawley Films, directed by Irwin Kerschner, and released in 1964. It was based on Brian MOORE's novel of the same name about an Irish immigrant in Montreal who wants to be a newspaperman above everything else. It starred Robert Shaw and Mary Ure and was a critical though not a commercial success (86 min., b & w.). Raymond Pannell's opera of the same name, with a libretto by Ronald Hambleton, was commissioned and produced in 1967 by the CANADIAN OPERA COMPANY.

Lucy (b.1915). Eskimo graphic artist at CAPE DORSET. She is best known for her prints of fanciful birds and whimsical flower designs done in bright colours.

Ludwig, Jack (b.1922). Novelist and journalist. Born in Winnipeg, he was educated at the University of Manitoba and UCLA and has taught for many years at the State University of New York. His lively and humorous novels about people with cultural and identity problems include *Confusions* (1963), *Above Ground* (1968), and *A Woman of Her Age* (1973). His fascination with the macho aspects of the sports world is evident in his reportage: *Hockey Night in Moscow* (1972), illustrated with cartoons by Christopher MOSHER; *Games of Fear and Winning: Sports with an Inside View* (1976); and *American Spectaculars* (1976).

Luktak (b.1928). Eskimo artist and printmaker at CAPE DORSET. He cuts and prints his own designs and is the son of KIAKSHUK.

Lumberman's strawberries. See CPR STRAWBERRIES.

Luncheon Date. CBC-TV's 60-minute five-day-a-week noon-hour interview show. Hosted by Elwood Glover (who was born in Moose Jaw in 1915), it started in 1956 as a radio program, switched to television in 1963, and finally signed off on 27 June 1975. Glover interviewed some 11,000 celebrity guests on this program.

Lund, Alan and **Blanche.** Dance team and choreographers. Born in Toronto in the

1920s, they were married in 1944. They were the first English-Canadian performers to sign a CBC-TV contract in May 1952, the year they began choreographing the CNE GRANDSTAND SHOWS. Alan Lund has been associated with the CHARLOTTETOWN SUMMER FESTIVAL since its founding and has been artistic director since 1968. They head the Alan and Blanche Lund School of Dance in Toronto.

Lundy's Lane, Battle of. An engagement in the WAR OF 1812 on the Niagara Peninsula, about a mile below the Falls. Both sides lost heavily in the two battles on 24-5 July 1814, when Gen. Gordon Drummond and Gen. Phineas Riall checked the advance of the American forces under Gen. Jacob Brown. The contest was inconclusive, but the Americans withdrew to FORT ERIE.

Lunge. See MASKINONGE.

Luscombe, George. See TORONTO WORKSHOP PRODUCTIONS.

Lyle, John M. (1872-1946). Architect. Born in Belfast, he was brought to Hamilton in 1877 and was trained at the Hamilton and then the Yale Art School, at the École des Beaux-Arts in Paris, and in the New York firm of Carrère and Hastings (1893-1907). He moved to Toronto, where his buildings included the ROYAL ALEXANDRA THEATRE (1907), UNION STATION (1913-20), and the original designs for the Bank of Nova Scotia at 44 King St W. (1929), built in 1949-51. He also designed the War Memorial Arch at the Royal Military College, Kingston (1921), and the Bank of Nova Scotia offices in Ottawa (1924), Calgary (1929), and Halifax (1937). His architecture developed towards a strong and simplified classicism.

Lyman, John (1886-1967). Painter. Born in Biddeford, Maine, but raised in Montreal, he studied art in Paris, working with Matisse for six months. He returned to Montreal and exhibited there—revealing his outstanding gifts as a bold, tasteful figure painter—but lived abroad from 1913 to 1931. He wrote a discerning art column for the *Montrealer* (1936-40), founded an organization of eastern artists, the CONTEMPORARY ART SOCIETY (1937-45), and taught in the Fine Art Department of McGill University from 1948 to 1957. One of his finest paintings is *Lady With a White Collar* (1936, NGC).

Lyon, George Seymour (1858-1938). Champion golfer. Born in the Toronto area, he excelled as a youth in a number of sports and represented Canada internationally in cricket. He began playing golf at 38 and proceeded to win many Canadian amateur titles. He won the golf championship in the 1904 Olympic Games at St Louis, defeating both the English and the American champion to be recognized as the world's best amateur golfer. In later years he was hailed as 'Canada's Great Old Man of Golf'.

Lyric Arts Trio. Chamber-music ensemble. Organized in Toronto in 1965 by flutist Robert AITKEN, with soprano Mary MORRISON and pianist Marion Ross, it specializes in unusual instrumental and vocal music, while performing chamber music of all periods and works commissioned from Canadian composers.

M

Mac-Paps, The. The popular name of the MACKENZIE-PAPINEAU BATTALION.

McArthur, Dan C. See DAN McARTHUR AWARDS.

McArthur, Peter (1866-1924). Author. Born in Ekfrid Township, Middlesex County, C.W. (Ont.), he attended the University of Toronto and worked in New York and London as a writer specializing in humorous sketches. Retiring in 1908 to a farm in Ekfrid Township, where he was known as the 'Sage of Ekfrid', he contributed humorous columns about the pastoral life to the Toronto *Globe* and the *Farmer's Advocate* that were collected in many volumes. Alex Lucas edited *The Best of Peter McArthur* (1967), which shows the author to be an aphorist of note.

MacAskill, Angus (1825-63). 'The Cape Breton Giant'. Born in Scotland, MacAskill was brought as a child to St Anne's, Cape Breton, and grew to a height of 7 ft 9 in. and a weight of 400 lb. Well known in his day, he is recalled as the subject of *The Cape Breton Giant: A Truthful Memoir* (1899), an inadvertently amusing biography by James P. GILLIS.

MacBlo. See MacMILLAN BLOEDEL LTD.

McBride, T.J. See VISTA-DOME CAR.

MacCallum, Dr James M. (1860-1943). Art patron. Born in Richmond Hill, Ont., he was a professor of pharmacology and then of ophthalmology at the University of Toronto while maintaining a private practice as an eye specialist. As a member of the ARTS AND LETTERS CLUB, Toronto, he met Lawren HARRIS around 1910 and through him other painters who would later be identified with the GROUP OF SEVEN. They were brought together by MacCallum's interest in painting and the artists' interest in northern Ontario, where MacCallum had a cottage on an island at Go Home Bay in the Georgian Bay region that he made available to his friends. Joining with Harris in erecting the STUDIO BUILDING, Toronto, he offered A.Y. JACKSON and Tom THOMSON space in it and guaranteed sales for a year. He bequeathed 134 paintings by Group members and others to the NATIONAL GALLERY OF CANADA.

McCarthy, D'Alton. See EQUAL RIGHTS ASSOCIATION, JESUITS' ESTATES ACT.

McCarthyites. See EQUAL RIGHTS ASSOCIATION.

McClelland, J.G. See McCLELLAND AND STEWART LIMITED.

McClelland and Stewart Limited. A leading trade and educational publishing house. Founded in Toronto in 1906 as a library supply house by John McClelland and Frederick Goodchild, former employees of the Methodist Book Room (later the RYERSON PRESS), it published its first book, John D. Rockefeller's *Random Reminiscences of Men and Friends*, in 1909. George Stewart joined the firm in 1914 and the company name was altered to McClelland, Goodchild & Stewart; so it remained until 1918, when Goodchild resigned and the company became simply McClelland & Stewart. In the early years the firm published such authors as Bliss CARMAN, Ralph CONNOR, Frederick Philip GROVE, Stephen LEACOCK, and Thomas H. RADDALL. An educational department was established in 1946. The NEW CANADIAN LIBRARY, the first Canadian quality paperback series, was launched in 1958. Under the supervision of the Institute of Canadian Studies at Carleton University, the CARLETON LIBRARY series of paperbacks in the humanities and social sciences

was initiated in 1963. Other M&S series include the CANADIAN CENTENARY SERIES (a comprehensive 18-volume history of Canada edited by W.L. MORTON and Donald CREIGHTON), the Canadian Centennial Library, the Canadian Illustrated Library, Canadian Favourites, and Canadian Classics, etc. These projects developed under the presidency of J.G. (Jack) McClelland, son of the founder. Born in Toronto in 1922, and president since 1954, he has aggressively promoted books by such authors as Margaret ATWOOD, Pierre BERTON, Leonard COHEN, Margaret LAURENCE, Irving LAYTON, Farley MOWAT, Peter C. NEWMAN, and Mordecai RICHLER. In 1971 M&S accepted a loan of close to $1 million, backed by the Ontario government, when the possibility of its sale was raised. This crisis—coming on the heels of the sale of the RYERSON PRESS to McGRAW-HILL and the purchase of W.J. GAGE LTD by Scott, Foresman and Company of Chicago—precipitated the appointment of the Ontario Royal Commission on Book Publishing.

McClung, Nellie L. (1873-1951). Feminist and author. Born in Chatsworth, Ont., and raised in the Souris Valley, Man., she was educated at the Winnipeg Normal School and taught school until 1898, when she married a Manitoba druggist and raised a family of five children. A popular and fiery lecturer, she took an active part in the work of the WCTU and in the struggle for legal and political equality for women. She was one of five Manitoba women to petition the government on the PERSONS CASE. The family moved to Alberta and she sat in the provincial legislature from 1921 to 1926. She spent her declining years in Victoria. As a writer she was lively, vivid, often sentimental—and widely read. Her principal novel is her first, *Sowing Seeds in Danny* (1908). Three autobiographical books—*In Times Like These* (1913), *Clearing in the West* (1935), and *The Stream Runs Fast* (1945)—give a good insight into the contemporary suffragette movement. The latter work includes details on the MOCK PARLIAMENT, when McClung ridiculed the position taken by Sir Rodmond Roblin, premier of Manitoba, at the Walker Theatre, Winnipeg, on 28 Jan. 1914.

McClure, Sir Robert. See NORTHWEST PASSAGE.

McColl-Frontenac Oil Company Limited. A Canadian-owned company that flourished from 1927 to 1959. Its history dates back to the partnership in 1873 of John B. McColl and William Anderson, manufacturers in Toronto of 'lubricating and fine illuminating oils'. The firm became McColl Brothers Limited in 1918 and sold oils, paints, varnishes, and gasoline nationally. In 1927 it merged with Frontenac Refineries Limited, a two-year-old Montreal company that sold a no-knock motor fuel called 'Cyclo Gasoline'. As McColl-Frontenac Oil Company Limited it sold 'Red Indian'-brand gasoline and lubricating oils from coast to coast. Controlling interests passed to an American company—what is now Texaco Inc.—in 1938, and within two years it was selling 'Sky Chief' products. The first fully integrated oil company in Canada, it was bought outright by the American company and renamed Texaco Canada Limited on 2 Feb. 1959.

McConnell, Rob (b.1935). Jazz trombonist, arranger, composer, and conductor. Born in Toronto, he studied under Gordon DELAMONT and in 1958 began a musical career that ranked him alongside Moe KOFFMAN and Guido BASSO. In 1968 he formed the Boss Brass, which plays popular songs to modified jazz and rock rhythms.

McConnell Foundation, The J.W. It was established in Montreal in 1936 by J.W. McConnell, publisher of the *Montreal Star*, to assist charities, education, health, social development, and the humanities.

McCord Museum. Non-profit general museum governed by McGill University and the Montreal Museum of Fine Arts. It was founded in 1919 on a gift of drawings, paintings, and objects relating to Canadian history donated to the university by David Ross McCord (1844-1930), a Montreal lawyer. Its collection includes Canadian ethnology, fine arts, costumes, toys, documents, and a reference library. Also part of the museum is the NOTMAN Photographic Archives.

McCourt, Edward (1907-72). Writer and teacher. Born in Ireland, he was brought to Canada in 1909. He was educated at the University of Alberta and Oxford and taught at the University of Saskatchewan from 1944 until his retirement. He wrote five prairie novels: *Music at the Close* (1947), *Home is the Stranger* (1950), *Walk Through the Valley* (1958), *The Wooden Sword* (1956), and *Fasting Friar* (1963). Among his non-fiction works are *The Canadian West in Fiction* (1949; rev. 1970); *Remember Butler* (1967), a biography of the author of *The* GREAT LONE LAND; and three travel books: *The Road Across Canada* (1965), *Saskatchewan* (1968), and *The Yukon and Northwest* (1969).

McCrea, John (1872-1918). Soldier and poet. Born in Guelph, Ont., and educated in medicine at the University of Toronto, he was a pathologist at the Montreal General Hospital when he enlisted to serve in the South African War (1899-1902). An assistant physician at the Royal Victoria Hospital and the author of *A Text-Book of Pathology* (1914), he enlisted as a medical officer in the First Canadian Contingent in 1914. He wrote one of the most famous war poems of all time, 'IN FLANDERS FIELDS', which appeared in *Punch* in 1915. He died of double pneumonia on 28 Jan. 1918 and is buried at the Wimereux Cemetery, Boulogne, France. A collection of his verse, *In Flanders Fields and Other Poems*, was published posthumously in 1919 with an introduction by Sir Andrew MacPhail. A light burns in his memory in the Memorial Gardens adjacent to the John McCrea House, a national historic site in Guelph, Ont.

McCready, Earl (b.1908). Champion wrestler. Born in Lansdowne, Ont., and raised in Saskatchewan, he won the Canadian heavyweight wrestling title at the age of 18. A scholarship took him to the Oklahoma Agricultural College and he became American college and amateur champion. He represented Canada at the 1930 British Empire Games in Hamilton, Ont., where he won a gold medal, and later turned professional. He is honoured in the Canadian and American Sports HALLS OF FAME.

McCulloch, Jack (1872-1918). All-round athlete. The Manitoba sportsman was proficient in hockey, cycling, rowing, paddling, and track athletics, but excelled in speed-skating. He became the Canadian champion speed-skater in 1893 and continued to win both American and world titles. He travelled widely, giving exhibitions of speed, fancy, and trick skating, and became a partner in the manufacture of the McCulloch Tube Skate, the favourite of many professional hockey players.

McCulloch, Thomas (1776-1843). Clergyman and author. Born at Ferenze, Scot., and educated at the University of Glasgow, he was ordained a Presbyterian minister in 1799. Four years later he settled in Pictou, N.S. He became president of Dalhousie University in 1838. McCulloch wrote the first work of Canadian humour, 'Letters of Mephibosheth Stepsure', which appeared in the *Acadian Recorder* in 1821-3. A witty satire on inertia and ostentation among the Nova Scotia settlers, the 22 letters first appeared in book form in 1862. Douglas Lochhead edited a modern edition, *The Stepsure Letters* (1960), with a preface by Northrop FRYE and a note by John A. Irving.

McCully, Jonathan (1809-77). A FATHER OF CONFEDERATION. Born in Nova Scotia, he trained as a lawyer. He was appointed to the legislative council in 1847 and in 1857 took up journalism. He was a delegate to all three Conferences that preceded Confederation. In 1867 he was appointed to the Senate and in 1870 he was made a puisne judge of the Supreme Court of Nova Scotia.

McCurdy, J.A.D. See AERIAL EXPERIMENT ASSOCIATION.

MacDermot, Galt (b.1929). Pop composer. Born in Montreal, he was educated at McGill University, where he contributed to the satiric revue MY FUR LADY. He is best known as the composer of *Hair: The American Tribal Love-Rock Musical* (1967), with words by James Rado and Gerome Ragni.

Macdonald, Andrew Archibald (1829-1912). A FATHER OF CONFEDERATION. Born in Prince Edward Island, he became a merchant and shipowner. He was elected to the legislative assembly in 1853 and was later appointed to the legislative and executive councils. He was a delegate to the QUEBEC CONFERENCE on Confederation, which the province rejected until 1873. He was lieutenant-governor from 1884 to 1889 and was appointed to the Senate in 1891.

Macdonald, Brian (b.1928). Dancer, choreographer, and teacher. Born in Montreal, he was a pupil of Gerald Crevier and Elizabeth Leese. He joined the NATIONAL BALLET OF CANADA at its inception in 1951 and from 1953 was a choreographer for variety shows in Montreal, Winnipeg, and Quebec, and of MY FUR LADY in 1957. He created six major works for CBS television and two series of children's television shows for the ROYAL WINNIPEG BALLET. He staged *Time out of Mind* for the Robert Joffrey Ballet; was choreographer and ballet master for the Royal Swedish Ballet, Stockholm; and became director of the Harkness Ballet in 1967 and of Les GRANDS BALLETS CANADIENS in 1974. His ballets include *Aimez-vous Bach?* (1958) and *Les* WHOOPS-DE-DOO (1959). His full-length ballet, ROSE LATULIPPE, was first performed at the STRATFORD FESTIVAL in 1966.

MacDonald, J.E.H. (1873-1932). Landscape painter and poet, member of the GROUP OF SEVEN. Born in Durham, Eng., of a Canadian father, he immigrated with his parents to Hamilton in 1887 and studied there and in Toronto, where he worked as a graphic designer with Grip Limited until 1911, when he followed the advice of Lawren HARRIS—who had seen a show of his sketches at the ARTS AND LETTERS CLUB, Toronto—and became a professional painter. Excited by a show of landscapes by Scandinavian artists in 1913, the two painters proceeded to interpret the Canadian North—Georgian Bay, Algoma, and the Rockies—and to attract other like-minded painters, who gave birth to the Group of Seven. MacDonald began teaching at the Ontario College of Art in 1921 and became principal in 1929. His best-known paintings are *The Tangled Garden* (1916, NGC), which was considered radical when it was first shown; *The* SOLEMN LAND (1921, NGC); and the poetic *Mist Fantasy, Sand River, Algoma* (c.1922, AGO). His *West by East and Other Poems* (1933) was published posthumously.

MacDonald, J.J. See James MacRAE.

Macdonald, Jock (1897-1960). Painter. J.W.G. Macdonald (he adopted the name Jock in 1954) was born in Thurso, Scot., trained there as a designer, and came to Canada in 1926 as head of design at the Vancouver School of Decorative and Applied Arts, where he remained until 1933. He became friendly with his colleague Fred VARLEY and took up painting under his tutelage. A great teacher, he taught in Calgary in 1946-7 and then was appointed to the Ontario College of Art, where he remained until his death. After Macdonald studied in the U.S. with Hans Hofmann, his painting took on new strength. The powerful, complex, richly coloured abstractions he painted in the last three years of his life revealed him as a painter of the first importance. The year he died the Art Gallery of Toronto gave him a retrospective—the first living Canadian, apart from members of the Group of Seven, to receive this honour. Among his finest works are *Fleeting Breath* (1959, AGO), the 6-ft tall *Heroic Mould* (1959, AGO), and *Nature Evolving* (1960, AGO).

Macdonald, Sir John A. (1815-91). First prime minister. Born in Glasgow, Scot., he trained as a lawyer in Kingston and was called to the bar in 1836. His election in 1844 as the Conservative member for Kingston began a 47-year career in Parliament. In 1856 he became premier. Faced with deadlock in the government of the Province of Canada in 1864, he became the chief architect of a confederation of all the provinces in British North America, entering into a coalition with George BROWN, a Liberal from Canada West (Ontario), who first proposed a federal system of government. Macdonald steered the discussions through the CHARLOTTETOWN CONFERENCE (Sept. 1864), the QUEBEC CONFERENCE (Oct. 1864), and the LONDON CONFERENCE

Macdonald

(Dec. 1866). He became the Dominion of Canada's first prime minister and the recipient of a knighthood on 1 July 1867. A colourful man, he was a relaxed though crafty politician (see the DOUBLE SHUFFLE), famous for his wit and humour and his drinking. Associated with his prime ministership are the purchase of RUPERT'S LAND from the HUDSON'S BAY COMPANY (1869); the creation of the provinces of Manitoba (1870) and British Columbia (1871); the trial-ridden building of the CPR with its attendant PACIFIC SCANDAL, which led to his resignation in 1873 (he was returned to power in 1878); a protective tariff called the NATIONAL POLICY (1879); and his indifferent treatment of the West, which brought about the NORTHWEST REBELLION of 1885 that led to his controversial decision to hang Louis RIEL. He fought and won his last election in Mar. 1891, three months before he died.

Macdonald, John Sandfield (1812-72). First premier of Ontario. He was born in St Raphael, U.C. (Ont.), and trained as a lawyer. He was elected to the legislative assembly of the Province of Canada in 1841 and headed two governments: the Macdonald-Sicotte ministry of 1862-3 and the Macdonald-Dorion ministry of 1863-4. At CONFEDERATION, to which he had been opposed, he became premier of Ontario, an office he held for four years.

Macdonald, Robert H. See ROSS AND MACDONALD.

MacDonald, Thoreau (b.1901). Artist. Born near Toronto, he studied painting with his father, J.E.H. MacDONALD, and developed a skill in wood-engraving. He became art editor of the CANADIAN FORUM in 1923 and over the next 40 years went on to illustrate and decorate over 150 books with distinguished graphics in the form of engravings and line drawings. Margaret E. Edison edited *Thoreau MacDonald: A Catalogue of Design and Illustration* (1973).

Macdonald, Sir William (1831-1917). Manufacturer and philanthropist. Born in Prince Edward Island, he became a tobacco manufacturer in Montreal (see MACDONALD TOBACCO INC.) and accumulated a fortune. A benefactor of McGill University ($11 million), he was also instrumental in starting domestic-science centres in major Canadian cities (1899-1900). The culmination of this philanthropy was the founding in 1903 of the Macdonald Institute on the Ontario Agricultural College campus at Guelph, Ont. (see UNIVERSITY OF GUELPH) and Macdonald College of McGill University at Ste Anne de Bellevue, Que. (1905). He was knighted in 1898.

See also Adelaide Hunter HOODLESS and MACDONALD PHYSICS LABORATORY.

MacDonald, Wilson (1880-1967). Poet. Born in Cheapside, Ont., he attended McMaster University, worked as a bank clerk and as an advertising copywriter and, from the 1920s on, supported himself by giving poetry readings at high schools and clubs across the country. These he enlivened by praising his own genius and castigating his critics and contemporaries. The last of the romantic versifiers, MacDonald wrote 'The Song of the Ski', a widely anthologized poem from his first collection, *Out of the Wilderness* (1926). More than a dozen collections followed. During his last years the Wilson MacDonald Poetry Society, with Canadian and American chapters, presented him annually with a new automobile. *Wilson MacDonald's Western Tour, 1923-4* (1976), edited by Stan Dragland, is a collage of letters, clippings, and poems, etc., that gives one a sense of the man and his message. In 1956-7 he toured Russia and China with J.S. WALLACE.

Macdonald Brier. The country's top curling award. It is presented annually to the winning rink at playdowns of the Canadian Curling Association. Sponsored since 1927 by the present MACDONALD TOBACCO COMPANY INC., the brier is actually a silver tankard, a symbol of which is an engraved silver tray that is presented to the winning rink.

Macdonald Physics Laboratory. Science laboratory at McGill University associated with the early work of Rutherford and Soddy. It was donated by Sir William MACDONALD, philanthropist and chancellor of McGill University. In charge of the laboratory and occupant of the chair of experimental physics from 1898 to 1907 was Ernest Rutherford (1871-1937), the New Zealand-born physicist who was later knighted. He collaborated with a number of scientists, chief among them being the British chemist Frederick Soddy (1877-1956), who worked at McGill from 1900 to 1905. Their research included work on the structure of the atom and the principles of radioactivity. Rutherford clearly anticipated the immense energy potential of atomic fission. For theoretical work done at McGill, Rutherford received the NOBEL PRIZE in chemistry in 1908; Soddy received it for related work in 1921.

Macdonald Tobacco Inc. Manufacturer of Canadian cigarettes. It was founded by William C. MACDONALD in 1858. Since that time profits from the Montreal company have endowed several Canadian educational institutions and cultural organizations. R.J. Reyn-

314

olds Tobacco Co. of Winston-Salem, N.C., purchased Macdonald's in 1974. Its most popular cigarettes are Export and Export A.

McDougald, Angus (Bud). See ARGUS CORPORATION LIMITED.

McDougall, William (1822-1905). A FATHER OF CONFEDERATION. Born in York (Toronto), he trained as a lawyer. In 1850 he founded a Clear GRIT paper, the *North American*, which amalgamated with the *Globe* in 1855; he was elected to the legislative assembly in 1858. He was provincial secretary in the GREAT COALITION and was a delegate to the QUEBEC and LONDON CONFERENCES on Confederation. He is best remembered for being refused entry into RUPERT'S LAND on the eve of the RED RIVER REBELLION when, as lieutenant-governor of that territory, he attempted to cross the American border at Pembina (North Dakota) to assume office in Oct. 1869.

Mace. Ceremonial sceptre, traditional symbol of royal authority. It is carried in and out of the Commons chamber by the SERGEANT-AT-ARMS. 'Gold and gleaming, elaborately chased and scrolled, it lies on the clerks' table when the House is in session, the heavy end, with the orb and cross, pointing to the Speaker's right at the people in power, the carrying end, to the left, at Her Majesty's Loyal Opposition and the other opposition groups.' (George Bain)

McEwen, Air Vice Marshal C.M. (1896-1967). RCAF commanding officer. Born in Griswold, Man., he was educated at the University of Saskatchewan. He enlisted in the 196th Battalion, Canadian Expeditionary Force, in 1916 and was commissioned in England as a lieutenant in 1917. In June 1917 he started training with the Royal Flying Corps, to which he was seconded as a pilot on 19 Oct., shooting down 22 enemy aircraft. He joined the fledgling Canadian Air Force, which became the ROYAL CANADIAN AIR FORCE on 1 Apr. 1924. He was promoted air commodore in 1941. He went to England in 1942 and was appointed Air Officer Commanding the No. 6 (RCAF) Group RAF Bomber Command in Feb. 1944, when he was made air vice marshal. His forceful, dynamic leadership of No. 6 Group won him high praise. He retired in 1946.

MacEwen, Gwendolyn (b.1941). Poet and novelist. Born in Toronto, she started to write poetry in her early teens. Her collections of verse—*The Rising Fire* (1963), *A Breakfast for Barbarians* (1966), *The Armies of the Moon* (1972), *The Magic Animals* (1974), *The Shadow-Maker* (1969), and *The Fire-Eaters*

(1976)—reflect beneath their brilliant surface the links she perceives between life now and the ancient past and the world of dreams, magic, and myth. These interests are also present in her two fantasy-novels—the allegorical *Julian the Magician* (1961) and the historical *King of Egypt, King of Dreams* (1969)—and in a collection of stories and sketches, *Noman* (1972).

McEwen, Jean (b.1923). Painter. Born in Montreal, he studied pharmacy at the University of Montreal before living in Paris and turning to a career in painting. Influenced by the AUTOMATISTES, he joined the Association des Artistes Non-Figuratifs de Montréal in 1956. From his early experiments with slashes of colour and white-on-white abstracts, he developed a refined colour-field style that employs both floating forms, textured by translucent layers of colour, and geometric shapes patterned to suggest spatial dimensions beyond the canvas. *Cellule noire* (1959, MMFA) is one of his most complex paintings. He has exhibited internationally and lives in Montreal.

McFadden, David (b.1940). Poet. Born in Hamilton, Ont., he attended primary and secondary schools there and joined the *Hamilton Spectator*, leaving in 1976 to become a free-lance writer. He captures the inanities and illuminations of everyday life in the pop poems that appear in his collections *Letters from the Earth to the Earth* (1969), *Poems Worth Knowing* (1971), *Intense Pleasure* (1972), and *A Knight in Dried Plums* (1975). Greg CURNOE illustrated his work of surreal fiction, *The Great Canadian Sonnet*, which was published in a two-part 'big little book' format in 1970 and 1971.

McGeachy, James B. (Hamish) (1899-1966). Newspaperman and broadcaster. Born near Glasgow, Scot., he came to Saskatchewan at the age of 14 and qualified as a Rhodes Scholar. With his 'rich, plummy voice' he was a broadcaster during the Second World War and was known as 'the voice of Canada in London'. He was an editorial writer on the *Globe and Mail*, Toronto (1946-56), and on the *Financial Post* (1956-65). During the 1950s he was the host of CBC Radio's NOW I ASK YOU. A selection of his columns appeared in *A Touch of McGeachy* (1962).

McGee, Frank (*c.*1880-1916). Hockey player. Even though he lost the sight of one eye, he became a member of the famed Ottawa Silver Seven hockey team and was renowned for his achievement during a STANLEY CUP match against a Dawson challenging team in 1904 when he scored 14 goals, eight of them consecutive, in little more than eight minutes. He was killed in action in the First World War.

McGee, Thomas D'Arcy (1825-68). A FATHER OF CONFEDERATION. Born in Ireland, he lived for two periods—1842-5 and 1848-58—in the United States before moving to Montreal. He was elected to the legislative assembly in 1858 and was in the GREAT COALITION ministry that preceded Confederation. A delegate to the CHARLOTTETOWN and QUEBEC CONFERENCES and a brilliant orator, he made some influential speeches in favour of Confederation. He was elected to the House of Commons in 1867 and spoke out strongly against the FENIANS. On 7 Apr. 1868 he was assassinated by a Fenian (Patrick James Whelan) in Ottawa. Among his many books, *The Poems of D'Arcy McGee* was published posthumously in 1869.

McGill, Frank (b.1893). Outstanding all-round athlete. The Montreal sportsman won Canadian championships in swimming, athletics, and waterpolo before 1914, and starred in both hockey and football in 1919 and 1920. During the Second World War he was appointed Vice Air-Marshall of the RCAF. He served on many sports associations and in 1965 was elected to the Football HALL OF FAME.

McGill Fence. See MID-CANADA LINE.

McGill Fortnightly Review. 'An independent journal of literature and opinion'. Founded by A.J.M. SMITH and F.R. SCOTT, it appeared twice monthly between Nov. 1925 and Apr. 1927. It published the earliest poems of Smith and Scott and the earliest criticism by Smith, along with contributions by Leon EDEL, A.B. Latham, Lew Schwartz, *et al.*

McGill-Queen's University Press. Scholarly publishing house with offices in Montreal and Kingston. McGill University Press, founded in 1960, merged with the newly formed Queen's University Press in 1969. The combined company publishes books of academic interest.

McGill University. Canada's most widely known institute of learning. It is named for the Hon. James McGill, a Montreal merchant who, at his death in 1813, bequeathed 46 acres of land in downtown Montreal and £10,000 to the Royal Institution of Advancement of Learning. A charter was granted in 1821 and the university opened its doors in 1829, specializing in the humanities and medicine. On McGill's campus in downtown Montreal may be found the Peter Redpath Museum of Natural History, constructed in 1882 as the first specially designed museum building in Canada; the OSLER Library of the History of Medicine; and the MACDONALD PHYSICS LABORATORY. More Nobel laureates have lectured on staff at McGill than at any other Canadian university. See also Sir John William DAWSON and Sir William MACDONALD.

McGillivray, William (1764?-1825). Fur trader. Born in Scotland, he came to Canada in 1784 and joined the NORTH WEST COMPANY, becoming its chief director in 1804. Fort William (now THUNDER BAY), the company's headquarters, was named after him in 1807.

McGraw-Hill Ryerson Ltd. General trade and educational publishers. It was formed in Dec. 1970 with the sale of the old established Canadian publishing house, the RYERSON PRESS, to McGraw-Hill, Inc., a New York publishing giant founded in 1909. The event galvanized the nationalist movement in Canadian publishing and led to the formation of the Independent Publishers' Association (now the ASSOCIATION OF CANADIAN PUBLISHERS). McGraw-Hill Ryerson distributes books published by the parent company and originates many Canadian titles in its Toronto offices.

MacInnes, Tom (1867-1951). Poet. Born in Dresden, Ont., and educated at the University of Toronto, he was called to the bar in 1893. He led a varied life (policing at Skagway during the KLONDIKE GOLD RUSH, helping to draft the immigration legislation of 1910, directing a tramway company in China in 1919-24, etc.) before settling near Vancouver. His verse, which is sometimes bizarre, with surreal touches, and often verges on doggerel—his two best-known poems are 'Zalinka' and 'The Tiger of Desire'—was collected in eight volumes, including *Complete Poems* (1923). He also wrote a book of prose sketches, *Chinook Days* (1926).

MacInnis, Joseph B. (b.1937). Marine scientist and explorer. Born in Barrie, Ont., he trained as a medical doctor. Since 1960 he has engaged in undersea research in the United States and Canada. He devised Sublimnos, Canada's first underwater habitat, a two-unit bathysphere, 8 ft in diameter, that was submerged in Georgian Bay in 1969-71 and acted as a base for marine scientists. He is the designer of Sub-Igloo, the first Arctic diving station, and the author of *Underwater Man* (1975).

McIntosh apple. Canadian-created red apple. John McIntosh (1777-1846), a Scottish-born farmer, first produced this sweet apple in 1811 on his farm near Dundela, Dundas Co., U.C. (Ont.). It is now grown extensively across North America.

McIntyre, James (1827-1906). Poetaster known as 'The Cheese Poet' from his 'Ode on the Mammoth Cheese', published in 1884 to celebrate the manufacture of a 7,000-lb. round of cheese in Ingersoll, Ont. McIntyre's verse is examined humorously by William Arthur DEACON in *The* FOUR JAMESES (1927).

McIntyre Mines Ltd. A major mining-investment company built on an important gold discovery in the Timmins area of northern Ontario. The original gold claims were staked at Porcupine, Ont., in 1909 by Sandy McIntyre, a fugitive from a disastrous marriage in Scotland, whose real name was Alexander Oliphant. McIntyre received little for his discovery but recognition for his adopted name in the corporate title. The company acquired many additional mines and by 1920 had diversified by purchasing the Blue Diamond Co. Ltd (widely used when Canadian homes were heated by coal). The original mine, almost depleted in the mid-1970s, is supplemented by new coal mines in the Smoky R. area of Alberta. McIntyre Mines also has a controlling share of FAL-CONBRIGE NICKEL. Control of the company has passed into the hands of the Keck family of the United States through their Superior Oil interests.

Mackasey flu. An imaginary illness that affects postal workers; euphemism for reporting in sick rather than working. This form of work stoppage gained ground in 1975 and took its name from that of Bryce Mackasey, the postmaster general.

McKay. Automobile manufactured from 1911 to 1914 by Nova Scotia Carriage, Kentville, N.S. The company produced Model 24, a two-passenger roadster that sold for $1,450.

McKee (Trans-Canada) Trophy. An award for meritorious services in the advance of aviation. Donated by J. Dalzell McKee, a wealthy American aviation enthusiast who made a cross-country flight from Montreal to Vancouver in 1928, it was given from 1927 to 1960.

Mackenzie, Ada (1893-1973). Champion golfer. Born near Toronto, she began winning golf championships in 1924 and continued to do so for more than 40 years; even in her seventies she was a member of an Ontario provincial team. She encouraged young golfers, donated trophies, and founded in Thornhill, near Toronto, a golf club reserved exclusively for women players.

Mackenzie, Sir Alexander (1764-1820). Fur trader and explorer. Born in Stornoway, Scot., he entered the fur trade in Montreal in 1779 and joined the NORTH WEST COMPANY in 1787. He made two great voyages of exploration. In 1789, by the Slave R. and Great Slave Lake, he explored the 'River of Disappointment' (so named because it did not reach the Pacific)—later named the Mackenzie in his honour. In 1793 he crossed the Rocky Mountains and reached the Pacific at Dean Channel. With a mixture of vermilion and grease he inscribed on a rock: 'Alex Mackenzie from Canada by land 22d July 1793'. His journal of these two expeditions, *Voyages from Montreal . . .*, was published in England in 1801 and he was knighted in 1802. He became a partner in the XY COMPANY in 1802 and in 1804 was elected to the legislative assembly of Lower Canada (Quebec), but after 1805 he was in Canada infrequently and did not return after 1810.

Mackenzie, Alexander (1822-92). Second prime minister of Canada. Born in Dunkeld, Scot., he came to Canada in 1842 and was a builder in Kingston, then Sarnia, C.W. (Ontario). He was elected to the legislative assembly in 1861 as a Reformer and, at CONFED-ERATION, to Parliament. After the Conservative defeat over the PACIFIC SCANDAL in 1873, he succeeded John A. MACDONALD as prime minister and formed a Liberal government that lasted until 1878. During his administration a Canadian Supreme Court was established and the secret ballot was introduced. He resigned as party leader in 1880.

MacKenzie, Gisèle (b.1927). Popular singer. Born Gisèle LaFlèche in Winnipeg, she trained as a violinist under Kathleen PARLOW at the Royal Conservatory of Music (1941-5). The possessor of a lilting voice, she became nationally known with her own CBC Radio show 'Meet Gisèle' (1946-9) and internationally known after being introduced to American audiences by Jack Benny in 1953. She starred in NBC-TV's 'Your Hit Parade' (1953-7). An American citizen since 1955, she lives in Encino, Calif.

McKenzie, Robert Tait (1867-1938). Physician and sculptor. Professor of anatomy and director of physical education at McGill University from 1895 to 1904, he spent the rest of his professional life at the University of Pennsylvania. As a sculptor, he won increasing recognition from 1902, culminating in 1928 with his membership in the ROYAL CANA-DIAN ACADEMY. His best-known sculptures and memorials depict a fascination with the human figure in sporting events, especially the early OLYMPIC GAMES in 1904 and 1912,

317

and he was frequently a competitor in the fine arts division of the games. In 1930 he and his wife restored an old grist mill near his birth-place, Almonte, Ont., as a summer home and named it the Mill of Kintail after McKenzie's Scottish ancestors. Today the mill is a museum that exhibits over 70 of his works, including *The Sprinter* (1902), *The Joy of Effort* (1912), and the *Scottish-American War Memorial* (1923-7).

Mackenzie, Sir William. See CANADIAN NORTHERN RAILWAY.

Mackenzie, William Lyon (1795-1861). Newspaper editor, politician, rebel leader in the REBELLION OF 1837. Born in Dundee, Scot., he came to York (Toronto) in 1820. As the editor of his own newspaper, the COLONIAL ADVOCATE, he took up the grievances of labourers and farmers and eventually gave vent to violent attacks on the governing clique of York. He was elected to—and expelled from—the legislative assembly several times and was the first mayor of Toronto for nine months in 1834-5. His political views became extreme and in Dec. 1837 he led some 750 rural supporters in an uprising that took the form of two skirmishes near and in Toronto. When they were put down, he escaped to the United States. He returned to Canada under the Act of Amnesty of 1849, was elected to the assembly in 1851, and retired from politics in 1858. He died in the house on Bond St, Toronto—now a museum—that a committee of friends had bought for him.

Mackenzie Eskimos. One of five groups of ESKIMOS. They inhabit the Arctic coast near the mouth of the MACKENZIE RIVER.

Mackenzie Highway. A northern highway. Originating in Edmonton, Alta, and presently constructed to Fort Simpson in the Northwest Territories, it is under construction to Fort Good Hope and will eventually connect with Inuvik on the Mackenzie delta.

Mackenzie-Papineau Battalion. Canadian volunteer battalion of the XVth International Brigade of the Spanish Republican Army. Named for William Lyon MACKENZIE and Louis-Joseph PAPINEAU and known as the Mac-Paps, it had as its motto '1837-1937—Fascism shall be destroyed'. It was formed in 1937 as part of the Popular Front against the Nationalist forces under Gen. Francisco Franco and served during the Spanish Civil War in numerous battles, including Jarama, Quinto, Belchite, Teruel, and the Ebro. Once the Spanish civil war was lost, the surviving volunteers returned to Canada in 1939. Op-

position to their return by the RCMP was overcome partly by the influence of an international committee, Friends of the Mackenzie-Papineau Battalion, whose sponsors included Albert Einstein, Eugene FORSEY, Ernest Hemingway, Upton Sinclair, and H.G. Wells. Official war records were destroyed in Spain. However, the final report of the Friends, issued in the spring of 1939, suggested that approximately 1,250 Canadians served in the war.

Mackenzie Rebellion. See REBELLION OF 1837.

Mackenzie River. Canada's longest river. Including the Peace R., its longest tributary, it measures over 2,635 mi. The Mackenzie proper flows and is navigable from Great Slave Lake northwesterly 1,065 mi. to the Beaufort Sea in the western Arctic Ocean. It was named after Sir Alexander MACKENZIE, its European discoverer. The Mackenzie R. drainage basin—including among other rivers the Peace, Athabasca, and Laird—is one of the world's largest river systems, vying with the Mississippi-Missouri as the largest in North America. It drains most of the Yukon, Alberta, northern Saskatchewan, the western Northwest Territories, and northeastern British Columbia.

Mackenzie Valley Pipeline. A proposed pipeline to convey natural gas from the Mackenzie delta and the Beaufort Sea areas of the Canadian and American Arctic down the Mackenzie Valley corridor to points in southern Canada and possibly the northern United States. A Royal Commission, chaired by Thomas Berger, Justice of the Supreme Court of British Columbia, was established on 21 Mar. 1974 to consider the ecological aspects of the proposal and the objections of the native peoples to it.

Mackie Rail. A once-popular term for steel railway track made shatter-free through a process devised by I.C. Mackie, chief metallurgist of the Dominion Steel and Coal Company of Sydney, N.S. Wondering why invisible fissures developed in railway track, he discovered that the problem arose in the cooling process and devised a system of controlled cooling, which is used to this day in the manufacture of shatter-free rails. He demonstrated its effectiveness at Sydney in July 1931, and the system went into international use. In Canada rails so manufactured are still stamped 'Mackie'.

McKim Advertising Limited. The first general advertising agency in Canada. It was founded in Montreal in 1889 by newspaper agent Anson McKim (1855-1917), incorporated as A. McKim Limited in 1907, and reorganized in its present form in 1945. It operates five branches across Canada. In 1892 the agency initiated publication of the *Canadian Newspaper Directory*, the country's first thorough listing of Canadian publications, which has appeared annually since 1942.

McKim, Mead and White. New York architectural firm formed by C.F. McKim (1847-1909), W.R. Mead (1846-1928), and Stanford White (1855-1906). Their manner of practice, with a large office taking on many varied commissions at the same time, and their Imperial style of Beaux Arts Classicism, were important influences on the development of Canadian architecture. Their works in Canada include the rebuilding and extension of the Bank of Montreal head office, Montreal (1904), one of their most important projects; the Royal Trust Building, Montreal (*c.*1914); and the Bank of Montreal, Winnipeg (1911).

Mackinac, Mackinac Island. See MICHILI-MACKINAC.

Mackinaw. A heavy woollen cloth from which the popular blanket is made. The word derives from Mackinac (see MICHILI-MACKINAC).

McKinnon, Catherine (b.1945). Singer and entertainer. Born in Saint John, N.B., she studied singing at the Royal Conservatory of Music and attracted a following with her appearances on SINGALONG JUBILEE in 1962. Her first album, *Voice of an Angel* (1968), made her the best-selling female recording artist in Canada at the time. In 1969 she married Don HARRON. Her signature song is 'FAREWELL TO NOVA SCOTIA'.

Mackinnon, Daniel (1876-1964). Sportsman and harness racer. Born near Charlottetown, P.E.I., he was actively involved in training, driving, and owning harness-racing horses and in promoting the sport in Canada. He was also aide-de-camp to the governor general.

McLachlan, Alexander (1818-96). Pioneer versifier. Born near Glasgow, Scot., he immigrated to Upper Canada (Ontario) in 1840, where he tried farming and tailoring. He died in Orangeville, Ont., having published four collections of poetry that convey appealingly his strength of character and honesty as he writes about nature, the pioneer experience, hypocrisy, etc., even though they have the sentimentality and crudeness of the work of a simple versifier. His best-known collection is *The Emigrant and Other Poems* (1861).

The Poetical Works of Alexander McLachlan appeared in 1900.

McLaren, Norman (b.1914). Famous animator and director of documentary films for the NATIONAL FILM BOARD. The Scottish-born film innovator was the discovery of John GRIERSON, who brought him to Canada in 1941 to continue his experiments in animation with the newly created NFB. McLaren's techniques include drawing directly onto the optical and sound tracks of his films, and 'pixillation'—the animated treatment of live actors. Among his many highly individual brief films are *Alouette* (1944), FIDDLE-DE-DEE (1947), BEGONE DULL CARE (1949), NEIGHBOURS (1953), BLINKITY BLANK (1955), A CHAIRY TALE (1957), LINES VERTICAL (1960), and PAS DE DEUX (1968). He won an Academy Award for *Neighbours*. In *The Eye Hears, The Ear Sees* (1971), a CBC-BBC television special on his work, McLaren said: 'The purpose of my films is to give the intellect a rest.' La Cinémathèque Canadienne published a study of his work entitled *Norman McLaren* (1965). *The Drawings of Norman McLaren* appeared in 1975.

MacLaren Advertising Limited. Largest of the Canadian-owned advertising agencies and the industry leader. Formed in Toronto in 1922 as the small branch office of the New York agency, Campbell-Ewald, to handle the General Motors account in Canada, it grew under the management of Jack MacLaren (1891-1955), a Toronto-born advertising executive who acquired the agency in 1935. A conversation between MacLaren and Conn SMYTHE in 1929 resulted in a special radio (then television) network's being created to carry HOCKEY NIGHT IN CANADA two years later. George G. SINCLAIR was elected chairman of the board in 1965 and the next year MacLaren's became Canada's first international agency with billings in excess of $50 million. In 1975 Sinclair and the president, H.M. (Bud) Turner, Jr, arranged a merger with another leading agency, Goodis, Goldberg, Soren, founded by Jerry GOODIS.

McLarnin, Jimmy (b.1907). Champion boxer. Born in Vancouver, B.C., he fought 57 times and became the world's welterweight boxing champion, retiring at the age of 29 to fame and fortune. In 1950 he was voted 'Canada's best boxer during the first half-century'.

McLauchlan, Murray (b.1948). Singer, guitarist, and composer. Born in Scotland and raised in Toronto, he began his career as a performer in Toronto in 1969 at the RIVERBOAT. Writing and singing with a rough-edged impact about the urban environment, he calls himself the 'Woody Allen of folk music'. His best-known singles are 'The Old Man's Song', 'Child's Song', and 'Jesus, Please Don't Save Me Till I Die'.

McLaughlin, R.S. (Sam) (1871-1972). Automobile manufacturer, sportsman, and philanthropist. He started in business as an apprentice in his father's carriage company, which in 1907 became the McLaughlin Motor Co. in Oshawa, Ont., and began producing the McLaughlin-Buick. The company's motto was 'One grade only and that the best'. In 1918 McLaughlin sold the company to General Motors and was appointed president and later chairman of General Motors of Canada. In his fifties he began buying and exhibiting show-horses. He founded Parkwood Stables on his estate 'Parkwood' outside of Oshawa and began breeding thoroughbreds, three of which won the historic King's Plate (see QUEEN'S PLATE).

McLean, Ross (b.1925). Television producer. Born in Guelph, Ont., and educated at the University of Toronto, he worked as a reporter and radio announcer before joining CBC Radio in 1948. Five years later he became CBC-TV's first supervisor of public affairs. As producer or executive producer of such stylish shows as TABLOID, 'Close-Up', QUEST, 'The Way It Is', TELESCOPE, MR PEARSON, etc., he gained a reputation as a discoverer of such talented performers as Elaine Grand and Jean Templeton. From 1961 to 1963 he was associated with the CTV Network and the PIERRE BERTON SHOW. Returning to the CBC, he has been program director of CBLT, the Toronto-area station, since 1974.

McLean Foundation. It was established in Toronto in 1945 by J.S. McLean, a meat-packing executive, to assist charitable, educational, and religious organizations.

Maclean-Hunter Limited. The name since Apr. 1968 of a periodicals publishing house and communications conglomerate. The Toronto-based operation was founded in 1887 by Col. John Bayne Maclean (1862-1950). Horace T. Hunter joined the company in 1903, became president in 1933, and chairman in 1952. Floyd S. Chalmers (see CHALMERS FOUNDATION) succeeded him in 1964 and was himself succeeded by Donald F. Hunter in 1969. *Canadian Grocer* (still going strong) was the new company's first publication, and the first of the many trade, business, and consumer publications Maclean founded or acquired. In 1905 he bought *Busy Man's Magazine* (the original digest-type periodical) and in 1911 turned it into MACLEAN'S. The FINANCIAL POST was launched in 1907 and

CHATELAINE in 1927. Publications no longer in existence include CANADIAN HOMES AND GARDENS and MAYFAIR. By the 1970s Maclean-Hunter published more than 50 consumer, trade, and business periodicals. It also arranges conventions and industrial and trade shows, operates press-clipping and mailing services, sells books by mail-order, and owns radio and television interests as well as a book publishing company—the MACMILLAN COMPANY OF CANADA, acquired in 1973.

Maclean's. 'Canada's Newsmagazine' (formerly 'Canada's National Magazine'), published by MACLEAN-HUNTER LIMITED. Known as *Busy Man's Magazine* when it appeared in 1905, it became *Maclean's Magazine* in 1911 and was published twice a month until 1967, when it changed to a monthly. In 1969 it changed its format from *Life* size (13½ in. by 10½ in.) to *Time* size (11 in. by 8¼ in.). On 6 Oct. 1975 it increased its frequency to 23 issues a year and became a newsmagazine. There are plans to publish *Maclean's* weekly in Oct. 1977. Notable features in the fifties and sixties have been: 'The Yellow Pages' (four—later eight—pages of topical articles at the front and back of the magazine), 1957-71; 'For the Sake of Argument' (later, 'Argument', a column on a controversial subject), 1956-68; 'LONDON LETTER' (a column by Beverley Baxter), 1935-60; 'Backstage at Ottawa' (coverage of Parliament Hill by Blair FRASER) 1943-68; 'Flashbacks' (great news stories from 'just over the hill of memory' of most readers), 1949-67; and 'Jasper' (a cartoon by James Simpkins), 1948-69 and 1971-5. Editors of the magazine include: W.A. Craik (1905-10); Roger Fry (1911-13); Thomas B. COSTAIN (1914-21); J. Vernon McKenzie (1921-6; H. Napier Moore (1926-45); W. Arthur Irwin (1945-50); Ralph ALLEN (1950-60); Blair Fraser (1960-8); Ken Lefolii (1962-4); Borden Spears (1964-9); Charles TEMPLETON (1969); Peter GZOWSKI (1969-70); and Peter C. NEWMAN (from 1971). *Le Maclean* (formerly *Le Magazine Maclean*), which differs almost totally from the English-language publication, has been published in Montreal since 1961.

Maclear. Popular public-affairs CTV Network program. Launched in the fall of 1974, it is seen weekly for 30 minutes and features news and investigative reporting by globe-trotting correspondent Michael Maclear, a Fleet St journalist who settled in Canada in 1954.

MacLellan, Gene (b.1939). Singer-composer. Born in Val d'Or, Que., and raised in Toronto, the country-rock performer, who plays the guitar and sports a black eye-patch, lives at Pownal, P.E.I. Anne MURRAY launched his career in 1970 when she made a hit of SNOWBIRD, the second song he had written. Since then he has gone on to write many more songs, including the popular hymn-like folksong 'Put Your Hand in the Hand'.

MacLennan, Hugh (b.1907). Novelist and essayist. Born in Glace Bay, Cape Breton, N.S., he was educated at Dalhousie University, Oxford, and Princeton, and in 1951 began a long association with the English department of McGill University. His social novels, in which the Canadian environment is an important influence on the lives of his characters, are unique in their attempt to explore through fiction the nature of the country's character; they do so with great breadth and occasionally memorable characterizations. The novels are BAROMETER RISING (1941); TWO SOLITUDES (1945); *The Precipice* (1948), about the ambivalence with which Canadians view the United States; *Each Man's Son* (1951), a Cape Breton novel; *The* WATCH THAT ENDS THE NIGHT (1959); and *Return of the Sphinx* (1967), about the interaction of generations and the relationship between French and English in contemporary Quebec. MacLennan is also a distinguished essayist in *Cross-Country* (1949), *Thirty and Three* (1954), and *Scotchman's Return and Other Essays* (1960). His *Seven Rivers of Canada* (1961) was revised and reissued, with photographs by John de Visser, as *Rivers of Canada* (1974). MacLennan also wrote the text for *The Colour of Canada* (1968) in the Canadian Illustrated Library.

Macleod, J.J.R. (1876-1935). Medical researcher. Born in Cluny, Scot., he graduated from the University of Aberdeen in 1898. He was appointed professor of physiology at the University of Toronto in 1918 and was head of the department when Dr Frederick G. BANTING coaxed from him eight weeks of laboratory time, one undergraduate assistant (Charles H. BEST), and 10 dogs for experimental purposes. Although Macleod was holidaying in Scotland in the summer of 1921, when Banting and Best isolated INSULIN, on his return he threw the resources of the laboratory behind the work of purifying the substance and brought in the biochemist J.B. COLLIP. Macleod and Banting were co-recipients of the 1923 NOBEL PRIZE for chemistry, Macleod sharing his cash award with Collip, and Banting his with Best. In 1928 Macleod returned to Scotland, where he took up the chair of physiology at Aberdeen University.

McLuhan, Marshall (b.1911). Communications theorist. Born in Edmonton, Alta, and educated at the University of Manitoba and Cambridge, he joined the English department of St Michael's College, University of Toronto, in 1946, and now heads that university's CENTRE FOR CULTURE AND TECHNOLOGY, which he founded in 1963. He published *The* MECHANICAL BRIDE: *Folklore of Industrial Man*, a satirical examination of popular culture, in 1951, and with Edmund Carpenter—who, like McLuhan, was influenced by the ideas of Harold Adams INNIS—he edited EXPLORATIONS (1953-9), a magazine that attracted contributors from many disciplines who were interested in communications theory. McLuhan's studies of mass communications and their impact on men's minds—beginning with The GUTENBERG GALAXY: *The Making of Typographic Man* (1964) and continuing with *Understanding Media: The Extensions of Man* (1964)—made him an international celebrity and one of the most influential thinkers of the 1960s. More popular expositions of his theory that modern electronic technology has altered man's view of himself and the world are *The Medium is the Massage* (with Quentin Fiore, 1967), *War and Peace in the Global Village* (with Quentin Fiore, 1968), *Through the Vanishing Point* (with Harley Parker, 1968), *Counterblast* (1969), *From Cliché to Archetype* (with Wilfred Watson, 1970), *Culture Is Our Business* (1970), and *Take Today* (with Barrington Nevitt, 1972). Eugene McNamara edited *Interior Landscape: The Literary Criticism of Marshall McLuhan, 1943-62* (1969). McLuhan is identified with the aphorism 'The MEDIUM IS THE MESSAGE'.

Maclure, Samuel (1860-1929). Architect. Born in New Westminster, B.C., he was largely self-taught. Working with Cecil Croker Fox, a pupil of the English architect C.F.A. Voysey, he designed many houses for the Anglo-Canadian aristocracy in Victoria and Vancouver—combining cottage-like forms of the English Arts and Crafts Movement with fine local craftsmanship and materials—including the Walter C. Nicol house (1912-13) at 140 The Crescent, Vancouver; the R.R. Sutherland house (1912-13), Victoria; and the atypical Hatley Park (1900), Victoria, for Robin Dunsmuir—now ROYAL ROADS MILITARY COLLEGE.

McMaster University. Created by an act of the legislature and named after Senator William McMaster—who had endowed funds for 'a Christian school of learning'—it was founded in Toronto in 1887 by a merger of the Toronto Baptist College and Woodstock College. It moved to Hamilton, Ont., in 1930. Formerly affiliated with the Baptist Convention of Ontario and Quebec, it became nondenominational in 1957—though the Baptist connection was continued through the separate incorporation and affiliation of a theological college, McMaster Divinity School.

McMichael Canadian Collection. A gallery of Canadian art and a memorial to the GROUP OF SEVEN. Some 1,200 paintings and other works of art are on display in a series of impressive galleries built of Douglas fir and barn boards and set amid 1,000 acres of Ontario countryside on the outskirts of Kleinburg, a village north of Toronto. Founded as the McMichael Conservation Collection in 1954—a personal tribute to the Group's spirit from the Toronto-born business executive Robert McMichael and his Danish-born wife Signe—it was presented by the McMichaels to the Ontario government on 8 July 1966, the 49th anniversary of Tom THOMSON'S death. On the grounds are Tom Thomson's shack, moved from behind the STUDIO BUILDING, Toronto, in 1962; and the graves of five members of the Group: Lawren HARRIS, A.Y. JACKSON (who spent his last years with the McMichaels), Frank JOHNSTON, Arthur LISMER, and F.H. VARLEY. The art critic Paul Duval has written an introduction to the catalogue, *A Vision of Canada: The McMichael Canadian Collection* (1973).

MacMillan, Sir Ernest (1893-1973). Conductor and composer. Born in Mimico, Ont., he studied organ in Toronto and Edinburgh and received a Doctor of Music degree from Oxford University in 1918. As conductor of the TORONTO SYMPHONY ORCHESTRA (1931-56) and the TORONTO MENDELSSOHN CHOIR (1942-57), principal of the ROYAL CONSERVATORY OF MUSIC, Toronto (1926-42), and Dean of Faculty of Music, University of Toronto (1927-52), he was at the centre of musical life in Canada for 25 years. His compositions for orchestra and choir show a mastery of contrapuntal forms and post-romantic harmonies. His best-known work is perhaps *Two Sketches Based on French Canadian Airs* (1927) for string orchestra. He was knighted in 1935.

MacMillan Bloedel Ltd. Canada's largest forest-products operation. The Vancouver-based company dates from the 1960 merger of companies founded by Harvey Reginald MacMillan in 1919 and by Prentice Bloedel in 1929.

Macmillan Company of Canada Ltd. Major publishing house. Founded in Toronto in 1905 as a subsidiary jointly owned by Macmillan & Company, London, and The Macmillan Company, New York, it developed a strong trade list under the energetic presidency of Hugh Eayrs (1894-1940). Among the well-known Canadian writers who have

been published by the firm are Marius BARBEAU, Morley CALLAGHAN, Donald CREIGHTON, Mazo DE LA ROCHE, Frederick Philip GROVE, Hugh MacLENNAN, W.O. MITCHELL, and E.J. PRATT. John Gray became manager in 1946 and president in 1956. At his retirement in 1969 he was succeeded by Hugh Kane. In 1973 the company was sold to MACLEAN-HUNTER; the president is George W. Gilmour.

Macnab, Sir Allan N. (1798-1862). Politician. Born at Niagara, he served in the WAR OF 1812 and was elected to the legislative assembly in 1830. He commanded the Gore militia in the REBELLION OF 1837, for which he was knighted. Elected to the assembly of the Province of Canada in 1841, he became leader of the MacNab-MORIN liberal-conservative ministry in 1854. He formed a ministry with Morin's successor, E.-P. Taché, in 1856 but was forced to resign later that year. He was created a baronet in 1858 and was elected to the legislative council in 1860.

McNaught, John. See James BANNERMAN.

McNaughton, Gen. A.G.L. (1887-1966). Army commander and distinguished public servant. Born in Moosomin, Sask., he was educated there, at Bishop's College School, Lennoxville, Que., and at McGill University. He was commissioned in 1909 and served overseas during the First World War, rising to the rank of brigadier-general in Nov. 1918. He had a distinguished career in the army between the two World Wars, and was joint inventor of the Cathode Ray Direction Finder (1926). In Sept. 1939 he was appointed General Officer Commanding the 1st Canadian Infantry Division; promoted lieutenant-general as GOC VIII Corps in 1940; appointed GOC Canadian Corps on its formation in 1941; appointed GOC First Canadian Army on 6 Apr. 1942; and promoted general in Sept. 1944. He retired from the army in Nov. 1944, when he became Minister of National Defence; he resigned the following year. He was chairman, Canadian Section, Permanent Joint Board on Defence (1945-59) and chairman, Canadian Section, International Joint Commission (1950-62).

McNaughton, Duncan A. (b.1910). Champion high-jumper. Born in Cornwall, Ont., but raised in Vancouver, he was living in Los Angeles when he was added at the last moment to the Canadian team in the 1932 Olympics in that city. He won the high-jump and was the only Canadian at those games to win a gold medal in track-and-field competition. After winning a DFC with Bar for service with the RCAF, he earned a doctorate in geology and founded his own petroleum consulting firm.

Macoun, John (1831-1920). Botanist and explorer. Born in County Down, Ire., he came to Upper Canada (Ontario) at the age of 13 and worked as a farm labourer while qualifying as a teacher. He taught at Albert College, Belleville, and worked as a botanist with CPR railway engineers in the 1870s, first crossing half the continent with Sandford FLEMING in 1872 and again exploring the Rockies in 1879-80. In 1882 he was appointed botanist to the GEOLOGICAL SURVEY OF CANADA. His report stating that the land in the so-called PALLISER'S TRIANGLE was not an arid belt but a fertile plain was a significant factor in the choice of a more southerly route for the CPR. His autobiography was published posthumously in 1922.

Macphail, Agnes (1890-1954). The first woman to sit in the Canadian House of Commons. Born in Ontario, she started her career as a schoolteacher and was elected to Parliament in 1921 as a candidate of the PROGRESSIVE PARTY; in subsequent elections she ran as an independent. After her defeat in 1940 she joined the CCF and won a seat in the Ontario legislature in 1943. She remained in provincial politics, though she did not always win a seat, until her death. She started her parliamentary career as a spokesman of farm interests, but was particularly noted for her demands for prison reform. She died in Toronto.

Macpherson, C.B. (b.1911). Political scientist. Born in Toronto and educated at the University of London, he has been a professor of political science at the University of Toronto since 1956. His important work, *The Political Theory of Possessive Individualism* (1962), studies the political ramifications of the psychological concept of ownership. Among his other publications are *Democracy in Alberta* (1953, 1962), *The Real World of Democracy* (1965), and *Democratic Theories: Essays in Retrieval* (1973). He is married to Kathleen (Kay) Macpherson, past president of the VOICE OF WOMEN.

McPherson, Donald (b.1945). Champion figure-skater. Stratford-born, he won the Canadian, North American, and world titles in figure-skating in 1963, at the age of 17, then retired from competitive skating and became a featured performer with a professional touring company.

Macpherson, Duncan (b.1924). One of the world's top political cartoonists. Born in Toronto, he revealed his skill in high school and after war service trained at the Boston Museum School of Fine Arts and the Ontario College of Art. He achieved his greatest fame after he became an editorial cartoonist on the *Toronto Star* in 1960; his brilliantly drawn and mordant cartoons are syndicated and sold in Europe, Scandinavia, and the United States. The recipient of many awards, he was given the Molson Prize in 1971. Numerous collections of his cartoons have been published by the *Star*.

Macpherson, Jay (b.1931). Poet. Born in England, she came to Canada as a child and was educated at Carleton College, Ottawa, and Victoria College, University of Toronto, where she is a professor of English. The short, witty poems in *The Boatman* (1957) form an intricate sequence that constructs a mythological world from Biblical and classical allusions. It was reissued as *The Boatman and Other Poems* (1968) and was followed by a privately printed collection, *Welcoming Disaster* (1974).

MacRae, James (1849-1900?). Poetaster who identified himself as 'A Native of County Glengarry'. MacRae's real name was J.J. MacDonald and his verse is examined humorously by William Arthur DEACON in *The FOUR JAMESES* (1927).

McRuer Commission. An Ontario Royal Commission inquiring into civil rights. It was established 'to examine, study and inquire into the laws of Ontario . . . assenting the personal freedoms, rights and liberties of Canadian citizens and other residents in Ontario for the purpose of determining how far there may be unjustified encroachment on those freedoms, rights and liberties by the Legislature', etc. Appointed on 21 May 1964, it was chaired by James Chalmers McRuer, then chief justice of the High Court of Ontario. It submitted its final report on 7 Feb. 1968.

MacSkimming, Roy (b.1944). Novelist and book reviewer. Born in Ottawa, he was educated at the University of Toronto and was an editor with CLARKE IRWIN from 1965 to 1968. His poems appeared with those of William Hawkins in *Shoot Low, Sheriff, They're Riding Shetland Ponies* (1964). With James Bacque and Dave GODFREY, he founded NEW PRESS in 1969. When it was acquired by GENERAL PUBLISHING in 1974 he accepted, in Oct. 1974, the position of book-review editor and columnist with the *Toronto Star*, which he resigned from in 1976. His novel *Formentera* was published in 1972.

McTavish, Simon (1750-1804). Merchant.

Born in Scotland, he worked in the fur trade in Albany, N.Y., in the early 1770s and in 1775 moved to Montreal, where he became one of the partners of, and the moving spirit behind, the NORTH WEST COMPANY, of which his firm—McTavish, Frobisher & Co.—was the Montreal agent. His house, built in 1785, still stands in OLD MONTREAL.

Mad Shadows. English title of the first novel of Marie-Claire BLAIS. It appeared in 1959 as *La Belle Bête*, and was translated the following year by Merloyd Lawrence. The story is about Isabelle Marie, a plain girl, her beautiful idiot brother Patrice, and their vain mother Louise, who scorns her daughter while smothering her son with affection and eventually abandons both for her lover. The author writes of a world in which evil predominates: Patrice causes the death of his mother's lover and is in turn disfigured by his sister, who hates him for his beauty.

Mad trapper, The. Sobriquet of Albert Johnson, of whom little is known other than that he was a somewhat demented sharpshooter and would murder prospectors for the gold in their teeth. He killed an RCMP officer sent to investigate his poaching of Indian traplines in the Fort McPherson area and this led to a massive manhunt in the Yukon near the Alaska border. Johnson was killed at a shoot-out in the Eagle River district on 17 Feb. 1932.

Madawaska. County in the northwest corner of New Brunswick settled in 1783. For half a century it had little contact with the provincial government and came to be called the 'Republic of Madawaska'.

Made Beaver. The pelt of an adult beaver used as a unit of exchange by the HUDSON'S BAY COMPANY. One Made Beaver was represented by a brass token—issued to trappers by the Company around 1854—on which Made Beaver is abbreviated as N.B.—a mistake of the die-cutter.

Made in Canada. Unofficial motto of the Canadian Manufacturers' Association during a 'Buy Canadian' campaign in 1903.

'Mae West et un Pepsi, Un'. Reference to the traditional lunch of the French-Canadian worker in Quebec in the 1940s and 1950s. A 'Mae West' is a sugar-roll and a 'Pepsi' is a bottle of Pepsi-Cola. Why a sugar-roll should be called after the Hollywood star is obscure, especially as the name of the buxom actress has been identified, since 1937, with an airman's inflatable lifejacket.

Magazine of the North. See *The* BEAVER.

Magdalen Islands. See ÎLES-DE-LA-MADELEINE.

Magdalen penny. First coin ever struck specifically for use in Canada. A copper coin, it was issued in 1815 by Sir Isaac Coffin for use on the ÎLES-DE-LA-MADELEINE, which he had been granted as a reward for public service.

Magee, Mike (b.1934). The creator of 'Fred Dobbs'. A broadcaster since 1954 and a 'colour man' for racing events, he created the cantankerous farmer from Beamsville, Ont., for CBC Radio. As written and delivered by Magee, the salty observations of Dobbs, 'the sage of the silo', were first heard on GERUSSI! in 1968. Since then Magee has appeared as Dobbs on numerous radio and television programs.

Maggie Muggins. See JUST MARY.

Magnetic Hill. Optical illusion and tourist attraction. On a gravel road 5 mi. north of Moncton, N.B., there is a hill 'where cars coast uphill without power'. A car, driven to the bottom of the hill, will appear to coast back up the same hill when the brakes are released. The phenomenon has nothing to do with magnetic forces; the countryside is so tilted that what appears to be an upgrade is really a downgrade. Locally known since the 1920s, the curiosity first attracted wide attention in 1933 when Stuart Trueman and other journalists wrote about it. There are similar natural illusions in other parts of North America, but New Brunswick's Magnetic Hill is by far the best known and annually attracts a million tourists.

Magnificent. Well-known aircraft carrier. The Belfast-built, 695-ft vessel was launched in 1944 and commissioned into the ROYAL CANADIAN NAVY in 1948, the first carrier actually owned by Canada. Used for training cruises and exercises, she took part in the Suez Crisis before being 'paid off' on 14 June 1957. Once described as 'a seagoing parking lot', she was popularly called 'Maggie'. She was replaced by the BONAVENTURE.

Magnussen, Karen (b.1952). Champion figure-skater. The Vancouver-raised skater won the Canadian women's senior title in 1968. At the 1972 Winter Olympics in Sapporo, Japan, she won the silver medal and the following year became the world's champion. She then travelled with the Ice Capades and was invested with the ORDER OF CANADA.

Mahoney, Michael. See KLONDIKE MIKE.

Mahovlich, Frank (b.1938). Hockey player. Born in Timmins, Ont., he played left wing with the TORONTO MAPLE LEAFS from 1956 and with the MONTREAL CANADIENS from 1970. Called 'The Big M' because of his size (6 ft 2 in.) and stick-handling ability, he joined the Toronto Toros as captain in 1974. His brother Peter Joseph (Pete) Mahovlich (b.1946) plays with the Montreal Canadiens.

Mail and Empire, The. A daily newspaper published in Toronto. An amalgamation in 1895 of the *Mail* (founded in 1872) and the *Empire* (founded in 1887), it was published until 1936, when it was merged with the GLOBE to form the GLOBE AND MAIL. See also 'KIT OF THE MAIL'.

Maillet, Antonine (b.1929). Acadian novelist. Born in Bouctouche, N.B., she was educated at the Université de Montréal and also at Laval, where she teaches literature and folklore. The author of a number of novels and folkloristic works, she is best known for *La* SAGOUINE (1971), 16 highly individual monologues in Acadian French that have been performed by Viola Leger.

Main, The. St Lawrence Blvd or boulevard St-Laurent, the main north-south artery in MONTREAL. Sometimes called St Lawrence Main, it runs straight north from the harbour, divides Montreal Island into the east end and west end, and is the point at which streets are numbered 'est' or 'ouest'.

Main John. Lumbering expression for a 'woods boss' or superintendent. It is said to be derived from the name of a well-known New Brunswick lumberman and senator, John B. Glasier (1809-94).

Maintiens le droit. Official motto of the ROYAL CANADIAN MOUNTED POLICE. The French phrase, which translated means 'Uphold the Right', was advocated for use in 1873 and adopted by the Force two years later.

Mair, Charles (1838-1927). Poet. Born in Lanarck, U.C. (Ont.), and educated at Queen's University, he was a founder of the CANADA FIRST movement and, after being sent to the RED RIVER SETTLEMENT as paymaster to a roadbuilding party, was a fomenter of discontent there; he was held prisoner by Louis RIEL from 7 Dec. 1869 to 9 Jan. 1870, when he escaped. After the RED RIVER REBELLION he returned to the West and died in Victoria, B.C. His two collections of verse—*Dreamland and Other Poems* (1868) and *Tecumseh: A Drama, and Canadian Poems* (1901)—are of little interest except for occasional effective passages inspired by Mair's sensitive appreciation of the Canadian wilderness. Norman Shrive wrote the standard biography, *Charles Mair: Literary Nationalist* (1965).

Maison du Canada. See CANADA HOUSE.

Maison du Radio-Canada. Multi-storey Montreal headquarters for the French and English networks of CBC Radio and CBC-Television. 25 acres were levelled to make way for the building, which was opened in 1974 as offices and studios for 3,300 people.

Maison Laurier. A national historic site at Laurentides (formerly St Lin), Que. The childhood home of Sir Wilfrid LAURIER, it is furnished in the style of the 1840s, the period of the prime minister's youth.

Maisonneuve, sieur de (1612-76). Founder of VILLE MARIE, first governor of the island of Montreal. Born in Neuville-sur-Vanne, France, Paul de Chomeday de Maisonneuve was appointed governor by the Société Notre-Dame de Montréal, the owners of the island. Maisonneuve arrived at Québec in the late summer of 1641 and at Ville Marie (Montreal) the following spring. Quoted by DOLLIER, the first historian of Montreal, as saying that he was determined to begin a colony at Montreal 'even if all the trees on this island were to be transformed into Iroquois', Maisonneuve distinguished himself not only as its heroic defender against the harassment of those very Indians, but as an organizer of the little settlement. He governed Montreal until 1665, when New France became a Crown colony and his commission was revoked.

Maîtres chez nous. 'Masters in our own house'. Semi-separatist slogan devised by René LÉVESQUE and identified with the so-called QUIET REVOLUTION that took place in Quebec between 1960 and 1966 under the Liberal administration of Jean LESAGE.

Maize. See CORN.

Maj. Official abbreviation of Major.

Major, André (b.1942). Quebec poet and novelist. Born in Montreal, he was expelled from the Collège des Eudistes because he wrote for leftist publications and was an early contributor to PARTI PRIS before breaking with it in 1965. His poetry, which oscillates between personal observation and political statement, has been seen as central to an understanding of the separatist movement in Quebec in the 1960s. Malcolm Reid discusses Major's life and work in *The Shouting Signpainters: A Literary and Political Account of Quebec Revolutionary Nationalism* (1972).

Major, Leon (b.1933). Director. Born in Toronto, he was educated at the University of Toronto, where he was associated with

Major

HART HOUSE THEATRE. He was the founder and artistic director of the NEPTUNE THEATRE in Halifax (1962-8). He has directed for the STRATFORD FESTIVAL and the CANADIAN OPERA COMPANY (1960-8) and has served as director of production at the University of Toronto's Graduate Centre for the Study of Drama (1968-70). Since then he has been artistic director of the ST LAWRENCE CENTRE.

Major Dan Cooper. Canadian comic-strip hero popular in many European countries but not carried by Canadian newspapers. The clean-cut, square-jawed pilot in the Canadian Armed Forces was created by Belgian cartoonist Albert Weinberg in 1956 and modelled on the flier 'Buzz' BEURLING. Major Dan Cooper is in love with Randi, a luscious Norwegian blonde.

Majority government. An administration with sufficient members in the provincial legislature or the federal House of Commons to pass legislation without the aid of the other parties. The opposite of MINORITY GOVERNMENT.

Make fish. Newfoundland expression for curing fish by drying it in the sun.

Makers of Canada Series, The. A series of biographies of historical figures published in Toronto between 1903 and 1911. The general editors—Duncan Campbell SCOTT and Pelham Edgar—were joined by William Dawson LeSueur. In 1926 the series of 21 volumes was reissued by the Oxford University Press in 12 volumes under the editorship of William Lawson Grant. Individual volumes are still being reprinted by the University of Toronto Press. The first series consisted of: *Champlain* (1905) by N.E. Dionne, *Bishop Laval* (1906) by A. LeBlond de Brumath, *Count Frontenac* (1906) by W.D. LeSueur, *Wolfe and Montcalm* (1905) by H.R. Casgrain, *Lord Dorchester* (1907) by A.G. Bradley, *Sir Frederick Haldimand* (1904) by Jean N. McIlwraith, *John Graves Simcoe* (1905) by Duncan Campbell SCOTT, *Mackenzie, Selkirk, Simpson* (1905) by George Bryce, *General Brock* (1904) by Lady Edgar, *Papineau: Cartier* (1904) by A.D. DeCelles, *William Lyon Mackenzie* (1908) by G.G.S. Lindsey, *Joseph Howe* (1904) by J.W. Longley, *Egerton Ryerson* (1903) by Nathanael Burwash, *Baldwin, Lafontaine, Hincks: Responsible Government* (1907) by Stephen LEACOCK, *Lord Sydenham* (1908) by Adam SHORTT, *Lord Elgin* (1903) by Sir John Bourinot, *Wilmot and Tilley* (1907) by James Hannay, *Sir John A. Macdonald* (1908) by George R. Parkin, *George Brown* (1906) by John Lewis, *Sir James Douglas* (1908) by R.H. Coats and R.E. Gosnell, *Index and Dictionary*

of Canadian History (1911) by A.G. DOUGHTY and L.J. Burpee.

For the 1926 edition the following changes were made: *Bishop Laval* by H.A. Scott and *Lord Elgin* by W.P.M. Kennedy replaced the earlier biographies. *Sir William Van Horne* by Walter Vaughan (first published in New York in 1920), *Lord Strathcona* by John Macnaughton, and *Sir Wilfrid Laurier and the Liberal Party: A Political History* by J.S. Willison (which was first published in 1903 in two volumes) were added. The title of the *Index* was changed to *The Oxford Encyclopaedia of Canadian History*.

Makers of Canadian Literature. A series of short studies of Canadian authors edited by Lorne PIERCE with Victor Morin. 11 volumes were published by the RYERSON PRESS between 1923 and 1926, and a twelfth in 1941. Each volume contained a biographical sketch, an appraisal of the author's work, selections from the author's writings, and a bibliography. The volumes are *Isabella Valancy Crawford* (1923) by 'Katherine Hale' (Amelia Beers Garvin), *Stephen Leacock* (1923) by Peter McARTHUR, *William Kirby* (1923) by W.R. Riddell, *Robert Norwood* (1923) by Albert Durrant Watson, *Peter McArthur* (1923) by W.A. DEACON, *Louis Fréchette* (1924) by 'Henri d'Arles' (Henri Beaudé), *Charles G.D. Roberts* (1925) by James Cappon, *Thomas Chandler Haliburton* (1925) by J.D. Logan, *Antoine Gérin-Lajoie* (1925) by Louvigny de Montigny, *François-Xavier Garneau* (French ed. 1926; English ed. 1927) by Gustave Lanctot, *John Richardson* (1923) by W.R. Riddell, and *Arthur Stringer: Son of the North* (1941) by Victor Lauriston.

Makpaaq. See Vital Makpa ARNASUNGNAK.

Mal de la Baie St-Paul. Euphemism for syphilis in an epidemic form, reported in 1785 in the Baie St-Paul area on the north shore of the St Lawrence below Quebec City.

Malabar Ltd. Costumers. Begun in Winnipeg in 1904 by Sarah Mallabar, a Quebec widow, the business of making and renting theatrical and other costumes and accoutrements is carried on by her family. Her son Harry Malabar (who dropped one l from his name when he moved to Toronto) opened the independent eastern operation in 1921. Malabar Ltd in Toronto supplies dance slippers to the NATIONAL BALLET, costumes to the CANADIAN OPERA COMPANY, 110 Santa Claus costumes at Christmas, etc. Over 30 costume-makers are employed at any one time. There are branches of Malabar's or Mallabar's in many large Canadian cities.

Malahat Review, The. 'An International Quarterly of Life and Letters'. It was founded by the novelist John Peter and Robin SKELTON and has been published by the University of Victoria since 1967. It includes all genres of writing and pays particular attention to modern British literature and contemporary art. It is named after a famous drive on the east coast of Vancouver Island.

Malahide. Township in Elgin Co., Ont., ruled over by Col. Thomas TALBOT. It was named for the village of Malahide, near Dublin, and Malahide Castle, where Talbot was born. Talbot named his Canadian log house Castle Malahide.

Malecite. See MICMAC.

Malemute. A dog bred by the Malemiut Eskimos of western Alaska. The word is variously spelled and was once used in the Yukon as a derogatory reference to an Eskimo. The first line of 'The Shooting of Dan McGrew' by Robert SERVICE, written in 1907, goes: 'A bunch of the boys were whooping it up in the Malamute saloon . . .'

Mallett, Jane (b.1904?). Actress. Born in London, Ont., she acted as a student at HART HOUSE THEATRE and with the Village Players in Toronto in the 1920s. She evolved into a versatile performer with an original manner, rather like that of Beatrice Lillie. She starred in the Toronto revue, *Town Tonics*, in 1934 and 1935, and made memorable appearances in SPRING THAW. She undertook a variety of roles with the NEW PLAY SOCIETY, the CREST THEATRE, and the JUPITER THEATRE, and first appeared on national radio in 1930 and on national television in 1952. She starred, as SARAH BINKS, in *Here Lies Sarah Binks*, Don HARRON's mini-musical that played for eight weeks in Toronto in 1968. In 1958 she founded the Actors' Fund of Canada to help indigent performers and is its president.

Malpeque oyster. An Atlantic oyster from Malpeque Bay in Prince Edward Island, known for its quality.

Malton. The name of the Toronto International Airport at Malton, Ont., from its founding in 1938 to 12 Jan. 1964, when it received its present name.

Man. Abbreviation of MANITOBA.

Man Alive. A weekly series of 30-minute CBC-TV programs on society and religion. Launched on 1 Oct. 1967, it is produced by Leo Rampen and hosted by Roy Bonisteel.

Man and His World. Annual fair in Montreal; its French name is Terre des Hommes.

Sometimes called 'Son of Expo', it consists of the remaining pavilions, boutiques, and restaurants of EXPO 67, including the Montreal Aquarium, on Île Sainte-Hélène. (The site has been physically altered to accomodate some events in the 1976 Olympics.) It is open from mid-June to Labour Day.

Man from Glengarry, The. Novel by Ralph CONNOR published in 1901. Based on the author's memories of life in Glengarry County, Ont., in the 1860s, and of the Highland pioneers and lumbermen there, it is one of his most successful mixtures of adventure, emotion, idealized characters, and strong local colour—qualities that have given it great popularity and make it rather irresistible today.

Man That Always Rides, The. Canvas by Paul KANE painted between 1849 and 1855. It is a romantic, European-inspired study of a picturesquely dressed Blackfoot chief on a rearing white horse set against a dramatically lighted sky. (ROM)

Manawaka. Fictional town created by Margaret LAURENCE as the setting for much of her fiction, located in the rolling hills of Manitoba about 100 mi. north of Winnipeg. The name includes syllables from Manitoba, the author's native province, and Neepawa, her birthplace. 'Manawaka' is also the name of her home on the Otonabee R. near Peterborough, Ont.

Mance, Jeanne (1606-73). Founder of the Hôtel-Dieu of Montreal. She arrived at Quebec in 1641 in the party of MAISONNEUVE and was with him at the founding of Ville Marie (Montreal). She began a hospital in the new settlement, a building for which was erected in 1645, and devoted the rest of her life to its interests.

Mandala. A five-man, rhythm-and-blues group centred in Toronto. It was the first such group in North America to make use of theatrical lighting and the first Canadian group to earn more than $1,000 for a performance in Canada. It flourished between 1965 and 1969.

Mandarins, Ottawa. See OTTAWA MANDARINS.

Mandel, Eli (b.1922). Poet and critic. Born in Estevan, Sask., he studied at the Universities of Saskatchewan and Toronto and since 1967 has been a professor of English and Humanities at York University. Both as a poet and as a critic he has been influenced by the 'mythopoetics' of Northrop FRYE. His poetry, which has become increasingly experimental in nature, has been collected in *Fuseli Poems* (1960), *Black and Secret Man* (1964), *An Idiot Joy* (1967), *Stony Plain* (1973), and *Crusoe* (1973), selected poems. *Criticism: The Silent-Speaking Words* (1966) is a collection of Mandel's radio talks and *Irving* LAYTON (1969) is a detailed analysis of that poet's themes. Mandel edited *Contexts of Canadian Criticism* (1971), an anthology of readings by various critics.

Mangeur du lard. See PORKEATER.

Manhattan. An American supertanker refitted to test the feasibility of a tanker route through the ice of the NORTHWEST PASSAGE in 1969 and 1970. It was accompanied by the Canadian icebreaker *John A. Macdonald*, but many felt that its voyage constituted a challenge to Canada's ARCTIC SOVEREIGNTY.

Manic 5. Popular name of the Daniel Johnson Dam, part of the Manicouagan-Outardes River hydro-electric project in northern Quebec. The fifth of seven dams, it was built across the MANICOUAGAN RIVER in 1968. Its official name honours the late premier of Quebec. It is the world's highest multiple-arch concrete dam.

Manicouagan River. A tributary of the St Lawrence, in Saguenay County, Que., this 310-mi. river drains the Canadian Shield east of Quebec City. Along the river are located several very large hydro-electric installations, notably Manic 3 and MANIC 5. The unusual shape of Lac Manicouagan, from which the river rises, is thought to be the result of a meteor impact millions of years ago.

Manion, Robert James (1881-1943). Leader of the Conservative Party and leader of the Opposition, 1938-40. A medical doctor, he served overseas during the First World War and was elected to the House of Commons as a Unionist in 1917. He served in the two MEIGHEN cabinets of the 1920s and was BENNETT's Minister of Railways and Canals. Selected as Bennett's successor at a national convention in 1938, he led the Tories to a disastrous defeat in the 1940 general election and shortly thereafter was unceremoniously dumped as leader by the party caucus.

Manitoba. The central province, bounded by Ontario on the east, the 49th parallel on the south, Saskatchewan on the west, and the 60th parallel on the north. Erected in 1870 around the nucleus of the RED RIVER SETTLEMENT as a result of the RED RIVER REBELLION, it was known as the 'postage stamp province' because of its size and shape. Its original boundaries of the 49th parallel on the south,

99° longitude on the west, 50° 33' latitude on the north, and 96° longitude on the east, were extended in 1881 westward and north to 52° 50' north, but some territory was lost in 1884 when the Ontario boundary was extended west to the North West Angle of Lake of the Woods. Its present boundaries were established in 1912. The federal government retained control of its public lands until 1930.

Its economy is more diversified than that of the other Prairie Provinces, with significant resources in the agricultural lands in the south; the minerals of the CANADIAN SHIELD—particularly nickel, zinc, and copper; hydroelectric installations on the Nelson and other rivers; and considerable forest-industry potential in the Boreal forest. Its manufacturing base, particularly in consumer products, is also varied and its marketing function extends to the west and north.

With a land area of 211,755 sq. mi. and a 1974 population of 1,008,000, Manitoba has, with Saskatchewan, the lowest population density of all the provinces (4.7 persons per sq. mi.). Its capital is WINNIPEG.

Manitoba Arts Council. Provincial arts body. Established in 1965 and composed of a chairman, vice-chairman, and 10 members, all appointed, it has the aim of promoting the study, enjoyment, production, and performance of works in the arts in Manitoba. It advises the city of Winnipeg on its cultural assistance and in 1971 helped establish the first Canadian Business and Arts Conference. It makes grants to individuals and institutions, including the MANITOBA THEATRE CENTRE and the ROYAL WINNIPEG BALLET.

Manitoba Defamation Act. The first 'group libel' law in Canada, passed in 1934. Until 1970 it was the only law in the country that permitted a member of a defamed group, although not personally affected, to sue for an injunction against the publisher or author of a libel against the group. (R.S.M. 1954, c. 60, s. 20)

Manitoba Museum of Man and Nature, The. Non-profit, natural-history museum in Winnipeg. It opened in 1970 as part of the Manitoba Centennial Centre; its Planetarium had opened in 1968. There are six permanent galleries that include material about the earth's history, a reconstruction of Winnipeg in 1920, a re-creation of a seventeenth-century ship, and an Arctic display.

Manitoba No. 1 Hard. Famous hard red spring wheat grown since the 1880s in the Prairie Provinces, each variety of which has its own name. There are six grades, the top grade being No. 1. 'I say to this Government,' A.R. McMaster, a Manitoba MP, declared in the House of Commons on 24 June 1919, 'trust the people; the heart of the Canadian people is as sound as our No. 1 Hard Manitoba wheat.'

Manitoba Schools Question. A national controversy over provincial grants to French Catholic schools in Manitoba. Protestant and Roman Catholic schools shared equally in grants until, by 1890, increased English-speaking immigration had changed the demography of Manitoba. The Manitoba government then abolished denominational schools and the use of the French language. French-speaking people in both Manitoba and Quebec were incensed. Heated political and legal debates over the right and responsibility of the federal government to intervene lasted until 1897, when Sir Wilfrid LAURIER arranged a compromise that recognized the province's right to determine its educational policies but also protected the rights of religious and linguistic minorities within the public system. This arrangement lasted until 1916, when English was adopted as the sole language of instruction. See also EQUAL RIGHTS ASSOCIATION.

Manitoba Theatre Centre. The first major regional theatre in Canada. It was founded in Winnipeg in 1958, with the amalgamation of two amateur groups, by John HIRSCH, artistic director, and Tom HENDRY, administrative director. Its first production, *A Hat Full of Rain*, opened on 16 July 1958, and it went on to become a model for all subsequent regional theatres in Canada. The MTC moved into its own building, a 786-seat theatre, on 2 Nov. 1970.

Manitou. Algonkian word for 'spirit'. *Mitchi Manitou* means 'evil spirit'; *Gitchi Manitou* means 'great spirit'. Christian missionaries equated the former with the devil and the latter with God. It is said that *Manitou* means the same as the Iroquoian word ORENDA and the Siouan word WAKANDA.

Manitoulin Island. Largest freshwater island in the world. It is 100 mi. long and 1,068 sq. mi. in area and lies in Lake Huron off northern Georgian Bay.

Mann, Sir Donald. See CANADIAN NORTHERN RAILWAY.

Mann Cup. A solid gold trophy emblematic of the senior amateur championship in LACROSSE. It was donated by Sir Donald Mann, builder of the CANADIAN NORTHERN RAILWAY, in 1910. It is valued at $2,500.

Manning, Ed. See ROLL BACK THE YEARS.

Manoir Richelieu. Resort hotel at Pointe au Pic, Que. The first hotel on the magnificent cliff-top site overlooking the St Lawrence R., between Quebec City and Tadoussac, was built by the Richelieu and Ontario Navigation Company in 1899 and was destroyed by fire in Sept. 1928. The Richelieu and Ontario, by then Canada Steamship Lines, opened a new hotel accommodating 600 guests—designed by John Archibald in a modified version of the CHÂTEAU STYLE—in 1929. The president of CSL, William H. Coverdale, collected some 3,000 items of Canadiana, which were displayed in the hotel. It was purchased by Warnock Hersey in 1968, by a business group in 1971, and by the Quebec government in 1975.

Manpower and Immigration, Department of. Federal government department. It recruits and develops manpower resources in line with the needs of the economy through the counselling and training of skilled workers and the introduction of new manpower through immigration. It administers the CANADA MANPOWER CENTRES, the Special Employment Plan, introduced in 1971, and the LOCAL INITIATIVES PROGRAM.

Maoists. See COMMUNIST PARTY OF CANADA (MARXIST-LENINIST).

Map Stamp. See IMPERIAL PENNY POSTAGE COMMEMORATIVE ISSUE OF 1898.

Maple. Any of numerous species of deciduous trees with lobed leaves and winged seeds, of which 13 species are native to Canada. The sugar maple, of central and eastern distribution, and the very similar black maple, are highly valued as hardwood timber and shade trees and are the chief sources of maple syrup. The silver maple, of the same geographical range, furnishes a softer fine-grained wood used for furniture. Also eastern are the red maple, a hardwood with striking scarlet autumn foliage, and the Norway maple, a lofty ornamental maple introduced from Europe. The broadleaf maple is a valuable timber tree scattered through the west-coast forest.

Maple Leaf. National emblem of Canada, so adopted in 1867. The second verse of the national anthem, 'O CANADA', makes reference to the land 'where pines and maples grow'. The NATIONAL FLAG OF CANADA, officially adopted on 15 Feb. 1965, bears a stylized red maple leaf and hence is popularly known as 'The Maple Leaf'. The leaf of the MAPLE tree, although not found in all regions of the country, was considered a suitable emblem as early as 1805. See also 'THE MAPLE LEAF FOREVER'. A quasi-official emblem of Canada is the BEAVER.

Maple Leaf

Maple Leaf, The. A newspaper published by the Canadian Army overseas. The 4- to 16-page tabloid appeared daily between Jan. 1944 and spring 1946 and was published in Naples, Rome, Caen, Brussels, Amsterdam, Delmenhorst (near Bremen, Germany), and London, Eng. The Army issued it as the counterpart of the American *Stars and Stripes*, the British *Union Jack*, and the French *La Patrie*. Managing editor at Brussels—when it was the first paper in the world to publish pictures of the signing of the armistice at Rheims—was J. D. MacFarlane, who helped create the paper's popular cartoon feature HERBIE.

'Maple Leaf Forever, The'. Patriotic song so popular that it attained semi-anthem status. It was written in 1867 by Alexander MUIR, a Scots-born public-school teacher. While walking through Leslie Gardens in Toronto in the fall, a maple leaf alighted on his sleeve. When he tried to brush it off and it clung, he jokingly remarked, 'The maple leaf forever.' Then he wrote the words of the song and fitted them to a tune of his own composition for his students to sing. He had 1,000 copies printed at a cost of $30 and sold four dollars' worth. The work was pirated by a music publisher who copyrighted it and promoted it widely. It was widely sung in English Canada from, roughly, the Boer War to the end of the Second World War, when its pro-British imagery was seen to be invidious in the light of French-Canadian sensibilities.

Maple Leaf Gardens. 'Canada's best-known building'. The Toronto sports arena was erected in six months at the height of the Depression and opened on 12 Nov. 1931 with a hockey match between the Chicago Black Hawks and the TORONTO MAPLE LEAFS (won by the former by 3 goals to 2). The present seating capacity for hockey exceeds 16,000, the only larger arena being the FORUM in Montreal. Under president Harold E. Ballard it offers many forms of entertainment, from the Ice Capades to rock concerts. The Gardens has also been called 'the house that Smythe built', a reference to Conn SMYTHE. It is the home of the Toronto Maple Leaf Hockey Club.

'Maple Leaf Rag'. A popular ragtime tune with no Canadian reference. Its title refers to the Maple Leaf Club in Sedalia, Mo., where its composer, Scott Joplin, once worked.

Maple syrup. A natural or processed syrup, made from the sap of the maple tree. After the trees are tapped in early spring, the sap is concentrated by boiling down. It takes 30-40 gallons of sap to produce one gallon of syrup. Maple syrup is often associated with Canadian cuisine, especially that of Quebec, which produces 90% of Canada's maple syrup.

Maple syrup pie. Custard-like pie made with maple syrup thickened with cornstarch. It is traditional in Quebec.

Maracle, Clifford (b.1944). Mohawk painter. Born on the Tyendinaga Reserve near Deseronto, Ont., he graduated from the Ontario College of Art in 1974. His canvases are bold, expressionistic depictions of contemporary Indian life embedded with satire or the macabre. His compositions are sometimes compared with those of the American artist Fritz Scholder. Maracle also works as a sculptor in pumice-stone. He lives in Toronto.

Marchand, J.-Omer (1873-1938). Architect. He was the first French-Canadian architect to study at the École des Beaux-Arts in Paris (1893-1903), and prior to his return to Canada he designed the Canadian pavilion at the Paris Exposition of 1900. In 1903 he formed a partnership with Stevens Haskell in Montreal that continued until the latter's death in 1913. Marchand was noted for his work for the Roman Catholic Church, including St Cunégonde (1906) in Montreal and St Boniface Cathedral in Manitoba (1907). These buildings are eclectic in their choice of Classical, Romanesque, and Byzantine details, used in rich tapestry-like façade compositions based on strict Beaux Arts planning. In other buildings by Marchand, such as the Bordeaux Jail near Montreal, there is a mannerist emphasis on shadow and relief that is characteristic of French Second Empire design.

Marchand, Jean (b.1918). Cabinet minister. Born in Quebec and educated at Université Laval, he was active in the labour movement, working with the Confederation of Canadian Catholic Workers from 1944 and becoming president of the CONFEDERATION OF NATIONAL TRADE UNIONS in 1961. A member of the Royal Commission on BILINGUALISM AND BICULTURALISM 1963-5, he entered federal politics in 1965, along with Pierre Elliott TRUDEAU and Gérard PELLETIER, the 'three wise men of Quebec', and was appointed Minister of Citizenship and Immigration. He held several other cabinet portfolios before his resignation in July 1976.

Marchbanks, Samuel. See SAMUEL MARCHBANKS.

'Marching Down to Old Quebec'. A marching song that celebrates the failure of the

Americans to take QUEBEC CITY and the death of Gen. Richard MONTGOMERY on 31 Dec. 1775. It begins: 'Oh, we're marching down to old Quebec/And the fifes and the drums are a-beating,/For the British boys have gained the day,/And the Yankees are retreating.'

'Marching with the workers'. A phrase identified with Canadian unionism. It comes from a celebrated letter written on 14 Apr. 1937 by David A Croll, when resigning as Minister of Labour, Public Welfare and Municipal Affairs, to Ontario premier Mitchell HEPBURN. Objecting to Hepburn's handling of the GM workers during the OSHAWA STRIKE, Croll wrote: 'My place is marching with the workers rather than riding with General Motors.'

Marco Polo. A 1,625-ton sailing ship built at Saint John, N.B., in 1851 and later, while engaged in the Australian passenger trade, billed as 'the fastest ship in the world'. She had been some years in Norwegian registry when, on 25 July 1883, she was wrecked off Cavendish, P.E.I.

Marcotte, Gilles (b.1925). Quebec critic and writer. Born in Sherbrooke, Que. and educated at the Université de Montréal, he is best known as the author of *Une Littérature qui se fait* (1962, 1971), a collection of critical essays, and *Le Temps des poètes* (1970), a survey. His novel *Le Poids de Dieu* (1962), about a young priest's spiritual crisis, appeared in translation by Elizabeth Abbott as *The Burden of God* (1964).

Maria Chapdelaine. (i) Classic novel of *habitant* life by Louis HÉMON completed in 1913. Set in the Lac Saint-Jean area of Quebec, it tells the moving story of Maria Chapdelaine who, on the death of François Paradis, the trapper she truly loves, must choose between two suitors: Lorenzo Suprenant, who will take her to a life of ease in Boston, and Eutrope Gagnon, a young farmer who can offer her only the life of the pioneer. She accepts the latter, for 'in this land of Quebec naught shall die and naught change'. Hémon's conclusion and his realistic depiction of *habitant* life were deplored by Quebec nationalists when the novel was published in Montreal in 1916, but it gradually found acceptance, particularly after it was praised in Europe. A translation by W.H. BLAKE, *Maria-Chapdelaine: A Tale of the Lake St. John Country*, appeared in 1921. (ii) A feature film based on the novel was produced in Paris in 1934. It was directed by Julien Duvivier for France Films and starred Madeleine Renaud, Jean Gabin, and Jean-Pierre Aumont, who spoke with Parisian accents. The exteriors were shot on location in the Lac Saint-Jean region of Quebec. 95 min., b & w.

Marie de l'Incarnation (1599-1672). Founder of the URSULINE order in New France. Born Marie Guyart, she married at 18, had a son, was widowed, and in 1633 became an Ursuline nun. She went to Quebec in 1639 and founded a monastery, of which she alternated as superior until her death, and a boarding school for girls. For 30 years she wrote many thousands of letters, most of them to her son, who was a Jesuit priest. They are vivid, detailed accounts of life in New France that have both historical and literary value. Some of them have been translated by Joyce MARSHALL in *Word from New France: The Selected Letters of Marie de l'Incarnation* (1967).

Mariposa. A township in Oxford County, Ont. The name was used by Stephen LEACOCK as the 'little town' in SUNSHINE SKETCHES OF A LITTLE TOWN (identified with Orillia, Ont.), and by the MARIPOSA FOLK FESTIVAL, which began in Orillia.

Mariposa Folk Festival. Well-known annual festival of folk music. It was first held on 6-8 July 1960 in Orillia, Ont. (the model for Mariposa in SUNSHINE SKETCHES OF A LITTLE TOWN), and was staged there until 1963. It changed locations three times between 1963 and 1968, when it settled on Centre Island, Toronto; it continues to be held there for three days in June every year. Mariposa was founded by Ian TYSON and attracts leading folksingers and some 20,000 fans annually.

Maritime Command. One of the five functional commands of the CANADIAN ARMED FORCES.

Maritime Provinces. New Brunswick, Nova Scotia, and Prince Edward Island. With Newfoundland they form the Atlantic Provinces.

Markings. See CANADA GRADING.

Markland. 'Land of forests' in Icelandic sagas. It has been identified with numerous locations in North America, the most likely of which is the east coast of Labrador, near Cape Porcupine, where it is believed the Viking explorer LEIF ERICSSON made a landfall in A.D. 1001. See also L'ANSE AUX MEADOWS.

Markle, Fletcher (b.1921). Film and television director. Born in Winnipeg, he was associated with the ACADEMY OF RADIO ARTS (1945-51) and directed for the CBC STAGE series. He worked in Hollywood and New York but returned to Canada to direct Walt

Disney's *The* INCREDIBLE JOURNEY (1963) and stayed. For CBC-TV he produced the stylish TELESCOPE (1963-9) and WHITEOAKS OF JALNA (1972), and served as head of the Television Drama Department from 1969 to 1972, when he became an executive producer. He returned to Hollywood in 1976.

Marquette, Jacques. See Louis JOLLIET.

Marquis wheat. A type of WHEAT developed in 1907 by Charles SAUNDERS. Because it was a faster-maturing wheat, it led to a great expansion of the wheat-growing area of the Prairies. By 1920 over 15 million acres were planted in Marquis.

Married Couple, A. Documentary film produced and directed by Allan KING; the assistant director was Richard LEITERMAN. It starred a non-professional couple, Billy and Antoinette Edwards, and recorded in *cinéma-vérité* style the disintegration of their marriage. Released in 1969, it was widely discussed but not commercially successful. 112 min., colour.

Marriott, Anne. See *The* WIND OUR ENEMY.

Marsh Report. An important document in the history of the development of the welfare state in Canada. It was written by Leonard Marsh (b.1906), director of social research at McGill University and research adviser for the Committee on Post-War Reconstruction. Published as *Report on Social Security for Canada* in 1943, it made recommendations that became the foundation of the government's post-war welfare programs.

Marshall, Joyce (b.1913). Novelist, short-story writer, and translator. Born in Montreal and educated at McGill University, she lives in Toronto and is the author of two novels—*Presently Tomorrow* (1946) and *Lovers and Strangers* (1957)—and a selection of fine stories, *A Private Place* (1975). As a skilled translator she is identified with several books by Gabrielle ROY; her selection and translation of the letters of MARIE DE l'INCARNATION, *Word from New France* (1967); and her abridgement and translation of a Canadian travel book by Eugène Cloutier, *No Passport: A Discovery of Canada* (1968).

Marshall, Lois (b.1924). Soprano. Born in Toronto, she trained at the Royal Conservatory of Music, studying singing under Weldon Kilburn. Her soaring voice and emotional interpretations captivated audiences while she was still a student, singing in oratorios and concerts. She won the Naumberg Musical Foundation Award, New York, in 1952 and the following year was chosen by

Arturo Toscanini to sing in his final performance and recording of Beethoven's *Missa Solemnis*. She went on to sing under other major conductors, including Sir Thomas Beecham, with whom she recorded Mozart's *Abduction from the Seraglio* in 1956, and to pursue a busy international concert career. She performs frequently in Canada, where she remains a much-loved singer.

Marshall, Tom (b.1938). Poet. Born in Niagara Falls and educated at the University of Toronto, he teaches English at Queen's University, where he edited QUARRY. Since 1973 he has served as poetry editor of the CANADIAN FORUM. His publications include a poetic quartet organized around the four elements: *The Silences of Fire* (1969), *Magic Water* (1971), *The Earth-Book* (1974), and *The White City* (1976).

Marshlands Inn. A family-run inn in Sackville, N.B. In 1935 Mr and Mrs H.W. Read turned their 30-room, nineteenth-century farm house—named after the nearby TANTRAMAR MARSHES—into a gracious inn filled with Canadian antiques and Edwardian furniture. There are 10 guest rooms. It is currently run by Mr and Mrs H.C. Read, who achieved a national reputation for the inn's cuisine by raising their own vegetables and chickens and serving their own preserves and canned foods.

Martin, Abraham. See PLAINS OF ABRAHAM.

Martin, Claire (b.1914). Quebec novelist and memoirist. Born in Quebec City and educated by the Ursulines and by the Soeurs de la Congrégation de Notre-Dame, she is the author of several novels but is best known for her two memoirs of an unhappy childhood in an oppressive society. They were translated by Philip STRATFORD and published in one volume as *In an Iron Glove* (1968). In 1975 these translations were republished in two volumes: *In an Iron Glove* and *The Right Cheek*.

Martin, Mungo (*c.*1881-1962). Master Kwakiutl carver. He was born at Fort Rupert, Vancouver Island, B.C. His Kwakiutl name was Naqapenkum (Ten Times Chief), and he was the last of the major totem-pole carvers. He carved poles for the University of British Columbia from 1947 and for the Provincial Museum in Victoria from 1952. Chanting traditional songs as he carved, he made the world's tallest cedar pole for Victoria's Beacon Hill Park—127 ft 6 in. high. The tradition is continued by his adoptive grandson, Tony HUNT.

Martyrs, Jesuit. See JESUIT MARTYRS.

Martyrs' Shrine. Twin-spired church built in 1926 near Midland, Ont., and Sainte-Marie-among-the-Hurons (see SAINTE-MARIE-AUX-HURONS) to commemorate the seventeenth-century Jesuits who were martyred in their missionary work with the Indians. Among them were five priests, canonized in 1930, who worked with the Huron Indians in HURONIA and were killed by Iroquois there: Jean de BRÉBEUF, Charles Garnier, Gabriel LALEMANT, Antoine Daniel, and Noël Chabanel. The other martyr-saints—Isaac JOGUES, René Goupil, and Jean de la Lande—were killed in what is now New York State.

Mary (or Marie) Celeste. Most famous of all mystery ships. The *Mary Celeste*—a twin-masted, 100-ft brigantine built at Spencer's Island, N.S., in 1861—was found abandoned on 5 Dec. 1872, drifting ghost-like at a point between the Azores and the Portuguese coast, her cargo intact. The mystery of her sudden abandonment on open waters and the disappearance of her captain and crew have never been explained, and speculation has continued to this day. In his short story, 'J. Habakuk Jephson's Statement', in *The Captain of the Pole-Star* (1890), A. Conan Doyle referred to the ship as the *Marie Celeste*, thus establishing the more poetic name.

Mask, The. Feature film produced and directed by Julian Roffman in 1961. It starred Paul Stevens, Claudette Nevins, Bill Walker, Anne Collings, and Martin Lavut. The story concerns a South American Indian mask that caused hallucinations and violent behaviour when Torontonians wore it. The hallucinatory sequences were shown in 3-D, and a voice on the screen notified the audience when it was time to put on its red-and-green goggles. This was the first and last Canadian 3-D feature. 95 min., colour.

Maskinonge. A large species of pike, weighing up to 80 lb., found principally in the GREAT LAKES. The accepted etymology is the Algonkian word (*mackinonge*) for pike. Variations of the name are lunge, muskellunge, and muskie.

Mason, Bill (b.1929). Film director. Born in Winnipeg, he worked as a painter and commercial artist before moving into animation with Crawley Films and then the NATIONAL FILM BOARD. A passionate naturalist, he has directed such films as PADDLE-TO-THE-SEA (1966), *Blake* (1969), and CRY OF THE WILD (1972)—an aggressively promoted feature that is probably the most commercially successful of all Canadian films.

Massasauga rattlesnake. The smallest of Canada's rattlesnakes, rarely exceeding 3 ft. It inhabits swamps along Georgian Bay, Lakes Huron, St Clair, and Erie, and Lake Ontario in the extreme southwest. Its venom is almost never fatal and it seldom bites unless attacked. Ojibwa for 'great river-mouth', its name derives from that of the Mississauga tribe.

Masses. Short-lived monthly magazine published by the COMMUNIST PARTY OF CANADA. Once referred to as 'the Communist answer to the socialistically inclined CANADIAN FORUM', it was published in Toronto and appeared irregularly between Apr. 1932 and Apr. 1934. Its title recalls that of the better-known New York magazine *New Masses*.

Massey, Raymond (b.1896). Actor. The brother of Vincent MASSEY, he was born in Toronto and made his theatrical début in London, Eng., in 1922. In 1938 he created the title role on Broadway of *Abe Lincoln in Illinois*—a characterization, it was said, that 'took the face off the penny and put it into the hearts of millions of Americans'. He became an American citizen in 1944. A veteran of many Hollywood films, he appealed to a generation of television viewers as Dr Gillespie, the mentor of *Dr Kildare* (1961-5). His autobiography, *When I Was Young*, appeared in 1976.

Massey, Vincent (1887-1967). First native-born GOVERNOR GENERAL of Canada. Born in Toronto, the elder brother of Raymond MASSEY, and educated at the University of Toronto and at Oxford, he lectured in modern history at the University of Toronto (1913-15), where he oversaw the construction of HART HOUSE. He was president of the family company, Massey-Harris (later MASSEY-FERGUSON), from 1921 to 1925. He served as the first Canadian minister in Washington (1926-30), was president of the National Liberal Federation (1932-5), and high commissioner in London (1935-46). In 1949 he was appointed chairman of the Royal Commission on National Development in the Arts, Letters, and Sciences (familiarly known as the MASSEY COMMISSION), which issued its famous *Report* in 1951. Governor general from 1952 to 1959, he was pleased when a newspaper noted that 'He made the Crown Canadian.' He published five collections of addresses, including *On Being Canadian* (1948), and his memoirs, *What's Past is Prologue* (1963). He lived at BATTERWOOD and died in London, Eng. See also MASSEY LECTURES, MASSEY MEDAL, and VINCENT MASSEY AWARDS.

Massey College. Residential college for senior scholars and graduate students within the UNIVERSITY OF TORONTO. Built in 1960-3 (to the design of Ron THOM) and furnished by the Massey Foundation, which was set up by Vincent MASSEY, it is not intended primarily for teaching but to provide study facilities and the associations of a collegiate life. Women students were admitted in 1974. The Master of the College is Robertson DAVIES.

Massey Commission. The Royal Commission on National Development in the Arts, Letters, and Sciences, 1949-51. It was chaired by Vincent MASSEY (later governor general). Also serving as commissioners were Dr Hilda NEATBY, Dr Arthur Surveyer, Dr Norman A.M. MacKenzie, and Dean Georges-Henri Lévesque. 1,200 individuals representing 462 different organizations made representations to the Commission. Its *Report* of 1951 made recommendations regarding radio, television, the NATIONAL FILM BOARD, libraries, galleries, museums, archives, historic sites and monuments, scholarships, scientific research, and representation abroad. Two actions taken by the federal government in response to the Commission were a program of unrestricted federal grants to universities and the establishment (in 1957) of the CANADA COUNCIL (for the encouragement of the Arts, Humanities, and Social Sciences).

Massey-Ferguson Limited. One of the world's major farm-implement manufacturers. It began in 1847 with a small foundry established by Daniel Massey (1798-1856) at Bond Head, C.W. (Ont.), and became the Massey Manufacturing Company in 1870 under his son Hart Massey (1823-96), who moved the headquarters to Toronto in 1878 and introduced the well-known Toronto Light Binder. In 1890 he merged his company with A. Harris and Son, founded in Beamsville, Ont., by Alanson Harris (1816-94), Massey's principal competitor and manufacturer of the Brantford Light Binder. Massey-Harris Ltd helped open up the West and developed an important export trade. Vincent MASSEY was president from 1921 to 1925. The company was merged with the Harry Ferguson Company in 1953, and was known as Massey-Harris-Ferguson until 1958, when the 'Harris' was dropped and it acquired its present name.

Massey Hall. Toronto concert auditorium. Built as the Massey Music Hall in 1894 to a design by George M. MILLER, it was presented to the city by Hart Massey (see MASSEY-FERGUSON LIMITED) as a memorial to his son Charles. It was planned as a general-purpose hall, with 2,765 seats, and many important events have been held there, including concerts by leading musicians and other performers from all over the world and the Toronto screenings of the first movie, the first talking picture, and the first colour film. Churchill spoke about his Boer War experiences there and Jack Dempsey held an exhibition match. It is the home of the TORONTO SYMPHONY ORCHESTRA.

Massey Lectures. CBC Radio's principal series of talks, named for the late governor general, Vincent MASSEY. Each year a noted scholar is asked to prepare and deliver a series of 30-minute radio talks. Resembling the annual Reith Lectures of the BBC, they were inaugurated in 1961 with Lady Barbara Ward Jackson's 'The Rich Nations and the Poor Nations'. Other distinguished speakers have included Northrop FRYE in 1962, Martin Luther King in 1967, George GRANT in 1969, and George Steiner in 1974.

Massey Medal, The. Awarded annually by the Royal Canadian Geographical Society 'for outstanding personal achievement in the exploration, development or description of the geography of Canada'. The silver gilt medal, established by the Massey Foundation, was first awarded in 1959 by Vincent MASSEY when he was governor general. See also VINCENT MASSEY AWARDS.

Massey's Magazine. See CANADIAN MAGAZINE.

Master Charge. A convenient banking and credit-card system whereby consumers may purchase goods or services from participating consumer outlets or obtain cash from branches of the Bank of Montreal by presenting their Master Charge card. Each month the cardholder is billed for the purchases made over the past month and has 25 days to pay this bill free of interest. If the cardholder chooses, he or she may hold over all or any part of the monthly bill at an interest rate of $1\frac{1}{2}\%$ per month or 18% per annum. Offered by the BANK OF MONTREAL and the BANQUE PROVINCIALE DU CANADA, the system has been in operation in Canada since 3 June 1973.

Masterpieces of Indian and Eskimo Art from Canada. An important exhibition of the arts of the native people of Canada. It was shown at the Musée de l'Homme in Paris in Nov. 1969 and at the National Gallery in Ottawa in Mar. 1970. Europeans for the first time were exposed to the indigenous art of the Indians and Eskimos from prehistory to the end of the nineteenth century, and the famous French cultural anthropologist, Claude Lévi-

Strauss said: 'I consider that the culture of the Northwest Indians produced an art on a par with that of Greece and Rome.' Of the more than 500 artifacts, 120 are reproduced in *Indian and Eskimo Art of Canada* (1970), with a text by Ian Christie Clark.

Masters in our own house. See MAÎTRES CHEZ NOUS.

Matchi Manitou. See MANITOU.

Mather, Bruce (b.1939). Composer. Born in Toronto, he studied piano and composition at the Royal Conservatory of Music and the University of Toronto. He also studied at the Paris Conservatoire with Darius Milhaud and Olivier Messiaen and later received his doctorate in music from the University of Toronto. He teaches at McGill University and the Université de Montréal. Among his compositions for orchestra, choir, voice, and piano, his five *Madrigals* (1967-73)—lyric, contemplative works for voice and instrumental ensemble inspired by the poems of Saint-Denys GARNEAU—are notable.

Mathews, Peter. See Samuel LOUNT.

Mathieu, Rodolphe (1890-1962). Composer, Born in Grondines, Que., he was a church organist in Montreal before studying and living in Paris, where he was influenced by the style of Debussy and Schoenberg's pre-serial experiments. After returning to Canada he founded the Institut Canadien de Musique. A pioneer of contemporary Canadian music, he is remembered especially for his *Sonate pour piano et violin* (1928) and *Quintette pour piano et cordes* (1942). His later years were devoted to teaching.

Matinée. See TRANS-CANADA MATINÉE.

Matriculation. Successful completion of secondary-school studies that satisfied the requirements for university entrance. As education is a provincial responsibility, the length of high-school instruction varies from province to province. In Ontario, Junior Matriculation was the completion of Grade XII, Senior Matriculation the completion of GRADE XIII. These terms are no longer in use, having been replaced by a credit system leading to a Secondary School Graduate Diploma or a Secondary School Honour Graduate Diploma.

Matton, Roger (b.1929). Composer. Born in Granby, Que., he studied at the Montreal Conservatoire and in Paris with Nadia Boulanger and Olivier Messiaen. In Quebec City he worked at the Archives de Folklore at Université Laval, where his discoveries altered

the focus of his music and led him to teach ethnomusicology. Of his compositions—which show great originality though solidly based in traditional structures—*Mouvement symphonique No 1* (1960), the cantata *Te Deum* (1967), and *Mouvement symphonique No 2* (1962) have been performed with success in both Canada and Europe. His music for the ballet *L'Horoscope* (1958) shows the influence of Acadian folklore.

Maudits anglais, Les. 'The damned English'. Phrase used by French Canadians to describe English Canadians.

Mavor, James (1854-1925). Political economist. Born at Stranraer, Scot., and educated at the University of Glasgow, he was professor of political economy at the University of Toronto from 1892 until his retirement in 1923. The author of several books and studies—including *An Economic History of Russia* (1914) and an autobiography, *My Windows on the Streets of the World* (1923)—he is mainly remembered for his role in negotiating with the Russian philosopher Prince Kropotkin and Clifford SIFTON the settlement of the DOUKHOBORS in the Northwest Territories.

Maxmobile. Automobile manufactured from 1900 to 1910 by D.A. Maxwell at Watford, Ont. It had a one-cylinder engine mounted under the seat.

Maxwell, E. and W.S. Architectural firm. Edward Maxwell (1868, retired 1923) was born in Montreal and trained in the Montreal office of A.F. Dunlop and in Boston. W.S. Maxwell (1874-1952) was born in Montreal and trained with his brother (1890-3), in the Boston office of Winslow and Wetherell (1893-6), and at the Boston Architectural Club; he also studied at the École des Beaux-Arts in Paris from 1899 to 1902. He practised with his brother from 1897 to 1899 and from 1902 to 1923, when he formed the firm Maxwell and Pitts. The brothers were committed to the ideals of Beaux Arts Classicism and their Montreal firm designed many buildings across the country, of which the finest are probably the Saskatchewan Legislative Building, Regina (1906-14); the MONTREAL MUSEUM OF FINE ARTS (c.1912-13); and the Hosmer House, Drummond St, Montreal (c.1900). Other works by the firm include extensions to WINDSOR STATION, Montreal (c.1900), in the Romanesque style of the original, and additions to the CHÂTEAU FRONTENAC in the CHÂTEAU STYLE (1920-4).

May the twenty-fourth. See VICTORIA DAY.

Mayfair. A monthly magazine established by

MACLEAN-HUNTER and published in Toronto between 1927 and 1956. A quality publication, edited in its last years by Robert FULFORD, it attempted, like the *New Yorker*, to cover the social, fashion, and cultural scenes.

Mayflower. Also called the trailing arbutus, this low-growing plant of the heath family, with spring-blooming white or pale pink flowers that grow in clusters, is found in eastern North America. The flower became Canada's first official provincial floral emblem when it was adopted by Nova Scotia in 1901. Prior to legislation it served in 1825 as the motif for Joseph HOWE's *Novascotian* and in the mid-nineteenth century as a decoration on military buttons and provincial stamps and coins.

Mayhew, Elza (b.1916). Sculptor. Born in Victoria, B.C., she was educated at the University of British Columbia. She took up sculpting in the 1950s and in 1962 received the Sir Otto Beit Medal from the Royal Society of British Sculptors. In 1964 she and Harold TOWN represented Canada at the Venice Biennale. Her bronze and stone columnar forms are reminiscent of pre-Columbian sculpture.

Mayne, Seymour (b.1944). Poet and editor. Born in Montreal and educated at McGill and the University of British Columbia, he helped found Very Stone House, a Vancouver-based poetry-publishing imprint, in 1965, and then Igluvik Publications in Montreal. He co-edited with Pat LANE *The Collected Poems of Red Lane* (1968) and with Dorothy LIVESAY *Forty Women Poets of Canada* (1971). He edited *Engagements: The Prose of Irving* LAYTON (1972) and *The A.M.* KLEIN *Symposium* (1975). His best-known poetry publications are *Mouth* (1970) and *Name* (1975). Since 1973 he has taught English at the University of Ottawa.

Mazzoleni, Ettore (1905-68). Conductor and music educator. Born in Brusio, Switz., and educated in England, he came to Toronto in 1929 and taught music and English at Upper Canada College until 1944. He was associate conductor of the TORONTO SYMPHONY ORCHESTRA (1943-8), principal of the ROYAL CONSERVATORY OF MUSIC (1945-68), director of the Opera School (1952-66), and a conductor of the CANADIAN OPERA COMPANY (1957-66).

MB. Initials that the holder of the MEDAL OF BRAVERY is entitled to place after his name.

MC. See MILITARY CROSS.

Mechanical Bride, The. The first book by Marshall McLUHAN, published in 1951. Subtitled *Folklore of Industrial Man*, it examines the impact of the mass media on our society through a juxtaposition of modern advertising illustrations, copy, and commentary. McLuhan discusses, among other things, 'a widely occurring cluster image of technology, sex, and death which contributes the mystery of the mechanical bride'—the media's image of sexuality.

Medal for Distinguished Conduct in the Field. Commonwealth decoration for acts of pre-eminent bravery, first awarded to non-commissioned officers and men of the British Army in 1854. The abbreviation is DCM.

Medal of Bravery. A Canadian honour awarded for acts of heroism, abbreviated as MB.

Medical Research Council. A federal CROWN CORPORATION to support medical research in Canadian universities and other institutions. Established in 1969, it has a president, a vice-president, and 20 members.

Medicare. Medical insurance plan put into operation by the Saskatchewan government in 1962. Although Medicare refers specifically to the Saskatchewan health plan, the word 'medicare' is used in Canada and the United States to refer to any health or hospital insurance plan sponsored by the federal government. Canadians enjoy comprehensive health- and hospital-insurance plans sponsored by the federal government and operated by the provincial governments on a cost-sharing basis. A national hospital-insurance plan has been in existence since 1961, and a national medical-care program, the Medical Care Act, since 1968. Medicare is known in each province under a different name—in Ontario, OHIP, etc.

Medicare Strike. See SASKATCHEWAN DOCTORS' STRIKE.

Medicine man. An Indian SHAMAN, curer, conjurer, or Eskimo ANGAKOK.

'Medium is the Message, The'. Famous phrase coined by Marshall McLUHAN in 1959 and elaborated in his *Understanding Media* (1964): ' "The Medium is the Message" because it is the medium that shapes and controls the scale and form of human association and action.'

Medley, E.S. (1838-1910). Architect and clergyman. Born in Exeter, Eng., he came to Fredericton, N.B., in 1845, when his father, John Medley (1804-92), was appointed Bishop. He trained in the London office of William Butterfield from 1853 to 1856, grad-

Mercantile Bank of Canada

uated from King's College, Fredericton, in 1862, and was ordained a priest in 1864 before returning to England in 1872. His wooden churches in New Brunswick—All Saint's, McKeen's Corner (1861); Church of St Mary the Virgin, New Maryland (1863-4); Christ Church, St Stephen (1863-4); and the Church of the Ascension, Apohaqui (1871-2)—represent a fusion of American board-and-batten techniques with the British traditions of half-timbering that aimed at creating a style specifically appropriate to Canadian conditions.

Meeting of the School Trustees, A. Canvas by Robert HARRIS painted in 1886. It shows a young teacher bravely explaining herself to four dour and sceptical trustees—residents of rural Prince Edward Island. (NGC)

Megantic Outlaw. Sobriquet of Donald Morrison (1858-94), a Scottish settler in Megantic county in the EASTERN TOWNSHIPS of Quebec. Cheated of the family farm, he accidentally killed an inspector who had been attempting to arrest him in 1888 on suspicion of having set it on fire. What followed was the longest manhunt in Canadian history, during which the Scottish settlers in the county conspired to protect Morrison from the law. Caught after three years and found guilty of manslaughter, he was sent to St Vincent de Paul Penitentiary, where he died. A ballad of Oscar Dhu and a novel by Bernard Epps recall the episode. It is also the subject of a 90-minute colour feature film written, produced, and directed by Ron KELLY and starring Gary McKeehan and Lloyd BOCHNER. *The Megantic Outlaw* was shown on CBC-TV on 27 Jan. 1970. The background music included 'Marion's Theme', a haunting melody composed by Doug Riley.

Meighen, Arthur (1874-1960). Ninth prime minister. Born in Perth County, Ont., he attended the University of Toronto, studied law in Winnipeg, Man., and practised in Portage la Prairie. He was elected to Parliament as a Conservative in 1908 and entered upon a political career that was marked by great personal abilities overshadowed by humiliating electoral defeats. He joined the cabinet of Sir Robert BORDEN's Union government in 1917. He was prime minister from July 1920 to Dec. 1921 and for 13 weeks in 1926 when Mackenzie KING resigned because the governor general, Lord BYNG, refused to dissolve Parliament. Defeated in the House and in the ensuing election, Meighen retired to private life. He joined the Senate in 1932. Becoming leader of the Conservative Party in 1941, he was once more defeated in a by-election and retired permanently from political life.

Melzack, Louis. See CLASSIC BOOKSHOPS.

Memoirs of Montparnasse. Novel-like memoir by John GLASSCO published in 1970, though it was written during and not long after the events described. Based on the author's recollections of his stay in Paris in the late 1920s, it is a vivid and entertaining account of what it was to be young in a city that was alive with creative people, literary expatriates, and eccentrics in pursuit of pleasure.

Memorial Day. Statutory holiday observed in Newfoundland on 1 July or the nearest Monday. As it commemorates the many Newfoundlanders who died at the Battle of Beaumont Hamel in 1916, it is sometimes called Commemoration Day.

Memorial University. Beginning as a college in St John's, Nfld, in 1925, it gained university status by an act of the provincial legislature in 1949. To the original Faculties of Arts and Science, Education, Engineering, and Applied Science was added Medicine in 1967. It has a well-known Department of Folklore, an Educational Television Centre, and Institutes of Social and Economic Research (1961) and Research in Human Abilities (1968). See also the FOGO PROCESS.

Mennonites. A religious sect named after Dutch Anabaptist leader, Menno Simons (1496-1561), who insisted on strict adherence to non-violence and to dictates of the Bible and placed the Christian conscience before government authority. There are 168,150 adherents in Canada (1971), ranging from German-speaking Old Order Mennonites, who reject the use of modern fashion and technology, to urban, almost totally assimilated Mennonites. Many live in the region of Kitchener, Ont.

Mental Health Canada. The name since 1975 of the Canadian Mental Health Association. A voluntary organization made up of those who are concerned with combatting mental illness in Canada, it was founded in Toronto in 1918 by Clarence E. Hincks (1883-1964), a psychiatrist who himself was subject to recurrent depression. In 1951 Hincks was succeeded as general director by Dr J.D.M. (Jack) Griffin, a psychiatrist, who retired in 1971. The CMHA sponsored the publication of the important report MORE FOR THE MIND.

Menzies spruce. The original name of a species of tall spruce found on the Pacific Coast and named after Archibald Menzies (1754-1842), who discovered it in 1792. It is now called the Sitka spruce.

Mercantile Bank of Canada. A foreign-

337

owned chartered bank with its head office in Montreal. A subsidiary of the First National City Bank of New York, it was incorporated in 1958 amid much controversy and with restrictions on its growth—the first foreign bank to receive a charter. It has 11 locations across the country.

Mercure, Pierre (1927-66). Composer. Born in Montreal, he studied at the Conservatoire in Montreal and later in Paris with Nadia Boulanger. He was a bassoonist with the Montreal Symphony Orchestra and produced music broadcasts for La Société RADIO-CANADA. His finest compositions include the electronic work *Structures métalliques* (1962); *Psaume pour abri* (1963) for choir and orchestra, which fuses electronic and traditional music; and *Lignes et points* (1964), commissioned by the Montreal Symphony Orchestra. He died accidentally in France.

Meredith, John (b.1933). Painter. The brother of William RONALD, he was born in Fergus, Ont., studied at the Ontario College of Art with Jock MacDONALD, and worked as a cartoonist for the *Brampton Conservator*. His use of intense colours, learned from the Abstract-expressionist style he rejected, is combined with mysterious symbols, similar to forms associated with eastern religions, that give his paintings a sacred aura. This is best seen in his triptych *Seeker* (1966, AGO), which shows the careful draughtsmanship and vibrant colours that characterize his highly personal style. He lives in Toronto and has been exhibited internationally.

Merril, Judith (b.1923). Science-fiction writer. Born in New York, she acquired a considerable reputation as a forward-looking editor of science-fiction anthologies, beginning with *Shot in the Dark* (1950). Settling in Toronto in Nov. 1968, she established the SPACED OUT LIBRARY at ROCHDALE COLLEGE in 1969. It was acquired by the Toronto Public Library System in 1970. She is a broadcaster and writer for CBC IDEAS and has published recently *Survival Ship and Other Stories* (1973) and *The Best of Judith Merril* (1976), a mass-market paperback.

Merrymaking. Famous canvas by Cornelius KRIEGHOFF painted in 1860. It is the best of the artist's storytelling paintings of *habitant* life, depicting an animated assemblage of people, horses, and sleighs outside the inn of J.-B. Jolifou after a night of partying. It is in the Beaverbrook Art Gallery, Fredericton, N.B.

'Message of the Carillon, The'. The title of an address delivered by Prime Minister W.L. Mackenzie KING on 1 July 1927. The occasion was the Diamond Jubilee of Confederation, when the newly installed carillons in the Peace Tower of the PARLIAMENT BUILDINGS were dedicated. The Bourdon bell, the largest of the 53 bells in the carillon, bears this inscription on its rim: 'Glory to God in the Highest and on Earth Peace, Goodwill Toward Men.' 'Such is the message of the carillon,' King declaimed. 'A message of rejoicing and thanksgiving known in Biblical lore as "The Angel's Song".' The passage appears in *The Message of the Carillon and Other Addresses* (1928).

Messer, Don. See DON MESSER'S JUBILEE.

Messina, Straits of. Three miles of sea that separate Sicily and the Italian mainland, the scene of a successful assault and crossing by Canadian troops on 3 Sept. 1943.

Metcalf, John (b.1938). Short-story writer. Born in Carlisle, Eng., and educated at the University of Bristol, he settled in Montreal, where he now teaches English at Concordia University. He has published two collections of well-constructed stories, *The Lady Who Sold Furniture* (1970) and *The Teeth of My Father* (1975), and one satirical novel about the teaching profession, *Going Down Slow* (1972). He has also edited several short-story anthologies.

Métis. French word for 'HALF-BREED'. It was used in the nineteenth century, largely on the Prairies, to refer to the offspring of marriages or liaisons between French-speaking fur traders and Cree and Ojibwa women. They were also called *bois-brûlés*. See also RED RIVER REBELLION, NORTHWEST REBELLION.

Metric Commission. A commission to advise the Minister of Industry, Trade and Commerce on plans for conversion to the metric system. Established in June 1971, it consists of a full-time chairman and up to 20 part-time members. The commission also provides the public with information on the metric system and may be written to c/o Box 4000, Ottawa, Ont. See also METRIC CONVERSION, SI SYSTEM.

Metric conversion. Plans for conversion from the imperial to the metric system in Canada were announced by the government on 16 Jan. 1970, when a White Paper on Metric Conversion was released. A METRIC COMMISSION was appointed to prepare and co-ordinate the adoption of the SI SYSTEM of metric measurement.

CONVERSION FACTORS
Imperial to Metric
1 inch = 2.540 cm

338

1 foot = 0.3048 m
1 mile = 1.609 km
1 acre = 0.405 ha
1 square mile = 259.1 ha
1 short ton = 2000 lbs = 0.907 tonne
(metric ton)
1 long ton = 2240 lbs = 1.016 tonne
(metric ton)

Metric to Imperial

1 cm = 0.3937 inch
1 m = 3.281 feet
1 km = 0.6214 mile
1 ha = 2.471 acres
1 km^2 = 0.386 square
mile
1 tonne (metric ton) = 1.1023 short ton
1 tonne (metric ton) = 0.9842 long ton

RULE-OF-THUMB METRIC CONVERSION
Kilometres to miles: multiply by 6 and knock
off one decimal point.
Kilogram: equivalent of 2.2 pounds.
Metre: 11/10 yard.
Litre: 11/10 quart.
Centimetre: 2.5 = 1 inch.
Gram: 33 = 1 pound.
Celsius to Fahrenheit: times 2 plus 32.
Fahrenheit to Celsius: minus 32, divide by 2.

Metro Toronto Zoo. A 710-acre zoological park in northeastern Metropolitan Toronto, the first phase of which opened in Aug. 1974. Some 3,500 animals, grouped in six zoo-geographical world regions, can be observed in settings simulating their natural environment. It is one of the largest public zoos in the world.

Metropolitan Opera Broadcasts. A weekly CBC Radio feature. Saturday-afternoon performances have been broadcast live from the stage of the Metropolitan Opera, New York, since Christmas Day 1931 (the production was *Hansel and Gretel*). In Canada the Met was first heard on a national network in 1933, when the CRBC made its first exchange plans with U.S. networks; the CBC continued coast-to-coast broadcasts after it was established in 1936. The opera broadcasts and intermission features have been sponsored by Texaco since 1940.

Metropolitan thesis. See J.M.S. CARELESS.

MGen. Official abbreviation of Major-General after UNIFICATION. Prior to unification it was Maj.Gen.

Michener, Daniel Roland (b.1900). GOVERNOR GENERAL of Canada from 1967 to 1974. Born in Lacombe, Alta, he was educated at the University of Alberta and at Oxford and was a corporation lawyer in Toronto before entering politics as a Conservative, occupying the Speaker's chair in the House of Commons from 1957 to 1962. He was high commissioner to India from 1964 to 1967 before his appointment as governor general. He is now a prominent Toronto lawyer.

Michilimackinac or **Mackinac.** An important centre in the nineteenth-century fur trade at the junction of Lake Michigan and Lake Huron. It refers to three areas in U.S. territory: the straits that join the two lakes; the island in the straits; and a point on the north shore. In 1670 a French mission was founded on the island; the area was surrendered to the British in 1761 and ceded to the United States in 1783. In 1784 a post on the island became the headquarters of a fur-trading company that became in turn a subsidiary of the NORTH WEST COMPANY in 1806. The territory was taken by the British in the WAR OF 1812 (see Battles of MICHILIMACKINAC) and returned to the United States under the TREATY OF GHENT. In Algonkian *michi* means 'great' and *macinac* means 'turtle'. The Ojibwa saw in the contour of Mackinac Island a turtle's back, hence the name.

Michilimackinac, Battles of. Two engagements in the WAR OF 1812. Capt. Charles Roberts took this fur-trading post on Mackinac Island in the Straits of Mackinac from American forces on 17 July 1812. Col. Robert MacDuall successfully repulsed an American attack on 4 Aug. 1814. The territory (in present-day Michigan) was returned to the United States under the TREATY OF GHENT.

Micmac. ALGONKIAN-speaking Indians occupying the Gaspé peninsula, present-day New Brunswick north of the St John R., and Nova Scotia. Allies of the French during the fur-trade wars, they were used to hunt down the BEOTHUK of Newfoundland but were in turn severely decimated by the IROQUOIS, allies of the British. The population in 1970 was 9,342, the majority living in Nova Scotia; 1,744 closely related Malecite occupy southern New Brunswick.

Mid. Official abbreviation of Midshipman.

Mid-Atlantic accent. Term used by broadcasting and theatre people to characterize an Anglo-Canadian manner of speech. Presumably merging the best British and American speech characteristics, the accent is associated with the GOLDEN AGE OF CANADIAN RADIO.

Mid-Canada Development Corridor. Belt of land extending across the continent immediately north of the great cities in the region of the boreal forest. The concept was presented and popularized in a study published in 1967 by Richard ROHMER, who foresaw Canada's development taking place along this 'corridor'.

Mid-Canada Line. A system of an unspecified number of unmanned warning stations north of settled areas across the Canadian North, generally following the 55th parallel. Part of a continental defence system developed at McGill University, the equipment is sometimes referred to as the 'McGill Fence'. Although entirely Canadian, the Mid-Canada Line was first announced in a joint communiqué of the Defence Departments of Canada and the United States on 27 Dec. 1954. It was discontinued in 1965. See also DEW LINE.

Midéwewin. ALGONKIAN word that has been translated 'Grand Medicine Lodge'. It was a secret society among the OJIBWA and neighbouring tribes involving four-to-eight grades (or lodges) of initiation, each conferring on the initiate increased insight and power.

Midnight. A weekly tabloid published in Montreal. It was founded in 1954 and featured sex and crime coverage of the local scene until 1959 when it started to include celebrity gossip. In 1969 *Midnight* was acquired by the Globe Newspaper Group of Montreal, which also publishes its French-language counterpart *Minuit* and the American tabloid *Police Gazette.*

Midnight Sun, Land of the. See LAND OF THE MIDNIGHT SUN.

Miles, Johnny (b.1905). Noted runner. A native of Sydney Mines, N.S., he specialized in distance running. He won the Boston Marathon in 1926 in record time and repeated the victory three years later, again in record time.

Military Colleges. See CANADIAN MILITARY COLLEGES.

Military Cross. Commonwealth army decoration for acts of courage, first awarded to commissioned officers of the British Army in 1914. The abbreviation is MC.

Military Medal. Commonwealth army decoration for acts of bravery, first awarded to non-commissioned officers and men of the British Army in 1916. The abbreviation is MM.

Mill of Kintail. See Robert Tait McKENZIE.

Millaire, Albert (b.1935). Actor and director. Born in Montreal, he joined the THÉÂTRE DU NOUVEAU MONDE in 1960 and became its associate artistic director in 1966. He has performed in both classical and contemporary plays, receiving acclaim as the star of John Coulter's RIEL at the National Arts Centre in 1975. He adapted Claude Confortes' play *The Marathon* as part of the cultural Olympics, directing and starring in it at the Théâtre du Nouveau Monde and, in John Van Burek's translation, at the St Lawrence Centre in 1976.

Millar Will. See STORK DERBY.

Miller, George M. (1854-1933). Architect. Born in Port Hope, Ont., and educated there, he began to practise in Toronto in 1885. At the turn of the century his was one of the largest and most productive architectural offices in Toronto, designing many churches, houses, and commercial buildings in various eclectic styles. His best buildings were done for the Massey family (see MASSEY-FERGUSON LIMITED) in Toronto: the MASSEY Music HALL (1894); renovations to Euclid Hall, Jarvis St, Toronto, for Hart Massey; additions to Chester Massey's house next door; Annesley Hall, Victoria College (1901-3); and the Lillian Massey Food Sciences Building, University of Toronto (1908-12).

Miller Medal. Awarded every two years by the ROYAL SOCIETY OF CANADA for outstanding research in any branch of the earth sciences, it was established in 1941 by 12 friends of Willet G. Miller, a distinguished geologist who died in 1925, and consists of a gold medal and $1,000.

Million Acre Farm. Sobriquet of PRINCE EDWARD ISLAND.

Mills, Alan (b.1914). Folksinger. Born in Lachine, Que., he began his career in 1935, touring, broadcasting, and composing his own songs and ballads. In 1951 he wrote the popular 'I Know an Old Lady Who Swallowed a Fly'. He recorded a nine-disc album, *Canadian Folk Songs*, in 1967.

Mills-Cockell, John. See SYRINX.

Mills of the Gods: Vietnam. A controversial CBC-TV documentary on the war in Vietnam. The 60-minute report, produced by Beryl FOX, was widely shown and won numerous international awards. First telecast on 5 Dec. 1965, it took a hard look at the American intervention and its effect on the Vietnamese people.

Milne, David (1882-1953). Painter. Born near Paisley, Ont., he went to New York to study painting in 1904 and exhibited in the famous Armory Show of 1913, which introduced post-Impressionist art to New York. He remained in the United States—except for war service in 1918-19—until 1929, when he returned to Canada. He lived and painted near Palgrave, Ont. (1930-3); at Six Mile Lake near Georgian Bay (1933-9); Toronto (1939-40); Uxbridge, Ont. (1940-52); and Bancroft, Ont., where he died. Particularly in watercolours, but also in oils and dry-points, he translated 'moments of vision' inspired by things around him—landscapes, his rooms, objects, and flowers—into a simplified arrangement of colours, forms, and spaces that give the viewer what the artist called a 'kick'—a quickening emotion that contains both intense feeling and aesthetic pleasure. In a career that was totally dedicated to painting, he produced many works of exhilarating technical mastery, among them PAINTING PLACE (1930, NGC); *Glass Jar, No. 1* (1946), formerly in the collection of Douglas DUNCAN and now in the Robert McLaughlin Art Gallery, Oshawa; and *Water Lilies, Temagami* (1929, NGC).

Miner, Jack (1865-1944). Ornithologist. Born in Dover Centre, Ohio, he settled in Canada with his parents in 1878. He opened his first bird sanctuary at Kingsville—the most southerly town in Canada, 30 mi. south of Windsor, Ont.—in 1904. To trace migratory paths, he banded his first bird in 1909. The Jack Miner Bird Foundation—a 2,000-acre sanctuary for migratory birds—was founded as a trust in 1932. Miner died at Kingsville, a greatly revered naturalist and widely quoted conservationist.

Minifie, James M. (1900-74). Broadcaster. Born in Burton, Eng., he was taken to Saskatchewan in 1912. He was educated there and qualified as a Rhodes Scholar. He was a correspondent for the New York *Herald-Tribune* from 1929 to 1953, when he joined the CBC as its correspondent in Washington; he remained there until his retirement in 1969. He wrote *Peacemaker or Powdermonkey* (1960), *Open at the Top* (1964), *Who's Your Fat Friend?* (1967), and two memoirs, *Homesteader* (1973) and *Expatriate* (1975).

Ministère des affaires culturelles du Québec. Ministry of culture and arts. Established by the Quebec government in 1961, it has aided the arts in the province since 1970. It has six principal branches: literary affairs, graphic arts, conservation, film and audiovisual, performing arts, and cultural relations. The ministry helps organizations and individuals, libraries, and museums. It sponsors the PRIX DAVID and the PRIX SCIENTIFIQUE DU QUÉBEC.

Ministry. A government; some of the elected members of a provincial or federal legislature appointed by a premier or a prime minister to head government departments or to act as ministers without portfolio. It is usual for most ministers to have a seat in the CABINET by virtue of their office, but occasionally ministers are not included in the cabinet.

Ministry of All the Talents. Sobriquet given the cabinet formed by Wilfrid LAURIER in 1896. Members of the cabinet included Sir Richard Cartwright, William S. Fielding, Sir Oliver MOWAT, William Mulock, and Clifford SIFTON. 'Ministry of All the Talents' was earlier used in Great Britain to describe the last administration of William Pitt the Younger.

Minor Adjustment. See LIKE FATHER, LIKE FUN.

Minority government. An administration with insufficient members in the provincial legislature or the federal House of Commons to ensure the passage of legislation without making special arrangements with the other parties. The opposite of MAJORITY GOVERNMENT.

Minto, Lord (1845-1914). GOVERNOR GENERAL of Canada from 1899 to 1904.

Minto Cup. A silver trophy emblematic of the junior amateur championship in LACROSSE. It was donated by Governor General Lord MINTO in 1901 and is awarded by the Canadian Lacrosse Association.

Mirabel International Airport. Montreal's second airport (after DORVAL). It was opened in Sept. 1975 at the village of St-Eustache, 34 mi. northwest of Montreal, and is the world's largest airport in area. It was named after a farm on the site whose name, in turn, is a contraction of the names of the farmer's two daughters, Miriam and Isabel. There are plans to make Mirabel the first supersonic jet airport in North America.

Miracle mile. Nickname of the celebrated one-mile race at the BRITISH EMPIRE AND COMMONWEALTH GAMES in Vancouver. It was won by Roger Bannister on 7 Aug. 1954. Both Bannister, a medical doctor from London, Eng., and John Landy, the runner-up, came in under four minutes, a world record.

Miramichi Folk Song Festival. A gathering held every summer since 1958 on the Miramichi R. at Newcastle, N.B. It attracts both professional and non-professional entertainers—woodsmen, housewives, etc.—who sing the campfire songs and folksongs they learned over the years. It was started by Dr Louise Manny, folklorist and historian.

341

Miron

Miron, Gaston (b.1928). Quebec poet. Born in Sainte-Agathe-des-Monts, Que., he helped found Les Éditions de l'Hexagone in 1953. An unsuccessful NDP candidate in the general elections of 1957 and 1958, he backed various separatist groups in the early sixties, wrote for PARTI PRIS, supported the RIN, and was detained during the OCTOBER CRISIS of 1970. That same year he published his important selection, *L'Homme rapaillé*, which established him, in the words of one critic, as 'the first bard of the Québécois nation'.

Mirvish, Edwin ('Honest Ed') (b.1914). Businessman and theatre owner. Born in Colonial Beach, Va, he came to Toronto with his family and took over his father's corner store at the age of 15. He opened Honest Ed's, the world's first discount department store, in 1948. In the late fifties he bought facing rows of nineteenth-century houses on neighbouring Markham St and created 'Mirvish Village', a community of antique shops, restaurants, etc. He acquired the ROYAL ALEXANDRA THEATRE when it was slated to be demolished, refurbished it, and has managed it successfully since 1963.

MISC. Acronym of Movement for an Independent Socialist Canada. See The WAFFLE.

Miss Canada. A female representation of Canada. The sweet but coy young lady was first depicted, with toque and sash, wearing an overcoat and long skirt, on skates, in a magazine illustration in 1912.

Miss Canada Pageant. Annual beauty contest. From a group of nearly 30 regional-award winners, a single girl is selected by a panel of judges on the basis of beauty, talent, personality, etc., and crowned 'Miss Canada'. The pageant originated in 1946 and is held in the last week in October or the first week in November. Each year the Miss Canada Pageant is broadcast live and in colour from the TV studios of CFTO in Toronto. The Miss Teen Canada Pageant, first presented in 1968 and telecast the following year, takes place in March. All participants in both pageants compete for prizes and merchandise. See also MISS DOMINION OF CANADA BEAUTY PAGEANT.

Miss Chatelaine. A magazine published seven times a year by MACLEAN-HUNTER in Toronto since 1963. Aimed at Canadian women between their late teens and early twenties, it focuses on fashion, grooming, careers, education, and sponsors an annual fiction contest. See also CHATELAINE.

Miss Dominion of Canada Beauty Pageant. Annual beauty contest. A 'Miss Dominion of Canada' has been crowned in the Grand Ballroom of the Sheraton-Brock Hotel, Niagara Falls, on 1 July every year since 1957. Contestants are judged on the basis of beauty and talent. See also MISS CANADA PAGEANT.

Miss Supertest III. Specially designed and powered speedboat that won the Harmsworth Trophy. Designed by James G. Thompson, of Supertest Petroleum Corporation, and driven by a former chicken farmer, R.D. (Bob) Hayward, the 30-ft, 3-ton speedboat took the Harmsworth Trophy on the Detroit R. on 4 July 1959. It defended the title in 1960 and 1961 when Hayward was killed and its career was curtailed. The orange-trimmed mahogany vessel, powered by a 2,000-h.p. aircraft engine, is on display at the ONTARIO SCIENCE CENTRE.

Miss Teen Canada Pageant. See MISS CANADA PAGEANT.

Mississaga. See GOLDEN HORSESHOE.

Mississauga rattlesnake. See MASSASAUGA RATTLESNAKE.

Mississippi River. A 105-mi. meandering river in southeastern Ontario that flows into Mississippi Lake and then northerly to the Ottawa R.

Mistaseni Rock. Immense boulder once located on a plain 90 mi. southwest of Saskatoon, Sask., said to be of religious importance to the CREE Indians. A 'Save the Rock' committee was formed in 1960 to move the boulder, which resembled a huge squatting buffalo, before it was submerged by the South Saskatchewan Dam project. When this proved too expensive, the 'medicine rock' was dynamited and sections were taken in 1965 to the nearby village of Elbow, where they formed part of an Indian monument.

Mistress in her own house. Phrase used by Lord Sankey of the JUDICIAL COMMITTEE OF THE PRIVY COUNCIL in the famous PERSONS CASE. Interpreting the constitution, he said about dominion-provincial relations: 'Their Lordships do not conceive it to be the duty of this Board—it is certainly not their desire—to cut down the provisions of the [BNA] Act by a narrow and technical construction, but rather to give it a large and liberal interpretation so that the Dominion to a great extent, but within certain fixed limits, may be mistress in her own house, as the Provinces to a great extent, but within certain fixed limits, are mistresses in theirs.' The phrase, used by

Lord Sankey in 1929, recalls the lines from Rudyard Kipling's poem 'OUR LADY OF THE SNOWS', published in 1897: 'Daugher am I in my mother's house,/But mistress in my own.'

Mitchell, Joni (b.1944). Folksinger. Born in Fort McLeod, Alta, she began singing in Toronto coffee houses in 1964. Fame followed when Judy Collins, Frank Sinatra, and others began recording her songs, especially 'Both Sides Now', written in 1968. She is now a top international folk artist based in California.

Mitchell, Peter (1824-99). A FATHER OF CONFEDERATION. Born at Newcastle, N.B., he trained as a lawyer. He was elected to the legislative assembly in 1856 and became premier of New Brunswick in 1866. He was a delegate to the QUEBEC and LONDON CONFERENCES on Confederation and was Minister of Marine and Fisheries in Sir John A. MACDONALD's first cabinet. In 1873 he became editor of the Montreal *Herald*, which he acquired in 1885. Defeated in 1878, he was returned to Parliament in 1882 and retired from politics in 1891.

Mitchell, W.O. (b.1914). Novelist and scriptwriter. Born in Weyburn, Sask., and educated at the Universities of Manitoba and Alberta, he travelled through England, France, and Spain before returning to Calgary, where he worked as an advertising salesman for the *Calgary Herald* in 1936 and as a program arranger for CFAC Radio. He taught school from 1942 to 1944, when he decided to become a free-lance writer. To a generation of MACLEAN'S readers and dévotés of the CBC, Mitchell remains the one writer who is able to capture the nuances of prairie life, which he recreated in the stories and scripts of JAKE AND THE KID (broadcast between 1949 and 1957, telecast in 1961, and published in story form in 1961), set in the fictitious community of CROCUS, Sask. He is the author of a Canadian classic about growing up on the prairies, the poetic WHO HAS SEEN THE WIND (1947). It was followed by two other novels: *The Kite* (1962) and *The Vanishing Point* (1973). His charm and skill as a raconteur have made him perhaps the most popular after-dinner speaker in English-speaking Canada.

Mittelmann, Norman (b.1932). Baritone. Born Norman Mittleman in Winnipeg, he studied singing in Philadelphia. He made his début with the CANADIAN OPERA COMPANY in 1958 as Marcello in *La Bohème* (appearing with Teresa STRATAS) and made his Metropolitan Opera début in 1962. He lives in Switzerland and is a member of the Zurich Opera.

MLA. Member of the LEGISLATIVE ASSEMBLY. Used to designate provincial parliamentarians in all provinces except Quebec and Ontario.

MLCR. Abbreviation of Montreal and Champlain Railroad.

MM. See MILITARY MEDAL.

MMFA. See MONTREAL MUSEUM OF FINE ARTS.

MMM. Member of the ORDER OF MILITARY MERIT.

Mobile Command. One of five functional commands of the CANADIAN ARMED FORCES.

Moccasin. Algonkian word for a flat-soled shoe made of soft leather, decorated originally with porcupine quills, and later also with beads and embroidery thread.

Moccasin flower. A pink and slightly fragrant variety of the LADY'S SLIPPER, also called Indian slipper or pink lady's slipper. Moccasin flower may also refer to any of the 18 varieties of lady's slipper.

Mock Parliament. Highly successful suffragette meeting held on the evening of 28 Jan. 1914 at the Walker Theatre, in Winnipeg. A mock Parliament was staged, with Nellie McCLUNG as 'premier' receiving a delegation of women acting as men seeking the vote for men from a Parliament of women. It was meant to ridicule the position of Premier Sir Rodmond Roblin, who was opposed to giving women the vote. Women were enfranchised in Manitoba in 1916.

Mohawk. See IROQUOIS.

Mohawk Chapel, Brantford. St Paul's Church of England, since 1906 a Chapel Royal, Her Majesty's Chapel of the Mohawks. Built in 1785, it is one of the oldest Canadian churches outside of Quebec. Its simple Georgian form has been altered in the style of the early Gothic Revival, but it still contains the carved and gilt Royal Arms presented by George III and the painted panels of the Ten Commandments in both Mohawk and English.

Moiseiwitsch, Tanya (b.1914). Costume designer. Born in London, Eng., she studied at the Abbey Theatre and the Old Vic Theatre and designed costumes for the Royal Shakespeare Festival in England. She accompanied Tyrone GUTHRIE to the STRATFORD FESTIVAL in 1953 and designed with him its famous thrust stage. There for five years she set a high standard for opulent costuming and imaginative stage design. She followed the director to the Tyrone Guthrie Theatre in Minnesota in 1963. The Festival opened a retrospective exhibition of her costumes and designs on 27 June 1974.

Molinari, Guido (b.1933). Painter. Born in Montreal, he studied there at the École des Beaux-Arts and the Montreal Museum of Fine Arts School, and was a founding member of the Association des Artistes Non-Figuratifs de Montréal in 1956. Influenced by the techniques of the AUTOMATISTES, his early work in the formal abstract manner developed into an analytic style concerned with colour properties. In the 1960s he began a series of large-scale paintings using uniform hard-edge vertical bands of colour to explore the interaction of colours by integrating them with the painting's simplified structure. *Bisériel orange-vert* (1967, NGC) is an example of the style he finally evolved. He has exhibited internationally and lives in Montreal.

Molson Breweries of Canada Limited. Canadian breweries. In 1786 John Molson (1763-1836) established a brewery in Montreal, which still operates on the same site. There are currently 11 Molson breweries across Canada, with the head office of their parent company, MOLSON COMPANIES LIMITED, in Montreal. They produce such popular beers as Molson's Canadian, Molson's Golden, Frontier Stout, and Export Ale. See also MOLSON FAMILY.

Molson Companies Limited, The. Canadian conglomerate. Among its holdings are MOLSON BREWERIES OF CANADA LIMITED, Aikenhead Hardware Limited, and Beaver Lumber Co. Ltd. See also MOLSON FAMILY.

Molson family. A prominent Montreal family with extensive brewing and financial interests. The dynasty was established by John Molson (1763-1836), an orphan from Lincolnshire, Eng., who in 1782 settled in Montreal, where he acquired a small brewery that four years later began to produce Molson's Ale. He built his own steamship, the ACCOMMODATION, and had three sons: William Molson (1793-1875), who established Molson's Bank (chartered in 1855, absorbed by the BANK OF MONTREAL in 1925); Thomas (1791-1863), distiller and brewer of Molson's Brewery Ltd; and John Molson (1787-1860), a director of the Bank of Montreal, whose son John Thomas Molson (1820-1907) continued his financial interests. John Thomas's son, Herbert Molson (1875-1938), was the father of Hartland de Montarville Molson (b.1907), a graduate of the Royal Military College in 1928, who became a chartered accountant, a sports enthusiast, and owner of the Montreal FORUM and the MONTREAL CANADIENS; he was summoned to the Senate in 1955. In *The Canadian Establishment* Peter C. NEWMAN notes that there is 'no higher-grade Old Money in the country than that of Senator Hartland de Montarville Molson', who is honorary chairman of the Toronto-based conglomerate, MOLSON COMPANIES LIMITED. See also MOLSON BREWERIES OF CANADA LIMITED, MOLSON FOUNDATION, MOLSON PRIZES.

Molson Foundation. It was established in Montreal in 1958 by T.H.P. Molson and H. de M. Molson, brewery executives, to make gifts, grants, contributions, and donations to hospitals, educational institutuions, and charitable institutions and organizations. It permits the CANADA COUNCIL to annually award three $20,000 MOLSON PRIZES. See also MOLSON COMPANIES LIMITED, MOLSON FAMILY.

Molson Prizes. Awarded annually by the CANADA COUNCIL to recognize outstanding contributions to the arts, humanities, and social sciences. Three prizes, now worth $20,000 each, are given annually. They are financed from a gift to the Canada Council by the MOLSON FOUNDATION and have been awarded since 1963. See also MOLSON COMPANIES LIMITED, MOLSON FAMILY.

Mon Oncle Antoine. Feature film directed by Claude JUTRA and produced by the NFB in 1971, with cinematography by Michel BRAULT. Written by Clément Perron, it depicts life in a small asbestos-mining town in Quebec, before the days of the miners' unions, as seen through the eyes of young Jacques. The boy helps his Uncle Antoine, who runs the general store and occasionally acts as the undertaker. It starred Jacques Gagnon, Lyne Champagne, and Jean Duceppe. A sensitive film, beautifully photographed and acted, it was commercially successful. 110 min., 20 sec.; colour.

'Mon Pays'. Title and first words of the most popular of contemporary Quebec songs. The words and music are by Gilles VIGNEAULT. It won first prize at the 1965 International Song Festival in Sopot, Poland, where it was sung by Monique LEYRAC. The refrain runs: *'Mon pays ce n'est pas un pays c'est l'hiver / Mon jardin ce n'est pas un jardin c'est la plaine / Mon chemin ce n'est pas un chemin c'est la neige / Mon pays ce n'est pas un pays c'est l'hiver.'* ('My country is not a country, it is winter / My garden is not a garden, it is a plain / My road is not a road, it is the snow / My country is not a country, it is winter.') Though Vigneault claims the song is neither separatist nor even nationalist—but rather a personal lament for the failure to share love and experience—it has become an unofficial anthem among Québécois.

Monarchy. The kings and queens of Canada since 1867 are Victoria, who acceded to the throne in 1837 and died in 1901, the last of the House of Hanover; Edward VII, who acceded in 1901 and died in 1910, of the House of Saxe-Coburg-Gotha; George V, who acceded in 1910 and died in 1936, the first of the reigning House of Windsor; Edward VIII, who acceded in 1936 and abdicated 325 days later in Dec. 1936; George VI, who acceded in 1936 and died in 1952; Elizabeth II, who acceded in 1952 and was crowned the following year. See also CROWN and ROYAL FAMILY.

Monastère des Ursulines, Le. See URSULINE CONVENT.

Monck, Lord (1819-1894). GOVERNOR GENERAL of British North America from 1861 to 1867 and of Canada from 1867 to 1868.

Money Bills. Bills to impose taxes or to appropriate public funds. Money bills differ from other bills in that they must be recommended by the GOVERNOR GENERAL; they must originate in the HOUSE OF COMMONS (the SENATE's right to amend them is disputed by the House of Commons); and they are presented to the governor general for assent in the name of the House of Commons alone.

Monk, Lorraine. Photography executive. Born in Montreal and educated at McGill University, she was appointed head of the Still Photography Division, NATIONAL FILM BOARD in 1960 and is now executive producer. Besides producing the *Image* series of 10 books presenting the work of leading Canadian photographers (1967-72), she was responsible for the celebrated CANADA / A YEAR OF THE LAND (1967), and other impressive photographic studies, including *Call Them Canadians* (1968), *Canada* (1973), *The Female Eye/Coup d'oeil féminin* (1975) (the NFB's salute to International Women's Year), and *Between Friends/Entre Amis* (1976), Canada's bicentennial gift to the United States of America.

Monk, Maria (1817?-49). The name assumed by a nortorious impostor who arrived in New York in a state of advanced pregnancy and claimed to be a nun who had 'escaped' from the Hôtel-Dieu, a Catholic convent in Montreal. Her memoirs, *The Awful Disclosures of Maria Monk, as Exhibited in a Narrative of Her Sufferings During a Residence of Five Years at the Hôtel-Dieu Nunnery at Montreal*—first pub-lished in 1836 as *The Hôtel-Dieu Nunnery Unveiled*—became a scandalous bestseller. They were ghosted by George Bourne (1780-1845), a Presbyterian minister of pronounced anti-Catholic views. Convicted of theft, she died in a New York prison.

Mons. Flemish town in Belgium, liberated by the CANADIAN CORPS under Gen. Sir Arthur CURRIE on 11 Nov. 1918, the day the armistice was signed that ended the FIRST WORLD WAR.

Mont Houy. Village in northern France liberated near the end of the FIRST WORLD WAR by the CANADIAN CORPS in Oct. 1918.

Montagnais-Naskapi. Wide-ranging ALGONKIAN-speaking Indians. The Montagnais territory comprised most of the semi-mountainous interior of Quebec, extending from the St Maurice R. to Sept-Îles and northward to the tree limit. They are so closely related to the Naskapi of Labrador that they are grouped together, but there are minor differences of language and custom. Their combined population in 1970 was 6,085.

Montane Forest Region. Forest area occupying a large part of the interior uplands of British Columbia, as well as part of the Kootenay Valley and a small area on the east side of the Rocky Mountains. Ponderosa pine, interior Douglas fir, lodgepole pine, and trembling aspen are generally present.

Montcalm, Marquis de (1712-59). French military officer, unsuccessful defender of Quebec in the Battle of the PLAINS OF ABRAHAM in the SEVEN YEARS' WAR. Louis-Joseph, Marquis de Montcalm, was appointed major-general in command of all the forces in New France in 1756 during the Seven Years' War. In spite of three victories—at Fort Oswego (1756), Fort William Henry (1757), and Fort Carillon (Ticonderoga, N.Y., 1758)—his career in New France was blighted by his disputes with the governor general, the Marquis de VAUDREUIL-CAVAGNAL, who was his superior; his contemptuous disregard for any military advice that did not conform with European military tactics; and his defeatist outlook and poor generalship during the siege of Quebec by the British forces under James WOLFE. Montcalm received a mortal wound while retreating from the Plains of Abraham and died shortly afterwards. He was buried in the Ursulines' Chapel at Quebec.

Monte Cassino. See CASSINO.

Montebello. See Le CHÂTEAU MONTEBELLO.

Monteregian Hills. The modern name of a range of peaks—old volcanic plugs—that are very conspicuous in the otherwise flat St Lawrence valley, extending from Montreal to the Appalachian Highlands. The name, given to them by Dr F.D. Adams, derives from the Latin name (*Mons Regius*) for the best known of them, MOUNT ROYAL. The other seven hills are Mount St Bruno, Beloeil Mountain, Rougemont, Yamaska Mountain, Shefford Mountain, Brome Mountain, and Mount Johnson.

Montgomery, Lucy Maude (1877-1942). Novelist. Born in Clifton, P.E.I., and educated at Prince of Wales College in Charlottetown and at Dalhousie University, she worked as a journalist in Halifax and as a teacher in Cavendish, P.E.I., before marrying a Presbyterian clergyman in 1911 and raising two children. She lived in Norval, Ont., and died in Toronto. She acquired an international following with her first book—a lively, warm novel for young girls, ANNE OF GREEN GABLES (1908)—and for its seven less-successful sequels. The complete series of the 'Anne books', arranged in terms of her life, follows: *Anne of Green Gables* (1908), she grows up; *Anne of Avonlea* (1909), she becomes a teacher; *Anne of the Island* (1915), she goes to college; *Anne of Windy Poplars* (1936), as a school principal she writes love letters to Gilbert Blythe; *Anne's House of Dreams* (1918), she marries and has her first child; *Anne of Ingleside* (1939), she bears five more children; *Rainbow Valley* (1919), she watches her children grow up; *Rilla of Ingleside* (1921), Anne's daughter has adventures of her own during the First World War. Montgomery's other novels for young girls were *Emily of New Moon* (1923) and *Pat of Silver Bush* (1933). A biography, *The Wheel of Things* (1975), was written by Mollie Gillen.

Montgomery, Richard (1738-75). Soldier. An Irish-born British officer, he was at the siege of LOUISBOURG in 1758 and at the capture of Montreal in 1760. He immigrated to the United States in 1772 and led an American attack on Canada in 1775, during the American Revolution. He captured Montreal on 13 Nov. but was killed while making an attack on Lower Town, Quebec, on 31 Dec.

Montgomery's Tavern. In the REBELLION OF 1837, an inn on the west side of Yonge St north of Toronto that was a rendezvous point of rebel groups in Upper Canada (Ontario). It was leased by John Montgomery. On 7 Dec. 1837 an armed group of rebels was dispersed half a mile south of the tavern by militia under Col. Allan MacNab. The tavern was later burned to the ground. The location

today, at Montgomery Ave and Yonge St, is the site of a post office building.

Montmorency Falls. A spectacular waterfall of 275 ft, over half again as high as Niagara, where the Montmorency R. meets the St Lawrence just east of Quebec City.

Montreal. With Toronto it is one of the two principal commercial, financial, and manufacturing centres of Canada. Associated with the Indian village of HOCHELAGA, which was visited by CARTIER, who named nearby MOUNT ROYAL (calling it Mont Royal), it was founded in 1642 by MAISONNEUVE as the colony of Ville-Marie, a name that eventually gave way to Montreal. Its early growth was related to the fur trade; subsequently its location at the head of navigation on the St Lawrence R., and at the convergence of the Ottawa R.-Great Lakes-Richelieu R. water routes, made Montreal, by the eighteenth century, the dominant city of North America in territorial influence. It grew steadily in the nineteenth century as the headquarters of the NORTH WEST COMPANY and as a seaport and railway terminus. Its three most important economic activities today relate to manufacturing, transportation, and finance. Its most distinctive characteristic is that it accommodates two major cultural groups, French and English, which do not merge but rather coexist. The English have traditionally dominated in business, but this situation has recently changed somewhat. In the past 15 years the city has undergone a great transformation, beginning with the construction of PLACE VILLE MARIE in 1962, followed by other multi-functioned office complexes such as PLACE BONAVENTURE and Place du Canada. The location in Montreal of EXPO 67 and the 1976 OLYMPIC GAMES has made it the best known of all Canadian cities. Its 1971 CMA population was 2,743,108. Its official motto is *Concordia salus* ('Salute to harmony'). See also BONSECOURS MARKET, CHÂTEAU DE RAMEZAY, CONCORDIA UNIVERSITY, HÔTEL DE VILLE, HÔTEL-DIEU DE MONTRÉAL, McGILL UNIVERSITY, The MAIN, MAN AND HIS WORLD, MONTREAL MUSEUM OF FINE ARTS, NOTRE-DAME-DE-BONSECOURS, NOTRE-DAME-DE-MONTRÉAL, OLD MONTREAL, PLACE D'ARMES, PLACE DES ARTS, ST JOSEPH'S ORATORY, UNIVERSITÉ DE MONTRÉAL, etc.

Montreal A.A.A. The Montreal Amateur Athletic Association, whose hockey team won the STANLEY CUP three times between 1892 and 1893 and 1900 and 1901.

Montreal Canadiens. The best-known hockey club in the country. One of the original members of the NATIONAL HOCKEY LEAGUE in 1917, it won the STANLEY CUP for the eighteenth time in 1976. Home ice is the Montreal FORUM. The club's colours are red, white, and royal blue.

Montreal Gazette, The. A morning newspaper published in Montreal. It is a direct descendant of *La Gazette littéraire*, which was first published in French and English on 3 June 1778. The publisher of the present paper, acquired by SOUTHAM PRESS in 1969, is Ross Munro (b.1913).

Montreal Herald, The. A daily newspaper once published in Montreal. Founded by William Gray in 1811, it reached its peak in circulation at the turn of the century under the management of James S. Brierley. When it folded in 1957 its assets were assumed by the MONTREAL STAR. The *Herald* was the model for the newspaper satirized in the novel and film WHY ROCK THE BOAT?

Montreal International Book Fair. 'First international publishers' fair in North America.' Organized by the Montreal publishing executive J.-Z. Léon Patenaude, the annual exhibition, with displays of books by European and North American publishing houses, was first held at the PLACE BONAVENTURE, Montreal, on 15-19 May 1975.

Montreal International Film Festival. Showcase for Canadian and world films, held at Loew's Theatre, Montreal, from 1960 to 1967. The purpose of the mid-summer festival was to exhibit Canadian films and promote the distribution of foreign films on the North American continent.

Montreal Main. Feature film produced and directed by Frank Vitale. Released in 1973, it starred Frank Vitale and featured John, Dave, and Anne Sutherland. It is a sensitive film about the friendship between a Montreal MAIN denizen and a typical suburban 12-year-old, told through unrehearsed monologues. 88 min., colour.

Montréal-Matin. A Sunday tabloid published in Montreal. It was founded in 1930 as an organ of the UNION NATIONALE Party. Since its acquisition by the POWER CORPORATION, it has specialized in sensational coverage of Quebec crime, politics, and society.

Montreal Museum of Fine Arts/Musée des beaux-arts de Montréal. It was founded in 1860 as the Art Association of Montreal, which grew out of the Montreal Society of Artists, organized in 1847. Its first gallery opened in 1879 on Phillips Square. The present gallery, designed by Edward and W.S. MAXWELL, opened in 1912 and included studio space for art classes where many of Montreal's leading painters taught and studied. With the development of a Decorative Arts section, the gallery acquired its present name in 1950. A new wing, including a 400-seat auditorium, was opened on 8 May 1976. Among the many gifts that have enlarged its holdings were 103 important paintings and numerous objects from the collection of Sir William VAN HORNE, bequeathed by his daughter, who died in 1941; Canadian paintings from the collection of A. Sydney Dawes; and from the Morrice family a selection of paintings by James Wilson MORRICE. The directors since 1947 have been Richard T. Davis (until 1952), John Steegman (1952-9), Evan H. Turner (1959-64), and David Giles Carter (from 1964).

Montreal Star, The. An evening newspaper published in Montreal. Founded in 1867 by Hugh Graham, later Lord Atholstan, it is the leading English-language newspaper in Quebec and among the most influential papers in Canada. It has both a slogan ('Canada's Greatest Newspaper') and a motto ('A Nation's Health is a Nation's Wealth'). Writers for the paper include Dominique Clift, Gerald Clark, John Richmond, Lawrence Sabbath, and W.A. (Bill) Wilson.

Montreal Symphony Orchestra. Founded in 1934 as the 'Société des Concerts symphoniques de Montréal', it acquired its present name in 1953. Its permanent conductors have been Désiré Defaw (1940-8), Igor Markevitch (1958-61), Zubin Mehta (1961-7), Franz-Paul Decker (1967-75), and Rafael Frühbeck de Burgos (from 1975). Its activities—centred in PLACE DES ARTS—include two major series, children's concerts, summer pop concerts, and opera productions.

Montrealer, The. A magazine published monthly by the Passing Show Publishing Company, Montreal, from Mar. 1924 to Jan. 1970. It was established as a society magazine and its format was modelled on the *New Yorker*. Under its last editor, the novelist Gerald Taaffe, it became an outlet for serious fiction and reportage.

Monts, Pierre du Gua, sieur de. See Samuel de CHAMPLAIN.

Moodie, Susanna (1803-85). Pioneer and author. Born in Bungay, Suffolk, Eng., a sister of Catharine Parr TRAILL and Samuel STRICKLAND, she married a half-pay officer and in 1832 immigrated with him to Upper Canada (Ontario), where they settled on a farm near Peterborough; they moved to Belleville, C.W. (Ont.), in 1840 and Mrs Moodie died in

Toronto. She wrote stories, sketches, serials, and poems about pioneer life for the LITERARY GARLAND. ROUGHING IT IN THE BUSH; or, Forest Life in Canada (1852, 1862) is an interesting book of anecdotes and character sketches dealing with her early life in Upper Canada and views; and Life in the Clearings versus the Bush (1853) describes her later life, which was easier and allowed her to recant her previous bad opinions of her adopted country. These books gave rise to Margaret ATWOOD'S The JOURNALS OF SUSANNA MOODIE (1970).

Moody, Rufus (b.1924). HAIDA carver. Born at Skidegate in the Queen Charlotte Islands, B.C., he is a descendant of Chief Skedans and follows a long line of carvers, including his grandfather Thomas, his father Arthur, and relatives Henry and Joseph. He was a logger until 1959, when he became a full-time carver. He quarries his own ARGILLITE and works equally well in silver. In 1973 he carved the world's tallest argillite totem pole (6 ft 8 in.), which he marked in his personal manner—with cross-hatches on the base.

Moogk, Edward. See ROLL BACK THE YEARS.

Moon, Wm Harold. See HAROLD MOON AWARD.

Mooneas. One of the Algonkian words for 'greenhorn' or 'white man'. It has various spellings, including moonias and moniyas. The latter is said to be the Cree word for 'Canadian', being an early Indian attempt to pronounce the word 'Montreal'.

Moontrap, The. Feature film directed by Michel BRAULT, Marcel Carrière, and Pierre PERRAULT for the NATIONAL FILM BOARD in 1964. It records the trapping of the white beluga whale by fishermen of l'Île-aux-Coudres, a small island in the St Lawrence where the practice died out in 1920. The title—Pour la suite du monde in French—refers to the influence the moon is held to have on the souls of the dead, who help catch the white whales. 83 min., 46 sec.; b & w.

Moore, Brian (b.1921). Novelist. Born in Belfast, he immigrated to Canada in 1948 and worked as a proofreader on the MONTREAL GAZETTE. He revealed himself as a brilliant novelist with his first novel, Judith Hearne (1955), set in Belfast. Though he lives in the United States, he retains his Canadian citizenship and many Canadian references and attitudes remain in his novels, which are: The Lonely Passion of Judith Hearne (U.S. title, 1956), The Feast of Lupercal (1957), The LUCK OF GINGER COFFEY (1960), An Answer from Limbo (1962), The Emperor of Ice-Cream (1965), I am

Mary Dunne (1968), Fergus (1970), Catholics (1972), The Great Victorian Collection (1975), and The Doctor's Wife (1976). He also wrote Canada (1963; rev. 1968) with the editors of Life and a documentary on the OCTOBER CRISIS, The Revolution Script (1971).

Moore, Dora Mavor. See Mavor MOORE, NEW PLAY SOCIETY.

Moore, Mavor (b.1919). Man-of-the-theatre. Born in Toronto, he was a radio and then television producer with the CBC (1941-54), an instructor at the ACADEMY OF RADIO ARTS (1945-51), and a founder with his mother, Dora Mavor Moore, of the NEW PLAY SOCIETY (1946-57). He was an originator of the Society's revue SPRING THAW (1947-66) and played the lead in John COULTER'S play RIEL (1950). He wrote SUNSHINE TOWN (1954), The OTTAWA MAN (1963), and the librettos for LOUIS RIEL (1967) and JOHNNY BELINDA (1968). The founder and director of the CHARLOTTETOWN SUMMER FESTIVAL (1964-7) and the first general director of the ST LAWRENCE CENTRE (1965-9), he was appointed head of the theatre department of YORK UNIVERSITY in 1969. As an actor, producer, director, writer, and teacher he displays enthusiasm and energy as well as discipline and talent.

Moore Corporation Limited. A Canadian-owned multinational corporation. Moore Business Forms, founded in Toronto in 1882, manufactures business forms, form-handling equipment, and paper boxes in nine plants in Canada. Through Reid Dominion Ltd it operates two more box plants and through Moore Corporation Limited it controls other subsidiaries in Mexico, the Caribbean, Central and South America, Europe, Australia, Africa, the United Kingdom, and Japan.

Moorside. See KINGSMERE.

Moose. A familiar Canadian mammal, the largest member of the deer family. It attains a height of 5½ to 6½ ft at the shoulders, often weighing over 1,000 lb. It is characterized by a short dark-brown spring coat that becomes longer and lighter in colour in the fall, long legs, a very short tail, a large head with a thick overhanging muzzle, and broadly palmated antlers in the male. It is much sought after as a hunting trophy. Formerly found throughout Canada in open woodlands and forests, its distribution range has gradually extended northward.

Moose Pasture. Slang term used for a worthless mining claim. In the North it describes terrain suitable only for browsing moose.

Moose River Disaster. Cave-in at the Moose R. gold mine, N.S. Dr D.E. Robertson and Hermann Magill of Toronto, who were inspecting the mine with the time-keeper, Alfred Scadding, were trapped from 12 to 22 Apr. 1936. Magill died of pneumonia in the mine, but Robertson and Scadding were rescued. The disaster was covered by radio broadcasts that put the whole country in a state of suspense. J. Frank WILLIS made hourly reports—the CRBC's first and most famous actuality program—from the Hotel Nova Scotia, Halifax, beginning on 20 Apr. Lasting for 69 hours, they reached 58 stations in Canada and 650 in the United States.

Moosemilk. A slang expression used in the North for either homebrew or a drink made with rum and a mixture of milk and cream.

Moraine. Rock debris carried and finally deposited during the retreat of both alpine and continental glaciers. Continental moraines are common in Ontario and the Prairies and are seen as narrow bands of low, irregular hills formed mainly of sand and gravel, with scattered small lakes.

Moraviantown. Community in Kent County, Ont., on the south bank of the Thames R. In 1792 Moravian missionaries, with their Delaware Indian converts, established the mission village of Schoenfeldt (Fairfield) on the north bank of the Thames. It was destroyed in the Battle of the THAMES in 1813. The mission was then re-established in the present location of Moraviantown; it is administered by the United Church of Canada.

Morawetz, Oskar (b.1917). Composer. Born in Svetla, Czech., he came to Canada in 1940 and received his music doctorate from the University of Toronto, where he teaches. Much of his recent work is neo-Romantic. He has written for orchestra, choir, voice, chamber groups, and piano; his showy piano music has been played by Glenn GOULD and Anton KUERTI. Three of his best-known compositions are two orchestral works—*Carnival Overture* (1946), which is popular internationally, and the *Passacaglia on a Bach Chorale* (1964), written in memory of John F. Kennedy—and *From the Diary of Anne Frank* (1970), for voice and orchestra.

More for the Mind. Influential report of the Tyhurst Commission on mental health in Canada, released in 1963. Eight psychiatrists, under the chairmanship of Dr J.S. Tyhurst, made 57 recommendations in the mental-health and psychiatric fields, stressing the need for the development of psychiatry in general hospitals and the continuance of care generally.

Morel, François (b.1926). Composer. Born in Montreal, Que., he was trained at the Quebec Conservatoire de Musique. In 1958 he helped found 'Musique de notre temps' in Montreal. His compositions—rooted in traditional techniques and forms yet personal and explorative—include *Trajectoire* (1967), commissioned by the CBC for Expo 67, and *Départs* (1969), written for the McGill Chamber Orchestra, among other orchestral pieces and chamber works.

Morenz, Howarth W. (Howie) (1902-37). Hockey player. Born in Mitchell, Ont., he played with the MONTREAL CANADIENS for almost 14 seasons and in one season averaged a goal a game. He was a three-time winner of the HART MEMORIAL TROPHY. He earned such sobriquets as 'Comet', 'Streak', 'Meteor', and 'Flash' for his brilliant and dashing plays. When he died six weeks after a hockey accident he was honoured with a funeral service in the Montreal FORUM. He was one of the first players elected to the Hockey HALL OF FAME in 1945.

Morgentaler case. A Quebec criminal case involving legal and ethical issues. Dr Henry Morgentaler, a Polish-born Montreal physician who admits to having performed 6,000 abortions under clinical conditions and to being a crusader for abortion reform, was charged with performing a single illegal abortion in 1973. He was acquitted by the Court of Queen's Bench on 13 Nov. 1973, but the verdict was overturned by the Quebec Appeal Court in 1974 and its decision was upheld by the SUPREME COURT OF CANADA. (An amendment to the Criminal Code preventing appeal courts from reversing 'not guilty' jury decisions was passed in Apr. 1976.) After serving 10 months of an 18-month sentence, Morgentaler was released. Because of technicalities a re-trial was ordered on 22 Jan. 1976.

Morin, A.N. (1803-65). Politician. Born at Saint-Michel-de-Bellechasse, L.C. (Que.), he trained as a lawyer and in 1830 was elected to the legislative assembly as a supporter of Louis-Joseph PAPINEAU. Elected to the assembly of the Province of Canada in 1841, he became leader of the BLEUS in 1851, when he formed a ministry with Francis HINCKS, which resigned in 1854; Morin then formed one with Sir Allan MacNAB. He resigned in 1855 to become a judge of the supreme court of Quebec.

Moriyama, Raymond (b.1930). Architect. Born in Vancouver, B.C., he was educated at the University of Toronto and McGill University. His works include the Japanese Cul-

Moriyama

tural Centre, Toronto (1962-4); the ONTARIO SCIENCE CENTRE (1965-9), an outstanding example of the use of reinforced concrete, terraced into the Don Valley; Scarborough Town Centre (opened 1973); and the Holiday Inn on Wynford Drive at Eglinton Ave E., Toronto.

'Morning on the Lièvre'. (i) A poem by Archibald LAMPMAN that first appeared in *Among the Millet* (1888). (ii) A 13-minute colour film based on that poem, produced by the NFB and directed by David Bairstow in 1961. Both the poem and the film capture the haunting beauty of the Lièvre R. in Quebec as it winds past maple-wooded hills in late September. The refrain runs: 'Softly as a cloud we go,/Sky above and sky below. . . .'

Morrice, James Wilson (1865-1924). Painter. Born in Montreal, he graduated from the University of Toronto and began to study law but gave it up in favour of painting. He moved to Paris in 1890 and remained there, though he made annual trips home up to 1914 and travelled extensively. He died in Tunis. A personality in the Parisian world of art and letters—Maugham used him for the alcoholic poet Cronshaw in *Of Human Bondage* (1915) and Arnold Bennett put him into *Buried Alive* (1908)—he was also a respected and well-known painter in his lifetime. In his early years he was influenced by Whistler and, after 1910, by the aesthetic possibilities of violent colour and rhythmical compositions that attracted the Fauves, notably his friend Matisse. With his paintings of Canadian subjects he introduced a way of treating the effects of nature that put aesthetic pleasure above pure representation or national feeling, as in his important *The* FERRY, QUEBEC (*c.*1909, NGC); and on his travels in North Africa and the West Indies he produced many softly colourful, sensual canvases that are as warm as *The Ferry* is cold.

Morris Gallery. Commercial art gallery in Toronto founded in 1962 by Jerrold Morris. It was among the first galleries to exhibit U.S. and international artists in Canada and now specializes in works by the GROUP OF SEVEN.

Morrison, Donald. The name of the MEGANTIC OUTLAW.

Morrison, Mary (b.1926). Soprano. Born in Winnipeg, Man., she trained at the Royal Conservatory of Music, Toronto, and was a founding member of, and soloist with, the CANADIAN OPERA COMPANY (1946-55). Also a founding member of the LYRIC ARTS TRIO, with Robert AITKEN and Marion Ross in 1964, she has performed religious, contemporary, and

classical music with major Canadian orchestras, CBC Radio and TV, and in chamber concerts. She is married to Harry FREEDMAN.

Morrisseau, Norval (b.1932). Ojibwa artist. Born in Fort William, Ont., he was raised at the Sandy Point Reserve on Lake Nipigon. He worked as a miner when a vision instructed him to depict his people's legends (although this had hitherto been taboo). Given art supplies by art historian Selwyn Dewdney, he evolved a personal, semi-abstract, 'x-ray' style in acrylic. He was then 'discovered' at Beardmore, Ont., by the art dealer Jack Pollock, who arranged a Toronto show that opened on 21 Sept. 1962 and was an outstanding success. Morrisseau, whose Indian name is Copper Thunderbird, has had an immense influence on other Indian artists. He wrote and illustrated *Legends of My People, the Great Ojibway* (1965), edited by Selwyn Dewdney, and illustrated Herbert T. Schwarz's *Windigo and Other Tales of the Ojibwas* (1969).

Morse, Barry (b.1918). Actor, director, producer. Born in London, Eng., he made his acting début there in 1936. He settled in Canada in 1951 and became one of the busiest of CBC Radio and TV actors. He was artistic director of the SHAW FESTIVAL in 1966, and achieved celebrity status for his role in the ABC television series 'The Fugitive' (1966-7). Now an international actor, he no longer lives in Canada but returns frequently to accept acting engagements.

Mortgaging the Homestead. Once-popular painting by George REID. A large showpiece painted by the Toronto artist in 1890, it depicts solemnly and with restrained sentiment a disconsolate family group, including the mother with an infant in her lap and the father signing away the ancestral farm in the presence of a self-righteous-looking banker. It was widely reproduced in school readers until the 1950s. (NGC)

Morton, Desmond (b.1937). Historian. Born in Calgary, he attended the Royal Military Colleges in Saint John, N.B., and Kingston, Ont.; Oxford; and the London School of Economics. He retired as a captain in the Royal Canadian Army Service Corps in 1964 and since 1969 has taught history at Erindale College, University of Toronto. Among his many publications are *Ministers and Generals: Politics and the Canadian Militia* (1970), *The Last War Drum* (1972), *Mayor Howland: The Citizens' Candidate* (1973), and *NDP: The Dream of Power* (1974).

Morton, W.L. (b.1908). Historian. Born in Gladstone, Man., he was educated at the University of Manitoba and Oxford. He taught history at the University of Manitoba from 1950 to 1965, when he became Vanier Professor of Canadian history at Trent University, Peterborough, Ont. A major Canadian historian, he has brought to his writings a strong sense of the cultural milieu of the prairie west and the plurality of Canadian life. Among his books are *The Progressive Party in Canada* (1950; rev. 1967); *Manitoba: A History* (1957; rev. 1967); *The Kingdom of Canada: A General History from the Earliest Time* (1964); and *The Critical Years: The Union of British North America* (1964). The latter volume appears in the CANADIAN CENTENARY SERIES of which Morton is executive director.

Mosaic. The image of Canada as a multicultural collage rather than as a unicultural melting pot. The word 'mosaic' was first used in this sense in *Romantic Canada* (1922) by the American travel writer Victoria Hayward.

Mosaic. 'A quarterly journal for the comparative study of literature and ideas'. Published by the University of Manitoba since 1967, each issue is devoted to a scholarly theme.

Mosher, Christopher Terry (b.1942). Caricaturist and political cartoonist. Born in Ottawa, he graduated from the École des Beaux-Arts in Quebec City and lives in Montreal. His work has appeared under the pen-name 'Aislin'—the name of his daughter—in many Canadian newspapers and magazines and has received gallery exhibitions in Montreal and Toronto. It has been published in four books of caricatures.

Mosport. A privately owned track for car racing, opened in 1958 near Orono, Ont. The 2.45-mi. track is on a 500-acre site.

Mosquito. A famous twin-engine fighter bomber in the Second World War. Designed by De Havilland, Eng., and built by DE HAVILLAND, Canada, of laminated plywood, the Mosquito was, at 425 m.p.h., the fastest plane of its type in the world.

Mosquito hawk. A dragon-fly or a night-hawk.

Most easterly city in Canada. Unofficial motto of ST JOHN'S, Nfld.

Most southerly city in Canada. Unofficial motto of Windsor, Ont., which is south of the northern tip of California.

Mother Carey's chicken. Name used in the Atlantic Provinces for the stormy petrel. The phrase may be an Anglicization of *Mater Cara*, Latin for 'dear mother', which is applied to the Virgin Mary, patroness of sailors.

Motion. A film magazine published every two months in Toronto. It was founded in 1972 by Peter M. Evanchuck and, while it specializes in articles on Canadian films, it also covers television and theatre in Canada. See also CINEMA CANADA.

Motion Picture Bureau. Bureau of the federal government established in 1917 to produce educational and promotional films. It was absorbed in 1941 by the newly formed NATIONAL FILM BOARD. One of its productions was LEST WE FORGET.

Mount Allison University. It evolved from the Mount Allison Academy for Boys, a Wesleyan Methodist residential high school established by Charles Frederick Allison in Sackville, N.B., in 1840, and a ladies' college that was added in 1854. In 1862 Mount Allison College was incorporated and given degree-granting powers. Here Grace Ann Lockhart was the first woman in the British Empire to be granted a Bachelor's degree (1875).

Mount Columbia. Highest peak in Canada outside of the Yukon and British Columbia. It is 12,294 ft high and lies in Alberta at the B.C. border in Jasper National Park.

Mount Logan. Canada's highest peak and the second-highest in North America. It rises 19,850 ft in the centre of the St Elias Range and the Logan-Hubbard Icefield in the southwestern Yukon.

Mount Lucania. Third-highest peak in Canada, rising from the Logan-Hubbard Icefield of the southwestern Yukon to a height of 17,174 ft.

Mount Revelstoke National Park. Established in 1914 on the western slopes of the Selkirk Mountains in British Columbia, it covers 101 sq. mi. of rolling mountain terrain that includes alpine meadows and lakes.

Mount Royal. An extinct volcano 764 ft above sea level dominating the centre of modern Montreal (it was once a day's journey from Old Montreal). First called *Mont Royal* by Jacques CARTIER, it has given its name to the city. An illuminated cross on its eastern flank, erected by the St-Jean-Baptiste Society in 1924 to commemorate MAISONNEUVE, is visible up to 50 mi. away. The top

Mount Royal

of the mountain, carefully preserved as a wooded park (designed by F.L. Olmstead) from which cars are banned, offers a fine view of the city. See also MONTEREGIAN HILLS.

Mount Royal Club, The. A nationally important luncheon club. Founded in 1899, it is housed in an imposing building on Sherbrooke St, Montreal. It has fewer than 500 members, largely English-speaking business executives. Peter C. Newman in *The Canadian Establishment: Volume One* (1975) calls it 'the most snobbish club in the country' and writes, 'The legend persists that the main reason Max Aitken, the future Lord BEAVERBROOK, left Montreal for England in 1910 was that he couldn't get into the Mount Royal.'

Mount Sorrel. Flemish village in Belgium, the scene of repeated German and Canadian attacks in the Ypres Salient during the FIRST WORLD WAR. The Third Canadian Division lost the village on 2 June 1916, but regained it on 13 June.

Mount Steele. Fourth-highest mountain in Canada at a height of 16,644 ft in the Yukon's St Elias Range.

Mount Stephen, Baron. See Sir George STEPHEN.

Mount Waddington. Second-highest peak outside the Yukon and the highest in southern Canada (south of the 58th parallel). It is 13,104 ft high and lies only about 175 mi. northwest of Vancouver in the glacier fields of the coastal range.

Mountain and the Valley, The. A highly regarded psychological novel by Ernest BUCKLER, published in 1952. Set on a farm in Nova Scotia, it shows how a lonely man's sensitivity to nature helps him to reconcile his personal conflicts and attain a sympathetic understanding of tangled family relationships.

Mountain beaver. A small greyish-brown rodent. Quite rare, it is found in secluded forests of the British Columbia and Alberta Rockies. Despite its name, it is not related to the beaver, being a 'living fossil' with no close relationship to any modern mammal.

Mountain oyster. Western slang for the testicle of a lamb or calf, regarded as a delicacy.

Mounties, The. See ROYAL CANADIAN MOUNTED POLICE.

Mousseau, Lac. See HARRINGTON LAKE.

Mowat, Farley (b.1921). Writer. Born in Belleville, Ont., he was educated at the University of Toronto and lived in the Canadian Arctic in 1947 and 1948 and in the Russian Arctic in 1966 and 1969. Many of his books eloquently convey his sympathy for all humans and animals that are oppressed or endangered by the inroads of modern civilization. He attracted considerable attention with his first book, PEOPLE OF THE DEER (1952), and its sequel *The Desperate People* (1959), which study the dying Ihalmuit or Inland Eskimos who live on the Barrens. (These books have been reissued in a uniform edition entitled *Death of a People.*) NEVER CRY WOLF (1963) and *A Whale for the Killing* (1972) study man's unnatural fear of animals and mammals. *Coppermine Journey* (1958) is an edited version of the narrative of Samuel HEARNE. Three other books composed of edited texts by Arctic explorers with a linking commentary were reissued as the 'Top of the World Trilogy' in 1973: *Ordeal by Ice* (1960), *The Polar Passion* (1967), and *Tundra* (1973). *The Regiment* (1955; rev. 1973) is a history of the Hastings and Prince Edward Regiment in the Second World War. *The Grey Seas Under* (1958) and *The Serpent's Coil* (1961) are two sea-rescue narratives. *Westviking: The Ancient Norse in Greenland and North America* (1965) is popular archaeology. *Sibir* (1970) bears the subtitle *My Discovery of Siberia*. *The Snow Walker* (1975) is a collection of short stories about Eskimos. Mowat wrote the text for three pictorial books: *The Rock Within the Sea* (photographs by John de Visser, 1968) and *Wake of the Great Sealers* (with David Blackwood's illustrations, 1968), both about Newfoundland, and *Canada North* (1967). He has also distinguished himself as a writer of books for children: *Lost in the Barrens* (1956) and its sequel *The Curse of the Viking Grave* (1966); *The Black Joke* (1962); *Owls in the Family* (1961); and *The* DOG WHO WOULDN'T BE (1957), the same kind of effective light narrative as *The Boat Who Wouldn't Float* (1969). In 1976 he published *Canada North Now*, an examination of living conditions in the Arctic.

Mowat, Sir Oliver (1820-1903). A FATHER OF CONFEDERATION and premier of Ontario. Born in Kingston, U.C. (Ont.), he studied law there under John A. MACDONALD and practised from 1841. He was elected to the legislative assembly in 1857. A member of the GREAT COALITION ministry of 1864, he was a delegate to the QUEBEC CONFERENCE on Confederation. As premier of Ontario from 1872 to 1896 he was a champion of provincial rights. Appointed to the senate in 1896, he was LAURIER's Minister of Justice for a year

352

until he was made lieutenant-governor of Ontario. He was knighted in 1892.

MP. Abbreviation of Member of Parliament. Parliamentarians are entitled to use these initials after their names.

MPP. Abbreviation of Member of Provincial Parliament. Provincial parliamentarians are entitled to use these initials after their names; in practice they are used in Ontario only.

Mr Canada. Sobriquet of John W. FISHER.

Mr Fix-it. Sobriquet of Peter Whittall. Called 'handyman to the nation', the former producer of farm programs starred on CBC-TV's weekly 15-minute segment devoted to home repairs that was inserted into other shows. He first appeared in 1952, built a recreation room in 1958, and a boat in 1962. He referred to himself as 'the five basic hand-tool man', a reference to his hammer, saw, plane, level, and square.

Mr Justice. See JUSTICE.

Mr. Member of Parliament. See QUENTIN JURGENS, M.P.

Mr North. Sobriquet of Thomas Lamb, early bush pilot. The father of six pilots, Lamb founded in 1935 Lamb Airways Limited at The Pas, Man., and is credited with opening up the north country through his flying service.

Mr. Pearson. A 100-minute film shown on CBC-TV. Written and directed by Richard Ballentine and photographed by D.A. Pennebaker, who used a *caméra-vérité* technique, it recorded a 'typical day' (identified as Monday, 7 Oct. 1963) in the life of Prime Minister Lester PEARSON. Thought by some to be partisan, by others to demean Pearson, it aroused a storm of controversy even before it was shown, with sound-track changes, on 20 Apr. 1969.

Mr Premier. Informal style of address of the premier of a province. The formal style of address in conversation is 'Sir'. (A female premier would be addressed as 'Madam Premier' and 'Madam'.) In formal usage a premier's name is preceded by 'The HONOURABLE'.

Mr Prime Minister. Informal style of address of the Prime Minister. The formal style of address in conversation is 'Sir'. (A female prime minister would be addressed as 'Madam Prime Minister' and 'Madam'.) In formal usage a prime minister's name is preceded by 'The RIGHT HONOURABLE'.

Mr. Sage. A series of 35 controversial political radio programs broadcast over the CRBC, the forerunner of the CBC, from 7 Sept. to 5 Oct. 1935. Carried by 21 stations from Quebec City to Vancouver and written by an advertising agency, they were so partisan in favour of the Conservatives during an election year that they were a factor leading to the formation of the CBC the year following. The part of Mr Sage, the wise old codger, was created by Rupert Lucas.

MTC. See MANITOBA THEATRE CENTRE.

Muckamuck. CHINOOK JARGON for 'food' or 'eat'. The phrase *hyiu muckamu 'k* means 'lots to eat', but it has been corrupted to *high muckamuck*, which means a 'leader' or 'bigshot'. A Chinook grace runs: *Typee papa mahsie kloshe muckamuck* ('Great Chief Father thanks for the good food').

Muddy York. See YORK.

Muir, Alexander (1830-1906). Composer of 'The MAPLE LEAF FOREVER'. Born in Lesmahagow, Scot., and brought to Canada as a child, he graduated from Queen's University and became a teacher and later principal of Gladstone Public School, Toronto. He composed the patriotic song 'The Maple Leaf Forever' in the fall of 1867 and published it himself. He died in Toronto, a noted sportsman and both Canadian and American champion in quoits.

Mukherjee, Bharati (b.1940). Novelist. Born in Calcutta, India, and raised in India, England, and Switzerland, she was educated at the Universities of Calcutta and Iowa. She teaches English at McGill University and is the author of two novels that draw on her Bengali background: *The Tiger's Daughter* (1972) and *Wife* (1975). With her husband, the novelist Clark BLAISE, she has written *Days and Nights*, a non-fiction account of a year spent in India, scheduled to appear in 1977.

Mukluk. Eskimo word used in the western Arctic for an ankle-length boot made of deerskin. The KAMIK is characteristic of the eastern Arctic.

Muktuk. Eskimo word for the skin of the NARWHAL and beluga. It is also known as blackskin and is eaten raw by Eskimos but cooked by whites.

Multinational corporation. A large company operating in two or more countries. The term 'multinational firm' was coined in 1958 by Howe Martyn, a Canadian economist, at the American University, Washington, D.C.

Municipality. A unit of local government—a city, town, or rural municipality. The legal term for a local government unit is the municipal corporation—an incorporated locality—but municipality is commonly used in Canada to refer to local governments.

Munk, Jens Eriksen (1579-1628). Danish sailor, explorer of Hudson Bay. Sent westward in 1619 by Christian IV to search for the NORTHWEST PASSAGE, he wintered at the mouth of the Churchill R. He made the first map depicting Hudson Bay, which he called Novum Mare Christian, as a single body of water.

Munro, Alice (b.1931). Short-story writer. Born in Wingham, Ont., and educated at the University of Western Ontario, she developed in the 1960s as a major writer of fiction, creating fine short stories about a small southern Ontario town and its environs that is similar to Wingham. Her stories have been collected in *Dance of the Happy Shades* (1968) and *Something I've Been Meaning to Tell You* (1974). Her novel, *Lives of Girls and Women* (1971), is really a sequence of linked stories.

Munsinger case. A widely reported sex scandal involving a woman from East Germany and a Conservative cabinet minister. On 7 Dec. 1960 the RCMP reported to the Minister of Justice, E. Davie Fulton, that the Associate Minister of National Defence, Pierre Sévigny, had been conducting an affair of two years' standing with Mrs Gerda Munsinger, a Montreal divorcée who had emigrated from East Germany in 1955. The RCMP believed there were security risks involved and Fulton informed Prime Minister John G. DIEFENBAKER who, on 13 Dec., confronted Sévigny, who terminated the affair. No other action was taken, a point at issue six years later when the matter surfaced in Parliament in a remark made by a Liberal minister during a heated debate and blossomed into a major national scandal that called into question the probity of the Diefenbaker administration. In Sept. 1966 a commission of inquiry under Mr Justice Wishart Spence tabled its report, which found some element of a 'security risk' and stated that the prime minister had erred in failing to dismiss his cabinet colleague.

Murchie's. 'Importers of Fine Tea, Coffee and Spices'. Started by John Murchie in New Westminster, B.C., in 1894, Murchie's Tea and Coffee Ltd is now a west-coast institution, with its head office in Vancouver. It blends Empress Afternoon Tea, named after Victoria's EMPRESS HOTEL.

Murdoch Case. A widely reported fight for property and women's rights. It centred on the attempt of Irene Murdoch, an Alberta farm woman, to secure as a divorce settlement a share in the 480-acre farm near Turner Valley established by herself and her husband over 25 years of marriage. In 1971 the Alberta Supreme Court disallowed her claim, maintaining that the farm was a business and that no formal contracts had been drawn up. In lieu of property interest, a monetary settlement of $200 a month was authorized. Her claim was also denied in a split decision by the Supreme Court of Canada in 1973. The Murdoch Case has been seen as a request for 'simple justice' and as a symbol of the inequalities of Canadian matrimonial property laws.

Murmansk 'mission'. Allied intervention in Russia during the FIRST WORLD WAR that included a Canadian contingent of some 100 troops. Two forces were dispatched in June 1918 to prevent German seizure of Murmansk and Archangel and remained to aid the cause of the White against the Red Russians. The Canadians were evacuated between June and Sept. 1919. See also VLADIVOSTOK 'MISSION'.

Murphy, Emily Gowan (1868-1933). Author, feminist; the first woman to be appointed a police magistrate in the British Empire. Born in Cooksville, Ont., and educated at Bishop Strachan School, Toronto, she married a clergyman in 1887. In 1903 they moved to Manitoba and then to Edmonton, Alta. Active in lobbying for married women's property rights and for a women's court for cases involving women, Emily Murphy was appointed the first magistrate of a newly created women's court in 1916. She was subsequently involved in the PERSONS CASE and became president of the Canadian Women's Press Club, vice-president of the National Council of Women, and president of the Federated Women's Institutes of Canada. She retired as a magistrate in 1931. She wrote for magazines under her maiden name, Ferguson, or her pen name, 'Janey Canuck'. Her books include: *The Impressions of Janey Canuck Abroad* (1901), *Janey Canuck in the West* (1910), *Open Trails* (1912), and *Seeds of Pine* (1914), sketches of life in Alberta.

Murray, Anne (b.1945). Country singer. Born in Springhill, N.S., she first gained national prominence on CBC-TV's SINGALONG JUBILEE in the 1960s. Her interpretation of Gene MacLELLAN's newly written song 'SNOWBIRD' in 1970 made it a hit and started her on the road to becoming an international pop star. She performs widely in clubs and on TV and has won major recording awards in Canada, the United States, and the United Kingdom.

Murray, Father Athol (1892-1975). Sports organizer. Born in Ontario, he became chancellor to the Archbishop of the Regina diocese in 1923. He organized a boys' athletic club that led to the founding of Notre Dame College in Wilcox, Sask., an institution that has been notable not only for its scholastic achievements but for the colourful personality of its founder and the excellence of its graduates in baseball, football and, especially, hockey.

Murray, Dr Gordon. See 'BLUE BABY' OPERATION and HEPARIN.

Murray, James (1722-94). British army officer, first British governor of Quebec. He took part in the siege of LOUISBOURG in 1758 and was one of Gen. WOLFE'S three brigadiers at Quebec in 1759, taking part in the Battle of the PLAINS OF ABRAHAM. He was military governor of Quebec when he was defeated by French forces under the duc de LÉVIS in the Battle of SAINTE-FOY on 28 Apr. 1760, retreating behind the city walls until the British fleet arrived. He became civil governor of Quebec in 1764 and adopted a conciliatory policy towards the French Canadians that was much resented by the British merchants. He left Quebec in 1766.

Murray, Rear Admiral Leonard Warren (1896-1971). Naval commander. Born in Granton, N.S., he was educated at Pictou Academy and was in the first class of the Royal Naval College of Canada in 1911. During the First World War he served mainly in the Royal Navy and was in the British Grand Fleet. He was a founding member of the Canada-United States Permanent Joint Board on Defence. In 1942 he was appointed Commanding Officer Atlantic Coast. In 1943, when the German submarine offensive was at its peak, he was appointed Commander-in-Chief, Canadian North West Atlantic. He was the only Canadian to hold an independent operational command during the Second World War. He retired from the RCN in Mar. 1946 and enrolled as a student at the Middle Temple, London. Called to the Bar in 1949, he practised law in Admiralty courts.

Murray, Robert (b.1936). Sculptor and painter. Born in Vancouver, he studied painting at the Regina College of Art and was strongly influenced by his experience at EMMA LAKE. He completed a welded steel sculpture fountain for the City Hall in Saskatoon in 1960, the year he moved to New York

City, where he studied and where he now teaches at the School of Visual Arts. His sculptures—monumental forms created from angled or curved sheets of steel or aluminum that are painted—have been exhibited internationally. They include two of our finest modern public monuments: *Cumbria* (1966) at the Vancouver airport and *Haida* (1973) in front of the Department of External Affairs, Ottawa.

Murray's Restaurants. Founded in Toronto in 1924 by Murray Crawley and Fred McCracken as a fast-food counter at Queen and Yonge Sts, it now operates 12 restaurants in Toronto, Hamilton, Ottawa, and Montreal. It serves plain, nutritious, economical meals to almost six million customers a year, and is now diversifying, with an emphasis on fast-food counters and industrial catering and cafeterias.

Museum of Contemporary Art/Musée d'Art Contemporain. Art museum in Montreal, Que. Founded in 1964, it exhibits local, national, and international contemporary work with the avowedly didactic purpose of creating an audience for new experiments in the arts. It is provincially funded.

Musgrave, Susan (b.1951). Poet. Born in California, she grew up in Victoria, has travelled widely, and lives part of the time in the Queen Charlotte Islands. Her poetry collections include: *Songs of the Sea-Witch* (1970), *Entrance of the Celebrant* (1972), *Grave Dirt and Selected Strawberries* (1973), and *The Impstone* (1976). *Gullband Thought Measles Was a Happy Ending* (1974) is a book for children.

Mush. A command to sled dogs to advance, associated with the North. It may derive from the French imperative *Marche donc!*

Mush ice. Northern expression for rotten or disintegrating ice.

Musical Ride. A ceremonial cavalry drill performed by members of the ROYAL CANADIAN MOUNTED POLICE to music. A troop of the North West Mounted Police (later the RCMP) first performed it in 1876 as a new part of their regular training, the cavalry drill. At first it was performed only in the West but became so popular it is now performed throughout Canada and in many other countries. The full Troop of the Ride is composed of 32 men and horses. Each member of the Ride performs for two years before returning to his regular duties. The Troop wears the scarlet tunic first used by the North West Mounted Police to obtain the respect of the Indians, to whom the force was known as the 'Redcoats'; a broad-brimmed hat, an adaptation of the cowboy's stetson worn as protection against the elements; breeches, originally grey or beige but changed in 1878 to blue-black with the yellow Cavalry stripe down the side; and Strathcona riding boots, used since 1901. Each member carries a lance made of bamboo that bears a red and white pennon. All the horses used in the Ride are black and are trained to walk, trot, and canter in intricate patterns in twos, fours, and eights. The highlight and finale of the Ride is the charge, a thrilling display of wheeling and turning performed at the gallop.

Musicamera. CBC-TV's showcase for operas, ballets, concerts, and musical dramas. The 60- or 90-minute specials were first shown on 28 Nov. 1973.

Musk ox. A shaggy hooved mammal of the Arctic tundra, with a characteristic musky odour. It stands about 5 ft at the shoulders, weighs up to 1,450 lb., and has a large broad head with low massive horns and long brown hair that is matted and curly at the shoulders. A gregarious animal, assembling in herds of 20 to 30, it is also suited to domestication, affording palatable meat and milk as well as wool.

Muskeg. Bogland in the northern forest and tundra formed in undrained basins and filled with living and dead vegetation, often to a considerable depth. Transportation across such areas during the summer is almost impossible. Its name is ALGONKIAN for 'swamp'.

Muskeg Express. Nickname of the HUDSON BAY RAILWAY.

Muskellunge. See MASKINONGE.

Muskie. See MASKINONGE.

Musson Book Company. See GENERAL PUBLISHING COMPANY LIMITED.

MWO. Official abbreviation of Master Warrant Officer.

My Country. A 30-minute weekly television series starring Pierre BERTON. With the aid of illustrations and artifacts, Berton tells true and colourful stories based on well-known or forgotten incidents in the Canadian past. Produced by Elsa FRANKLIN for the GLOBAL TELEVISION NETWORK, which has showed 52 episodes since the series' first program was broadcast in Jan. 1974, it is now nationally syndicated. 18 episodes from past programs are written up in Berton's *My Country* (1976).

'My Financial Career'. Stephen LEACOCK'S most popular short story. It is the humorous first-person account of a young man's attempt to open his first bank account and begins, 'When I go into a bank I get rattled.' First appearing in *Literary Lapses* (1910), it has been frequently reprinted. It was turned into a film directed by Grant Munro and Gerald Potterton for the NFB in 1962 (6 min., 38 sec.; colour).

My Fur Lady. Musical comedy that originated as a McGill University satiric revue and subsequently toured the country. When it opened in Montreal on 7 Feb. 1957 it was a smash hit. With words by Tim Porteous and others, and music by James de B. Domville and others (including Galt MacDERMOT), it was directed and choreographed by Brian MACDONALD. Called 'a song and dance enquiry into Canadian manners and foibles, ranging in scope from national defence to poetry', it concerns Aurora, the Eskimo princess of Mukluko, who must marry before she turns 21 or her Arctic principality 'somewhere off Baffin Island' will revert to Canada.

My Remarkable Uncle and Other Sketches. A collection of humorous stories by Stephen LEACOCK published in 1942 that includes a celebrated account of the author's eccentric uncle, Edward Philip Leacock.

Myers, Barton (b.1934). Architect. Born in Norfolk, Va, he was educated at the U.S. Naval Academy, Annapolis, Md, and at the University of Pennsylvania, where he studied with Louis Kahn, before coming to Canada in 1968. In the firm of A.J. DIAMOND and Barton Myers he was partner-in-charge of the design work for the Ontario Medical Association building (1968); the student housing at the University of Alberta, Edmonton (1969); and the Dundas-Sherbourne project, Toronto (1973-6)—all of which stress the importance of infill construction that respects the character of the urban fabric without compromising its own contemporary character. His independent work has developed the strongly modern idiom—e.g., the Myers House (1970) and the Wolf House (1972), both in Toronto—and his interest in the concept of the community and its relation to new architecture is exemplified by the Lincoln Park Community, Calgary (begun 1975-6).

Myers, Martin (b.1928). Novelist. Born in Toronto, he was educated at the University of Toronto and Columbia University and is associated with Baker Lovick Ltd, an advertising agency. Known throughout the business for his brilliance and inventiveness, he has written two satiric novels that are infectiously humorous: *The Assignment* (1971) and *Frigate* (1975).

Mysterious East, The. A radical monthly published in the Maritimes between 1969 and 1972. Edited and published by Donald CAMERON, Robert Campbell, and Russell Hunt, it grew out of student unrest at the University of New Brunswick in Saint John,

where the editors were on the academic staff, and acted as an 'opposition press' for the Atlantic provinces. The editors regularly presented Rubber Duck Awards to the 'worst newspapers' published in the Maritimes. It was called *The Mysterious East* 'not because there is anything particularly inscrutable about the Maritimes, but because the most suitable editorial stance seems to be one of puzzlement'.

N

N.B. Abbreviation of NEW BRUNSWICK.

N.B. See MADE BEAVER.

N.F. Unofficial abbreviation of NEWFOUNDLAND, the official one being 'Nfld'.

N.S. Abbreviation of NOVA SCOTIA.

N.W.T. Abbreviation of NORTHWEST TERRITORIES.

NAC. See NATIONAL ARTS CENTRE.

Nahani. ATHAPASCAN-speaking Indians occupying the Nahanni R. watershed of the southern Yukon Territory and northern British Columbia. They are now known as Kaska. Their population in 1970 was 1,112.

Nahanni National Park. Established in 1972, along the South Nahanni R. in the southwest corner of the Northwest Territories, it covers 1,840 sq. mi. of largely inaccessible wilderness with deep canyons and spectacular falls.

Naismith, James A. (1861-1939). Inventor of basketball. He was born in Lanark Co., near Almonte, Ont. As a student at McGill he was active in gymnastics, lacrosse, wrestling, and football. He graduated in theology and became a YMCA instructor at a training school in Springfield, Mass., where the need for a competitive indoor team sport led him to devise, in Dec. 1891, a game played under 13 basic rules with a ball and two round baskets. He took a medical degree and became professor of physical education at Kansas University. He was elected to the Sports HALL OF FAME.

Nakumara, Kazuo (b.1926). Painter. Born in Vancouver, he studied at Central Technical School, Toronto, and was a founding

member of PAINTERS ELEVEN. His early watercolour and oil paintings of stylized landscapes culminated in a series of delicate works concerned with water reflections. *Waves* (1957, Norman MacKenzie Art Gallery) represents the brooding, empty landscape style that later evolved into 'string paintings'—minimal paintings based on string shapes organized in subtle patterns. He has exhibited internationally and lives in Vancouver.

Nakoowamik. Eskimo word used in the eastern Arctic for 'thank you'.

Namko. Fictitious community of Indians and white settlers. Created by Paul ST PIERRE for the CBC-TV series CARIBOO COUNTRY, it is located in the Chilcotin Plateau region of British Columbia.

Nanabozho. The trickster hero (also known as Nanabush) of the OJIBWA and other ALGONKIAN-speaking Indians. His father was the West Wind and his mother was Wenonah, granddaughter of the Moon. He was 'more than human' and changed himself at birth into a hare and then into a handsome brave. He stole fire for man, raised the CANADIAN SHIELD, refashioned the world following the Flood, fought his enemies the Windigos, entered the belly of the Great Sturgeon, made an ally of the THUNDERBIRD, created the MIDÉWEWIN, and invented rock art. He lived near Kakabeka Falls in northern Ontario and, on the low rocky promontory of Thunder Cape, near THUNDER BAY, fell into a long sleep from which he has yet to awaken (see the SLEEPING GIANT). Except for his crude buffoonery, he is not unlike GLOOSCAP. Many of his exploits are attributed to the semi-legendary HIAWATHA by Henry Wadsworth Longfellow in his famous poem, owing to a confusion of the two figures in his source, a scholarly work by Henry Rowe Schoolcraft.

Nanaimo Strikes. A series of strikes by coalminers for union recognition. The mines at Nanaimo, B.C., were owned by the Dunsmuir family, which was opposed to unionization. Major strikes broke out in 1877, 1904, and 1912-14. The latter, lasting from 17 Sept. 1912 to 19 Aug. 1914, was accompanied by the introduction of Orientals as strike-breakers and of the militia as reinforcements. The union won recognition, but claims were not settled until 1919.

Nancy. A 75-foot schooner launched at Detroit for a firm of local merchants in 1789. In 1812 she was requisitioned as a supply ship to become the only British naval vessel on the upper Great Lakes. On 14 Aug. 1814 an American flotilla of three ships destroyed her in the Nottawasaga R. Her hull, retrieved in 1927, is now housed in the Museum of the Upper Lakes at Wasaga Beach, Ont.

Nanogak, Agnes (b.1924). Eskimo graphic artist at HOLMAN. She illustrated *Tales from the Igloo* (1972), a collection of stories edited and translated by Maurice Metayer. Her drawings are playful in spirit, yet assured in handling.

Nanook of the North. Documentary film classic photographed, produced, and directed by Robert FLAHERTY. Filmed in nothern UNGAVA in 1921-2, and sponsored by REVILLON FRÈRES, it was released in 1922 by Jesse Lasky. It was the world's first feature-length documentary and has set a style and a standard for real-life features ever since. Nanook (the name means 'the bear'), who was an actual hunter whom Flaherty befriended in the eastern Arctic, became the world's best-known Eskimo. Flaherty learned of his death the year of the film's release. 6 reels, b & w.

NAR. Abbreviation of Northern Alberta Railways.

Narizzano, Silvio (b.1924). Film director. Born in Montreal, he directed for the stage and, with the arrival of television, became a CBC-TV producer in Toronto in the 1950s before leaving, with Sydney NEWMAN, in 1955-6 for London, Eng., where his BBC-TV drama productions were well received. Among his feature films are *Under Two Flags* (co-director, 1960), *Fanatic* (1965), *Georgy Girl* (1966), *Blue* (1967), *The Man Who Had Power Over Women* (1969), *Loot* (1970), and *Why Shoot the Teacher?* (1976).

Narwhal. An Arctic whale, the male of which has a long, straight, spirally grooved tusk, which gave rise to its popular name, sea unicorn. In 1955 the handle of the mace of the Northwest Territories was made from a narwhal tusk by Eskimos at Cape Dorset.

Nascopie. Supply ship of 2,500 tons launched for the HUDSON'S BAY COMPANY at Newcastle-on-Tyne in 1911. During the First World War she made a number of trips to Russia with munitions. She served the Company's northeastern Canadian outposts until 21 July 1947, when she struck a reef off Dorset harbour. She could not be saved and her hulk slipped off and disappeared in Oct. 1948.

Nashwaak-Miramichi Trail. Well-known hunting and fishing tour of the interior of New Brunswick. The scenic route begins at Fredericton and proceeds through lumber country along the Miramichi R. to Escuminac on the Gulf of St Lawrence.

Naskapi. See MONTAGNAIS-NASKAPI.

Nathanson, N.L. See ALLEN'S THEATRES, FAMOUS PLAYERS LTD, ODEON THEATRES (CANADA) LTD.

National, The. The national newscast on CBC-TV, televised nightly at 11:00 p.m. It was called CBC NATIONAL NEWS from 1952 to 1966 and was identified with the newscasters Larry Henderson (1954 to 1959), Earl CAMERON (1959 to 1966), and Stanley BURKE (1966 to 1970). In Aug. 1970 the present title and a new reader, Lloyd Robertson, were introduced. 'The National' consists of 19 minutes of the day's news read by an announcer, backed by clips and graphics. Until 1976 it was followed by VIEWPOINT.

National Advisory Council on Fitness and Amateur Sport. It was established in 1961 to encourage participation in physical recreation and amateur sport activities ranging from day camps to the Olympics. Up to 30 appointed members advise the Minister of National Health and Welfare on how to achieve the aims of the Amateur Sport Program of 1961.

National Anthem. See ANTHEM.

National Arts Centre. Centre for the performing arts in CONFEDERATION SQUARE, Ottawa, that opened in 1969. It includes three auditoriums: an opera house and concert hall (2,300 seats), a theatre (800 seats), and an experimental studio (300 seats)—plus a salon for recitals (120 seats); there are also restaurants and boutiques. The impressive building, designed by Fred Lebensold, is notable for its striking interior decoration employing painting, sculpture, and wall hangings. The NAC, which is the residence of the NATIONAL ARTS CENTRE ORCHESTRA, is operated by the National Arts Centre Corporation, established in 1966.

National Arts Centre Orchestra, The. Resident ensemble of the NATIONAL ARTS CENTRE, Ottawa. Founded in 1969 under conductor Mario BERNARDI, it is a 45-member orchestra that is known particularly for its superb performances of eighteenth-century works, though its repertoire goes beyond this period. It tours internationally, and has made three records for the RCA 'Red Seal' label.

National Assembly. See ASSEMBLÉE NATIONALE.

National Ballet of Canada, The. With the ROYAL WINNIPEG BALLET in the West and the success of the Canadian Ballet Festivals in 1948, 1949, and 1950, it was inevitable that some Torontonians sought a ballet company for the East. At the suggestion of Ninette de Valois, Celia FRANCA was invited from London to advise on the formation of a national ballet for Canada. As a result the National Ballet of Canada was formed in 1951, with a board of directors and Franca as artistic director and Betty OLIPHANT as ballet mistress. It found a home in ST LAWRENCE HALL, Toronto. The first performance was at the Eaton Auditorium in Nov. 1951. It has since become one of the leading ballet companies in the world, regularly touring Canada and the United States; it has also performed in London, Eng. The early years were concentrated upon establishing standard classics from the Russian and Diaghilev repertoires— *Swan Lake, Nutcracker, Coppelia, Giselle,* and *Les Sylphides*—to which were added such ballets as Antony Tudor's *Lilac Garden* and *Dark Elegies*. Later the National developed a repertoire of native Canadian choreographies from David ADAMS, Grant STRATE, Ray Powell, and others. The company performs at the O'Keefe Centre in Toronto. Erik BRUHN, Rudolf Nureyev, and Mikhail Baryshnikov have been guest artists with the company, Nureyev creating a highly successful new version of *The Sleeping Beauty* and Bruhn creating a new *Swan Lake*. (Bruhn was for a time resident producer.) Franca retired as artistic director in 1975 and was succeeded briefly by David Haber and in 1976 by the English character dancer Alexander Grant. The company has had its own school—the

NATIONAL BALLET SCHOOL—since 1959, with Betty Oliphant as principal and director.

National Ballet School. Founded in 1959 by Celia FRANCA and Betty OLIPHANT, who became principal and director, it is affiliated with the NATIONAL BALLET OF CANADA and offers both dancing instruction and academic courses to selected students.

National Battlefields Park. A 235-acre national historic park in Quebec City that includes the PLAINS OF ABRAHAM, where WOLFE led his forces against those of MONTCALM in 1759 and sealed the fate of New France.

National Capital Commission. Federal body concerned with public lands in the Ottawa area. Established in 1959 to replace the Federal District Commission, the NCC has been responsible for public lands, municipal projects, and the siting and appearance of federal buildings in the 1,800-sq.-mi. NATIONAL CAPITAL REGION.

National Capital Region. Area of 1,800 sq. mi. around Ottawa. In 1951 the Gréber Plan —a comprehensive master plan for the redevelopment of the cities of Ottawa, Ont., and Hull, Que., and their surrounding areas— was tabled in the House of Commons. Accordingly, in 1959 the NATIONAL CAPITAL COMMISSION was created 'to prepare plans for and assist in the development, conservation and improvement of the National Capital Region in order that the nature and character of the seat of the Government of Canada may be in accordance with its national significance.'

National Club, The. An important luncheon club in Toronto. Founded in the 1870s to house the CANADA FIRST group, it has quarters on Bay St in downtown Toronto. One of the larger of the businessmen's clubs, it has over 1,000 members.

National Defence, Department of. Federal government department responsible for the CANADIAN ARMED FORCES and all matters relating to national defence. The Chief of the Defence Staff is the senior military adviser to the Minister.

National Design Council. Federal body concerned with the design of Canadian products. Established in 1961, the NDC makes recommendations to the Minister of Industry, Trade and Commerce on improving the design of the products of Canadian industry, both private and public. Programs recognized by the Council bear the identification 'Design Canada'.

National Dream, The. The title of the first volume of Pierre BERTON'S two-volume history of the building of the CPR. *The National Dream: The Great Railway, 1871-1881* appeared in 1970; *The Last Spike: The Great Railway, 1881-1885* appeared in 1971. Together the two volumes constitute a remarkably readable and detailed account of the politicians and financiers, surveyors and contractors who struggled to bring the project to completion. The two volumes became the basis of a popular CBC-TV series called 'The National Dream'. Subtitled 'Building the Impossible Railway', it was written by Timothy FINDLEY and William Whitehead, produced by James Murray, and directed by Eric TILL and James Murray. It starred William HUTT as Sir John A. MACDONALD and John COLICOS as Sir William VAN HORNE. Berton acted as consultant and narrator. The series opened on Sunday evening (from 9 to 10 p.m.) on 3 Mar. 1974. It was sponsored by Royal Trust. The eight episodes were 'The Great Lone Land', 'The Pacific Scandal', 'The Horrid B.C. Business', 'The Great Debate', 'The Railway General', 'The Sea of Mountains', 'The Desperate Days', and 'The Last Spike'.

National Emergency Planning Establishment. A federal agency to mitigate the effects of disasters in Canada. Derived from the CANADA EMERGENCY MEASURES ORGANIZATION, it was established on 1 Apr. 1974 to work under the PRIVY COUNCIL OFFICE. The NEPE has offices in each provincial capital to co-ordinate arrangements for emergency measures with the provinces.

National Energy Board. Federal board concerned with the use of energy resources. Established in 1959, the NEB regulates such matters as oil and gas pipelines under federal jurisdiction, the export and import of gas, the export of electric power, and the construction of power lines. The nine-man board also functions as an energy review agency, reporting to Parliament through the Minister of Energy, Mines and Resources.

National Farm Radio Forum. An important and long-running series of adult-education programs on CBC Radio. With the co-operation of the Canadian Federation of Agriculture and the CANADIAN ASSOCIATION FOR ADULT EDUCATION, the CBC broadcast on Monday evenings, beginning in Jan. 1939, 60-minute programs written and produced for rural audiences that gathered in small groups (called 'Farm Forums') in neighbours' homes to listen to, discuss, and possibly act on the ideas presented. 'Inquiry into Co-operation' was the general title of the first programs, and a monthly guide was distributed. The motto of the series, supervised by Neil M. Morrison, was 'Read-Listen-Discuss-Act'. Its summer replacement was called 'Summer Fallow'. The self-help element gradually disappeared and by 1960 the series was reporting international farming news. On 1 Nov. 1965 it was incorporated as a segment of COUNTRY MAGAZINE. See also CITIZENS' FORUM.

National Film Board. Public film-production agency. Established by John GRIERSON for propaganda purposes in 1939, it absorbed the MOTION PICTURE BUREAU in 1941. The NFB is headed by a Government Film Commissioner and reports to Parliament through the Secretary of State. The largest government film unit in the world, the NFB is authorized to produce and distribute films in the national interest, especially those 'designed to interpret Canada to Canadians and to other nations'. It has produced many award-winning short features and, since 1963, some feature-length films. The head office is in Ottawa; its studios are in Montreal. Its French name is Office national du film.

National Flag of Canada, The. Once derisively nicknamed 'Pearson's pennant', it is popularly called the MAPLE LEAF. After much debate in the House of Commons, the act creating a distinctive and new Canadian flag was passed on 15 Dec. 1964 and was given royal assent on 28 Jan. 1965. It was first flown from PARLIAMENT HILL at the inauguration ceremony at noon of 15 Feb. 1965. The National Flag of Canada is officially described in the proclamation of 28 Jan. 1965 as 'a red flag of the proportions two by length and one by width, containing in its centre a white square the width of the flag, bearing a single red maple leaf, or, in heraldic terms, described as Gules on a Canadian pale Argent a maple leaf of the first.' The maple leaf was a symbol for Canada as early as 1805; it was used for decorative purposes for the ROYAL VISIT of the Prince of Wales in 1860; it is part of the CANADIAN COAT-OF-ARMS, which was officially granted in 1921; and it has long been used as a symbol and mark of identity by the armed forces and sports teams abroad. Red and white are the colours of Canada, being part of the Canadian Coat-of-Arms. Earlier flags include: ST GEORGE'S BANNER, ROYAL FLAG OF FRANCE, FIRST UNION FLAG, UNION JACK, CANADIAN RED ENSIGN.

National Gallery of Canada, The. The country's principal art gallery, in Ottawa, Ont. In 1880 it began with donations from the first Royal Canadian Academy Exhibition. Since then it has had various temporary quarters until moving into the Lorne Building—also temporary—in 1960. The original collection grew slowly until the government established an Advisory Arts Council in 1907 to supervise acquisitions. 1910 marked the appointment of Eric Brown as the first full-time Director; he served until 1939. Under him the gallery began building a representative collection of European and Canadian works. It has been expanded by subsequent directors: Harry Orr McCurry (1939-55), who made the gallery's first acquisitions of modern French art, expanded its staff, and published its first scholarly catalogue; Alan JARVIS (1955-9), who concentrated on twentieth-century works and developed the gallery's programs; Charles COMFORT (1960-5); William Dale, Acting Director (1965-6); and Jean Sutherland BOGGS (1966-76), who acquired the gallery's first contemporary American art and continued to develop its programs, sponsoring exhibitions of the works of living Canadians abroad. Major bequests include the donations by Dr James MacCALLUM of over 100 paintings by Tom THOMSON and the GROUP OF SEVEN; by Vincent MASSEY of 88 English paintings and over 100 Canadian works; and by Douglas M. DUNCAN of almost 700 works, the gallery's largest gift.

National Health and Welfare, Department of. Federal government department established in 1944. There are two deputy ministers: the Deputy Minister of Health is responsible for all matters concerning health, fitness, and medical services; and the Deputy Minister of Welfare administers all welfare programs, including the CANADA PENSION PLAN and the CANADA ASSISTANCE PLAN.

National Heritage Day. See HERITAGE DAY.

National Historic Parks and Sites. System of federal parks of historic interest established and maintained by Parks Canada within the Department of Indian Affairs and Northern Development. Canada's National Historic Parks and Sites preserves, restores, and reconstructs sites and artifacts commemorating persons, places, or events of major significance in the historical development of Canada. From 1911 to 1975 the system has grown to include 44 National Historic Parks and Sites, in addition to 28 NATIONAL PARKS. The 44 major National Historic Parks and Sites are divided into five regions:

Western Region: ROCKY MOUNTAIN HOUSE, FORT ST JAMES, FORT LANGLEY, ST ROCH, FORT RODD HILL.

Prairie Region: YORK FACTORY, FORT PRINCE OF WALES, LOWER FORT GARRY, BATOCHE, BATTLEFORD, FORT WALSH, YUKON HISTORIC SITES.

Ontario Region: FORT WELLINGTON, BELLEVUE HOUSE, FORT GEORGE, QUEENSTON HEIGHTS AND BROCK'S MONUMENT, WOODSIDE, FORT MALDEN, FORT ST JOSEPH.

Quebec Region: NATIONAL BATTLEFIELDS PARK, CARTIER-BRÉBEUF PARK, QUEBEC CITY WALLS AND GATES, ARTILLERY PARK, LES FORGES DU SAINT-MAURICE, FORT LENNOX, FORT CHAMBLY, MAISON LAURIER, CÔTEAU-DU-LAC, FORT TÉMISCAMINGUE.

Atlantic Region: CAPE SPEAR, SIGNAL HILL, CASTLE HILL, Fortress of LOUISBOURG, Alexander Graham Bell Museum (see BADDECK), Halifax CITADEL, PRINCE OF WALES MARTELLO TOWER, YORK REDOUBT, PORT ROYAL, FORT ANNE, GRAND PRÉ, FORT AMHERST, FORT BEAUSÉJOUR, CARLETON MARTELLO TOWER, ST ANDREWS BLOCKHOUSE.

National History Project. A two-year study of the teaching of Canadian history and social studies in public schools by A.B. Hodgetts, published under the title *What Culture? What Heritage?* (1968). His report documented the inadequate treatment given to Canadian studies at all levels of schooling throughout the country.

National Hockey League. An association of professional hockey clubs, founded in Montreal on 22 Nov. 1917 with Frank CALDER as first president. The first NHL game was played on 19 Dec. 1917; the first season's champion team was the Toronto Arenas (forerunner of the TORONTO MAPLE LEAFS). In 1943 there was a regular playing schedule for the 'big six'—the Boston Bruins, Chicago Black Hawks, Detroit Red Wings, MONTREAL CANADIENS, New York Rangers, Toronto Maple Leafs—which competed for the PRINCE OF WALES TROPHY and the STANLEY CUP. The 'big six' became the Eastern Division, with expansion in 1967 and the creation of a brand-new Western Division: the Los Angeles Kings, Minnesota North Stars, Oakland Seals, Philadelphia Flyers, Pittsburgh Penguins, and St Louis Blues. The Eastern Division competed for the Prince of Wales Trophy, the Western Division for the Clarence Campbell Bowl (named after the popular NHL president), the championship-winning team taking the Stanley Cup. Further expansion in 1970 added the Vancouver Canucks and the Buffalo Sabres. In 1972 a second league, the WORLD HOCKEY ASSOCIATION, was formed. Following the Stanley Cup playoff game the NHL makes these annual presentations: ART ROSS TROPHY, BILL MASTERSON MEMORIAL TROPHY, CALDER MEMORIAL TROPHY, CLARENCE S. CAMPBELL BOWL, CONN SMYTHE TROPHY, HART MEMORIAL TROPHY, JAMES NORRIS MEMORIAL TROPHY, LADY BYNG MEMORIAL TROPHY, LESTER PATRICK TROPHY, PRINCE OF WALES TROPHY, STANLEY CUP, VÉZINA TROPHY.

National Library of Canada. The national collection of books and other materials published in or relating to Canada. It grew out of some of the holdings of the LIBRARY OF PARLIAMENT and was formally established on 1 Jan. 1953 by an Act of Parliament. The first National Librarian was W. Kaye LAMB. Since 1953 the law has required that copies of all publications—including books, maps, periodicals, pamphlets, records, and audio tapes—be deposited with the National Library, which now holds the most extensive collection of Canadian books in the world. It also publishes *Canadiana*, a monthly catalogue of new publications relating to Canada, and maintains the Canadian Union Catalogue, which records the holdings of major libraries across Canada. The National Library itself has more than 500,000 volumes. Since 20 June 1967 it has shared quarters in Ottawa with the PUBLIC ARCHIVES OF CANADA.

National Library of Quebec. The Bibliothèque nationale du Québec is a legal-deposit library in Montreal for all books and documents issued by Quebec publishers. It grew out of the Bibliothèque Saint-Sulpice, in existence since 1844, and was officially established under its present name in 1968. It collects and preserves documents published in or about Quebec and issues bibliographies, including, since 1969, the checklist of current publications, *Bibliographie du Québec*. Work is under way to publish a retrospective bibliography of Laurentiana, a generic term used to designate any document printed in Quebec; any document printed outside Quebec but that deals primarily with Quebec; any French-language document printed in Canada; and any document printed outside of Quebec that deals with French Canada.

National Museum of Man. One of the four museums under the NATIONAL MUSEUMS OF CANADA. It is located in Ottawa and includes the Canadian Centre for Folk Culture Studies, the Archaeological Survey of Canada, the CANADIAN WAR MUSEUM, and three divisions: ethnology, which carries out work on Indian, Eskimo, and Métis culture; history, which studies Canadian society and material culture since the beginning of European colonization; and communications, which is responsible for the exhibition program, including travelling exhibits such as 'Canada's Multicultural Heritage'.

National Museum of Natural Sciences. One of the four museums under the NATIONAL MUSEUMS OF CANADA. It is located in Ottawa and covers the natural sciences of botany, zoology, geology, mineralogy, and paleonto-

logy. It supports research such as the POLAR CONTINENTAL SHELF PROJECT and the work of some NATIONAL RESEARCH COUNCIL post-doctoral fellows. It also maintains the Canadian Oceanographic Identification Centre, which identifies approximately 400,000 specimens a year.

National Museum of Science and Technology. The newest of the four museums under the NATIONAL MUSEUMS OF CANADA, it opened in 1967. It is located in Ottawa and includes exhibits of all forms of transportation, meteorology, astronomy, time pieces, and a model workshop. It also administers the National Aeronautical Collection of over 90 aircraft from the earliest beginnings of aviation in Canada.

National Museums of Canada. CROWN CORPORATION to centralize the management of four federal museums, established in 1968. The museums, located in Ottawa, are the NATIONAL GALLERY OF CANADA, the NATIONAL MUSEUM OF MAN (including the CANADIAN WAR MUSEUM), the NATIONAL MUSEUM OF NATURAL SCIENCES, and the NATIONAL MUSEUM OF SCIENCE AND TECHNOLOGY (including the National Aeronautical Collection). One purpose of the NMC is 'to demonstrate the products of nature and the works of man, with special but not exclusive reference to Canada, so as to promote interest therein throughout Canada and to disseminate knowledge thereof'. Jean Sutherland BOGGS, the Director of the National Gallery since 1966, resigned in 1976 mostly because of the encroachment on Gallery autonomy by the NMC.

National Newspaper Awards. Given to raise standards of newspaper work and to inspire members of the profession. Established by the Toronto Men's Press Club (since 1975 the Toronto Press Club) and presented annually since 1949 for work published by newspaper people in Canadian dailies during the previous year, the awards are accompanied by $500 cheques. There are nine categories: Editorial, Feature, Critical, and Sports Writing; Spot News and Editorial Reporting; Spot News and Feature Photography; and Cartooning.

National Parks. System of federal parklands established and maintained by Parks Canada within the Department of INDIAN AFFAIRS AND NORTHERN DEVELOPMENT. Canada's National Parks preserve areas representative of the natural heritage of the country for purposes connected with conservation, education, and recreation. The system, begun in 1885, had grown by 1975 to include 28 National Parks covering more than 55,000 sq. mi. in addition to 44 major NATIONAL HISTORIC PARKS AND SITES. The 28 National Parks are divided into five administrative regions:

Western Region: PACIFIC RIM, MOUNT REVELSTOKE, GLACIER, YOHO, KOOTENAY, WATERTON LAKES, BANFF, JASPER, ELK ISLAND.

Prairie Region: KLUANE, NAHANNI, WOOD BUFFALO, PRINCE ALBERT, RIDING MOUNTAIN.

Ontario Region: PUKASKWA, GEORGIAN BAY ISLANDS, POINT PELÉE, ST LAWRENCE ISLANDS.

Quebec Region: LA MAURICIE, BAFFIN ISLAND, FORILLON.

Atlantic Region: KOUCHIBOUGUAC, FUNDY, PRINCE EDWARD ISLAND, KEJIMKUJIK, CAPE BRETON HIGHLANDS, GROS MORNE, TERRA NOVA.

National Parole Board. A board with the power to grant parole for all prisoners sentenced under federal law except those who have been committed for murder. The Board was established in Jan. 1959 and is responsible to the SOLICITOR GENERAL.

National Policy. First advocated by Sir John A. MACDONALD in the House of Commons on 12 Mar. 1878, it was a three-part policy of (i) protective tariffs to foster local agriculture, mining, and manufacturing; (ii) transcontinental railway building to promote a national economy; and (iii) immigration to the West to build up home markets for Canadian manufactured products. It appealed to members of the CANADA FIRST movement and was close in spirit to ECONOMIC NATIONALISM. See also RECIPROCITY.

National Research Council of Canada. Federal agency that promotes scientific and industrial research, established in 1916. As well as undertaking research in its science and engineering laboratories in Ottawa, Halifax, and Saskatoon, the NRC gives financial support to research conducted by universities and industrial laboratories across the country. It maintains the main physical standards, and co-ordinates research on problems of national interest. It has awarded the STEACIE MEMORIAL FELLOWSHIP annually since 1963.

National Research Council Official Time Signal. The name since 1 Apr. 1970 of the Dominion Observatory Time Signal. Time signals for the use of telegraphers were introduced by the Dominion Observatory in Jan. 1905, and the early CNR radio stations began to broadcast them twice a week at 9:00 p.m. in 1924, substituting an 800-cycle tone for the irritating buzzer first used to identify the correct time. The present 30-second sounding at 1:00 p.m. of the Dominion Observatory Time Signal was first broadcast on 5 Nov. 1939.

The timing was originally controlled by the sighting of certain stars, then by crystal oscillators, and since 1963 by atomic-frequency standards and an electric digital system.

National Resources Mobilization Act. Contentious measure passed by Parliament in June 1940 whereby able-bodied males were conscripted into the CANADIAN ARMY for compulsory service at home but not abroad. The government acquired a mandate through a national plebiscite, held on 27 Apr. 1942, to amend the Act to permit the sending of conscripts overseas. Under the Act 157,841 men were conscripted, but none was sent overseas until 1944. See also CONSCRIPTION.

National Revenue, Department of. Department of the federal government concerned with the assessment and collection of duties and taxes. Established under its present name in 1927, it consists of two divisions: the Customs and Excise Division, which is responsible for the assessment and collection of customs and excise duties as well as of sales and excise taxes; and the Taxation Division, which is responsible for the assessment and collection of income taxes, for the old-age security tax, parts of the CANADA PENSION PLAN, and the premiums and administration of some parts of the Unemployment Insurance Act.

National School Broadcasts. A long-running CBC Radio series of weekly programs for primary and secondary students. School broadcasting got under way in 1942 with 'Heroes of Canada', a series of sixteen 30-minute programs, each of which consisted of a historical drama plus a current newscast called 'What's in the News' read by Lamont Tilden. Such series as 'Kindergarten of the Air', 'It's Fun to Draw', 'Music for Young Folk', etc. followed, under the executive producer R.S. Lambert. School broadcasting and telecasting continue to this day.

National Science Library. Central collection of scientific and technological information in Ottawa. The NATIONAL RESEARCH COUNCIL's library, established in 1924, was named the National Science Library in 1966. Located in the NRC building in Ottawa since 1974, the collection will eventually house over two million publications. The NSL originates a current-awareness service (CAN-SDI) on a subscription basis and an inquiry service (CAN/OLE) on a computer basis. On-going projects include the publication of select bibliographies and the English translation of the Russian journal *Problemy Severa* ('Problems of the North').

National Social Christian Party. See PARTI NATIONAL SOCIAL CHRÉTIEN.

National Theatre School of Canada. Founded in Montreal on 2 Nov. 1960, it provides young actors, designers, and technicians with professional training in the theatre. Associated with the School have been Michel Saint-Denis, Jean GASCON, James de B. Domville, Powys Thomas, Tom PATTERSON, and Douglas RAIN. The school is co-lingual rather than bilingual, for there are separate but similar three-year programs of instruction in English and French.

National Trades and Labour Congress. An association to unite all labour organizations of the Dominion and to organize national labour unions. It was founded in Berlin (now Kitchener), Ont., in Sept. 1902, mainly by the KNIGHTS OF LABOUR following their expulsion from the TRADES AND LABOUR CONGRESS. It barred all international unions. The NTLC changed its name in 1908 to CANADIAN FEDERATION OF LABOUR.

National Transcontinental. The eastern division of the GRAND TRUNK RAILWAY.

National Unity Party. See PARTI NATIONAL SOCIAL CHRÉTIEN.

National War Memorial. Imposing memorial in CONFEDERATION SQUARE, Ottawa. The gigantic arch through which bronze soldiers and horses pass was sculpted by Vernon March and commemorates the more than 60,000 Canadians who died in the FIRST WORLD WAR. The arch is surmounted by allegorical figures of Peace and Freedom. It was unveiled by George VI and Queen Elizabeth in May 1939, four months before the outbreak of the SECOND WORLD WAR. It is the scene of ceremonies on REMEMBRANCE DAY.

National Youth Orchestra, The. Seasonal non-professional symphony orchestra. It selects by annual competition 100 members aged 14 to 24 for four weeks of intensive training under experienced conductors and instrumental coaches to prepare them for Canadian and foreign tours. It was founded by Walter SUSSKIND in 1960 and its resident and guest conductors have included Brian Priestman, Seiji Ozawa, Franz-Paul Decker, Lukas Foss, and Victor FELDBRILL. It has been described by musicians and critics as the best youth orchestra in the world.

Nation's Business, The. A series of CBC-TV 'free-time political telecasts' on which a parliamentarian holds forth on questions of the day. It was launched from Ottawa on 16 Apr. 1956 and has been shown since then for 15 minutes each week. The title predates both television and the CBC, for this was the name of a similar series of radio programs first heard in May 1929, when broadcasting in Canada was in the hands of the CNR.

Native peoples. Collective term for the Indians and Eskimos of Canada. According to the 1971 census, there are 297,000 Indians and 18,000 Eskimo people living in Canada. All but 40,000 of the Indian population are registered under the Indian Act by the Department of Indian Affairs and Northern Development and comprise 560 bands that occupy some 2,200 reserves across the country. About two-thirds of the Eskimos reported in the 1971 census live in communities in the Northwest Territories; the remainder live in New Quebec, Labrador, and northern Ontario. See also ESKIMOS, INUIT, INDIANS.

Native Sons of Canada. A right-wing fraternal society founded to foster Canadian nationalism. It was begun in Winnipeg on 12 Apr. 1921 and had strong local chapters during the forties and fifties, when it began to die out. The Toronto chapter disbanded in 1963.

NATO. Acronym of the North Atlantic Treaty Organization. A military alliance concerned with collective security and mutual defence against aggression in Europe and North America. The North Atlantic Treaty, which established NATO, was signed at Washington, D.C., on 4 Apr. 1949 by Belgium, Canada, Denmark, France, Iceland, Italy, Luxembourg, the Netherlands, Norway, Portugal, the United Kingdom, and the United States. See also ATLANTIC COMMUNITY, SACEUR, SACLANT, and SHAPE.

NATO Fellowship Programme. A fellowship awarded annually by NATO through the offices of the ROYAL SOCIETY OF CANADA to enable the winning candidate, who must be a national of a NATO member state, to undertake research into the history, status, or future of the Alliance. Consisting of a grant of 23,000 Belgian francs a month for up to six months, the award was first made in 1967.

Nature of Things, The CBC-TV's award-winning science series. The only science series on North American television, the 30-minute weekly programs were first telecast on 6 Nov. 1960. The originator is John Livingston, the executive producer is James Murray, and the chief writer is William Whitehead. Individual episodes—some of them 60-minute specials—explore topics like pollution. Lister SINCLAIR wrote the impressive series on 'Charles Darwin and the Galapagos', which ran from 4 Sept. to 2 Oct. 1966.

Nautilus. See NORTHWEST PASSAGE.

Navy Hall. Part of the first capital of UPPER CANADA at Newark, now NIAGARA-ON-THE-LAKE. The group of four buildings on the Niagara R. near FORT GEORGE was built in 1787 to house naval stores. In 1792 the first legislative assembly met there in a council chamber that was added to by Gov. John Graves SIMCOE. Most of the buildings were burned in 1813. In 1864 the remaining building was moved by the Erie and Niagara Railroad several hundred feet from its original site. It came under the jurisdiction of the Niagara Parks Commission in 1934 and reconstruction began several years later, when the building was moved back to its original site. Now administered by the federal government, Navy Hall houses an extensive military museum.

NAWAPA. Acronym of NORTH AMERICAN WATER AND POWER ALLIANCE.

Naylor, Bernard (b.1907). Composer. Born in Cambridge, Eng., he studied at the Royal College of Music under Ralph Vaughan Williams. He came to Canada in 1932, was conductor of the Winnipeg Philharmonic until 1936, and founded the Little Symphony Orchestra in Montreal in 1942. He has devoted himself to composition since 1959 and lives in Victoria, B.C. His principal works are for choir and solo voice. They include the cycle *Nine Motets* (1952), his best-known work; *Six Poems from Miserere* (1960); and *Stabat Mater* (1961).

Nazi Eyes on Canada. A CBC Radio series devoted to wartime propaganda. Well-known figures—including Orson Welles, Quentin Reynolds, Vincent Price, and House Jamieson—reported incidents involving espionage during the Second World War. Produced by J. Frank WILLIS, it was heard for 30 minutes each week from 11 Oct. to 4 Nov. 1942.

NC Press. See NEW CANADA PRESS.

NCC. See NATIONAL CAPITAL COMMISSION.

NDHQ. Abbreviation of National Defence Headquarters. It was created in Ottawa in 1972 by the merging of the civil and military sectors of the Department of National Defence.

NDP. Abbreviation of the New Democratic Party, a socialist political party founded in 1961 by the CCF and the NEW PARTY clubs, with the support of the CANADIAN LABOUR CONGRESS. Its first leader was T.C. DOUGLAS, at that time premier of Saskatchewan. The NDP has never received a majority of seats in any federal election, nor has it ever received enough seats to form the official Opposition. But at the provincial level it has been more successful: in 1969 Manitoba elected an NDP government under Ed Schreyer; in 1971 Allan Blakeney was elected to power in Saskatchewan; in 1972 the NDP under Dave Barrett was elected in British Columbia; in 1973 Schreyer was re-elected in Manitoba; and in 1975 the NDP formed the official Opposition in Ontario under Stephen Lewis.

Nearctic. One of the major zoo-geographical regions of the world. It comprises all of Canada, Greenland, the United States, and northern Mexico. Often grouped with Europe and Siberia, whose fauna it closely parallels, into a greater Haloarctic Region, it also exhibits similarities (the raccoon, etc.) with the animals of South America.

Neatby, Hilda (1904-75). Historian and educator. Born in Sutton, Eng., she grew up in Saskatchewan and was educated there and at the University of Minnesota. She taught at the University of Saskatchewan. She was best known for her controversial book, SO LITTLE FOR THE MIND: *An Indictment of Canadian Education* (1953), and for her contribution as a member of the MASSEY COMMISSION (1951). She also wrote *Quebec: The Revolutionary Age, 1760-1791* (1966).

NEB. See NATIONAL ENERGY BOARD.

Neel, Boyd (b.1905). Conductor. Born in London, Eng., he became a medical doctor before founding the Boyd Neel Orchestra in London in 1933 and touring with it extensively. He was Dean of the ROYAL CONSERVATORY OF MUSIC from 1953 to 1971, when he retired. He founded the HART HOUSE ORCHESTRA in 1954 and toured with it in North America and Europe.

Neepawa. See MANAWAKA.

Neighbourly News. A long-running CBC Radio series popular with rural audiences and broadcast in regional editions. The Ontario program was produced by Reid Forsee and originally consisted of Andy Clarke reading selections with appropriate comments from Canadian weekly newspapers. The 30-minute weekly program—first heard on 7 Jan. 1940—created a national reputation for Clarke, a Toronto newspaper columnist, who was known as 'the mayor of little places' for his appreciation of the subtleties of rural living. *Andy Clarke and His Neighbourly News* was published in 1949, the year after his

Neighbourly News

death. For 15 years thereafter Arthur L. PHELPS was associated with the program, which is still popular in its regional editions.

Neighbours. A famous short film made by Norman McLAREN. It is the parable of two men who come to blows over the possession of a flower that grows mid-way between their houses. Shot in 16 mm and released by the NFB in 1952, it received an Academy Award the following year. McLaren photographed live action frame by frame to create the effect of animation. 8 min., colour.

Nellie. See ACTRA AWARDS.

Nelligan, Émile (1879-1941). Quebec poet. Born in Montreal of an Irish father and a French-Canadian mother, he began to write symbolist poems at 16, achieving recognition from other young writers, but sank into a permanent depression four years later and spent the rest of his life in mental institutions. His poems, which are considered to be the beginning of modern literature in French Canada, were collected in *Poésies complètes* (1952) edited by Luc Lacourcière. P.F. Widdows translated the best-known poems, including 'Le Vaisseau d'or' ('The Ship of Gold'), in the *Selected Poems* (1960) of Nelligan.

Nelson, Wolfred (1792-1863). Rebel. Born in Montreal, he trained as a surgeon. He was a member of the legislative assembly from 1827 to 1830 and from 1834 until the REBELLION OF 1837, of which he was one of the leaders in Lower Canada (Quebec). He led a band of PATRIOTES in the engagement at SAINT-DENIS. He was captured, however, and exiled to Bermuda. Returning to Canada from the United States in 1843, he sat in the assembly from 1844 to 1851 and was mayor of Montreal from 1854 to 1856.

Nelson River. It flows 400 mi. from the northwestern corner of Lake Winnipeg to Hudson Bay at YORK FACTORY. An important hydro-electric installation is located near Kettle Rapids. The Nelson R. drainage basin, extending for 1,600 mi., includes the Bow, Saskatchewan (South and North), Assiniboine, and Red Rivers, and Lakes Winnipegosis and Winnipeg, draining a large area of southern Alberta, Saskatchewan, Manitoba, and the north-central United States.

Nelsova, Zara (b.1918). Cellist. Born in Winnipeg and famous as a child prodigy, she studied cello with Pablo Casals, among others. She went on to have a distinguished career, playing with major orchestras and undertaking extensive solo concert tours,

sometimes performing with her husband, the pianist Grant Johannesen. Since 1962 she has been teaching at the Juilliard School of Music, New York.

Nelvana of the Northern Lights. Beautiful comic-book heroine conceived, written, and drawn in black and white by the Toronto artist Adrian Dingle between 1940 and 1945. The statuesque Nelvana, 'daughter of the Northern Lights', had long raven-black hair, sported a cape, and wore a fur-trimmed mini-skirt. The protector of the Eskimo people, she possessed the power to disappear in the face of her enemies and 'to cause the caribou to roam again'. Dingle maintained she was based on an Eskimo legend heard by the painter Franz JOHNSTON. See also CANADIAN WHITES.

Nepean Point. Promontory overlooking the OTTAWA RIVER with a striking view of the PARLIAMENT BUILDINGS in Ottawa. It was named in honour of Sir Evan Nepean (1751-1822), secretary of the admiralty. There is a Nepean Township in Carleton County, surveyed in 1798.

Neptune Theatre. (i) The name of the first theatrical activity in North America. On 14 Nov. 1607 Marc LESCARBOT's masque, *Le Théâtre de Neptune dans la Nouvelle France*, was staged at PORT ROYAL to greet the return of the sieur de POUTRINCOURT. Lescarbot himself referred to it as 'some jovial spectacle'. (ii) The name of a regional repertory theatre founded in Halifax on 28 June 1962, with Leon MAJOR as artistic director and John Gray as administrative director. It opened in 1963 in the renovated and renamed 525-seat Garrick Theatre with Shaw's *Major Barbara*.

Neshtow. An Algonkian term of endearment, meaning literally 'brother-in-law'.

Netchek. Eskimo word used in the eastern Arctic for 'seal'. It is more properly spelled *nattsiq*. A baby seal is called a *nattiak*.

Neuchâtel Junior College. A co-educational private school for North Americans in Neuchâtel, Switz. Popular with Canadians, it is located on Lac de Neuchâtel and was founded in 1956 by Leonard Wilde, an Englishman and former master of Shawnigan Lake School in British Columbia. The total enrolment of secondary-school students is 100, of whom 95 are Canadians.

Neutrals. See IROQUOIAN.

Never Cry Wolf. Farley MOWAT's vivid account of a wolf family in the North and of misunderstandings about the nature of the wolf. Published in 1963 and written for adults but adopted by children, it places Mowat with Ernest Thompson SETON and Charles G.D. ROBERTS among the finest writers about animals.

New Age, The. The general title chosen by the Montreal writer Hugh HOOD for his projected series of linked novels that will document and dramatize Canadian social history for a period of 75 years. The first novel, *The Swing in the Garden*, was published in 1975. The proposed titles of the succeeding novels and their planned publication years follow: *A New Athens* (1977), *Reservoir Ravine* (1979), *Black and White Keys* (1982), *The Scenic Art* (1984), *The Motor Boys in Ottawa* (1986), *Property and Value* (1988), *Tony's Book* (1991), *Be Sure to Close Your Eyes* (1993), *Dead Men's Watches* (1995), *Great Realizations* (1997), and a title to be announced (1999).

New Ancestors, The. Novel by Dave GODFREY published in 1970. Set in 'Lost Coast', Africa (Ghana and Mali, prior to the revolution of 1966), it focuses on the lives of Michael Burdener, an English representative of colonial days; his mission-educated native wife Ama; and First Samuels, principal agent of the 'Redeemer', a political leader. It gives a vivid impression of the seething undercurrents in an emerging African nation.

New Brunswick. One of the Atlantic provinces, it is bounded by Maine on the west, Quebec on the north, and is connected to NOVA SCOTIA by the narrow CHIGNECTO ISTHMUS. When the mainland of Nova Scotia was ceded to Britain in 1713, France retained the area north of the isthmus, where ACADIANS had settled along the rivers, and built forts to protect them. These forts were taken by the British in 1755 and the Acadians were expelled (some returned in 1786 and were given land). The area was then settled by New Englanders and British immigrants, including disbanded regiments after the conclusion of peace between England and France. Settlement was augmented after the American Revolution by the arrival of LOYALISTS, and in 1784 the province of New Brunswick was created. In 1865 an election resulted in defeat for the supporters of CONFEDERATION, but they returned to power in 1866 to enable New Brunswick to become one of the founding provinces of the Dominion of Canada in 1867.

The present economy is a diverse one. Forest covers 85% of the province, supporting a substantial lumber and pulp-and-paper industry. Mining is now largely based on lead, copper, and zinc deposits in the vicinity of Bathurst in the north-east. Fishing has a long tradition, although New Brunswick is experiencing the same problem of depleted fish stocks as the rest of Atlantic Canada. Agriculture includes cash crops such as potatoes, dairying, and mixed farming. Secondary manufacturing has grown considerably in recent years, with SAINT JOHN and Moncton the main centres.

New Brunswick has a land area of 27,835 sq. mi. and in 1971 a population of 634,557 of which 31% is French-speaking. Its capital is FREDERICTON and its motto is *Spem Reduxit* ('She [England] restored hope').

New Brunswick Chapbooks. A series of poetry booklets published by FIDDLEHEAD magazine at the University of New Brunswick. Kent Thompson, Robert Gibbs, and others began publishing them in 1967.

New Caledonia. Meaning 'New Scotland', Caledonia being Latin for the northern part of Britain. It was the early name for Nova Scotia and a nineteenth-century name, used in the fur trade, for the interior of British Columbia.

New Canada Press. Publishing house founded in 1967 in Toronto to publish and distribute books and pamphlets of a revolutionary nature. It is the publishing wing of the Canadian Liberation Movement, which is concerned with 'the struggle for national independence and socialism in Canada and throughout the world'. Among its earliest publications was Garce Maurice's translation of Léandre Bergeron's neo-Marxist and separatist study, *The History of Quebec: A Patriote's Handbook* (1971). In the spring of 1976 NC Press gave birth to a competitor, Steel Rail Publishing.

New Canadian. An immigrant who has applied for citizenship or has recently received it. Its earliest use seems to be in *New Canada and the New Canadians* (1907) in which H.A. Kennedy equates the new Canadian settlers with the 'New Canada' (i.e., the West). 'New Canadian' was a vogue phrase in the 1950s and fell out of fashion some time around 1967, when it was replaced by 'ethnic'.

New Canadian Library. A paperback reprint series of books by Canadian authors. It was launched in 1957 by McCLELLAND & STEWART with Frederick Philip GROVE's *Over Prairie Trails*. With approximately 150 titles in print in 1976, it is edited by Malcolm Ross, professor of English, Dalhousie University, and includes critical introductions.

New Democracy. The name under which SO-CIAL CREDIT fought the federal election of 1940. Led by W.D. Herridge, R.B. BENNETT's brother-in-law, who was the former Canadian minister in Washington, New Democracy ran a pro-conscriptionist campaign, the only party in 1940 to do so. Ten members were elected, all in Alberta, but Herridge was not, and the party reverted to the name Social Credit soon after.

New Democratic Party. See NDP.

New Denmark. The name given in 1619 to the western coast of HUDSON BAY by the Danish sailor Jens MUNK, who had sailed west for Christian IV of Denmark.

New France. The name given to the French possessions in North America—the territories discovered, explored, settled or claimed from the sixteenth to the eighteenth centuries. At its zenith in 1712, New France stretched from the Gulf of St Lawrence to beyond Lake Superior and included NEW-FOUNDLAND, ACADIA, the Iroquois country, and the Mississippi valley as far as the Gulf of Mexico—nearly three quarters of the North American continent. It began to disintegrate when the TREATY OF UTRECHT was signed in 1713 and ceased to exist as a political entity in 1763 under the terms of the TREATY OF PARIS. LOUISIANA, the last French colony on mainland North America, was sold to the United States in 1803.

New Frontier. A short-lived quarterly devoted to culture and the arts sponsored by the COMMUNIST PARTY OF CANADA. Published in Toronto in 1936-7, it carried stories, poetry, and articles about the poor and underprivileged. It was revived as NEW FRONTIERS.

New Frontiers. A quarterly devoted to culture and the arts edited by Margaret FAIRLEY and sponsored by the COMMUNIST PARTY OF CANADA. It was published in Toronto from 1952 to 1957 as a successor to NEW FRONTIER and carried work by Milton ACORN and George RYGA. It promoted peace, socialism, and people's culture.

New Horizons Research Foundation. Parapsychology research centre. Established in 1969 by Donald C. (Ben) Webster, a Toronto stockbroker, it encourages and co-ordinates research in extrasensory perception and related subjects. It has been called a 'parapsychology think-tank' and is run by Dr George Owen, a scientist from Cambridge University. A 1975 experiment in psychic phenomena by a group of researchers at the Foundation is described in *Conjuring Up Philip: An*

Adventure in Psychokinesis (1976) by Iris M. Owen and Margaret Sparrow.

New Ireland. The name proposed for Prince Edward Island in 1780 when it was still known as the Island of St John.

New Liberty. See LIBERTY.

New Manitoba. Part of the old district of Keewatin added to Manitoba in 1912.

New nationality. Political and social phrase associated with CONFEDERATION. It was used as early as 1858 by Alexander Morris and Thomas D'Arcy McGEE, but it came into prominence in 1865 when Governor General Lord Monck, in his Speech from the Throne, urged the creation of a 'new nationality'. In another Speech from the Throne, on 7 Nov. 1867, he was able to congratulate Canadians on having 'laid the foundation of a new nationality'.

New North, The. Unofficial motto of the NORTHWEST TERRITORIES.

New Ontario. Part of the northern region added to OLD ONTARIO when the province was extended to Hudson Bay in 1912.

New Outlook, The. See UNITED CHURCH OBSERVER.

New Party. Name given to the clubs organized in 1958 by the CCF, the CANADIAN LABOUR CONGRESS, and other interested groups to discuss the formation of a new socialist party. The New Party clubs were disbanded in 1961 when the NDP was founded.

New Play Society. An important professional Toronto theatrical group, founded in 1946 by Dora Mavor Moore. It staged plays until 1954, when it focused on drama education, specializing in children's plays from 1957 to 1965. The annual revue SPRING THAW began in 1948. Company actors included Lloyd BOCHNER, Bernie BRADEN, Lorne GREENE, Barbara Kelly, Bud Knapp, and Donald and Murray Davis (see DAVIS FAMILY). Its productions of new plays included works by Morley CALLAGHAN, Fletcher MARKLE, Len PETERSON, and Lister SINCLAIR.

New Press. Publishing company founded in Toronto in 1969 by James W. Bacque, Dave GODFREY, and Roy MacSKIMMING. Specializing in topical and literary books, it was acquired by GENERAL PUBLISHING COMPANY LTD in 1974.

New Quebec. The northern part of Quebec, especially the Ungava peninsula, which was added to the province in 1912. For a list of art co-operatives in New Quebec (Nouveau-

Québec), see La FÉDÉRATION DES CO-OPÉRATIVES DU NOUVEAU-QUÉBEC.

New Quebec Crater. Popularly called the Chubb Crater—after Frederick W. Chubb, a prospector who discovered it in July 1950, along with Ken MacTaggart and Victor Ben Meen—it is perhaps Canada's most visually impressive meteorite crater. In northwest Quebec, it has a diameter of over 2 mi. and a depth of over 1,360 ft. It is also known as Ungava Crater or Cratère du Nouveau-Québec.

New School of Art. Independent non-profit art school founded in Toronto in 1965 by Dennis BURTON, Robert Hedrick, and John Sime. A division of the THREE SCHOOLS, it is open to people over 18 and requires no academic prerequisites. It offers informal part-time instruction by practising artists in painting, sculpture, and design, where the emphasis is on individual guidance. Its director is appointed annually.

New Year's Day. Statutory holiday observed throughout Canada on 1 Jan. to mark the beginning of the new year.

Newark. See NAVY HALL and NIAGARA-ON-THE-LAKE.

Newfeld, Frank (b.1928). Book designer and illustrator. Born in Brno, Czech., he was educated in England at the Central School of Arts and Crafts, London, and moved to Toronto in 1954. He was associated with McCLELLAND AND STEWART LIMITED for 12 years, latterly as Vice-President, Publishing. The recipient of 141 national and international design awards, he is also the author and illustrator of two children's books: *The Princess of Tomboso* (1960) and *Simon and the Golden Sword* (1976). Other books he has illustrated are *Alligator Pie* (1974) and *Nicholas Knock and Other Poems* (1974), both by Dennis LEE.

Newfie. A slang reference to a native of Newfoundland.

Newfie Bullet. Nickname of the narrow-gauge Newfoundland Railway. Finished in 1898, it travelled across the interior of the island from St John's to Port-aux-Basques. It was taken over by the CNR in 1949 and was replaced by a standard-gauge line in 1968-9. In its day it was affectionately regarded as 'the slowest train in North America'.

Newfie joke. A variation of the standard ethnic joke. Using a Newfoundlander as the humorous butt, the Newfie joke swept the mainland in 1968, stereotyping the Newfie as an outsider from the mainstream of English Canada. Many of these jokes have been collected and published by Robert Tulk of New-

foundland in a series of booklets beginning with *Newfie Jokes* (1971).

Newfiejohn. Slang reference to St John's, the capital of Newfoundland.

Newfoundland. The most easterly province of Canada includes the island of Newfoundland, adjacent islands (except ST PIERRE AND MIQUELON) and LABRADOR. An international fishery developed off the coast of Newfoundland on the GRAND BANKS during the sixteenth century. By 1588 France and England were the only serious contenders for control of the fisheries, and this struggle was ended in 1713 when Newfoundland was ceded to Britain, except for a FRENCH SHORE on which the French were permitted to dry fish. Britain extinquished these rights by purchase in 1904. Settlement was slow to develop. The first resident governor was not appointed until 1817; the first HOUSE OF ASSEMBLY was elected in 1825. Proposals to join CONFEDERATION were defeated, and Newfoundland remained a colony of Great Britain. In 1932 economic collapse led to a suspension of the constitution and the province was ruled directly by the British colonial office until J.R. SMALLWOOD led the campaign to join Canada. It became the tenth province on 31 Mar. 1949.

The present economy is largely resource-based, with mining, forestry, and fishing the principal activities. Although it is famous for its cod fisheries, it is mining, particularly iron ore from the Gagnon area of the LABRADOR TROUGH, that contributes most to the economy of Newfoundland. The rugged CANADIAN SHIELD in Labrador and the hills of the island that are a continuation of the Canadian APPALACHIANS, together with the cool climate, have almost eliminated commercial agriculture. The largest hydro-electric installation in Canada is at Churchill Falls in Labrador.

The land area is 143,045 sq. mi. and the 1971 population was 522,104. 99% speak English and almost 96% were born in Newfoundland—unique characteristics among Canadian provinces. Because of the island's isolation, there are several distinct dialects—similar to the speech of Great Britain in the early 1800s—based on a mixture of Devonshire, Dorset, and Irish dialects. They are now dying out, though some words unique to Newfoundland remain in common usage—for example *swiles* for 'seals'. In the capital city, ST JOHN'S, the speech has had a distinct Irish flavour, but it too is becoming standardized. The province's motto is *Quaerite Prime Regnum Dei* ('Seek Ye First the Kingdom of God').

Newfoundland dog. The only dog indigenous to Canada. A native of Newfoundland, it is a large and powerfully built domesticated dog that normally has thick black to brown fur. It averages 4-5 ft in length and can weigh up to 170 lb. Renowned for its life-saving instincts and aquatic prowess, as well as for its gentle disposition, the Newfoundland was a companion to the early settlers and sailors of North America and today ranks as one of the largest breeds of show dogs.

Newfoundland National Memorial. Imposing memorial to the Newfoundland war dead at King's Beach in St John's, near Sir Humphrey GILBERT'S landfall. It was unveiled by Field Marshal Earl Haig on 1 July 1924, the anniversary of the Battle of BEAUMONT HAMEL and also DOMINION DAY. With its life-like bronze figures set in a semi-circular wall of granite, it recalls the former colony's achievements by land and sea and commemorates those who died in the effort to realize them.

Newfoundland Scene. A notable short film produced by Crawley Films for IMPERIAL OIL. A sympathetic and informative picture of many facets of life in Newfoundland, it was directed by F.R. CRAWLEY with music by William McCauley and narration by Frank Peddie. 35 min., colour.

Newlove, John (b.1938). Poet. Born in Regina, Sask., he attended the University of Saskatchewan and has lived in Vancouver, Toronto, and Montreal, working as an editor or teacher. He conveys the 'joyless pleasures' of contemporary life. He is the author of the well-known poem 'The Pride' about the defeat and dispersal of the Indians of western Canada. His full-length collections of verse are *Black Night Window* (1968), *The Cave* (1970), and *Lies* (1972).

Newman, Peter (b.1929). Journalist and editor. Born in Vienna of Czechoslovakian parents who brought him to Canada in 1940, he attended Upper Canada College and the University of Toronto. He worked for the *Financial Post* (1951-6), *Maclean's* (1956-64), and from 1964 to 1969 was the nationally syndicated Ottawa editor of the *Toronto Star*, of which he was editor-in-chief from 1969 to 1971. He was appointed editor of *Maclean's* in 1971, overseeing its rebirth as a nationalistic newsmagazine. He was a founder of the COMMITTEE FOR AN INDEPENDENT CANADA (1970) and co-authored several CBC-TV series, including the TENTH DECADE (1965). He is the author of *Flame of Power* (1959), *Renegade in Power: The Diefenbaker Years* (1963, 1973), *The Distemper of Our Times: Canadian Politics in Transition, 1963-1968* (1968), *Home Country: People, Places and Power* (1973), and the first volume of a socio-economic study *The Canadian Establishment* (1975).

Newman, Sydney (b.1917). Television and film producer. Born in Toronto, he joined the NATIONAL FILM BOARD in 1941 as a 'splicer-boy'. Working under John GRIERSON, he produced the CANADA CARRIES ON series in 1945 and rose to become executive producer (1947 to 1952). He was a television drama producer for the CBC from 1952 to 1958, when he settled in London, Eng. He was BBC-TV's chief drama editor from 1963 to 1968 and introduced the 'kitchen-sink' dramatists on television. He was Commissioner of the NFB from 1970 to 1975, when he was succeeded by André LAMY.

Newmark, John (b.1904). Pianist, accompanist. Born in Bremen, Germany, he came to Canada in 1944, settling in Montreal, where he became the leading accompanist in Canada. He has accompanied many famous musicians—mainly singers—and is himself a fine interpreter, particularly of chamber music.

Newsmagazine. See CBC NEWSMAGAZINE.

Next Year Country. Unofficial motto of ALBERTA. It alludes to the optimistic spirit of the settlers at the turn of the century in the face of innumerable difficulties, such as poor harvests, crop diseases, etc.: 'Things will be better next year.'

NFB. See NATIONAL FILM BOARD.

Nfld. Abbreviation of NEWFOUNDLAND.

NGC. See NATIONAL GALLERY OF CANADA.

Niagara Escarpment. A limestone ridge extending from Tobermory to Niagara Falls, Ont. It runs parallel to the south shore of the Lake Ontario to Hamilton, where it winds northward to the Blue Mountains at Collingwood. It travels west then northward along the east shore of the BRUCE PENINSULA on Georgian Bay, where it dips under the water to re-emerge along the north coast of Manitoulin Island. Essentially it is a product of erosion, formed over hundreds of millions of years. Its rugged beauty and steep slopes make it a favourite spot for outdoor recreation, particularly skiing and hiking. See also BRUCE TRAIL.

Niagara Falls. Two picturesque waterfalls on the NIAGARA RIVER (on the international border) caused by the drop of the NIAGARA ESCARPMENT. While 7 ft shorter than the American Falls, the Canadian (or Horseshoe) Falls, 160 ft high, channels nearly 90% of the total flow of over 120 million gallons per minute. Many Canadian waterfalls are higher than Niagara, but none approaches it in volume. The Falls were first described by Louis HENNEPIN in 1678. The city of Niagara Falls, Ont., calls itself 'The Honeymoon Capital of the World' and 'The World's Most Famous Address'.

Niagara-on-the-Lake. Town on Lake Ontario near the mouth of the NIAGARA RIVER. Originally settled by Loyalists and known as Niagara, it was named Newark by John Graves SIMCOE. It was the capital of Upper Canada (Ontario) from 1792 to 1796, after which it reverted to its original name until 1906, when it became Niagara-on-the-Lake. It was occupied by American troops during the WAR OF 1812 and largely destroyed. Today it is an attractive and much-visited community, with restored stately homes, pioneer museums, and historic sites that include FORT GEORGE and NAVY HALL. It is the home of the SHAW FESTIVAL.

Niagara River. In its 35 mi. course it links Lake Erie and Lake Ontario and forms part of the boundary between the State of New York and the Province of Ontario. It drops 326 ft over NIAGARA FALLS (somewhat more than half) and a series of heavy rapids. The hydroelectric potential of the river, shared with the United States, is developed in two large downstream plants: Robert Moses in the U.S. and Sir Adam Beck 1 and 2 in Ontario.

Nichol, bp (b.1944). Poet. Born in Vancouver, based in Toronto, an associate of THERAFIELDS, he is the country's chief concrete and sound poet. He is a member of the FOUR HORSEMEN, a sound-poetry collective, and the subject of *Sons of Captain Poetry*, a 16 mm experimental film by Michael ONDAATJE. Nichol's publications include *Journeying and the Returns* (1967), *ABC: The Aleph Beth Book* (1971), *The Martyrology* (1972), and *Love: A Book of Remembrance* (1974). He edited the anthology *The Cosmic Chef: An Evening of Concrete* (1970).

Nicholson, James. See DICTIONARY OF CANADIAN BIOGRAPHY.

Nickel. An important mineral used chiefly as an alloy with steel to produce stainless steel. In 1971 Canada produced 45% of the world's output, chiefly from mines in the area of Sudbury, Ont., and at Thompson, Man. It is second to copper in total value of production: $978 million in 1974.

Nickel belt. The Sudbury district of Ontario, site of the world's most productive NICKEL mines. It is also the name of a federal constituency.

Nicol, Eric (b.1919). Humorist and dramatist. Born in Kingston, Ont., he graduated from the University of British Columbia and has been a columnist for the *Vancouver Province* since 1951. Quick with a quip, he writes regularly for CBC Radio's variety programs. When his play LIKE FATHER, LIKE FUN, which was successful in Vancouver, Toronto, and Montreal, flopped on Broadway (where it was called *Minor Adjustment*), on 6 Oct. 1967, he wrote *A Scar is Born* (1968). A series of short books illustrated by Peter WHALLEY—including *An Uninhibited History of Canada* (1959), *Say Uncle* (1961), *Russia, Anyone?* (1963), and *100 Years of What?* (1966)—were bestsellers. Nicol's columns have been collected in *A Herd of Yaks* (1962), *Still a Nicol* (1972), and *Best of Eric Nicol* (1975). He wrote about his hometown in *Vancouver* (1970). *Beware the Quickly Who* (1967) is a popular play. *Letter to My Son* (1974), illustrated by Roy PETERSON, is a recent 'advice' book.

Night-Blooming Cereus. Three-act chamber opera by John BECKWITH, with a libretto by James REANEY. It was commissioned by CBC Radio and first heard on 4 Mar. 1959. The first stage production was at HART HOUSE THEATRE, on 5 Apr. 1960, with the orchestra directed by Ettore MAZZOLENI. The title refers to the central image, a plant that blooms once a year at night and has an unexpected effect on life in a small Ontario town.

Nijmegen. Dutch city near the Rhine R., scene of fighting during the SECOND WORLD WAR. Wintering along the Mass R., Canadians and their Allies made a successful attack from a salient near Nijmegen on 8 Feb. 1945 and then proceeded to crack the Siegfried Line.

Nikka Yuko. North America's largest Japanese garden, in Lethbridge, Alta, built as a joint centennial project of the city and of Japanese-Canadians relocated there during the Second World War. It contains a five-tiered pagoda and a ceremonial bell that symbolizes Japanese-Canadian friendship.

Nikki, Wild Dog of the North. Feature film produced in 1960 by Walt Disney on location near Banff, Alta. Directed by Don Haldane and J. Couffer, it was based on James Oliver

371

Nikki, Wild Dog of the North

Curwood's *Nomads of the North* (1919). It starred Jean Couteau and Émile Genest. 73 min., colour.

Nile Expedition. Volunteer corps of Canadian VOYAGEURS that went to the Sudan in 1884 under Lt-Col. Frederick Denison to rescue Gen. C.G. Gordon at Khartoum. The expedition—commanded by Gen. Lord Wolseley, commander of the RED RIVER EXPEDITION of 1870—approached the besieged city of Khartoum on 28 Jan. 1885, two days after it had been stormed by Moslems, who killed Gordon.

Nimmons, Philip (b.1923). Composer. Born in Kamloops, B.C., he studied the piano, the clarinet, and composition at the Juilliard School of Music, New York, and the Royal Conservatory of Music, Toronto. He was the founder in 1953 of a jazz ensemble, 'Nimmons and Nine', and later 'Nimmons and Nine Plus Six', which appeared frequently on CBC radio and television. He composed the film scores for *A* DANGEROUS AGE (1957) and *A* COOL SOUND FROM HELL (1959). In 1960 he co-founded the Advanced School of Contemporary Music in Toronto with Oscar PETERSON and Ray Brown (it was dissolved in 1963). Since then he has made numerous recordings—including *Take Ten* (1964) and *Strictly Nimmons* (1956)—performed across Canada, and in 1972 served as director of a jazz workshop in the Faculty of Music, University of Toronto.

Nine-Hour Day. Slogan associated with the resolution adopted by the TORONTO TRADES ASSEMBLY in 1872 that 'Fifty-four hours be a legal week's work'. The number of hours was to be reduced to 54, or nine hours a day, six days a week. With the formation of the Nine-Hour League, strikes were organized in Montreal and Toronto, Hamilton, Brantford, St Catharines, and other Ontario centres, most of which were successful.

Ninety-two Resolutions. See Louis-Joseph PAPINEAU.

Niosi brothers. Three musical brothers from London, Ont., whose parents were Sicilian-born immigrants. In 1928 Bert (b.1909), who plays the flute and trumpet, etc., formed a nine-piece dance band that included Joe (b.1906), who plays bass, and John (1916-67), who played drums. A 15-man Niosi band, plus a vocalist, played the Palais Royale in Toronto from 1932 to 1950. Bert was called 'Canada's King of Swing'; Joe was a well-loved member of CBC Radio's the HAPPY GANG; and John was a master percussionist.

Nisei. Japanese word for 'second generation', applied to someone born in Canada of parents who were born in Japan. See also ISSEI and KIKANISEI.

Niska. See TSIMSHIAN.

Niviaksiak (1908-59). Eskimo sculptor and graphic artist at CAPE DORSET. One of the first Inuit to make a print, whose work is highly prized, he specialized in carving and drawing bears and died, under mysterious circumstances, in the presence of a bear. There are those who believe his death was caused by 'bear spirits' offended by his extreme interest in them.

No. 1 Hard. See MANITOBA NO. 1 HARD.

'No Truck Nor Trade With the Yankees!' Anti-RECIPROCITY slogan. The memorably worded political phrase has been attributed to Sir George E. Foster, Conservative cabinet minister in 1911, when Robert BORDEN defeated the Liberals under Sir Wilfrid LAURIER, who favoured reciprocity with the U.S.

Noah, William (b.1943). Eskimo graphic artist at BAKER LAKE. The son of Jessie OONARK, he is known for his striking single figures—a wolf, a muskox, a shaman. He prints his own designs and those of others, including his wife Martha (b.1943).

Nobel Prize Laureates, Canadian. Four Canadians have been recipients of Nobel Prizes. These international awards for achievement—four (physics, chemistry, literature, and physiology or medicine) given at Stockholm, and one (for the promotion of peace) given at Oslo—have been awarded each December since 1901. Dr Frederick BANTING and Professor J.J.R. MACLEOD jointly received the prize for Medicine—for the isolation of INSULIN—in 1923. Banting shared his monetary reward with his co-worker Charles H. BEST, and Macleod shared his with his colleague Dr J.B. COLLIP. Lester B. PEARSON was awarded the prize for Peace in 1957 for his success at the United Nations in establishing the UN Emergency Force to separate the belligerents following the 1956 Suez Crisis. Dr Gerhard HERZBERG, a German-born scientist since 1948 identified with the NATIONAL RESEARCH COUNCIL, received the prize in Chemistry in 1971 for studies in Spectroscopy.

Two scientists born in Canada but working in the United States as American citizens are Nobel laureates. Canadian-born Dr William F. Giauque (b.1895) of the University of California, the discoverer of tumour-inducing viruses, received the prize for Chemistry in 1949. Dr Charles B. Huggins (b.1901), a native of Halifax working at Chicago University Hospital on the hormonal treatment of prostatic cancer, was jointly awarded the prize for Medicine in 1966 with an American colleague, Dr Peyton Rous.

Four scientists have received Nobel Prizes for work that was partly furthered by their professional careers in Canada. Guglielmo Marconi (1874-1937), who sent wireless messages across the Atlantic from SIGNAL HILL in 1901, was co-recipient of the prize for Physics in 1909 along with Ferdinand Braun. Sir Ernest Rutherford and Frederick Soddy, both researchers at McGill's MACDONALD PHYSICS LABORATORY at the turn of the century, received Chemistry awards—Sir Ernest's in 1908, Soddy's in 1921. Har Gobind Khorana (b.1922), a native of India, worked on cell synthesis at the British Columbia Research Council between 1952 and 1959; he continued that work at the University of Wisconsin and shared with two others the prize for Medicine in 1968.

Nobody Waved Good-bye. Feature film directed by Don OWEN and produced by the NFB in 1964. It was shot in Toronto by the director (who was thought to be preparing a documentary). It is the story of a youth who rebels against his parents' middle-class values but whose need for money leads him to juvenile delinquency. The youngster was well played by Peter Kastner in his first role. 80 min., b & w.

Nolan, Dick (b.1939). Folk-singer. Born in Corner Brook, Nfld, he has performed professionally since the early 1960s, touring the east coast and Canada with songs about the sea, some traditional and some his own compositions. A popular guest on television variety programs, and one of the few Canadians to have performed at Nashville's Grand Ol' Oprey (in 1973), he has recorded over 20 albums and received three Gold Records.

Non-Partisan League. A farmers' party that sprang up on the Prairies in 1916. It originated in North Dakota on a platform of agrarian reform. Carried over the border to Saskatchewan in 1916, it emphasized radical reform and quickly captured a following. Its influence was likely responsible for forcing reluctant Prairie farm leaders to go into politics as PROGRESSIVES after the First World War: they had to enter the political arena or risk the loss of their followers to the League.

Nonsuch. Square-rigged ketch that proved the commercial feasibility of the fur trade.

Under Capt. Zachariah Gillam, Sieur de GROSEILLIERS left Gravesend, Eng., on 3 June 1668 and arrived at the mouth of the Rupert R. on the east coast of James Bay on 29 Sept. He wintered there and returned the following August, arriving in England loaded with beaver in Oct. The HUDSON'S BAY COMPANY was chartered on 2 May 1670. See also NONSUCH II.

Nonsuch II. Replica of the original NONSUCH. To mark its 300th anniversary, the HUDSON'S BAY COMPANY ordered the construction at Appledore, Devon, of a replica of the 54-ft square-rigged ketch, with the addition of a 90-h.p. diesel engine and radar. Completed in 1969, and after showing her paces along the British coast, she was brought to Canada aboard a freighter and sailed in eastern and western Canadian waters from 1970 to 1972. She is now housed in the MANITOBA MUSEUM OF MAN AND NATURE in Winnipeg, the home of the Bay's Canadian headquarters.

Nootka. Indians of the west coast of Vancouver Island (and Cape Flattery near the end of the Olympic Peninsula) who speak three closely related WAKASHAN languages: Makah on the Olympic Peninsula, Nitinat south of Barkley Sound, and what might be called Nootka proper north of the latter. They once formed a unique whale-hunting society and built sea-going dugout canoes up to 60 ft in length. Their population in 1970 was 3,409.

NORAD. The North American Air Defence Command. A joint Canadian-American air defence alliance, it was formed 12 Sept. 1957 to integrate air reconnaissance and defence systems for the United States and Canada. Of NORAD's 200,000 personnel, 16,000 are Canadian. Its Combat Operations Centre is located deep inside Cheyenne Mountain the outskirts of Colorado Springs, Colo. Integral parts of the system are the DEW LINE, MID-CANADA LINE, and PINE TREE LINE. See also BOMARC, ICBM, and IRBM.

Noranda Mines Ltd. A major corporation with extensive interests in mines, metallurgical plants, fertilizer, lumber, and other forest products. It founded in 1922 the company town (now the city) of Noranda in northern Quebec, near the Ontario border, to work a copper-gold discovery—one of the richest mineral claims in Canadian history—made by the Nova Scotian prospector Ed Horne in 1920. The name 'Noranda' is said to have originated in a law-office error when a clerk dropped the 'c' from the company's intended name 'Norcanda', a contraction of 'Northern Canada'.

Nordair. Regional airline. Established in 1957, with its headquarters at Dorval, Que., Nordair Ltée-Ltd operates scheduled services in Quebec, Ontario, and the Northwest Territories, as well as North American charter flights.

Norman incident. The suicide of Herbert Norman (1909-57), Canadian ambassador to Egypt. The career diplomat leapt from a nine-storey apartment building in Cairo on 4 Apr. 1957, after a six-month investigation by the RCMP and six years of character assassination by the U.S. Senate Sub-Committee Investigating 'The Scope of Soviet Activity in the United States'. Born to Canadian parents in Japan in 1909 and a scholar who spoke six languages, Norman joined the Department of External Affairs in 1939 and became its far-eastern adviser in 1951. The Senate Sub-Committee accused Norman of having joined the Communist Party of Canada in 1940 but, following his suicide, withdrew the charge. (There is the possibility that the Senate Sub-Committee was passed incorrect information by the RCMP.) Jack GRAY's play *Bright Sun at Midnight* (1957) deals with the tragic incident. Norman's papers were edited by John W. Dower and published as *Origins of the Modern Japanese State* (1975).

Norman Mackenzie Art Gallery, The. Art gallery of the University of Regina. Built from the legacy of Norman Mackenzie—a Regina lawyer who left the university his art collection in 1936, along with funds for the construction of a gallery—it opened in 1953, with additions in 1957. It exhibits European paintings from the fifteenth to the nineteenth centuries and contemporary Canadian and American art. In addition to popularizing the work of Saskatchewan artists, it operates a satellite gallery in a Regina shopping centre and a community arts program.

Norman Wells. A small town on the Mackenzie R. just south of the Arctic Circle. It was the first (in 1920) and remains the only oil-producing area in the Northwest Territories.

Normandy Invasion. The successful Allied landing on the coast of Normandy, a turning-point in the SECOND WORLD WAR. On 6 June 1944 Allied forces landed on the German-held beaches of this French province on the English Channel. The vitally important naval task in this invasion was called Operation Neptune, in which some 100 warships of the ROYAL CANADIAN NAVY participated. Nearly all of some 40 ROYAL CANADIAN AIR FORCE squadrons stationed in the United Kingdom flew in a large number of sorties on the night of 5-6 June and during 6 June in support of the sea and land forces. The 3rd Canadian Infantry Division and the 2nd Canadian Armoured Brigade fought under the Second British Army and landed at 'Juno' Beach in the British sector. Securing this sector of the beachhead, Canadian troops suffered 1,000 casualties the first day on the beach and in later bridgehead battles. Many of the dead are buried at the Beny-sur-Mer Canadian War Cemetery near the village of Reviers, close to CAEN, the ultimate objective of the Normandy Invasion, which was taken the following month. The successful assault, known as Operation Overlord—said to be the bitter fruit of the abortive DIEPPE raid two years earlier—was dramatized by Cornelius Ryan in his bestselling novel *The Longest Day* (1959) and filmed by Darryl F. Zanuck in 1962. D-Day is the first day of any major military operation. This was the most publicized D-Day of the Allies.

Noronic. Cruise ship. Built at Port Arthur, Ont., this 6,905-ton vessel entered service in 1914. She inaugurated the new WELLAND CANAL in 1931. Her usual run was between Detroit and Duluth, but it was during a rare visit to Toronto, on 17 Sept. 1948, that she was destroyed by fire with the loss of 118 passengers. This disaster sounded the death knell of the Great Lakes passenger trade.

Norris, Len (b.1913). Cartoonist. Born in England, he trained at the Ontario College of Art, Toronto, before becoming a staff-member in 1950 of the *Vancouver Sun*, where his witty and elegantly drawn cartoons have achieved great popularity. Besides cartooning, he illustrates magazines and children's books.

Norris Memorial Trophy. See JAMES NORRIS MEMORIAL TROPHY.

Norseman. The world's first freight-carrying bush aircraft. Capable of being fitted with floats, wheels, or skis, it was designed for bush flying by Bob Noorduyn of Noorduyn Aviation and built in his Montreal plant in 1935. It was flown in the northern regions by Canadian Airways and other transportation companies.

North, The. An all-inclusive term for the sparsely settled areas north of the large cities, especially the ARCTIC and sub-Arctic regions.

North American Air Defence Command. See NORAD.

North American Indian Travelling College. See ONAKE CORP.

North American Water and Power Alliance. A scheme to divert Canadian waters for American use. The NAWAPA plan, proposed by the Frank M. Parsons Company of Los Angeles in 1964, calls for the erection of huge dams across rivers in Alaska and the Yukon to direct surplus water through the Rocky Mountain Trench, a natural defile, and for a sequence of dams and tunnels to two destinations: to the upper reaches of the Mississippi and Missouri Rivers for American use; and to Lake Superior for Canadian use. There has been Canadian opposition to the proposed scheme from the first.

North Atlantic Treaty Organization. See NATO.

North Atlantic Triangle. A term used to describe Canada's trade relationship with the United States and the United Kingdom between the First and Second World Wars. The subject is studied by John Bartlet Brebner in *North Atlantic Triangle* (1945).

North-nord. A journal of information and opinion on life and activity in Canada's North. It has been published six times a year since 1954 by the Department of Indian Affairs and Northern Development.

North of Sixty. The region north of the 60th parallel—that is, the NORTHWEST TERRITORIES, YUKON TERRITORY, and Alaska.

North of Superior. A travelogue about northern Ontario. Produced, directed, and photographed by Graeme FERGUSON, it was shot in the IMAX PROCESS for showing in the Cinesphere Theatre at ONTARIO PLACE, Toronto, in 1971. (This theatre has a curved screen six storeys high and 80 ft wide surrounded by 57 speakers; the projector uses 70 mm film placed on its side.) With many stomach-gripping visual effects, its initial popularity has endured. 18 min., colour.

North Poles. Two very different points in the Arctic. The north geographic pole is situated in the polar ice cap north of Ellesmere Island and is the northern point of the earth's rotation on its axis. It was first reached by the American explorer Robert E. Peary on 6 Apr. 1909, though another American explorer, Frederick A. Cook, claimed to have reached it on 21 Apr. 1908. This claim was disallowed at a scientific congress in Copenhagen, but even today it is accepted by some, including Farley MOWAT.

The north magnetic pole is the north pole of the earth's magnetic field to which compass needles point. It 'wanders'; that is, it shifts position, often as much as 200 mi. in a few decades. At present writing it is located on Bathurst Island in the Northwest Territories.

North Shore. One of three shorelines: the part of New Brunswick that faces the Gulf of St Lawrence and the Northumberland Strait; the part of Quebec that lies on the north shore of the Gulf of St Lawrence and the St Lawrence R.; the part of Burrard Inlet opposite Vancouver, B.C.

North Shore, Lake Superior. Canvas painted by Lawren HARRIS in 1926 (nicknamed *The Grand Trunk*), the best known of his Lake Superior canvases. His interest in the transcendental found expression in translating the stark features of the Lake Superior landscape into semi-abstract forms denoting the spiritual forces in nature. A tall, hollow tree stump is set against the lake and mountainous clouds that are lit up by the sun's rays. The unintentional phallic symbolism of the stump—the *Grand Trunk*—is not out of keeping with the elemental significance Harris wished his painting to convey. (NGC)

North Star. The DC-4, a four-prop passenger aircraft flown by TCA from 1947 to 1961. Built by Canadair Limited, Montreal, as a modified version of the U.S. Douglas DC-4, it had the first pressurized cabin in Canada and was capable of carrying from 40 to 57 passengers at 230 m.p.h.

'North Star West'. Well-known poem by Earle BIRNEY that recreates the experience of a flight on a TCA NORTH STAR in 1951. The cities evoked are Montreal, Toronto, Winnipeg, Edmonton, and Vancouver. In an impressionistic yet panoramic fashion Birney comments on life ('our destinies fixed but our seats adjustable') and on Canada ('the fling of a nation'). It first appeared in *Trial of a City and Other Verse* (1952).

North West Company. Fur-trade association. The name was officially adopted by a group of partnerships trading in the Northwest in 1783. While its headquarters were in Montreal, trade was conducted by the 'wintering partners' on Lake Superior—at GRAND PORTAGE until 1805, then at Fort William. There was strong competition with the HUDSON'S BAY COMPANY, which attracted Indians to their posts on the Bay instead of going out to meet them as the Nor'Westers did. (The HBC called their rivals 'pedlars'.) In 1814-16 the NWC opposed the RED RIVER SETTLEMENT, which was on land granted to Lord SELKIRK by the HBC. The NWC, however, united with

North West Company

the HBC in 1821. Three Nor'Westers who undertook important explorations were Alexander MACKENZIE, Peter POND, and David THOMPSON.

North West Mounted Police. A police force that came into existence by a statute of 23 May 1873 to police the Northwest Territories. In 1904 it became the ROYAL NORTH WEST MOUNTED POLICE, which in turn became the ROYAL CANADIAN MOUNTED POLICE in 1920. See also 'RIDERS OF THE PLAINS'.

North West Rebellion. Armed revolt of MÉTIS and Indians in the Saskatchewan district of the Northwest Territories. Métis were angered by the government's procrastination over giving them land grants and by its failure to recognize them as a distinct people. The Cree Indians—whose leaders were BIG BEAR and POUNDMAKER—had lost their means of livelihood, the buffalo, which had been driven away by settlement. These disaffected people asked Louis RIEL to help them and he arrived at BATOCHE in July 1884. After forwarding a petition of grievances to Ottawa in December, he resorted to arms when, in Mar. 1885, there was a brief skirmish at DUCK LAKE. The government sent troops into action. One force, under Gen. Frederick Middleton, was intercepted by Métis under Gabriel DUMONT at FISH CREEK on 24 Apr. On 9 May Middleton attacked Batoche, which held out for three days. Riel fled, but gave himself up the next day. Other engagements took place at FROG LAKE, Fort Pitt, CUT KNIFE HILL, and BATTLEFORD.

North Wind. See KEEWATIN.

Northerly point, The most. Cape Columbia, Ellesmere Island, N.W.T., 83° 07' N., which except for Greenland is the most northerly land area in the northern hemisphere.

Northern allowance. Bonus paid by government or industry to employees engaged in the FAR NORTH as compensation for the high cost of living.

Northern Dancer. Most successful thoroughbred in Canadian racing history. The energetic stock bay colt was sired by Nearctic and delivered of Natalma in May 1961 on E.P. TAYLOR's Windfields Farm, north of Toronto. On 2 May 1964 he became the first Canadian horse to win the Kentucky Derby. Later that year he won the Preakness, finished a poor third in the Belmont Stakes, but took the QUEEN'S PLATE, thus winning the TRIPLE CROWN. As a reward for winning $580,000 in prizes, Northern Dancer was put out to stud on the Windfields Farm in Maryland. By 1970

he was the world's leading sire, having produced Northfield, Laurie's Dancer, True North, Once for All, Minsky, Nijinsky, and other champion thoroughbreds.

Northern Development, Department of. See Department of INDIAN AFFAIRS AND NORTHERN DEVELOPMENT.

Northern Games. A summer event for the Indian and Eskimo people, held in a different northern community each year. Since the first games at Inuvik, N.W.T., in 1970, participants from the Yukon, Northwest Territories, and Alaska have engaged in traditional games, skills, and contests, including harpoon-throwing, blanket-tossing, dog-racing, and drum-dancing. Among its unique features are the Good Woman events—muskrat- and seal-skinning, fish-cleaning, geese-plucking, etc. In 1976 the games were held in Coppermine, N.W.T. See also ARCTIC WINTER GAMES.

Northern Indian. Term used in early accounts to refer to a Chipewyan Indian, and sometimes to a neighbouring Athapaskan, to distinguish him or her from a Cree.

Northern Journey. A literary quarterly published in Montreal. It was founded by Fraser SUTHERLAND in the fall of 1971 to publish lively prose, poetry, and criticism by younger writers. It ceased publication in 1976.

Northern Lights. See AURORA BOREALIS.

Northern Messenger. The longest-running series on CBC Radio. Called the 'party line of the North', it predates the CBC itself, having been first broadcast by its forerunner, the CRBC, since 2 Dec. 1933. It carried messages of 25 words or less from 'the outside' to 'residents of the Northwest Territories and the Canadian Arctic not in touch by regular means of communication such as air mail, telephone, or telegraph'. It was heard on various evenings of the week and lasted until 1964, when the need ended for this type of news service.

Northern Miner, The. A tabloid of interest to the mining and investment communities. It has appeared weekly since 25 May 1915 and was published from Cobalt, Ont., until 1928, when the operation was shifted to Toronto. Since 1956 it has been written, edited, printed, and sorted under one roof. It supplies mining news, market information, and financial services to some 30,000 subscribers. Each issue carries a drawing of a surveyor's level; surmounting it is the motto 'On the Level'.

Northern Review. An important magazine 'of writing and the arts in Canada' edited by John SUTHERLAND. Published six times a year and then quarterly, first from Montreal and then from Toronto, it appeared between Dec. 1945 and the summer of 1956, the result of a merger of the cosmopolitan-minded PREVIEW and the more nationalistic FIRST STATEMENT. It published many of the best writers of the day.

Northern Service. The CBC's radio and television service to the Canadian North. In 1958 the CBC extended its transmission facilities northward and opened stations in the NORTH-WEST TERRITORIES and the YUKON TERRITORY to service 80,000 Canadians spread across two million square miles. National network programs, special features, and local productions are carried in English and French and in Indian and Eskimo dialects.

Northey, William H. (1872-1963). Well-known sportsman. Born in Montreal, he became a life-member of both the Montreal Amateur Athletic Association and the Canadian Amateur Hockey Association. He supervised the erection of the Montreal FORUM in 1924 and was for many years its managing director. He was elected a member of the Hockey HALL OF FAME in 1947.

Northumberland Strait. The part of the Gulf of St Lawrence separating the province of Prince Edward Island from mainland Canada.

Northwest, The. A reference to one of two unpopulated areas of Canada. In the eighteenth and early-nineteenth centuries 'the great northwest' defined the region north and west of Lake Superior, what is now called the Canadian West. Since the late-nineteenth century 'the Northwest' has referred to the region north of the WESTERN PROVINCES and west of Hudson Bay—the NORTHWEST TERRITORIES and YUKON TERRITORY.

Northwest Coast Indians. A reference to the native people of the Pacific coast of North America from Yakutat Bay to northern California. The many Indian tribes in this region of British Columbia are divided into seven groups—sometimes referred to as 'nations'—based on language divisons. They are, from north to south, the TLINGIT, TSIMSHIAN, HAIDA, KWAKIUTL, BELLA COOLA, NOOTKA, and COAST SALISH.

Northwest Mounted Police. Feature film produced by Paramount and directed by Cecil B. DeMille. Released in 1940, it was said to be based on R.C. Fetherstonhaugh's *Royal Cana-*

dian Mounted Police (1938), yet it played fast and loose with historical and even human details. The epic starred Gary Cooper, Madeleine Carroll, Paulette Godard, and Robert Preston. In the DeMille version of Canadian history, Cooper saves the Mounties from the onslaughts of the treacherous MÉTIS, commanded by Louis RIEL. 125 min., colour.

Northwest Passage. A route between the Atlantic and Pacific Oceans, through or south of the islands between Baffin Island and the Beaufort Sea. Among the early explorers who searched for the passage (as a presumed route to Asia) were Sir Humphrey GILBERT, Martin FROBISHER, John DAVIS, Henry HUDSON, and William BAFFIN. The northerly route is Davis Strait, Baffin Bay, Lancaster Sound, Barrow Strait, Viscount Melville Sound, McClure Strait into the Beaufort Sea. It was established in 1850 when Cmdre Robert McClure (1807-73), entering from the Pacific, found Banks Island, which had been sighted on a westward voyage by F.W. Beechey in 1819. The southerly route is by Hudson Strait, Foxe Channel and Basin, Fury and Hecla Strait, the Gulf of Boothia, Bellot Strait, Franklin Strait, Victoria Strait, Queen Maude Gulf, Dease Strait, Coronation Gulf, Dolphin and Union Strait, and Amundsen Gulf leading into the Beaufort Sea. It was first negotiated in 1903-6 by Roald AMUNDSEN. In 1940-2 Sgt Henry Larsen, RCMP, crossed it from west to east in the ST ROCH. In 1958 the American submarine *Nautilus* passed from the Atlantic to the Pacific in four days.

Northwest Staging Route. Aviation corridor developed primarily for military operations during the Second World War that opened up the Northwest Territories and Alaska. A pioneer flight over the route from Edmonton to Aklavik via Fort St John and Fort Nelson, was piloted by C.H. 'Punch' Dickins in 1929. The Yukon Southern Transport Company flew the route two years later, and in 1938 added the Vancouver-Fort St John leg. In 1940 Edmonton became the first and most important stop-over point on the Northwest Staging Route and facilitated a military build-up in Alaska, eventually permitting the rapid construction in 1942 of the ALASKA HIGHWAY.

Northwest Territories. The area east of the Yukon Territory, west of Hudson Bay, and north of the 60th parallel, including all the Arctic islands north of the mainland of Canada and all the islands in HUDSON BAY, JAMES BAY, Hudson Strait, and UNGAVA Bay. The name once applied to all the HUDSON'S BAY

Northwest Territories

COMPANY lands and Rupert's Land, which were united with Canada in 1870. The Northwest Territories were organized into provisional districts in the following years: KEEWATIN (1876), ALBERTA (1882), ASSINIBOIA (1882), ATHABASKA (1882), SASKATCHEWAN (1882), Franklin (1895), Mackenzie (1895), Ungava (1895), and YUKON (1895). In 1880 the Territories were augmented by the addition of all the North American Arctic islands claimed by Great Britain. In 1898 the Yukon District was made a separate territory. In 1905 the provinces of Alberta and Saskatchewan were created. By 1912 the Northwest Territories were limited to their present boundaries. An Order in Council, effective 1 Jan. 1920, defined the boundaries of the districts of Mackenzie, Keewatin, and Franklin as they now exist.

From an economy in which furs and fish were the only resources of value, the opening up of such mines as PINE POINT (lead and zinc) in 1964 and the discovery of significant oil and natural gas deposits in the Mackenzie delta region and the northern islands (Melville, King Christian, and Ellef Ringnes) have resulted in many changes. These have brought problems, particularly in relation to the native people and the somewhat fragile ecosystems of the northern environment.

The territories contain approximately one-third of the total land area of Canada—1,304,903 sq. mi.—and a population in 1974 of 38,000, confined to a few larger settlements (YELLOWKNIFE, Hay River, INUVIK, and Frobisher Bay) and remote outposts. Their administrative headquarters is Yellowknife. See also COMMISSIONER, TERRITORIAL GOVERNMENT.

Northwester. A fur trader employed by the NORTH WEST COMPANY; a native of the Northwest. The word is sometimes shortened to Nor'Wester.

Northwoods. Mythical region, familiar to film-goers, identified with Canada. Rather than produce films about Canada specifically, Pierre BERTON wrote in Hollywood's Canada (1975), 'Hollywood preferred to stick to that vast, mythical region, never geographically defined, which it invented and called the Northwoods. It wasn't necessary to mention Canada at all if you talked about the Woods, the Northwoods, the Northwest Woods, or the Great Woods.' It was the setting for films produced from 1912 to the late-1950s and extended from the 49th parallel to the Arctic Circle.

Nor'Wester. See NORTHWESTER.

No-see-'ems. Popular name for a tiny winged insect that bites and is most plentiful in the North.

Notary. In Quebec a Notaire; in the rest of Canada a Notary Public. The first has the powers of a lawyer but cannot plead in court. The second merely has the authority to take oaths and certify documents.

Notman, William (1826-91). Photographer. Born in Paisley, Scot., he immigrated to Montreal in 1856 and opened a photographic studio on Bleury St; in due course branch studios opened in Ottawa (bought by W.J. Topley), Halifax, and Toronto; and in New York, Boston (two), Albany, and several other centres in the northeastern states. A second Montreal studio was opened in the Windsor Hotel in 1878. (His brother James opened his own gallery in Saint John, N.B., in 1871.) Notman was a portraitist of widespread fame: virtually every celebrity who came to Montreal visited his studio, as well as ordinary citizens and Canadian dignitaries. The studio was known for its much-admired 'composites'—large group pictures for which a background was designed and painted and each subject was photographed separately in a predetermined pose; the resulting prints were cut out and pasted onto the background and the whole composite was rephotographed. Notman and his sons, William and Charles, also made landscape studies, providing a valuable and in many cases beautiful record of late-nineteenth-century Canada from coast to coast. His sons took over the business when their father died. There are almost 400,000 photographic prints and negatives in the Notman Archives, McCord Museum, McGill University, representing photographs taken by Notman himself, his sons, his studios, and photographs he acquired and published.

Notre-Dame-de-Bonsecours. Historic church in OLD MONTREAL. This beautiful chapel—first built between 1657 and 1678, rebuilt in 1771-3, remodelled in 1886-92—includes many paintings and artifacts of historic and artistic interest.

Notre-Dame-de-la-Paix de Québec. The Quebec Basilica. It is on the site of Notre-Dame-de-Recouvrance, built in 1633 by CHAMPLAIN, who was buried there. It was destroyed by fire in 1640 and the church of Notre-Dame-de-la-Paix was built in 1647-50; it became the first cathedral in North America in 1674. It was embellished with a tower and clocher in 1684-7; rebuilt in 1744-9 to designs of CHAUSSEGROS DE LÉRY; but it was destroyed in 1759. Repairs, changes—notably interior decoration by François BAILLAIRGÉ (1785-1802) and a new façade by Charles BAILLAIRGÉ (1843-4)—and additions, which took place over the next century, resulted in a building that is strongly reminiscent of that of Chaussegros de Léry. The interior was destroyed by fire in 1922 and largely reconstructed.

Notre-Dame-de-Montréal, Church of. Designed in a Gothic-Revival style by James O'Donnell, it was built on Place d'Armes in 1824-8 beside La Paroisse, the old parish church of Notre-Dame (1672, remodelled 1722-5), which was demolished in 1830. The new church was given a twin-towered façade and a monumental entrance porch and was for some time the largest church in North America. The uncompleted interior was renovated by Victor Bourgeau, beginning in 1872, and the Chapelle du Sacré Coeur—with its colourful High Victorian Gothic interior executed in wood—was built in 1888 by Henri-Maurice Perrault and Albert Mesnard.

Notre-Dame-des-Victoires. Historic church in Place Royale, Quebec City, built in 1688 near the site of CHAMPLAIN's Habitation. It was originally called Notre-Dame-de-la-Victoire and commemorated the defeat of Sir William PHIPS in 1690; it was renamed Notre-Dame-des-Victoires after the defeat of Sir Hovenden Walker in 1711. It was damaged during the bombardment of 1759 and has been restored several times. From the church ceiling is suspended the model of a sailing vessel.

Notre Dame du Saguenay. Statue to the Virgin Mary erected on the promontory of Cape Trinity overlooking the SAGUENAY RIVER. It was commissioned by a pedlar named Charles-Napoléon Robitaille, who in the late winter of 1878 broke through the ice and almost drowned. With the financial assistance of those in the district he commissioned Louis JOBIN to sculpt from wood a 30-ft-high statue that was erected in 1881 and is now a celebrated sight.

Notre maître, le passé. See Lionel-Adolphe GROULX.

Nouveau Journal, Le. Daily French-language newspaper once published in Montreal. Appearing between 5 Sept. 1961 and 21 June 1962, it was edited by Jean-Louis Gagnon. It offered readers and advertisers a modernistic format and coverage of world and Quebec news and the arts from a moderate leftist and somewhat separatist perspective, but it failed to attract a large enough readership and sufficient advertising.

Nouvelle France, La. See NEW FRANCE.

Nouvelle Relève. See *La* RELÈVE.

Nouvelles Soirées Canadiennes, Les. See *Les* SOIRÉES CANADIENNES.

Nova Scotia. One of the Atlantic provinces, it consists of two parts: peninsular Nova Scotia, separated from the mainland by the Bay of Fundy and connected by the narrow CHIGNECTO ISTHMUS, and CAPE BRETON ISLAND. First settled by France, it was known as ACADIA and included what is now NEW BRUNSWICK. The British name Nova Scotia dates from 1621 when a Scot, Sir William Alexander, was given a charter for colonization. French influence dominated the territory until 1710, when the British captured PORT ROYAL and renamed it ANNAPOLIS ROYAL; in 1713 the mainland was ceded to Britain and the French built the fortress of LOUISBOURG on Île-Royale (Cape Breton). The French-speaking ACADIANS were caught in the conflict between the two countries until they were expelled in 1755 and 1758. Louisbourg was captured by the British in 1758. HALIFAX was founded in 1749, and its small population was augmented by the arrival of LOYALISTS in 1783-4. This led to the erection of New Brunswick and Cape Breton as separate colonies (the latter was re-annexed in 1820). Nova Scotia was one of the founding provinces of the Dominion of Canada in 1867.

As in the other Atlantic provinces, resource-based industries—primary steel, fish processing, and wood processing—are important, although secondary manufacturing is more developed. Halifax (the capital) and Sydney, Cape Breton, are the principal industrial cities. Agriculture is restricted by the rugged, rocky Atlantic uplands mainly to the ANNAPOLIS-CORNWALLIS VALLEY, the Chignecto Isthmus, and southern Cape Breton.

Nova Scotia has a land area of 20,402 sq. mi. and a population in 1971 of 788,960—over 70% of British origin and approximately 12% French-speaking.

Nova Scotia Song. See 'FAREWELL TO NOVA SCOTIA'.

Novascotian, The. A weekly newspaper published in Halifax between 29 Dec. 1824 and 1926. It was acquired in 1828 by Joseph HOWE, who edited and printed it, first as a literary paper and then as a reform paper in which he attacked abuses of the appointed magistrates. Arrested for libel, he pleaded his own case and won in May 1835; he was carried home from the courtroom in triumph on the shoulders of a rejoicing people. Howe sold the paper in 1842 but continued to serve as editor from 1844 to 1847, arguing for equal rights, RESPONSIBLE GOVERNMENT, and the abolition of class privileges. He contributed regularly to the paper until 1856.

November the Eleventh. See REMEMBRANCE DAY.

Now I Ask You. A literary quiz program on CBC Radio. Aired for 30 minutes on Saturday nights (and originally called 'International Quiz Show' and then 'Beat the Champs'), it was christened 'Now I Ask You' on 3 Nov. 1950 and ran until 4 Oct. 1969. In its heyday it featured J.G. McGEACHY as moderator of a panel that included Ralph ALLEN, James BANNERMAN, and Morley CALLAGHAN. Listeners sent in questions that were checked by quiz master Ron Hambleton. The program began with 'Hamish' McGeachy saying, in his thick Scots accent, 'Well, gentlemen, now I ask you.'

Now That April's Here. A feature film based on four stories from Morley CALLAGHAN's collection *Now That April's Here and Other Stories* (1936). It was produced by William Davidson and Norman Klenman in Toronto in 1958 and directed by Davidson. The actors included Don Borisenko, John DRAINIE, Michael Mann, and Raymond MASSEY, who was also narrator. The stories dramatized were 'Silk Stockings', 'Rocking Chair', 'The Rejected One', and 'A Sick Call'. The film was well made but seemed somewhat artificial to the critics. 84 min., b & w.

Nowlan, Alden (b.1933). Poet and fiction writer. Born in Windsor, N.S., he has worked as a newspaper editor and, since 1969, as a creative-writing instructor and a free-lance writer in Fredericton and Saint John, N.B. He writes straightforward, compassionate poems and stories that reveal as much about human nature as they do about life in New Brunswick and Nova Scotia. Among his poetry collections are *Bread, Wine and Salt* (1966), *The Mysterious Naked Man* (1969), *Between Tears and Laughter* (1971), and *I'm a Stranger Here Myself* (1974). *Miracle at Indian River* (1968) is a collection of stories and

Various Persons Named Kevin O'Brien (1973) is a novel. He has also written a local history, *Campobello* (1975), and, with Walter Learning, *Frankenstein* (1976), a play based on Mary Shelley's novel.

NPD. See NUCLEAR POWER DEMONSTRATION.

NRU. The initials of National Research Universal, an atomic reactor at CHALK RIVER, Ont. It was started up on 3 Nov. 1957. The word 'universal' signifies that the reactor has a wide range of applications, including the production of cobalt 60 for cobalt therapy units.

NRX. National Research Experimental, an early heavy-water-cooled atomic reactor at CHALK RIVER, Ont. It was started up on 22 July 1947. A widely reported accident that put it out of commission for 14 months occurred on 'Black Friday', 12 Dec. 1952.

NTLC. See NATIONAL TRADES AND LABOUR CONGRESS.

NTR. Initials of the National Transcontinental Railway, now CANADIAN NATIONAL RAILWAYS.

Nuclear Power Demonstration. An electrical power-generating station fuelled by a CANDU reactor. The first in a series of NPD stations in Ontario and Quebec was built on the Ottawa R. at Rolphton, Ont., near CHALK RIVER. It began producing electrical power on 4 June 1962.

Nunavut. Eskimo for 'our land'. The name for an area comprising much of the NORTHWEST TERRITORIES and the Arctic Islands, proposed by the INUIT TAPIRISAT OF CANADA in a land claim presented to the federal government on 27 Feb. 1976.

Nunny-bag. In Newfoundland, a haversack made of sealskin often filled with food.

NWMP. See NORTH WEST MOUNTED POLICE.

Nymph and the Lamp, The. Historical romance by Thomas RADDALL published in 1950. With the background provided by the author's experiences as a wireless operator on Cape Sable, N.S., it tells the story of a love affair between a light-house keeper and a girl from the mainland on an isolated, wind-swept island in the Atlantic.

O

'O Canada'. The national anthem. The stately melody was composed by Calixa LA-VALLÉE in 1880. The French version of the lyrics was written by Sir Adolphe-Basile ROUTHIER earlier that year, and the English version by R. Stanley WEIR in 1908. Parliament did not officially recognize 'O Canada' as the national anthem until 1975, when it formally accepted a modified English text, the melody and the French lyrics having been officially recognized some years previously. The French and English lyrics appear in *Colombo's Canadian Quotations* (1974). 'O Canada' is the national anthem; 'GOD SAVE THE QUEEN' is the royal anthem.

'O God! O Montreal!' Refrain from a satiric poem by the English novelist Samuel Butler. In 1875, when he caught sight of the naked Discobolus more or less hidden in a Montreal museum, the British author was inspired to write 'A Psalm of Montreal', which includes the above refrain. The poem appeared in *The Note-Books of Samuel Butler* (1926) edited by Henry Festing Jones and can be read in *The BLASTED PINE* (1957; rev. 1967) edited by F.R. SCOTT and A.J.M. SMITH.

OAC. Initials of the Ontario Agricultural College. See UNIVERSITY OF GUELPH.

Oak Island. One of some 300 islands in Mahone Bay off the Atlantic coast of Nova Scotia. Only a mile long, it has been associated with buried treasure—some have thought Capt. Kidd's or Sir Henry Morgan's—and searches for it have been made since 1795, but none has ever been found.

Oakes murder case. The unsolved slaying of the millionaire mining magnate Sir Harry Oakes (1874-1943). As an American-born prospector he made a major gold strike near Kirkland Lake, Ont., in 1912 and found Tough-Oakes Mines and Lake Shore Mines. From 1928 to 1934 he resided in Oak Hall, a 37-room mansion at Niagara Falls, Ont., which has been open as a museum since 1964. He settled near Nassau, Bahamas, for tax reasons in 1935 and was knighted in 1939. An associate, Harold Christie, found Sir Harry's charred, beaten corpse in the bedroom of his villa on 8 July 1943. His son-in-law, Count Alfred de Marigny, was charged, tried, and acquitted of the murder, but the sensational case was never closed. In *King's X* (1972) the American lawyer Marshal Houts claimed that Oakes was slain by the Mafia at the instigation of Meyer Lansky who, with the tacit agreement of the Duke of Windsor, then governor general of the Bahamas—but against Sir Harry's wishes—was extending his gambling monopoly to the Bahamas.

Oath of Allegiance. Oath required by the Canadian Citizenship Act of 1952 before non-Canadians are granted CITIZENSHIP. It is administered by the Department of the SECRETARY OF STATE and, in its 1975 amended form, reads: 'I, A.B., do swear that I will be faithful and bear true allegiance to Her Majesty Queen Elizabeth the Second, Her Heirs and Successors, according to law, and that I will faithfully observe the laws of Canada, and fulfil my duties as a Canadian citizen. So help me God.'

Oban Inn. Beautifully restored nineteenth-century inn at NIAGARA-ON-THE-LAKE, Ont. It was built *c*.1824 by Capt. Duncan Malloy and later served as a hostelry and, during the First World War, as an officer's mess. The inn declined until 1962 when the Burroughs family bought and completely refurbished it, restoring its elegant Victorian décor. It has 22 guest rooms and a dining room that seats 300.

Oberon Press. A family-owned publishing company that specializes in fiction and poetry collections. It was founded in Ottawa in 1966 by Michael Macklem, a former teacher and encyclopaedia editor, and his wife Anne Hardy, who still run it from their Ottawa home. Each year Hardy and Macklem travel together across the country selling their list, which includes such perennials as WHERE TO EAT IN CANADA and Oberon's annual short-story anthologies, both of which were initiated in 1971.

Objectif. Quebec film magazine. Published quarterly in Montreal from 1960 to 1967, it devoted serious attention to Quebec films. Among its editors were Jean-Pierre LEFÈBVRE, Jacques Leduc, and Robert Daudelin.

O'Brien, Lucius R. (1832-99). Artist. Born in Shanty Bay, U.C. (Ont.), and educated at Upper Canada College, Toronto, he trained in an architect's office and entered business in Orillia. He did not become a professional painter until 1872. The first president of the ROYAL CANADIAN ACADEMY, he showed at the first exhibition in 1880 SUNRISE ON THE SA-

381

GUENAY (1880), a favourite painting in the National Gallery of Canada.

OBU. See ONE BIG UNION.

OC. Officer of the ORDER OF CANADA.

OCA. Initials of the ONTARIO COLLEGE OF ART.

O/Cdt. Official abbreviation of Officer-Cadet.

Ocean to Ocean. A patriotic and influential travel book by George Monro GRANT, the full title of which is *Ocean to Ocean: Sandford* FLEMING's *Expedition Through Canada in 1872* (1873). The phrase 'ocean to ocean' is sometimes used in the sense of 'From sea to sea', the English translation of A MARI USQUE AD MARE, the official motto of Canada.

October Crisis. On 5 Oct. 1970 a cell of the FLQ kidnapped James Cross, a British trade commissioner in Montreal. Among the demands of the cell were that the FLQ manifesto be issued (it was subsequently broadcast on Radio-Canada) and that 23 terrorists held in custody be released. While the government was negotiating with the kidnappers, another cell of the FLQ seized Pierre Laporte, Quebec Minister of Labour, on 10 Oct. On 16 Oct. the government invoked the WAR MEASURES ACT, banning the FLQ, and sent troops into Quebec. On 17 Oct. the body of Pierre Laporte was found in the trunk of a car at St Hubert airport. He had been strangled. The Montreal police and the RCMP discovered the whereabouts of the first cell, and James Cross was released on 3 Dec. in return for the provision of safe passage to Cuba for the kidnappers and some relatives. Members of the second cell were captured later that month and charged with murder.

Odeon Theatres (Canada) Ltd. Canada's second-largest theatre chain. It was set up in 1941 as a subsidiary of Britain's Rank Organization by N.L. Nathanson (who, in 1920, had set up FAMOUS PLAYERS LTD, now the country's largest theatre chain). The present chain owns or controls approximately 138 theatres in Canada, which take in 19% of the national box-office receipts. It is fully owned by the Rank Organization.

Odjig, Daphne (b.1925). Odawa artist. Born and raised on the Wikwemikong Reserve, Manitoulin Island, Ont., she has lived in British Columbia and northern Manitoba. She is self-taught and works in pastels, oils, prints, pen-and-ink, acrylic, and collage. She depicts, in a graceful and fluid manner, the legends of her people, and sometimes paints in a non-objective manner. Her work was represented in the Canadian Pavilion at Expo 70 in Osaka, Japan, and she illustrated *Tales from the Smoke House* (1974) by Herbert T. Schwarz.

Office national du film. The French name of the NATIONAL FILM BOARD.

Office of the Auditor General. See AUDITOR GENERAL.

Office of the Prime Minister. See PMO.

Official Languages Act. An Act making French and English the official languages of Canada. The right to use French or English in the federal houses of Parliament and in federal courts was guaranteed under the BNA ACT. The Official Languages Act, 1969, extends the use of both languages to all federal government services, to the NATIONAL CAPITAL REGION, and to districts determined by the BILINGUAL DISTRICTS ADVISORY BOARD.

OFY. See OPPORTUNITIES FOR YOUTH.

Ogdensburg, Battle of. An engagement in the WAR OF 1812. On 22 Feb. 1813 British forces, led by Lt-Col. George Macdonell, captured the town and fort of Ogdensburg on the St Lawrence R., in present-day New York State.

Ogdensburg Agreement. Important declaration signed by Prime Minister Mackenzie KING and President Roosevelt on 17-18 Aug. 1940, at Ogdensburg, N.Y., a port city on the St Lawrence R. It established the Permanent Joint Board of Defence 'to consider in the broad sense the defence of the north half of the Western Hemisphere'. The Joint Board outlasted the Second World War, which occasioned its creation.

Ogema. Former Algonkian word for 'chief'. In the nineteenth century it came to be applied to a white man who was an important official or boss. There are numerous variations in spelling. Ogema is the name of a town near Weyburn, Sask.

Ogopogo. The name given by the Shushwap Indians to a fabulous sea serpent. Seen by early settlers in the waters of the North Saskatchewan R. near Rocky Mountain House, Alta, and in the waters of Lake Okanagan at Penticton, B.C., it is still reportedly sighted every year or so. The Rocky Ogopogo was described in 1939 as a 'fish fifty feet long, and as big around as an elephant'. Austin F. Cross wrote in *Cross Roads* (1936) of the Penticton Ogopogo that 'he would sooner be in a myth than a museum'. Another native sea serpent is CADBOROSAURUS.

O'Grady, Standish (c.1793-1841). Poet. Born in Ireland, a graduate of Trinity College, Dublin, and a clergyman in the Church of Ireland, he settled on a farm at Sorel, L.C. (Que.), in 1836. He published *The Emigrant: A Poem in Four Cantos* privately in 1841. An amateurish work written in over 1,000 heroic couplets, it is nevertheless a realistic, vigorous portrait of the difficult life of an immigrant farmer in Lower Canada.

O'Hagan, Howard (b.1902). Fiction writer and essayist. Born in Lethbridge, Alta, he grew up in the Yellowhead region of the Rockies. He graduated in law from McGill but preferred the active life and has lived in Australia, California, and Sicily; he now lives in Victoria, B.C. Best known for his fine mythic novel *Tay John* (1939), he has collected his stories in *The Woman Who Got on at Jasper and Other Stories* (1963) and his essays about the Northwest in *Wilderness Men* (1958).

O'Hara, Geoffrey (1882-1966). Tin Pan Alley composer. Born in Chatham, Ont., he is remembered for two First World War songs: 'K-K-K-Katy', a stammering song that was the hit of 1918, and his arrangement of 'There Is No Death', which is associated with the first Armistice Day.

OHMS. Initials of 'On His [Her] Majesty's Service', which were perforated on postage stamps supplied to Dominion government departments for prepayment of postage on official mail ineligible for franking purposes. The abbreviation was used in this way between 1939 and 1949 and appeared on post boxes until the mid-1960s. See also G.

Oil Centre of Canada. Unofficial motto of ED-MONTON, near which oil was discovered in 1947.

Oil Springs. Village in Enniskillen Township, south of Sarnia, Ont., the site of the first commercial oil well in North America. Charles and Henry Tripp of Woodstock, Ont., digging an ordinary well to the depth of 30 ft, struck oil, which they marketed in 1852. James Miller Williams, a Hamilton carriage-maker, assumed their operation in 1856 and drilled the first successful oil well in North America in the summer of 1857, two years before Edwin L. Drake successfully drilled for oil in Pennsylvania. Williams also built the first Canadian oil refinery. A replica of one of Williams' wells stands near the Oil Museum of Canada, which opened in 1959 at Oil Springs.

OISE. Acronym of the ONTARIO INSTITUTE FOR STUDIES IN EDUCATION.

Ojibwa or **Ojibway.** A group of ALGONKIAN-speaking Indian bands occupying a large area from the Ottawa R. valley west to the Prairies and as far north as CREE territory. They include the Ottawa at the eastern end, the Salteaux around Sault Ste Marie, and the Mississauga in southern Ontario. They are known for the multitude of uses they put birchbark to—for canoes, to cover wigwams, and for utensils—as well as for their rich folklore. Some of the tales of the trickster-hero NANABOZHO of the central Ojibwa influenced Longfellow's narrative poem about HIAWATHA (an Iroquois name). The legendary hero of the Salteaux was Wiskedjak (WHISKEY JACK). The western-Ontario Ojibwa have a religious society known as the MIDÉWEWIN. Their population in 1971 was 50,431. They are known as Chippewa in the U.S.

Oka. A strong-smelling soft cheese, made by Trappist monks since 1881 at the village of Oka, Que. See also Les TROIS CHAPELLES.

Okanagan. INTERIOR SALISH Indians in the Okanagan Valley of British Columbia, closely related to the Lake people of the upper Columbia R. and Arrow Lakes. Their population in 1974 was 743.

Okanagan Valley. An area in southern British Columbia, between the Fraser plateau and the Columbia Mountains, famed for its fruit production.

O'Keefe Brewery. See CARLING O'KEEFE BREWERIES.

O'Keefe Centre. A centre for the performing arts in Toronto. The 3,155-seat theatre on Front St, designed by Morgan, Page, and Steele for the O'Keefe Brewing Company, opened on 1 Oct. 1960 with the world première of *Camelot*, a musical by Lerner and Lowe starring Richard Burton, Julie Andrews, and Robert GOULET. It was operated by O'Keefe's until Aug. 1968, when it was turned over to the Metropolitan Toronto Council. The performing home of the CANADIAN OPERA COMPANY and the NATIONAL BALLET OF CANADA, it also houses a succession of touring shows.

Oktoberfest. A German beer-drinking festival held each October. The first such affair was held in Munich in 1810. Since 1969 Kitchener, Ont., has hosted an annual Oktoberfest, which features nine days of parades and festivities centred on local food and drink, all prepared in the German or Pennsylvania Dutch manner in Waterloo County.

Ol'Antoine. Memorable television character created by Paul ST PIERRE and played by Chief

Ol'Antoine

Dan GEORGE. Ol'Antoine, a dignified Indian chief who has fallen on bad days, first appeared in the notable CBC-TV series CARIBOO COUNTRY in 1960 and in *The Education of Phyllistine*—a two-part drama first shown on CBC-TV on 12 and 19 Mar. 1964—as the guardian of a 10-year-old Indian girl 'borrowed' by white settlers to make a quorum of students to start a school. When Ol' Antoine died in *Antoine's Wooden Overcoat*, a 60-minute episode from 'Cariboo Country' seen on 13 May 1966 (and broadcast separately in 1967), the selection of his coffin and burial place became significant events in the lives of the inhabitants of the fictitious Cariboo community of NAMKO. He also made an appearance in HOW TO BREAK A QUARTER HORSE, a CBC-TV production shown on 19 Jan. 1966.

Old Age Security Pension. A plan to pay pensions to all Canadians aged 65 and over who have fulfilled certain residence requirements. The first Old Age Pension Plan was introduced in 1927 and provided federal grants to those provinces that agreed to pay pensions. The pension was subject to a means test and payable to anyone over 70. A Joint Parliamentary Committee of the House of Commons and the Senate studied the question of old-age security in 1950, and in 1951, after agreement with the provinces, an amendment to the BNA ACT was passed enabling the federal government to enact the Old Age Security Act. An amendment passed in 1966 provides for the payment of the Guaranteed Income Supplement to pensioners who have no other income. The Old Age Security program is administered by the Department of NATIONAL HEALTH AND WELFARE through its regional offices. See also CANADA PENSION PLAN.

Old Chieftain, The. (i) Sobriquet of Sir John A. MACDONALD. (ii) The subtitle of the second volume of Donald CREIGHTON's biography of Macdonald, published in 1955.

Old Country, The. A reference to Europe, especially the British Isles, as the place of one's origin.

Old Man Ontario. Sobriquet of Leslie M. Frost, premier of Ontario from 1949 to 1961. It was given to Frost for his sense of small-town values by the advertising executive (and later Senator) Alistair Grossart.

'Old Man, the Old Flag, the Old Policy, The'. Slogan of the Conservative Party in the election of 1891. The 'old man' was Sir John A. MACDONALD; the 'old flag' was the UNION JACK; the 'old policy' was Macdonald's NATIONAL POLICY.

Old Montreal. Bounded by McGill St on the west, St Jacques and the Champs-de-Mars on the north, Berri on the east, and Commune and Commissaires on the south, it is the old centre of Montreal. Its streetscapes, squares, and many of its old buildings retain much of their nineteenth-century appearance. Preservation and restoration of the area are controlled by the Jacques-Viger Commission, set up by the city. Its centre is BONSECOURS MARKET.

Old Ontario. A reference to the settled areas of southern Ontario, especially since 1912 when Northern or NEW ONTARIO was added to the province.

'Old Ontario Strand, The'. A college song evocative of the traditional values of Ontario and Upper Canada. The word 'strand' refers specifically to the northern shoreline of Lake Ontario. The chorus of this song, first sung at Queen's University in 1866, runs: 'On the Old Ontario Strand, my boys,/Where Queen's forever shall stand!/For has she not stood/Since the time of the flood/On the Old Ontario Strand!' With variations in the wording, it is the official song of Victoria College, University of Toronto.

Old Originals, The. (i) The first 500 men recruited by the NORTH WEST MOUNTED POLICE in 1873. (ii) The members of the first contingent of the First Canadian Division of the First World War.

Old Régime. The period of French rule in North America—the period of NEW FRANCE.

'Old Tomorrow'. A nickname for Sir John A. MACDONALD, a reference to his putting problems off repeatedly until tomorrow.

O'Leary Commission. The Royal Commission on Publications. Chaired by journalist (later Senator) Grattan O'Leary (1889-1976), it was established in 1960 by the DIEFENBAKER government and reported in May 1961 on 'the position and prospects of Canadian magazines . . . with special attention to foreign competition'. The Commission urged the removal of the tax deduction for advertisements in foreign periodicals directed at the Canadian market, a proposal aimed directly at TIME CANADA and READER'S DIGEST. This action was not taken by the Diefenbaker government.

Oliphant, Betty (b.1918). Ballet teacher and ballet mistress. Born in London, Eng., she danced in musicals there. She came to Canada in 1947 and in 1949 opened her own school in Toronto, which became large and successful. She taught at the first Summer

School of the NATIONAL BALLET OF CANADA and was first ballet mistress of the company and then director and principal of the highly respected NATIONAL BALLET SCHOOL, which she co-founded with Celia FRANCA. She also served as the associate-director of the company. In 1967, at Erik BRUHN's invitation, she went to Stockholm to advise on the reorganization of the Royal Swedish Ballet School.

Olympic Bobsled Team. Championship Canadian four-man bobsled team. The gold medal in the four-man event at the 1964 Winter Olympics at Innsbruck, Austria, was won by a crew composed of Victor Emery, John Emery, Douglas Anakin, and Peter Kirby. The following year, at St Moritz, Switz., the world title was won by another Canadian crew: Victor Emery, Peter Kirby, Michael Young, and Gerald Presley. Both crews had to train in Europe, as Canada had no bobsled run at the time.

Olympic Games. Games of the XXI Olympiad held in Montreal, 17 July to 1 Aug. 1976—the first such games ever staged in Canada. The prime mover of the Montreal Olympics was Mayor Jean DRAPEAU. The buildings and pageantry cost $1.4 billion. Over 250,000 people watched the feats of athletic skill in the $800-million stadium—which professional teams will eventually use as a sports centre—and at other sites. The Olympic Village, built to house 10,000 athletes and many officials, will be converted into apartments.

The spirit of the Games was marred by the federal government's late refusal to permit the participation of Taiwan as the Republic of China; and by the last-minute boycott of almost 30 African and other nations in protest over the participation of New Zealand, which, in June 1976, had permitted its rugby team to compete against South Africa (excluded from Olympic membership in 1970 because of its apartheid policy), despite Olympic boycott threats from the Supreme Council of Sport in Africa.

The program for the XXI Olympiad included 21 sports: Archery, Athletics (track and field), Basketball, Boxing, Canoeing, Cycling, Equestrian Sports, Fencing, Football (soccer), Gymnastics, Handball, Hockey (field), Judo, Modern Pentathlon, Rowing, Shooting, Swimming, Volleyball, Weightlifting, Wrestling, Yachting. The Canadian Olympic Association delegated its powers to the organizing committee known as COJO (Comité Organisateur des Jeux Olympiques). The official symbol consisted of five rings topped by the Olympic podium, as designed by Georges Huel. The podium represents 'the spirit of chivalry' as well as the letter 'M' for Montreal. At the centre of the design is the oval of the Olympic stadium. The five entwined rings represent world brotherhood and correspond to the five sections of the world. Transmission of the Games was facilitated by ORTO (Olympics Radio and Television Organization), created by the CBC to supply all radio, television, and film services for world-wide coverage to reach an estimated billion people. The ancient Greek event was revived in Athens in 1896 and Games have been held at four-year intervals ever since (except for 1916, 1940, and 1944).

Olympic Grand Prix Jumping Team. Three-man Canadian equestrian team. The gold medal for the Grand Prix jumping competition at the 1968 Olympics in Mexico City was won by Jim Elder, Tom Gayford, and Jim Day. They competed against teams from 15 nations and in the presence of 80,000 spectators on the final day of the XIX Olympiad.

Olympic Medal Winners, Canadian. A list follows of the competitions won by Canadians (the names of single winners, not of team-members, are given) Gold, Silver, and Bronze medals are awarded to those who place first, second, and third.

SUMMER OLYMPICS

I. 1896, Athens
Canada not represented.

II. 1900, Paris
2,500-metre steeplechase/George Orton/First (Orton, a Canadian, competed for the U.S.)

III. 1904, St Louis
Throwing 56-pound weight/Etienne DESMARTEAU/First
Senior eights rowing/Toronto Argonauts/Second
Association football/Galt Football Club/First
Golf/George S. LYON/First
International lacrosse/Shamrock Club, Winnipeg/First

IV. 1908, London
100-metre/Robert KERR/Third
200-metre/Robert KERR/First
Running long jump/C. BRICKER/Third
Pole vault/E. Archibald/Third
Hop, step and jump/Garfield McDonald/Second
Hammer throw/Con Walsh/Second
Wrestling/Bantamweight/A. Cote/Third
Army Gun/Team shooting/Third
Clay pigeon shooting/W.H. EWING/First/G. Beattie/Second
Cycling/Team pursuit/Third
Lacrosse/First

385

Olympic Medal Winners

V. 1912, Stockholm
10,000-metre walk/George GOULDING/First
Running long jump/C.D. BRICKER/Second
Pole vault/William Happeny/(tied) Third
Hammer throw/Duncan Gillis/Second
Pentathlon/Frank Lukeman/Third
400-metre swim/George HODGSON/First
1,500-metre swim/George HODGSON/First
Single-sculls rowing/E.B. Butler/Third

VII. 1920, Antwerp
110-metre hurdles/Earl Thompson/First
Boxing/Bantamweight/C.G. Graham/Second
Boxing/Lightweight/C. Newton/Third
Boxing/Welterweight/T. Schneider/
First
Boxing/Middleweight/Prudhomme/Second
400-metre swim/George Vernot/ Third
1,500-metre swim/George Vernot/Second
Ice hockey/Winnipeg Falcons/First

VIII. 1924, Paris
Boxing/Welterweight/Douglas Lewis/Third
Rowing/Fours without coxswain/Vancouver
Rowing Club/Second
Rowing/Eights/University of Toronto/
Second
Shooting/Team event/Second

IX. 1928, Amsterdam
100-metre/Percy WILLIAMS/First
200-metre/Percy WILLIAMS/First
400-metre/James BALL/Second
1,600-metre relay/Third
100-metre/Women/F. ROSENFELD/Second
400-metre relay/Women/First
High jump/Women/Ethel CATHERWOOD/First
Wrestling/Bantamweight/James TRIFUNOV/
Third
Wrestling/Light middleweight/
M. Letchford/Third
Wrestling/Middleweight/D. Stockton/Second
Boxing/Welterweight/Raymond Smilie/
Third
Swimming/800-metre relay/Third
Rowing/Double sculls/Argonaut Rowing
Club/Second
Rowing/Eights/Argonaut Rowing Club/Third

X. 1932, Los Angeles
400-metre/Alexander Wilson/Third
800-metre/Alexander Wilson/Second/
Philip Edwards/Third
1,500-metre/Philip Edwards/Third
1,600-metre relay/Third
High jump/D. McNAUGHTON/First
100-metre/Women/Hilda STRIKE/Second
400-metre relay/Women/Second
High jump/Women/Eva Dawes/Third
Wrestling/Light middleweight/Daniel
MacDonald/Second
Boxing/Bantamweight/Horace GWYNNE/First
Rowing/Double sculls/Third
Rowing/Eights/Hamilton Leanders/Third

Yachting/6-metre R-class/Third
Yachting/8-metre International class/Second

XI. 1936, Berlin
800-metre/Dr Philip Edwards/Third
400-metre hurdles/John Loaring/Second
80-metre hurdles/Women/Elizabeth
Taylor/Third
400-metre relay/Women/Third
Wrestling/Light middleweight/Joseph
Schleimer/Third
Canoeing/1,000-metre single/Francis
AMYOT/First
Canoeing/1,000-metre doubles/Third
Canoeing/10,000-metre doubles/Second
Art/Dr Tait McKENZIE/Third
Basketball/Second

XIV. 1948, London
400-metre relay/Women/Third
Canoeing/Singles/1,000-metre/
D. Bennet/Second
Canoeing/Singles/10,000-metre/N. Lane/
Third
Music/Instrumental and chamber/
J. WEINZWEIG/Second

XV. 1952, Helsinki
Weight-lifting/Welterweight/G. Gratton/
Second
Clay-Pigeon Shooting/G. GENEREUX/First
Canoeing/Doubles/10,000-metre/Second

XVI. 1956, Melbourne
Rowing/Fours without coxswain/University
of British Columbia/First
Rowing/Eights/University of British
Columbia/Second
Shooting/Small-Bore rifle prone/
G. OUELETTE/First
Shooting/Small-Bore rifle prone/G. BOA/
Third
Women's Diving/3-metre springboard/Irene
MacDonald/Third
Equestrian/Three-day event/Third

XVII. 1960, Rome
Rowing/Eights/University of British
Columbia/Second

XVIII. 1964, Tokyo
100-metre run/Harry JEROME/Third
800-metre run/Bill CROTHERS/Second
Rowing/Coxswainless pairs/G. HUNGERFORD,
R. JACKSON/First

XIX. 1968, Mexico City
Swimming/Men/400-metre free-style/Ralph
Hutton/Second
Swimming/Women/200-metre backstroke/
Elaine TANNER/Second
Swimming/Women/800-metre free-style/
Elaine TANNER/Second

Swimming/Team/400-metre free-style relay/Third
Equestrian/Grand Prix/First

XX. 1972, Munich
Swimming/Men/100-metre-butterfly/Bruce Robertson/Second
Swimming/Women/200-metre backstroke/Donna Marie Gurr/Third
Swimming/Women/400-metre individual medley/Leslie Cliff/Second
Swimming/Team/400-metre medley relay/Third
Yachting/International sailing class/Third

XXI. 1976, Montreal
Canoeing/Men/500-metre Canadian singles/John Wood/Second
Equestrian/Individual jumping/Michel Vaillancourt/Second
Swimming/Men/Team/4 x 100-metre medley relay/Second
Swimming/Women/100-metre backstroke/Nancy Garapick/Third
Swimming/Women/200-metre backstroke/Nancy Garapick/Third
Swimming/Women/400-metre free-style/Shannon Smith/Third
Swimming/Women/400-metre individual medley/Cheryl Gibson/Second/Becky Smith/Third
Swimming/Women/Team/400-metre free-style relay/Third
Swimming/Women/Team/400-metre medley relay/Third
High jump/Men/Greg Joy/Second

WINTER OLYMPICS

I. 1924, Chamonix
Ice Hockey/Toronto Granites/First

II. 1928, St Moritz
Ice Hockey/University of Toronto Grads/First

III. 1932, Lake Placid
Figure Skating/Men/Montgomery Wilson/Third
Speed Skating/500-metre/Alex. Hurd/Third
Speed Skating/1,500-metre/Alex. Hurd/Second/William Logan/Third
Speed Skating/5,000-metre/William Logan/Third
Speed Skating/10,000-metre/Frank STACK/Third
Speed Skating/Women/500-metre/Jean WILSON/First
Speed Skating/Women/1,000-metre/Hattie Donaldson/Second
Speed Skating/Women/1,500-metre/Jean WILSON/Second
Sled-Dog Racing/Emil St Godard/First/'Shorty' Russick/Third
Curling/Manitoba Rink/First
Ice Hockey/First

IV. 1936, Garmisch-Partenkirchen
Ice Hockey/Second

V. 1948, St Moritz
Figure Skating/Women's individual/Barbara Ann SCOTT/First
Figure Skating/Pairs/Suzanne Morrow, Wallace Diestelmeyer/Third
Ice Hockey/RCAF Flyers/First

VI. 1952, Oslo
Speedskating/500-metre/G. Audley/Third
Ice Hockey/Edmonton Mercurys/First

VII. 1956, Cortina-D'Ampezzo
Skiing/Women/Downhill race/Lucille WHEELER/Third
Figure Skating/Pairs/Frances Dafoe, Norris Bowden/Second
Ice Hockey/Kitchener-Waterloo/Third

VIII. 1960, Squaw Valley
Skiing/Women's slalom/Anne HEGGTVEIT/First
Figure Skating/Men's individual/D. JACKSON/Third
Figure Skating/Pairs/Barbara WAGNER, Bob PAUL/First
Ice Hockey/Kitchener-Waterloo/Second

IX. 1964, Innsbruck
Figure Skating/Women's individual/Petra BURKA/Third
Figure Skating/Pairs/D. Wilkes, G. Revell/Third
Bobsled/4-man bob/First

X. 1968, Grenoble
Skiing/Women's giant slalom/Nancy GREENE/First
Skiing/Women's slalom/Nancy Greene/Second
Ice Hockey/Third

XI. 1972, Sapporo
Figure Skating/Women's individual/Karen MAGNUSSEN/Second

XII. 1976, Innsbruck
Skiing/Women's giant slalom/Cathy KREINER/First
Speed Skating/Women/500-metre/Cathy Priestner/Second
Figure Skating/Men's singles/Toller CRANSTON/Third

Olympic Women's 400-metre Relay Team. 1928 Olympics winner. Fanny ROSENFELD, Ethel Smith, Jane Bell, and Myrtle Cook, good individual sprinters, combined to form the Canadian women's 400-metre relay team, which won the gold medal at the 1928 Olympics in Amsterdam, establishing a world record.

Ombudsman

Ombudsman, Canadian. Citizen's defender against bureaucratic abuse. The office originated in Sweden in 1809 when a commissioner was appointed by the legislature to assist the citizenry in its dealings with the government and public services. An ombudsman makes recommendations to appropriate officials but has no power to enforce decisions. There is no federal ombudsman in Canada, but the following provincial governments have each appointed one: *Alberta:* George B. McClelland, former commissioner of the RCMP, 1967, succeeded by Randall Ivany, former Anglican cleric, in 1975. *New Brunswick:* W.T. Ross Flemington, former president of Mount Allison University, 1967, succeeded by Charles Léger, a lawyer, in 1971; office vacant since Apr. 1976. *Quebec:* Dr Louis Marceau, former dean of law, Université Laval, 1969, succeeded by Luce Patenaude, professor of law, Université de Montréal, 1 Sept. 1976. *Manitoba:* George Maltby, former Winnipeg police chief, 1969. *Newfoundland:* Ambrose Piddel, 1975. *Nova Scotia:* Dr Harry D. Smith, former president of King's College, 1970. *Ontario:* Arthur Maloney, former criminal lawyer, 1975. *Saskatchewan:* W.K. Barker (acting). The first international meeting for some 60 ombudsmen from round the world was held in Edmonton on 7-10 Sept. 1976.

OMM. Officer of the ORDER OF MILITARY MERIT.

'On His [Her] Majesty's Service'. See OHMS.

On to Ottawa. The slogan and name of a mass trek of unemployed men in 1935. It began on 3 June 1935 when 1,000 men boarded CPR transcontinental freight cars at Vancouver and headed east. They reached Calgary, Alta, on 7 June and arrived at Swift Current, Sask., on 12 June. On 14 June about 2,000 entered Regina, where they remained while their leaders went ahead to meet Prime Minister R.B. BENNETT in his Ottawa office. Following the abortive meeting on 22 June, a riot broke out in Regina, on 1 July, thus ending the trek.

Onake Corp. A cultural and educational association formed 12 July 1974 to fund the North American Indian Travelling College. The word *onake* means 'birch-bark' and by extension 'currency' in Mohawk. Based at Cornwall Island, Ont., the Travelling College sends Indians into Canadian schools with traditional artifacts, brochures, slides, art, photographs, and films to lecture and conduct workshops among native and non-native students in the interests of correcting misinformation in history texts about Canada's native peoples.

Ondaatje, Michael (b.1943). Poet. Born in Ceylon, he was educated in England and settled in Canada in 1962. He received an M.A. from Queen's University and teaches English at York University, Toronto. He is married to the painter Kim Ondaatje. His poetry—with its striking use of sometimes macabre imagery and embracing Ondaatje's many interests, including animals, birds, myths, and social history—has been collected in *The Dainty Monsters* (1967), *The Man with Seven Toes* (1969), *The* COLLECTED WORKS OF BILLY THE KID (1970), and *Rat Jelly* (1973). He based his 16 mm experimental film, *Sons of Captain Poetry*, on bp NICHOL and edited *The Broken Arc* (1971), an anthology of poems about animals, illustrated by Tony URQUHART.

One Big Union. A labour association founded in Mar. 1919 in Calgary, Alta, largely by unions in western Canada. The OBU's objective was to establish new industrial unions to displace the old craft unions, and efforts were made to recruit members among the miners of Nova Scotia in 1924-5. But the OBU was eventually eliminated when its last few members joined the CANADIAN LABOUR CONGRESS in 1957.

One Flag, One Fleet, One Throne. An inscription formerly placed in all Ontario elementary school readers under a full-coloured picture of the UNION JACK opposite the title page. The Department of Education was so imperialist-minded that it also developed 24 May, (Queen Victoria's birthday, into Empire Day (see VICTORIA DAY), at the suggestion of Clementina Fessenden.

One Hundred Associates. See COMPANY OF NEW FRANCE.

One Million Children. The widely read report of the Commission on Emotional and Learning Disorders in Children, released in June 1970. CELDIC, representing seven Toronto-based voluntary associations, made more than 100 specific recommendations for changes in the treatment of handicapped children as learners and in the prevalent attitude that the problem could be solved in a piecemeal fashion. The title is a reference to the estimated number of handicapped children in Canada with some degree of emotional or learning disorder.

Oneida. See IROQUOIS.

ONF. Office national du film, the French name of the NATIONAL FILM BOARD.

Onley, Toni (b.1928). Painter. Born on the Isle of Man, Eng., he studied at the Douglas School of Art and came to Canada in 1943. He lives in Vancouver, where he teaches at the University of British Columbia. After painting stark, contemplative landscapes of prehistoric-like land formations, he concentrated on shapes to explore abstract landscapes in subdued acrylic colours. This evolved into a collage style in which paper cut-outs in geometric shapes are pasted on canvas and painted with accents of delicate colour. *Polar 12* (1962, AGH) is a powerful rendition of the almost mystical space that characterizes his work. Onley is exhibited and collected internationally.

Only living Father of Confederation. Popular sobriquet applied to Joseph R. (Joey) SMALLWOOD, who brought Newfoundland into Confederation in 1949.

Onondaga. See IROQUOIS.

Onontio. Iroquois name—meaning 'Great Mountain'—given to governors of New France. It was first given to the sieur de Montmagny (1583-1653), who succeeded Samuel de CHAMPLAIN as governor in 1636.

ONR. Abbreviation of ONTARIO NORTHLAND RAILWAY.

Ont. Abbreviation of ONTARIO.

'Ontar-i-ar-i-ar-io'. Theme song from *A PLACE TO STAND*, a documentary film directed by Christopher CHAPMAN for the Ontario Pavilion at EXPO 67. The words are by Richard Morris, the music by Dolores Claman.

Ontario. The province that links Quebec and the Atlantic provinces with Manitoba and the western provinces. During the French régime, what is now Ontario remained largely unsettled except for the building of a few forts. Settlement began only with the arrival of the LOYALISTS; the area west of the Ottawa R. was formed into the Province of Upper Canada by the CONSTITUTIONAL ACT OF 1791. Settlement continued with the arrival of the 'late loyalists' and with British immigration in the nineteenth century, until by 1840 the population was about 400,000. At that time, as a result of the REBELLION OF 1837 and the financial difficulties of the province, the ACT OF UNION was passed and in 1841 Upper Canada became the administrative district of CANADA WEST in the PROVINCE OF CANADA. In 1867, at CONFEDERATION, it became the Province of Ontario.

With its mineral deposits and the forests of the CANADIAN SHIELD in the north and the productive agricultural plains in the south, Ontario leads all other provinces in manufacturing, electrical generation, and service industries (particularly finance). Second to Alberta in total value of mineral production, Ontario is the leading producer of nickel, zinc, and gold; and second in copper and iron ore. The industrial base of the province is diversified: food and beverages, primary metals (particularly iron and steel), and transportation are the most important industries. The majority of the population and consequently most economic activity is concentrated in the south, particularly in the GOLDEN HORSESHOE centring on TORONTO.

Ontario is the third-largest province in area—the land area is 344,092 sq. mi.—and the largest in population—8,094,000 in 1971. 60% of the population is of British origin, 10% French, 6% German, 6% Italian, and 3% Dutch. Its capital is Toronto and its motto is *Ut incepit fidelis sic permanent* ('Loyal she began, loyal she remains').

Ontario Agricultural College. See UNIVERSITY OF GUELPH.

Ontario Arts Council. Provincial arts body. Established in 1962 as the Province of Ontario Council for the Arts (POCA), but known since 1973 as the Ontario Arts Council (OAC), it consists of a chairman, a vice-chairman, and 10 other members, all appointed. It was formed to promote the study, enjoyment, and production of works of art in the province and makes grants to individuals and institutions, including the TORONTO SYMPHONY ORCHESTRA and the STRATFORD FESTIVAL. The director is Louis APPLEBAUM (from 1971).

Ontario College of Art. It was founded in 1876 under the sponsorship of the Ontario Society of Artists. Over the years it has undergone many location and name changes until, in 1911, it was reorganized as the OCA and located near the Art Gallery of Toronto. The aim of the college is to train professional artists and designers. A diploma is granted upon graduation from the four-year program.

Ontario Crafts Council. A 3,000-member non-profit organization fostering the development of Canadian crafts. Formed in Jan. 1976 as the result of a merger between the Canadian Guild of Crafts (Ontario), founded in 1931, and the Ontario Craft Foundation, founded in 1966, it is the Ontario successor of the Canadian Handicrafts Guild, established in 1906. The Council runs a gallery and Guild Shop in Toronto, sponsors annual crafts exhibitions, and publishes its own magazine, the *Craftman*. Associated with the

Ontario Crafts Council

Council is the Canadian Guild of Crafts shop in Montreal.

Ontario Film Institute. Founded in 1969 by Gerald PRATLEY and located in the ONTARIO SCIENCE CENTRE, it provides information about all aspects of film and encourages film appreciation, with regular screenings under the name of the Ontario Film Theatre in the 482-seat auditorium of the Ontario Science Centre. The Institute's library includes approximately 5,000 books and journals related to film and over 2,000 soundtrack recordings. It also runs a program of regional Film Theatres with weekly screenings in Windsor and Brockville. Each September it presents the Stratford International Film Festival in collaboration with the STRATFORD FESTIVAL.

Ontario Hydro. The name of the Hydro-Electric Power Commission of Ontario since 4 Mar. 1974. The largest power-producing and distributing organization in Canada—possibly the largest in the world—and the first such utility to be nationalized, the company was created by Sir Adam Beck (1857-1925) on 7 May 1906 to bring hydro-electric generated power from NIAGARA FALLS to southern Ontario communities. Beck, a former manufacturer and a prominent cabinet minister, was the first chairman, and a strong advocate of 'the people's power'. The motto of Ontario Hydro is *Dona Naturae Pro Populo Sunt* ('The Gifts of Nature are for the People').

Ontario Institute for Studies in Education, The. OISE was established in 1965 as an independent post-secondary institution for research into education, development of learning skills and materials, and graduate studies. It is affiliated with the University of Toronto and grants a Master of Education degree. See also CANADA STUDIES FOUNDATION.

Ontario Northland Railway. A provincially owned railway that serves North Bay, Moosonee, Timmins, Ont., and Noranda, Que. Opened on 15 Jan. 1905, it has operated since the 1960s a popular one-day return excursion train in the summer from Cochrane to Moosonee, known as the POLAR BEAR EXPRESS.

Ontario Place. An amusement complex opened by the Ontario government on 22 May 1971. Designed by Craig, Zeidler & Strong and located on 96 acres of man-made islands on the Toronto waterfront adjoining the CNE, it consists of the Cinesphere, an 800-seat theatre containing a six-storey movie screen where the IMAX film NORTH OF SUPERIOR was first shown; the Forum, a 2,000-seat out-door amphitheatre that can accommodate an additional 6,000 spectators on the surrounding lawns; the Children's Village; a 350-boat marina; restaurants; and the HMCS HAIDA. It is open from late spring to late fall.

Ontario Science Centre. The Centennial Centre of Science and Technology in Don Mills, Ont. Set in an 18-acre park on the slopes of the Don Valley, the futuristic three-building complex was designed by Raymond MORIYAMA and opened in 1969. On display are more than 550 interpretative exhibits of scientific principles and technological achievements in the areas of space and earth sciences, communications, physics, genetics, and engineering, many of them participatory and audio-visual. It also houses the ONTARIO FILM INSTITUTE.

Ontario Society of Artists. Founded by a group of seven painters in 1872, it is the oldest existing professional arts society in Canada. It is described as 'an organization of artists to promote art and the concerns of art, the fostering of original art in the province, the holding of annual exhibitions, and the formation of an art library and museum . . .'. The OSA was instrumental in the founding of the ONTARIO COLLEGE OF ART and the ART GALLERY OF ONTARIO.

Ookpik. An Arctic owl made of sealskin that became a popular symbol of the Canadian North. Jeannie Snowball, an Eskimo widow living in Fort Chimo, sewed the first Ookpik doll, which was a hit at the Philadelphia Trade Fair in Nov. 1963. It was then manufactured commercially as a souvenir. *Ookpik* means 'happy little Arctic owl' in Eskimo.

Oolichan. CHINOOK JARGON for a small fish, referring to a fish of the smelt family native to the Pacific Coast. Its edible oil was prized by the Indians of the west coast.

Oonark, Jessie (b.1906). Eskimo graphic artist at BAKER LAKE. She is equally renowned for her graphic images and her brilliantly imaginative wall-hangings, one of which is displayed in the lobby of the NATIONAL ARTS CENTRE in Ottawa. She illustrated *I Breathe a New Song* (1971), an anthology edited by Richard Lewis. She is the mother of William NOAH.

Open Grave, The. A controversial 60-minute CBC-TV drama written by Charles E. Israel. Produced and directed by Ron KELLY and telecast on 25 Mar. 1964, it had as its theme the effect of the resurrection of Christ on today's society. The fact that it was produced in a documentary manner gave it great immediacy—and made it seem blasphemous to some. Anchorman for the production was J. Frank WILLIS.

Open House. A popular 30-minute weekday program on CBC-TV. Produced in Toronto with Anna Cameron and Fred DAVIS as hosts, and later with Max FERGUSON and Gwen Grant, it had a wide following. It was seen from 8 May 1957 to 29 June 1962.

Open Letter. A journal devoted to avant-garde literary theory, criticism, poetry, and reviews. Founded in 1965 by Frank DAVEY when he was teaching at Royal Roads Military College, Victoria, it was mimeographed and distributed free; it lapsed after five issues. It was revived in Toronto on a three-issues-a-year basis in 1971. The design and printing are handled by COACH HOUSE PRESS.

Opeongo Road. Colonization road extending nearly 100 mi. between Farrell's Landing on the Ottawa R. and Lake Opeongo, Renfrew Co., Ont. It was opened in 1854.

Operation Neptune. See NORMANDY INVASION.

Operation Overlord. See NORMANDY INVASION.

Operations Centre. A crisis-management centre located in the East Block of the Parliament Buildings in Ottawa. Developed by the Department of EXTERNAL AFFAIRS, it is a briefing room with offices and has elaborate communications and gaming facilities. In the OCTOBER CRISIS of 1970 it was the heart of the government's planning process, with staff drawn from External Affairs, the Prime Minister's Office, the RCMP, and other departments.

OPP. Initials of the Ontario Provincial Police, which was formed in 1909.

Opportunities for Youth. A program to create summer employment for students between the ages of 16 and 25. Launched by the Department of the SECRETARY OF STATE in Mar. 1971, OFY funded a variety of projects, some of a cultural nature, for up to 16 weeks each year. It was terminated in 1975.

Opportunity Knocks. A popular CBC Radio series that encouraged and developed Canadian talent. Each week for 30 minutes amateur singers and performers competed among themselves for audience votes. The talent hunt, which began in July 1947 and went into its last season on 24 Sept. 1950, was hosted by John ADASKIN.

Opposition, The. The party or parties that do not have a majority of seats in the House of Commons or a provincial legislature. The official Opposition is the largest minority party, and its leader is called 'the Leader of the Opposition'. It has been said that 'the duty of the Opposition is to oppose', and its aim is to defeat the government and obtain a majority in the next general election. Because the government is answerable to Parliament, the role of the Opposition is important in criticizing, and proposing amendments to, government bills.

Opthof, Cornelis (b.1930). Baritone. Born in Rotterdam, Holland, he came to Canada in 1944 and studied at the Royal Conservatory of Music Opera School, Toronto, in 1957-9. A frequent singer of leading roles in the CANADIAN OPERA COMPANY, he toured Australia with Joan Sutherland in 1965. He made his Metropolitan Opera début with Sutherland and Luciano Pavarotti in *I Puritani* in 1976.

Opting-out Formula. A procedure whereby a provincial government may 'opt out' of a federal plan by assuming its administrative burden and receiving appropriate tax concessions. During the 1960s the Quebec government opted out of a number of federal schemes.

Orangemen's Day. Anniversary of the Battle of the Boyne, Northern Ireland, which took place on 12 July 1690. On that date William, the Protestant Prince of Orange, was victorious over his father-in-law James II, the Catholic King of England, Scotland and Ireland. It is observed by members of the lodges of The Loyal Orange Association of British America. The Orangemen's Parade and other festivities take place on 12 July or the nearest Saturday (or, in Newfoundland, on the nearest Monday). There were parades in Toronto as early as the 1820s.

Order-in-Council. The formal instrument of decisions made by the Committee of the PRIVY COUNCIL or CABINET acting as the GOVERNOR IN COUNCIL. An Act of the Canadian Parliament may delegate authority to enact subordinate legislation—ranging from regulations concerning technical details to blanket powers in emergencies—and such legislation is enacted by orders-in-council.

Order of Canada. An HONOUR awarded to Canadians for outstanding achievement and service to their country or to humanity. Instituted on 1 July 1967, there were two levels of membership, revised to three in 1972: Companions of the Order, limited to 150, who are entitled to use CC after their names; officers

(OC); and members (CM). Non-Canadians may be appointed as honorary members at any of the three levels.

Order of Good Cheer/Ordre de Bon Temps. An informal order of chivalry. Samuel de CHAMPLAIN founded it to keep spirits high during the winter of 1606-7 at PORT ROYAL. Its members took turns providing game for the table. The food was ceremoniously presented by the 'Chief Steward' of the day, and entertainment followed the meal.

Order of Military Merit. A Canadian HON-OUR awarded to members of the Canadian Armed Forces to recognize exceptional merit. Established in 1972, it has three levels of membership: Commander (CMM); Officer (OMM); and Member (MMM).

Order Paper and Notices. Printed document setting out the order of business for each day in the HOUSE OF COMMONS.

Orders of the Day. See ROUTINE PROCEEDINGS AND ORDERS OF THE DAY.

Ordre Patriotique des Goglus. A fascist party headed by Adrien ARCAND, who named it after his anti-semitic newspaper *Le Goglu* ('The Bobolink'). It was founded in Montreal in Nov. 1929 to promote racism, Quebec nationalism, and Catholicism. It was succeeded in Feb. 1934 by the NATIONAL SOCIAL CHRISTIAN PARTY.

Ordres, Les. Feature film written and directed by Michel BRAULT. Released in 1973, it starred Hélène Loiselle, Jean Lapointe, Guy Provost, and others. One of the best Quebec and Canadian movies ever made, it mixes fact and fiction in a quasi-documentary fashion as it recounts what happened to a group of Québécois arrested under the WAR MEASURES ACT during the OCTOBER CRISIS of 1970. It shared the Grand Prize at the Cannes Film Festival in 1975. 180 min., colour.

Oregon dispute. See 'FIFTY-FOUR FORTY, OR FIGHT'.

Orenda. Iroquoian word for 'spirit'. It is said to mean the same as the Algonkian word MANITOU and the Siouan word WAKANDA.

Orenda. A series of turbojet engines produced in Canada. They were designed and built by A.V. ROE at Malton, Ont., in 1948. The engine was first testflown in 1950. The Orenda series powered the CF-100S and the CANADAIR-built F-86 (Sabres).

Orford String Quartet. It was established in 1965 under the auspices of Les JEUNESSES MUSICALES, from whose camp at Mount Orford,

Que., it took its name. The members are violinists Andrew Dawes and Kenneth Perkins, violist Terence Helmer, and cellist Marcel St Cyr. Artists in residence at the University of Toronto since 1968 and champions of new Canadian music, the Orford won top honours in the European Broadcasting Union's quartet competition in 1974 and made a successful 1975 European tour funded by the Department of External Affairs.

Orignal. The French word for MOOSE.

Orr, Bobby (b.1948). Popular hockey defenceman. Born in Parry Sound, Ont., he was captain of the Oshawa Generals from 1964 to 1966, when he joined the Boston Bruins. In 1976 he signed a 10-year contract with the Chicago Blackhawks for $3 million. He won the CALDER MEMORIAL TROPHY in 1967 and the JAMES NORRIS MEMORIAL TROPHY in 1968.

Orthokeratology. Corrective eye care through contact lenses. Advances in the therapeutic use of contact lenses were made by Dr Ned Paige, a Toronto optometrist who in 1969 introduced the PLI system now used by practitioners in many countries. The initials stand for Plus Lens Increment and the system consists of using a series of contact lenses to reshape the cornea to aid vision. It has been of special benefit to those professionals requiring good sight without glasses or contact lenses (police, pilots, etc.).

Ortona. Small seaport in Italy, the scene of fierce hand-to-hand fighting during the SECOND WORLD WAR. Canadian infantry, led by the Loyal Edmonton Regiment and the Seaforth Highlanders, attacked this German stronghold on the Adriatic on 21 Dec. 1943. After seven days of 'blaze and blood', the Germans abandoned the town.

OS. Official abbreviation of Ordinary Seaman.

Osborne Collection of Early Children's Books. A reference collection of children's books published in England before 1910. It has grown from the gift of 2,000 books presented in 1949 to the Toronto Public Library's BOYS AND GIRLS HOUSE by Dr Edgar Osborne, an English librarian and collector. Two catalogues of the collection were published in 1958 and 1975. Also housed in Boys and Girls House on St George St, Toronto, is the Lillian H. Smith Collection of Children's Books, named after the librarian who established the children's services of the TPL and administered them for many years. Founded in 1962, it begins where the Osborne Collection leaves off, bringing together the best books for children published since 1910 in Canada, the United States, and the United Kingdom. The two collections exceed 12,500 titles.

Osgoode Hall. Neo-Classical building on Queen St W. in downtown Toronto, the home of the Law Society of Upper Canada and the Supreme Court of Ontario. It housed the Law School from 1873 to 1968, when much of the instruction was shifted to the main campus of YORK UNIVERSITY. The east wing was built in 1829-32 and named for William Osgoode (1754-1824), first chief justice of Upper Canada (1792-4). The west wing was built in 1844-6 and joined to the east wing by an arcade surmounted by two storeys and a dome. This central portion was replaced in 1857-60 by a larger building bearing the façade we see today; it was designed by Frederick William CUMBERLAND.

Oshawa. 'The Go Ahead City', 'The Detroit of Canada'. An Ontario village in 1850, a city in 1925, Oshawa has been closely identified with the fortunes of the automobile manufacturer R. S. McLAUGHLIN. Oshawa is an Indian word said to mean 'that point of the stream where the canoe was exchanged for the trail'. Its motto is 'Labour and Prosperity'. The city boasts the Canadian Automotive Museum, unique in the country, and the ROBERT McLAUGHLIN ART GALLERY. Its population in 1971 was 91,587.

Oshawa Strike. A widely reported strike of auto workers at General Motors in Oshawa, Ont., from 8 to 26 Apr. 1938. It grew out of the demand for union agreement, wage increases, and other benefits. The Ontario Premier Mitchell HEPBURN pictured it as a strike led by 'foreign agitators' and organized a force of police and military (the so-called HEPBURN'S HUSSARS) to deal with the violence-prone situation. He faced the resignation of two senior ministers, David A. Croll (see 'MARCHING WITH THE WORKERS') and Arthur W. Roebuck. The strike ended without gains on either side.

Osler, Sir William (1849-1919). Doctor and medical teacher. Born at Bond Head, C.W. (Ont.), he graduated in medicine from McGill University in 1872 and studied in Europe for two years before returning to McGill to teach physiology and pathology. He then taught at the University of Pennsylvania (from 1884), Johns Hopkins University Hospital (from 1889), and Oxford University (from 1905), where he occupied the Regius Chair of Medicine, established in 1546, until his death. He was made a baronet in 1911

and he willed to McGill his personal library, the catalogue of which, *Bibliotheca Osleriana* (1929), includes 7,600 titles. Osler has been called 'the most influential physician in history', both for his intuitive bedside manner and for his humanistic and inspirational addresses. He was the author of *The Principles and Practice of Medicine* (1892), which went through 100 reprints and editions and until the 1950s was the standard text on clinical medicine. Many of Osler's addresses were published in book form—during his lifetime and posthumously. W.B. Bean edited *Aphorisms from His Bedside Teachings and Writings* (1950), preserving his witty observations on man and medicine. See *The Life of Sir William Osler* (2 vols, 1925) by Harvey Cushing.

Osmond, Dr Humphrey. See PSYCHEDELIC.

Osowetuk (b.1923). Eskimo sculptor and printmaker at CAPE DORSET. A prolific artist, since the 1950s he has produced a great many imaginative sculptures of humans, animals, and birds, some in white quartz.

Ossawippi. The name of the fictional river that flows into 'Lake WISSANOTTI', on which is located MARIPOSA, the town in SUNSHINE SKETCHES OF A LITTLE TOWN (1912) by Stephen LEACOCK.

Ostrich fern. See FIDDLEHEAD.

Oswego, Battle of. An engagement in the WAR OF 1812. On 6 May 1813 the American fort, at the east end of Lake Ontario in present-day New York State, was stormed and taken by a British force under Cmdre Sir James Yeo.

Other Place, The. Euphemism for the SENATE in the HOUSE OF COMMONS and for the House of Commons in the Senate.

Ottawa. The capital city of Canada. It began as the headquarters of the Royal Engineers under Col. John BY, who built the RIDEAU CANAL between 1826 and 1832. Incorporated as Bytown in 1850, it was renamed Ottawa in 1855 and was chosen as the capital of the Province of Canada in 1857 and the Dominion of Canada in 1867. Development has been largely related to the growth of federal-government and related administrative activities, which together dwarf all other urban activities, including manufacturing and commerce. While the Ottawa metropolitan area includes a great variety of governmental jurisdictions, it is unique in Canada in that the federal government, through the NATIONAL CAPITAL COMMISSION, is concerned with the integration of planning for the entire region.

One of the accomplishments of this authority has been the purchase for $40 million of a 42,000-acre greenbelt completely surrounding Ottawa. The 1971 CMA population was 602,510 (including the city of Hull). Its official motto is 'Advance-Ottawa-En Avant'. See also CARLETON UNIVERSITY, CHÂTEAU LAURIER, CONFEDERATION SQUARE, EARNSCLIFFE, GOVERNMENT HOUSE, LAURIER HOUSE, NATIONAL ARTS CENTRE, NATIONAL GALLERY OF CANADA, NATIONAL LIBRARY OF CANADA, NATIONAL MUSEUMS OF CANADA, PARLIAMENT BUILDINGS, PEACE TOWER, PUBLIC ARCHIVES OF CANADA, ROYAL CANADIAN MINT, STORNOWAY, TULIP FESTIVAL, UNIVERSITY OF OTTAWA.

Ottawa. Northern ALGONKIAN-speaking Indians, they were associated with the OJIBWA in a confederacy. They originally occupied the BRUCE PENINSULA and perhaps MANITOULIN ISLAND in Ontario. They were strongly influenced by the neighbouring HURON, adapting to village life and some agriculture early in the seventeenth century, and were also active fur traders. They now live mainly on Manitoulin Island and in 1970 had a population of 1,632.

Ottawa Citizen, The. An evening newspaper published in Ottawa. Describing itself as 'An independent paper founded in 1844', it was known for many years as a left-of-centre champion of social reform. It was acquired by SOUTHAM PRESS in 1897 and is the chain's flagship publication, being the 'home paper' of Charles Lynch, chief of Southam News Services, and Jim Coleman, sports editor and columnist.

Ottawa-Hull. Term used to refer to the urban complex of OTTAWA, Ont., and Hull, Que. The hybrid first appeared in *The Guide to Canada's Capital* (1974), a publication of the NATIONAL CAPITAL COMMISSION, and caused a controversy. Its use has no official sanction.

Ottawa Journal, The. An evening newspaper published in Ottawa. Founded in 1885 and for some time a Unionist paper called the *Ottawa Journal-Press*, it has been owned by FP PUBLICATIONS since 1959. Its motto is 'An independent Conservative newspaper'. P.D. Ross (1858-1949), E. Norman Smith (1871-1957), Grattan O'Leary (1889-1976), and I. Norman Smith (b.1909) have been associated with it as publisher/editor/writer.

Ottawa Lowland Fault. A series of several dozen (and about five major) earthquake sliplines running the length of the Ottawa Valley from Pembroke to beyond Cornwall, primarily on the Ontario side of the provincial border. Several faults underlie the Na-

tional Capital Region, one directly beneath downtown Ottawa.

Ottawa Man, The. An adaptation by Mavor MOORE of Nikolai Gogol's *The Inspector General* (1837). It opened at the CREST THEATRE, Toronto, on 21 May 1958, and was successfully revived at the CHARLOTTETOWN SUMMER FESTIVAL on 7 July 1966. A satire on the Ottawa bureaucracy, it is set in 1875 in a town in northwest Manitoba where the townsfolk learn that Ottawa is sending an inspector, who turns out to be a NORTH WEST MOUNTED POLICE officer in disguise.

Ottawa mandarins. A phrase somewhat facetiously used to characterize top-ranking federal government officials. The allusion is to the civil-servant class that ran the bureaucracy of ancient China.

Ottawa River. Rising in northern lakes and forming the boundary between Ontario and Quebec for more than half its length of approximately 700 mi., it flows into the St Lawrence R. at MONTREAL. In the seventeenth century it was used by northern Indians who went to Montreal to trade in furs and it was a major route to the north and west for explorers, fur traders, and missionaries. Lumber was transported down the river in the nineteenth century.

Ottawa Rough Riders. Popular professional football team, founded in 1907. Since 1938 it has won the Eastern Football Conference title 10 times and the GREY CUP eight times.

Otter. A short-legged, long-tailed animal with aquatic habits found along watercourses throughout Canada. Its thick dark-brown fur is highly valued commercially.

Otter. A large, single-engine utility transport. It was designed and built by DE HAVILLAND in 1951 to handle a larger load than the BEAVER. The STOL-type craft seated 12 or carried more than a ton of freight. See also CARIBOU and TWIN OTTER.

Otter, Gen. Sir William (1843-1929). First Canadian soldier to attain the rank of general. Born near Clinton, Ont., and educated at the Toronto Model School and Upper Canada College, he joined the Volunteer Militia in 1861 and the Permanent Active Militia in 1883. He wrote and published *The Guide*, a manual of military interior economy that was reprinted many times. He commanded the column that marched on BATTLEFORD in the NORTHWEST REBELLION (1885) and the first Canadian contingent sent to the SOUTH AFRICAN WAR in 1899. He was the first Chief of the

General Staff, Ottawa, from 1908 to 1910, when he became Inspector-General Canadian Militia. He retired in 1912 and was knighted in 1913.

Ouananiche. Algonkian word for a species of small fresh-water salmon native to Lac Saint-Jean, Que., and other lakes in Ontario and Quebec. It is sometimes spelled the way it is pronounced in English: 'Wananish'.

Ouellet, Fernand (b.1926). Quebec historian. Born in Lac-Bouchette, Lac Saint-Jean, Que., he was educated at Université Laval and has taught in the history department of Carleton University since 1965. Using the tools of the social sciences, he has analysed the foundations of Quebec society in socio-economic terms. His principal work is *Histoire économique et sociale du Québec, 1760-1850* (1968).

Ouellette, Fernand (b.1930). Quebec poet. Born in Montreal and educated at the Université de Montréal, he is a producer with Radio-Canada and a co-founder of LIBERTÉ. He has written a study of *Edgar Varèse* (1966), and numerous books of verse, notably *Les Actes retrouvés* (1970), for which he was awarded but declined the Governor General's Award.

Ouellette, Gerald R. (Gerry) (1934-75). Champion rifleman. At the 1956 Olympics at Melbourne, he fired a perfect score of 600 in the small-bore rifle shooting event and won the gold medal. He won many other honours at Bisley, Eng., and the Pan-American Games before his single-engine plane crashed in 1975. He left his widow Jennifer, who was herself a six-time member of Canada's Bisley Team.

Our Generation. Current title of a monthly periodical published in Montreal. It first appeared in 1961 as *Our Generation Against Nuclear War*, published by the Combined Universities for Nuclear Disarmament (CUCND). It acquired its present name in 1966, when it began to appear under the auspices of the Student Union for Peace Action. The magazine has consistently opposed the proliferation of atomic weaponry.

'Our Lady of the Snows'. A poem about Canada by Rudyard Kipling, first published in 1897, the year Canada introduced an Imperial Preference policy—lower tariffs on goods imported from Great Britain. It begins: 'A Nation spoke to a Nation,/A Throne sent word to a Throne:/"Daughter am I in my mother's house,/But mistress in my own."' Many resented the British writer's implication that Canada was a land of ice and snow.

Kipling was familiar with the church of Notre-Dame des Neiges in the Montreal district of Côte des Neiges, and possibly with Thomas D'Arcy McGEE's poem 'Our Ladye of the Snow' about this church. Kipling's poem appears in *Rudyard Kipling's Verse: Definitive Edition* (1940).

'Our political masters'. Sarcastic phrase used by civil servants from the 1940s to the 1960s to describe government members of the House of Commons, especially cabinet ministers.

Outaouais. The French name for a group of OJIBWA Indians—from an Algonkian word meaning 'to trade'—that was applied to the tributary of the St Lawrence R., called the Ottawa in English, after which the city was named. *Un Outaouais* is a resident of Ottawa.

Outarde. The French word for 'bustard' or 'buzzard', used historically to refer to a wild goose, especially the CANADA GOOSE.

Outports. Originally the term referring to all places outside St John's, Nfld, it now applies to villages situated on the sea. Although 385 settlements have closed down since 1950, there are some 500 outports today.

Outremont. A Montreal municipality of 944 acres on the northern slope of Mount Royal. Founded in 1875, and one of the most beautiful areas of Montreal, it is inhabited mainly by upper-middle-class French Canadians and is now considered 'richer than WESTMOUNT'.

Outside, The. The settled and civilized parts of Canada seen from the vantage-point of unsettled areas, especially the North.

Over Prairie Trails. A collection of nature essays by Frederick Philip GROVE published in 1922, based on his experiences of the country around Gladstone, Man. It was his first published book.

Overlanders of '62. A group that travelled overland to the Cariboo country during the FRASER RIVER GOLD RUSH. 138 men, two women, and two children left FORT GARRY in 1862 in RED RIVER CARTS and made their way to Fort Edmonton, where they transferred their belongings to mules and pack horses and crossed the Rocky Mountains, reaching Fort George, near the present city of Prince George, B.C.

Owen, Don (b.1934). Film director. Born in Toronto, he began as a writer for Westminster Films and then for the NATIONAL FILM

BOARD. Now a free-lance film-maker, he directed such short features as *High Steel* (1965), *Ladies and Gentlemen, Mr. Leonard Cohen* (with Donald BRITTAIN, 1966), *Gallery: A View of Time* (1969), and *Cowboy and Indian* (1972). His first feature-length film, NOBODY WAVED GOOD-BYE (1964), represented a watershed in English-Canadian cinema. He also directed *The Ernie Game* (1967) and *Partners* (1976).

Owl, Arctic or **Snowy.** A large carnivorous bird with a wing span of 45-55 in. and, unlike most owls, active during the day. Normally an inhabitant of the tundra, every four to five years, owing to a change in its food supply, it migrates and can be seen as far south as Mexico and Bermuda. The plumage is a basic white with brown feather-tips and is retained year round.

Oxford. Automobile manufactured from 1913 to 1915 by Oxford Motor Cars and Foundries, Montreal. Built by French-Canadian interests, a four-cylinder Model A sold for $1,600.

Oxford Companion to Canadian History and Literature, The. Standard reference work written by Norah Story and published by the OXFORD UNIVERSITY PRESS in 1967. It includes some 2,000 alphabetically arranged entries on historical and literary figures and subjects with bibliographies. The *Supplement to The Oxford Companion to Canadian History and Literature* edited by William Toye was published in 1973.

Oxford University Press Canada. Book publishers. Established in Toronto in 1904 by the Oxford University Press—a department of the University of Oxford founded in 1478—it has published in Canada many trade and educational titles, including books by some of the leading Canadian poets; well-known anthologies, such as *The Oxford Book of Canadian Verse* (1960) edited by A.J.M. SMITH; and such reference books as Norah Story's *The* OXFORD COMPANION TO CANADIAN HISTORY AND LITERATURE (1967). Managers of the Canadian business have been S.B. Gundy (1904-36), W.H. Clarke (1936-49), C.C. Johnson (1949-63), I.M. Owen (1963-73), and L.M. Wilkinson (from 1973).

P

P1. Official abbreviation of Petty Officer, 1st Class.

P2. Official abbreviation of Petty Officer 2nd Class.

P.E.I. Abbreviation of PRINCE EDWARD ISLAND.

P.O. Official abbreviation of Petty Officer before the rating was divided into two classes.

P.Q. Abbreviation of the Province of QUEBEC.

Paardeberg, Battle of. See SOUTH AFRICAN WAR.

Pablum. The first pre-cooked, vitamin-enriched cereal; the name is derived from the Greek word for food, *pabulum*. It was created by Drs Frederick Tisdall, T.G.H. Drake, and Alan BROWN at the Hospital for Sick Children, Toronto, during the late 1920s, and was first marketed internationally by Mead Johnson in 1930. Pablum's sale has generated substantial royalties for the hospital's Pediatric Research Foundation.

PAC. See PUBLIC ARCHIVES OF CANADA.

Pacey, Desmond (1917-75). Literary critic. Born in Dunedin, N.Z., and educated at the University of Toronto and at Cambridge, he began his long association with the University of New Brunswick in 1944 when he joined the English department, eventually becoming vice-president of the university. His pioneering work, *Creative Writing in Canada* (1952; rev. 1961), remains the only readable survey of its kind. He is the author of numerous other books, including *Essays in Canadian Criticism: 1938-1968* (1969), which stress the influence of biography and geography on literature. His work on behalf of Frederick Philip GROVE resulted in the appearance of a biography (1945), a collection of critical essays (1970), an edition of Grove's stories, *Tales from the Margin* (1971), and *The Letters of Frederick Philip Grove* (1976), which appeared posthumously and has been called the first complete scholarly edition of the letters of any Canadian author.

Pachter, Charles. See QUEEN ON MOOSE.

Pacific Express. The first regular passenger

train in transcontinental service in Canada. Operated by the CANADIAN PACIFIC RAILWAY, it left Montreal at 8:00 p.m. on 28 June 1886 and arrived at Port Moody, B.C., exactly on time, at 12:00 noon on 4 July. It carried the sleeping car 'Honolulu' and the dining car 'Holyrood'. In its day it offered the longest continuous scheduled train trip on earth.

Pacific Great Eastern. See BRITISH COLUMBIA RAILWAY.

Pacific National Exhibition. An exhibition held annually in Vancouver's Exhibition Park. The 17-day fair, which closes on LABOUR DAY, is the fifth largest in North America. It dates from the Vancouver Exhibition, opened by Sir Wilfrid LAURIER in Sept. 1910, and received its present name in 1946. Important features are the major shows (called 'star spectaculars'), Playland (the fun centre), and the sports events in Empire Stadium (which seats 39,000).

Pacific Northwest. The part of Canada west of the Rockies, corresponding to British Columbia. In North American terms the designation includes, as well, the Pacific coast of Alaska, the two northern Pacific states (Washington and Oregon), and sometimes three landlocked states (Idaho, Montana, and Wyoming).

Pacific Rim National Park. Established in 1971 on the west coast of Vancouver Island, it covers 150 sq. mi. and includes three distinct areas: Long Beach, including 7 mi. of beach; the Broken Group Islands, more than 100 small islands in Barkley Sound; and the West Coast Trail, a 45-mi. trail from Bamfield to Port Renfrew.

Pacific Scandal. Famous corruption case of 1873. The Liberal charge that the charter to build the CANADIAN PACIFIC RAILWAY had been given to Sir Hugh ALLAN in return for massive campaign contributions was shown to be true by a royal commission: Allan had given $179,000 to the Conservatives in the 1872 election. In Parliament, on 3 Nov. 1873, the prime minister, Sir John A. MACDONALD, spoke movingly in his own defence for nearly five hours but resigned two days later.

Pacific Western Airlines Ltd. Regional airline. Established in 1951, with headquarters at Vancouver, it operates scheduled flights in British Columbia, Alberta, Saskatchewan, and the Northwest Territories, as well as North American charter flights. It was acquired by the Alberta government in 1974 and its headquarters were moved to Calgary.

Paddle-to-the-Sea. A popular children's book with a Canadian locale written and illustrated by the American author Holling C. Holling and published in 1941. It tells of the travels of a tiny wooden Indian in a canoe carved by an Indian boy and released near Lake Nipigon. It crosses the Great Lakes (tumbling over Niagara Falls), and sails down the St Lawrence R. into the Gulf, where it is rescued by a fisherman and taken to France. The journey of *Paddle-to-the-Sea* takes four years and is fraught with many adventures. It was filmed by the NFB in 1966.

Padlock Law. The popular title of an Act of the Quebec legislature 'to Protect the Province against Communist Propaganda' that gave the attorney-general authority, without trial, charge, or conviction, to evict anyone from a building or to close (or padlock) a building for one year if it was suspected of being used to propagate Communism. Passed unanimously in 1937 by the UNION NATIONALE government of Maurice DUPLESSIS, it was challenged but upheld in the Quebec courts. However, it was opposed by F.R. SCOTT and others and found to be *ultra vires* by the Supreme Court of Canada in 1957 on the grounds that any restriction on freedom of speech belonged to the criminal law, which was a matter of exclusive federal jurisdiction.

Page, John Percy (1877-1973). Basketball coach of the famed EDMONTON GRADS. Born in Rochester, N.Y., and raised in Bronte, Ont., he graduated from Queen's University and taught at McDougall Commercial High School in Edmonton, where he began coaching girls' basketball teams. Success came early and stayed late, for the Edmonton Grads basketball teams between 1915 and 1940 won every possible title in North America and Europe and once had a string of 148 consecutive victories. The Grads retired, but their coach remained active, becoming a member of the Alberta legislature for seven years, then lieutenant-governor of the province for another seven.

Page, P.K. (b.1916). Poet. Born in Swanage, Eng., she was brought to Red Deer, Alta, as a child. She was associated with PREVIEW in 1942 and with its successor, NORTHERN REVIEW, from which she resigned in 1947. An accomplished artist and the author of a novel—*The Sun and the Moon* (1944; rev. 1973)—she is best known as a poet who writes brilliant, intense poems rich with metaphysical imagery. Her poetry collections are *As Ten as Twenty* (1946), *The Metal and the Flower* (1954), *Cry Ararat!* (1967), and *Poems*

Selected and New (1974). In 1950 she married W. Arthur Irwin (b.1898), the editor of *Maclean's* from 1945 to 1950; High Commissioner to Australia and Ambassador to Brazil and Mexico; and then publisher of the *Victoria Daily Colonist*.

Paige, Dr Ned. See ORTHOKERATOLOGY and WENDO.

Painters Eleven. The group name of Toronto-area artists who exhibited together from 1954 to 1959 in Toronto, Ottawa, Montreal, and by invitation at the Twentieth Annual Exhibition of Abstract Art in New York (1956). Though influenced by the New York abstract expressionists, they had no common manifesto. The 11 painters were: Jack BUSH, Oscar Cahen, Hortense Gordon, Tom Hodgson, Alexandra Luke, J.W.G. (Jock) MACDONALD, Ray Mead, Kazuo NAKAMURA, William RONALD, Harold TOWN, and Walter YARWOOD. The major collection of their work is owned by the ROBERT McLAUGHLIN GALLERY.

Painting Place. Canvas by David MILNE painted at Palgrave, Ont., in 1930. It is the third version of a painting first executed in 1926 while he was summering at Big Moose in the Adirondacks. It is a powerful arrangement of the artist's materials in the foreground set against evergreens and a tree-stump overlooking a still expanse of water and, in the distance, a rolling pattern of Adirondack hills. (NGC) At Palgrave in 1930-1 Milne also created a black-and-green drypoint of the same subject (with the elements transposed), re-engraving it enough times to produce some 3,000 copies, which were bound into *The Colophon: A Book Collectors' Quarterly*, Part Five, published in New York in 1931. He called it *Hilltop: A Drypoint in Two Colours*.

Palliser, John. See PALLISER'S TRIANGLE.

Palliser's Triangle. An area that includes most of the southern part of present-day Alberta and Saskatchewan. Captain John Palliser (1807-87), backed by the Royal Geographical Society and the British Colonial Office, led an expedition that explored the Prairies in 1857-60 and divided the region into two parts: a 'fertile belt' and an 'arid belt' or 'triangle' roughly coincident with the grasslands or true prairie. This latter region is the driest part of the Prairies and was considered by him to be unsuitable for farming. The heart of the arid belt has proved difficult for agriculture and is very thinly settled, while its outer margins contain some of the best grain-growing land in the country. See also John MACOUN.

Palmer, Edward (1809-89). A FATHER OF CONFEDERATION. Born in Charlottetown P.E.I., he studied law and was elected to the legislative assembly of Prince Edward Island in 1835 and was appointed to the legislative council in 1860. He was a delegate to the CHARLOTTETOWN and QUEBEC CONFERENCES on Confederation, to which he was opposed until 1873, when the province joined the Dominion. In 1874 he was made Chief Justice of the Supreme Court of P.E.I.

Pan American Games. A series of competitions held for athletes from North and South America. Scheduled at four-year intervals since 1951, they were first hosted by Canada in Winnipeg in 1967.

Panarctic Oils Ltd. A consortium of private oil and gas companies, individuals, and the federal government. Formed in 1967, it explores for oil and gas in the Arctic area. The government holds 45% of the shares.

Pangnark, John (b.1920). Eskimo sculptor at Eskimo Point, N.W.T. He specializes in abstract figures, mainly of humans. He was one of four Inuit artists to travel to Osaka, Japan, for Expo 70.

Pangnirtung. Eskimo settlement in the Northwest Territories off Cumberland Sound in the eastern part of Baffin Island. One of the most recent art centres, it published its first collection of prints in 1973.

Pannell, Raymond (b.1935). Composer. Born in London, Ont., he represented Canada as pianist in the Tchaikovsky Competition in Moscow in 1962. His works include *Concerto for Piano and Orchestra* (1966-7); *The* LUCK OF GINGER COFFEY (1967), an opera; and *Exiles* (1973), a stage piece. He lives in Toronto, where he is active in elementary music-education projects.

Panneton, Philippe. See THIRTY ACRES.

Panoramic Camera. Canada's best-known contribution to the world of photography. Capable of photographing a 360° circle in a single exposure, it was patented by John R. Connon of Elora, Ont., in 1887. The camera is widely used today for photographing large groups or scenes.

Paperback Hero. Feature film produced by John F. BASSETT and directed by Peter PEARSON. Released in 1973, it starred Keir Dullea, Elizabeth Ashley, John Beck, and others. It is the story of a rowdie in a small prairie town whose passions are hockey and fighting. The hockey sequences are especially vivid, but the film did not repay its investment. 94 min., colour.

PaperJacks. A line of mass-market paperbacks published by GENERAL PUBLISHING COMPANY LIMITED.

Papineau, Louis-Joseph (1786-1871). Rebel leader in the REBELLION OF 1837 in Lower Canada (Quebec). Born in Montreal and trained as a lawyer, he was elected to the legislative assembly in 1814 and was Speaker for three periods until 1837. An opponent of the ACT OF UNION (1841), he gradually became hostile to the colonial government. His powers of oratory attracted radicals around him who came to be called PATRIOTES, of whom a committee in the assembly, with his assistance, drew up Ninety-two Resolutions, comprised of numerous grievances and recommending an elected upper house. They fomented an uprising in Lower Canada, though Papineau himself fled to the United States before the first major engagement at SAINT-DENIS. He returned to Montreal under the amnesty of 1844 and re-entered politics as a member of the assembly. In 1854 he retired to his manor house, Montebello (see Le CHÂTEAU MONTEBELLO), on the Ottawa R.

Papineau-Couture, Jean (b.1916). Composer. Born in Montreal, he studied with Nadia Boulanger and graduated from the New England Conservatory of Music. He has taught piano and administrated many musical organizations, including the Canadian Music Centre, Les Jeunesses Musicales du Canada, the Canadian League of Composers, and the Société de Musique Contemporaine de Quebec. From 1968 to 1973 he was Dean of the music faculty at the Université de Montréal. His music is structuralist and polyphonic, showing the influence of both Stravinsky and the French Renaissance. Major works include *Églogues* (1942), *Psaume 150* (1954), and *Sextuor* (1967) for instrumental ensemble (the first two with voice), and *Contraste* (1970) for voice and orchestra.

Papoose. Algonkian word for an Indian baby.

Paradise Hill. Musical comedy with lyrics, music, and dialogue by Pierre BERTON. It is based on an incident that took place during the KLONDIKE GOLD RUSH when a Norwegian prospector attempted to buy a dancehall girl for her weight in gold. Choreographed by Alan LUND, it opened at the CHARLOTTETOWN SUMMER FESTIVAL on 3 July 1967 and was not a success.

Parallel. A short-lived magazine devoted to literature, politics, and the arts. It was edited in Montreal by Peter Desbarats (see CANADIAN ILLUSTRATED NEWS), who called it 'the first magazine ever published in this country which could conceivably interest a non-Canadian'. Three issues were published in 1966-7.

Para-thor-mone. Trade name of the aqueous extract of the parathyroid glands of cattle. It is used in medicine to correct irregularities in calcium and phosphorus absorption. The active principle of the parathyroid glands was first isolated and given the name para-thormone in 1926 by Dr J.B. COLLIP after two years of research at the University of Alberta.

Parent Commission. Royal Commission on Education, Quebec, 1961. Headed by Mgr A.M. Parent, vice-rector of Université Laval, it made recommendations, which were implemented, that became the rationale for a radical overhaul of the Quebec educational system, changing its philosophy, curriculum, administration, and organization.

Parfleche. A piece of rawhide, usually buffalo hide, or an envelope of rawhide so folded as to protect valuables. The French-Canadian word *parflèche* (from the French *parer*, 'to parry'; *flèche*, 'arrow') signifies the use of rawhide as a shield.

Paris Crew. See The ST JOHN FOUR.

Parish. A unit of ecclesiastical administration. In British North America parishes were established in what are now Quebec, Ontario, and the Maritimes, each with its own church and clergyman. Today in Quebec a parish may also be a rural MUNICIPALITY similar to a TOWNSHIP, but with the same geographical area as the original parish.

Parisian. Steamship operated by the ALLAN LINE. Built in Glasgow, Scot., in 1881, she was outfitted with four masts and two funnels and sailed between Liverpool and North American ports. Called the finest ship in the Canadian trade, she was scrapped in 1914 after a successful career.

Parka. A hooded coat or jacket made of fur or deerskin worn by the Eskimos. The Aleuts of Alaska introduced the word 'parka', which is Russian for 'pelt'.

Parker. Automobile manufactured from 1921 to 1923 by the Parker Motor Car Company, Montreal. It had a six-cylinder 70-h.p. engine and closely resembled the U.S.-built Birmingham.

Parker, Sir Gilbert (1862-1932). Novelist. Born in Camden Township East, C.W.

(Ont.), educated at the University of Toronto, and ordained a deacon in the Church of England in 1882, he settled in England in 1889 and sat in the British House of Commons (1900-18). A strong imperialist and among the most popular novelists of his day, he set his romantic historical fiction mainly in Canada. Among his books are PIERRE AND HIS PEOPLE (1882), tales of the North, and The SEATS OF THE MIGHTY (1896), about the last days of the Old Régime in Quebec. The Works of Gilbert Parker (1912-23) appeared in 23 volumes.

Parker, Jackie (b.1932). Football player. Born in Mississippi, the quarterback played on All-American teams before joining the Edmonton Eskimos in 1954. He played with the team for nine years, helping it take three GREY CUPS, and received the CANADIAN SCHENLEY FOOTBALL AWARD as top footballer three years in a row. Since then he has been associated with the Toronto Argos and the B.C. Lions as a coach. Parker, who is said to be flatfooted, is a member of the Football HALL OF FAME.

Parkin, John B. (1911-75). Architect. Born in Toronto, he was educated at the University of Toronto. Until 1969, when he transferred his practice to Los Angeles, he was a senior partner in John B. Parkin Associates with John C. PARKIN (no relation). The work of the firm with which he was particularly connected included Terminal One and the master plan for the Toronto International Airport (1957-63); the Simpson's Tower, Bay St, Toronto (1969); and the TORONTO DOMINION CENTRE (completed 1969) in association with Mies van der Rohe.

Parkin, John C. (b.1922). Architect. Born in England, he grew up in Winnipeg and was educated at the University of Manitoba and at Harvard, where he studied with Walter Gropius and Marcel Breuer. Formerly senior partner in charge of design in John B. PARKIN Associates, and now heading his own firm, his work includes the headquarters building of the Ontario Association of Architects, 50 Park Rd, Toronto (1953-4); the DON MILLS Shopping Centre (c.1957); the New Ottawa Union Station (c.1966-7); Terminal One of the Toronto International Airport (1957-63); and the rebuilding of the ART GALLERY OF ONTARIO, Toronto (c.1973). Parkin's strongest work has been done in the International Style, concentrating on exact proportions, fine materials, and expressive detailing.

Parkman, Francis (1823-93). American historian. Born in Boston, Mass., he conceived his master plan, while still a student, to write

'the history of the American forest' and, although of delicate health, he became an adept hunter and ranger. He was almost blind by the time he completed his eight-volume epic, to which he gave the general title 'France and England in the New World'. These histories, unsurpassed in narrative power though outmoded in scholarship, are The Conspiracy of Pontiac (1851), Pioneers of France in the New World (1865), The Jesuits in North America in the Seventeenth Century (1867), La Salle and the Discovery of the Great West (1860; rev. 1879), The Old Régime in Canada (1874), Count Frontenac and New France and Louis XIV (1877), Montcalm and Wolfe (1884), and A Half Century of Conflict (1892). A two-volume edition of The Journals of Francis Parkman was published in 1947. The Parkman Reader (1955) was edited by Samuel Eliot Morison.

Parks Canada. See NATIONAL HISTORIC PARKS and NATIONAL PARKS.

Parkwood. The 10-acre estate of R.S. McLAUGHLIN of McLaughlin-Buick fame. The estate land outside Oshawa, Ont., was bought in 1915, when 'Colonel Sam' began to build his 50-room mansion, with Italian garden, using masons from Scotland. Parkwood's stables bred prize-winning horses. The house is now open as a museum.

Parliament Buildings. A group of three buildings on Parliament Hill, a promontory overlooking the Ottawa R. in downtown Ottawa; the seat of the federal government. The East and West Blocks, designed by Augustus Laver and Thomas Stent, and the original Centre Block (including the LIBRARY OF PARLIAMENT), designed by Thomas FULLER (with Augustus Laver), were built in 1860-6. The Centre Block was destroyed by fire on 3 Feb. 1916, except for the Library, and was rebuilt in a much-enlarged form with similar massing and more correct but somewhat less adventurous Gothic detail by J.A. PEARSON (1916-24). It contains the House of Commons and the Senate Chamber as well as the Library; standing in front of it is the soaring PEACE TOWER. The East Block housed the offices of the Privy Council and the prime minister and his cabinet until mid-1976, when these offices were moved to the LANGEVIN BLOCK. The West Block is mainly offices.

Parliament Hill. A promontory overlooking the Ottawa R. in downtown Ottawa upon which are situated the PARLIAMENT BUILDINGS. 'Parliament Hill' is also another way of saying 'seat of government'.

Parliamentary Guide, Canadian. A basic reference work for those concerned with contemporary politics. The red-covered book of over 900 pages, published annually in Ottawa, includes biographies of the members of the upper and lower houses in the federal and provincial governments, names of members of the press gallery, Supreme Court judges, and lists of consular representatives at home and abroad, etc.

Parliamentary Internships. A program designed to provide university graduates with a sense of Parliament, and backbench MPS with qualified assistants. The Canadian Political Science Association established the program in 1969-70 with funds provided initially by the Donner Canadian Foundation and since 1973 by Canadian life-insurance companies. Each year 10 interns are chosen in competition. In September they are assigned to assist MPS of the party of their choice—five to the government, three to the opposition, and one each to the remaining parties. In February a second allocation takes place and the interns move to the opposite side of the chamber.

Parliamentary Press Gallery. An association of reporters who cover events in the federal and provincial Parliaments. All members of the press gallery must be accredited representatives of newspapers, magazines, news chains, and TV and radio stations. The association elects a president and other officers annually, and this board deals with applications for membership in the press gallery, among other things. There are under 150 members in the parliamentary press gallery in Ottawa (fewer in the provincial capitals). Some foreign newspapers and news agencies have resident correspondents in Ottawa; e.g., the London *Times*, the *New York Times*, Tass. The reporters sit above the Speaker's chair in both Houses. Press rooms, news releases, and typewritten copies of all speeches made in the House are some of the privileges enjoyed by members, in addition to their seat in the gallery. Members also sponsor the annual Press Gallery Dinner (held in Ottawa each April), which features skits and speeches lampooning the parliamentarians and the press itself. By tradition these proceedings go unreported in the press.

Parliamentary secretary. Member of Parliament appointed to assist a cabinet minister. Since 1959 parliamentary secretaries have been appointed by the prime minister to hold office for 12 months. A parliamentary secretary is not formally considered part of either the cabinet or the ministry and is not directly accountable to Parliament for the department to which he or she is assigned.

Parlow, Kathleen (1890-1963). Violinist. Born in Calgary, Alta, she studied in San Francisco and St Petersburg (with Leopold Auer), played a command performance before Queen Alexandra in London in 1905, and made her public début in Berlin in 1906. After a world-wide concert career, she became a teacher at the Toronto Conservatory of Music in the 1940s. She was co-founder with Sir Ernest MacMILLAN and Zara NELSOVA of the Canadian Trio (1941) and of the Parlow String Quartet (1943).

Parochial schools. Private schools that receive no tax support. Most parochial schools are maintained by religious or ethnic groups as an alternative to the public, tax-supported school system. See also SEPARATE SCHOOLS.

Parr (c.1889-1969). One of the earliest and most famous of all Eskimo artists. A CAPE DORSET engraver, he worked in ivory in the traditional style and was one of the first Inuits to experiment with etching techniques. A noted hunter, he frequently depicted hunting scenes in his many prints, which were done in a characteristically spare but powerful style.

Parry, Sir Edward (1790-1855). Seaman and Arctic explorer. He commanded the ships *Hecla* and *Griper* on an expedition of 1819-20 that sailed through Lancaster Sound, proving it was not landlocked—an important discovery in the search for the NORTHWEST PASSAGE. He also discovered other waterways and named 20 islands, including Devon, Somerset, Cornwallis, Melville, and Banks. He wintered on Melville Island. On his expedition of 1821-3 he discovered Fury and Hecla Strait off the northern tip of Melville Peninsula—an important link in the southerly route of the Passage.

Parti National Social Chrétien. A fascist party headed by Adrien ARCAND. It was established in Montreal in Feb. 1934 with the same aims as its predecessor, L'ORDRE PATRIOTIQUE DES GOGLUS. When the new party's activities were restricted in May 1938, it reappeared as the National Unity Party. This group was declared illegal in Sept. 1939, and Arcand himself was interned during the Second World War.

Parti pris. A political, social, and cultural review published in Montreal between 1963 and 1968. Founded by Pierre Maheu, André MAJOR, Paul CHAMBERLAND, and other Quebec intellectuals, as a reaction against the genera-

Parti pris

tion of intellectuals that preceded them (particularly those associated with CITÉ LIBRE), it advocated, among other things, economic and political independence for Quebec. The name *parti pris*—literally, 'positions taken'—remains as the imprint of the socialist and separatist publishing house Les Éditions Parti Pris, founded in 1964.

Parti Québécois. Quebec political party dedicated to SEPARATISM, founded on 12-15 Oct. 1968 out of the Mouvement Souveraineté-Association and the Ralliement Nationale. The aims of the party are to declare unilaterally that Quebec is a separate state and to make French the sole official language. The president is René LÉVESQUE. At the last provincial election in 1973 the PQ obtained 30.1% of the popular vote and 6 seats, forming the official Opposition. See also RIN.

Partridge berry. A tart red berry, also called lingonberry, that grows on evergreen shrubs in Newfoundland and Nova Scotia.

Pas de deux. A famous short film by Norman McLAREN. Two ballet dancers, Margaret Mercier and Vincent Warren, perform a *pas de deux* to a Romanian folksong, 'Song of the River Olt', arranged by Maurice Blackburn and played on pan pipes by Dobré Constantin. By exposing each frame as many as 11 times, McLaren was able to create multiple images of each dancer that appear and disappear. The film was cited as 'a magnificent demonstration of the use of staggered, synthesized multiple images derived from the live-action record of a dance movement' by Roger Manville in *The International Encyclopedia of Film* (1972). Many think that this film, which was released by the NFB in 1967, is McLaren's masterpiece. 13 min., 22 sec.; b & w.

Passchendaele. Flemish village in Belgium, the scene of vicious fighting, in the most appalling mud, during the First World War. All four divisions of the CANADIAN CORPS stormed the German stronghold from 26 Oct. to 10 Nov. 1917, when it was finally taken, with a loss of 16,000 Canadian lives. The village was abandoned to the Germans in 1918.

Patents. Proprietary claims. Patents for inventions are issued under the provisions of the Patent Act. Applications for patents for inventions are addressed to the Commissioner of Patents, Bureau of Intellectual Property, Department of Consumer and Corporate Affairs, Ottawa.

Patrick, Lester (1883-1960). Hockey player. Born in Drummondville, Que., he became a

professional player with Brandon in 1903. He and his brother Frank Patrick moved to British Columbia, where they played, coached, managed and built artificial-ice arenas in Vancouver and Victoria, assembled teams, and formed leagues. In 1926 Lester became manager of the New York Rangers and led them to three STANLEY CUP championships. He later became vice-president of the New York Rangers and league governor. He was the father of two sons who also became professional hockey players. See also LESTER PATRICK TROPHY.

Patrie, La. A Sunday tabloid published in Montreal by the POWER CORPORATION. The title recalls the daily newspaper launched on 24 Feb. 1879 by Honoré Beaugrand and Israël Tarte, prominent Liberals, and an even earlier biweekly, published from 26 Sept. 1854 to 17 July 1858.

Patriote, Le. A 300-seat 'song-box' and theatre on Ste-Catherine St in Montreal. Established in 1965 on a shoestring by Yves Blais and Percival Broomfield, it provides a stage for promising young singers, monologists, and musicians. Virtually every Quebec 'pop' artist has appeared there for a fee of $5.00 a night. Robert CHARLEBOIS performed there in JOUAL and Michel TREMBLAY's *Les BELLES SOEURS* was first produced there.

Patriotes. The name given the followers of Louis-Joseph PAPINEAU and other radical reformers who fomented the REBELLION OF 1837 in Lower Canada (Quebec).

Patrons of Industry. A farmers' political party of the 1890s. The Patrons originated in the United States and entered Canada at the beginning of the 1890s, catching on with some rapidity and spreading into the West. The party platform called for rigid economy, tariff reform, simplification of the laws, and the abolition of the Senate. It ran a few federal candidates in 1891 and several more in 1896 without notable success. But in the Ontario election of 1894 it won 11 seats.

Patterson, Tom (b.1920). Founder of the STRATFORD FESTIVAL. Born in Stratford, Ont., and educated at the University of Toronto, he was consumed with the idea of creating an international theatre in his home town from the age of 14. Failing in his attempt to do this in 1946, he joined MACLEAN-HUNTER. In Jan. 1952, however, he succeeded in committing the Stratford city council to the scheme, which was greatly aided by the support of Tyrone GUTHRIE. The Stratford Shakespearian Festival—the middle word was dropped a few years later—was incorporated in Nov. 1952 and opened on 13 July 1953. Patterson was associated with the DAWSON CITY GOLD RUSH FESTIVAL and is now planning consultant for the Stratford Festival.

Paul, Robert (b.1937). Champion figure-skater. Born in Toronto, he joined forces in 1954 with Barbara WAGNER, with whom he won that year the Canadian pairs junior figure-skating championship. In 1957 they captured the Canadian, North American, and World titles in the space of sixteen days. They retained all three honours for three years. At the 1960 Winter Olympics at Squaw Valley, Calif., they won the gold medal and then retired from amateur competition to perform in touring ice-shows.

Paupers, The. The first Canadian rock group to land a major American recording contract. An electronic rock group that was formed in Toronto in 1965, it disbanded two years later when its first American-released album, *Magic People* (1967), flopped.

Pauta (b.1916). Eskimo sculptor and graphic artist at CAPE DORSET. His work often depicts graceful seals and massive polar bears. His 'dancing bear' motif is very popular; his stone cuts and copper engravings are widely collected. There is a limestone polar bear by Pauta in HIGH PARK, Toronto.

Pays, Le. French word for 'land' or 'country-side' that in French Canada has a strong secondary meaning of 'homeland' or 'country'. See also 'MON PAYS'.

Pays d'en haut. French phrase meaning 'up country'. In nineteenth-century Quebec it referred to the Canadian NORTHWEST; in twentieth-century Quebec it refers to the north-western part of the province, and in particular the deep forests of the Témiscamingue region.

Pays sauvages. French phrase meaning 'Indian country', the fur-trade area of the NORTHWEST.

PCO. See PRIVY COUNCIL OFFICE.

Peace Bridge. A 360-ft truss bridge that spans the Niagara R. between Fort Erie, Ont., and Buffalo, N.Y. It was dedicated in 1927 to peace between Canada and the United States.

Peace River. One of Canada's longest rivers. Part of the MACKENZIE RIVER system, it flows 1,195 mi. from the Rockies of central British Columbia northeast to join the Slave R. at the juncture of Lake Claire and southwest Lake Athabasca. The Peace is dammed for hydro-electric power in British Columbia, forming Williston Lake.

Peace River Country. The fertile valley of the Peace R. in northern Alberta and neighbouring British Columbia.

Peace Tower. One of the most symbolic of Canadian images, the Gothic-style tower rises above the Centre Block of the PARLIAMENT BUILDINGS and is the focal point of the PARLIAMENT HILL complex. Designed by J. A. PEARSON, it was begun in 1919—the cornerstone was laid by the Prince of Wales—and dedicated in 1927. It is 291 ft high and includes a carillon of 53 bells. The lower level of the tower is a Memorial Chamber with an Altar of Sacrifice upon which are displayed the Books of Remembrance, completed in 1926 and 1957. Inscribed in them are the names of the 111,542 Canadians who died on active service in the two world wars.

Peace-keeping, Canadian. See UNITED NATIONS.

Peameal bacon. Pickled but unsmoked pork loin rolled in cornmeal. This distinctive Canadian cut is sometimes confused with smoked back bacon, commonly referred to as CANADIAN BACON.

Pearl, Bert. See The HAPPY GANG.

Pearson, John A. (1867-1932). Architect. Born in England, he attended the University of Sheffield before coming to Toronto in 1888 to work with Darling & Curry. He joined Frank DARLING in the firm of Darling and Pearson. After Darling's death in 1923, Pearson continued the work of the firm and was responsible for the rebuilding of the Centre Block of the PARLIAMENT BUILDINGS in Ottawa (1916-24); for the PEACE TOWER (dedicated 1927); and, with York & Sawyer of New York, for the design of the main office of the Bank of Commerce (1929-31) at 25 King St W., Toronto.

Pearson, Lester (1897-1972). Fourteenth prime minister of Canada. Born in Newtonbrook, near Toronto, Lester Bowles Pearson was educated at the University of Toronto and—after service abroad in the First World War—at Oxford University. He lectured in history at Toronto from 1923 to 1927, when he entered the newly formed Department of External Affairs as a foreign-service officer; in 1941 he became Assistant Under-Secretary. The next year he moved to Washington to assist the head of the Canadian Legation there; it was designated an embassy in 1945 and Pearson became Canada's first ambassador to Washington. Made Under-Secretary of State for External Affairs in 1946, he was appointed Minister of External Affairs in 1948 and was elected to a seat in Parliament for Algoma East as a Liberal. He took an active part in the United Nations Organization—he was elected president of the General Assembly in 1952—and distinguished himself in its dealings with such crises as Palestine, Korea, and Suez. For his peacekeeping efforts in the Suez crisis of 1956, which led to the creation of a UN Emergency Force, he was awarded the Nobel Peace Prize in 1957, the year in which the Liberal government of Louis ST LAURENT was defeated and Pearson became leader of the Opposition. With a change in government in the election of 1963, he became prime minister. Accomplishments associated with his term of office are the adoption of a Canadian flag; the successful realization of the CENTENNIAL YEAR celebrations; the introduction of the CANADA PENSION PLAN, the CANADA ASSISTANCE PLAN, and MEDICARE; the UNIFICATION of the armed forces; and the establishment of the Royal Commission on BILINGUALISM AND BICULTURALISM. Pearson retired from political life in 1968. The wide use of his nickname 'Mike' by press and public alike was evidence of the affection felt for him.

Pearson, Peter (b.1938). Film director. Born in Toronto and a cousin of Lester B. PEARSON, he studied film-making in Rome and worked on CBC-TV'S THIS HOUR HAS SEVEN DAYS before joining the NATIONAL FILM BOARD. Since 1969 he has been a free-lance film-maker in Toronto. Among his best-known films are *Saul Alinsky Went to War* (with Donald BRITTAIN, 1968), *The* BEST DAMN FIDDLER FROM CALABOGIE TO KALADAR (1968), PAPERBACK HERO (1973), and *Only God Knows* (1974). For CBC-TV he produced such dramas as *The Insurance Man from Ingersoll* (1976).

Pearson College of the Pacific. A United World College near Victoria, B.C. Named after the late Lester B. PEARSON, this secondary school is the third in a world-wide series dedicated to promoting international understanding and fellowship. It opened in Sept. 1974. Students are selected on the basis of merit and are supported by scholarships. Approximately half are Canadian; the rest come from many countries of the world. Two earlier United World Colleges are in Glamorgan, South Wales, and Singapore, Malaysia. In addition, two are planned for Italy and West Germany in 1976-8.

Peck. Automobile manufactured from 1911 to 1913 by Peck Electric, Toronto. An electric vehicle, it came as a coupé or a roadster. The slogan of the company was 'Keeps Pecking'.

Peden, William John (Torchy) (b.1906). 'King of the Six-Day Cyclists'. Born in Vancouver, B.C., he represented Canada as a cyclist in the 1928 Olympic Games at Amsterdam. He toured Great Britain and Europe with success and, sometimes partnered with his brother Doug, was the featured winner in many North American six-day bicycle races. Before the craze passed he had established a world record for a paced mile, averaging 74 mi. an hour.

Pedlars. The name given to fur traders from Quebec and then to traders of the NORTH WEST COMPANY by officers of the HUDSON'S BAY COMPANY, who attracted Indians to their posts on Hudson Bay instead of going out to meet them, as the Nor'Westers did.

Peel, Paul (1860-92). Painter. Born in London, Ont., he studied painting in Philadelphia and Paris, where he settled. He was a rather facile academic painter who nevertheless produced several famous works, including AFTER THE BATH (1890, AGO) and *A Venetian Bather* (1889), the first nude to be exhibited publicly in Toronto.

Peg, The. A slang reference to Winnipeg.

Peggy's Cove. Small fishing community 27 mi. south of Halifax, N.S. A quaint rustic village with weatherbeaten frame houses and wharves, fishing boats in the harbour, and a lighthouse that stands above granite rocks, it is one of the most photographed and painted spots in Canada.

Peguis Publishers. A regional publishing company. Founded in Winnipeg in 1967 by Mary Scorer, a retired bookseller, it specializes in publishing books of interest to Manitobans. It was named after a nineteenth-century chief of the Saulteaux Indians.

Pélican. 44-gun French warship built in 1692. On 5 Sept. 1697, under the command of IBERVILLE, she defeated three HUDSON'S BAY COMPANY ships in a battle near the mouth of the Hayes R. in Hudson Bay. Her adversaries were the *Hampshire,* which was sunk; the *Hudson's Bay,* which was captured; and the *Dering,* which escaped. The *Pélican* was damaged by the *Hampshire*'s guns and had to be abandoned.

Pellan, Alfred (b.1906). Painter. Born in Quebec City, he began painting at 14 and sold a work to the National Gallery of Canada at 17. He won a provincial bursary in 1925 to study in Paris, where he became part of the art scene, and returned to Canada in 1940. Quebec and Montreal were greatly surprised by a retrospective show of his work that revealed him as French Canada's first modernist in paintings such as the cubist-inspired *Jeune Comédien* (c.1935, NGC) and *La Fenêtre ouverte* (1936, Hart House, University of Toronto), among other colourful paintings that were inspired by Parisian Surrealists, particularly Miró and Léger. As a teacher at Montreal's École des Beaux-Arts from 1940 to 1952, Pellan's advocacy of modernism provoked the authorities, while giving him a loyal student following. His greatest creative period began in the fifties with paintings of high technical accomplishment and originality in which calligraphic shapes, playfully but skilfully abstracted figures, Surrealist forms, and bright colours all played a part.

Pellegrini, Maria (b.1940). Soprano. Born in Pescara, Italy, she arrived in Ottawa in 1958 and in 1965 won recognition at the Metropolitan Opera Auditions. She has sung leading roles with opera companies in Europe and North America, as well as with the CANADIAN OPERA COMPANY, where she is particularly known for her Butterfly in *Madama Butterfly*.

Pelletier, Denise (1928-76). Actress. Born in St Jovite, Que., she first acted professionally with Les COMPAGNONS DE ST LAURENT and was a founding member of the THÉÂTRE DU NOUVEAU MONDE. In the 1950s she played Cécile in the PLOUFFE FAMILY, the longrunning CBC-TV series. An aristocratic actress of great range and power who performed with distinction in both French and English, she played opposite Jean GASCON in a memorable STRATFORD FESTIVAL production of Strindberg's *Dance of Death* in 1966. When she died she was appearing in a highly successful one-woman play, *The Divine Sarah*. Written especially for her by Montreal Playwright Jacques Beyderwellen, it was first performed at the NATIONAL ARTS CENTRE in Aug. 1975.

Pelletier, Gérard (b.1919). Former cabinet minister, Canadian ambassador to France. Educated at the Université de Montréal, he worked as a journalist for *Le* DEVOIR, *La Presse*, and on radio and TV. He entered federal politics in 1965 along with TRUDEAU and MARCHAND, the 'three wise men of Quebec', and was appointed to the cabinet as minister without portfolio in 1968. Later that year he was made Secretary of State, a position he held until 1972, when he became Minister of Communications. He was appointed ambassador in 1975.

Pelletier, Wilfrid (b.1896). Conductor. Born in Montreal, he studied music, piano, and opera in Montreal and Paris and embarked on a distinguished North American career based in New York. He joined the Metropolitan Opera Company as coach in 1917 and was assistant conductor from 1922 until 1932, when he became principal conductor. His career has included many associations with the musical life of Montreal—he was founder and conductor of Les Concerts Symphoniques de Montréal (1934-8)—Quebec City, and indeed of the province. The concert hall at PLACES DES ARTS, Montreal, bears the name Salle Wilfrid-Pelletier. He married the celebrated contralto Rose Bampton in 1937.

Peltrie, Marie-Madeleine de la (1603-71). Secular foundress of the URSULINES of Quebec. With MARIE DE L'INCARNATION, among others, she sailed for Quebec in 1639, on a vessel she chartered. She was buried in the Ursuline chapel.

Pemmican. Preserved buffalo or caribou meat, food staple of the fur trade and the Plains Indians. It was prepared by pounding strips of dried meat with animal fat and berries. The name 'pemmican' is Cree.

Penfield, Wilder (1891-1976). Surgeon and author. Born in Spokane, Wash., he studied medicine at Princeton University and Oxford. He settled in Montreal in 1928 as professor of neurology and neurosurgery at McGill University. He established the Montreal Neurological Institute and served as its director from 1934 until his retirement in 1960. Penfield's early studies of epilepsy encouraged him to undertake a systematic mapping of the human brain, work that was continued by the Neurological Institute, which became world famous. He was also the first director of the VANIER INSTITUTE OF THE FAMILY. His historical novels—*No Other Gods* (1954), the story of Moses, and *The Torch* (1960), the story of Hippocrates—found a wide readership. *The Second Career* (1964) is a collection of essays that point out the advantages of preparing for retirement with another career in mind. In *Second Thoughts* (1970) the much-honoured physician and scientist expressed his views 'on science and man in a conflicting world'.

Penitentiaries. Correctional institutions operated by the federal government under the SOLICITOR GENERAL, in which sentences of from two years to life imprisonment are served. What follows is a regionally arranged list of the larger penitentiaries, with locations, security arrangements (maximum or medium), and approximate prison populations.

Penitentiaries

Atlantic. Dorchester, Dorchester, N.B., max., 450; Springhill, Springhill, N.S., med., 432.

Quebec. Archambault, Ste-Anne-des-Plaines, max., 429; Cowansville, Cowansville, med., 432; Leclerc, Ville de Laval, med., 484.

Ontario. Collins Bay, Kingston, med., 400; Joyceville, Kingston, med., 450; Millhaven, max., 429; Warkworth, Campbellford, med., 432.

Prairies. Stony Mountain, Stony Mountain, Man., med., 379; Saskatchewan Penitentiary, Prince Albert, Sask., max., 407; Drumheller, Alta., med., 432.

Pacific. British Columbia Penitentiary, New Westminster, max., 570; Matsqui, Abbotsford, med., 337.

The federal government also operates Community Correctional Centres that act as 'half-way houses' for prisoners completing their sentences. What follows is a regionally arranged list of these centres (which have inmate populations ranging from 6 to 60), with locations.

Atlantic. Carleton, Halifax, N.S.; The Parr Town, Saint John, N.B.

Quebec. St Hubert, Montreal; Duvernay, Ville de Laval.

Ontario. King St (women), Toronto; Montgomery, Toronto; Portsmouth, Kingston.

Prairies. Altadore, Calgary, Alta; Grierson, Edmonton, Alta; Osborne, Winnipeg, Man.; Oskana, Regina, Sask.; Scarboro, Calgary, Alta.

Pacific. Burrard, Vancouver; Pandora, Victoria; Robson, Vancouver.

Penticton V's. A senior amateur hockey team from Penticton, B.C. It won the ALLAN CUP in 1954 and, in Feb. 1955, at Krefeld, West Germany, defeated the Soviet national team 5-0, thereby winning the World Hockey Championship. The hard-hitting team was led by the three Warwick brothers—Bill, Dick, and Grant—who were former professionals.

Pentland, Barbara (b.1912). Composer. Born in Winnipeg, Man., she began composing as a child and later studied in Paris and at the Juilliard Graduate School, New York. She has taught at the Royal Conservatory of Music, Toronto, and the University of British Columbia. A prolific composer, she works with avant-garde modes, including serial music, and has written much for piano and chamber groups as well as orchestral works and songs.

People of the Deer. Farley MOWAT's first book, published in 1952. It is an eloquent expression of indignation at the plight of the cari-

bou-hunting aborigines of the Barren Lands whose way of life was disrupted by contact with white civilization.

Pépin, (Jean-Josephat) Clermont (b.1926). Composer. Born in Saint-Georges-de-Beauce, Que., he was a child prodigy. He studied with Claude CHAMPAGNE in Montreal, at the Curtis Institute of Music in Philadelphia, the Royal Conservatory of Music, Toronto, and in Paris. In 1955 he was appointed to the Montreal Conservatoire to teach composition and was director from 1967 to 1972. Though his choral, orchestral, and chamber works use contemporary techniques, they are generally associated with the classical tradition of music. Pépin has composed theatrical scores for the Théâtre-Club in Montreal and the Théâtre du Nouveau Monde. He was national president of Les Jeunesses Musicales du Canada from 1969 to 1972.

Péquiste. Member of the separatist PARTI QUÉBÉCOIS.

Percé Rock. Island off the eastern tip of the Gaspé Peninsula, named by Samuel de CHAMPLAIN in 1607 on his first voyage to Canada. The limestone rock is 1,500 ft long, 288 ft high, and is pierced (*percé*) by a central arch-shaped opening 60 ft high and 100 ft wide. A bird sanctuary since 1919, it is a popular tourist attraction.

Père Chopin, Le. Feature film produced in Quebec in 1944. Directed by Fedor Ozep of Renaissance Films and released by France-Film, it is a comedy about a rich brother and a poor brother who emigrate from France to Quebec. Its importance lies in the fact that it was the first of 18 feature films produced in Montreal between 1944 and 1954 starring French-Canadian radio talent that eventually moved to television—which ended this particular movie boom. 108 min., b & w.

Perkins, Simeon (1735-1812). Shipbuilder and diarist. Born in Norwich, Conn., he immigrated to Liverpool, N.S., in 1762. He sat in the House of Assembly from 1765 to 1799 and was also a judge of probate. His diary, begun in 1766 and having a wealth of information about life in the period, was published by the Champlain Society as *The Diary of Simeon Perkins, 1766-90* (3 vols, 1948-61). It describes the building of his house, also begun in 1766, which still stands; with eighteenth-century furnishings, it is a museum owned by the Nova Scotia government.

Permafrost. Subsoil and rock that remain below 0°C for longer than one year, usually beneath a layer of thawing topsoil. Continuous permafrost never rises above −5°C and occurs throughout the tundra; discontinuous permafrost occurs in a wide band looping into the provinces and extending as far south as the southern end of James Bay. Coined in 1943, it combines part of the word *perma*nent and *frost*.

Perrault, Pierre (b.1927). Film director. Born in Montreal, he is a poet, dramatist, and lawyer whose films are social and cultural documents of the Québécois. He wrote the commentary for the 13-part series *Au pays de Neuve-France*, directed by René Bonnière for CBC-TV in 1959-60. He directed *Pour la suite du monde* (see The MOON TRAP) (with Michel BRAULT, 1963), *Le Règne du jour* (1966), *Les Voitures d'eau* (1969), *Un Pays sans bon sens* (1970), *L'Acadie, L'Acadie* (with Michel Brault, 1971), and *Un Royaume vous attend* (1975). He won a Governor General's Award for his collections of poetry: *Au Coeur de la rose* (1964) and *Chouennes* (1975).

Persons case. Celebrated decision of the Privy Council of Great Britain that women are persons and are eligible to be summoned to the Senate. Five women from Alberta—Emily MURPHY, Nellie McCLUNG, Louise McKinney, Irene Parlby, and Henrietta Edwards—petitioned the Supreme Court of Canada and then the Privy Council of Great Britain for a ruling on Section 24 of the BNA ACT: 'The Governor General shall . . . summon qualified persons to the Senate.' The landmark decision—'the word persons includes members of the male and female sex'—was rendered on 18 Oct. 1929 by Lord Chancellor Sankey. The first woman appointed to the Senate was Cairine Wilson in 1930.

Perspectives. See WEEKEND MAGAZINE.

Perth County Conspiracy. A pop musical group from Perth Co., Ont. Composed of young people who live communally and perform at rock concerts and appear on radio and television, it was formed in 1968 by Cedric Smith, a singer, writer, composer, and actor. The full name of the lively group is 'The Perth County Conspiracy (does not exist)'.

Peter Dwyer Scholarships. Series of scholarships given annually to the most promising students enrolled in the NATIONAL BALLET SCHOOL and the NATIONAL THEATRE SCHOOL. Totalling $10,000, they were established in 1973 by the CANADA COUNCIL to honour its former director, the late Peter M. DWYER.

'Peter Emberly'. A tragic ballad popular in lumber camps in eastern Canada and the eastern United States. It is the true story of a young man who left his native Prince Edward Island to work in the woods of the Miramichi R. region of New Brunswick and was fatally injured when struck by falling logs. This lament was written shortly after his death in 1881 by the New Brunswick balladeer John Calhoun.

Peter Jackson Trophy. An award to the winner of the Men's Annual Canadian Open Golf Championship in July of each year. First presented by Imperial Tobacco Limited in 1971, it consists of an Eskimo sculpture and a cheque for $40,000.

Peter Martin Associates. Book publishers. It was founded in Toronto in 1965 by Peter and Carol Martin as an outgrowth of their READER'S CLUB OF CANADA. PMA was a founding member of the Independent Publishers' Association (see ASSOCIATION OF CANADIAN PUBLISHERS), of which Peter Martin was the first president in 1971.

Peter Puck. A cartoon character created by the Toronto sportswriter and broadcaster Brian McFarlane. Drawn by the Hanna-Barbera Studios, he first appeared to teach hockey basics and safety tips to young hockey fans as an intermission feature on CBC-TV'S HOCKEY NIGHT IN CANADA in the fall of 1975. McFarlane produced a book about him, *Peter Puck*, in 1975.

Peterborough canoe. World-famous canoe constructed with wooden planks. Patterned after Indian birchbark canoes, 'Peterboroughs' were first built in 1870 in Peterborough, Ont., by the Peterborough Canoe Company, which flourished from 1883 to 1961.

Peterborough Petroglyphs. Prehistoric rock-carvings at a secluded site 34 mi. north of Peterborough, Ont. A large outcropping of crystalline limestone shows over 900 images of unknown significance, believed to be carved by Algonkian Indians between A.D. 900 and 1400. The carvings were discovered in 1954 and have been part of the Petroglyphs Provincial Park since 1972.

Peterson, Len (b.1917). Playwright. Born in Regina, Sask., the Toronto-based writer is best known for his many CBC Radio plays and adaptations. He anticipated many theatre-of-the-absurd techniques with his half-hour radio play BURLAP BAGS, produced in 1946 and published in 1972. His play about retribution among the Eskimos, *The Great Hunter*, was originally produced by the Arts Theatre in Toronto in Nov. 1960, published in 1967, and broadcast on CBC STAGE on 18 and 25 Feb. 1968. He wrote ALL ABOUT US for the CANADIAN PLAYERS' tour of 1964.

Peterson, Oscar (b.1925). Jazz pianist. Born in Montreal and discovered on the Ken Sobel Amateur Hour, he has recorded and worked with many of the great names of jazz. He is known for his dazzling technique on the piano and has been one of the world's reigning jazz kings since the 1950s. There have been various Oscar Peterson Trios, but the one best remembered played from 1959 to 1965 and was composed of Peterson on the piano, Ray Brown on bass, and Ed Thigpen on drums.

Peterson, Roy (b.1936). Cartoonist. Born in Winnipeg, Man., he began work as a freelance cartoonist in 1962. Besides drawing editorial cartoons for the *Vancouver Sun*, he has illustrated articles in Canadian and international magazines such as *Maclean's*, the *New York Times*, and the *Spectator* and *Punch* in England. He placed first in the 1973 International Salon of Cartoons and illustrated *Frog Fables and Beaver Tales* (1973) and *The Day of the Glorious Revolution* (1974), with texts by Stanley BURKE.

Petit Journal, Le. A Sunday tabloid published in French in Montreal since 1926. It treats local news events sensationally and artistic events intelligently. Its editor is the poet André MAJOR and its owner is the POWER CORPORATION.

Petit Nord, Le. French name for the FRENCH SHORE of Newfoundland.

'Petit rocher'. A French-Canadian folksong popular among the VOYAGEURS. Called the first song about a Canadian incident, 'Little Rock' is the lament of Jean Cadieux, who succeeded in saving his family from an Iroquois attack on the Ottawa R. in 1709. The story goes that the trapper, although mortally wounded, lived long enough to dig his own grave and write his lament in his own blood on a piece of birchbark.

Petite Aurore l'Enfant Martyre, La. An immensely popular Quebec film produced in 1952. Directed by Jean-Yves Bigras and produced by the Alliance Cinématographique Canadienne, it was based on Émile Asselin's play of the same name and starred Yvonne LaFlamme, Lucie Mitchell, and Paul Desmarteaux. It is about an actual incident, the turn-of-the-century murder trial of a psychotic mother whose hatred of her daughter led her to torture and murder. It concentrates on the evil mother, the ineffectual father, and a priest who discovers the evil in time to administer the last sacrament to the dying daughter. 104 min., b. & w.

Petro-Canada. Crown corporation formed in Calgary in 1975 to develop petroleum and oversee Canada's oil needs. It is commonly known as Petrocan.

Petun. See IROQUOIAN.

Pflug, Christiane (1936-72). Painter. She was born in Berlin and came to Toronto in 1959. Influenced by the Dutch realists, she infused fragments of her surroundings with sad and lonely mystery, as in *Kitchen Door with Esther* (1965), a large canvas in which a small girl sits on a doorstep in front of a paradisial garden. She took her own life.

PFRA. See Department of REGIONAL ECONOMIC EXPANSION.

PGE. Abbreviation of the Pacific Great Eastern, now the BRITISH COLUMBIA RAILWAY.

Phantom bank notes. Fraudulent bills issued during the early part of the nineteenth century. They were imprinted with the names of fictitious institutions, like 'Canadian Banking Company' and 'The Commercial Bank of Fort Erie'—names that suggested those of well-established Canadian chartered banks. Usually printed in New York, the notes were accepted by unsuspecting Americans and Canadians and are avidly collected today.

Phelps, Arthur L. (1888-1970). Educator and broadcaster. Born in Columbus, Durham Co., and raised in Lindsay, Ont., he taught English literature at United College, Winnipeg (1921-45), and at McGill University (1947-53). He began broadcasting on CBC Radio in Winnipeg in 1935 and, from 1945 to 1947, was head of the CBC International Service. For 15 years his was the voice of CBC Radio's NEIGHBOURLY NEWS.

Phillips, Nathan. See TORONTO CITY HALL.

Phips, Sir William (1651-95). American ship's captain. Born in Woolwich (Maine), he was sent by Massachusetts against the French settlements in Acadia in 1690 and took PORT ROYAL. In October of that year he arrived in the St Lawrence to take Quebec. FRONTENAC, the governor, rejected his summons to surrender, which Phips's bombardment failed to effect; he left Quebec a week after his arrival. He later became the first governor of Massachusetts.

Pickering Generating Station. Nuclear power plant in Pickering, Ont. Opened in 1971, it operates on natural uranium fuel. The total capacity of 2.16 million kilowatts produces enough electricity to supply more than one million homes.

Pickersgill, John Whitney (b.1905). Civil servant, cabinet minister, and author. Educated at the University of Manitoba and at Oxford, he entered the Department of External Affairs as a civil servant in 1937 but was seconded to the office of the prime minister and worked closely with Mackenzie KING and subsequently Louis ST LAURENT. In 1953 he entered federal politics and was appointed Secretary of State. He held several portfolios in subsequent Liberal administrations, the last being Minister of Transport. In 1967 he left federal politics and was appointed President of the Canadian Transport Commission, retiring in 1972. King had appointed him his literary executor, and Pickersgill edited four volumes of his diaries for publication under the title *The Mackenzie King Record* (1960-70). His memoirs appeared in 1975.

Pickford, Mary (b.1893). Film star. Born Gladys Mary Smith in Toronto, she made her début at the age of five on the stage of the Princess Theatre. Under the guidance of her widowed mother, the child actress joined David Belasco, who changed her name and gave her work on Broadway in 1907. Introduced to films by D. W. Griffith, she became the most popular movie actress of her day—one of the most famous of all stars—appearing in such silent films as *Pollyana* (1919) and *Little Annie Rooney* (1925), and in a few talkies. The wife of Douglas Fairbanks and then of Buddy Rogers, 'America's Sweetheart' lives in seclusion at 'Pickfair' in Hollywood, still a Canadian citizen. On 27 May 1973 a plaque marking the site of her childhood home, now occupied by the Hospital for Sick Children, was unveiled in the presence of her husband.

Pickthall, Marjorie. (1883-1922). Poet and novelist. Born in Gunnersbury, Eng., she was brought to Toronto as a child and educated at Bishop Strachan School; she worked for a time in the library of Victoria College, University of Toronto. She lived in England from 1912 to 1919 but spent her last years in Vancouver. Beginning with *A Drift of Pinions* (1913), she published several collections of delicate, sometimes moving verse, of which 'Père Lalement', 'Resurgam', and 'Quiet' are three effective examples. She also wrote seven works of fiction—children's novels, historical romances, and collections of

stories. Lorne PIERCE edited the *Selected Poems of Marjorie Pickthall* (1957).

Picture Gallery of Canadian History, The. A three-volume set of historical drawings by C. W. JEFFERYS. In over 2,000 pen-and-ink drawings Jefferys depicted Eskimo, Indian, French, and British artifacts, as well as carefully researched reconstructions of important incidents in Canadian history. These scenes became familiar to generations of students through wide reproduction in history texts. The volumes were published by the Ryerson Press: *Volume I (Discovery to 1763)* in 1942; *Volume II (1763 to 1830)* in 1945; *Volume III (1830 to 1900)* in 1950.

Picture Loan Society. Co-operative artistic venture. Financed by Douglas DUNCAN, it was founded by Duncan and Rick Kettle, Erma Lennox, Norah McCullough, Gordon Macnamara, Pegi Nicol, and Gordon Webber to assist artists by means of picture rentals and exhibitions. It opened in Toronto on 14 Nov. 1936 and Duncan ran it until his death in 1968.

Pierce, Lorne (1890-1961). 'The dean of Canadian publishing'. Born in Delta, Ont., and educated at Queen's University, he was a Doctor of Divinity from the Montreal Theological College. A long-time editor of The RYERSON PRESS (1920-59), he initiated the MAKERS OF CANADIAN LITERATURE series and the 'Canadian Books of Prose and Verse'. He maintained a correspondence and friendship with many leading writers of his generation and donated his library and papers to Queen's University. At the age of 36 he donated the LORNE PIERCE MEDAL to the ROYAL SOCIETY OF CANADA to be awarded for distinguished service to Canadian literature. Among the works he edited were *Canadian Poetry in English* (1954) with Bliss CARMAN and V. B. Rhodenizer. His essay *A Canadian Nation* (1960) foresaw a distinct culture arising from the intermingling of the best ethnic strains that make up Canadian society. Pierce's wife, Edith Chown, was a noted collector of Canadian glass.

Pierre and His People. A collection of romantic and melodramatic short stories of the Canadian Northwest by Sir Gilbert PARKER published in 1882. Immensely successful, it went through 27 printings and was the basis of a Hollywood film.

Pierre Berton Show, The. A 30-minute weekly television series hosted by Pierre BERTON. It originated from Toronto and other world centres and had Berton interviewing Canadian and internationally known personalities. It was produced by Elsa FRANKLIN and syndicated by Screen Gems (Canada) Ltd from 1962 to 1973. *The Cool Crazy Committed World of the Sixties: Twenty-One Television Encounters* (1966), edited by Berton, was based on the show, which was dubbed 'the program that comes to you from the major capitals of the world'.

Pierre le Canadien. The name given Peter Dmytruk, a young flier of Ukrainian ancestry from Wynyard, Sask., murdered by the Germans at Martres-de-Veyre, France, on 10 Dec. 1943. Since 1972 the French village and Canadian town have been twinned.

Pig War. War almost broke out between Britain and the United States in 1859 over the ownership of San Juan Island in the Straits of Georgia, lying between Vancouver Island and the mainland, on which both sides had settled people and animals in token possession. When an American farmer shot a British pig that had invaded his potato patch, war might actually have occurred had both Britain and the United States not been involved in other conflicts. Only in 1871 did they submit to the arbitration of Emperor Wilhelm I of Germany, who ceded San Juan to the United States.

Pile o'Bones. A translation of *Wascana*. It was the original name of REGINA, Sask., and refers to a pile of buffalo bones near Wascana Creek.

Pilgrims of the Wild. A nature chronicle by GREY OWL, published in 1934. It is a humorous and touching description of his and his wife's experiences with the beaver and of how he turned from hunting it to protecting it.

Pilon, Jean-Guy (b.1930). Quebec poet. Born at Saint-Polycarpe, Que., he graduated in law from the Université de Montréal in 1954 and is a producer for Radio-Canada and a founding editor of *Liberté*. Known as a spokesman for Quebec poetry at international conferences, especially in the world of *francophonie*, he co-edited with Eli MANDEL *Poetry 62/Poésie 62* (1961). A selection of his frequently allusive yet moving verse, *Comme Eau retenue: poèmes 1954-1963*, was published in 1970.

Pine, Jack. Species of cone-bearing evergreen tree. Found in the BOREAL FOREST REGION, the Jack pine (*P. Banksiana Lamb.*) is often considered the characteristic Canadian pine or fir tree (the MAPLE tree performing the same function for deciduous trees). See also *The* JACK PINE by Tom Thomson.

'Pine-clad hills'. Phrase evocative of Newfoundland from the provincial anthem, 'Ode to Newfoundland', written by Sir Cavendish Boyle while serving as governor from 1901 to 1904.

Pine Hill Divinity Hall. The theological college of the United Church of Canada in the Atlantic Provinces, it was formed by the amalgamation of the Presbyterian College at Halifax, N.S., and the Theological Department of MOUNT ALLISON UNIVERSITY at Sackville, N.B., in 1926.

Pine Point Mines Ltd. The owner and developer of lead-zinc mines on the south shore of Great Slave Lake in the Northwest Territories. Incorporated in 1951, the company went into production in 1965 and has expanded through the development of mineral discoveries nearby. Pine Point is controlled by COMINCO LTD, a major metal producer based at Trail, B.C.

Pine Tree Line. A system of 30 warning, tracking, and interceptor stations constructed and maintained by Canada and the United States. Part of a continental radar defence system, it straddles the 49th parallel. It was first announced by an exchange of notes on 1 Aug. 1951 and was completed in 1954. See also DEW LINE.

Pingoes. Mounds of ice found in Arctic areas. Formed by the pressure of expanding ice in the subsoil, they are sometimes as high as 150 ft.

Pink-eye. See CALGARY RED-EYE.

Pinsent, Gordon (b.1930). Actor and writer. Born in Grand Falls, Nfld, he left for the mainland in 1948 and acted with the MANITOBA THEATRE CENTRE. In 1959 he settled in Toronto, where he married the actress Charmion King. He came to national attention playing the lead in QUENTIN DURGENS, M.P. (1966). He also appeared in the Hollywood films *Colossus: The Forbin Project* (1969) and *The Thomas Crown Affair* (1968). He wrote and starred in *The* ROWDYMAN (1972), a successful independent feature film that drew on his Newfoundland youth. A novel based on the film was published in 1974, and a second novel *John and the Missus*, was published in 1975 and produced as a play at the NEPTUNE THEATRE in 1976.

Pipe. A measure of distance used by the VOYAGEURS. The term derived from the practice of stopping at roughly two-hour intervals for a rest and a smoke. See also POSE.

Pipeline, Natural gas. See MACKENZIE VALLEY PIPELINE.

Pipeline Debate. A debate in the House of Commons in May 1956 about the funding of a pipeline, which developed into a controversy about parliamentary procedure. Trans-Canada Pipelines Ltd, a company controlled by American financial interests, was given a charter to construct a pipeline to take surplus natural gas for export from Alberta to Montreal by an all-Canadian route north of the Great Lakes. The Liberal government under Louis ST LAURENT wanted the project completed before the next general election. In late April 1956 the company announced that it could not raise the $80 million needed to complete the line from Alberta to Winnipeg. The government was prepared to lend the money under security, but the company had to have it by 7 June if it was to meet its construction deadline. C. D. HOWE introduced the bill to the House of Commons on 13 May; the bill would have to be passed by the Commons on 31 May and by the Senate by 1 June to receive Royal Assent by 7 June. In order to keep the debate in the Commons within the 14 days available, the government announced that it would impose CLOSURE at each stage of debate on the bill. This was only the second time a Liberal government had ever imposed closure, and never before in parliamentary history had closure been announced before debate had begun. Uproar broke out in the House of Commons at every reading of the bill. It was finally passed by the Commons on 1 June, with the assistance of the Speaker, who appeared to be favouring the Liberals, and the company received the money by the deadline. But 'the longest pipeline in the world' was not completed on schedule because a steel strike in the U.S. held up delivery of the pipe. The Liberals were defeated, after 22 years in power, in the election of 1957.

Pitcher plant. Any of several carnivorous plants with leaves adapted for trapping insects, the common North American species being the sidesaddle plant of central and eastern distribution. The leaves are modified to form pitcher-like structures in which rainwater collects and that attract insects. An insect entering the pitcher becomes trapped by its lining of downward-slanting bristles, drowns, and is digested. The plant bears a single dull red flower and has been the floral emblem of Newfoundland since 1954.

Pitseolak. See Pitseolak ASHOONA.

Pitseolak, Peter (1900-73). Eskimo sculptor, photographer, and graphic artist at CAPE DOR-SET. His carvings are realistic and depict a variety of subjects, including animals and figures. He made drawings of the fantasy or spirit world but most of his graphics depict legends. His photographs illustrate *People From Our Side* (1975), his life story woven into a history of Cape Dorset, told to Dorothy Eber by the artist.

Place. French word for 'place' or 'square', as in PLACE DES ARTS.

Place Bonaventure. Commercial and exhibition area in Montreal. Opened in 1967 as the second-largest commercial establishment in the world, it has 3 million sq. ft of offices, entertainment centres, exhibition halls, and 'indoor streets' that connect it underground with PLACE VILLE MARIE. It was designed by Raymond Affleck of Arcop Associates.

Place d'Armes. Historic square in the heart of OLD MONTREAL. On this site, where MAISON-NEUVE founded the colony of Ville-Marie, stands a monument to him and his companions by Louis-Philippe HÉBERT. NOTRE-DAME-DE-MONTRÉAL, built in 1824-8, and the Seminary of St-Sulpice, the oldest building in Montreal, both face Place d'Armes.

Place des Arts. Arts centre in Montreal. Opened in 1965, it has three main buildings: the Salle Wilfrid-PELLETIER, a 3,000-seat concert hall; the 1,300-seat Théâtre Maisonneuve; and the smaller Théâtre Port-Royal. The complex was designed by Raymond Affleck and decorated by some of Quebec's most talented artists. L'Opéra du Québec and Les GRANDS BALLETS CANADIENS perform there.

Place to Stand, A. One of the great promotional films of all time, it celebrates the beauty and variety of life in Ontario. It was produced, directed, photographed, and edited by Christopher CHAPMAN; the executive producer was David Mackay; and its catchy theme song, 'ONTAR-I-AR-I-AR-IO', became popular in its own right. A 70-mm colour film, it made spectacular use of the multi-image technique, compressing over 100 viewing hours into 17½ minutes. It was first shown at the Ontario Pavilion at EXPO 67 and won numerous prizes, including an Academy Award and a CANADIAN FILM AWARD.

Place Ville Marie. Largest integrated office and shopping complex in North America, located in downtown Montreal. Designed by I. Mario Pei for William Zeckendorf and the Royal Bank of Canada, it opened in 1962 on a 7-acre site at a cost of $105 million. Its plaza is three times as large as New York's Rocke-

Place Ville Marie

feller Plaza, and the entire complex contains more rental space than the Empire State Building. Its most prominent feature is the 42-storey cruciform Royal Bank building. Under the plaza are stores, theatres, movie houses, restaurants, and walkways to the Queen Elizabeth Hotel and the railway station. Its daytime 'population' is 25,000.

Plains. A stretch of open land, as the PLAINS OF ABRAHAM; a vast stretch of level land, as the PRAIRIES.

Plains Cree. See CREE.

Plains Indians. Collective name for the several tribes of Indians inhabiting the PRAIRIES, such as the Assiniboine, Blackfoot, Cree, etc.

Plains of Abraham. A plain that stretches to the west of Quebec, beyond the old walls. Named after Abraham Martin (1589-1664), a ship's pilot, to whom the land was granted in two parcels in 1635 and 1645 (it was sold to the Ursulines in 1667), the area was the scene of one of the famous battles of history on 13 Sept. 1759, when British forces under WOLFE defeated French forces under MONTCALM, and of the Battle of SAINTE-FOY on 28 Apr. 1760, when French forces under the duc de LÉVIS defeated the British under James MURRAY, causing them to retire to Quebec; they were saved by the arrival of the British fleet. The site has been designated a National Historic Park. See also WOLFE'S COVE.

Plamondon, Antoine Sebastien (1802-95). Early Quebec artist. Born near Quebec City, he was apprenticed to Joseph LÉGARÉ and then studied classical portrait painting in Paris, returning in 1830 to Quebec, where he opened a studio. His most popular paintings—among the finest of the period in Canada—are one of a series of young nuns, *Soeur Saint-Alphonse* (1841, NGC), and a genre painting, *La Chasse aux tourtes* (1853, AGO), a study of three boys with a rifle and dead pigeons.

Plano culture. See CLOVIS CULTURE.

Platform for the Arts. Touring office established in Toronto in 1974 to arrange national tours for members of the LEAGUE OF CANADIAN POETS, WRITERS' UNION OF CANADA, and PLAYWRIGHTS CO-OP.

Plattsburg, Battle of. An engagement in the WAR OF 1812. On 11 Sept. 1814 a large British force under Sir George Prevost was badly defeated by a smaller American force at Plattsburg, N.Y., on the western shore of Lake Champlain. In a naval engagement

some days later (often called the Battle of Lake Champlain), Capt. George Downie, commanding the British flotilla, was defeated by Cmdre Thomas Macdonough. Downie lost his life.

Plaunt, Alan B. See CANADIAN RADIO LEAGUE.

Playhouse, The. A 763-seat multi-purpose theatre built in 1964 in Fredericton, N.B., by Lord BEAVERBROOK. After extensive design renovations by Arcop Associates of Montreal in 1971, it re-opened in May 1972 and has hosted a variety of productions, from performances by the NATIONAL BALLET OF CANADA and the CANADIAN OPERA COMPANY to rock music concerts and evangelical meetings. Since 1969 it has been the home of Theatre New Brunswick, under the artistic direction of Walter Learning. It is funded by the Beaverbrook Canadian Foundation.

Playhouse Theatre. Regional theatrical group formed in Vancouver in 1962. Its first production, Brendan Behan's *The Hostage*, was mounted in 1962 in the 647-seat Queen Elizabeth Playhouse. Malcolm Black became its first artistic director in 1963.

Playwrights Co-op. Non-profit publisher and agent for Canadian playwrights. Inexpensive editions of original drama scripts were issued as early as 1969, using funds provided by LOCAL INITIATIVE PROGRAM grants, but it was not until the Co-op was incorporated in Jan. 1972 by Tom HENDRY, Carol BOLT, and Daryl Sharp that publication began in earnest. It is now funded by various arts councils, and has almost 200 new plays in print.

Pleistocene epoch. Geological epoch that began one million years ago and ended 10,000 years ago. During this time four glacial advances and retreats took place and almost all of Canada was covered by ice.

Plouffe, Les. A popular novel by Roger LEMELIN published in French in 1948. Set in Lower Town, a working-class district of Quebec City, during the Second World War, it dramatized the domestic life of the Plouffe family. *Les Plouffe* was translated into English by Mary Finch and published as *The PLOUFFE FAMILY* (1950), which gave the name to a CBC-TV serial.

Plouffe Family, The. A popular CBC-TV series about a poor family in Quebec City's Lower Town. The characters were based by Roger LEMELIN on the characters in his novel *Les PLOUFFE* (1948). Long popular on the French-language radio network and a hit on French-language television—the characters were dubbed 'the first family of Quebec television'—'Les Plouffe' was the first original dramatic series by a Canadian author on Canadian television. An English-language version, 'The Plouffe Family', was seen on CBC-TV from 4 Oct. 1954 to 19 June 1959. It appeared concurrently with the French series and was played by the same cast, which included Amanda Alarie and Paul Guevremont as M. and Mme Plouffe, with Émile Genest, Jean-Louis ROUX, Janine Mignolet, and Denise PELLETIER as their children. Production in the Montreal studios was under Jean-Paul Fugère.

Plummer, Christopher (b.1929). Actor. Born in Toronto and raised in Senneville, Que., he made his stage début in Ottawa at the age of 17 and acted with the Montreal Repertory Theatre. He was associated with the JUPITER THEATRE in 1952-3 and with the STRATFORD FESTIVAL for five seasons in the fifties and sixties. Now a star in London and Broadway plays and in films, he has been described as 'like aluminum: light but metallic'.

PMO. Office of the Prime Minister. It is a secretariat, under the PRIVY COUNCIL OFFICE, responsible for providing assistance to the prime minister by arranging his appointments, releasing his public statements, and providing general secretarial assistance.

P/O. Official abbreviation of Pilot Officer.

Poets' Corner of Canada. A reference to FREDERICTON in general and to the University of New Brunswick in particular, both being associated with a group of poets. The idea of a monument to poets originated with Dr Alfred G. Bailey, of the university, himself a poet, who proposed it to Dr J.C. Webster, then chairman of the Historic Sites and Monuments Board of Canada. The phrase was Dr Webster's and appears on a bronze plaque in front of the Harriet Irving Library on the UNB campus, unveiled on 15 May 1947. The poets, who were born in the area and attended UNB, are Bliss CARMAN, Sir Charles G.D. ROBERTS, and Francis Joseph Sherman. The ashes of the first and the bodies of the second two are buried at Forest Hill Cemetery, Fredericton.

Poets of the Sixties. A group of poets born between 1860 and 1862. It includes Bliss CARMAN, Archibald LAMPMAN, Sir Charles G.D. ROBERTS, and Duncan Campbell SCOTT. Their work appears in *Poets of the Confederation* (1960), edited by Malcolm Ross.

Pogey. Hobo slang for 'workhouse', with the specific meanings in Canada since the DEPRESSION of a hostel for indigents; a welfare office; food and clothing, etc., for the indigent; unemployment insurance payments.

Pogue carburetor. A device to save gasoline and revolutionize the automobile industry. Charles N. Pogue of Winnipeg publicly claimed in Jan. 1936 that he had invented an automobile carburetor that would drive a car 200 mi. on a single gallon of gasoline; the device preheated and vapourized the fuel before it entered the engine cylinders. That August he claimed his working models had been stolen from his workshop, but it was rumoured that he had been 'bought off' by major oil interests.

Point blanket. Popular woollen blanket sold by the HUDSON'S BAY COMPANY since 1779. In the past the blue or red marks or 'points' woven into the fabric signified the exchange value of the blanket in terms of beaver skins. Today the points indicate the sizes the blankets come in: 2 points (54 by 72 in.), 3½ points (60 by 86 in.), 4 points (72 by 90 in.), and 6 points (90 by 100 in.).

Point Frederick. Peninsula in the St Lawrence R. just east of Kingston, Ont., comprising the grounds of the ROYAL MILITARY COLLEGE OF CANADA.

Point Pelee. The southernmost tip of Canada's mainland, a long thin stretch of sand and shifting shoal extending into Lake Erie from southwestern Ontario. It is at the same latitude as northern California. Point Pelee National Park, established in 1918, covers 6 sq. mi. of marsh, forest, and beach and is a birdwatcher's paradise, the site of two annual bird migration flyaways. It is the smallest of the national parks. See also the most SOUTHERLY POINT.

.08%. A formula commonly used to describe the offence of driving with more than .08% alcohol content in the blood. Section 236 of the CRIMINAL CODE OF CANADA reads: 'Every one who drives a motor vehicle or has the care and control of a motor vehicle, whether it is in motion or not, having consumed alcohol in such a quantity that the proportion thereof in his blood exceeds 80 milligrams of alcohol in 100 millilitres of blood, is guilty of an offence punishable on summary conviction and is liable to a fine of not less than fifty dollars and not more than one thousand dollars or to imprisonment for not more than six months, or both.' See also BLOOD, BREATH, SPIT AND URINE.

Pointe Claire Cemetery

Pointe Claire Cemetery. See LAST POST FUND.

Poke. British dialect word meaning 'bag', used in the KLONDIKE for a small sack for carrying gold dust or nuggets.

Polar bear. One of three groups of bears found in Canada (the other two are the BLACK BEAR and the brown or GRIZZLY BEAR). Yellowish- to creamy-white, this Arctic animal weighs up to 1,600 lb. and vies with the Kodiac bear as the world's largest carnivore. Inhabiting all of Canada's north coast, including Hudson Bay and the Arctic islands, polar bears often ride ice-floats as far south as the St Lawrence and Anticosti Island.

Polar Bear Express. A popular one-day excursion train to the shore of James Bay. Operated by ONTARIO NORTHLAND RAILWAY daily during the summer, it travels across 186 mi. of muskeg and bush country from Cochrane to Moosonee and its twin community Moose Factory in northern Ontario. The only alcoholic beverage served is Doran's Northern Ale.

Polar Continental Shelf Project. A program of Arctic investigation. Undertaken by the Department of Energy, Mines and Resources through its Science and Technology Sector, it is an integrated program of Arctic research that has a special interest in aeromagnetic, geodetic, and topographic surveys of Arctic regions.

Polar Route. Aviation corridor linking Vancouver and Amsterdam. The 4,821-mi. route, which is misnamed because it does not pass within 1,000 mi. of the North Pole, was inaugurated by CP Air on 3 June 1955. Vancouver is also on the projected 14,000-mi. route from Buenos Aires to Hong Kong.

Pollock Gallery Ltd. Commercial art gallery in Toronto. Founded in 1960 by Jack Pollock in an old warehouse, and occupying different premises at each stage of its growth, it helped to establish Toronto's commercial-art world. It originally showed contemporary Canadian and Indian art (Pollock discovered Norval MORRISSEAU), but now concentrates on nineteenth- and twentieth-century European and American art, and Canadian Indian art.

Pollution Probe. Research organization concerned with monitoring man's influence on the environment. It was founded in 1969 by a group led by Donald A. Chant, head of the Department of Zoology, University of Toronto.

Polymer Corporation. See POLYSAR LIMITED.

Polysar Limited. The name of the Polymer Corporation since its acquisition by the CANADA DEVELOPMENT CORPORATION on 22 Mar. 1973. Polymer was established in Sarnia, Ont., as a CROWN CORPORATION in 1942 to build and operate a plant for the production of synthetic rubber, greatly in demand during the Second World War. It now produces and sells synthetic rubber, latex, resins, and chemicals, and operates six plants in Canada, 18 in the United States, and three in Europe. 'Polysar' is a contraction of 'Polymer' and 'Sarnia'.

Pond, Peter (1740-1807). American fur trader and explorer. He established the first post in the Athabaska country in 1778 and may have travelled as far west as Great Slave Lake. In 1783 he became a partner in the NORTH WEST COMPANY but sold his shares in 1790 after being connected for the second time with a killing in the Northwest. He returned to the United States.

Pontiac (*c.*1720-69). Ottawa chief, the central figure in the Indian uprisings against the English in the American Middle West in 1763-5, often called Pontiac's Conspiracy.

Pontifical Institute of Medieval Studies. Founded in Toronto in 1929, and given pontifical status in 1939, it is a small academic community affiliated with the School of Graduate Studies of the University of Toronto that seeks to conduct historical research in the thought, culture, writings, and institutions of medieval society. It is managed by the Basilian Fathers. Étienne Gilson, who inspired the institute, was a member of the original faculty. Jacques Maritain lectured there annually from 1932 to 1945 and as a visiting philosopher from 1949 to 1955. A close relationship is maintained with St Michael's College and the TORONTO SCHOOL OF THEOLOGY.

Pool, The. See WHEAT POOLS.

'Poor Little Girls of Ontario, The'. Title and refrain of a folksong popular in Ontario since the 1880s. The song is the complaint of women whose men were leaving them for 'the Great North-West'. In the words of the refrain: 'One by one they all clear out,/Thinking to better themselves, no doubt,/Caring little how far they go/From the poor little girls of Ontario.'

Popcorn Man, The. Children's musical with words and music by Pat Patterson and Dodi Robb, Toronto broadcasters. Commissioned by the YOUNG PEOPLE'S THEATRE, it opened in Toronto on 14 Mar. 1970. The story concerns a vendor who sells hot buttered popcorn to a boy and an old lady in the park and angers the park superintendent.

Pope, William (1825-79). A FATHER OF CONFEDERATION. Born at Bedeque, P.E.I., he trained as a lawyer. He was made colonial secretary of the Island in 1859 and was elected to the legislative assembly in 1863. He was a delegate to the CHARLOTTETOWN and QUEBEC CONFERENCES on Confederation and was made a judge in 1873, the year Prince Edward Island joined the Dominion.

Pope of Methodism. Sobriquet of Egerton RYERSON.

Poppy. Small red plant or flower with narcotic properties. It has been associated with the war dead since John McCRAE described the poppies blowing near Ypres, Belgium, in his popular poem 'IN FLANDERS FIELDS'. Each REMEMBRANCE DAY the ROYAL CANADIAN LEGION organizes a poppy campaign 'to honour the dead and help the living'.

Population. The population of Canada, as determined by the Dominion CENSUS on 1 June 1971, was 21,568,310.

Porcépic, Press. Small publishing house founded in 1972 by Dave GODFREY, Tim Inkster, and Eldon Garnet, producing attractive editions of literary books of limited commercial appeal. The printing was originally done by Tim and Elke Inkster, who in 1975 established their own Porcupine's Quill imprint in Erin, Ont. 'Porcépic' is French for porcupine, the Press's identifying symbol.

Porkeater. In its earliest use, a VOYAGEUR employed by the NORTH WEST COMPANY. It refers to the diet of pork eaten by the French-Canadian boatmen; the French term is *mangeur du lard*. It later came to mean voyageurs who were newcomers to the Northwest.

Port Arthur. See THUNDER BAY.

Port Hope Conference. Important meeting of representatives of the LIBERAL PARTY of Canada at BATTERWOOD, the home in Port Hope, Ont., of Vincent MASSEY, who was President of the Liberal Federation from 1932 to 1935. The purpose of the conference, which was held in the summer of 1933, was to dedicate the party to the evolution of social change. The proceedings were published.

Port Radium. A mining community on the east coast of Great Bear Lake, N.W.T. It came into being following the discovery of pitchblende there on 16 May 1930 by Gilbert LaBine of ELDORADO NUCLEAR LIMITED.

Port Royal. The first permanent white settlement in Canada. It was founded in 1605 by the sieur de POUTRINCOURT in ACADIA, on the north shore of the Équille R. in the Annapolis Basin (N.S.). Its HABITATION, which was lived in by Samuel de CHAMPLAIN and Marc LESCARBOT, was destroyed in 1613 in an English raid under Samuel Argall. In 1629 William Alexander, with Claude de LA TOUR, erected Charles Fort nearby. Acadia was returned to France in 1632 and in 1636 Charles de Menou d'Aulnay built a new Port Royal on the south side of the Équille R. It changed hands several times until 1710, when it became British. It was renamed Fort Anne and the settlement was called ANNAPOLIS ROYAL, N.S.

A modern reconstruction of the Habitation has been built near the original site in Port Royal National Historic Park, a 20-acre park at Lower Granville, the name of which has been changed to Port Royal.

Portage. A French-Canadian word for the place where a canoe and supplies are carried, or the carrying of such, between two waterways or around rapids that make navigation impossible.

Portage and Main. The intersection of Portage Ave and Main St in Winnipeg, dominated by the Bank of Montreal (1911, by McKIM, MEAD AND WHITE), has the reputation of being the coldest and windiest place in the country.

Pose. Word used in the FUR TRADE for a resting place and temporary deposit. A portage was often measured by the number of its poses. It derives from the French verb *poser*, to rest, to set down. See also PIPE.

Postage Stamp Province. An epithetical description of the rectilinear shape of Manitoba from its creation in 1870 to 1881, when its boundaries were extended.

Postal code. A system to facilitate the movement of mail. The Canada Post Office introduced its new postal code between Apr. 1971 and Nov. 1973 after studying other automated mail-sorting systems, including the U.S. zip code and the British postcode. Under the Canadian system a six-character code is added as the last item of the postal address, thereby allowing mechanical sorting of mail. The six alpha-numeric characters of the code permit 7.2 million combinations, only 10% of which are currently employed. The postal code of the governor general's residence is K1A 0A1. The first three characters (K1A) identify the geographical area for sorting purposes and the last three characters (0A1) identify the specific locality for de-

Postal code

livery purposes. The code identifies 18 geographical divisions, each with its initial identifying letter:

A Newfoundland	M Metropolitan Toronto
B Nova Scotia	N Southwestern Ontario
C Prince Edward Island	P Northern Ontario
E New Brunswick	R Manitoba
G Quebec East	S Saskatchewan
H Montreal Metropolitan	T Alberta
J Quebec West	V British Columbia
K Eastern Ontario	X Northwest Territories
L Central Ontario	Y Yukon Territory

Postpak. A procedure whereby the Post Office delivers at low cost up to 66 lb. of separate packages from one destination to another in a single mailbag.

Potash. The name for certain potassium compounds, particularly potassium carbonate used in fertilizers. Canada's production of potash—second only to the U.S.S.R.'s in 1971—is entirely in the province of Saskatchewan, notably at Esterhazy, Belle Plaine, and Viscount. In Nov. 1975 the provincial government announced its intention to nationalize a substantial part of the potash industry to regulate production, ensure expansion, secure greater revenue, and repatriate control.

Potlatch. The word in CHINOOK JARGON for 'gift' or 'a giving'. It was the practice of the KWAKIUTL and other Pacific-coast Indians to hold a ceremonial festival at which the hosts lavishly bestowed gifts on guests in a show of wealth and as payment for their bearing witness to, and thereby validating, the ceremonial prerogatives displayed and therefore claimed by the host group. As the potlatch was an institution based on reciprocity, the host group would be invited to other potlatches and would receive payment as befitted their rank—which was established by means of the potlatch series. The custom was prohibited in 1884 as being socially disruptive, but in 1951 the ban was lifted. There is no evidence that the expression 'Indian giver' originated with this custom.

Potts, Nadia (b.1947). Dancer. Born in London, Eng., she came to Canada with her parents in 1951 and began studying with Betty OLIPHANT as a private pupil in 1954 and then at the NATIONAL BALLET SCHOOL. She has produced consistently polished and elegant work since she became soloist with the NATIONAL BALLET OF CANADA in 1966 and is now one of the company's leading ballerinas. In 1970 she won a first award at the Varna International Ballet Competition.

Poudrière, La. A small theatrical company in Montreal. Founded by Jeanine C. Beaubien

in 1956, it is located on the Île Sainte-Hélène in an old gunpowder magazine dating from 1822 and refurbished with 180 seats. The company has mounted productions in five languages: French, English, German, Italian, and Spanish.

Poundmaker (1838-86). Cree chief. In the NORTH WEST REBELLION he attacked BATTLEFORD with his Indians in Mar. 1885 and defeated Col. William OTTER at CUT KNIFE HILL on 2 May. He surrendered to Gen. Frederick Middleton later in the month, was tried, and sentenced to three years' imprisonment. Released the next year, he died soon afterwards.

Pour la suite du monde. See *The* MOONTRAP.

Poutines rapée. Potato dumplings made with pork fat. This Acadian dish is popular in New Brunswick and is sold there in several drive-in restaurants on a take-out basis.

Poutrincourt, Jean de Biencourt de, Baron de Saint-Just (1557-1615). Leader of the first permanent settlement in ACADIA. In 1604 he accompanied Pierre du Gua de Monts, governor of Acadia, on a colonizing expedition. After a winter spent at Dochet's Island (Maine) on the Sainte-Croix R., the colony moved to PORT ROYAL, which was given to Poutrincourt as a grant on the condition that he colonize the surrounding land. Poutrincourt brought more settlers to Port Royal in 1606, but it was abandoned in 1607 when the Monts's monopoly was revoked. Poutrincourt, with his son Biencourt and Claude de LA TOUR, re-established the colony in 1610, though he returned to France in 1611. Port Royal was destroyed by Samuel Argall in 1613. When Poutrincourt saw its ruins in 1614 he decided to abandon the post and ceded the title to his lands in Acadia to Biencourt.

Povungnituk. Eskimo settlement at the mouth of the Povungnituk R. on the east side of Hudson Bay in NEW QUEBEC. Carving was introduced there in 1949, printmaking in 1964. Povungnituk sculpture is noted for its wild, fantastic, shamanistic imagery. Povungnituk prints usually depict incidents from Eskimo mythology and invariably reproduce the external contours of the stone. Eskimo artists who work there include Davidialuk AMIITUK, Leah QUMALUK, Levi SMITH, and Joe TALIRUNILIK.

Power Corporation of Canada, Limited. Powerful investment and management company. Incorporated in Montreal in 1925, it began to attract national attention during the 1960s under Paul Desmarais, the owner and chairman, who was born in Sudbury in 1927 and educated at the University of Ottawa. It owns or controls The Investors Group, CANADA STEAMSHIP LINES, Montreal Trust Company, Great-West Life Assurance Company, and Laurentide Financial Corporation Ltd, etc. Since 1967, through Gesca Ltée and Les Journaux Trans-Canada, it has acquired the following newspapers: La PRESSE, MONTRÉAL-MATIN, La Tribune (Sherbrooke), La Nouvelliste (Trois-Rivières), La Voix de l'est (Granby); and the following tabloids: La PATRIE, Immeubles, and Le PETIT JOURNAL. As a result of its attempt to gain control of the ARGUS CORPORATION between 1972 and 1975, the federal government appointed the Royal Commission on Corporate Concentration in 1975.

Power Politics. A sequence of brilliant short poems by Margaret ATWOOD, published in 1971, in which the war between the sexes receives a relentlessly honest and memorable examination.

Pow-wow. Algonkian word for an Indian ceremony or conference, especially one that includes dancing or revelry.

PQ. Abbreviation of PARTI QUÉBÉCOIS.

Prairie chicken. A common game bird of Manitoba, it is marinated before cooking.

Prairie Dog Sanctuary. A quarter section of prairie, east of the town of Val Marie, Sask., leased by the Natural History Society of Saskatchewan since 1965 to protect the black-tailed prairie dog, a burrowing animal that has been likened in appearance to a gopher and whose call resembles the bark of a dog. It is sometimes called a 'barking squirrel'.

Prairie Farm Rehabilitation Administration. A farm-aid agency of the federal government. It was established in 1935 to assist in the rehabilitation of agricultural lands seriously affected by drought and drifting soil in Manitoba, Saskatchewan, and Alberta. The PFRA is an entity within the Department of REGIONAL ECONOMIC EXPANSION (DREE).

Prairie grass. The original flora of the Prairies that included a variety of high grasses and wild grain-plants. Owing to the turning-over of almost all the Prairies to wheat and other crops, only a few scattered acres of the native prairie grasses remain extant.

Prairie oyster. A popular western drink, made by adding one raw egg to a pint of beer.

Prairie Provinces. Alberta, Manitoba, and Saskatchewan. With British Columbia, they form the Western Provinces.

Prairies. The southern areas of Alberta and Saskatchewan, and of southwestern Manitoba. A continuation of the Great Plains of the United States, they are not flat but are gently rolling hill country rising gradually towards the west and cut deeply by river canyons, particularly in the west. Before European settlement these vast open grasslands grew a wide variety of mixed wild flora and supported large herds of buffalo. They were later converted into the largest continuous agricultural area in Canada devoted primarily to wheat, other grains, oilseeds, and cattle. Contrary to their popular name, the PRAIRIE PROVINCES have less than a third of their areas occupied by such open grassland agriculture: most of the prairie land is forested. 'Prairies' is the plural form of the French noun for 'meadow'. The word used in the United States for 'prairies' is 'plains'.

Pratley, Gerald (b.1923). Film enthusiast. Born in London, Eng., he immigrated to Canada in 1946 after reading a pamphlet about the NATIONAL FILM BOARD. He joined CBC Radio in Toronto in Apr. 1948 as film critic and commentator, and his programs included 'This Week at the Movies' and 'The Movie Scene', begun in 1948, and 'Music from the Films', launched in 1949. These were succeeded by the popular and long-running 'Pratley at the Movies'. He reorganized the CANADIAN FILM AWARDS in 1968, founded the ONTARIO FILM INSTITUTE at the ONTARIO SCIENCE CENTRE in 1969, and brought back the Stratford International Film Festival in 1971. He has written books on the cinema of John Frankenheimer, David Lean, Otto Preminger, and John Houston.

Pratt, Christopher (b.1935). Painter. Born in St John's, Nfld, he studied engineering at Memorial University and art at Mount Allison University and the Glasgow School of Art. Showing the influence of his teacher Alex COLVILLE, the austere images of isolation in his acrylic, oil, and watercolour paintings are idealized subjects rather than detailed correspondences to reality. An aura of detached stillness pervades both the subdued mood studies of the female figures he painted in the 1960s and the sharply rendered but eerily evocative unpopulated landscapes, dominated by architectural forms, of his more recent work. *Institution* (1970, NGC), one of his finest paintings, uses the limited colour palette that has become associated with his style. He lives in St Mary's Bay, Nfld.

Pratt

Pratt, E.J. (1882-1964). Poet. Born in Western Bay, Nfld, he was educated at the Methodist College, St John's, and at Victoria College, University of Toronto, where he received his Ph.D. in theology in 1917. He taught in the English department there (1920-53) and edited *Canadian Poetry Magazine* (1936-42), gradually coming to prominence as a 'national poet', a master of both the short lyric and the long narrative. His principal publications are: *Newfoundland Verse* (1923); *The Witches' Brew* (1925), a satire on prohibition; *Titans* (1926), which includes 'The Cachalot', an important longer poem; *The Iron Door: An Ode* (1927); *The Roosevelt and the Antinoë* (1930), about a rescue at sea; *Verses of the Sea* (1930); *Many Moods* (1932); *The* TITANIC (1935), about the loss of the 'unsinkable' ship; *The Fable of the Goats and Other Poems* (1937); *Still Life and Other Verse* (1943); *Dunkirk* (1941); *Collected Poems* (1944); *They are Returning* (1945); *Behind the Log* (1947); BRÉBEUF AND HIS BRETHREN (1940); and TOWARDS THE LAST SPIKE (1952). Northrop FRYE edited and introduced the second edition of Pratt's *Collected Poems* (1958).

Pratt, Walter (Babe) (b.1916). Hockey player. Born in Stoney Mountain, Man., he became a professional player with a Philadelphia team at the age of 20. He joined the New York Rangers in 1936 and the TORONTO MAPLE LEAFS in 1942. In recent years he has been an executive member of, and commentator for, the Vancouver Canucks. His son Tracy is also a successful professional hockey player.

Precambrian Period. The earliest geological era ending approximately 600 million years ago and referring to all previous time in earth history extending back to the origins of the earth 4.5 billion years ago. As rock formations characteristic of this period remain exposed in Canada, notably in the CANADIAN SHIELD, nineteenth-century American geologist James Dwight Dana called it the 'Canadian Period'. The accepted term today is 'Precambrian', meaning 'early Cambrian', Cambria being the medieval name of Wales, where such ancient rock formations were first observed.

Precambrian Shield. See CANADIAN SHIELD.

Pre-Loyalist. Someone from New England who settled in Nova Scotia prior to the American Revolution of 1776. See also LOYALIST.

Premier. The head of a provincial government, and in practice the leader of the party in power in the provincial legislature.

Premiers, Provincial. For each province are listed the names of the premiers and their terms of office, commencing with each province's entry into Confederation.

Alberta. Alex Rutherford, 1905-10; A.L. Sifton, 1910-17; Charles Stewart, 1917-21; Herbert Greenfield, 1921-5; John Edward Brownlee, 1925-34; Richard Gavin Reid, 1934-5; William ABERHART, 1935-43; E.C. Manning, 1943-68; H.E. Strom, 1968-71; P. Lougheed, 1971-.

British Columbia. J.F. McCreight, 1871-2; A. DE COSMOS, 1872-4; G.A. Walkem, 1874-6; A.C. Elliott, 1876-8; G.A. Walkem, 1878-82; R. Beavan, 1882-3; W. Smithe, 1883-7; A.E.B. Davie, 1887-9; J. Robson, 1889-92; T. Davie, 1892-5; J.H. Turner, 1895-8; C.A. Sembin, 1898-1900; Jos. Martin, 28 Feb. 1900-14 June 1900; J. Dunsmuir, 1900-2; E.G. Prior, 1902-3; R. McBride, 1903-15; William J. Bowser, 1915-16; Harlan C. Brewster, 1916-18; John Oliver, 1918-27; John Duncan MacLean, 1927-8; Simon Fraser Tolmie, 1928-33; T.D. Pattullo, 1933-41; John Hart, 1941-7; B.I. Johnson and H. Anscomb, 1947-52; Byron I. Johnson, 18 Jan. 1952 - 1 Aug. 1952; William A.C. BENNETT, 1952-72; David Barrett, 1972-5; Bill Bennett, 1975-.

Manitoba. A. Boyd, 1870-1; N.A. Girard, 1871-2; H.J.H. Clarke, 1872-4; N.A. Girard, 8 July 1874-2 Dec. 1874; R.A. Davis, 1874-8; John Norquay, 1878-87; D.H. Harrison, 1887-8; T. Greenway, 1888-1900; H.J. Macdonald, 8 Jan. 1900-29 Oct. 1900; R.P. Roblin, 1900-15; T.C. Norris, 1915-22; John BRACKEN, 1922-43; S.S. Garson, 1943-8; D.L. Campbell, 1948-58; Dufferin Roblin, 1958-67; Walter Weir, 1967-9; Edward Schreyer, 1969-.

New Brunswick. A.R. Wetmore, 1867-70; G.E. King, 1870-1; George Hathaway, 1872; G.E. King, 1872-8; J.J. Fraser, 1878-82; D.L. Hannington, 1882-3; A.G. Blair, 1883-96; Jas. Mitchell, 1896-7; H.R. Emmerson, 1897-1900; L.J. Tweedie, 1900-7; Wm. Pugsley, 6 Mar. 1907-15 Apr. 1907; C.W. Dolinson, 1907-8; J.D. Hazen, 1908-11; James K. Flemming, 1911-14; George J. Clarke, 1914-17; James A. Murray, 1 Feb. 1917-4 Apr. 1917; Walter E. Foster, 1917-23; Peter J. Veniot, 1923-5; John B.M. Baxter, 1925-31; Chas. D. Richards, 1931-3; L.P.D. Tilley, 1933-5; A. Allison Dysart, 1935-40; J.B. Flemming, 1952-60; Louis J. Robichaud, 1960-70; Richard B. Hatfield, 1970-.

Newfoundland. Joseph R. SMALLWOOD, 1949-72; Frank D. Moores, 1972-.

Nova Scotia. H. Blanchard, 4 July 1867-3 Nov. 1867; William Annand, 1867-75; P.C. Hill, 1875-8; S.H. Holmes, 1878-82; J.S.D. Thompson, 25 May 1882-3 Aug. 1882; W.T. Pipes, 1882-4; W.S. Fielding, 1884-96;

George H. Murray, 1896-1923; Ernest Howard Armstrong, 1923-5; Edgar N. Rhodes, 1925-30; Gordon S. Harrington, 1930-3; Angus L. Macdonald, 1933-40; A.S. MacMillan, 1940-5; A.L. Macdonald, 1945-54; Harold Connolly, 13 Apr. 1954-30 Sept. 1954; Henry D. Hicks, 1954-6; Robert L. STANFIELD, 1956-67; George I. Smith, 1967-70; Gerald A. Regan, 1970-.

Ontario. J.S. MACDONALD, 1867-71; Edward BLAKE, 1871-2; Oliver MOWAT, 1873-96; A.S. Hardy, 1896-9; G.W. Ross, 1899-1905; J.P. Whitney, 1905-14; William Howard Hearst, 1914-19; Ernest Charles Drury, 1919-23; G.H. Ferguson, 1923-30; G.S. Henry, 1930-4; Mitchell F. HEPBURN, 1934-42; G.D. Grant, 1942-3; H.C. Nixon, 18 May 1943 - 17 Aug. 1943; George A. DREW, 1943-8; T.L. Kennedy, 1948-9; Leslie Frost, 1949-61; John P. Robarts, 1961-71; William G. Davis, 1971-.

Prince Edward Island. J.C. Pope, Apr.-Sept. 1873; L.C. Owen, 1873-6; L.H. Davies, 1876-9; W.W. Sullivan, 1879-89; N.McLeod, 1889-91; F. Peters, 1891-7; A.B. Warburton, 1897-8; D. Farquharson, 1898-1901; A. Peters, 1901; F.L. Hasyard, 1908-11; H. James Palmer, 16 May 1911-2 Dec. 1911; John A. Mathieson, 1911-17; Aubin E. Arsenault, 1917-19; J.H. Bell, 1919-23; James D. Stewart, 1923-7; Albert C. Saunders, 1927-30; Walter M. Lea, 1930-1; James D. Stewart, 1931-3; William J.P. MacMillan, 1933-5; Walter M. Lea, 1935-6; Thane A. Campbell, 1936-43; J. Walter Jones, 1943-53; Alexander W. Matheson, 1953-9; Walter R. Shaw, 1959-66; Alexander B. Campbell, 1966-.

Quebec. P.J. Chauveau, 1867-73; G. Ouimet, 1873-4; C.E.B. de Boucherville, 1874-8; H.G. Joly, 1878-9; J.A. Chapleau, 1879-82; J.A. Mousseau, 1882-4; J.J. Ross, 1884-7; L.O. Taillon, 25 Jan. 1887 - 27 Jan. 1887; H. Mercier, 1887-91; C.E.B. de Boucherville, 1891-2; L.O. Taillon, 1892-6; E.J. Flynn, 1896-7; F.G. Marchand, 1897-1900; S.N. Parent, 1900-5; L. Gouin, 1905-20; Louis Alexandre Taschereau, 1920-36; Adélard Godbout, 11 June 1936-26 Aug. 1936; Maurice DUPLESSIS, 1936-9; J.A. Godbout, 1939-44; Maurice Duplessis, 1944-59; J.P. Sauvé, 1959-60; Antonio Barrette, 8 Jan. 1960 - 15 June 1960; Jean LESAGE, 1960-6; Daniel Johnson, 1966-8; J. Jacques Bertrand, 1968-70; Robert Bourassa, 1970-.

Saskatchewan. Walter Scott, 1905-16; W.M. Martin, 1916-22; C.A. Dunning, 1922-6; James G. Gardiner, 1926-9; J.T.M. Anderson, 1929-34; James G. Gardiner, 1934-5; William J. Patterson, 1935-44; Thomas C. DOUGLAS, 1944-61; W.S. Lloyd, 1961-4; W. Ross Thatcher, 1964-71; A.E. Blakeney, 1971-.

Prent, Mark (b.1947). Sculptor. Born in Montreal, where he lives, he studied at Sir George Williams University. Primitive archetypes underlie the brutal satire of his grotesque, mixed-media sculpture and fibreglass studies of deformed human figures, presented in environmental stage-like sets to confront the viewer with an indictment of man's savagery. One of his strongest works is *From Love's First Fever to Her Plague* (1971, private coll.), a fibreglass sculpture of a dead pregnant drawf enclosed in a wooden crib. He has exhibited internationally. While showing his work in 1972, the ISAACS GALLERY, Toronto, was charged with exhibiting disgusting objects contrary to the Criminal Code of Canada. The case was dismissed.

Preparatory Commission for Metric Conversion. See METRIC COMMISSION.

Presbyterian Church. Continuing Presbyterians—after two-thirds of the Church membership joined Methodists and Congregationalists in church union in 1925—number 872,335 adherents (1971) and are largely Scottish in ethnic origin. From their Calvinist background, there is a strong emphasis on individual morality, prayer, and scholarly preaching.

Presbyterian College. The first classes in this Montreal church college were held in 1867. It is adjacent to McGILL UNIVERSITY and participates in the university's Faculty of Religious Studies. Ordinands complete two years in the McGill faculty and one at the College.

President's Medals of the University of Western Ontario. Annual awards made to the authors of the best poem, short story, scholarly article, and general article submitted for competition and published in a Canadian periodical during the previous year. They have been made since 1951, each winner receiving a medal and $100.

Press Bill. A phrase used by Mr Justice Canon of the Supreme Court of Canada to refer to Bill No. 9 of the Alberta legislature: 'An Act to ensure the Publication of Accurate News and Information (1938)'. It was designed to control the press to the extent that any newspaper, when required to do so by the chairman of the Social Credit Board, had to publish any reply furnished by the chairman relating to any policy or activity of the government described by that newspaper. Failure to comply could result in suspension of the newspaper's right to publish. The Alberta Bill was disallowed by the GOVERNOR GENERAL IN COUNCIL.

Press gallery

Press gallery. See PARLIAMENTARY PRESS GALLERY.

Presse, La. An evening newspaper published in Montreal. Founded in 1884, it had the largest circulation at the turn of the century of any newspaper, French or English, in the country. It describes itself as *Le plus grand quotidien français d'Amérique* ('North America's largest French-language daily') and has been called the largest French-language paper published outside France. The editor-in-chief since 1973 has been Roger LEMELIN. To celebrate the paper's ninetieth anniversary the following year, Lemelin established Le prix de l'Éditeur de *La Presse*, an annual award of $5,000 to a young writer of promise for the best book published the previous year.

Preview. A Montreal poetry magazine. Appearing irregularly in 23 issues between Mar. 1942 and Dec. 1944 (with one undated issue in 1945), it was founded by F.R. SCOTT, Bruce Ruddick, Neufville Shaw, Margaret Day, and Patrick ANDERSON, the most influential member of the group. P.K. PAGE joined the magazine in Issue 2 and A.M. KLEIN in Issue 19, although his verse began to appear in Issue 5 (July 1942). Cosmopolitan in its interests, it merged with FIRST STATEMENT to form NORTHERN REVIEW in Dec. 1945.

Preview Commentary. A three-minute analysis of the news on CBC Radio. It is heard five mornings a week following the national news at 8:00 a.m. and seeks 'to provide a free expression of opinions from informed observers'. The counterpart of CBC-TV's 'Commentary', the program began in Nov. 1957 but was cancelled in June 1959 after Prime Minister John DIEFENBAKER criticized it for being partisan. 32 producers went out on strike and threatened to resign unless the program was reinstated. It was, and is still being heard.

Prévost, André (b.1934). Composer. Born in Hawkesbury, Ont., he studied at the Conservatoire in Montreal and in Paris. His early work explored the serial technique and small ensemble forms. He is now concerned with composition on a larger scale, and since returning from Paris in 1962 has favoured somber philosophical themes for such orchestral works as *Fantasmes* (1963) and *Diallèle* (1968).

Price, Art (b.1918). Sculptor. Born in Edmonton, Alta, he took courses at the Ontario College of Art, Toronto, and then joined the Merchant Navy. He was encouraged in his interest in Northwest Coast Indian art and French-Canadian folklore by his father-in-law Marius BARBEAU, and these motifs found their way into his early metal work and cast sculpture in the 1950s. His large bronze and cast-aluminum figures and abstract sculptures have been commissioned by many companies and institutions. They include a 24-ft abstract sculpture for the Ottawa Postal Terminal Building and sculpture for the Coliseum at the Canadian National Exhibition, Toronto.

Price, Bruce (1846-1903). American architect. He was trained in the office of Henry Hobson Richardson. In his designs of hotels and stations for the CPR he was a formative influence on the development of the CHÂTEAU STYLE. His work in Canada includes the original section of WINDSOR STATION (1888-9) and Place Viger Station (1896-8), both in Montreal; the first BANFF SPRINGS HOTEL, (1886-8, destroyed 1925); and original sections of the CHÂTEAU FRONTENAC in Quebec City (1892-3, additions 1897-9).

Price, Frank Percival (b.1901). Carillonneur. Born and educated in Toronto, he was appointed the first Dominion Carillonneur in 1927. He was the first to sound the great carillons in the PEACE TOWER on the occasion of Canada's Diamond Jubilee, 1 July 1927. Settling in the United States, he founded the Guild of Carillonneurs in North America and won a Pulitzer Prize in 1934 for his symphony *St Laurent*.

Price, Harry I. (b.1896). Sports organizer. Born in Toronto, he became director of the Ontario Athletic Commission and chairman of the sports committee of the CANADIAN NATIONAL EXHIBITION after the First World War. First chairman of both the Canadian Horse Show Association and the Sports HALL OF FAME, he also founded his own insurance business.

Price Spreads Commission. A royal commission established by the government of R.B. BENNETT in 1934 on the recommendation of a select special committee of the House of Commons. The House committee, guided by H.H. Stevens, had found evidence of monopolies, combines, and unfair practices in certain industries, and the royal commission was created to further its work. Before the completion of its report, however, Bennett and Stevens had quarrelled and broken relations, and the Tory opportunity to use the findings in the election of 1935 was lost. The report nonetheless contained substantial evidence of sweatshop conditions and of the dubious practices of large chainstores.

Pricket, Abacuk. See Henry HUDSON and Sir Thomas BUTTON.

Prime minister. The head of the federal government of Canada, and in practice the leader of the party in power in the HOUSE OF COMMONS.

Prince Albert. A city in Saskatchewan on the North Saskatchewan R. It has the distinction of having elected three prime ministers: Sir Wilfrid LAURIER (1896-1911), W.L. Mackenzie KING (1921-6, 1926-30, 1935-48), and John G. DIEFENBAKER (1957-63), who would boast, 'As Prince Albert goes, so goes the nation.'

Prince Albert National Park. Established in 1927 north of Prince Albert, Sask., it covers 1,496 sq. mi. of transitional land, from northern forests to prairie grassland. GREY OWL, who settled in a cabin beside Ajawaan Lake in 1931, is buried there.

Prince Edward Island. Known as 'the Garden of the Gulf', it is separated from New Brunswick and Nova Scotia by Northumberland Strait, 10 to 25 mi. wide. Visited by CARTIER in 1534, it was named Île-Saint-Jean by the French. Although some fishing ports were established, settlement was not really begun until 1720 and proceeded only slowly, reaching about 5,000 by 1758. The island came under British control in 1763, was called the Island of St John, and annexed to Nova Scotia until 1769, when it was given its own legislature. Its name was changed to Prince Edward Island in 1799 in honour of the Duke of KENT. Although the CHARLOTTETOWN CONFERENCE was held there in 1864, opinion in the island was hostile to the proposals for British North American union, and they were rejected by the legislature in 1865. The province did not enter CONFEDERATION until 1873.

Agriculture is the principal economic activity, followed by manufacturing and fishing. Tourism is also a major contribution to the economy. The province, however, is very dependent on financial assistance from the federal government.

P.E.I. is the smallest province, with a land area of 2,184 sq. mi. and a population of 111,641 in 1971. Its motto is *Parva sub Ingenti* ('The Small under the Protection of the Great'). The capital is CHARLOTTETOWN.

Prince Edward Island National Park. Established in 1937, it comprises a long coastal strip on the GULF OF ST LAWRENCE. It covers 7 sq. mi. that include dunes, cliffs, salt marshes, and beaches. Green Gables is a museum in the park (see ANNE OF GREEN GABLES).

Prince of Wales Martello Tower. One of several forts in Point Pleasant Park, Halifax, N.S. Built in the 1790s by the Duke of KENT, as part of the harbour defencework, it has been restored and is a national historic site.

Prince of Wales Trophy. Presented annually to 'the team finishing in first place in the Eastern Division at the end of the regular championship schedule' by the NATIONAL HOCKEY LEAGUE. The trophy was donated by the Prince of Wales—later Edward VIII, then Duke of Windsor—in 1924. The Prince of Wales Trophy is to the Eastern Division what the CLARENCE S. CAMPBELL BOWL is to the Western Division.

Prince's Lodge. The Duke of KENT built a suburban residence for Julie de Montgenet on Bedford Basin, N.S., of which all that remains is the Rotunda. It was started in 1794 and finished about 1800.

Princess Louise's. See 8TH CANADIAN HUSSARS.

Princess Patricia's Canadian Light Infantry. Canadian army regiment. It was organized in 1914 and served in the FIRST WORLD WAR with the Canadian Corps as part of the 7th Infantry Brigade. During the SECOND WORLD WAR it was part of the 2nd Infantry Brigade in Sicily and Italy. It has distinguished itself in many battles, including YPRES (1915, 1917), VIMY (1917), and Northwest Europe (1945). Since then it has served in Korea and Germany. The colonel-in-chief was Princess Patricia—the daughter of the Duke of Connaught, governor general from 1911 to 1916, and a granddaughter of Queen Victoria—who designed the regimental badge and colours, known as the 'Ric-a-dam-doo'. It has been called the last military unit to be raised by a private individual (35-year-old Maj. Andrew Hamilton Gault) for service under the Crown. It is familiarly known as the 'Princess Pats'.

Princess Sophia. A Scottish-built CPR passenger steamship. On 23 Oct. 1918, while sailing from Skagway, Alaska, to Vancouver, she struck a reef in the Lynn Canal. Two days later during a violent storm, she slipped off the reef and sank. The only survivor of the disaster was a small dog that managed to swim to shore—all 343 people on board were lost.

Printed in Canada. Identification required by law on all publications manufactured in Canada for resale outside the country and for copyright protection.

Prism International. A literary magazine published by the Creative Writing Department of the University of British Columbia. Launched in 1959 as *Prism*, a quarterly edited by Jacob Zilber and others, it became attached to UBC in 1964 as *Prism International* and has appeared three times a year since 1968. It specializes in original poems and stories and translations. The editor since 1973 has been Michael BULLOCK.

Private bill. A measure introduced to Parliament to deal with the law relating to a particular locality or to a person or body of persons. Examples of private bills are bills for the incorporation of a company or for authorizing the extension of a railway line. Private bills may originate in either the SENATE or the HOUSE OF COMMONS, but in practice they are usually introduced in the Senate first. They are presented in the form of a petition, and a fee must be paid for presenting them. See also PUBLIC BILL, MONEY BILL.

Private schools. Primary and secondary schools operated for and by private bodies and not by the provincial governments. Private schools are exclusive, they charge tuition fees, and they espouse specific religious, educational, or social principles. See also PUBLIC SCHOOLS, CANADIAN JUNIOR COLLEGE, and NEUCHÂTEL JUNIOR COLLEGE. A list of English-Canadian schools, with year of founding and 1975 enrolment figures, follows:

Co-educational schools
Albert College, Belleville, Ont., 1857, 170
Bishop's College School, Lennoxville, Que., 1836, 266
Brentwood College School, Mill Bay, B.C., 1923, 280
Halifax Grammar School, Halifax, N.S., 1958, 230
Hillfield-Strathallan Colleges, Hamilton, Ont., 1901, 650
St George's School of Montreal, Montreal, Que., 1930, 425
St John's Ravenscourt School, Winnipeg, Man., 1820, 440
Strathcona-Tweedsmuir School, Okotoks, Alta, 1934, 350
Weston School, Montreal, Que., 1917, 100

Boys' schools
Appleby College, Oakville, Ont., 1911, 360
Ashbury College, Ottawa, Ont., 1891, 355
Crescent School, Willowdale, Ont., 1913, 285
De La Salle College 'Oaklands', Toronto, Ont., 1870, 900
King's College School, Windsor, N.S., 1788, 160

Lakefield College School, Lakefield, Ont., 1879, 233
Lower Canada College, Montreal, Que., 1909, 585
Pickering College, Newmarket, Ont., 1842, 150
Ridley College, St Catharines, Ont., 1889, 480
Rothesay Collegiate School, Rothesay, N.B., 1877, 130
St Andrew's College, Aurora, Ont., 1899, 360
St David's School for Boys, Squamish, B.C., 1971, 75
St George's College, Toronto Ont., 1961, 346
St George's School, Vancouver, 1931, 600
St John's Cathedral Boys' School, Selkirk, Man., 1961, 100
St John's School of Alberta, Stony Plain, Alta, 1967, 100
St Michael's College School, Toronto, Ont., 1852, 900
St Michael's University School, Victoria, B.C., 1910, 445
Selwyn House School, Montreal, Que., 1908, 430
Shawnigan Lake School, Shawnigan, B.C., 1916, 220
Stanstead College, Stanstead, Que., 1817, 211
Trinity College School, Port Hope, Ont., 1865, 360
UPPER CANADA COLLEGE, Toronto, Ont., 1829, 888

Girls' schools
Alma College, St Thomas, Ont., 140
Balmoral Hall School, Winnipeg, Ont., 240
Bishop Strachan School, Toronto, Ont., 670
Branksome Hall, Toronto, Ont., 670
Convent of the Sacred Heart, Montreal, Que., 340
Crofton House School, Vancouver, B.C., 340
Miss Edgar's and Miss Cramp's School, Montreal, Que., 260
Edgehill School, Windsor, N.S., 80
Elmwood School, Ottawa, Ont., 160
Halifax Ladies' College, Halifax, N.S., 160
Havergal College, Toronto, Ont., 620
Loretto Abbey, Toronto, Ont., 500
Loretto College School, Toronto, Ont., 380
Netherwood (Rothesay School for Girls), Rothesay, N.B., 75
Norfolk House, Victoria, B.C., 240
Ontario Ladies' College, Whitby, Ont., 115
Queen of Angels Academy, Dorval, Que., 160
Queen Margaret's School, Duncan, B.C., 185

St Clement's School, Toronto, Ont., 330

St Joseph's College School, Toronto, Ont., 730

St Joseph's Convent High School, Toronto, Ont., 720

St. Margaret's School, Victoria, B.C., 240

St Mildred's-Lightbourn School, Oakville, Ont., 345

Strathcona Lodge School, Shawnigan Lake, B.C., 120

The Study, Montreal, Que., 240

Trafalgar School for Girls, Montreal, Que., 240

York House School, Vancouver, B.C., 330

Privy Council. A body to aid and advise the CROWN. The Queen's Privy Council for Canada was constituted by the BNA ACT in 1867, and its members are chosen by the governor general on the advice of the prime minister. All cabinet ministers must first become members of the Canadian Privy Council, which has also included from time to time various members of the Royal Family, Commonwealth prime ministers, provincial premiers, speakers of the Senate and the House of Commons, the Chief Justice, the leader of the Opposition, and other distinguished people. Since membership in the Privy Council is for life for federal cabinet ministers (members of provincial cabinets continue only so long as they are ministers), it includes past as well as present federal cabinet members and prime ministers. A member of the Privy Council is styled 'Honourable' and may use the initials 'PC' after his name. Governors general and prime ministers of Canada are also appointed to the United Kingdom Privy Council. A member of the U.K. Privy Council is styled 'Right Honourable'. The Canadian Privy Council as a whole has met on only a few ceremonial occasions. Its constitutional responsibilities—to advise the Crown on matters respecting the government of Canada—are discharged by the Committee of the Privy Council, whose membership is identical to that of the CABINET. Its instrument is the ORDER-IN-COUNCIL, which is approved by the governor general. The president of the Privy Council since 1968 has been the GOVERNMENT LEADER in the House of Commons.

Privy Council Office. Secretariat providing staff support for cabinet, etc. Headed by the Clerk of the Privy Council, it consists of a cabinet secretariat and the Office of the Prime Minister (PMO). The cabinet secretariat handles matters pertaining to cabinet meetings and committees. In addition the Privy Council Office receives submissions to the GOVERNOR IN COUNCIL, prepares draft orders

and regulations, and circulates and publishes approved ORDERS-IN-COUNCIL in the CANADA GAZETTE.

Prix Benjamin-Sulte. Annual prize of $100, with a medal depicting the historian Benjamin Sulte (1841-1923), awarded since 1972 by the SOCIÉTÉ SAINT-JEAN-BAPTISTE de Trois-Rivières to a writer who lives in the area, whether a journalist or the author of a book, for work completed in the previous year.

Prix Champlain. Annual prize of $500 awarded by the Conseil de la Vie française en Amérique for the best study, published or unpublished, submitted by a Franco American or a French Canadian living in Quebec, on the subject of French values in North America. The award, named after Samuel de CHAMPLAIN, was first made in 1957.

Prix David. Highest award given by the Ministère des Affaires Culturelles du Québec to an author on the merit of his or her work as a whole. It was named after Laurent-Olivier David (1840-1926), a Quebec senator and writer, and carries a prize of $5,000. It has been awarded annually since 1968 to a Canadian citizen domiciled in Quebec or to a citizen domiciled outside Quebec if he or she writes in French.

Prix de l'Actuelle. Annual prize of $1,000 awarded since 1971 to the author of the best French literary work (excluding novels) in French submitted for publication to the Montreal magazine L'Actuelle. The magazine also sponsors the Prix de l'Actuelle Jeunesse for writers who are students; this prize is $250 and a return ticket to France courtesy of Air France.

Prix du Cercle du Livre de France. Annual prize of $1,000 awarded since 1950 to the French-Canadian author of the best novel, collection of stories, or popular biography submitted for publication to Le Cercle du Livre de France, a Montreal publishing house.

Prix Duvernay. Annual award made to a French-Canadian writer or thinker whose work expresses the best aspects of Quebec life. The prize of $1,000 has been awarded since 1944 by the SOCIÉTÉ SAINT-JEAN-BAPTISTE de Montréal. It was named after Ludger Duvernay (1799-1852), editor and founder of the society.

Prix Études Françaises. Annual award made to writers of literary works in French who live in countries other than France. The prize of $2,000 has been awarded since 1968 by the magazine Études françaises, published by the Université de Montréal.

Prix France-Canada

Prix France-Canada. Annual literary award made to the author of a book published the previous year in French. The prize of 1,000 French francs was first awarded in 1961 by the Association France-Canada and the Ministère des Affaires Culturelles du Québec.

Prix France-Québec Jean-Hamelin. Annual literary award made to the author of a book published the previous year in French. The prize of 2,000 French francs was first presented in 1965 by the Association des Écrivains de la Mer et de l'Outre-Mer and the Ministère des Affaires Culturelles du Québec. It honours the Quebec writer and historian Jean Hamelin (b.1920).

Prix Jean Béraud-Molson. Annual prize of $1,000 awarded since 1968 to the author of the best French novel or romance submitted for publication to Le Cercle du Livre de France, a Montreal publishing house.

Prix Marie-Claire Daveluy. Annual prize of $100 awarded by the Ministère des Affaires Culturelles du Québec since 1970. It succeeds the Prix Maxime, which was first awarded in 1965, and goes to the author 14 to 20 years of age who submits the best book-length French-language manuscript written for children. It was named after a Quebec historian, writer, and librarian.

Prix Marie-Lemelin. Annual prize of $200 awarded since 1966 by the Société des poètes canadiens-français to the author of the best unpublished French-language poem submitted by a member. The award is named after a friend of the society.

Prix Michelle-Le Normand. Annual prize of $250 awarded since 1971 by the Société des écrivains canadiens to an author who writes for children in French.

Prix scientifique du Québec. Highest award made by the Ministère des Affaires Culturelles du Québec to a scientist for work as a whole or for a single exceptional achievement in the pure or applied sciences. Presented to Quebec-based scientists since 1967, the $5,000 prize is awarded in rotation to the natural, chemical, biological, and physical sciences.

Prochain Épisode. Hubert AQUIN's first novel, published in 1965 while the author was detained at a psychiatric hospital. It uses the device of a story within a story to reveal the emotions of a young man held for a subversive act. It was translated by Penny Williams and published in English under the same title in 1967.

Producers' Strike of 1959. See PREVIEW COMMENTARY.

Progress Books. A Canadian-owned publishing house. Established in Toronto about 1929, it distributes English-language books and periodicals issued by Progress Publishers in Moscow and other Soviet publishers. Over the years it has published several notable books, including Margaret FAIRLEY's *Spirit of Canadian Democracy* (1945), Stanley B. RYERSON's *Unequal Union* (1968), and Peter H. Weinrich's *A Select Bibliography of Tim* BUCK (1974).

Progressive Conservative Party. The name (since 1942) of the oldest continuing Canadian political party. The Conservatives were the party of nation-building, the party that has retained credit for creating and fulfilling CONFEDERATION, for establishing the NATIONAL POLICY that led to the growth of manufacturing, the settlement of the West, and the construction of the transcontinental railway. Its foundation and subsequent success owed much to John A. MACDONALD, who assumed leadership in 1856 of the coalition of conservatives, moderate reformers, and Quebec BLEUS, created by Sir Allan MacNAB and A.-N. MORIN in 1854. Under Macdonald's skilful direction a GREAT COALITION was formed in 1864 to press for the union of British North America, and upon its success Macdonald became the first prime minister of Canada in 1867. Office turned many of the coalition members into Conservatives. With the exception of the Alexander MACKENZIE Liberal interregnum, the TORIES held power under Macdonald until his death in 1891, and for five years after his death his shade kept a disintegrating machine in office. But since 1896 Canada has been Liberal in orientation.

The Tories have sought constantly to retrieve the Macdonald style. Leaders suffered from the attacks of their followers because they lacked it, and the party changed its name and often its tactics with bewildering speed. Only Sir Robert BORDEN (1911-20), Arthur MEIGHEN (1920-1, 1926), R.B. BENNETT (1930-5), and John DIEFENBAKER (1957-63) led the party to power; none of these was venerated by his followers and all but Borden were virtually hounded from the leadership. The party's difficulties stemmed from its too-close identification with high finance, its inability—thanks to its support for conscription in both world wars—to establish a solid base in Quebec, and its reputation for being right-wing. None of these complaints is entirely fair (many Liberals supported conscription, the GRITS have enjoyed more big-business support than the Tories, and the party's record includes much of Canada's progressive legislation), but the Tory reactionary label is hard to shake. The chief flaw has been generalship. At every turn the Conservatives have suffered from the unfailing ability of the Liberals to find the right man. Mackenzie KING was opposed by Meighen, Bennett, MANION, BRACKEN; ST LAURENT by DREW; PEARSON by Diefenbaker; TRUDEAU by STANFIELD and CLARK (elected leader at the Ottawa convention on 22 Feb. 1976). Only when Liberalism grew tired could the Tories find a road to power. Unfortunately for the Conservatives, in the twentieth century those Liberal lapses were relatively few.

Progressive Party. A former political party. It was founded in 1920 by T.A. CRERAR in order to obtain law tariffs for western farmers. In 1921, 64 members connected with the farmers' parties in the western provinces were elected to the federal Parliament and held the balance of power, although they refused to form the official Opposition. But within a year there were splits within the ranks of the party, most notably with the formation of the GINGER GROUP in 1924. Its representation was greatly reduced in the election of 1925, and was all but wiped out in the election of 1926. Only the Ginger Group remained after 1930, and they merged with the CCF before the next election. See also UNITED FARMERS OF ALBERTA, UNITED FARMERS OF MANITOBA, UNITED FARMERS OF ONTARIO.

Prohibition. The name given to the period after 1916 when the sale of alcoholic beverages was prohibited. The period of prohibition varied from province to province, but it was in effect throughout Canada between 1916 and 1917 except in Quebec, where it was adopted for hard liquor in 1919. It was a period of great lawlessness, with gangsters engaged in bootlegging, rum-running, battles with police, and even murder. During the 1920s all but two provinces (which followed suit later) returned to local option and the sale of liquor under provincial licence in government stores. See also CANADA TEMPERANCE ACT.

Promenade des Gouverneurs, La. Walkway on the southeast side of the CITADEL, Quebec, linking DUFFERIN TERRACE to NATIONAL BATTLEFIELDS PARK. The Governors' Promenade was named in honour of the two dozen governors of New France.

Promenade Symphony Concerts. The 'Prom Concerts' were organized in 1933 by Reginald Stewart (b.1900) and the Toronto Musical Protective Association to keep its

members working during the summer. They were presented weekly in Varsity Arena, University of Toronto, to audiences of six or seven thousand, some of whom sat on floor cushions, until 1956. Reginald Stewart was conductor from 1934 to 1941. Celebrated soloists and, after Stewart left, distinguished guest conductors performed. In 1938 the CBC picked up the event; the broadcast transmitted from a booth under the roof was then a considerable technical achievement. From 1954 to 1956 the concerts were broadcast on the Trans Canada network. In Montreal the CBC enabled listeners to 'sit in' for the broadcasts at the Chalet on Mount Royal.

Province. One of the 10 political divisions of Canada. In figurative terms, a 'realm' is divided into 'provinces'. The concept of a province's having certain rights, and sharing others with a federal government, dates from CONFEDERATION. A list of the provinces of Canada follows (with the year of entry into Confederation): ALBERTA (1905), BRITISH COLUMBIA (1871), MANITOBA (1870), NEW BRUNSWICK (1867), NEWFOUNDLAND (1949), NOVA SCOTIA (1867), ONTARIO (1867), PRINCE EDWARD ISLAND (1873), QUEBEC (1867), SASKATCHEWAN (1905). In addition Canada has two territories that have not achieved the status of provinces and are administered directly by the federal government: NORTHWEST TERRITORIES and YUKON TERRITORY. The Yukon Territory was established in 1898; the Northwest Territories were established in their present form in 1905, when Alberta and Saskatchewan were created as separate provinces.

Province House (Charlottetown). Historic building where the legislative assembly of Prince Edward Island convenes. It was the scene of the CHARLOTTETOWN CONFERENCE in Sept. 1864, held in the Confederation Chamber. Prior to 1867 it was known as the Colonial Building. It was built in 1843-7 and designed by Isaac Smith.

Province House (Halifax). Legislative building of Nova Scotia. An outstanding example of fine Georgian architecture in Canada, it was finished in 1819 under the architect-builder Richard Scott, though its cornerstone was laid on 12 Aug. 1811. Its dramatic interior has remained unaltered.

Province of Canada. The name given the combined districts of Canada West and Canada East—the former provinces of Upper and Lower Canada—created by the ACT OF UNION of 1841. It ceased with CONFEDERATION on 1 July 1867 when the two districts became the provinces of Ontario and Quebec.

Provincial

Provincial. Under the jurisdiction of one of the provinces of Canada; provincial as opposed to DOMINION or FEDERAL.

Provincial autonomy. Areas in which the provincial legislatures have exclusive powers. The provinces are autonomous and not subject to the federal government in the fields of property and civil rights, education, justice within the province, incorporation of companies in the province, provincial taxation, public lands, provincial social services, and municipal institutions, according to the BNA ACT of 1867. The phrase 'provincial autonomy' is particularly identified with the province of Quebec, which has sought an extension of its powers, notably under Maurice DUPLESSIS (1936-9, 1944-59) and Jean LESAGE (1960-6).

Provincial government. The legislative authority within a province. Under sections 92, 93 and 95 of the BNA ACT the provinces have legislative authority in certain areas (see PROVINCIAL AUTONOMY). In each of the provinces the CROWN is represented by a LIEUTENANT-GOVERNOR appointed by the GOVERNOR GENERAL in Council. The lieutenant-governor acts on the advice of the PREMIER and the EXECUTIVE COUNCIL. Each province has a legislature consisting of one house, which is elected for a maximum of five years but may be dissolved by the lieutenant-governor within that period on the advice of the premier. The name of the legislature and the number of members vary from province to province. *Alberta:* legislative assembly of 75 members; *British Columbia:* legislative assembly of 55 members; *Manitoba:* legislative assembly of 57 members; *New Brunswick:* legislative assembly of 58 members; *Newfoundland:* House of Assembly of 42 members; *Nova Scotia:* House of Assembly of 46 members; *Ontario:* legislative assembly of 117 members; *Prince Edward Island:* legislative assembly of 32 members; *Quebec:* Assemblée Nationale of 110 members; *Saskatchewan:* legislative assembly of 60 members.

Provincial Workmen's Association. A union of miners of Nova Scotia and New Brunswick. Founded in 1879 and incorporated in 1881, it was in conflict with the United Mine Workers of America in 1906. (See GLACE BAY AND SPRINGHILL STRIKES.) It joined the CANADIAN FEDERATION OF LABOUR in 1910 and finally dissolved in 1927.

Psychedelic. Neologism coined from the Greek words for 'mind' and 'expanding' by Dr Humphrey Osmond and Dr Abram Hoffer, two psychiatrists studying the effects on humans of hallucinogenic drugs in Saskatoon, Sask. Osmond administered mescaline, a natural form of LSD, to Aldous Huxley, who described the experience in *The Doors of Perception* (1954). The word 'psychedelic' first appeared in print in 1957 in an article by Osmond.

Ptarmigan. Any of several species of medium-sized birds of the grouse family inhabiting the Arctic tundra and northern Rockies. An important game bird, its brown summer plumage turns white in winter.

Pte. Official abbreviation of Private.

PTR. Initials of the Pool Test Reactor, an atomic pile in a cooling tank the shape of a swimming pool. It was constructed at CHALK RIVER, Ont., in 1958 to test the absorbent properties of various materials.

Public Archives of Canada. National collection of documents relating to the history of Canada. The PAC, which has shared quarters in Ottawa with the NATIONAL LIBRARY OF CANADA since 1967, has holdings in excess of 150 million items in the form of documents, maps, photographs, paintings, books, and other materials that record the development of Canada. It is also responsible for MAISON LAURIER. The first archivist, Douglas Brymner, appointed in 1872, worked under the jurisdiction of the Department of Agriculture. The task of preserving federal-government records, entrusted to the Keeper of the Records in the Department of the Secretary of State, was transferred in 1903, and the title Dominion Archivist and Keeper of the Records was created. The PAC acquired its present name and status as a government department in 1912. An illustrated guide to the holdings was published as *Archives: Mirror of Canada Past / Archives: miroir du passé du Canada* (1972).

Public Bill. A measure introduced in either the HOUSE OF COMMONS or the SENATE to deal with a matter of public or general nature. There are two kinds of public bills: those introduced by a cabinet minister or parliamentary assistant, and known as government bills; and those introduced by a private member. See also PRIVATE BILL, MONEY BILL.

Public schools. Non-denominational primary and secondary schools that are supported by provincial taxes. See also PRIVATE SCHOOLS, SEPARATE SCHOOLS.

Public Service Commission. Central staffing agency of the federal government. The first civil-service commission was created in 1908 and introduced the merit system in person-

426

nel administration in the public service. The Act of 1918 gave the Commission authority to control the recruitment, selection, appointment, classification, and organization of government personnel. In 1961 the Civil Service Act strengthened the principles of the merit system and gave staff associations the right to be consulted. An Investigation Branch was established in 1972 to inquire into charges of discrimination in the civil service.

Public Works, Department of. Federal-government department concerned with public buildings, roads (including the TRANS-CANADA HIGHWAY), and bridges. It has been in existence since 1867 and has regional offices in Halifax, Montreal, Ottawa, Toronto, Edmonton, and Vancouver.

Pudlo (b.1916). Eskimo sculptor and graphic artist at CAPE DORSET. A sculptor for many years, he became a successful graphic artist after printing was introduced at Cape Dorset.

Pugwash Conferences. Annual meetings on science and world affairs, attended by scientists from both communist and capitalist countries. Following publication of a paper by Bertrand Russell and Albert Einstein urging a thinker's conference on science and world peace, the first conference was held in July 1957 and attended by 22 famous scientists. They were guests at the summer home of Cyrus Eaton (b.1883)—a wealthy Cleveland industrialist, owner of Ungava Iron Ores Co. Ltd, and benefactor of many subsequent conferences—whose birthplace and home in the small fishing village of Pugwash, N.S., gave the conferences their name.

Puisne judge. A puisne judge is junior in appointment to a chief judge or presiding judge of a high court. The word derives from the Old French *puîné* ('petty') and is pronounced 'puny'.

Pukaskwa National Park. Established in 1971 on the northern shore of Lake Superior in the wilderness area of northern Ontario, it covers 752 sq. mi. of rugged terrain that is rich in wildlife.

Pulford, Harvey (1875-1940). Sports champion. Born in Toronto, he moved to Ottawa where he excelled in seven sports: hockey, football, lacrosse, boxing, paddling, squash, and rowing. He is best remembered for his hockey career, during which he starred with the Ottawa Senators, later voted 'the best Canadian team of the first half-century'.

Pulhems. Acronym for a system of medical classification introduced by the Director General of Medical Services for the Canadian Army during the Second World War. It divides the body into seven functional parts and activities: P (physique); U (upper extremities); L (lower extremities); H (ears and hearing); E (eyes and eyesight); M (mental capacity); S (stability). The system was prepared by Dr Brock Chisholm (1896-1971), a psychiatrist, who was the first director-general of the World Health Organization (and strongly disapproved of encouraging children to believe in Santa Claus).

Punkydoodles Corners. A community near the intersection of Perth, Waterloo, and Oxford Counties, between Kitchener and Stratford, Ont. No one knows the origin of the name, but local tradition attributes it to the pumpkins grown and sold in the area, or to a Germanized version of 'Yankee Doodle'. Local radio announcers have been known to comment on the state of affairs in 'the heart of beautiful downtown Punkydoodles Corners'.

Purcell, Jack (b.1904). Champion badminton player. Born in Guelph, Ont., he became Ontario badminton champion while still in his teens and held the title for five consecutive years. In 1929, after winning Canadian honours, he toured England until 1933, when he became a professional and won the world title; he retired undefeated. In 1950 he was elected Canada's outstanding athlete of the half century in the 'miscellaneous category'.

Purdy, Al (b.1918). Poet. Born of Loyalist stock at Wooller, near Ameliasburg, the small Ontario town where he now lives, he was a casual labourer until the late fifties, when he was able to support himself as a free-lance writer. His characteristic style—colloquial, sometimes melancholy, often comic, as he tells of his daily experiences and his visits to distant places—has evolved from book to book: *The Enchanted Echo* (1944); *The Crafte so Longe to Lerne* (1959); *Poems for all the Annettes* (1956; rev. 1968; rev. 1973); *Emu, Remember!* (1957); *The Blur in Between* (1962); *The Cariboo Horses* (1965); *North of Summer* (1967), with illustrations by Frederick VARLEY; *Wild Grape Wine* (1969); *Love in a Burning Building* (1970); *Selected Poems* (1972); *Hiroshima Poems* (1972); *Sex and Death* (1973); *In Search of Owen Roblin* (1974), with photos by Bob Waller; and *Sundance at Dusk* (1976). Purdy has edited four anthologies: *The New Romans* (1968), *Fifteen Winds* (1969), *Storm Warning* (1971), and *Storm Warning II* (1976).

'Push on, brave York Volunteers!'

'Push on, brave York Volunteers!' Popularly believed to be the dying words of Sir Isaac BROCK, who fell in the Battle of QUEENSTON HEIGHTS on 13 Oct. 1812. Historians maintain that the rallying cry to the York (Toronto) Militia was made more than a mile from where the hero was mortally wounded.

Put Canada First. A slogan coined by the LABOUR PROGRESSIVE PARTY and employed by Tim BUCK as the title of two pamphlets published in 1953 and 1954 during a period of increased economic penetration of the Canadian economy by American capital.

Put-in Bay, Battle of. See Battle of LAKE ERIE.

PWA. See PROVINCIAL WORKMEN'S ASSOCIATION.

Q

Q-Book. The popular name of a publication distributed to all Eskimo families by the Department of Northern Affairs and National Resources. The 300-page volume—covering such subjects as civics, education, health, safety, etc.—appeared in English and Eskimo, and in three scripts (Eskimo syllabic, Eskimo Roman, and English Roman). Its Eskimo title is *Quajivaallirutissat*; its English title, *Eskimo Book of Wisdom*. It ceased publication in 1973.

QC. Queen's Counsel (or KC for King's Counsel). A barrister is accorded this title by the government of a province or of Canada in recognition of his or her merit and ability as counsel. It is sometimes suggested that, as with other honours, political effort rather than professional excellence determines the appointment. Originally a QC or KC (when the monarch is a king) represented the CROWN in court cases. The holder is entitled to wear a silk gown in court; hence the expression 'to take silk' means 'to become a QC'

Qimmik. Eskimo word for 'dog'. The *qimmik*, or *kimik*, usually has wolf blood in its background and is referred to as a HUSKY by southern Canadians, et al. Used as a beast of burden and not as a pet, it is well known for turning on man, particularly unknowing newcomers to the North. It generally travels in packs when loose and howls as a wolf does. Nowadays few real *qimmiks* survive owing to their displacement by the SKIDOO.

QPP. Initials of the QUEBEC PROVINCIAL POLICE.

Quadra. A 573-ton lighthouse tender owned by the Department of Marine and Fisheries.

Built in Paisley, Scot., in 1891, she was rammed on 26 Feb. 1916 by the Canadian Pacific steamer *Charmer* at the entrance to Nanaimo harbour and was beached to prevent her foundering. She was sold as a wreck to a local salvage and dredging company.

Quality Records. A record company established in Toronto in 1949. Founded by Harold P. Carson, an automobile tycoon, it distributes American labels in Canada and records some Canadian talent. Ian TYSON records for Broadlands, its country-and-western label.

Quarry. A literary magazine devoted to contemporary prose, poetry, and reviews. Originally founded in 1951 as a publication for students at Queen's University, it became in 1965—under the editorship of Tom MARSHALL, Tom Eadie, and Colin Norman—a magazine of national interest. Now an independent publication, it is issued three times a year and distributed by OBERON PRESS.

Quarter-section. In the Prairie Provinces the land was surveyed in 'sections', each of one square mile with road allowances between them. Under the Free Land Homestead Act of 1872 a settler was entitled to a free grant of a quarter-section (160 acres) provided that he occupied and improved it within a specified period, at which point he could obtain another quarter-section nearby for a nominal sum. Land in the West is still bought and sold in quarter-sections.

Que. Abbreviation of QUEBEC.

Quéant. See DROCOURT-QUÉANT.

Quebec. The oldest and largest Canadian province, it extends from 45° N to 62° N and is bounded by Ontario on the west, Hudson Strait and Ungava Bay on the north, and Labrador, New Brunswick, and the U.S. on the east and south. It possesses more northern territory than any other province, although this is very sparsely inhabited and—until the JAMES BAY PROJECT developed—largely unexploited. The Province of Quebec was created by the Proclamation of 1763; it extended west of the Ottawa R. to include land that is now part of Ontario. The British merchants who had arrived after the Conquest demanded British law, and in 1774 the QUEBEC ACT adopted both British criminal law and French civil law. In order to meet the demands of the LOYALISTS who had settled west of the Ottawa R. after the American Revolution, the CONSTITUTIONAL ACT OF 1791 was passed and the area east of the Ottawa R. was erected into the Province of Lower Canada. As a result of the REBELLION OF 1837 the ACT OF UNION (1841) was passed, by which Lower Canada became Canada East in the PROVINCE OF CANADA. In 1867, at CONFEDERATION, it became the province of Quebec. Nationalism in Quebec—the desire to evolve a separate destiny for French-speaking citizens of the province—developed in the 1860s but was partly kept in check by the regressive conditions caused by the power of the Church in secular matters, the domination of business and finance by English Canadians, and corruption in provincial governments. With the accession of Jean LESAGE as premier in 1960, the social structure of the province was reorganized in what is known as the QUIET REVOLUTION. This led to the desire for a SPECIAL STATUS within Confederation and to increasing demands for self-determination, many of which have been met by the federal government and some of which point to SEPARATISM: the formation of a sovereign state of Quebec.

An economy that was once dominated by agriculture and forestry has become greatly diversified during the past several decades with the opening up of many mines and hydro-electric installations in the CANADIAN SHIELD. The former include the iron-ore mines at Schefferville and Gagnon; copper, zinc, and silver production at Mattagami, Chibougamau, Murdochville, and elsewhere; and in the Appalachian regions asbestos production at Asbestos and Thetford Mines. These natural resources have led to the development of secondary manufacturing in the southern cities; among the most important are food and beverages, pulp and paper, electrical products, textiles and clothing, and chemicals.

With a land area of 523,860 sq. mi. and a 1971 population of 6,027,764, Quebec is unique among Canadian provinces in that just over 80% of the population is French speaking, being descended mainly from the 70,000 French colonists who were in NEW FRANCE when the Treaty of Paris was signed in 1763. Its capital is QUEBEC CITY and its motto is *Je me souviens* ('I remember').

Quebec. Feature film produced by Paramount in 1951. Directed by George Templeton, it starred John Barrymore Jr and was produced partly on location in Quebec City. A Hollywood version of the REBELLION OF 1837 in Lower Canada (Quebec), it also starred Corinne Calvet as a female Louis-Joseph PAPINEAU. 84 min., colour.

Quebec Act. The act of the British Parliament by which Quebec—the Canada of the day—was governed from 1774 to 1791. The area delineated included all the territory north to the HUDSON'S BAY COMPANY lands (later RUPERT'S LAND), as well as Indian territories in the southwest as far as the junction of the Mississippi and Ohio Rivers—a claim that angered the Thirteen Colonies and helped to precipitate the American Revolution in 1776. The liberal terms of the Act also specified the introduction of British criminal law, the retention of French civil law, and protected the rights of Roman Catholics. See also the CONSTITUTIONAL ACT OF 1791.

Quebec Angel of Peace. Colossal statue proposed but never built on the heights of Quebec City. It was to tower 152 ft above the Quebec ramparts (and thus stand 6 in. taller than the Statue of Liberty in New York). Its erection was proposed by Governor General Lord GREY who, in an address to the Women's Canadian Club of Montreal in 1908, saw the angelic figure 'offering her welcoming outstretched arms to clasp the whole of the old world to her bosom'.

Quebec Bridge. Spanning the St Lawrence R. 6 mi. above Quebec, it was designed as the world's longest cantilever bridge. It was begun in 1900, but as it neared completion in Aug. 1907 one of the cantilevers collapsed, killing 75. In Sept. 1916 the central span collapsed, killing 13. The bridge was finally completed in 1917. With a span of 1,800 ft, it was the greatest achievement in Canadian bridge-building for half a century.

Quebec Chronicle-Telegraph, The. A daily newspaper published in Quebec City. It traces its history back to the founding of the *Quebec Gazette* in 1764, thus claiming to be 'the oldest continuing newspaper in North

Quebec Chronicle-Telegraph

America'. It is the result of a merger in 1926 of the *Morning Chronicle* (founded in 1847) and the *Quebec Telegraph* (founded in 1872).

Quebec City. The oldest continuously inhabited settlement in North America and the capital of QUEBEC. Associated with the Indian village of STADACONA, visited by CARTIER, and founded as a fur-trading post in 1608 by Samuel de CHAMPLAIN, it played a crucial role in the development of NEW FRANCE as its capital (1663). After the British captured it in 1759 and gained official possession in 1763, it remained the political and military centre of Canada for some years, with timber and ship-building as its major industries. Its economic and political position began to change in the mid-nineteenth century with the growth of Montreal and Toronto, so that today its principal functions are related to its role as provincial capital and to tourism. It is the only walled city in North America. Picturesquely situated at a narrowing of the St Lawrence R., with its Upper Town on CAPE DIAMOND and its Lower Town below, with many historic buildings and narrow cobbled streets, and with the PLAINS OF ABRAHAM nearby, the scene of WOLFE'S famous victory over MONTCALM in 1759, it attracts many thousands of visitors annually. Its 1971 CMA population was 480,502. Its official motto is *Don de Dieu Feray Valoir* ('God's Gift to Make the Most'). See also ARTILLERY PARK, BREAK-NECK STAIRS, CARTIER-BRÉBEUF PARK, CHÂTEAU FRONTENAC, CHÂTEAU ST LOUIS, the CITADEL, DUFFERIN TERRACE, HABITATION, HÔTEL-DIEU DE QUÉBEC, JACQUET HOUSE, NATIONAL BATTLEFIELDS PARK, NOTRE-DAME-DE-LA-PAIX DE QUÉBEC, NOTRE-DAME-DES-VICTOIRES, PROMENADE DES GOUVERNEURS, QUEBEC CITY WALLS AND GATES, QUEBEC CONFERENCE, QUEBEC MUSEUM, QUEBEC WINTER CARNIVAL, UNIVERSITÉ LAVAL, URSULINE CONVENT, WOLFE'S COVE.

Quebec City Walls and Gates. A national historic park in QUEBEC CITY, the only walled city in North America. The walls originally had five handsome gates—St-Louis (1693), St-Jean (1693), Palace (1750), Hope (1786), and Prescott (1797)—which were torn down in 1871. The three gates standing today—St-Louis, St-Jean, and Kent—were constructed in the late 1870s and the 1880s as part of a building program inspired by Governor General Lord Dufferin. St-Louis and Kent Gates were designed by Charles BAILLAIRGÉ. Kent Gate, built in 1879 on the site of an old postern, was paid for by Queen Victoria in memory of her father, the Duke of KENT, who had been stationed in Quebec from 1791 to 1793.

Quebec Conference. (i) The second conference, held in Oct. 1864—following the CHARLOTTETOWN CONFERENCE of the month before—to discuss the federal union of the colonies of British North America. SEVENTY-TWO RESOLUTIONS were adopted, which formed the basis of the BNA ACT, 1867, on which CONFEDERATION is founded. (ii) Top-level meetings held in Quebec City during the Second World War. The first conference was held in Aug. 1943, the second in Sept. 1944. Both conferences, held in the CHÂTEAU FRONTENAC, were attended by Prime Minister Churchill and President Roosevelt as Combined Chiefs of Staff. Since Canada was not represented, Prime Minister Mackenzie KING attended as 'host'.

Quebec Department of Cultural Affairs. See MINISTÈRE DES AFFAIRES CULTURELLES DU QUÉBEC.

Quebec heater. A cast-iron heating stove with a tall, cylindrical firebox, manufactured in Quebec in the late-nineteenth century.

Quebec lieutenant. A spokesman for Quebec's special interests. In the federal government the position, unofficial but traditional, is invariably filled by a French-speaking minister of cabinet rank who represents a Quebec constituency.

Quebec Museum/Musée du Québec. Provincially funded museum in National Battlefields Park, Quebec City. It was designed by Wilfrid Lacroix in 1927 and opened in 1933. Representing the evolution of Quebec culture from the seventeenth century onward, the collection includes historical and ethnological material, masterpieces of Quebec art from early times to the present, sculpture and graphics, and natural-science exhibitions.

Québec Nordiques. See WORLD HOCKEY ASSOCIATION.

Quebec North Shore and Labrador Railway. Owned by the Iron Ore Company of Canada, it is its main freight line for iron ore from mines at Schefferville, Que., near the Quebec-Labrador border, to the town of Sept-Îles on the St Lawrence R. The QNS&L was opened in 1954.

Quebec Provincial Police A provincial law-enforcement body established on 1 Feb. 1870. It now numbers some 4,000. The French name is Sûreté du Québec.

Quebec Tercentenary. A celebration in Quebec City from 20 to 31 July 1908 that marked the anniversary of the founding of Quebec by Samuel de CHAMPLAIN 300 years earlier. A military and naval occasion, it was climaxed by a historical pageant. A series of commemorative stamps, the Quebec Tercentenary Issue of 1908, appeared to mark the anniversary.

Quebec Winter Carnival. Week-long festivity held annually in Quebec City. The first *Carnaval* was held in 1894, but the current festivities date from 1954. A pre-Lenten festival held in late February or early March, it features JEAN BONHOMME—also called *Bonhomme Carnaval*—'the only talking snowman in the world'.

Québecair. Regional airline. Established in 1946 with headquarters in Montreal, and known under its present name since 1953, Québecair offers scheduled services in Quebec and Labrador, as well as North American charter flights.

Quebecker. A native or resident of QUEBEC. In contemporary usage, a Quebecker is likely to be an English-speaking person, QUÉBÉCOIS being reserved for a French-speaking person.

Québécois. A native or resident of QUEBEC; the people of Quebec. In contemporary usage, a Québécois (the feminine form is Québécoise) is always French speaking, the word QUEBECKER being reserved for an English-speaking person.

Queen Anne's War (1702-13). North American phase of the War of the Spanish Succession between England and France. Fighting broke out between Acadia and New England—including three attacks on PORT ROYAL, the last in 1710, when it fell—and in Newfoundland. It was ended by the TREATY OF UTRECHT in 1713.

Queen Charlotte Islands. A large chain of islands about 200 mi. long just south of the Alaska boundary. Although so far north, they enjoy mild winters, with rare clinging snow, owing to warming ocean currents. HAIDA Indians work the ARGILLITE quarries found there.

Queen City. The nickname of TORONTO and other Canadian cities. Toronto may have been called 'the Queen City' because of its loyalty to British institutions in the mid-nineteenth century. REGINA (the name itself is the Latin for 'queen') has been called 'the Queen City of the Plains'. VICTORIA (named after the British queen) is known as 'the Queen City of British Columbia'.

Queen of the Coast. Unofficial motto of VANCOUVER, from the poem entitled 'A Toast' by Pauline JOHNSON.

Queen on Moose. An acrylic sketch of Queen Elizabeth II riding a moose. It was drawn by Charles Pachter (b.1942), a Toronto artist who studied at the Sorbonne and the University of Toronto, and it formed the centerpiece of 'Monarchs of the North', an exhibition of Pachter's work that opened in Toronto in June 1973 during a Royal Visit. The controversial show included numerous images based on a Canadian child's recollection of royal visits. *Queen on Moose* has been reproduced as a silkscreen and as a lithograph in red, pink, blue, beige, green and grey.

Queen's Bench. Legal term for the SUPERIOR COURT of a province with power to try the most serious cases, both civil and criminal. Its judges exercise supervisory authority over the judges of lower courts.

Queen's Birthday. See VICTORIA DAY.

Queen's Bush. The name given the backwoods of Canada West (Ontario) near Lake Huron and Georgian Bay, north of the HURON TRACT, when a region of two million acres was opened for colonization in Apr. 1847. It included present-day Bruce, Dufferin, Grey, and Wellington Counties.

Queen's Counsel. See QC.

Queen's Fellowships. Awarded annually to three Canadian graduate students specializing in the field of Canadian studies at an M.A. level. The fellowships were created by the Government of Canada to commemorate the visit to this country of Queen Elizabeth II in 1973. Worth up to $5,000 each, plus tuition and travel, they are administered by the CANADA COUNCIL.

Queen's Own Rifles of Canada, The. Canadian army regiment. Organized in Toronto in 1860, it served in France and Flanders during the FIRST WORLD WAR, distinguishing itself at YPRES, the SOMME, and VIMY. In the SECOND WORLD WAR it served as part of the 8th Infantry Brigade in the NORMANDY INVASION and later in numerous battles with the 3rd Canadian Infantry Division. Battalions have since served in Korea and Germany.

Queen's Park. A reference to the Ontario legislature, located in downtown Toronto. The pink sandstone Romanesque Revival Parliament Building—designed by the American architect R.A. Waite and occupying the site of a lunatic asylum (demolished in the

1880s)—was formally opened on 4 Apr. 1893. The park behind the Parliament Building—named after Queen Victoria—was opened in 1860 by her son, the Prince of Wales, later Edward VII, and contains an equestrian statue of him that once stood in Edward Park, Delhi.

Queen's Plate. The oldest continuously run turf event in North America. It dates from 1859 when Queen Victoria arranged for an annual grant of 50 guineas to be presented to the winner of a horse race to be run at Toronto or some other location in what is now Ontario. The first race was on 27 June 1860, on Carlton Track in Toronto. It continued there for four years until the site was moved to several provincial towns and then returned to Toronto in 1883, where it has been held ever since. The length of the race, now held in late June, has varied but is firmly established at New Woodbine as one and a quarter miles. The annual event remains among the most popular horse-races on the continent. It has had numerous royal visits and the winning owner receives the Queen's personal gift of 50 gold sovereigns and a gold cup. A list follows of winners (with owners, jockeys, and time) since the race moved to the New Woodbine in 1956:

1956 Canadian Champ, Mr W.R. Beasley, D. Stevenson, 1 min., 55 sec.
1957 Lyford Cay, Mr E.P. TAYLOR, A. Gomez, 2 min., 2 and 3/5 sec.
1958 Caledon Beau, Mr C. SMYTHE, A. Coy, 2 min., 4 and 1/5 sec.
1959 New Province, WINDFIELDS Farm, R. Ussery, 2 min., 4 and 4/5 sec.
1960 Victoria Park, Windfields Farm, A. GOMEZ, 2 min., 2 sec.
1961 Blue Light, K.R. Marshall, H. Dittfach, 2 min., 5 sec.
1962 Flaming Page, Windfields Farm, J. Fitzsimmons, 2 min., 4 and 3/4 sec.
1963 Canebora, Windfields Farm, M. Ycaza, 2 min., 4 sec.
1964 NORTHERN DANCER, Windfields Farm, W. Hartack, 2 min., 2 and 1/5 sec.
1965 Whistling Sea, Olivier Ranches, T. Inouye, 2 min., 3 and 4/5 sec.
1966 Titled Hero, P.K. Marshall, A. GOMEZ, 2 min., 3 and 3/5 sec.
1967 Jammed Lovely, C. SMYTHE, J. Fitzsimmons, 2 min., 3 sec.
1968 Merger, Golden West Farm, W. Harris, 2 min., 5 and 2/5 sec.
1969 Jumpin Joseph, Warren Beasley, A. GOMEZ, 2 min., 4 and 1/5 sec.
1970 Almoner, Parkview Stable, S. HAWLEY, 2 min., 4 and 4/5 sec.
1971 Kennedy Road, Mrs A. Stollery, S. HAW-LEY, 2 min., 3 sec.
1972 Victoria Song, Green Hills Farm, R. Platts, 2 min., 3 and 1/5 sec.
1973 Royal Chocolate, Stafford Farms, Ted Colangelo, 2 min., 8 sec.
1974 Amber Herod, Stafford Farms, R. Platts, 2 min., 9 and 1/5 sec.
1975 L'Enjoleur, J.L. Levesque, S. HAWLEY, 2 min., 2 and 3/5 sec.
1976 Norcliffe, Charles Baker, Jeff Fell, 2 min., 5 sec.

Queen's Printer. The deputy minister of either the federal or a provincial government responsible for the publication and distribution of documents and records. The title and function of the federal Queen's Printer were assumed by INFORMATION CANADA from 1970 to 1976, when the Department of Supply and Services took over. The Queen's Printer for Canada prints and publishes almost as many titles as all the commercial publishers in Canada combined.

Queen's Quarterly. Academic journal published by QUEEN'S UNIVERSITY, Kingston, since 1893. It includes learned articles on current affairs and scholarly articles on the humanities as well as original prose and poetry and reviews of current books.

Queen's University. Located in Kingston, Ont., it began as an institution of the Presbyterian Church and was issued a charter by Queen Victoria in 1841. Denominational control was lifted in 1912. Queen's has one of the major law faculties in the province and an important faculty of education. It publishes QUEEN'S QUARTERLY. See also George Munro GRANT.

Queen's York Rangers, The. Canadian army regiment. Also known as the 1st American Regiment after a Loyalist regiment of the American Revolutionary War, it originated in 1866 and provided companies for service in the NORTHWEST REBELLION and the SOUTH AFRICAN WAR. In the FIRST WORLD WAR it served in numerous battles in Europe, including YPRES, VIMY, and AMIENS. During the SECOND WORLD WAR it was on active service for local protection.

Queenston Heights, Battle of. An engagement in the WAR OF 1812. On 13 Oct. 1812 Gen. Sir Isaac BROCK was mortally wounded leading an attack on the heights south of Queenston, which were occupied by American forces under Gen. Stephen Van Rensselaer. Later that day Gen. Roger Sheaffe drove the American invaders from the heights in a successful attack. See also QUEENSTON HEIGHTS AND BROCK'S MONUMENT.

Queenston Heights and Brock's Monument.
National historic park at Queenston, Ont.
On these slopes the Battle of QUEENSTON
HEIGHTS was fought in the WAR OF 1812 on 13
Oct. 1812. The American invaders were
turned back, but Gen. Sir Isaac BROCK was
killed. He lies buried beneath the 184-ft monument that towers over the surrounding
countryside and the Niagara R. Built in 1824,
it was blown up during the REBELLION OF 1837
and a new monument was erected in 1854 to
the design of William THOMAS—a tall fluted
Corinthian column in the tradition of Nelson's monument in Trafalgar Square and superbly sited.

Quelques arpents de neige. 'A few acres of
snow'. This phrase was made famous by
Voltaire in *Candide* (1759) when he wrote that
the French and the English 'have been at war
over a few acres of snow near Canada, and
that they are spending on this fine struggle
more than Canada itself is worth.' An arpent
is about one and a quarter acres.

Quentin Durgens, M.P. A popular CBC-TV series about a bachelor backbencher who rights
as many wrongs as he can. It starred Gordon
PINSENT as the Member from Moose Falls, a
fictitious Ontario constituency, and was
created and written by George ROBERTSON.
Directed by David Gardner and Peter
Boretski, it first appeared on 7 Oct. 1965 as a
six-part drama under the title 'Mr. Member
of Parliament'. It was retitled and seen from
6 Dec. 1966 to 4 Feb. 1969.

Quest. An adventurous CBC-TV series on the
arts. Created and produced by Ross McLEAN
and hosted by Andrew ALLAN, it made its
début (as 'Q for Quest') on 3 Jan. 1961 with
the television première of Len PETERSON'S
BURLAP BAGS. After the first season it was produced by Daryl DUKE and premièred Jules
Feiffer's play *Crawling Arnold* and George
RYGA'S *Indian*. 'Quest' commissioned *One
Time Around*, the film biography of Hugh
Hefner, directed by Richard Ballentine and
Gordon Sheppard, in 1962. The series was
concluded on 10 Mar. 1964 (with a program
on Bob Dylan) when Duke left to produce the
'Steve Allen Show' in New York.

Question Period. A CTV Network program.
Produced in Ottawa since the fall of 1968, it
features for 30 minutes each week a politician
in the news who is questioned by three panelists (two regulars, Charles Lynch and Doug
Fisher, plus a special guest); it is moderated
by Bruce Phillips. It has been called 'television's most quoted news program'.

Quiet Canadian, The. Sobriquet of Sir William Stephenson (b.1896), inventor, and coordinator of British and American intelligence operations during the Second World
War. Born in Manitoba, he served in the Canadian Army during the First World War.
After the war he went into business in England and in 1924 invented the wireless
photo-transmission process. In 1940 he was
appointed Winston Churchill's chief espionage agent in North America and was
knighted for his services in 1945. He is the
subject of two post-war biographies: *The
Quiet Canadian: The Secret Service Story of Sir
William Stephenson* (1962) by H. Montgomery
Hyde and *A Man Called Intrepid* (1976) by William Stevenson, a journalist. He is retired
and lives in Bermuda.

Quiet diplomacy. A phrase used to describe
Canada's foreign policy towards the United
States, and the implementation of it on a private and non-confrontational basis. Specifically associated with the policies of the PEAR
SON government during the 1960s, it
assumed a special relationship with the U.S.
based on economic and geographic ties. It
was expounded in *Canada and the United
States: Principles for Partnership* (June 1965) by
A.D.P. Heeney and Livingston T. Merchant.
It was attacked by Canadian nationalists and
others who held anti-American views regarding the Vietnam War and deplored the
Canadian government's lack of public censure concerning it.

Quiet Revolution. Political phrase associated
with the Liberal administration of Premier
Jean LESAGE in the province of Quebec. Between 1960 and 1966 Lesage made major educational and social reforms and pressed
Quebec's case for SPECIAL STATUS within Confederation.

Quilico, Louis (b.1926). Baritone. Born in
Montreal, he studied there and in New York.
He is well known in Canada through many
appearances in concert and with the CANA
DIAN OPERA COMPANY, but pursues a brilliant
international career. He has sung with the
Paris Opera; at Covent Garden; and with the
Vienna, Bolshoi, San Francisco, and New
York City Centre Operas. In 1974 he made
his début at the Metropolitan Opera, where
one of his great roles is Rigoletto. Between
engagements he teaches in the Faculty of
Music of the University of Toronto.

Quill & Quire. Magazine of the Canadian
book trade. Founded as a quarterly in 1935,
Quill & Quire has appeared on a monthly
basis since 1971. The tabloid is owned by
Greey de Pencier Publications and each issue

contains articles on the book trade, information about the world of Canadian publishing, and book reviews.

Quintal. In Newfoundland, a quantity of fish weighing 122 lb., or a container for dried and salted cod of that weight.

Quinze, Les Éditions. A writer's co-operative established in Montreal in Oct. 1975 to publish members' manuscripts. Founded by Gérard BESSETTE, Marie-Claire BLAIS, Jacques GODBOUT, and others, the publishing house

was called *quinze,* or fifteen, in the hope that it would issue a new book every 15 days. It publishes *Interventions,* a new literary magazine.

Qumaluk, Leah (b.1934). Eskimo artist at PO-VUNGNITUK. Her drawings and prints show a brooding dreamwork of fantasy and legendary images, characteristic of other Povungnituk artists.

Qurunnamik. The widely used Eskimo word for 'many thanks'.

R

Racan Photo-Copier Fraud. A classic case of fraud perpetrated by Elias Rabbiah, a Lebanese immigrant, who supposedly designed and built 'a revolutionary new photo-copy machine'. He founded a public company in Toronto in 1962 to promote his invention—which later turned out to be a competitor's machine with the nameplate removed—and collected over four million dollars in fees. Through manipulation, Racan stock rose from $3.50 to $26.00 and fell again. Charged with fraud in 1965, Rabbiah jumped bail and disappeared. The Racan promotion was a contributing factor in the failure of ATLANTIC ACCEPTANCE.

Rachel, Rachel. See *A* JEST OF GOD.

Radar. Acronym of RAdio Detection And Ranging, an electronic system devised in the United Kingdom prior to the Second World War by Sir Robert Watson-Watt (1892-1973), who later moved to Thornhill, north of Toronto, where he developed the commercial possibilities of his invention.

Raddall, Thomas H. (b.1903). Novelist. Born in Hythe, Eng., he was brought to Halifax in 1913. He is best known for his historical romances, which are informed by a rich knowledge of Nova Scotia history: HIS MAJESTY'S YANKEES (1942), *Roger Sudden* (1944), *Pride's Fancy* (1946), *The* GOVERNOR'S LADY (1960), and *Hangman's Beach* (1966). *The* NYMPH AND THE LAMP (1950), *Tidefall* (1953), and *Wings of the Night* (1956) are three novels with a contemporary setting. He is also the author of *Halifax: Warden of the North* (1948, 1965); *At the*

Tide's Turn and Other Stories (1959), a selection from four volumes of short stories; and *Footsteps on Old Floors* (1968), a collection of yarns and sketches. *In My Time,* his autobiography, appeared in 1976.

Radials. The name in southern Ontario for electrical-powered inter-urban streetcars. Radiating out of Toronto—one went as far north as Lake Simcoe—they operated from the 1890s and continued into the 1940s.

Radio-Canada, La Société. The French name of the CANADIAN BROADCASTING CORPORATION.

Radio Canada International. Since 1972, the name of the International Service of the CBC, unofficially called the 'Voice of Canada'. It consists of the CBC's shortwave radio service of news reports, commentaries, features, and music, prepared in Montreal in 11 languages (a drop from 16 in 1960) and beamed from CBC transmitters at Sackville, N.B. Now serving broadcasting organizations around the world through tape-recordings distributed by its transcription service, it was inaugurated on 25 Feb. 1945.

Radio Television Canada. Proposed name for the CANADIAN BROADCASTING CORPORATION.

Radio Television News Directors Association of Canada. See CHARLES EDWARDS AWARDS and DAN McARTHUR AWARDS.

'Radishes and Gooseberries'. Sobriquets given by young history students to two seventeenth-century explorers, Pierre-Esprit RA-

DISSON and Médard Chouart, sieur des GRO-
SEILLIERS.

Radisson, Pierre-Esprit (*c*.1640-1710).
Colourful explorer and coureur de bois, one
of the originators of the HUDSON'S BAY COM-
PANY. He was brought to Trois-Rivières in
1651. As a boy he was captured by the Mohawks (1651), escaped, was captured again
and escaped in 1653. In 1659, with his
brother-in-law GROSEILLIERS, he journeyed to
Lake Superior. (On his return in 1660 he
found the bodies of DOLLARD DES ORMEAUX
and his companions on the Ottawa R.) After
their furs were seized and they were fined
for going west without permission, they left
the colony, Radisson going to New England
and in 1665 to London, where in 1668 he was
engaged with Groseilliers by a group of merchants, the nucleus of the Hudson's Bay
Company. They made several fur-trading expeditions to Hudson Bay between 1670 and
1675, the year they deserted England for
France. They returned to the Bay in 1682 for
some Canadian merchants and established
Fort Bourbon on the Hayes R., which Radisson captured in 1684 after he had gone back
to the HBC's service; it was renamed YORK FAC-
TORY. Radisson lived in Hudson Bay from
1685 to 1687, the year he became a British
subject. His account of his voyages, in im-
perfect but vivid English, can be read in *The
Explorations of Pierre Esprit Radisson* . . . (1961)
edited by A.T. Adams. See also ADVENTURES
OF PIERRE RADISSON and RADISHES AND GOOSE-
BERRIES.

RAdm. Official abbreviation of Rear-Admi-
ral.

Railrodder, The. Short film starring Buster
Keaton produced by the NATIONAL FILM BOARD
in 1965. One of the last films made by the
famous silent-film star, it was produced by
Julian Biggs and directed by Gerald Potterton. Keaton is seen crossing Canada from
east to west on a railway track scooter. Not a
word is spoken but there are many sight
gags. (24 min., 47 sec.; colour). The actual
filming of *The Railrodder* was the subject of a
second film, *Buster Keaton Rides Again* (55
min., 25 sec.; b & w), a documentary directed
by John Spotton and produced by Julian
Biggs. It includes interviews with Keaton
and his wife and clips from his early films.

Rain, Douglas (b.1928). Actor. Born in Winnipeg, Man., he studied at the Banff School
of Fine Arts (BANFF CENTRE) (1948-9) and the
Old Vic, London (1950-3). He understudied
Alec Guinness at the first STRATFORD FESTIVAL
in 1953, and played many important roles

with distinction at the Festival in the years
following, appearing most recently as An-
gelo in *Measure for Measure* (1975, 1976). He
created the title role in *Hadrian VII* at the
Mermaid Theatre, London, in 1968, and his
was the off-screen voice of HAL 9000, the ma-
levolent computer, in *2001: A Space Odyssey*
(1968). Since 1974 he has taught at the NA-
TIONAL THEATRE SCHOOL. He is married to the
actress Martha HENRY.

Rainbow. The first ship commissioned (on 4
Aug. 1910) in the ROYAL CANADIAN NAVY. A
3,600-ton cruiser, she had been launched for
the Royal Navy in 1891. Apart from two
small submarines, she alone defended Canada's Pacific coast during the First World
War. She was sold for scrap in 1920.

Rainbow Bridge. A suspension bridge that
spans the Niagara R. between Niagara Falls,
Ont., and Niagara Falls, N.Y. The 950-ft
arch-span bridge was built to replace the
HONEYMOON BRIDGE and was officially opened
on 1 Nov. 1941.

Rainmaker, The. Sobriquet of Keith DAVEY.

Ralliement des Créditistes, Le. Official name
of the Quebec wing of the SOCIAL CREDIT
PARTY. It is sometimes abbreviated to 'the
Rally'.

Rambler. An early light aircraft first flown in
1929. Only 36 were designed and manufactured by Curtiss-Reid, Montreal. None is
known to have survived.

Ramezay, Claude de. See CHÂTEAU DE RAME-
ZAY.

Rand Formula. A reference to the famous
and influential settlement effected by Mr Justice Ivan Rand of the Supreme Court of Canada in a labour dispute involving the Ford
Motor Company in Jan. 1946. Both labour
and management agreed to accept the principle—or 'formula'—of union security,
whereby management deducted the equivalent of union dues from the pay of non-union
workers, since it was said that they benefited
from the union's bargaining activities.

Rang **system.** A system of land division, also
known as the long lots of Quebec, established during the seventeenth and eighteenth centuries to give colonists access to a
river, notably the St Lawrence. The lots had
a small river frontage ranging from 490 to 820
ft and originally an indeterminate depth.
When these waterfront lots were used up a
second *rang* or tier of lots was established behind the first. See also SEIGNEURIAL TENURE.

Rapee pie

Rapee pie. An Acadian dish popular in the Maritime provinces and Quebec. It combines fowl and rabbit or pork with potatoes and onions. The name is derived from the French word *râpé* for 'grated'.

Rapido. Fast inter-city train introduced by CN on its Montreal-Toronto run on 31 Oct. 1965. It covers the 335-mi. distance in 4 hours, 59 minutes. See also TURBO.

Rapoport, Janis (b.1946). Poet. Born in Toronto and educated at Neuchâtel and New College, University of Toronto, she worked in publishing in London, Eng., before returning to Toronto in 1970. She is a member of the editorial board of the TAMARACK REVIEW and an effective reader of her own poetry, some of which has been collected in *Within the Whirling Moment* (1967) and *Jeremy's Dream* (1974).

Raquette. The French word for SNOWSHOE.

Rasky, Frank (b.1924). Journalist and author. Born in Toronto, a brother of the TV producer Harry RASKY, he is a graduate of the University of Toronto. From 1954 to 1962 he edited *New* LIBERTY and then spent eight years writing on theatre for the *New York Herald-Tribune* and on film for *Variety*. He returned to Toronto in 1970 as a features writer for the TORONTO STAR. He is the author of *Gay Canadian Rogues, Swindlers, Gold-Diggers and Spies* (1958), *Great Canadian Disasters* (1961), *The Taming of the Canadian West* (1967), and *The Polar Voyageurs* (1976).

Rasky, Harry (b.1928). Television producer. Born in Toronto, the brother of Frank RASKY, he worked as a reporter for four years and in 1956 as a producer for CBC-TV's 'Newsmagazine'. From 1956 to the early 1970s he worked in television in New York, producing such award-winning documentaries as 'Upon This Rock' (1969). For CBC-TV he has produced important documentaries on Jerusalem, Bernard Shaw, and Marc Chagal.

Rasmussen, Knud (1879-1933). Danish explorer. Born in Greenland, the son of a Danish missionary and an Eskimo woman, he began his ethnological studies of the Eskimo in 1902. From the scientific station he established at Thule, Cape York, Greenland, in 1910, he led four scientific expeditions to northern Greenland. The fifth THULE Expedition (1921-4) took him to the Canadian Arctic with Kaj Birket-Smith, Therkel Mathiassen, and Peter Freuchen, who studied the eastern Arctic while Rasmussen went on to visit the Eskimos of the Mackenzie R. and Alaska. His account of this journey appeared in *Across Arctic America* (1927). Rasmussen died before completing his famous *Report of the Fifth Thule Expedition,* which was published in 10 volumes in 1931-4.

Rattenbury, Francis Mawson (1867-1935). Architect. Born in Leeds, Eng., and trained in the firm of Lockwood and Mawson, he came to Canada in 1892 and settled in Victoria, B.C. His most important work is the Parliament Building, Victoria, designed in 1892 and built in 1894-7, which has the exuberance of contemporary Edwardian baroque design in England and the strong sense of material characteristic of the Romanesque Revival in eastern Canada. He also designed (in Victoria) the more completely Romanesque Bank of Montreal (1896) and the EMPRESS HOTEL (1904-8) in a simplified version of the CHÂTEAU STYLE.

Raven. The trickster hero / culture hero of the HAIDA, TSIMSHIAN, and other Northwest Coast Indian groups. Robert Ayre calls him by his Tahltan name in his imaginative retelling of the cycle, *Sketco, the Raven* (1961). Raven was born 'beyond the rim of the world, in the high North, in the North beyond the North'. Assuming bird form or human form at will, he stole the sun, moon, and stars for the Indian people, who had formerly huddled in the darkness and cold. He descended to the sea floor to battle the Shark People and to the mountaintops to defeat the Thunder Man. He inveigled fire from the Snowy Owl and brought civilization to the Indians. But one day 'he rose higher on his broad black wings and vanished into the North, content to be remembered in their tales.' See also the ARTS OF THE RAVEN.

Ravenscrag. Montreal mansion of the Allan family. Built about 1865 by J. W. Hopkins for Sir Hugh ALLAN, it was named after a knoll of moorland in Allan's native Ayrshire, Scot. It was also the home of his son, Sir Hugh Montague ALLAN who, lacking an heir, donated it to the Royal Victoria Hospital in 1943. It now houses the Neurological Institute of the Royal Victoria Hospital.

Rawhide. Radio character created and impersonated by broadcaster and writer Max FERGUSON. 'Old Rawhide', first heard on CBC Halifax in 1946, was such a success that he became the mainstay of 'The Max Ferguson Show', which was heard over CBC Radio from Toronto between 1949 and 1961.

Ray, Carl (b.1943). Ojibwa artist. Born on the Sandy Lake Reserve in northern Ontario, the grandson of a Cree medicine man, he worked as a trapper, fisherman, and miner before teaching himself how to paint while recovering from tuberculosis in the sanatorium at Thunder Bay. His painting and printmaking owe something to Norval MORRISSEAU, who has called him 'little brother'. Ray's acrylics, pen-and-ink drawings, and prints depict the legends of the Cree-Ojibwa people and are done in bright colours in a free-flowing manner. He illustrated James Stephen's *Sacred Legends of the Sandy Cree* (1971).

Rayner, Gordon (b.1935). Painter. Born in Toronto, he is largely self-taught. He worked as a commercial artist and now teaches at the NEW SCHOOL OF ART, Toronto. An exceptionally versatile painter of both landscapes and geometric shapes in oil and acrylic, he has used both realistic and abstract-expressionist techniques to explore the abstract elements of landscape forms. Mysteriously lush paintings like *Magnetawan No 2* (1965, NGC) show his interest in the northern Ontario landscape. His strength as a colourist is seen in both hard-edge experiments and in his Turneresque washes of colour. He has exhibited internationally.

Razilly, Isaac de (1587-1635). French naval officer, colonizer, and governor of ACADIA. As the result of a report he wrote for Cardinal Richelieu in 1626, the COMPANY OF NEW FRANCE was formed as a colonizing company. Razilly was made lieutenant-general of New France in 1632 and sailed with supplies, workmen, and colonists to Acadia, landing on the south shore of Nova Scotia at La Hève (now La Have), where he established a colony and where he died.

RCA. See ROYAL CANADIAN ACADEMY OF ARTS.

RCAF. See ROYAL CANADIAN AIR FORCE.

RCMP. See ROYAL CANADIAN MOUNTED POLICE.

RCMP. A television series on the ROYAL CANADIAN MOUNTED POLICE produced for CBC-TV and British television by Crawley Films. It made its début on 28 Oct. 1959 to a measure of popular acclaim. There were 39 half-hour episodes starring Gilles Pelletier as Corporal Jacques Gagnier, Don Francks as Constable Mitchell, and John Perkins as Constable Scott, members of the three-man detachment at the fictitious French community of Shamattawa. The action was photographed near Aylmer, Que. The executive producer was F. R. (Budge) CRAWLEY, the producer Harry Horner, the writer George SALVERSON.

RCN, RCNR. See ROYAL CANADIAN NAVY.

RDIA. See Department of REGIONAL ECONOMIC EXPANSION.

Readers' Club of Canada. The only Canadian-owned book club. It was established by Peter and Carol Martin of PETER MARTIN ASSOCIATES, a Toronto publishing house, in 1959. It publishes the *Canadian Reader*, a monthly bulletin, for its more than 3,000 members.

Reader's Digest, The. The largest paid-circulation magazine in Canada. The monthly publication was founded in the United States in 1922, and until 1943 the American edition was sold in Canada. That year the CANADIAN EDITION was established in Montreal, and in 1947 the French edition, *Sélection du Reader's Digest*, was founded. English circulation in 1975 was 1,220,000; French circulation, 255,000. The Canadian edition is edited and printed in Montreal and differs from the American edition in that approximately one-fifth of the articles in any single issue have been specially commissioned from Canadian authors. *The Reader's Digest* is published in 13 languages in 26 editions around the world.

'Ready, aye, ready'. Traditional British answer to the call to arms (and the motto of the Napiers, an old English family). The jingoistic phrase was used in the House of Commons by Sir George Foster in 1896; by Sir Wilfrid LAURIER in 1914; and by Arthur MEIGHEN, the Conservative leader, in a speech in Toronto during the Chanak crisis of 1922, when Britain cabled Ottawa to ask for troops if war broke out with Turkey. No reply was given, and the crisis came to nothing, but Meighen declared: 'When Britain's message came, then Canada should have said: "Ready, aye ready; we stand by you." '

Reaney, James (b.1926). Poet and playwright. Born on a farm near Stratford, Ont., and educated at the University of Toronto, he joined the English Department of the University of Manitoba in 1949 and since 1961 has been at the University of Western Ontario, where he is a professor. He is an ingenious and imaginative writer of poetry and plays, strongly interested in the illuminating powers of symbol and myth. The poems from his early volumes—*The Red Heart* (1949), *A Suit of Nettles* (1958), *Twelve Letters to a Small Town* (1962), and *The Dance of Death at London, Ontario* (1963)—are collected in *Poems* (1972), edited by Germaine Warkentin. His *Selected Longer Poems* (1975) and *Selected Shorter Poems* (1976) followed. Since 1960, the year that saw the production of his chamber opera NIGHT-BLOOMING CEREUS and his poetic entertainment *One-Man Masque*,

Reaney

Reaney has concentrated on writing for the theatre. His plays, long and short ones, have been both widely produced and published: *The KILLDEER and Other Plays* (including 'Night-Blooming Cereus', 'The Sun and the Moon', 'One-Man Masque', 1962); *Colours in the Dark* (1969); *Apple Butter and Other Plays for Children* ('Names and Nicknames', 'Geography Match', 'Ignoramus', 1972, *Listen to the Wind* (1972); *Masks of Childhood* ('The Easter Egg', 'Three Desks', 'The Killdeer', 1972); and the trilogy on the DONNELLYS: *Sticks and Stones* (1975), *The St Nicholas Hotel* (1975), and *Handcuffs* (1975). Reaney edited, handset, and printed his own magazine, ALPHABET (1961-71), and wrote a children's book about William Lyon MACKENZIE, *The Boy with an R in His Hand* (1965).

Rebellion Losses Bill. A controversial measure introduced into the legislative assembly of the Province of Canada in 1849. It provided funds to compensate those in Canada East (Quebec) who sustained losses in the suppression of the REBELLION OF 1837. Its opponents referred to it as the 'rebel rewarding bill' and it aroused a mob to burn the Parliament buildings in Montreal. The fact that Governor Lord ELGIN signed it into law on the advice of his ministers—an early manifestation of the principle of RESPONSIBLE GOVERNMENT—made it a landmark in Canadian constitutional history. See also ANNEXATION MANIFESTO.

Rebellion of 1837. Insurrections led by Louis-Joseph PAPINEAU in Lower Canada (Quebec) and by William Lyon MACKENZIE in Upper Canada (Ontario). Both men led groups of radical PATRIOTES (L.C.) and REFORMERS (U.C.) that took violent action to express their grievances against the anti-democratic governing establishment. Among other things, they wanted the appointed councils to be responsible to the elected legislative assemblies and they were opposed to the system of granting Crown lands (see CLERGY RESERVES). Abortive uprisings took place in Lower Canada at SAINT-CHARLES, SAINT-DENIS, and SAINT-EUSTACHE; and in Upper Canada at MONTGOMERY'S TAVERN, Toronto. See also Battle of the WINDMILL.

Receiver General of Canada. The national treasurer responsible for all public money on deposit, called the CONSOLIDATED REVENUE FUND. See also the Department of SUPPLY AND SERVICES.

Reciprocity. Economic movement favouring the mutual abolition or reduction of customs duties between Canada and the United States. A treaty establishing free trade in nat-

ural products existed from 1854 to 1866. Another agreement was reached in 1911, but when the Liberals, under Sir Wilfrid LAURIER, were defeated in the so-called Reciprocity Election later that year, the matter was dropped.

Recollets. Members of the Recollet branch of the Franciscan Order who served in Quebec from 1625 to 1629 and in other missions in New France after 1670.

Reconstruction Party. A political organization formed and led by H. H. Stevens for the 1935 election. Reconstruction was essentially a conservative small-business-oriented party that was created by Harry Stevens after his resignation from the R. B. BENNETT government in 1934. Although Reconstruction garnered 385,000 votes, it won only one seat—Stevens' own—and disappeared forthwith. Stevens rejoined the Conservative Party in 1938.

Recreation Canada. See SPORT CANADA.

Red Barn Theatre. A summer-stock company located in a red barn built in 1878-9 on farm land near Jackson's Point, 40 mi. north of Toronto. Since 1949 various producers—including Brian DOHERTY and Donald and Murray Davis (see DAVIS FAMILY)—have leased the theatre for eight weeks each summer to produce light comedies for vacationers. Marigold Charlesworth and Jean Roberts co-directed it from 1959 to 1964, and had a winter season at the Central Library Theatre, Toronto. In 1974 the 290-seat theatre was taken over by the Lake Simcoe Arts Foundation and productions have become part of the Festival of Theatre and Music.

Red Chamber. Traditional name for the SENATE, derived from the colour of the carpeting and other appointments.

Red Deer Badlands. See BADLANDS.

Red Ensign. See CANADIAN RED ENSIGN.

Red Fife wheat. See FIFE WHEAT.

Red Indian. A name (like 'Redskin' and 'Red Man') formerly applied to the North American Indian, derived from the appearance of the BEOTHUK of Newfoundland—the first aborigines seen by Europeans—who painted themselves with red ochre.

Red Maple, The. Canvas by A. Y. JACKSON. Painted in Nov. 1914 from a sketch made the previous month in Algonquin Park, Ont., it is a study of a rushing stream and its brown-coloured shore seen through a striking pattern of almost-bare branches to which brilliant red maple leaves cling. (NGC).

Red River. A river in Manitoba associated with MÉTIS settlers. An American river for most of its length, it enters Canada at the border directly south of Winnipeg, joining the Assiniboine R. at Winnipeg for the short distance north to Lake Winnipeg. As it is noted for its severe spring flooding, particularly in and around Winnipeg, a diversion channel has been constructed enabling floodwaters to bypass the city. See also RED RIVER SETTLEMENT.

Red river cart. A two-wheeled, horse-drawn cart associated with the RED RIVER SETTLEMENT. It was made entirely of wood and SHAGANAPPI and its ungreased axle gave forth a piercing sound as it bounced over the plains.

Red River Expedition. A military force of British troops and Canadian militia from Ontario and Quebec under Col. Garnet Wolseley sent to put down the RED RIVER REBELLION in May 1870. Facing many difficulties, Wolseley and his troops arrived at FORT GARRY on 24 Aug. 1870 to find that the rebellion was over, Riel having fled to the United States.

Red River Rebellion. An uprising of 1870 at the RED RIVER SETTLEMENT that preceded the founding of the province of Manitoba. The proposed sale of HUDSON'S BAY COMPANY territories to Canada threatened the MÉTIS, who were particularly aggravated when their lands, to which they had no legal title, were surveyed. Acts of resistance on the part of their leader, Louis RIEL, led to his occupying FORT GARRY (Nov. 1869), to the taking of prisoners, including Thomas SCOTT, and to the declaration of a Provisional Government (Jan. 1870). With the arrival of an expeditionary force under Gen. Garnet Wolseley in August, Riel fled and the rebellion collapsed. In March a small delegation had left for Ottawa with a Bill of Rights, many of the clauses of which were incorporated in the Manitoba Act (12 May 1870) under which the new province was created; an area of 1,400,000 acres was set aside for the half-breeds.

Red River Settlement. A colony at the junction of the Red and Assiniboine Rivers in ASSINIBOIA (Man.), on land granted by the HUDSON'S BAY COMPANY to Lord SELKIRK. It was founded in 1812, the year Fort Douglas was built. The settlers were harassed by the NORTH WEST COMPANY, whose opposition to the settlement climaxed in fighting at SEVEN OAKS (1816), after which the North West Company gained control of Fort Douglas.

The colony grew after 1817, when Selkirk regained control. FORT GARRY, which replaced Fort Douglas, was built in 1817-18. See also RED RIVER REBELLION.

'Red River Valley, The'. The best-known folksong in the West. Its refrain is: 'Then come sit here awhile e'er you leave us, / Do not hasten to bid us adieu, / Just remember the Red River Valley, / And the cowboy who loves you so true.'

Red Rose Tea. Brand name of the most popular tea in the country. It was first blended, branded, and packaged by T.H. Estabrooks and W.R. Miles, wholesale general merchants in Saint John, N.B., who, in 1894, began importing black teas from India and Ceylon instead of the more common green teas from China and Japan. The company, which also packaged Red Rose Coffee, was acquired by BROOKE BOND CANADA LIMITED in 1932. Red Rose Tea is exported in quantity to the United States.

Red Serge, The. A reference to the red jackets made of heavy wool serge worn by the ROYAL CANADIAN MOUNTED POLICE. This was the title of a collection of stories about the RCMP by Harwood Steele (1961).

'Red Tory'. 'A Conservative who prefers the CCF-NDP to the Liberals, or a socialist who prefers the Conservatives to the Liberals.' The phrase was first used in this sense by the political scientist Gad Horowitz in the *Canadian Journal of Economics and Political Science*, May 1966.

Red, White and Blue Days. CN's fare plan. Launched in 1962, and widely imitated, it promotes railway travel by offering lower fares on specific days of the week and in seasons of the year when travelling is not at its peak. Red days are the cheapest, white days the average, and blue days the most expensive.

Red Wing. A biplane produced by the AERIAL EXPERIMENT ASSOCIATION. It was built by Thomas Selfridge and first flown on 12 Mar. 1908. It carried F.W. (Casey) Baldwin 319 ft at a height of 10 ft before crashing into Lake Keuka, N.Y. Baldwin thus became the first Canadian to fly a heavier-than-air craft.

Redcoats. Sobriquet of the NORTH WEST MOUNTED POLICE, so called because of their scarlet jackets.

Redeemed Children. Displaced youngsters from Europe who were given new homes in Canada after the SECOND WORLD WAR. The 'Redeemed Children' numbered 1,116 Jewish

Redeemed Children

war orphans who, between Sept. 1947 and Mar. 1952, were settled by the Canadian Jewish Congress in eight of the ten provinces.

Redinger, Walter (b.1940). Sculptor. Born in Wallacetown, Ont., he studied in Detroit and at the Ontario College of Art. His large-scale fibreglass works are in non-objective blob-like shapes sometimes reminiscent of totemistic forms. Redinger has exhibited internationally, including the Venice Biennale in 1972, and has received commissions for sculptured pieces from the ROYAL WINNIPEG BALLET (1970).

Reeve. In Ontario and the West, the chairman of a village, TOWNSHIP, or municipal-district council.

Reeve, Edward H. (Ted) (b.1902). Athlete and sports-writer. The Toronto-born sports editor in his youth played on two GREY CUP champion football teams and three Dominion champion lacrosse teams. During the Second World War he served as gunner in Conn SMYTHE'S Sportsman's Battery and after three years was invalided home. Later he was a successful football coach with Balmy Beach and Queen's University. He is still active, writing a widely read and respected sports column for the *Toronto Sun*, where he is affectionately known as 'The Moaner' after one of his fictitious creations, 'Moaner McGuffy'.

Reformers. Supporters of moderate reform in Upper Canada (Ontario) in the 1830s. They wanted the colonial system of government to be modelled after the British cabinet system, which in British North America evolved as RESPONSIBLE GOVERNMENT. See also William Warren BALDWIN and Robert BALDWIN.

Refus Global. An important document by Paul-Émile BORDUAS—400 mimeographed copies of which were published on 9 Aug. 1948—that marked the beginning of modern French Canada, preaching liberation from all strictures and from all compromises with the controlling forces of society. As a result of it Borduas lost his teaching position at the École du Meuble in Montreal.

Regal. Automobile manufactured from 1914 to 1917 by Regal Motor Company, Berlin (Kitchener), Ont. It came with a four-cylinder or a V-8 engine.

Regenstreif, Peter (b.1936). Political scientist and pollster. Born in Montreal and educated at McGill and Cornell, he has taught at the University of Rochester since 1961 and been professor of Political Science and Canadian

Studies since 1970. The author of *The Diefenbaker Interlude: Parties and Voting in Canada* (1965), since 1962 he has taken political polls to predict the outcome of federal elections for the *Montreal Star* and the *Toronto Star*.

Regent Park. Housing complex in downtown Toronto, the first public-housing project in Canada. Bounded by Gerrard St on the north, River St on the east, Shuter St on the south, and Parliament St on the west, it is divided into two separate housing projects at Dundas St E. The northern project—begun by the City of Toronto as slum clearance in 1948—replaced several bocks of deteriorated mid- and late-nineteenth-century housing. It was influenced by British concepts of public housing that gave it an institutional character; the design, by J.E. Hoare, mixes two-storey housing with six-storey apartment blocks. The southern section of the project—designed by J.E. Hoare Jr with Page and Steele in 1957 and sponsored by the CENTRAL MORTGAGE AND HOUSING CORPORATION and a federal-provincial partnership—replaced some blighted areas of CABBAGETOWN with large-scale high-rise buildings. Though these apartments may fall behind current dwelling standards, they have more open tracts of land and recreation facilities than are presently required. However, the heavy concentration of people has contributed to social problems associated with the area.

Régiment de Trois-Rivières, Le. Canadian army regiment. Organized in 1871 as the 'Three Rivers Provisional Battalion of Infantry', it was redesignated its present name in 1949. During the FIRST WORLD WAR it was part of the 10th Reserve Battalion that provided reinforcements to the Canadian Corps. In the SECOND WORLD WAR it served as a tank battalion in England, and as part of the 1st Canadian Armoured Brigade in Sicily.

Regina. The capital of Saskatchewan. The site of a buffalo-hunting camp called PILE O' BONES, it was renamed Regina and made the capital of the Northwest Territories in 1882, when the CPR reached this point. Incorporated as a city in 1903, it was made the provincial capital in 1906. It was the headquarters of the NORTH WEST (later ROYAL CANADIAN) MOUNTED POLICE from 1882 until 1920. It is primarily a government city, although it also serves as the principal market town and service centre for the surrounding agricultural population of the wheat-growing Regina Plain. Its 1971 CMA population was 140,734. Its official motto is *Floreat Regina* ('Let Regina flourish'). See also WASCANA CENTRE.

Regina Five. An exhibition of abstract art that toured Canada in 1961. It was organized by Ronald BLOORE, then director of the NORMAN MACKENZIE ART GALLERY at the University of Saskatchewan, and included the work of five Regina-based painters influenced by the EMMA LAKE experience: Bloore, Ted Godwin, Kenneth Lochhead, Arthur McKay, and Douglas Morton. They were interested in simplified forms and colours. The exhibition's national tour was arranged by the National Gallery of Canada.

Regina Leader-Post. An evening newspaper published in Regina, Sask. Founded in 1883, it was purchased, along with the SASKATOON STAR-PHOENIX, in 1925 by Sir Clifford SIFTON. It is now owned by Armadale Publishers Ltd.

Regina Manifesto. The party platform of the CCF. It was first drafted by F.H. UNDERHILL and revised by other members of the LEAGUE FOR SOCIAL RECONSTRUCTION, then presented to the national executive of the CCF in Regina in 1933. After further revision it was adopted at the Regina Conference of the party in Aug. 1933. With close affinities to the manifesto of the LSR, it stated that 'The principle regulating production, distribution and exchange will be the supplying of human needs and not the making of profits. We aim to replace the present capitalist system, with its inherent injustice and inhumanity, by a social order . . . in which economic planning will supersede unregulated private enterprise and competition. . . .' It called for increased public ownership, and welfare measures that have since been put into effect by other parties: unemployment insurance and socialized medicine for all.

Regina Trench. Codeword for the German trench that was the objective of the CANADIAN CORPS fighting during the First World War at COURCELETTE, France, in Sept. 1916. Along with the Sudbury Trench and the Kenora Trench, it was taken in Nov. 1916.

Regional Development Incentives Act. See Department of REGIONAL ECONOMIC EXPANSION.

Regional Economic Expansion, Department of. Department of the federal government concerned with regional economic disparities. Established in 1969, DREE's function is to ensure that industrial growth is dispersed widely across Canada to bring employment and earning opportunities in the slow-growth regions as close as possible to those in the other parts of the country without interfering with a high over-all rate of national growth. The Department is responsible for programs under the Agricultural and Rural Development Act (ARDA), the Fund for Rural Economic Development (FRED), the Prairie Farm Rehabilitation Act (PFRA), and the Regional Development Incentives Act (RDIA).

Registered Home Ownership Savings Plan. Federal plan that came into effect in 1975. It permits the accumulation of savings of $1,000 per year tax-free towards the purchase of a residence (house or condominium) as long as the intended purchaser does not own residential property in the year of application.

Registered Retirement Savings Plan. A federal-government plan to allow tax-deductible savings for retirement. It was first introduced in 1957, and following certain changes in 1972 it permits a percentage of earned income to be set aside each year, tax-free, towards purchasing an annuity from a Canadian insurance company. The plan is operated through trust companies, banks, credit unions, investment firms, and insurance companies.

Reichswald. Forest in Holland near the Rhine, scene of fighting during the SECOND WORLD WAR. The First Canadian Army and British troops, fighting successfully in the pine forests and water-logged countryside, eventually cracked the Siegfried Line on 21 Feb. 1945.

Reid, George A. (1860-1947). Painter. Born near Wingham, C.W. (Ont.), he studied painting in Philadelphia with Thomas Eakins and in Paris in 1888-9. After settling in Toronto he became known for large genre paintings that appealed to the taste of the time. Two of his paintings—MORTGAGING THE HOMESTEAD (1890, NGC) and a picture of a boy reading *The Arabian Nights* in a hay loft, *Forbidden Fruit* (1889, AGH)—are two of the best-known images associated with nineteenth-century Canadian painting.

Reid, Kate (b.1930). Actress. Born in London, Eng., she graduated from the University of Toronto and performed with the HART HOUSE THEATRE and the CREST THEATRE. An actress of tremendous power and presence, she has successfully undertaken a wide variety of roles on the stage and in television and films in Canada and the United States. She has appeared in seven seasons of the STRATFORD FESTIVAL. On Broadway she played opposite Alec Guinness in *Dylan* (1964) and, opening on 13 Oct. 1962, undertook the taxing role of Martha in the matinée company of Edward Albee's *Who's Afraid of Virginia*

Woolf? She was in the film of Albee's *A Delicate Balance* (1974) and created the role of Adeline Whiteoak in the CBC-TV production of *The* WHITEOAKS OF JALNA (1972). At the Shaw Festival in 1976 she achieved a triumph in *Mrs Warren's Profession.* From 1953 to 1962 she was married to Austin WILLIS.

Reid, William (Bill) (b.1920). Master HAIDA carver. Born in British Columbia, a relative of Charles EDENSHAW and a grandson of Charles GLADSTONE, he worked as an announcer for CBC Radio in Vancouver (1935-48) and in Toronto (1948-51). In 1948 he decided he would try to emulate his grandfather and other Haida silver- and goldsmiths and by 1959 emerged as a master carver himself. His work is distinguished by its sculptural relief. A retrospective exhibit at the Vancouver Art Gallery opened on 5 Nov. 1974 and included over 200 pieces of sculpture and jewellery carved in cedar, ivory, argillite, gold, silver, and abalone. Reid wrote the text of *Out of the Silence* (1971), a collection of photographs of totem poles by Adelaide de Menil.

Reindeer. See CARIBOU.

Réjeanne Padovani. Feature film produced by Jean-Pierre LEFÈBVRE and written and directed by Denys ARCAND. Released in 1973, it starred Jean Lajeunesse, Luce Guibault, and Roger Lebel. Seemingly based on the activities of Quebec public figures of the recent past, it is about political corruption and organized crime that include beatings, bribery, and murder. It became a hit despite its initially unfavourable reception. 94 min., colour.

Relations of Capital and Labour, Royal Commission on. The popular name for the royal commission appointed in 1886, with James Armstrong as chairman, 'to inquire into and report on the subject of Labour, its relation to capital, the hours of labour and the earnings of labouring men and women'. The evidence gathered by the commission from 1,800 witnesses in four provinces constitutes a major source of information on working conditions in late-nineteenth-century Canada.

Relève, La. A French-language journal published in Montreal. Founded in 1934 by a group of writers in sympathy with the Christian revival in France, it was edited by Jean LE MOYNE. From Sept. 1941 to Sept. 1948 it appeared as *Nouvelle Relève.*

Relief Camps. A system of work camps established by the federal government in 1932. To cope with unemployment among single males, camps were opened across the country by the Department of National Defence. They were located in isolated and harsh environments and were under military control. The British Columbia government established similar camps with a higher rate of pay, but when these camps were transferred to National Defence, the old rate of 20 cents a day for each day worked was established and dissension resulted. The WORKERS UNITY LEAGUE was active in these camps and helped form the Relief Camp Workers Union, which in 1938 organized the VANCOUVER SIT-INS and the ON TO OTTAWA trek.

'Remember Butler'. Terse cable sent to Col. Garnet Wolseley by William Francis BUTLER, who was eager to join the RED RIVER EXPEDITION of 1870 being organized by Wolseley. Edward McCourt explains the incident in *Remember Butler: The Story of Sir William Butler* (1967).

'Remember the Caroline'. See CAROLINE.

Remembrance Day. Statutory holiday observed throughout Canada on 11 Nov. to honour the dead of both the First and Second World Wars. It commemorates the Armistice that ended the First World War on that day in 1918. On the steps of cenotaphs and other war monuments throughout the Commonwealth, ceremonies of a patriotic and memorial nature are held, and a two- or three-minute silence is observed to mark the actual signing, which took place at 11:00 a.m., when the hostilities officially ceased. Originally called Armistice Day (as it continues to be known in Newfoundland), it was merged with THANKSGIVING DAY from 1921 to 1931, when it was renamed Remembrance Day and its observance reverted to 11 Nov.

Remittance man. Term used in the West, with derogatory connotations, for a person living in Canada on money remitted from his family in England, usually to ensure that he would not return home to become a source of embarrassment. In the 1890s, one account says, 'Remittance men were as plentiful as gophers and just as unpopular.'

Renaud, Jacques (b.1943). Quebec novelist. Born in the Montreal working-class district of Rosemont, he left high school to hold down a variety of jobs before becoming associated with PARTI PRIS soon after the magazine was founded in 1963. Renaud is mainly known for his first novel, *Le Cassé* (1964), about Ti-Jean, who has been called the most alienated character in Quebec literature. It was written in JOUAL and translated by Gérald Robitaille as *Flat Broke and Beat* (1968).

Reno, Ginette (b.1947). Quebec singer. Born in the east end of Montreal, Reno (derived from Raynault) emerged as a song stylist with 'the husky, high-voltage voice'. She has been popular since 1960, when her recording of 'J'aime Guy' was released.

'Rep by pop'. See REPRESENTATION BY POPULATION.

Repatriation of the Constitution. Transferring the power to amend the BNA ACT from the British Parliament to the Canadian Parliament. The proper word is 'patriation', as the BNA Act is a British statute and the power to amend it has never been vested in the Canadian government. Numerous attempts have been made to secure agreement among all the provinces and the federal government on a method by which amendments could be effected in Canada, including the FULTON-FAVREAU FORMULA.

Répertoire de l'édition au Québec. See CANADIAN BOOKS IN PRINT.

Reppen, Jack (1933-64). Toronto-born artist. His cartoons appeared in the *Toronto Star* from 1952 until his untimely death. His mural work, especially that influenced by Mexican motifs, was unusual and attracted much attention.

Representation by population. The concept that political representation should be determined in direct proportion to the size of the population. The slogan 'Rep by Pop' was advocated by George BROWN in his Toronto newspaper the *Globe* after the census of 1851 showed that Canada West (Ontario) had a larger population than Canada East (Quebec), whose identity was guaranteed by equal representation of each province. The BNA ACT established that representation in the HOUSE OF COMMONS was to be based on population. Quebec was always to have 65 members, and the other provinces would have a greater or lesser number of representatives in proportion as their populations were greater or lesser than the population of Quebec, the size of the populations to be determined by the decennial census. Because of shifts in population since Confederation, it was established in 1952 that, while the other provinces would still receive representation in proportion to their population, the smaller provinces would be guaranteed a minimum number of seats, and that the Territories would each receive one representative.

Republic of Madawaska. See MADAWASKA.

Reserve. A tract of land set aside for a specific purpose by the government. See CLERGY RESERVES and INDIAN RESERVE.

Residence requirement. The legal requirement, as defined by the Immigration Act of 1962, that an immigrant reside or be domiciled in Canada for a period of five years with LANDED IMMIGRANT STATUS before applying for CITIZENSHIP.

Residual powers. See DISTRIBUTION OF POWERS.

Responsible government. A system of government in which the executive (CABINET) must maintain the confidence of the elected branch of the legislature (HOUSE OF COMMONS) in order to remain in office. The idea that Upper Canada (Ontario) should be granted a provincial ministry that would be removed if it was defeated in the legislative assembly was first put forward by Dr William Warren BALDWIN in 1828 and developed by his son Robert BALDWIN in 1836. It was recommended in the *Report* (1839) of Lord DURHAM. In 1848 responsible-government ministries were formed in the PROVINCE OF CANADA (the ministry of Robert Baldwin and Louis-H. LAFONTAINE) and in Nova Scotia (the James Boyle Uniacke ministry), where Joseph HOWE had been the best-known supporter of the principle.

Restigouche salmon. Atlantic salmon caught in the Restigouche R., N.B. Though they spawn during the fall, some enter fresh water in spring or early summer and are called 'early run' fish. Restigouche salmon is a delicacy when caught during this early-run period.

RETP. Abbreviation of Reserve Entry Training Plan whereby male members of the Reserve Forces are provided military and academic training at the CANADIAN MILITARY COLLEGES. Reserve Entry cadets receive the same education and training as Regular Officer Training Plan cadets, but they are required to pay a fee that includes tuition, clothing, books, instruments, food, and lodging. On graduation and commissioning they may be required to serve on a part-time basis in the Reserve Force. See also ROTP.

Revanche du berceau. See REVENGE OF THE CRADLE.

Revell, Viljo (1910-64). Finnish architect. Born in Vaasa, Finland, he studied with Alvar Aalto and had a distinguished career in Europe. The architect of the TORONTO CITY HALL, which opened in 1965, he won the commission in competition in 1958.

Revenge of the Cradle. English translation of the French phrase *Revanche du berceau*. Associated with Quebec before the First World War, it implied that the French-Canadian birthrate would exceed the growth, through natural means, of English Canada.

Reversing Falls. On the Saint John R. at Saint John, N.B., this phenomenon, caused by the ebb and flow of ocean tides over a high ledge, occurs twice daily and is a major tourist attraction.

Revillon. A traditional French-Canadian meal served after midnight mass on Christmas Eve.

Revillon Frères Trading Company. A fur-trade company based in Paris and operating in Canada from 1905 to 1936, when it was absorbed by the HUDSON'S BAY COMPANY.

Revue Canadienne, La. A serious but popular French-language monthly devoted to philosophy, history, law, literature, and political economics. It was published in Montreal between 1864 and 1922 and revived in Ottawa from 1951 to 1956.

Rhapsody in Two Languages. A brilliant experimental film about a day in the life of Montreal. Released in 1934, it was directed by Gordon Sparling for Associated Screen News' CANADIAN CAMEO series. It made excellent use of multiple exposures and was well edited to the musical score. 10 min., b & w.

Rhine, Battle of the. The German river, the boundary between Holland and Germany, was the scene of fighting during the Second World War. On 23 Mar. 1945 British troops crossed the Rhine and captured Rees. On the following day the 3rd Canadian Infantry Division crossed the Rhine at Rees and began the liberation of The Netherlands.

Rhinoceros Party. A quasi-political party founded by the novelist Jacques FERRON in Montreal. A short-lived movement, it was established in 1972 to ridicule the lack of policies of the candidates in the federal election of that year. It was named after an incident in Rio de Janeiro in which, to demonstrate voter dissatisfaction with the candidates, a rhinoceros was elected as a city councillor.

Rhodes Scholarship. An academic trust established in 1902 for study at Oxford University under the terms of the will of Sir Cecil Rhodes (1853-1902). It is open to unmarried male Commonwealth citizens aged 19 to 25 who combine 'quality of both character and intellect' with 'literary and scholastic attainments'. Normally tenable for two years, the scholarships are awarded in Canada as follows: two each to Ontario and Quebec and one each to the rest of the provinces. The award is valued at £2,000 ($4,000) per year.

RHOSP. See REGISTERED HOME OWNERSHIP SAVINGS PLAN.

Riccio, Pat (b.1921). Jazz arranger, bandleader, alto saxophonist. Born in Toronto, he was musical director and arranger of the RCAF's Streamliners (1942-6), which toured Britain and Europe. Returning to Toronto, he played in orchestras with Bert NIOSI, Maynard FERGUSON, Art Hallman, and Mart Kenney, and has led various jazz groups of his own.

Richard, Maurice (b.1921). Hockey star, nicknamed 'The Rocket' for his speed, shooting-power, and general brilliance. Born in Montreal, he played professional hockey with the MONTREAL CANADIENS for 18 seasons and was widely acclaimed for his dedication, fiery temperament, and scoring excellence. A member of the famed 'Richard-Lach-Blake line', he once scored all five goals in a STANLEY CUP match. He retired about 1960. His brother Henri also starred with the Montreal Canadiens for 19 years until his retirement in 1974.

Richardson, John (1796-1852). Novelist, poet, historian. Born in Queenston, U.C. (Ont.), he was a gentleman volunteer in the British army during the WAR OF 1812 and from 1815 to 1838 served as an officer in Paris, Spain, the West Indies, and London, where he contributed anonymously to various literary journals. He returned to Canada in 1838 as a correspondent for the London *Times*. He owned and edited the *New Era*, a literary weekly in Brockville from 1840 to 1842, and moved to New York in 1850, where he died in poverty. The author of numerous books, including several novels, he achieved some fame with WACOUSTA (1832), a frontier tale about the capture of Fort Detroit. He also wrote *Tecumseh* (1828), a poem in four cantos about the Shawnee chief with whom Richardson had served, and *War of 1812* (1842), a vivid history of the British-American conflict partly drawn from his own experiences and based on articles he had written for the *New Era*.

Richardson Rink, The. Notable curling rink. Four members of the Richardson family—Ernie, Arnold, Garnet, and Wes—born near the village of Stoughton, Sask., formed an almost unbeatable rink and in one season (1958-9) won 45 matches, losing only three.

The quartet has been called 'the greatest curling rink ever'.

Richelieu River. Named in honour of Cardinal Richelieu, it rises in Lake Champlain, flowing north for 80 mi. and emptying into Lake St Peter, a widening of the St Lawrence R., at Sorel. In the seventeenth and eighteenth centuries it was the highway for Iroquois moving north to attack the French settlements, for French punitive expeditions headed for Mohawk villages in the south, and for war parties during the French-English struggle to control North America and during the American Revolution. Of the numerous forts built on it, FORT CHAMBLY still stands. Today it is a direct route from Montreal to the Hudson R. and New York City via the Champlain Canal.

Richler, Mordecai (b.1931). Novelist. Born in Montreal and educated at Sir George Williams (now Concordia) University, he worked for the CBC from 1952 to 1959, when he settled in England. In London he contributed to the screenplays of *No Love for Johnny* (1961), *Room at the Top* (1959), *Tiara Tahiti* (1963), and received full screenplay credit for *Life at the Top* (1965). He returned to Montreal in 1972. After his first two novels— *The Acrobats* (1954) and *A Choice of Enemies* (1957)—he revealed himself as a brilliant, sometimes deliberately shocking writer of satirical fiction. *Son of a Smaller Hero* (1955) and *The* APPRENTICESHIP OF DUDDY KRAVITZ (1959) are set in the predominately Jewish community of Montreal's ST URBAIN district, where he grew up. They were followed by *The Incomparable Atuk* (1963), *Cocksure* (1968), and ST URBAIN'S HORSEMAN (1971). Richler's journalism, in which he is an aggressive social critic and moralist, has been collected in *Hunting Tigers under Glass* (1968) and *Shovelling Trouble* (1972). Some of his accomplished short stories, also drawn from his boyhood experiences, were collected in *The Street* (1969). Richler edited the anthology *Canadian Writing Today* (1970). In 1976 he was made a judge of the Book-of-the-Month Club.

Rideau Canal. It was built between 1826 and 1832 by the Royal Engineers under Col. John BY from a point 100 mi. above Montreal— now Ottawa—to Kingston on Lake Ontario. Originally planned after the WAR OF 1812 as a route to Lake Ontario through which troops could be moved without passing close to the international boundary, it was never used for military purposes. It is a 125-mi. waterway with 49 locks and 12 mi. of artificial channels. The 4½ mi. stretch through the heart of Ot-tawa is used by about 500,000 skaters every winter.

Rideau Club. A nationally important luncheon club. Founded by Sir John A. MACDONALD in 1865, it is located on Wellington St across from the Parliament Buildings in Ottawa. It has close to 1,000 members, all male, most of whom are connected with the government, the civil-service, or business.

Rideau Hall. The popular name for GOVERNMENT HOUSE.

Rideau River. A river in southeastern Ontario with many rapids. It empties into the Ottawa R. over the Rideau Falls at Ottawa. The French name *rideau*, meaning 'curtain' or 'screen', was suggested by the falls.

'Riders of the Plains'. A once-popular anonymous poem about the exploits of the RCMP when it was called the NORTH WEST MOUNTED POLICE. All 17 stanzas are reproduced by Charles Pelham Mulvaney in *The History of the North-West Rebellion of 1885* (1885).

Ridgeway, Battle of. On 2 June 1866 a band of about 800 FENIANS under 'General' John O'Neill attacked Ridgeway (about 9 mi. west of Fort Erie, Ont). 10 militia-men were killed and 30 were wounded before he was pushed back. The most serious of the Fenian raids, it gave impetus to the Confederation movement.

Riding Mountain National Park. Established in 1929 on the summit of the Manitoba escarpment, 165 mi. northwest of Winnipeg, it covers 1,149 sq. mi. at the meeting-point of northern and eastern forests and western grasslands.

Ridout, Godfrey (b.1918). Composer. Born in Toronto, he studied with Healey WILLAN and later joined the staffs of the University of Toronto and the Royal Conservatory of Music. He has conducted for the CBC and directed Toronto's Eaton Operatic Society. A versatile composer known for traditional lyricism reminiscent of Shostakovich and Britten, he works in all genres, including orchestral, solo, choral, and chamber music. One of his finest compositions is *Cantiones Mysticae* (1953), a setting of Donne's poems dedicated to Lois MARSHALL. FALL FAIR (1961), a lively piece of program music, is the most frequently performed Canadian orchestral work.

Riel. A historical drama by John COULTER based on the fall of Louis RIEL. It was largely responsible for the revival of interest—in English-speaking Canada at least—in Riel as

Riel

a symbol of minority rights. Mavor MOORE played the lead in the première staged by the NEW PLAY SOCIETY on 17 Feb. 1950. It was broadcast by CBC Radio on 9 May 1951 and telecast by CBC-TV, starring Bruno GERUSSI, on 23 and 30 Apr. 1961. The script was published the following year. The first full-scale production was mounted by the NATIONAL ARTS CENTRE in Ottawa on 13 Jan. 1975, starring Albert MILLAIRE. Coulter's pageant-like drama influenced Mavor Moore's libretto for LOUIS RIEL, the opera by Harry SOMERS. Coulter's short play, The TRIAL OF LOUIS RIEL, focuses on the events that took place in the Regina courtroom in 1885.

Riel, Louis (1844-85). Central figure in the RED RIVER REBELLION and the NORTH WEST REBELLION. Born near St Boniface (Man.), he became the leader of a group of MÉTIS who felt threatened by plans for the Province of Canada to acquire the HUDSON'S BAY COMPANY territories. His acts of resistance included the occupation of FORT GARRY (Nov. 1869), the declaration of a Provisional Government (Dec.), and the taking of prisoners, including Thomas SCOTT. In March a Bill of Rights was sent to Ottawa with three delegates, but as an expeditionary force under Gen. Wolseley approached the fort in August, Riel fled. In Feb. 1874 he was elected to the House of Commons for the Manitoba constituency of Provencher but was not able to take his seat. In 1875 he was given an amnesty, conditional upon a five-year banishment. His mental state necessitated confinement in a hospital in 1876-8. He became an American citizen in 1883 and was teaching in St Peter's, Montana, when a delegation from the North Saskatchewan country pressed him to become their leader in finding redress for their grievances. He arrived at BATOCHE in July 1884. Convinced that his mission to lead the Métis was divinely inspired, he entered upon the NORTH WEST REBELLION in Mar. 1885. It failed. Riel surrendered in May, was tried in July, found guilty of high treason, and hanged on 16 Nov. His rise and fall—covering only fifteen years and arousing extremists on both sides in a religious and racial conflict between Ontario and Quebec—ensured Riel a place in Canadian history as the Father of Manitoba and an authentic people's hero. See also EXOVEDATE, and RIEL for the dramas based on his career.

Riel Rebellions, The. See RED RIVER REBELLION, NORTH WEST REBELLION.

Right Honourable, The. Style of address, in Canada, of the PRIME MINISTER of Canada, the CHIEF JUSTICE of Canada, and all members of the United Kingdom PRIVY COUNCIL. It precedes the name of the official and is generally abbreviated to 'The Rt Hon.'. See also The HONOURABLE.

Rights, Canadian Bill of. See CANADIAN BILL OF RIGHTS.

Riley, Conrad (Con) (1875-1950). Noted oarsman and coach. Born in Winnipeg, Man., he became a talented rower and coach with the Winnipeg Rowing Club. Under his tutelage WRC singles, doubles, fours, and eights won titles in Canada, the United States, and England. He rose in the Hudson's Bay Company to become a senior director.

RIN. Rassemblement pour l'Indépendance Nationale, a Quebec SEPARATIST political party that was formed on 10 Sept. 1960. Its best-known member was Marcel Chaput, author of Pourquoi je suis séparatiste (1962), who became president. Chaput was employed by the federal government's Defence Research Board. Refused permission by the Board to attend a conference on Confederation at Laval, he went—and was suspended by the Board for neglecting his work. Chaput resigned, complaining that he was being persecuted for his separatist views. At a meeting of the RIN almost immediately following the founding of the PARTI QUÉBÉCOIS in 1968, the RIN voted to dissolve and join the PQ so that there would be only one separatist party in the province. See also FLQ.

Rindisbacher, Peter (1806-34). Artist. Born in Switzerland, he travelled with his parents via Hudson Bay to the RED RIVER SETTLEMENT in 1821, where he lived until 1826. The first white man to make drawings of the Indians of the Canadian Prairies, he painted richly detailed watercolours that give a naïve, appealing view of forts, transport canoes, and Indian life. He left Canada in 1826 and died in St Louis, Mo.

Ringuet. Pseudonym of Philippe Panneton, author of THIRTY ACRES.

Rio Algom Ltd. The Canadian arm of the giant Rio Tinto-Zinc Corp. of the United Kingdom. It was incorporated in 1960 in Toronto as an amalgamation of the uranium mines and other Canadian interests owned by Joseph Hirshhorn (b.1899). The Latvian-born American mining magnate opened a Toronto office in 1933 and in 1955 financed one of the biggest uranium strikes in the western hemisphere (Algom Uranium Mines Ltd, Milliken Lake, Ont.). His associate in the major discovery was the San Francisco-born, Victoria-raised geologist Franc Joubin (b.1911). Hirshhorn amassed a major collection of modern art; the Hirshhorn Gallery opened in Washington, D.C., in 1974.

Riopelle, Jean-Paul (b.1923). Painter. Born in Montreal, he was a student of Paul-Émile BORDUAS at the École du Meuble and came together with the small group of advanced painters in Montreal known as Les AUTOMATISTES. He left for Paris in 1946 and remained there, establishing an international reputation in exhibitions in Paris and New York as well as in Canada. He is known for his visually exciting 'action paintings'—richly coloured, dynamic, three-dimensional mosaics built up with a palette knife. Two of his best-known works are *Knight Watch* (1953, NGC) and *Pavane* (1954, NGC), a triptych.

Ristigouche Salmon Club. A sportsmen's hideaway. This exclusive club, owned by a group of North American business executives, is located on its own preserve at Matapedia on the Quebec side of the Restigouche R., which it persists in spelling 'Ristigouche'.

Ritchie, Al (1890-1966). Hockey and football coach. Born in Midland, Ont., he moved to Regina in 1911 and played on, coached, and managed hockey and football teams that became junior Canadian champions. In 1919 he managed and coached the Regina Rough Riders, frequent GREY CUP challengers.

Ritchie, John W. (1808-90). A FATHER OF CONFEDERATION. Born at Annapolis, N.S., he trained as a lawyer and in 1864 was made a member of the legislative council and solicitor-general of the province. He was a delegate to the LONDON CONFERENCE on Confederation and was appointed to the Senate in 1867. He was a judge of the Supreme Court of Nova Scotia from 1873 to 1882.

Ritz-Carlton Hotel. Famous hotel in Montreal. Designed by Warner & Wetmore of New York and Winnipeg, it opened in 1912, with 230 guest rooms. In 1957 a new wing was added, with 67 rooms and suites. Between 1970 and 1973 extensive renovations were undertaken, that included refurbishing the elegant décor of the reception and guest rooms for which the hotel is noted.

Rivard affair. The Montreal hood, Lucien Rivard, charged by the U.S. attorney general with narcotics smuggling, was arrested on 19 June 1964 and taken to Bordeaux Jail to await his bail hearing. Attempts were made to arrange bail by bribing the lawyer who was acting on behalf of the U.S. government. When

these failed, Rivard—offering to water the jail's skating rink in above-zero weather—scaled the wall and escaped on 2 Mar. 1965. Caught in the Laurentians three months later, he was finally extradited and sentenced in Laredo, Tex., to a 20-year prison sentence (of which he served 10) for 'masterminding a giant narcotics ring'. See also the DORION REPORT.

'River of Disappointment'. See Sir Alexander MACKENZIE.

River Route. A picturesque tour of New Brunswick that follows the valley of the Saint John R. It begins at Edmundston and, passing through rich farmland, proceeds south to Fredericton and then to Saint John.

Riverboat, The. Coffee house devoted to popular singers. Since it was opened by Bernie Fiedler on Yorkville Ave, Toronto, in 1964, the 117-seat Riverboat has been the centre of the modern folk movement in Canada. Many famous performers have played there, usually early in their careers.

RMC. Initials of the ROYAL MILITARY COLLEGE OF CANADA.

RNWMP. Initials of the ROYAL NORTH WEST MOUNTED POLICE.

Robb Wave Organ. The world's first commercial electronic organ. As early as 1927 Belleville-born Morse Robb (b.1902) was able to demonstrate an organ of his own design that was electronic rather than electric in that it worked on the principle of reproducing a natural rather than a synthetic waveform. He founded the Robb Wave Organ Company Limited in Belleville, Ont., in 1934 and produced a few electronic organs but went broke two years later. In contrast the well-financed Laurens Hammond of Hammond, Indiana, produced his first successful electric organ only in 1935, and his first electronic organ only in 1939.

Robert McLaughlin Gallery. Small public art gallery in Oshawa, Ont. Founded in 1968 as the Art Gallery of Oshawa, it moved in 1968 to its present location in the Oshawa Civic Centre, which Ewert McLaughlin built in memory of his grandfather Robert McLaughlin (the father of R.S. McLAUGHLIN). It specializes in contemporary Canadian work and owns the most important collection of PAINTERS ELEVEN. (Alexandra Luke [1901-67], one of the group's original members, was the wife of Ewert McLaughlin.) In addition to its promotion of young artists it prepares exhibitions, which have included major retrospectives and travelling shows.

Roberts

Roberts, Sir Charles G.D. (1860-1945). Man-of-letters. Born in Douglas, N.B., a brother of Theodore Goodridge ROBERTS and a cousin of Bliss CARMAN, he was educated at the University of New Brunswick. He edited Goldwin SMITH's periodical *The* WEEK in 1883-4, taught English at King's College, Windsor, N.S., lived in New York and London, and returned to Canada in 1925, spending his last two decades in Toronto. Knighted in 1935, he made a distinguished contribution to Canadian letters as the author of over 50 books of poetry, fiction, and historical writings, and as an editor. *Orion, and Other Poems* (1880) struck a responsive chord in Archibald LAMPMAN and encouraged a group of young poets to write about the Canadian landscape. Roberts' next collection, *In Divers Tones* (1886)—including some of his best reflective nature verse, descriptive of the New Brunswick countryside, and poems in a patriotic vein—was followed by 16 other collections. Some well-known Roberts poems are 'The TANTRAMAR REVISITED', 'The Solitary Woodsman', and his sonnets 'The Potato Harvest', 'The Pea Fields', 'The Sowing', and 'The Mowing'. *The Selected Poems of Charles G.D. Roberts* (1956) was edited by Desmond Pacey. As a writer of fiction Roberts made a distinct contribution to the animal story—beginning with *Earth's Enigmas* (1896) and *The* KINDRED OF THE WILD (1902)—in which animals are endowed with human feelings and the power of reason. A selection appears in *The Last Barrier and Other Stories* (1958) edited by Alec Lucas and *King of Beasts* (1967) edited by Joseph Gold. Roberts combined fiction and history in such ACADIAN romances as *The Forge in the Forest* (1896) and *A Sister to Evangeline* (1898). He supported the idea of an autonomous dominion in *A History of Canada* (1897). He edited the first of the series *The* CANADIAN WHO'S WHO (1910) and translated AUBERT DE GASPÉ's *Les* ANCIENS CANADIENS, which appeared in English as CANADIANS OF OLD (1890).

Roberts, David (*c.*1830-1907). Architect. He may have been born in Yorkshire and brought to Toronto with the rest of William Gooderham's family in the 1830s. His first known work, more that of an engineer than an architect, was the main distillery building in the Gooderham and Worts complex, Trinity St, Toronto, built in 1859-61 of Kingston limestone. Roberts was also probably responsible for the buildings of the complex, completed *c.*1870-5, which ranks as one of the most important nineteenth-century industrial sites in Canada and is now owned by HIRAM WALKER-GOODERHAM AND WORTS LTD. His other Toronto buildings for the Gooder-ham family included 135 St George St (1890, now the York Club), 504 Jarvis St (*c.*1890), and the Gooderham Building at Wellington and Church Sts (1891-2), better known as the Flat Iron Building. These later designs are among the finest Romanesque Revival buildings in the city.

Roberts, Goodridge (1904-75). Painter. The son of Theodore Goodridge ROBERTS and the nephew of Sir Charles G.D. ROBERTS, he was born in Barbados but brought up in Fredericton, N.B. After studying painting in Montreal and New York, he taught at Queen's University (1953-6) and in Montreal. Encouraged and influenced by John LYMAN, he began in the forties to build his reputation as a painter of figures, still-lifes, and landscapes—harmonious post-Impressionist compositions showing a strong sense of the relation of strongly modelled forms and of colour to colour. His *Lake Orford* (1945, NGC) is one of his finest landscapes and *Yellow Nude on a Red Carpet* (1960, private coll.) is a notable figure painting.

Roberts, Theodore Goodridge (1877-1953). Novelist and poet. A brother of Sir Charles G.D. ROBERTS and a cousin of Bliss CARMAN, he was born and educated in Fredericton, N.B., served as a Spanish-American War correspondent, and edited *Newfoundland Magazine* before turning to a literary career in 1900. He wrote some 30 historical romances—many of which are set in the Maritime provinces—including *The House of Isstens* (1900), an adventure tale about Newfoundland, and composed poetry that was collected in *The Leather Bottle* (1934). He was the father of Goodridge ROBERTS.

Roberts Gallery. Toronto's oldest commercial art gallery. Established in 1842 by the Roberts family, it was purchased in 1948 by S.L. Wildredge, a Toronto businessman, whose son Jack has been owner and director since 1957. It was the first gallery to exhibit work of PAINTERS ELEVEN in three annual exhibitions from 1952 to 1955 and has specialized in Canadian art since 1958.

Robertson, George (b.1929). Television and film writer. Born in Vancouver, he has worked for the NATIONAL FILM BOARD (1951-3), CBC Radio (1953-7), and CBC-TV (1960-6). He wrote the script for the film *Son of Raven, Son of Deer* (1967) and was joint author of the NFB-CBC co-production WAITING FOR CAROLINE (1967). He also created QUENTIN DURGENS, M.P. (1966-9).

Robertson, Heather (b.1942). Writer. Born in Winnipeg and educated at the University of

Manitoba and Columbia University, she has worked for the *Winnipeg Tribune* (1964-6), produced CBC public affairs programs (1968-71), and written for *Maclean's* (1971-5). In *Reservations Are for Indians* (1970), *Grass Roots* (1973), with photographs by Myfanwy Phillips, and *Salt of the Earth* (1974), she has recreated the Indian, prairie, and immigrant experiences of many Canadians.

Robertson, John Ross (1841-1918). Journalist. Born in Toronto, he attended Upper Canada College and entered journalism, founding the *Evening Telegram* in 1876. His philanthropies included the founding of the Hospital for Sick Children and the creation of the John Ross Robertson collection of historical pictures, given to the Toronto Public Library in 1912. He was a member of Parliament from 1896 to 1900. He published *Robertson's Landmarks of Toronto* (6 vols, 1894-1914).

Robertson Galleries. Commercial art gallery in Ottawa, Ont. Founded by John K.B. Robertson in 1953, it specializes in Eskimo arts and crafts. An active member of the CANADIAN ESKIMO ARTS COUNCIL, Robertson has used his knowledge of Eskimo art as an advisor to such institutions as the National Gallery of Canada and the National Arts Centre.

Robertson raft. A huge cigar-shaped raft once used for transporting logs. It was devised by Hugh Robertson of Saint John, N.B., in 1886.

Roberval, sieur de (1500?-60). Courtier, lieutenant-general in Canada. Charged by Francis I to begin a colony in Canada, Jean-François de la Roque, sieur de Roberval, set out from France in 1542, a year after Jacques CARTIER, who was part of the expedition. Cartier was returning to France when he met Roberval at St John's, Nfld. Roberval sailed up the St Lawrence to the mouth of the Cap Rouge R., where Cartier had built two forts. He wintered there, explored the river, and returned to France in 1543. The town of Roberval, Que., was named after him. See also Marguerite de LA ROQUE.

Robichaud, Michel (b.1939). Fashion designer. Born in Montreal, he studied fashion design in Paris and worked at Nina Ricci's before presenting his first collection in Montreal in 1963. A designer who strives for elegant simplicity, he has designed clothes for Elizabeth Taylor and uniforms for Expo '67 and Air Canada. In 1971 he opened an exclusive boutique for men's wear and two years later promoted 'Brunante', the first Canadian

perfume. He co-founded the FASHION DESIGNERS ASSOCIATION OF CANADA, INC. and served as its first president.

Robinson, Sir John Beverley (1791-1863). Chief justice of Upper Canada (Ontario). Born at Berthier, L.C. (Que.), he was a pupil of John STRACHAN at the Cornwall Grammar School and studied law in York (Toronto)—where he took part in the WAR OF 1812 as a member of the militia—and later in England. He was appointed attorney general of Upper Canada in 1818 and was elected to the legislative assembly in 1821. A member of the Tory establishment in York that William Lyon MACKENZIE called the FAMILY COMPACT, he was a highly respected man of great ability whose term as chief justice lasted from 1829 to 1862. He was created a baronet in 1854.

Robson, Fred J. (1879-1944). Champion speed-skater. The Toronto-born athlete participated in rowing and cycling but concentrated on speed-skating. When he was 19 he held three world records in speed-skating, and later held nine world records at the same time, many of which were unbroken for 40 years.

Rochdale College. A former student residence in Toronto. Named after the birthplace of the co-operative movement in Lancashire, Eng., Rochdale College on Bloor St W. was opened in Sept. 1968 to provide students with both low-cost housing and an 'alternative' to the system of instruction at the University of Toronto nearby. Rochdale helped subsidize COACH HOUSE PRESS, SPACED-OUT LIBRARY, and THÉÂTRE PASSE MURAILLE but, reduced to selling its 'degrees', it became a 'hippie haven' and drug centre. That phase ended with the eviction of long-time residents in May 1975, when the building was taken over by CENTRAL MORTGAGE AND HOUSING for mortgage arrears. Negotiations are currently under way for the sale of the building to Metropolitan Toronto for possible use as a senior citizens' residence.

Rockcliffe Park. An incorporated village and adjoining city park in Ottawa, named after Rockcliffe House, which was first built in 1835 by Duncan Rynier MacNab and rebuilt in 1868 and 1928. The area is a prestigious residential district for senior civil servants and diplomatic personnel.

Rocket Robin Hood. An animated action-adventure television series set in the future, starring a space-age super-hero modelled on Robin Hood. The 52 half-hour weekly episodes were produced for Canadian and

American television stations in 1968-9 and have been rerun on an irregular basis ever since. Perhaps the most ambitious animated cartoon series ever undertaken, it was produced by The Guest Group, a Toronto studio run by Al Guest (b.1933), a Winnipeg-born artist, and Jean Mathieson (b.1942), a Toronto-born animator, employing a staff of 150. Based on a concept created by Tony Peters of Instant Miracles, a New York company, the series was produced in Toronto by Bernard Cowan. Although a critical success, it resulted in a $2 million loss for the studio.

Rocky Mountain House National Historic Park. At Rocky Mountain House, Alta, this park is the site of a series of fur-trading posts operated by the NORTH WEST COMPANY and the HUDSON'S BAY COMPANY between 1799 and 1875.

Rocky Mountains. The easternmost range of mountains comprising the WESTERN CORDILLERA, they extend from the Liard R. in the north into the United States in the south and are bordered by the Foothills in the east and the Rocky Mountain Trench in the west. The mountains are highest in the south, with many peaks over 9,842 ft. A significant barrier to east-west transportation, they are crossed by four major passes: CROW'S NEST (4,452 ft), KICKING HORSE (5,338 ft), YELLOWHEAD (3,730 ft), and Pine (2,851 ft). Relatively young mountains, they have been severely glaciated and are renowned for their natural beauty. Several large national parks are located in the Rocky Mountains, of which BANFF and JASPER are the best known.

Rodden, M.J. (Mike) (b.1891). Sportsman. Born in Mattawa, Ont., he was a prominent hockey, baseball, football, and lacrosse player in his youth. He later coached many championship football teams, two of which were GREY CUP winners. He refereed over 2,800 hockey games and later served as sports editor of the Toronto *Globe and Mail* and the *Kingston Whig-Standard*.

Rodman Hall Arts Centre. Housing 25 cultural and service organizations incorporated under the name of the St Catharines and District Arts Council, it opened in St Catharines, Ont., in 1960. It is located in a 30-room mansion built in 1853 by Thomas Rodman Merritt and serves the Niagara region.

Rodriguez, Percy (b.1918). Actor. Born in St Henri, Que., a suburb of Montreal, he was a Canadian lightweight boxing champion before he received recognition as a performer in 1950 by winning a DOMINION DRAMA FESTIVAL award for the lead in *Emperor Jones*. He has

acted in both French and English productions for CBC Radio and TV. In 1966 he played opposite Irene Worth in the Broadway production of *Toys in the Attic* and he has appeared in such films as *The Heart is a Lonely Hunter* and *Peyton Place*. Called Canada's most successful black actor, he has lived in the United States since the late 1960s.

Roffman, Julian (b.1919). Producer and director. Born in Montreal, he worked for the NATIONAL FILM BOARD before directing commercial films. His many film credits include *The Bloody Brood* (1959) and *The MASK* (1961). The latter, a 3-D horror film produced by Nat Taylor, is sometimes revived as *Eyes of Hell*.

Rogers, E.S. (Ted). See CFRB.

Rogers, Robert. See ROGERS' RANGERS.

Rogers Chocolates Ltd. Famous candy manufacturer in Victoria, B.C. It was founded in 1885 by Charles Rogers (d.1927), who moved across Government St in 1903 to the present store, the interior of which—with its glass-fronted oak shelves and counters and stained-glass details—remains unchanged. The business was purchased by Americans on Rogers' death and in 1968 by its present Canadian owners. Rogers' large pure-cream chocolates, in their bright red boxes, are shipped all over the world.

Rogers Pass. A 92-mi. route through the Selkirk Mountains in British Columbia, from Revelstoke to Golden and passing through GLACIER NATIONAL PARK. Named after Major A.B. Rogers, who explored it in 1882 for the CANADIAN PACIFIC RAILWAY, the route was adopted for the Trans-Canada Highway in 1956. It is 4,354 ft above sea level and has an average annual snowfall of 342 in. Because of the threat of snowslides, the 6-mi. CONNAUGHT TUNNEL was built through Mount MacDonald in 1916.

Rogers' Rangers. Several companies of guerilla-type soldiers commanded by Massachusetts-born Robert Rogers (1731-95). Organized in 1755, they served in the SEVEN YEARS' WAR, fighting against the French.

Rohmer, Richard (b.1924). Novelist and lawyer. Born in Hamilton, Ont., and a graduate of the University of Western Ontario and Osgoode Hall, he holds the rank of Brigadier General in the Canadian Armed Forces. A prominent lawyer, he served as chairman of the Ontario Royal Commission on Book Publishing (1971-2) and is also known for his advocacy of the MID-CANADA DEVELOPMENT CORRIDOR. He has found a wide public for his novels, which deal futuristically with Canadian social problems: ULTIMATUM (1973), EXX-ONERATION (1974), *Exodus/UK* (1975), and *Separation* (1976).

Roi nègre. Catch-phrase coined by André LAURENDEAU to describe the English-speaking ruling élite in Quebec, likening them to British administrators in Africa who backed a native ruler so long as he governed in their favour. The so-called 'Black King' theory was popularized in an editorial that appeared in *Le* DEVOIR on 4 July 1958, when no English-language paper in Quebec reported Maurice DUPLESSIS's expulsion of a *Le Devoir* reporter from a press conference.

Roll Back the Years. A CBC Radio series of half-hour programs devoted to old recordings. The records were collected by Ed Manning, the professional name of Edward B. Moogk, who was born in Weston, Ont., in 1914. Manning conceived, wrote, and announced the series of nostalgic programs, which was first carried by CKCR in Kitchener in 1943 and was then broadcast by CBC Radio from 1950 to 1970. In 1972 his collection formed the basis of the Recorded Sound Section of the NATIONAL LIBRARY, whose first publication was *Roll Back the Years: History of Canadian Recorded Sound and Its Legacy* (1975).

Rolph, Ernest. See SPROATT AND ROLPH.

Rolph, John (1793-1870). Physician and politician. Born in England, he trained there as a lawyer and a doctor. After settling in Charlotteville, U.C. (Ont.), he practised both law and medicine until 1829, when he gave up law. Elected to the legislative assembly in 1824, he became a leading Reformer. As a secret supporter of William Lyon MACKENZIE during the REBELLION OF 1837, he fled to the United States before the rebellion was quelled. Returning to Canada in 1843, he founded the Toronto School of Medicine and became active again in politics, helping to found the Clear GRIT Party and sitting in the assembly from 1851 to 1857.

ROM. See ROYAL ONTARIO MUSEUM.

Roman, Stephen B. (b.1921). Mining executive. Born in Slovakia and educated at a Czechoslovakian agricultural college until his departure for Canada in 1937, he served with the Canadian Army and then began an investment career. In 1953 he acquired North Denison Mines Ltd, a speculative venture incorporated in 1938, when it was named after Denison Township in northern Ontario, where it held nickel claims. Roman acquired uranium properties in the Algoma District of northern Ontario, renamed the company Consolidated Denison in 1954, then Denison Mines Limited, and worked the largest uranium reserves ever discovered. The residential community of ELLIOT LAKE, in the heart of the uranium area, was created in 1954. (The town of Blind River on Lake Huron's North Channel is strategically located near the uranium fields.) Denison became the base for many of Roman's other activities. In 1970 the Trudeau administration disallowed the proposed sale of Denison to Continental Oil of Delaware. Roman lives at Romandale, his 1,200-acre estate at Unionville, Ont.

Roman Catholic Church. It has the largest number of adherents of any Canadian religious body—9,974,895, according to the 1971 census. Despite the declining birth rate in French-speaking Quebec, its membership has continued to grow mainly because of vast immigration from Roman Catholic areas of the world. Radical changes have occurred in recent years, with the translation of the liturgy into the vernacular, ecumenical cooperation, and a greater participation of the laity in worship and church life. The Roman Catholic Church is divided into two rites and bodies: the Western or Latin rite and the Eastern rite, which is composed of numerous groups, including adherents of the Ukrainian-Byzantine rite, the largest Eastern Catholic sect in Canada.

Romance of Canada, The. The first series of radio dramas produced in Canada. The 60-minute programs, which dramatized events in early Canadian history, were produced live in Montreal each week by the CRBC, the forerunner of the CBC. Tyrone GUTHRIE was the producer and Merrill DENISON the scriptwriter. A series of 16 episodes was launched on 22 Jan. 1931 with a program on the last voyage of Henry HUDSON. A second series of eight episodes, produced by Esmé Moonie, was launched on 11 Feb. 1932.

Romanelli brothers. Three conductors of popular dance bands in Toronto from the 1920s to the 1950s. They were born into a family of 10 musical sons and daughters of Italian immigrants and were all talented conductors and violinists. Luigi (1885-1942), who was born in Belleville, Ont., directed the dance band of the King Edward Hotel, Toronto, for 25 years, and was a pioneer in the broadcasting of dance music. Toronto-born Don (1891-1960) was in the same period the musical director of the Royal York Hotel. Also born in Toronto, Leo (1902-61) was musical director of the Old Mill and the King Edward Hotel for 20 years and led an orchestra for many summers at the MANOIR RICHELIEU.

Ronald

Ronald, William (b.1926). Painter. The brother of John MEREDITH, he was born in Stratford, Ont., studied at the Ontario College of Art, and worked as a display artist at Robert Simpson Co., which he persuaded to sponsor an exhibition of non-figurative painting in 1953 that was the impetus of PAINTERS ELEVEN. He has exhibited internationally and now teaches at York University. His dedication to abstract expressionism in the 1950s resulted in a direct style of bold, jagged brushstrokes that focus on a central image. The highly structured *Central Black* (1955, Robert McLaughlin Gallery) is a beautiful example of this style, dominated by its powerful black images against a white ground. The controlled organization of large space characterizes his strikingly colourful paintings—such as *Gypsy* (1959, private coll.)—which currently include experimentation with acrylic and with oil on cotton. As a broadcasting personality Ronald has hosted numerous programs, including 'Umbrella' for CBC-TV in 1966; 'AS IT HAPPENS' for CBC-Radio from 1969 to 1971, when he was co-host with Barbara FRUM until 1972; and 'Free for All' for CITY-TV from 1972 to 1974.

Roncarelli case. A famous civil-liberties case in Quebec. On 4 Dec. 1946 the fashionable Crescent St restaurant owned by Frank Roncarelli in Montreal was raided and its liquor licence cancelled. Represented by Montreal lawyers A.L. Stein and F.R. SCOTT, Roncarelli sued on 10 May 1950 and 16 days later was awarded minimal damages. An appeal for further damages was dismissed on 12 Apr. 1956. A suit against Maurice DUPLESSIS, as premier of Quebec, was successful when, on 27 Jan. 1959, the Supreme Court of Canada awarded Roncarelli, then a labourer in the United States, a total of $33,123 in damages. Stein and Scott were able to prove (in the words of the majority decision of the Court) 'gross abuse of legal power expressly intended to punish' Roncarelli for acting as bondsman to the Jehovah's Witnesses, a group being persecuted by the Quebec government.

Rose, Wild. A flat-faced, deep-pink, five-petalled wild flower with prickly stems, common throughout most areas of North America. It was adopted as the provincial flower of Alberta in 1930. The winter bud may be eaten raw and is high in vitamin C; its flowers may be brewed for tea.

Rose-Belford's Canadian Magazine. See CANADIAN MONTHLY AND NATIONAL REVIEW.

Rose Latulippe. A three-act ballet created by Brian MACDONALD for the ROYAL WINNIPEG BAL-LET, called 'the first full-length ballet by a Canadian on a Canadian theme'. Based on the French-Canadian legend of 'the girl who danced with the devil' but whose soul is saved by the power of love, it is set in Quebec in 1740. The music is by Harry FREEDMAN and the scenario is by William Solly and Macdonald. It had its première at the STRATFORD FESTIVAL on 16 Aug. 1966.

Rose-Marie. Operetta about love among the Mounties. With music by Rudolf Friml and lyrics by Otto Harbach and Oscar Hammerstein II, it was the hit of the 1924 Broadway season. It was made into three films: a silent version with Joan Crawford (1928), a memorable and highly popular version with Jeanette MacDonald and Nelson Eddy (1936), and an undistinguished version with Anne Blyth and Howard Keel (1954). The well-remembered second film, *Rose-Marie*, produced by MGM, was directed by W.S. Van Dyke and is probably the best-known and most popular movie ever made with a Canadian theme or setting—and the epitome of Hollywood's notion of Canada. To this day a soft assignment is known in ROYAL CANADIAN MOUNTED POLICE ranks as 'a Rose Marie posting'.

Rosedale. Toronto residential district above Bloor St and east of Yonge, lived in since the 1820s, when it was several miles north of York (Toronto). It took its name from the house of William Botsford Jarvis and was developed as a select neighbourhood of splendid houses, some of them with large grounds, between the 1880s and the 1930s.

Rosenblatt, Joe (b.1933). Poet. Born in Toronto and a protégé of Milton ACORN, he specializes in a comic vision of the subhuman worlds and in sound-poetry presentations. He is the author of *Voyage of the Mood* (1962), *LSD Leacock* (1966), *Winter of the Luna Moth* (1968), *The Bumblebee Dithyramb* (1972), *The Blind Photographer* (1973), *Dream Craters* (1974), and *Vampires and Virgins* (1975)—some of which are illustrated with his pen-and-ink drawings. He is the editor of JEWISH DIALOGUE, a literary quarterly.

Rosenfeld, Fanny (Bobbie) (1903-69). Canada's first celebrated all-round female athlete. Born in Russia and brought to Canada as an infant, she competed in hockey, softball, tennis, basketball, and athletics. She was a member of the girls' winning relay team at the 1928 Olympic games in Amsterdam and won a silver medal in the 100-metre race. Later severe arthritis restricted her activities to coaching and sportswriting. Voted 'Canada's best woman athlete of the first

452

half-century', she was elected to the Sports HALL OF FAME.

Ross, Arthur H. (1886-1964). Hockey player and sports executive. Born in Naughton, Ont., he played hockey in Westmount, Brandon, Kenora, Montreal, Haileybury, and Ottawa before retiring in 1918. In 1924 he became manager-coach of the Boston Bruins and continued in that association for 40 years. He designed the Ross nets and pucks that are standard equipment today.

Ross, Sinclair (b.1908). Novelist and short-story writer. Born near Prince Albert, Sask., he joined the staff of the Royal Bank of Canada and ultimately moved to Montreal. He retired to Greece in the late sixties and then to Spain. In his highly praised first novel, AS FOR ME AND MY HOUSE (1941), and his short stories, the best known of which are 'The Lamp at Noon' and 'The Painted Door', he portrayed the isolated, lonely existences of people who lived through drought and the Depression on the Prairies in the 1930s. His other novels are *The Well* (1958), *A Whir of Gold* (1970), and *Sawbones Memorial* (1974). Ross's stories have been collected in *The Lamp at Noon and Other Stories* (1968).

Ross, W.W.E. (1894-1966). Poet. Born in Peterborough, Ont., and educated at the University of Toronto, he joined the staff of the Dominion Magnetic Observatory in Toronto as a geophysicist in 1924. His sharp imagist poems, published privately in the thirties, were collected by Raymond SOUSTER and John Robert Colombo in *Shapes and Sounds: Selected Poems of W.W.E. Ross* (1968). He was married to the journalist Mary Lowrey Ross.

Ross and Macdonald. Montreal architectural firm, formed in 1913. George Allan Ross (1879-1946) was born in Montreal and educated at the Massachusetts Institute of Technology and the École des Beaux-Arts in Paris and in the firms of Parker and Thomas, Boston, and Carrère and Hastings, New York. Robert H. Macdonald (1875-1942) was born in Melbourne, Australia, and came to Canada to train with Robert Findlay of Montreal. The firm of Ross and Macdonald was among the first in Canada to adopt the American method of using a large office to handle a wide variety of commissions at the same time. They worked in a wide range of period styles. Their buildings included, in Toronto, Eaton's College Street Store (1928-33, with SPROATT AND ROLPH), the ROYAL YORK HOTEL (1929), MAPLE LEAF GARDENS (1931), and the UNION STATION (1914-27, with John M. LYLE as design architect); in Montreal, the Château

Apartments (c.1925, in a variation on the CHÂTEAU STYLE), the Mount Royal Hotel (1927), and the Dominion Square Building (1928-9). They replanned the port of Halifax after the 1917 explosion.

Ross Bay Cemetery. Established in 1872 on the outskirts of Victoria, B.C., the 27½-acre cemetery has been called 'the history of the province written in stone and marble and granite'. Buried there are James DOUGLAS, Matthew BEGBIE, 10 premiers of British Columbia, Emily CARR, and Billy Barker (see BARKERVILLE), *et al.*

Ross Rifle. After failing to have a British company manufacture the British Army Lee-Enfield rifle in Canada, the Canadian government signed a contract with the Ross Rifle Company to manufacture in Quebec City a rifle designed by Sir Charles Ross. The Canadian militia received the first 1,000 rifles in 1905. Although an accurate target rifle, it was soon found to have many defects and became the subject of widespread controversy. The original design was modified nearly 100 times and manufacturing was accelerated when war was declared. The First Canadian Contingent was equipped with the Ross rifle but the First Canadian Infantry Division discarded it in June 1915—after the Battle of YPRES in April—when it was found to jam during rapid fire; the backsight was easily broken or misaligned and the breech mechanism was more susceptible to clogging by mud and dust than the Lee-Enfield. The Ross rifle was withdrawn from the other Canadian divisions in June 1916 and replaced by the Lee-Enfield rifle.

Ross Trophy. See ART ROSS TROPHY.

Ross's goose. The popular name of a small white goose that breeds in the FAR NORTH. It was named after Bernard R. Ross, a Hudson's Bay Company factor who died in 1874.

Rotary snowplough. Canada's most important contribution to world railroading. The basic patent on the 'revolving snow shovel' to replace the wedge-plough then used by railroads was taken out by a Toronto dentist, J.W. Elliott, in 1869. Supervised by an inventor named Orange Jull, and built in 1883-4 by Leslie Brothers of Orangeville, Ont., the Elliott-Jull snowplough became standard equipment on North American railway lines against drifts, avalanches, and other obstructions. The basic plough now in use derives from the Elliott-Jull design, which was standardized in 1911.

Rothmans Tennis Championship

Rothmans Canadian Open Tennis Championship. Cash awards totalling $155,000 are presented to winners of the men's and ladies' singles, and the men's and ladies' doubles, in the annual Canadian Open Tennis Tournament every August. The awards have been made by ROTHMANS OF PALL MALL CANADA LIMITED since 1972.

Rothmans Merit Award for Literature. An annual prize honouring a writer who has made a significant contribution to Canadian letters. The $1,000 award was first made in 1975 by the CANADIAN AUTHORS ASSOCIATION with funds provided by ROTHMANS OF PALL MALL CANADA LIMITED.

Rothmans of Pall Mall Canada Limited. A cigarette company—part of the Rothmans Multinational Corporation, which has its headquarters in South Africa—noted for its sponsorship of sports, cultural, and social programs and awards since 1965. In the sports field Rothmans sponsors tennis tournaments (including the International and the Canadian Open), equestrian events, sailing competitions (including the Olympic Seeker Program), and police curling bonspiels. In the cultural area it aids performing arts groups (by designing and printing souvenir programs), art galleries (with subsidized tours of international art exhibitions), and literature (through the CAA's annual writer's award). In the social sphere it sponsors the Outstanding Citizens of the Year Awards (with the Canadian Jaycees) and operates the Craven Foundation (named after Craven A), which maintains a collection of antique and vintage cars and was established in June 1972.

ROTP. Initials of the Regular Officer Training Plan whereby students are enrolled as Officer Cadets in the CANADIAN ARMED FORCES and receive a free education with pay at one of the CANADIAN MILITARY COLLEGES. See also RETP.

Rotstein, Abraham (b.1930). Political economist and economic nationalist. Born in Montreal and educated at McGill, the University of California, and Columbia, he teaches political economy at the University of Toronto. He was an author of the WATKINS REPORT, a founding member of the COMMITTEE FOR AN INDEPENDENT CANADA, the editor of the CANADIAN FORUM when it published the then-secret GRAY REPORT, and a prime mover of the UNIVERSITY LEAGUE FOR SOCIAL REFORM. Among his books is *The Precarious Homestead* (1973), a selection of essays.

Rouges. Members of the *Parti rouge* (red party), formed in Canada East (Quebec) in 1848. A radical group of liberals influenced by Louis-Joseph PAPINEAU, it was led by A.-A. Dorion. (It was the counterpart of the moderate reformers called BLEUS, supporters of Louis-H. LAFONTAINE.) The *Rouges* were one of the founding groups of the Liberal Party in 1873.

Roughing It in the Bush. A famous book about pioneering in Upper Canada (Ontario) by Susanna MOODIE, published in 1852. Written chiefly in the form of anecdotes and character sketches, it is a disenchanted but vivid account of the hardships and cultural deprivations the author encountered in her early years in Upper Canada.

Routhier, Sir Adolphe-Basile (1839-1920). Jurist and author. Born in St Placide, L.C. (Que.), educated at Université Laval, and called to the bar in 1861, he was a leading Conservative and a prominent jurist, being chief justice of the superior court of Quebec from 1904 to his retirement in 1906. Routhier wrote more than a dozen books—essays, novels, travel books, speeches—but is best known as the author of a 32-line verse, 'Chant national', which he published in *Les Échos* (1882). Calixa LAVALLÉE set it to music for a concert in Quebec City on 24 June 1880. It is known in R. Stanley Weir's translation as 'O CANADA'.

Routine Proceedings and Orders of the Day. Printed document setting out the order of business for each day in the HOUSE OF COMMONS; now called ORDER PAPER AND NOTICES.

Roux, Jean-Louis (b.1923). Actor. Born in Montreal, he acted with Les COMPAGNONS DE ST LAURENT from 1939 to 1944, moved to Paris, and on his return co-founded the THÉÂTRE DU NOUVEAU MONDE in 1951. Since then the thin, mercurial actor has been associated with the NATIONAL THEATRE SCHOOL and the STRATFORD FESTIVAL.

Rowdyman, The. Feature film written by and starring Gordon PINSENT. Released in 1971 and directed by Peter Carter, it starred—in addition to Pinsent—Will Geer, Frank Converse, and Linda Goranson. Set in Corner Brook, Nfld, it tells the story of a happy-go-lucky Newfoundlander, Will Cole, whose irresponsibility causes the death of his best friend. 94 min., colour.

Rowe, Terry (b.1936). Poet and singer. Born in Peterborough, Ont., he left home at 13. He has travelled throughout North America and western Europe and is now based in

Toronto. His poems about love and loss have been collected in the bestselling *To You with Love* (1971), *The Warmth of Christmas* (1973), and *You and I, and Love* (1973). An album, *To You with Love*, was released in 1973. He has been called 'Canada's own Rod McKuen'.

Rowell-Sirois Commission. The name by which the Royal Commission on Dominion-Provincial Relations (1937-40) is usually known. Newton Rowell was the original chairman when it was charged with the mandate of examining the economic and financial basis of Confederation, the distribution of legislative responsibility, and the financial relations between governments. After Rowell resigned in 1938 because of ill health, Joseph Sirois headed the Commission until its report was given to the Mackenzie KING government in 1940. Its findings, based on a series of splendid scholarly studies, proposed substantial alterations in federal-provincial relations and financing, including a scheme of national-adjustment grants designed to maintain a national minimum of services across the country. The coming of the Second World War and the opposition of Alberta, Ontario, and British Columbia prevented any agreement, but wartime exigency led Ottawa unilaterally to implement some financial aspects of the Commission's proposals.

Roxborough, Henry H. (b.1891). Sportsman and author. Born in Toronto, he participated in many sports and judged many national and international athletic events. He refereed at the British Empire games in London in 1934 and was official observer at the 1936 Olympic Games in Berlin. His principal books are *Great Days in Canadian Sport* (1957), *Olympic Hero* (1960), *Canada at the Olympics* (1963), *Stanley Cup Story* (1964), and *One Hundred—Not Out* (1966).

Roy, Gabrielle (b.1909). Novelist. Born in Saint-Boniface, Man., she taught in rural Manitoba schools but moved to Montreal and began a realistic, compassionate novel about the poor there during the Depression and the early years of the Second World War. She achieved immediate prominence and acclaim with the publication of *Bonheur d'occasion* (1945), which appeared in English as *The* TIN FLUTE (1947), translated by Hannah Josephson. *Alexandre Chenevert* (1955) was translated by Harry Binsse as *The Cashier* (1955). Three collections of semi-fictional linked narratives, set in Manitoba and written with great delicacy, are *La Petite Poule d'eau* (1950), translated by Harry Binsse as WHERE NESTS THE WATER HEN (1951); *Rue Des-*

CHAMBAULT (1955), translated by Harry Binsse as *Street of Riches* (1957); and *La Route d'Altamont* (1966), translated by Joyce MARSHALL as *The Road Past Altamont* (1966). Two novels about the Far North are *La Montagne secrète* (1961), translated by Harry Binsse as *The Hidden Mountain* (1962), and *Windflower* (1970), a translation by Joyce Marshall of part of *La Rivière sans repos* (1970). *Cet Été qui chantait* (1972), reminiscences of a summer in Charlevoix Co., Que., was translated by Joyce Marshall as *The Enchanted Summer* (1976).

Royal, The. See the ROYAL AGRICULTURAL WINTER FAIR.

Royal 22e Régiment. Canadian army regiment—the 'Vandoos'. It was organized in 1914 and redesignated its present name in 1928. During the FIRST WORLD WAR it served as part of the 5th Infantry Brigade in France, distinguishing itself at the SOMME (1916, 1918), VIMY (1917), and YPRES (1917). In the SECOND WORLD WAR it served as a unit of the 3rd Infantry Brigade in England, Sicily, and Italy. Since then its battalions have served in Korea and Germany. 'Vandoos' is a playful version of the regimental number, *vingt-deuxième*.

Royal Academy of Dancing/Canada, The. Established in London, Eng., in 1920, the Royal Academy started activity in Canada in 1939. With the appointment of Bettina Byers as the first Canadian organizer, a tour of lectures and demonstrations by Dame Adeline Genée in 1940, and first ballet examinations for 33 candidates in 1941, the RAD/Canada came into being. By 1976 membership was over 1,100; over 5,000 candidates are examined yearly in both dancing and teaching.

Royal Agricultural Winter Fair. 'Canada's Show Window of Agriculture' and the Royal Horse Show—commonly called 'The Royal'. Annual events in the Coliseum on the grounds of the Canadian National Exhibition, they have been held every November since 1922, except for the war years.

Royal Alexandra Theatre. An attractive Edwardian theatre in Toronto. Designed by John LYLE and built for Cawthra Mulock, a young Toronto millionaire, it opened on 20 Aug. 1907. It was slated to be demolished when it was acquired by Edwin ('Honest Ed') MIRVISH, who had it beautifully restored and refurbished and reopened it on 9 Sept. 1963. It has 1,497 seats.

Royal Anthem. See ANTHEM.

Royal Assent. The final stage in the passing of a bill, the point at which it becomes law. Constitutional usage requires that assent be given in the presence of both Houses of Parliament. Assent may be given by the sovereign in person or by her representative; or the governor general or lieutenant-governor may sign a commission appointing a deputy and setting forth the bills to which assent is to be given. It is not necessary for the sovereign or her representative to sign every bill—assent given in the presence of both Houses is what makes a bill statutory. The clerks of both Houses then endorse the day on which assent was given on each bill, and 'the date of such assent shall be the date of the commencement, if no other date of commencement is therein provided.'

Royal Bank Award. A medal and cash grant of $50,000 awarded annually since 1967 by an independent selection committee meeting under the auspices of the ROYAL BANK OF CANADA. The largest award of its kind in the country, it seeks to honour 'a Canadian citizen or person domiciled in Canada whose outstanding achievement is of such importance that it is contributing to human welfare and the common good'.

Royal Bank of Canada. A chartered bank with its head office in Montreal. It was incorporated in 1869 as the Merchant Bank of Halifax; the present name was adopted in 1901. In 1976 it had 1,382 branches in Canada and 88 outside the country. The Royal is the largest chartered bank in Canada.

Royal Canadian Academy of Arts/Academie Royale des Arts du Canada. The oldest national society in the visual and environmental arts. Founded in 1880 by HRH the Princess Louise and her husband, the Marquis of Lorne, then governor general, it encourages the visual arts in Canadian society. Its membership—which is honorary—includes painters, sculptors, architects, film-makers, and graphic, typographic, and industrial designers. Full members can use the initials RCA after their name. See also WINDFIELDS.

Royal Canadian Air Cadets. See CADETS.

Royal Canadian Air Force. Although many Canadians served in the Royal Flying Corps, Royal Naval Air Service, and Royal Air Force during the FIRST WORLD WAR, Canada did not try to form an air force until early 1918 in England; it was disbanded early in 1920. An effort to form a Royal Canadian Naval Air Service in Canada in the summer of 1918 was equally short-lived. In 1919 the government established an Air Board to control all aeronautics in the Dominion. In 1920 a non-permanent Canadian Air Force was formed, whose sole role was to conduct refresher courses for former officers and airmen. In 1923 the Department of National Defence was created and the Air Board ceased as a separate department. On 1 Apr. 1924 the Royal Canadian Air Force became a permanent component of Canada's defence forces under the Army Chief of the General Staff.

The RCAF's major effort was directed towards civil air operations until 1934, when the purchase of 10 service aircraft marked a new trend and the Force continued to grow and improve its military training. In 1938 the Senior Air Officer became Chief of the Air Staff, on an equal footing with the Navy and Army chiefs of staff. The start of the SECOND WORLD WAR and the agreement to establish the BRITISH COMMONWEALTH AIR TRAINING PLAN resulted in rapid expansion. The strength rose from 4,000 permanent and auxiliary in 1939 to 215,000 in 1943. Over 40 home-defence squadrons and 48 overseas squadrons were formed, the latter based in the U.K., Iceland, Northwest Europe, North Africa, Italy, and Southeast Asia. Casualties totalled 17,101 killed and 1,416 wounded. (See also NORMANDY INVASION.)

The post-war regular air force, originally set at 16,000, began to grow as a result of the Cold War. By 1954 its strength was 46,000 and in 1963 it was 53,000. In 1951 Canada contributed an air division to NATO that was initially based in France and Germany and from 1967 in Germany only. Maritime Air Command east-coast squadrons flew daily operational patrols in support of NATO Atlantic Command. In 1957 the RCAF began to operate closely with the United States Air Force in North American Air Defence. Air Transport Command provided airlifts for United Nations peacekeeping operations in the Middle East, the Congo, Cyprus, and Pakistan. Search and rescue operations in Canada were another important role. On 1 Feb. 1968 the Royal Canadian Air Force was unified with the ROYAL CANADIAN NAVY and the CANADIAN ARMY to form the CANADIAN ARMED FORCES.

Royal Canadian Armoured Corps. Army corps. Authorized in 1940, it has served as an administrative and training organization—it has had no combat role.

Royal Canadian Army Cadets. See CADETS.

Royal Canadian Corps of Signals, The. Army corps. It was authorized in 1919 as the 'Canadian Signalling Instruction Staff' and was redesignated its present name in 1948.

During the FIRST WORLD WAR it served as part of the Canadian Engineers in France. In the SECOND WORLD WAR it served at home and abroad. Since then it has served in the Far East, Europe, the Middle East, and Indo-China.

Royal Canadian Dragoons, The. Army regiment. It originated in 1883 with the 'Cavalry School Corps'—it served in the NORTH WEST REBELLION of 1885—and was redesignated its present name in 1893. During the FIRST WORLD WAR it served as infantry with the 1st Canadian Division in 1915, and later as cavalry. In the SECOND WORLD WAR it served as an armoured car regiment to the 1st Canadian Corps, and was important in battles in Sicily and on mainland Italy. Since then its squadrons have served in Korea, Europe, and the Middle East.

Royal Canadian Geographical Society. See MASSEY MEDAL.

Royal Canadian Infantry Corps. Army corps. It was authorized in 1942 to serve as an administrative organization during the SECOND WORLD WAR.

Royal Canadian Legion, The. A club for ex-service people. It grew out of a conference of veterans' groups held in Winnipeg on 25-6 Nov. 1925 and was originally called The Canadian Legion of the British Empire Service League. It was renamed Canadian Legion in 1949 and The Canadian Legion in 1951; the Royal prefix was granted in 1959. Some 1,800 branches, ranging from halls to community centres, are maintained in Canada and the United States. Membership in 1975 was approximately 445,000 ex-service people and a Ladies Auxiliary of 80,000. The Legion organizes annual POPPY campaigns on REMEMBRANCE DAY. It represents the interests of veterans at Ottawa and through ACTION (A Commitment To Improve Our Nation), a program that addresses itself to social questions. The Legion's motto is *Memoriam forum retinebimus* ('We will remember them').

Royal Canadian Mint. A CROWN CORPORATION for producing coins, plaques, and other devices. First established as a branch of the Royal Mint in 1870, it has been in operation since 1908, becoming a Crown agency corporation in 1969. The Mint, which makes a small profit, has a seven-man board of directors: the Master of the Mint, the Chairman, and five others. In 1975 a branch was opened in Winnipeg.

Royal Canadian Mounted Police. Federal civilian police force. Established in 1873 as the NORTH WEST MOUNTED POLICE for service in the Northwest, it was granted the prefix 'Royal' in 1904. In 1920 it absorbed the DOMINION PO-LICE, transferred its headquarters from Regina to Ottawa, and changed its title to Royal Canadian Mounted Police. The motto of the force is *Maintiens le droit* (in English, 'Uphold the Right'). The reputation of the Mounties has stood so high that it has been said 'THEY ALWAYS GET THEIR MAN'. Responsible to the SOLICITOR GENERAL of Canada, the force is managed by a commissioner who holds the rank and status of deputy minister. All provinces except Ontario and Quebec (which have their own provincial police forces) have entered into contracts with the Royal Canadian Mounted Police to enforce the CRIMINAL CODE OF CANADA and provincial laws under the direction of the respective attorneys general. In addition, the force provides police services to 161 municipalities in those eight provinces and polices exclusively the Yukon Territory and Northwest Territories. Apart from Headquarters Division and the Office of the Commissioner, which are located in Ottawa, there are 12 operational divisions located in the provincial capitals, in Montreal, and in Ottawa. The criminal investigation services of the force are available to police services throughout Canada. The French name for the force, Gendarmerie royale du Canada, came into use in 1970-1. See also MUSICAL RIDE, The RED SERGE, SCARLET AND STETSON, SECURITY SERVICE.

Royal Canadian Navy. Established by an Act of Parliament on 4 May 1910, it had two training cruisers, HMCS *Niobe* on the east coast and HMCS *Rainbow* on the west coast, at the outbreak of the FIRST WORLD WAR. While its personnel quickly grew to about 7,000, most of whom served in British warships, the fleet remained small until, in 1917, anti-submarine patrols became necessary in the Atlantic. In 1923 the Royal Canadian Naval Reserve and the Royal Canadian Naval Volunteer Reserve were formed, and the fleet started to increase from six fighting ships in 1928 to 11 in 1939, manned by 1,047 officers and men. By 1945 there were over 900 ships in the RCN, of which 375 were armed for offensive action, and a total personnel of about 95,000, all volunteers. The formation of RCNVR units across Canada in the 1920s and 1930s greatly facilitated this large increase. Canada's principal naval effort in the SECOND WORLD WAR was directed against German U-boats in the Battle of the Atlantic: the protection of troop and cargo ship convoys. A part of this vital link between North America and the United Kingdom was the Canadian North-West Atlantic Command, under

Royal Canadian Navy

RAdm L.W. MURRAY. Canadian warships escorted the Anglo-American invasion force to North Africa late in 1942. Over 100 Canadian vessels, including landing craft, took part in Operation Neptune, the naval support for Operation Overlord. (See also NORMANDY INVASION.) During the Second World War the RCN commissioned ships in the following categories (the classes are in parentheses): Cruisers; Armed Merchant Cruisers; Aircraft Carriers; Destroyers (River, Town, Tribal); Destroyer Escorts (St Laurent, Restigouche, Mackenzie, Annapolis, Iroquois); Fast Hydrofoil Escorts; CORVETTES (Flower, Castle); Frigates (River, Loch); Minesweepers (Basset, Bangor, Algerine, Llewellyn, Lake, Bay); Anti-Submarine Trawlers (Western Iles); Armed Yachts; Submarines; Motor Craft; Arctic Patrol Vessels; and Operational Support Ships.

In 1946 the RCNR and the RCNVR were reorganized to form the Royal Canadian Naval Reserve. RCN strength increased owing to the Cold War and the Korean War (1950-3), in which Canada provided three destroyers on a rotational basis; by 1962 it was 21,500. On 1 Feb. 1968 the Royal Canadian Navy was unified with the CANADIAN ARMY and the ROYAL CANADIAN AIR FORCE to form the CANADIAN ARMED FORCES.

Royal Canadian Regiment, The. Army regiment. Originating in 1883 when the 'Infantry School Corps' was authorized, it was redesignated its present name in 1901. It served in the NORTH WEST REBELLION in 1885 and in the SOUTH AFRICAN WAR in 1899-1902. During the FIRST WORLD WAR it joined the Canadian Corps in France and also served in the 3rd Canadian Division, distinguishing itself at YPRES (1915, 1917), the SOMME (1916), and VIMY (1917). In the SECOND WORLD WAR it was part of the Second British Expeditionary Force in France, and also served in numerous battles in Sicily and on mainland Italy. Since then its battalions have served in Korea and Germany.

Royal Canadian Sea Cadets Corps. See CADETS.

Royal Canadian Yacht Club. Pioneer water club. Founded in Toronto in 1852 as the Boat Club, it became the Canadian Yacht Club; the prefix 'Royal' was added in 1854. The first clubhouse was a scow moored to a wharf at the foot of York St. It now enjoys handsome quarters on Toronto Island—open for about half the year—with a private ferry service from the mainland. In 1974 it amalgamated with the Carleton Club (Hayden St) and is now a year-round club. The RCYC

offers the Prince of Wales Trophy, which was first presented in 1860 by the Prince of Wales for an annual competition on Lake Ontario.

Royal Canadians, The. See LORD STRATHCONA'S HORSE.

Royal City. The unofficial motto of Guelph, Ont., which was named by John GALT in 1827, after the family name of the Royal Family. It is also the sobriquet of New Westminster, B.C.

Royal Commission. A commission appointed by a government to make an impartial inquiry into a problem. Royal Commissions are appointed by either the federal or a provincial government, Commissioners, who hold their commissions from the CROWN, are appointed because they are experts in the problem to be investigated, are free from bias on the matter, or have a wide experience in matters allied to the investigation. They have power to hear witnesses, hold public hearings, and commission studies by experts. At the end of their study, which may take some years, they transmit a report with recommendations for action to the government, but the government is not obliged to act on the report. There have been hundreds of Royal Commissions since CONFEDERATION. Some of the best known are those on Dominion-Provincial Relations (ROWELL-SIROIS COMMISSION), Canada's Economic Prospects (GORDON COMMISSION), BILINGUALISM AND BICULTURALISM, the STATUS OF WOMEN, the RELATIONS OF CAPITAL AND LABOUR; and the HONG KONG INQUIRY, the PRICE SPREADS COMMISSION, the O'LEARY COMMISSION, the HALL COMMISSION, the CARTER COMMISSION, and the MASSEY COMMISSION.

Royal Conservatory of Music. The country's leading school of music. The Toronto Conservatory of Music was incorporated as a private company in 1886. The trusteeship passed in 1921 to the University of Toronto, which has administered it ever since, and 'Royal' was substituted for 'Toronto' in the name in 1946—the year of its Diamond Jubilee. Its comprehensive range of instruction, high standards, and system of examinations, especially in piano and theory, have stimulated a vigorous musical life from coast to coast. A diploma of Associateship (ARCT) is awarded successful candidates in performance, teaching, and composition. The principals have been Dr Edward Fisher (from 1886), Dr A. S. VOGT (from 1913), Ernest MacMILLAN (from 1926), Norman Wilks (from 1943), Dr Ettore MAZZOLENI (from 1946), and Dr David Ouchterlony (from 1968).

Royal Conservatory Opera School. Opera School of the ROYAL CONSERVATORY OF MUSIC, Toronto. It was founded in 1946 and in 1948 Herman GEIGER-TOREL was invited to Canada to direct it. It is now a department of the Faculty of Music, University of Toronto.

Royal Family. The immediate family of the reigning monarch. The Queen of Canada, Elizabeth II, was born to the Duke and Duchess of York on 21 Apr. 1926. Her father, who became George VI, was the second son of George V; her mother, the former Lady Elizabeth Bowes-Lyon, is now the Queen Mother. Her sister, Princess Margaret, was born in 1930. Princess Elizabeth's marriage to Philip Mountbatten, Duke of Edinburgh, was celebrated on 20 Nov. 1947. She acceded to the throne as Elizabeth II on the death of her father in 1952; her coronation was held in Westminster Abbey on 2 June 1953. The Queen and her consort have four children: Prince Charles, Prince of Wales, born in 1948; Princess Anne, born in 1950; Prince Andrew, born in 1960; and Prince Edward, born in 1964. For the official title of the sovereign, see ROYAL STYLE AND TITLE. For a list of the British kings and queens of Canada, see MONARCHY.

Royal Horse Show. See the ROYAL AGRICULTURAL WINTER FAIR.

Royal Military College of Canada. A tri-service cadet college. Established at Kingston, Ont., by an Act of Parliament in 1874, it opened in 1876 to impart an education for 'the military profession'—originally for army officers. After 1948, when it was reorganized as a Canadian Services College, cadets were trained for all armed services. In 1959 the province empowered the college to confer degrees in arts, science, and engineering. Each year RMC graduates at the baccalaureate level some 200 Officer Cadets. It is the oldest of three CANADIAN MILITARY COLLEGES. See also Le COLLÈGE MILITAIRE ROYAL DE SAINT-JEAN, ROYAL ROADS MILITARY COLLEGE.

Royal North West Mounted Police. Former federal police force for western Canada. Originally the NORTH WEST MOUNTED POLICE, formed in 1873, it received the 'Royal' prefix in 1904. It became a dominion-wide force, the ROYAL CANADIAN MOUNTED POLICE, in 1920.

Royal Ontario Museum. Canada's largest public museum, located on Queen's Park Crescent in Toronto. Its west-wing galleries—designed by Frank DARLING and John PEARSON and built from 1910 to 1913—originally incorporated five museums: the Royal Ontario Museums of Archaeology, Geology, Mineralogy, Paleontology, and Zoology. The wing on Queen's Park Crescent was added in 1933. In 1947 the museums merged and became part of the University of Toronto, separating from it in 1955. The primary art and archaeological collections of the ROM resulted from the efforts of Sir Edmund WALKER and Charles Trick Currelly, the first curator and Director of Archaeology from 1914 to 1917. Known internationally for its collection of Chinese artifacts, gathered in the 1920s and 1930s by George Crofts and William Charles White, Anglican Bishop of Honan, the ROM also houses, in a separate building, the Sigmund Samuel Collection of early Canadiana donated by Dr Samuel in 1951. In 1964 the ROM received a gift from Col. R. S. McLAUGHLIN to build the Planetarium that bears his name; it opened in 1968. The museum's directors have included Theodore A. Heinrich (1955-62), F. M. Turner (acting director, 1962-3), William Elgin Swinton (1963-6), Peter C. Swann (1966-72), Walter M. Tovell (1972-5), and James E. Cruise (from 1975).

Royal Regiment of Canadian Artillery. Army regiment. It originated in 1871 with two batteries of garrison artillery and took its present name in 1883. Its units served in both the FIRST and SECOND WORLD WARS and it was prominent in the DIEPPE raid. Since then it has served in Korea, Europe, and the Middle East.

Royal Roads Military College. A tri-service cadet college. Originally it was HMCS *Royal Roads*, a naval training establishment set up in 1941 on the 650-acre Hatley Park estate of the Honourable James Dunsmuir overlooking the Strait of Juan de Fuca, B.C., which the Canadian government purchased for $75 million. Each year it graduates at the baccalaureate level some 100 Officer Cadets. It is now one of three CANADIAN MILITARY COLLEGES. See also Le COLLÈGE MILITAIRE ROYAL DE SAINT-JEAN, ROYAL MILITARY COLLEGE OF CANADA.

'Royal Salute'. An abbreviated combination of 'O CANADA' and 'GOD SAVE THE QUEEN' that is played on semi-official occasions.

Royal Society of Canada. A national academy whose aim is the promotion of learning and research in the arts and sciences in Canada. Founded in 1882 by the Governor General the Marquis of Lorne, it is organized in three academies: L'Academie des lettres et des sciences humaines; Academy of Humanities and Social Sciences; and the bilingual

Academy of Science. It holds its annual meetings in conjunction with those of other LEARNED SOCIETIES; every second year these are held in Ottawa. The Society publishes its *Transactions*, STUDIA VARIA, and *Proceedings of Symposia*. The elected membership exceeds 600 men and women of academic distinction. Members are entitled to use the initials FRSC after their name. The Society oversees the following distinctions: BANCROFT AWARD, CHAUVEAU MEDAL, FLAVELLE MEDAL, HARRISON PRIZE, HENRY MARSHALL TORY MEDAL, INNIS-GÉRIN MEDAL, LORNE PIERCE MEDAL, MILLER MEDAL, NATO FELLOWSHIP PROGRAMME, RUTHERFORD MEMORIAL SCHOLARSHIP, SIR ARTHUR SIMS SCHOLARSHIP, TYRRELL MEDAL.

Royal Style and Title. The official designation of the sovereign. Following the accession to the throne of Elizabeth II, Parliament approved the official Royal Style and Title on 3 Feb. 1953: 'Elizabeth the Second, by the Grace of God, of the United Kingdom, Canada and Her other Realms and Territories, Queen, Head of the Commonwealth, Defender of the Faith.' Similar designations apply in the United Kingdom, Australia, and New Zealand.

Royal Visit. The progress of the monarch or a member of the ROYAL FAMILY through a dominion or colony. The first Royal Visit to Canada of a reigning monarch was that of King George VI, who crossed the country with Queen Elizabeth from 17 May to 15 June 1939. Previous visits by future monarchs were those of the Prince of Wales, later Edward VII, in 1860; by the Duke and Duchess of York, later George V and Queen Mary, in 1901; by the Prince of Wales, later Edward VIII, in 1919, 1924, and 1927; and by the Duke of York, later George VI, in 1927. As Princess Elizabeth, Elizabeth II visited Canada in 1951; as a reigning monarch she made Royal Visits in 1957, 1959, 1964, 1967, 1970, 1974, and 1976.

Royal William. Paddle steamer built in Quebec and launched there on 29 Apr. 1831. She began a Quebec-Halifax service that fall, but it was decided in 1833 to send her to Europe for sale. She left Quebec on 4 Aug., was coaled at Pictou, N.S., and arrived at Gravesend, Eng., on 11 Sept.; the trip was made under steam alone for three days out of every four. She had been partly owned by Samuel Cunard, and her successful Atlantic crossing—the first entirely under steam—may have inspired him with the idea of a transatlantic steam service. She was sold to Spain in 1834 and became a naval frigate, the *Isabella Segunda*.

Royal Winnipeg Ballet, The. Canada's first and oldest continuing ballet company. It was founded in 1938 by Gweneth LLOYD and her partner Betty Hall Farrally as the Winnipeg Ballet Club, an extension of their ballet school. Its first presentation was a pair of new ballets choreographed by Gweneth Lloyd and inspired by the local scene: *Kilowatt Magic* and *Grain*. The company became fully professional in 1949 and danced a Command Performance for Princess Elizabeth and Prince Philip in 1951. After appearing again before Elizabeth, now Queen, it was granted the use of 'Royal' in 1953, three years before Sadler's Wells became the Royal Ballet. A disastrous fire in 1954 destroyed all its property and most of its records and delayed performances until 1956. Arnold SPOHR was appointed artistic director in 1958.

The RWB has continued to build a worldwide reputation featuring its own repertoire of ballets with indigenous and contemporary themes—35 of which were choreographed by Gweneth Lloyd during her tenure as director. The company has produced 14 works by Brian MACDONALD, a visiting choreographer from 1964 to 1970. John Neumeier and Oscar Araiz have choreographed numerous works for it since then. It has undertaken many international tours, including nine American tours since 1964; England in 1965; Paris, Russia, and Czechoslovakia in 1968; Italy and France in 1970, when their four weeks in Paris became the longest commercial engagement of any Canadian dance company outside Canada; Australia in 1972; Latin America in 1974; and Israel in 1975. Some of the RWB's notable ballets are SHADOW ON THE PRAIRIE (Lloyd), *Pas d'Action* (Brian Macdonald), *The Rehearsal* (Agnes de Mille), and *The* ECSTASY OF RITA JOE (Norbert Vesak). The company's ballet school was formed in the early 1960s and developed a dance style based on the teachings of Vera Volkova; 20 of the 25 dancers in the 1976 RWB company were trained there.

Royal York Hotel. The Commonwealth's largest hotel, located in Toronto and operated by the CPR. Officially opened in 1929, the 27-storey building was designed by ROSS AND MACDONALD in a symmetrical Beaux Arts version of the Romanesque style. With additions and renovations, it now has 1,600 guest rooms.

Royalite No. 1. See DINGMAN'S DISCOVERY.

RPM Weekly. The trade magazine of the Canadian recording industry and allied arts. Founded by Walt Grealis in Toronto in 1964, it sponsored the JUNO AWARDS until 1975. It contains news, industry charts on best-selling records, radio-station play lists, etc., along with a section devoted to country music.

RRMC. See ROYAL ROADS MILITARY COLLEGE.

RRSP. See REGISTERED RETIREMENT SAVINGS PLAN.

RSC. Abbreviation of the Revised STATUTES OF CANADA. The Statutes are collected and reprinted in a consolidated form every 20 years or so.

RSC. See ROYAL SOCIETY OF CANADA.

Rt Hon., The. See The RIGHT HONOURABLE.

RTNDA. Initials of the Radio Television News Directors Association of Canada. See the CHARLES EDWARDS AWARDS and the DAN McARTHUR AWARDS.

Rubaboo. Algonkian word for 'soup', 'broth', or 'stew' eaten by fur traders. It might include PEMMICAN, flour, wild onions, sugar, vegetables, and salt pork. *Rubaboo* (or *rubbaboo*) has the meaning today of 'miscellany' or 'mixed bag'.

Rubenstein, Louis (1861-1931). Champion figure-skater. Born in Montreal, he won the Canadian and American figure-skating championships and then went on to become the world's first recognized figure-skating champion at St Petersburg (now Leningrad) in 1890. The day prior to the competition he was ordered out of the country by the Russian police because of his Jewish ancestry, but intervention by the British ambassador prevented his deportation and ensured his participation. He presided over Canadian associations in cycling, bowling, curling, fig-ure- and speed-skating, etc., and was alderman of Montreal's St Louis ward for 17 years.

Rubes, Jan (b.1920). Bass. Born in Volyne, Czech., he studied singing there and in Switzerland and was an opera singer in Europe before coming to Toronto in 1949. Since 1950 he has sung leading bass roles with the CANA-DIAN OPERA COMPANY, of which he is now Director of Touring and Program Development. Through his skilled performances in opera, light opera, and on radio and television, he is one of Canada's best-known singers.

Ruby Foo's. North America's largest restaurant. Founded in Montreal in 1945, it now has five dining rooms in Oriental décor with a seating capacity of 1,000. Famous for its Chinese cuisine, it also serves French and American food. A motor hotel was added in 1962.

Rugby-football. A name for a distinctive variety of football developed in Canada in the late nineteenth century from the English game rugby (or rugger). It is sometimes called simply 'rugby'. Since the 1930s it has largely been displaced by the American term 'football'.

Rule, Jane (b.1931). Novelist. Born in Plain-field, N.J., she settled in Canada in 1956 and now teaches creative writing at the University of British Columbia. She wrote *Lesbian Images* (1975), a collection of short essays relating the lives and work of famous lesbian authors, and lesbianism is in part the subject of her three novels: *The Desert of the Heart* (1964), *This Is Not for You* (1970), and *Against the Season* (1971). A new novel, *The Young in One Another's Arms*, is scheduled for publication in 1977. *Theme for Diverse Instruments* (1975) is a collection of short stories.

Rupert's House. The oldest trading-post of the HUDSON'S BAY COMPANY. It was built in 1668 by Zachariah Gillam, commander of the *Nonsuch* (which had GROSEILLIERS on board), at the mouth of the Rupert R. on the east coast of James Bay. Originally called Fort Charles, it became a fort of the HBC when the Company was founded in 1670, though it was in French hands from 1686 to 1713. The Company re-established it in 1777 and it is still in operation.

Rupert's Land. An area comprising all those territories drained by rivers flowing into Hudson Bay. This territory was granted by Charles II in 1670 to Prince Rupert and 17 associates who formed the HUDSON'S BAY COM-PANY. In 1870 Rupert's Land and the NORTH-WEST TERRITORIES became part of the Dominion of Canada.

Rush-Bagot Agreement. Signed in 1817 by Richard Rush for the United States and by Sir Charles Bagot for Great Britain, it limited armed vessels on the border lakes to four under 100 tons: one each on Lake Ontario and Lake Champlain and two on the upper lakes. With later modifications, it has remained in force.

Russell. An automobile manufactured from 1905 to 1915 by Canada Cycle and Motor Company, Toronto. Four models were produced, each available in touring or runabout versions, that ranged in price from $1,475 to $4,500. The company's motto was 'Made up to a standard—not down to a price'. See also CCM.

461

Russell, Anna (b.1913). Concert comedienne. Born in London, Eng., she learned the French horn at the Royal College of Music and made her British début in a one-woman revue in 1924. With her Canadian-born mother she settled in Cooksville, Ont., in 1939, making her concert début in Toronto in 1944, her Broadway début in 1948, and appearing with SPRING THAW in 1953. Apart from some years of residence in Australia, she has made her home in Unionville, Ont. Through concerts and recordings she has acquired a wide following for her exuberant, irreverent, and brilliant parodies of singers—folk, opera, and concert—and especially for her take-offs on German opera. She has been called 'the funniest woman in the world'.

Rutherford, Ernest, Baron Rutherford of Nelson. See MACDONALD PHYSICS LABORATORY, RUTHERFORD MEMORIAL SCHOLARSHIP.

Rutherford Memorial Scholarship. Awarded annually since 1952 by the ROYAL SOCIETY OF CANADA, it enables a student of experimental physics and chemistry who holds a NATIONAL RESEARCH COUNCIL Post-doctorate Overseas Fellowship to broaden his experience and outlook through further training in another country. Named after the great nuclear physicist Lord Rutherford, some of whose work was done at McGill at the turn of the century, the scholarship consists of a $750 grant. See also MACDONALD PHYSICS LABORATORY.

Ryan, Norman (Red) (1895-1936). Celebrated bank robber. Born in Toronto, he stole a bike at the age of 12 and thereafter was seldom out of jail. Sentenced to life imprisonment for a succession of daring bank robberies, he was a model prisoner and won the confidence of an influential Catholic chaplain. Agitation by the Toronto press and the belief that Ryan was a changed man led to his parole after some 11 years. Ten months later, on 24 May 1936, he was killed in a gunbattle while trying to rob a liquor store in Sarnia, Ont. It was then discovered that he had masterminded a succession of robberies since his release. Ryan's behaviour toughened the parole board's stand and his story inspired Morley CALLAGHAN's novel *More Joy in Heaven* (1937).

Ryan, Thomas F. (1872-1961). The inventor of five-pin bowling. Born in Guelph, Ont., and raised in Toronto, he was a notable baseball player and later racehorse owner. In 1908-9 he made a popular contribution to alley bowling when he devised the game of five-pins, a precursor of the standard 10-pins, which could have been very profitable had he ever decided to patent it. He eventually prospered as an auctioneer and a dealer in antiques.

'Ryans and the Pittmans, The'. Alternate title of 'WE'LL RANT AND WE'LL ROAR'.

Ryder, Gus (b.1899). Amateur athlete and swimming instructor. The Toronto sportsman was chosen Canada's Man of the Year after he coached Marilyn BELL in her marathon swim across Lake Ontario on 9 Sept. 1954. He is widely respected for his many years of work with handicapped children.

Rye whisky. A blended whisky derived from Alberta rye grain. By law the aging process must take at least three years, though its golden colour is produced by artificial colouring, usually caramel. Canadian rye is one of the world's most popular whiskies and many brands are distributed internationally. SEAGRAM'S V.O. and Hiram Walker's CANADIAN CLUB are the two best known.

Ryerson, Egerton (1803-82). Clergyman and educator. Born in Charlotteville, U.C. (Ont.), of a United Empire Loyalist family, he entered the Methodist ministry in 1825. He became editor of the *Christian Guardian*, a Methodist newspaper, in 1829, and in 1841 became the first principal of Victoria College, Cobourg. As chief superintendent of education in Canada West (Ontario) from 1844 to 1876, he was able to lay the basis for the Ontario educational system. *The Story of My Life* (1883), edited by J.G. Hodgins, was published posthumously. *My Dearest Sophie: Letters from Egerton Ryerson to his Daughter* (1955) was edited by C.B. Sissons.

Ryerson, Stanley (b.1911). Historian. Born in Toronto and educated at UPPER CANADA COLLEGE, he studied at the University of Toronto and the Sorbonne. He was active as the Educational Director of the LABOUR PROGRESSIVE PARTY and editor of the *Marxist Quarterly*, which he renamed *Horizons*. Among his publications are *1837—Rebirth of a Canadian Democracy; French Canada: A Study of Canadian Democracy* (1943); a two-volume Marxist history, *The Founding of Canada: Beginnings to 1815* (2nd ed. 1963); and *Unequal Union: Confederation and the Roots of Conflict in the Canadas, 1815-73* (1968).

Ryerson Polytechnical Institute. A college in downtown Toronto named after Egerton RYERSON. The Ryerson Institute of Technology was created by an act of the provincial legislature in 1948; it achieved degree-granting status and a name-change in 1971. The academic program encompasses the applied arts, arts, business, community services, and technology.

Ryerson Press, The. For many years the leading English-Canadian publishing house. It was founded in Toronto in 1829 as the Methodist Book Room and Publishing House. Under William Briggs (1836-1922), who was Book Steward from 1879 to 1919, it acquired a modest reputation for publishing trade books, including Robert SERVICE's *The Spell of the Yukon* (1907). Under the long editorship of Lorne PIERCE (1920-59), The Ryerson Press (named after Egerton RYERSON in 1921) developed an active and varied trade program, publishing writers—especially poets—who would later become well known. Pierce initiated the MAKERS OF CANADIAN LITERATURE series (11 short biographies of writers, published in 1923-6, with a twelfth in 1941); the 'Ryerson Poetry Chapbooks' (200 booklets of contemporary verse issued between 1925 and 1962); the 'Canadian Books of Prose and Verse' (a series of five primary-school readers launched in 1927, some of which are still in print); and 'The Ryerson Fiction Award' (given for a 'distinguished novel' from 1942 to 1949). Called 'the mother publishing house' for its role in training staff that left to found competing firms, Ryerson was the oldest publishing house in Canada when, in Dec. 1970, it was sold by the UNITED CHURCH OF CANADA to the American publishing company, McGraw-Hill, Inc., to become McGRAW-HILL RYERSON LTD.

Ryga, George (b.1932). Playwright and novelist. Born to Ukrainian parents in Deep Creek, Alta, he attended school for seven years before turning his hand to a variety of jobs. Since 1962 he has written full time for radio, television, and the stage. He lives in Summerland, B.C. His first success was *Indian*, a 30-minute play, seen on CBC-TV in 1962, about the despair of an Indian labourer and his relations with a government official. His best-known work is *The* ECSTASY OF RITA JOE, a 'lyrical documentary play' that had its première at the Vancouver Playhouse in 1967; it was turned into a ballet for the ROYAL WINNIPEG BALLET in 1971. *Captives of the Faceless Drummer*, which is in essence the dialogue between a guerrilla leader and a government captive, was commissioned by the Vancouver Playhouse but was rejected; it was performed instead at the VANCOUVER ART GALLERY in Apr. 1971 and the next year at the ST LAWRENCE CENTRE in Toronto, and at FESTIVAL LENNOXVILLE. Ryga has published not only plays—*Captives of the Faceless Drummer* (1971), *The Ecstasy of Rita Joe and Other Plays* (1970, 1974), *Sunrise on Sarah* (1974)—but also three novels: *Hungry Hills* (1963), *Ballad of a Stone-Picker* (1966), and *Night Desk* (1976).

S

S. The abbreviation of 'section'. Chapters of the STATUTES OF CANADA are formed of sections.

S sgt. Official abbreviation of Staff Sergeant.

Sable Island. A treeless strip of sand and submerged shoals 22 mi. long, 190 mi. east of Halifax, N.S. It is known as the 'graveyard of the Atlantic' because many ships have been wrecked there owing to unexpected shallows and to the great storms common in the area. In 1598 the marquis de La Roche tried to start a colony there with 50 settlers, only 11 of whom were living in 1603, when they were removed. It is the home of about 200 wild horses.

Sabre, The. See CL-13.

SACEUR. Acronym of Supreme Allied Commander EURope, a military appointment created by NATO on 18 Dec. 1950.

Sachem. Algonkian word for the chief of a tribe.

Sackett's Harbour, Battle of. An engagement in the WAR OF 1812. British forces under Sir George Prevost, embarking from ships under the command of Cmdre Sir James Yeo, assaulted the American naval base on Lake Ontario on 29 May 1813, but failed to take the objective.

SACLANT. Acronym of Supreme Allied Commander AtLANTic, a naval appointment created by NATO on 10 Apr. 1952.

Sad Song of Yellow Skin

Sad Song of Yellow Skin. A documentary film about the Vietnamese people, produced by the NATIONAL FILM BOARD in 1970. Directed by Michael Rubbo, it takes its title from a Vietnamese folksong heard in the film. It depicts the beauty of Saigon and the suffering of the people of Vietnam. 58 min., 5 sec.; colour.

Saddleback justice. A phrase used to describe the rough-and-ready manner in which justices of the peace, in the days of pioneer settlement, dealt with charges against citizens in rural areas of the Canadian Prairies.

Safdie, Moshe (b.1938). Architect. Born in Haifa, Israel, he came to Canada in 1954 and was educated at McGill University. He also worked with the American architect and teacher, Louis Kahn, in 1962-3. Safdie's most important building is HABITAT, Montreal (1966-7), in which he experimented with precast modular elements for on-site assembly. His later projects for San Juan, Puerto Rico, and New York City have developed from this concept.

Sagakomi. Algonkian word for the 'smoking-leaf berry'—the bearberry, which is used alone or mixed with tobacco for smoking.

Sagamité. Algonkian word for a broth or soup of boiled meat, fish, etc. Among Huron Indians it referred to a kind of porridge made from maize (see CORN).

Sagamore. Algonkian word for a chief (or SA-CHEM) or any important person.

Sagard-Théodat, Gabriel (*active* 1614-36). Recollet friar, the first religious historian of Canada. Arriving in New France as a missionary in 1623, he served in HURONIA, returning to France the following year. He wrote two descriptive works of historical importance: *Le Grand Voyage au pays des Hurons* (1632), translated in 1939 as *The Long Journey to the Country of the Hurons*, and *L'Histoire du Canada . . .* (1636).

SAGE. Acronym of Semi-Automatic Ground Environment, a central-combat control centre utilizing high-speed computers and high-performance radar. Announced for construction in Sept. 1958, the SAGE installation at NORAD's regional headquarters at North Bay, Ont., gives a visual display of air-traffic and possible tactical solutions to hostile situations.

Sage of Ekfrid. The sobriquet of Peter MacARTHUR, who was born on a homestead in Ekfrid Township, Middlesex, Co., Ont. In 1908, at the age of 42, he returned to the fam-

ily farm and made rural life the subject of his humorous essays.

Sager. An automobile manufactured in 1910-11 by United Motors, Welland, Ont. Named after Frederick Sager, pioneer car salesman, the four-cyclinder 30 h.p. touring car sold for $1,650.

Sagouine, La. A memorable character created by the Acadian writer Antonine MAIL-LET. La Sagouine ('The Slattern')—a 72-year-old-charlady, a former prostitute, the wife of an Acadian fisherman—recites grievances, recollections, anecdotes, and homilies in a rich argot that is descended from sixteenth-century French, traces of which still survive among the ACADIANS of New Brunswick. Her 16 monologues, collected in *La Sagouine* (1971), have been performed to much acclaim by Violet Leger on stage, radio, and television.

Saguenay, Kingdom of. An undefined fabulous region, perhaps between the SAGUENAY and OTTAWA RIVERS, described to Jacques CAR-TIER on his voyages of 1534 and 1535. The Indians reported that the 'kingdom' contained precious metals and stones. The promising samples Cartier found on his third voyage, in 1541-2, turned out to be not gold and diamonds but iron pyrites and quartz; they gave rise to the expression 'false as Canadian diamonds'. But the myth of the riches of the Saguenay was still alive in 1609, when Marc LE-SCARBOT wrote of this region, 'where is infinite gold, rubies and other riches, and where the men are as white as in France, and clad in wool'.

Saguenay River. Rising in Lac Saint-Jean, Que., it flows 475 mi. into the St Lawrence R. at TADOUSSAC, passing through a mountainous canyon in the Laurentian Shield. Its picturesque scenery has been a tourist attraction since 1849, when boat trips were introduced. In its upper course it has been dammed for the production of hydro-electric power.

Saidye Bronfman Centre, The. The cultural centre of the YM-YWHA in Montreal. It was opened in 1967 and named in honour of Saidye Bronfman, the wife of Sam Bronfman (see SEAGRAM CORPORATION), whose children provided funds for the centre, which includes a theatre seating 350, studios, exhibition areas, and classrooms. To enrich the lives of Montrealers and meet the cultural and educational needs of the Jewish people, it sponsors courses and lectures in dance, music, drama, visual arts, and Judaica.

St Andrew's Banner. The flag of Scotland, showing a diagonal white cross on a blue field. With the addition of ST GEORGE'S BANNER, it became the FIRST UNION FLAG of 1606. With the addition of ST PATRICK'S BANNER in 1801, it became the UNION JACK.

St Andrews Blockhouse. One of three blockhouses erected at St Andrews, N.B., at the outbreak of the WAR OF 1812, the so-called West Point blockhouse is the only one to survive, and is now a national historic site.

St Andrew's College. Incorporated in 1912-13 as the Presbyterian Theological College, Saskatoon, by the Saskatchewan legislature, it underwent a name-change in 1924 in anticipation of church union. In 1972 the College was made responsible for providing academic training for all United Church ordinands on the Prairies and, to ensure an ecumenical outlook, it was affiliated with the Faculty of Theology of St Thomas More College (Roman Catholic). Today both are participants in the School of Religious Studies of the UNIVERSITY OF SASKATCHEWAN.

Saint-Charles. A Quebec village on the Richelieu R., the scene of activity during the REBELLION OF 1837. A famous meeting of PATRIOTES was held there on 23 Oct. 1837. On 25 Nov. rebel forces under Thomas Storrow Brown failed to stop a column of regulars led by Lt-Col. Charles Wetherall and the village was occupied.

Saint-Denis. A Quebec village on the Richelieu R., the scene of fighting during the REBELLION OF 1837. PATRIOTES led by Wolfred NELSON stopped a column of regulars led by Col. Charles Gore on 23 Nov. 1837. But on 1 Dec. the village was sacked and burned in reprisal for the death of Lt John Weir.

Saint-Denis, Michel (1897-1971). Anglo-French theatre director and educator. Born in Beauvais, France, he founded the Old Vic School (1946-52) in London and Le Centre de l'Este (1952-7) in Strasbourg. After serving as the bilingual adjudicator of the DOMINION DRAMA FESTIVAL in 1937, 1950, 1952, 1958, and 1959, he exerted a paramount influence on the organization of the NATIONAL THEATRE SCHOOL, which he helped found in Montreal in 1960.

Saint-Denys-Garneau. See Hector de Saint-Denys-GARNEAU.

St Elias. Canada's second-highest mountain peak. Located at the international border in the southwest Yukon, it rises to a height of 18,008 ft.

St Elias Range. The most northwestern extent of the ROCKY MOUNTAINS in Canada, it is in northwest British Columbia and the southwest Yukon. Not all its peaks have been climbed or precisely measured, but it easily contains Canada's 15 highest mountains and its largest mainland glacier fields. Much of the range is included in Kluane National Park.

St Eloi. A Flemish village in Belgium, it was the scene of fighting during the FIRST WORLD WAR in the winter of 1915-16. The Second Canadian Division suffered the loss of 2,000 men in attempting but failing to hold the muddy pock-marked line between St Eloi and the Menin Road.

Saint-Eustache. A Quebec village near the lower end of the Lake of Two Mountains, north of Montreal Island, the scene of fighting during the REBELLION OF 1837. Dr Jean-Olivier Chénier and some PATRIOTES barricaded themselves in the stone church, which was shelled and set on fire by troops under Sir John COLBORNE on 14 Dec. 1837. Chénier and 70 others died. This marked the last major battle of the Rebellion in Lower Canada (Quebec).

St Francis Xavier University. A Roman Catholic educational institution, it was founded in Nova Scotia in 1853 and moved to its present location in Antigonish, N.S., in 1855. Originally a school for the training of priests, it became a community centre for higher learning. Full university powers were granted by the legislature in 1866 and Nova Scotia's first engineering school was established there in 1899. It was affiliated with Mount Saint Bernard College for women in 1883—to become the first co-educational Roman Catholic college in North America. Degrees were granted to women in 1894. An affiliated junior college, Xavier College, was founded in Sydney in 1951; it amalgamated with the Nova Scotia Eastern Institute of Technology in 1974. See also ANTIGONISH MOVEMENT.

St George's Banner. A seafarer's insignia that represented England and shows a red cross on a white field. With the addition of ST ANDREW'S BANNER, it bcame the FIRST UNION FLAG of 1606; with the addition of ST PATRICK'S BANNER in 1801 it became the UNION JACK. See also ROYAL FLAG OF FRANCE.

St George's Day. A holiday observed in Newfoundland. It is celebrated on the Monday closest to 23 Apr., the day sacred to the saint who suffered martyrdom about A.D. 303 after slaying the dragon that lived in a lake near Libya.

St James' Cathedral

St James' Cathedral. The Mother Church of the Toronto Diocese of the Anglican Church of Canada. Located at King and Church Sts, it is on the site of York's first church, a small wooden structure that was completed in 1807, enlarged in 1818-19, and replaced by a stone church in 1833. It burned down in 1839 and was replaced in the same year by a church that was destroyed by fire in 1849. The present Gothic Revival building (by Frederick William CUMBERLAND) was begun in 1850, opened in 1853, and finally completed by Henry LANGLEY in 1874, the year the spire was built. The grounds are a city park.

St James's Club, The. A nationally important luncheon club. Founded in 1857, it is located on Union St in downtown Montreal. It has about 800 members, almost all of whom are business executives.

St James St/rue Saint-Jacques. It dates from 1674 and was the financial centre of Montreal until the late 1960s, when banks and finance companies moved to Dorchester Blvd; the headquarters of the BANK OF MONTREAL are still there. Once called 'Canada's Wall Street', St James St and BAY ST in Toronto came to symbolize the financial power of central Canada.

Saint-Jean-Baptiste. The patron saint of Quebec and of Canada, according to the canon of the Catholic Church. It was on the birthday of St John the Baptist, 24 June, which happens to be Midsummer's Day, that John CABOT made his historic (and unspecified) landfall in eastern Canada in 1497. Since then, 'the voice of one crying in the wilderness' has been held in special honour in Canada and especially in Quebec, where the birthday of St John is a festive holiday. St John is the only saint whose birthday—and not his date of death—is celebrated. The non-statutory holiday is observed in Quebec on 24 June (or on the following Monday when 24 June falls on a Sunday). Two SOCIÉTÉS SAINT-JEAN-BAPTISTE—one in Montreal, the other in Quebec City—were named after him.

Saint-Jean-Baptiste Society. See SOCIÉTÉ SAINT-JEAN-BAPTISTE.

Saint John. It was called the 'Loyalist City' in recognition of the United Empire LOYALISTS, who came in 1783 to this location at the mouth of the St John R., N.B. In its early years Saint John—which was incorporated as a city in 1785, the year after the province of New Brunswick was created—developed lumber and shipbuilding industries. As these and the port function grew, so did the com-

mercial importance of Saint John. Today it is predominantly a city of heavy industry: pulp mills, sugar and oil refineries, and the port are the largest employers in the metropolitan area. Its 1971 CMA population was 106,744. Its official motto is *O, Fortunati, quorum jam moenia surgunt* ('O fortunate ones whose walls are now raised up').

St John Four, The. Championship four-oared rowing crew from New Brunswick. Composed of three fishermen (Samuel Hutton, Robert Fulton and George Price) and a lighthouse-keeper (Elijah Ross), it took the world title for four-oared racing at a meet in Paris in 1867. The four oarsmen met with a tumultous welcome on their return to Saint John. They lost the title in 1870 but regained it the following year before 20,000 spectators. The surprising success of the St John Four, also called the Paris Crew, stirred national pride in the new Dominion and encouraged participation in all sports.

St John the Baptist. See SAINT-JEAN-BAPTISTE, SOCIÉTÉ SAINT-JEAN-BAPTISTE.

St John's. The capital of Newfoundland, the most easterly city in Canada. It is one of the oldest inhabited towns in North America, the site of a marker placed in 1583 by Sir Humphrey GILBERT claiming possession of Newfoundland for England. The early history of the settlement revolved almost entirely around the fishing industry, and by 1801 there were 3,420 inhabitants. As it prospered during the nineteenth century, the importance of St John's grew: it became the principal commercial, judicial, and administrative centre for Newfoundland. It was incorporated as a city in 1888, when it had a population of about 30,000. In 1892 over 75% of the city was destroyed by fire. The economy of St John's is based largely on commerce and administration. Despite an excellent natural harbour, the amount of cargo handled is relatively small; it serves mainly as a supply and repair depot for international and domestic fishing fleets. With SIGNAL HILL at the harbour entrance and with its brightly painted houses and Anglican Cathedral clustering on hills facing the waterfront, St John's (sometimes called 'Newfiejohn') is a picturesque city much enjoyed by visitors. It is the home of MEMORIAL UNIVERSITY. Its 1971 CMA population was 131,814.

St John's Daily News. A morning newspaper published in St John's, Nfld. Founded in 1894, it describes itself as 'The daily newspaper of Newfoundland and Labrador'. Among its contributors are W.R. Callahan, James R. Thoms, and Albert B. Perlin.

St John's Day. See DISCOVERY DAY.

St John's Evening Telegram, The. An evening newspaper published in St John's, Nfld. Founded in 1879, it has the motto 'The People's Paper' and has been a publication of THOMSON NEWSPAPERS since 1 Aug. 1970. Among its contributors are the playwright Michael Cook, the satiric columnist Ray GUY, and the editor Michael Harrington.

St Joseph's Oratory. A domed Renaissance-style basilica on MOUNT ROYAL. Known also as 'Brother André's Shrine', the Oratory, which can hold 16,000 persons, is on the site of a chapel built by Brother ANDRÉ in 1904. Its construction began in 1924, and it was completed in 1967 with the help of a public subscription.

St Julien Memorial. An impressive monument northeast of YPRES, Belgium, to the Canadian soldiers who died during German gas attacks on 22-4 Apr. 1915. It marks the battlefield and the cemetery where 2,000 Canadians are buried. Designed by Frederick Clemesha of Regina, Sask., it is a tall shaft of granite surmounted by the bust of a brooding helmeted soldier.

St Laurent, Louis (1882-1973). The twelfth prime minister of Canada, 1948 to 1957. Born in Compton, Que., he was educated at Université Laval and trained as a lawyer. Virtually unknown outside the legal profession, he was called in late 1941 to become Minister of Justice in the government of William Lyon Mackenzie KING in succession to Ernest Lapointe, the righthand man to King since 1921. St Laurent established a reputation for probity and enormous ability with astonishing quickness, and proved his worth to King when he remained in the government during the CONSCRIPTION crisis of 1944. In 1946 he became Secretary of State for External Affairs, the first time anyone other than the prime minister had held this portfolio, and led the effort to involve Canada in world affairs; his speeches included the first call for a North Atlantic Treaty. He was chosen to succeed King in 1948. For the next nine years the St Laurent government led the country through its period of fastest growth and greatest prosperity, ruling by right, very competently, but without much flair. 'Uncle Louie' was a benevolent paterfamilias to the country, and his cabinets contained as much talent as had ever served in Ottawa. The collapse began with the great PIPELINE DEBATE of 1956, and with the increasing fatigue of the prime minister. In the election of 1957 John DIEFENBAKER led the Tories to a narrow victory, and St Laurent retired from the Liberal leadership as soon as he decently could.

St Lawrence Centre for the Performing Arts, The. Toronto's civic theatre and concert hall. It was officially opened on 31 Dec. 1969, with Mavor MOORE as general director. The first production—Jacques LANGUIRAND's *Man Inc.*, in Moore's translation, with music by Norman SYMONDS—opened on 26 Feb. 1970. In 1970 Leon MAJOR became general director, supervising Toronto Arts Productions, which co-ordinates activities that include a drama series and Music at the Centre, the overall name for several impressive concert series arranged by Franz Kraemer, music director. The Centre consists of a 830-seat theatre, a resident repertory company, and a 480-seat Town Hall that is used for concerts and civic discussions. The building on Front St E. was designed by Gordon Adamson Associates.

St Lawrence Hall. The social and cultural centre of Toronto in the 1850s. Designed by William THOMAS and built on King St E. in 1850, the handsome three-storey Neo-Classical building—housing shops, an assembly room, and a market—fell into disuse in the 1890s but was restored in 1967 as a Centennial project. Now the permanent home of the CANADIAN NATIONAL BALLET, its assembly room is available for public use.

St Lawrence Islands National Park. Established in 1904 in the picturesque THOUSAND ISLANDS region of the St Lawrence R. in Ontario, it covers less than 2 sq. mi. and is Canada's smallest national park. It includes 18 heavily treed islands and 80 rocky islets in the St Lawrence, as well as some mainland area.

St Lawrence River. The river proper extends 650 mi. from Kingston, Ont., to the Gulf of St Lawrence—forming the international boundary between Canada and the United States for 114 mi.—while the St Lawrence R. drainage system includes the Great Lakes for a total of 2,480 mi. (The most westerly source of the drainage system is the St Louis R. in Minnesota.) It was discovered in 1535 by Jacques CARTIER, who gave the name Saint-Laurent to Pillage Bay on the north shore of the gulf—a name that came to be applied to both gulf and river. Its main tributaries are the OTTAWA, Saint-Maurice, and SAGUENAY Rivers flowing from the north and the RICHELIEU, St Francis, and Chaudière Rivers flowing from the south. The river between Kingston and Montreal has been greatly altered by the construction of the canals, locks, and dams of the ST LAWRENCE SEAWAY.

St Lawrence Seaway. A shipping route that provides navigation to a depth of 27 ft from Montreal to the head of the Great Lakes and installations for the production of hydroelectric power. The rapids in the upper ST LAWRENCE impeded navigation on the river until canals were built to bypass them in the eighteenth and nineteenth centuries. The modern St Lawrence Seaway, a joint enterprise of Canada and the United States, involved deepening the river and some old canals (including the WELLAND CANAL) and building new canals, dams, and power stations. In the International Rapids section, where the river marks the boundary between Canada and the U.S., a total of 2,200,000 horsepower is divided equally between the Ontario Hydro-Electric Power Commission (ONTARIO HYDRO) and the Power Authority of the State of New York. The Seaway was officially opened in 1959. Because of the winter freeze-up it is used only from 1 Apr. to 18 Dec., but it is a major route for world trade.

St Lawrence Seaway Authority. A corporation to construct and maintain the ST LAWRENCE SEAWAY between the Port of Montreal and Lake Erie. Established in 1956, it is under the Ministry of Transport.

St Nicholas Hotel, The. See The DONNELLYS.

St Patrick's Banner. The flag of Ireland, showing a diagonal red cross on a white field. With the addition of ST ANDREW'S BANNER and ST GEORGE'S BANNER in 1801, it became the UNION JACK.

St Patrick's Day. A holiday observed in Newfoundland. Celebrated on the Monday closest to 17 Mar., it is dedicated to the patron saint of Ireland, who died about A.D. 461. According to legend the Irish will be judged on the Last Day by St Patrick himself.

St Pierre, Paul (b.1923). Television writer. Born in Chicago, Ill., of Nova Scotian parents, he was raised in Dartmouth, N.S., and in 1945 settled in Vancouver, where he wrote for the *Vancouver Sun* for 20 years. From 1968 to 1972, he was a Member of Parliament for Coast-Chilcotin, an area that roughly corresponds to the Cariboo region of British Columbia. He recreated the region in CARIBOO COUNTRY—a series shown on CBC-TV in 1960-1, 1964, and 1966—which included three memorable plays by St Pierre: *The Education of Phyllistine* (also broadcast separately in 1965 and 1967); HOW TO BREAK A QUARTER HORSE (broadcast separately in 1966 and 1971); and *Antoine's Wooden Overcoat* (broadcast separately in 1966 and 1967). *How to*

Break a Quarter Horse was the basis of a novel, *Breaking Smith's Quarter Horse* (1966), which itself gave rise to the Walt Disney movie *Smith* (1969). St Pierre has written other novels, including *Boss of the* NAMKO *Drive* (1965) and *The Chilcotin Holiday* (1970), and a play, *Sister Balonika* (1973).

St Pierre and Miquelon. Small islands in the North Atlantic 15 mi. south of Newfoundland. An Overseas Territory of France until July 1976, when they were made a metropolitan department, they are all that remains of France's once-extensive empire in North America. They were occupied by the French in the seventeenth century and claimed by Britain several times in the eighteenth; they became an undisputed French possession in 1763 under the TREATY OF PARIS and were colonized. They are inhabited by 6,000 descendants of Breton, Norman, and Basque fishermen.

St Roch. A 104-ft motor schooner built as an Arctic patrol vessel for the ROYAL CANADIAN MOUNTED POLICE in 1928 in North Vancouver. In 1940-2, sailing from west to east under the command of Sgt Henry Larsen, she became the second (first Canadian) ship to traverse the NORTHWEST PASSAGE, repeating the feat from east to west in 1944. She was presented to the city of Vancouver in 1951. Restored, she is exhibited at the Maritime Museum there as a Maritime Historic Site. *The Big Ship: An Autobiography* (1967) is an account of the ship's career by Larsen, with F. R. Sheer and E. Omholt-Jensen. See also GJOA.

St Thomas University. Originally a Basilian Fathers high school and junior college for boys in Chatham, N.B., founded in 1910, it received a university charter in 1934; the present name was adopted in 1960 when high-school courses were dropped. In 1964, after federation with the UNIVERSITY OF NEW BRUNSWICK was achieved, new buildings were established in Fredericton on the main university campus. St Thomas continues to grant its own degrees in Arts and Education.

St Urbain St. A rundown street in Montreal's ethnic area near the MAIN, which found its Balzac in Mordecai RICHLER, who was born in the neighbourhood. There are descriptions of it in Richler's The APPRENTICESHIP OF DUDDY KRAVITZ (1959), in which Baron Byng High School is described as Fletcher's Field, *The Street* (1969), and ST URBAIN'S HORSEMAN (1971). It was settled at the turn of the century by Jews of East European origin whose children moved out, leaving room for the Greeks and Portuguese who now live there.

St Urbain's Horseman. A novel by Mordecai RICHLER published in 1971. It penetrates the dissatisfactions, guilt, and fears of middle-aged Jake Hersch, a London film director, who seeks relief from his inner turmoil in a fantasy that his scounderly cousin Joey, a fine horseman—the central symbol of the novel—will avenge the Jews by killing a Nazi war criminal who had escaped to South America.

Sainte-Anne-de-Beaupré. Well-known Catholic shrine on the St Lawrence R. north-east of Quebec City, dedicated to the mother of the Virgin Mary. In 1658 three ship-wrecked Breton sailors who had been washed ashore at Beaupré erected a chapel to thank Sainte Anne for their deliverance. The present modern Romanesque-style basilica is the eighth place of worship to occupy the site. Miraculous cures have been claimed by some of the million-odd pilgrims who have visited the shrine, which has been called 'the Lourdes of North America'.

Sainte-Foy, Battle of. A battle of 28 Apr. 1760 that took place on the PLAINS OF ABRA-HAM. The French forces under the duc de LÉVIS were victorious, causing the British under James MURRAY to retreat behind the walls of Quebec, where they remained until the arrival of the British fleet.

Sainte-Marie, Buffy (b.1941). Singer-composer. Born Beverley Sainte-Marie at the Pia-pot Reserve near Regina, Sask., she was raised in Wakefield, Mass., by adoptive parents. The raven-haired singer played the guitar and sang her own songs in Greenwich Village, New York. Her lament, 'Universal Soldier', caught on in 1963 as 'the battle hymn of the draft-card burners'. The royal-ties from such albums as *Changing Woman* (1974) have been earmarked for foundations she established, such as the Nehewan Foun-dation and the Native North American Women's Association.

Sainte-Marie-aux-Hurons. The first Euro-pean settlement in inland North America, headquarters of the Jesuit mission to the Huron Indians. Founded in 1639 by Jérôme LALEMANT in HURONIA, near present-day Mid-land, Ont., it was a palisaded settlement with numerous log buildings—including res-idences, workshops, a hospital, and a church—and a canal with three locks. After the 1648-9 Iroquois raids on the other HURON MISSIONS, it was destroyed by fire in 1649 by the Jesuits. It has been reconstructed under the guidance of Wilfrid Jury, and as Sainte-Marie-among-the-Hurons it is a popular tourist site operated by the Ontario Ministry of Natural Resources.

Saints. The first North American saints to be recognized by the Catholic Church were JE-SUIT MARTYRS—the eight Jesuit missionaries martyred by the Hurons who were canon-ized on 29 June 1930 and proclaimed patron saints of Canada on 16 Oct. 1940: Jean de BRÉBEUF, Noël Chabanel (1613-49), Antoine Daniel (1601-48), Charles Garnier (1606-49), René Goupil (1608-42), Isaac JOGUES, Jean de La Lande (d.1646), and Gabriel LALEMANT. Although not yet canonized, Kateri TEKAK-WITHA has been declared 'venerable'. Marie Marguerite d'YOUVILLE, founder of the GREY NUNS, was declared 'venerable' in 1890. Brother ANDRÉ has inspired devotion in Que-bec. St Joseph, the husband of Mary, whose feast day is 19 Mar., has special significance among Quebec Catholics because CHAMPLAIN held him in reverence. See also SAINTE-ANNE-DE-BEAUPRÉ, SAINT-JEAN-BAPTISTE.

'Salesmen of Death'. One of the most widely read magazine articles of all time. Written by Lt-Col. George A. DREW, it first appeared in MACLEAN'S on 1 Aug. 1931 and was reprinted in pamphlet form and ultimately translated into 30 languages. The article indicts Sir Basil Zaharoff and other munitions salesmen as 'warmakers'.

Salina Sea. A prehistoric sea. 400-425 million years ago it extended south into Manitoba and in a wide arc throughout Quebec into southern Ontario. During this era the Atlan-tic Ocean had not yet formed and life had not yet emerged onto land.

Salishan. The largest linguistic family of In-dians on the Pacific coast. It is composed of three sub-families: the COAST SALISH, who oc-cupy the Fraser delta and coastland and the opposite shores of Vancouver Island, includ-ing much of Juan de Fuca Strait; the INTERIOR SALISH, who occupy much of the dry interior plateaux and river and lake valleys between the Coast Range and the Rockies; and the Puget Sound Salish of the State of Washing-ton. The total Salishan population in 1970 was 20,989.

Salmon. Any of several related varieties of pink-fleshed fish living in salt water but spawning in fresh water. The Pacific varie-ties, which die after spawning, are COHO, SOCKEYE, Chinook, Chum, and Pink. They are used for most of Canada's smoked salmon. The Atlantic varieties—of which the RESTIGOUCHE SALMON is the best known—are related to the trout family and spawn several times. They have a more delicate taste than the Pacific varieties.

Salomonie, Joanassie (b.1936). Eskimo sculptor at CAPE DORSET. His stylized ptarmigans have been widely exhibited. He starred in The WHITE DAWN, the 1974 film version of James HOUSTON's novel, and the same year won the Zagreb Film Festival Award for a short animated film, called Animation from Cape Dorset, that used cardboard cutouts.

Salt-chuck. CHINOOK JARGON for 'salt-water'. It refers not only to the ocean but to all saltwater inlets, canals, and bays affected by tidewater.

Salterton. Fictitious community based on Kingston, Ont., used by Robertson DAVIES as the setting for the novels Tempest-Tost (1951), LEAVEN OF MALICE (1954), and A Mixture of Frailties (1958).

Saltzman, Percy (b.1915). TV personality. Born in Winnipeg, he trained as a meteorologist and worked for the Dominion Meteorological Service (1948-68). On 8 Sept. 1952 he made his début as a weather forecaster, first person to appear on live English-language television in Canada, on CBC-TV's CBLT. Since July 1973 he has been interviewer, host, and weatherman on a succession of shows, including CANADA A.M.

Salverson, George (b.1916). Writer. Born in 1916 in St Catharines, Ont., the son of Laura Goodman SALVERSON, he was a writer and announcer with CKRC in Winnipeg (1942-8) before becoming a free-lance scriptwriter for radio and television. He wrote for the CBC STAGE series and created the CBC-TV series HATCH'S MILL, which had its première on 7 Mar. 1966.

Salverson, Laura Goodman (1890-1970). Novelist. Born in Winnipeg to parents who were emigrants from Iceland, she was raised in poverty in Winnipeg and educated there. Her best-known novels are The Viking Heart (1923) and The Dark Weaver (1937), both about Icelandic immigrants in Manitoba. Her autobiography, Confessions of an Immigrant's Daughter (1939), was widely read. She was the mother of George SALVERSON.

Sam Slick. Memorable and internationally famous comic character created by Thomas Chandler HALIBURTON in 1835, when the author turned to writing satire. A Yankee pedlar of clocks who speaks in a comical dialect, Sam Slick first appeared in 21 sketches in the Novascotian, which were reprinted in The Clockmaker; or the Sayings and Doings of Sam Slick of Slickville (1836). This was followed by three other Sam Slick books. The sketches are presented as a dialogue between Sam and a traveller, and Sam's views are expressed in a series of anecdotes, tall tales, pungent sayings, and shrewd comments on human nature.

Sam the Record Man. A chain of record outlets. It was started in 1951 by the music promoter Sam Sniderman, who was born in Toronto in 1920. In 1976 the chain included 39 stores from coast to coast and accounted for 10% of record sales in Canada. The principal store on Yonge St, Toronto, has been called the largest record store in North America.

Samuel French (Canada) Limited. Play publishers and authors' representatives. The Canadian office of the multi-national operation was opened in Toronto in 1933. The company itself was founded in 1854 by Samuel French, a New York publisher and theatre enthusiast, who acquired a British firm begun in London in 1813 by the actor Thomas Lacey. The Canadian office, which during the first decade of its operation published 'The Canadian Playwrights Series', sells playscripts to, and collects royalties from, amateur and professional companies. The office's cable address is 'Theatrical, Toronto'.

Samuel Marchbanks. A literary character created by Robertson DAVIES in the 1940s while he was editor of the Peterborough Examiner. Davies attributed to the curmudgeon all manner of witty observations on life, criticisms of contemporary manners, and attacks on stupidity, narrow-mindedness, and philistinism. The 'Marchbanks' books, written in a style of humorous hyperbole, are The Diary of Samuel Marchbanks (1947), The Table Talk of Samuel Marchbanks (1949), and Samuel Marchbanks' Almanack (1968).

Sanctuaire de Notre-Dame-du-Cap. Stone chapel at Cap-de-la-Madeleine, Que. Built by the Oblate Fathers in 1714, the Shrine of Our Lady is one of the oldest and best-preserved chapels in Quebec. When its statue of the Blessed Virgin of the Holy Rosary appeared to three witnesses to become animated in 1888, it was considered miraculous. Designated a Catholic shrine and a place of pilgrimage in 1909, it is Canada's national Marian shrine.

Sandwell, B.K. (1876-1954). Editor and author. Born in Ipswich, Eng., he was brought to Canada as a child and educated at Upper Canada College and the University of Toronto. A journalist and drama critic for the

MONTREAL HERALD (1905-11), and then editor of the FINANCIAL TIMES (1911-18), he taught economics at McGill and then English at Queen's University before becoming editor of SATURDAY NIGHT (1932-51). His witty essays appeared in *The Privacy Agent* (1928) and *The Diversions of Duchesstown* (1955), introduced by Robertson DAVIES. On the appointment of Vincent MASSEY as governor general in 1952, Sandwell published his famous ditty: 'Let the Old World, where rank's yet vital, / Part those who have and have no title. / Toronto has no social classes— / Only the Masseys and the masses.'

Sangster, Charles (1822-93). Poet. Born in Kingston, U.C. (Ont.), he left school at 15 and worked in his home town as a clerk, a newspaper editor, and a civil servant. He published two collections of ambitious poems: *The St. Lawrence and the Saguenay* (1856) and *Hesperus and Other Poems and Lyrics* (1860). The title poem of the first volume is made up of 110 Spenserian stanzas with lyrical interludes; the title poem of the second is a masque, 'A Legend of Stars', written in blank verse with lyrical interludes. Sangster struck a patriotic note in 'Brock', an ode written for the dedication on 13 Oct. 1859 of the new monument to Sir Isaac BROCK at Queenston, which begins: 'One voice, one people, one in heart / And soul, and feeling, and desire!'

Sansei. Japanese word for 'third generation', applied to someone born in Canada to Canadian-born parents whose own parents were born in Japan.

Sapp, Allen (b.1929). Painter. Born on the Red Pheasant Reserve, Sask., he had to withdraw from the Onion Lake Anglican Residential School in Grade 2 when he developed meningitis. He is a self-taught artist who depicts realistically scenes of life on the reserve. He has had successful exhibitions at the Zachary Waller Gallery, Los Angeles, Calif. He was also part of Canadian Indian Art '74.

SARAH Beacon. Acronym for Search And Rescue And Homing, a battery-operated beacon designed and produced in Canada in the 1960s for use as safety equipment in aircraft.

Sarah Binks. A tongue-in-cheek fictional satire of poetasters and prairie life by Paul HIEBERT published in 1947. Something of a classic, it features Sarah Binks (1906-29), 'the Sweet Songstress of Saskatchewan', who was born at 'Willows', Sask., and won the 'Wheat Pool Medal' for such verses as 'Hi,

Sooky, Ho, Sooky', 'The Farmer is King', and her epic, 'Up from the Magma and Back Again: Canto I, The Great Ice Age'. Hiebert took the same approach to Sarah's contemporaries in the sequel *Willows Revisited* (1967). *Sarah Binks* was the basis of a radio play written by Tommy TWEED, with music by Lucio AGOSTINI, broadcast by CBC Radio in 1948. Don HARRON turned the play into a 'mini-musical' called *Here Lies Sarah Binks*. Directed by Robert CHRISTIE and starring Jane MALLET, it ran for eight weeks in Toronto in Feb. and Mar. 1968.

Sarrazin, Michael (b.1940). Actor. Born in Quebec City, he worked with TORONTO WORKSHOP PRODUCTIONS in the early 1960s, then with CBC-TV on the WOJECK series in 1966. Now a movie star in Hollywood, he appeared in *The Flim-Flam Man* (1967) and *They Shoot Horses, Don't They?* (1969) among other films.

Sask. Abbreviation of SASKATCHEWAN.

Saskatchewan. One of the three prairie provinces, situated between Manitoba and Alberta and extending from the 49th to the 60th parallel. Created a province on 1 Sept. 1905 because of the increasing population of the area owing to immigration, it derived its name from one of the administrative districts of the NORTHWEST TERRITORIES. It was provided with a single-chamber legislature, but its public lands and resources were retained under the control of the federal government until 1930.

Situated on a great continental plain, the province has been dependent on agriculture—mainly wheat—since its first settlement. In recent years, however, mining, particularly POTASH, and oil and gas have contributed to the development of secondary manufacturing and service industries.

With a land area of 220,182 sq. mi. and a 1974 population of 907,000, Saskatchewan is unusual in that its present population has been declining since the 1961 census, largely as a result of a substantial drop in the farm population. Its capital is REGINA and its unofficial motto is 'Wheat Province'.

Saskatchewan. Feature film produced by Universal Pictures in 1954. Directed by Raoul Walsh, it starred Alan Ladd, Shelley Winters, J. Carrol Naish, and Hugh O'Brien. The exteriors were photographed in the Canadian Rockies, although the film was ostensibly about the Prairies. In this last major Hollywood epic set in Canada, a stranger, Alan Ladd, breaks up an alleged conspiracy of the Cree, led by Sitting Bull, to take over western Canada. 87 min., colour.

'Saskatchewan'. An amusing song about a farmer's life on the Prairies during the DE-PRESSION. Written by William W. Smith of Swift Current in the 1930s, it begins: 'Saskatchewan, the land of snow,/Where winds are always on the blow,/Where people sit with frozen toes,/And why we stay here no one knows.'

Saskatchewan, District of. A provisional district of the NORTHWEST TERRITORIES created in 1882. In 1905 most of its territory was absorbed into the province of SASKATCHEWAN.

Saskatchewan Arts Board. Provincial arts body. Established in 1949, it consists of between 7 and 15 voluntary members, all appointed, and a staff of 5. It assists established organizations and individuals and gives aid to such bodies as the Saskatchewan Summer School of the Arts and the NORMAN MACKENZIE ART GALLERY.

Saskatchewan Doctors' Strike. A 'withdrawal' of all but essential services by the province's doctors. To protest the introduction of MEDICARE, in the form of the Medical Care Insurance Act promised by the CCF government in 1959, the College of Physicians and Surgeons of Saskatchewan authorized the strike, which lasted from 1 to 23 July 1962. Services remained suspended until a 29-point compromise agreement was reached that, among other things, permitted doctors to practise outside the insurance scheme.

Saskatchewan River, North and South. The most important and largest of prairie rivers. The North branch rises near Banff, flowing through Edmonton; the South branch rises in southern Alberta. The two meet just east of Prince Albert to flow into Cedar Lake and then Lake Winnipeg. The overall length of its drainage system is 1,205 mi.

Saskatoon. The second-largest city in Saskatchewan. It was founded in 1882 as a temperance colony on land granted along the South Saskatchewan R., and was incorporated as a city in 1906. Referred to as the 'POTASH Capital of the World' or 'POW Country' (potash, oil, wheat), it has an economy that is closely tied to local natural resources. Its 1971 CMA population was 126,449. Its official motto is 'Commerce, Industry, Education'. It is the home of the UNIVERSITY OF SASKATCHEWAN.

Saskatoon berry. A small purple berry that grows on the shad bush in the Prairies. Also called the Juneberry, it was used in the preparation of PEMMICAN. The word 'saskatoon'

comes from the Cree for 'fruit of the tree of many branches'.

Saskatoon Star-Phoenix. An evening newspaper published in Saskatoon, Sask. Founded in 1902, it was purchased, along with the REGINA LEADER-POST, in 1925 by Sir Clifford SIFTON. It is still privately owned.

Sasquatch. Mysterious ape-like creature said to inhabit the remoter regions of the Pacific Northwest. The word 'Sasquatch' is Salish for 'wild men' or 'hairy men'. In Northern California the 8-ft being is known as Big Foot (or Bigfoot). Evidence for the existence of the Sasquatch in British Columbia and Alberta (references in Indian myth and iconography, in passages from the writings of David THOMPSON and Paul KANE, and sightings from the earliest times to the present day) is considered in *Sasquatch* (1973) by Don Hunter and René Dahinden and in *Bigfoot: The Yeti and Sasquatch in Myth and Reality* (1972) by John Napier, a British biologist. The elusive ape-man is called the Yeti or the Abominable Snowman in the Himalayas and the Far East.

Satellites. See ALOUETTE, ANIK, COMMUNICATIONS TECHNOLOGY SATELLITE (CTS), and SATELLITES FOR IONOSPHERIC STUDIES (ISIS).

Satellites for Ionospheric Studies. Series of two satellites, known as ISIS I and ISIS II, designed and built in Canada and launched by NASA at Cape Kennedy to explore the upper atmosphere. ISIS I was sent into a circular orbit 625 mi. above the earth on 28 Jan. 1969; ISIS II orbits 756 mi. above the earth and was sent up on 31 Mar. 1971. They have been called 'orbiting laboratories'.

Saturday Night. A monthly publication devoted to society and the arts published in Toronto since 1887. Over the years it has changed owners, format, and periodicity (until 1962 it was fortnightly; since then it has been a monthly), but it has remained an important general publication of cultural interest. Editors of SN have been Edmund E. Sheppard (1887-1906), Joseph T. Clark (1906-9), Frederick Paul (1909-26), Hector CHARLESWORTH (1926-32), B.K. SANDWELL (1932-51), Robert Farquharson (1951-3), C. Gwyn Kinsey (1953-7), Robert Marjoribanks (1957-8), Arnold EDINBOROUGH (1958-62), Arthur Lowe (1962-3), Arnold Edinborough (1963-8), and Robert FULFORD (since 1968). A *Saturday Night Scrapbook* (1973) was edited by Morris Wolfe, with an introduction by Fulford.

Sault, The. A reference to Sault Ste Marie, Ont. 'Sault' is the French word for 'rapids' or 'waterfall' and is widely used in place names. The phonetic spelling 'Soo' is sometimes used as a nickname for Sault Ste Marie.

Saulteaux. See OJIBWA.

Saunders, Sir Charles Edward (1867-1937). Cerealist. Born in London, Ont., he was educated at the University of Toronto and Johns Hopkins University. Appointed Dominion cerealist in 1903 at the Experimental Farms at Ottawa, he developed Garnet, MARQUIS, Reward, and Ruby wheats. He received numerous honours and was knighted in 1933.

Saunders, Marshall. See BEAUTIFUL JOE.

Sauvage. Early French reference to the Indian.

Savanna. In the Atlantic Provinces, a tract of peat bog or a boggy barren.

Sawchuck, T.G. (Terry) (1929-70). Goalkeeper. Born in Winnipeg, Man., he played more games and more seasons and recorded more shutouts than any other goalkeeper in NHL history. During his 20-year career with teams in Detroit, Boston, Toronto, Los Angeles, and New York, he was elected to seven first or second all-star teams and was credited with more than 100 shutouts.

SC. See STATUTES OF CANADA.

SC. Initials that the holder of the STAR OF COURAGE is entitled to place after his name.

SCA. See SOCIETY OF CANADIAN ARTISTS.

Scadding, Henry (1813-1901). Clergyman and author. Born in England, he came to Canada in 1821 and was educated at UPPER CANADA COLLEGE and Cambridge University. He taught at UCC and, after ordination, became first rector of the Church of the Holy Trinity, Toronto, in 1847, retiring in 1875. The author of several books, he is best known for *Toronto of Old* (1873), a readable and detailed account of the city between 1818 and 1841. His house on Trinity Square, near Holy Trinity, still stands.

Scammell, Arthur M. See 'SQUID-JIGGIN' GROUND'.

Scarlet and Stetson. A reference to the red jackets and broad-brimmed hats worn by the ROYAL CANADIAN MOUNTED POLICE. It is the title of a history of the RCMP by Vernon Kemp published in 1964.

Schaefer, Carl (b.1903). Landscape painter. Born in Hanover, Ont., he studied at the Ontario College of Art (1921-4) under Arthur LISMER and J.E.H. MacDONALD. After a period as an official war artist (1943-6), he returned to the College as a teacher (1948-69). His outstanding achievement lies in the depiction of the Ontario countryside around his home town—lyrical, rhythmic, rather ominously coloured landscapes in oil and watercolour that often convey a breathtaking sense of space, and still lifes of fruit and vegetables. Two of his best-known paintings are *Storm Over the Fields* (1937, AGO) and *Ontario Farmhouse* (1934, NGC).

Schafer, R. Murray (b.1933). Composer and educator. Born in Sarnia, Ont., he studied at the Royal Conservatory of Music before working in England from 1956 to 1961. He was artist-in-residence at Memorial University, St John's, from 1963 to 1965, when he joined the staff of Simon Fraser University. His highly personal style is dissonant rather than serial and often uses mythological and mystical texts. His best-known and perhaps finest works are for the stage: *Loving (Toi)* (1965), an opera, and *Patria* (1972), a trilogy of which the third part is still in progress: Part II, *Requiems for the Party-Girl*, was performed in 1972 at the Stratford Festival. *Son of Heldenleben* (1968) for orchestra and *Threnody* (1966) for choir and orchestra have also contributed to his international reputation as Canada's most successful composer. Schafer is the author of several books including *British Composers in Interview* (1963), *The Composer in the Classroom* (1971), and *The New Soundscape* (1971).

Schefferville. See IRON ORE COMPANY OF CANADA LTD.

Scheldt, Battle of the. A series of assaults on the German-held estuary of the Scheldt R. to clear the sea approaches to the Belgian port of Antwerp during the SECOND WORLD WAR. Many Canadian lives were lost when the Allied troops fought at Breskens Pocket, Woensdrecht, South Beveland, and Walcheren, from 2 Oct. to 6 Nov. 1944. On 28 Nov. the first convoy entered the harbour of Antwerp. The Canadian-built SS *Fort Cataraqui* was the leading ship of this convoy.

Schenley Football Awards, Canada. See CANADIAN SCHENLEY FOOTBALL AWARDS.

Schmidt, Milt C. (b.1918). Hockey star. Born in Kitchener, Ont., he played professional hockey with the Boston Bruins and centred the notable 'Bauer-Schmidt-Dumart' line, also called the KRAUT LINE because the three players were of German ancestry and came from Waterloo Co., Ont. After playing for 18 years, he coached with the Boston team and became general manager. He was known as an aggressive, rugged, clever player.

Scholes, Lou F. (1880-1942). Champion oarsman. The Toronto-born athlete won the Canadian and United States sculling titles in 1902. Two years later he won the prestigious Diamond Sculls and was hailed as the world's best amateur oarsman. On his return to Toronto he was welcomed by a massive street-lined parade and given civic honours. The sculler was but one member of a Toronto sports-minded family. Lou's older brother John (Jack) Scholes won the world boxing championship in England in 1901. Their father, John F. Scholes, was himself an all-round athlete who held the world record for snowshoe racing in the late 1870s. Three world championships in three different sports in a single family is probably a world's record in itself.

Schramek, Tomas (b.1944). Dancer. Born in Bratislava, Czech., he was a principal with the Slovak Dance Company before he came to Canada in 1968. He became a principal dancer with the NATIONAL BALLET OF CANADA in 1973.

Schroeder, Andreas (b.1946). Writer. Born in Hoheneggelsen, Germany, he was raised in Berlin, Winnipeg, and Agassiz, B.C. He is a graduate of the creative-writing program of the University of British Columbia and lives near Mission, B.C., where he edits CONTEMPORARY LITERATURE IN TRANSLATION. His books include *The Ozone Minotaur* (1969), a collection of poems; *The Late Man* (1972), a collection of stories; and *Shaking It Rough: A Prison Memoir* (1976). In 1976 he was elected national chairman of the WRITERS' UNION OF CANADA.

Schull, Joseph (b.1910). Writer and historian. Born in Watertown, S. Dak., he was brought to Moose Jaw, Sask., in 1913, and educated at the University of Saskatchewan and Queen's University. A free-lance writer since 1945, he has written many radio and television plays and adaptations for the CBC and several commissioned works, including *The Far Distant Ships* (1950), a history of Canadian naval operations during the Second World War. His principal books are *Laurier: The First Canadian* (1965); *Rebellion: Rising in French Canada, 1837* (1971); and a two-volume biography of *Edward Blake* subtitled *The Man of the Other Way* (1975) and *Leader and Exile* (1976).

Schultz, Sir John Christian (1840-96). Lieutenant-governor of Manitoba. Born in Amherstburg, U.C. (Ont.), he trained as a doctor

and practised in the RED RIVER SETTLEMENT, where he also kept a store. Opposed to Louis RIEL, he and some armed supporters were imprisoned by Riel in Fort Garry, but Schultz escaped in Jan. 1870. He went to Toronto, where he spoke publicly against the execution of Thomas SCOTT. He returned to Manitoba in 1870, was elected to the House of Commons in 1871, and was appointed to the Senate in 1882. He was lieutenant-governor of the province from 1888 to 1895, the year he was knighted.

Science and Technology, Ministry of State for. Federal government department to foster the development and application of science and technology. It was established in Aug. 1971.

Science Council of Canada. Advisory body on science and technology. Established in 1966, the SCC became a CROWN CORPORATION in 1969 with an appointed board of 29 members. It assesses in a comprehensive manner Canada's scientific and technological resources, requirements, and potentialities, and makes recommendations to Parliament through the designated minister.

Scotch Line. A CONCESSION road, near Perth, Ont., where many Scots settled in the early-nineteenth century.

Scott, Barbara Ann (b.1928). Famous figure-skater. At the age of 11 the Ottawa-born skater became junior ladies champion. In 1948, in less than a month—at Prague, St Moritz, and Davos—she won the European, Olympic, and World ladies figure-skating championships. Upon her return to Ottawa she was welcomed by 70,000 onlookers and presented with a gold key and the freedom of the city and a motorcar with the licence number 48VI, signifying the 1948 Sixth Winter Olympics. With no more amateur worlds to conquer, she joined an ice show, where her skill and personality charmed capacity crowds. In 1955 she married a Chicago publicist.

Scott, Duncan Campbell (1862-1947). Poet and short-story writer. Born in Ottawa, he joined what later became the Department of Indian Affairs in 1879, rising to deputy superintendent and retiring in 1932. He was a fine poet whose lyrics catch the essentially hostile quality of the northern landscapes and whose narrative poems depict the Indians as the most enduring of people—in such poems as 'At the Cedars', 'The FORSAKEN', and 'The Onondaga Madonna'. His poetry collections are *Labour and the Angel* (1898), *New World Lyrics and Ballads* (1905), *Via*

Borealis (1906), Lundy's Lane and Other Poems (1916), Beauty and Life (1921), The Poems of Duncan Campbell Scott (1926), The Green Cloister: Later Poems (1935), and The Circle of Affection (1947). He also wrote effective short stories, collected in In the Village of Viger (1896) and The Witching of Elspie (1923). A volume of Selected Stories appeared in 1972. With Pelham Edgar, Scott edited the MAKERS OF CANADA series, to which he contributed a volume on John Graves SIMCOE in 1905. He was Archibald LAMPMAN's literary executor and, with E.K. BROWN, he edited Lampman's At the Long Sault and Other New Poems (1943). See also 'AT THE MERMAID INN'.

Scott, F.R. (b.1899). Poet and social philosopher. Born in Quebec City—the son of Canon Frederick George SCOTT, himself a poet—Francis Reginald Scott attended Bishop's College, Oxford, and McGill University. He was called to the bar in 1927 and taught in the Faculty of Law at McGill, serving as its dean from 1961 until his retirement in 1964. He was a founder of the LEAGUE FOR SOCIAL RECONSTRUCTION in 1932, a contributor to SOCIAL PLANNING FOR CANADA (1935), and national chairman of the CCF from 1942 to 1950. An authority on constitutional law and a strong advocate of civil liberties and minority rights, he fought and won two important cases in Quebec in the 1950s relating to the PADLOCK LAW and the RONCARELLI CASE and defended D.H. Lawrence's Lady Chatterley's Lover against a charge of obscenity. He was a member of the Royal Commission on BILINGUALISM AND BICULTURALISM. While a law student he founded with A.J.M. SMITH the McGILL FORTNIGHTLY REVIEW in 1925 and with others PREVIEW in 1942. The author of many well-known poems that express the Canadian identity, he has produced a rich body of poetry embracing social and political satire, nature and love poems, metaphysical and found poems, and translations from the French. They have been collected in Overture (1945), Events and Signals (1954), The Eye of the Needle (1957), Signature (1964), Selected Poems (1966), Trouvailles: Poems from Prose (1967), and The Dance is One (1973). He co-edited New Provinces: Poems from Several Authors (1936) and The BLASTED PINE (1957; rev. 1967). Saint-Denys-Garneau & Anne Hébert: Translations/Traductions appeared in 1962. He is married to Marian SCOTT.

Scott, Frederick George (1861-1944). Clergyman and poet. Born in Montreal, educated at Bishop's College, and ordained in the Anglican ministry in 1886, he was appointed a canon of the Anglican Cathedral at Quebec in 1906 and archdeacon in 1925. He was se-

nior chaplain of the First Canadian Division and wrote his reminiscences in The Great War as I Saw It (1922), a work with an almost epic sweep. He was the author of 11 books of religious, nature, and patriotic verse; his Collected Poems appeared in 1933. He was the father of F.R. SCOTT.

Scott, Marian (b.1906). Painter. Born Marian Dale in Montreal, she studied at the Art Association of Montreal, the École des Beaux-Arts, and the Slade School in London. In 1940 she created a well-known mural, Endocrinology, for the McGill University medical building, that led her into abstraction. Her widely exhibited paintings are the result of a 'non-ending journey of visual experience' that reflects various phases in her use of acrylic colours and of forms, textures, and transparencies. She is married to F.R. SCOTT.

Scott, Thomas (c.1840-70). Irish-Canadian anti-Métis labourer. During the RED RIVER REBELLION he was taken prisoner by Louis RIEL, tried by a court-martial of Riel's Provisional Government at Fort Garry, and condemned to death. He was shot on 4 Mar. 1870—an execution that inflamed public opinion in Ontario, especially among Orangemen, and created racial and religious animosity in Ontario and Quebec.

Scott Act. The popular name of the CANADA TEMPERANCE ACT of 1878. It was introduced by Richard William Scott (1825-1913), who was at that time Secretary of State.

Scrap-book Debates. The unofficial scrap-book records of debates in the House of Commons and the Senate covering the period 1867 to 1874. Consisting of clippings from the newspapers of the time, which were mounted in scrapbooks in the LIBRARY OF PARLIAMENT, they are available on microfilm. They were succeeded by the COTTON DEBATES, which were succeeded by HANSARD.

Screech. A strong low-grade rum popular in Newfoundland. The name derives from 'screigh', a Scottish dialect word for whisky.

Screening agency. See FOREIGN INVESTMENT REVIEW AGENCY.

Sculping. In Newfoundland, removing the skin and adhering fat from a seal. The process is also known as 'sealing'.

Sculpture/Inuit. The first major travelling exhibition of Eskimo sculpture. It opened in Vancouver in 1971; was shown in Paris, Copenhagen, Moscow, Leningrad, London, Philadelphia, and Montreal; and closed in Ottawa in 1973. Organized by the CANADIAN

ESKIMO ARTS COUNCIL, it showed 450 pieces of art, from archaeological to contemporary times. The catalogue, *Sculpture/Inuit: Sculpture of the Inuit: Masterworks of the Canada Arctic* (1971), was edited by George Swinton.

Scurvy. A deficiency disease caused by a lack of fresh meat, fruit, and vegetables, characterized by swollen gums and limbs, decaying teeth, and weakness. It is associated with the privations suffered by the early explorers, especially Jacques CARTIER's men during the winter spent at Stadacona (1535-6). They were told by the Indian Domagaya to drink a brew made from white cedar, which contains ascorbic acid (vitamin C), and when they did they recovered.

SDPC. See SOCIAL DEMOCRATIC PARTY OF CANADA.

SDU. See STUDENTS FOR A DEMOCRATIC UNIVERSITY.

Sea otter. A large aquatic mammal of the weasel family, found on the northern Pacific coast. Hunted for its dark, lustrous fur, it faced extinction at one time and is now protected by international treaty.

Sea unicorn. See NARWHAL.

Seaforth Highlanders of Canada, The. Canadian army regiment. It originated in 1910 and served in the FIRST WORLD WAR with the 72nd Battalion in France and Flanders, distinguishing itself in many battles. During the SECOND WORLD WAR it landed in Sicily as part of the 2nd Infantry Brigade and then participated in numerous battles in Northwest Europe.

Seagram Corporation, The. The name since 1974 of the world's largest distillers. It was founded as the Distillers Corporation in Montreal in 1924 by Samuel Bronfman (1891-1971). Born in Brandon, Man., and at one time a hotelkeper in Winnipeg, in 1927 he acquired the ailing firm of Joseph E. Seagram & Sons and the following year united them as Distillers Corporation—Seagram's Limited. Finding a ready outlet for whisky in the Prohibition-dry United States, the House of Seagram, as it came to be known, expanded to command the lead position after the Second World War with Seven Crown and SEAGRAM'S V.O., the world's bestselling brands. Earnings of the Seagram Corporation and related interests are controlled by Cemp Investments. 'Cemp' is an acronym of the names of the four children of Sam and Saidye Bronfman: Charles (b.1931), president of the Seagram Company in Montreal and owner of the Montreal Expos since 1968;

Edgar (b.1928), president of the American operation; Minda, the wife of Baron Alain de Gunzburg; and Phyllis Lambert, an architect and architectural historian.

Seagram's Five Star. Canadian rye whisky. SEAGRAM's largest-selling brand in Canada.

Seagram's V.O. Canadian rye whisky. SEAGRAM's largest-selling brand in the United States and the largest-selling Canadian whisky in the world.

Seal, Harp. A medium-sized sea mammal inhabiting coastal waters from the Maritimes to Baffin Island. The mainstay of the eastern sealing industry, it has rapidly declined in numbers. The campaign against the annual slaughter of pups has received wide publicity. See SEAL HUNT.

Seal flipper pie. A casserole popular in Newfoundland. It is made with seal flippers (the seal's forepaws), salt pork, potatoes, and a pastry crust covering.

Seal hunt. The annual spring slaughter of the harp or Greenland seals for their pelts and blubber on the ice floes north and east of Newfoundland. Since 1965 national and international protests have decried the commercial hunts for reasons of cruelty and conservation.

Search-for-a-New-Alberta-Novelist Competition. Annual contest open to Alberta authors who have written unpublished first novels. The winner receives a prize of $1,000 and an advance of $1,500 against future royalties from MACMILLAN OF CANADA. The competition was established by the Culture, Youth and Recreation Department of the Alberta Government in 1974.

Search for America, A. Autobiographical novel by Frederick Philip GROVE published in 1927. Based on Grove's travels in North America, it views life in the United States at the turn of the twentieth century panoramically, and rejects its values in the end.

Seasons, The. The first film made by Christopher CHAPMAN. Shot over the course of a year on the shore of a lake in Ontario, it captured the seasonal changes. The 16 mm film was produced, directed, photographed, and edited by Chapman and sold to IMPERIAL OIL in 1952. It has been in circulation ever since. 18 min., colour.

Seats of the Mighty, The. Historical novel by Sir Gilbert PARKER published in 1896. Setting it in Quebec in 1757-9 and using the memoirs of Robert STOBO for the exploits of its main character, Parker blended fact and fancy in handling real and imaginary characters, love interest, and intrigue to produce an implausible but entertaining romance.

Seaway. A large-scale CBC-TV series. It was produced to much acclaim by Maxine Samuels and made its début on 16 Sept. 1963. It starred Austin WILLIS as a troubleshooter on the ST LAWRENCE SEAWAY. Although sold to British television, it was dogged by poor scripts and was too expensive to continue without an American network as co-sponsor.

Seaweed, Willie (c.1873-1967). Master Kwakiutl artist. Born at Blunden Harbour, B.C., he was a high-ranking chief whose Indian name was Hey'hlamas (Right Maker) or, more familiarly, Kwa'ghitola (Smokey Top). He is well known for the strong, flamboyant, innovative nature of his work, particularly the many cannibal-bird (*hâmatsa*) masks that he made.

2Lt. Official abbreviation of Second Lieutenant.

Second World War. 'The Hitler War'. The Canadian Parliament declared war on Germany on 10 Sept. 1939, seven days after the British declaration of war. A total of 730,625 Canadians saw service in the CANADIAN ARMY, the ROYAL CANADIAN NAVY, and the ROYAL CANADIAN AIR FORCE. Of this number, 630,052 were volunteers, the balance being conscripted under the NATIONAL RESOURCES MOBILIZATION ACT. The German government surrendered in the French cathedral city of Reims at 8:00 a.m. on 5 May 1945. The Japanese surrender was taken at Tokyo Bay on 2 Sept. 1945. Canadian occupation forces remained in Germany until Apr. 1946. For specific engagements and related matters, see: AGIRA, ARNHEM, BAYEUX MEMORIAL, BOULOGNE, BRITISH COMMONWEALTH AIR TRAINING PLAN, BROOKSIDE CEMETERY, BROOKWOOD MILITARY CEMETERY, CAEN, CALAIS, COMMONWEALTH AIR FORCES OTTAWA MEMORIAL, DIEPPE, FALAISE, FIRST CANADIAN ARMY, HALIFAX MEMORIAL, HOCHWALD RIDGE, HONG KONG, KAPELSCHE VEER, KISKA, LE HAVRE, MESSINA, NEWFOUNDLAND NATIONAL MEMORIAL, NIJMEGEN, NORMANDY INVASION, ORTONA, REICHSWALD, RHINE, SCHELDT, SPITSBERGEN, VERRIÈRES RIDGE.

Secord, Laura (1775-1868). Heroine of the WAR OF 1812. Born Laura Ingersoll in Massachusetts, she came to Upper Canada (Ontario) with her Loyalist family and married James Secord. In June 1813, while living at Queenston, she learned of a planned attack on BEAVER DAM from American soldiers bil-

leted on her. She walked 19 mi. to tell Lt James FitzGibbon who, already forewarned by Indians, scored an important victory. Laura Secord's undeniable courage and her largely symbolic deed went unrewarded until the Prince of Wales, later Edward VII, learning of her trek, awarded her £100 in 1861. There are monuments to Laura Secord at Drummond Hill Cemetery (dedicated in 1901) and at Queenston Heights (dedicated in 1910). In 1969 the LAURA SECORD candy company bought and restored her frame house at Queenston Heights. See also QUEENSTON HEIGHTS AND BROCK'S MONUMENT.

Secret of Heroism, The. A tribute to the spirit of idealism and sacrifice written by W.L. Mackenzie KING and published in 1906. In this short work, occasioned by the tragic death of his young assistant Henry Albert Harper, King discovered the 'secret of heroism' to lie in the life of self-sacrifice. See also SIR GALAHAD.

Secretary of State, Department of the. Department of the federal government concerned with civic and cultural affairs. The Secretary of State's Department includes branches for Citizenship, Citizenship Registration, Education Support, Bilingualism Development Programs, Arts and Culture, State Protocol and Special Events, and a Translation Bureau. The Minister is responsible for matters pertaining to multiculturalism and reports to Parliament on behalf of the CANADA COUNCIL, the PUBLIC ARCHIVES, the CANADIAN BROADCASTING CORPORATION, the PUBLIC SERVICE COMMISSION, and various cultural bodies.

Secretary of State for External Affairs. See Department of EXTERNAL AFFAIRS.

Section. A unit of land survey of one square mile in the prairie west. See QUARTER-SECTION.

Section 93. This section of the BNA ACT gives exclusive jurisdiction for the administration of education to the provincial legislatures. Assurance is also given that denominations may retain the separate schools in operation at the time of the Act's passage (1867)—thus establishing a precedent for others to follow, given provincial readiness to do so.

Section 98. A controversial section of the CRIMINAL CODE OF CANADA that declared unlawful any association that advocated the use of force to change society. Originally adopted during the First World War, it was broadened as a result of the WINNIPEG GENERAL STRIKE. It provided for the arrest of anyone suspected of SEDITIOUS CONSPIRACY and increased the maximum penalty for those charged and found guilty from 2 to 20 years' imprisonment. At the same time, an amendment to the Immigration Act provided for the immediate deportation, without trial or hearing, of any immigrant, including a British subject, regardless of citizenship status or length of stay in Canada. Section 98 and the Immigration Act amendment were not repealed until 1936.

Sector theory. First enunciated by Senator Pascal Poirier in 1907, it was based on a suggestion by Capt. J.E. BERNIER that all the territory between the Canadian north coast and the North Pole enclosed by longitudinal lines drawn from the east and west extremities of the coast line should be claimed by Canada.

Security and Intelligence, Interdepartmental Committee on. See SECURITY PANEL.

Security Panel. A secret body concerned with national security. The advisory panel consisted of selected deputy ministers and two officials of the PRIVY COUNCIL OFFICE charged 'to advise on the co-ordination of the planning, organization and execution of security measures which affect government departments, and to advise on such other security questions as might be referred to it'. Originally formed in 1946 and reconstituted in 1963, since the publication of the Report of the Royal Commission on Security in 1969 it has been reconstituted again and renamed the Interdepartmental Committee on Security and Intelligence. The role of the new body is the 'co-ordination of security and intelligence activities'.

Security Service. Department of the ROYAL CANADIAN MOUNTED POLICE established by the GOVERNOR IN COUNCIL 'to maintain and operate such security and intelligence services as may be required'. It was known as the Directorate of Security and Intelligence until June 1971, when it acquired its present name. It is concerned with the defence of Canada against espionage and clandestine, conspiratorial, subversive, and other illegal activities from within. To this end it undertakes security-clearance investigations, briefings, debriefings, etc.

Seditious conspiracy. Phrase from SECTION 98 of the CRIMINAL CODE OF CANADA, which specifically outlawed any group or association that advocated social change through force. Leaders of the WINNIPEG GENERAL STRIKE were charged with seditious conspiracy. The section was repealed in 1936.

Sedna. Ruler of the lower depths among the CENTRAL ESKIMOS. The subject of tales collected by Franz BOAS, Sedna disobeyed her father and married a dog-husband. When he deserted her the father took Sedna into a boat and cast her overboard. She clung to the gunwales but he chopped her fingers off. She descended into the sea and her fingertips turned into seals, walruses, and the sea mammals.

SEFACAN. Acronym for SEgregator, FAcer, CANceller, a semi-automatic machine to increase the efficiency of the postal service. The mechanized sorter, of British design and Canadian modification, was installed in post offices in 1963. SEFACAN 'segregates' mail by size, 'faces' letters in a single direction, then 'cancels' the stamps, all in a continuous operation.

Segal, Y.Y. (1896-1954). Yiddish poet. Born in Poland, he was brought to Montreal at the age of 14. He learned tailoring, taught in a Jewish parochial school, and wrote on Jewish subjects for the Yiddish-language newspaper, *Canader Odler* ('Canadian Eagle'). He produced numerous collections of his lyrical poems, influenced by Yiddish folksongs, which movingly and simply capture the Jewish milieu in Quebec. A few in effective translations by Miriam WADDINGTON appear in *A Treasury of Yiddish Poetry* (1969) edited by Irving Howe and Elizer Greenberg and in VOLVOX (1971) edited by J. Michael Yates.

Seigneur, seigneury. See SEIGNEURIAL TENURE.

Seigneurial tenure. A system of land settlement in New France. The Crown granted concessions of land *(seigneuries)* to individuals *(seigneurs)*, who in turn had to settle a number of *habitants (censitaires)* on them. Other obligations of the *seigneur* were the building of a mill and the establishment of a court of law for minor disputes, while the *habitants* had to clear the land and pay modest annual dues *(cens et rentes)* to the seigneur. The system survived until 1854. See also RANG SYSTEM.

Seigniory Club. See Le CHÂTEAU MONTEBELLO.

Seitz, Ernest. See 'The WORLD IS WAITING FOR THE SUNRISE'.

Selke, Frank (b.1893). Hockey executive. Born in Berlin (now Kitchener), Ont., he moved to Toronto in 1918. He was associated with Conn SMYTHE in the erection of MAPLE LEAF GARDENS in 1931 and in helping to manage the TORONTO MAPLE LEAFS to STANLEY CUP championships. In 1946 he was general manager of the MONTREAL CANADIENS for six NHL titles. He is chairman of the Hockey HALL OF FAME's selection committee, to which he was elected a hockey builder in 1960.

Selkirk, Lord (1771-1820). Philanthropic sponsor of settlements. A Scot, Thomas Douglas Selkirk established settlers at Orwell Bay, P.E.I. (1803), at BALDOON near Lake St Clair, U.C. (Ont.) (1804), and on the Red River in 1812 (see RED RIVER SETTLEMENT) on lands owned by the HUDSON'S BAY COMPANY, in which he had substantial interests. The opposition of the NORTH WEST COMPANY to the Red River Settlement brought him many trials and eventually broke his health.

Selye, Hans (b.1907). Medical research scientist and authority on STRESS. Born in Vienna and educated at the German university at Prague, the University of Paris, and the University of Rome, he taught biochemistry at McGill University from 1932. Since 1945 he has been associated with the Institute of Experimental Medicine and Surgery at the Université de Montréal. In addition to his scientific publications on endocrinology and related subjects, he has popularized through his books and speeches the concept of stress in *The Stress of Life* (1956), *From Dream to Discovery* (1964), and *Stress Without Distress* (1974).

Séminaire de Québec. See UNIVERSITÉ LAVAL.

Semple, Robert. See Massacre of SEVEN OAKS.

Senate, The. The upper house of the federal legislature; the House of Parliament whose members are appointed, not elected. SENATORS are appointed by the GOVERNOR GENERAL on the advice of the prime minister. There are 102 senators, who are appointed proportionally to represent the provinces: 4 members from Prince Edward Island; 6 members each from Alberta, British Columbia, Manitoba, Newfoundland, and Saskatchewan; 10 each from Nova Scotia and New Brunswick; and 24 each from Ontario and Quebec. Members were originally appointed for life, but those appointed since 1965 retire at age 75. Deliberations are presided over by the SPEAKER, and government business in the Senate is sponsored by the GOVERNMENT LEADER. The Senate's powers are those of the HOUSE OF COMMONS, except that MONEY BILLS must originate in the Commons. Concurrence of the Senate is necessary before any piece of legislation, public or private, can become law. The role of the Senate, which has been called the RED CHAMBER,

has been justified because it offers a forum for the discussion of public issues and the airing of grievances, and takes a 'sober second look' at legislation originating in the House of Commons.

Senator. A member of the SENATE. The formal style of address in conversation is 'sir' or 'madam', the informal style is 'senator'. In formal usage a senator's name is preceded by 'The HONOURABLE'.

Senator for Kicking Horse Pass. See Dave BROADFOOT.

Seneca. See IROQUOIS.

Senior A. One of two hockey series for non-professional players organized by the Canadian Amateur Hockey Association. Players first competed for the ALLAN CUP when the series was established in 1907-8. See also JUNIOR A.

Senior Matriculation. See MATRICULATION.

Separate schools. Denominational schools on the primary and secondary levels, especially those operated for and by Roman Catholics. Separate schools are tax-supported in Alberta, Ontario, Saskatchewan, and the two Territories. The phrase 'separate Church Schools' goes back as far as 1852. See also PUBLIC SCHOOLS, PAROCHIAL SCHOOLS.

Separatism. The political concept of a province withdrawing from CONFEDERATION and existing as a separate and independent state, strongly identified with QUEBEC since the early 1960s. The PARTI QUÉBÉCOIS is dedicated to bringing about an independent Quebec.

September Gale, Georgian Bay, A. Canvas by Arthur LISMER sketched at Go Home Bay, Ont., and painted in the fall of 1920. Its boldly delineated forms of wind-bent trees and grass, of waves, heavy clouds, and thrusting rocks produce a dynamic close-up of the gale's impact. Lismer sketched it at the same time as F.H. VARLEY made his sketch for STORMY WEATHER, GEORGIAN BAY (1920, NGC). With Tom THOMSON'S WEST WIND (1917, AGO), these paintings of similar subjects are the best-known images of the northern landscape. (NGC)

Sergeant-at-Arms. The official charged with ceremonial functions and security duties in the HOUSE OF COMMONS. The Sergeant-at-Arms carries the MACE in front of the SPEAKER.

Serpent Mounds. Prehistoric Indian burial site. Now a provincial park, the Serpent

Serpent Mounds

Mounds are located on the shore of Rice Lake, 3 mi. south of Keene, near Peterborough, Ont. Constituting the largest serpentine burial tumuli ever discovered, they have been excavated intermittently since 1895 and have yielded skeletons and implements dating back to the Hopewellian culture that flourished in eastern North America 2,000 years ago.

Service, Robert W. (1874-1958). 'The poet of the Yukon'. Born in Preston, Eng., and raised in Glasgow, where he worked briefly at the Commercial Bank of Scotland, he left in 1894 for the Canadian West and in 1902 entered the Bank of Commerce in Vancouver; he was transferred to Whitehorse, Y.T., in 1904 and to Dawson in 1906. There, out of boredom, he began to write popular ballads in imitation of 'On the Road to Mandalay', 'Casey at the Bat', and 'The Face on the Bar-Room Floor', which in Yukon mining towns following the KLONDIKE GOLD RUSH were recited as the main form of public entertainment. Service sent a collection of his ballads to the Methodist Book Room (the forerunner of The RYERSON PRESS) to be printed at his own expense, but the publisher, William Briggs, offered to issue them on a royalty basis. *Songs of a Sourdough* (1907) included the sentimental favourites 'The SHOOTING OF DAN McGREW' and 'The CREMATION OF SAM McGEE' and was an immediate hit. *The Spell of the Yukon* (1909), *Ballads of a Cheechako* (1909), etc., followed. The royalties permitted Service to spend the next two years in a Dawson cabin (built in 1898 by a prospector named Sam McGee and now open to the public as the Robert Service Cabin), where he wrote his first novel, *The Trail of '98: A Northland Romance* (1911). Thereafter Service left the Yukon far behind him and lived in Hollywood, the south of France, and Monaco. He wrote more than a dozen collections of verse, six melodramatic novels, and a two-volume autobiography: *The Ploughman of the Moon* (1945) and *Harper of Heaven* (1948). His poetry is reprinted in *Collected Verse* (1930), *More Collected Verse* (1949), and *Later Collected Verse* (1963). Selections from his prose and verse appear in *Rhyme and Romance: A Robert Service Anthology* (1958). He is buried at Lancieux, Brittany, France.

Serviceberry. See SASKATOON BERRY.

Services Colleges. See CANADIAN MILITARY COLLEGES.

Seton, Ernest Thompson (1860-1946). Naturalist, author, and artist. Born in South Shields, Durham, Eng., he was six when his parents brought him to Lindsay, C.W. (Ont.), and then to Toronto, where he was educated at the Ontario College of Art and, by his own admission, in the parks of Toronto. Appointed naturalist to the Manitoba government, he wrote and illustrated *The Birds of Manitoba* (1891) and *Life-Histories of Northern Animals* (2 vols, 1909). *The Arctic Prairies* (1911) was written after a trip to the BARREN LANDS. *Lives of Game Animals* (1925-8) is a comprehensive work in four volumes. He founded the Woodcraft League in New York in 1902 and was chief of the Boy Scouts of America from 1910 to 1915. His famous children's classic *Two Little Savages: Being the Adventures of Two Boys Who Live as Indians and What They Learned* (1903) is set in the bush country around Lindsay. Seton also reached a very large public as a prolific writer and illustrator of animal stories, many of which are enjoyed by children. These include *Wild Animals I Have Known* (1898), *The Biography of a Grizzly* (1900), and *Lives of the Hunted* (1901). *Trail of an Artist-Naturalist* (1940) is his autobiography. In 1930 he established the Seton Institute, a school for children interested in woodcrafts and wildlife, at Sante Fe, New Mexico, where he died. His wife Julia Seton compiled *Ernest Seton's America* (1954), an anthology of his writings.

Settlers of the Marsh. The first naturalistic Canadian novel in English, written by Frederick Philip GROVE and published in 1925. Set in northern Manitoba, it is about an idealistic young Swedish farmer and man's struggle against nature. It contains references to sex that aroused great disapproval at the time the book was published and damaged sales.

Seul ou avec d'autres. Feature film that appeared in 1962 and marked the beginning of the Quebec cinema boom. Produced with professional help and directed by Dénis HÉROUX, Denys ARCAND, and Stephane Venne, it starred students at the Université de Montréal and enjoyed a commercial run. It is a portrait of student life focusing on a love affair. 65 min., b & w.

Seven Days. See THIS HOUR HAS SEVEN DAYS.

700,000,000, The. A 70-minute CBC-TV documentary about Red China. It was produced by Patrick WATSON, written by Roy Faibish, and photographed by Erik Durschmeid, with a narration by Bud Knapp. The first television documentary made in Mainland China since the revolution in 1949, it was shown on 4 Nov. 1964 and was notable for its even-

Shaking Tent

handed presentation of life in the Communist country. It was bought by both the BBC and NET in New York.

Seven-O-One. See TABLOID.

Seven Oaks, Massacre of. A skirmish that took place on 19 June 1816 when MÉTIS and Indians under the halfbreed Cuthbert GRANT—supported by the NORTH WEST COMPANY—killed Robert Semple, governor of ASSINIBOIA, and 20 settlers of the RED RIVER SETTLEMENT.

Seven Sisters. Waterfalls on the Winnipeg R., Man.; a group of majestic Douglas-fir trees in STANLEY PARK, Vancouver, B.C. The name may have come from William Wordsworth's poem 'The Seven Sisters'.

Seven Years' War. Britain declared war on France on 15 May 1756. In North America the conflict began 26 months earlier (Feb. 1754) in the Ohio valley and ended when New France was ceded to Great Britain by the Treaty of Paris in 1763. Significant battles were at Fort William Henry (1757) and Fort Carillon (Ticonderoga, N.Y., 1758), in which the French forces under MONTCALM were victorious; at LOUISBOURG, which fell to the British in 1758; and at Quebec, where British forces under WOLFE defeated French forces under Montcalm on the PLAINS OF ABRAHAM on 13 Sept. 1759. The Battle of SAINTE-FOY took place there the following April; the French, under LÉVIS, were victorious but failed to take Quebec. VAUDREUIL-CAVAGNAL, the governor general of New France, capitulated in Sept. 1960 at Montreal. The final engagement in North America took place at St John's, Nfld, which was held by the French from June to Sept. 1762.

Seventeen, The. See DOLLARD DES ORMEAUX.

Seventy-two Resolutions. A draft constitution accepted at the QUEBEC CONFERENCE (Oct. 1864) by the Province of Canada, Nova Scotia, and New Brunswick that became the basis of the BNA ACT of 1867. The seven-week discussion of them in the Canadian legislature in Feb. 1865 is known as the Confederation Debates. They were approved by a vote of 91 to 33.

Seymour, Lynn (b. 1939). Dancer. Born in Wainwright, Alta, she studied in Vancouver with Jean Jepson and Nicolai Svetlanoff, then at the Sadler's Wells, London, in 1954-6. She danced with the Covent Garden Opera Ballet in 1956, toured with the Royal Ballet in 1957, and was soloist with the Royal in 1958-60, with Kenneth MacMillan as direc-

tor; she is MacMillan's main subject for his ballets. She was guest artist with the NATIONAL BALLET OF CANADA in 1964, dancing *La Sylphide* to Erik BRUHN'S James, and with the Festival Ballet in 1969 and 1970, the year she returned to the Royal Ballet as ballerina. In the Queen's birthday honours of 1976 she was made a Companion of the Order of the British Empire (CBE).

SG. Official abbreviation of Surgeon in the ROYAL CANADIAN NAVY.

Sgt. Official abbreviation of Sergeant.

Shad. A food fish found on the Atlantic coast.

Shad berry. See SASKATOON BERRY.

Shadbolt, Jack (b.1909). Painter. Born in Shoeburyness, Eng., he was raised in Victoria, B.C., where Emily CARR influenced his work. He studied in Europe and at the Vancouver School of Art, where he later taught. His stylistic versatility appears in evocative watercolours of the west coast and mixed-media paintings that use non-objective fantasy images. *Winter Theme No. 7* (1961, NGC) is a visually exciting example of the burst of colour and form that characterizes his best work.

Shad-fly. In the Maritime provinces, the May fly.

Shadow on the Prairie. A ballet choreographed by Gweneth LLOYD and first produced by the ROYAL WINNIPEG BALLET in 1952. With music by Robert FLEMING and designed by John Graham, it presents 'the grandeur and loneliness of the prairie winter and the agony of nostalgia driving a young wife to her death'.

Shaffer, Ivan (b.1928). Popular writer with a business background. Born in Ottawa, he is the author of *The Stock Promotion Business* (1967) and of three novels: *The Midas Compulsion* (1969), *Business Is Business?* (1974), and *The Medicine Man* (1975).

Shaganappi. Algonkian word for a piece of rawhide or a thong made of rawhide (a BABICHE). It has overtones in the West of 'inexperienced' or 'inferior', as in 'shaganappi pony', which may be untrained or undersized.

Shaking Tent, The. A rite of the Montagnais-Naskapi, Cree, and Ojibwa Indians, as witnessed and described by European fur traders at the close of the eighteenth century. A naked medicine man, bound and wrapped in a robe, was left on the floor of a teepee or

481

specially constructed tent. After some time the teepee or tent would shake, as if rocked by winds, and noises and voices could be heard, as during a séance. This would continue for some hours. When unbound, the perspiring medicine man would expound on what the spirits had told him. Explanations of the Shaking Tent mystery range from the spiritualistic—the medicine man had contacted the spirit world—to the realistic—the conjurer had, Houdini-like, loosened his bonds, supplied the effects, then rebound himself, possibly in a trance-like state.

Shaman. Sacred priest of shamanism. This complex religious system—common to hunting and gathering societies—uses ecstatic states, animal transformations, hallucinogenic plants, and communication with the spirits of the dead to divine events, cure disease, and affirm the social order. Shaman have existed in most early cultures across the world: Canadian Eskimos and the Indians of the plains and the northwest coast in particular relied on this figure. The Shaman is referred to as a 'medicine man', a term that suggests only his healing powers. His relationship with the supernatural and the collective unconscious was often at the very centre of pre-agricultural societies. The practice of shamanism was outlawed by the Revised Statutes of Canada in 1927.

Shanawdithit, Nancy. See BEOTHUK.

SHAPE. Acronym of Supreme Headquarters Allied Powers in Europe, an integrated NATO force under SACEUR. It became operational at Rocquencourt, near Paris, on 2 Apr. 1951, and moved to Brussels on 31 Mar. 1967, after France had ceased participation in NATO integrated military commands.

Sharon Fragments. Popular a cappella choral piece composed by John BECKWITH in 1966. Based on texts by David WILLSON, which Beckwith first used in Canada Dash, Canada Dot (1965-7), its themes come from two nineteenth-century hymn tunes of the Children of Peace sect at SHARON TEMPLE.

Sharon Temple. A religious building unique in Canada, begun in 1825 at Sharon, Ont., and designed by David WILLSON and Ebenezer Doan to house the ritual festivals of the Children of Peace (or Davidites), a music-loving group of former Quakers. It is a handsome frame building 60 ft square and rises in three tiers to a lantern 12 ft square; the complete design symbolizes the beliefs of the Children of Peace. The group's meeting house (since destroyed) and Willson's study formed part of the complex. The temple fell

into neglect after Willson's death in 1866 and the decline of the sect, but it was restored and is preserved by the York Pioneer and Historical Society.

Shatner, William (b.1932). Actor. Born in Montreal, he acted with the Canadian Repertory Theatre in Ottawa and for three years with the STRATFORD FESTIVAL and the CANADIAN PLAYERS. In 1958 he appeared on Broadway in The World of Suzie Wong and in the Hollywood feature The Brothers Karamazov. He is best known internationally as Captain Kirk on NBC-TV's Star Trek (1966-9) and in Canada as the television pitchman for LOBLAW COMPANIES LTD ('By gosh, the price is right!').

Shaw Festival. A summer theatre for the production of plays by Bernard Shaw and his contemporaries located at NIAGARA-ON-THE-LAKE, Ont. Founded in 1962 by Brian DOHERTY, it mounted its first production in the historic Court House (1848), which was provided with a seating capacity of 361, on 29 June 1962. The artistic directors have been Andrew ALLAN (1963-5), Barry MORSE (1966), and Paxton WHITEHEAD, who was appointed in 1967. On 12 June 1973 it opened an 813-seat theatre designed by Ron THOM. The Festival now includes concerts, and the theatre building remains in use throughout the winter for the Festival's International Concert Series and other presentations. A list of theatre productions follows:

1962 'Don Juan in Hell' from Man and Superman, Candida
1963 You Never Can Tell, How He Lied to Her Husband, The Man of Destiny, Androcles and the Lion
1964 Heartbreak House, Village Wooing, The Dark Lady of the Sonnets, John Bull's Other Island
1965 Pygmalion, The Shadow of a Gunman (O'Casey), The Millionairess
1966 Man and Superman, Misalliance, The Apple Cart
1967 Arms and the Man, The Circle (Maugham), Major Barbara
1968 Heartbreak House, The Importance of Being Oscar (MacLiammoir), The Chemmy Circle (Feydeau/Grossman)
1969 The Doctor's Dilemma, Back to Methuselah: Part I, Five Variations for Corno Di Bassetto, The Guardsman (Molnar/Marcus)
1970 Candida, G.K.C.: The Wit and Wisdom of Gilbert Keith Chesterton (van Bridge), Forty Years On (Bennett)
1971 The Philanderer, Summer Days (Weingarten), Tonight at 8:30 (Coward), A Social

Success, O'Flaherty, V.C., Press Cuttings (Beerbohm)
1972 *The Royal Family* (Kaufman & Ferber), *Getting Married, Misalliance*
1973 *The Philanderer, You Never Can Tell, The Brass Butterfly* (Golding), *Fanny's First Play*
1974 *The Devil's Disciple, The Admirable Bashville, Too True to be Good, Rosmersholm* (Ibsen), *Charley's Aunt* (Thomas)
1975 *Pygmalion, Caesar and Cleopatra,* LEAVEN OF MALICE (DAVIES), *The First Night of Pygmalion* (Huggett), *G.K.C.: The Wit and Wisdom of Gilbert Keith Chesterton* (van Bridge)
1976 *The Admirable Crichton* (Barrie), *Mrs Warren's Profession, Arms and the Man, The Apple Cart*

Shea, Sir Ambrose (1815-1905). A FATHER OF CONFEDERATION. Born in St John's, Nfld, he was elected to the House of Assembly in 1848. He was a delegate to the QUEBEC CONFERENCE on Confederation, which Newfoundland rejected. He was knighted in 1883 and was governor of the Bahamas from 1887 to 1895.

Shearwater. See CANADIAN FORCES BASE SHEARWATER.

Shebib, Don (b.1938). Film director. Born in Toronto, he graduated in sociology from the University of Toronto before enrolling in the film school of the University College of Los Angeles. He then worked with CBC-TV, CTV, and the NATIONAL FILM BOARD. His favourite film remains *Good Times, Bad Times* (1969), a CBC-TV documentary on hospitalized war veterans. His first feature was GOIN' DOWN THE ROAD (1970), a remarkable film based on a script by William FRUET. His subsequent features include *Rip-Off* (1971), *Between Friends* (1973), and *Second Wind* (1976).

Shedd, Marjory (b.1926). Champion badminton player. Born in Toronto, she played basketball and volleyball but excelled in badminton and won several national titles between 1953 and 1963. She competed in the important all-England tournament. In 1970 she was elected to the Sports HALL OF FAME.

Shediac oyster. A well-known oyster from Shediac, N.B.

Sheepskin Coats, Men in. A reference to immigrants in the Northwest between 1896 and 1900—mainly Ukrainians and DOUKHOBORS—who were resented by those who wanted the country peopled by Anglo-Saxons. Brought out by Clifford SIFTON, Minister of the Interior, as part of the immigration policy of the

LAURIER government, they justified Sifton's determined effort to develop the agricultural potential of the Northwest.

Sherlock Holmes Society. See the BOOTMAKERS OF TORONTO.

Sherring, William J. (1877-1964). Champion distance-runner. A native of Hamilton, Ont., he defeated 57 competitors from 12 countries at the 1906 International Games in Athens and was recognized as the world's champion distance-runner. He entered public life in Hamilton as a controller.

Sherritt Gordon Mines Ltd. An important nickel, copper, and zinc producer. It dates back to 1913, when Indian prospectors found copper in the Kississing Lake area of northwestern Manitoba, following which the property passed through various hands, including those of Carl Sherritt, a prospector, and J.P. Gordon, a civil engineer. The Toronto-based company was incorporated in 1927 and went into production in 1931. The original copper deposit ran out in 1951 but the company discovered minerals at Lynn Lake, Man., and at the Ruttan and Fox mines southeast of Lynn Lake. Sherritt has been a pioneer in the chemical treatment of ores and has an extensive metal and chemical operation at Fort Saskatchewan, Man.

Shield, The. See CANADIAN SHIELD.

Shilling, Arthur (b.1941). Ojibwa artist. Born at the Rama Reserve near Orillia, Ont., he attended the New School of Art and the University of Toronto. He has been called 'the Indian VARLEY' for his bold brush-work and his sensitive portraits of the young and the old. In 1968 he produced textile designs with brightly coloured Ojibwa motifs, but he is mainly noted for his portraits of Indians.

Shin plasters. A derogatory name for paper currency, used in the United States in the 1820s. It came to be applied to 25-cent bank notes issued in Canada in 1870, 1900, and 1923.

Shiners. A name for Irish labourers in Bytown (Ottawa) in the 1830s and 1840s. Its origin is obscure.

Shining mountains, The. An early description of the ROCKY MOUNTAINS, the snow-covered crests of which shine in the sun. It is said to be a translation of the Cree name for the Rockies and is associated with Anthony HENDAY, the first European to see the mountains (between June 1754 and June 1755).

Shinny

Shinny. A game played in Britain with a ball and curved sticks, similar to hockey. In nineteenth-century Canada it was played by children on ice or grass. Today it is an informal game of hockey played without referees.

'Shooting of Dan McGrew, The'. A popular ballad by Robert SERVICE, published in *The Spell of the Yukon* (1907). It tells, in rollicking metre and rhyme, how 'a man with a foot in the grave' entered 'the Malamute saloon' and shot and killed 'Dangerous Dan McGrew', the love of whose life was 'the lady that's known as Lou'.

Shopsy's. Trade name of a popular brand of Jewish-style packaged meats. Shopsy's Foods Ltd was opened in 1950 by Sam (Shopsy) Shopsowitz, who was born in Toronto in 1920. Since 1946 he has run Shopsy's Delicatessen—founded in Toronto in 1921 by his Polish-born father and mother, Harry and Jenny Shopsowitz—which is popular with showbusiness people. The company—which packages all-beef wieners, corned beef, salami, pastrami, baby beef, etc.—was acquired by Lever Brothers Ltd in 1971.

Shore, Edward W. (b.1902). Hockey player. Born in Fort Qu'Appelle, Sask., he was a vigorous hockey defenceman who played in Edmonton, Regina, and Edmonton again, then joined the Boston Bruins in 1926 and remained for 13 seasons. He was a four-time winner of the HART MEMORIAL TROPHY, awarded annually to the most valuable player on a team in the entire NHL. He was elected to seven all-star NHL teams.

Short, Richard (active 1759-64). Naval officer and military draughtsman. He came to North America with the forces of James WOLFE in 1759 and produced two sets of drawings—6 of Halifax and 12 of Quebec after the bombardment of 1759—that were published as engravings in 1761. They became famous as fine early records of the Canadian scene.

Short administration. The shortest ministry on record was that of George BROWN and Antoine-Aimé Dorion, which lasted four days, 2-6 Aug. 1858.

Shortt, Adam (1859-1931). Economist and historian. Born at Kilworth, C.W. (Ont.), and educated at Queen's and the Universities of Glasgow and Edinburgh, he taught philosophy and then political science at Queen's. From 1918 until shortly before his death he was chairman of the Board of Historical Publications of the PUBLIC ARCHIVES OF CANADA. Among his scholarly publications in eco-nomic history are *The Early History of Canadian Banking* (1898) and his edition of *Documents Relating to Canadian Currency, Exchange, and Finance during the French Régime* (1926). With the Dominion Archivist A.G. DOUGHTY he edited *Documents Relating to the Constitutional History of Canada: 1759-91* (1907; rev. 1918) and the 23-volume reference work, CANADA AND ITS PROVINCES (1913-17).

Shouldice Surgery. A world-renowned treatment centre for hernia cases. The clinic opened in Toronto in 1945, the hospital in nearby Thornhill in 1953. Both make use of a fast technique of operating on hernias that allows quick recovery. It was devised by Dr Earle Shouldice (1891-1965), who was born in Chesley, Ont., and taught clinical surgery at the University of Toronto for 25 years before opening his clinic.

Showtime. A popular but short-lived CBC-TV variety series. It started on 7 July 1957 as a summer replacement for the 'Shirley Harmer Show', produced by Drew Crossan and later Norman JEWISON. It starred Robert GOULET, Joyce Sullivan, Shayne Rimmer, Ken Steele, Barbara Franklin, and Howard CABLE and his orchestra. The series ended in June 1959.

Shulman, Morton (b.1925). Doctor, social activist, and media personality. Born in Toronto, he took his medical degree at the University of Toronto, and served as chief coroner of Metropolitan Toronto from 1963 to 1967. A self-made investment millionaire, controversial advocate of various causes, and former NDP member of the Ontario legislature, he became host of 'The CITY Show' for CITY-TV in 1975. His bestselling books include: *Anyone Can Make a Million* (1966), *The Billion Dollar Windfall* (1969), *Anyone Can Still Make a Million* (1972), and *Coroner* (1975). He was the model for WOJECK.

Shuster, Frank. See WAYNE AND SHUSTER.

Shuswap. The most widespread of the INTERIOR SALISH Indians. They live in a territory approximately north of the Thompson R., between the Fraser R. and the Rockies. Their population in 1970 was 3,862.

Shutout. A term used in hockey for a game in which the opposing team fails to score even a single goal.

SI System, The. The short name for *Le Système International d'Unités* (The International System of Units), the modernized metric system of measurement established in 1960. The metric system was originally devised in France in 1795. Most countries have converted, or are preparing to convert, to the newer SI System. In Canada a METRIC COMMISSION was appointed to prepare and co-ordinate METRIC CONVERSION. A summary of common units in the system follows.

LENGTH		
kilometre	1 km	= 1000 m
metre	1 m	= 10 dm
decimetre	1 dm	= 10 cm
centimetre	1 cm	= 10 mm
millimetre		

AREA		
square kilometre	1 km^2	= 100 ha
hectare	1 ha	= 10 000 m^2
square metre	1 m^2	= 100 dm^2
square decimetre	1 dm^2	= 100 cm^2
square centimetre		

VOLUME		
cubic metre	1 m^3	= 1000 dm^3
cubic decimetre	1 dm^3	= 1000 cm^3
cubic centimetre		
kilolitre	1 kl	= 1000 l
litre	1 l	= 1000 ml
millilitre		

MASS		
tonne	1 t	= 1000 kg
kilogram	1 kg	= 1000 g
gram	1 g	= 1000 mg
milligram		

Sicily. See AGIRA.

Sick Heart River. A novel by John Buchan (Lord TWEEDSMUIR), posthumously published in 1941. Of this imaginary river within the Arctic Circle, one of the characters says, 'We have each of us to travel to his own Sick Heart River.' The U.S. title is *Mountain Meadow* (1941).

Sicotte, Louis-Victor (1812-89). Politician. Born in Boucherville, L.C. (Que.), he trained as a lawyer and was elected to the legislative assembly of the PROVINCE OF CANADA in 1851. A reformer, he formed a ministry with John Sandfield MACDONALD in 1862, but resigned the next year and was appointed a judge of the superior court.

Sidbec. A partial acronym for Siderurgie du Québec, an integrated iron-and-steel complex created by the Quebec government in 1964. Four years later Sidbec acquired controlling interest in Dosco (Dominion Steel and Coal Company, with plants in Quebec and Ontario), which it operates as Sidbec-Dosco Ltd.

Sifton, Sir Clifford (1860-1929). Minister of the Interior. Born in London, C.W. (Ont.), he trained as a lawyer and was a member of

the Manitoba legislature from 1888 to 1896, when he entered federal politics, becoming Minister of the Interior under Wilfrid LAURIER. He pursued a vigorous immigration policy (see Men in SHEEPSKIN COATS) in the face of much opposition. Resigning from the ministry in 1905, he organized a revolt over the RECIPROCITY treaty with the United States that helped defeat Laurier's government in 1911. He then left the Liberal Party. In 1917 he was prominent in the formation of the coalition UNION GOVERNMENT to see the country through the First World War. He was owner of the WINNIPEG FREE PRESS, which was edited by John W. DAFOE.

Sifton's Sheepskins. See Men in SHEEPSKIN COATS.

Sigmund Samuel Canadiana Building. Art gallery and archives established in Toronto in 1940 by Sigmund Samuel (1867-1962) and the ROYAL ONTARIO MUSEUM. Dr Samuel's extensive collection of Canadiana—including oil paintings, prints, watercolours, books, and maps—was first housed in a wing of the ROM until 1951, when the Sigmund Samuel Canadiana Building opened. The gallery also houses collections of early Canadian glass, furniture, silver, utensils, ceramics, and pottery.

Signal Hill. Rising 500 ft above the harbour of ST JOHN'S, Nfld, it is a national historic park. It contains the ruins of fortifications, begun in the eighteenth century, called the Queen's Battery. From the crest of Signal Hill, using an aerial flown from a kite, Guglielmo Marconi received the first transatlantic wireless message on 12 Dec. 1901. Included in the 260-acre park is the CABOT MEMORIAL TOWER.

Silent Force, The. A phrase used to describe the ROYAL CANADIAN MOUNTED POLICE. It is the title of a book about the RCMP by T.M. Longstreth published in 1927.

Silk trains. Crack CPR freight trains that crossed the continent from Vancouver to New York, between the First and Second World Wars, loaded with raw silk that came from Japan on the EMPRESS LINE. They travelled at high speeds to deter possible hijackers and to lessen demurrage, so valuable was their cargo.

Silver. A mineral used for a variety of purposes, including coinage, jewelry, photography, and by the electronics industry. In 1971 Canada produced 15% of the world's output. The largest mines are at Timmins, Ont.; Kimberley, B.C.; and in the Mayo District, Y.T.

Silver Dart

Silver Dart. A famous biplane produced by the AERIAL EXPERIMENT ASSOCIATION. Designed and flown by J.A.D. McCURDY at Baddeck, N.S., it carried him nearly half a mile at an elevation of 30 ft on 23 Feb. 1909, marking the first flight of a heavier-than-air machine in the British Empire, six years after the Wright Brothers' test flight at Kitty Hawk. It crashed during a demonstration flight at Petawawa, Ont., on 2 Aug 1909, and was scrapped, though the engine was preserved and is in the National Aviation Museum. A replica of the *Silver Dart,* made for the 50th anniversary of the flight, is displayed in the National Aeronautical Collection.

Silver Jubilee. See JUBILEE.

Silver thaw. On both the east and west coasts, freezing rain that covers all exposed surfaces with glistening ice, or the ice that results from such freezing rain.

Silverheels, Jay (b.1920). Mohawk actor. Born Harry Jay Smith at the Six Nations Reserve near Brantford, Ont., the brother of the potter Elda SMITH, he changed his name to make it 'more Indian-sounding'. He was discovered by Joe E. Brown in 1949 and performed throughout the 1950s on radio and television as Tonto, the 'faithful Indian companion' of the Lone Ranger in the program of that name. He lives in California.

Simard, René (b.1960). Quebec pop singer. Born in Montreal, he has been a popular singer of ballads since he was 13. His recordings of 'Ave Maria' and 'L'Oiseau' have sold more copies than any other Canadian record at any time.

Simard fortune. Industrial wealth controlled by the influential Simard family of Quebec. The basis of the family's fortune is Marine Industries Inc., a 'billion-dollar duchy' devoted to shipbuilding founded at Sorel, Que., by Joseph-Arthur Simard (1888-1963) and his brothers Ludger and Edouard. The latter is the father of Andrée Simard who, in 1958, married Robert Bourassa (b.1933), premier of Quebec since 1970. The Quebec government is the sole owner of General Investment Corporation (GIC), a holding company with 57% of Marine Industries, the remaining 43% being owned by six Simard nieces and nephews, including Andrée and her brother Claude (who is an MLA), through such holding and trust companies as La Compagnie de Charlevoix, Clauremiand Ltée, and Simcor Inc. Provincial and federal revelations of possible conflicts of interest brought the family fortune into prominence in the mid-1970s.

Simcoe, Elizabeth Posthuma (1766-1850). The wife of John Graves SIMCOE, she wrote a famous diary about her stay in Upper Canada (Ontario) from 1792 to 1796. It was first published in 1911 as *The Diary of Mrs John Graves Simcoe,* with illustrations that included reproductions of 90 sketches by Mrs Simcoe. A modern edition edited by Mary Quayle Innis appeared in 1965.

Simcoe, John Graves (1752-1806). The first lieutenant-governor of UPPER CANADA and founder of YORK (Toronto). In 1792 he arrived at NIAGARA (ON-THE-LAKE), which he renamed Newark and which served as the capital of Upper Canada until 1797, when it was transferred to York, which Simcoe founded in 1793. He left Canada in 1796. See also Elizabeth Posthuma SIMCOE.

Simcoe Day. An anniversary marked in Toronto on the statutory holiday called CIVIC HOLIDAY, the first Monday in August. It commemorates the afternoon of 30 July 1793 when John Graves SIMCOE arrived at the site of the future capital of York (later TORONTO). The anniversary was first celebrated in 1861 but was first observed officially in 1968.

Simeon Perkins House. See Simeon PERKINS.

Simon, James (b.1956). Ojibwa artist. Born on the Wikwemikong Reserve, Manitoulin Island, Ont., he started painting at the Indian Art Club of the Manitoulin Secondary School. His canvases treat in a semi-surreal manner the traditional images of his Ojibwa ancestors. His paintings are on permanent display at the McMICHAEL CANADIAN COLLECTION.

Simon Fraser University. Named after the fur trader and overland explorer Simon FRASER, it was created by an act of the British Columbia legislature in 1963 and opened in 1965. It is situated atop the 1,200-ft Burnaby Mountain, east of Vancouver, and is famous for the striking contemporary architecture of its buildings, designed by Arthur ERICKSON and Geoffrey Massey.

Simonds, Lt-Gen. G.G. (1903-74). Army commander. Born in Bury St Edmunds, Eng., he was educated at Ashbury College, Ottawa, and the ROYAL MILITARY COLLEGE. He assumed command of the 1st Canadian Infantry Division—the first to see active service in the Second World War—on 29 Apr. 1943, and continued to command this division in Italy until Nov. 1943, when he became GOC, 5th Canadian Armoured Division, in Italy. In Jan. 1944 he was promoted lieutenant-general to command the 2nd Canadian Corps, which was then in England preparing for the NORMANDY INVASION. He originated the armoured personnel carrier, a turretless tank to carry assaulting infantry, and employed it successfully for the first time in the attack south of CAEN on the night of 7 Aug. 1944. Owing to the illness of Gen. H.D.G. CRERAR, he commanded the First Canadian Army during the Battle of the SCHELDT late in 1944. He was Chief of the General Staff from 1951 to 1955, when he retired.

Simoneau, Léopold (b.1918). Tenor. Born in Quebec city, he made his operatic début in Montreal in *Mignon* and went on to a distinguished international career, singing with the Paris Opéra and Opéra Comique (1949-54), La Scala (1953), Glyndebourne, Salzburg, the Metropolitan Opera, New York (1964), among other companies, and making numerous recordings, including *Così fan tutte* under Karajan, a fine memento of his superlative interpretations of Mozart. He married the coloratura soprano Pierette ALARIE in 1946.

Simpson, Sir George (1787-1860). Governor-in-chief of the HUDSON'S BAY COMPANY territories. Born in Scotland, he joined the Hudson's Bay Company in 1820. He was made governor of the department of RUPERT'S LAND in 1821 and governor-in-chief of all the Company's territories in 1839. An autocratic but efficient administrator—he was called 'the little emperor'—he reorganized the Company and developed its trade to the Pacific coast. He was knighted in 1841. From 1833 he lived at Lachine, L.C. (Que.), where he died.

Simpsons, Limited. Department-store chain. It has grown from the single store that was opened in Toronto in 1872 by the Scots-born draper, Robert Simpson (1834-97). The year following his death the company was acquired by a group of financiers who expanded the operation. It has been in the mail-order business since 1894, when it issued its first catalogue. In 1952 Simpsons, Limited went into partnership with the American firm Sears-Roebuck to create Simpson-Sears, which assumed all the company's mail-order services and now owns and operates 56 retail stores, 4 catalogue centres, and 646 sales offices. In 1976 Simpsons, Limited owned and operated 19 department stores in Toronto (8), Montreal (4), Halifax (2), and one each in Regina, London, Ottawa, Windsor, and Kitchener.

Simpsons-Sears. See SIMPSONS, LIMITED.

Sims Scholarship. See SIR ARTHUR SIMS SCHOLARSHIP.

SIN. Acronym for Social Insurance Number. Every taxpayer is issued his or her individual SIN Number. A nine-digit numbering system (e.g., 111 111 111) has been in use since 1964, when the numbering system used by the Unemployment Insurance Commission began to run out of digits. The SIN system—which is used for unemployment insurance, pensions, income tax, medical plans, etc.—permits 99 million combinations. The first digit identifies one of five regional registration offices (1 is Atlantic region; 2 is Quebec; 4 is Ontario; 6 is Prairies; 7 is Pacific); the final digit is a check number. The seven middle digits have no significance other than to identify a specific number-holder.

Sinclair, George G. (b.1916). Advertising executive. Born in Toronto, the brother of Gordon SINCLAIR, he worked as a reporter on the *Toronto Star* in 1937 and then acted as publicity manager for the DIONNE QUINTUPLETS. After serving with the RCAF, he joined MACLAREN ADVERTISING LIMITED in 1946 and was elected chairman of the board in 1965. As head of the country's largest Canadian agency and past president of the Institute of Canadian Advertising, Sinclair is considered the spokesman for the industry.

Sinclair, Gordon (b.1900). Broadcaster and newspaperman. Born in Toronto, he was nationally known as a brash young roving correspondent and travel writer for the *Toronto Star* from 1923 to 1936 and wrote a number of books for young readers about his adventures. In 1943 he joined CFRB in Toronto and embarked on a new career as a broadcaster, eventually acquiring the largest following for his opinionated 'news and comments', heard daily at 11:45 a.m. and 5:45 p.m. In 1957 he became a controversial CBC-TV personality as one of the original panelists on FRONT PAGE CHALLENGE. He has written two volumes of memoirs, the titles of which allude to a phrase used on an American television show: *Will the Real Gordon Sinclair Please Stand Up?* (1962) and *Will Gordon Sinclair Please Sit Down?* (1975). See also GORDON SINCLAIR AWARD.

Sinclair, Lister (b.1921). CBC producer and playwright. Born in Bombay, India, he graduated from the University of British Columbia in 1942 and taught at the ACADEMY OF RADIO ARTS in Toronto. Something of a polymath, he has written and produced programs for CBC Radio and CBC-TV on a great range of specialized subjects, including the award-winning 'Darwin and the Galapagos', seen on The NATURE OF THINGS on 4 Sept. and 2 Oct. 1966. His original plays include *Socrates* (1957) and *The* BLOOD IS STRONG, (1956). His *A Play on Words and Other Radio Plays* (1948) includes the popular satire *We All Hate Toronto*. He was executive vice-president of the CBC from 1972 to 1974.

Singalong Jubilee. CBC-TV's summer replacement for 'DON MESSER'S JUBILEE'. The Halifax-produced musical-variety show was seen from 1961 to 1974, with singer-instrumentalist Bill Langstroth as host. The program introduced announcer Jim Bennet and singer Anne MURRAY, whom Langstroth later married.

Singing Stars of Tomorrow. A once-popular CBC Radio program. Young Canadian singers under 26 competed each week for an annually awarded prize of a $1,000 musical scholarship. The 60-minute series was broadcast each week before a live audience at the Fairlawn Theatre in Toronto from 1943 to 1956. The orchestra was conducted by Rex BATTLE. It was sponsored by C-I-L.

Siouan. Large linguistic family of Indians extending from the American plains northward into the Saskatchewan and Manitoba Prairies. Siouan-speaking Indians are represented in Canada by the closely related ASSINIBOINE and Dakota Sioux. Their population in 1970 was 6,212.

Sir Arthur Sims Scholarship. Awarded annually by the ROYAL SOCIETY OF CANADA since 1952 to a graduate of a Canadian university who is a British subject and shows outstanding merit and promise in the humanities, social sciences, or natural sciences, it makes possible postgraduate work in Great Britain. The scholarship is awarded for two years and has an annual value of £650.

Sir Galahad. A statue of the brave knight of the Round Table that stands on PARLIAMENT HILL in OTTAWA. It commemorates Henry Albert Harper, a young assistant and friend of W.L. Mackenzie KING who drowned in 1901 in a vain attempt to rescue a little girl who was skating. The romantic statue, sculpted by Ernest Wise Keyser and unveiled in 1905, is a favourite of Ottawans. See also *The* SECRET OF HEROISM.

Sir George Williams University. See CONCORDIA UNIVERSITY.

Sir John A. A familiar reference to Sir John A. MACDONALD.

Sir John A. Macdonald. General title of the standard two-volume biography of Canada's first prime minister by Donald CREIGHTON. The two parts are *The Young Politician* (1952) and *The Old Chieftain* (1955).

Sisters of Charity. See Mère d'YOUVILLE.

Sitka. Tlingit word for 'Alaska', which has lent its name to the Sitka deer, the Sitka grouse, the Sitka spruce, and to the town in Alaska.

Sitka spruce. See MENZIES SPRUCE.

SIU. Initials of the Seafarers International Union. See CANADIAN SEAMEN'S UNION.

Sivuraq, Thomas (b.1941). Eskimo artist at BAKER LAKE. He does massive carvings and is also very productive as a graphic artist and printer.

Siwash. CHINOOK JARGON for a west-coast Indian, derived from the French word *sauvage*. Today it is derogatory slang.

Siwash Rock. Imposing rock in Stanley Park. In *Legends of Vancouver* (1911) Pauline JOHNSON, whose ashes were buried near Siwash Rock, tells the legend of the young Indian who was turned into this rock. See also SIWASH.

'Six Months' Hoist'. A procedure in the HOUSE OF COMMONS for defeating a bill. An amendment may be passed on the second reading of a bill—that it be read 'this day six months'; that is, beyond the probable duration of the session—thus in effect killing it.

Six Nations, League of. See IROQUOIS.

Six Nations Confederacy. See IROQUOIS.

Six Nations Reserve. Also known as the Tuscarora Reserve, it is a 78-sq.-mi. tract on the Grand R. near Brantford, Ont., set aside by the government and settled in 1784 by Joseph BRANT and the Six Nations of the IROQUOIS Confederacy. Its governing centre is at Ohsweken. In 1924 a controversy arose when followers of the hereditary chiefs attempted unsuccessfully to oust Ottawa's elected council. Today its population of 9,500 is administered by the Department of Indian Affairs and Northern Development, although the Six Nations never signed a treaty agreement with the Canadian government.

Sixty-Eight Publishers. A Czech-Canadian publishing house established in Toronto in 1971 by Josef SKVORECKY and his wife Zdena Salivarova. It originates and reprints paperback editions of literary works written in the

Czech language, many subsequently translated and published by other houses around the world, and maintains a Readers' Club of some 5,000 members, 1,500 in Canada. It issued 42 titles in its first five years. Its name commemorates the year of the Soviet occupation of Prague.

Skeena. See GITKSAN.

Skelton, Robin (b.1925). Man-of-letters. Born in Easington, Eng., he was educated at Cambridge and lectured in English at Manchester University until 1963, when he assumed a teaching post at the University of Victoria and founded the Creative Writing Department there. In 1967, with the novelist John Peter, he founded the MALAHAT REVIEW. A scholar of Synge, Yeats, and Ruskin, and an anthologist, he is the author or editor of over 40 books, including numerous collections of his lyrical meditations and love lyrics, which have appeared most recently in *Selected Poems: 1947-1967* (1968) and *Time Light* (1974).

Ski-doo. World-famous motor vehicle that operates on snow. The Ski-doo was invented by the Quebec manufacturer Joseph Armand Bombardier. The notion of devising a little tractor to run on snow came to him in 1926, but it was not until 1959 that the famous Ski-doo (originally called Ski-dog) rolled off his assembly line at Valcourt, near Sherbrooke, Que.

Skookum. CHINOOK JARGON meaning powerful, strong, big, brave. *Skookumchuck* means 'rapids' or 'tides', *skookum tumtum* means 'strong hearted', *skookum wawa* means 'strong talk'.

Skraelings. In Icelandic sagas, the word for 'pygmies'. Of obscure origin, Mercator added it to his map of the unexplored northern regions in 1569. It has been suggested that the Skraelings were early Eskimos of the DORSET culture.

Skvorecky, Josef (b.1924). Novelist. Born in Nachod, Czech., he graduated from Charles University, Prague, in 1951. He was a leading translator of American novels into the Czech language and the editor of the magazine *World Literature* when he fell into official disfavour in 1958 two weeks after the publication and subsequent banning of the Czech edition of his novel *The Cowards*, which deals frankly with disaffection among Czech youth. With his wife, the novelist Zdena Salivarova, he escaped during the Soviet occupation of Prague in the summer of 1968 and settled in Toronto. A professor of English at the University of Toronto, he is the author of the following novels: *The Cowards* (1970), translated by Jeanne Nemcova; *The Mournful Demeanour of Lieutenant Boruvka* (1973), translated by Rosemary Kavan, Kaca Polackova, and George Thiner; and *Miss Silver's Past* (1974), translated by Peter Kussi. A former scriptwriter, he chronicled the rise of Czech film-making in *All the Bright Young Men and Women* (1971), translated by Michael Schonberg. With his wife he founded SIXTY-EIGHT PUBLISHERS in Toronto to issue Czech-language books.

Sky pilot. In the West, a colloquial name for a travelling missionary. A clergyman is the hero of Ralph CONNOR's novel *The Sky Pilot: A Tale of the Foothills* (1898), an emotional and dramatic tale set in a foothills town of the West in the 1880s and 1890s and dealing with the conflicts that arise from the primitive, untamed qualities of the land versus encroaching civilization, progress, and morality.

S/L. Official abbreviation of Squadron Leader.

Slade, Bernard (Bernie) (b.1930). Born in St Catharines, Ont., and raised in England, he first acted with a London repertory company in 1948. The following year he returned to Canada, where he played in summer stock. In 1953 he married the actress Jill Foster, who starred in his stage play *Simon Says Get Married*, which opened at the CREST THEATRE on 8 Dec. 1961. Slade's light comedies, commissioned by CBC-TV for GM PRESENTS and FESTIVAL, were resold to the major American television networks. In 1964 Slade settled in Brentwood, Calif., as the story editor of 'Bewitched'. He is responsible for such television series as 'The Flying Nun', 'The Partridge Family', and 'Bridget Loves Bernie'. His amusing two-character sex comedy, *Same Time, Next Year*, opened on Broadway in Apr. 1975 to land-office business.

Slave. A group of ATHAPASKAN-speaking Indians who were given this nickname by the more aggressive CREE. They lived at the west end of Great Slave Lake and moved down the Mackenzie R. Mainly forest hunters, they seldom ventured into the tundra for caribou. Their population in 1970 was 3,334.

Slave River. A short but important link in the MACKENZIE RIVER drainage system. Only 258 mi. long, it connects Lake Athabasca (and thus the Peace and Athabasca Rivers) to Great Slave Lake, from which flows the Mackenzie.

Sleeping Giant

Sleeping Giant. A rocky promontory of land on Lake Superior visible from THUNDER BAY, Ont. Its profile resembles a reclining man with his hands folded on his chest; the Ojibwa thought it was once their creator-magician NANABOZHO. Called variously Sleeping Indian or Giant's Tomb, the promontory is 1,000 ft high and 7 mi. long and lies 18 mi. offshore. It was described by Sir Richard Bonnycastle in 1841 as 'very like an enormous grave . . . as wild as imagination can picture it'.

Slick, Sam. See SAM SLICK.

Slough. On the Prairies, a pothole or pond; on the west coast, a marsh. In western Canada it is pronounced 'slu'. In eastern Canada, when used at all, it is pronounced 'slau' and means 'marsh'.

SLPC. See SOCIALIST LABOUR PARTY OF CANADA.

SLt. Official abbreviation of Sub-Lieutenant.

Small, Ambrose (1867-1919?). Famous missing person. Born at Bradford, Ont., he was the millionaire owner of a chain of theatres across Canada when, on 2 Dec. 1919, he disappeared from downtown Toronto and was never seen again. Although presumed murdered for reasons unknown, Small's disappearance has always puzzled the police and the public.

Smallwood, Joseph Roberts (b.1900). Former premier of Newfoundland and 'the only living father of Confederation'. Born in St John's, Nfld, and educated there and in New York, he took up a career in journalism. In 1946 he was elected to a national convention to debate the issue of Newfoundland's joining Canada, and 'Joey' Smallwood emerged as the leading advocate of union. The day after Newfoundland entered Confederation, which occurred on 31 Mar. 1949, he was appointed premier and led the provincial Liberal Party to power in the elections of 1951, 1956, 1959, 1962, 1966, and 1969. Finally defeated in 1971, he resigned as premier and retired as leader of the party in 1972. In 1974 he stood for re-election as party leader, and when he did not win formed the Liberal Reform Party in 1975, which contested the election that year, winning four seats. He edited *The Book of Newfoundland* (2 vols, 1937; 2 vols, 1967) and wrote his lively memoirs, *I Chose Canada* (1973).

Smeaton, J. Cooper (b.1890). Hockey referee. Born in Carleton Place, Ont., he moved to Montreal where he starred in amateur baseball, football, basketball, and hockey.

After the First World War he became the NHL's referee-in-chief and in 1946 was appointed a STANLEY CUP trustee.

Smiles 'n Chuckles. Brand name of a variety of chocolates, manufactured in Kitchener, Ont. since the 1930s. It was taken over by LAURA SECORD CANDY SHOPS LTD in 1964.

Smith, A.J.M. (b.1902). Poet, critic, anthologist. Born in Montreal and educated at McGill and the University of Edinburgh, he taught English at Michigan State University from 1936 until his retirement in 1972. While a student at McGill he founded with F.R. SCOTT the McGILL FORTNIGHTLY REVIEW (1925-7). An accomplished lyric poet whose work embraces a wide variety of themes and styles with subtlety, elegance, and wit, he has had a salutary influence on the appreciation of Canadian poetry through his application of discriminating and cosmopolitan standards in a long career of writing criticism and producing important anthologies. His poems have been collected in *News of the Phoenix* (1943), *A Sort of Ecstasy* (1954), *Collected Poems* (1962), and *Poems: New and Collected* (1967). His most notable poetry anthologies are *A Book of Canadian Poetry* (1943; rev. 1948, 1957), *The Oxford Book of Canadian Verse* (1960), and *Modern Canadian Verse* (1967). The first volume of *The Book of Canadian Prose* appeared in 1965. In 1973 it and its companion volume appeared as *The Book of Canadian Prose: Volume I, English-Canadian Writing Before Confederation* and *The Canadian Century: English-Canadian Writing Since Confederation* and in a one-volume abridgement: *The Canadian Experience: A Brief Survey of Canadian Prose*. With F.R. Scott he co-edited *New Provinces: Poems by Several Authors* (1936, 1976) and the well-known anthology of satirical verse, *The BLASTED PINE* (1957; rev. 1967). Smith's *Towards a View of Canadian Letters: Selected Critical Essays 1928-1971* appeared in 1973.

Smith, Cedric. See The PERTH COUNTY CONSPIRACY and TEN LOST YEARS.

Smith, Donald A. (1820-1914). Financier, politician, diplomat. Born in Scotland, he joined the HUDSON'S BAY COMPANY in 1838 and rose steadily in its ranks, becoming land commissioner in 1874. He was a member of Parliament from 1871 to 1880 and from 1887 to 1896. The possessor of a fortune, acquired partly through railway investments, he rescued the CPR from financial collapse and in 1885 was given the honour of driving in the LAST SPIKE. He was president of the Bank of Montreal in 1882 and 1887. On his retirement from politics in 1896 he was made high com-

490

missioner to Great Britain, an appointment he held until 1913. Knighted in 1886, he was raised to the peerage as Baron Strathcona and Mount Royal in 1897. Around 1880 he built one of the most impressive mansions in Montreal, at 1157 Dorchester Blvd; it was demolished in 1941.

Smith, Eden (1858-1949). Architect. He was born in England and trained in several English architectural offices before immigrating to Manitoba in 1885 and settling in Toronto in 1888 to practise. He designed over 2,000 medium- and small-sized houses, which showed the emphasis on craftsmanship and form of the English architecture of the Arts and Crafts Movement. Among his finest houses are 32 Clarendon Ave (*c*.1915). He also designed three Toronto churches: St John's Portland St (1892, demolished), St Thomas's Huron St (1892), and Grace Church on the Hill (*c*.1912), in which the Gothic forms of English country churches are used as the complement to Smith's concept of domestic architecture. The Bain Ave and Spruce Court Apartments (1914), built as low-cost housing for the Toronto Housing Company, represent a pioneering attempt to bring the comfort and attractive environment of middle-class housing to the working classes. The STUDIO BUILDING, designed at the same time (1913) for Lawren HARRIS, is equally innovative in its straightforward, unornamented approach to studio housing.

Smith, Elda (b.1919). Mohawk ceramist. Born on the SIX NATIONS RESERVE near Brantford, Ont., she augmented her schoolteacher husband's income by making and selling beaded bags, leather jackets, etc. In 1961 she turned to ceramics and set up her own Mohawk Pottery at Hagersville, Ont., where she bases her work on ancient Iroquois designs and colours. She signs her work 'E.M.S.' She is the sister of Jay SILVERHEELS.

Smith, Goldwin (1823-1910). Born in Reading, Eng., and educated at Eton and Oxford, he became a well-known English intellectual. He was professor of history at Oxford from 1846 to 1866 and taught at Cornell University from 1868 to 1870. He settled in Toronto in 1871 and involved himself in the CANADA FIRST movement, but eventually repudiated it to support the unpopular idea of Canada's political and economic union with the United States. A prolific journalist (who signed his articles 'A Bystander') and a famous stylist, he was the author of many books on a variety of subjects. His impact was felt through the publications he was associated with: the BYSTANDER, the WEEK, and the farmer's newspa-

per the *Weekly Sun*. In 1875 he married the widow of Henry Boulton, owner of the GRANGE, Toronto.

Smith, John Ivor (b.1927). Sculptor. Born in London, Eng., he moved to Canada in 1940 and was educated at McGill University and the School of Art and Design in the Montreal Museum of Fine Arts. A self-taught sculptor, he has won numerous awards and is represented in many Canadian collections. Two of his commissions for Expo 67 are still on the site at MAN AND HIS WORLD. He was made head of the sculpture department at Sir George Williams (Concordia) University in 1966.

Smith, Levi (b.1927). Eskimo sculptor at POVUNGNITUK, well known for his fantastic mythological subjects.

Smith, Lillian H. See BOYS AND GIRLS HOUSE.

Smith, Lois (b.1929). Dancer. Born in Vancouver, B.C., she was a pupil of McBirney and Loring and also studied at the Royal Ballet School, London. She toured North America in *Song of Norway* in 1946. She joined the NATIONAL BALLET OF CANADA in 1951, was prima ballerina from 1956 to 1969, and was awarded the Centennial Medal in 1967. She danced in the film of *Swan Lake* (1967) with Erik BRUHN and the National. She now runs the Lois Smith School of Dance in Toronto.

Smith, Willian W. See SASKATCHEWAN.

Smyth, Coke (1808-82). Artist. John Richard Coke Smyth was drawing master in the household of Lord DURHAM. While he was in Upper and Lower Canada in 1838 he produced 23 picturesque lithographs of Canadian scenes—including Niagara Falls, Montreal, and Quebec—that were published in book form as *Sketches in the Canadas* (1840).

Smyth, Hervey (1734-1811). British officer-artist. An aide-de-camp to Gen. James WOLFE, he executed a series of sketches that were engraved and published in 1760 by Thomas Jefferys, London, as *Six Views of the Most Remarkable Places of the Gulf and River St Lawrence*. The best-known engraving is probably *A View of the Fall of Montmorency*, showing the unsuccessful British attack of 31 July 1759.

Smythe, Conn (b.1895). All-round sportsman. The Toronto-born athlete, coach, manager, financier, horseowner and breeder, and philanthropist is particularly identified with MAPLE LEAF GARDENS, which he founded and built in 1931. In the Second World War he assembled the Sportsman's Battery and led them in Europe, where he was wounded. He was a founder of the Hockey HALL OF FAME of which he has been a member since 1958. He is an active promoter of the Ontario Society for Crippled Children. See also CONN SMYTHE TROPHY.

Sniderman, Sam. See SAM THE RECORD MAN.

Snorri Thorfinnsson. See Snorri THORFINNS- SON.

Snow, A few acres of. See QUELQUES ARPENTS DE NEIGE.

Snow, Hank (b.1917). Country-and-western singer and composer. Born in Nova Scotia, he has been one of the biggest names in country music since 1936 when he recorded his hit tune 'I'm Movin' On'. Since 1950 he has reigned over the Grand Ole Opry in Nashville, Tenn. It has been estimated that Snow has recorded over 1,600 songs and sold over 66 million records.

Snow, Michael (b.1929). Painter and film- maker. Born in Toronto, he studied at the Ontario College of Art and lived in New York from 1962 to 1971. An innovative artist in several media, including music (he is a jazz pianist and trumpeter), he turned from for- mal abstract painting to minimal painting in 1961 with a long series of inventive and witty variations of the silhouetted WALKING WOMAN figure, which dominated his work until 1967. He achieved international recognition with his experimental films, notably *New York Eye and Ear Control* (1964, 35 min.), WAVELENGTH (1966), *Back and Forth* (1968-9, 55 min.), *La Région centrale* (1970-1, 3 hrs), and *Rameau's Nephew* (1975, 4 hrs. 30 min.). In 1976 the Museum of Modern Art, New York, had a five-week retrospective of his films with an exhibition of his photographs. He lives in Toronto with his wife Joyce WIELAND.

Snow apple. A late fall apple, native to Can- ada, having a deep-red skin or red stripes. The name derives from the apple's bright white granulated flesh. In French it is known as *Pomme de neige* or *Fameuse*. For many years it was the staple of the Quebec apple in- dustry.

Snow glasses. See EEGAK.

'Snowbird'. A popular song written by Gene MacLELLAN in 1970. This country ballad conso- lidated MacLellan's status and launched the career of its singer, Anne MURRAY.

Snows, Our Lady of the. See OUR LADY OF THE SNOWS.

Snowshoe. Footgear used for walking on deep snow. It is a light, wooden, usually oval frame, strung with leather strips and strengthened by crossbars. The French word for snowshoe is *raquette*, alternatively spelled *racquette*.

Snowshoe hare. A medium-sized member of the rabbit family averaging 3-5 lb. in weight. The most important small game mammal in Canada, it is found throughout the forest, prairie, and tundra regions. In winter its rusty- or greyish-brown summer coat turns white.

Snye. A channel that bypasses a falls or rapids, or the sluggish tributary of a river. It derives from the French for 'channel', *chenal*.

So Little for the Mind. A book subtitled *An Indictment of Canadian Education* and written by the historian Hilda NEATBY that created a sensation when it was published in 1953 for its castigation of the 'anti-intellectual' and 'anti-cultural' trends in Canadian education that were leading to mediocrity and very lit- tle training and discipline of the mind.

Soapstone. A soft stone, grey or greenish grey in colour, the use of which is limited to Eskimo craftsmen who employ it for soap- stone carvings and engraving plates for prints. The coarse, heavy, easily worked stone is a variety of talc rock, known as stea- tite, and has a smooth 'soapy' feel. The pop- ular name 'soapstone' derives from the fact that, on occasion, the softer varieties have been used as soap.

Social Credit. A monetary theory involving the redistribution of purchasing power; pro- vincial and federal parties holding this theory. The Social Credit scheme was devel- oped in the 1920s by Maj. C.H. Douglas, an English engineer. Simplified for use in Al- berta by William ABERHART, it seemed a pan- acea that could resolve the problems of the DEPRESSION. Aberhart formed the Social Credit Party and swept to power in Alberta in 1935. He retained power to his death in 1944, and his successor Ernest Manning won every election until he stepped down in 1968. Under Harry Strom, however, Social Credit lost to the Conservatives in 1971.

In neighbouring British Columbia, W.A.C. BENNETT led a coalition of 'outs' into power under the Social Credit label in 1952 and re- tained office for 20 years. His son, Bill Ben- nett, returned the party to power in 1975.

None of these leaders practised the undi- luted economic principles of Maj. Douglas; nor did the federal Social Creditors, who had limited success in Alberta and Quebec and held the balance of power in the minority governments between 1962 and 1968. By the end of the 1960s only the Quebec Créditistes held seats in Parliament, mostly because of the charisma of party leader Réal CAOUETTE and careful fence-mending in economically depressed constituencies.

Social Democratic Party of Canada. A political group founded in Winnipeg in 1910 to organize workers into a political party and transform private property into collective property. The SDPC joined the International Socialist Bureau. Many members joined the COMMUNIST PARTY OF CANADA when it was formed in 1921.

Social Insurance Number. See SIN.

Social Planning for Canada. Influential book written by the Research Committee of the LEAGUE FOR SOCIAL RECONSTRUCTION. Published in the autumn of 1932, it constituted a thoroughgoing critique of Canada along socialist and reformist lines. It was the 'pooled product' of Eugene FORSEY, J. King Gordon, Leonard Marsh, J.F. Parkinson, F.R. SCOTT, Graham SPRY, and F.H. UNDERHILL. The foreword was written by J.S. WOODSWORTH. The first half surveyed and analysed the social, economic, resource, and manufacturing climate of Canada; the second half explained in Canadian terms 'what Socialist Planning really means'. It had a marked influence on the REGINA MANIFESTO and has been influencial in leftist and left-liberal thought to this day. It was reissued with a new preface in 1975.

Social Science Research Council of Canada. An advisory association that promotes the interests of the social sciences in Canada. It was founded in 1940 and reorganized in 1969 as a federation of LEARNED SOCIETIES. The Council is made up of representatives of nine learned societies and 15 members-at-large from government and universities. See also its parallel organization, the HUMANITIES RESEARCH COUNCIL OF CANADA.

Socialist Labour Party of Canada. Political party devoted to the Marxist-De Leonist program. As early as 1904 it ran four candidates in the Ontario provincial election. Its program was identical with that of the Socialist Labour Party of America—founded in 1890—to which it was linked organizationally while it developed as a national party in Canada. Owing to political problems and witch hunting in the early years of the Second World War, it became an autonomous organization

in 1940. Its program still resembles that of the American party.

Société nationale des Acadiens. An association to represent all the ACADIANS, not only those in the Maritimes but also those scattered across the rest of Canada and the United States. It was formed in Moncton, N.B., in 1955 and has been especially active in the 1970s.

Société Radio-Canada. French name of the CANADIAN BROADCASTING CORPORATION.

Société Saint-Jean-Baptiste. There are two independent organizations named after St John the Baptist, the patron saint of Quebec and of Canada, both of which promote the culture of French Canadians. La Société Saint-Jean-Baptiste de Montréal was founded in that city in 1834; it involves itself in banking, insurance, and charitable activities, and makes the following annual awards for achievement: Prix de Musique Calixa-LAVALLÉE; PRIX DUVERNAY; Prix de Journalisme Olivar-Asselin; Prix des Arts Plastiques Philippe-HÉBERT; Prix de Théatre Victor-Morin. La Société Saint-Jean-Baptiste de Québec, founded in Quebec City in 1843, concerns itself mainly with promoting the traditions and language of French Canadians by extending aid to students, etc. See also SAINT-JEAN-BAPTISTE.

Society of Canadian Artists. Founded in Toronto in 1957 as the Society of Co-operative Artists, it offered younger artists, often those rejected by the ONTARIO SOCIETY OF ARTISTS and other older associations, an exhibition gallery and opportunity to exhibit. Its name was changed in 1967 to reflect the society's attempt to exhibit nationally and internationally. A year later members' open-juried exhibitions began, together with the annual Open-Juried SCA Show. It has exhibited its 100 member artists across Canada; in Florence, Italy; and in Honolulu, Hawaii. From 1969 to 1973 it published *Art* magazine. The gallery and the Open-Juried Show were discontinued in 1968 and 1973 respectively.

Sockeye salmon. A species of Pacific fish that ranges from Alaska to Japan and is plentiful in the Fraser R., B.C. The name is said to derive from the COAST SALISH word for 'red fish'. Among the Northwest Coast Indians, only the Coast Salish STRAIT harvested the Fraser R. sockeye salmon, using a technique called reef netting.

Socred. A member of the SOCIAL CREDIT Party. See also CRÉDITISTE.

Sod hut

Sod hut. A crude dwelling of turf, raised by prairie settlers in the late-nineteenth and early-twentieth centuries as temporary living quarters.

Soddy, Frederick. See MACDONALD PHYSICS LABORATORY.

Soeurs Grises, Les. See Mère d'YOUVILLE.

Soft sawder. Sweet talk or blarney, associated with the fast-talking Yankee pedlar SAM SLICK, created by Thomas Chandler HALIBURTON.

Soirées Canadiennes, Les. A journal of Quebec writing published in Quebec City from 1861 to 1865. It was founded by Abbé H.-R. Casgrain and others as an outlet for Quebec authors willing to popularize legends, historical incidents, and other subjects of French-Canadian interest. Two related periodicals are *Le Foyer Canadien* (1863-6) and *Les Nouvelles Soirées Canadiennes* (1882-8).

Solemn Land, The. Famous painting by J.E.H. MacDONALD of the Montreal R. in the Algoma district of northern Ontario. It depicts a monumental landscape of simplified forms—rocky headlands, a rounded sunlit cliff plunging into a lake, and heavy clouds pressing down over all. (1921, NGC)

Solicitor General, Department of the. Government department concerned with correction and law enforcement. The present department was created in 1966, when the Solicitor General was given the rank of cabinet minister. The Solicitor General is responsible for the ROYAL CANADIAN MOUNTED POLICE and the Canadian Penitentiary Service, and he reports to Parliament for the NATIONAL PAROLE BOARD.

Solomon Grundy. Fillet of salt herring, marinated in vinegar, onions, and sugar. It is popular in Nova Scotia. The name, that of a nursery rhyme, obtained currency as a playful version of *salmagundi*, a mixed dish of chopped meat, eggs, onions, etc.

Solway, Larry (b.1928). Broadcaster and interviewer. The Toronto-born former journalist and radio writer gained notoriety in Nov. 1971 when, on *Speak Your Mind*—the popular hot-line show he hosted on CHUM in Toronto from 1966—he tried to talk openly about sex. He wrote *The Day I Invented Sex* (1971) about the experience. He now conducts the syndicated *Larry Solway Show*, a television interview series.

Some Hon. Members. A CBC-TV series of interviews or discussions with backbench or frontbench MPs. The weekly half-hour current-affairs program was moderated by Patrick WATSON and produced by Cameron Graham in Ottawa. It had its première on 23 Oct. 1973 and ended on 7 May 1974.

Somers, Harry (b.1925). Composer. Born in Toronto, he studied piano and composition at the Royal Conservatory, Toronto, and with Darius Milhaud in Paris. His music shows diverse influences, including baroque, contemporary, and electronic. He has composed for orchestra, chamber groups, solo and choral voice, and solo instruments. His best-known work is the opera LOUIS RIEL (1967), which has been performed to acclaim in two seasons of the Canadian Opera Company and uses folk material, atonal writing, diatonic writing, and combinations of these—sometimes with electronic sounds. His numerous commissions include pieces for the Toronto Symphony Orchestra (*Stereophony*, 1963), the National Ballet of Canada (*The House of Atreus*, 1963), the Hungarian String Quartet (*String Quartet No 3*, 1959), and the Koussevitsky Foundation (*Lyric for Orchestra*, 1960). *Harry Somers* (1975) by Brian Cherney is so far the only book on a Canadian composer.

Somerville, C. Ross (Sandy) (b.1903). Champion golfer. Born in London, Ont., he excelled in his school years in cricket, hockey, athletics, and rugby football. Achieving particular success in golf, he not only won many Canadian titles but also, in 1932, captured the United States amateur golf championship. In 1950 he was named 'Canada's best golfer of the last half-century'.

'Something to Sing About'. A popular patriotic song by Oscar BRAND. Written for a Bell Canada television special in 1963, the refrain runs: 'From the Vancouver Island to the Alberta Highland,/'Cross the prairie, the lakes, to Ontario's towers./From the sound of Mount Royal's chimes out to the Maritimes,/Something to sing about, this land of ours.' See also THIS LAND IS YOUR LAND.

Somme, The. River in northern France, the scene of many bloody battles during the FIRST WORLD WAR. See ANCRE HEIGHTS, COURCELETTE.

Sonar. Acronym of SOund NAvigation Ranging, the American name for ASDIC.

'Song for Canada'. A patriotic song with words by Peter GZOWSKI and music by Ian TYSON, written in 1965. The refrain runs: 'Just one great river always flowing to the sea,/One single river rolling in eternity;/Two nations in the land that lies along each shore,/But just one river rolling free.'

'Song My Paddle Sings, The'. Poem by Pauline JOHNSON. It appeared in her second book, *The White Wampum* (1895), is frequently reprinted, and rythmically celebrates the sights and sounds of nature associated with a journey by canoe down an unnamed northern river.

Songs of the Great Dominion. Widely read anthology of Canadian poetry of a nationalistic nature. It was compiled for a British publisher by William Douw Lighthall (1857-1954) and published in 1889 with the subtitle *Voices from the Forests and Waters, the Settlements and Cities of Canada.* The poems were arranged in nine sections: 'The Imperial Spirit', 'The New Nationality', 'The Indian', 'The Voyageur and Habitant', 'Settlement Life', 'Sports and Free Life', 'The Spirit of Canadian History', 'Places', and 'Seasons'.

Sono Nis Press. Small poetry-publishing house founded in Vancouver in 1968 by J. Michael YATES. It derives its name (Spanish for 'sound' and 'nothing') from that of a character in Yates's *Man in the Glass Octopus* (1968). Many of the press's books are examples of what one critic has called 'West Coast Surrealism'.

Sons of Freedom. See DOUKHOBORS.

Sons of Liberty. See FILS DE LA LIBERTÉ.

Soo, The. A phonetic abbreviation of Sault Ste Marie, Ont.

Soucy, Elzéar (1876-1970). Sculptor. Beginning as a woodcarver's apprentice at the age of 16, he sculpted both woodcarvings of religious subjects and bronze commemorative statues. His best-known pieces are the Sir George-Étienne CARTIER monument on Fletcher's Field (1919) and the Westmount War Memorial (1926), both in Montreal.

Sourdough. A fermented bread dough, popular in the days of the KLONDIKE GOLD RUSH. Starter-dough was saved from a previous baking in order to avoid the need for fresh yeast. Before the Gold Rush of 1898 experienced prospectors called themselves sourdoughs and the newcomers cheechakos.

Sourdough City. Unofficial sobriquet of Whitehorse, capital of the YUKON TERRITORY. See also SOURDOUGH.

Souster, Raymond (b.1921). Poet. Born and educated in Toronto, where he works for the Canadian Imperial Bank of Commerce, he has been writing poetry for some 30 years, mainly about life in Toronto, about which he writes unpretentious, colloquial lyrics ex-

pressing joy, nostalgia, and sometimes anger. He has published more than 20 collections of verse, the best known of which are *The Colour of the Times* (1964), *As Is* (1967), and *Selected Poems* (1972). His most recent collections are *Rain-Check* (1975) and *Change-Up* (1976). The author of two novels—*The Winter of Time* (1949) and *On Target* (1973)—he has edited such anthologies as *Poets 56* (1956), *New Wave Canada* (1966), and *Made in Canada* (1970), with Douglas Lochhead. He has also edited a number of 'little magazines', including *Contact* (1952-4) and *Combustion* (1957-60). He helped found CONTACT PRESS (1952-66), an important co-operative publishing venture, with Louis DUDEK and Irving LAYTON, whose poems appeared with his in *Cerberus* (1952). Souster was the prime mover of the LEAGUE OF CANADIAN POETS, established in 1966.

South African War. War between the British and the Boers in South Africa, 1899-1902. Canada (and other members of the British Empire) participated in the South African (or Boer) War by raising, equipping, and sending a force of 1,000 volunteers to Cape Town. The Royal Canadian Regiment, under Lt-Col. W.D. OTTER, fought the Battle of Paardeberg on 18-26 Feb. 1900 and the Battle of Leliefontain on 7 Nov. 1900.

South Beveland. See Battle of the SCHELDT.

South of the border. South of the Canadian-American border. The periphrastic expression refers to the UNITED STATES, which is situated geographically below the FORTY-NINTH PARALLEL.

South Shore. The south shore of the St Lawrence R. and Gulf of St Lawrence; the southeast shore of the Nova Scotia peninsula, from Halifax to Yarmouth.

Southam Fellowships for Journalists. Five annual fellowships to working journalists under 40 years of age. They have been awarded annually on the basis of professional competence by SOUTHAM PRESS since 1962. Each recipient is given a year's leave of absence to study as a fellow-at-large at the University of Toronto in a program of his or her own choosing. Each fellowship pays the equivalent of $18,000 plus tuition and expenses.

Southam Press Limited. A chain of newspapers, business publications, and printing companies. It was founded in 1877 when William Southam (1843-1932) acquired a half-interest in the *Hamilton Spectator* and was expanded by him and his six sons. There

495

Southam Press Limited

were major reorganizations in 1927 and again in 1964 when the company acquired its present name. In 1976 it published 17 newspapers and 101 business and related publications. It has a half-interest in the CANADIAN MAGAZINE. The newspapers in the chain are: *Brantford Expositor, Burlington Gazette,* CALGARY HERALD, EDMONTON JOURNAL, FINANCIAL TIMES, *Hamilton Spectator, Medicine Hat News,* MONTREAL GAZETTE, *North Bay Nugget,* OTTAWA CITIZEN, *Owen Sound Sun-Times, Pointe Claire News and Chronicle, Prince George Citizen, Sault Ste Marie Star,* VANCOUVER PROVINCE, *Windsor Star,* and WINNIPEG TRIBUNE.

Southerly point, The most. Middle Island in Lake Erie, Ont., 41° 41' N—the same latitude as Rome. See also POINT PELEE.

Sovereign. See MONARCHY.

Spaced-Out Library. The world's largest collection of 'imaginative literature'. It was established by the science-fiction author and anthologist Judith MERRIL at ROCHDALE COLLEGE in 1969 and the following year was acquired by the Toronto Public Library. It opened on 6 Apr. 1971 as a separate branch. It now consists of 15,000 items covering in depth such areas as science-fiction, speculative fantasy, and innovative and imaginative writing. The Spaced-Out Library subscribes to 60 specialized periodicals, and includes special collections devoted to futurology and Jules Verne.

Spacemaster. The name of CP Air's jetliner. Its first Douglas DC8-63 was delivered for use on 18 Jan. 1968.

Spanish Civil War. See the MACKENZIE-PAPINEAU BATTALION.

Sparshott, Francis (b.1926). Poet and philosopher. Born in Chatham, Eng., and educated at Oxford University, he has lectured in philosophy at Victoria College, University of Toronto, since 1950. An elegant clarity and a donnish wit enhance both his poetry, collected in *A Divided Voice* (1965) and *A Cardboard Garage* (1969), and his philosophical works, which include *An Enquiry into Goodness* (1958) and *The Concept of Criticism* (1967) and for which he uses his initials: F. E. Sparshott.

'Speak White'. A poem by Michèle LALONDE. Copies were distributed by French students who protested English instruction at McGill University in Montreal in Feb. 1969. Associated with the American race issue, the phrase 'speak white', when used by Québécois, implies the identification of the French with the Blacks. The poem appears in both French and English in *How Do I Love Thee* (1970), edited by John Robert Colombo.

Speaker. Title of the Speaker of the House of Commons or the Senate. The Speaker of the Senate is appointed by the GOVERNOR GENERAL. The Speaker of the HOUSE OF COMMONS is elected by the members at the beginning of each newly elected Parliament to act as its presiding officer and conduct its business. By tradition the Speaker is unwilling to assume his post and must be 'assisted' into the chamber by the Prime Minister at the opening of a new Parliament. The formal style of address is 'sir' or 'madam', the informal 'Mr (Madam) Speaker'.

Special status. Political and social term for the demand of Quebec not to be treated like the other provinces but to be granted 'special status'. This demand is associated with the premiership of Jean LESAGE (1960-6).

Speech from the Throne. Formal address delivered by the GOVERNOR GENERAL on behalf of the Queen in the Senate chamber to both Houses of Parliament (or by the Queen if she happens to be in Canada). The Speech from the Throne is written by the government and states those measures it proposes to put before Parliament in the coming session. A provincial legislature is opened by a Speech from the Throne read by the LIEUTENANT-GOVERNOR.

Speers, James (1882-1955). Race-horse breeder. Born in Ontario, he built his own race track at St Boniface, Man., in 1923, and the Polo Park Track in Winnipeg the following year. He introduced pari-mutuel betting to Canada and, in 1931, the daily-double system to North America. He developed a racing empire of his own, becoming the country's leading breeder of race horses in St Boniface.

Spell of the Yukon, The. A collection of ballads by Robert W. SERVICE, published in 1907. The poems celebrate life in the YUKON during the KLONDIKE GOLD RUSH of the 1890s.

Spence Commission. See MUNSINGER CASE.

Spencer Inquiry. It came to light on 2 Nov. 1965 that George Victor Spencer, a Vancouver postal clerk dying of cancer, had been fired for supplying the Soviet Embassy in Ottawa with non-classified information (such as tombstone inscriptions, useful in the preparation of false documents). Spencer was concerned with the loss of his pension rights and it appeared that the government was persecuting an innocent man. An inquiry was ordered when the incident became a national issue. Spencer's death was reported on 10 Apr. 1966 before the Commission of Inquiry under Mr Justice D.C. Wells could table its report. It established that, although Spencer had committed no offences under the Official Secrets Act, he had acted in a manner incompatible with his loyalty oath as a civil servant.

Spitsbergen. Island in the Arctic Ocean belonging to Norway, the scene of a bloodless expedition during the Second World War. A small Canadian-British naval force sailed there in the autumn of 1941 to destroy wireless and meterological stations and coal-mining facilities lest they fall into German hands.

Splendid isolation. An expression of British Empire solidarity. This once-popular phrase was first heard in the House of Commons on 16 Jan. 1896 when Sir George E. Foster, the Conservative finance minister, explained that 'the great mother Empire stands splendidly isolated in Europe'. The phrase echoed throughout the Empire.

Spohr, Arnold (b.1929). Dancer and choreographer. Born in Rhein, Sask., he studied dance in London, Eng., receiving the advanced certificate with Solo Seal of the Royal Academy of Dancing, and in New York and Hollywood. He joined the Winnipeg Ballet in 1947 and was its leading male dancer until 1954, dancing a large repertoire, including his own ballets *Ballet Premier* and *Intermede* in 1951. A choreographer and dancer for CBC television, he also partnered Alicia Márkova in *Where the Rainbow Ends* in London in 1956-7. He was appointed Artistic Director of the ROYAL WINNIPEG BALLET in 1958.

Sport Canada. Part of a national sports policy and program established by the Department of National Health and Welfare in Mar. 1970, the other part being Recreation Canada. Sport Canada exists to encourage competitive excellence in sports, Recreation Canada to encourage mass participation. Sport Canada supports the SPORTS FEDERATION OF CANADA and such special projects as the ARCTIC WINTER GAMES, the CANADA GAMES, and the Canada Fitness Award.

Sports Federation of Canada. An association of some 100 nationally organized sport and recreation bodies, originally established as the Canadian Sports Advisory Council in 1951. It acquired its present name and constitution in 1972 and promotes participation in amateur sport and acts as a liaison with government agencies, including SPORT CANADA, its source of subsidy. The Sports Federation

of Canada offers five prizes on an annual basis: The Norton H. Crow Memorial Trophy (for the most outstanding male athlete of the year); the Velma Springstead Memorial Trophy (for the most outstanding female athlete of the year); the Elaine TANNER Trophy (for the most outstanding junior [under 20] female athlete of the year); the Viscount Alexander Trophy (for the most outstanding junior [under 20] male athlete of the year); and the Tom LONGBOAT Memorial Trophy (for the outstanding Indian of the year who, besides athletic achievement, has contributed to the betterment of his people).

Sports Hall of Fame. See HALLS OF FAME.

Spring Thaw. A long-running annual revue of topical satire and music. Named by Andrew ALLAN and launched by the NEW PLAY SOCIETY in Toronto on 1 Apr. 1948, it has featured such performers as Dave BROADFOOT, Robert GOULET, Barbara HAMILTON, Don HARRON, Budd Knapp, Jane MALLETT, Peter Mews, and Drew Thompson. For the 1952 edition Harron created CHARLIE FARQUARSON and Broadfoot the Senator for Kicking Horse Pass. Hamilton and Broadfoot took the 1964 show on a national tour. Harron wrote the entire production in 1967. *Thaw* was last produced in 1971.

Springstead Memorial Trophy, The Velma. See SPORTS FEDERATION OF CANADA.

Sproatt and Rolph. Toronto architectural firm, formed in 1899. Henry Sproatt (1866-1934) was born in Toronto and trained there in the office of A.R. Dennison. Ernest Rolph (1871-1958) was born in Toronto and trained in the office of David ROBERTS. The Toronto buildings of the firm—of which Sproatt was the designer and Rolph the constructor—span a wide range of styles, from the Beaux-Arts Classicism of the Canada Life Building, University Ave (1929-31), and the Manufacturers Life Assurance Building, 100 Bloor St E. (1924-6), to the English collegiate Gothic of Burwash Hall (1909-12), the Carnegie-Birge Library (1908-11), and Emmanuel College (1929), all for Victoria College, University of Toronto. Their finest work is HART HOUSE and Soldiers' Tower at the University of Toronto (1912-25), which won for the firm the American Institute of Architects Gold Medal for 1925.

Spruce beer. A Canadian brew, popular in the Maritime provinces. It is made with molasses, ginger, and spruce essence.

Spry, Graham (b.1900). National broadcasting enthusiast. Born in St Thomas, Ont., he was a Rhodes Scholar, and the National Secretary of the ASSOCIATION OF CANADIAN CLUBS from 1926 to 1932. Along with Alan B. Plaunt (1904-41), he formed the Canadian Radio League in Ottawa in 1930 to promote the use of radio as an instrument of national unity, culture, and entertainment, not as a medium for merchandising. Spry also launched The CANADIAN NATION and arranged lecture tours for Frederick Philip GROVE. He is a co-author of SOCIAL PLANNING FOR CANADA (1934) and the father of the film-maker Robin SPRY. In 1967 he retired from the post of Agent-General for Saskatchewan in London. See also CANADIAN BROADCASTING LEAGUE.

Spry, Robin (b.1939). Film director. Born in Toronto, the son of Graham SPRY, he spent his youth in England and was educated at Oxford and the London School of Economics. He joined the NATIONAL FILM BOARD in 1965 and has directed *Flowers on a One-Way Street* (1968) and two feature films, *Prologue* (1969) and ACTION: THE OCTOBER CRISIS (1975).

Spud Island. Slang reference to PRINCE EDWARD ISLAND.

Squamish. One of the COAST SALISH Indian groups. They live along the shores of Howe Sound and on a portion of the north shore of Burrard Inlet, B.C. Their population in 1970 was 1,232.

Square Mile. The most exclusive residential area of Montreal from 1860 until the stock market collapse of 1929. Hugh MacLENNAN has defined the boundaries of the area as University St on the east, Pine Ave and Cedar Ave on the north, Côte des Neiges Rd and Guy St on the west, and Dorchester St on the south. Most of its mansions have been taken over by McGill University or have disappeared.

Squaw. Former Algonkian word for a married woman. Today it is a derogatory word meaning 'prostitute'. A 'squawman' was a white man married to an Indian woman, especially one who followed Indian ways.

Squaw winter. In the Northwest, a cold snap followed by INDIAN SUMMER.

'Squid-Jiggin' Ground, The'. A ballad, especially popular in Newfoundland, descriptive of fishing for squid. It was written by Arthur Scammell in 1944. The title identifies the place where fishermen fish with a jig—a fishhook that is bobbed up and down.

Stacey, C.P. (b.1906). Historian. Born in Toronto and educated at the University of Toronto and at Oxford and Princeton, he served as director of the historical section of

the Canadian Army in Ottawa from 1945 until his retirement in 1959, when he joined the history department of the University of Toronto. A distinguished military historian, he has written numerous books, including *The Canadian Army, 1939-1945: An Official Historical Summary* (1948) and *Quebec: The Siege and the Battle* (1959). His most recent book, *A Very Double Life: The Private World of Mackenzie King* (1976), lays bare the late prime minister's relationships with women and spiritualists.

Stack, Frank (b.1906). Speed-skater. Born in Winnipeg, he began winning competitions at the age of 13 and in the next 35 years won the Canadian championship six times. He won the Canadian speed-skating title for the last time in 1954 and retired from competition, though he continued to coach.

Stadacona. Iroquois village on the site of Quebec City (probably on Cape Diamond). It was visited by Jacques CARTIER on his second voyage of 1535.

Stadacona Hall. The Ottawa home of Sir John A. MACDONALD from 1877 to 1883, when he bought EARNSCLIFFE. Built in 1871 for John A. Cameron, a lumber merchant, on Laurier Ave E., it is now the residence of the Ambassador of Belgium.

Stage Series. See CBC STAGE.

Stampeders. A rock group established in Calgary, Alta, in 1964. The three performers—Richard Dobson, Ronnie King, and Kim Berly—recorded an internationl hit with 'Sweet City Woman' in 1970 and remain a popular performing and recording group.

Stamps, Rare. Some Canadian stamps issued in the nineteenth century are very rare and fetch large prices at sales, some in the thousands of dollars. The following is a short list of the rarest: 1851 12d black; 1855-7 7½d green; 1855-7 ½d rose; 1855-7 6d reddish purple; 1859-64 10¢ black and brown; 1868 2¢ green (perhaps the rarest of all Canadian stamps—a used copy could be worth $25,000, one in mint state $50,000); 1868 1¢ brown and red; 1851 New Brunswick 1s dull violet; 1860 Newfoundland 1s orange. One recent stamp has become a collector's rarity: the 1959 5c red-and-blue stamp issued on 26 June 1959 to commemorate the opening of the St Lawrence Seaway. Owing to an error in the printing, a copy of this stamp could be worth several thousand dollars. A useful reference is *The Guidebook and Catalogue of Canadian Stamps* (2nd ed. 1973) edited by Glenn F.

Hansen. See also THREE-PENCE BEAVER, 'WEEP-ING PRINCESS'.

'Stand fast, Craigellachie'. The text of a telegram sent by George STEPHEN, president of the CPR, to Donald A. SMITH, a director of the railway, in 1884. Stephen had gone to England in a desperate effort to raise funds for the railway, which was in financial trouble. The telegram exhorted Smith not to give up the fight, for Craigellachie was the rock in Banffshire, Scot. (near where both men had been born), that was the rallying point for the Clan Grant in battle against other clans. William VAN HORNE, the general manager of the CPR, had heard Stephen refer to the rock before and had already decided in 1880 that the spot where the LAST SPIKE of the railway was driven would be marked by a station named Craigellachie. The site in British Columbia is marked by a commemorative plaque.

Standard Time. International system for determining local time. The suggestion that the world should be divided into 24 equal time zones to standardize the telling of time was first made in Toronto in 1879 by Sandford FLEMING. The engineer saw his resolution adopted at a Washington conference in 1884. Canada occupies seven of the 24 time zones, the only nation to do so. Greenwich, Eng., is accepted as the mean, so when Greenwich Mean Time is 12:00, it is the following times in these Canadian zones: Newfoundland, 3:30; Atlantic, 4:00; Eastern, 5:00; Central 6:00; Mountain, 7:00; Pacific, 8:00; Yukon, 9:00. Although time-setting is a provincial responsibility, DAYLIGHT SAVING TIME, which is one hour ahead of Standard Time, is a federal responsibility and was first introduced in the summer of 1918.

Standards Council of Canada. Federal body concerned with the adoption of uniform technical standards. Established in 1970, it encourages voluntary standardization of procedures and products in construction, manufacturing, and other industries. The SCC is responsible for the development of standards in the metric SI SYSTEM.

Standing Order 43. The rule by which a motion may be made in the House of Commons without prior notice providing the matter is of some urgency.

Standing Orders. Rules by which Parliament conducts its business.

Stanfield, Robert L. (b.1914). Former leader of the Opposition. Born in Truro, N.S., he was educated at Dalhousie University, where he won a Governor General's gold medal, and at Harvard. He was first elected to the Nova Scotia legislature as a Progressive Conservative in 1949, and became premier in 1956. Elected leader of the Progressive Conservative Party of Canada on 9 Sept. 1967, he resigned as premier of Nova Scotia on 13 Sept. and entered the House of Commons as leader of the Opposition on 15 Nov. He resigned as leader of the PCs and was replaced at a leadership convention on 22 Feb. 1976 by Charles Joseph (Joe) CLARK.

Stanfields. Long underwear manufactured by Stanfield's Ltd. The knitting mill in Truro, N.S., is owned by the family of Robert L. STANFIELD.

Stanley, G.F.G. (b.1907). Historian. Born in Calgary, Alta, and educated at the University of Alberta and at Oxford, he taught history at the Royal Military College from 1949 to 1969, when he moved to Mount Allison University, where he became director of Canadian Studies. He is highly respected as both a prairie and a military historian. His books include *The Birth of Western Canada* (1936; rev. 1961); *Louis Riel* (1963), an authoritative biography; *Canada's Soldiers* (1954; rev. 1960); *New France: The Last Phase, 1744-1760* (1968) in the CANADIAN CENTENARY SERIES; and *Canada Invaded: 1775-76* (1973).

Stanley, Lord (1841-1908). GOVERNOR GENERAL of Canada from 1888 to 1893.

Stanley Cup, The. Highest award in professional hockey, presented annually by the NATIONAL HOCKEY LEAGUE to its championship team. The Stanley Cup is the oldest trophy competed for by professional athletes in North America. The sterling bowl was purchased for 10 guineas (approximately $55) in 1893 by Governor General Lord Stanley as a challenge cup for amateur-hockey champions. Since 1910 it has been associated with professional hockey; since 1926 with NHL teams; since 1946 with the NHL exclusively. It is said to be 'symbolic of the World's Hockey Championship' (the ALLAN CUP is its amateur counterpart). It bears the names of all the members of the winning teams and is on permanent display at the Hockey HALL OF FAME in Toronto. A list of winners follows:

1892-3—MONTREAL A.A.A.; 1893-4—Montreal A.A.A.; 1894-5—Montreal Victorias; 1895-6—Winnipeg Victorias (Feb.); 1895-6—Montreal Victorias (Dec.); 1896-7—Montreal Victorias; 1897-8—Montreal Victorias; 1898-9—Montreal Shamrocks; 1899-1900—Montreal Shamrocks; 1900-1—Winnipeg Victorias; 1901-2—Montreal A.A.A.; 1902-3—Ottawa

Stanley Cup

Silver Seven; 1903-4—Ottawa Silver Seven; 1904-5—Ottawa Silver Seven; 1905-6—Montreal Wanderers; 1906-7—Kenora Thistles (Jan.); 1906-7—Montreal Wanderers (Mar.); 1907-8—Montreal Wanderers; 1908-9—Ottawa Senators; 1909-10—Montreal Wanderers; 1910-11—Ottawa Senators; 1911-12—Quebec Bulldogs; 1912-13—Quebec Bulldogs; 1913-14—Toronto Blueshirts; 1914-15—Vancouver Millionaires; 1915-16—MONTREAL CANADIENS; 1916-17—Seattle Metropolitans; 1917-18—Toronto Arenas; 1918-19—No decision; 1919-20—Ottawa Senators; 1920-1—Ottawa Senators; 1921-2—Toronto St Pats; 1922-3—Ottawa Senators; 1923-4—Montreal Canadiens; 1924-5—Victoria Cougars; 1925-6—Montreal Maroons; 1926-7—Ottawa Senators; 1927-8—New York Rangers; 1928-9—Boston Bruins; 1929-30—Montreal Canadiens; 1930-1—Montreal Canadiens; 1931-2—TORONTO MAPLE LEAFS; 1932-3—New York Rangers; 1933-4—Chicago Black Hawks; 1934-5—Montreal Maroons; 1935-6—Detroit Red Wings; 1936-7—Detroit Red Wings; 1937-8—Chicago Black Hawks; 1938-9—Boston Bruins; 1939-40—New York Rangers; 1940-1—Boston Bruins; 1941-2—Toronto Maple Leafs; 1942-3—Detroit Red Wings; 1943-4—Montreal Canadiens; 1944-5—Toronto Maple Leafs; 1945-6—Montreal Canadiens; 1946-7—Toronto Maple Leafs; 1947-8—Toronto Maple Leafs; 1948-9—Toronto Maple Leafs; 1949-50—Detroit Red Wings; 1950-1—Toronto Maple Leafs; 1951-2—Detroit Red Wings; 1952-3—Montreal Canadiens; 1953-4—Detroit Red Wings; 1954-5—Detroit Red Wings; 1955-6—Montreal Canadiens; 1956-7—Montreal Canadiens; 1957-8—Montreal Canadiens; 1958-9—Montreal Canadiens; 1959-60—Montreal Canadiens; 1960-1—Chicago Black Hawks; 1961-2—Toronto Maple Leafs; 1962-3—Toronto Maple Leafs; 1963-4—Toronto Maple Leafs; 1964-5—Montreal Canadiens; 1965-6—Montreal Canadiens; 1966-7—Toronto Maple Leafs; 1967-8—Montreal Canadiens; 1968-9—Montreal Canadiens; 1969-70—Boston Bruins; 1970-1—Montreal Canadiens; 1971-2—Boston Bruins; 1972-3—Montreal Canadiens; 1973-4—Philadelphia Flyers; 1974-5—Philadelphia Flyers; 1975-6—Montreal Canadiens.

Stanley House. A meeting-place for artists and scholars operated by the CANADA COUNCIL. Originally built as a fishing lodge for Lord Stanley, governor general from 1888 to 1893, this rustic retreat near New Richmond, Que., was deeded to the Canada Council by Miss Olivia Terrell in 1961. It has since been operated by the Council as a summer meeting-place where, during July and August, small groups hold four- or five-day seminars to discuss subjects that lie within the broad interests of the Council.

Stanley Park. Beautiful 1,000-acre park at the entrance to Burrard Inlet, Vancouver, B.C. Roads and trails wind through its forested areas past Prospect Point, Beaver Lake, Lost Lagoon, Big Tree, and SIWASH ROCK, Pauline JOHNSON's memorial, a zoo, an aquarium, and an impressive stand of Indian totem poles. It was named after Lord Stanley, governor general from 1888 to 1893, and was officially opened by him in 1888.

Star of Courage. A Canadian HONOUR awarded for outstandingly courageous actions. The abbreviation is SC.

Star Weekly, The. A weekend supplement to the TORONTO STAR that was also sold separately across Canada from 1910 to 1969. From the twenties to the forties, it had a distinctive and entertaining character all its own, publishing feature articles by such journalists for the daily paper as Gregory CLARK, Ernest Hemingway, and Gordon SINCLAIR, along with a rotogravure section, coloured comics—including BIRDSEYE CENTRE—and an abridged novel.

Starlost, The. Science-fiction series on the CTV NETWORK. Created by Harlan Ellison and starring Keir Dullea, it was set in A.D. 2873 aboard a gigantic 'space ark'. CTV's and NBC's answer to 'Star Trek', the 16 one-hour episodes were produced in the Toronto studios of Glen-Warren Productions and shown from Sept. to Dec. 1973.

Starr Medal. 'The Victoria Cross of Canadian medicine'. It has been awarded annually by the Canadian Medical Association since 1935 in honour of Dr Frederick Newton Gisborne Starr (1867-1934), a prominent Toronto surgeon especially concerned with postgraduate medical education. Made possible by his widow, it is given to a person whose 'achievements should be so outstanding as to serve as an inspiration to the medical profession of Canada'.

Staryk, Steven (b.1933). Violinist and teacher. Born in Toronto, he left his second-string position with the TORONTO SYMPHONY ORCHESTRA in 1955 for a career as a concert and recording soloist and as concertmaster of the London Royal Philharmonic (under Sir Thomas Beecham), the Amsterdam Concertgebouw, and the Chicago Symphony. Since his return to Canada in 1970 he has continued his solo career while holding various teaching positions.

StatCan. See STATISTICS CANADA.

States-General. A short-lived popular assembly for Quebec. Based on the Estates-General that assembled at Versailles in 1789, which precipitated the French Revolution, the States-General of French Canada had no legislative authority. It was established at Lévis, Que., on 6 Apr. 1964, by the SOCIÉTÉ SAINT-JEAN-BAPTISTE and appointed Abbé Lionel GROULX its honorary chairman. Its aims were 'to locate and analyze the actual reality of the French-Canadian nation; to define its vital operations; to lead it into such action which may allow it to fulfill itself.' It rejected biculturalism but fell short of endorsing separatism at its annual conventions, the last of which was held in 1969.

Statistics Canada. The central statistical agency for Canada, the new name for the Dominion Bureau of Statistics, which was established in 1918. It compiles and publishes statistical information on all aspects of the economy and social conditions of Canada. It also conducts the decennial CENSUS. Its head is the Chief Statistician of Canada.

Statten, Taylor. See TAYLOR STATTEN CAMPS.

Status of Women, Royal Commission on. A commission to 'inquire and report upon the status of women in Canada, and to recommend what steps might be taken by the federal government to ensure for women equal opportunities with men in all aspects of Canadian society.' It was appointed on 16 Feb. 1967. The chairperson was Mrs Florence Bird and there were six other commissioners, two of them men. It held public hearings in cities across Canada and received many briefs and letters. Its report was released in 1970 and contained 167 recommendations. In May 1973 the federal government set up an Advisory Council on the Status of Women to see that the recommendations of the Commission are implemented.

Statute of Westminster. Enacted in 1931 by the British Parliament, it formally recognized the autonomous status of the British Dominions by translating into statute law principles previously enunciated in the BALFOUR REPORT of 1926 and long established in practice. Specifically, it repealed the obsolete Colonial Laws Validity Act of 1865, which had ruled that Dominion legislation contradicting legislation of the British Parliament could be nullified.

Statutes of Canada. The laws that govern Canada. The statutes take the form of annual volumes, bound in black, containing the leg-islation passed by the Parliament of Canada in any one year. Each statute is referred to as a Chapter, and these are cited as follows: 'The Canadian Bill of Rights, SC 1960, c. 44'. When a specific Section of a Chapter is being referred to, a number is added, as follows: 'The Canadian Bill of Rights, SC 1960, c. 44, s. 3'. About every 20 years the annual volumes are collected and reprinted in a consolidated form, rendering it possible for the industrious and intelligent, with effort, to understand the law. These revised collections are cited as 'RSC'.

Steacie Memorial Fellowship. An annual award made by the NATIONAL RESEARCH COUNCIL since 1963 to 'an outstanding young researcher working in one of the fields of science supported by the NRC' whose development could be helped by from two to three years freed for research purposes. It honours E.W.R. Steacie (1900-62), president of the NRC from 1952 to 1962.

Stead, Robert (1880-1959). Novelist. Born in Middleville, Lanark Co., Ont., he was raised on a homestead near Cartwright, Man. He worked with the Department of Immigration in the publicity department from 1919 until his retirement in 1946. He wrote seven realistic novels about life before and after the turn of the century in Manitoba and the Alberta foothills, the most important of which is GRAIN (1926).

Steatite. See SOAPSTONE.

Steelhead. A subspecies of rainbow trout, common along the coast of British Columbia. It averages 16 lb. and is considered an important game fish.

Steenman, L.F. See 'The COBALT SONG'.

Steeves, Wiliam H. (1814-73). A FATHER OF CONFEDERATION. Born at Hillsborough, N.B., he became a businessman and was elected to the legislative assembly of New Brunswick in 1846 and was a member of the legislative council from 1851 to 1867. He was a delegate to the CHARLOTTETOWN and QUEBEC CONFERENCES on Confederation and in 1867 was appointed to the Senate.

Stefanschi, Sergiu (b.1941). Dancer. Born in Romania, he was a soloist with the Bucharest Ballet Company and danced with the Bolshoi and the Kirov in Russia before arriving in Toronto in 1971 to become a principle with the NATIONAL BALLET OF CANADA.

Stefansson, Vilhjalmur (1879-1962). Arctic explorer. Born in Gimli, Man., and raised in North Dakota from the age of three, he was educated at the Universities of North Dakota, Iowa, Harvard, and in Iceland, where he studied anthropology. He lived among the Mackenzie Eskimos and learned to hunt and survive in the North on the Anglo-American Arctic expedition of 1906-7. He studied the Eskimos of the Central Arctic on the Canadian-American Expedition of 1908-12. He commanded the Canadian Arctic Expedition of 1913-18 and, following the loss of his flagship KARLUK, captained by Bob BARTLETT, proved his thesis that there was life in the Beaufort Sea. As an advocate of the North he was an effective speaker and a rigorous, interesting writer. His account of the Anglo-American Arctic expedition appears in *Hunters of the Great North* (1922); of the Canadian-American Expedition in *My Life with the Eskimo* (1913); and of the Canadian Arctic Expedition in his best-known book, *The Friendly Arctic* (1921), the thesis of which is that the North is more 'friendly' than forbidding. Other extremely readable works are *The Northward Course of Empire* (1922), *Unsolved Mysteries of the Arctic* (1938), *Ultima Thule: Further Mysteries of the Arctic* (1940), and *Discovery* (1964), his posthumously published autobiography.

Steinberg, David (b.1941). Comedian. Born in St Boniface, Man., the son of a Romanian rabbi, he studied theology in Israel and English at the University of Chicago, then wrote for and performed with the Second City Revue. His irreverent Old Testament skit on the *Smothers Brothers Comedy Hour* led CBS to cancel the TV show in Apr. 1969. Steinberg, who is in demand for his stage appearances and guest-hosting of TV comedy and talk shows, counterpoints a relaxed deadpan manner with nimble and surreal satire. Although he lives in Beverley Hills, Calif., he launched from Toronto a CTV Network comedy series, produced by fellow Winnipeger Perry Rosemond, in Sept. 1976.

Steinberg's Limited. A large retail operation for food and general merchandise. It was founded by Hungarian-born Ida Steinberg (1885-1942), who opened a delicatessen in Montreal in 1917 and a self-service groceteria in 1938. Her philosophy was 'always give the customer a little more'. The business, which quickly expanded throughout Quebec and into Ontario in 1959, is headed by her second son Sam (b.1905). In 1969 Steinberg's Limited became the first Canadian chain to begin discounting food prices. In 1976 it operated some 140 Steinberg's food stores in Quebec and 58 Miracle Food Mart stores in Ontario, in addition to the Quebec-based Cardinal Distributors (catalogue showrooms)

and Beaucoup (food and general-merchandise outlets).

STELCO. Acronym of the STEeL COmpany of Canada, a merger of five steel companies that took place under the direction of Max Aitken (the future Lord BEAVERBROOK) in 1910.

Stellar coal. A kind of soft coal found in Nova Scotia in 1798. The town Stellarton, N.S., was named after the 'oil coal' that gives off sparks like stars when ignited. It was last mined in 1957.

Stephen, Sir George (1829-1921). Financier. Born in Banffshire, Scot., he came to Canada in 1850 and entered a woollen-goods business, which he eventually controlled. He became a director of the Bank of Montreal, its president (1876-81), and one of the financiers and entrepreneurs of the CANADIAN PACIFIC RAILWAY, of which he was president from 1881 to 1888, the year he moved to England. He was knighted in 1886 and made Baron Mount Stephen in 1891. His Renaissance-style mansion on Drummond St, Montreal—designed by William T. THOMAS and built in 1880—became the Mount Stephen Club in 1926.

Stephenson, Sir William. See The QUIET CANADIAN.

Stewart, Marlene. See Marlene Stewart STREIT.

Stewart, Reginald. See PROMENADE SYMPHONY CONCERTS.

Sticks and Stones. See The DONNELLYS.

StLAR. Abbreviation of the St Lawrence & Atlantic Railway.

Stobo, Robert (1726-70). Military officer. A Scots-born Virginian, he led a highly adventurous life in North America (1742-60). He was for a time on the staff of Gen. James WOLFE and claimed in his 'Memoirs'—which he probably did not write—that he told Wolfe about WOLFE'S COVE, but there is no convincing evidence that this was so.

Stoddard, Jack. See GENERAL PUBLISHING COMPANY LIMITED.

STOL. Acronym for Short Take-Off and Landing. Since the 1940s Canada has pioneered in the manufacture of low-speed, low-flying aircraft (20-30,000 ft) capable of landing on runways of less than 2,000 ft. The Department of Transport authorized the development of a demonstration STOL commuter service in 1971, and since 1973 Airtransit has operated half-hourly flights between Ottawa and Montreal. The aircraft used are 12-passenger de Havilland Twin Otters.

Stone Angel, The. Popular novel by Margaret LAURENCE published in 1964. Its central character—90-year-old Hagar Shipley, a proud and bitter woman who struggles to maintain her independence from her son and daughter-in-law—is one of the most memorable characters of modern literature.

Stone of Remembrance. Official name for the memorial stone found in cemeteries for the war dead. It was designed by the British architect Sir Edwin Lutyens for the Imperial (since 1960, Commonwealth) War Graves Commission. The 12-ft altar-shaped stone is inscribed with the following line, taken by Rudyard Kipling from the aprocryphal scripture *Ecclesiasticus* (44:14): 'Their name liveth for evermore'.

Stonehookers. Vessels whose owners made an often precarious living grappling stones from the bottom of Lake Ontario for building material. From about 1830 to the turn of the century there were some 40 of these craft in operation at any given time. About half were from Port Credit, the rest from various ports between Whitby and Port Nelson.

Stoney Creek, Battle of. An engagement in the WAR OF 1812. British regulars under Lt-Col. John Harvey made a surprise attack on 6 June 1813 on a much larger American force under Gen. John Chandler and Gen. William Winder, both of whom were captured. The Americans were camped at Stoney Creek, near Burlington Bay on Lake Ontario.

Stoneys. See ASSINIBOINE.

Storey, R.A. (Red) (b.1918). Athlete and referee. Born in Barrie, Ont., he played hockey, lacrosse, and baseball. At 20 he joined the Toronto Argonauts when that football team won the GREY CUP. He is remembered for scoring three touchdowns in the final quarter of another Grey Cup game. He later refereed in lacrosse, football, and more than 2,000 hockey matches. He was elected to the Hockey HALL OF FAME as a builder.

Stories with John Drainie. A popular CBC Radio series. Original stories of less than 2,000 words by Canadian writers were read by the actor John DRAINIE in the early afternoon five days a week from 1959 to 1965. A selection of the best-received stories, edited by Drainie, was published under the series title in 1963.

Stork derby. A bizarre contest to claim the legacy of the millionaire Toronto lawyer Charles Millar, who died in 1926. His eccentric will provided two-thirds of a million dollars 'to the mother who has since my death given birth in Toronto to the greatest number of children'. After 10 years of litigation, the legacy was divided among four sets of parents, each with nine children, some born out of wedlock.

Storm, William G. (1826-92). Architect. Born in Burton-upon-Strather, Eng.—the son of Thomas Storm, who came to Toronto in 1830—he was first trained in his father's business and in 1844 was articled to William THOMAS. In 1850 he joined the office of Cumberland & Ridout as draughtsman on the ST JAMES' CATHEDRAL project (1849-50) and in 1852 he formed a partnership with Frederick William CUMBERLAND that lasted until 1865. Storm's later buildings include St Andrew's Presbyterian Church at King and Simcoe Sts, Toronto (1875) in a heavy version of the Scottish Baronial style, and the main building for Victoria College, University of Toronto (1890-2)—his last work—which is completely within the Romanesque style and notable for the use of baronial elements and for its picturesque massing.

Stormont, Dundas and Glengarry Highlanders. Canadian army regiment. Organized in 1868, it served in the FIRST WORLD WAR for local protective duty and contributed to several battalions that participated in many battles, including YPRES and AMIENS. During the SECOND WORLD WAR it served as a unit of the 4th Infantry Brigade in the NORMANDY INVASION and in other crucial battles.

Stormy Weather, Georgian Bay. Canvas by F.H. VARLEY sketched at Go Home Bay, Ont., and painted in the fall of 1920. It depicts a windblown pine tree on the edge of a wave-strewn bay, with smooth water under sunny storm clouds in the distance. Varley sketched it at the same time as Arthur LISMER made his sketch for SEPTEMBER GALE, GEORGIAN BAY (1920, NGC). With Tom THOMSON'S WEST WIND (1917, AGO), these paintings of similar subjects are the best-known images of the northern landscape. (NGC)

Story, Norah (b.1902). Archivist and historian. Former head of the Manuscript Division of the Public Archives of Canada, she is the author of a standard work of reference, *The* OXFORD COMPANION TO CANADIAN HISTORY AND LITERATURE (1967).

Strachan, John (1778-1867). First Anglican bishop of Toronto. Born and educated in

Aberdeen, Scot., he immigrated to Kingston, U.C. (Ont.), where he was employed as a tutor. In 1803 he was ordained in the Church of England and moved to Cornwall, Ont., where he taught school. He was appointed rector of York (Toronto) in 1812 and became headmaster of the grammar school there. He was a pillar of the Tory establishment called the FAMILY COMPACT and his influence broadened as his pupils began to assume positions of power. He was appointed archdeacon in 1827 and bishop of Toronto in 1839. In 1851 he founded Trinity College, Toronto, an Anglican university, and became its first chancellor.

Strait. A linguistic group of COAST SALISH Indians. The same language is spoken by the Saanich, Songhee, and Sooke on Vancouver Island; the Klallam on the southern shore of Juan de Fuca Strait and at Beecher Bay on Vancouver Island; and the Semiahmoo, Lummi, and Samish on the mainland of British Columbia south of the Fraser R. The Strait were unique in being the only group on the Northwest Coast to harvest the huge Fraser SOCKEYE SALMON, using a technique called reef netting.

Strait of Anian. A mythical waterway. It appeared on a map as early as 1566 in the position of Bering Strait, but by the late seventeenth century it had moved south as an opening to the Pacific, near 50° N. Its origin is obscure. It was used as an image by Earle BIRNEY in his collection of poems called *The Strait of Anian* (1948).

Strait of Belle Isle. A body of water separating the island of Newfoundland from the mainland (Labrador).

Strait of Georgia. The salt-water extension of the Pacific Ocean separating lower Vancouver Island from mainland British Columbia. It connects with the sea in the north by Johnstone and Queen Charlotte Straits, and in the south by the Strait of Juan de Fuca.

Strait of Juan de Fuca. The salt-water arm of the Pacific Ocean separating the southern part of Vancouver Island from mainland United States (State of Washington). Juan de Fuca was the assumed name of Apostolos Valerianos, a Greek navigator who claimed to have discovered it in 1592 while sailing for Spain.

Strange Manuscript Found in a Copper Cylinder, A. A utopian novel by James DE MILLE, published posthumously in 1888. Both an imaginative adventure story and a satirical examination of human nature, it is set in the South Polar land of the Kosekin, a race of cannibals to whom darkness, poverty, and death represent the highest good. The wealthy Kohen is among the lowest of men; the most influential and highly respected citizens are the paupers.

Stratas, Teresa (b.1938). Soprano. Born Anastasia Stratakis in Toronto, she studied singing with Irene Jessner at the Royal Conservatory of Music. She made her début as Mimi in the Canadian Opera Company production of *La Bohème* and the following year, in 1954, joined the Metropolitan Opera, New York, where she became a popular leading singer. Renowned for her acting ability and her temperament as well as for her voice, she has not performed recently.

Strate, Grant (b.1927). Dancer and choreographer. Born in Cardston, Alta, he was a pupil of Betty OLIPHANT and Celia FRANCA in the National Ballet School and joined the company in 1951; he became a soloist in 1953, resident choreographer 1956, and assistant to Celia Franca from 1960. He studied in the United States and Europe and taught at the Juilliard School of Music in 1962. He taught at the National Ballet School from 1967 to 1970, when he became associate professor and director of the Programme in Dance at York University, Toronto. Among the ballets he has choreographed is Harry SOMERS' *The House of Atreus*, the Canadian première of which was on 13 Jan. 1964.

Stratford, Philip (b.1927). Translator. Born in Chatham, Ont., he was educated at the Universities of Western Ontario, Bordeaux, Paris, and London, and teaches at the Université de Montréal. Editor of *Stories from Quebec* (1974), he is best known as a translator and has compiled, with Maureen Newman, a *Bibliography of Canadian Books in Translation* (1975). Among his translations are books by André LAURENDEAU, Jean LeMOYNE, and Claire MARTIN. With Francine Dufresne he wrote *Cooking Fish and Wild Game, French-Canadian Style* (1975).

Stratford Festival. Canada's leading theatrical company. It was founded in Stratford, Ont., by Tom PATTERSON—who was supported by the encouragement and advice of the Irish director Tyrone GUTHRIE—for the production of William Shakespeare's plays. The Stratford Shakespearean Festival—the middle word was eventually dropped—was incorporated in Nov. 1952. Guthrie directed three plays the next year in a specially designed tent on the Avon R. in downtown

Stratford, opening with Alec Guinness in *Richard III* on 13 July 1953, an evening which, according to the critic Herbert WHITTAKER, was 'the most exciting night in the history of Canadian theatre'. The Festival Theatre, designed by Robert Fairfield, with a seating capacity of 2,258, came into use in 1957. The pillared, porticoed thrust stage, designed by Tanya MOISEIWITSCH and Tyrone Guthrie, is a striking feature of the permanent building, as it was of the tent. The Avon Theatre—a reconditioned movie house with 1,102 seats, used since 1956—was acquired in 1963; the Third Stage, a small theatre for original drama and music, opened in 1971. The Festival season—from June to October—does not restrict itself to plays by Shakespeare and includes concerts, operas, seminars, and film festivals. The International Film Festival, first held in 1956 and now organized by Gerald PRATLEY, invites entries from world film festivals. The artistic directors of the Stratford Festival have been Tyrone GUTHRIE (1953-4), Michael LANGHAM (1955-67), Jean GASCON (1968-74), and the English director Robin Phillips (from 1974). A list of plays performed follows:

1953 *Richard III, All's Well That Ends Well*
1954 *Measure for Measure, The Taming of the Shrew, Oedipus Rex* (Sophocles)
1955 *The Merchant of Venice, Julius Caesar, Oedipus Rex* (Sophocles)
1956 *Henry V, The Merry Wives of Windsor*
1957 *Hamlet, Twelfth Night*
1958 *Henry IV: Part I, A Winter's Tale, Much Ado About Nothing*
1959 *Othello, As You Like It*
1960 *King John, A Midsummer Night's Dream, Romeo and Juliet*
1961 *Coriolanus, Henry VIII, Love's Labour's Lost, The Canvas Barricade* (Jack)
1962 *Macbeth, The Taming of the Shrew, The Tempest, Cyrano de Bergerac* (Rostand)
1963 *Troilus and Cressida, Cyrano de Bergerac, The Comedy of Errors, Timon of Athens*
1964 *Richard II, Le Bourgeois Gentilhomme* (Molière), *King Lear, The Country Wife* (Wycherley)
1965 *Henry IV (Henry IV: Part One), Falstaff (Henry IV: Part Two), Julius Caesar, The Cherry Orchard* (Chekhov)
1966 *Henry V, Henry VI, Twelfth Night, The Last of the Tsars* (Bawtree), *The Dance of Death* (Strindberg)
1967 *Antony and Cleopatra, Richard III, The Merry Wives of Windsor, The Government Inspector* (Gogol/Raby), *Colours in the Dark* (REANEY)
1968 *Romeo and Juliet, A Midsummer Night's Dream, Tartuffe* (Molière/Wilbur), *The Three Musketeers* (Dumas/Raby), *The*

Seagull (Chekhov), *Waiting for Godot* (Beckett)
1969 *Hamlet, The Alchemist* (Jonson), *Measure for Measure, Tartuffe, Hadrian VII* (Rolfe/ Luke) *Satyricon* (Silverman/HENDRY)
1970 *The Merchant of Venice, The School for Scandal* (Sheridan), *Hedda Gabler* (Ibsen/Hampton), *Cymbeline, The Architect and the Emperor of Assyria* (Arrabal), *The Friends* (Wesker), *Vatzlav* (Mrozek/Manheim), *The Sun Never Sets* (Crean)
1971 *Much Ado About Nothing, The Duchess of Malfi* (Webster), *Macbeth, Volpone* (Jonson), *An Italian Straw Hat* (Labiche & Marc-Michel), *There's One in Every Marriage* (Feydeau/Grossman & WHITEHEAD), *The Red Convertible* (Buenaventura/Bawtree & Sampson)
1972 *As You Like It, Lorenzaccio* (de Musset/Lewin), *King Lear, She Stoops to Conquer* (Goldsmith), *The Threepenny Opera* (Brecht & Weill), *La Guerre, Yes Sir!* (CARRIER/Grossman), *Mark* (Wylie), *Pinocchio* (Collodi/Wood)
1973 *The Taming of the Shrew, She Stoops to Conquer* (Goldsmith), *Othello, Pericles, A Month in the Country* (Turgenev/Mac-Andrew), *The Marriage Brokers* (Gogol/Berkman), *The Collected Works of Billy the Kid* (ONDAATJE), INOOK AND THE SUN (Beissel)
1974 *The Imaginary Invalid* (Molière/Frame), *Love's Labour's Lost, Pericles, King John, La Vie Parisienne* (Offenbach/Gibson), *Walsh* (Pollock), *Ready Steady Go* (Jones)
1975 *Saint Joan* (Shaw), *Twelfth Night, Measure for Measure, Trumpets and Drums* (Brecht), *The Two Gentlemen of Verona, The Comedy of Errors, The Crucible* (Miller)
1976 *Hamlet, The Way of the World* (Congreve), *The Tempest, The Merchant of Venice, Antony and Cleopatra, The Importance of Being Earnest* (Wilde), *Measure for Measure, Eve* (Fineberg), *A Midsummer Night's Dream, Three Sisters* (Chekhov)

Stratford Strike. A strike by woodworkers in Stratford, Ont., that began on 14 Sept. 1933. Supported by the TRADES AND LABOUR CONGRESS, furniture workers led by the WORKERS UNITY LEAGUE struck for the 44-hour week and union recognition. There was mass picketing and the introduction of troops, machineguns, and even tanks. It ended on 18 Oct. with wage increases and the recognition of shop committees.

Strathcona, Lord. See Donald A. SMITH.

Straw Hat Players. A summer-stock company that tours Ontario summer resorts. Donald and Murray Davis (see DAVIS FAMILY) and Brian DOHERTY have been among the producers who have mounted summer productions at Port Carling and Muskoka, Ont., since 1948. The Muskoka Summer Theatre, established in 1973, now operates the Straw Hat Players.

Streit, Marlene Stewart (b.1934). Champion golfer. Born in Cereal, Alta, but raised in Fonthill, Ont., she caddied as a youngster and was tutored by the Lookout Point golf pro, Gordon McInnes. She matured so quickly that at 17 she won the Canadian women's open championship. In 1953 she won the coveted British title. Later she added the championships of the United States and Australia to become the only golfer ever to win these four national honours.

Stress. 'The rate of all the wear and tear caused by life', a subject identified with Hans SELYE, who so described his specialty. The Vienna-born, Montreal-based medical researcher published his first paper on stress in 1936 and since then has undertaken extensive research in the area. In *The Stress of Life* (1956) he defined stress as 'the state manifested by a specific syndrome which consists of all the nonspecifically induced changes within a biologic system.'

Strickland, Samuel (1804-67). Pioneer and author. The brother of Susanna MOODIE and Catherine Parr TRAILL, he immigrated to Upper Canada (Ontario) in 1825, finally settling near Peterborough. He wrote *Twenty-seven Years in Canada West: The Experiences of an Early Settler* (1853).

Strike, Hilda (b.1910). Runner. Born in Montreal, she was a double winner at the 1932 Olympics in Los Angeles, where she won two silver medals and equalled the Olympic record in the 100-metre event. Later that year she was chosen 'Canada's outstanding women's athlete'. A double medallist at the 1934 British Empire Games in London, she retired the next year from competition but continued to coach.

Strikes. Some strikes of national importance: ASBESTOS STRIKE, BRANDON STRIKE, CORBIN STRIKE, ESTEVAN STRIKE, FLIN-FLON STRIKE, FORT WILLIAM STRIKE, GLACE BAY AND SPRINGHILL STRIKES, KIRKLAND LAKE STRIKE, LETHBRIDGE STRIKE, NANAIMO STRIKES, OSHAWA STRIKE, STRATFORD STRIKE, SYDNEY STRIKES, VANCOUVER SIT-IN, WINDSOR STRIKES, WINNIPEG GENERAL STRIKE.

Structurist. An art publication issued annually since 1960 by the University of Saskatchewan at Saskatoon and edited by Eli Borenstein. It includes articles and illustrations about creation in art and nature. 'The Structurist view accepts man as capable of expanding his visible knowledge of nature and art even further.'

Students for a Democratic University. During the 1960s on several university campuses groups of Canadian students carried on public demonstrations against university administrations because of their close connections with United States government and with multi-national corporations involved in the war in Vietnam. The SDU was the counterpart of the Students for a Democratic Society in the United States.

Studia Varia. Latin for 'varied studies', the general title of a series of publications designed for the general reader and composed largely of contributions to interdisciplinary symposia at the annual meetings of the ROYAL SOCIETY OF CANADA. It was temporarily and informally discontinued in 1971. Papers presented at symposia held by the RSC are now published in English and French in *Proceedings of Symposia*.

Studio Building. A three-storey atelier designed by Eden SMITH and built by Lawren HARRIS and Dr James MacCALLUM in Toronto's Rosedale Ravine in 1913-14. Originally called 'The Studio Building of Canadian Art', it was intended as working and living quarters for like-minded artists—some of whom exhibited together as the GROUP OF SEVEN—who would pay a nominal rent. The first artists to move into it were A.Y. JACKSON, who shared a studio with Tom THOMSON (and lived there until 1954), William Beatty, J.E.H. MacDONALD, Arthur Heming, Curtis Williamson, and Harris. In the fall of 1915 Thomson moved into a shack behind the building. The Studio Building is still in use: Harold TOWN rents studio space there.

Subalpine Forest Region. Coniferous forest area. It is located on the mountain uplands of Alberta and British Columbia, from the Rocky Mountain range through the interior of British Columbia to the Pacific Coast inlets. Characteristic species include Engelmann spruce, alpine fir, and lodgepole pine.

Subject Guide to Canadian Books in Print. See CANADIAN BOOKS IN PRINT.

Subways. There are two subway systems in Canada. The Toronto subway—running under Yonge St from Union Station to Eglinton (12 stations)—opened on 30 Mar. 1954. Further extensions opened in 1963 (University Ave), 1966 (Bloor-Danforth line from Woodbine to Keele), 1968 (Bloor-Danforth line extension from Keele to Islington and from Woodbine to Warden), 1973 (Yonge line extension from Eglinton to York Mills), and 1974 (Yonge line extension from York Mills to Finch). The Spadina extension (Bloor to Lawrence) will open in late 1977. The Métro in Montreal opened in Oct. 1966 with 26 stations, each decorated by a different artist, and is being extended. The entrance to Place Victoria station was designed by Hector Guimar in 1905 for the Paris Métro and was a gift from the city of Paris. The trains run quietly on rubber tires.

Such, Peter (b.1939). Novelist. Born in London, Eng., he came to Canada in 1953 and graduated from the University of Toronto in 1960. He has taught at the Ryerson Polytechnical Institute and, since 1972, at Atkinson College, York University. He is the author of *Soundprints* (1972), a personal and useful study of contemporary Canadian composers, and of two 'documentary novels': *Fallout* (1969) and *Riverrun* (1973). He founded *Impulse Magazine* in 1972 and edited it until 1975, the year he joined BOOKS IN CANADA as managing editor.

Such is My Beloved. Novel by Morley CALLAGHAN published in 1934. Depression conditions in the 1930s serve as the background for this moral tale about a priest who befriends two prostitutes. Father Dowling's struggle with wealthy, respectable people who lack compassion and charity leads to a breakdown that symbolizes the individual's conflict with society. Many consider this to be Callaghan's finest novel.

Sudbury basin. A structural rock basin approximately 35 mi. long east to west and 16 mi. wide north to south. Within the basin are some of the world's largest deposits of nickel, copper, and platinum. Discovered in 1883 when the CPR was built through the region, these deposits are the principal economic support for the city of Sudbury and a number of smaller communities.

Sudbury trench. See REGINA TRENCH.

Sugar bush. A grove of sugar maple trees.

Sugaring-off. The process of boiling sap that has been collected from maple trees. Maple syrup and maple sugar result from evaporation and crystallization.

Sulpicians. The Société des Prêtres de Saint-Sulpice, founded in Paris in 1641, sent four Sulpicians to New France in 1657. They were the first religious order to be given a large land grant in Montreal: they became its actual seigneurs—Les Messieurs de St-Sulpice—and in 1694 began the first building of a complex two miles from OLD MONTREAL (on the north side of Sherbrooke St, between Atwater and Guy) that became the Grande Séminaire and the Collège de Montréal. The Domain Sulpice is perhaps the largest single privately owned property in a North American city. Sulpicians erected the first Parish Church of Notre-Dame in Montreal, 'La Paroisse', between 1670 and 1683 (see NÔTRE-DAME-DE-MONTRÉAL). They also served in various outlying missions, including OKA, founded in 1710.

Summer Games. See CANADA GAMES.

Sun dance. A three-day religious event held among the Indians of the western Prairies, particularly the Blackfoot and the Assiniboine, in an enormous lodge having a central sacred pole. It was composed of dances and banqueting and (among the Blackfoot) a ceremony of voluntary self-torture in honour of the Great Spirit, in which a young warrior whose shoulders or breasts were attached by a thong to the pole, danced round it until he broke loose or was freed.

Sundance Sea. An extremely shallow, marsh-like sea of the Jurassic or dinosaur period, some 135-180 million years ago. A giant arm of the Arctic Ocean separated from the Pacific by the then newly rising Rockies, it covered the Yukon, Alberta, and Saskatchewan, and extended as far south as Arizona. See also CRETACEOUS INLAND SEA.

Sunday. CBC-TV's replacement for THIS HOUR HAS SEVEN DAYS. A public-affairs program with a magazine format, it was shown Sunday evenings from 6 Nov. 1966 to 16 Apr. 1967. It was produced by Daryl DUKE and hosted by Ian TYSON, Peter Reilly, Robert Hoyt, and Larry ZOLF. It made use of 'the bear-pit', in which individuals in the news were interrogated.

Sunday Magazine. A popular CBC Radio news program. An in-depth analysis of the week's major news stories, it was heard for 30 min., later increased to 55 min., on Sunday mornings from 1961 to 1 Nov. 1976, when it was replaced by a three-hour news show.

Sunday Morning, #2. Painting by Jack CHAMBERS of two small boys seated in their living room, their heads turned to watch a TV set, with a cold suburban landscape visible through a window in the background. It is perhaps Chambers' best-known work, in which the meticulously realistic interpretation of a familiar scene is invested with emotional significance. (1969-70, Mr & Mrs E.A. Schwendau Collection)

Sunday Night. See CBC TUESDAY NIGHT.

Sunrise on the Saguenay. Painting by Lucius R. O'BRIEN. Great cliffs softened by a pink sunrise loom over boats that rest tranquilly in the Saguenay R. It is a serene, luminous celebration of the sublime in nature. One of the first works in the collection of the NATIONAL GALLERY OF CANADA, where it was deposited as O'Brien's diploma piece for membership in the Royal Canadian Academy of Arts, it is today one of the Gallery's most popular paintings. (1880)

Sunshine Sketches of a Little Town. The most popular collection of humorous sketches by Stephen LEACOCK, published in 1912. It depicts life in MARIPOSA—Orillia, Ont., where the author spent his summers and where some citizens were outraged by the unflattering picture it presented of the foibles and hypocrisies of small-town life. See also SUNSHINE TOWN.

Sunshine Town. Musical comedy in two acts with lyrics and music by Mavor MOORE, based on Stephen Leacock's SUNSHINE SKETCHES OF A LITTLE TOWN. Set in MARIPOSA in 1911, it concerns a rich man's son who must prove himself to win the hand of his girl. It began as a radio play for 'CBC Wednesday Night' (see CBC TUESDAY NIGHT) on 31 Mar. 1954 called 'The Hero of Mariposa', and appeared on CBC-TV as 'Sunshine Town' on 26 Dec. 1954. The stage première was mounted by the NEW PLAY SOCIETY on 10 Jan. 1955, and it was successfully revived by the CHARLOTTETOWN SUMMER FESTIVAL on 29 July 1968.

Super Continental, The. The transcontinental train service offered by CANADIAN NATIONAL RAILWAYS. Each day Super Continentals leave Montreal, Toronto, and Vancouver and travel across the country with full complements of observation and sleeping cars. The Super Continental was introduced on 24 Apr. 1955, replacing The CONTINENTAL LIMITED.

Superior court. A court with more jurisdiction than an INFERIOR COURT. Superior courts include the SUPREME COURT OF CANADA, the FEDERAL COURT OF CANADA, all provincial appeal courts, and provincial Supreme Courts and Courts of QUEEN'S BENCH.

Supply, Committee of. Members of the House of Commons acting as a financial committee to consider expenditures proposed by the government. It was abolished in 1968. All estimates of expenditure are now scrutinized by standing committees.

Supply and Services, Department of. A federal government department that provides the goods and services required by governments and agencies, makes payments on behalf of a federal department, and maintains the fiscal and public accounts of Canada. Established in 1969, it is organized into two major administrations: Supply and Services. The Minister of Supply and Services is also the RECEIVER GENERAL OF CANADA.

Supreme Court of Canada. Highest appeal court in the land. Established in 1875, it consists of the Chief Justice of Canada and eight PUISNE (junior) judges, appointed by the GOVERNOR IN COUNCIL. The court sits in Ottawa and exercises appellate jurisdiction throughout Canada in civil and criminal cases. It is required to advise on questions referred to it by the Governor in Council and may also advise the Senate and the House of Commons on PRIVATE BILLS. Appeals may be brought to it from any final judgment of the highest court of final resort in a province in any case where the value of the matter in dispute exceeds $10,000. The judgement of the Supreme Court of Canada is final and conclusive. See also CHIEF JUSTICE OF CANADA.

Surmeyan, Hazaros (b.1943). Dancer. Born in Skoplje, Yugoslavia, he joined the Yugoslav Skoplje Ballet in 1960 and the Cologne Ballet in 1963-6. He became a principal dancer with the NATIONAL BALLET OF CANADA in 1966. His first role was Romeo in John Cranko's *Romeo and Juliet* and he has danced as principal in most of the National's classical repertoire.

Surrey, Phillip (b.1910). Painter. Born in Calgary, Alta, he studied painting at the Winnipeg School of Art and at the Vancouver School of Art under F.H. VARLEY. He worked as photographic editor and features editor of *Weekend Magazine* from 1937 to 1964, when he became associate editor. He is a painter of Montreal whose cityscapes in oil and watercolour are evocative and personal. Representative paintings are *The Crocodile* (1940, AGO) and the colourful *Girouard Avenue* (1968, private coll.), one of a series of night scenes painted in the 1960s.

Survival. (i) A catchword among those concerned with Canadian sovereignty. (ii) The title of Margaret ATWOOD's examination of the 'victim' theme in Canadian literature, published in 1972, which gave the word currency in a literary context. (iii) The French *la survivance* has long been a rallying cry among French Canadians concerned about the erosion of their cultural identity on an English-speaking continent.

Survivance, La. See SURVIVAL.

Susannah, A Little Girl with the Mounties. A once-popular children's novel about a nine-year-old girl who 'joins' the North West Mounted Police in Regina in 1896. It was written by Winnipeg-born Muriel DENISON and published in 1936. It was turned into a film, SUSANNAH OF THE MOUNTIES (1939), that starred Shirley Temple, and was succeeded by three sequels.

Susannah of the Mounties. Feature film directed by William A. Seiter for 20th Century-Fox and released in 1939. It starred Randolph Scott, Margaret Lockwood, and Shirley Temple as the heroine of Muriel DENISON's novel SUSANNAH, A LITTLE GIRL WITH THE MOUNTIES (1936). 78 min., b & w.

Sussex Drive. Important thoroughfare in Ottawa on which are located the ROYAL CANADIAN MINT, EARNSCLIFFE, 24 SUSSEX DRIVE, and GOVERNMENT HOUSE.

Susskind, Walter (b.1913). Conductor and pianist. Born in Prague, Czech., he had an impressive European and Australian career before coming to Canada in 1956 to conduct the TORONTO SYMPHONY ORCHESTRA (1956-65). During his influential Canadian career he also conducted the CANADIAN OPERA COMPANY (1957-64), the TORONTO MENDELSSOHN CHOIR (1960-4), and the NATIONAL YOUTH ORCHESTRA, which he founded in 1960. He was director of the St Louis Symphony for seven years, resigning in Sept. 1975, and is now a free-lance conductor.

Sutherland, Donald (b.1935). Film actor. Born in Saint John, N.B., and raised in Bridgewater, N.S., he acted with the STRAW HAT PLAYERS and HART HOUSE THEATRE, graduating from the University of Toronto in 1958. He then studied at the London Academy of Music and Dramatic Art. The lanky 6 ft 4 in. actor got his start in England in 1964, and since then has appeared in ACT OF THE HEART (1970), *M.A.S.H.* (1969), *Alien Thunder* (1973), and *The Day of the Locust* (1975), etc. Formerly married to Jean Douglas, the daughter of Tommy DOUGLAS, he is now married to Francine Racette, a Quebec actress, and lives in Paris.

Sutherland, Fraser (b.1946). Poet and editor. Born in Pictou, N.S., and educated at the University of King's College in Halifax and at Carleton University, Ottawa, he has lived since 1971 in Montreal, where he edited and published NORTHERN JOURNAL. He writes 'hyper-real' poetry-inventive, imaginative, and influenced by European writers—that has been included in *Strange Ironies* (1972) and *In the Wake Of* (1974). He has also written a comparative study of Morley CALLAGHAN and Ernest Hemingway: *The Style of Innocence* (1972).

Sutherland, James T. (Cap). (c.1860-1955). Hockey official. Born in Kingston, Ont., he played in a four-team hockey league in 1885 and became president of the Ontario Hockey Association in 1915. Four years later he became president of the Canadian Amateur Hockey Association. He helped to build Kingston's Hockey HALL OF FAME.

Sutherland, John (1919-56). Poet and editor. Born in Liverpool, N.S., he attended McGill University and while there founded FIRST STATEMENT (1942-5), a mimeographed poetry magazine that stressed the need for a more down-to-earth language and imagery than were used by the metaphysically minded contributors to its rival PREVIEW. First Statement Press issued a number of important chapbooks, beginning with Irving LAYTON's *Here and Now* (1945). *First Statement* merged with *Preview* to become NORTHERN REVIEW, which Sutherland edited from Dec. 1945 to the summer of 1956. When Robert FINCH received the Governor General's Award for his *Poems* (1946), Sutherland's savage review of the book so alienated its contributing editors that many of them resigned. Sutherland also edited *Other Canadians: An Anthology of the New Poetry of Canada, 1940-46* (1947) and wrote the critical essay *The Poetry of E.J. Pratt: A New Interpretation* (1956). Miriam WADDINGTON edited and warmly introduced *John Sutherland: Essays, Controversies, and Poems* (1972).

Suttles, Duncan (b.1945). Canadian chess champion, 1969. Born in San Francisco, he now resides in Vancouver. In 1972 he was awarded the title of International Grand Master for his performance at the San Antonio International Tournament. He ranks first on Canada's chess rating list and is recognized as the world's foremost authority on the Pirc Defence.

'Suzanne'. A hit song by Leonard COHEN written in 1966. The lyrics tell of the poet's love for a half-mad girl, 'our lady of the harbour', who 'wears rags and feathers from Salvation Army counters' and 'feeds you tea and oranges that come all the way from China' until 'she's touched your perfect body with her mind'.

Suzuki, David (b.1936). Geneticist and broadcaster. Born in Vancouver of Japanese ancestry and interned with his family during the Second World War, he was an authority on the fruit fly and a professor of zoology at the University of British Columbia from 1963 to 1975, when he decided to devote himself full time to the popularization of science. His half-hour weekly CBC-TV series 'Suzuki on Science' began on 10 Jan. 1971. He has written and hosted numerous science programs since then.

Sverdrup Basin. A sedimentary basin that extends from Melville Island to Ellesmere Island in the high Arctic. Significant natural gas and some oil discoveries have been made there, notably at Drake Point, King Christian Island, and Romulus on Ellesmere Island. It was named after the Norwegian Arctic explorer Otto Neumann Sverdrup (1855-1930).

Swastika Clubs. Fascist-style youth groups in Toronto in the 1930s. A number of these clubs for teenage boys sprang up briefly in the East End of Toronto in 1933. They adopted the Nazi swastika emblem as a badge.

Sweet Substitute. Feature film produced and directed by Lawrence KENT, released in 1964. It is about student sexuality and aroused a greater furor than Kent's earlier film, BITTER ASH. It starred Robert Howay and Angela Gann and won a Special Feature award at the Canadian Film Awards in 1965. For American distribution, under the title *Caressed*, a nude scene was added. 90 min., b & w.

Sydenham, Lord (1799-1841). Governor general of the Canadas, 1839-41. Born Charles Poulett Thomson, he was appointed governor general of Upper and Lower Canada in 1839, succeeding Lord DURHAM. He was created Baron Sydenham of Kent in England and of Toronto in Canada for assisting the accomplishment of a legislative union of the Canadas. Reappointed governor of the Province of Canada, he only partially implemented RESPONSIBLE GOVERNMENT, to which he was opposed. He died from a fall off a horse in Kingston.

Sydney Strikes. A series of strikes by steelworkers and miners on Cape Breton Island, N.S., between 28 June and 1 Aug. 1923.

Steelworkers struck for higher wages, the eight-hour day, and union recognition. Protest strikes were threatened when the homes of strike leaders were searched for evidence of sedition. Civil disorder resulted, and when the militia was called in, the miners struck in protest. The strikers refused a back-to-work order from the union, and the district charter of the United Mine Workers was revoked and the officers removed. Dissatisfaction continued with sporadic strikes well into 1925.

Syllabics. A system of writing in syllables devised for the use of Indians and Eskimos. A wholly new alphabet derived from shorthand notation was devised for the Cree Indians by the Methodist missionary James EVANS about 1840; in a modified form it was introduced to the Eskimos on Baffin Island by the Anglican missionary E.J. Peck in 1894. The Eskimo syllabic system used across the Arctic today (excluding the Labrador and Mackenzie Eskimos, who use Roman orthography) has 11 symbols for the different consonants found in Eskimo speech patterns. These are rotated into four patterns to represent the four possible vowel combinations.

INUKTITUUT SYLLABARY

	▽ ai	△ i	▷ o	◁ a	(finals) lightly sounded
P	∨ pai	∧ pee	> po	< paw	‹ p
T	∪ tai	∩ tee	⊃ to	⊂ taw	⸓ t
K	ᕴ kai / ᕴ hkai	ᖸ kee / ᖸ hkee	ᑯ ko / ᑯ hko	ᖳ kaw / ᖳ hkaw	ᐟ k
G	ᖴ ngai	ᖽ ngee	⅃ ngo	ᒧ ngaw	∟ ng
M	⅂ mai	Γ mee	⅃ mo	⌐ maw	∟ m
N	⌐ nai	σ nee	ᕪ no	ᕬ naw	ᐠ n
S	ᕽ shai	ᖀ shee	ᖅ sho	ᕼ shaw	ᕀ s
L	⊃ lai	⊂ lee	⊃ lo	⊂ law	ᕐ l
Y	ᐸ yai	ᐳ yee	ᐘ yo	ᐳ yaw	
V	∨ vai	ᐱ vee	> vo	< vaw	‹ v
R	∪ hrai	∩ hree	⊃ hro	ᕲ hraw	ᕐ r

Symonds, Norman (b.1920). Composer. Born in Nelson, B.C., he taught himself the clarinet while serving in the Royal Canadian Navy from 1939 to 1946 and played with a local Halifax jazz group in 1940-1. He continued his training at the Royal Conservatory of Music, Toronto, while working in the dance-band field as performer and arranger. Usually employing jazz idioms, he has written, on commission, works for stage, radio, television, and symphony orchestra.

Symons, Scott (b.1933). Novelist. Born in Toronto and educated at the University of Toronto, he was curator of the Sigmund Samuel Canadiana Building of the Royal Ontario Museum from 1962 to 1965 and then Quebec correspondent for the *Toronto Telegram*. He is the author of two stream-of-consciousness novels, *Place d'Armes* (1967) and *Civic Square* (1969), and of *Heritage: A Romantic Look at Early Canadian Furniture* (1971), with photographs by John de Visser.

Syncrude Canada Limited. A consortium of multi-national oil companies established to extract oil from the ATHABASCA TAR SANDS. Conceived in 1963, approved by the Alberta government in 1973, and scheduled to begin operations in 1976, Syncrude encountered financial difficulties in 1974 (when Atlantic Richfield bowed out) that were overcome in 1975 when the consortium of Imperial Oil, Gulf Oil, and Cities Service received an infusion of new capital from the federal government and the provinces of Alberta and Ontario.

Syrinx. An experimental rock group formed in Toronto in 1970. It is led by the composer John Mills-Cockell (b.1943), who performs on a Moog Synthesizer, which permits a blending of styles from African primitive to rock. Syrinx has appeared on television, on stage, and in concert.

Szep, Paul (b.1941). Well-known American editorial cartoonist. Born in Hamilton, Ont., and a graduate of the Ontario College of Art, he joined the Boston *Globe* in 1966. His finely drawn editorial cartoons, influenced by Duncan MACPHERSON, won him the Pulitzer Prize in 1974.

T

T.O. A playful abbreviation of TORONTO, dating from the 1960s.

Tabloid. The earliest and most influential of CBC-TV's public-affairs shows. It was created and stylishly produced by Ross McLEAN and made its début on CBLT in Toronto on 2 Mar. 1953. The 30-minute, five-day-a-week show starred Elaine Grand, Dick McDougal, Gil Christy, and Percy SALTZMAN, and was billed as 'facts with fun'. Because a pharmaceutical firm had copyrighted the commercial use of the word 'tabloid', the title was changed on 12 Sept. 1960 to 'Seven-O-One' (a reference to the time slot, following a 60-second news recap at 7:00 p.m.). Joyce Davidson, John O'Leary, and Max FERGUSON were regulars on this program, which was replaced on 12 Sept. 1966 by TBA, a similar program taking for its title the TV term for 'To Be Announced'; it ended on 22 Sept. 1967.

Taché, Alexandre-Antonin (1823-94). Bishop of St Boniface. Born in Rivière-du-Loup, L.C. (Que.), he entered the Oblate Order in 1844 and was sent to the RED RIVER SETTLEMENT, where he was ordained. He was made bishop in 1871. Sympathetic to the MÉTIS, he attempted to arrange a settlement of their grievances prior to the RED RIVER REBELLION, during which he was out of the country. After the NORTH WEST REBELLION he took the view that RIEL was insane. A staunch believer in denominational schools, he promoted this cause during the MANITOBA SCHOOLS QUESTION.

Taché, Sir Étienne-Paschal (1795-1865). A FATHER OF CONFEDERATION. Born in Saint-Thomas-de-Montmagny, L.C. (Que.), he studied medicine. He sat in the legislative assembly from 1841 to 1846 and was appointed to the legislative council in 1848. He led the Canada East (Quebec) section in the ministries of A.N. MacNAB and John A. MACDONALD and in 1864 became premier of the GREAT COALITION. He died shortly after presiding over the QUEBEC CONFERENCE on Confederation. He was knighted in 1858.

Tadoussac. A Quebec village on the east shore of the SAGUENAY RIVER, near its mouth. Visited by CARTIER in 1535 and by ROBERVAL in 1542, it became a French trading post. 16

men were left there by the fur trader Pierre Chauvin to spend the winter of 1600-1. This attempt at a colony was disastrous, but Tadoussac became increasingly important in the fur trade. A wooden chapel built in 1747 still stands.

Taft, Sammy (b.1913). 'World-famous hatter'. Born in Toronto, he has sold hats and ties from his well-known store at 303 Spadina Ave, Toronto, since 1935. In the thirties he developed the 'slouch hat', which became associated with Hollywood gangsters; during the late thirties and early forties he sold some 9,000 of these hats a year. The 'slouch hat', first known as 'the Sammy', has been called the 'Chicago block', the 'Boston block', the 'pork-pie slouch', and the 'turn-down slouch'—different names for different creases. A 'slouch-hat' revival was launched in the 1970s by such Hollywood films as *The Sting, Chinatown*, and *The Great Gatsby*.

Tahltan. ATHAPASKAN-speaking Indians of the mountain interior east of the Alaskan Pan Handle. They were primarily salmon eaters, and were strongly influenced by the adjacent Pacific Coast cultures. Their population in 1970 was 702.

Taiga. The great boreal coniferous forest of Canada. From northern Alberta east of the Rockies, it stretches in a wide arc to the Maritimes—north of the Prairies and deciduous woodland, and south of the tundra—comprising the single largest ecological system on the continent, and the third-largest continuous forest in the world (after Siberia's similar taiga and the Amazonian rainforest). The principal species include spruce, balsam fir, jack pine, and tamarack. Taiga is a Russian word of Turkish origin meaning 'rocky mountainous terrain'.

Taignoagny. See DONNACONA.

Take One. An international film magazine founded in Montreal in 1966 and published every two months. It is edited and published by Peter Lebensold with Joe Medjuck. Circulated widely in the United States, it has not concentrated on Canadian films and has thus spurred a number of nationalistic magazines like CINEMA CANADA and MOTION.

Take 30. Long-running afternoon CBC-TV show. A 30-minute program of interviews, talks, and special features of interest to housewives, it was first seen on 17 Sept. 1962. The hosts were Anna Cameron and Paul Soles. Adrienne CLARKSON replaced Anna Cameron on 20 Sept. 1965, and she in turn was succeeded by Mary Lou Finlay on 3 Sept. 1975. It is telecast five days a week.

Takeover. The acquisition of a Canadian business by a foreign (especially an American) business organization. See also MULTINATIONAL CORPORATION.

Talbot, Thomas (1771-1853). Founder of the Talbot Settlement. Born in Ireland, he joined the British army and was first in Canada in 1790-4. Returning in 1801, he was granted 5,000 acres in Upper Canada (Ontario), on land fronting on Lake Erie, and founded his settlement, building roads (including the TALBOT ROAD), establishing townships, and acting as the autocratic patriarch of some 6,000 settlers, until his powers were finally curtailed in 1848.

Talbot Road. Historic road in southwestern Ontario built at the instigation of Thomas TALBOT. Constructed in 1809-11 and later extended and improved, it followed the north shore of Lake Erie from the Niagara R. at Fort Erie to the Detroit R. at Sandwich (Windsor). Highway No. 3 follows much of the same route.

Talbot Settlement. See Thomas TALBOT.

Talc. See SOAPSTONE.

Talirunilik, Joe. (b.1899). Eskimo sculptor and printmaker at POVUNGNITUK. He is known for his finely detailed depictions of the whale hunt. His masterpiece is *The Migration*, a carving of an UMIAK with 40 people aboard. It—and a well-known print called *Return of the Survivors from the Floating Ice*—is drawn from a dramatic journey of his infancy when 13 families paddled to safety in an *umiak* through threatening ice-floes.

Talon, Jean (1626-94). First and best-known INTENDANT of New France. During his two administrations—1665-8 and 1670-2—he encouraged agriculture, industry, crafts, and education in the colony on the St Lawrence; gave it order and justice; stimulated trade; increased the population; and aided settlers. He changed the face of New France, enlarging its extent by the encouragement of exploration and the establishment of far-flung trading posts. He is sometimes referred to as the Great Intendant, the title of a biography of him by Thomas Chapais published in 1914.

Talonbooks. A publishing house devoted to experimental poetry, fiction, and drama. Founded in Vancouver in 1967 by two writers, Jim Brown and David Robinson, it specializes in fine design. A series of 'Talonplays' is edited by Peter Hay.

Tamarack. A species of larch pine, the only deciduous coniferous tree in Canada. It grows 40-70 ft high and is widely distributed from Newfoundland to northeastern British Columbia. In the early years of European settlement its strong, heavy wood was used in shipbuilding and for posts and railway ties.

Tamarack Review, The. A literary quarterly devoted to new stories, poems, essays, and reviews by established and new Canadian writers. It was founded in Toronto in 1956 and was modelled to some extent on the *London Magazine*. The founding editors were Robert WEAVER, with Kildare DOBBS, Millar MacLure, Ivon Owen, William Toye, and Anne WILKINSON. Weaver and Toye are still on the editorial board, which was joined by John Robert Colombo in 1960 and Janis RAPOPORT in 1974.

Tanabe, Takao (b.1926). Painter. Born in Prince Rupert, B.C., he studied at the Winnipeg School of Art and is director of painting at the BANFF CENTRE School of Fine Arts. Using the west-coast landscape as an inspiration, he painted lyrical, pale-coloured impressions of it before turning to a hard-edge abstract style based on geometric and calligraphic shapes. He is exhibited and collected internationally.

Tanner, Elaine (b.1951). Swimmer. Born in Vancouver, she started racing at 13 and two years later not only won the American championships in backstroke and butterfly events but also set the world's record in '220 yards individual medley'. She won four gold and three silver medals in the 1966 British Commonwealth games in Kingston, Jamaica. Then she won two gold medals and three silver medals at the 1967 Pan-American Games in Winnipeg. After winning three medals—two silver and one bronze—in the 1968 Olympics in Mexico City, she retired from competition and returned to school at the age of 18. She has been dubbed 'The Mighty Mouse'.

Tanner Trophy, The Elaine. See SPORTS FEDERATION OF CANADA.

Tantramar Marshes. 80 sq. mi. of land near Sackville, N.B. Sometimes called the world's biggest hayfield, this fertile land—full of wildlife—is shielded from the sea by old Acadian dikes. The marshes inspired some of the lyrical nature poetry of Charles G.D. ROBERTS and are immortalized in one of his best poems, 'The Tantramar Revisited'.

Tapp, Gordie (b.1920). Country-and-western singer. Born in London, Ont., he studied

at the ACADEMY OF RADIO ARTS in 1946. As an emcee and band leader he acquired a national following in the 1950s with CBC-TV's 'Country Hoedown', delighting audiences with his impersonation of the country yokel Cousin Clem, a character he created in 1947. For his smooth professional manner Tapp has been called 'the country gentleman'.

Tapscott, Carl. See CARL TAPSCOTT SINGERS.

Tar Sands. See ATHABASCA TAR SANDS.

Tariff. Schedule of customs duties. The Canadian tariff consists of three sets of rates on imported goods. British Preferential status, the lowest rate, is extended to Commonwealth countries. Most-Favoured-Nations status, the next lowest rate, is extended to most other non-Commonwealth countries. General status, the highest rate, applies to a negligible number of countries.

Tarragon Theatre. A Toronto theatrical group that specializes in the production of new Canadian plays. Under the resident director William GLASSCO, the first production in its 180-seat theatre was David Freeman's CREEPS on 5 Oct. 1971. It is also known for its production of James REANEY's theatrical trilogy *The* DONNELLYS in 1973-4-5, and for presenting Michel TREMBLAY's *Hosanna* in translation in 1974.

Tassie's School. The nickname of the Galt Grammar School, established in 1852 in Galt, C.W. (Ont.). It was named after William Tassie, its Dublin-born headmaster from 1853 to 1881, and is said to have attracted students from across the continent.

Tax-sharing agreement. See EQUALIZATION PAYMENTS.

Tay. A township in Simcoe Co., Ont., named in 1822 after one of the three pet dogs of Lady Sarah, the wife of Sir Peregrine Maitland, the lieutenant-governor of UPPER CANADA from 1818 to 1828. See also FLOS and TINY.

Taylor, E.P. (b.1901). Capitalist and sportsman. Born in Ottawa, he graduated from McGill University in mechanical engineering in 1922. He became president of Canadian Breweries Limited in 1930 and nine years later established the ARGUS CORPORATION, which he headed until 1969. During the Second World War he held many advisory positions concerned with the manufacturing of munitions and supplies. An outspoken critic of socialism, big government, and economic nationalism, Taylor (whose initials stand for Edward Plunket) has been dubbed 'Excess

Profits' Taylor. In 1936 he began breeding thoroughbreds at Windfield Farms Limited, Oshawa—named after his estate WINDFIELDS, in North York, Toronto—and he has headed the Breeders of North America since 1974. Since his retirement in 1969 he has lived at Lyford Cay, Bahamas. He is now chairman of the New Providence Development Company Ltd in Nassau. See also NORTHERN DANCER.

Taylor, Fred (Cyclone) (b.1883). Hockey player. Born in Tara, Ont., he played hockey in Listowel, Thessalon, Portage La Prairie, Houghton (Michigan), Renfrew, Ottawa, and finally Vancouver, where his career ended in 1921. A brilliant player, he was chosen to perform the sod-turning for the Hockey HALL OF FAME in Toronto in 1960.

Taylor Statten Camps. Prestigious summer camps for boys and girls between 8 and 16, located in ALGONQUIN PROVINCIAL PARK. Camp Ahmek for boys and Camp Wapomed for girls were established in 1921 by Dr Taylor Statten, a Toronto-born psychiatrist who taught at McGill University.

TBA. See TABLOID.

TCA. See TRANS-CANADA AIR LINES.

Teach-Ins, The International. A series of topical conferences organized by students of York University and the University of Toronto in the 1960s. The first annual two-day affair attracted some 6,000 observers, and an estimated 100,000 listened to the addresses and debates over the 'International Teach-In Radio Network' that covered North America. Held on 8-10 Oct. 1965 and called 'Revolution and Response', the first Teach-In was really about U.S. involvement in Vietnam. Subsequent topics were 'China: Co-existence or Containment?' (1966); 'Religion and International Affairs' (1967); and 'Exploding Humanity: The Crisis of Numbers' (1968). Some of the proceedings have been published.

Teach Me How to Cry. Play by Patricia Joudry (b.1921) about young love in a prairie town. It was broadcast on CBC-TV on 13 Oct. 1953 and opened at the CREST THEATRE, Toronto, in a production directed by Leon MAJOR, on 4 Apr. 1955. In 1958 it failed in London— where it was called *Noon Has No Shadows*— and in New York. As *The Restless Years* it was filmed in Hollywood in 1958.

Team Canada. The name of two all-star hockey teams mounted by the NATIONAL HOCKEY LEAGUE and the WORLD HOCKEY ASSOCI-

ATION in 1972 and 1974 respectively to compete against Soviet 'amateur' teams in Moscow and in several North American cities. The two series of eight games each were billed as 'the hockey series of the century'. The NHL's Team Canada 72 won their series by four games to three with one game tied— on the strength of a single goal scored by Paul Henderson in the final game on 27 Sept. 1972. The WHA's team lost their series by four games to one with three games tied. Team Canada 76 was formed from Canadian players in the NHL and WHA to compete in a six-team tournament—representing six countries—in Sept. 1976. These games will be played in Montreal, Toronto, Ottawa, Winnipeg, Quebec City, and Philadelphia. The winning team will be decided by a play-off between the two top teams.

Technical and Vocational Training Assistance Act. By virtue of this Act of 1960 the federal government agreed to share costs of technical and vocational training with provincial governments—75% of capital costs of new facilities and 50% of operating costs of technician training. As a result, within nine years COMMUNITY COLLEGES were established in most provinces and the number of technical students rose from 8,300 to 80,000.

Teck Corporation Limited. A Vancouver-based company with extensive gold, silver, lead, zinc, oil, and gas interests. The operation had its origin in a company incorporated in 1913 to develop the Teck-Hughes gold mine in Teck Township near Kirkland Lake in northern Ontario, staked by two brothers, Billy and Jim Hughes. This company later developed the Lamaque mine in Bourlamaque Township in the Val d'Or region of Quebec. Following the acquisition of the original company in 1959 by Dr Norman B. Keevil, a geophysicist turned miner and financier, it began to diversify. Teck is developing a new columbium mine in Quebec, a copper and smelting complex in British Columbia, and a zinc mine in Newfoundland.

Tecumseh (1768-1813). Shawnee chief. Born in the Ohio country, he became influential over a large group of tribes and supported the British in the WAR OF 1812. He was put in charge of Indian troops and fought courageously until his death in the Battle of the THAMES.

Teepee. Siouan word for a conical structure of poles covered with buffalo hide or canvas used by the Indians of the Prairies. See also the Algonkian WIGWAM and the Eskimo TUPEK.

Tekahionwake. See Pauline JOHNSON.

Tekakwitha, Kateri (1656-80). Saintly Christian Mohawk, known as Lily of the Mohawks. Persecuted after her baptism in 1675, she fled to CAUGHNAWAGA, Que., where she was revered after her death. Her relics lie in a tomb in the Mission Church of St Francis Xavier there. She was declared venerable in 1943 and is being considered for beatification. She appeared in visions to the central character in Leonard COHEN's novel BEAUTIFUL LOSERS (1966).

Téléglobe Canada. The name given the Canadian Overseas Telecommunication Corporation in 1976 to symbolize its concern with 'world communications'. The CROWN CORPORATION was established in 1950 to maintain and operate Canada's external telecommunications services, which include telegraph, telephone, telex, and other transmissions outside the country.

Telegraph votes, To. Slang for the practice of voting more than once in a Quebec election by impersonating other voters—as in the election of 1877 contested by Wilfrid LAURIER in Drummond-Arthabaska, in which 3,800 votes were cast in a constituency where there were only 3,200 registered voters. (Laurier lost.) The French verb is *télégrapher*. The origin of the expression is obscure.

Telephone. See Alexander Graham BELL.

Telephone City. Unofficial motto of Brantford, Ont., where Alexander Graham BELL conceived the idea of the telephone in 1874.

Telesat Canada. A corporation to establish satellites to provide telecommunication services, incorporated in 1969. Its shareholders are the federal government and the commercial telecommunications carriers.

Telescope. A popular 30-minute CBC-TV series. Seen from 1 July 1963 to 21 Dec. 1972, it was produced and hosted by Fletcher MARKLE. In its early years it presented topics of social and cultural interest; in its later years it profiled well-known people in the arts and show business.

Temperance beer. A weak brew, legally bottled and sold during the PROHIBITION years in Canada.

Templeton, Charles (b.1915). Journalist, author, broadcaster. Born in Toronto, he has been a sports cartoonist (1932-6), an evangelist (1938-56), a television personality (1957-60), a newspaper editor (1960-4), a television executive (1967-9), and editor of MACLEAN'S (Feb.-Sept. 1969); at present he is a radio broadcaster. He is the author of *Jesus* (1973), a retelling of the Gospels, and *The Kidnapping of the President* (1974), a thriller.

Ten-B-X. See FIVE-B-X.

Ten Lost Years. A collection of interviews, with the subtitle *Memoirs of Canadians who Survived the* DEPRESSION, taped by Barry BROADFOOT, published in 1973. It was adapted for the stage by Cedric Smith and Jack WINTER for TORONTO WORKSHOP PRODUCTIONS the following year.

Ten Women, Two Men and a Moose. A two-hour entertainment based on writings by Canadian authors, mostly women, selected and performed by Mia Anderson in 1972 at FESTIVAL LENNOXVILLE and then on a national tour and on radio and television.

Tennant, Veronica (b.1946). Dancer. Born in London, Eng., she trained at the Arts Educational School in London and then in 1955 at the National Ballet School in Toronto. Since 1967 she has been a principal dancer with the NATIONAL BALLET OF CANADA, distinguishing herself particularly as Juliet in John Cranko's *Romeo and Juliet*.

Tennis Championship, Canadian Open. See ROTHMANS CANADIAN OPEN TENNIS CHAMPIONSHIP.

Tenth Decade, The. An eight-part series of CBC-TV documentaries on Canadian political life from 1957 to 1967. The one-hour programs were researched by Peter C. NEWMAN, produced by Cameron Graham, and narrated by Jon Granik. The series was launched on 27 Oct. 1971.

Teperman and Sons Ltd. A firm of wrecking contractors whose orange-and-black signs are a common and frequently ominous sight throughout Ontario and Quebec. Founded in Toronto in 1933 by Samuel Teperman, the firm has been run by his grandson Marvin since 1965. Teperman's largest single contract was for demolishing the town of Morrisburg, Ont., in 1958 to make way for the ST LAWRENCE SEAWAY. It took four and a half months to level the 280 buildings.

Tercentenary, The. See the QUEBEC TERCENTENARY.

Terra Nova. Latin for 'new land', an early name for NEWFOUNDLAND. It appeared on Johann Ruysch's *Mappimundi* in 1507 and designated the area he considered to be the easternmost border of Asia. In the sixteenth century the name was also used to refer to both North and South America.

Terra Nova National Park. Established in 1957 on the northeastern coast of Newfoundland, it is the most easterly of Canada's national parks. It includes 153 sq. mi. of spectacular inlets, rocky points, and a boreal forest.

Terre des Hommes. See MAN AND HIS WORLD.

Territorial government. The power or authority within a TERRITORY. No jurisdiction or powers are allocated to a territory under the BNA ACT, and a territorial government has only the authority allocated to it by the federal government. In the NORTHWEST TERRITORIES the government consists of a COMMISSIONER and a deputy commissioner appointed by the federal government, and a council of 10 elected and four appointed members. In the YUKON TERRITORY the government consists of a commissioner appointed by the federal government, an elected council of seven members, and an executive committee comprising the commissioner and four members, two of whom are members of the council. The council has authority to legislate on all matters that come under provincial jurisdiction except natural resources. The role of the commissioner in the Yukon Territory is similar to that of a LIEUTENANT-GOVERNOR—he calls the council into session, and gives his assent to legislation passed by it.

Territory. A region in Canada that has not achieved the status of a PROVINCE. There are two territories in Canada: the NORTHWEST TERRITORIES and YUKON TERRITORY. See also TERRITORIAL GOVERNMENT.

Terroir, Le. A school of writing in Quebec that celebrated the French Canadians' attachment to 'the homeland' and 'the soil'. It began in the late nineteenth century and was at its height between 1915 and 1920. Typical of le terroir were the poems of Nérée Beauchemin (1850-1931) and L'Appel de la terre (1919), a novel by Damase Potvin (1881-1964). Such writing was encouraged by the ÉCOLE LITTÉRAIRE DE MONTRÉAL.

Texasgulf Inc. A minerals company incorporated in Texas in 1909 with origins in sulphur production, but best known as the discoverer (in Apr. 1964) and developer of the Kidd Creek copper and zinc mine at Timmins, Ont. This is one of the richest mines in the world. Texasgulf holds extensive interests in natural gas and oil and other mining concerns in Canada, the United States, and Australia. In 1973, the CANADA DEVELOPMENT CORPORATION acquired effective control of Texasgulf by purchasing a 30% interest in the company.

Thames, Battle of the. An engagement in the WAR OF 1812. On 5 Oct. 1813 the American Gen. William Harrison, leading a raiding party on the Thames R., defeated British forces at the mission village of Fairfield (MORAVIANTOWN, near Chatham, U.C. [Ont.]). Col. Henry Procter escaped with his life but his ally, TECUMSEH, died in the raid, which is sometimes known as the Battle of Moraviantown.

Thanksgiving Day. Statutory holiday observed throughout Canada since 1957 on the second Monday in October as the day on which thanks are given for a bountiful harvest. The first formal service of thanksgiving on the North American continent was observed by Sir Martin FROBISHER in the eastern Arctic in 1578. The citizens of Halifax proclaimed a day of thanksgiving in 1763 to celebrate the TREATY OF PARIS. It was only in 1879 that Parliament set aside a day of thanksgiving, on 6 Nov. Until 1957 it was celebrated on various days in October and November. In the United States, Thanksgiving Day, observed since 1789 on the last Thursday in November, celebrates the landing of the Pilgrim Fathers in 1681.

That Summer in Paris. Memoir by Morley CALLAGHAN published in 1963. A nostalgic account of the author's experiences during the summer of 1929, it recalls his friendship with Hemingway and Fitzgerald and other English and American expatriate writers who formed a kind of literary village in Paris at the time.

Thayendanegea. See Joseph BRANT.

Theatre Calgary. Regional theatre founded in Calgary in 1968. It was formed by Christopher Newton, artistic director, out of the amalgamation of two amateur companies. Its first production was Neil Simon's *The Odd Couple* in 1968 in a 493-seat theatre in the Allied Arts Centre.

Theatre Canada. A successor to the DOMINION DRAMA FESTIVAL. It was founded in 1970 to arrange non-competitive theatrical festivals in six regions and one national festival each year devoted to plays produced by amateur and semi-professional theatres across the country. The first such festival was held in Ottawa in the week of 17 May 1971.

Théâtre du Nouveau Monde. Quebec's leading repertory theatre. It was founded in Montreal in 1951 by Jean GASCON, Jean-Louis

ROUX, and the actor Guy Hoffman. The first production, in Oct. 1961 in the old Orpheum Theatre, was Molière's *L'Avare*. The company made a favourable impression at the Second International Festival of Dramatic Art in Paris in 1955 and played on Broadway in 1958. It moved to the 823-seat Théâtre Port-Royale in the PLACE DES ARTS in 1967. The TNM is the home of Les Jeunes Comédiens, an award-winning troupe of students of the NATIONAL THEATRE SCHOOL, which was first sent on a tour of western Canada in Oct. 1963.

Théâtre du Rideau Vert. Quebec's oldest repertory theatre. The 'Theatre of the Green Curtain' was founded on 30 Nov. 1948 in Montreal by the actress-director Yvette BRIND'AMOUR, with Mercedes Palomino as administrative director. It has a reputation for light commercial plays, which it produces along with classical plays.

Theatre New Brunswick. Regional theatre in Fredericton, N.B. It was founded in 1968, with Walter Learning as artistic director and Brian Swarbrick as administrator. It operates out of the Playhouse, the popular name of the 800-seat Beaverbrook Auditorium. TNB's first production was John Van Druten's *Bell, Book and Candle*.

Theatre of Freedom, The. A series of live 'inspirational dramas' on CBC Radio during the Second World War. The 60-minute Sunday-night programs, produced from 2 Feb. to 27 Apr. 1941 by Rupert Lucas, presented adaptations of British and American plays and starred Broadway and Hollywood performers who donated their talent for the war effort.

Theatre of Neptune. See Marc LESCARBOT.

Théâtre Passe Muraille. An underground theatrical collective established in Toronto in 1968 through ROCHDALE COLLEGE to produce offbeat plays. *Passe muraille* is French for 'passing beyond walls'. It was created largely by University of Toronto students, with Tim Gerrard as its founding artistic director. He was succeeded by Paul Thompson in 1970.

Theatre Under the Stars. A series of plays and musical comedies presented in the open air at the Malkin Bowl in Vancouver's STANLEY PARK. TUTS (as it was called) arranged summer programs from 1939 to 1961.

Thélus. See VIMY.

Therafields. A psychotherapeutic movement in Toronto. The name, chosen by a practising lay psychotherapist named Lea Hindley-Smith, combines the words 'therapy' and 'fields' to describe both the curing process and the farm in southern Ontario where a group meets for weekend retreats, discussion, psychotherapy, and 'theradramas'. Therafields Corporation was chartered as a charitable foundation in 1967, and Therafields Environmental Centre (York) Limited was founded as a company with share capital in 1970 to maintain the real estate, etc., of the movement.

Thériault, Yves (b.1915). Quebec novelist. Born in Quebec City of French and Montagnais descent, he quit school at 15 and had various jobs before he became a writer for the National Film Board (1943-5) and Radio-Canada (1945-50). The most prolific writer in Canada, the closest equivalent to Jack London that Quebec has produced, Thériault has written over 1,300 radio and television scripts and some 50 books. In 1967 he published six works—one play, four novels, and a collection of 18 stories. AGAGUK (1958), translated by Miriam Chapin in 1967, is an ambitious, vigorous, yet sensitive account of an Eskimo's coming to maturity. ASHINI (1960), translated by Gwendolyn Moore in 1972, is a lyrical novel about the last chief of the Montagnais to live according to ancestral customs. N'Tsuk (1968), translated by Gwendolyn Moore in 1972, is about a century-old Montagnais woman who is anxious to relate her life story and her thoughts to a white woman. In 1969 Thériault novelized Dénis Héroux's sexploitation film, VALÉRIE (1968).

They always get their man. Expression associated with the ROYAL CANADIAN MOUNTED POLICE. This unofficial slogan dates from 13 Apr. 1877 when an approximation of these words appeared in the *Fort Benton Record*, published by John J. Healy, an American whisky-trader. The official motto of the Force is MAINTIENS LE DROIT.

Third option. See CONTRACTUAL LINK.

Thirty Acres. Title of the English translation of *Trente arpents* (1938), a classic novel of *habitant* life by Ringuet, the pseudonym of Philippe Panneton (1895-1960), a professor of medicine at the Université de Montréal and later Canadian ambassador to Portugal. Translated by Felix and Dorothea Walter, *Thirty Acres* (1940) chronicles the fall of Euchariste Moison, a hard-working farmer who inherits 30 acres of land and loses everything through his blindness to the need for social change. It marked the end of French-Canadian pastoral novels extolling *habitant* life.

Thirty Thousand Islands. The name given to the islands of eastern Georgian Bay on eastern Lake Huron.

This Country in the Morning

This Country in the Morning. A popular CBC Radio program. Heard weekday mornings from 9:15 to 12:00 from 4 Oct. 1971 to 28 June 1974, the nationalistic talk-and-music show was produced by Alex Frame and hosted by Peter GZOWSKI, with such regulars as Andrew ALLAN, Danny Finkleman, Helen Hutchison, and Larry ZOLF. Gzowski edited a bestselling compendium of material used on the show called *Peter Gzowski's This Country in the Morning* (1974). A new producer, Anne Gibson, and a new host, Michael Enright, kept the program going from 3 Sept. 1974 to 27 June 1975, when Judy LaMARSH took over as host of the 'Judy' show.

This Hour Has Seven Days. Controversial and popular CBC-TV public-affairs show. Watched each week by an estimated 3.2 million viewers, it was produced by Patrick WATSON and Douglas LEITERMAN and starred, in addition to the producers, John DRAINIE, Laurier LaPIERRE, Warner Troyer, Larry ZOLF, Robert Hoyt, Ken Lefolii, and Dinah Christie. It was seen Sunday evenings from 10 to 11 p.m. from 4 Oct. 1964 to 8 May 1966. It invented the 'hot seat' or 'bear pit' and introduced to Canadian television the techniques of investigative and advocacy journalism. Of the 50 or so shows that aired some 300 items, approximately 20 became national issues, one of them being whether the program would continue. It was terminated by CBC management and succeeded by SUNDAY.

'This Land Is Your Land'. The Canadian adaptation of an American song of the same title written in 1956 by Woody Guthrie. The adaptation was made shortly after by Martin Bochner for the TRAVELLERS and proved exceptionally popular. The Canadian words begin: 'This land is your land, this land is my land,/From Bona Vista to Vancouver Island,/From the Arctic Islands to the Great Lakes waters;/This land was made for you and me.' See also SOMETHING TO SING ABOUT.

This Magazine. A militant publication concerned with schools and teaching and also trade unions, politics, and culture. It was founded as *This Magazine Is About Schools* in Toronto in 1966 by Satu Repo, a former teacher and social worker, who edited the anthology *This Book Is About Schools* (1970). Since then the magazine, which appears six times a year, has concerned itself with socialism as much as with education.

Thom, Ron (b.1923). Architect. Born in Penticton, B.C., he trained at the Vancouver School of Art. His first works included houses in Vancouver (designed in associa-

tion with Thompson, Berwick, Pratt and Partners) that drew on traditional Japanese design, and on the works of Frank Lloyd Wright, to create a style appropriate to the west coast (the D.H. Copp house, 4755 Belmont Ave, 1951; and 1143 Eyremount Dr., 1962-3). The same creative eclecticism can be seen in the Prince Hotel, Toronto (1972-3) and MASSEY COLLEGE, on the University of Toronto campus (1960-3), which creates an environment in the manner of an Oxford College without specific stylistic references. Among his other buildings are TRENT UNIVERSITY, Peterborough (1964-9); the SHAW FESTIVAL Theatre, Niagara-on-the-Lake (1969-72); and the LESTER PEARSON COLLEGE OF THE PACIFIC, Pedder Bay, B.C. (1971-4).

Thomas, Audrey (b.1935). Novelist. Born in Binghampton, N.Y., and educated at Smith College in Massachusetts, she came to Canada in 1959 and attended the University of British Columbia, where she has taught. She has lived in England and Ghana (1964-6), settings for the stories in *Ten Green Bottles* (1964). Her compelling novels, in which she often writes about women wounded by society, are *Mrs. Blood* (1969), *Munchmeyer and Prospero on the Island* (1971), *Songs My Mother Taught Me* (1973), and *Blown Figures* (1974).

Thomas, Ian (b.1950). Pop composer and singer. Born in Dundas, Ont., he made an impact with Tranquillity Base (1966-71), the Hamilton Philharmonic's resident pop group. Performing solo since 1973, he enjoyed an international success with 'Painted Ladies', recorded that year.

Thomas, Jacob E. (b.1922). Cayuga carver. Born on the SIX NATIONS RESERVE near Brantford, Ont., he learned from his father David how to carve in the traditional Iroquois manner. He specializes in false-face and ceremonial masks and what are called 'broken-nose masks'. At least three of his 10 children—Thomas Jr (b.1947), Milton (1953-74), Gene (1960)—have produced important masks. Since 1970 he has recorded three albums of traditional songs and has been in demand as a lecturer on Iroquois lore. Since 1974 he has been associated with the North American Indian Travelling College (see ONAKE CORP.).

Thomas, Powys (b.1925). Actor. Born in Wales, he studied at the Old Vic school (1948-51), toured with the Young Vic, and appeared at the Stratford-on-Avon Festival (1952-4). In 1956 he came to Canada and performed at the CREST THEATRE; the following year he joined the STRATFORD FESTIVAL as a character actor and has appeared in 10 seasons since then. He was a founder of the NA-TIONAL THEATRE SCHOOL and its first English-language artistic director (1960-5). He appeared in the film of *The* LUCK OF GINGER COFFEY (1964).

Thomas, William (1800-60). Architect and engineer. Born in Stroud, Eng., he opened his practice in Toronto in Apr. 1841. A friend of Sir Charles Barry and the author of *Designs for Monuments and Chimney Pieces* (London, 1843), he designed buildings in a sober classical style (e.g., the Commercial Bank of the Midland District, Toronto, 1845) and was also the leading exponent of the Decorated Gothic style in Canada West (St Paul's—formerly St Andrew's—Presbyterian Church, Hamilton, 1854). His other buildings include Brock's Monument (see QUEENSTON HEIGHTS AND BROCK'S MONUMENT), Queenston (1854); St Paul's, London (1845); and in Toronto, ST LAWRENCE HALL (1849-50), St Michael's Cathedral and Bishop's Palace (1845), and Oakham Hall, his own house at Church and Gould Sts (1848). He was the father of William T. THOMAS, also an architect.

Thomas, William T. (d.1893). Architect. The son of William THOMAS, he was trained in Toronto by his father, acting first as his Clerk of Works in 1848 at Christ Church, Hamilton. After his father's death in 1860 he moved to Montreal, where he practised with his brother C.P. Thomas (who later moved to Chicago). His work includes St George's Church, Montreal; the Town Hall, Prescott, Ont.; and Trinity Church, Saint John, N.B. His commercial work—such as the Caverhill Block on rue St Pierre, Montreal, and the George STEPHEN house (now the Mount Stephen Club) on Drummond St, Montreal—are in an exuberantly ornamental Renaissance style.

Thompson. INTERIOR SALISH people named after the river that flows into the Fraser from the east. Their population in 1974 was 5,187.

Thompson, David (1770-1857). Explorer and geographer. Born in London, Eng., he joined the HUDSON'S BAY COMPANY at 14 and was sent to Churchill. As his interest in exploring and surveying developed, he joined the NORTH WEST COMPANY in 1797 and was made a partner in 1804. In 1807 he built the first trading post on the Columbia R. and in 1811 descended and charted that river to its mouth. He surveyed and mapped almost two million square miles of western North America. He named the Fraser R. after Simon FRASER, who had named the Thompson R. for him. *David Thompson's Narrative of his Explorations in*

Western North America 1784-1812 (1916; rev. ed. 1963) is an important travel document.

Thompson, Gordon V. (1885-1965). Songwriter and publisher. Born in Toronto, he penned patriotic songs like 'I Want to Kiss Daddy Goodnight' in 1916 and 'For the Glory of the Grand Old Flag' in 1918 before turning to music publishing. When Ross Parker and Hughie Charles, two English songwriters, were unable to find a British publisher for a patriotic song they had written, they sent it to Gordon V. Thompson Ltd, which in 1939 became the first publisher of 'There'll Always Be an England'.

Thompson, Sir John Sparrow David (1844-1894). Fourth prime minister of Canada. Born in Halifax, he trained as a lawyer and was elected to the Nova Scotia House of Assembly in 1877, becoming premier in 1882. Entering the federal cabinet as Minister of Justice in 1885, he became leader of the Conservative Party on the resignation of Sir John Abbott in 1892 and was prime minister from 1892 to 1894. He died at Windsor Castle while a guest of Queen Victoria.

Thompson River. A major tributary of the Fraser R. Its north branch is 304 mi. long and its south branch 206 mi. It was named by Simon FRASER for David THOMPSON.

Thomson, Charles Poulett. See Lord SYDENHAM.

Thomson, Earl (b.1895). Hurdler. Born at Birch Hills, Sask., he trained at various American universities. He won a gold medal in 110-metre hurdles and set a new record at the 1920 Olympics in Antwerp. After graduating from Dartmouth University he became a track-and-field coach and served for many years with the United States Naval Academy.

Thomson, Heather (b.1941). Soprano. Born in Vancouver, B.C. she first sang with the CANADIAN OPERA COMPANY in 1962 and the following year sang Mimi in *La Bohème* when she was 22. As a prima donna of the Canadian Opera Company she sings leading lyric-soprano roles and has performed also in Europe and the United States.

Thomson, Roy (1894-1976). Newspaper publisher. Born in Toronto, the son of a barber, he left school at 14, and it was not until he was 37 that his career began properly to unfold. In 1931 he acquired a small North Bay radio station, and in 1934 the Timmins *Press*, the first of his newspapers, for $200 down. This sparked a chain reaction of acquisitions

Thomson

that led to the formation of THOMSON NEWSPA-
PERS LIMITED, which publishes 46 newspapers
in Canada and controls Thomson News Inc.,
which publishes 58 American newspapers.
With the estrangement of his long-time
partner, Jack Kent COOKE, and the death of
his wife, Thomson grew restless and established residence in Edinburgh, where he acquired The Scotsman in 1953 and founded ITV
(Independent Television) in Scotland in 1957
(occasioning his celebrated quip: 'A TV franchise is a licence to print money'). A rash of
acquisitions resulted in the family company,
the Thomson Organization, becoming what
is perhaps the world's largest communications conglomerate. Ownership of the Sunday Times came in 1959 and of the prestigious
flagship newspaper, The Times of London, in
1967. He was created a baron (Lord Thomson
of Fleet and of Northbridge in the City of Edinburgh) in 1964. The standard biography,
Russell Braddon's Roy Thomson of Fleet Street
(1965), is supplemented by After I Was Sixty
(1975), Thomson's own account of his British
experiences, written with warmth and insight. His Canadian and American interests
are managed in Toronto by his only son Kenneth, born in Toronto in 1923, who inherited
the peerage on his father's death on 4 Aug.
1976.

Thomson, Tom (1877-1917). Painter. Born at
Claremont and raised near Owen Sound,
Ont., he was virtually self taught. He
worked in commercial art studios in Seattle
and Toronto, where he was employed at
Grip Limited, though when he discovered
the northern woods he found his true home
in ALGONQUIN PARK, where he could paint,
fish, and guide. He visited the Park for the
first time in May 1912, and drowned there in
July 1917. If he had lived past his fortieth
year he would have become the leading
member of the GROUP OF SEVEN, for these
other painters were greatly impressed by his
developing gifts. Because of the mysterious
circumstances of his death; the short period
of his brilliant productivity—his first major
canvas, Northern River in the NATIONAL GAL-
LERY OF CANADA, was done in 1914-15; and the
fact that two brilliant canvases from the last
year of his life, The WEST WIND (1917, AGO) and
The JACK PINE (1916-17, NGC), are perhaps the
most frequently reproduced of all Canadian
paintings—he has become a legend. The
shack he lived in behind the STUDIO BUILDING,
Toronto, has been preserved and restored on
the grounds of the McMICHAEL CANADIAN COL-
LECTION, Kleinburg, Ont., where many other
Thomsons, including his brilliant oil
sketches, may be seen.

Thomson Newspapers Limited. The largest
newspaper chain in Canada. Begun in 1934
with the acquisition of the Timmins Press by
Roy THOMSON (later Lord Thomson of Fleet),
by 1976 it owned 46 weeklies, semi-weeklies,
tri-weeklies, and dailies. The Canadian company operates Thomson News Inc., which
publishes 58 newspapers throughout the
United States and controls two West Indian
newspapers. The Thomson family owns both
the Canadian and American companies as
well as the Thomson Organization Ltd,
which is perhaps the world's largest communications conglomerate, with extensive
publishing and broadcasting interests
throughout the western world, including
ownership of The Times of London. What follows is a list by province of the Canadian
daily newspapers published by the Thomson
chain:

British Columbia: Kamloops Daily Sentinel,
Kelowna Daily Courier, Nanaimo Daily Free
Press, Penticton Herald, Vernon Daily News.

Saskatchewan: Moose Jaw Times-Herald,
Prince Albert Daily Herald.

Ontario: Barrie Examiner, Belleville Intelli-
gencer, Brampton Daily Times, Cambridge Daily
Reporter, Chatham Daily News, Cornwall Stan-
dard-Freeholder, Guelph Mercury, Kirkland Lake
Northern Daily News, Niagara Falls Review,
Orillia Daily Packet and Times, Oshawa Times,
Pembroke Observer, Peterborough Examiner, St.
Thomas Times-Journal, Sarnia Observer, Sud-
bury Star, Thunder Bay Times-News/Chronicle-
Journal, Timmins Daily Press, Welland Evening
Tribune, Woodstock Daily Sentinel-Review.

Nova Scotia: New Glasgow Evening News,
Sydney Cape Breton Post, Truro News.

Prince Edward Island: Charlottetown
Guardian/The Evening Patriot.

Newfoundland: Corner Brook Western Star,
St. John's Evening Telegram.

The two West Indian newspapers are:
Bridgetown Advocate (Barbados), Port of Spain
Guardian and Evening News (Trinidad).

Thorfinnsson, Snorri (born c.1005-13). The
first white child born on the North American
continent. As reported in the Saga of Eric the
Red, he was the son of Thorfinnr Karlsefni
Thordarson and his wife Guidridr, who set
out on a colonizing expedition between 1003
and 1015. Snorri was born at a place called
Straumfjord (Bay of Strong Currents, possibly Baie des Sept Îles in the St Lawrence).
The colony—which was probably further
south, near Cape Cod—lasted three years.
Snorri lived out his life in Iceland.

Thousand Islands. The island cluster at the
outlet of the St Lawrence R., at the eastern
end of Lake Ontario, formed where the St

Lawrence crosses the Canadian Shield. It is a popular resort area for Canadians and Americans. There are more than 1,500 islands.

Three-pence Beaver. The first Canadian postage stamp. The Province of Canada issued the red Three-pence Beaver on 23 Apr. 1851. Designed by Sandford FLEMING, it depicted a beaver building a dam. A 15-cent commemorative issue incorporating the original design was issued 100 years later. See also Rare STAMPS.

Three principal pillars of the temple of justice, The. A reference to the appointment, tenure, and salaries of judges. It was made by Lord Atkin in the British Privy Council in the case of Toronto Corporation vs York Corporation in 1938. He said: 'These are three principal pillars of the temple of justice, and they are not to be undermined.'

Three Schools, The. An organization of independent non-profit schools offering full- and part-time instruction in the performing, visual, and literary arts, including dance, theatre, design, and writing. Founded in Toronto in 1950 as the Artist's Workshop by Ruth Faux, Cleeve HORNE, William Winter, Barbara Wells, and others, it is comprised of the Workshop, The Other Place, the NEW SCHOOL OF ART, the New School of Theatre, and the Hockley Valley School. It also operates the Poor Alex Theatre and several retail outlets. It is supported by the Toronto Board of Education and various arts councils, including the CANADA COUNCIL. The president and director is John Sime.

Throne Speech. See SPEECH FROM THE THRONE.

Thule. The name given the Eskimo culture that followed the DORSET and flourished in the Central Arctic between A.D. 1000 and 1900. The Thule culture was described in *The Report of the Fifth Thule Expedition, 1921-24* (1931). The expedition was organized by Knud RASMUSSEN who earlier, in 1910, applied the ancient Greek word for 'the most northerly region of the world' to the tiny trading and scientific station he established on the northwest coast of Greenland.

Thunder Bay. A city and large port at the head of navigation on Lake Superior. Formed in 1970 from an amalgamation of Fort William and Port Arthur, Ont., it is at the mouth of the Kaministikwia R., which empties into Thunder Bay. A fur-trade post was built there by Daniel Greysolon Dulhut in 1679, rebuilt in 1717, and abandoned by the French about 1756. The headquarters of the NORTH WEST COMPANY were begun there around 1805 and named Fort William in 1807 after William McGILLIVRAY, the chief director of the company. (It is being reconstructed as it was in 1816.) Thunder Bay is the home of LAKEHEAD UNIVERSITY. See also NANABOZHO and the SLEEPING GIANT.

Thunderbird. A mythic bird, the subject of stories told by the OJIBWA and other ALGONKIAN-speaking Indians. It is a gigantic creature of immense power that is either a curse or a blessing to the Indian people. Thunderbirds with straight beaks have mild tempers; those with crooked beaks, bad tempers. When angry, bolts of lightning flash from their eyes; thunder crashes from the flapping of their wings. In current Indian art Thunderbirds are frequently depicted at war with Water Serpents, which they stun and then devour in their nests in the hills or mountains. Norval MORRISSEAU describes these fearsome birds in *Legends of My People, the Great Ojibway* (1965).

Thunderbird Park. 'One of the most photographed spots in British Columbia'. It was established in Victoria, B.C., in 1940 and includes a collection of Haida, Kwakiutl, Tsimshian, Bella Coola, Nootka, and Coast Salish totem poles, along with house posts, house fronts, dugout canoes, and the house of the master carver Mungo MARTIN.

Ti-Jean. A boy in Quebec legends and children's adventure tales. 'Ti' is short for *petit*. Like the lumberjack Paul BUNYAN, he may not be a pure part of folklore, since most tales about him were circulated in print rather than orally, and have been adapted in a literary fashion. Paul Wallace based his popular children's book *Baptiste Larocque, Legends of French Canada* (1923) on a selection of tales collected by Marius BARBEAU. Wallace's Ti-Jean is a lazy, shrewd, prankish boy who inhabits a magical world of unicorns and princesses and outsmarts everyone he meets, finally arriving in heaven where he challenges God to a game of cards with a marked deck. He is expelled and never heard from again. These similarities to the folklore trickster figure are not present in the Ti-Jean stories in *The Golden Phoenix and Other French-Canadian Fairy Tales* (1958), retold by Marius Barbeau and Michael Hornyansky, in which Ti-Jean is the youngest child of a poor family who conquers adversity and eventually marries a princess. The NATIONAL FILM BOARD produced three short films based on Ti-Jean's adventures between 1953 and 1958.

Tickle. In NEWFOUNDLAND, a narrow straight between an island and the mainland, or the narrow entrance into a harbour.

Ticktala, Irene (b.1941). Eskimo graphic artist and sculptor at BAKER LAKE who is also known for her many imaginative wall-hangings.

Tidal bore. An unusual rise of water caused by the rushing of incoming tides from a wide-mouthed estuary into a narrow channel. This phenomenon is particularly well illustrated in Canada by the tides of the Bay of Fundy, which are forced into narrow river valleys, such as the valley of the Petitcodiac R., and can be observed from Bore View Park in Moncton, N.B. Here the tidal bore creates a 2.5-ft wave up and down the river.

Tiger Moth. A two-seater biplane ideal for primary training. The British-designed aircraft was modified for Canadian needs and assembled by DE HAVILLAND AIRCRAFT OF CANADA in Toronto in 1937; the original design continued to be built by De Havilland in England and was used by the BRITISH COMMONWEALTH AIR TRAINING PLAN. It was an improved version of the GYPSY MOTH.

Tiktak (b.1916). Well-known Eskimo sculptor at Rankin Inlet. He was the first Inuit artist to have a one-man retrospective exhibition, which was held at the University of Manitoba in 1970.

Tilden Rent-a-car. The trade name of Canada's largest car-rental agency. It was founded in Montreal in 1925 by the business executive Samuel F. Tilden (1896-1973), and is now managed by his sons Ted and Walter. Not only is Tilden 'number one' in Canadian car rentals, but it is the only Canadian-owned national car-rental service of any size, with over 10,000 vehicles at 350 locations.

Till, Eric (b.1929). Television and film director. Born in London, Eng., he came to Toronto in 1954 as manager of the NATIONAL BALLET OF CANADA and began directing for CBC-TV's 'Festival' series. A notable success was *Pale Horse, Pale Rider* (1964). His feature films—made in Canada, the U.K., and the U.S.— include: *A Great Big Thing* (1967), *Hot Millions* (1968), *The Walking Stick* (1971), *A Fan's Notes* (1972), and *All Things Bright and Beautiful* (1975). With James Murray he co-directed for CBC-TV *The* NATIONAL DREAM (1974).

Tilley, Sir Samuel Leonard (1818-96). A FATHER OF CONFEDERATION. Born at Gagetown, N.B., he became a druggist. He sat in the legislative assembly of New Brunswick in 1850-1, 1854-6, and 1857-65, becoming premier in 1861. He was a delegate to the CHARLOTTETOWN and QUEBEC CONFERENCES on Confederation, on the platform of which his government was defeated in 1865, though it returned to power the next year. Tilley attended the LONDON CONFERENCE and in 1867 was elected to the House of Commons, becoming minister of customs. He had two terms as lieutenant-governor of New Brunswick: 1873-8 and 1885-93. In between he was minister of finance in the federal government. He was knighted in 1879.

Tillicum. A word in CHINOOK JARGON for 'one's people' or 'friend'.

Time. See DAYLIGHT SAVING TIME, STANDARD TIME.

Time Canada. The CANADIAN EDITION of 'The Weekly Newsmagazine'. The first issue of *Time*, published in New York, was dated 3 Mar. 1923. The U.S. edition, with international advertising, was sold in Canada until the first issue with Canada-only advertising appeared, dated 3 May 1943. Later that year publication began of an edition of *Time* with Canadian editorial matter; this was printed in Canada from 1962. The last issue of *Time Canada* (which had a Canadian circulation of 510,000) was 2 Mar. 1976. It featured on the cover Joe CLARK, newly elected Conservative leader. Latterly the five-page Canadian news section was written and edited in Montreal and was based on stories filed from bureaus in Vancouver, Toronto, Montreal, and Ottawa.

Timmins. Mining city in northern Ontario. It began in the early 1900s as the gold-mining centre of the Porcupine area, and was named after the Timmins brothers, Noah and Henry, who developed one of Canada's greatest gold mines there. As gold declined in importance, a new ore body was discovered in the early 1960s that became the Kidd Creek mine. This area produces a substantial portion of the copper, lead, zinc, and silver mined in Canada. The 1971 population of Timmins was 28,542. See also HOLLINGER MINES LIMITED.

Timmy. A name conferred by the Ontario Society for Crippled Children on a handicapped youngster chosen to represent each Easter crippled children helped through the sale of Easter Seals. From 1947 to 1965 Timmy was the star of 'Timmy's Easter Parade of Stars' on CBC-TV and appeared alongside professional entertainers who devoted their talents to the fund-raising campaign.

Tin Flute, The. Title of the English translation of Gabrielle ROY'S first novel. It was published as *Bonheur d'occasion* in 1945 and Hannah Josephson's translation appeared in 1947. About a family living in a working-class district of Montreal during the Depression and early years of the Second World War, it memorably portrays the dreams and aspirations of the poor.

Tiny. A township in Simcoe Co., Ont., named in 1822 after one of the three pet dogs of Lady Sarah, the wife of Sir Peregrine Maitland, the lieutenant-governor of UPPER CANADA from 1818 to 1828. See also FLOS and TAY.

Tipi. See TEEPEE.

Tish. A mimeographed poetry newsletter issued by a group of poets while still students of English at the University of British Columbia. The title (an anagram) identifies the Vancouver school that included Frank DAVEY, *Tish's* first editor, George BOWERING, and Lionel Kearns, all of whom were influenced by American poets associated with Black Mountain College in North Carolina (Charles Olson and others). *Tish* appeared monthly from 1961 to 1963 and irregularly until 1968, when it was discontinued. Frank Davey's OPEN LETTER is regarded as its successor.

Tit-Coq. Perhaps the most famous of Canadian plays. It was written and directed by Gratien GÉLINAS, who played the lead in both the French and English productions. It opened at the Monument National in Montreal on 22 May 1948 and ran for 200 performances. The English production opened in Montreal at the Gésu Theatre on 6 Nov. 1950. The title is French for 'little rooster', the nickname of 'a little soldier without a family who came out of nowhere'. Tit-Coq returns to Montreal from fighting overseas to find his girl has succumbed to parental pressure and married another man. The French script was published in 1952; the English translation, by Mavor MOORE, in 1967. The Broadway production was a critical success, as was the film version released by France-Film in 1953. It was directed by René Delacroix and starred—in addition to Gélinas—Monique Miller, Juliette Béliveau, Paul Dupuis, and Denise PELLETIER. 101 min., b & w.

Titanic, The A powerful narrative poem of the sea by E.J. PRATT, published in 1935. It describes the liner's ill-fated voyage, the iceberg that threatened it, and shows the strengths and weaknesses of its passengers in the face of death, which confronted them when the ship began to sink in the Atlantic off the coast of Newfoundland on 15 Apr. 1912.

TLC(C). Initials of the TRADES AND LABOUR CONGRESS OF CANADA.

Tlingit. A linguistic group of Indians occupying the Alaskan Pan Handle, represented in Canada by the Tagish of the Teslin R. (B.C.) and the Chilkat, expert weavers known for their CHILKAT BLANKETS. The Tlingit population in 1970 was 491.

TNM. Initials of the THÉÂTRE DU NOUVEAU MONDE.

TNOR. Initials of the Temiskaming & Northern Ontario Railway, now the ONTARIO NORTHLAND RAILWAY.

To the Wild Country. A series of privately produced CBC-TV specials on the Canadian wilderness. The one-hour programs, the first of which was shown on 18 Nov. 1973, were photographed by the husband-and-wife team of John and Janet Foster and narrated by Lorne GREENE. Still photographs taken on location were published in book form under the series title in 1975.

Tobacco. Plants of the nightshade family prepared for smoking. In Canada tobacco was cultivated by the Huron-Iroquois tribes for use in rituals. Its use for pipe smoking was largely a European invention. French settlers on the St Lawrence cultivated it for this purpose as early as 1700. Most of Canada's tobacco is now grown in southern Ontario, though there are crops in Quebec and British Columbia.

Toboggan. Algonkian word for a long flat-bottomed sleigh, made of hardwood by MICMAC and other Indians for sliding over snow.

'Today's Child'. An award-winning newspaper feature. It first appeared six days a week in the *Toronto Telegram* in 1964 and is now a thrice-weekly feature in the TORONTO STAR and widely syndicated. Conceived and written by Helen Allen, a Toronto journalist, it features photographs and biographies of homeless children who may be adopted. It has been responsible for finding permanent homes for a large number of children, many of them mentally and physically handicapped.

Todd, Robert (1809-65). Painter. Born in England, he immigrated to Quebec in 1834 and set up business as a 'house, carriage and ornamental painter'. His famous *Ice Cone, Montmorency Falls* (c.1845, NGC), with its red sleigh drawn by prancing horses in the foreground, was one of several paintings of the falls that were perhaps done as souvenirs. Todd moved to Toronto in 1854.

Tolpuddle Martyrs. Farmers exiled from England in 1834 for seeking farm-labour organization at Tolpuddle, Dorsetshire. Five of the six Tolpuddle Martyrs eventually settled on farms near London, C.W. (Ont.), in 1844. The grave of their leader, George Loveless, is in the Siloam Cemetery in London Township, Ont.

Tomahawk. Algonkian word for a light war-club or hatchet. It has been suggested that tomahawks were not used by the Indians prior to European contact. To 'bury the tomahawk [or hatchet]' is to declare peace. To 'throw the tomahawk [or hatchet] to the sky' is to pledge peace. See also CASSE-TÊTE À CALUMET.

Tommy. The world's first rock ballet. Choreographed by Fernand Nault and first performed by the GRANDS BALLETS CANADIENS in Quebec City on 2 June 1971, this striking work has successfully toured North America. Nault based his rock ballet on the rock opera of the same name, which was created by Peter Townsend of the Guess Who and first performed by the British rock group in 1969. It tells the story of the cure of a deaf, dumb, and blind young man who becomes a pinball champion. Ken Russell directed a film version of the opera that was released in 1975.

Tompkins, Father J.J. See ANTIGONISH MOVEMENT.

Tonto. See Jay SILVERHEELS.

Tonty, Henri (de) (1650?-1704). Explorer and fur-trader. Born in France of Italian parents—his father invented the 'tontine', a system of life annuity—he served in the French army. In Sicily his right hand was blown off by a grenade. (Because of his hook-shaped artificial arm, the Indians in New France called him *Bras de fer*.) Arriving at Quebec in 1678 as the lieutenant of LA SALLE, he superintended the building of the GRIFFON, went to the Illinois R. with La Salle, and descended the Mississippi R. with him in 1682. That year he built Fort Saint-Louis in the Illinois country and was put in command by La Salle, whom he never saw again. In 1700 he worked with IBERVILLE in establishing the fur-trade in Louisiana, where he died of yellow fever.

Tookoome, Simon (b.1934). Eskimo artist, cutter, and printer at BAKER LAKE. He repro-

duces his own drawings in the medium of stonecut and stencil. His vividly coloured human-animal forms and multiple faces show evidence of shamanism.

Toolooktook, Paul. Eskimo sculptor at BAKER LAKE. He spent six months carving in the Canadian Pavilion at Expo 70 in Osaka, Japan.

Toque. French word for a long woolen stocking-like cap with a tassel, associated with woodsmen and voyageurs; a shorter woollen cap with a tassel. An alternative spelling is 'tuque'.

Tories. A popular reference to the PROGRESSIVE CONSERVATIVE PARTY and its predecessor, the Conservative Party. In colonial times supporters of the *status quo* and, in Upper Canada (Ontario), opposers of the REFORMERS and their desire for a greater measure of self-government. Sir John A. MACDONALD found his party 'satisfac-Tory'. Bob Edwards found it a 'no-Tory-ous party'. If the Conservatives are Tories, the Liberals are GRITS.

Torngak. The singular form of TORNIT.

Tornit. Eskimo word for devils or spirits, the singular of which is *Torngak*. The *Tornit*, a race of mighty giants with power over the elements, were presided over by Torngarsuk (literally, the 'great spirit'). The word is less commonly but more correctly spelled and pronounced *Tungait* (pl.) and *Tungak* (sing.).

Toronto. The capital of Ontario and, with Montreal, one of the two dominant urban centres of Canada. The first permanent settlement began in 1793, when the site was chosen as the capital of the new province of Upper Canada (Ontario), called York. Its name was changed to Toronto upon incorporation in 1834. In 1953 Toronto and its adjoining 12 municipalities formed the Municipality of Metropolitan Toronto and in 1966 the 13 were reduced to six: the City of Toronto and the boroughs of Etobicoke, North York, Scarborough, York, and East York. The composition of the population changed from being 70% to 45% British between 1951 and 1971, with the influx of large numbers of immigrants—particularly Italians, Germans, Portuguese, and more recently West Indians—who have done much to alter the character of the city. Supporting numerous educational and cultural institutions and a complex array of manufacturing, commercial, and service activities that have both national and international markets, Toronto has experienced a rate of economic expansion in recent years greater than that of any other North American city. The 60- to

70-storey office complexes that have arisen in the city centre are dwarfed by the 1,800-ft freestanding CN TOWER which, together with the TORONTO CITY HALL complex, will undoubtedly be civic symbols for many years. Its 1971 CMA population was 2,628,043. Its official motto is 'Industry, Intelligence, Integrity'. See also ART GALLERY OF ONTARIO, BLACK CREEK PIONEER VILLAGE, CABBAGETOWN, CANADIAN NATIONAL EXHIBITION, CASA LOMA, FORT YORK, The GRANGE, HART HOUSE, HIGH PARK, KENSINGTON MARKET, MASSEY HALL, METRO TORONTO ZOO, O'KEEFE CENTRE, ONTARIO PLACE, ONTARIO SCIENCE CENTRE, OSGOODE HALL, QUEEN'S PARK, ROSEDALE, ROYAL AGRICULTURAL WINTER FAIR, ROYAL ALEXANDRA THEATRE, ST JAMES' CATHEDRAL, ST LAWRENCE CENTRE, ST LAWRENCE HALL, TORONTO ISLAND, TORONTO MAPLE LEAFS, TORONTO MENDELSSOHN CHOIR, TORONTO SYMPHONY ORCHESTRA, TORONTO THE GOOD, UNION STATION, UNIVERSITY OF TORONTO, YONGE ST, YORK UNIVERSITY.

Toronto Book Award, City of. See BOOK AWARD OF THE CITY OF TORONTO.

Toronto Centred Region (TCR). A large area centred on Toronto and extending as far as Peterborough in the east, Orillia in the north, and Kitchener-Waterloo in the west. It was established by the provincial government in 1970 together with a broad plan outlining the way in which the government would like to see this area developed.

Toronto City Hall. Designed by the Finnish architect Viljo REVELL, who won the commission in competition in 1958, it opened in 1964. With two curved towers (27 and 20 storeys respectively) that surround a domed council chamber, which rests on a podium, it has become a famous landmark. It stands on Nathan Phillips Square, named after the mayor whose enthusiasm contributed greatly to the project in its early days.

Toronto Club, The. A nationally important luncheon club. Founded in 1835, it is housed in a Victorian brick structure at the corner of Wellington and York Sts in downtown Toronto. With fewer than 400 business-executive members, it is considered the most difficult club to join in the country.

Toronto Dance Theatre. Modern dance company. Established in 1968 by three Toronto dancers trained by Martha Graham—Peter Rondazzo, David Earle, and Patricia Beatty, now its co-directors and choreographers—it produces innovative dance-dramas that first met with rejection but are now applauded throughout the country. It has made European and American tours.

Toronto-Dominion Bank, The. A chartered bank with its head office in Toronto. (See TORONTO-DOMINION CENTRE.) Formed in 1955 by the merger of the Bank of Toronto and the Dominion Bank, in 1976 it had 874 branches in Canada and six elsewhere.

Toronto-Dominion Centre. Large office complex in downtown Toronto containing the head office of the TORONTO-DOMINION BANK. Designed by Mies van der Rohe and John B. PARKIN Associates, it was built in 1967-74 and is the most complete monument of the International style in Canada. It is composed of a single-level Banking Pavilion and three towers, the tallest of which is the 56-storey Toronto-Dominion Bank Tower, which houses an Observation Gallery.

Toronto Drama Bench. See CHALMERS AWARD.

Toronto Globe and Mail. See the GLOBE AND MAIL.

Toronto Island. Protecting Toronto's Inner Harbour and made up of several islands, it was once called the Peninsula and was joined to the eastern mainland by a sandbar that was washed away in 1858. The Gibraltar Point lighthouse (1806) at the western end is the oldest building in the City of Toronto. In the second half of the nineteenth century Centre Island, Hanlan's Point, and Ward's Island developed into highly popular pleasure-grounds, containing hotels, amusements, two yacht clubs, and many summer residences. In 1954 the islands were taken over by the Metropolitan Toronto Parks Commission and most of the 650 residences and all the hotels and amusement centres were demolished. (The small residential community remaining on Algonquin and Ward's Islands is one of the most distinctive and closely knit neighbourhoods in the city.) The 552 acres have been turned into parkland.

Toronto Maple Leafs. One of the best-known hockey clubs in the country. Originally formed as the Toronto Arenas, it was one of the original members of the NATIONAL HOCKEY LEAGUE in 1917. The club won its twelfth STANLEY CUP in 1967. Its home ice is MAPLE LEAF GARDENS. The club's colours are blue and white.

Toronto Mendelssohn Choir. Formed in 1894, under the direction of Augustus VOGT, the 100-member non-professional choir soon established a continental reputation. Under its subsequent directors, including Sir Ernest MacMILLAN (1942-57) and Walter SUSSKIND

Toronto Mendelssohn Choir

(1960-4) and international guest conductors such as Leopold Stokowski and Fritz Reiner, the choir improved its technique and broadened its repertoire. In 1964 Elmer ISELER became its director and in 1968 the FESTIVAL SINGERS OF CANADA became the Choir's professional corps, bringing about an expansion in its repertoire to include works of modern composers. It made a successful European tour in 1971-2.

Toronto Printer's Strike. A strike by Toronto printers in 1872 to obtain a nine-hour day. The committee members of the Typographical Union were arrested because unions had not been made legal in Canada. After Sir John A. MACDONALD passed laws that year legalizing unions, the prosecution was dropped and the strikers won.

Toronto School of Theology. In this school, unique in North America, the main currents of Anglican, Protestant, and Roman Catholic thought and tradition are offered by seven Toronto theological colleges and faculties: St Augustine's, EMMANUEL, KNOX, St Michael's, Regis, TRINITY, and WYCLIFFE. Incorporated in 1970 and affiliated with the University of Toronto, it succeeds a loose pooling of resources, called the Toronto Graduate School of Theological Studies, that had been in existence since 1944. McMaster Divinity School in Hamilton and Waterloo Lutheran University became affiliated after 1970.

Toronto Star, The. An evening newspaper, with Canada's largest circulation, published in Toronto. Founded by striking printers in 1894, it came under the control of the publisher and philanthropist Joseph E. Atkinson (1865-1946) in 1899. Known as 'Holy Joe', Atkinson was respected for his social conscience and pursued a policy that was continued by his son-in-law, the colourful Harry Comfort Hindmarsh (1887-1955). The present publisher is Beland H. Honderich (b.1915). The *Star* created a legend in the 1920s and 1930s with a 'flying squad' of journalists who were ready to give on-the-spot coverage of events in the Hearst tradition. The comedian Dave BROADFOOT has described the *Star's* present character as 'small-l Conservative'. From 1910 to 1969 the *Star* published the STAR WEEKLY. In 1965, with SOUTHAM PRESS, it founded the CANADIAN MAGAZINE as its Saturday supplement. The paper's advertising slogan is 'Reach for the *Star*—Most People Do'. Among former *Star* employees are Morley CALLAGHAN, Fred Griffin, Ernest Hemingway, Gregory CLARK, and Gordon SINCLAIR; associated with it more recently have been Pierre BERTON, Robert FUL-

FORD, Peter GZOWSKI, and Peter C. NEWMAN. Among those currently writing for the paper are George Bain, Dalton CAMP, Robert Duffy, Richard Gwyn, Gary Lautens, and Anthony Westell.

Toronto Sun, The. A morning newspaper published in Toronto. Founded amid the ashes of the TORONTO TELEGRAM in 1971, it is an independently owned tabloid, appearing six days a week (it does not appear on Saturday). Its motto is 'Toronto's Other Voice'. Writers and columnists include Doug Fisher, Trent Frayne, Paul Hellyer, McKenzie Porter, Morton Shulman, Joan Sutton, Peter Worthington, and Lubor J. Zink.

Toronto Symphony Orchestra. Between 1908 and 1922 what became the TSO was an informal group of Toronto Conservatory and theatre players under the leadership of Frank Welsman; in 1922, under Dr Luigi von Kunits (1922-32), it became the New Symphony Orchestra and in 1927 the Toronto Symphony Orchestra. When talking pictures replaced silent films, theatre musicians became unemployed. This made it possible for the newly appointed conductor, Dr Ernest MacMILLAN (1931-56), to arrange formal orchestral programs and concerts. He introduced 'pop' concerts, subscriptions series, school concerts, and a women's committee for fund raising. In 1956 Walter SUSSKIND became musical director, followed in 1965 by Seiji Ozawa, in 1969 by Karl Ancerl, and in 1974 by Andrew Davis as musical director designate. Davis became musical director in 1975. Until 1976 the TSO was the opera-house orchestra for the CANADIAN OPERA COMPANY seasons. It now plays a summer season at ONTARIO PLACE, Toronto. Its home is MASSEY HALL.

Toronto Telegram, The. A daily evening newspaper once published in Toronto. Appearing between 1876 and 1971, it is recalled for its combination of conservatism and sensationalism. In its long life it had but three publishers: John Ross ROBERTSON, the founder, whose trust continued the paper following his death; C. George McCullagh (1905-52), who owned both the *Tely* in 1948-52 and the GLOBE AND MAIL; and John W. BASSETT, who acquired it in 1952 and discontinued it after many circulation battles with the TORONTO STAR. During the 1930s it was so influential in local politics that its city editor, Bert Wemp, was also Toronto's mayor.

Toronto the Good. Sobriquet given to Toronto in the nineteenth century because of its alleged piety, reflected in its many churches and its puritanical laws. It was used sarcastically in the title of a book, *Of Toronto the Good* (1898), by C.S. Clark who, with the intention of writing a sociological study and promoting reform, described with some avidity certain 'unpalatable' aspects of the city, including poverty, crime, drunkenness, and prostitution.

Toronto Toros. See WORLD HOCKEY ASSOCIATION.

Toronto Trades and Labour Council. An early association of unions organized mainly to campaign for political representation. Founded in June 1881, it admitted the KNIGHTS OF LABOUR to membership in 1883 and founded the Canadian Trades and Labour Congress, which took the name TRADES AND LABOUR CONGRESS in 1892.

Toronto Trades Assembly. An association of unions founded in Toronto in Apr. 1871. The first city central assembly in Canada, the TTA was an association of printers', coopers', and painters' unions, along with the Knights of St Crispin. The TTA played a leading role in promoting the NINE-HOUR DAY in 1872 and in forming the CANADIAN LABOUR UNION in 1873.

Toronto Workshop Productions. A group theatre established for the production of new Canadian plays, founded in 1959 by George Luscombe, a Toronto-born director-manager who had worked with Joan Littlewood (1953-6). First performing in a warehouse, it moved to a 320-seat theatre in 1968. It has employed a dramaturge, Jack WINTER, off and on since 1961. TWP's greatest success was Winter's dramatization of TEN LOST YEARS, which opened on 7 Feb. 1974.

Tortière. A minced pork and potato pie of French-Canadian origin. The dish was originally prepared with passenger pigeons or *tourtes*, a now-extinct bird that provided its name.

Tory. See TORIES.

Tory, Henry Marshall (1862-1947). Educator. Born in Guysborough Co., N.S., and educated at McGill University, from which he received a D.Sc. in 1903, he was ordained into the Methodist Church. He was the first principal of McGill College, Vancouver (the forerunner of the University of British Columbia), the first president of the UNIVERSITY OF ALBERTA, and the president of the NATIONAL RESEARCH COUNCIL from 1928 to 1935. From 1942 until his death he was president of Carleton College (now CARLETON UNIVERSITY). See also KHAKI COLLEGE, HENRY MARSHALL TORY MEDAL.

Totem. Southern Ojibwa word for a spirit that presides over a clan; the stylized form of a bird, animal, or plant that represents this spirit. See also TOTEM POLE.

Totem pole. Among certain west-coast Indians—notably the HAIDA and TSIMSHIAN—a red cedar log carved and painted with stylized representations of ancestral spirits. One of the best-known totem-pole carvers in modern times was Mungo MARTIN, who carved the tallest totem pole in the world (127 ft, 6 in.), in Beacon Hill Park, Victoria, B.C.

Touring Office. Branch of the CANADA COUNCIL concerned with touring the performing arts in Canada. Opened in Ottawa in Apr. 1973, it provides subsidies, technical assistance, and support services to encourage and coordinate tours by Canadian performing artists and companies and to make their performances accessible to a wider audience. With the Cultural Affairs Division of the Department of External Affairs, it co-ordinates Canadian performing tours abroad. On occasion the Touring Office will import outstanding foreign attractions.

Tousignant, Claude (b.1932). Painter. Born in Montreal, he studied at the Montreal Museum of Fine Arts School and in Paris. With other Montreal artists, including Guido MOLINARI, he concentrated on formal abstract painting that he simplified to geometric shapes in the late 1950s, when his watercolours introduced diagonal bands of intense, clear colours. This style evolved into his bichromatic hard-edge colour paintings that use the target form of concentric circles. *Oeil de boeuf* (1964, NGC) is one of his finest paintings. He has exhibited internationally and lives in Montreal.

Towards the Last Spike. Narrative poem by E.J. PRATT published in 1952. Written in stately blank verse, it recounts the difficulties encountered in building Canada's first transcontinental railway, the CPR, and pays tribute to the men who helped bring the project to completion against monumental odds.

Town, Harold (b.1924). Painter and printmaker. Born in Toronto, he studied at the Ontario College of Art, worked as a commercial artist, and was one of the founding members of PAINTERS ELEVEN. A highly productive artist of great versatility and inventiveness, he has successfully explored drawing, painting, printmaking, collage, and sculpture. In the 1950s he established his reputation for remarkably fluent draughtsmanship and a striking sense of design as a graphic artist with his single autographic

527

Town

prints (1955-7). While developing a personal style of abstract expressionism in the late fifties, he used action-painting techniques for a huge abstract mural (1958) in the Robert H. Saunders Generating Station near Cornwall, Ont. He was at the height of his powers in the 1960s, painting a series in black, silver, and white called *The Tyranny of the Corner* and creating the richly textured yet detailed surface of his best-known canvas, GREAT DIVIDE (1965). Known also for his witty, opinionated, iconoclastic journalism, he is a prominent figure in the Canadian art world. He has exhibited internationally and has published several books, including *Enigmas* (1965), *Drawings* (1969), *Silent Stars, Sound Stars, Film Stars* (1971), and *Albert* FRANCK: *Keeper of the Lanes* (1974).

Town Above, The. A CBC-TV series set in Quebec City's Upper Town. Written by Roger LEMELIN, it replaced The PLOUFFE FAMILY as a weekly 30-minute situation comedy. The Plouffes were working class, the Chevaliers of 'The Town Above' were upper-middle class. The series was seen on the French television network from 1954 to 1960 and on the English network from 1959 to 1960. It starred Roland Chenail and Denise PELLETIER as Mr and Mrs Chevalier, the antics of whose sons Pierre and Denis and daughter Diane were the cause of their pleasures and pains.

Town Below, The. Title of the English translation of Roger LEMELIN's first novel. *Au pied de la pente douce* was published in 1944, and Samuel Putnam's English translation in 1948. It is considered a landmark in French-Canadian literature for its realistic depiction of contemporary life in a LOWER TOWN working-class parish of Quebec City.

Townie. In Newfoundland, someone who lives in St John's. The opposite of a townie is a BAYMAN.

Township. A land-survey area. As settlement spread in British North America and across the West, the land was surveyed and divided into townships, which were then subdivided into lots for settlers. The area of each township varied—in Quebec, for example, the land north of the seigneuries was divided after the Conquest into townships of approximately 100 sq. mi., while in what is now Alberta a township was 36 sq. mi. divided into 36 sections. Today the township is also a MUNICIPALITY in Quebec and Ontario.

Trade and Commerce. See Department of INDUSTRY, TRADE AND COMMERCE.

Trades and Labour Congress of Canada. An association created to work for the passage of new laws in the interests of the working class. It was founded at the TORONTO TRADES AND LABOUR COUNCIL's convention of Dec. 1883 but was not reconvened until Sept. 1886. In the 1890s it became closely associated with the AMERICAN FEDERATION OF LABOUR and in 1902 it amended its constitution along the lines of the AFL to permit only one union in each trade or craft; as a result the KNIGHTS OF LABOUR, and purely Canadian unions that overlapped with international unions affiliated with the AFL, were expelled and formed the NATIONAL TRADES AND LABOUR CONGRESS. The TLC finally merged with the CANADIAN CONGRESS OF LABOUR in June 1956 to form the CANADIAN LABOUR CONGRESS.

Trail of '98, The. A reference to the CHILKOOT PASS and other northern trails scaled by goldseekers during the KLONDIKE GOLD RUSH of 1898. It gave Robert W. SERVICE the title of his first novel, published in 1911. It is also the unofficial motto of Whitehorse, Y.T.

Trailing arbutus. See MAYFLOWER.

Traill, Catharine Parr (1802-99). Pioneer and author. Born in London, Eng., a sister of Susanna MOODIE and Samuel STRICKLAND, she published her first book for children at the age of 16. In 1832 she married a half-pay officer and they immigrated to Upper Canada (Ontario), where they settled in Douro Township. A contributor to the LITERARY GARLAND, she is remembered for numerous books that advise would-be immigrants and describe the botanical world about her. *The Backwoods of Canada* (1836, 1966), written in epistolary form, was widely read and has endured to this day. *The Female Emigrant's Guide* (1854) went through numerous editions. As an informed and ardent naturalist, she wrote *Rambles in the Canadian Forest* (1859), *Canadian Wild Flowers* (1869), and *Studies of Plant Life in Canada* (1885), among other volumes. She also wrote several children's books, including *The Canadian Crusoes* (1852), reprinted as *Lost in the Backwoods* (1882), and *Lady Mary and Her Nurse: A Peep into the Canadian Forest* (1856), which was reissued under various titles.

Traîneau. French word for 'sled'.

Trained seals. A phrase coined by George DREW in 1956 to describe the behaviour of partisan backbenchers. See also LOOSE FISH.

Training Command. See CANADIAN ARMED FORCES.

'Tramp, tramp, tramp, the boys are marching!' Refrain of 'An Anti-Fenian Song' sung during the FENIAN invasions of 1865. The refrain runs: 'Tramp, tramp, tramp, the boys are marching!/Cheer up, comrades, let them come, / For beneath the Union Jack we will drive the Fenians back, / And we'll fight for our belov'd Canadian home.' It is a variation on the American Civil War song of the same name.

Trans-Atlantic Ferry Service. Second World War scheme to organize flights across the North Atlantic. From 10 Nov. 1940 to 1945, planes, men, supplies, and equipment from North America were ferried from such airports as GANDER and GOOSE BAY, over the 'northern route' (above Labrador, Greenland, and Iceland), to such British airports as Prestwick in Scotland and Aldergrove in Ireland. Proposed by Lord BEAVERBROOK, it was initially operated by Canadian Pacific Airlines.

Trans-Canada Air Lines. The name of the government-owned airline from its founding in 1937 until 1965, when its name changed to AIR CANADA.

Trans-Canada Air Pageant. A memorable air show designed to interest Canadians in flying. Organized by flying clubs across the country, members of which presented aerobatic and other displays, the pageant opened in Hamilton, Ont. on 1 July 1931. Air shows were staged by two touring groups in 20 cities before the pageant was disbanded on 12 Sept.

Trans-Canada Highway. A modern highway system that links the 10 provinces. The Trans-Canada Highway stretches from St John's to Victoria and has been called 'the longest highway in the world'. Construction began on the federal-provincial undertaking soon after the Trans-Canada Highway Act received Royal Assent, on 10 Dec. 1948. The 4,860-mi. roadway was declared officially open on 3 Sept. 1962, at a ceremony at Rogers Pass, Glacier National Park, Alta. Edward McCOURT has described a motor trip along it in *The Road Across Canada* (1965).

Trans Canada Limited. The name of the CANADIAN PACIFIC RAILWAY's transcontinental passenger train on the Montreal-Toronto-Vancouver run. Service on the all-sleeping-car train was inaugurated on 1 June 1919.

Trans-Canada Matinée. Long-running afternoon CBC Radio program. With features mainly of interest to women, it made its début on 29 Sept. 1952. The 30-minute, five-day-a-week program, which changed its name to 'Matinée' with the disappearance of the Trans-Canada Network in 1962, is identified with the radio personality Pat Patterson.

Trans-Canada Network. See CBC RADIO NETWORK.

Trans-Canada Pipeline. A natural-gas pipeline that extends from the Alberta border to Montreal and Toronto. See also PIPELINE DEBATE.

Transair. Regional airline. Established in 1969, with headquarters at Winnipeg, Transair Limited operates scheduled services in Manitoba, Saskatchewan, Ontario, and the Northwest Territories, as well as North American charter flights.

Transcontinental. Extending across a continent; the word often refers to a railway train (CPR, CNR) that does this.

Translation Prizes. Annual awards made to encourage the translation of Canadian books from one official language to the other. Amounting to $2,500 each, the two prizes—for the best English-to-French and French-to-English translations—are awarded annually. They were instituted by the CANADA COUNCIL in 1974.

Transport, Ministry of. A ministry of the federal government. Known until 1970 as the Department of Transport, it is a structure that embodies CROWN CORPORATIONS and agencies in all fields of transportation—land, sea, air. The ministry is responsible for the Canadian Coast Guard, the ST LAWRENCE SEAWAY AUTHORITY, AIR CANADA, CANADIAN NATIONAL RAILWAYS, and other Crown corporations and agencies.

Travellers, The. Pioneer folksong group. It was formed at Camp New World, a leftist Jewish trade-unionist summer camp in northern Ontario, during the summer of 1954. The original group consisted of Sydney Dolgay (leader and bass mandolin player), Jerry Gray (lead singer and banjo player), Simone Cook (singer), Jerry Goodis (singer), and Marty Meslin (singer), all of whom were fully employed outside showbusiness. Later members have included Ray Woodley, Joe Lawrence, Oscar Ross, Ted Roberts, Don Vichery, and Pam Fernie, with Jerry Gray (a full-time dentist) remaining the sole link. In the late 1950s their manager, Martin Bochner, adapted Woody Guthrie's 'This Land Is Your Land' as a signature song. The Travellers was the first group in Canada to perform songs that were topical and patriotic. Besides performing nationally, it toured the Soviet Union in 1962, the United Kingdom in 1964, and appeared at Expo 70 in Japan.

Traverse. French word for a 'way across'. An open stretch of water or a journey across it; or, on the Prairies, an expanse of open land situated between bluffs or a journey across it.

Travois. An Indian conveyance—from the French word *travail*, 'a shaft'—consisting of two poles joined by a platform or net and dragged by a dog, pony, or horse.

Treasure Trail. Popular 30-minute weekly quiz program produced by private radio stations. Starting in 1937 and continuing through the war into the 1950s, it was developed by Jack Murray for Wrigley's Gum, who paid for productions in Vancouver, Winnipeg, Toronto, and Montreal (in French). It helped many announcers in their careers, including Laurie Irving and Barney Potts in Vancouver; Earl CAMERON, Thom Benson, and Wilf Carpentier in Winnipeg; and Cy Strange and Jack Dennet in Toronto.

Treasury Board. Central management agency of government. Established in 1867 as a committee of the PRIVY COUNCIL, it has been a separate department of the federal government with its own minister since 1966. It is composed of the President of the Treasury Board, the Minister of Finance, and four other privy councillors. The staff is divided into five branches: Administrative, Planning, Personnel Policy, Official Languages, and Program.

Treaty of Aix-la-Chapelle. Signed in 1748, it ended the War of the Austrian Succession (see KING GEORGE'S WAR). Île-Royale (Cape Breton Island), including LOUISBOURG, which had been captured by the British, was returned to France.

Treaty of Ghent. Peace treaty signed by Great Britain and the United States at Ghent, Belgium, on 24 Dec. 1814, bringing an end to the WAR OF 1812.

Treaty of Paris. Signed on 10 Feb. 1763, it ended the SEVEN YEARS' WAR. Under its terms France ceded to Great Britain all her possessions in northern North America excepting ST PIERRE AND MIQUELON.

Treaty of Ryswick. Signed in 1697, it provided for the return of all conquests made by France and England in KING WILLIAM'S WAR, including portions of ACADIA and posts on Hudson Bay.

Treaty of Utrecht. Signed in 1713, it ended QUEEN ANNE'S WAR. France gave up to England: Newfoundland, Hudson Bay, and ACADIA except for Île-Royale (Cape Breton Island).

Tree line. The approximate limit of continuous forest, more or less the northern limit of the Boreal forest. It is also found at high altitudes in major mountain systems.

Tremblay, Gilles (b.1932). Composer. Born in Arvida, Que., he studied at the Conservatoire in Montreal and at the Université de Montréal before taking courses at the Marlboro School of Music in Vermont, the Paris Conservatoire, and the Ferienkurse für neue Musik in Darmstadt. In 1959 he began working with electro-acoustics. He now teaches at the Montreal Conservatoire. His works, which have been performed internationally, show a special interest in winds and percussion.

Tremblay, Michel (b.1942). Quebec playwright. Born and raised in the east end of Montreal, he trained as a graphic artist and became a typographer. For three years he was unable to find a producer for his first play, *Les* BELLES-SOEURS, which, when it was produced by the THÉÂTRE DU RIDEAU VERTE in 1968, made him an overnight celebrity. It was produced in English at the ST LAWRENCE CENTRE, Toronto, in 1973 to great acclaim and published in 1974. *À Toi pour toujours, Marie-Lou* was produced in English under the title *Forever Yours, Marie-Lou* at the TARRAGON THEATRE, Toronto, in 1972. Tarragon also produced *Hosanna* (1974), a dark comedy about a homosexual couple. The role of Hosanna—a young man dressed as Elizabeth Taylor in *Cleopatra*—was superbly created, in both French and English productions, by Richard Monette. *Bonjour là, bonjour,* produced in English in 1975, dramatizes in a technically adroit manner and in rich language the breakdown in communications and the breakup of a middle-class Montreal family. The English translations of Tremblay's plays are by his English-language director, Bill GLASSCO, and John Van Burek. Tremblay has steadfastly refused to allow any of these English versions of his plays to be produced in Quebec where, he feels, English-speaking audiences should attend the French productions.

Trent crisis. Tensions created by Britain's official neutrality and unofficial sympathy for the South, during the American Civil War, reached a danger point when, on 8 Nov. 1861, two Confederate agents were forcibly removed from the British mail packet *Trent*, en route to England, by the captain of the USS *San Jacinto*. In the war fever stirred by this insult to British shipping rights 15,000 troops were dispatched to BRITISH NORTH AMERICA. The American decision to release the captured Southerners ended the immediate crisis, but the incident suggested the need for some sort of union of the British North American colonies in order to ensure their safety.

Trent University. Picturesquely located in a wooded 1,400-acre campus on the Otonabee R., on the northern edge of Peterborough, Ont., and named after the nearby Trent Canal, it was created by an act of the provincial legislature in 1963. It is known particularly for its low ratio of students to staff, for its tutorial and seminar system, patterned after Oxford's, and for its Canadian Studies program. It publishes the JOURNAL OF CANADIAN STUDIES.

'Trial of a City'. A poetic drama by Earle BIRNEY celebrating the past, present, and future of Vancouver. Broadcast by CBC Radio, it was included in *Trial of a City and Other Verse* (1952).

Trial of Louis Riel, The. A one-act play by John COULTER based on the trial of Louis RIEL for treason. It makes use of transcripts of the actual trial that was held in a courtroom in Regina in 1885. Commissioned by the City of Regina, the play has been produced each summer in the same courtroom since 1967. See also Coulter's full-length drama, RIEL.

Tribal Class. A British-designed class of 27 destroyers bearing the names of various Commonwealth aboriginal tribes. The four that served with the ROYAL CANADIAN NAVY during the Second World War, and the four built later, all bore Indian tribal names: *Athabasca I* and *II*, *Cayuga*, HAIDA, *Huron*, *Iroquois*, *Micmac*, and *Nootka*. These RCN ships saw much action on Russian convoys, in the English Channel and the Bay of Biscay in 1944, and later in Korean waters.

Tribune of Nova Scotia, The. Sobriquet of Joseph HOWE, who championed his province's interests.

Trifunov, James (b.1903). Wrestler. Born in Serbia, he was brought to Canada at the age of seven. He won a bronze medal at the 1928 Olympics in Amsterdam and a gold medal at the 1930 British Empire Games in Hamilton, Ont. Then he turned to coaching and the presidency of the Manitoba Wrestling Association.

Trillium, White. A three-petalled wild flower of north-central and eastern North America. Usually white, it turns pink with age. The provincial flower of Ontario since 1937, it won its status against competition from the shamrock, thistle, dandelion, and orange lily.

Trillium Home Furniture Awards. Annual awards made by the Ontario government and the Ontario Furniture Manufacturers Association. They were established in 1974 and are presented to Ontario manufacturers of products designed by Canadians on the basis of design, mass appeal, value, serviceability, and ingenuity in the development of the product. The award itself is a stylized trillium composed of three pieces of brushed metal on a polished stone base.

Trinity College. Anglican college federated with the University of Toronto. It was founded by Bishop John STRACHAN and inaugurated in 1852. Originally built to the southwest of Toronto—at present-day Queen St and Strachan Ave—it moved to the university campus in 1925, when the present building was erected. It is a member of the TORONTO SCHOOL OF THEOLOGY. Its chapel—designed by Sir Giles Gilbert Scott and dedicated in 1955—is one of the most important examples of Gothic Revival architecture on the continent.

Triple Crown Series, The. Annual horse races at the Woodbine Race Track, Toronto. Inaugurated in 1959, the three races in this series include the QUEEN'S PLATE, the Prince of Wales Stakes, and the Breeders Stakes. Its three-sided gold trophy has been won only twice—by E.P. TAYLOR's New Providence in 1959 and Canebora in 1963. Only Canadian-born horses are eligible.

Triple Crown Trophy. A senior golfing award. A piece of sculpture and a cheque for $25,000 go to the professional male golfer who in the same year wins the British Open, the U.S. Open, and the Canadian Open Golf Championships. It has been presented by Imperial Tobacco Limited since 1971.

Trois Chapelles, Les. Three stone chapels built on the side and summit of a mountain at OKA, Que., in 1740-2 as Stations of the Cross. They are all that remain of seven chapels erected by a Supilcian priest. A procession to the three chapels is made on Holy Cross Day, 14 Sept.

Trotskyists. See LEAGUE FOR SOCIALIST ACTION.

Trottier, Pierre (b.1925). Quebec poet. Born in Montreal and educated in law at the Université de Montréal, he entered the Department of External Affairs and since the late 1960s has been second-in-command at the Canadian Embassy in Moscow. His elegant and detached poetry was collected as *Sainte-Mémoire* (1972). His imaginative essays appear in *Mon Babel* (1963).

Trudeau, Pierre Elliott (b.1919). Fifteenth prime minister of Canada. Born in Montreal, he was educated at the Université de Montréal, Havard University, the École des Sciences Politiques in Paris, and the London School of Economics. In 1950 he was one of the founders of CITÉ LIBRE, a monthly magazine advocating democracy and civil liberties in opposition to the Union Nationale régime of Maurice DUPLESSIS. During the 1950s he practised law and was involved in civil-liberties cases, labour law, and political activity in Quebec. It was during this period that he edited a collection of essays, *La Grève de l'amiante* (1956), on the ASBESTOS STRIKE—translated by James Boake and published in English as *The Asbestos Strike* (1974). He entered federal politics as a Liberal in 1965 and was appointed Minister of Justice in 1967. Elected leader of the Liberal Party of Canada on 6 Apr. 1968 to replace Prime Minister Lester PEARSON, who was retiring, he was sworn in as prime minister on 20 Apr. He led his party to a substantial majority in the election on 25 June of that year and retained power in subsequent elections. Among his books are *Federalism and the French Canadians* (1968) and *Conversations with Canadians* (1972). He wrote a series of essays, *Les Cheminements de la Politique* (1970) and, with Jacques Hébert, *Deux Innocents en Chine-rouge* (1961), which were translated by Ivon Owen and published in English as *Approaches to Politics* (1970) and *Two Innocents in Red China* (1968).

Trudel, Marcel (b.1917). Quebec historian. Born in Saint-Narcisse, Que., and educated at Université Laval and Harvard, he was appointed chairman of the history department at the University of Ottawa in 1966. With his vast knowledge of archival papers, he has expanded the perspective on New France and the years immediately following its collapse. Among his many scholarly works are *Atlas de la Nouvelle France/An Atlas of New France* (1968) and *The Beginnings of New France: 1524-1663* (1973), translated by Patricia Claxton for the CANADIAN CENTENARY SERIES. He was associate editor of the first volume of the DICTIONARY OF CANADIAN BIOGRAPHY.

True Nature of Bernadette, The. See *La* VRAIE NATURE DE BERNADETTE.

True North, The. Canada as a northern ideal. The noble phrase was the inspiration of Alfred Lord Tennyson who in 1873, in the Epilogue to *The Idylls of the King,* referred to Canada as 'That True North, whereof we lately heard'. R. Stanley Weir made use of the phrase in his version of 'O CANADA' in 1908. The line runs: 'The True North, strong and free'.

True North Records. A record company established in Toronto in 1970. It is owned and managed by Bernie Finkelstein and Bernie Fiedler (owner of the RIVERBOAT). Bruce COCKBURN, Murray McLAUCHLAN, John Mills-Cockell, and other leading Canadian performers appear on the True North label.

Truscott murder case. A controversial case revolving around 14-year-old Steven Truscott, who was sentenced to hang for the rape-murder of 12-year-old Lynne Harper of Clinton, Ont., in 1959. The sentence was commuted to life imprisonment. Through the efforts of Toronto writer Isabel Lebourdais, the author of *The Trial of Steven Truscott* (1966), the Supreme Court reviewed the case in 1967 but confirmed the original decision. Truscott, who always maintained his innocence, was paroled in 1969 and is married with a family and living somewhere in Canada under a new name.

Tsimshian. A group of Indian tribes living in northern British Columbia, on the Nass and Skeena Rivers and on the coast between the Nass and Milbank Sound. They form three cultural groups speaking two related languages. The Nass R. Niska and Skeena R. GITKSAN speak dialects of Nass-Gitksan, to which the Tsimshian language of the Coast Tsimshian is closely related. The Tsimshian population in 1970 was 7,730.

TTA. Initials of the TORONTO TRADES ASSEMBLY.

TTLC. Initials of the TORONTO TRADES AND LABOUR COUNCIL.

Tudhope. Automobile manufactured from 1906 to 1924 by Tudhope Carriage Company, Orillia, Ont. It came with a two-cylinder or four-cylinder air-cooled engine. The owner, J.P. Tudhope, changed the name of his operation to Fisher Motor Company in 1913.

Tudlik (*c.*1890-1960). Well-known Eskimo sculptor at CAPE DORSET. He specialized in soapstone carvings of small owls but also made a few prints before his death. His son LATCHOLASSIE is also a sculptor.

Tudluq. See Marion Tudluq ANGUHADLUK.

Tuesday Night. See CBC TUESDAY NIGHT.

Tugboat Annie, Adventures of. See ADVEN-TURES OF TUGBOAT ANNIE.

Tuktu Series. 13 short films for children about Tuktu, an Eskimo boy, produced by the NATIONAL FILM BOARD in 1966-8. It was edited from colour footage taken of the Net-silik Eskimos before acculturation. Produced by Lawrence Hyde and directed by David Bairstow, each film depicts a different aspect of the boy's life. 14 min., 15 sec.; colour.

Tukummik, Simon (b.1934). Eskimo graphic artist and printmaker at BAKER LAKE. His graphics depict shamanistic and other vi-sionary subjects.

Tulip Festival. Annual floral display in Ot-tawa, the largest in North America. Held when the tulips bloom in late May, the Festi-val centres on PARLIAMENT HILL and includes concerts and special exhibitions. It dates from the end of the Second World War when Queen Juliana of the Netherlands, who had spent the war years in Ottawa, showed her gratitude by making a gift to the city of 100,000 Dutch bulbs. Over one million tulips bloom each year. It is now known as the Fes-tival of Spring.

Tully, Kivas (1820-1905). Architect. Born in Queen's Co., Ire., he came to Toronto in 1844 after training in London and in Limerick as an architect-engineer. Victoria Hall, Co-bourg, Ont. (1857), shows his precise sense of material, scale, and fine detailing in the Classical-Renaissance manner. The first Trinity College, Toronto (1851, demolished c.1955), was an important example of the pic-turesque vein in the Gothic Revival. Tully was appointed architect to the Province of Ontario in 1869 and his last works were asy-lums in London, Hamilton, Brockville, and Mimico.

Tump. Algonkian word for a 'pack strap'. A tump or tumpline is a leather harness that crosses the forehead and is attached to a pack supported on the back.

Tumtum. CHINOOK JARGON for the beating of the heart and having the meaning 'heart', 'affection', 'mind', or 'opinion'.

Tundra. The Arctic prairie occurring in the north Yukon, extreme northern Quebec, and much of the Northwest Territories and non-glacial Arctic Archipelago. Although tree-less, it supports a wide variety of animal life and in summer an equally varied range of flowering and lichen-type flora. The word is Lapp for 'hill'. See also the BARREN LANDS.

Tundra Books of Montreal. A publishing house that specializes in art and children's books. It was founded in 1967 by May Ebbitt Cutler, a journalist. Many of its books—not-ably several by William KURELEK—have been co-published with foreign houses and have won awards for design and production.

Tunit. Eskimo word for 'people earlier than ourselves'. According to Eskimo tradition, the *Tunit* (or *Tunnik*) were an ancient warlike race of giants, inhabitants of Baffin Island, who held the Eskimos enthralled. Stone IN-UKSHUKS have been described as monuments to the Eskimo victory over the *Tunit*.

Tupek. Eskimo word for a 'tent made of skin'. During the summer months the Es-kimos used to live in a *tupek*; during the winter months in an IGLOO. A *tupek*, or *tupirk*, is the northern equivalent of a TEEPEE or WIG-WAM.

Tupilaq. Eskimo word for 'hell animal'. Bones from various animals, arranged to simulate an animal's skeleton, are wrapped in an animal's skin. After much conjuring by the shaman, the *tupilaq* is said to come alive and run or swim across the path of the hunter, who is doomed to die.

Tupper, Sir Charles (1821-1915). A FATHER OF CONFEDERATION. Born in Amherst, N.S., he became a doctor. He was elected to the House of Assembly in 1855, taking the seat away from Joseph HOWE. He became premier in 1864. He headed the Nova Scotia delega-tion to all three conferences on Confedera-tion, triumphing over anti-Confederation sentiment in the province. He was elected to Parliament in 1867 and headed several minis-tries. After being High Commissioner in London from 1884 to 1896, he returned to Ot-tawa to lead the Conservative Party and suc-ceeded Sir Mackenzie BOWELL as prime min-ister, a post he held for only two months before his party met with defeat at the polls. He led the Opposition until 1900, when he was defeated in his constituency.

Turbinia. The first turbine-engined ship on the Great Lakes. Built on the Tyne in 1904, she was advertised as 'the fastest ship on the Lakes', though she proved slower than the conventionally powered *Cayuga*. After serv-ing in the First World War as a cross-Channel troopship, she returned to Canada and the Toronto-Hamilton run in 1924, served on the lower St Lawrence in 1926-7, and was laid up and scrapped about 1937.

Turbo

Turbo. Fastest inter-city train in North America. CN introduced its Turbo on the Montreal-Toronto run on 17 Dec. 1973 after trial runs in 1971 and 1972. It covers the 335-mi. route in 4 hours and 10 minutes. The name refers to the seven-turbine engines that supply its power. See also RAPIDO.

Turcotte, Ron (b.1941). Jockey. Born in Grand Falls, N.B.—the brother of Noel, Ruddy, and Roger, all jockeys—he found his height (5 ft 2 in.) an asset in finding work with a trainer at Woodbine Racetrack, Toronto, and he learned to ride. He became the regular jockey of Secretariat, riding her in 1973 to the first TRIPLE CROWN in 25 years. On 5 Mar. 1976 he rode six winners in one day at the New York Aqueduct.

Turgeon, Bernard. Baritone. Born in Edmonton, Alta, he studied singing at the Royal Conservatory of Music, Toronto, from 1951 to 1955. He has been a guest soloist with the Sadler's Wells Opera, the Glyndebourne Festival, and other musical organizations in Europe, but has mainly made his career in Canada. He has sung with the CANADIAN OPERA COMPANY since 1952 and is particularly associated with having created the title role in Harry SOMERS' *Louis Riel* (1967). Since 1969 he has been head of the vocal and opera department at the University of Alberta.

Turnbull, Wallace Rupert. See VARIABLE-PITCH PROPELLER.

Turner, David (b.1903). Soccer player. Born in Scotland, he settled in Edmonton, then British Columbia, where he played soccer with the New Westminster Royals, who won four Dominion championships. When his active playing career ended he took two university degrees, then joined the B.C. Department of Lands and Forests. From 1957 until his retirement in 1968 he was Deputy Minister of Recreation and Conservation.

Turner Valley. A village southwest of Calgary, Alta, where the first major discovery of oil in Canada was made in 1914 and of gas in 1924.

Turofsky, Lou (1891-1959). Sports photographer. Born in Chicago, the elder brother of Nat Turofsky, he began taking pictures with a box camera at the age of 12. He was brought to Toronto shortly thereafter and started Alexandra Studio in 1919. Within 10 years he and Nat were the preferred photographers of hockey, racing, baseball, and other sporting events. Their photos, especially action shots, illustrated books, magazines, and newspapers for many years. Ted

REEVE wrote the commentary to *Sports Seen: Fifty Years of Camera Work by Lou and Nat Turofsky* (1960). The opera singer Riki TUROFSKY is Lou's daughter.

Turofsky, Riki (b.1944). Soprano. Born in Toronto, the daughter of the sports photographer Lou TUROFSKY, she studied privately and at the Vancouver Opera School and made her professional début with the Vancouver Opera Association in 1970. Two years later she made her début with the New York City Opera and in 1976 her European début at the Holland Festival singing Curley's wife in Carlisle Floyd's *Of Mice and Men*. Tall and blonde, with great presence, she has sung with the CANADIAN OPERA COMPANY and the FESTIVAL SINGERS OF CANADA and is a popular concert performer.

Turvey. A novel by Earle BIRNEY published in 1949. It is a picaresque tale of the adventures of Thomas Leadbeater Turvey from 'Skookum Falls', B.C., a private in the 'Kootenay Highlanders' during the Second World War. An unauthorized edition was published in 1960 as *The Kootenay Highlander*. The novel was republished in 1976 in an 'unexpurgated' edition.

Tuscarora. See IROQUOIS.

Tutela Heights. See Alexander Graham BELL.

Tuvavouteet. In the eastern Arctic, the Eskimo way of saying 'goodbye'. It means literally 'stay as you are', the implied meaning being 'remain in good health'.

TV Ontario. A provincially owned regional television network. Established in 1970 as the Ontario Educational Communications Authority (OECA), it is funded by the provincial government's Department of Culture and Recreation. It broadcasts out of Toronto; uses transmitters in Chatham, Windsor, Paris, Kitchener, and London; and provides a cable package for viewers in nine communities not reached by the network.

TvA. The call letters of Television Associates Network, a privately owned network of 14 stations—three in English and 11 in French—located in Montreal, Quebec City, Chicoutimi, Sherbrooke, Trois-Rivières, and Ottawa.

Tweed, Tommy (1908-71). Actor and writer. Born in Medicine Hat, Alta, he worked in Winnipeg as an actor from 1934 to 1941, when he joined CBC Radio in Toronto and played leading roles in CBC STAGE productions. As well as narrating *The* LOON'S NECK-

LACE (1950) and appearing in Walt Disney's *The* INCREDIBLE JOURNEY (1963), he wrote and acted in a great many CBC Radio programs on historical subjects. See also SARAH BINKS.

Tweedsmuir, Lord (1875-1940). GOVERNOR GENERAL of Canada, novelist. Born John Buchan in Scotland, educated at Glasgow University and Oxford, and called to the bar in 1901, he was elected as a Conservative to the British House of Commons (1927-35). He served with distinction as governor general of Canada from 1935, when he was created first Baron Tweedsmuir, until his death in Ottawa. He was the first chief executive to visit the Arctic and he established the GOVERNOR GENERAL'S LITERARY AWARDS. The author of many first-rate thrillers such as *The Thirty-Nine Steps* (1915) and *Greenmantle* (1916), he made reference to his feelings about Canada in his autobiography, *Memory Hold-the-Door* (1940; U.S. title: *Pilgrim's Way*). Two works of fiction, published posthumously, have a Canadian setting: SICK HEART RIVER (1941) and a collection of stories for young readers, *Lake of Gold* (1941; U.S. title: *The Long Traverse*).

Twentieth century belongs to Canada, The. The most celebrated of Canadian aphorisms. This assertion derives from an address delivered by Prime Minister Sir Wilfrid LAURIER to the Canadian Club of Ottawa on 18 Jan. 1904, and has been a touchstone of national aspiration and progress ever since.

24 Sussex Drive. The official residence in Ottawa of the prime minister. The grey stone mansion, built by Joseph Merrill Currier in 1867, was acquired by the Canadian government in 1949. Its first prime-ministerial occupant was Louis ST LAURENT in 1951.

Twenty-fourth of May. See VICTORIA DAY.

Twin Cities. A reference to the neighbouring cities of Kitchener and Waterloo in Waterloo Co., Ont., locally abbreviated to 'Kit-Wat'. Also a reference to Port Arthur and Fort William, Ont., before they amalgamated as THUNDER BAY on 1 Jan. 1970.

Twin Otter. The name of a utility transport aircraft. It was built by DE HAVILLAND in 1966 and equipped with two turboprop engines that permitted it to carry 14 to 20 passengers or 2 tons of freight at 210 m.p.h. It is widely used for both scheduled and charter operations. See also OTTER.

Two Canadas, The. A reference to UPPER CANADA and LOWER CANADA (from 1791 to 1841), or to CANADA WEST and CANADA EAST (from 1841 to 1867).

'Two-key' arrangement. A provision for the shared control of nuclear weapons. When American nuclear weapons are stored in another country, an American stationed in that country and a member of the host country both have a key, and both keys must be inserted and turned at the same time before the weapons can be activated. The arrangement was worked out when the weapons stored in Canada under the NORAD agreement were to be equipped with nuclear warheads; the Americans also have 'two-key' arrangements with members of NATO.

'Two nations warring in the bosom of a single state'. See Lord DURHAM.

Two Sketches on French-Canadian Airs. Skilful arrangements for string orchestra or quartet composed in 1927 by Ernest MacMILLAN. It has often been performed by the TORONTO SYMPHONY ORCHESTRA in its pop concert series.

Two Solitudes. A novel by Hugh MacLENNAN published in 1945, an ambitious fictional study of French-English conflicts in Quebec. This subject was not much written about at the time and the novel was very widely read. The title has entered the language as an image of the mutual alienation of the founding peoples of Canada. The phrase comes from a letter to a young poet written by Rainer Maria Rilke in 1904.

Tyee. In CHINOOK JARGON, an Indian chief or an important person.

Tyndall stone. A kind of blue-grey limestone used for ornamental purposes on buildings. It has been quarried at Tyndall, near Garson, Man., since 1896.

Tyrone Guthrie Awards. Scholarships given annually since 1953 by the STRATFORD FESTIVAL to senior members of the company to honour the Festival's first artistic director, Sir Tyrone GUTHRIE. See also JEAN A. CHALMERS THEATRE APPRENTICE AWARDS.

Tyrrell Medal. Awarded annually or biennially by the ROYAL SOCIETY OF CANADA for the furtherance of the knowledge of the history of Canada. The medal was endowed by J.B. Tyrrell (1858-1957), geologist and historian, in 1927. It consists of a gold medal and $1,000.

Tyson, Ian and Sylvia. Folk singers and composers. Ian Tyson, born in British Columbia in 1935, and Sylvia Fricker, born in Chatham, Ont., in 1941, formed a team—Ian and Sylvia—in Toronto in 1956. Their first album, *Four Strong Winds* (1963), established them as leading composers and performers. Married in 1964, they have toured with the Great Speckled Band and appeared together on CTV's 'Ian Tyson Show' in 1969. Since then they have performed separately. In 1974 Sylvia starred in 'Touch the Earth', her own CBC Radio show, and made a solo album, *Woman's World* (1975).

U

UBC. See UNIVERSITY OF BRITISH COLUMBIA.

UBC Medal for Popular Biography. Annual award made by the University of British Columbia for the best biography of a popular nature published during the previous year. The eligible book must have been written by or about a Canadian. The medal was designed by Bill REID and has been awarded since 1952.

Ultimatum. A political thriller by Richard ROHMER published in 1973. The United States president issues an ultimatum to the Canadian government to share its energy reserves on a continental basis or be annexed. The consequences are traced in the author's best-selling sequel EXXONERATION (1974).

Ultramontane. In late nineteenth-century Quebec, a supporter of the principle that the Church had authority over legislators and electors as the guardian of the moral law. The clergy opposed the Liberals and supported the right-wing Conservative CASTORS. Clerical intervention in elections was forbidden by a papal encyclical in 1897.

Ulu. Eskimo word for a woman's knife. The *ulu* (pronounced 'ooloo') is an all-purpose knife with a crescent-shaped blade and a bone or wood handle. A *suvik*, a man's knife, is shaped like a long butcher knife.

Umiak. Eskimo word for a seal-skin, flat-bottomed, CANOE-like craft to carry freight and passengers, traditionally rowed by Eskimo women. It can be 40 ft long, 5 ft wide, and 3 ft deep. It is an enlarged version of the single-passenger KAYAK.

Uncle Louie. Sobriquet of Louis ST LAURENT.

Uncle Tom. See Josiah HENSON.

Uncrowned King of Alberta. Sobriquet of Henry Wise WOOD.

Under Attack. A weekly 60-minute panel show created for television by Elsa FRANKLIN and Dan Enright for Screen Gems (Canada) Ltd. A well-known public figure is questioned, first by a moderator, then by a selected panel of student experts, and finally by an audience of college students. Created for the CTV Television Network, it was first broadcast in Sept. 1967. The moderators have included Pierre BERTON, Fred DAVIS, and Bill Walker.

Under the Volcano. Famous novel by Malcolm LOWRY published in 1947. The exotic and sinister aspects of Mexico—where Lowry lived briefly—are symbols for the tormented world of the novel's hero, Geoffrey Firmin, an alcoholic former British consul. The story takes place on the Day of the Dead, 2 Sept. 1938, and chronicles Firmin's unsuccessful reunion with his estranged wife Yvonne and his half-brother Hugh (who is in love with Yvonne), culminating in Firmin's murder by the chief of Rostrums, a small Mexican town. The account of Firmin's degeneration in part embodies Lowry's understanding of his own alcoholism and his desire to conquer the darker parts of himself.

Underground railroad. The code name for the secret routes taken by southern slaves seeking freedom in the northern states or in Canada before the American Civil War. The 'conductors', who led them through unknown territory, risked arrest, as did the 'station agents' in whose homes ('stations') they stopped along the way. Following the passage in 1850 of the American Fugitive Slave Act, which made it illegal to harbour runaway slaves anywhere in the United States, the final termini became, of necessity, Canadian border communities, such as Buxton, Ont. See also Josiah HENSON.

Underhill, Frank H. (1889-1971). Historian, political journalist, and teacher. Born in Stouffville, Ont., and educated at the University of Toronto and Oxford, he taught history at the University of Saskatchewan before going to the University of Toronto, where he taught from 1927 until 1955, when he became curator of LAURIER HOUSE, Ottawa. A social theorist who specialized in writing incisive, epigrammatic, frequently indignant short essays, he helped found the CANADIAN FORUM in 1929, the LEAGUE FOR SOCIAL RECONSTRUCTION in 1932, and wrote the first draft of the REGINA MANIFESTO. His later modification of his socialist views is described in his collection of articles and addresses, *In Search of Canadian Liberalism* (1960).

Unemployment Insurance. A plan to assist those who are unemployed. The Unemployment Insurance Act was first passed in 1940. In 1971 all members of the work force who receive salary or wages were brought into the scheme. Employers and employees both contribute to the scheme, the employer paying a larger share than the employee. A claimant can draw benefits for a maximum of 51 weeks, depending on circumstances. Benefits are payable in some cases when earnings are interrupted by sickness. See also UNEMPLOYMENT INSURANCE COMMISSION.

Unemployment Insurance Commission. Federal commission to administer the Unemployment Insurance Act. Established in 1940, the UIC, subject to regulations, ensures that weekly payments are made to unemployed persons for a limited time. Consisting of three commissioners in Ottawa and five regional and numerous district offices, it reports to Parliament through the Minister of Manpower and Immigration. See also UNEMPLOYMENT INSURANCE.

Ungava. Eskimo word, said to mean 'an unknown, faraway land'. It refers to the northern Quebec area around Fort Chimo, which is on Ungava Bay.

Unicity. A reference to Greater Winnipeg. The incorporation of the City of Winnipeg and its 11 boroughs—Charleswood, East Kildonan, Fort Garry, North Kildonan, Old Kildonan, St Boniface, St James-Assiniboia, St Vital, Transcona, Tuxedo, and West Kildonan—took place in Jan. 1972.

Unicorn, Sea. See NARWHAL.

Unification. The ROYAL CANADIAN NAVY, the CANADIAN ARMY, and the ROYAL CANADIAN AIR FORCE became the world's first unified fighting force, called the CANADIAN ARMED FORCES, on 1 Feb. 1968. The Minister of National Defence responsible for the controversial action, undertaken in the interests of efficiency

and economy, was Paul Hellyer. Unification was preceded by a period of integration in 1966-7 during which the three services retained their separate identities but cooperated to promote efficiency and economy, particularly in administration.

Union Government. A coalition government under Sir Robert BORDEN, formed on 12 Oct. 1917 and lasting until 10 July 1920.

Union Jack. The official flag of Great Britain associated with the early history of Canada. Proclaimed the official flag of Great Britain in 1801, it symbolizes the union of England, Scotland, and Ireland through the union of the crosses of the patron saints of these countries: ST GEORGE'S BANNER (a red cross on a white field), ST ANDREW'S BANNER (a diagonal white cross on a blue background), and ST PATRICK'S BANNER (a diagonal red cross on a white field). The resulting flag is officially called the 'Royal Union Flag'. The red, white, and blue colours of the Union Jack were widely flown in Canada until the CANADIAN RED ENSIGN was recognized as the official flag in 1945; this was succeeded in 1965 by the NATIONAL FLAG OF CANADA.

Union Nationale. A Quebec political party created and dominated by Maurice DUPLESSIS. It was formed in 1935 by Duplessis's Conservatives and the members of L'Action Libérale Nationale under Paul Gouin in an attempt to topple the corrupt Liberal administration of Alexandre Taschereau. The coalition was initially reformist and nationalist and it had enough force almost to topple the provincial government in the election of Nov. 1935. The next year Duplessis effectively drove out Gouin, and the UN won a sweeping victory in the 1936 election. It held power from 1936 to 1939 and from 1944 to 1960. Duplessis's death in 1959 and the death shortly after of his successor, Paul Sauvé, left the party in ruins. It came to power again in 1966 under Daniel Johnson, but was defeated in 1970.

When in power under Duplessis the UN was generally perceived as near-repressive in its actions, with the government controlling freedom of religion and dissent with the PADLOCK LAW and allying with the Church to slow the pace of change. PROVINCIAL AUTONOMY was the watchword, and the Duplessis régime resisted every effort of Ottawa to increase the federal government's powers. Under Johnson the UN led Quebec towards a special status within Confederation and laid the groundwork for SEPARATISM.

Union Station

Union Station. Toronto railway station designed by John LYLE and built mainly in 1915-20, though it was not officially opened until 6 Aug. 1927. This impressive building on Front St is a monument to the early twentieth-century belief that the railway station, as the symbol of progress, deserved an imposing architectural form. It drew on the grandeur of classical architecture, expressed by the immense ticket lobby or Great Hall, with its vaulted ceiling 88 ft high.

Unit B. An important film production unit within the NATIONAL FILM BOARD. With a reorganization of the Board in 1950, production was divided among five units or studios identified by the letters A through E. (In the late fifties a Quebec unit was added.) Unit B, under the executive producer Tom DALY, attracted innovative film-makers (like Colin LOW, Stanley Jackson, Wolf KOENIG, Roman KROITER, and Guy Côté), who went on to contribute to the CANDID EYE series. The Science Film Unit and the Animation Department were then attached to Unit B, which disappeared in a major NFB reorganization in 1964.

United Canada. A reference to the union of the provinces of UPPER CANADA and LOWER CANADA by the ACT OF UNION, which came into effect on 10 Feb. 1841 and created the PROVINCE OF CANADA.

United Church Observer, The. A widely read monthly magazine published in Toronto by the UNITED CHURCH OF CANADA. It was founded by Egerton RYERSON in 1829 as the *Christian Guardian* and was the voice of the Methodist Church in Canada. At Church union in 1925 it was renamed the *New Outlook*; it received its present name in 1939. It comments on Canadian life and includes national and international church news, etc. Since 1955 it has been edited by the Rev. Al Forrest, who has often sided with the Arab cause in the Arab-Israeli disputes of the last two decades.

United Church of Canada. The largest Protestant religious denomination in Canada, with 3,768,805 adherents (1971). It was formed by a union of Methodists, Presbyterians, and Congregationalists in 1924-5. The first United Church service was celebrated in Toronto on 10 June 1925 in the Mutual St Arena (now The Terrace), Toronto.

United Empire Loyalists. See LOYALISTS.

United Farmers of Alberta. An association that formed itself into a provincial party in 1919. The president at that time was Henry

Wise WOOD. The central idea of the party was that occupational groups should be represented in Parliament and the provincial legislatures and that the UFA would look after the interests of the farmers. The party sent 11 PROGRESSIVE PARTY members to Parliament in 1921 and won power in Alberta the same year. It was defeated in 1935. The UFA combined with labour groups to help form the CCF in 1932. See also UNITED FARMERS OF MANITOBA, UNITED FARMERS OF ONTARIO.

United Farmers of Manitoba. A provincial political party formed to represent farmers' interests. It won the Manitoba election of 1922 and remained as the government until 1958, although after 1926 the members were calling themselves Liberal-Progressives because of connections with the remnants of the PROGRESSIVE PARTY, which had formed an alliance with the Liberals. See also UNITED FARMERS OF ALBERTA, UNITED FARMERS OF ONTARIO.

United Farmers of Ontario. An association formed in 1913-14 and converted into a political party. The central idea was that occupational groups should be represented in Parliament and the provincial legislature and that the UFO would look after the interests of farmers. In 1919 the party won 43 seats in Ontario, but this was not a majority and the premier, E.C. Drury, formed a union with labour and independent members in a People's Party. Drury was defeated in 1923. See also UNITED FARMERS OF ALBERTA, UNITED FARMERS OF MANITOBA, PROGRESSIVE PARTY.

United Nations. 'An effective international organization for the maintenance of international peace and security.' Canada is one of 50 founding nations that approved the UN charter at San Francisco, 25 Apr.-26 June 1945, and has taken part in more UN peace-keeping operations—called 'the most revolutionary development in the field of international organizations since the end of the Second World War'—than any other country.

United Press International. A merger of two foreign-owned news agencies: British United Press (formed in 1907) and International News Service (formed in 1909). The Canadian wing of UPI is the country's major news service after CANADIAN PRESS. It has operated in Canada since 1922.

United Way. The name since 15 May 1975 of the United Appeal. In Toronto and other cities a combined fund-raising campaign for voluntary health and welfare services is held each October. The United Appeal, so named in Oct. 1956, was originally called the Community Chest, which, with its 'Red Feather campaign', goes back to 1918.

United World College. See PEARSON COLLEGE OF THE PACIFIC.

Unitt, Doris (b.1909) and **Peter** (b.1913). Publishers of antique guides. The British-born couple—Doris was a librarian and researcher, Peter a watchmaker turned photographer—settled in Peterborough, Ont., in 1954, opened an antique shop for Canadiana, and in 1968 founded Clock House Publications to issue standard reference books for collectors. They have compiled, written, and published such titles as *Unitt's Canadian Guide to Antiques and Collectables* (4 vols, 1968-75), *Canadian Silver, Plate, and Related Glass* (1970), *Bottles in Canada* (1972), *American and Canadian Goblets* (1975), and *Antiques in Ontario* (1975).

Unity Bank of Canada. A chartered bank with its head office in Toronto. Incorporated in 1972 with a board composed of representatives of numerous ethnic groups, it had 22 branches in Ontario, Manitoba, Alberta, and British Columbia in 1976.

Unity Party. See COMMUNIST PARTY.

Universe. Documentary film produced by the NATIONAL FILM BOARD in 1960. Directed by Roman KROITER and Colin LOW under the production of Tom DALY, it recreates an awesome picture of the universe as it would appear to a voyager travelling through space past the sun and milky way into galaxies as yet unfathomed. It has won a record 23 awards and its special effects influenced Stanley Kubrick's *2001: A Space Odyssey*. 26 min., 10 sec.; b & w.

Université de Montréal. The largest French-language university in the world outside of France. Strikingly sited on the northern slope of Mount Royal, it was founded for Catholic instruction in 1870 as a branch of the UNIVERSITÉ LAVAL and became independent in 1920. With over 30 affiliated colleges throughout Quebec, it is noted for its faculty of medicine and its institute of town planning.

Université Laval. North America's oldest French-language university. Located in Quebec City, it was founded for Catholic instruction in 1852 by the Séminaire de Québec, a college of fine arts and theology founded in 1663 by Bishop LAVAL. It was granted a royal charter by Queen Victoria in 1852 and a pontifical charter by Pope Pius IX in 1876. Laval is

noted for its faculty of modern languages and has the oldest Canadian school of social studies, which was founded in 1938 by the Dominican, Georges-Henri Lévesque, who taught there until 1963, when he left to teach in Africa.

University Alumnae Dramatic Club. The oldest surviving theatrical organization in Toronto. The 'Women's Alumnae' was founded by theatre enthusiasts at the University of Toronto in 1919. Especially active in the 1950s and 1960s, it staged the Canadian premières of Samuel Beckett's *Waiting for Godot* and James REANEY'S *The Killdeer* in 1958. In 1972 the group moved into permanent quarters in the Firehall Theatre.

University College. An original part of the UNIVERSITY OF TORONTO. From the college's opening in 1859 until 1887, it housed both the teaching and administrative divisions of the univeristy. With the federation of denominational colleges after 1887, its instruction was limited to subjects assigned to the colleges (e.g., English, philosophy, classics, and languages). A reorganization of the university's teaching facilities in 1975 changed this arrangement. The building, designed by Frederick William CUMBERLAND and built in 1857-8 (restored after a fire in 1890), is one of the finest Victorian monuments in the city.

University League for Social Reform. A group of professors concerned with developing reform ideas and with finding solutions to current social and economic problems of Canada founded the ULSR at the University of Toronto in Oct. 1962. It was modelled to some extent on the old LEAGUE FOR SOCIAL RECONSTRUCTION. Collections of articles edited for the ULSR include:
The Prospect of Change: Proposals for Canada's Future (1965) edited by Abraham ROTSTEIN, *Nationalism in Canada* (1966) edited by Peter Russell, *An Independent Foreign Policy for Canada?* (1968) edited by Stephen Clarkson, *Agenda 1970: Proposals for a Creative Politics* (1968) edited by Trevor Lloyd and Jack McLeod, *Close the 49th Parallel etc.: The Americanization of Canada* (1970) edited by Ian Lumsden, *The City: Attacking Modern Myths* (1972) edited by Alan Powell, *Thinking about Change* (1974) edited by David P. Shugarman, *Domination* (1976) edited by Alkis Kontos.

University of Alberta. Created by an act of the legislature in 1906, it is located in Edmonton, on the south bank of the North Saskatchewan R. The earliest faculties were arts, applied science, law, and medicine. Several colleges are affiliated with the university, including the Collège Universitaire Saint-Jean (1970), where 70% of the instruction (arts, science, and education) is in French. Today there are associated Junior Colleges in Medicine Hat, Camrose, Red Deer, and Grande Prairie.

University of Alberta National Awards. An annual award given to Canadians 'who have made distinguished contributions over a period of time to the development of Letters, Music, and Painting and the Related Arts in Canada'. From 1951 to 1961 three gold medals were presented each year at the Banff School of Fine Arts (BANFF CENTRE) on behalf of the Board of Governors of the University of Alberta. Since then a single medal has been awarded each year in a different category.

University of British Columbia. Located at West Point Grey, Vancouver, B.C. An attempt was made to create a provincial university by an act of the British Columbia legislature in 1890, but the measure failed owing to the lack of a quorum. It succeeded nine years later when the Vancouver High School became affiliated with McGILL UNIVERSITY. UBC gained status as an independent university in 1915. Its Institute of Oceanography, established in 1949 and directly funded by the federal government, is known around the world. The university publishes CANADIAN LITERATURE and PRISM INTERNATIONAL, the latter being issued by the CREATIVE WRITING DEPARTMENT.

University of British Columbia Medal. See UBC MEDAL FOR POPULAR BIOGRAPHY.

University of Calgary. Founded in 1945 as a branch of the Faculty of Education of the University of Alberta, it gained full autonomy in 1966. There are faculties of arts and science, business, fine arts, medicine, environmental design, and graduate studies, as well as schools of social welfare, nursing and physical education. It is located on a 314-acre campus in the northwest section of Calgary.

University of Guelph. Created by an act of the Ontario legislature in 1964, it is an amalgam of three well-known local institutions: the Ontario Agricultural College (established as the Ontario School of Agriculture in 1874 and as OAC in 1882); the Ontario Veterinary College (established in Toronto in 1864, moved to Guelph in 1922); and the Macdonald Institute (founded in 1903 for the instruction of women in the domestic sciences). Formerly affiliated with the University of Toronto, the University of Guelph now grants its own degrees in humanities, sciences, and social sciences, while maintaining its emphasis on veterinary medicine, biology, and family studies. It operates three agricultural research stations: Elora for field crops, dairy and beef cattle; Arkell for poultry and swine; and Cambridge for horticultural crops. See also Sir William MACDONALD.

University of King's College. Founded as an Anglican college at Windsor, N.S., in 1802 under the Royal Charter of King George III, it moved to Halifax in 1920. Since 1930 it has been in partnership with DALHOUSIE UNIVERSITY. They maintain joint faculties of the arts and sciences, but Dalhousie grants the degrees (except for theology).

University of Lethbridge. It evolved from the university section of the Lethbridge Junior College, which had been affiliated with the UNIVERSITY OF ALBERTA. It was given university status by the Alberta legislature in 1967. The university year is organized in three semesters. A significant component of the university's research is devoted to regional studies for the southern Alberta community.

University of Manitoba. The oldest university in western Canada, located in the Winnipeg borough of Fort Garry, it was created by the legislature in 1877 to grant degrees to students graduating from the three church colleges: St Boniface (Roman Catholic), St John's (Anglican), and Manitoba (Presbyterian). The Manitoba Medical College became part of the university in 1882. In 1904 the university began teaching on its own by providing science courses not offered in the colleges. Over the years other colleges have become affiliated: Wesley in 1888 (later joined with Manitoba to become United College), the Manitoba College of Pharmacy in 1902, St Paul's (Roman Catholic) and Brandon College in 1938, and St Andrew's College (Greek Orthodox) in 1964. United College has since become the UNIVERSITY OF WINNIPEG and Brandon College BRANDON UNIVERSITY.

University of New Brunswick. Founded in 1785 in Fredericton by the governor and council of New Brunswick as the Provincial Academy of Arts and Sciences, it underwent several name changes before it was reconstituted in 1859 as a provincial university. The Brydone Jack building, erected in 1851—the oldest astronomical observatory in Canada—today also contains the offices of *The* FIDDLEHEAD. A branch of the university operates in

Saint John as a two-year college of arts and sciences.

University of Ottawa/Université d'Ottawa. A bilingual university located in downtown Ottawa, it was founded as the College of By-town in 1848 by the Missionary Oblates of Mary Immaculate and in 1866 was raised to university status by an Act of the Parliament of the Province of Canada. In 1889 it received pontifical recognition as a full university by decree of Pope Leo XIII. The Faculty of Law prepares lawyers to practise under Canada's two legal systems. A Faculty of Medicine was established in 1945 and the Faculty of Science and Engineering in 1948.

University of Prince Edward Island. Located in Charlottetown, it was formed in 1969 by the union of Prince of Wales College (founded in 1834) and St Dunstan's University (founded in 1855). Courses are offered leading to degrees in arts, sciences, business administration, education, and music. The university operates on a semester system.

University of Regina. Regina College, a residential school of the Methodist Church, was founded in 1911. In 1925 it became an affiliated Junior College of the University of Saskatchewan and in 1934 turned non-denominational. In 1965 buildings on a new site were opened as part of the province's plan to make the college an independent degree-granting university, which it became in 1974. Federated with the university are Campion College (Roman Catholic) and Luther College (Lutheran).

University of Saskatchewan. It was created by an act of the provincial legislature in 1907 and located in Saskatoon. Affiliated colleges are St Thomas More (since 1936), Emmanuel College (since 1909)—now the College of Emmanuel and St Chad—ST ANDREWS (since 1913), and Lutheran Theological Seminary. Regina College was affiliated in 1934 but became the UNIVERSITY OF REGINA in 1974.

University of the Air. See CBC IDEAS.

University of Toronto. The largest university in Canada. Located in downtown Toronto, it dates back to the granting in 1827 of a royal charter to King's College (founded by John STRACHAN), which opened in 1843 as an Anglican college but, after much public controversy over one denomination's receiving public funding to the exclusion of others, was secularized by the government in 1849. Today the U of T consists of a federation (dating from 1887) of various colleges and faculties. The earliest colleges were VICTORIA

(originally a Methodist college but now United Church, 1841), TRINITY (Anglican, 1851), ST MICHAEL'S (Roman Catholic, 1852), and UNIVERSITY COLLEGE (non-denominational 1859). There are three affiliated colleges that offer only theological instruction: KNOX (Presbyterian, 1843), Wycliffe (Anglican, 1877), and EMMANUEL (United Church, 1928). A unique feature of university theological learning is the TORONTO SCHOOL OF THEOLOGY. In the 1960s and 1970s the university was augmented by additional colleges: Erindale, Innis, MASSEY, New, Scarborough, and Woodsworth. Associated with the U of T are the DAVID DUNLAP OBSERVATORY, HART HOUSE, the John P. Robarts Research Library, the Thomas Fisher Rare Book Library, the PONTIFICAL INSTITUTE OF MEDIEVAL STUDIES, the CENTRE FOR CULTURE AND TECHNOLOGY, the Graduate Centre for the Study of Drama, and the Research Program in Canadian Theatre History.

University of Toronto Press. A department of the UNIVERSITY OF TORONTO, established in 1901, the first university press to be founded in North America. UTP issues 120 to 150 new titles annually—the largest book program in Canada. It also prints and publishes 18 academic journals, mostly quarterlies. Some 1,300 titles, or upwards of 11% of all Canadian books in print in English, now bear this imprint. It publishes the DICTIONARY OF CANADIAN BIOGRAPHY. The director is Marsh Jeanneret.

University of Toronto Quarterly, The. A leading academic journal published four times a year by the UNIVERSITY OF TORONTO since 1931. It publishes scholarly articles on the humanities, with special emphasis on English studies. *UTQ* reviews all worthwhile books published in Canada during the previous year in 'LETTERS IN CANADA', a useful supplement in the Summer issue.

University of Victoria. Located in Victoria, B.C., it was created in 1903 as Victoria College, an affiliate branch of McGILL UNIVERSITY (a beginning common to some other western universities), which functioned until 1915, when the University of British Columbia was established. A new Victoria College was set up in 1920 in affiliation with UBC to provide the first two years of an arts and science program. After 1945 the college began its evolution to university status: a faculty of education was added in 1956; the first B.A. was granted in 1961; and full university status was achieved in 1963. The university sponsors the publication of the internationally known quarterly, *The* MALAHAT REVIEW.

University of Waterloo

University of Waterloo. It was incorporated in 1959, although classes were first held in 1957 with the introduction of a pioneering co-operative engineering program, whereby students worked a semester in industry between each academic semester. Federated with Waterloo are the University of St Jerome's College (Roman Catholic), Renison College (Anglican), Conrad Grebel College (Mennonite), and St Paul's College (United).

University of Western Ontario. Located in London, Ont., it is noted for its School of Business Administration and its Faculty of Education (which publishes the *History and Social Science Teacher*). There are three associated colleges: Brescia (a Roman Catholic women's college), Huron (Anglican), and King's (Roman Catholic).

University of Windsor. Assumption College, founded by the Basilian Fathers in 1857, was granted independent university status in 1953. A decade later the non-denominational University of Windsor was formed, with Assumption University as a federated member. Also affiliated with the university are Holy Redeemer College (Roman Catholic), Canterbury College (Anglican), and Iona College (United Church).

University of Windsor Review, The. A literary quarterly founded in 1965 by the UNIVERSITY OF WINDSOR to publish scholarly articles in the arts, sciences, politics, and social sciences. Each issue includes fiction, poetry, and reviews.

University of Winnipeg. Located in downtown Winnipeg, it was formerly United College, an affiliate of the UNIVERSITY OF MANITOBA, until university status was achieved in 1967. Programs are offered in the arts, sciences, and theology; a collegiate division is also maintained. In 1968 the Institute of Urban Studies was established.

Unknown Country, The. A popular romantic study of Canada by Bruce HUTCHISON. Published in 1942 and revised in 1948, it was the first modern book to foster a nationalistic sentiment as it celebrated the beauties and possibilities of the nation and optimistically claimed that the English- and French-speaking language groups were growing together in understanding.

Unrestricted reciprocity. See RECIPROCITY.

UPI. See UNITED PRESS INTERNATIONAL.

Uplands. The original name of the Ottawa International Airport. It was founded as the Uplands Air Field in the late 1920s by a pri-

vate flying club and purchased in 1936 by Laurentian Air Services, which sold it to the Department of Transport in 1938. Known as Uplands Airport until 1960, when its name was changed to Ottawa Airport, it was designated Ottawa International Airport in 1964.

Upper Canada. The area west of the Ottawa R.—present-day Ontario—formed by the CONSTITUTIONAL ACT OF 1791. Upper Canada became CANADA WEST in 1841 as a result of the ACT OF UNION; it became Ontario in 1867.

Upper Canada College. Private boys' school in Toronto. Founded by Sir John COLBORNE in 1829, it moved in 1891 from King and Simcoe Sts to its present location on Lonsdale Rd, its clocktower facing Avenue Rd. It was rebuilt in a Georgian-style design by Mathers and Haldenby in 1958; the redesigned tower preserves the silhouette and the important landmark quality of the original building. The school offers instruction for grades one through 13 and has approximately 900 students.

Upper Canada Village. A museum community of nineteenth-century buildings and artifacts situated in CRYSLER'S FARM Battlefield Park, 7 mi. east of Morrisburg, Ont. Assembled in 1950s from parts of historic Canadian villages threatened by development of the ST LAWRENCE SEAWAY, it opened in 1961. The 65-acre site contains over 40 buildings of the period 1785 to 1860. It is administered by the St Lawrence Parks Commission.

Upper chamber. See SENATE.

Upper Fort Garry. See FORT GARRY.

Upper house. Body of members appointed to advise the governor of a colony; the House of Parliament whose members are appointed, not elected. In colonial times the upper house was called the LEGISLATIVE COUNCIL. Since Confederation the upper house of the federal Parliament has been known as the SENATE. See also LOWER HOUSE.

Upper Lakes. A reference to Lake Huron and Lake Superior, the most northerly of the GREAT LAKES in relation to the St Lawrence R.

Upper Town. That part of QUEBEC CITY on the plateau of Cape Diamond. See also LOWER TOWN.

Uranium. Radioactive metallic element used in the production of nuclear energy. Canada produces 18.1% of the world's output (outside of the U.S.S.R.) from mines around ELLIOT LAKE, Ont., and Uranium City, Sask. See also CHALK RIVER and ELDORADO NUCLEAR LIMITED.

Urban Affairs, Ministry of State for. Federal government department concerned with urban policies and programs. It was established in June 1971.

Urquhart, Tony (b.1934). Painter. Born in Niagara Falls, Ont., he studied at the Albright Art School in Buffalo and at the University of Buffalo. His abstract, allegorical landscapes—painted in a watercolour technique that subtly conveys the texture of the earth's surface—suggest nature's renewal. *In Hiding* (1960, NGC) is one of his finest paintings. Recently he has turned to photography and prepared a series about decayed French funerary sculpture shown in rural settings. His interest in landscape is also present in his collage constructions: boxes painted with landscape motifs having various elements superimposed on them. He has exhibited internationally.

Ursuline Convent. Founded in 1639 by Madame de la PELTRIE, with MARIE DE L'INCARNA-TION as the first Superior, it was the first private school for girls in North America. The first building was erected in 1641, but it was reconstructed after fires in 1650 and 1686. It is now a complex of buildings in Quebec's Upper Town, of which the Ste Famille and St Augustine wings date from the reconstruction that took place in 1686. The chapel was built in 1715-22 and remodelled in 1902. (It contains the skull of MONTCALM.) Later wings were built in 1836, 1853 (the girl's school), and 1859 or 1865 (the Parlour Wing). See also URSULINES.

Ursulines. Roman Catholic religious order. Founded in Italy in 1540, it spread to other European countries, including France in 1612. In 1639 a branch was founded in Quebec for educational purposes by Madame de la PELTRIE, with three nuns, one of whom was MARIE DE L'INCARNATION. Today the order maintains convents in Ontario and Saskatchewan as well as in Quebec City. See also URSULINE CONVENT.

V

VAdm. Official abbreviation of Vice-Admiral.

Vaillancourt, Armand (b.1931). Sculptor. Born in Quebec City, he studied at the Montreal Museum of Fine Arts School and at L'École des Beaux-Arts. He has achieved many commissions and awards for his abstract designs, which are generally made from welded scrap metal and steel. His public commissions for Toronto's HIGH PARK and San Francisco caused civic controversy in both cities; the uncompleted Toronto piece was removed. The Chicoutimi War Memorial is perhaps his finest work.

Valcartier. See CANADIAN FORCES BASE VALCARTIER.

Valdy (b.1946). Singer-composer. Born Vladimir Horsdal in Ottawa, he was first heard singing his casual, folk-like compositions on THIS COUNTRY IN THE MORNING. His third album, *Family Gathering* (1975), was quite successful. Valdy has roots in opposite ends of the country, owning farms at Sook, Vancouver Island, B.C., and on Woody Island, Placentia Bay, Nfld.

Valenciennes. A town in northern France, liberated in the last phase of the FIRST WORLD WAR by the CANADIAN CORPS on 1-2 Nov. 1918.

Valérie. Feature film directed by Dénis HÉROUX and released in 1968. Starring Danielle Ouimet and Guy Godin, it concerns the amorous adventures of a girl who leaves a convent and is saved from a life of prostitution by true love. It was the first Quebec sexploitation film to break box-office records. 95 min., b & w.

Vallières, Pierre (b.1938). Quebec writer. Born in Montreal's East End, its working-class district, he knew Jacques FERRON as a youngster. He began writing for Le DEVOIR and CITÉ LIBRE, which he edited in the 1960s until it became apparent to Pierre Elliott TRUDEAU that his notion of social change was more revolutionary than the future prime minister's. Arrested for demonstrating before the United Nations in New York on behalf of the FLQ, Vallières was incarcerated in the Manhattan House of Detention for Men (The Toombs) in 1966-7 and there wrote much of *Nègres blancs d'Amérique* (1968), which was published in English as *White Niggers of America* (1971) translated by Joan Pinkham. Deported to Montreal, he spent almost four years in jail on charges connected with his FLQ activities. In 1971 he identified himself with the newly formed PARTI QUÉBÉCOIS. This development is the subject of *L'Urgence de choisir* (1971), or *Choose!* (1971) in its English translation by Penny Williams. In 1975 Vallières was operating La Relève, an art gallery in downtown Montreal.

Valour, Cross of. See CROSS OF VALOUR.

Valuation Day. The day—27 Dec. 1972—on which all Canadians were required to value their property for purposes of the Capital Gains Tax imposed under the Tax Reform Bill, 1971-2-3. Within the legal profession Valuation Day is referred to as V.D. or Fiscal V.D.

van Hamel, Martine (b.1945). Dancer. Born in Brussels, she studied at the Hague Conservatorium in 1956-7 and with Henry Danton in Caracas in 1957-9. She continued her training at the National Ballet School and in 1963 joined the NATIONAL BALLET OF CANADA as soloist. She won first prizes for junior-class dancing and artistic interpretation at the Third International Ballet Competition in Varna, Bulgaria, in 1966, partnered by Earl KRAUL. The National's principal dancer between 1967 and 1969, she was inundated with offers from companies around the world and finally left for New York in 1969. Her career faltered for the next four years, but in 1974 she emerged as one of the leading ballerinas of the American Ballet Theatre and was guest artist with the Royal Swedish Ballet and the Joffrey Ballet.

Van Horne, Sir William (1843-1915). President of the CANADIAN PACIFIC RAILWAY. Born in Chelsea, Ill., he worked for American railways until 1882, when he was appointed general manager of the CPR, whose construction had been bedevilled by countless difficulties. Van Horne capably oversaw the expeditious completion of the railway in 1885. He was made president in 1888. He lived in a mansion on Sherbrooke St, Montreal—demolished in 1973—that contained one of the great private art collections in North America. He was knighted in 1894.

Vancouver. The third-largest city in Canada, it has no rival in terms of the physical beauty of its setting. The first permanent settlement occured in 1856 as a result of the discovery of gold in the Fraser R., but the site was not surveyed until 1870, when it was known as Granville. Little growth took place until 1885, when it was chosen as the western terminus of the CPR. The following year it was incorporated as a city and renamed Vancouver. Its economic base has been shaped by its principal functions as a transportation terminus and major port and as the financial, service, and manufacturing centre for the rich resource-based economy of British Columbia. Vancouver's Chinatown is considered to be the second-largest Chinese community in North America (next to San Francisco's). The 1971 CMA population was 1,082,352. Its official motto is *Splendor Sine Occasu* ('Splendour Undiminished'). See also CAPILANO SUSPENSION BRIDGE, GASTOWN, GROUSE MOUNTAIN, LIONS GATE BRIDGE, SIMON FRASER UNIVERSITY, STANLEY PARK, UNIVERSITY OF BRITISH COLUMBIA, VANCOUVER ART GALLERY, VANCOUVER INTERNATIONAL FESTIVAL.

Vancouver, George (1757-98). Navigator. He sailed on two voyages with Capt. James COOK, on the second of which, in 1778, Nootka Sound, Vancouver Island, was visited. In 1791 Vancouver returned to the west coast in command of the *Discovery* on a British expedition to take over the Nootka Sound territory from the Spaniards.

Vancouver Art Gallery. Founded in 1931, it has a permanent collection of national and international works and owns the most important collection of paintings by Emily CARR. It publishes *Vanguard* and *Criteria*, two newsletters concerning both regional and national aspects of the arts.

Vancouver Blazers. See WORLD HOCKEY ASSOCIATION.

Vancouver Club, The. A nationally important luncheon club. Founded in 1893, it is housed in its own five-storey building in Vancouver. It has 1,200 members, mainly British Columbia business executives.

Vancouver International Festival. An ambitious two-week-long arts festival. It was launched to celebrate the centennial of the mainland colony of British Columbia, and opened, under the artistic direction of Nicholas Goldschmidt, on 19 July 1958. The events—which included operas, concerts, art shows and a film festival—were held in the Vancouver Civic Auditorium. The Peking Opera made its North American début at the Festival on 10 Aug. 1960. The eleventh and last season concluded on 18 Aug. 1968.

Vancouver Island. Canada's largest Pacific island, 285 mi. long, across the Strait of Georgia from the southwestern mainland of

British Columbia. Mountainous and heavily forested, it is actually the top of a partially submerged mountain system. Visited by Capt. James COOK and George VANCOUVER in 1778 and held after 1818 by both Great Britain and the United States under a treaty of joint occupation, it became British territory under the terms of the Oregon treaty of 1846. In 1849 Britain released the island to the HUDSON'S BAY COMPANY on the condition that the Company establish a colony there. It was annexed to the mainland colony of British Columbia in 1866. In 1868 the capital was moved from New Westminster to VICTORIA.

Vancouver News-Herald, The. A morning newspaper published in Vancouver. Founded in 1933, it was acquired by the THOMSON PRESS. It folded in 1957.

Vancouver Province, The. A morning newspaper published in Vancouver. Founded in 1898, it has been owned by SOUTHAM PRESS since 1923. It is now published by Southam's for Pacific Press Ltd.

Vancouver Sit-ins. A 1938 sit-down strike by RELIEF CAMP workers and others in the Vancouver Post Office and other public buildings. The workers allowed the public to use the buildings during the day. The sit-ins were peaceful until the police attempted to evict the strikers from the post office, using considerable force, on BLOODY SUNDAY.

Vancouver Sun, The. An evening newspaper published in Vancouver. Dating back to 1886 and the end-product of mergers and renamings, it has been part of FP PUBLICATIONS since 1957. It is printed and published by Pacific Press Ltd. The publisher is Stuart Keate and the editorial director Bruce HUTCHISON. Columnists include Allan Fotheringham, Eric NICOL, Paul ST PIERRE, and Jack Wasserman.

Vandoos. The popular name of the ROYAL 22e RÉGIMENT, derived from *vingt-deux*, 'twenty-two'.

Vanguard. A turboprop aircraft in the service of TRANS-CANADA AIRLINES from 1961 to 1972. Built by Vickers in Britain as a successor to the VISCOUNT, it carried 108 passengers at 415 m.p.h.

Vanier, Georges (1888-1967). GOVERNOR GENERAL of Canada from 1959 to 1967. Born in Montreal, he studied law at Université Laval. In the First World War he served in the ROYAL 22e REGIMENT, which he commanded from 1925 to 1928. He had a distinguished career as a public servant and diplomat—he was ambassador to France from 1944 to 1953—before he was appointed governor general.

Vanier, Jean. See L'ARCHE.

Vanier Institute of the Family. An organization founded to study the Canadian family. One recommendation of the Canadian Conference on the Family in 1965, the Institute was founded in Ottawa on 18 Mar. 1965 under the sponsorship of Governor General and Madam Georges VANIER, with Wilder PENFIELD as President.

Vanier Medal. Gold medal awarded annually by the Institute of Public Administration of Canada to mark either distinctive leadership or a significant contribution in the field of public administration in Canada. It was named after Governor General Georges VANIER and was first awarded in 1962.

Vannelli, Gino (b.1952). Pop singer. Born in Montreal of Italian parents, he started in show business as a drummer at the age of 11 and recorded his first single at 16. Backed by a five-piece band, led by his brother Joe, that creates a 'layered sound'—a combination of rock, pop, jazz, soul, Latin American, and electronic music—he became a strong performing and recording star in the 1970s.

Variable-pitch propeller. A propeller with a mechanism to alter the slant of its blades while in motion, making the air-transport industry possible. It was invented by Wallace Rupert Turnbull (1870-1954), an aeronautical engineer born in Saint John, working in his private laboratory at Rothesay, N.B. Completed in 1916, it was first publically demonstrated at Camp Borden, Ont., in 1923. Turnbull, who has been called the 'father of aeronautical research in Canada', had earlier, in 1902, built Canada's first wind tunnel.

Variations on a Cellophane Wrapper. A well-known 'personal' film directed by David Rimmer of Vancouver in 1970. A loop film, it repeats a visual image that is gradually transformed until it disintegrates. 8 min., colour.

Varley, F.H. (1881-1969). Landscape and portrait painter, member of the GROUP OF SEVEN. Frederick Horseman Varley was born in Sheffield, Eng., and studied art there and in Antwerp. He worked as a commercial artist in England and in 1912 moved to Toronto, where he worked as a designer for Grip Limited (for three weeks) and then Rous and Mann. He painted his well-known *Some Day the People Will Return* (NGC) after a visit to the Front in 1918 as a war artist. In 1926 he moved to Vancouver, where he taught and painted for 10 years. He was less interested in landscapes than in portraits, but in 1920, the year of the founding of the

Group of Seven, he painted the famous STORMY WEATHER, GEORGIAN BAY (NGC), and in 1927-8 *The Cloud, Red Mountain, B.C.* (AGO). Among his very fine portraits are VERA (*c.*1930, NGC) and DHÂRÂNA (1932, AGO).

Vaudreuil, Marquis de (*c.*1643-1725). Governor of New France. Born in France, Philippe de Rigaud, Marquis de Vaudreuil, came to New France in 1687 as commander of the troops in Canada and led several expeditions against the Iroquois in the 1690s. He was made governor of Montreal in 1694, administrator of the government in Canada in 1703, and governor of New France in 1705. One of his four sons was François-Pierre de Rigaud, marquis de VAUDREUIL-CAVAGNAL, who became the last governor of New France.

Vaudreuil-Cavagnal, Pierre de Rigaud, marquis de (1698-1778). Last governor of New France. Born in Montreal, the son of Philippe de Rigaud, Marquis de VAUDREUIL, he became governor of Trois-Rivières in 1733, governor of Louisiana in 1742, and governor general of New France in 1755, when he entered upon the defence of Canada in the SEVEN YEARS' WAR. His authority and advice were constantly challenged by the vain, disputatious MONTCALM, who arrived in 1756. After the battle of the PLAINS OF ABRAHAM and Montcalm's death, Vaudreuil surrendered Quebec to the British, and a year later surrendered Montreal. He and the colonial officials were held accountable in France for the loss of Quebec, though a combination of Montcalm's poor generalship and superior British forces were the real cause. He was imprisoned in the Bastille and tried for maladministration of the colony but was cleared of blame for the defeat and awarded a pension.

VC. See VICTORIA CROSS.

Vedette. The first aircraft designed and built in Canada. The single-engine, three-seater flying boat was manufactured by Canadian Vickers at Maisonneuve, near Montreal, in 1924, and commissioned by the RCAF for forest patrol work. Two years earlier the RCMP had commissioned for use on civil projects the British-built, Canadian-owned Viking.

Vera. One of the best-known portraits by F.H. VARLEY, painted about 1930. The subject is Vera Weatherbie, an art student and friend of Varley's. Her strikingly beautiful oval face, with its clear-eyed gaze and sensuous lips, is crowned by free-flowing straight red hair. The face is lighted by tinges of green—suggesting spirituality—and green is the predominant colour of the shapeless clothes. NGC

Verchères, Madeleine de (1678-1747). Heroine of New France. She was the fourth of 12 children of François Jarret de Verchères, who had a seigneury on the south shore of the St Lawrence (30 mi. from Montreal), with a fort for protection against the Iroquois. In 1692, when Madeleine was 14 and her parents were absent, Iroquois captured some settlers in the fields surrounding the fort. Madeleine was seized but escaped, gained the fort, and proceeded to take command, alarming the Indians with a round of gunfire and causing them to withdraw on the second day. As an adult she wrote two accounts of her childhood triumph, which has entered the mythology of New France, and LA POTHERIE and CHARLEVOIX contributed their versions, creating some confusion about details. An arresting bronze statue of the heroine by Louis-Philippe HÉBERT was erected at Verchères, Que., in 1913.

Verigin, Peter Vasil'evich (1859-1924). Celebrated leader of the DOUKHOBORS, called Peter the Lordly. Born in Russia, he was acclaimed leader of the sect in 1887 and was immediately arrested and exiled to a northern province for five years. In 1894 he was sent to Siberia for refusing to take an oath of allegiance to the tsar and for his resistance to a military-service law. On his release in 1902 he immigrated to Canada and assumed control of the Doukhobor settlement in Saskatchewan. Both there, and in a second settlement established in British Columbia in 1908, he succeeded against political and geographical odds in creating a strong community organization. He was killed near Grand Forks, B.C., on 29 Oct. 1924 when the railway coach in which he was travelling blew up; the explosion was likely planned. In 1917 Verigin built a handsome white meeting-house at Verigin, Sask., that is still in use.

Vernon, John (b.1932). Actor. Born in Regina of Polish parents—his given name was Adolphus Vernon Agopsowicz—he attended the Royal Academy of Dramatic Art in 1952 and supplied the deep voice of Big Brother for the British film *Nineteen Eighty-Four* (1956). As a stage actor he appeared at the CREST THEATRE and the STRATFORD FESTIVAL. He played the lead in CBC-TV's WOJECK series, first shown in 1966, and has since appeared as a 'heavy' in numerous Hollywood films, including Hitchcock's *Topaz* (1969), and television plays.

Verrazzano, Giovanni da (*c.*1485-*c.*1528). Italian navigator and the first explorer to discover that North America was a continent. Sailing in the service of France, he left the Madeiras in Jan. 1524, coasted the continent from North Carolina to Nova Scotia, reached Newfoundland, and left for France in July.

Verrières Ridge. A ridge in Normandy, France, the scene of repeated fighting during the SECOND WORLD WAR. Canadian and British troops met German reserves at the Ridge on 20 and 25 July 1944, but succeeded in taking their objective, FALAISE, on 14 Aug. 1944.

Vertical Mosaic, The. Subtitled *An Analysis of Social Class and Power in Canada,* it is an influential work by John Porter, a sociologist at Carleton University, published in 1965.

Vertical Take-Off and Landing. Description of an aircraft (the CL-84) designed and built in Canada by DE HAVILLAND that, in addition to flying normally, can hover and take off and land vertically in the manner of a helicopter. The VTOL was first built in 1973.

Very Stone House. Publishing operation founded in Vancouver by Patrick LANE and Seymour MAYNE to publish avant-garde poetry. It flourished between 1966 and 1971.

Veterans Affairs, Department of. Federal-government department concerned exclusively with the welfare of veterans, and with the dependants of veterans and of those who died or were injured on active service. Established in 1944, it provides treatment, welfare services, education assistance, and other services.

Vézina, Georges (1888-1926). Hockey goalkeeper. Nicknamed 'The Chicoutimi Cucumber' for his coolness under fire, he was born in Chicoutimi, Que. He became a professional in 1910 with the MONTREAL CANADIENS and was a member of two teams that won the STANLEY CUP. He died of tuberculosis. The VÉZINA TROPHY is awarded annually to the NHL goalkeeper on the team with fewest 'goals against'.

Vézina Trophy. Presented by the NATIONAL HOCKEY LEAGUE annually 'to the goalkeeper(s) having played a minimum of 25 games for the team with the fewest goals scored against it'. The trophy was presented by former owners of the MONTREAL CANADIENS in 1926-7 in memory of Georges VÉZINA, outstanding goalkeeper of the Canadiens who collapsed during a League game in 1925 and died a few months later. The overall winner receives $1,500; the runner-up $750.

Vickers, Jon (b.1926). Tenor. Born in Prince Albert, Sask., he studied singing at the Royal Conservatory of Music, Toronto, from 1949 to 1956. He is a dramatic tenor whose brute strength and austere dedication to every aspect of acting and singing the great operatic roles—of which he knows more than 40—have made him one of the top three operatic tenors in the world (with Luciano Pavarotti and Placido Domingo). Though he is in demand in many countries for recordings and live performances, he is particularly associated with Covent Garden, London (since 1957), and the Metropolitan Opera, New York (since 1960). He is identified especially with the title roles in *Peter Grimes, Parsifal, Otello,* and with Florestan in *Fidelio,* Siegmund in *Die Walküre,* Canio in *Pagliacci,* and Tristan in *Tristan und Isolde.*

Vicky Metcalf Award. Annual award for 'a body of writing inspirational to Canadian youth'. It was established in 1963 by Vicky Metcalf of the CANADIAN AUTHORS ASSOCIATION, which administers the $1,000 award.

Victor Lynch-Staunton Awards. Three annual Senior Arts Grants of the CANADA COUNCIL. Since 1973 three successful candidates in competition for the Senior Arts Grants of the Canada Council have been recipients of Victor Lynch-Staunton Awards. They honour the memory of the Montreal lawyer who died in 1967 and left a bequest to the Council of $700,000.

Victoria. The capital of British Columbia. On the southern tip of Vancouver Island, it was the site chosen by James DOUGLAS for a HUDSON'S BAY COMPANY fort, built in 1843. The settlement grew quickly as a result of the FRASER RIVER GOLD RUSH of 1858 and was incorporated as a city in 1862. Today Victoria's economy is primarily dependent on government, tourism, and on its agreeableness as a haven for retired people. Called the 'garden city' of Canada, it is regarded with envy by many Canadians because of the beauty of its physical surroundings, its mild winters (Jan. average 4°C), and its leisurely way of life. Its 1971 CMA population was 195,800. See also ART GALLERY OF GREATER VICTORIA, BEACON HILL PARK, EMPRESS HOTEL, FORT RODD HILL NATIONAL HISTORIC PARK, ROGERS CHOCOLATES, ROYAL ROADS MILITARY COLLEGE, THUNDERBIRD PARK, UNIVERSITY OF VICTORIA.

Victoria Bridge. Nineteenth-century engineering feat. Spanning the St Lawrence R. from Montreal to Longueuil, and built in 1854-9, it was the first large bridge with a metal superstructure in North America. It was designed as a tubular bridge by the famous English engineer Robert Stephenson and was officially opened in 1860 by the

Prince of Wales, later Edward VII. The tube was replaced with an open truss and the bridge was widened in 1897-8.

Victoria College. A federated college of the UNIVERSITY OF TORONTO. It was founded as the Upper Canada Academy, a Methodist school, in 1836 in Cobourg, Ont., and changed its name to Victoria College in 1841, when it granted its first degrees. In 1892 it moved into its present Victorian Gothic building, designed by W.G. STORM and located on Queen's Park Crescent. A union of Victoria College as the arts faculty and a separate Faculty of Divinity (named EMMANUEL COLLEGE in 1928) led to the creation of Victoria University in 1884. The combined colleges still bear this name. Victoria College is an affiliate of the UNITED CHURCH OF CANADA.

Victoria Cross. The highest military decoration in the Commonwealth, first awarded for valour by Queen Victoria in 1856. The abbreviation is VC.

Victoria Daily Colonist, The. A morning newspaper published in Victoria. British Columbia's oldest paper, it was founded by Amor DE COSMOS in 1858. Since 1950 it has been owned by FP PUBLICATIONS, which prints and publishes the *Colonist* along with the VICTORIA TIMES. It appears seven days a week and has two mottos: 'An Independent Newspaper—the Organ of No Clique or Party' and 'Vancouver Island's Leading Newspaper since 1858'.

Victoria Day. Statutory holiday observed throughout Canada to celebrate Queen Victoria's birthday on 'the twenty-fourth of May'. It is observed on the Monday before 25 May and is also known as the Queen's Birthday and as Commonwealth Day. The custom of celebrating this event originated in CANADA WEST (Ontario) in 1845, but it was not until 1896 that Clementina Fessenden determined that the anniversary of Queen Victoria's birth would be the ideal day on which to salute the British Empire. The following year the world's first Empire Day was celebrated in Canada West, and the custom spread throughout the Empire. 'The Queen's Birthday' or 'the twenty-fourth of May' was declared a holiday by the Canadian Parliament in 1901.

Victoria Times, The. An evening newspaper published in Victoria. Founded in 1872, it has been owned by FP PUBLICATIONS since 1949. It is printed and published along with the VICTORIA COLONIST.

Victorian Order of Nurses. The country's oldest national nursing organization, specializing in pre- and post-natal care. It was founded in Ottawa in 1897 with the help of Lady Aberdeen, wife of the governor general, at the request of the National Council of Women, which saw the need for a group of visiting nurses to bring medical care to sparsely settled areas of the country and to urban slums. The VON was named to commemorate Queen Victoria's Diamond Jubilee and was modelled on the Queen's Jubilee Nurses.

Victory Theatre. Landmark in the Spadina 'garment district' of Toronto. Built in 1915 as a legitimate Jewish theatre and called the Standard, it became the New Strand in the 1930s, the Victory movie theatre in the 1940s, and the Victory Burlesk in the 1950s. It was turned into a Chinese restaurant in 1976.

Vie des Arts. A quarterly in French devoted to the visual arts, music, photography, and film, with special emphasis on the fine arts. Published since 1956 in Montreal, it pays particular attention to Quebec and to French art and artists. The magazine is well illustrated and an English summary of the French text appears in every issue.

Vie heureuse de Léopold Z, La. Feature film directed by Gilles CARLE and produced by the NATIONAL FILM BOARD in 1965. It is a comedy about a Montreal snow remover, a happy-go-lucky fellow who manages to satisfy his wife, himself, and even attend midnight Mass on Christmas Eve. It was the first NFB feature to achieve popular success in Quebec cinemas. 68 min., 20 sec., b & w.

Viewpoint. The longest-running public-access show on CBC-TV. The six-minute program of 'free opinion' on the topics of the day, prepared and delivered by free-lance observers, followed the NATIONAL and was hosted by Earl CAMERON. First seen on 28 Oct. 1957, it was phased out on 5 Jan. 1975 to some controversy. Its radio counterpart is PREVIEW COMMENTARY.

Vigneault, Gilles (b.1928). Poet and singer. Born in Natashquan, Que., he was educated at Université Laval. He founded Éditions de L'Arc, dedicated to poetry publishing, and began his successful career as a chansonnier in 1960. He is known as 'Le troubadour de Natashquan', for he writes about his native region with deep affection in poems that have appeared in numerous collections. *Avec les vieux mots* (1964) included his lyric 'MON PAYS', made famous by Monique LEYRAC at the International Song Festival in Sopot, Poland, in 1965. A bilingual edition of a collection of fables, translated by Paul Allard, appeared as *Tales (Sur la pointe des pieds)* (1972).

Viirlaid, Arved (b.1922). Emigré poet and novelist who writes in Estonian. He was born in Estonia and settled in Toronto in 1954. He is the author of a number of novels, but only *Year of Storms* (1949) and *Graves Without Crosses* (1952; translated by Ilse Lehiste, 1972) have appeared in English. A selection of his poems, translated by Astrid Ivask and Taimi Ene Moks, appears in VOL-VOX (1971), edited by J. Michael Yates.

Viking. See VEDETTE.

Viking, The. Early Canadian feature film. Made by the Newfoundland-Labrador Film Company, it was produced by Varick Frissell, directed by George Melford, and released in 1931. It is a drama about two seal hunters, rivals for a woman, who are caught in a blizzard and lost on the ice. The power of the film lies in the documentary sequences of the seal hunt. While additional footage was being shot, the SS *Viking* exploded, killing 27 men, including Frissell. Completed by the Hollywood director George Melford, it was probably the first sound film made on location outside a studio anywhere in the world. Sir Wilfred GRENFELL introduces the film and Capt. Bob BARTLETT makes a cameo appearance. 8 reels, b & w.

Ville Marie. The original seventeenth-century name of MONTREAL, which gradually replaced the name Ville Marie after the settlement was founded in 1642.

Vimy. A village in northern France, the scene of a brilliant assault during the FIRST WORLD WAR by all four divisions of the CANADIAN CORPS under Lt-Gen. Julian BYNG. Vimy rests at the foot of a chalky ridge that was a German bastion extending several miles from the coal fields of Lens (see HILL 70) in the north to the city of ARRAS in the south. On Easter Monday, 9 Apr. 1917, the Canadians took Thélus, Hill 145, and Vimy Ridge itself. Vimy, marked by great *esprit de corps*, remains the most celebrated of Canadian battles. See also VIMY MEMORIAL.

Vimy Memorial. Canada's most impressive monument to the war dead. It stands on the crest of a chalk ridge overlooking the village of VIMY and the Douai Plain of northern France, where a German bastion was captured by the CANADIAN CORPS on Easter Monday, 9 Apr. 1917. Vimy Memorial consists of a 250-acre park, presented to Canada by France, on the site of the battlefield, and the imposing monument itself, with soaring

twin pylons that have been likened to 'a gate leading to a better world'. Designed by the Toronto sculptor Walter S. ALLWARD, it took ten years to build and was dedicated by Edward VIII on 26 July 1936.

Vincent Massey Awards. Awards 'for excellence in the urban environment'. Sponsored by the CANADA COUNCIL, the Massey Foundation, and CENTRAL MORTGAGE AND HOUSING CORPORATION, and established in 1971, the Vincent Massey Awards for Excellence in the Urban Environment are given—up to 15 every two to four years—for recent projects that have made significant contributions to the amenity of urban life. A travelling jury awards certificates to the people of the communities in which the projects exist and distinctive bronze markers are erected on the winning sites. The awards honour the late Governor General Vincent MASSEY.

Vinland or **Vineland.** 'Land of vines' in Icelandic sagas, named by LEIF ERICSSON. Vinland has been identified with numerous locations on the east coast of North America. The weight of evidence favours Newfoundland because archaeological excavations on the northwestern coast have located the site of a Viking colony, settled about A.D. 1001, at present-day L'ANSE AUX MEADOWS (pronounced 'Lancy Meadows').

Violet. Any of various species of low-growing herbs with solitary, usually bluish-purple flowers. New Brunswick officially adopted the purple violet as its floral emblem in 1936. However, botanists were quick to point out that no such classification of a violet exists and that the flower intended in the legislation was probably one of the blue violets common throughout the Maritimes.

Violin, The. A popular short film directed by George Pastic. 'Love of the violin brings together an eccentric old man and two young boys, out of which evolves a short-lived but intense friendship.' The old man was played by violinist Maurice Solway. The film was shot on TORONTO ISLAND by Sincinkin Productions in 1971. (It was turned into a children's book, *The Violin* [1976], with a text by Robert Thomas ALLEN, the original scriptwriter.) 25 min., colour.

Viscount. The world's first turboprop aircraft, introduced to North America by TRANS-CANADA AIR LINES and in service from 1955 to 1974. Built by Vickers in Britain, it carried from 40 to 54 passengers at 315 m.p.h. Its Rolls-Royce Dart engines reached a unprecedented 9,000-hour interval between overhauls of basic components.

Visites Interprovinciales

Visites Interprovinciales. A government-funded, non-profit educational service that facilitates the summer exchange of students between Quebec and Ontario homes. Begun in 1936, it has involved over 60,000 students in exchanges that are for a minimum of two weeks each. In 1968 the organization introduced six-day visits for groups of 40 students each.

Visiteur du soir, Le. Canvas by Jean-Paul LE-MIEUX painted in 1956. The most famous of his simplified, dream-like images, it shows a tall triangular figure on the right standing before a severely straight horizon line, with a short thin ribbon of land on the left, that divides an even expanse of white below from the sky above. (NGC)

Visitor status. Legal status of a tourist or visitor admitted to Canada for a period of not more than three months, as defined by the Immigration Act of 1962. No tourist or visitor may request LANDED IMMIGRANT STATUS.

Vista-dome car. A double-deck railway passenger car with glass sides and ceiling for observation purposes. An early model—the McBride Observation Car, named after the Winnipeg inventor, T.J. McBride—was in use on the Rocky Mountain run as early as 1896; the CPR built four in 1904. The vista-dome car, however, had to await the advent of air conditioning on trains to become truly popular. See also The CANADIAN.

'Vive la Canadienne'. Title and first words of a popular French-Canadian folksong. 'Here's to "La Canadienne" ' is a toast to the beauty of the ideal woman who has 'sweet eyes so gay, gay, gay'.

Vive le Québec libre! Separatist slogan given wide currency by Charles de Gaulle when the French President included it in his address to a crowd of 10,000 from the balcony of Montreal's city hall—the HÔTEL DE VILLE—on 24 July 1967.

Vizinczey, Stephen (b.1933). Author. Born in Budapest, a student of George Lukacs, he left Hungary in 1956 and spent a year in Italy before immigrating to Canada in 1957. He edited EXCHANGE (1961-2) in Montreal and worked as a program producer for CBC Radio in Toronto. He achieved a measure of notoriety with *In Praise of Older Women* (1965), a widely translated episodic novel about a young man's progress towards sexual and social maturity. Since 1965 he has lived in England, where he is a reviewer for the *London Telegraph*. His second book, *The Rules of Chaos* (1969), is a collection of elegantly written philosophical reflections.

Vladivostok 'mission'. Allied intervention in Russia during the First World War that included a Canadian contingent of nearly 5,000 men. Dispatched in Oct. 1918 to aid the cause of the White against the Red Russians, the Canadian contingent, which included a cavalry squadron of the Royal North West Mounted Police, was recalled between Apr. and June 1919. See also MURMANSK 'MISSION'.

Vogt, Augustus Stephen (1861-1926). Organist and conductor. He was born in Washington, C.W. (Ont.), and studied music in Boston and Leipzig. The founder of the TORONTO MENDELSSOHN CHOIR, he was its conductor from 1894 to 1907. He taught at the Toronto Conservatory from 1913 and was dean of the Faculty of Music of the University of Toronto from 1919 until his death.

Voice of Canada, The. The early nickname of RADIO CANADA INTERNATIONAL.

Voice of Women, The. A national organization to 'unite women in concern for the future of the world' and to 'crusade against the possibility of nuclear war'. Founded in Toronto on 28 July 1960 by Kay Macpherson, Thérèse F. Casgrain, and other committed women, the non-partisan group spoke out on such social and international issues as the proliferation of atomic arms, Canada's joining the 'nuclear club', abortion reform, the admission of Communist China to the United Nations, and fighting in Vietnam. The VOW was responsible for the UN's designating 1963 International Cooperation Year (ICY).

Volkoff, Boris (1902-74). Dancer, choreographer, director, founder, teacher. Born in Tula, Russia, he had a successful career as a character dancer with major ballet companies in the U.S.S.R. and the United States. He arrived in Toronto in 1929, directed ballet at the Uptown Theatre, and in 1936 founded the Boris Volkoff School of the Dance, which was a centre of ballet instruction in Toronto before the founding of the NATIONAL BALLET SCHOOL. His Volkoff Dancers represented Canada at the XII Olympiad in Berlin in 1936. In 1939 he founded and began to direct the Volkoff Canadian Ballet. Awarded the Service Medal of the Order of Canada in 1972, he was known as 'the Father of Canadian Ballet'.

Voltaire. See QUELQUES ARPENTS DE NEIGE.

Voltigeur. French word for a light-infantry soldier. Various militia detachments in English and French Canada during the nineteenth century were called *Voltigeurs*.

Volvox. An anthology having as its subtitle *Poetry from the Unofficial Languages of Canada in English Translation.* It was edited by J. Michael YATES and published in 1971. Taking its name from a 'small freshwater organism', it is the first comprehensive collection of poems by Canadians who write in languages other than French and English.

Von Schoultz, Nils Szolteocky. See Battle of the WINDMILL.

VOR. Abbreviation of Visual Omni Range, an aviation device that permits pilots to select desired courses at will rather than follow a given course. VOR, introduced between Montreal and Windsor in 1955, is now used on all transcontinental routes. Supplementary radio-guidance systems include GCA (Ground Controlled Approach), ILS (Instrument Landing System), LF (Low Frequency), LORAN (Long Range Aids to Navigation), NDB (Non-Directional Beacon), PAR (Precision Approach Radar), SSR (Secondary Surveillance Radar), and VHF (Very High Frequency).

Voyageurs. Canoemen. They worked in the western fur trade of New France and, after the Conquest, until 1821 paddled the large canoes of the Montreal fur companies, leaving LACHINE for the western trading posts in the spring and returning in the autumn. They were formerly called COUREURS DE BOIS.

Vraie nature de Bernadette, La. Feature film produced by Pierre Lamy and directed, scripted, and edited by Gilles CARLE. Released in 1972, it starred Micheline Lanctot and Donald Pilon. Bernadette leaves her husband and his affluent life style for life in the country, where her generosity, including love, is misunderstood and commercialized. At the end she exchanges love for violence as a means of changing the world. 96 min., colour.

V/STOL. Abbreviation of Vertical Short Take-Off and Landing—a STOL aircraft with a helicopter-like lift.

VTOL. Initials of VERTICAL TAKE-OFF AND LANDING.

W

W5. The CTV Network's long-running television news and public-affairs show. Launched on 11 Sept. 1966, it is seen for 60 minutes each Sunday and combines 'visual information and fact'. Hosts have included Peter Reilly, Allan Anderson, Charles TEMPLETON, Ken Cavanaugh, Michael MACLEAR, and Carole Taylor. The title refers to the journalist's five 'w's': who, what, when, where, and why.

WAAC. Acronym of the former Women's Auxiliary Army Corps and the name of a member.

Wabush Mines. A company founded to develop and mine the iron-ore deposits in the Wabush Lake area of Labrador. It was established by a consortium of Canadian, American, and Italian steel companies; production started in 1965 after a capital expenditure of more than $270 million. The iron properties were initially explored by Canadian Javelin Ltd, which had obtained extensive mineral concessions from the Newfoundland government. The Canadian partners are STELCO

and DOFASCO. The principal production property is named the Scully Mine in honour of Vincent Scully, the former president of Stelco.

Wacousta; or, The Prophecy. A historical romance by John RICHARDSON subtitled *A Tale of the Canadas* and published in 1832. Popular in Europe during the mid-nineteenth century, it has as its background the PONTIAC wars of 1763 and tells the story of Wacousta—a white man who lives as an Indian—and his revenge on the governor of Fort Detroit. A sequel, *The Canadian Brothers; or, The Prophecy Fulfilled*, was published in 1840.

Waddington, Miriam (b.1917). Poet. Born in Winnipeg and educated at the University of Toronto and the Pennsylvania School of Social Work, she was a social worker in Montreal during the 1940s and contributed poems to FIRST STATEMENT and PREVIEW. Since 1964 she has been a member of the English department at York University, Toronto. Waddington has been called the finest lyric poet in the country, writing poems about the

Waddington

Canadian landscape, love and loss, and foreign travels that can be both romantic and tough-minded and on occasion somewhat surreal. Her collections are *Green World* (1945), *The Second Silence* (1955), *The Season's Lovers* (1958), *The Glass Trumpet* (1966), *Call Them Canadians* (1968), *Say Yes* (1969), *Dream Telescope* (1972), *Driving Home: Poems New and Selected* (1972), and *The Price of Gold* (1976). An interesting literary critic, she has written a study of A.M. KLEIN (1970), edited his *Collected Poems* (1975), and edited *John* SUTHERLAND: *Essays, Controversies, Poems* (1973).

Waffle, The. A group of ultra-nationalist members of the NEW DEMOCRATIC PARTY formed in the spring of 1969. The name was apparently coined by one of its members, Ed BROADBENT, in the group's 'Manifesto for an Independent Socialist Canada' in which it was stated that if the group waffled on any issue it would 'waffle to the left'. The group was dissolved in the summer of 1972, after having been rejected by the NDP. James Laxer and Mel Watkins, two founders, went on to found their Movement for an Independent Socialist Canada (MISC).

Waghorne, Fred C. (1866-1956). Early sports official. Born in Tunbridge, Eng., he came in his youth to Toronto where he excelled as a hockey and lacrosse referee. He initiated many new hockey rules and, in 1911, founded the Toronto Hockey League, which became the largest of its kind in the world.

Wagner, Barbara (b.1938). Champion figure-skater. Born in Toronto, she joined forces in 1954 with Robert PAUL, with whom she won that year the Canadian pairs junior figure-skating championship. In 1957 they captured the Canadian, North American, and World titles in the space of 16 days. They retained all three honours for three years. At the 1960 Winter Olympics at Squaw Valley, Calif., they won the gold medal and then retired from amateur competition to perform in touring ice-shows.

Waiting for Caroline. Feature film directed by Ron KELLY and produced by the NFB in a co-production arrangement with the CBC. The script was by George ROBERTSON. It starred Alexandra Stewart as a girl torn between two cultures: the English-speaking community of Vancouver where she grew up and the French-speaking milieu of Quebec City where the film opens. 84 min., 8 sec.; colour.

Wakanda. Siouan word for 'spirit'. It is said to mean the same as the Iroquoian word ORENDA and the Algonkian word MANITOU.

Wakashan. Linguistic family of Indians, living on Vancouver Island and the British Columbia mainland, to which the NOOTKA and KWAKIUTL belong. The Wakashan population in 1970 was 8,217.

Walcheren. See Battle of the SCHELDT.

Wald, Susana. See Ludwig ZELLER.

Walker, David (b.1911). Novelist. Born in Scotland and educated at Sandhurst, Eng., he came to Canada in 1938 as an aide-de-camp to Lord TWEEDSMUIR and now lives in St Andrews, N.B. His most popular novels are *Geordie* (1950), about a stubborn Highlander, and *Come Back Geordie* (1966), both of which were made into successful films. *Where the High Winds Blow* (1960) and *Mallabec* (1965) are set in the Canadian North and New Brunswick respectively. His latest novel is a somewhat autobiographical work called *Ash* (1976).

Walker, Sir Edmund (1848-1924). Financier and founder of cultural institutions. Byron Edmund Walker was born in Seneca township, C.W. (Ont.), He had a distinguished career in banking that culminated in the presidency of the Canadian Bank of Commerce from 1907 to 1924. An art connoisseur and collector, he was instrumental in establishing the NATIONAL GALLERY OF CANADA, of which he was the first Chairman of the Board of Trustees; the ROYAL ONTARIO MUSEUM; and helped found the Art Museum of Toronto (later the ART GALLERY OF ONTARIO). He also founded the CHAMPLAIN SOCIETY; served as honorary president of the TORONTO MENDELSSOHN CHOIR; and chaired the Board of Governors of the UNIVERSITY OF TORONTO from 1919 to 1923, when he was elected its chancellor. He was knighted in 1910.

Walker, Hiram. See HIRAM WALKER-GOODERHAM AND WORTS LTD.

Walker, Horatio (1850-1938). Painter. Born in Listowell, C.W. (Ont.), he took up residence in New York in 1878, though he built a home for himself on the Île d'Orléans, where he retired, and it was the life and scenery there that inspired such paintings as *Oxen Drinking* (1899, NGC). His large, richly coloured pastoral scenes sold well in New York—he was the highest-paid Canadian painter in the first decade of the century.

Walking Woman. The stylized profile of a woman walking used in an extensive and important series of works by the artist Michael SNOW between 1961 and 1967. The image was given a wide variety of treatments—many of them involving film-like repetition—that culminated in its appearance in 11 monumental stainless-steel cutouts scattered in the Ontario Pavilion of Expo 67. Snow's first important film, *New York Eye and Ear Control* (1964), combines cutouts of the Walking Woman with live action scenes filmed in New York, and a soundtrack of memorable New York jazz. 35 min., b & w.

Wallace, J.S. (Joe) (1890-1975). Communist versifier. Born in Toronto and raised in Nova Scotia, he attended St Francis Xavier University and opened a Halifax advertising agency before devoting himself to the Communist cause. This included working for the CANADIAN LABOUR DEFENCE LEAGUE, writing for the *Daily Clarion*, and composing verse, which appeared in volumes issued in Moscow in editions of 10,000 copies each in English, Russian, and Chinese. With Wilson MacDONALD he toured Russia and China in 1956-7. He died in Vancouver. Among Wallace's publications are *Night is Ended* (1943); *All My Brothers* (1953); *Hi, Sister, Hi, Brother!* (1956); *The Golden Legend* (1957); and *A Radiant Sphere* (1964), selected poems.

Wallace, W. Stewart (1884-1970). Historian. Born in Georgetown, Ont., and educated at the University of Toronto and at Oxford, he taught history at a number of Canadian universities and was Librarian of the University of Toronto from 1923 to 1954. Editor of the CANADIAN HISTORICAL REVIEW (1920-39) and secretary of the CHAMPLAIN SOCIETY (1943-8), he was general editor and principal author of the ENCYCLOPEDIA OF CANADA (1935-6; rev. 1948), which provided the basis of many entries in the ENCYCLOPEDIA CANADIANA (1958). He also edited *The Dictionary of Canadian Biography* (1926; rev. 1948), which was enlarged and renamed *The Macmillan Dictionary of Canadian Biography* (1963) to distinguish it from the DICTIONARY OF CANADIAN BIOGRAPHY project. Among his many other scholarly works are two volumes and one translation for the CHRONICLES OF CANADA series. Wallace was a meticulous scholar and the inspiration for Norah Story, who wrote *The* OXFORD COMPANION TO CANADIAN HISTORY AND LITERATURE (1967).

Wallis, Sir Provo (1791-1892). Naval officer. Provo William Parry Wallis was born in Halifax, N.S., and joined a Royal Navy frigate in 1804. During the WAR OF 1812 he was second lieutenant of the HMS *Shannon* when it captured the U.S. frigate *Chesapeake* off Boston on 1 June 1813. As the captain was wounded and the first lieutenant killed, Wallis took command of the two ships and brought them to Halifax. He had a long and illustrious career, attaining in 1877 the Royal Navy's highest rank, Admiral of the Fleet, which he retained until his death at the age of 101.

Walsh, Maj. James Morrow. See FORT WALSH.

Walter, Arnold (1902-73). Music educator and composer. Born in Hannsdorf, Moravia, he studied music in Berlin after receiving a doctorate in law from Prague University. He came to Canada in 1937 and directed the Royal Conservatory Senior School, Toronto, from 1945 to 1952, founding the Conservatory's Opera School in 1946. He directed the Faculty of Music, University of Toronto, from 1952 to 1968; was president of the Canadian Music Council and the International Society for Music Education; and founded the Canadian Association of University Schools of Music in 1965. As a composer he wrote traditional romantic works as well as atonal and electronic pieces.

Walters, Capt. Angus (b.1881). Lunenberg-born skipper of the famous schooner BLUENOSE.

Walton, Dorothy Mackenzie (b.1909). Badminton player. Born in Swift Current, Sask., she won local and provincial honours in a variety of sports. After her marriage she lived in Toronto and concentrated on tennis and badminton. In the latter she soon was dominant in both Canada and the United States. Her continental supremacy was crowned in 1939 when whe won the prestigious all-England tournament to become recognized as the world's best women's badminton player. The following year she was named 'Canada's outstanding female athlete'.

Wampum. Algonkian word for a 'white string' or a string of white and purple shell beads. It was used by the Indians of the eastern woodlands as a form of currency. Worked into a belt with significant designs, the beads recorded decisions, treaties, etc.

Wandering Spirit. See Massacre of FROG LAKE.

Wanigan. Algonkian word for a 'trap' or 'box for odds and ends'. A lumberman's name for a storage chest, an accounts office, a supply boat, etc.; in the North, a mobile shed. It is also a short laced boot.

Wanzer Lamp. A once-popular oil lamp. The chimneyless cooking and illuminating lamp, which employed an artificial forced draft to keep the oil-burning flame alight, was

Wanzer Lamp

named after its inventor, R.M. Wanzler, an immigrant from Pennsylvania in 1860 who, the following year, began manufacturing Wanzer Lamps in Hamilton, C.W. (Ont.).

Wapiti. A large deer, the male of which has branching antlers, known also as the American Elk. The race of eastern wapiti found in southern Quebec and Ontario at the time of settlement is now extinct. The name is an Algonkian word for 'a light-coloured animal'.

Wapoose. Algonkian word for a rabbit, especially the white hare.

War for Men's Minds. A short film released by the NFB in 1943 in its WORLD IN ACTION series. Produced by Stuart Legg, with narration by Lorne GREENE, it studied the techniques of psychological warfare and contrasted the axis and allied uses of information and propaganda, making use of much 'found' footage. 21 min., b & w.

War Measures Act. An Act to give the government emergency powers in the event of 'war, invasion, or insurrection, real or apprehended'. It rests on a section of the BNA ACT that states that the federal government has the power to make laws for 'peace, order, and good government' and it gives the federal cabinet authority to override provincial authority and civil liberties for the duration of the emergency. It was invoked in the two World Wars. The only time it has been invoked in peacetime was during the OCTOBER CRISIS of 1970, when its use provoked considerable controversy. The government justified its course by saying that a state of apprehended insurrection existed, but in Dec. 1970 it replaced the Act with a temporary emergency measures Act that was allowed to lapse on 30 Apr. 1971.

War of 1812. A war between Great Britain and the United States, fought mainly in Upper Canada (Ontario). The United States—objecting to Britain's searching American ships for arms and British subjects during the Napoleonic Wars—declared war on 19 June 1812. A series of campaigns, invasions, and raids by land and sea followed, with both sides claiming victories. Hostilities ceased with the signing, on 24 Dec. 1814, of the TREATY OF GHENT. The following engagements are of special interest or importance: BEAVER DAM, CHÂTEAUGUAY, CHIPPEWA, CRYSLER'S FARM, DETROIT, FORT ERIE, FORT GEORGE, FORT NIAGARA, LAKE ERIE, LUNDY'S LANE, MICHILIMACKINAC, OGDENSBURG, OSWEGO, PLATTSBURG, QUEENSTON HEIGHTS, SACKETT'S HARBOUR, STONEY CREEK, THAMES, YORK.

War resisters. Synonym for 'draft-dodgers' and 'draft-evaders'. War resisters are conscientious objectors who emigrated from the United States rather than be drafted by the U.S. armed forces to fight in Vietnam. It has been estimated by AMEX CANADA that between 20,000 and 25,000 Americans of draft age applied for LANDED IMMIGRANT STATUS in Canada from the escalation of the war in Vietnam in 1965 to the limited amnesties of 1975. The terms 'draft-dodger' and 'war resister' came into current use in 1966.

Warden, John. Fashion designer. Born near Niagara Falls, Ont., and educated at the Parsons School of Design in New York City, he settled in Montreal in the mid-1960s and took an active part in its developing fashion world. He has designed uniforms for CP Air and the Canadian Olympic team, and designs commercially for both men and women. In 1974 he co-founded the FASHION DESIGNERS ASSOCIATION OF CANADA, INC.

Warden of the Plains. The title given the officer at the RED RIVER SETTLEMENT charged with keeping law and order on the Prairies. The first Warden was Cuthbert GRANT, who was appointed in 1828 by the HUDSON'S BAY COMPANY.

Warrendale. Documentary film produced by Patrick WATSON and directed by Allan KING in 1966. It featured the staff of Warrendale, a Toronto-area treatment centre for disturbed children—John Brown, director from 1953 to 1966; Terry Adler, Robyn Rice, Ena Brocklehurst, and Martin Fisher—and the children themselves. Having commissioned the film, CBC-TV refused to telecast it for reasons of language. In its commercial release it quickly became a classic of its kind for its moving depiction of unrehearsed situations captured in cinéma-vérité style. 100 min., b & w. See also BROWNDALE.

Wars, World. See FIRST WORLD WAR and SECOND WORLD WAR.

Wartime Elections Act. Contentious Act passed by the Unionist Government of Sir Robert BORDEN during the First World War. Passed in 1917, it disenfranchised conscientious objectors and aliens who had become naturalized Canadians after 1902, and gave the vote to women who were over 21 years of age and British subjects with a close relative serving in the armed forces of Canada or Britain. The bill was designed to achieve support for the Union Government in the next election.

Wartime Prices and Trade Board. A board to control the economy of Canada during the Second World War. Established on 3 Sept. 1939, it had power to control the price, supply, and distribution of all goods and services. In 1941 it instituted a freeze on prices and wages and in 1942 the rationing of some essential goods. Decontrol began after the war in 1946, and was complete by 1950.

Wascana Centre. A park of some 2,000 acres located in the heart of REGINA, Sask. It includes not only the Legislative Building but also the city campus of the University of Saskatchewan, a centre for the performing arts, a museum of natural history, an art gallery, and recreational facilities. Part of the park is Wascana Lake, an artificial body formed by the damming of Wascana Creek. The word 'Wascana' is derived from the Cree *Oskana*, which means PILE O' BONES, the original name of Regina.

Washington of the North. Sobriquet applied to Ottawa, attributed to Wilfrid LAURIER in 1893.

Watch That Ends the Night, The. Novel by Hugh MacLENNAN published in 1959. Set in Montreal, it is the story of Jerome Martell, a brilliant surgeon and idealist (who bears resemblances to Norman BETHUNE); his ailing wife Catherine; and George Stewart, his closest friend, who marries Catherine when Martell is reported dead. It is a study of moral courage in the face of psychological disaster, climaxed by Martell's return home.

Watchee. In the North, a traditional greeting. It is said to be the Cree version of the English words 'What cheer?'

Water sky. A dark and cloudy Arctic sky over open (unfrozen) water.

Water-tight compartments. A picturesque phrase used in 1937 by Lord Atkin of the JUDICIAL COMMITTEE OF THE PRIVY COUNCIL. When giving judgement in a dispute between Ontario and Canada over the interpretation of Canada's constitution, he concluded that any federal legislation that affects the provinces must represent the 'co-operation between the Dominion and the Provinces. While the ship of state now sails on larger ventures and into foreign waters she still retains the water-tight compartments which are an essential part of her original structure.'

Waterton Lakes National Park. Established in 1895 in southwestern Alberta, it covers 203 sq. mi. and is distinctive in that it includes both Rocky Mountains and prairie grasslands. The first warden, George 'Kootenai' Brown, is buried in the park. In 1932 Waterton Lakes National Park was linked with Glacier National Park in Montana and the whole is known as Waterton-Glacier International Peace Park. Charles Waterton was an English naturalist.

Watkins, Kathleen Blake. See KIT OF THE MAIL.

Watkins Fellowships. The designation of three CANADA COUNCIL fellowships. Since 1973 two successful candidates in the Leave Fellowships competition, and one in the Doctoral Fellowships competition, have been chosen annually for Watkins Fellowships. In accordance with the terms of the bequest of the late John B.C. Watkins—former ambassador to Norway, Iceland, and Denmark—the candidates must conduct their programs in Norway, Iceland, Denmark, or Sweden.

Watkins Report. The popular name of the controversial report of a government task force, chaired by Melville Watkins, on the state of foreign ownership in Canadian business and industry. Entitled *Foreign Ownership and the Structure of Canadian Industry* and released in Feb. 1968, it aroused public alarm at the extent of foreign ownership in Canada (mostly American) and sparked the rise of a small but vociferous group of nationalists whose aim was the reduction of that ownership and the 'repatriation' of the economy.

Watson, Homer (1855-1936). Painter. Born at Doon, Ont., he lived most of his life there. An early landscape painting, *The Pioneer Mill* (1880), was purchased for Queen Victoria by her daughter Princess Louise and is in the Windsor Castle collection. Acclaimed as the 'Canadian Constable' by Oscar Wilde on a visit to Toronto in 1882, Watson had at that time never seen a Constable painting. His landscapes became popular in England and he had a successful one-man show in London in 1899. The next year he painted *The* FLOOD GATE (1900, NGC). Another of his outstanding landscapes is *Before the Storm* (1887, private coll.). His Doon home is a museum.

Watson, Kenneth (b.1906). Curler and authority on curling. The Manitoba high-school teacher not only skipped his rink to victory in six consecutive Manitoba Bonspiel championships, he also took three MACDONALD BRIER titles representing Canadian supremacy. His book, *Ken Watson on Curling* (1950), has sold 150,000 copies. He retired from major competition in 1971.

Watson, Patrick (b.1929). TV personality and writer. The Toronto-born broadcaster came to national prominence as producer and host of CBC-TV's hour-long Sunday evening public-affairs show THIS HOUR HAS SEVEN DAYS (1964-6). More recently he produced and hosted the imaginative series WITNESS TO YESTERDAY (1974). He is the author of three books. His views on the mass media are found in *Conspirators in Silence* (1969). *Fasanella's City* (1973) is his study of an American primitive painter. His *Zero to Air Time*, a political thriller, appeared in 1974.

Watson, Sheila. The author of *The* DOUBLE HOOK.

Watson, Whipper Billy (b.1918). Wrestler. He was born in Toronto as William Potts and, wrestling in Europe in 1936, was called 'The Whip'. He devised the 'Canadian avalanche' (in which he performs cartwheels before the opponent) and the 'Canuck Commando Unconscious' (a hold on the opponent's carotid artery). He was twice world heavyweight champion (1946, 1956) and has been honoured for his work for crippled and underprivileged children.

Watson-Watt, Sir Robert. See RADAR.

Wavelength. An experimental film made by the artist Michael SNOW. It is a continuous zoom across an 80-ft New York artist's loft, accompanied by an electronically produced soundtrack that begins low and works up to an intensity of 12,000 cycles per second. A classic of the sixties' 'underground' cinema, it has been described as 'probably the most rigorously composed movie in existence'. 1966-7, 45 min., colour.

Wawa. In CHINOOK JARGON, the word for 'talk', 'speech', 'language', 'words'. In Algonkian, *wawa* or *wavey* is the word for 'snow goose'.

Wayman, Tom (b.1945). Poet. Born in Hawkesbury, Ont., he grew up in Prince Rupert, B.C., and studied at the University of British Columbia. One of the few poets to be a member of the INDUSTRIAL WORKERS OF THE WORLD, he burst on the scene in the early seventies, effectively reciting his comic and satirical poems at readings. These have been collected in *Waiting for Wayman* (1973), *For and Against the Moon* (1974), and *Money and Rain: Tom Wayman Live!* (with cassette, 1975).

Wayne and Shuster. Television comedians. Johnny Wayne (b.1918) and Frank Shuster (b.1916) are Toronto-born graduates of Harbord Collegiate and the University of Toronto. They joined the CBC in 1939, and during the war they wrote and performed in various army shows. They launched 'The Wayne and Shuster Show' on CBC Radio in 1948 and on CBC-TV in 1954. They specialize in skits that offer parody, lampoons, and gentle satire. The first of their many appearances on 'The Ed Sullivan Show' took place in New York on 4 May 1958, when they presented their memorable skit on the assassination of Julius Caesar. Aside from 'Holiday Lodge'—a situation comedy series launched by CBS and CBC-TV on 10 June 1961 and carried for a single season—their successes have been consistent. Wayne is the short one.

Ways and Means, Committee of. Members of the House of Commons acting as a body to devise ways and means of raising revenue through taxes, duties, etc. Abolished in 1968, its business is now conducted through a standing committee.

W/C. Official abbreviation of Wing Commander.

WCTU. Abbreviation of the WOMEN'S CHRISTIAN TEMPERANCE UNION.

WEA. See WORKERS' EDUCATIONAL ASSOCIATION OF CANADA.

Weaver, Robert (b.1921). Editor and broadcaster. Born in Niagara Falls, Ont., he was educated at the University of Toronto and joined CBC Radio as a program organizer for Public Affairs. He originated CRITICALLY SPEAKING and STORIES WITH JOHN DRAINIE and assumed responsibility for CBC TUESDAY NIGHT and ANTHOLOGY. He was the prime mover behind the founding of the TAMARACK REVIEW in 1956. He is also a well-known anthologist, editing two series of *Canadian Short Stories* (1960, 1968); *Ten for Wednesday Night* (1961); *The First Five Years* (1962), selections from *The Tamarack Review;* and (with William Toye) *The Oxford Anthology of Canadian Literature* (1973). Head of CBC Radio Arts since 1971, he has been called 'a one-man Canada Council'.

Webb, Phyllis (b.1927). Poet. Born in Victoria, B.C., and educated at the University of British Columbia and at McGill, she has taught at UBC and produced CBC IDEAS in Toronto from 1964 to 1969, when she returned to the west coast. Writing 'lonely poems' darkly coloured by a despairing view of self and existence, she has moved from an emotional, somewhat metaphysical expression of this vision to a more objective, spare, abstract poetry, as in her memorable sequence of haiku-like lyrics, *Naked Poems* (1965). Her other collections are *Even Your*

Right Eye (1956), *The Sea Is Also a Garden* (1962), and *Selected Poems* (1971), which contains all of *Naked Poems*.

Webster, Jack (b.1918). Journalist and broadcaster. Born in Glasgow, he worked on Fleet St before joining the *Vancouver Sun* as an investigative reporter in 1947. His career as a radio broadcaster began in 1953. Known for his hearty Scots burr, withering wit, and abrupt manner, he became the country's leading hot-liner in the 1960s with a five-day-a-week three-hour show carried in Vancouver, Kamloops, Kelowna, and Prince George, B.C.

Webster, John C. See JOHN C. WEBSTER MEMORIAL TROPHY.

Webster-Ashburton Treaty. Concluded in Aug. 1842 by a joint commission headed by Daniel Webster for the United States and Lord Ashburton for Great Britain, it ended the so-called AROOSTOOK (or Lumbermen's) WAR, waged by lumbermen from Maine and New Brunswick over disputed forest tracts. The boundary between Maine and New Brunswick was by this treaty clearly and permanently fixed.

Wedding in White. Feature film written and directed by William FRUET. Released in 1972, it was photographed by Richard LEITERMAN and starred Doris Petrie, Carol Kane, and Donald Pleasance. It is set on the Prairies during the Second World War and tells what happens to a young girl who is raped by a family friend and is then married off to a bachelor in his fifties to save the father from dishonour. 103 min., b & w.

Wednesday Night. See CBC TUESDAY NIGHT.

Weed/Flower Press. Small poetry-publishing operation founded by Nelson Ball in 1965. The Toronto-based house issued booklets, many designed by Barbara Caruso, until 1974.

Week, The. 'A Canadian journal of politics, society, and literature'. Founded in Toronto by Goldwin SMITH and initially edited by Charles G.D. ROBERTS, it appeared between 6 Dec. 1883 and 20 Nov. 1896. It published the stories, poems, and essays of the leading authors of the day for the purpose of 'stimulating our national sentiment'.

Weekend Magazine. The weekly supplement to the Saturday editions of 21 newspapers, with a total circulation of two million copies. Founded in Montreal in 1951, it publishes illustrated articles of topical interest. Recent editors include Frank Lowe and Sheena Pat-

terson. In 1959 *Weekend Magazine* began to publish *Perspectives,* a weekly supplement for French-language newspapers which, in 1976, enjoyed a circulation of 75,000.

'Weeping Princess'. The popular name of a flawed one-cent stamp issued in 1935. A small flaw in the engraving plate that resembles a teardrop appears under the eye of the young Princess Elizabeth, giving the illusion that the future queen is weeping. See also Rare STAMPS.

Weintraub, William. See WHY ROCK THE BOAT?

Weinzweig, John (b.1913). Composer. Born in Toronto, he studied at the University of Toronto, where he founded its symphony orchestra, and later at the Eastman School of Music in Rochester, N.Y. An extremely influential teacher, he was appointed to the Faculty of Music, University of Toronto, in 1952. He was the teacher of Harry SOMERS, Samuel Dolin, Murray ADASKIN, Harry FREEDMAN, Philip NIMMONS, Murray SCHAFER, John BECKWITH, Norma BEECROFT, and Srul Irving GLICK. He was Canada's first composer to advocate the 12-tone technique, influencing the course of contemporary Canadian music. His many works for orchestra, choir, instrumental ensemble, and piano include numerous commissions for Canadian cultural organizations. In 1949 he wrote the music for the ballet *Red Ear of Corn* and a suite for orchestra based on it.

Weir, R. Stanley. See 'O CANADA'.

'We'll Rant and We'll Roar'. A popular Newfoundland fisherman's song. The words were written around 1880 by W.H. LeMessurier. Two of the verses go: 'Farewell and adieu to ye fair ones of Valen, / Farewell and adieu to ye girls in the Cove; / I'm bound to the westward, to the wall with the hole in, / I'll take her from Toslow the wild world to rove.' 'We'll rant and we'll roar like true Newfoundlanders, / We'll rant and we'll roar on deck and below, / Until we see bottom inside the two sunkers, / When straight through the Channel to Toslow we'll go!'

Welland Canal. Artificial watercourse across the Niagara Peninsula. Lake Ontario and Lake Erie are connected for navigational purposes by the Welland Ship Canal which, through a system of eight locks and 28 mi. of canal, allows for the 326-ft difference in height between Lake Erie and Lake Ontario caused by Niagara Escarpment. The canal connects Port Colborne and Port Weller, Ont., and runs parallel with the Niagara R., bypassing NIAGARA FALLS; it includes the largest inland lock in the world, near Port Colborne.

The present canal, which permits the accommodation of ocean-going vessels, is actually the fourth such canal in the Niagara Peninsula. The first was built by the industrialist William Hamilton Merritt as the Upper Canadian response to American initiative in constructing the Erie Canal following the War of 1812. Merritt's canal was commenced in 1824 and completed in 1829; dates of the two subsequent canal systems are 1842-5 and 1875-87. Construction on the Welland Ship Canal was begun in 1913; it opened in 1933. Since that time the canal has been deepened to ST LAWRENCE SEAWAY standards, from 25 to 27 ft. A bypass of 8.3 mi. was opened in 1973 to take the canal around rather than through the city of Welland.

Wells Gallery. Commercial art gallery in Ottawa. Founded in 1965 by Barbara Ensor, it has actively promoted the work of Canadian artists through one-man shows of painting, sculpture, and graphics. Canadian crafts have recently been included in its exhibition policy.

Wendigo. 'Evil spirit' or 'cannibal' of the ALGONKIAN Indians. The Wendigo has been described as the phantom of hunger that stalks the forests in search of lone Indians to consume. It takes the form of a cannibalistic Indian breathing flame or a supernatural creature with a heart of ice that flies through the night in search of victims to satisfy its craving for human flesh. Algernon Blackwood, the British horror-story writer who lived in Toronto at the turn of the century, published his celebrated story called 'The Wendigo' in *Selected Tales* (1943), in which victims of the Wendigo escaped with their lives but were rendered completely lacking in individuality.

Wendo. A system of self-defence for women. It was devised in the early 1960s by Dr Ned Paige, a Toronto optometrist who is a brown belt in ju-jitsu and a black belt in karate, as a physical way for a woman to overcome any feelings of passivity she might experience when faced with a male assailant. The word *Wendo* is composed of two Chinese roots—*wen* meaning 'circular' and *do* meaning 'way'. The system is now taught throughout North America. A development of Wendo is Yuen-Do, properly known as Yuen-Do Contemplation-Meditation (YCM), 'an active mental self-defence system' devised in 1975 by Dr Paige.

Weslock, Nick (b.1918). Well-known amateur golfer. Born in Poland, he won several titles in Ontario and Canadian championships and was repeatedly the top amateur in Canadian open tournaments. He represented Ontario and Canada in important team contests and continues to win senior honours.

West, Benjamin. See *The* DEATH OF WOLFE.

West, The. Western Canada, the part of Canada west of the Great Lakes. The West, or the Western Provinces, includes the Prairie Provinces and British Columbia.

West Block. See PARLIAMENT BUILDINGS.

West coast. The Pacific or western coast of Canada, especially southwestern British Columbia. The term embraces Vancouver Island and the Queen Charlotte Islands. British Columbia is composed of the west coast and the INTERIOR.

West Coast Review. A literary quarterly published at SIMON FRASER UNIVERSITY, Burnaby, B.C. Founded in 1966, it publishes stories, poems, plays, essays, drawings, photographs, and reviews. A special feature is a continuing bibliography of avant-garde literature.

West Indian fish. A slang term used in Newfoundland for the poorest grade of cod. It was once sent to the islands of the Caribbean.

West Wind, The. Famous painting by Tom THOMSON. It is based on a sketch made at Lake Cauchon, Algonquin Park, Ont., in 1916. The branches of a lone pine tree bent by the wind curve tortuously against a background of white-capped water and storm-laden clouds, which move from right to left across the canvas. It is perhaps the best-known image in Canadian painting. (1917, AGO). See also *The* JACK PINE.

Westerly point, The most. The meridian of longitude 141° W, which forms the boundary between the Yukon Territory and the state of Alaska. The most westerly settlement is Mirror Creek, Y.T., at 140° 57' W by 62° 31' N.

Western Brook Pond. A spectacular prehistoric landscape on the west coast of Newfoundland. At the base of the Long Range Mountains, it displays spruce trees partly buried by sand-dunes, a twisting fjord, and rocky plateaux above 2,000-ft cliffs.

Western Canada. Geographic division. It consists of the four Western Provinces: Manitoba, Saskatchewan, Alberta, and British Columbia.

Western or **Canadian Cordillera.** One of five principal GEOGRAPHICAL REGIONS of Canada, it includes the westernmost part of Alberta, all of British Columbia, and most of the Yukon Territory. Characterized by a rugged landscape and breathtaking scenery, the region can be divided into an eastern mountain area that includes the COLUMBIA and ROCKY MOUNTAINS; interior plateaux, of which the Fraser and Nechako are the most important; and the COAST MOUNTAINS in the west. The natural resources of this region—forests, mines, fish, farmland, and water-power—are of great importance. The majority of the population is concentrated in a few cities in the southwest, of which Vancouver and Victoria are by far the most important.

Western Provinces. The three Prairie Provinces (Alberta, Manitoba, Saskatchewan) and British Columbia.

Western Sea. Fabulous body of water and route to the Orient sought after by LA VÉRENDRYE and other French explorers. Indians at Lake Nipigon in 1727 assured him its shores were beyond the Lake of the Woods (Ont.).

Western Townships. A term once used for those townships in southeastern Upper Canada (Ontario) settled by Loyalists in the late eighteenth century. See also EASTERN TOWNSHIPS.

Westgate, Murray (b.1918). Broadcaster. Born in Regina, Sask., he attended the Radio Actors Workshop conducted by CBR, Vancouver, in the spring of 1947, and joined CBC Radio later that year. He appeared as Jake in CBC-TV's revival of JAKE AND THE KID, beginning on 4 July 1961, but is best known as the gravel-voiced actor who promoted Esso products on HOCKEY NIGHT IN CANADA from 1952 to 1968.

Westinghouse Presents. See DON WRIGHT CHORUS.

Westmain, The. The western shore of Hudson Bay. Used in the FUR TRADE, the term dates from 1680. See also The EASTMAIN.

'Westminster in the Wilderness'. Facetious nineteenth-century epithet for the PARLIAMENT BUILDINGS in Ottawa. The reference is to Westminster Palace in London, where the British Parliament met prior to the erection of the present Houses of Parliament.

Westmount. A residential district in Montreal with a population of about 40,000. It has long been considered the symbol of well-to-do Anglo-Saxon conservatism, but in fact, while the majority of the population is English-speaking, people of all income levels live there. Westmount has been a pioneer in local government, with a professional manager. It has its 'own' mountain—a spur of MOUNT ROYAL.

Weston, W. Garfield (b.1898). Bread and biscuit manufacturer. Born in Toronto, he was educated at Harbord Collegiate Institute. In 1921 he entered his father's biscuit-manufacturing firm (incorporated in 1910), and inherited it three years later. It was incorporated under the name George Weston Ltd in 1928. In 1929 Garfield Weston expanded into the United States and in 1933 into Great Britain, where he moved his headquarters, establishing Allied Bakeries Ltd, with world-wide interests. From 1939 to 1945 he sat as a Conservative in the British House of Commons. The W. Garfield Weston Charitable Foundation in England owns 52% of George Weston Ltd which, managed by Garfield's son Galen Weston, controls Weston Bakeries Ltd, McCormick's Ltd, McLarens Foods Ltd, E.B. EDDY CO., LOBLAW COMPANIES LTD, G. Tamblyn Ltd, B.C. Packers Ltd, etc.

WHA. See WORLD HOCKEY ASSOCIATION.

Whalebone. A horny and porous substance, yellowish-white in colour, that grows in place of teeth in certain whales. Although the supply of whalebone is necessarily limited, it is becoming increasingly popular among Eskimo craftsmen, who use it for sculptures.

Whalley, Peter (b.1921). Artist and illustrator. Born is Brockville, Ont., and educated at the Nova Scotia College of Art, he has lived and worked since 1948 as a free-lance cartoonist in Morin Heights, Que. He is best known as the illustrator of *An Uninhibited History of Canada* (1959) and other books of humour by Eric NICOL.

Wheat. The world's foremost grain and food crop, cultivated in Egypt as early as 5000 B.C. Thousands of varieties exist. In Canada the Prairie Provinces account for 95% of the national harvest. Mainly bread wheat is grown, although small areas produce Winter Wheat and Durum, which are used for pastry flour. About 90% of Canadian wheat is made up of the Hard Red Spring strains. In the 1840s Ontario farmer David Fife developed European seedlings into Red FIFE. Introduced into the West in 1884, it remained the lead crop until 1908, when it was supplanted by MARQUIS, a cross of Red Fife and Hard Red Calcutta (from India), grains bred by Charles SAUNDERS. Dozens of other strains followed—each replacing, at least partially, a previous strain in rapid succession—among them Thatcher (1935), Apex and Renown (1937), Regent (1939), Redman (1946), Selkirk (1953), and Pembina (1959). New wheats—the most widely planted, crosses of Thatcher or Selkirk—continue to be developed. The most sought-after traits are early maturation to escape frosts and resistance to rust disease. Depending upon the crop yield, which varies greatly, Canada produces 4% and 6.5% of the world harvest and accounts for 20% and 30% of world trade in wheat in a given year. See also MANITOBA NO.1 HARD.

Wheat Pools. Farmers' co-operatives. There are three co-operatives in western Canada: the Alberta Wheat Pool, formed in 1923; the Manitoba Pool Elevators, formed in 1925; and the Saskatchewan Wheat Pool, formed in 1924. They began as grain-handling co-operatives, and an important aspect of their activities was the acquisition of country and terminal GRAIN ELEVATORS and the marketing of grain, although the latter is now handled through the CANADIAN WHEAT BOARD. Today they have diversified and now provide services in marketing other farm products, although each pool still handles about 65% of the grain produced in the three Prairie Provinces through the elevators they control directly and those controlled by their local co-operative elevator associations.

Wheeler, Lucile (b.1935). Skier. Born into a ski-oriented family at St Jovite, Que., where her parents were lodge-owners who catered to winter sportsmen, she became the first Canadian skier to win an Olympic medal. This was at the 1956 Winter Olympics at Cortina, Italy. Two years later she became title-holder of the women's world championship in both the downhill and giant slalom.

Whelan, Edward (1824-67). A FATHER OF CONFEDERATION. Born in Ireland, he immigrated to Nova Scotia and was encouraged to move to Prince Edward Island by Joseph HOWE, under whom he learned printing. He became Queen's Printer in 1852. He was elected to the legislative assembly in 1846 and was appointed to the legislative council in 1858. He was a delegate to the QUEBEC CONFERENCE on Confederation, which he advocated but which the province rejected until 1873.

Where Nests the Water Hen. Title of the English translation of a novel by Gabrielle ROY, *La Petite Poule d'eau* (1950). Translated by Harry Binsse in 1951, it is a tender and poetic fictional account of life in the isolated rural areas of northern Manitoba, based on the au-

thor's memories of her own childhood, on her observations as a teacher, and on the experiences of her father, an official with the Department of Immigration.

Where to Eat in Canada. Food guide published annually since 1971. As opinionated as the *Guide Michelin*, it is researched and written by Anne Hardy and published by Oberon Press. It includes entries of praise and blame on over 400 restaurants across Canada. The author states that 'nobody can buy space in this guide and nobody can buy his way out.'

Whig. Political term used to describe both a particular party and its politics, in England and the United States, and an interpretation of history. In the former sense it is associated with the liberalism of the great landed magnates—not to be confused with twentieth-century liberalism. In the latter sense it denotes an evolutionary concept of history that ascribes moral value to the achievement of liberty and material progress. In England the Whig principle of free government dates from the Revolution of 1688. The term was used in the United States and sometimes in Upper Canada (Ontario) with respect to the reform party. (The *British Whig*, for example, was a reform newspaper founded in Kingston in the 1830s.) Its importance to Canada increased with the Whig appointment of Lord DURHAM as governor general in 1837. Though some historians have argued that Durham's emphasis on RESPONSIBLE GOVERNMENT directly contributed to the Liberal or GRIT view of Canadian history as a crusade to achieve autonomous nationhood from colonial status, others have debated and rejected the identification of Whig history with Liberal history.

Whiskey Howl. A rock jazz band formed in Toronto in 1960. Its five original members, who first came together in a Toronto suburban basement, started one of Canada's most successful blues-based performing bands. The group disbanded in 1975.

Whiskey Jack. An anglicized form of Wisekedjak, the name of NANABOZHO among the CREE and Saulteaux. Since the Ojibwa trickster hero Nanabozho is sometimes confused with the Micmac culture hero GLOOSCAP, the name Whiskey Jack is sometimes mistakenly used to refer to Glooscap.

Whisky, Canadian. See RYE WHISKY.

Whisky post. An illegal trading-post for liquor; for instance, FORT WHOOP-UP.

White coal. A reference to water used to generate hydro-electric power.

White Dawn, The. One of the few authentic feature films set in the Canadian Arctic, released in 1974. Produced by Martin Ransohoff for Paramount Pictures and directed by Philip Kaufman from a screenplay partly written by James HOUSTON and based on his novel *The White Dawn: An Eskimo Saga* (1971), it was photographed on BAFFIN ISLAND and cast both professional actors—including Timothy Bottoms and Warren Oates—and local Eskimos in starring roles. The film dramatizes a historical incident in 1896 when three whalers were shipwrecked and rescued by a group of Eskimos whose way of life was consequently disrupted.

White Empresses. See EMPRESS LINE, CANADIAN PACIFIC STEAMSHIP CO.

White Niggers of America. Title of the English edition—published in a translation by Joan Pinkham in 1971—of Pierre VALLIÈRES'S *Nègres blancs d'Amérique* (1968). Written in the Manhattan House of Detention while the author was awaiting deportation for demonstrating on behalf of the FLQ in front of the United Nations, it is a memoir of disenchantment with Quebec in the 1960s and a Marxist argument for Quebec independence. Vallières likens the condition of the Québécois in Canada to that of the Blacks in the United States.

White paper. A document prepared by the government and tabled in the HOUSE OF COMMONS. The purpose of a white paper is to present government policy that is to be translated into legislation. Set also GREEN PAPER.

White Pass and Yukon Railway. A privately owned, narrow-gauge railway line from Skagway, Alaska, to Whitehorse, Y.T. The 111-mi. railway follows the Dead Horse Trail of the KLONDIKE GOLD RUSH. The WPYR has been in continuous operation since 1900 and (a rare distinction) has never received a government subsidy. Passengers have often joked about the intials WP&YR: 'Wait Patiently and You'll Ride'.

White passion. A phrase used in Britain to describe the fascination of the Arctic following the disappearance there of Sir John FRANKLIN in 1847.

White power. A phrase associated with the generation of electricity through hydro (or water) power about 1910. It probably derives from the whitish appearance of falling water at Niagara Falls.

White-tailed deer. See White-tailed DEER.

White water. A description of rapids. A 'white-water man' is an expert canoeman or a logger who specializes in negotiating rapids or in clearing log jams.

White Wing. A biplane constructed by the AERIAL EXPERIMENT ASSOCIATION. It was designed and flown by F.W. (Casey) Baldwin at Baddeck, N.S., on 18 May 1908.

Whitehead Paxton (b.1937). Actor and director. Born in England, he studied at the Webber-Douglas School in London and performed with the Royal Shakespeare Company. After appearing on Broadway, he made his Canadian début in 1965 at the MANITOBA THEATRE CENTRE. He acted with the SHAW FESTIVAL in 1966 and became its artistic director the following year, overseeing its growth and recent expansion. He has distinguished himself with the festival as both actor and director.

Whitehorse. The capital since 1952 of the YUKON TERRITORY, and its largest settlement, with a population in 1971 of 11,217. It came into being during the KLONDIKE GOLD RUSH and has long been the Yukon's main communications and transportation centre.

Whiteoaks of Jalna, The. CBC-TV's dramatization of the JALNA novels by Mazo DE LA ROCHE. The 13-part series of one-hour episodes, launched on 23 Jan. 1972, starred Kate REID as Adeline Whiteoak and Paul Harding as her grandson Renny. Produced by John Trent and principally written by Timothy FINDLEY, the series was neither a critical nor a commercial success. Each episode ran two stories concurrently and confused viewers.

White-out. A phenomenon encountered in the Arctic, occurring when the landscape is enveloped in mist or drifting snow and visibility diminishes, or when a cloudy sky and a snowy landscape appear to merge into an overall whiteness, banishing all shadows and even the horizon.

Whitepainters. A word given currency by Harry Bruce, writing in *Maclean's*, 18 Apr. 1964, for 'people who buy a moldy downtown house and then spend several thousand dollars to clean out the cockroaches, replace the plumbing and generally exploit the building's sweet possibilities.'

Whittaker, Byng (1914-70). Broadcaster. Born in Dundela, near Ottawa, he worked as an announcer and scriptwriter for CKCR, Kitchener, in 1935 and joined CBC Radio in 1937. Called 'the expert of the day', he ap-

Whittaker

peared regularly on COURT OF OPINION, hosted 'Byng's Choice', and covered the ROYAL VISITS as the CBC's chief commentator.

Whittaker, Herbert (b.1911). Drama critic and director. Born in Montreal, he wrote for the *Montreal Gazette* before being appointed the Toronto *Globe and Mail*'s drama critic in 1949, a position from which he retired in Sept. 1975. He has directed many plays for amateur and professional organizations, including the JUPITER THEATRE and the CREST THEATRE, and was on the executive committee of the DOMINION DRAMA FESTIVAL. He is the author of *The Stratford Festival: 1953-57* (1958) and *Canada's National Ballet* (1967).

Whittall, Peter. See MR. FIX-IT.

Who Has Seen the Wind. Popular novel by W.O. MITCHELL published in 1947. It is the sensitive story of a young boy growing up to maturity on the Prairies during the Depression. The title is from a poem by Christina Rossetti. Allan KING is directing a film based on the novel, scheduled for release in 1977.

Who Owns Canada? Title of a pamphlet first published in 1934 and reissued in 1947. Published by the CCF under the pseudonym 'Watt Hugh McCollum' ('what you may call'em), it gave details of foreign ownership of Canadian industry and on the resources concentrated in a few hands.

Whooping crane. The symbol of conservationists in both Canada and the United States. This large, white, long-legged, long-necked bird barely escaped extinction and now breeds only in WOOD BUFFALO NATIONAL PARK, journeying over 2,000 mi. to winter in Texas.

Whoops-de-Doo, Les. A short ballet created by Brian MACDONALD for the ROYAL WINNIPEG BALLET. Based on the prairie whoop-up, the ballet of comedy and games was first performed in Flin Flon, Man., on 3 Oct. 1959.

Whoop-up. See FORT WHOOP-UP.

Whore's eggs. Popular Newfoundland name for sea urchins, a small shell-fish covered with sharp spines. They are not eaten.

Who's Who in Canada. 'Illustrated Biographical Record of Men and Women of the Time'. First published in 1911 and edited since 1961 by Ernest W. Whelpton, it includes approximately 3,000 entries and photographs and appears every 30 months. It is not to be confused with the CANADIAN WHO'S WHO.

Why Rock the Boat? Feature film directed by John Howse and produced by William Weintraub for the NFB in 1974. Based on the Weintraub novel about the comic adventures of a novice reporter who works for a tyrannical editor on a Montreal newspaper in the 1940s, it was one of the more successful Canadian features, at least critically. It starred Stuart Gillard as the young reporter and Tiiu Leek, an Estonian-Canadian starlet, as his girl friend. 112 min., 13 sec.; colour. See also the MONTREAL HERALD.

Wiebe, Rudy (b.1934). Novelist. Born near Fairholme, Sask., he was educated at the Mennonite High School in Carsdale, Alta, and at the Universities of Alberta and Tübingen, West Germany. He is a professor of English at the University of Alberta and writes strong, realistic prairie novels and short stories. *Peace Shall Destroy Many* (1962) and *The Blue Mountains of China* (1970) have the Mennonite immigration to western Canada as a background. The Indian in the West is the subject of *First and Vital Candle* (1966) and *The Temptations of Big Bear* (1973) is an imposing historical novel of the NORTHWEST REBELLION, written synoptically and expressionistically. *Where Is the Voice Coming From?* (1974) is a volume of short stories. Wiebe has edited *The Story-Makers* (1970), *Stories from Western Canada* (1972), and *Double Vision* (1976). See also ALMIGHTY VOICE.

Wieland, Joyce (b.1931). Painter and filmmaker. Born in Toronto, she studied at the Central Technical School. Her early work concentrated on the human figure until abstract expressionism interested her in painting free, richly coloured forms with blurred, translucent textures, such as the lyrical *Time Machine Series* (1961, AGO). Two other well-known paintings of the sixties, both done as a checkerboard of figures—one a hand that turns into a flower then into a penis, the other images of a sailboat that becomes submerged—are *Nature Mixes* (1963, private coll.) and *Boat Sinks* (1964, AGO). In 1962 she and her husband, Michael SNOW, moved to New York, where they stayed for ten years. Like Snow an innovative film-maker, Wieland made *La Raison avant la passion* there. This title, in English, was given to a famous work in yet another medium: *Reason Over Passion* (1968)—titled after a maxim of Prime Minister Trudeau—is one of her handsome large quilts, wittily designed in the pop-art style; it was purchased by the National Gallery of Canada. A Wieland retrospective in 1971 at the National Gallery was called *True Patriot Love,* suggesting her strong attachment to her country. Her romanticism, love of symbolism, of Canadian myths, of Canada itself came together in her feature-length film *The Far Shore* (1976), in which one of the three leading characters is a Tom THOMSON figure.

Wigwam. Algonkian word for a dwelling or lodge. It is a dome-shaped structure of poles covered with hide or bark, once used by Indians from the Atlantic Provinces to Manitoba. The Siouan word is TEEPEE, the Eskimo word TUPEK.

Wild rice. Canada's only exclusively native cereal, also known as 'riz sauvage' and 'zizanie'. Found in swampy land from New Brunswick to Saskatchewan, the plants may reach a height of 8 ft. It has a nutty taste and should be cooked only to crunchy texture.

Wilderness Award. Presented annually by the CBC to recognize outstanding achievement in films made for CBC-TV, English and French. It was established in 1963 to honour three television film-makers—producer Norman Caton and cameramen Len Macdonald and Charles Riegler—who were killed on 25 Feb. 1963 in a plane crash while making a film entitled *Wilderness* for CBC-TV's 'Camera Canada'. The Award was initiated by CBC personnel and takes the form of a gold-bearing Canadian rock specimen, donated by Kerr-Addison Mines, mounted on an oak pedestal. It remains on display for a year at the CBC production centre responsible for the winning film. Principal artists and technicians who worked on the winning film or on other films entered are given Wilderness Medals, which were designed by Gert Pollmer of CBC Graphics and executed by Dora DE PÉDERY-HUNT.

Wilkinson, Anne (1910-61). Poet. Born in Toronto, raised in London, Ont., and educated abroad, she wrote sensuous, graceful, witty poetry filled with riddles and puns. It was collected and introduced by A.J.M. SMITH for *The Collected Poems of Anne Wilkinson* (1968), which also includes a fine prose memoir, 'Four Corners of My World'. She wrote *Lions in the Way* (1956), a history of the Osler family, of which she was a member, and *Swann & Daphne* (1960), a fantasy for children, and was a founding editor of *The TAMARACK REVIEW*.

Will Pay to the Bearer on Demand. Familiar wording on bank notes issued by the Bank of Canada from 1935, the year the Bank commenced operations. In 1969 the line was replaced by the wording 'This Note is Legal Tender'.

Willan, Healey (1880-1968). Composer. Born in Balham, Eng., he was organist in several London churches before coming to Canada in 1913. He taught at the Royal Conservatory of Music, Toronto, where he was vice-principal, and at the University of Toronto. He also served as the University Organist from 1932 to 1964. He had an important influence on church music in Canada and the United States with his advocacy of Plainsong after he became precentor of St Mary Magdalene's Church, Toronto—a post he held from 1921 until his death. His early religious music shows the influence of late nineteenth-century romanticism, which remained a major characteristic of his work. His finest compositions include *Introduction, Passacaglia and Fugue* (1916) for organ, *An Apostrophe to the Heavenly Hosts* (1921) for choir, and two operas: *Transit Through Fire* (1942) and DEIRDRE (1945; rev. 1962, 1965).

Williams, Percy (b.1908). 'World's fastest human'. Born in Vancouver, he overcame rheumatic fever to become the gold medallist in both the 100-metre and 200-metre races at the 1928 Olympics in Amsterdam. He returned home to tumultuous welcomes. After winning the 100-yard race at the 1930 British Empire Games in Hamilton, Ont., he suffered a pulled muscle and never regained his former speed and power.

Williams, Richard (b.1933). Film animator. Born in Toronto, he trained with George DUNNING at the NATIONAL FILM BOARD before settling in London, Eng., in 1955. There he produced the most influential of modern cartoons, *The Little Island* (1958), which introduced absurd and often violent humour. Williams established a studio that turned out imaginative television commercials as well as titles and inserts to *Casino Royale* (1967), *What's New Pussycat?* (1965), and *The Return of the Pink Panther* (1975), among other films.

Williams, Saul (b.1955). Ojibwa artist. Born at North Caribou Lake, some 300 mi. north of Thunder Bay, he studied art at Elliot Lake in 1971 for a total of three weeks. His stylized drawings, like those of Norval MORRISSEAU, are bold in colour and imagery. A favourite subject is the stylized conflict between the Snake and the THUNDERBIRD.

Willingdon, Lord (1866-1941). GOVERNOR GENERAL of Canada from 1926 to 1931.

Willis, Austin (b.1916). Born in Halifax, N.S., the younger brother of J. Frank WILLIS, Austin became known as an actor-announcer with CBC Radio, taking part in such productions as CARRY ON, CANADA, COMRADES IN ARMS, and FIGHTING NAVY. His was 'The Victory Loan Voice'. He was a story-teller on TRANS-CANADA MATINÉE from 1959 to 1963 and appeared as Admiral Fox in the CBC-TV series SEAWAY (1965-6). Since then the silver-haired actor has worked in the United States on stage and screen. He was married to Kate REID from 1953 to 1962.

Willis, J. Frank (1909-69). Radio producer. Born in Halifax, N.S., the elder brother of Austin WILLIS, he was a novice CRBC radio announcer in Halifax when 'the news story of the half-century' broke: the MOOSE RIVER DISASTER, which he covered at hourly intervals for 69 hours, beginning on 20 Apr. 1936. He was maritime director of the CRBC and its successor the CBC at Halifax (1933-8), director of radio features in Toronto (1939-58), and of documentaries (1958-69). He was producer of such wartime programs as COMRADES IN ARMS and CARRY ON, CANADA.

Willison's Monthly. 'A national magazine devoted to the discussion of public affairs affecting Canada and the Empire'. It was founded and edited in Toronto by Sir John Willison (1856-1927) in 1925 and continued by the journalist's son, Walter Willison, until 1929, when it ceased publication.

Willows. Fictional birthplace in southern Saskatchewan of SARAH BINKS.

Wills, Frank (1819?-57). Architect. Born in Exeter, Eng., he came to Fredericton, N.B., in 1845 with the Rt Rev. John Medley, first Bishop of Fredericton. Wills was responsible for the basic design of Medley's cathedral, Christ Church, which was later completed after designs by William Butterfield. He also built for Medley St Anne's Chapel, Fredericton (1846-7)—described as the 'finest small North American parish church of its date in the English Gothic Revival style'. In 1848 Wills moved to New York City.

Willson, David (1778?-1866). Religious enthusiast. Born in New York State, he came to Canada in 1801 and, in 1812, organized a short-lived religious sect—a dissident Quaker group—called 'The Children of Peace'. His SHARON TEMPLE, a handsome architectural curiosity, still stands at Sharon, Ont. (north of Toronto).

Willson, Thomas. See CARBIDE.

Wilmot, Robert Duncan (1809-91). A FATHER OF CONFEDERATION. Born in Fredericton, N.B., he entered the milling and shipping business. He was elected to the legislative assembly in 1846 and joined several minis-

tries. He changed from opposing to approving Confederation and was a delegate to the LONDON CONFERENCE. Appointed to the Senate in 1867, he resigned in 1880 to become lieutenant-governor of New Brunswick.

Wilson, Ethel (b.1890). Novelist and short-story writer. Born in Elizabeth, South Africa, and brought to Vancouver as a child, she was educated in England and taught school in Vancouver from 1907 to 1920. The following year she married a medical doctor. Nearly 60 when her first novel was published, she created in her urbane fiction a world in which her whimsical, sensitively observed characters seem to accept unquestioningly the unexpected, sometimes catastrophic or surreal occurrences that beset them. Her novels, which were acclaimed internationally, are *Hetty Dorval* (1947), *The Innocent Traveller* (1949), *The Equations of Love* (1952), *Swamp Angel* (1954), and *Love and Salt Water* (1956). Her stories were collected in *Mrs. Golightly and Other Stories* (1961).

Wilson, J. Tuzo (b.1908). Internationally known geophysicist. Born in Ottawa, he was professor of geophysics at the University of Toronto. He served three terms as president of the International Union of Geodesy and Geophysics and is the author of *One Chinese Moon* (1959), *I.G.Y.: The Year of the New Moons* (1961), and *Unglazed China* (1973), an account of scientific and private visits to China in 1958 and 1971. He has been director-general of the ONTARIO SCIENCE CENTRE since 1974.

Wilson, Jean (1910-33). Speed-skater. Born in Glasgow and raised in Toronto, she was a successor to the famed Lela BROOKS, becoming North American female champion speed-skater in 1931. She broke one world record and finished first in another skating event at the 1932 Winter Olympics at Lake Placid, N.Y., where the events were still termed exhibitions. Her promising skating career ended abruptly in 1933 when she succumbed to a rare muscular disease.

Wind chill index. A measurement of the combined effects of the temperature and speed of the wind on the human body. In winter it is not the cold but the wind that causes discomfort. At a wind chill count of 2,400, exposed flesh begins to freeze. The index dates from 1949 and is based on a Canadian-American study undertaken at a testing station at Churchill, Man.

Wind Our Enemy, The. A brief sequence of poems by Anne Marriott (b.1913) inspired by the tragedy of drought and dust storms on the Prairie. It was published in 1939. The 10 poems are written in a free-verse, documentary manner and form the first of several books by Marriott, who was born and raised in Victoria, B.C.

Windfall Commission. An Ontario Royal Commission 'to investigate trading in the shares of Windfall Oils and Mines, Ltd'. Justice Arthur Kelly was appointed to inquire into the activities of the small Toronto mining exploration company, headed by Viola MacMillan, which held properties in the Timmins area at the time of the TEXASGULF discovery of Apr. 1964. Rumours sent Windfall stock from 57 cents to $5.60 and down again. The Windfall Commission's report, published in 1965, found instances of illegal insider trading. It resulted in tougher exchange regulations and marked the end of the era of public involvement in the financing of mining exploration.

Windfields. The name of E.P. TAYLOR's estate in North York, Toronto. 30 acres have been donated to the borough of North York, and the remaining 20 will be divided between the borough and the ROYAL CANADIAN ACADEMY OF ARTS for use as an art centre on Taylor's death. Taylor's two breeding farms—Windfield Farms Limited, in Oshawa, Ont., and Maryland—are named after the estate.

Windmill, Battle of the. A raid on Upper Canada (Ontario) by American sympathizers after the REBELLION OF 1837 on 12-16 Nov. 1838. Under Nils von Schoultz they landed at Windmill Point, near Prescott, Ont., and took possession of a stone windmill, where they eventually surrendered. They were tried and Von Schoultz was hanged on 8 Dec. See also HUNTERS' LODGES.

Windsor, House of. See MONARCHY.

Windsor-Detroit Tunnel. See DETROIT-WINDSOR TUNNEL.

Windsor Station. Montreal railway station. Built by the CPR in 1888-9, it is the terminus of the transcontinental line and still houses its administrative headquarters. The impressive stone structure was designed by Bruce PRICE in the ornate Romanesque Revival manner and was extended about 1900 by the firm of E. and W.S. MAXWELL.

Windsor Strikes. A series of three strikes, exemplifying poor labour relations, by auto workers at Windsor, Ont. In 1942 a strike in support of equal pay for equal work was ended by arbitration. In 1943 a strike to protest a speed-up order was also settled by arbitration. In 1944 a strike regarding grievance procedures, which lasted from 20 Apr. to 14 May, was ultimately referred to the National Labour Board for arbitration.

Winnipeg. The capital of Manitoba. Originally a fur-trading post, it developed on the site of the RED RIVER SETTLEMENT, established in 1812, and FORT GARRY. Though growth was slow, it was made the capital of the new province of Manitoba in 1870 and was incorporated as a city in 1873 with a population of 1,869. Its position as 'Gateway to the West' was guaranteed in 1881 when the CPR was built through Winnipeg. Accommodating various manufacturing, transportation, and service industries, and having an ethnically and culturally diverse population, it supports numerous musical and theatre groups, including the widely acclaimed ROYAL WINNIPEG BALLET. The 1971 CMA population was 540,262. Its official motto is *Unum cum Virtute Multorum* ('One with the Strength of Many'). See also GOLDEN BOY, MANITOBA MUSEUM OF MAN AND NATURE, MANITOBA THEATRE CENTRE, PORTAGE AND MAIN, UNIVERSITY OF MANITOBA, UNIVERSITY OF WINNIPEG.

Winnipeg. Automobile manufactured from 1920 to 1923 by Winnipeg Motor Cars, Winnipeg. It came in touring, sport, and sedan models and had a four-cylinder engine. The slogan of the company was 'As good as the wheat'.

Winnipeg Free Press, The. An evening newspaper published in Winnipeg. Founded in 1872 and called the *Manitoba Free Press* until 1931, it has traditionally championed the western viewpoint. It gained national renown under the long editorship (1901-44) of John W. DAFOE. Acquired by Clifford SIFTON in 1898, it was the flagship newspaper of FP PUBLICATIONS (to which it lent its initials) until the chain acquired the Toronto GLOBE AND MAIL. Once published by Richard S. Malone, it is now published by his son Richard Malone. Its motto is 'Freedom of Trade, Liberty of Religion, Equality of Civil Rights'.

Winnipeg General Strike. The only general strike in Canada. After a strike began in the metals and building trades in Winnipeg over issues of union recognition and collective bargaining, a general sympathetic strike was called for Thursday, 15 May 1919. Over 22,000 workers responded, including civic and government employees, initially paralysing the city. Only the police and a skeleton staff at the waterworks were asked to stay on duty; permits were later issued by the strike committee to allow essential services to be maintained. Ranged against the

565

Winnipeg General Strike

strikers were not only the employers but three levels of government—municipal, provincial, and federal—convinced that the strike was Communist-inspired, largely because the Marxist-oriented ONE BIG UNION was being formed at that time. The city police, sympathetic to the strikers, were replaced by a special force, and the authorities placed the Royal North West Mounted Police and the military on standby. The policy of the strikers was non-violent—even peaceful picketing was discouraged—and there were few incidents until 21 June, since known as Bloody Saturday, when the special police informed the mayor they could not handle the crowds gathering for a parade. The Mounted Police were called in just as the crowd was attacking a streetcar run by anti-strikers. A horse tripped, its rider was attacked by the crowd, and the rest of the force fired into the crowd: two strikers were killed and 20 injured. The strike was called off on 26 June.

The collapse of the strike was caused by government intervention and by the strikers' lack of experience in organizing a general strike. In the aftermath, SEDITIOUS CONSPIRACY charges were laid against the strike leaders, who included J.S. WOODSWORTH, and amendments to SECTION 98 of the Criminal Code were rushed through Parliament, widening the meaning of sedition and increasing the penalties for it.

The strike was a landmark not only in the dispute between the old craft-based unions of eastern Canada and the new industrial-based unions of the West, but in the growth of radicalism in the West: Woodsworth became the first socialist in the House of Commons in 1921.

Winnipeg goldeye. A small tasty fresh-water fish of the shad family, usually smoked. It has largely disappeared from Manitoba and Saskatchewan waters owing to overfishing and is now imported from northern Minnesota.

Winnipeg Jets. See WORLD HOCKEY ASSOCIATION.

Winnipeg Tribune, The. An evening newspaper published in Winnipeg. Founded in 1890, it has been owned by SOUTHAM PRESS since 1920. It narrowed the traditionally large gap between itself and its rival, the WINNIPEG FREE PRESS, by modernizing its design and outlook in 1975. The *Tribune*'s motto is 'That's My Kind Of Paper'.

Winspear Foundation. It was established in Edmonton in 1961 by Francis G. Winspear, an accountancy executive, to aid education,

health, social development, humanities, international activities, religion, and national development.

Winter, Jack (b.1936). Playwright. Born in Montreal and educated at McGill and the University of Toronto, he worked as dramaturge of TORONTO WORKSHOP PRODUCTIONS (1962-7), which produced his plays *Before Compiègne* (1964) and *Hey, Rube* (1966). The Studio Theatre of the NATIONAL ARTS CENTRE was opened with his experimental *Party Day* in 1969. *Selling Out* (1971), his short film about a Prince Edward Island farmer selling his farm, was directed by Tadeusz Jaworski and nominated for an Academy Award. Winter is the author of *The Island* (1972), a collection of sketches about P.E.I., and the co-adapter of TEN LOST YEARS (1974).

Winter Carnival. See QUEBEC WINTER CARNIVAL.

Winter Games. See CANADA GAMES.

Winter Kept Us Warm. Feature film produced and directed by David Secter. Made while Secter was a student at the University of Toronto, it is the sensitive study of campus friendships that lapse with maturity and graduation. It was released in 1964. 81 min., b & w.

Winter Studies and Summer Rambles in Canada. A vivid account by Anna JAMESON of her eight-month stay in Canada, published in 1838. Containing lively, sometimes caustic descriptions of life in Toronto and southwestern Ontario and of colonial pretensions, and offering a splendid evocation of landscape and character, it is a classic among early Canadian travel books.

Wisekedjak. See WHISKEY JACK.

Wiseman, Adele (b.1928). Novelist. Born in Winnipeg, Man., she was educated at the University of Manitoba and travelled extensively before teaching at McGill University's Macdonald College and Sir George Williams (now Concordia) University. She has written two novels about Jewish life in Winnipeg's North End, exploring the psychology of uprooted people: *The Sacrifice* (1956), an imaginative and austere retelling of the Abraham-Isaac legend, and *Crackpot* (1974). She has also written many short stories and articles, and the text for *Old Markets, New Worlds* (1964), illustrated by Joe Rosenthal. She lives in Toronto.

Wissanotti, Lake. The fictional name of Lake Couchiching in Stephen LEACOCK'S SUNSHINE SKETCHES OF A LITTLE TOWN (1912).

Without fear, favour or affection. Memorable phrase from the oath of office of the ROYAL CANADIAN MOUNTED POLICE. Dating from the founding of the Force in 1874, the oath enjoins the recruit to 'well and truly obey and perform all lawful orders or instruction . . . without fear, favour or affection of or toward any person or party whomsoever.' The phrase was used by Vernon Kemp for the title of his memoirs of 35 years with the Force, published in 1959.

Witness to Yesterday. A 30-minute weekly television series starring Patrick WATSON, who questions historical figures impersonated by well-known actors. The 20 episodes were created by Watson for GLOBAL TELEVISION NETWORK and broadcast from Jan. to May 1974. They have since been nationally syndicated. Notable programs included William HUTT as Columbus, Robert MARKLE as Rembrandt, Mavor MOORE as Socrates, Barry MORSE as Shakespeare, Denise PELLETIER as Sarah Bernhardt, Kate REID as Queen Victoria, and Watson interviewing himself as da Vinci.

Wizard of the North. Sobriquet given Sir John A. MACDONALD in recognition of his political acumen.

WO. Official abbreviation of Warrant Officer.

WO1. Official abbreviation of Warrant Officer, Class 1.

WO2. Official abbreviation of Warrant Officer, Class 2.

Wobblies. See INDUSTRIAL WORKERS OF THE WORLD.

Woensdrecht. See Battle of the SCHELDT.

Wojeck. A CBC-TV series about a fighting coroner in a big city. Created by Toronto writer Phillip Hersch, produced by Ron Weyman, and starring John VERNON as Dr Steve Wojeck, the series of 10 one-hour episodes was launched on 13 Sept. 1966, following the showing of the pilot on 9 Mar. The character of Wojeck was modelled on that of Dr Morton SHULMAN.

Wolf. Famous wild canine varying in length from 59 to 81 in. and weighing between 57 and 174 lb. Once common throughout Canada, from the Arctic tundra to the southern Prairies and woodland, it has been extensively hunted and now runs wild only in the more inaccessible regions of the North. Contrary to popular belief, it does not attack man. It is also called timber wolf and grey wolf.

Wolfe, James (1727-59). Army officer, victorious commander of the siege of Quebec and the Battle of the PLAINS OF ABRAHAM in the SEVEN YEARS' WAR. A brigade commander in the successful siege of LOUISBOURG, he was put in charge of the land forces for the expedition against Quebec. His first attack, on a French redoubt west of the Montmorency R. on 31 July 1759, was a failure. His second, made above Quebec on the advice of his brigadiers, was a success—a result of good luck and French ineptitude rather than good planning, for Wolfe, a sickly man, was an indecisive planner. Early in the morning of 13 Sept. his troops landed at WOLFE'S COVE (Anse au Foulon) about two miles above the town, climbed the cliffs, and formed on the Plains of Abraham, to the surprise of the French commander MONTCALM, who attacked prematurely and with ruinous loss. Quebec surrendered, but Wolfe had been fatally shot. He was buried at Greenwich, Eng. There is a tradition that Wolfe recited, or heard an officer recite, Thomas Gray's 'Elegy, Written in a Country Church-yard' the evening before the engagement, remarking, 'Gentlemen, I would rather have written those lines than take Quebec tomorrow', or a variation of those words.

Wolfe's Cove. Originally called Anse au Foulon, it is on the north shore of the St Lawrence R. about two miles above Quebec. On the night of 12-13 Sept 1759, British troops led by Gen. James WOLFE made a landing there, followed a track up the cliffs, and formed on the PLAINS OF ABRAHAM. A short battle ensued that was a victory for the British and occasioned the eventual surrender of Quebec.

Wolverine. A large carnivorous mammal of the weasel family once widely distributed in Canada but now restricted to remoter areas of the tundra and Rockies. The wolverine, or carcajou, figures prominently in the folklore and trapping yarns of both French and English Canada owing to its habit of breaking into the caches of hunters and explorers, gorging on the food, ripping apart the supplies, and spoiling any remains beyond use. Its fur is highly prized by northern peoples for use in parkas because of its resistance to frost.

Women's Alumnae. See UNIVERSITY ALUMNAE DRAMATIC CLUB.

Women's Christian Temperance Union. A prohibition-minded association formed in Owen Sound, Ont., in 1874. It has its headquarters in Toronto and operates as a social-service agency. Nellie McCLUNG used to joke that the WCTU did *not* stand for 'Women Continually Torment Us'.

Women's Institutes. A national organization to help farm women in household science. It was founded as the result of a speech delivered by Adelaide Hunter HOODLESS, who had lost a child because of contaminated milk, before the Farmers' Institute at Stoney Creek, Ont., on 19 Feb. 1897. The Federated Women's Institutes of Canada was organized in Winnipeg in 1919 by Judge Emily MURPHY, who served as the first national president. The WI has spread to many other countries and remains active in such areas as home economics, citizenship, agriculture, and industry.

Women's Press, The. See CANADIAN WOMEN'S EDUCATIONAL PRESS.

Women's suffrage. Women's franchise movement. Influenced by the struggle to gain votes for women in Great Britain and the United States, the Canadian suffrage movement had to challenge not only the prevailing view of the inequality of the sexes, but the issue of FRANCHISE itself, which was more restrictive in Canada than in either the U.S. or England. The suffrage movement did not gain a popular following until 1910, when western Canada took the lead in demanding equal voting rights for women under feminists such as Nellie L. McCLUNG. Manitoba was the first province to grant women the vote, in 1916, and Quebec the last, in 1940. Complete federal enfranchisement for women was in effect by 1918. The right of women to sit in the House of Commons was permanently granted in 1920. See also PERSONS CASE.

Wood, Elizabeth Wyn (1903-66). Sculptor. Born in Orillia, Ont., she was educated at the Ontario College of Art and the Art Students' League in New York. She married the sculptor Emanuel HAHN in 1926. She was interested in transferring the landscape forms into three-dimensional sculpture, using as a motif the Precambrian Shield, which was also popular with the GROUP OF SEVEN. One of her best-known portrait commissions is the 10-ft statue of King George VI near Niagara Falls, Ont.

Wood, Henry Wise (1860-1941). Prairie farm leader. Born in Munroe City, Mo., he became a farmer. He settled in Alberta in 1905 and in 1916 became leader of the UNITED FARMERS OF ALBERTA, which established the master pattern for a Canadian farm movement. He made the UFA a major force not only in Al-

berta but in the nation. Under Wood the theory of group government was developed and tested, with the eventual result that the PROGRESSIVE PARTY was destroyed; under his grudging direction the farmers entered politics at provincial and national levels; and under his leadership the Alberta WHEAT POOLS became a major economic force. A man of enormous influence on Canadian social and political life, Wood is nevertheless little known.

Wood Buffalo National Park. Established in 1922, it straddles the Alberta-Northwest Territories border between Lake Athabasca and Great Slave Lake. Wood Buffalo is the world's largest national park. Comprising 17,300 sq. mi. of forests and open plains, it is the home of the largest remaining herd of bison on the continent and the breeding ground of the rare WHOOPING CRANE.

Woodbine Race Track. The largest race track in North America (780 acres), located in Metropolitan Toronto and opened in 1956. Each June it holds the continent's oldest continuously run horse race, the QUEEN'S PLATE.

Woodcock, George (b.1912). Man-of-letters. Born in Winnipeg and educated in England, where he edited two anarchist publications, he returned to western Canada in 1949 and lived in isolation at Sooke on the southwest coast of Vancouver Island. He joined the English department of the University of British Columbia in 1956, founded CANADIAN LITERATURE in 1959, and has been a full-time editor and writer since 1963. Writing informally, lucidly, and knowledgeably about a very wide range of subjects, he has produced over 40 biographical and literary studies, travel books, histories, and collections of verse between 1940 and 1976. Of special interest or importance are the following: *Ravens and Prophets: An Account of Journeys in British Columbia, Alberta and Southern Alaska* (1952); *Incas and Other Men: Travels in the Andes* (1959); *Anarchism: A History of Libertarian Ideas and Movements* (1962); *The Crystal Spirit: A Study of George Orwell* (1966); *The Doukhobors* (1968), written with Ivan Avakumovic; *Canada and the Canadians* (1970); *Odysseus Ever Returning: Essays on Canadian Writing* (1970); *Victoria* (1971), with photographs by his wife Ingeborg Woodcock; *Gabriel DUMONT* (1975), the first biography of the Métis leader; and *Notes on Visitations: Poems 1936-1975* (1976).

Woodhouse and Hawkins. Radio comedy team. Two Calgary hardware-shop clerks, Frank Deaville (b.1905) from Victoria and Art McGregor (b.1906) from Scotland, made their radio début as Woodhouse and Hawkins, a comedy duo, on 'Nit Wit Court' in Calgary in 1931. They were heard Friday evenings at 8:30 impersonating a variety of characters and accents. They travelled east to Toronto via Winnipeg, where music was added to their show in 1941. When the CBC eventually dropped them, CFRB Toronto carried them until the late 1940s.

Woodlot Improvement Act. See DEMONSTRATION WOODLOT.

Woods Cree. See CREE.

Woods, Gordon & Co. See CLARKSON, GORDON & CO.

Woodside National Historic Park. A 12-acre park in Kitchener, Ont., that is the site of Woodside, the home of W.L. Mackenzie KING in the 1890s. The grey brick house was built in 1853 and restoration work was begun in 1943.

Woodsworth, James Shaver (1874-1942). Founding leader of the Co-operative Commonwealth Federation (CCF). Born in Ontario, he was ordained as a Methodist minister in 1896. He was one of the new breed of clergy who believed in working with the people and he held a variety of jobs, including those of teacher, longshoreman, and lecturer. He broke with his church during the First World War and played a major role during the WINNIPEG GENERAL STRIKE of 1919. In 1921 he was elected to the House of Commons for Winnipeg North and in 1932, after a distinguished career in Parliament that included credit for forcing the implementation of old-age pensions in 1926, he became the first leader of the CCF. For the next eight years he attacked government inaction during the Depression and crusaded for neutrality in the coming war. In one of the memorable moments in Canadian history the frail Woodsworth rose during the emergency session of 1939 to say that he opposed Canadian participation in the war against Germany, a position that was disavowed by his own followers.

Woodward Stores Limited. A chain of department stores in British Columbia and Alberta. It dates back to 1892 when Charles Woodward (1852-1937), a merchant from Ontario, opened a drygoods store in Vancouver. The expansion that began in 1948 is particularly identified with the chairmanship (since 1964) of Charles Namby Wynn Woodward (b.1924), grandson of the founder. Woodward's sells 85% Canadian-made merchandise and in 1976 operated from 22 loca-

tions in western Canada. The company maintains a branch office in London, Eng., on a 98-ft barge moored in the Thames near the Houses of Parliament.

Woolf, George (1910-46). Jockey. Known as 'The Iceman', he rode on American tracks and twice led all jockeys in the value of winning purses. In 1946, after winning 721 races, and on the verge of retirement, he was killed when a mount stumbled. In his memory a full-sized bronze statue was erected on the Santa Anita course, and the George Woolf Memorial Award was offered for annual competition 'to the most sportsmanlike jockey', won in 1951 by his friend and fellow Canadian, Johnny LONGDEN.

Woolsey Family, The. Early masterpiece of Canadian painting. William BERCZY painted this family group in 1808 as a commission from John William Woolsey, a Quebec merchant. A favourite painting in the National Gallery of Canada, it shows John and Julie Woolsey, their four children, his mother and her brother, and a dog. (Each figure cost ten pounds; the dog was free.) Painted in the Neo-classical style, the figures are formally placed, more-or-less side by side, near an open window through which the St Lawrence R. can be seen.

'Work! For the Night Is Coming.' Popular evangelical hymn written by Annie Louisa (Walker) Coghill and published anonymously in Montreal in 1861. The musical arrangement was made without the poet's knowledge in 1864 by Lowell Mason.

Workers' Educational Association of Canada. An organization to educate workers and reflect the problems and interests of the unions. Modelled on the WEA in Great Britain, it was founded as a provincial organization—the WEA of Ontario—by the Toronto District TRADES AND LABOUR CONGRESS, with assistance from the University of Toronto, in 1917. It has been a national organization since 1936. With the decline of university support in 1942, it has since been supported by organized labour.

Workers Party of Canada. The name of the COMMUNIST PARTY OF CANADA from 1922 to 1925, stressing its concern with labour and unions during this early period.

Workers' Unity League. Founded in 1929 to organize workers and to lead a program of revolutionary struggle, it fought many strikes and obtained improved wage offers. It was active in the RELIEF CAMPS and also organized the ON TO OTTAWA trek in 1935.

World at Six

World at Six, The World at Eight, The World at Nine, The. CBC Radio news broadcasts heard nationally at 6:00 p.m., 8:00 p.m., and 9:00 p.m. Monday to Friday. Although CBC NATIONAL NEWS has scheduled national news reports since 1941, the present half-hour news programs, heard five days a week, made their début on 31 Oct. 1966.

World Hockey Association. Professional hockey league formed in Nov. 1971 with headquarters at Newport Beach, Calif. The WHA, a result of North American hockey expansion, mounted its first series in 1972-3 and checked the growth of the NATIONAL HOCKEY LEAGUE. Of the 15 teams that are franchised, five are Canadian: the Edmonton Oilers, Québec Nordiques, Toronto Toros, Vancouver Blazers, and Winnipeg Jets. Players from the WHA were chosen to form TEAM CANADA, which played the Soviet Union in 1974. The WHA awards the AVCO WORLD TROPHY and makes the following presentations: Ben Hatskin Trophy (best goaltender), Dennis A. Murphy Award (best defensemen), Gary L. Davidson Trophy (most valuable player), Howard Baldwin Award (coach of the year), Lou Kaplan Award (rookie of the year), Paul Deneau Award (most gentlemanly player), and the W.D. (Bill) Hunter Trophy (scoring champion). Team Canada 76 is made up of both WHA and NHL players.

World in Action. A series of propaganda newsreels released monthly during the Second World War by the NFB. These one- and two-reel compilation films, with broader themes of international moment than the CANADA CARRIES ON series, were distributed by United Artists to 5,000 theatres around the world. The first of the 29 films was *Inside Fighting Russia* (released in Apr. 1942) and the last was *Now—the Peace* (released in May 1945). Some of the better-known films were *The Mask of Nippon* (1942), *Battle Is Their Birthright* (1943), WAR FOR MEN'S MINDS (1943), and *Our Northern Neighbour* (1944). The series producer was John GRIERSON, the writer-director Stuart Legg, the principal editor Tom DALY, and the narrator Lorne GREENE.

'World is Waiting for the Sunrise, The'. Immensely popular song, published in 1919, that caught the mood of the post-war years. The music was composed in 1918 by Ernest Seitz (b.1892). Born in Hamilton, Ont., he became a distinguished concert pianist and was for many years the leading piano teacher at the Toronto Conservatory of Music before he retired to become vice-president of his family's auto-dealership, Gorries. The words

were by Gene Lockhart (1891-1957). Born in London, Ont., he was a pianist who became a well-known Hollywood actor.

World Wars. See FIRST WORLD WAR and SECOND WORLD WAR.

Worts, James. See HIRAM WALKER—GOODERHAM AND WORTS LTD.

WPC. Initials of the WORKERS PARTY OF CANADA.

WPYR. See WHITE PASS AND YUKON RAILWAY.

WRCNS. Initials of the former Women's Royal Canadian Naval Service, which was active in the ROYAL CANADIAN NAVY during the Second World War.

Wright, Alonzo. See KING OF THE GATINEAU.

Wright, Don. See DON WRIGHT CHORUS.

Wright, Jack (1903-49). Tennis champion. Born in British Columbia, he studied medicine at McGill University and became a three-time winner of the Canadian tennis championship. He represented Canada in Davis Cup competitions for 10 years. Selected as Canada's outstanding tennis player of the first half-century, he was elected to membership in the Sports HALL OF FAME.

Wright Jr, Joseph (b.1906). A distinguished oarsman—like his father Joseph WRIGHT Sr—he won the Diamond Sculls at Henley, Eng., the greatest honour in amateur sculling. 'Little Joe' was a member of the Toronto Argonauts when that football team won the GREY CUP in 1933.

Wright Sr, Joseph (1864-1950). All-round athlete and oarsman of distinction. He raced in singles, pairs, fours, and eights, winning 150 events before retiring from active participation at 51. He then found success as a coach with the Toronto Argonauts and the University of Pennsylvania, and served as an alderman. In 1950 he was named 'Canada's greatest oarsman of the half-century'. He was called 'Big Joe' to distinguish him from his son Joseph WRIGHT Jr, who was called 'Little Joe'.

Wright, Philemon (1760-1839). 'Father of the Ottawa'. Born in Massachusetts, he founded the settlement of Wrightville (officially Hull), L.C. (Que.), on the Ottawa R. in 1800. He built mills, a tannery, and developed a timber industry. The *Union of Ottawa*, the first steamboat on the river, was built for him.

Wright, Richard (b.1937). Novelist. Born in Midland, Ont., a graduate of the Ryerson Polytechnic Institute, Toronto, and of Trent University, Peterborough, he has worked as a traveller for a book publisher, as an advertising copywriter, and, since 1975, as a teacher at Ridley College, St Catharines, Ont., where he is head of the English department. He has written two highly praised novels that deal with the 'thundering ironies' of life: *The Weekend Man* (1971) and *In the Middle of a Life* (1973). His recent *Farthing's Fortunes* (1976) is a comic novel.

Writer's Union of Canada, The. National association of prose writers founded in Toronto on 3 Nov. 1973. Its purpose 'is to unite Canadian writers for the advancement of their common interests'. The first chairperson was the novelist Marian ENGEL.

Wrong, G.M. (1860-1948). Historian. Born in Grovesend, Elgin Co., C.W. (Ont.), and educated at the Universities of Toronto, Oxford, and Berlin, he was ordained in the Anglican ministry in 1883. He was head of the department of history at the University of Toronto from 1894 to his retirement in 1927, and once defined his hiring policy in this way: 'What I want is a scholar and a gentleman, and if he knows any history, so much the better.' He founded the *Review of Historical Publications Relating to Canada* (1897-1918), which was superseded by the CANADIAN HISTORICAL REVIEW, which he edited until 1927. Secretary of the CHAMPLAIN SOCIETY from 1905 to 1922, he was joint editor with H.H. Langton of the CHRONICLES OF CANADA. Among his many books are *A Canadian Manor and Its Seigneurs* (1908; rev. 1938), *The Rise and Fall of*

New France (1928), and *The Canadians: The Story of a People* (1938).

WUL. Initials of the WORKERS UNITY LEAGUE.

Wycliffe College. Founded in 1877 as the Protestant Episcopal Divinity School, it held classes in St James' Cathedral, Toronto. The present name was adopted in 1879. It acquired its present building on the campus of the UNIVERSITY OF TORONTO, with which it federated in 1889, in 1891. It is a participating member of the TORONTO SCHOOL OF THEOLOGY and continues to train candidates for ministry within the Anglican Church.

Wyers, Jan G. (b.1891). Primitive painter of prairie scenes. Born in Steendern, Holland, he immigrated in 1916 and began painting at his farm at Windhorst, Sask., in 1935. He painted during the winters, in a personal yet direct manner, scenes of the farming life around him.

Wyle, Florence (1881-1968). Sculptor. Born in Trenton, Ill., she studied at the Art Institute of Chicago after becoming interested in anatomy while studying medicine at the University of Illinois. She came to Toronto in 1913 to join Frances LORING, with whom she lived for 60 years; they were known as 'the Girls' to the Canadian art community. Wyle accepted large-scale commissions for animal and portrait sculptures, working in bronze, wood, and stone. She was known especially for her fountains. In 1928 she helped found the Sculptors Society of Canada. Her works are exhibited in public collections in Ottawa, Winnipeg, Toronto, and Chicago.

X

XWA. The call letters of Canada's first radio station, licensed in 1919. The Marconi station in Montreal transmitted the first scheduled radio broadcast in North America—the proceedings of a ROYAL SOCIETY OF CANADA meeting in Ottawa—on 20 May 1920, almost half a year before any other station. X stood for 'experimental'. The station is now known as CFCF.

XY Company. The popular name for the New North West Company, a fur-trading company whose bales were marked XY to differentiate them from those of the NORTH WEST COMPANY. Formed in 1798, it was later expanded by the addition of new partners, including Sir Alexander MACKENZIE in 1802. It was reorganized and acquired Mackenzie's name in 1803, but was absorbed by the North West Company in 1804.

Y

Y.T. Abbreviation of YUKON TERRITORY.

Yale Convention. A meeting of 26 delegates from the colony of British Columbia to express popular support for union with Canada, held at Yale (B.C.) on 14 Sept. 1868. The head of the eight-man delegation from Vancouver Island was Amor DE COSMOS.

Yaneff, Chris (b.1928). Graphic designer and consultant. Born in Toronto and educated at the Central Technical School and the Ontario College of Art, he was art director of the FINANCIAL POST from 1949 to 1956. A design consultant for a number of publications, including *Executive Magazine* and *Maclean's*, since 1956, he now heads Chris Yaneff Ltd, which specializes in creating expressive trademarks for corporations.

Yanofsky, Daniel Abraham (b.1925). One of Canada's foremost chessplayers. Born in Poland, he now lives in Winnipeg. He held the Canadian Championship in 1941, 1943, 1945, 1947, 1953, 1959, 1963, and 1965; the British Championship in 1953 (his only attempt); and the U.S. Open Championship in 1942. Awarded the title of International Grandmaster in 1964, on the strength of his showing in the Sixteenth Chess Olympics at Tel Aviv that year, he is the author of several books, including *100 Years of Chess in Canada* (1967), *Chess the Hard Way* (1953), and *How To Win the Endgames* (1957).

Yanovsky, Zalman (b.1945). Pop musician. Born in Toronto, the son of Avrom Yanovsky, a Toronto artist, he dropped out of Downsview Collegiate and re-emerged in 1964 as the founder, lead guitarist, and chief clown of the Lovin' Spoonful, the top rock group in North America in 1964 and 1967. He composed the score for the film NORTH OF SUPERIOR (1971).

Yarwood, Walter (b.1917). Sculptor. Born in Toronto, he studied there at the Western Technical School. He was an advertising artist before turning to sculpture in 1960. His sculptures are done in cast bronze, welded steel, and bolted aluminum. Important public commissions include sculpture for the Winnipeg Airport (1963) and an abstract sculptural relief for an exterior wall of Sydney Smith Hall, University of Toronto (1964).

Yates, J. Michael (b.1938). Poet. Born on Victoria Island in the Northwest Territories, he studied at the Universities of Missouri and Michigan and was a member of the CREATIVE WRITING DEPARTMENT at the University of British Columbia from 1967 to 1971, when he settled, until 1974, in the Queen Charlotte Islands. His poetry has been collected in several books, including: *Great Bear Lake Meditations* (1970), *Nothing Speaks for the Blue Moraines: New and Selected Poetry* (1974), and *The Qualicum Physics* (1975). He founded the SONO NIS PRESS, which published the important anthology VOLVOX.

'Yellow Pages, The'. See MACLEAN'S.

Yellowhead Interprovincial Highway. Picturesque highway connecting JASPER NATIONAL PARK with southern Manitoba via Edmonton.

Yellowhead Pass. A pass through the Rocky Mountains on the British Columbia-Alberta border west of Jasper, Alta, 3,711 ft above sea level. It was favoured by Sandford FLEMING in his railway surveys of 1870, was rejected by the CPR, and later became the route of the CNR main line. It is said to be named after François Decoigne, a fair-haired Nor'wester who was in charge of Jasper House in 1814 and whose nickname was Tête-Jaune ('Yellowhead').

Yellowknife. The capital since 1967 of the NORTHWEST TERRITORIES and its largest settlement, with a population in 1971 of 6,122. It originated with a gold discovery in 1935, was largely abandoned during the war years, and grew again in 1944, the result of a renewed gold rush. It became a city in 1970. Its motto is *Multum in Parvo* ('Much from Little').

Yellowknife. A once-powerful band of ATHAPASKAN-speaking people. They were also called the Copper Indians, after the copper they found on the Coppermine R., which they hammered into points and axes. In the early 1820s they were nearly decimated by their Athapaskan neighbours.

Yerxa, Leo (b.1947). Ojibwa artist. Born on the Couchiching Reserve near Fort Frances, Ont., a brother of Wayne YERXA, he lived there until 1967. He paints with acrylic in a semi-impressionistic manner. He won the design competition for the fourth series of Olympic coins, devoted to track and field, which he executed in the traditional manner of Algonquin quill-work. He illustrated *What They Used to Tell About: Indian Legends from La-*

brador (1969) by Peter Desbarats, and had his first one-man show in Toronto in 1975.

Yerxa, Wayne (b. 1945). Ojibwa artist. Born on the Couchiching Reserve near Fort Frances, Ont., a brother of Leo YERXA, he spends much of his time as a guide or hunter. Executing colourful pen-and-ink drawings of animal life in its natural habitat, he also interprets Ojibwa legends and lore. He took part in the Canadia Indian Art '74 exhibition at the Royal Ontario Museum. His first one-man show of drawings and acrylics was held in Toronto in 1975.

Yes. A poetry magazine, published in Montreal by Michael Gnarowski and Glen Siebrasse, that appeared irregularly from 1956 to 1970.

Yesno, Johnny (b.1941). Broadcaster. An Ojibwa Indian, born at Fort Hope on the Albany R. in northern Ontario, he acted with TORONTO WORKSHOP PRODUCTIONS in the early 1960s and appeared in Walt Disney's film *Biography of a Grizzly* (1970). A spokesman for the Canadian Indian, he became the host in 1967 of the CBC Radio program 'Indian Magazine', founded in 1963 and renamed 'Our Native Land' in 1972. It is the only continuing national radio program for Canada's native peoples.

Yesterday the Children Were Dancing. The English title of *Hier, les enfants dansaient*, a play by Gratien GÉLINAS. The French version was first produced by the COMÉDIE-CANA-DIENNE on 11 Apr. 1966, with Gélinas playing the father and his own two sons, Yves and Alain, playing the sons in the play. Mavor MOORE'S translation, published in 1967, was performed at the CHARLOTTETOWN SUMMER FESTIVAL in July 1967. Set in Montreal in 1964, it is about the complications that arise when Pierre Gravel, a middle-aged lawyer who has political ambitions, learns that his sons are engaged in separatist activities.

Yeti. See SASQUATCH.

Yoho National Park. Established in 1886 with an area of 10 sq. mi., it now covers 507 sq. mi. on the west slope of the Rocky Mountains in British Columbia and includes peaks, glaciers, waterfalls, lakes, and two valleys (Yoho and Kicking Horse). The extremely picturesque park derives its name from the Cree word for 'wonder' or 'astonishment'.

Yonge St. Famous Toronto thoroughfare. Begun in 1794 at Eglinton Ave to provide an overland fur-trade link with the Upper Great Lakes, it was for many years the principal link between Toronto and northern Ontario.

It is one of Toronto's principal north-south arteries, under which the first Canadian subway was built in 1954. It was named for Sir George Yonge, a friend of John Graves SIM-COE. It has been called 'the longest street in the world'.

York. The capital of Upper Canada (Ontario), the scene of an engagement in the WAR OF 1812. Founded in 1793 by John Graves SIM-COE, it was named after George, Duke of York, son of George III. On 27 Apr. 1813 an American force under Gen. Henry Dearborn, embarking from ships commanded by Cmdre Isaac Chauncey, occupied the town. The American invaders withdrew four days later after destroying the Parliament Building and other properties. The town was reoccupied on 31 July and 1 Aug., when the Americans withdrew for good. On 6 Mar. 1834 York was incorporated as the city of TORONTO.

York boat. A shallow-draft, open-decked freight boat used in the nineteenth century in the fur trade. Equipped with a square sail and oars, its was named after YORK FACTORY.

York Club, The. A nationally important luncheon club. Founded in 1909, it is housed in the former Gooderham mansion at the corner of St George and Bloor Sts, Toronto, designed by David ROBERTS. The club has 300 members, mostly business executives, though some are academics from the University of Toronto nearby.

York Factory. HUDSON'S BAY COMPANY post. In 1682 RADISSON and GROSEILLIERS, on a French expedition, built Fort Bourbon on the Hayes R., which flows into Hudson Bay. In 1684, working for the HBC, Radisson took the fort; it was rebuilt and called York Fort, and later York Factory. It changed hands several times in the seventeenth and eighteenth centuries, but after 1713 it became an important HBC depot and remained in use until 1957. The remains of the post are part of York Factory National Historic Park.

York Fort. See YORK FACTORY.

York Redoubt. A fortified coastal defence battery near Halifax, N.S. First built in 1796, it was employed during the Second World War as a defence against German submarines. It is now a national historic site.

York University. Founded as an affiliate of the University of Toronto in 1959, it became independent six years later. The main Downsview campus is on the northwest outskirts of Toronto; Glendon campus is in North Toronto. Its colleges include Atkinson

York University

(evening and part-time courses), Bethune, Calumet, Founders, McLaughlin, Stong, Vanier, Winters, and the OSGOODE HALL Law School. The Glendon campus, situated in a parkland setting on the edge of the Don R. valley, is the location of Glendon College, where the academic emphasis is on public affairs and bilingualism.

York Volunteers. See PUSH ON, BRAVE YORK VOLUNTEERS!

Yorkton International Film Festival. The oldest continuing film festival in North America. Held every other year at Yorkton, Sask. (population 14,000), it is open to all films under 60 minutes in length shot in 16 mm (and 8 mm, including Super8, in the amateur category). 20 awards are offered, including the Golden Sheaf for the best film of the festival. The first festival—held in 1950 and limited to documentary films—was sponsored by the Yorkton Film Council, with the assistance of the NATIONAL FILM BOARD'S district representative, Jim Lysyshyn.

Yorkville. Formerly a village north of Toronto—laid out in 1830 by Joseph Bloor, a brewer, and Sheriff William Botsford Jarvis—it gave its name to Yorkville Ave, two blocks north of Bloor St between Yonge and Avenue Road. Many of its nineteenth-century houses survive as boutiques, restaurants, and cafés. In the middle 1960s the street had a reputation as a meeting place for hippies.

'You Asked Us'. A popular write-in column. Appearing weekly in The CANADIAN MAGAZINE since 15 Apr. 1967, it consists of questions submitted by readers and answers supplied by researchers and writers. A selection of material, ranging from obscure Canadiana to the personal lives of Hollywood stars, was published in You Asked Us (1971).

Young, George (1910-72). Toronto-born marathon swimmer, the only swimmer to complete the marathon distance from Catalina Island to the California mainland in 1927. He claimed the $25,000 prize and returned to Toronto to a tumultuous welcome. 'The Catalina Kid' continued racing but met with little success and soon retired. He was elected to the Sports HALL OF FAME.

Young, Sir John (1807-76). GOVERNOR GENERAL of Canada from 1869 to 1872. He was created Baron Lisgar in 1870.

Young, Neil (b.1945). Folk and rock singer and composer. Born in Toronto, the son of the Toronto Globe and Mail columnist Scott Young, he joined the Buffalo Springfield, a well-known American rock group, at 17 and

went on to join—and to have his name added to—Crosby, Stills, and Nash. Between 1973 and 1976 he sold out Carnegie Hall, Massey Hall, and Maple Leaf Gardens.

Young Canada's Book Week. Annual program to encourage children to read books. The first Young Canada's Book Week, or Semaine du livre pour la jeunesse canadienne, was held across Canada from 12 to 19 Nov. 1949. Activities over the years have included puppet shows, story hours, films, contests, displays, etc. The last event was held from 15 to 22 Nov. 1973. Sponsored by the Canadian Library Association with the Canadian Book Publishers' Council, it was discontinued for financial reasons.

Young People's Theatre. A theatrical group founded by Susan Douglas Rubes in 1966. The Toronto-based group commissions short plays suitable for children from Canadian playwrights and then takes them on tour to schools and theatres throughout Ontario.

Young Politician, The. Subtitle of the first volume, published in 1952, of the two-part biography John A. Macdonald by Donald CREIGHTON. The second volume is The Old Chieftain (1955).

Youville, Mère d' (1701-71). Founder of the Grey Nuns (Les Soeurs Grises) of Montreal. Born at Varennes, Marie-Marguerite Dufrost de la Jemmerais married in 1722, was widowed in 1730, and thereupon devoted herself to charity. She was joined by three other widows and a grey habit was adopted as their distinctive dress. While head of the Hôpital-Général, Montreal, she founded the Order of Sisters of Charity (usually referred to as the Grey Nuns) in 1755.

Ypres. Flemish town in Belgium near which—at St Julien—the Allied front line formed a salient. The Germans attacked this salient on 22 Apr. 1915 when they first used chlorine gas, causing some French colonial troops to retreat in disorder. The gallantry and determination of the 1st Canadian Division during the first three days of this, its first battle, saved the situation despite heavy casualties.

Yukon Historic Sites. Sites in the Yukon Territory associated with the KLONDIKE GOLD RUSH that are being developed as part of the KLONDIKE GOLD RUSH INTERNATIONAL HISTORIC PARK. The Canadian sites include BONANZA CREEK, CHILKOOT PASS, SS KENO, and TRAIL OF '98.

Yukon River. Fifth-largest river in North America with a total length of about 2,300 mi. and a drainage basin that covers 330,000 sq. mi., about one-half of this area lying in Canada. Although its source is in British Columbia, the river proper is formed by the confluence of the Lewes and Pelly Rivers at Fort Selkirk in the Yukon. Its chief tributaries are the White, Stewart, Klondike, Porcupine, Chandler, and Tanana Rivers.

Yukon Territory. The most northwesterly part of Canada, bounded by Alaska on the west, the 60th parallel on the south, the NORTHWEST TERRITORIES on the east, and the Beaufort Sea on the north. Canada acquired the former HUDSON'S BAY COMPANY territory in 1870 and incorporated it in the Northwest Territories. It was made a provisional district in 1895. In 1896 gold deposits were found on BONANZA CREEK, precipitating the KLONDIKE GOLD RUSH of 1898, and in that year the district was made a separate territory.

With little or no manufacturing and agriculture, very limited forestry and trapping, the economy of the Yukon Territory is based principally on mining and tourism. The former has grown rapidly in recent years with the opening of an asbestos mine near Clinton Creek and a lead-zinc mine at Faro. In addition copper, silver, gold, nickel, and coal are being mined, and exploration is continuing for new deposits of these resources and for petroleum and natural gas.

Much of the territory is unpopulated. In a land area of 205,346 sq. mi. the majority of the 1971 population of 18,388 is found in the principal town, WHITEHORSE. See also TERRITORIAL GOVERNMENT.

Z

Z. See ZED.

Zacks, Ayala and Sam. Art collectors. Major institutions, including Queen's University in 1963 and the Art Gallery of Ontario in 1970, have received bequests of Canadian and world art from the private collection of Ayala Zacks (b.1912) and Samuel Zacks (1904-70) a Kingston-born, Toronto-based business executive. The AGO bequest, made shortly before the latter's death, consisted of 385 paintings, drawings, and sculpture by such twentieth-century artists as BORDUAS, Dufy, Matisse, Moore, and Picasso, collected over a 25-year period.

Zarou, Jeanette (b.1936). Soprano. Born in Ramallah, Palestine, she settled in Cornerbrook, Nfld, in 1947, and studied singing at the Royal Conservatory of Music and the Faculty of Music, University of Toronto. She has performed many times with the CANADIAN OPERA COMPANY—she sang the title role in Healey WILLAN'S DEIRDRE in 1966—and is a member of the Deutsche Oper am Rhein in Düsseldorf, Germany.

Zed. Anglo-Canadian pronunciation of the last letter of the alphabet. The American pronunciation is 'zee'.

ZED-2. Zero Energy Deuterium, an atomic reactor. The forerunner of the better-known CANDU reactor, it was started up at CHALK RIVER on 7 Sept. 1960.

ZEEP. Acronym for Zero Energy Experimental Pile, Canada's first atomic reactor. Designed by a team of Canadian, British, and Frer.ch scientists and engineers working under the NATIONAL RESEARCH COUNCIL in 1942, this nuclear chain reactor went into production at CHALK RIVER, Ont., on 5 Sept. 1945 and provided data for the design of the powerful NRX reactor. Transmuting uranium 235 into plutonium and moderated by heavy water, it produced a single watt of heat. It ceased operation in July 1970.

Zeller, Ludwig (b.1927). Artist. Born at Rio Loa in northern Chile and educated at Antofagasta and the University of Chile in Santiago, he worked for the ministry of education as an arts organizer from 1953 to 1968. In 1971 he settled in Toronto, where he has exhibited his strange, menacing collages and published *Woman in Dream* (1975), a surreal poem translated from the Spanish by Estella Lorca and illustrated with drawings by Zeller's wife, the Budapest-born ceramist and art teacher, Susana Wald (b.1937).

Zeller's Limited

Zeller's Limited. A chain of small department stores for family apparel, accessories, and home needs. It was founded in 1931 by Walter P. Zeller (1890-1957), a variety-store manager born in Waterloo County, Ont. In 1976 there were 156 Zeller's stores in all the provinces. Two-thirds are concentrated in Ontario and Quebec.

Zend, Robert (b.1920). Poet. Born in Budapest, Hungary, where he worked as a cartoonist and columnist, he settled in Toronto in 1956 and joined the CBC. Since 1968 he has produced programs for CBC IDEAS. His witty and surreal poems, co-translated by John Robert Colombo, appear in *From Zero to One* (1973).

Zinc. A mineral used to galvanize steel and to make die castings, copper alloys, etc. In 1971 Canada produced 23% of the world's output, chiefly from mines at Bathurst, N.B.; Maltagami, Que.; Timmins, Ont.; Manitouwadge, Ont.; the area of Flin Flon, Man.; Kimberley, B.C.; Faro, Y.T.; and Pure Point, N.W.T.

Znaimer, Moses (b.1942). Television performer and executive. Born in Kubat, Tajikistan, U.S.S.R., he was brought to Montreal in 1948. He took an M.A. in Russian studies at Harvard and joined CBC Radio as a public-affairs producer in 1965, appearing as an interviewer on THIS HOUR HAS SEVEN DAYS, 'The Way It Is', and TAKE 30. He produced *Revolution Plus Fifty*, a 13-part television series on Russia today that was first shown on 8 Jan. 1967. He left broadcasting for business but re-emerged as general manager of Toronto's innovative CITY-TV station, which opened on 28 Sept. 1972.

Zolf, Larry (b.1934). Author and personality. Born in the North End of Winnipeg, he was educated at the University of Toronto and OSGOODE HALL where, in 1956-7, he was debating champion. He has written for CBC Radio and Television since 1962 and is now a current-affairs producer and political pundit for such programs as AS IT HAPPENS and TAKE 30. The author of *Dance of the Dialectic* (1973), he has been called both a 'gadfly' and a 'guru' for his incisive intelligence and rococo manner.

Zombie. A soldier conscripted for home defence and not service overseas during the Second World War. The West Indian term for a supernaturally animated corpse was applied to those men who did not volunteer for overseas service. They were drafted in Oct. 1940 for service under the NATIONAL RESOURCES MOBILIZATION ACT (NRMA) in 1940, and many of them later volunteered for active duty overseas.

Zones of Compass Unreliability. Undefined areas of the world, particularly in the Canadian North, where compass readings are unreliable. Near the Magnetic NORTH POLE (which is constantly shifting position), the earth's magnetic field is vertical, rendering the magnetic compass useless.

Zorra, Men of. Champion tug-of-war team. In the early 1880s five sturdy farmers—Bill Munro, Ira Hummason, Sandy Clark, Bob MacLeod, and Bob McIntosh—from East and West Zorra Townships, near Woodstock, Ont., formed a tug-of-war team. The Men of Zorra won numerous titles and took the world-championship title at the Chicago World's Fair on 4 July 1893. Their slogan was the anti-Fenian boast, 'They'll No Tak' Zorra!'